HARPER'S
Topical
Concordance
of the Bible

REVISED AND ENLARGED EDITION

HARPER'S Topical Concordance

of the Bible

compiled by

Charles R. Joy

1817

HARPER & ROW, PUBLISHERS, SAN FRANCISCO

New York, Cambridge, Philadelphia, St. Louis
London, Singapore, Sydney, Tokyo

TO MY WIFE

LUCY ALICE

And To My Children

ALICE, LUCY, ROBERT, NANCY

"Love is strong as death."
"Many waters cannot quench love,
Neither can the floods overwhelm it."

HARPER'S TOPICAL CONCORDANCE. Copyright 1940 by Harper & Row, Publishers, Inc. All rights reserved. Printed in the United States of America. No part of this book may be used or reproduced in any manner whatsoever without written permission except in the case of brief quotations embodied in critical articles and reviews. For information address Harper & Row, Publishers, Inc., 10 East 53rd Street, New York, N.Y. 10022. Published simultaneously in Canada by Fitzhenry & Whiteside Limited, Toronto.

Revised and Enlarged Edition published in 1962.

First Harper & Row paperback edition published in 1976.

STANDARD BOOK NUMBER: ISBN: 0-06-064229-7

LIBRARY OF CONGRESS CATALOG CARD NUMBER: 62-11129

89 90 91 92 93 HAD 10 9 8 7 6 5 4 3 2 1

PREFACE

It is a noteworthy fact that no adequate topical concordance has ever hitherto been published. For centuries preaching from texts has been a Christian custom, yet in the search for these texts clergymen have had to depend upon their own knowledge, the ordinary concordance, and the fragmentary subject-indices usually appended to the Bible. The Bible is a vast and complex literature. No student ever feels that he has mastered it. There are many vivid texts to adorn his discourses that elude his search at the moment he needs them, either because his memory is not sufficiently agile, or because that particular use of the text has not occurred to him before.

In the old days, most preaching was expository. The clergyman selected a Biblical passage, and then prepared a sermon to expound the meaning and implications of it. Preaching in modern times has become increasingly topical. The clergyman selects a subject, suggested by the spiritual needs of his people, or by the contemporaneous scene, and he then searches for some text appropriate to that theme. How much time can be consumed in such a search, every Biblical student, every preacher knows.

Most prefaces belong in the literature of apologetics. This preface is not among them. The preparation and publication of this book need no defense. Had such a book as this been available to me a quarter of a century ago, when I began my ministry, it would have been of inestimable value. It is a task that has needed doing for long generations. I have undertaken it because I needed such a volume myself, and because other clergymen and Bible students have told me how indispensable such a book would be. The completion of the work gives me great satisfaction. The book should fill a gap in the library of all Bible students as an important work of reference.

This concordance of subjects should not be confused with the usual concordance. The latter enables one to find a particular verse under the principal words which it contains. The present work will help one to find appropriate texts for a topic, even though the topic itself is not among the words of the text. If, for instance, a text is desired for the subject of Honesty, the ordinary concordance would not readily yield the striking verse, Deuteronomy 25:13, "Thou shalt not have in thy bag divers weights, a great and a little." If the topic is Forgiveness, how would a student find Joel 2:25, the verse reading, "I will restore to you the years that the locust hath eaten"? If the topic is Inconstancy, what key word would be likely to come to mind to lead one to the text, Hosea 6:4, "Your goodness is as a morning cloud, and as the early dew it goeth away"? What finer text for a sermon on Compensation could be found than that of Ezekiel 1:1, "As I was among the captives, . . . the heavens were opened, and I saw visions of God!" Yet the older concordances do not help one to find such texts. In them one would find for the topic Determination such a text as "Solomon determined to build an house for the name of the Lord," 2 Chronicles 2:1, but he would not find that more vivid and unusual text, Ezekiel 1:12,

"Whither the spirit was to go, they went; and they turned not when they went."

There are many words in common use today which do not occur in the King James version, words such as Ambition, Audacity, Aspiration, Responsibility. These have their important place in the present topical concordance, though they do not occur in the older text-finding volumes.

The common concordance, while far from being complete in listing every unimportant word in the Bible, is necessarily filled with many words that have no homiletical value. A concordance that happens to be before me at the moment lists such words as Another, As, Because, Before, Over, Upon. Such words have no place in a topical concordance, and in the present volume only comprehensive topics in their substantive form occur. Necessarily, also, a good concordance of the traditional arrangement will list every instance in which a particular word appears. Many of these instances are repetitious, or devoid of all significance. The concordance before me lists over three hundred texts containing the word Behold, three hundred and sixty containing the word Blood, two hundred and seventy containing the word Babylon. In the present book, texts are not classified in accordance with some particular word common to them, but in harmony with their subject or sentiment. Only significant and vivid verses are included.

In the usual concordance Biblical proper names are listed. The concordance to which I refer begins with Aaron (more than 100 texts) ; Children of Aaron; Aaron, with Moses; Aaron, with sons; Aaronites; Abaddon; Agatha; Abana; Abarim. The present book includes no proper names among its topics, except those that have symbolic significance, like Babel, and Jerusalem, and Zion.

By the omission of all this unimportant matter, the present volume is much more compact, and much more usable than the older concordance, and the larger type makes the book a pleasure to handle and read.

This book has another great advantage over the usual concordance. Because of the necessity of including so much matter, the usual concordance must contract and abbreviate. Often the omissions are not indicated, so that the reader cannot be sure he has the complete text without referring to the Bible itself. Often the text is not given at all, but only the reference. In the present volume, there are no references without the text; omissions, if they occur, are clearly indicated; and otherwise the quotations are complete and accurate. No turning the pages of the Bible is necessary to verify a given text.

No liberties whatever are taken with the text except in an occasional change of punctuation made necessary by the indicated abridgements. For instance, in Proverbs 21:4, we find these words, "A high look, and a proud heart, and the plowing of the wicked, is sin." Under Plow in the present book we find the following quotation, "The plowing of the wicked is sin," the comma before "sin" being omitted.

The present volume is, then, not an abridged concordance of the older kind. It is a wholly new work.

The plan of the book is very simple, practical, and convenient. All subjects are arranged in their alphabetical order. Under each subject the verses appear in their Biblical order. The King James Bible is used without exception, and the spelling, hyphenization, and punctuation conform with early seventeenth-century standards.

Every effort has been made to exclude from the book any theological bias. It would be an unpardonable impertinence in such a work as this to let a particular type of religious thought and conviction color one's judgment in the selection and exclusion of texts. The book is as comprehensive as the Bible itself, because it is the Bible, just as it is given to us, with all its treasury of riches. The present volume is not compiled to sustain any sectarian viewpoint.

All verses in the present volume have been carefully verified. In addition to the professional proofreading, every quotation has been double-checked by a competent assistant and myself. The reader may count upon the accuracy of the entire book.

The adequacy of the volume is evident in the fact that 25,000 verses have here been arranged under more than 2100 topics. The reader will find under the various subjects, not only the obvious texts that one would expect to find there, but also a surprising number of unusual texts, vivid, full of beauty and spiritual value. Finally a thorough system of cross references will aid the student who is looking for a text with some exact shade of meaning, some precise emphasis.

The first concordance to the whole English Bible was printed in London in 1550. It was compiled by John Marbeck, whose story is told in Fox's *Book of Martyrs*, although Marbeck himself escaped martyrdom. He was too poor to purchase Thomas Matthews' Bible, when it was published in 1537, so he borrowed a copy, and began to write it all out for himself by hand. A friend remonstrated with him, saying "Tush! thou goest about a vain and tedious labour. But this were a profitable work for thee, to set out a concordance in English."

"A concordance," said he, "what is that?" The friend replied that it was a book to find out any word in the whole Bible by the letter, and that there was one in Latin already. But Marbeck said that he had no learning to go about such a thing. The friend insisted. "Enough," said he, "for that matter, for it requireth not so much learning as diligence. And seeing thou art so painful a man, and one that cannot be unoccupied, it were a good exercise for thee."

The present compiler, as he looks back upon this long and laborious task, is convinced that these words describe it well. It has been a task requiring not so much learning, as diligence, and judgment, and patience. If this work proves to be a helpful reference book for students of the Bible, and a revealing anthology of the most marvelous literature in the long history of religious aspiration, the toil of many months will seem in retrospect short and light.

CHARLES R. JOY

August 18, 1940

PREFACE TO THE ENLARGED EDITION

More than two decades have passed since the first edition of *Harper's Topical Concordance* appeared. The book is still as useful today as it was when it was issued. It has become a standard reference book for all lovers of the Bible.

The present greatly enlarged edition springs from the conviction, however, that the book can be made even more helpful.

625 new topics have been added, making a total of 2,775. These new topics include many subjects that have become important to those concerned with spiritual, ethical, and social problems in our time. For instance, we find in this new edition such subjects as Integration, Segregation, Morale, Reverence for Life, Well-Being, Unemployment, Secularism, Stoicism. These topics reflect some of the present interests of the church. The number of new texts added is about 8,200, and the total in the book is now about 33,200.

Another of the pulpit problems that concern the preacher today is to find appropriate texts for church holy days and national holidays. Here then are topics like Lincoln's Birthday, Washington's Birthday, Lent, Ash Wednesday, Whit-Sunday, Mother's Day, Father's Day, Graduation Day, Flag Day, United Nations Day.

This book can serve many purposes. It can be used for private devotions. The various texts found under a single topic offer rich material for meditation and prayer. New Scriptural readings from the old Bible can be arranged by using, instead of a single consecutive passage, a dozen or more verses related to the same subject. The preacher can not only find texts for his sermon topics but even suggestions for the topics themselves. The different verses grouped together here under one heading will also reveal new paths which the preacher's thought may take, new side-lights on his theme, new illustrative material for his use.

It is with confidence and faith that this enlarged edition of the Concordance goes forth.

CHARLES R. JOY

January 1, 1961

TABLE OF ABBREVIATIONS

The Books of the Old Testament

Genesis . . . . . . Ge.	Proverbs . . . . . Pr.
Exodus . . . . . . Ex.	Ecclesiastes . . . . . Ec.
Leviticus . . . . . . Le.	Song of Solomon . . . . S. of S.
Numbers . . . . . . Nu.	Isaiah . . . . . . Is.
Deuteronomy . . . . . De.	Jeremiah . . . . . Je.
Joshua . . . . . . Jos.	Lamentations . . . . La.
Judges . . . . . . Ju.	Ezekiel . . . . . Eze.
Ruth . . . . . . Ru.	Daniel . . . . . Da.
1 Samuel . . . . . . 1 S.	Hosea . . . . . Ho.
2 Samuel . . . . . . 2 S.	Joel . . . . . Jo.
1 Kings . . . . . . 1 K.	Amos . . . . . Am.
2 Kings . . . . . . 2 K.	Obadiah . . . . . Ob.
1 Chronicles . . . . . 1 Ch.	Jonah . . . . . Jon.
2 Chronicles . . . . . 2 Ch.	Micah . . . . . Mi.
Ezra . . . . . . Ezr.	Nahum . . . . . Na.
Nehemiah . . . . . Ne.	Habakkuk . . . . Hab.
Esther . . . . . . Es.	Zephaniah . . . . Zph.
Job . . . . . . Jb.	Haggai . . . . . Hag.
Psalms . . . . . . Ps.	Zechariah . . . . Zch.

Malachi . . . . . . Mal.

The Books of the New Testament

Matthew . : : . . . Mat.	2 Thessalonians . . . 2 Th.
Mark . . . . . . Mk.	1 Timothy . . . . 1 Ti.
Luke . . . . . . Lu.	2 Timothy . . . . 2 Ti.
John . . . . . . Jn.	Titus . . . . . Tit.
Acts . . . . . . Ac.	Philemon . . . . Phm.
Romans . . . . . . Ro.	Hebrews . . . . He.
1 Corinthians . . . . 1 Co.	James . . . . . Ja.
2 Corinthians . . . . 2 Co.	1 Peter . . . . 1 Pe.
Galatians . . . . . Ga.	2 Peter . . . . 2 Pe.
Ephesians . . . . . Ep.	1 John . . . . 1 Jn.
Philippians . . . . . Ph.	2 John . . . . 2 Jn.
Colossians . . . . . Col.	3 John . . . . 3 Jn.
1 Thessalonians . . . 1 Th.	Jude . . . . . Jude

Revelation . . . . . Re.

Harper's Topical Concordance of the Bible

A

Abandonment

God forbid that we should forsake the Lord, to serve other gods. *Jos.* 24: 16.

Thou wilt not leave my soul in hell. *Ps.* 16: 10.

Leave me not, neither forsake me, O God of my salvation. *Ps.* 27: 9.

When my father and my mother forsake me, then the Lord will take me up. *Ps.* 27: 10.

I have been young, and now am old; yet have I not seen the righteous forsaken. *Ps.* 37: 25.

Forsake me not utterly. *Ps.* 119: 8.

In that day every man shall cast away his idols of silver, and his idols of gold. *Is.* 31: 7.

For a small moment have I forsaken thee; but with great mercies will I gather thee. *Is.* 54: 7.

Let the wicked forsake his way, and the unrighteous man his thoughts. *Is.* 55: 7.

Leave thy fatherless children, I will preserve them alive. *Je.* 49: 11.

Repent, and turn yourselves from your idols. *Eze.* 14: 6.

He that loveth father or mother more than me is not worthy of me. *Mat.* 10: 37.

He that loseth his life for my sake shall find it. *Mat.* 10: 39.

That day shall not come, except there come a falling away first. *2 Th.* 2: 3.

See also

Renunciation; Resignation; Surrender.

Abasement

How long wilt thou refuse to humble thyself before me? *Ex.* 10: 3.

He humbled thee. *De.* 8: 3.

Look on every one that is proud, and bring him low. *Jb.* 40: 12.

Now mine eye seeth thee. Wherefore I abhor myself. *Jb.* 42: 5, 6.

Thus saith the Lord God; Remove the diadem, and take off the crown. *Eze.* 21: 26.

Those that walk in pride he is able to abase. *Dan.* 4: 37.

All the proud, yea, and all that do wickedly, shall be stubble: and the day that cometh shall burn them up. *Mal.* 4: 1.

Whosoever shall exalt himself shall be abased. *Mat.* 23: 12.

He hath put down the mighty from their seats. *Lu.* 1: 52.

Make me as one of thy hired servants. *Lu.* 15: 19.

The publican, standing afar off, would not lift up so much as his eyes unto heaven, but smote upon his breast, saying, God be merciful to me a sinner. *Lu.* 18: 13.

O wretched man that I am! *Ro.* 7: 24.

I . . . will bring to nothing the understanding of the prudent. *1 Co.* 1: 19.

As having nothing, and yet possessing all things. *2 Co.* 6: 10.

For if a man think himself to be something, when he is nothing, he deceiveth himself. *Ga.* 6: 3.

I know . . . how to be abased. *Ph.* 4: 12.

Humble yourselves in the sight of the Lord, and he shall lift you up. *Ja.* 4: 10.

See also

Christ, Humiliation of; Christ, Humility of; Disgrace; Dishonor; Humiliation; Humility; Ignominy; Reproach; Shame.

Abbreviation

Jacob served seven years for Rachel, and they seemed unto him but a few days; for the love he had to her. *Ge.* 29: 20.

Are not my days few? *Jb.* 10: 20.

Man that is born of a woman is of few days. *Jb.* 14: 1.

Man . . . cometh forth like a flower, and is cut down. *Jb.* 14: 1, 2.

How oft is the candle of the wicked put out! *Jb.* 21: 17.

What pleasure hath he in his house after him, when the number of his months is cut off in the midst? *Jb.* 21: 21.

The days of his youth hast thou shortened. *Ps.* 89: 45.

A thousand years in thy sight are but as yesterday when it is past. *Ps.* 90: 4.

The days of our years are threescore years and ten; and if by reason of strength they be fourscore years, yet is their strength labour and sorrow; for it is soon cut off, and we fly away. *Ps.* 90: 10.

So teach us to number our days. *Ps.* 90: 12.

He shortened my days. *Ps.* 102: 23.

The years of the wicked shall be shortened. *Pr.* 10: 27.

The bed is shorter than that a man can stretch himself on it. *Is.* 28: 20.

He will finish the work, and cut it short in righteousness. *Ro.* 9: 28.

This I say, brethren, the time is short. *1 Co.* 7: 29.

See also

Life, the Short; Brevity.

Abeyance

I cannot do any thing till thou be come hither. *Ge.* 19: 22.

Moses delayed to come down out of the mount. *Ex.* 32: 1.

The sun stood still, and the moon stayed. *Jos.* 10: 13.

Howbeit the hair of his head began to grow again after he was shaven. *Ju.* 16: 22.

Till I know what God will do for me. *1 S.* 22: 3.

Rest in the Lord, and wait patiently for him. *Ps.* 37: 7.

Now, Lord, what wait I for? *Ps.* 39: 7.

My salvation shall not tarry. *Is.* 46: 13.

The Lord is good unto them that wait for him. *La.* 3: 25.

Blessed is he that waiteth. *Da.* 12: 12.

The vision is yet for an appointed time, but at the end it shall speak, and not lie: though it tarry, wait for it. *Hab.* 2: 3.

My lord delayeth his coming. *Mat.* 24: 48.

Tarry ye here, and watch with me. *Mat.* 26: 38.

Occupy till I come. *Lu.* 19: 13.

If I will that he tarry till I come, what is that to thee? *Jn.* 21: 22.

But if we hope for that we see not, then do we with patience wait for it. *Ro.* 8: 25.

The Lord direct your hearts into the love of God, and into the patient waiting for Christ. *2 Th.* 3: 5.

Let patience have her perfect work. *Ja.* 1: 4.

Where is the promise of his coming? *2 Pe.* 3: 4.

That which ye have already hold fast till I come. *Re.* 2: 25.

See also

Delay; Wait.

Abhorrence

Neither shalt thou bring an abomination into thine house, lest thou be a cursed thing like it: but thou shalt utterly detest it. *De.* 7: 26.

I abhor myself, and repent in dust and ashes. *Jb.* 42: 6.

The Lord will abhor the bloody and deceitful man. *Ps.* 5: 6.

The wicked . . . blesseth the covetous, whom the Lord abhorreth. *Ps.* 10: 3.

He deviseth mischief upon his bed; he setteth himself in a way that is not good; he abhorreth not evil. *Ps.* 36: 4.

Their soul abhorreth all manner of meat. *Ps.* 107: 18.

I hate and abhor lying. *Ps.* 119; 163.

Fools despise wisdom. *Pr.* 1: 7.

He that despiseth his neighbour sinneth. *Pr.* 14: 21.

As for them whose heart walketh after the heart of their detestable things and their abominations, I will recompense their way upon their own heads. *Eze.* 11: 21.

Abhor that which is evil; cleave to that which is good. *Ro.* 12: 9.

Despise ye the church of God? *1 Co.* 11: 22.

See also

Animosity; Antagonism; Antipathy; Aversion; Hatred; Malevolence; Malice.

Ability

God is my strength and power. *2 S.* 22: 33.

They gave after their ability. *Ezr.* 2: 69.

We after our ability have redeemed our brethren. *Ne.* 5: 8.

Power belongeth unto God. *Ps.* 62: 11.

Such as had ability in them to stand in the king's palace. *Da.* 1: 4.

All things are possible to him that believeth. *Mk.* 9: 23.

They said unto him, We can. *Mk.* 10: 39.

She hath done what she could. *Mk.* 14: 8.

If it be possible, as much as lieth in you, live peaceably with all men. *Ro.* 12: 18.

As every man hath received the gift, even so minister the same one to another. *1 Pe.* 4: 10.

The ability which God giveth. *1 Pe.* 4: 11.

See also

Aptitude; Capacity; Energy; Force; Power; Skill; Strength; Talent.

Abnegation

Ye have this day rejected your God. *1 S.* 10: 19.

He is despised and rejected of men. *Is.* 53: 3.

Because thou hast rejected knowledge, I will also reject thee. *Ho.* 4: 6.

How shall I give thee up, Ephraim? *Ho.* 11: 8.

If any man will come after me, let him deny himself, and take up his cross, and follow me. *Mat.* 16: 24.

The stone which the builders rejected, the same is become the head of the corner. *Mat.* 21: 42.

He that denieth me before men shall be denied before the angels of God. *Lu.* 12: 9.

The cock shall not crow this day, before thou shalt thrice deny that thou knowest me. *Lu.* 22: 34.

We have renounced the hidden things of dishonesty. *2 Co.* 4: 1, 2.

Obedient unto death, even the death of the cross. *Ph.* 2: 8.

He hath denied the faith, and is worse than an infidel. *1 Ti.* 5: 8.

See also

Denial; Rejection; Renunciation; Self-Denial.

Abnormality

Behold every form of creeping things, and abominable beasts. *Eze.* 8: 10.

The first was like a lion, and had eagle's wings. *Da.* 7: 4.

Behold another beast, a second, like to a bear, and it raised up itself on one side, and it had three ribs in the mouth of it between the teeth of it. *Da.* 7: 5.

Another, like a leopard, which had upon the back of it four wings of a fowl; the beast had also four heads. *Da.* 7: 6.

Behold a fourth beast, dreadful and terrible, and strong exceedingly; and it had great iron teeth: . . . and it had ten horns. *Da.* 7: 7.

He gave them power against unclean spirits. *Mat.* 10: 1.

There was in their synagogue a man with an unclean spirit. *Mk.* 1: 23.

The unclean spirits went out, and entered into the swine: and the herd ran violently down a steep place into the sea. *Mk.* 5: 13.

Mary called Magdalene, out of whom went seven devils. *Lu.* 8: 2.

Have not I chosen you twelve, and one of you is a devil? *Jn.* 6: 70.

Round about the throne, were four beasts full of eyes before and behind. *Re.* 4: 6.

The four beasts had each of them six wings about him. *Re.* 4: 8.

In the midst of the throne . . . stood a Lamb as it had been slain, having seven horns and seven eyes. *Re.* 5: 6.

I saw three unclean spirits like frogs come out of the mouth of the dragon. *Re.* 16: 13.

See also

Abomination; Strangeness; Unnaturalness.

Abode

I know thy abode, and thy going out, and thy coming in. *2 K.* 19: 27.

He shall abide before God for ever. *Ps.* 61: 7.

Abide with us: for it is toward evening, and the day is far spent. *Lu.* 24: 29.

If a man love me, he will keep my words: and my Father will love him, and we will come unto him, and make our abode with him. *Jn.* 14: 23.

Abide in me, and I in you. *Jn.* 15: 4.

We know that if our earthly house of this tabernacle were dissolved, we have a building of God, an house not made with hands, eternal in the heavens. *2 Co.* 5: 1.

Let them learn first to shew piety at home. *1 Ti.* 5: 4.

Now, little children, abide in him. *1 Jn.* 2: 28.

See also

Dwelling; Habitation; Home; House; Residence; Roof; Shelter; Sojourn.

Abolition

The idols he shall utterly abolish. *Is.* 2: 18.

My righteousness shall not be abolished. *Is.* 51: 6.

Ye are not under the law, but under grace. *Ro.* 6: 14.

Being then made free from sin. *Ro.* 6: 18.

Thou art no more a servant, but a son. *Ga.* 4: 7.

He . . . hath broken down the middle wall of partition between us. *Ep.* 2: 14.

Jesus Christ . . . hath abolished death, and hath brought life and immortality to light through the gospel. *2 Ti.* 1: 10.

The former things are passed away. *Re.* 21: 4.

See also

Annulment; Cancellation; Slavery.

Abomination

All that do unrighteously, are an abomination unto the Lord thy God. *De.* 25: 16.

A false balance is abomination to the Lord. *Pr.* 11: 1.

Lying lips are abomination to the Lord. *Pr.* 12: 22.

It is abomination to fools to depart from evil. *Pr.* 13: 19.

The sacrifice of the wicked is an abomination to the Lord. *Pr.* 15: 8.

The thoughts of the wicked are an abomination to the Lord. *Pr.* 15: 26.

Every one that is proud in heart is an abomination to the Lord. *Pr.* 16: 5.

An unjust man is an abomination to the just: and he that is upright in the way is abomination to the wicked. *Pr.* 29: 27.

Turn away your faces from all your abominations. *Eze.* 14: 6.

That which is highly esteemed among men is abomination in the sight of God. *Lu.* 16: 15.

See also

Corruption; Defilement; Depravity; Lust; Vileness; Wickedness.

Absence

The Lord watch between me and thee, when we are absent one from another. *Ge.* 31: 49.

Intreat me not to leave thee. *Ru.* 1: 16.

His disciples were gone away alone. *Jn.* 6: 22.

It is expedient for you that I go away. *Jn.* 16: 7.

Absent in body, but present in spirit. *1 Co.* 5: 3.

Wherefore we labour, that, whether present or absent, we may be accepted of him. *2 Co.* 5: 9.

As ye have always obeyed, not as in my presence only, but now much more in my absence. *Ph.* 2: 12.

See also

Departure; Destitution; Parting; Want; Withdrawal.

Absolution

Thy sins be forgiven thee. *Mat.* 9: 2.

The Son of man hath power on earth to forgive sins. *Mat.* 9: 6.

Who can forgive sins, but God alone? *Lu.* 5: 21.

If the Son therefore shall make you free, ye shall be free indeed. *Jn.* 8: 36.

Whosoever believeth in him shall receive remission of sins. *Ac.* 10: 43.

To declare his righteousness for the remission of sins that are past, through the forbearance of God. *Ro.* 3: 25.

Being then made free from sin. *Ro.* 6: 18.

Without shedding of blood is no remission. *He.* 9: 22.

See also

Christ, Forgiveness of; Deliverance; Forgiveness; God, Forgiveness of; Pardon; Penance; Remission.

Abstinence

Wine is a mocker, strong drink is raging: and whosoever is deceived thereby is not wise. *Pr.* 20: 1.

Look not thou upon the wine when it is red. *Pr.* 23: 31.

After long abstinence Paul stood forth in the midst of them. *Ac.* 27: 21.

Be not drunk with wine, wherein is excess. *Ep.* 5: 18.

Abstain from all appearance of evil. *1 Th.* 5: 22.

Abstain from fleshly lusts, which war against the soul. *1 Pe.* 2: 11.

See also

Avoidance; Continence; Control; Forbearance; Moderation; Self-Control; Sobriety; Temperance.

Abundance

Your threshing shall reach unto the vintage, and the vintage shall reach unto the sowing time. *Le.* 26: 5.

The Lord thy God will make thee plenteous in every work of thine hand, in the fruit of thy body, and in the fruit of thy cattle, and in the fruit of thy land, for good. *De.* 30: 9.

In thy presence is fulness of joy. *Ps.* 16: 11.

For thou, Lord, art . . . plenteous in mercy. *Ps.* 86: 5.

The thoughts of the diligent tend only to plenteousness. *Pr.* 21: 5.

He that tilleth his land shall have plenty of bread. *Pr.* 28: 19.

A faithful man shall abound with blessings. *Pr.* 28: 20.

The stretching out of his wings shall fill the breadth of thy land. *Is.* 8: 8.

The earth shall be full of the knowledge of the Lord, as the waters cover the sea. *Is.* 11: 9.

Then shall he give the rain of thy seed, that thou shalt sow the ground withal; and bread of the increase of the earth, and it shall be fat and plenteous. *Is.* 30: 23.

I brought you into a plentiful country. *Je.* 2: 7.

I . . . will reveal unto them the abundance of peace and truth. *Je.* 33: 6.

Behold, the days come, saith the Lord, that the plowman shall overtake the reaper, and the treader of grapes him that soweth seed; and the mountains shall drop sweet wine, and all the hills shall melt. *Am.* 9: 13.

Sufficient unto the day is the evil thereof. *Mat.* 6: 34.

Out of the abundance of the heart the mouth speaketh. *Mat.* 12: 34.

Whosoever hath, to him shall be given, and he shall have more abundance. *Mat.* 13: 12.

Good measure, pressed down, and shaken together, and running over. *Lu.* 6: 38.

I am come that they might have life, and that they might have it more abundantly. *Jn.* 10: 10.

Where sin abounded, grace did much more abound. *Ro.* 5: 20.

Always abounding in the work of the Lord. *I Co.* 15: 58.

Therefore, as ye abound in every thing, in faith, and utterance, and knowledge, and in all diligence, and in your love to us, see that ye abound in this grace also. *2 Co.* 8: 7.

God is able to make all grace abound toward you. *2 Co.* 9: 8.

The abundance of the revelations. *2 Co.* 12: 7.

The fulness of him that filleth all in all. *Ep.* 1: 23.

But I have all, and abound: I am full. *Ph.* 4: 18.

My God shall supply all your need according to his riches in glory by Christ Jesus. *Ph.* 4: 19.

An entrance shall be ministered unto you abundantly into the everlasting kingdom of our Lord. *2 Pe.* 1: 11.

See also

Adequacy; Ampleness; Fertility; God, Wealth of; Goods; Plenty; Productivity; Riches; Satiety; Substance; Sufficiency; Wealth.

Abuse

If a man smite his servant, or his maid, with a rod, and he die under his hand; he shall be surely punished. *Ex.* 21: 20.

Ye shall not afflict any widow, or fatherless child. *Ex.* 22: 22.

Thou shalt not revile the gods, nor curse the ruler of thy people. *Ex.* 22: 28.

The Lord opened the mouth of the ass, and she said unto Balaam, What have I done unto thee, that thou hast smitten me three times? *Nu.* 22: 28.

Draw thy sword, and thrust me through therewith; lest these uncircumcised come and thrust me through, and abuse me. *I S.* 31: 4.

Her priests have violated my law. *Eze.* 22: 26.

Woe unto him that giveth his neighbour drink, that puttest thy bottle to him. *Hab.* 2: 15.

Blessed are ye, when men shall revile you. *Mat.* 5: 11.

Whoso shall offend one of these little ones which believe in me, it were better for him that a millstone were hanged about his neck, and that he were drowned in the depth of the sea. *Mat.* 18: 6.

They that passed by reviled him. *Mat.* 27: 39.

Being reviled, we bless. *I Co.* 4: 12.

Know ye not that the unrighteous shall not inherit the kingdom of God? . . . abusers of themselves with mankind. *I Co.* 6: 9.

They that use this world, as not abusing it. *I Co.* 7: 31.

That I abuse not my power in the gospel. *I Co.* 9: 18.

Who, when he was reviled, reviled not again. *I Pe.* 2: 23.

See also

Affront; Injury; Reviling.

Abyss

Thou has laid me in the lowest pit, in darkness, in the deeps. *Ps.* 88: 6.

Her guests are in the depths of hell. *Pr.* 9: 18.

Hell from beneath is moved for thee to meet thee at thy coming. *Is.* 14: 9.

Thou shalt be brought down to hell, to the sides of the pit. *Is.* 14: 15.

I cast him down to hell with them that descend into the pit. *Eze.* 31: 16.

See also

Deep; Depth; Hell; Pit.

Accent

The whole earth was of one language, and of one speech. *Ge.* 11: 1.

Go to, let us go down, and there confound their language, that they may not understand one another's speech. *Ge.* 11: 7.

Therefore is the name of it called Babel. *Ge.* 11: 9.

Then said they unto him, Say now Shibboleth: and he said Sibboleth: for he could not frame to pronounce it right. *Ju.* 12: 6.

Speak, I pray thee, to thy servants in the Syrian language; for we understand it. *2 K.* 18: 26.

The mountains and the hills shall break forth before you into singing. *Is.* 55: 12.

O Lord, Thou art, in the midst of us, and we are called by thy name. *Je.* 14: 9.

I have pronounced the word, saith the Lord. *Je.* 34: 5.

They bring unto him one that was deaf, and had an impediment in his speech. *Mk.* 7: 32.

Thou art a Galilæan, and thy speech agreeth thereto. *Mk.* 14: 70.

They shall speak with new tongues. *Mk.* 16: 17.

They were all filled with the Holy Ghost, and began to speak with other tongues. *Ac.* 2: 4.

Now hear we every man in our own tongue. *Ac.* 2: 8.

Every knee shall bow to me, and every tongue shall confess to God. *Ro.* 14: 11.

Do all speak with tongues? *1 Co.* 12: 30.

Though I speak with the tongues of men and of angels, and have not charity, I am become as sounding brass. *1 Co.* 13: 1.

See also

Babel; Language; Speech; Tongue.

Acceptance

The Lord thy God accept thee. *2 S.* 24: 23.

Let the words of my mouth, and the meditation of my heart, be acceptable in thy sight, O Lord, my strength, and my redeemer. *Ps.* 19: 14.

To do justice and judgment is more acceptable to the Lord than sacrifice. *Pr.* 21: 3.

They shall come up with acceptance on mine altar. *Is.* 60: 7.

To proclaim the acceptable year of the Lord. *Is.* 61: 2.

Your burnt offerings are not acceptable, nor your sacrifices sweet unto me. *Je.* 6: 20.

I will say to them which were not my people, Thou art my people; and they shall say, Thou art my God. *Ho.* 2: 23.

No prophet is accepted in his own country. *Lu.* 4: 24.

Jesus of Nazareth, a man approved of God. *Ac.* 2: 22.

I beseech you therefore, brethren, by the mercies of God, that ye present your bodies a living sacrifice, holy, acceptable unto God, which is your reasonable service. *Ro.* 12: 1.

Behold, now is the accepted time; behold, now is the day of salvation. *2 Co.* 6: 2.

Proving what is acceptable unto the Lord. *Eph.* 5: 10.

This is a faithful saying, and worthy of all acceptation, that Jesus Christ came into the world to save sinners. *1 Ti.* 1: 15.

Study to shew thyself approved unto God. *2 Ti.* 2: 15.

If, when ye do well, and suffer for it, ye take it patiently, this is acceptable with God. *1 Pe.* 2: 20.

See also

Approval; Receptivity.

Access

Lift up your heads, O ye gates; and be ye lift up, ye everlasting doors; and the King of glory shall come in. *Ps.* 24: 7.

Come ye near unto me, hear ye this. *Is.* 48: 16.

Come unto me, all ye that labour and are heavy laden, and I will give you rest. *Mat.* 11: 28.

By whom also we have access by faith into this grace wherein we stand. *Ro.* 5: 2.

A door was opened unto me of the Lord. *2 Co.* 2: 12.

Through him we both have access by one Spirit unto the Father. *Ep.* 2: 18.

In whom we have boldness and access with confidence by the faith of him. *Ep.* 3: 12.

Let us therefore come boldly unto the throne of grace. *He.* 4: 16.

Behold, I have set before thee an open door, and no man can shut it. *Re.* 3: 8.

If any man hear my voice, and open the door, I will come in to him, and will sup with him, and he with me. *Re.* 3: 20.

Behold, a door was opened in heaven: and the first voice which I heard . . . said, Come up hither. *Re.* 4: 1.

The Spirit and the bride say, Come. And let him that heareth say, Come. *Re.* 22: 17.

See also

Christ, Coming to; Christ, the Door; Door; God, Access to; Hospitality; Welcome.

Accident

The day of their calamity is at hand. *De.* 32: 35.

Eli . . . fell from off the seat backward by the side of the gate, and his neck brake, and he died. *1 S.* 4: 16, 18.

Behold, I saw Absalom hanged in an oak. *2 S.* 18: 10.

They prevented me in the day of my calamity: but the Lord was my stay. *2 S.* 22: 19.

Therefore shall his calamity come suddenly; suddenly shall he be broken without remedy. *Pr.* 6: 15.

Woe to him that is alone when he falleth. *Ec.* 4: 10.

Ofttimes he falleth into the fire, and oft into the water. *Mat.* 17: 15.

Judas . . . purchased a field with the reward of iniquity; and falling headlong, he burst asunder in the midst. *Ac.* 1: 16, 18.

See also

Calamity; Chance; Disaster; Misfortune.

Acclamation

All the people shouted, and said, God save the king. *1 S.* 10: 24.

God is gone up with a shout, the Lord with the sound of a trumpet. *Ps.* 47: 5.

Even from everlasting to everlasting, thou art God. *Ps.* 90: 2.

Let them shout from the top of the mountains. *Is.* 42: 11.

Let them give glory unto the Lord, and declare his praise. *Is.* 42: 12.

I will say to them which were not my people, Thou art my people. *Ho.* 2: 23.

So shall ye know that I am the Lord your God. *Jo.* 3: 17.

Forthwith he came to Jesus, and said, Hail, master. *Mat.* 26: 49.

They bowed the knee before him, and mocked him, saying, Hail, King of the Jews! *Mat.* 27: 29.

Hail, thou that art highly favoured, the Lord is with thee. *Lu.* 1: 28.

See also

Applause; Approval; Assent; Shout.

Accomplice

The rulers take counsel together, against the Lord. *Ps.* 2: 2.

They commune of laying snares privily. *Ps.* 64: 5.

They have consulted together with one consent: they are confederate against thee. *Ps.* 83: 5.

Depart from me, ye evildoers. *Ps.* **119: 115.**

The poor and the deceitful man meet together. *Pr.* **29: 13.**

Be ye not unequally yoked together with unbelievers. *2 Co.* **6: 14.**

What concord hath Christ with Belial? *2 Co.* **6: 15.**

See also

Alliance; Ally; Association.

Accomplishment

And God saw every thing that he had made, and, behold, it was very good. *Ge.* **1: 31.**

So the house of the Lord was perfected. *2 Ch.* **8: 16.**

When he had . . . cut down all the idols throughout all the land of Israel, he returned to Jerusalem. *2 Ch.* **34: 7.**

Teach me, O Lord, the way of thy statutes; and I shall keep it unto the end. *Ps.* **119: 33.**

I have sworn, and I will perform it. *Ps.* **119: 106.**

The Lord will perfect that which concerneth me. *Ps.* **138: 8.**

Cry unto her, that her warfare is accomplished. *Is.* **40: 2.**

When they had performed all things according to the law of the Lord. *Lu.* **2: 39.**

Which of you, intending to build a tower, sitteth not down first, and counteth the cost, whether he have sufficient to finish it? *Lu.* **14: 28.**

Jesus . . . said, It is finished. *Jn.* **19: 30.**

Now therefore perform the doing of it; that as there was a readiness to will, so there may be a performance also out of that which ye have. *2 Co.* **8: 11.**

That the man of God may be perfect, throughly furnished unto all good works. *2 Ti.* **3: 17.**

There came a great voice out of the temple of heaven, from the throne, saying, It is done. *Re.* **16: 17.**

See also

Achievement; Attainment; Completion; Fulfilment; Success.

Accord

Can two walk together, except they be agreed? *Am.* **3: 3.**

These all continued with one accord in prayer and supplication. *Ac.* **1: 14.**

The people with one accord gave heed unto those things which Philip spake, hearing and seeing the miracles which he did. *Ac.* **8: 6.**

Fulfil ye my joy, that ye be likeminded, having the same love, being of one accord, of one mind. *Ph.* **2: 2.**

See also

Agreement; Assent; Compact; Compatibility; Concord; Consent; Contract; Covenant; God, Unity of; Harmony; Oneness; Treaty; Unanimity; Unity.

Account

So shall my righteousness answer for me in time to come. *Ge.* **30: 33.**

Howbeit there was no reckoning made with them of the money that was delivered into their hand, because they dealt faithfully. *2 K.* **22: 7.**

It [wisdom] cannot be valued with the gold of Ophir. *Jb.* **28: 16.**

What then shall I do when God riseth up? and when he visiteth, what shall I answer him? *Jb.* **31: 14.**

Lord, what is man, . . . that thou makest account of him! *Ps.* **144: 3.**

Every idle word that men shall speak, they shall give account thereof in the day of judgment. *Mat.* **12: 36.**

Therefore is the kingdom of heaven likened unto a certain king, which would take account of his servants. *Mat.* **18: 23.**

Which of you, intending to build a tower, sitteth not down first, and counteth the cost? *Lu.* **14: 28.**

Give an account of thy stewardship. *Lu.* **16: 2.**

How much owest thou unto my lord? *Lu.* **16: 5.**

There was also a strife among them, which of them should be accounted the greatest. *Lu.* **22: 24.**

We shall all stand before the judgment seat of Christ. *Ro.* **14: 10.**

Let a man so account of us, as of the ministers of Christ, and stewards of the mysteries of God. *1 Co.* **4: 1.**

The doctrine . . . of eternal judgment. *He.* **6: 2.**

As they that must give account. *He.* **13: 17.**

So speak ye, and so do, as they that shall be judged by the law of liberty. *Ja.* **2: 12.**

Be ready always to give an answer to every man that asketh you a reason of the hope that is in you. *1 Pe.* **3: 15.**

The answer of a good conscience toward God. *1 Pe.* **3: 21.**

The judgment of the great day. *Jude* **1: 6.**

Fear God, and give glory to him; for the hour of his judgment is come. *Re.* **14: 7.**

See also

Christ, the Judge; Cost; Fable; God, the Judge; Judgment; Judgment, the Last; Responsibility.

Accumulation

David . . . died in a good old age, full of days, riches, and honour. *1 Ch.* **29: 26, 28.**

He heapeth up riches, and knoweth not who shall gather them. *Ps.* **39: 6.**

Behold, these are the ungodly, who prosper in the world; they increase in riches *Ps.* **73:12.**

That our garners may be full, affording all manner of store: that our sheep may bring forth thousands and ten thousands in our streets. *Ps.* **144: 13.**

So shall thy barns be filled with plenty. *Pr.* **3: 10.**

Though he heap up silver as the dust, and prepare raiment as the clay; He may prepare it, but the just shall put it on, and the innocent shall divide the silver. *Jb.* **27: 16, 17.**

I will pull down my barns, and build greater; and there will I bestow all my fruits and my goods. *Lu.* **12: 18.**

I will say to my soul, Soul, thou hast much goods laid up for many years; take thine ease. *Lu.* **12: 19.**

So is he that layeth up treasure for himself, and is not rich toward God. *Lu.* **12: 21.**

See also

Goods; Harvest; Mass; Riches; Store.

Accuracy

Ye shall do no unrighteousness in judgment, in meteyard, in weight, or in measure. *Le.* 19: 35.

Just balances, just weights, a just ephah, and a just hin, shall ye have. *Le.* 19: 36.

Thou shalt have a perfect and just weight, a perfect and just measure shalt thou have. *De.* 25: 15.

He weigheth the waters by measure. *Jb.* 28: 25.

Let me be weighed in an even balance, that God may know mine integrity. *Jb.* 31: 6.

The judgments of the Lord are true and righteous altogether. *Ps.* 19: 9.

As a faithful witness in heaven. *Ps.* 89: 37.

A false balance is abomination to the Lord: but a just weight is his delight. *Pr.* 11: 1.

A faithful witness will not lie. *Pr.* 14: 5.

A just weight and balance are the Lord's. *Pr.* 16: 11.

Falsifying the balances by deceit. *Am.* 8: 5.

Shall I count them pure with the wicked balances, and with the bag of deceitful weights? *Mi.* 6: 11.

I lifted up mine eyes again, and looked, and behold a man with a measuring line in his hand. *Zch.* 2: 1.

With what measure ye mete, it shall be measured to you again. *Mat.* 7: 2.

Thou hast been faithful over a few things, I will make thee ruler over many things. *Mat.* 25: 21.

Good measure, pressed down, and shaken together, and running over. *Lu.* 6: 38.

Who then is that faithful and wise steward? *Lu.* 12: 42.

I know that the witness which he witnesseth of me is true. *Jn.* 5: 32.

He that saw it bare record, and his record is true. *Jn.* 19: 35.

The measure of the stature of the fulness of Christ. *Ep.* 4: 13.

We also bear record; and ye know that our record is true. *3 Jn.* 12.

These are the true sayings of God. *Re.* 19: 9.

See also

Balance; Measure; Truth; Weight.

Accusation

Thou chargest me to day with a fault concerning this woman. *2 S.* 3: 8.

Hearest thou not how many things they witness against thee? *Mat.* 27: 13.

The chief priests accused him of many things. *Mk.* 15: 3.

Do violence to no man, neither accuse any falsely. *Lu.* 3: 14.

If I have taken any thing from any man by false accusation, I restore him fourfold. *Lu.* 19: 8.

Woman, where are those thine accusers? hath no man condemned thee? *Jn.* 8: 10.

What accusation bring ye against this man? *Jn.* 18: 29.

Then they suborned men, which said, We have heard him speak blasphemous words against Moses, and against God. *Ac.* 6: 11.

See also

Charge; Condemnation; Denunciation.

Achievement

Thus the heavens and earth were finished. *Ge.* 2: 1.

The desire accomplished is sweet to the soul. *Pr.* 13: 19.

Thy builders have perfected thy beauty. *Eze.* 27: 4.

The Lord will do great things. *Jo.* 2: 21.

How am I straitened till it be accomplished! *Lu.* 12: 50.

My meat is to do the will of him that sent me, and to finish his work. *Jn.* 4: 34.

Jesus knowing that all things were now accomplished, that the scripture might be fulfilled, saith, I thirst. *Jn.* 19: 28.

I have fought a good fight, I have finished my course, I have kept the faith. *2 Ti.* 4: 7.

Therefore, . . . let us go on unto perfection. *He.* 6: 1.

See also

Accomplishment; Attainment; Completion; Fulfilment; Success.

Acquaintance

Acquaint now thyself with him, and be at peace. *Jb.* 22: 21.

It was not an enemy that reproached me: . . . But it was thou, a man mine equal, my guide, and mine acquaintance. *Ps.* 55: 12, 13.

Thou . . . art acquainted with all my ways. *Ps.* 139: 3.

Acquainting mine heart with wisdom. *Ec.* 2: 3.

He is despised and rejected of men; a man of sorrows, and acquainted with grief. *Is.* 53: 3.

He answered and said, Verily, I say unto you, I know you not. *Mat.* 25: 12.

She calleth her friends and her neighbours together, saying, Rejoice with me. *Lu.* 15: 9.

He denied him, saying, Woman, I know him not. *Lu.* 22: 57.

All his acquaintance . . . stood afar off, beholding these things. *Lu.* 23: 49.

See also

Companionship; Fellowship; Friendship; Knowledge.

Acquiescence

If sinners entice thee, consent thou not. *Pr.* 1: 10.

With her much fair speech she caused him to yield. *Pr.* 7: 21.

Yielding pacifieth great offences. *Ec.* 10: 4.

He giveth his cheek to him that smiteth him. *La.* 3: 30.

He consented to them in this matter, and proved them ten days. *Da.* 1: 14.

Agree with thine adversary quickly. *Mat.* 5: 25.

I say to this man, Go, and he goeth; and to another, Come, and he cometh; and to my servant, Do this, and he doeth it. *Mat.* 8: 9.

Didst not thou agree with me for a penny? *Mat.* 20: 13.

Render therefore unto Caesar the things which are Caesar's. *Mat.* 22: 21.

Why call ye me, Lord, Lord, and do not the things which I say? *Lu.* 6: 46.

Ye allow the deeds of your fathers. *Lu.* 11: 48.

The Jews also assented, saying that these things were so. *Ac.* 24: 9.

Yield yourselves unto God. *Ro.* 6: 13.

Wives, submit yourselves unto your own husbands. *Ep.* 5: 22.

See also

Affirmation; Agreement; Confirmation; Consent.

Acquisition

It is he that giveth thee power to get wealth. *De.* 8: 18.

Doth Job fear God for nought? *Jb.* 1: 9.

Through thy precepts I get understanding. *Ps.* 119: 104.

So are the ways of every one that is greedy of gain. *Pr.* 1: 19.

Wisdom is the principal thing; therefore get wisdom: and with all thy getting get understanding. *Pr.* 4: 7.

He that is greedy of gain troubleth his own house. *Pr.* 15: 27.

How much better is it to get wisdom than gold! and to get understanding rather to be chosen than silver! *Pr.* 16: 16.

He coveteth greedily all the day long. *Pr.* 21: 26.

He that by usury and unjust gain increaseth his substance, he shall gather it for him that will pity the poor. *Pr.* 28: 8.

A time to get, and a time to lose; a time to keep, and a time to cast away. *Ec.* 3: 6.

He that getteth riches, and not by right, shall leave them in the midst of his days. *Je.* 17: 11.

The prince asketh, and the judge asketh for a reward. *Mi.* 7: 3.

What is a man profited, if he shall gain the whole world, and lose his own soul? *Mat.* 16: 26.

So is he that layeth up treasure for himself, and is not rich toward God. *Lu.* 12: 21.

Lord, thy pound hath gained ten pounds. *Lu.* 19: 16.

Go to now, ye that say, To day or to morrow we will go into such a city, and continue there a year, and buy and sell, and get gain. *Ja.* 4: 13.

See also

Avarice; Covetousness; Gain; Greed; Riches; Wealth; Worldliness.

Acquittal

Who ever perished, being innocent? or where were the righteous cut off? *Jb.* 4: 7.

Thou wilt not acquit me from mine iniquity. *Jb.* 10: 14.

Judge me, O Lord, according to my righteousness. *Ps.* 7: 8.

I shall be innocent from the great transgression. *Ps.* 19: 13.

Thou hast cast all my sins behind thy back. *Is.* 38: 17.

Before him innocency was found in me. *Da.* 6: 22.

Thou wilt cast all their sins into the depths of the sea. *Mi.* 7: 19.

The Lord is slow to anger, and great in power, and will not at all acquit the wicked. *Na.* 1: 3.

If ye had known what this meaneth, I will have mercy, and not sacrifice, ye would not have condemned the guiltless. *Mat.* 12: 7.

The governor said, Why, what evil hath he done? *Mat.* 27: 23.

He took water, and washed his hands before the multitude, saying, I am innocent of the blood of this just person. *Mat.* 27: 24.

And now, brethren, I wot that through ignorance ye did it. *Ac.* 3: 17.

There is laid up for me a crown of righteousness, which the Lord, the righteous judge, shall give me at that day. *2 Ti.* 4: 8.

See also

Innocence; Judgment; Sinlessness.

Action

And Lot . . . said, Up, get you out of this place. *Ge.* 19: 14.

Go now ye that are men, and serve the Lord. *Ex.* 10: 11.

Your eyes have seen all the great acts of the Lord which he did. *De.* 11: 7.

Up; for this is the day. *Ju.* 4: 14.

The Lord is a God of knowledge, and by him actions are weighed. *1 S.* 2: 3.

Arise therefore, and be doing, and the Lord be with thee. *1 Ch.* 22: 16.

Praise him for his mighty acts. *Ps.* 150: 2.

Jesus saith unto him, Rise, take up thy bed, and walk. *Jn.* 5: 8.

Moses, . . . mighty in word and deed. *Ac.* 7: 22.

Not by works of righteousness which we have done, but according to his mercy he saved us. *Tit.* 3: 5.

Be ye doers of the word, and not hearers only. *Ja.* 1: 22.

If any be a hearer of the word, and not a doer, he is like unto a man beholding his natural face in a glass: For he beholdeth himself, and goeth away, and straightway forgetteth what manner of man he was. *Ja.* 1: 23, 24.

Faith, if it hath not works, is dead. *Ja.* 2: 17.

Let us not love in word, neither in tongue; but in deed. *1 Jn.* 3: 18.

See also

Activity; Christ, Work of; Deed; Happening; Motion; Occupation; Operation; Service; Task; Toil; Work.

Activity

If thou knowest any men of activity among them, then make them rulers. *Ge.* 47: 6.

Fulfil your works, your daily tasks. *Ex.* 5: 13.

Six days shalt thou labour, and do all thy work. *Ex.* 20: 9.

As thy servant was busy here and there, he was gone. *1 K.* 20: 40.

The people had a mind to work. *Ne.* 4: 6.

It is vain for you to rise up early, to sit up late, to eat the bread of sorrows. *Ps.* 127: 2.

Seest thou a man diligent in his business? he shall stand before kings. *Pr.* 22: 29.

Great in counsel, and mighty in work: . . . to give every one according to his ways, and according to the fruit of his doings. *Je.* 32: 19.

As they went, they were cleansed. *Lu.* 17: 14.

I must work the works of him that sent me, while it is day. *Jn.* 9: 4.

Let us not be weary in well doing: for in due season we shall reap, if we faint not. *Ga.* 6: 9.

That ye might walk worthy of the Lord, . . . being fruitful in every good work. *Col.* 1: 10.

Study to shew thyself approved unto God, a workman that needeth not to be ashamed. *2 Ti.* 2: 15.

See also

Action; Business; Busybody; Diligence; Quickness.

Adaptation

I was eyes to the blind, and feet was I to the lame. *Jb.* 29: 15.

To every thing there is a season, and a time to every purpose under the heaven: A time to be born, and a time to die; a time to plant, and a time to pluck up that which is planted. *Ec.* 3: 1, 2.

Doth the plowman plow all day to sow? doth he open and break the clods of his ground? *Is.* 28: 24.

John the Baptist came neither eating bread nor drinking wine; . . . The Son of man is come eating and drinking. *Lu.* 7: 33, 34.

All things are lawful unto me, but all things are not expedient. *1 Co.* 6: 12.

For though I be free from all men, yet have I made myself servant unto all, that I might gain the more. *1 Co.* 9: 19.

I am made all things to all men, that I might by all means save some. *1 Co.* 9: 22.

Addition

Ye shall not add unto the word which I command you, neither shall ye diminish ought from it. *De.* 4: 2.

They took no gain of money. *Ju.* 5: 19.

Add iniquity unto their iniquity. *Ps.* 69: 27.

Let the beauty of the Lord our God be upon us. *Ps.* 90: 17.

Length of days, and long life, and peace, shall they add to thee. *Pr.* 3: 2.

He that is greedy of gain troubleth his own house. *Pr.* 15: 27.

The heart of the wise teacheth his mouth, and addeth learning to his lips. *Pr.* 16: 23.

Precept must be upon precept, precept upon precept; line upon line, line upon line; here a little, and there a little. *Is.* 28: 10.

The Lord hath added grief to my sorrow. *Je.* 45: 3.

Seek ye first the kingdom of God, and his righteousness; and all these things shall be added unto you. *Mat.* 6: 33.

The Lord added to the church daily such as should be saved. *Ac.* 2: 47.

Much people was added unto the Lord. *Ac.* 11: 24.

The law . . . was added because of transgressions. *Ga.* 3: 19.

Add to your faith virtue. *2 Pe.* 1: 5.

See also

Coherence; Gain; Increase; Profit.

Adept

Skilful to work. *2 Ch.* 2: 14.

Play skilfully with a loud noise. *Ps.* 33: 3.

He . . . guided them by the skilfulness of his hands. *Ps.* 78: 72.

The work of our hands establish thou it. *Ps.* 90: 17.

The race is not to the swift, . . . nor yet favour to men of skill. *Ec.* 9: 11.

They all hold swords being expert in war. *S. of S.* 3: 8.

I am now come forth to give thee skill and understanding. *Da.* 9: 22.

I know thee to be expert in all customs and questions which are among the Jews. *Ac.* 26: 3.

See also

Aptitude; Expert; Mastery; Skill; Workmanship.

Adequacy

The land, behold it is large enough for them. *Ge.* 34: 21.

The stranger, and the fatherless, and the widow, which are within thy gates, shall come, and shall eat and be satisfied. *De.* 14: 29.

The Lord shall make thee plenteous. *De.* 28: 11.

The Lord shall open unto thee his good treasure. *De.* 28: 12.

I shall be satisfied, when I awake, with thy likeness. *Ps.* 17: 15.

The Lord . . . plentifully rewardeth the proud doer. *Ps.* 31: 23.

The Lord is . . . plenteous in mercy. *Ps.* 103: 8.

He satisfieth the longing soul, and filleth the hungry soul with goodness. *Ps.* 107: 9.

Thou openest thine hand, and satisfieth the desire of every living thing. *Ps.* 145: 16.

The righteous eateth to the satisfying of his soul: but the belly of the wicked shall want. *Pr.* 13: 25.

He that tilleth his land shall have plenty of bread. *Pr.* 28: 19.

There are three things that are never satisfied, yea, four things say not, It is enough: The grave; and the barren womb; the earth that is not filled with water; and the fire that saith not, It is enough. *Pr.* 30: 15, 16.

All the rivers run into the sea; yet the sea is not full. *Ec.* 1: 7.

He that loveth silver shall not be satisfied with silver. *Ec.* 5: 10.

He . . . is as death, and cannot be satisfied. *Hab.* 2: 5.

Sufficient unto the day is the evil thereof. *Mat.* 6: 34.

The harvest truly is plenteous. *Mat.* 9: 37.

In my father's house are many mansions. *Jn.* 14: 2.

Shew us the Father, and it sufficeth us. *Jn.* 14: 8.

Our sufficiency is of God. *2 Co.* 3: 5.

He which soweth bountifully shall reap also bountifully. *2 Co.* 9: 6.

God is able to make all grace abound toward you; that ye, always having sufficiency in all things, may abound to every good work. *2 Co.* 9: 8.

My grace is sufficient for thee. *2 Co.* 12: 9.

On the east three gates; on the north three gates; on the south three gates; on the west three gates. *Re.* 21: 13.

See also

Fullness; Plenty; Satisfaction; Sufficiency.

Administration

O that my ways were directed to keep thy statutes! *Ps.* 119: 5.

Commit thy works unto the Lord. *Pr.* 16: 3.

The government shall be upon his shoulder. *Is.* 9: 6.

I will direct their work in truth. *Is.* 61: 8.

There are differences of administration, but the same Lord. *1 Co.* **12: 5.**

This grace . . . is administered by us to the glory of the same Lord. *2 Co.* **8: 19.**

This abundance . . . is administered by us. *2 Co.* **8: 20.**

The administration of this service . . . is abundant also by many thanksgivings unto God. *2 Co.* **9: 12.**

See also

Conduct; Dispensation; Execution; Operation; Supervision.

Admiration

I will extol thee, O Lord. *Ps.* **30: 1.**

Beautiful for situation, the joy of the whole earth, is mount Zion. *Ps.* **48: 2.**

Let another man praise thee, and not thine own mouth. *Pr.* **27: 2.**

He hath made every thing beautiful in his time. *Ec.* **3: 11.**

The people were astonished at his doctrines. *Mat.* **7: 28.**

All they that heard it wondered. *Lu.* **2: 18.**

He shall come to be glorified in his saints, and to be admired in all them that believe. *2 Th.* **1: 10.**

Having men's persons in admiration. *Jude* **16.**

I wondered with great admiration. *Re.* **17: 6.**

See also

Esteem; Praise; Regard; Reverence; Wonder.

Admission

This is none other than the house of God; and this is the gate of heaven. *Ge.* **28: 17.**

I had rather be a doorkeeper in the house of my God, than to dwell in the tents of wickedness. *Ps.* **84: 10.**

Enter into his gates with thanksgiving. *Ps.* **100: 4.**

The entrance of thy words giveth light. *Ps.* **119: 130.**

Open ye the gates, that the righteous nation which keepeth the truth may enter in. *Is.* **26: 2.**

The glory of the Lord came into the house by the way of the gate. *Eze.* **43: 4.**

Enter ye in at the strait gate. *Mat.* **7: 13.**

Strait is the gate, and narrow is the way, which leadeth unto life. *Mat.* **7: 14.**

Not every one that saith unto me, Lord, Lord, shall enter into the kingdom of heaven. *Mat.* **7: 21.**

It is easier for a camel to go through the eye of a needle, than for a rich man to enter into the kingdom of God. *Mat.* **19: 24.**

While they went to buy, the bridegroom came; and they that were ready went in with him to the marriage: and the door was shut. *Mat.* **25: 10.**

Trouble me not: the door is now shut. *Lu.* **11: 7.**

Strive to enter in at the strait gate: for many, I say unto you, will seek to enter in, and shall not be able. *Lu.* **13: 24.**

I am the door. *Jn.* **10: 9.**

For yourselves, brethren, know our entrance in unto you, that it was not in vain. *1 Th.* **2: 1.**

An entrance shall be ministered unto you abundantly into the everlasting kingdom of our Lord and Saviour Jesus Christ. *2 Pe.* **1: 11.**

I . . . have the keys of hell and of death. *Re.* **1: 18.**

Blessed are they that do his commandments, that they may have right to the tree of life, and may enter in through the gates into the city. *Re.* **22: 14.**

See also

Avowal; Door; Entrance; Reception.

Admonition

How have I hated instruction, and my heart despised reproof. *Pr.* **5: 12.**

The law is light; and reproofs of instruction are the way of life. *Pr.* **6: 23.**

He that refuseth reproof erreth. *Pr.* **10: 17.**

If thou warn the wicked, and he turn not from his wickedness, nor from his wicked way, he shall die in his iniquity; but thou hast delivered thy soul. *Eze.* **3: 19.**

What I say unto you I say unto all, Watch. *Mk.* **13: 37.**

All these things . . . are written for our admonition. *1 Co.* **10: 11.**

Bring them up in the nurture and admonition of the Lord. *Ep.* **6: 4.**

See also

Caution; Rebuke; Reproof; Warning.

Adoption

As many as received him, to them gave he power to become the sons of God, even to them that believe on his name. *Jn.* **1: 12.**

Ye have received the Spirit of adoption, whereby we cry, Abba, Father. *Ro.* **8: 15.**

The Spirit itself beareth witness with our spirit, that we are the children of God: And if children, then heirs; heirs of God, and joint-heirs with Christ. *Ro.* **8: 16, 17.**

We ourselves groan within ourselves, waiting for the adoption, to wit, the redemption of our body. *Ro.* **8: 23.**

I will receive you, And will be a Father unto you, and ye shall be my sons and daughters, saith the Lord Almighty. *2 Co.* **6: 17, 18.**

God sent forth his Son, . . . To redeem them that were under the law, that we might receive the adoption of sons. *Ga.* **4: 4, 5.**

Thou art no more a servant, but a son; and if a son, then an heir of God through Christ. *Ga.* **4: 7.**

Having predestinated us unto the adoption of children by Jesus Christ to himself, according to the good pleasure of his will. *Ep.* **1: 5.**

Behold, what manner of love the Father hath bestowed upon us, that we should be called the sons of God. *1 Jn.* **3: 1.**

See also

Heir; Son.

Adoration

Put off thy shoes from off thy feet, for the place whereon thou standest is holy ground. *Ex.* **3: 5.**

I fell down before the Lord. *De.* **9: 18.**

Worship the Lord in the beauty of holiness. *1 Ch.* **16: 29.**

O come, let us worship and bow down: let us kneel before the Lord our maker. *Ps.* **95: 6.**

O sing unto the Lord a new song: sing unto the Lord, all the earth. *Ps.* **96: 1.**

Exalt the Lord our God, and worship at

his holy hill; for the Lord our God is holy. *Ps.* **99: 9.**

Bless the Lord, O my soul: and all that is within me, bless his holy name. *Ps.* **103: 1.**

Holy and reverend is his name. *Ps.* **111: 9.**

Not unto us, O Lord, not unto us, but unto thy name give glory. *Ps.* **115: 1.**

Both young men, and maidens; old men, and children: let them praise the name of the Lord. *Ps.* **148: 12, 13.**

Holy, holy, holy, is the Lord of hosts: the whole earth is full of his glory. *Is.* **6: 3.**

We have seen his star in the east, and are come to worship him. *Mat.* **2: 2.**

These all continued with one accord in prayer. *Ac.* **1: 14.**

I will therefore that men pray every where, lifting up holy hands. *1 Ti.* **2: 8.**

To the only wise God our Saviour, be glory and majesty, dominion and power, both now and ever. Amen. *Jude* **1: 25.**

Holy, holy, holy, Lord God Almighty, which was, and is, and is to come. *Re.* **4: 8.**

And they sung a new song, saying, Thou art worthy. *Re.* **5: 9.**

The temple was filled with smoke from the glory of God, and from his power. *Re.* **15: 8.**

I fell at his feet to worship him. *Re.* **19: 10.**

See also

Adulation; Awe; Christ, Worship of; Devotion; God, Adoration of; God, Worship of; Honor; Respect; Reverence; Veneration.

Adornment

Put on thy beautiful garments, O Jerusalem. *Is.* **52: 1.**

To give unto them . . . the garment of praise for the spirit of heaviness. *Is.* **61: 3.**

He hath clothed me with the garments of salvation. *Is.* **61: 10.**

I have caused thine iniquity to pass from thee, and I will clothe thee with change of raiment. *Zch.* **3: 4.**

How camest thou in hither not having a wedding garment? *Mat.* **22: 12.**

Jesus, moved with compassion, put forth his hand, and touched him. *Mk.* **1: 41.**

I will therefore that . . . women adorn themselves in modest apparel. *1 Ti.* **2: 8, 9.**

Shewing all good fidelity; that they may adorn the doctrine of God our Saviour in all things. *Tit.* **2: 10.**

Whose adorning let it not be that outward adorning of plaiting the hair, and of wearing of gold, or of putting on of apparel; But let it be the hidden man of the heart, in that which is not coruptible, even the ornament of a meek and quiet spirit. *1 Pe.* **3: 3, 4.**

See also

Beauty; Ornament.

Adulation

They flatter with their tongue. *Ps.* **5: 9.**

With flattering lips and with a double heart do they speak. *Ps.* **12: 2.**

The words of his mouth are smoother than butter. *Ps.* **55: 21.**

With much fair speech she caused him to yield. *Pr.* **7: 21.**

Behold, thou art fair, my love; behold thou art fair. *S. of S.* **4: 1.**

Thou art beautiful, O my love, as Tirzah,

comely as Jerusalem, terrible as an army with banners. *S. of S.* **6: 4.**

They loved the praise of men more more than the praise of God. *Jn.* **12: 43.**

See also

Adoration; Commendation; Eulogy; Homage; Honor; Praise; Reverence; Veneration.

Adult

As the man is, so is his strength. *Ju.* **8: 21.**

David . . . died in a good old age, full of days, riches, and honour. *1 Ch.* **29: 26, 28.**

He is green before the sun. *Jb.* **8: 16.**

Are thy days as the days of man? *Jb.* **10: 5.**

Man goeth forth unto his work and to his labour until the evening. *Ps.* **104: 23.**

That our sons may be as plants grown up in their youth. *Ps.* **144: 12.**

Length of days, and long life, and peace, shall they add to thee. *Pr.* **3: 2.**

Train up a child in the way he should go: and when he is old, he will not depart from it. *Pr.* **22: 6.**

Jesus himself began to be about thirty years of age. *Lu.* **3: 23.**

He is of age; ask him. *Jn.* **9: 23.**

What man knoweth the things of a man, save the spirit of man which is in him? *1 Co.* **11.**

When I became a man, I put away childish things. *1 Co.* **13: 11.**

See also

Age; Man; Maturity; Woman.

Adulteration

Ye shall do no unrighteousness in judgment. *Le.* **19: 35.**

Their wine is the poison of dragons. *De.* **32: 33.**

They that go to seek mixed wine. *Pr.* **23: 30.**

Thy silver is become dross, thy wine mixed with water. *Is.* **1: 22.**

The Lord our God hath . . . given us water of gall to drink. *Je.* **8: 14.**

As the toes of the feet were part of iron, and part of clay, so the kingdom shall be partly strong, and partly broken. *Da.* **2: 42.**

Iron is not mixed with clay. *Da.* **2: 43.**

See also

Abasement; Counterfeit; Defilement; Taint.

Adultery

Thou shalt not commit adultery. *Ex.* **20: 14.**

The eye also of the adulterer waiteth for the twilight. *Jb.* **24: 15.**

Whosoever looketh on a woman to lust after her hath committed adultery with her already in his heart. *Mat.* **5: 28.**

For out of the heart proceed . . . adulteries. *Mat.* **15: 19.**

Know ye not that the unrighteous shall not inherit the kingdom of God? *1 Co.* **6: 9.**

Let not the wife depart from her husband. *1 Co.* **7: 10.**

Walk in the Spirit, and ye shall not fulfil the lust of the flesh. *Ga.* **5: 16.**

See also

Carnality; Debauchery; Lust; Sensuality.

Advance

Speak unto the children of Israel, that they go forward. *Ex.* **14: 15.**

Arise, take thy journey before the people. *De.* 10: 11.

Now therefore arise, go over this Jordan, thou, and all this people. *Jos.* 1: 2.

The people went up into the city, every man straight before him, and they took the city. *Jos.* 6: 20.

Get you early on your way. *Ju.* 19: 9.

I will surely go forth with you myself also. 2 *S.* 18: 2.

He . . . went . . . forty days and forty nights unto Horeb the mount of God. *1 K.* 19: 8.

O God, when thou wentest forth before thy people, when thou didst march through the wilderness. *Ps.* 68: 7.

He . . . made his own people to go forth like sheep. *Ps.* 78: 50, 52.

They shall march every one on his ways, and they shall not break their ranks. *Jo.* 2: 7.

Thou wentest forth for the salvation of thy people. *Hab.* 3: 13.

Arise, let us go hence. *Jn.* 14: 31.

This I say then, Walk in the Spirit. *Ga.* 5: 16.

See also
Evolution; Future; Growth; Progress.

Advancement

I will promote thee unto very great honour. *Nu.* 22: 17.

The trees went forth on a time to anoint a king over them. *Ju.* 9: 8.

It is the Lord that advanced Moses and Aaron. *1 S.* 12: 6.

I took thee from the sheepcote, . . . to be ruler over my people. 2 *S.* 7: 8.

Lead me to the rock that is higher than I. *Ps.* 61: 2.

Promotion cometh neither from the east, nor from the west, nor from the south. But God is the judge. *Ps.* 75: 6, 7.

I will make him my firstborn, higher than the kings of the earth. *Ps.* 89: 27.

The stone which the builders refused is become the head stone of the corner. *Ps.* 118: 22.

The last shall be first. *Mat.* 20: 16.

I will make thee ruler over many things. *Mat.* 25: 21.

Friend, go up higher. *Lu.* 14: 10.

He that humbleth himself shall be exalted. *Lu.* 14: 11.

See also
Advance; Evolution; Improvement; Progress.

Advantage

Turn ye not aside: for then should ye go after vain things, which cannot profit. *1 S.* 12: 21.

To obey is better than sacrifice. *1 S.* 15: 22.

Can a man be profitable unto God, as he that is wise may be profitable unto himself? *Jb.* 22: 2.

What profit shall I have, if I be cleansed from my sin? *Jb.* 35: 3.

Wisdom is better than rubies. *Pr.* 8: 11.

Riches profit not in the day of wrath. *Pr.* 11: 4.

In all labour there is profit. *Pr.* 14: 23.

What profit hath a man of all his labour which he taketh under the sun? *Ec.* 1: 3.

A good name is better than precious ointment. *Ec.* 7: 1.

Thy love is better than wine. *S. of S.* 1: 2.

She . . . was nothing bettered, but rather grew worse. *Mk.* 5: 26.

For what is a man advantaged, if he gain the whole world, and lose himself, or be cast away? *Lu.* 9: 25.

I made myself servant unto all, that I might gain the more. *1 Co.* 9: 19.

To live is Christ, and to die is gain. *Ph.* 1: 21.

What things were gain to me, those I counted loss for Christ. *Ph.* 3: 7.

Godliness is profitable unto all things. *1 Ti.* 4: 8.

Chastening . . . yieldeth the peaceable fruit of righteousness. *He.* 12: 11.

See also
Benefit; Gain; Profit.

Advent

Art thou he that should come, or do we look for another? *Mat.* 11: 3.

This is he, of whom it is written, Behold, I send my messenger before thy face, which shall prepare thy way before thee. *Mat.* 11: 10.

Tell ye the daughter of Sion, Behold, thy King cometh unto thee. *Mat.* 21: 5.

Hosanna to the son of David: Blessed is he that cometh in the name of the Lord; Hosanna in the highest. *Mat.* 21: 9.

Then shall they see the Son of man coming in a cloud with power and great glory. *Lu.* 21: 27.

Lift up your heads; for your redemption draweth nigh. *Lu.* 21: 28.

This generation shall not pass away, till all be fulfilled. *Lu.* 21: 32.

I am the voice of one crying in the wilderness, Make straight the way of the Lord. *Jn.* 1: 23.

After me cometh a man which is preferred before me. *Jn.* 1: 30.

This same Jesus . . . shall so come in like manner as ye have seen him go into heaven. *Ac.* 1: 11.

The sun shall be turned into darkness, and the moon into blood, before that great and notable day of the Lord come. *Ac.* 2: 20.

Judge nothing before the time, until the Lord come. *1 Co.* 4: 5.

As often as ye eat this bread, and drink this cup, ye do shew the Lord's death till he come. *1 Co.* 11: 26.

The day of the Lord will come as a thief in the night. *2 Pe.* 3: 10.

Behold, the Lord cometh with ten thousands of his saints. *Jude* 1: 14.

Behold, he cometh with clouds; and every eye shall see him. *Re.* 1: 7.

See also
Approach; Coming; Second.

Adventure

The Lord went before them by day in a pillar of a cloud, to lead them the way; and by night in a pillar of fire, to give them light. *Ex.* 13: 21.

Sing ye to the Lord, for he hath triumphed gloriously; the horse and his rider hath he thrown into the sea. *Ex.* 15: 21.

We gat our bread with the peril of our lives. *La.* 5: 9.

Sirs, I perceive that this voyage will be with hurt and much damage. *Ac.* **27: 10.**

When they had taken up the anchors, they committed themselves unto the sea. *Ac.* **27: 40.**

So it came to pass, that they escaped all safe to land. *Ac.* **27: 44.**

As it is written, For thy sake we are killed all the day long. *Ro.* **8: 36.**

Nay, in all these things we are more than conquerors through him that loved us. *Ro.* **8: 37.**

Howbeit whereinsoever any is bold, . . . I am bold also. *2 Co.* **11: 21.**

In journeyings often, in perils of waters, in perils of robbers, in perils by mine own countrymen, in perils by the heathen, in perils in the city, in perils in the wilderness, in perils in the sea. *2 Co.* **11: 26.**

He was caught up into paradise, and heard unspeakable words. *2 Co.* **12: 4.**

Endure hardness as a good soldier of Jesus Christ. *2 Ti.* **2: 3.**

In the last days perilous times shall come. *2 Ti.* **3: 1.**

Abraham . . . went out, not knowing whither he went. *He.* **11: 8.**

Who through faith subdued kingdoms, wrought righteousness, obtained promises, stopped the mouths of lions, Quenched the violence of fire, escaped the edge of the sword, out of weakness were made strong, waxed valiant in fight, turned to flight the armies of the aliens. *He.* **11: 33, 34.**

See also

Courage; Danger; Heroism; Pilgrim; Pioneer.

Adversary

The Lord is departed from thee, and is become thine enemy. *1 S.* **28: 16.**

The hand of our God was upon us, and he delivered us from the hand of the enemy. *Ezr.* **8: 31.**

Satan came also among them. *Jb.* **1: 6.**

Oh . . . that mine adversary had written a book. *Jb.* **31: 35.**

If thine enemy be hungry, give him bread to eat; and if he be thirsty, give him water to drink. *Pr.* **25: 21.**

Who is mine adversary? Let him come near to me. *Is.* **50: 8.**

The adversary hath spread out his hand upon all her pleasant things. *La.* **1: 10.**

Agree with thine adversary quickly, whiles thou art in the way with him. *Mat.* **5: 25.**

I say unto you, Love your enemies. *Mat.* **5: 44.**

A man's foes shall be they of his own household. *Mat.* **10: 36.**

He that is not with me is against me. *Mat.* **12: 30.**

Thou couldest have no power at all against me, except it were given thee from above. *Jn.* **19: 11.**

He must reign till he hath put all enemies under his feet. *1 Co.* **15: 25.**

The last enemy that shall be destroyed is death. *1 Co.* **15: 26.**

Put on the whole armour of God, that ye may be able to stand against the wiles of the devil. *Ep.* **6: 11.**

Give none occasion to the adversary to speak reproachfully. *1 Ti.* **5: 14.**

Whosoever therefore will be a friend of the world is the enemy of God. *Ja.* **4: 4.**

Your adversary the devil, as a roaring lion, walketh about, seeking whom he may devour. *1 Pe.* **5: 8.**

See also

Antagonism; Antichrist; Enemy; Foe; Opponent; Opposition; Satan.

Adversity

Ye shall sow your seed in vain, for your enemies shall eat it. *Le.* **26: 16.**

Therefore shalt thou serve thine enemies which the Lord shall send against thee, in hunger, and in thirst, and in nakedness, and in want of all things: and he shall put a yoke of iron upon thy neck, until he have destroyed thee. *De.* **28: 48.**

They shall be burnt with hunger, and devoured with burning heat, and with bitter destruction. *De.* **32: 24.**

God did vex them with all adversity. *2 Ch.* **15: 6.**

Shew me wherefore thou contendest with me. *Jb.* **10: 2.**

Man that is born of a woman is of few days, and full of trouble. *Jb.* **14: 1.**

Many are the afflictions of the righteous: but the Lord delivereth him out of them all. *Ps.* **34: 19.**

God is our refuge and strength, a very present help in trouble. *Ps.* **46: 1.**

Thou shalt not be afraid for the terror by night; nor for the arrow that flieth by day. *Ps.* **91: 5.**

It is good for me that I have been afflicted. *Ps.* **119: 71.**

A friend loveth at all times, and a brother is born for adversity. *Pr.* **17: 17.**

In the day of prosperity be joyful, but in the day of adversity consider. *Ec.* **7: 14.**

They shall look unto the earth; and behold trouble and darkness, dimness of anguish. *Is.* **8: 22.**

I will give thee the treasures of darkness. *Is.* **45: 3.**

I have chosen thee in the furnace of affliction. *Is.* **48: 10.**

I will give . . . the valley of Achor for a door of hope. *Ho.* **2: 15.**

In the world ye shall have tribulation: but be of good cheer; I have overcome the world. *Jn.* **16: 33.**

Rejoicing in hope, patient in tribulation. *Ro.* **12: 12.**

Remember them that are in bonds, as bound with them. *He.* **13: 3.**

My brethren, count it all joy when ye fall into divers temptations; Knowing this, that the trying of your faith worketh patience. *Ja.* **1: 2, 3.**

Rejoice, inasmuch as ye are partakers of Christ's sufferings. *1 Pe.* **4: 13.**

These are they which came out of great tribulation. *Re.* **7: 14.**

See also

Affliction; Calamity; Catastrophe; Depression; Disaster; Distress; Gloom; Grief; Misery; Misfortune; **Suffering;** Trial; Tribulation; Trouble.

Advice

The thing that thou doest is not good. *Ex.* 18: 17.

I will give thee counsel, and God shall be with thee. *Ex.* 18: 19.

He forsook the counsel of the old men. *1 K.* 12: 8.

Who is this that darkeneth counsel by words without knowledge? *Jb.* 38: 2.

We took sweet counsel together, and walked unto the house of God in company. *Ps.* 55: 14.

He that hearkeneth unto counsel is wise. *Pr.* 12: 15.

Hear counsel, and receive instruction. *Pr.* 19: 20.

Come now, and let us reason together, saith the Lord. *Is.* 1: 18.

Therefore hear the counsel of the Lord. *Je.* 49: 20.

If thou warn the righteous man, that the righteous sin not, and he doth not sin, he shall surely live, because he is warned; also thou hast delivered thy soul. *Eze.* 3: 21.

Teaching and admonishing one another in psalms and hymns and spiritual songs. *Col.* 3: 16.

Admonish him as a brother. *2 Th.* 3: 15.

See also

Admonition; Counsel; Exhortation; Instruction.

Advocate

He bare the sin of many, and made intercession for the transgressors. *Is.* 53: 12.

The Spirit itself maketh intercession for us with groanings which cannot be uttered. *Ro.* 8: 26.

He ever liveth to make intercession for them. *He.* 7: 25.

We have such an high priest, who is set on the right hand of the throne of the Majesty in the heavens. *He.* 8: 1.

If any man sin, we have an advocate with the Father, Jesus Christ the righteous. *1 Jn.* 2: 1.

See also

Intercession.

Affectation

I hate every false way. *Ps.* 119: 104.

What shall be done unto thee, thou false tongue? *Ps.* 120: 3.

An hypocrite with his mouth destroyeth his neighbour. *Pr.* 11: 9.

When ye fast, be not, as the hypocrites, of a sad countenance. *Mat.* 6: 16.

Beware of the scribes, which . . . for a pretence make long prayers. *Mk.* 12: 38, 40.

That ye may be sincere and without offence till the day of Christ. *Ph.* 1: 10.

The one preach Christ of contention, not sincerely. *Ph.* 1: 16.

Whose adorning let it not be that outward adorning of plaiting the hair, and of wearing of gold, or of putting on of apparel; But let it be the inward man of the heart. *1 Pe.* 3: 3.

See also

Hypocrisy; Insincerity; Pretension.

Affection

Thy love to me was wonderful, passing the love of women. *2 S.* 1: 26.

How excellent is thy lovingkindness, O God! *Ps.* 36: 7.

Because thy lovingkindness is better than life, my lips shall praise thee. *Ps.* 63: 3.

Better is a dinner of herbs where love is, than a stalled ox and hatred therewith. *Pr.* 15: 17.

His banner over me was love. *S. of S.* 2: 4.

Love is strong as death. *S. of S.* 8: 6.

Many waters cannot quench love, neither can the floods drown it. *S. of S.* 8: 7.

I will mention the lovingkindnesses of the Lord. *Is.* 63: 7.

I have loved thee with an everlasting love. *Je.* 31: 3.

I drew them with cords of a man, with bands of love. *Ho.* 11: 4.

Where your treasure is, there will your heart be also. *Mat.* 6: 21.

God so loved the world, that he gave his only begotten Son, that whosoever believeth in him should not perish, but have everlasting life. *Jn.* 3: 16.

Be kindly affectioned one to another with brotherly love. *Ro.* 12: 10.

Set your affection on things above, not on things on the earth. *Col.* 3: 2.

Above all these things put on charity. *Col.* 3: 14.

Be thou an example of the believers, in word, in conversation, in charity. *1 Ti.* 4: 12.

Giving all diligence, add . . . to godliness brotherly kindness; and to brotherly kindness charity. *2 Pe.* 1: 5, 7.

If we love one another, God dwelleth in us. *1 Jn.* 4: 12.

See also

Attachment; Caress; Cherishment; Christ, Love of; Devotion; God, Love of; God, Love to; Kindness; Kiss; Love; Loving-kindness; Tenderness.

Affirmation

Let the whole earth be filled with his glory; Amen, and Amen. *Ps.* 72: 19.

Let all the people say, Amen. *Ps.* 106: 48.

Another confidently affirmed, saying, Of a truth this fellow also was with him. *Lu.* 22: 59.

Verily, verily, I say unto thee. *Jn.* 3: 3.

Jesus, which was dead, whom Paul affirmed to be alive. *Ac.* 25: 19.

All the promises of God in him are yea, and in him Amen. *2 Co.* 1: 20.

These things I will that thou affirm constantly. *Ti.* 3: 8.

See also

Acquiescence; Agreement; Announcement; Assent; Declaration; Profession; Protest.

Affliction

I was at ease, but he hath broken me asunder: he hath also taken me by my neck, and shaken me to pieces, and set me up for his mark. *Jb.* 16: 12.

When he giveth quietness, who then can make trouble? *Jb.* 34: 29.

Thou hast enlarged me when I was in distress. *Ps.* 4: 1.

This poor man cried. *Ps.* 34: 6.

None of them that trust in him shall be desolate. *Ps.* 34: 22.

We are consumed by thine anger, and by thy wrath are we troubled. *Ps.* 90: 7.

I have eaten ashes like bread, and mingled my drink with weeping. *Ps.* 102: 9.

Thou hast lifted me up, and cast me down. *Ps.* 102: 10.

If thou faint in the day of adversity, thy strength is small. *Pr.* 24: 10.

Behold, I have taken out of thine hand the cup of trembling; . . . thou shalt no more drink it again. *Is.* 51: 22.

For a small moment have I forsaken thee; but with great mercies will I gather thee. *Is.* 54: 7.

O thou afflicted, tossed with tempest, and not comforted, behold, I will lay thy stones with fair colours. *Is.* 54: 11.

The angel of his presence saved him. *Is.* 63: 9.

He doth not afflict willingly nor grieve the children of men. *La.* 3: 33.

We will return and build the desolate places. *Mal.* 1: 4.

Blessed are ye, when men shall revile you, and persecute you. *Mat.* 5: 11.

Who shall separate us from the love of Christ? shall tribulation, or distress, or persecution? *Ro.* 8: 35.

We are troubled on every side, yet not distressed. *2 Co.* 4: 8.

Our light affliction, which is but for a moment, worketh for us a far more exceeding and eternal weight of glory. *2 Co.* 4: 17.

I take pleasure in infirmities, in reproaches, in necessities, in persecutions, in distresses for Christ's sake. *2 Co.* 12: 10.

Pure religion . . . is this, To visit the fatherless and widows in their affliction. *Ja.* 1: 27.

See also
Adversity; Calamity; Chagrin; Depression; Disaster; Distress; Grief; Misery; Misfortune; Suffering; Trial; Tribulation; Trouble; Wretchedness.

Affront

How long will this people provoke me? *Nu.* 14: 11.

There came forth little children out of the city, and mocked him, and said unto him, Go up, thou bald head; go up, thou bald head. *2 K.* 2: 23.

When thou mockest, shall no man make thee ashamed? *Jb.* 11: 3.

Blessed is the man that walketh not in the counsel of the ungodly, . . . nor sitteth in the seat of the scornful. *Ps.* 1: 1.

Thou makest us a reproach to our neighbours, a scorn and a derision to them that are round about us. *Ps.* 44: 13.

How oft did they provoke him in the wilderness. *Ps.* 78: 40.

How long, ye simple ones, will ye love simplicity? and the scorners delight in their scorning? *Pr.* 1: 22.

A brother offended is harder to be won than a strong city. *Pr.* 18: 19.

Yielding pacifieth great offences. *Ec.* 10: 4.

Hear the word of the Lord, ye scornful men. *Is.* 28: 14.

I am in derision daily, every one mocketh me. *Je.* 20: 7.

They shall scoff at the kings, and the princes shall be a scorn unto them. *Hab.* 1: 10.

They shall mock him, and scourge him. *Mk.* 10: 34.

He shall be delivered unto the Gentiles, and shall be mocked, and spitefully entreated, and spitted on. *Lu.* 18: 32.

Give none offence. *1 Co.* 10: 32.

Charity . . . is not easily provoked. *1 Co.* 13: 4, 5.

Your zeal hath provoked very many. *2 Co.* 9: 2.

Be not deceived; God is not mocked. *Ga.* 6: 7.

Whatsoever a man soweth, that shall he also reap. *Gal.* 6: 7.

There shall come in the last days scoffers. *2 Pe.* 3: 3.

See also
Abuse; Provocation; Reviling.

Aftermath

They that plow iniquity, and sow wickedness, reap the same. *Jb.* 4: 8.

They that sow in tears shall reap in joy. *Ps.* 126: 5.

He that soweth iniquity shall reap vanity. *Pr.* 22: 8.

They have sown the wind, and they shall reap the whirlwind. *Ho.* 8: 7.

Ye shall hear of wars and rumours of wars: see that ye be not troubled: for all these things must come to pass, but the end is not yet. *Mat.* 24: 6.

There shall be famines, and pestilences, and earthquakes, in divers places. *Mat.* 24: 7.

His blood be upon us, and on our children. *Mat.* 27: 25.

First the blade, then the ear, after that the full corn in the ear. *Mk.* 4: 28.

He which soweth sparingly shall reap also sparingly; and he which soweth bountifully shall reap also bountifully. *2 Co.* 9: 6.

In due season we shall reap, if we faint not. *Ga.* 6: 9.

Babylon the great is fallen, is fallen. *Re.* 18: 2.

Therefore shall her plagues come in one day, death, and mourning, and famine; and she shall be utterly burned with fire. *Re.* 18: 8.

See also
Consequence; Result.

Age

Then shall ye bring down my gray hairs with sorrow to the grave. *Ge.* 42: 38.

And Moses said unto them, I am an hundred and twenty years old this day. *De.* 31: 2.

All the increase of thine house shall die in the flower of their age. *1 S.* 2: 33.

I am young, and ye are very old; wherefore I was afraid, and durst not shew you mine opinion. *Jb.* 32: 6.

So the Lord blessed the latter end of Job more than his beginning. *Jb.* 42: 12.

Mark the perfect man, and behold the upright: for the end of that man is peace. *Ps.* 37: 37.

Mine age is as nothing before thee. *Ps.* 39: 5.

Cast me not off in the time of old age. *Ps.* **71: 9.**

We spend our years as a tale that is told. *Ps.* **90: 9.**

So teach us to number our days, that we may apply our hearts unto wisdom. *Ps.* **90: 12.**

They shall still bring forth fruit in old age . . . To shew that the Lord is upright. *Ps.* **92: 14, 15.**

The hoary head is a crown of glory. *Pr.* **16: 31.**

We all do fade as a leaf. *Is.* **64: 6.**

Your old men shall dream dreams. *Jo.* **2: 28.**

When thou shalt be old, thou shalt stretch forth thy hands, and another shall gird thee, and carry thee whither thou wouldest not. *Jn.* **21: 18.**

Rebuke not an elder, but intreat him as a father. *1 Ti.* **5: 1.**

See also

Adult; Era; Generation; Life, the Long; Oldness; Senior; Time.

Age, Golden

The Lord God planted a garden eastward in Eden; and there he put the man whom he had formed. *Ge.* **2: 8.**

There were giants in the earth in those days. *Ge.* **6: 4.**

The word of the Lord was precious in those days. *1 S.* **3: 1.**

The wolf also shall dwell with the lamb, and the leopard shall lie down with the kid; and the calf and the young lion and the fatling together; and a little child shall lead them. *Is.* **11: 6.**

They shall not hurt nor destroy in all my holy mountain: for the earth shall be full of the knowledge of the Lord, as the waters cover the sea. *Is.* **11: 9.**

He shall feed his flock like a shepherd: he shall gather the lambs with his arm, and carry them in his bosom, and shall gently lead those that are with young. *Is.* **40: 11.**

Behold, I create new heavens and a new earth: and the former shall not be remembered, nor come into mind. *Is.* **65: 17.**

I will say to them which were not my people, Thou art my people; and they shall say, Thou art my God. *Ho.* **2: 23.**

They that dwell under his shadow shall return; they shall revive as the corn, and grow as the vine. *Ho.* **14: 7.**

It shall come to pass afterward, that I will pour out my spirit upon all flesh. *Jo.* **2: 28.**

It shall come to pass in that day, that the mountains shall drop down new wine, and the hills shall flow with milk. *Jo.* **3: 18.**

They shall build the waste cities and inhabit them; and they shall plant vineyards, and drink the wine thereof; they shall also make gardens, and eat the fruit of them. *Am.* **9: 14.**

In the last days it shall come to pass. *Mi.* **4: 1.**

They shall beat their swords into plowshares, and their spears into pruninghooks. *Mi.* **4: 3.**

They shall sit every man under his vine and under his fig tree; and none shall make them afraid. *Mi.* **4: 4.**

At that time will I bring you again, even in the time that I gather you. *Zph.* **3: 20.**

The streets of the city shall be full of boys and girls playing in the streets thereof. *Zch.* **8: 5.**

In that day shall there be upon the bells of the horses, HOLINESS UNTO THE LORD. *Zch.* **14: 20.**

All nations shall call you blessed: for ye shall be a delightsome land. *Mal.* **3: 12.**

That in the dispensation of the fulness of times he might gather together in one all things in Christ. *Ep.* **1: 10.**

Behold, the days come, saith the Lord, when I will make a new covenant. *He.* **8: 8.**

And I saw thrones, and they sat upon them. *Re.* **20: 4.**

See also

Civilization; Climax; Future; Kingdom, the Coming; Land, the Promised; Millennium; World, the New.

Agent

Bless ye the Lord, all ye his hosts; ye ministers of his, that do his pleasure. *Ps.* **103: 21.**

A faithful ambassador is health. *Pr.* **13: 17.**

Whom shall I send, and who will go for us? Then said I, Here am I; send me. *Is.* **6: 8.**

Follow me, and I will make you fishers of men. *Mat.* **4: 19.**

Behold, I send you forth as sheep in the midst of wolves. *Mat.* **10: 16.**

Thou art Peter, and upon this rock I will build my church. *Mat.* **16: 18.**

Go ye therefore, and teach all nations. *Mat.* **28: 19.**

God so loved the world, that he gave his only begotten Son. *Jn.* **3: 16.**

The Father . . . hath given him authority to execute judgment. *Jn.* **5: 26, 27.**

The living Father hath sent me. *Jn.* **6: 57.**

So shall ye be my disciples. *Jn.* **15: 8.**

We are ambassadors for Christ. *2 Co.* **5: 20.**

I am an ambassador in bonds. *Ep.* **6: 20.**

Who maketh ·his angels spirits, and his ministers a flame of fire. *He.* **1: 7.**

See also

Ambassador; Instrument.

Aggressiveness

How long will this people provoke me? *Nu.* **14: 11.**

Then will they turn unto other gods, and serve them, and provoke me, and break my covenant. *De.* **31: 20.**

They . . . provoked the Lord to anger. *Ju.* **2: 12.**

Harden not your heart, as in the provocation. *Ps.* **95: 8.**

Frowardness is in his heart, he deviseth mischief continually; he soweth discord. *Pr.* **6: 14.**

The righteous are bold as a lion. *Pr.* **28: 1.**

There arose no small stir about that way. *Ac.* **19: 23.**

Whereinsoever any is bold, . . . I am bold• also. *2 Co.* **11: 21.**

Let all bitterness, and wrath, and anger, and clamour, and evil speaking, be put away from you. *Ep.* **4: 31.**

With all boldness, as always. *Ph.* 1: 20.
See also
Activity; Audacity; Boldness; Energy; Provocation; Zeal.

Agitation

The nations . . . shall tremble, and be in anguish because of thee. *De.* 2: 25.
Fear came upon me, and trembling, which made all my bones to shake. *Jb.* 4: 14.
God . . . Which shaketh the earth out of her place. *Jb.* 9: 2, 6.
Why do the heathen rage? *Ps.* 2: 1.
The mountains shake. *Ps.* 46: 3.
Thou hast made the earth to tremble. *Ps.* 60: 2.
God . . . Which stilleth the noise of the seas, the noise of their waves, and the tumult of the people. *Ps.* 65: 5, 7.
Thou hidest thy face, they are troubled. *Ps.* 104: 29.
They cry unto the Lord in their trouble, and he bringeth them out of their distresses. *Ps.* 107: 28.
My flesh trembleth for fear of thee; and I am afraid of thy judgments. *Ps.* 119: 120.
They shall look unto the earth; and behold trouble and darkness, dimness of anguish. *Is.* 8: 22.
The earth shall quake before them; the heavens shall tremble. *Jo.* 2: 10.
I will make Jerusalem a cup of trembling. *Zch.* 12: 2.
An angel went down at a certain season into the pool, and troubled the water. *Jn.* 5: 4.
God is not the author of confusion, but of peace. *I Co.* 14: 33.
Work out your own salvation with fear and trembling. *Ph.* 2: 12.
Where envying and strife is, there is confusion, and every evil work. *Ja.* 3: 16.
Be not afraid of their terror, neither be troubled. *I Pe.* 3: 14.
See also
Disorder; Disturbance; Trouble; Tumult; Turmoil.

Agnosticism

They will not believe me, nor hearken unto my voice. *Ex.* 4: 1.
Because they believed not in God, and trusted not in his salvation. *Ps.* 78: 22.
If ye have faith, and doubt not. *Mat.* 21: 21.
He marvelled because of their unbelief. *Mk.* 6: 6.
Lord, I believe; help thou mine unbelief. *Mk.* 9: 24.
If I tell you, ye will not believe. *Lu.* 22: 67.
Ye worship ye know not what. *Jn.* 4: 22.
Except ye see signs and wonders, ye will not believe. *Jn.* 4: 48.
Ye neither know me, nor my Father. *Jn.* 8: 19.
Though ye believe not me, believe the works. *Jn.* 10: 38.
Except I shall see in his hands the print of the nails, . . . I will not believe. *Jn.* 20: 25.
He hath denied the faith, and is worse than an infidel. *I Ti.* 5: 8.
Take heed, brethren, lest there be in any of you an evil heart of unbelief. *He.* 3: 12.

See also
Christ, Denial of; Christ, Doubt of; Denial; Doubt; Faithlessness; God, Denial of; Heresy; Unbelief.

Agony

I will speak in the anguish of my spirit. *Jb.* 7: 11.
The wicked man travaileth with pain all his days. *Jb.* 15: 20.
Reproach hath broken my heart; and I am full of heaviness. *Ps.* 69: 20.
The pains of hell gat hold upon me. *Ps.* 116: 3.
Trouble and anguish have taken hold on me. *Ps.* 119: 143.
He shall see of the travail of his soul. *Is.* 53: 11.
I have heard a voice as of a woman in travail, and the anguish as of her that bringeth forth her first child. *Je.* 4: 31.
Being in an agony he prayed more earnestly. *Lu.* 22: 44.
His sweat was as it were great drops of blood falling down to the ground. *Lu.* 22: 44.
We know that the whole creation groaneth and travaileth in pain together until now. *Ro.* 8: 22.
Out of much affliction and anguish of heart I wrote unto you with many tears. *2 Co.* 2: 4.
They gnawed their tongues for pain. *Re.* 16: 10.
See also
Christ, Cross of; Christ, Suffering of; Pain; Suffering; Torment; Travail.

Agreement

Make an agreement with me by a present. *2 K.* 18: 31.
Your covenant with death shall be disannulled, and your agreement with hell shall not stand. *Is.* 28: 18.
Agree with thine adversary quickly, whiles thou art in the way with him. *Mat.* 5: 25.
If two of you shall agree on earth as touching any thing that they shall ask, it shall be done for them of my Father which is in heaven. *Mat.* 18: 19.
They lifted up their voice to God with one accord. *Ac.* 4: 24.
There are three that bear witness in earth, the spirit, and the water, and the blood: and these three agree in one. *I Jn.* 5: 8.
See also
Accord; Acquiescence; Affirmation; Assent; Bargain; Compact; Compatibility; Concord; Consent; Contract; Harmony; Oneness; Unanimity; Unity.

Aid

The God of my father . . . was mine help. *Ex.* 18: 4.
The Lord raised up a deliverer. *Ju.* 3: 9.
I have commanded the ravens to feed thee. *I K.* 17: 4.
The ravens brought him bread and flesh in the morning, and bread and flesh in the evening. *I K.* 17: 6.
Lord, it is nothing with thee to help, whether with many, or with them that have no power: help us, O Lord our God; for we rest on thee. *2 Ch.* 14: 11.
Our soul waiteth for the Lord: he is our help and our shield. *Ps.* 33: 20.

He shall deliver the needy when he crieth; the poor also, and him that hath no helper. *Ps.* 72: 12.

Come over into Macedonia, and help us. *Ac.* 16: 9.

Helping together by prayer for us. *2 Co.* 1: 11.

In the day of salvation have I succoured thee. *2 Co.* 6: 2.
See also
Assistance; Help; Relief; Service; Succor; Support.

Ailment

The Lord will take away from thee all sickness. *De.* 7: 15.

If thou wilt not observe to do all the words of this law that are written in this book . . . Then the Lord will make all thy plagues wonderful, . . . Moreover he will bring upon thee all the diseases of Egypt. *De.* 28: 58-60.

What aileth the people that they weep? *1 S.* 11: 5.

Ye are all physicians of no value. *Jb.* 13: 4.

The Lord will strengthen him upon the bed of languishing. *Ps.* 41: 3.

Who healeth all thy diseases. *Ps.* 103: 3.

What ailed thee, O thou sea, that thou fleddest? *Ps.* 114: 5.

Hope deferred maketh the heart sick. *Pr.* 13: 12.

Is there no balm in Gilead; is there no physician there? *Je.* 8: 22.

Jesus went about all Galilee, . . . healing . . . all manner of disease among the people. *Mat.* 4: 23.

They that be whole need not a physician, but they that are sick. *Mat.* 9: 12.

He gave them power . . . to heal all manner of sickness and all manner of disease. *Mat.* 10: 1.

I was sick, and ye visited me. *Mat.* 25: 36.

Physician, heal thyself. *Lu.* 4: 23.

The prayer of faith shall save the sick. *Ja.* 5: 15.
See also
Disease; Illness; Infirmity; Sickness.

Aim

Ponder the path of thy feet, and let all thy ways be established. *Pr.* 4: 26.

Turn not to the right hand nor to the left: remove thy foot from evil. *Pr.* 4: 27.

A man's heart deviseth his way: but the Lord directeth his steps. *Pr.* 16: 9.

This is the purpose that is purposed upon the whole earth. *Is.* 14: 26.

To this end was I born, and for this cause came I into the world, that I should bear witness unto the truth. *Jn.* 18: 37.

I ask therefore for what intent ye have sent for me? *Ac.* 10: 29.

He . . . exhorted them all, that with purpose of heart they would cleave unto the Lord. *Ac.* 11: 23.

To the end ye may be established. *Ro.* 1: 11.

Christ is the end of the law. *Ro.* 10: 4.

The things that I purpose, do I purpose according to the flesh? *2 Co.* 1: 17.
See also
Ambition; Aspiration; Christ, Purpose of; End; Intention; Purpose.

Aimlessness

They grope in the dark without light. *Jb.* 12: 25.

A leaf driven to and fro. *Jb.* 13: 25.

Let me not wander from thy commandments. *Ps.* 119: 10.

They have wandered as blind men in the streets. *La.* 4: 14.

Therefore they shall be as the morning cloud, and as the early dew that passeth away, as the chaff that is driven of the whirlwind out of the floor, and as the smoke out of the chimney. *Ho.* 13: 3.

Withal they learn to be idle, wandering about from house to house; and not only idle, but tattlers also and busybodies, speaking things which they ought not. *1 Ti.* 5: 13.

He that wavereth is like a wave of the sea driven with the wind and tossed. *Ja.* 1: 6.
See also
Wandering.

Air

Let them have dominion . . . over the fowl of the air. *Ge.* 1: 26.

There is a path which no fowl knoweth. *Jb.* 28: 7.

To make the weight for the winds. *Jb.* 28: 25.

The Lord answered Job out of the whirlwind. *Jb.* 38: 1.

What profit hath he that hath laboured for the wind? *Ec.* 5: 16.

A man shall be as an hiding place from the wind. *Is.* 32: 2.

The birds of the air have nests. *Mat.* 8: 20.

What manner of man is this, that even the winds and the sea obey him! *Mat.* 8: 27.

In time past ye walked according to the course of this world, according to the prince of the power of the air. *Ep.* 2: 2.
See also
Atmosphere; Breath; Wind.

Alarm

He put a trumpet into every man's hand. *Ju.* 7: 16.

God himself is with us for our captain, and his priests with sounding trumpets to cry alarm against you. *2 Ch.* 13: 12.

Except the Lord keep the city, the watchman waketh but in vain. *Ps.* 127: 1.

Awake, awake, put on strength, O arm of the Lord; awake, as in the ancient days. *Is.* 51: 9.

Cry aloud, spare not, lift up thy voice like a trumpet. *Is.* 58: 1.

Arise, cry out in the night. *La.* 2: 19.

He that taketh warning shall deliver his soul. *Eze.* 33: 5.

Blow ye the trumpet in Zion, and sound an alarm in my holy mountain. *Jo.* 2: 1.

The Lord God shall blow the trumpet. *Zch.* 9: 14.

If the trumpet give an uncertain sound, who shall prepare himself to the battle? *1 Co.* 14: 8.

Awake thou that sleepest, and arise from the dead, and Christ shall give thee light. *Ep.* 5: 14.
See also
Dread; Fear; Terror; Trembling.

Alertness

Be ready in the morning. *Ex.* 34: 2.

My soul waiteth for the Lord more than they that watch for the morning. *Ps.* 130: 6.

Blessed is the man that heareth me, watching daily at my gates, waiting at the posts of my doors. *Pr.* 8: 34.

Watch therefore: for ye know not what hour your Lord doth come. *Mat.* 24: 42.

Watch and pray. *Mat.* 26: 41.

Let your loins be girded about, and your lights burning. *Lu.* 12: 35.

Blessed are those servants, whom the lord when he cometh shall find watching. *Lu.* 12: 37.

Lord, I am ready to go with thee, both into prison, and to death. *Lu.* 22: 33.

Watching . . . with all perseverance. *Ep.* 6: 18.

Watch thou in all things, . . . make full proof of thy ministry. *2 Ti.* 4: 5.

Ready to every good work. *Tit.* 3: 1.

Be watchful. *Re.* 3: 2.

See also

Readiness; Vigilance; Wait; Watch.

Alien

I am a stranger and a sojourner with you. *Ge.* 23: 4.

I have been an alien in a strange land. *Ex.* 18: 3.

Love ye therefore the stranger: for ye were strangers in the land of Egypt. *De.* 10: 19.

Thy people shall be my people, and thy God my God. *Ru.* 1: 16.

At that time ye were without Christ, being aliens from the commonwealth of Israel, and strangers from the covenants of promise. *Ep.* 2: 12.

Being alienated from the life of God through the ignorance that is in them. *Ep.* 4: 18.

Where there is neither Greek nor Jew, circumcision nor uncircumcision, Barbarian, Scythian, bond nor free. *Col.* 3: 11.

By faith he sojourned in the land of promise, as in a strange country, dwelling in tabernacles. *He.* 11: 9.

Turned to flight the armies of the aliens. *He.* 11: 34.

Be not forgetful to entertain strangers: for thereby some have entertained angels unawares. *He.* 13: 2.

See also

Foreigner; Gentile; Immigration; Stranger.

All

His kingdom ruleth over all. *Ps.* 103: 19.

The Lord is good to all. *Ps.* 145: 9.

The profit of the earth is for all: the king himself is served by the field. *Ec.* 5: 9.

He giveth to all life, and breath, and all things. *Ac.* 17: 25.

The gospel of Christ . . . is the power of God unto salvation to every one that believeth. *Ro.* 1: 16.

All have sinned, and come short of the glory of God. *Ro.* 3: 23.

All are yours. *1 Co.* 3: 22.

Are all apostles? are all prophets? are all teachers? *1 Co.* 12: 29.

As in Adam all die, even so in Christ shall all be made alive. *1 Co.* 15: 22.

One God and Father of all, who is above all, and through all, and in you all. *Ep.* 4: 6.

Christ is all, and in all. *Col.* 3: 11.

All shall know me, from the least to the greatest. *He.* 8: 11.

Every one that loveth is born of God, and knoweth God. *1 Jn.* 4: 7.

Whosoever will, let him take the water of life freely. *Re.* 22: 17.

See also

Whole.

All Saints

He will keep the feet of his saints. *1 S.* 2: 9.

O love the Lord, all ye his saints. *Ps.* 31: 23.

Precious in the sight of the Lord is the death of his saints. *Ps.* 116: 15.

Called to be saints. *1 Co.* 1: 2.

All the saints salute you. *2 Co.* 13: 13.

Unto me, who am less than the least of all saints, is this grace given, that I should preach . . . the unsearchable riches of Christ. *Ep.* 3: 8.

Giving thanks unto the Father, which hath made us meet to be partakers of the inheritance of the saints. *Col.* 1: 12.

These all died in faith, not having received the promises, but having seen them afar off. *He.* 11: 13.

These all, having obtained a good report through faith, received not the promise: God having provided some better thing for us, that they without us should not be made perfect. *He.* 11: 39, 40.

We also are compassed about with so great a cloud of witnesses. *He.* 12: 1.

Behold, the Lord cometh with ten thousands of his saints. *Jude* 1: 14.

Hurt not the earth, neither the sea, nor the trees, till we have sealed the servants of our God in their foreheads. *Re.* 7: 3.

I heard as it were the voice of a great multitude, and as the voice of many waters, and as the voice of mighty thunderings, saying, Alleluia: for the Lord God omnipotent reigneth. *Re.* 19: 6.

Blessed are they which are called unto the marriage supper of the Lamb. *Re.* 19: 9.

See also

Holiness; Saint.

All Souls

All nations shall call him blessed. *Ps.* 72: 17.

He preserveth the souls of his saints. *Ps.* 97: 10.

The glory of the Lord shall be revealed, and all flesh shall see it together. *Is.* 40: 5.

Mine house shall be called a house of prayer for all people. *Is.* 56: 7.

Behold, I am the Lord, the God of all flesh. *Je.* 32: 27.

Behold, all souls are mine. *Eze.* 18: 4.

Come unto me, all ye that labour and are heavy laden, and I will give you rest. *Mat.* 11: 28.

Behold, I bring you good tidings of great joy, which shall be to all people. *Lu.* 2: 10.

All flesh shall see the salvation of God. *Lu.* 3: 6.

And hath made of one blood all nations of men for to dwell on all the face of the earth. *Ac.* 17: 26.
See also
Soul; Universality.

Allegiance

Take good heed therefore unto yourselves, that ye love the Lord your God. *Jos.* 23: 11.

As for me and my house, we will serve the Lord. *Jos.* 24: 15.

The soul of Jonathan was knit with the soul of David, and Jonathan loved him as his own soul. *1 S.* 18: 1.

My lord, O king, according to thy saying, I am thine, and all that I have. *1 K.* 20: 4.

All the ends of the world shall remember and turn unto the Lord. *Ps.* 22: 27.

Thou art my God. *Ps.* 31: 14.

Stablish thy word unto thy servant, who is devoted to thy fear. *Ps.* 119: 38.

Faithful are the wounds of a friend. *Pr.* 27: 6.

Thou shalt worship the Lord thy God, and him only shalt thou serve. *Mat.* 4: 10.

Thou shalt love the Lord thy God with all thy heart, and with all thy soul, and with all thy mind. *Mat.* 22: 37.

Blessed is that servant, whom his lord when he cometh shall find so doing. *Mat.* 24: 46.

Ye cannot serve God and mammon. *Lu.* 16: 13.

Christ Jesus . . . was faithful to him that appointed him. *He.* 3: 1, 2.

Honour the king. *1 Pe.* 2: 17.
See also
Constancy; Devotion; Faithfulness; Fidelity; Loyalty; Service.

Allegory

A man of understanding shall attain unto wise counsels: To understand a proverb, and the interpretation. *Pr.* 1: 5, 6.

Say now to the rebellious house, Know ye not what these things mean? *Eze.* 17: 12.

Thou canst make interpretations, and dissolve doubts. *Da.* 5: 16.

If thou canst read the writing, and make known to me the interpretation thereof, thou . . . shalt be the third ruler in the kingdom. *Da.* 5: 16.

The angel that talked with me answered and said unto me, Knowest thou not what these be? *Zch.* 4: 5.

Which things are an allegory. *Ga.* 4: 24.
See also
Fable; Parable.

Alleluia

All the people shall answer and say, Amen. *De.* 27: 15.

Praise the Lord; for his mercy endureth for ever. *2 Ch.* 20: 21.

Blessed be the Lord God of Israel from everlasting, and to everlasting. Amen, and Amen. *Ps.* 41: 13.

Let all the people say, Amen. Praise ye the Lord. *Ps.* 106: 48.

Praise ye the Lord from the heavens: praise him in the heights. *Ps.* 148: 1.

Continually in the temple, praising and blessing God. Amen. *Lu.* 24: 53.

Again they said, Alleluia. *Re.* 19: 3.

The four and twenty elders and the four beasts fell down and worshipped God that sat on the throne, saying, Amen; Alleluia. *Re.* 19: 4.
See also
Hallelujah; God, Praise of; Praise.

Alleviation

Thou has strengthened the weak hands. *Jb.* 4: 3.

Though I speak, my grief is not assuaged: and though I forbear, what am I eased. *Jb.* 16: 6.

Withhold not thou thy tender mercies from me, O Lord. *Ps.* 40: 11.

The Lord will strengthen him upon the bed of languishing. *Ps.* 41: 3.

The Lord . . . will make all his bed in his sickness. *Ps.* 41: 3.

Thou hast taken away all thy wrath. *Ps.* 85: 3.

Then shall the lame man leap as an hart. *Is.* 35: 6.

For a small moment have I forsaken thee; but with great mercies will I gather thee. *Is.* 54: 7.

To give unto them beauty for ashes, the oil of joy for mourning ,the garment of praise for the spirit of heaviness. *Is.* 61: 3.

Mine eye runneth down with water, because the comforter that should relieve my soul is far from me. *La.* 1: 16.

The diseased have ye not strengthened, neither have ye healed that which was sick. *Eze.* 34: 4.

I . . . will bind up that which was broken. *Eze.* 34: 16.

I . . . will strengthen that which was sick. *Eze.* 34: 16.

Whom God hath raised up, having loosed the pains of death. *Ac.* 2: 24.
See also
Moderation; Relief.

Alliance

These forty years the Lord thy God hath been with thee; thou hast lacked nothing. *De.* 2: 7.

The Lord, he it is that doth go before thee; he will be with thee, he will not fail thee. *De.* 31: 8.

Be not afraid, neither be thou dismayed: for the Lord thy God is with thee whithersoever thou goest. *Jos.* 1: 9.

The Lord do so to me, and more also, if ought but death part thee and me. *Ru.* 1: 17.

Fear not: for they that be with us are more than they that be with them. *2 K.* 6: 16.

Thou shalt be in league with the stones of the field. *Jb.* 5: 23.

Some trust in chariots and some in horses: but we will remember the name of the Lord our God. *Ps.* 20: 7.

The Lord God is my strength. *Hab.* 3: 19.

Where two or three are gathered together in my name, there am I in the midst of them. *Mat.* 18: 20.

Who shall separate us from the love of Christ? *Ro.* 8: 35.
See also
Accomplice; Ally; Association; Collaboration; Cooperation; Covenant; League; Nations, League of.

Allotment

I will give unto thee . . . the land of Canaan, for an everlasting possession; and I will be their God. *Ge.* 17: 8.

This land shall be your possession before the Lord. *Nu.* 32: 22.

I must die in this land, I must not go over Jordan: but ye shall go over, and possess that good land. *De.* 4: 22.

These are the statutes and judgments, which ye shall observe to do in the land, which the Lord God of thy fathers giveth thee to possess it. *De.* 12: 1.

His allowance was a continual allowance given him of the king, a daily rate for every day, all the days of his life. *2 K.* 25: 30.

The Lord is the portion of mine inheritance. *Ps.* 16: 5.

The lines are fallen unto me in pleasant places. *Ps.* 16: 9.

These are their portions, saith the Lord God. *Eze.* 48: 29.

Grant that these my two sons may sit, the one on thy right hand, and the other on thy left, in thy kingdom. *Mat.* 20: 21.

He divided their land to them by lot. *Ac.* 13: 19.

See also

Part; Portion; Share.

Allurement

Entice him, and see wherein his great strength lieth. *Ju.* 16: 5.

If sinners entice thee, consent thou not. *Pr.* 1: 10.

Behold, there met him a woman with the attire of an harlot, and subtil of heart. *Pr.* 7: 10.

Such is the way of an adulterous woman. *Pr.* 30: 20.

With lovingkindness have I drawn thee. *Je.* 31: 3.

I will allure her, and bring her into the wilderness, and speak comfortably unto her. *Ho.* 2: 14.

This I say, lest any man should beguile you with enticing words. *Col.* 2: 4.

Every man is tempted, when he is drawn away of his own lust, and enticed. *Ja.* 1: 14.

They allure through the lusts of the flesh. *2 Pe.* 2: 18.

See also

Attraction; Enticement; Temptation.

Ally

If God will be with me, . . . then shall the Lord be my God. *Ge.* 28: 20, 21.

We be come from a far country: now therefore make ye a league with us. *Jos.* 9: 6.

Joshua made peace with them, and made a league with them, to let them live. *Jos.* 9: 15.

As for me and my house, we will serve the Lord. *Jos.* 24: 15.

Whither thou goest, I will go; and where thou lodgest, I will lodge. *Ru.* 1: 16.

The Lord do so to me, and more also, if ought but death part thee and me. *Ru.* 1: 17.

They that be with us are more than they that be with them. *2 K.* 6: 16.

The Lord opened the eyes of the young man; and he saw: and, behold, the mountain was full of horses and chariots of fire round

about Elisha. *2 K.* 6: 17.

They were among the mighty men, helpers of the war. *1 Ch.* 12: 1.

The Lord of hosts is with us. *Ps.* 46: 7.

Happy is he that hath the God of Jacob for his help. *Ps.* 146: 5.

Woe to them that go down to Egypt for help. *Is.* 31: 1.

As birds flying, so will the Lord of hosts defend Jerusalem. *Is.* 31: 5.

He that is not with me is against me. *Mat.* 12: 30.

Lo, I am with you alway. *Mat.* 28: 20.

Be ye followers of me, even as I also am of Christ. *1 Co.* 11: 1.

The Lord is my helper, and I will not fear. *He.* 13: 6.

See also

Alliance; Association.

Almighty

I am the Almighty God; walk before me, and be thou perfect. *Ge.* 17: 1.

Despise not thou the chastening of the Almighty. *Jb.* 5: 17.

Is it any pleasure to the Almighty, that thou art righteous? *Jb.* 22: 3.

There is a spirit in man: and the inspiration of the Almighty giveth them understanding. *Jb.* 32: 8.

He that dwelleth in the secret place of the most High shall abide under the shadow of the Almighty. *Ps.* 91: 1.

Ye do err, not knowing the scriptures, nor the power of God. *Mat.* 22: 29.

They were all amazed at the mighty power of God. *Lu.* 9: 43.

Who are kept by the power of God. *1 Pe.* 1: 5.

Holy, holy, holy, Lord God Almighty, which was, and is, and is to come. *Re.* 4: 8.

Alleluia: for the Lord God omnipotent reigneth. *Re.* 19: 6.

I saw no temple therein: for the Lord God Almighty and the Lamb are the temple of it. *Re.* 21: 22.

See also

Deity; God, the Almighty; God, Omnipotence of; God, Power of; God, Sovereignty of; God, Strength of; God, Supremacy of.

Almsgiving

Thou shalt not . . . gather every grape of thy vineyard; thou shalt leave them for the poor. *Le.* 19: 10.

If thy brother be waxen poor, and fallen in decay with thee; then thou shalt relieve him: yea, though he be a stranger, or a sojourner; that he may live with thee. *Le.* 25: 35.

Thou shalt not harden thine heart, nor shut thine hand from thy poor brother. *De.* 15: 7.

Thou shalt open thine hand wide unto thy brother. *De.* 15: 11.

I was a father to the poor. *Jb.* 29: 16.

He that giveth unto the poor shall not lack. *Pr.* 28: 27.

When thou doest alms, let not thy left hand know what thy right hand doeth. *Mat.* 6: 3.

Then shall the righteous answer him, saying, Lord, when saw we thee an hungred, and fed thee? *Mat.* 25: 37.

This poor widow hath cast more in, than

all they which have cast into the treasury. *Mk.* 12: 43.

Give alms of such things as ye have. *Lu.* 11: 41.

Sell all that thou hast, and distribute unto the poor, and thou shalt have treasure in heaven. *Lu.* 18: 22.

Thy prayers and thine alms are come up for a memorial before God. *Ac.* 10: 4.

Though I bestow all my goods to feed the poor, . . . and have not charity, it profiteth me nothing. *1 Co.* 13: 3.

To do good and to communicate forget not: for with such sacrifices God is well pleased. *He.* 13: 16.

See also

Charity; Contribution; Help; Philanthropy; Poor; Poverty; Relief.

Alpha

The beginning of the word of the Lord by Hosea. *Ho.* 1: 2.

The beginning of the gospel of Jesus Christ, the Son of God. *Mk.* 1: 1.

The firstborn of every creature. *Col.* 1: 15.

His dear son . . . is before all things, and by him all things consist. *Col.* 1: 13, 17.

He is . . . the beginning, the firstborn from the dead; that in all things he might have the pre-eminence. *Col.* 1: 18.

When he bringeth in the firstbegotten into the world, he saith, And let all the angels of God worship him. *He.* 1: 6.

I am Alpha and Omega, the beginning and the ending, saith the Lord, which is, and which was, and which is to come. *Re.* 1: 8.

These things saith the Amen, the faithful and true witness, the beginning of the creation of God. *Re.* 3: 14.

See also

Beginning; Christ, the Creator; Commencement; First; Genesis; Omega.

Altar

This is none other but the house of God, and this is the gate of heaven. *Ge.* 28: 17.

He erected there an altar. *Ge.* 33: 20.

Put off thy shoes from off thy feet, for the place whereon thou standest is holy ground. *Ex.* 3: 5.

Who shall stand in his holy place? *Ps.* 24: 3.

I have seen thee in the sanctuary. *Ps.* 63: 2.

Thy way, O God, is in the sanctuary. *Ps.* 77: 13.

Then flew one of the seraphim unto me, having a live coal in his hand, which he had taken . . . from off the altar. *Is.* 6: 6.

I dwell in the high and holy place, with him also that is of a contrite and humble spirit. *Is.* 57: 15.

I saw the Lord standing upon the altar. *Am.* 9: 1.

The hour cometh, when ye shall neither in this mountain, nor yet at Jerusalem, worship the Father. *Jn.* 4: 21.

See also

God, House of; Ground, Holy; Sanctuary; Temple; Worship.

Alteration

My covenant will I not break, nor alter the thing that has gone out of my lips. *Ps.* 89: 34.

As a vesture shalt thou change them, and they shall be changed. *Ps.* 102: 26.

Can the Ethiopian change his skin, or the leopard his spots? *Je.* 13: 23.

According to the law of the Medes and Persians, which altereth not. *Da.* 6: 8.

One jot or one tittle shall in no wise pass from the law, till all be fulfilled. *Mat.* 5: 18.

The fashion of his countenance was altered. *Lu.* 9: 29.

Who changed the truth of God into a lie, and worshipped and served the creature more than the Creator. *Ro.* 1: 25.

Behold, I shew you a mystery; We shall not all sleep, but we shall all be changed. *1 Co.* 15: 51.

See also

Change; Conversion; Transformation.

Altitude

Behold a ladder set up on the earth, and the top of it reached to heaven. *Ge.* 28: 12.

Is not God in the height of heaven? and behold the height of the stars, how high they are. *Jb.* 22: 12.

If I ascend up into heaven, thou art there. *Ps.* 139: 8.

Praise ye the Lord from the heavens: praise him in the heights. *Ps.* 148: 1.

The heaven for height, and the earth for depth. *Pr.* 25: 3.

The mountain of the Lord's house shall be established in the top of the mountains. *Is.* 2: 2.

Ask thee a sign of the Lord thy God; ask it either in the depth, or in the height above. *Is.* 7: 11.

Thou hast said in thine heart, I will ascend into heaven, I will exalt my throne above the stars of God. *Is.* 14: 13.

I will ascend above the height of the clouds; I will be like the most High. *Is.* 14: 14.

The tree grew, and was strong, and the height thereof reached into heaven. *Da.* 4: 11.

Though they climb up to heaven, thence will I bring them down. *Am.* 9: 2.

Though thou exalt thyself as the eagle, and though thou set thy nest among the stars, thence will I bring thee down, saith the Lord. *Ob.* 4.

See also

Heaven; Height; Hill; Mountain.

Altruism

Thou shalt love thy neighbour as thyself. *Le.* 19: 18.

And David said unto him, Fear not: for I will surely shew thee kindness for Jonathan thy father's sake. *2 S.* 9: 7.

Now these are thy servants and thy people, whom thou hast redeemed by thy great power, and by thy strong hand. *Ne.* 1: 10.

The Lord turned the captivity of Job, when he prayed for his friends. *Jb.* 42: 10.

They helped every one his neighbour; and every one said to his brother, Be of good courage. *Is.* 41: 6.

With what measure ye mete, it shall be measured to you again. *Mat.* 7: 2.

He saved others; himself he cannot save. *Mat.* 27: 42.

As ye would that men should do to you, do

ye also to them likewise. *Lu.* 6: 31.

Simon, son of Jonas, lovest thou me more than these? He saith unto him, Yea, Lord; thou knowest that I love thee. He saith unto him, Feed my lambs. *Jn.* 21: 15.

Remember the words of the Lord Jesus, how he said, It is more blessed to give than to receive. *Ac.* 20: 35.

Let every one of us please his neighbour. *Ro.* 15: 2.

For even Christ pleased not himself. *Ro.* 15: 3.

All things are lawful for me, but all things are not expedient. *1 Co.* 10: 23.

Look not every man on his own things, but every man also on the things of others. *Ph.* 2: 4.

See also

Almsgiving; Beneficence; Benevolence; Brotherhood; Charity; Clemency; Generosity; Philanthropy; Unselfishness; Will, Good.

Amazement

I have seen God face to face. *Ge.* 32: 30.

Sanctify yourselves: for to morrow the Lord will do wonders among you. *Jos.* 3: 5.

Stand in awe, and sin not. *Ps.* 4: 4.

I am as a wonder unto many. *Ps.* 71: 7.

I will remember thy wonders of old. *Ps.* 77: 11.

Shall thy wonders be known in the dark? *Ps.* 88: 12.

Open thou mine eyes, that I may behold wondrous things out of thy law. *Ps.* 119: 18.

His name shall be called Wonderful. *Is.* 9: 6.

How great are his signs! and how mighty are his wonders! *Da.* 4: 3.

This is the Lord's doing, and it is marvellous in our eyes? *Mat.* 21: 42.

They were all amazed, and glorified God. *Mk.* 2: 12.

They were sore amazed in themselves beyond measure, and wondered. *Mk.* 6: 51.

All bare him witness, and wondered at the gracious words which proceeded out of his mouth. *Lu.* 4: 22.

As they were afraid, and bowed down their faces to the earth, they said unto them, Why seek ye the living among the dead? *Lu.* 24: 5.

They were filled with wonder and amazement at that which had happened unto him. *Ac.* 3: 10.

There appeared a great wonder in heaven. *Re.* 12: 1.

See also

Astonishment; Awe; Marvel; Surprise; Wonder.

Ambassador

He shall send his angel before thee. *Ge.* 24: 7.

I will speak of thy testimonies also before kings, and will not be ashamed. *Ps.* 119: 46.

A faithful ambassador is health. *Pr.* 13: 17.

A faithful messenger . . . refresheth the soul of his masters. *Pr.* 25: 13.

I heard the voice of the Lord saying, Whom shall I send, and who will go for us? Then said I, Here am I; send me. *Is.* 6: 8.

I ordained thee a prophet unto the nations. *Je.* 1: 5.

The priest's lips should keep knowledge,

. . . for he is the messenger of the Lord of hosts. *Mal.* 2: 7.

I will send my messenger, and he shall prepare the way before me. *Mal.* 3: 1.

He called his twelve disciples together, and gave them power and authority. *Lu.* 9: 1.

I will send my beloved son: it may be they will reverence him. *Lu.* 20: 13.

He shall send Jesus Christ, which before was preached unto you. *Ac.* 3: 20.

Depart: for I will send thee far hence unto the Gentiles. *Ac.* 22: 21.

I have appeared unto thee for this purpose, to make thee a minister and a witness. *Ac.* 26: 16.

Woe is unto me, if I preach not the gospel. *1 Co.* 9: 16.

I delivered unto you first of all that which I also received. *1 Co.* 15: 3.

We are ambassadors for Christ, as though God did beseech you by us. *2 Co.* 5: 20.

See also

Agent; Errand; Forerunner; Messenger; Missionary; Prophet.

Ambition

Let us make us a name. *Ge.* 11: 4.

Absalom prepared him chariots and horses, and fifty men to run before him. *2 S.* 15: 1.

Oh that I were made judge in the land. *2 S.* 15: 4.

I will build me a wide house and large chambers. *Je.* 22: 14.

The last shall be first, and the first last. *Mat.* 20: 16.

Grant that these my two sons may sit, the one on thy right hand, and the other on thy left, in thy kingdom. *Mat.* 20: 21.

Whosoever will be great among you, let him be your minister. *Mat.* 20: 26.

By the way they had disputed among themselves, who should be the greatest. *Mk.* 9: 34.

Whosoever of you will be the chiefest, shall be servant of all. *Mk.* 10: 44.

I will pull down my barns, and build greater. *Lu.* 12: 18.

Strive to enter in at the strait gate. *Lu.* 13: 24.

He marked how they chose out the chief rooms. *Lu.* 14: 7.

How can ye believe, which receive honour one of another, and seek not the honour that cometh from God only? *Jn.* 5: 44.

When Jesus therefore perceived that they would come and take him by force, to make him a king, he departed again into a mountain himself alone. *Jn.* 6: 15.

I have strived to preach the gospel, not where Christ was named, lest I should build upon another man's foundation. *Ro.* 15: 20.

So run, that ye may obtain. *1 Co.* 9: 24.

Every man that striveth for the mastery is temperate in all things. *1 Co.* 9: 25.

Covet earnestly the best gifts. *1 Co.* 12: 31.

Seek that ye may excel to the edifying of the church. *1 Co.* 14: 12.

This one thing I do, forgetting those things which are behind, and reaching forth unto those things which are before, I press toward the mark for the prize. *Ph.* 3: 13, 14.

The servant of the Lord must not strive. *2 Ti.* 2: 24.

Avoid . . . contentions, and strivings. *Tit.*
3: 9.
See also
Aspiration; First; Honor; Pride.

Amen

Let the whole earth be filled with his glory;
Amen, and Amen. *Ps.* 72: 19.
Blessed be the Lord God of Israel from
everlasting to everlasting: and let all the people say, Amen. *Ps.* 106: 48.
For thine is the kingdom, and the power,
and the glory, for ever. Amen. *Mat.* 6: 13.
They . . . were continually in the temple,
praising and blessing God. Amen. *Lu.* 24: 52,
53.
Christ, . . . who is over all, God blessed
for ever. Amen. *Ro.* 9: 5.
All the promises of God in him are yea,
and in him Amen, unto the glory of God by
us. 2 *Co.* 1: 20.
See also
Yea.

Amendment

If ye will not be reformed by me . . . Then
will I also walk contrary unto you. *Le.* 26:
23, 24.
My covenant will I not break, nor alter the
thing that is gone out of my lips. *Ps.* 89: 34.
Consider the work of God: for who can make
that straight, which he hath made crooked?
Ec. 7: 13.
Amend your ways and your doings, and I
will cause you to dwell in this place. *Je.* 7: 3.
Can the Ethiopian change his skin, or the
leopard his spots? *Je.* 13: 23.
Turn ye again now every one from his evil
ways. *Je.* 25: 5.
According to the law of the Medes and
Persians, which altereth not. *Da.* 6: 8.
Turn thou to thy God. *Ho.* 12: 6.
I am the Lord, I change not. *Mal.* 3: 6.
Bring forth therefore fruits meet for repen-
tance. *Mat.* 3: 8.
Except ye be converted, and become as
little children, ye shall not enter into the
kingdom of heaven. *Mat.* 18: 3.
He answered and said, I will not: but after-
ward he repented, and went. *Mat.* 21: 29.
Repent ye, and believe the gospel. *Mk.* 1: 15.
Her sins, which are many, are forgiven; for
she loved much. *Lu.* 7: 47.
We shall all be changed. 1 *Co.* 15: 51.
Let not the sun go down upon your wrath.
Ep. 4: 26.
All scripture . . . is profitable for doctrine,
for reproof, for correction. 2 *Ti.* 3: 16.
See also
Betterment; Change; Conversion; Correction;
Improvement; Reform.

Amends

He should make full restitution. *Ex.* 22: 3.
He shall make amends for the harm that
he hath done. *Le.* 5: 16.
According to his substance shall the restitu-
tion be. *Jb.* 20: 18.
The Lord . . . will comfort all her waste
places; and he will make her wilderness like
Eden, and her desert like the garden of the
Lord. *Is.* 51: 3.
In a little wrath I hid my face from thee

for a moment; but with everlasting kindness
will I have mercy on thee, saith the Lord thy
Redeemer. *Is.* 54: 8.
To give unto them beauty for ashes, the
oil of joy for mourning, the garment of praise
for the spirit of heaviness. *Is.* 61: 3.
Amend your ways and your doings, and I
will cause you to dwell in this place. *Je.* 7: 3.
He that scattered Israel will gather him,
and keep him, as a shepherd doth his flock.
Je. 31: 10.
I will restore to you the years that the
locust hath eaten. *Jo.* 2: 25.
Blessed are ye that hunger now: for ye shall
be filled. *Lu.* 6: 21.
If I have taken any thing from any man by
false accusation, I restore him fourfold. *Lu.*
19: 8.
See also
Compensation; God, Reward of; Payment;
Recompense; Reparation; Restitution. Restora-
tion; Return; Reward.

Amnesty

The Lord said, If I find in Sodom fifty
righteous within the city, then will I spare all
the place for their sakes. *Ge.* 18: 26.
The Lord hearkened to Hezekiah, and
healed the people. 2 *Ch.* 30: 20.
The beasts of the field shall be at peace
with thee. *Jb.* 5: 23.
The wolf also shall dwell with the lamb,
and the leopard shall lie down with the kid.
Is. 11: 6.
They shall not hurt nor destroy in all my
holy mountain. *Is.* 11: 9.
Speak ye comfortably to Jerusalem, and cry
unto her, that her warfare is accomplished,
that her iniquity is pardoned. *Is.* 40: 2.
I will pardon all their iniquities. *Je.* 33: 8.
In that day will I raise up the tabernacle of
David that is fallen, and close up the breaches
thereof; and I will raise up his ruins, and I
will build it as in the days of old. *Am.* 9: 11.
I will bring again the captivity of my people
of Israel, and they shall build the waste cities,
and inhabit them; and they shall plant vineyards, and drink the wine thereof; they shall
also make gardens, and eat the fruit of them.
Am. 9: 14.
See also
Forgiveness; Pardon; Peace.

Ampleness

Ye shall come . . . to a large land: for God
hath given it into your hands; a place where
there is no want of any thing that is in the
earth. *Ju.* 18: 10.
They found fat pasture and good, and the
land was wide, and quiet, and peaceable.
1 *Ch.* 4: 40.
The earth is the Lord's, and the fulness
thereof. *Ps.* 24: 1.
Thou hast set my feet in a large room. *Ps.*
31: 8.
Thou, O God, didst send a plentiful rain.
Ps. 68: 9.
So shall thy barns be filled with plenty, and
thy presses shall burst out with new wine. *Pr.*
3: 10.
Riches and honour are with me. *Pr.* 8: 18.
Hast thou found honey? eat so much as is
sufficient for thee. *Pr.* 25: 16.

In that day shall thy cattle feed in large pastures. *Is. 30: 23.*

Let judgment run down 'as waters, and righteousness as a mighty stream. *Am. 5: 24.*

Behold, the days come, saith the Lord, that the plowman shall overtake the reaper, and the treader of grapes him that soweth seed; and the mountains shall drop sweet wine, and all the hills shall melt. *Am. 9: 13.*

Their portion is fat, and their meat plenteous. *Hab. 1: 16.*

Our sufficiency is of God. *2 Co. 3: 5.*

My grace is sufficient for thee. *2 Co. 12: 9.*

Trust . . . in the living God, who giveth us richly all things to enjoy. *1 Ti. 6: 17.*

See also

Abundance; Fullness; Plenty; Riches; Sufficiency: Wealth.

Amusement

God hath made me to laugh. *Ge. 21: 6.*

The people sat down to eat and to drink, and rose up to play. *Ex. 32: 6.*

My glory was fresh in me, and my bow was renewed in my hand. *Jb. 29: 20.*

Then was our mouth filled with laughter, and our tongue with singing. *Ps. 126: 2.*

Let them praise his name in the dance. *Ps. 149: 3.*

Let the saints be joyful in glory: let them sing aloud upon their beds. *Ps. 149: 5.*

A merry heart maketh a cheerful countenance. *Pr. 15: 13.*

Every man should eat and drink, and enjoy the good of all his labour, it is the gift of God. *Ec. 3: 13.*

A man hath no better thing under the sun, than to eat, and to drink, and to be merry. *Ec. 8: 15.*

A feast is made for laughter, and wine maketh merry. *Ec. 10: 19.*

The voice of my beloved! behold, he cometh leaping upon the mountains, skipping upon the hills. *S. of S. 2: 8.*

Let us eat and drink; for to morrow we die. *Is. 22: 13.*

The streets of the city shall be full of boys and girls playing in the streets thereof. *Zch. 8: 5.*

Blessed are ye that weep now: for ye shall laugh. *Lu. 6: 21.*

Bring hither the fatted calf, and kill it; and let us eat, and be merry. *Lu. 15: 23.*

They that dwell upon the earth shall rejoice over them, and make merry. *Re. 11: 10.*

See also

Dance; Feast; Festival; Gaiety; Laughter; Merriment; Mirth; Play.

Anarchy

It came to pass, when the judge was dead, that they returned, and corrupted themselves more than their fathers. *Ju. 2: 19.*

He that hath no rule over his own spirit is like a city that is broken down, and without walls. *Pr. 25: 28.*

When the wicked beareth rule, the people mourn. *Pr. 29: 2.*

All thy rulers are fled together. *Is. 22: 3.*

Violence in the land, ruler against ruler. *Je. 51: 46.*

And makest men as the fishes of the sea, as the creeping things, that have no ruler over them. *Hab. 1: 14.*

See also

Chaos; Confusion; Lawlessness; Rebellion.

Anathema

I shall bring a curse upon me, and not a blessing. *Ge. 27: 12.*

If thou wilt not hearken unto the voice of the Lord thy God, . . . all these curses shall come upon thee. *De. 28: 15.*

Cursed shalt thou be when thou comest in, and cursed shalt thou be when thou goest out. *De. 28: 19.*

The Lord shall make the pestilence cleave unto thee. *De. 28: 21.*

Thy heaven that is over thy head shall be brass, and the earth that is under thee shall be iron. *De. 28: 23.*

If ye will not hear, and if ye will not lay it to heart, to give glory unto my name, saith the Lord of hosts, I will even send a curse upon you, and I will curse your blessings. *Mal. 2: 2.*

Depart from me, ye cursed, into everlasting fire. *Mat. 25: 41.*

No man speaking by the Spirit of God calleth Jesus accursed. *1 Co. 12: 3.*

If any man love not the Lord Jesus Christ, let him be Anathema Maranatha. *1 Co. 16: 22.*

See also

Curse; Excommunication.

Ancestor

The same became mighty men which were of old, men of renown. *Ge. 6: 4.*

I . . am a jealous God, visiting the iniquity of the fathers upon the children unto the third and fourth generation of them that hate me. *Ex. 20: 5.*

I will . . . remember the covenant of their ancestors. *Le. 26: 45.*

The fathers shall not be put to death for the children, neither shall the children be put to death for the fathers. *De. 24: 16.*

The Lord our God be with us, as he was with our fathers. *1 K. 8: 57.*

The Lord is the portion of mine inheritance. *Ps. 16: 5.*

I have a goodly heritage. *Ps. 16: 6.*

Our fathers trusted in thee: they trusted, and thou didst deliver them. *Ps. 22: 4.*

I have considered the days of old, the years of ancient times. *Ps. 77: 5.*

One generation shall praise thy works to another. *Ps. 145: 4.*

The memory of the just is blessed. *Pr. 10: 7.*

The fathers have eaten a sour grape, and the children's teeth are set on edge. *Je. 31: 29.*

Think not to say within yourselves, We have Abraham to our father: for I say unto you, that God is able of these stones to raise up children unto Abraham. *Mat. 3: 9.*

They are not all Israel, which are of Israel: neither because they are the seed of Abraham, are they all children. *Ro. 9: 6, 7.*

They without us should not be made perfect. *He. 11: 40.*

See also

Descent; Father; Genealogy; Generation; Heritage.

Anchor

My covenant shall stand fast. *Ps.* 89: 28.

He shall not be afraid of evil tidings: his heart is fixed, trusting in the Lord. *Ps.* 112: 7.

They cast four anchors out of the stern, and wished for the day. *Ac.* 27: 29.

Stand fast in the faith. *1 Co.* 16: 13.

Stand fast therefore in the liberty wherewith Christ hath made us free. *Ga.* 5: 1.

Now we live, if ye stand fast in the Lord. *1 Th.* 3: 8.

Prove all things; hold fast that which is good. *1 Th.* 5: 21.

Stand fast, and hold the traditions which ye have been taught. *2 Th.* 2: 15.

Hold fast the confidence and the rejoicing of the hope firm unto the end. *He.* 3: 6.

Hope we have as an anchor of the soul, both sure and stedfast. *He.* 6: 19.

Let us hold fast the profession of our faith without wavering. *He.* 10: 23.

That which ye have already hold fast till I come. *Re.* 2: 25.

See also

Steadfastness.

Angel

The Lord . . . shall send his angel before thee. *Ge.* 24: 7.

Behold the angels of God ascending and descending on it. *Ge.* 28: 12.

And he said, Let me go, for the day breaketh. And he said, I will not let thee go, except thou bless me. *Ge.* 32: 26.

He shall give his angels charge over thee, to keep thee in all thy ways. *Ps.* 91: 11.

Bless the Lord, ye his angels. *Ps.* 103: 20.

My God hath sent his angel, and hath shut the lions' mouths. *Da.* 6: 22.

Behold, angels came and ministered unto him. *Mat.* 4: 11.

They . . . are as the angels of God in heaven. *Mat.* 22: 30.

They had also seen a vision of angels. *Lu.* 24: 23.

All . . . saw his face as it had been the face of an angel. *Ac.* 6: 15.

The Lord himself shall descend from heaven . . . with the voice of the archangel. *1 Th.* 4: 16.

Be not forgetful to entertain strangers: for thereby some have entertained angels unawares. *He.* 13: 2.

Which things the angels desire to look into. *1 Pe.* 1: 12.

See also

Forerunner; Messenger.

Anger

O Lord, rebuke me not in thine anger. *Ps.* 6: 1.

His anger endureth but a moment. *Ps.* 30: 5.

Who may stand in thy sight when once thou art angry? *Ps.* 76: 7.

A soft answer turneth away wrath: but grievous words stir up anger. *Pr.* 15: 1.

He that is slow to anger is better than the mighty; and he that ruleth his spirit than he that taketh a city. *Pr.* 16: 32.

The discretion of a man deferreth his anger; and it is his glory to pass over a transgression. *Pr.* 19: 11.

Wrath is cruel. *Pr.* 27: 4.

I . . . will be no more angry. *Eze.* 16: 42.

It displeased Jonah exceedingly, and he was very angry. *Jon.* 4: 1.

Whosoever is angry with his brother without a cause shall be in danger of the judgment. *Mat.* 5: 22.

Let not the sun go down upon your wrath. *Ep.* 4: 26.

Slow to wrath. *Ja.* 1: 19.

See also

Christ, Wrath of; Displeasure; Fury; God, Anger of; God, Wrath of; Indignation; Passion, Rage; Resentment; Vexation; Wrath.

Angler

There dwelt men of Tyre also therein, which brought fish. *Ne.* 13: 16.

The fishers also shall mourn, and all they that cast angle into the brooks shall lament, and they that spread nets upon the waters languish. *Is.* 19: 8.

They shall be broken in the purposes thereof, all that make sluices and ponds for fish. *Is.* 19: 10.

I will put hooks in thy jaws, and I will cause the fish of thy rivers to stick unto thy scales. *Eze.* 29: 4.

Follow me, and I will make you fishers of men. *Mat.* 4: 19.

Go thou to the sea, and cast an hook, and take up the fish that first cometh up. *Mat.* 17: 27.

Launch out into the deep, and let down your nets for a draught. *Lu.* 5: 4.

Peter saith unto them, I go a fishing. *Jn.* 21: 3.

Cast the net on the right side of the ship, and ye shall find. *Jn.* 21: 6.

Bring of the fish which ye have now caught. *Jn.* 21: 10.

See also

Fisher.

Anguish

He delivered them out of their distresses. *Ps.* 107: 6.

The pains of hell gat hold upon me. *Ps.* 116: 3.

Trouble and anguish have taken hold on me. *Ps.* 119: 143.

When your fear cometh as desolation, and your destruction cometh as a whirlwind; . . . Then shall they call upon me. *Pr.* 1: 27, 28.

He was wounded for our transgressions, he was bruised for our iniquities. *Is.* 53: 5.

There appeared an angel unto him from heaven, strengthening him. And being in an agony he prayed more earnestly: and his sweat was as it were great drops of blood falling down to the ground. *Lu.* 22: 43, 44.

Tribulation and anguish, upon every soul of man that doeth evil. *Ro.* 2: 9.

Out of much affliction and anguish of heart. *2 Co.* 2: 4.

Neither shall there be any more pain. *Re.* 21: 4.

See also

Affliction; Agony; Distress; Hell; Pain; Torment.

Animal

That ye may put difference between . . . unclean and clean. *Le.* 10: 10.

This is the law of the beasts. *Le.* 11: 46.

In that day will I make a covenant for them with the beasts of the field. *Ho.* 2: 18.

The beasts of the field shall be at peace with thee. *Jb.* 5: 23.

Thou hast put all things under his feet. *Ps.* 8: 6.

Thou preservest man and beast. *Ps.* 36: 6.

Every beast of the forest is mine. *Ps.* 50: 10.

A righteous man regardeth the life of his beast: but the tender mercies of the wicked are cruel. *Pr.* 12: 10.

A little child shall lead them. *Is.* 11: 6.

The beasts of the field cry also unto thee. *Jo.* 1: 20.

Be not afraid, ye beasts of the field. *Jo.* 2: 22.

Are not five sparrows sold for two farthings, and not one of them is forgotten before God? *Lu.* 12: 6.

I have never eaten anything that is common or unclean. *Ac.* 10: 14.

If meat make my brother to offend, I will eat no flesh. *1 Co.* 8: 13.

See also
Beast; Brute.

Animosity

Esau hated Jacob because of the blessing. *Ge.* 27: 41.

Thou shalt not hate thy brother in thine heart. *Le.* 19: 17.

They that hate thee shall be clothed with shame. *Jb.* 8: 22.

Consider mine enemies; for they are many; and they hate me with cruel hatred. *Ps.* 25: 19.

I will beat down his foes before his face, and plague them that hate him. *Ps.* 89: 23.

Many a time have they afflicted me from my youth: yet they have not prevailed against me. *Ps.* 129: 2.

Blessed are ye, when men shall hate you. *Lu.* 6: 22.

Marvel not, my brethren, if the world hate you. *1 Jn.* 3: 13.

See also
Antipathy; Enemy; Hatred; Hostility; Opposition.

Annals

This is the book of the generations of Adam. *Ge.* 5: 1.

All Israel were reckoned by genealogies. *1 Ch.* 9: 1.

The book of the records of thy fathers. *Ezr.* 4: 15.

On that night could not the king sleep, and he commanded to bring the book of records of the chronicles. *Es.* 6: 1.

Lo, I come: in the volume of the book it is written of me. *Ps.* 40: 7.

Of making many books there is no end. *Ec.* 12: 12.

The book of the generation of Jesus Christ, the son of David. *Mat.* 1: 1.

All the generations from Abraham to David are fourteen generations; and from David until the carrying away into Babylon are fourteen generations; and from the carrying away into Babylon unto Christ are fourteen generations. *Mat.* 1: 17.

Many have taken in hand to set forth in order a declaration of those things which are most surely believed among us. *Lu.* 1: 1.

There are also many other things which Jesus did, the which, if they should be written every one, I suppose that even the world itself could not contain the books that should be written. *Jn.* 21: 25.

Fellowlabourers, whose names are in the book of life. *Ph.* 4: 3.

This is the record, that God hath given to us eternal life. *1 Jn.* 5: 11.

See also
History; Past.

Annihilation

Every thing that is in the earth shall die. *Ge.* 6: 17.

All in whose nostrils was the breath of life, of all that was in the dry land, died. *Ge.* 7: 22.

He that sacrificeth unto any god, save unto the Lord only, he shall be utterly destroyed. *Ex.* 22: 20.

Behold, I am bringing such evil upon Jerusalem and Judah, that whosoever heareth of it, both his ears shall tingle. *2 K.* 21: 12.

I will wipe Jerusalem as a man wipeth a dish, wiping it, and turning it upside down. *2 K.* 21: 13.

At destruction and famine thou shalt laugh. *Jb.* 5: 22.

Thou turnest man to destruction. *Ps.* 90: 3.

Thou shalt not be afraid . . . for the destruction that wasteth at noonday. *Ps.* 91: 5, 6.

Bless the Lord, O my soul, . . . Who redeemeth thy life from destruction. *Ps.* 103: 2, 4.

Pride goeth before destruction. *Pr.* 16: 18.

Who shall be punished with everlasting destruction from the presence of the Lord. *2 Th.* 1: 9.

See also
Destruction; Overthrow; Ruin.

Anniversary

It came to pass the third day, which was Pharaoh's birthday, that he made a feast unto all his servants. *Ge.* 40: 20.

This is my name for ever, and this is my memorial unto all generations. *Ex.* 3: 15.

This day shall be unto you for a memorial; and ye shall keep it a feast to the Lord throughout your generations. *Ex.* 12: 14.

Ye shall observe the feast of unleavened bread. *Ex.* 12: 17.

Thy name, O Lord, endureth for ever; and thy memorial, O Lord, throughout all generations. *Ps.* 135: 13.

The memory of the just is blessed. *Pr.* 10: 7.

The memory of them is forgotten. *Ec.* 9: 5.

Wheresoever this gospel shall be preached in the whole world, there shall also this, that this woman hath done, be told for a memorial of her. *Mat.* 26: 13.

I will keep the passover at thy house with my disciples. *Mat.* 26: 18.

Herod on his birthday made a supper to his lords. *Mk.* 6: 21.

Many shall rejoice at his birth. *Lu.* 1: 14.

This do in remembrance of me. *Lu.* 22: 19.

One man esteemeth one day above another: another esteemeth every day alike. *Ro.* 14: 5.

He that regardeth the day, regardeth it unto the Lord; and he that regardeth not the day, to the Lord he doth not regard it. *Ro.* **14: 6.**

Ye observe days, and months, and times, and years. *Ga.* **4: 10.**

Call to remembrance the former days. *He.* **10: 32.**

Have these things always in remembrance. *2 Pe.* **1: 15.**

I stir up your pure minds by way of remembrance. *2 Pe.* **3: 1.**

See also

Celebration; Commemoration; History; Memory; Wedding.

Announcement

Proclaim liberty throughout all the land unto all the inhabitants thereof. *Le.* **25: 10.**

Proclaim in the ears of the people, saying, Whosoever is fearful and afraid, let him return. *Ju.* **7: 3.**

The Lord gave the word: great was the company of those that published it. *Ps.* **68: 11.**

The Lord shall cause his glorious voice to be heard. *Is.* **30: 30.**

The Lord hath anointed me to preach good tidings. *Is.* **61: 1.**

Stand in the gate of the Lord's house, and proclaim there this word. *Je.* **7: 2.**

We declare unto you glad tidings. *Ac.* **13: 32.**

Whom therefore ye ignorantly worship, him declare I unto you. *Ac.* **17: 23.**

Every man's work shall be made manifest: for the day shall declare it. *1 Co.* **3: 13.**

I declare unto you the gospel. *1 Co.* **15: 1.**

See also

Affirmation; Declaration; Herald; News, Good; Proclamation; Publicity; Tidings.

Annoyance

Thou shalt neither vex a stranger, nor oppress him. *Ex.* **22: 21.**

The Lord shall send upon thee cursing, vexation, and rebuke. *De.* **28: 20.**

His soul was vexed unto death. *Ju.* **16: 16.**

Art thou he that troubleth Israel? *1 K.* **18: 17.**

In those times there was no peace to him that went out, nor to him that came in. *2 Ch.* **15: 5.**

There the wicked cease from troubling. *Jb.* **3: 17.**

How long will ye vex my soul, and break me in pieces with words? *Jb.* **19: 2.**

The Almighty . . . hath vexed my soul. *Jb.* **27: 2.**

Lord, how are they increased that trouble me! *Ps.* **3: 1.**

O lord, heal me; for my bones are vexed. *Ps.* **6: 2.**

God is angry with the wicked every day. *Ps.* **7: 11.**

Behold, all is vanity and vexation of spirit. *Ec.* **1: 14.**

Better is an handful with quietness, than both the hands full with travail and vexation of spirit. *Ec.* **4: 6.**

The little foxes, that spoil the vines. *S. of S.* **2: 15.**

Is it a small thing for you to weary men, but will ye weary my God also? *Is.* **7: 13.**

They rebelled, and vexed his holy Spirit. *Is.* **63: 10.**

Ye have wearied the Lord with your words. Yet ye say, Wherein have we wearied him? *Mal.* **2: 17.**

Why troublest thou the Master? *Mk.* **5: 35.**

Lord, trouble not thyself: for I am not worthy. *Lu.* **7: 6.**

Trouble me not: the door is now shut. *Lu.* **11: 7.**

Because this widow troubleth me, I will avenge her, lest by her continual coming she weary me. *Lu.* **18: 5.**

Ye have not injured me at all. *Ga.* **4: 12.**

See also

Disturbance; Offence; Trouble; Vexation.

Annulment

Wilt thou also disannul my judgment? *Jb.* **40: 8.**

The Lord bringeth the counsel of the heathen to nought. *Ps.* **33: 10.**

The Lord . . . maketh the devices of the people of none effect. *Ps.* **33: 10.**

My covenant will I not break. *Ps.* **89: 34.**

Thou hast made void the covenant of thy servant. *Ps.* **89: 39.**

They have made void thy law. *Ps.* **119: 126.**

The idols he shall utterly abolish. *Is.* **2: 18.**

The Lord of hosts hath purposed, and who shall disannul it? *Is.* **14: 27.**

Your covenant with death shall be disannulled. *Is.* **28: 18.**

Your agreement with hell shall not stand. *Is.* **28: 18.**

My salvation shall be for ever, and my righteousness shall not be abolished. *Is.* **51: 6.**

Thus have ye made the commandment of God of none effect by your tradition. *Mat.* **15: 6.**

What if some did not believe? shall their unbelief make the faith of God without effect? *Ro.* **3: 3.**

Do we then make void the law through faith? God forbid: yea, we establish the law. *Ro.* **3: 31.**

The law of the Spirit of life in Christ Jesus hath made me free from the law of sin and death. *Ro.* **8: 2.**

Though it be but a man's covenant, yet if it be confirmed, no man disannulleth. *Ga.* **3: 15.**

This I say, that the covenant, that was confirmed before of God in Christ, the law, which was four hundred and thirty years after, cannot disannul. *Ga.* **3: 17.**

If ye be led of the Spirit, ye are not under the law. *Ga.* **5: 18.**

He . . . hath broken down the middle wall of partition between us. *Ep.* **2: 14.**

Having abolished in his flesh the enmity, even the law of commandments contained in ordinances. *Ep.* **2: 15.**

Our Saviour Jesus Christ . . . hath abolished death. *2 Ti.* **1: 10.**

Now once in the end of the world hath he appeared to put away sin by the sacrifice of himself. *He.* **9: 26.**

See also

Abolition; Cancellation.

Annunciation

The angel came in unto her. *Lu.* **1: 28.**

Hail, thou that art highly favoured, the Lord is with thee. *Lu.* **1: 28.**

Behold, thou shalt . . . bring forth a son, and shalt call his name Jesus. *Lu.* 1: 31.

The Holy Ghost shall come upon thee, and the power of the Highest shall overshadow thee. *Lu.* 1: 35.
See also
Proclamation.

Anointing

The Lord thy God hath chosen thee to be a special people unto himself. *De.* 7: 6.

He shall give strength unto his king, and exalt the horn of his anointed. *1 S.* 2: 10.

He poured the oil on his head. *2 K.* 9: 6.

Who then is willing to consecrate his service this day unto the Lord? *1 Ch.* 29: 5.

Thou anointest my head with oil. *Ps.* 23: 5.

The Lord hath anointed me to preach good tidings. *Is.* 61: 1.

They shall consecrate themselves. *Eze.* 43: 26.

A woman in the city, which was a sinner, . . . kissed his feet, and anointed them with the ointment. *Lu.* 7: 37, 38.

God anointed Jesus of Nazareth with the Holy Ghost and with power. *Ac.* 10: 38.

He which . . . hath anointed us, is God. *2 Co.* 1: 21.

Chosen of God, and precious. *1 Pe.* 2: 4.
See also
Consecration; Dedication; Oil; Ointment.

Answer

They cry, but none giveth answer. *Jb.* 35: 12.

He shall call upon me, and I will answer him. *Ps.* 91: 15.

Then shall they call upon me, but I will not answer. *Pr.* 1: 28.

Every man shall kiss his lips that giveth a right answer. *Pr.* 24: 26.

All that heard him were astonished at his understanding and answers. *Lu.* 2: 47.

O man, who art thou that repliest against God? *Ro.* 9: 20.

Be ready always to give an answer to every man that asketh you a reason of the hope that is in you. *1 Pe.* 3: 15.
See also
Prayer, Answer to; Reply.

Antagonism

Cain rose up against Abel his brother, and slew him. *Ge.* 4: 8.

Let not thine anger burn against thy servant. *Ge.* 44: 18.

Every man's sword was against his fellow, and there was a very great discomfiture. *1 S.* 14: 20.

Rebellion is as the sin of witchcraft, and stubbornness is as iniquity and idolatry. *1 S.* 15: 23.

Against whom hast thou exalted thy voice, and lifted up thine eyes on high? even against the Holy One of Israel. *2 K.* 19: 22.

When the wicked, even mine enemies and my foes, came upon me to eat up my flesh, they stumbled and fell. *Ps.* 27: 2.

Thou hast lifted me up, and hast not made my foes to rejoice over me. *Ps.* 30: 1.

I will beat down his foes before his face. *Ps.* 89: 23.

They shall fight every one against his brother, and every one against his neighbour;

city against city, and kingdom against kingdom. *Is.* 19: 2.

A man's foes shall be they of his own household. *Mat.* 10: 36.

For from henceforth there shall be five in one house divided, three against two, and two against three. *Lu.* 12: 52.

The Lord said unto my Lord, Sit thou on my right hand, Until I make thy foes thy footstool. *Ac.* 2: 34, 35.
See also
Adversary; Animosity; Antipathy; Enemy; Foe; Hatred; Hostility; Opponent; Opposition.

Anthem

They ministered . . . with singing. *1 Ch.* 6: 32.

Sing unto him, sing psalms unto him, talk ye of all his wondrous works. *1 Ch.* 16: 9.

He appointed singers unto the Lord, and that should praise the beauty of holiness. *2 Ch.* 20: 21.

Praise the Lord with harp: sing unto him with the psaltery. *Ps.* 33: 2.

My tongue shall sing aloud of thy righteousness. *Ps.* 51: 14.

Sing forth the honour of his name. *Ps.* 66: 2.

Let the nations be glad and sing for joy. *Ps.* 67: 4.

Sing us one of the songs of Zion. *Ps.* 137: 3.

I gat me men singers and women singers. *Ec.* 2: 8.

We will sing my songs to the stringed instruments all the days of our life in the house of the Lord. *Is.* 38: 20.
See also
Hymn; Psalm.

Antichrist

Ye have heard that antichrist shall come, even now are there many antichrists. *1 Jn.* 2: 18.

He is antichrist, that denieth the Father and the Son. *1 Jn.* 2: 22.

Every spirit that confesseth not that Jesus Christ is come in the flesh is not of God: and this is that spirit of antichrist. *1 Jn.* 4: 3.
See also
Devil; Lucifer; Satan.

Anticipation

The expectation of the poor shall not perish. *Ps.* 9: 18.

Wait thou only upon God; for my expectation is from him. *Ps.* 62: 5.

Lord, I have hoped for thy salvation. *Ps.* 119: 166.

The earnest expectation of the creature waiteth for the manifestation of the sons of God. *Ro.* 8: 19.

If we hope for that we see not, then do we with patience wait for it. *Ro.* 8: 25.

Charity . . . hopeth all things. *1 Co.* 13: 4, 7.

While we look not at the things which are seen, but at the things which are not seen. *2 Co.* 4: 18.

I press toward the mark. *Ph.* 3: 14.

Looking for that blessed hope, and the glorious appearing of the great God and our Saviour Jesus Christ. *Tit.* 2: 13.

There remaineth therefore a rest to the people of God. *He.* 4: 9.

Unto them that look for him shall he appear the second time. *He.* 9: 28.

Looking for and hasting unto the coming of the day of God. *2 Pe.* 3: 12.

We . . . look for new heavens and a new earth. *2 Pe.* 3: 13.

See also

Christ, Hope in; Expectancy; Future; God, Hope in; Hope; Progress; Wait.

Antidote

He went forth unto the spring of the waters, and cast the salt in there, and said, Thus saith the Lord, I have healed these waters. *2 K.* 2: 21.

The wrath of God arose against his people, till there was no remedy. *2 Ch.* 36: 16.

Suddenly shall he be broken without remedy. *Pr.* 6: 15.

He, that being often reproved hardeneth his neck, shall suddenly be destroyed, and that without remedy. *Pr.* 29: 1.

Is there no balm in Gilead? *Je.* 8: 22.

Thou hast no healing medicines. *Je.* 30: 13.

I will bring it health and cure, and I will cure them. *Je.* 33: 6.

In vain shalt thou use many medicines; for thou shalt not be cured. *Je.* 46: 11.

Take balm for her pain, if so be she may be healed. *Je.* 51: 8.

The fruit thereof shall be for meat, and the leaf thereof for medicine. *Eze.* 47: 12.

The leaves of the tree were for the healing of the nations. *Re.* 22: 2.

See also

Balm; Medicine; Physician; Remedy.

Antipathy

He teareth me in his wrath, who hateth me. *Jb.* 16: 9.

All my inward friends abhorred me. *Jb.* 19: 19.

The Lord trieth the righteous: but the wicked and him that loveth violence his soul hateth. *Ps.* 11: 5.

They hate me with cruel hatred. *Ps.* 25: 19.

How long will ye imagine mischief against a man? *Ps.* 62: 3.

They have rewarded me evil for good, and hatred for my love. *Ps.* 109: 5.

My soul hath long dwelt with him that hateth peace. *Ps.* 120: 6.

The Lord was as an enemy. *La.* 2: 5.

Thou hast had a perpetual hatred. *Eze.* 35: 5.

I am come to set a man at variance against his father, and the daughter against her mother, and the daughter in law against her mother in law. *Mat.* 10: 35.

Every city or house divided against itself shall not stand. *Mat.* 12: 25.

That which I do I allow not: for what I would, that do I not; but what I hate, that do I. *Ro.* 7: 15.

See also

Animosity; Antagonism; Enemy; Foe; Hatred; Hostility; Opposition.

Antiquity

Giants dwelt therein in old time. *De.* 2: 20.

The word of the Lord was precious in those days. *1 S.* 3: 1.

As saith the proverb of the ancients. *1 S.* 24: 13.

With the ancient is wisdom; and in length of days understanding. *Jb.* 12: 12.

I have considered the days of old, the years of ancient times. *Ps.* 77: 5.

Remove not the ancient landmark, which thy fathers have set. *Pr.* 22: 28.

Say not thou, What is the cause that the former days were better than these? for thou dost not inquire wisely concerning this. *Ec.* 7: 10.

The ancient and honourable, he is the head. *Is.* 9: 15.

Is this your joyous city, whose antiquity is of ancient days? *Is.* 23: 7.

Remember the former things of old: for I am God. *Is.* 46: 9.

It is a mighty nation, it is an ancient nation. *Je.* 5: 15.

One like the Son of man came with the clouds of heaven, and came to the Ancient of days. *Da.* 7: 13.

Hath this been in your days, or even in the days of your fathers? *Jo.* 1: 2.

Now I will not be unto the residue of this people as in the former days. *Zch.* 8: 11.

Woe unto you, scribes and Pharisees, hypocrites! because ye build the tombs of the prophets, . . . And say, If we had been in the days of our fathers, we would not have been partakers with them in the blood of the prophets. *Mat.* 23: 29, 30.

Call to remembrance the former days. *He.* 10: 32.

See also

Descent; Heritage; Inheritance; Old; Past; Time, Past.

Antithesis

God called the light Day, and the darkness he called Night. *Ge.* 1: 5.

The heaven for height, and the earth for depth. *Pr.* 25: 3.

A time to kill, and a time to heal; a time to break down, and a time to build up. *Ec.* 3: 3.

A time to get, and a time to lose; a time to keep, and a time to cast away. *Ec.* 3: 6.

A time to rend, and a time to sew; a time to keep silence, and a time to speak. *Ec.* 3: 7.

A time to love, and a time to hate; a time of war, and a time of peace. *Ec.* 3: 8.

Till heaven and earth pass away. *Mat.* 5: 18.

Swear not at all: neither by heaven; for it is God's throne: Nor by the earth; for it is his footstool. *Mat.* 5: 34, 35.

Five of them were wise, and five were foolish. *Mat.* 25: 2.

There was a certain rich man, . . . And there was a certain beggar. *Lu.* 16: 19, 20.

Two men went up into the temple to pray; the one a Pharisee, and the other a publican. *Lu.* 18: 10.

God, I thank thee, that I am not as other men are. *Lu.* 18: 11.

I saw a new heaven and a new earth. *Re.* 21: 1.

See also

Extreme; Opposition.

Anvil

They did beat the gold into thin plates.
Ex. 39: 3.

There was no smith found throughout all
the land of Israel. *1 S.* 13: 19.

They shall beat their swords into plowshares,
and their spears into pruninghooks. *Is.* 2: 4.

The carpenter encouraged the goldsmith,
and he that smootheth with the hammer him
that smote the anvil. *Is.* 41: 7.

The smith with the tongs both worketh in
the coals, and fashioneth it with hammers
and worketh it with the strength of his arms.
Is. 44: 12.

I have created the smith that bloweth the
coals in the fire, and that bringeth forth an
instrument for his work. *Is.* 54: 16.

Of their silver and their gold have they
made them idols. *Ho.* 8: 4.

See also
Blacksmith.

Anxiety

Though I walk through the valley of the
shadow of death, I will fear no evil. *Ps.* 23: 4.

Fret not thyself because of evildoers. *Ps.* 37:
1.

I am troubled; I am bowed down greatly; I
go mourning all the day long. *Ps.* 38: 6.

He shall give his angels charge over thee, to
keep thee in all thy ways. *Ps.* 91: 11.

He that keepeth Israel shall neither slumber
nor sleep. *Ps.* 121: 4.

Which of you by taking thought can add
one cubit unto his stature? *Mat.* 6: 27.

Why take ye thought for raiment? *Mat.* 6: 28.

Take therefore no thought for the morrow:
for the morrow shall take thought for the
things of itself. *Mat.* 6: 34.

The cares of this world . . . choke the word,
and it becometh unfruitful. *Mk.* 4: 19.

Martha, Martha, thou art careful and
troubled about many things. *Lu.* 10: 41.

When they bring you unto the synagogues,
and unto magistrates, and powers, take ye no
thought how or what thing ye shall answer,
or what ye shall say. *Lu.* 12: 11.

Why are ye troubled? and why do thoughts
arise in your hearts? *Lu.* 24: 38.

I would have you without carefulness. *1 Co.*
7: 32.

We are troubled on every side. *2 Co.* 4: 8.

Be careful for nothing: but in every thing
by prayer and supplication with thanksgiving
let your requests be made known unto God.
Ph. 4: 6.

Casting all your care upon him. *1 Pe.* 5: 7.

See also
Concern; Fretfulness; Solicitude; Tension;
Torment; Trial; Trouble; Vexation; Worry.

Apathy

The tender and delicate woman among you,
. . . her eye shall be evil toward the husband
of her bosom, and toward her son, and toward
her daughter. *De.* 28: 56.

She is hardened against her young ones, as
though they were not her's. *Jb.* 39: 16.

Harden not your heart. *Ps.* 95: 8.

I looked on my right hand, and beheld,
but there was no man that would know me.
Ps. 142: 4.

No man cared for my soul. *Ps.* 142: 4.

Hear now this, thou that art given to
pleasures, that dwellest carelessly. *Is.* 47: 8.

They are all dumb dogs, they cannot bark;
sleeping, lying down, loving to slumber. *Is.*
56: 10.

They shall not lament for him, saying, Ah
my brother! or, Ah sister! they shall not
lament for him, saying, Ah Lord! or, Ah his
glory! *Je.* 22: 18.

They are not grieved for the affliction of
Joseph. *Am.* 6: 6.

This is the rejoicing city that dwelt carelessly. *Zph.* 2: 15.

Let not thine hands be slack. *Zph.* 3: 16.

How often would I have gathered thy children together, even as a hen gathereth her
chickens under her wings, and ye would not!
Mat. 23: 37.

I would have you without carefulness. *1 Co.*
7: 32.

I have no man likeminded, who will
naturally care for your state. *Ph.* 2: 20.

All seek their own, not the things which are
Jesus Christ's. *Ph.* 2: 21.

See also
Callousness; Dullness; Indifference.

Apocalypse

The heavens were opened, and I saw visions
of God. *Eze.* 1: 1.

I saw in my vision by night. *Da.* 7: 2.

I Daniel alone saw the vision. *Da.* 10: 7.

Except I shall speak to you . . . by revelation. *1 Co.* 14: 6.

Caught up to the third heaven. *2 Co.* 12: 2.

And I went up by revelation. *Ga.* 2: 2.

Behold, he cometh with clouds; and every
eye shall see him. *Re.* 1: 7.

I was in the Spirit on the Lord's day, and
heard behind me a great voice, as of a trumpet.
Re. 1: 10.

After this I looked, and behold, a door was
opened in heaven. *Re.* 4: 1.

There appeared a great wonder in heaven.
Re. 12: 1.

I saw a new heaven and a new earth. *Re.* 21:
1.

I John saw the holy city, new Jerusalem,
coming down from God out of heaven. *Re.* 21:
2.

See also
Christ, Revelation of; God, Revelation of;
God, Vision of; Manifestation; Revelation;
Vision.

Apocrypha

The words of the wise, and their dark sayings. *Pr.* 1: 6.

I will give thee the treasures of darkness,
and hidden riches of secret places. *Is.* 45: 3.

I have shewed thee new things from this
time, even hidden things, and thou didst not
know them. *Is.* 48: 6.

We speak the wisdom of God in a mystery,
even the hidden wisdom. *1 Co.* 2: 7.

The Lord . . . will bring to light the hidden
things of darkness. *1 Co.* 4: 5.

See also
Secrecy.

Apostasy

The backslider in heart shall be filled with his own ways. *Pr.* 14: 14.

They have forsaken the Lord. *Is.* 1: 4.

Hast thou seen that which backsliding Israel hath done? *Je.* 3: 6.

Return, thou backsliding Israel, saith the Lord. *Je.* 3: 12.

They . . . went backward, and not forward. *Je.* 7: 24.

Thou hast forsaken me, saith the Lord, thou art gone backward. *Je.* 15: 6.

Jerusalem . . . sigheth, and turneth backward. *La.* 1: 8.

Israel slideth back as a backsliding heifer. *Ho.* 4: 16.

I will heal their backsliding. *Ho.* 14: 4.

Judas Iscariot, which also was the traitor. *Lu.* 6: 16.

No man, having put his hand to the plow, and looking back, is fit for the kingdom of God. *Lu.* 9: 62.

He that denieth me before men, shall be denied before the angels of God. *Lu.* 12: 9.

In the last days perilous times shall come. For men shall be . . . traitors. *2 Ti.* 3: 1, 2, 4.

See also

Backsliding; Christ, Denial of; Denial; Estrangement; God, Denial of; Refusal; Rejection; Renunciation; Treachery.

Apostle

They straightway left their nets, and followed him. *Mat.* 4: 20.

The disciple is not above his master. *Mat.* 10: 24.

They forsook all, and followed him. *Lu.* 5: 11.

If any man . . . hate not . . . his own life, . he cannot be my disciple. *Lu.* 14: 26.

He that followeth me shall not walk in darkness. *Jn.* 8: 12.

If ye continue in my word, then are ye my disciples indeed. *Jn.* 8: 31.

He . . . began to wash the disciples' feet. *Jn.* 13: 5.

Herein is my Father glorified, that ye bear much fruit; so shall ye be my disciples. *Jn.* 15: 8.

Art not thou also one of this man's disciples? *Jn.* 18: 17.

Be ye followers of me. *1 Co.* 4: 16.

Am I not an apostle? am I not free? *1 Co.* 9: 1.

Are all apostles? are all prophets? *1 Co.* 12: 29.

I . . . am not meet to be called an apostle. *1 Co.* 15: 9.

An apostle of Jesus Christ by the will of God. *2 Co.* 1: 1.

He gave some, apostles; and some, prophets; and some, evangelists. *Ep.* 4: 11.

Who is he that will harm you, if ye be followers of that which is good? *1 Pe.* 3: 13.

See also

Christ, Disciple of; Christ, Follower of; Disciple; Follower; Messenger; Missionary.

Apparel

They were both naked, the man and his wife, and were not ashamed. *Ge.* 2: 25.

Thy raiment waxed not old upon thee. *De.* 8: 4.

The Lord your God . . . loveth the stranger, in giving him food and raiment. *De.* 10: 17, 18.

My flesh is clothed with worms. *Jb.* 7: 5.

Drowsiness shall clothe a man with rags. *Pr.* 23: 21.

Can a maid forget her ornaments, or a bride her attire? *Je.* 2: 32.

I counsel thee to buy me . . . white raiment, that thou mayest be clothed. *Mat.* 3: 18.

Is not the life more than meat, and the body than raiment? *Mat.* 6: 25.

Why take ye thought for raiment? *Mat.* 6: 28.

Even Solomon in all his glory was not arrayed like one of these. *Mat.* 6: 29.

If God so clothe the grass of the field, which to day is, and to morrow is cast into the oven, shall he not much more clothe you, O ye of little faith? *Mat.* 6: 30.

If so be that being clothed we shall not be found naked. *2 Co.* 5: 3.

Having food and raiment let us be therewith content. *1 Ti.* 6: 8.

If there come unto your assembly a man with a gold ring, in goodly apparel, and there come in also a poor man in vile raiment; And ye have respect to him that weareth the gay clothing, . . . Are ye not then partial in yourselves? *Ja.* 2: 2-4.

Be clothed with humility. *1 Pe.* 5: 5.

I counsel thee to buy of me . . . white raiment, that thou mayest be clothed. *Re.* 3: 18.

What are these which are arrayed in white robes? and whence came they? *Re.* 7: 13.

Appeal

I call heaven and earth to witness against you this day. *De.* 4: 26.

Call ye on the name of your gods, and I will call on the name of the Lord. *1 K.* 18: 24.

Let thine ear now be attentive, and thine eyes open, that thou mayest hear the prayer of thy servant. *Ne.* 1: 6.

Call now, if there be any that will answer thee; and to which of the saints wilt thou turn? *Jb.* 5: 1.

Oh that I might have my request; and that God would grant me the thing that I long for! *Jb.* 6: 8.

Hear me when I call, O God of my righteousness. *Ps.* 4: 1.

Consider and hear me, O Lord my God. *Ps.* 13: 3.

The Lord fulfil all thy petitions. *Ps.* 20: 5.

Save with thy right hand, and hear me. *Ps.* 60: 5.

The Lord is nigh unto all them that call upon him, to all that call upon him in truth. *Ps.* 145: 18.

Seek ye the Lord while he may be found, call ye upon him while he is near. *Is.* 55: 6.

It shall come to pass, that before they call, I will answer; and while they are yet speaking, I will hear. *Is.* 65: 24.

I was constrained to appeal unto Caesar. *Ac.* 28: 19.

The same Lord over all is rich unto all that call upon him. *Ro.* 10: 12.

I therefore, the prisoner of the Lord, beseech you that ye walk worthy of the vocation wherewith ye are called. *Ep.* 4: 1.

Let your requests be made known unto God.
Ph. 4: 6.
Ye ask, and receive not, because ye ask
amiss. *Ja.* 4: 3.
See also
Entreaty; Petition; Plea; Request; Supplica-
tion.

Appearance
The angel of the Lord appeared unto him
in a flame of fire out of the midst of a bush.
Ex. 3: 2.
I will appear in the cloud upon the mercy
seat. *Le.* 16: 2.
Man looketh on the outward appearance, but
the Lord looketh on the heart. *1 S.* 16: 7.
When shall I come and appear before God?
Ps. 42: 2.
When the Lord shall build up Zion, he shall
appear in his glory. *Ps.* 102: 16.
The Lord hath appeared of old unto me.
Je. 31: 3.
When ye fast, be not, as the hypocrites, of a
sad countenance. *Mat.* 6: 16.
There appeared unto them Moses and Elias
talking with him. *Mat.* 17: 3.
Ye are like unto whited sepulchres, which
indeed appear beautiful outward, but are
within full of dead men's bones. *Mat.* 23: 27.
Judge not according to the appearance. *Jn.*
7: 24.
There appeared unto them cloven tongues
like as of fire. *Ac.* 2: 3.
We must all appear before the judgment
seat of Christ. *2 Co.* 5: 10.
Unto them that look for him shall he appear the second time without sin unto salvation. *He.* 9: 28.
If any man among you seem to be religious,
and bridleth not his tongue, but deceiveth
his own heart, this man's religion is vain. *Ja.*
1: 26.
When the chief Shepherd shall appear, ye
shall receive a crown of glory that fadeth not
away. *1 Pe.* 5: 4.
When he shall appear, we shall be like him.
1 Jn. 3: 2.
See also
Apocalypse; Christ, Revelation of; Christ,
Second Coming of; Coming, Second; God, Revelation of; God, Vision of; Look; Manifestation; Revelation; Vision.

Appetite
Of the tree of the knowledge of good and
evil, thou shalt not eat of it. *Ge.* 2: 17.
Let me not eat of their dainties. *Ps.* 141: 4.
Put a knife to thy throat, if thou be a man
given to appetite. *Pr.* 23: 2.
Be not among winebibbers; among riotous
eaters of flesh. *Pr.* 23: 20.
The drunkard and the glutton shall come to
poverty. *Pr.* 23: 21.
Let us eat and drink; for to morrow we shall
die. *Is.* 22: 13.
The Son of man came eating and drinking,
and they say, Behold a man gluttonous, and a
winebibber. *Mat.* 11: 19.
Woe unto you that are full! for ye shall
hunger. *Lu.* 6: 25.
Take thine ease, eat, drink, and be merry.
Lu. 12: 19.

The kingdom of God is not meat and drink.
Ro. 14: 17.
It is evil for that man who eateth with of-
fence. *Ro.* 14: 20.
Even unto this present hour we both hunger,
and thirst. *1 Co.* 4: 11.
Be not drunk with wine, wherein is excess.
Ep. 5: 18.
I am instructed both to be full and to be
hungry. *Ph.* 4: 12.
When we walked in . . . excess of wine
revellings, banquetings. *1 Pe.* 4: 3.
See also
Desire; Drunkenness; Food; Gluttony;
Hunger; Intoxication; Longing; Lust; Passion.

Applause
O clap your hands, all ye people; shout unto
God with the voice of triumph. *Ps.* 47: 1.
Let the floods clap their hands: let the hills
be joyful together. *Ps.* 98: 8.
When a man's ways please the Lord, he
maketh even his enemies to be at peace with
him. *Pr.* 16: 7.
All the trees of the field shall clap their
hands. *Is.* 55: 12.
This is my beloved Son, in whom I am well
pleased. *Mat.* 3: 17.
Let your light so shine before men, that
they may see your good works, and glorify
your Father which is in heaven. *Mat.* 5: 16.
Well done, thou good and faithful servant.
Mat. 25: 21.
Inasmuch as ye have done it unto one of the
least of these my brethren, ye have done it unto
me. *Mat.* 25: 40.
She hath wrought a good work upon me.
Mat. 26: 10.
Wheresoever this gospel shall be preached
in the whole world, there shall also this, that
this woman hath done, be told for a memorial
of her. *Mat.* 26: 13.
Mary hath chosen that good part, which
shall not be taken away from her. *Lu.* 10: 42.
Praise the Lord, all ye Gentiles; and laud
him, all ye people. *Ro.* 15: 11.
Worthy of the Lord unto all pleasing. *Col.*
1: 10.
See also
Acclamation; Approval; Assent.

Appointment
Thy servants are ready to do whatsoever my
Lord the king shall appoint. *2 S.* 15: 15.
He chose David also his servant, and took
him from the sheepfolds. *Ps.* 78: 70.
I heard the voice of the Lord, saying, Whom
shall I send, and who will go for us? Then said
I, Here am I; send me. *Is.* 6: 8.
Thou shalt go to all that I shall send thee,
and whatsoever I command thee thou shalt
speak. *Je.* 1: 7.
See, I have this day set thee over the na-
tions and over the kingdoms. *Je.* 1: 10.
Who is a chosen man, that I may appoint
over her? *Je.* 49: 19.
Son of man, stand upon thy feet, and I will
speak unto thee. *Eze.* 2: 1.
The Lord took me as I followed the flock,
and the Lord said unto me, Go, prophesy unto
my people Israel. *Am.* 7: 15.
The Lord appointed other seventy also, and

sent them two and two before his face into every city and place, whither he himself would come. *Lu.* 10: 1.

Go your ways: behold, I send you forth as lambs among wolves. *Lu.* 10: 3.

He is a chosen vessel unto me. *Ac.* 9: 15.

There stood a man of Macedonia, and prayed him, saying, Come over into Macedonia, and help us. *Ac.* 16: 9.

Called to be an apostle. *Ro.* 1: 1.

He that is called in the Lord, being a servant, is the Lord's freeman: likewise also he that is called, being free, is Christ's servant. *1 Co.* 7: 22.

No man should be moved by these afflictions: for yourselves know that we are appointed thereunto. *1 Th.* 3: 3.

I am appointed a preacher, and an apostle, and a teacher of the Gentiles. *2 Ti.* 1: 11.

His Son, whom he hath appointed heir of all things. *He.* 1: 2.

See also

Choice; Direction; Election; Establishment; Office; Order.

Appraisal

My soul was precious in thine eyes. *1 S.* 26: 21.

Thou art worth ten thousand of us. *2 S.* 18: 3.

I will give thee the worth of it in money. *1 K.* 21: 2.

Oh that my grief were throughly weighed. *Jb.* 6: 2.

Ye are all physicians of no value. *Jb.* 13: 4.

Who will make me a liar, and make my speech nothing worth? *Jb.* 24: 25.

Wisdom . . . cannot be valued with the gold of Ophir. *Jb.* 28: 12, 16.

Let me be weighed in an even balance. *Jb.* 31: 6.

The heart of the wicked is little worth. *Pr.* 10: 20.

Many waters cannot quench love, neither can the floods drown it: if a man would give all the substance of his house for love, it would utterly be contemned. *S. of S.* 8: 7.

Thou art weighed in the balances, and art found wanting. *Da.* 5: 27.

Ye are of more value than many sparrows. *Mat.* 10: 31.

They took the thirty pieces of silver, the price of him that was valued. *Mat.* 27: 9.

I seek not your's, but you. *2 Co.* 12: 14.

See also

Price; Value; Worth.

Appreciation

God saw every thing that he had made, and, behold, it was very good. *Ge.* 1: 31.

I will call on the Lord, who is worthy to be praised. *2 S.* 22: 4.

She is more precious than rubies. *Pr.* 3: 15.

A virtuous woman is a crown to her husband. *Pr.* 12: 4.

Let another man praise thee, and not thine own mouth. *Pr.* 27: 2.

A good name is better than precious ointment. *Ec.* 7: 1.

I will make a man more precious than fine gold. *Is.* 13: 12.

Ye are of more value than many sparrows. *Mat.* 10: 31.

Among them that are born of women there hath not risen a greater than John the Baptist. *Mat.* 11: 11.

Let each esteem other better than themselves. *Ph.* 2: 3.

Esteem them very highly in love for their work's sake. *1 Th.* 5: 13.

See also

Perception; Praise; Value; Worth.

Apprehension

God speaketh once, yea twice, yet man perceiveth it not. *Jb.* 33: 14.

He heard me, and delivered me from all my fears. *Ps.* 34: 4.

Fears shall be in the way. *Ec.* 12: 5.

The Lord shall give thee rest from thy sorrow, and from thy fear. *Is.* 14: 3.

I will put my fear in their hearts, that they shall not depart from me. *Je.* 32: 40.

Who is wise, and he shall understand these things? prudent, and he shall know them? *Ho.* 14: 9.

We were troubled on every side; without were fightings, within were fears. *2 Co.* 7: 5.

I count not myself to have apprehended. *Ph.* 3: 13.

That ye might be filled with the knowledge of his will . . . and spiritual understanding. *Col.* 1: 9.

Lay hold on eternal life, whereunto thou art also called. *1 Ti.* 6: 12.

That . . . we might have a strong consolation, who have fled for refuge to lay hold upon the hope set before us. *He.* 6: 18.

Through faith we understand that the worlds were framed by the word of God. *He.* 11: 3.

See also

Anxiety; Concern; Fear.

Approach

Let us draw near hither unto God. *1 S.* 14: 36.

The king approached to the altar, and offered thereon. *2 K.* 16: 12.

Be ye lift up, ye everlasting doors; and the King of glory shall come in. *Ps.* 24: 7.

It is good for me to draw near to God. *Ps.* 73: 28.

They draw near unto the gates of death. *Ps.* 107: 18.

Open ye the gates, that the righteous nation which keepeth the truth may enter in. *Is.* 26: 2.

I will camp against thee round about. *Is.* 29: 3.

Come near, ye nations, to hear; and hearken, ye people. *Is.* 34: 1.

They take delight in approaching to God. *Is.* 58: 2.

I will cause him to draw near, and he shall approach unto me. *Je.* 30: 21.

The priests that approach unto the Lord. *Eze.* 42: 13.

Enter ye in at the strait gate: for wide is the gate, and broad is the way, that leadeth to destruction. *Mat.* 7: 13.

Say unto them, The kingdom of God is come nigh unto you. *Lu.* 10: 9.

They rehearsed all that God had done with them, and how he had opened the door of faith unto the Gentiles. *Ac.* 14: 27.

The light which no man can approach unto *1 Ti.* 6: 16.

Let us draw near with a true heart and full assurance of faith. *He.* 10: 22.

Draw nigh to God, and he will draw nigh to you. *Ja.* 4: 8.

All nations shall come and worship before thee. *Re.* 15: 4.

See also

Access; Advance; Christ, Coming to; Christ, the Door; Door; Way.

Approval

The Lord taketh pleasure in his people. *Ps.* 149: 4.

The Lord is well pleased for his righteousness' sake. *Is.* 42: 21.

This is my beloved Son, in whom I am well pleased. *Mat.* 3: 17.

Blessed is that servant, whom his lord when he cometh shall find so doing. *Mat.* 24: 46.

Well done, thou good and faithful servant. *Mat.* 25: 21.

He that is faithful in that which is least is faithful also in much. *Lu.* 16: 10.

With such sacrifices God is well pleased. *He.* 13: 16.

If ye fulfil the royal law, . . . ye do well. *Ja.* 2: 8.

The praise of them that do well. *1 Pe.* 2: 14.

We . . . do those things that are pleasing in his sight. *1 Jn.* 3: 22.

See also

Acceptance; Acclamation; Acquiescence; Assent; Confirmation.

Aptitude

Apt for war. *2 K.* 24: 16.

And shall make him of quick understanding. *Is.* 11: 3.

I long to see you, that I may impart unto you some spiritual gift. *Ro.* 1: 11.

A bishop then must be . . . apt to teach. *1 Ti.* 3: 2.

Neglect not the gift that is in thee. *1 Ti.* 4: 14.

See also

Ability; Capacity; Endowment; Expert; Gift; Skill; Talent.

Arbitration

The Lord judge between me and thee. *Ge.* 16: 5.

The God of Abraham . . . judge betwixt us. *Ge.* 31: 53.

The Lord therefore be judge . . . between me and thee. *1 S.* 24: 15.

Come now, and let us reason together, saith the Lord. *Is.* 1: 18.

He shall judge among the nations. *Is.* 2: 4.

And now, . . . judge, I pray you, betwixt me and my vineyard. *Is.* 5: 3.

He said unto him. Man, who made me a judge or a divider over you. *Lu.* 12: 14.

See also

Judgment.

Archangel

At that time shall Michael stand up, the great prince which standeth for the children of thy people. *Da.* 12: 1.

I am Gabriel, that stand in the presence of God; and I am sent to speak unto thee. *Lu.* 1: 19.

The angel Gabriel was sent from God unto a city of Galilee, named Nazareth, To a virgin. *Lu.* 1: 26, 27.

For the Lord himself shall descend from heaven with a shout, with the voice of the archangel. *1 Th.* 4: 16.

I saw the seven angels which stood before God. *Re.* 8: 2.

There was war in heaven: Michael and his angels fought against the dragon. *Re.* 12: 7.

I saw another sign in heaven, great and marvellous, seven angels having the seven last plagues. *Re.* 15: 1.

I heard the angel of the waters say, Thou are righteous, O Lord, which art, and wast, and shalt be. *Re.* 16: 5.

I heard another out of the altar say, Even so, Lord God Almighty, true and righteous are thy judgments. *Re.* 16: 7.

There came one of the seven angels which had the seven vials, and talked with me. *Re.* 17: 1.

After these things I saw another angel come down from heaven, having great power; and the earth was lightened with his glory. *Re.* 18: 1.

I saw an angel standing in the sun. *Re.* 19: 17.

Architecture

The two doors also were of olive tree. *1 K.* 6: 32.

Let the house of God be builded in his place. *Ezr.* 5: 15.

He built his sanctuary like high palaces. *Ps.* 78: 69.

Strength and beauty are in his sanctuary. *Ps.* 96: 6.

Except the Lord build the house, they labour in vain that build it: except the Lord keep the city, the watchman waketh but in vain. *Ps.* 127: 1.

Through wisdom is an house builded. *Pr.* 24: 3.

The glory of Lebanon shall come unto thee, the fir tree, the pine tree, and the box together, to beautify the place of my sanctuary. *Is.* 60: 13.

Behold, the days come, saith the Lord, that the city shall be built to the Lord. *Je.* 31: 38.

The city that men call The perfection of beauty. *La.* 2: 15.

Thy borders are in the midst of the seas, thy builders have perfected thy beauty. *Eze.* 27: 4.

He is like a man which built an house. *Lu.* 6: 48.

The gate of the temple which is called Beautiful. *Ac.* 3: 2.

As a wise masterbuilder, I have laid the foundation, and another buildeth thereon. *1 Co.* 3: 10.

We have a building of God, an house not made with hands, eternal in the heavens. *2 Co.* 5: 1.

He looked for a city which hath foundations, whose builder and maker is God. *He.* **11: 10.**

See also

Art; Builder.

Ardor

He was zealous for my sake among them. *Nu.* **25: 11.**

The zeal of thine house hath eaten me up. *Ps.* **69: 9.**

Not slothful in business; fervent in spirit; serving the Lord. *Ro.* **12: 11.**

Whether we be beside ourselves, it is to God: or whether we be sober, it is for your cause. *2 Co.* **5: 13.**

Your fervent mind. *2 Co.* **7: 7.**

It is good to be zealously affected always in a good thing. *Ga.* **4: 18.**

Our God is a consuming fire. *He.* **12: 29.**

The effectual fervent prayer of a righteous man availeth much. *Ja.* **5: 16.**

See that ye love one another with a pure heart fervently. *1 Pe.* **1: 22.**

See also

Eagerness; Earnestness; Enthusiasm; Fervor; Zeal; Zest.

Argument

How forcible are right words! but what doth your arguing reprove? *Jb.* **6: 25.**

Surely I would speak to the Almighty, and I desire to reason with God. *Jb.* **13: 3.**

Should he reason with unprofitable talk? or with speeches wherewith he can do no good? *Jb.* **15: 3.**

I would order my cause before him, and fill my mouth with arguments. *Jb.* **23: 4.**

Debate thy cause with thy neighbour himself; and discover not a secret to another. *Pr.* **25: 9.**

The Lord hath a controversy with the nations. *Je.* **25: 31.**

O ye of little faith, why reason ye among yourselves. *Mat.* **16: 8.**

Lest there be debates, envyings, wraths, strifes, backbitings, whisperings, swellings, tumults. *2 Co.* **12: 20.**

See also

Cause; Controversy; Debate; Dispute; Reason; Speech.

Aridity

They went three days in the wilderness, and found no water. *Ex.* **15: 22.**

My flesh longeth for thee in a dry and thirsty land, where no water is. *Ps.* **63: 1.**

He turneth the wilderness into a standing water, and dry ground into watersprings. *Ps.* **107: 35.**

Better is a dry morsel, and quietness therewith, than an house full of sacrifices with strife. *Pr.* **17: 1.**

Whoso boasteth himself of a false gift is like clouds and wind without rain. *Pr.* **25: 14.**

As the heat in a dry place. *Is.* **25: 5.**

A man shall be as . . . rivers of water in a dry place. *Is.* **32: 2.**

The parched ground shall become a pool. *Is.* **35: 7.**

O ye dry bones, hear the word of the Lord. *Eze.* **37: 4.**

The unclean spirit . . walketh through dry places, seeking rest, and findeth none. *Mat.* **12: 43.**

If they do these things in a green tree, what shall be done in the dry? *Lu.* **23: 31.**

See also

Barrenness; Desert; Dryness; Sand.

Aristocracy

Take you wise men, . . . and I will make them rulers over you. *De.* **1: 13.**

I . . . have made thee a great name, like unto the name of the great men that are in the earth. *2 S.* **7: 9.**

He that ruleth over men must be just, ruling in the fear of God. *2 S.* **23: 3.**

These also are the chief of the mighty men whom David had. *1 Ch.* **11: 10.**

Let now our rulers of all the congregation stand. *Ezr.* **10: 14.**

Put not forth thyself in the presence of the king, and stand not in the place of great men. *Pr.* **25: 6.**

I will get me unto the great men, and will speak unto them; for they have known the way of the Lord. *Je.* **5: 5.**

The rich men thereof are full of violence. *Mi.* **6: 12.**

I am among you as he that serveth. *Lu.* **22: 27.**

Do not rich men oppress you, and draw you before the judgment seats? *Ja.* **2: 6.**

Go to now, ye rich men, weep and howl for your miseries that shall come upon you. *Ja.* **5: 1.**

The kings of the earth, and the great men, and the rich men, and the chief captains, and the mighty men . . . hid themselves; . . . For the great day of his wrath is come. *Re.* **6: 15, 17.**

Thy merchants were the great men of the earth. *Re.* **18: 23.**

See also

Best; Chief; Greatness; Nobility.

Ark

Come thou and all thy house into the ark. *Ge.* **7: 1.**

There went in two and two unto Noah into the ark. *Ge.* **7: 9.**

He took and put the testimony into the ark. *Ex.* **40: 20.**

Joshua . . . fell to the earth upon his face before the ark of the Lord. *Jos.* **7: 6.**

The glory is departed from Israel: for the ark of God is taken. *1 S.* **4: 22.**

What shall we do with the ark of the God of Israel? *1 S.* **5: 8.**

If ye send away the ark of the God of Israel, send it not empty. *1 S.* **6: 3.**

They lifted up their eyes, and saw the ark, and rejoiced to see it. *1 S.* **6: 13.**

By faith Noah . . . prepared an ark to the saving of his house. *He.* **11: 7.**

Arm

The greatness of thine arm. *Ex.* **15: 16.**

Underneath are the everlasting arms. *De.* **33: 27.**

Hast thou an arm like God? *Jb.* **40: 9.**

Neither did their own arm save them: but thy right hand, and thine arm. *Ps.* **44: 3.**

Thou hast with thine arm redeemed thy people. *Ps.* **77: 15.**

His holy arm hath gotten him the victory.
Ps. **98:** 1.

Great is our Lord, and of great power. *Ps.*
147: 5.

He shall gather the lambs with his arm.
Is. **40:** 11.

I have made the earth . . . by my outstretched arm. *Je.* **27:** 5.

All day long I have stretched forth my
hands unto a disobedient and gainsaying
people. *Ro.* **10:** 21.

Who are kept by the power of God through
faith unto salvation. *1 Pe.* **1:** 5.

See also

Might; Power; Strength; Support; Weapon.

Armistice

Comest thou peaceably? And he said,
Peaceably. *1 S.* **16:** 4, 5.

Shall the sword devour for ever? knowest
thou not that it will be bitterness in the latter
end? *2 S.* **2:** 26.

Thus saith the king, Is it peace? *2 K.* **9:** 19.

If ye be come peaceably unto me to help
me, mine heart shall be knit unto you. *1 Ch.*
12: 17.

Thou shalt not build an house unto my
name, because thou hast shed much blood
upon the earth in my sight. *1 Ch.* **22:** 8.

Thus saith the Lord, Ye shall not go up,
nor fight against your brethren. *2 Ch.* **11:** 4.

He maketh wars to cease. *Ps.* **46:** 9.

He breaketh the bow, and cutteth the spear
in sunder; he burneth the chariot in the fire.
Ps. **46:** 9.

I am for peace: but when I speak, they are
for war. *Ps.* **120:** 7.

Nation shall not lift up sword against
nation, neither shall they learn war any more.
Is. **2:** 4.

Lord, thou wilt ordain peace for us. *Is.* **26:**
12.

Her warfare is accomplished. *Is.* **40:** 2.

All thy children shall be taught of the Lord;
and great shall be the peace of thy children.
Is. **54:** 13.

I know the thoughts that I think toward
you, saith the Lord, thoughts of peace, and
not of evil. *Je.* **29:** 11.

I will make a covenant of peace with them.
Eze. **37:** 26.

Nation shall not lift up a sword against
nation, neither shall they learn war any more.
Mi. **4:** 3.

Jerusalem shall be inhabited as towns without walls. *Zch.* **2:** 4.

The counsel of peace shall be between them
both. *Zch.* **6:** 13.

Blessed are the peacemakers. *Mat.* **5:** 9.

Have peace one with another. *Mk.* **9:** 50.

On earth peace, good will toward men. *Lu.*
2: 14.

He sendeth an ambassador, and desireth
conditions of peace. *Lu.* **14:** 32.

See also

Peace.

Armor

David . . . became his armourbearer. *1 S.*
16: 21.

He is my shield. *2 S.* **22:** 3.

He is our help and our shield. *Ps.* **33:** 20.

The Lord God is a sun and shield. *Ps.* **84:**
11.

Let us put on the armour of light. *Ro.* **13:**
12.

Put ye on the Lord Jesus Christ. *Ro.* **13:** 14.

By the word of truth, by the power of God,
by the armour of righteousness. *2 Co.* **6:** 7.

Put on the whole armour of God. *Ep.* **6:** 11.

Above all, taking the shield of faith. *Ep.* **6:**
16.

God hath not given us the spirit of fear:
but of power, and of love, and of a sound
mind. *2 Ti.* **1:** 7.

See also

Breastplate; Buckler; Defence; Helmet; Protection; Shield.

Army

Behold, the mountain was full of horses
and chariots of fire round about Elisha. *2 K.*
6: 17.

Terrible as an army with banners. *S. of S.*
6: 4.

They shall beat their swords into plowshares, and their spears into pruninghooks.
Is. **2:** 4.

Woe to them that . . . trust in chariots, because they are many; and in horsemen, because
they are very strong. *Is.* **31:** 1.

How then wilt thou . . . put thy trust on
Egypt for chariots and for horsemen? *Is.* **36:** 9.

They . . . stood up upon their feet, an
exceeding great army. *Eze.* **37:** 10.

I . . . will save them by the Lord their
God, and will not save them by bow, nor by
sword, nor by battle, by horses, nor by horsemen. *Ho.* **1:** 7.

Beat your plowshares into swords, and your
pruninghooks into spears; let the weak say, I
am strong. *Jo.* **3:** 10.

Endure hardness as a good soldier of Jesus
Christ. *2 Ti.* **2:** 3.

See also

Belligerent; Host; Soldier.

Arrest

Bring my soul out of prison. *Ps.* **142:** 7.

They shall be gathered together, as prisoners
are gathered in the pit, and shall be shut up
in the prison. *Is.* **24:** 22.

John was cast into prison. *Mat.* **4:** 12.

When they sought to lay hands on him,
they feared the multitude. *Mat.* **21:** 46.

They cast them into prison, charging the
jailor to keep them safely. *Ac.* **16:** 23.

Many of the saints did I shut up in prison.
Ac. **26:** 10.

See also

Captivity; Delay; Imprisonment; Prison.

Arrogance

I will break the pride of your power. *Le.*
26: 19.

Let not the foot of pride come against me.
Ps. **36:** 11.

Pride compasseth them about as a chain.
Ps. **73:** 6.

Pride, and arrogancy, . . . do I hate. *Pr.* **8:**
13.

Pride goeth before destruction. *Pr.* **16:** 18.

I am come to great estate, and have gotten
more wisdom than all they that have been
before me in Jerusalem. *Ec.* **1:** 16.

I will cause the arrogancy of the proud to cease. *Is.* 13: 11.

Thou hast said in thine heart, I will ascend into heaven, I will exalt my throne above the stars of God *Is.* 14: 13.

Woe to the crown of pride. *Is.* 28: 1.

All the proud, yea, and all that do wickedly, shall be stubble. *Mal.* 4: 1.

He hath scattered the proud in the imagination of their hearts. *Lu.* 1: 51.

Casting down . . . every high thing that exalteth itself. *2 Co.* 10: 5.

Who . . . exalteth himself above all that is called God. *2 Th.* 2: 4.

Men shall be lovers of their own selves, covetous, boasters, proud. *2 Ti.* 3: 2.

God resisteth the proud, but giveth grace unto the humble. *Ja.* 4: 6.

See also

Boasting; Braggart; Conceit; Disdain; Haughtiness; Ostentation; Presumption; Pride.

Arrow

The arrow of the Lord's deliverance. *2 K.* 13: 17.

The arrows of the Almighty are within me. *Jb.* 6: 4.

God shall shoot at them with an arrow. *Ps.* 64: 7.

Thou shalt not be afraid for the terror by night; nor for the arrow that flieth by day. *Ps.* 91: 5.

As arrows are in the hand of a mighty man; so are children of the youth. *Ps.* 127: 4.

A man that beareth false witness against his neighbour is . . . a sharp arrow. *Pr.* 25: 18.

Their tongue is as an arrow shot out; it speaketh deceit. *Je.* 9: 8.

Art

The work was perfected by them. *2 Ch.* 24: 13.

Blessed be the Lord God of our fathers, which hath put such a thing as this in the king's heart, to beautify the house of the Lord. *Ezr.* 7: 27.

The firmament sheweth his handywork. *Ps.* 19: 1.

Play skilfully with a loud noise. *Ps.* 33: 3.

The glory of Lebanon shall come unto thee, the fir tree, . . . and the box together, to beautify the place of my sanctuary; and I will make the place of my feet glorious. *Is.* 60: 13.

Thy builders have perfected thy beauty. *Eze.* 27: 4.

God gave them knowledge and skill in all learning and wisdom. *Da.* 1: 17.

Every good gift and every perfect gift is from above. *Ja.* 1: 17.

See also

Architecture; Calling; Profession; Readiness; Skill; Workmanship.

Artisan

I have filled him with the spirit of God, . . . in all manner of workmanship. *Ex.* 31: 3.

They were craftsmen. *1 Ch.* 4: 14.

All manner of cunning men for every manner of work. *1 Ch.* 22: 15.

Establish thou the work of our hands upon us; yea, the work of our hands establish thou it. *Ps.* 90: 17.

If I forget thee, O Jerusalem, let my right hand forget her cunning. *Ps.* 137: 5.

Working with our own hands. *1 Co.* 4: 12.

Study to show thyself . . . a workman that needeth not to be ashamed. *2 Ti.* 2: 15.

See also

Hand; Labor; Skill; Toil; Work; Workmanship.

Ascension

Who shall ascend into the hill of the Lord? *Ps.* 24: 3.

If I ascend up into heaven, thou art there. *Ps.* 139: 8.

While he blessed them, he was parted from them, and carried up into heaven. *Lu.* 24: 51.

No man hath ascended up to heaven, but he that came down from heaven. *Jn.* 3: 13.

I ascend unto my Father, and your Father. *Jn.* 20: 17.

When he ascended up on high, he led captivity captive. *Ep.* 4: 8.

Seeing then that we have a great high priest, that is passed into the heavens, Jesus the Son of God, let us hold fast our profession. *He.* 4: 14.

Christ is not entered into the holy places made with hands, which are the figures of the true; but into heaven itself, now to appear in the presence of God for us. *He.* 9: 24.

Who is gone into heaven, and is on the right hand of God; angels and authorities and powers being made subject unto him. *1 Pe.* 3: 22.

See also

Christ, Ascension of; Climbing; Hill; Mountain.

Asceticism

Ye shall not make any cuttings in your flesh for the dead. *Le.* 19: 28.

Now he is dead, wherefore should I fast? *2 S.* 12: 23.

I set my face unto the Lord God, to seek by prayer and supplications, with fasting, and sackcloth, and ashes. *Da.* 9: 3.

The people of Nineveh believed God, and proclaimed a fast, and put on sackcloth. *Jon.* 3: 5.

Shall I give my firstborn for my transgression, the fruit of my body for the sin of my soul? *Mi.* 6: 7.

John had his raiment of camel's hair, and a leathern girdle about his loins; and his meat was locusts and wild honey. *Mat.* 3: 4.

The foxes have holes, and the birds of the air have nests; but the Son of man hath not where to lay his head. *Mat.* 8: 20.

He withdrew himself into the wilderness, and prayed. *Lu.* 5: 16.

If any man come to me, and hate not his father, and mother, and wife, and children, and brethren, and sisters, yea, and his own life also, he cannot be my disciple. *Lu.* 14: 26.

I fast twice in the week. *Lu.* 18: 12.

The voice of one crying in the wilderness. *Jn.* 1: 23.

If ye through the Spirit do mortify the deeds of the body, ye shall live. *Ro.* 8: 13.

They that are Christ's have crucified the flesh. *Ga.* 5: 24.

See · also
Abstinence; Chastity; Fast; Renunciation;
Self-Sacrifice.

Ash Wednesday
I have taken upon me to speak unto the
Lord, which am but dust and ashes. *Ge.* 18:
27.
Tamar put ashes on her head. 2 *S.* 13: 19.
I am become like dust and ashes. *Jb.* 30: 19.
I abhor myself, and repent in dust and
ashes. *Jb.* 42: 6.
Deliver me from all my transgressions. *Ps.*
39: 8.
As the heaven is high above the earth, so
great is his mercy toward them that fear
him. *Ps.* 103: 11.
He shall be holden with the cords of his
sins. *Pr.* 5: 22.
Though your sins be as scarlet, they shall
be as white as snow. *Is.* 1: 18.
The Lord hath anointed me . . . to give
unto them beauty for ashes. *Is.* 61: 1, 3.
Gird you with sackcloth, lament and howl:
for the fierce anger of the Lord is not turned
back from us. *Je.* 4: 8.
He hath covered me with ashes. *La.* 3: 16.
I set my face unto the Lord God, to seek by
prayer and supplications, with fasting, and
sackcloth, and ashes. *Da.* 9: 3.
He said unto them, Where is your faith?
Lu. 8: 25.
If ye through the Spirit do mortify the deeds
of the body, ye shall live. *Ro.* 8: 13.
My grace is sufficient for thee: for my
strength is made perfect in weakness. 2 *Co.*
12: 9.
Put on the new man. *Ep.* 4: 24.
See also
Contrition; Penance; Penitence; Regret;
Remorse.

Ashes
I have taken upon me to speak unto the
Lord, which am but dust and ashes. *Ge.* 18:
27.
He hath cast me into the mire, and I am
become like dust and ashes. *Jb.* 30: 19.
I abhor myself, and repent in dust and
ashes. *Jb.* 42: 6.
To give unto them beauty for ashes. *Is.* 61: 3.

Aspiration
Let us build us a city, and a tower, whose
top may reach unto heaven. *Ge.* 11: 4.
Lift up your heads, O ye gates; even lift
them up, ye everlasting doors; and the King
of glory shall come in. *Ps.* 24: 9.
Unto thee, O Lord, do I lift up my soul.
Ps. 25: 1.
As the hart panteth after the water brooks,
so panteth my soul after thee, O God. *Ps.* 42: 1.
My soul thirsteth for God, for the living
God. *Ps.* 42: 2.
Truly my soul waiteth upon God. *Ps.* 62: 1.
I will lift up mine eyes unto the hills. *Ps.*
121: 1.
But mine eyes are unto thee, O God the
Lord. *Ps.* 141: 8.
Lift up your eyes on high. *Is.* 40: 26.
Blessed are they which do hunger and thirst
after righteousness: for they shall be filled.
Mat. 5: 6.

Friend, go up higher. *Lu.* 14: 10.
Not as though I had already attained, either
were already perfect: but I follow after, if
that I may apprehend that for which also I
am apprehended of Christ Jesus. *Ph.* 3: 12.
Forgetting those things which are behind,
and reaching forth unto those things which
are before, I press toward the mark. *Ph.* 3:
13, 14.
If ye then be risen with Christ, seek those
things which are above. *Col.* 3: 1.
Set your affection on things above. *Col.* 3: 2.
See also
Ambition; Desire; God, Aspiration for; Inspiration; Longing; Yearning.

Ass.
Thou shalt not covet thy neighbour's . . .
ass. *Ex.* 20: 17.
If thou meet thine enemy's ox or his ass
going astray, thou shalt surely bring it back
to him again. *Ex.* 23: 4.
The ass saw the angel of the Lord standing
in the way. *Nu.* 22: 23.
With the jaw of an ass have I slain a
thousand men. *Ju.* 15: 16.
Vain man would be wise, though man be
born like a wild ass's colt. *Jb.* 11: 12.
They drive away the ass of the fatherless.
Jb. 24: 3.
The ox knoweth his owner, and the ass his
master's crib. *Is.* 1: 3.
He shall be buried with the burial of an
ass. *Je.* 22: 19.
Thy King cometh unto thee: he is just, and
having salvation; lowly, and riding upon an
ass, and upon a colt the foal of an ass. *Zch.*
9: 9.
Doth not each one of you on the sabbath
loose his ox or his ass from the stall, and lead
him away to watering? *Lu.* 13: 15.
Fear not, daughter of Sion: behold, thy
King cometh, sitting on an ass's colt. *Jn.* 12:
15.
The dumb ass speaking with man's voice
forbad the madness of the prophet. 2 *Pe.* 2:
16.

Assassin
Cain rose up against Abel his brother, and
slew him. *Ge.* 4: 8.
In their anger they slew a man. *Ge.* 49: 6.
He looked this way and that way, and when
he saw that there was no man, he slew the
Egyptian, and hid him in the sand. *Ex.* 2: 12.
Thou shalt not kill. *Ex.* 20: 13.
Then Jael Heber's wife took a nail of the
tent, and took an hammer in her hand, and
went softly unto him, and smote the nail into
his temples, and fastened it into the ground.
Ju. 4: 21.
How much more, when wicked men have
slain a righteous person in his own house
upon his bed? 2 *S.* 4: 11.
In the night will they come to slay thee.
Ne. 6: 10.
The murderer rising with the light killeth
the poor and needy. *Jb.* 24: 14.
In the secret places doth he murder the
innocent. *Ps.* 10: 8.
They slay the widow and the stranger, and
murder the fatherless. *Ps.* 94: 6.

Herod . . . slew all the children that were in Bethlehem. *Mat.* 2: 16.

Out of the heart proceed . . . murders. *Mat.* 15: 19.

The thief cometh not, but for to steal, and to kill, and to destroy. *Jn.* 10: 10.

And killed the Prince of life, whom God hath raised from the dead. *Ac.* 3: 15.

Wilt thou kill me, as thou diddest the Egyptian yesterday? *Ac.* 7: 28.

See also

Murder; Slaughter; Treachery.

Assault

Let us go up at once, and possess it; for we are well able to overcome it. *Nu.* 13: 30.

Go up and possess the land which I have given you. *De.* 9: 23.

Shout; for the Lord hath given you the city. *Jos.* 6: 16.

Which of us shall go up first to the battle? *Ju.* 20: 18.

Fight for your master's house. *2 K.* 10: 3.

Be not ye afraid of them: remember the Lord, which is great and terrible, and fight for your brethren, your sons, and your daughters, your wives, and your houses. *Ne.* 4: 14.

Though an host should encamp against me, my heart shall not fear. *Ps.* 27: 3.

Fight against them that fight against me. *Ps.* 35: 1.

They be many that fight against me, O thou Most High. *Ps.* 56: 2.

A wise man scaleth the city of the mighty, and casteth down the strength of the confidence thereof. *Pr.* 21: 22.

There was a little city, and few men within it; and there came a great king against it, and besieged it, and built great bulwarks against it. *Ec.* 9: 14.

See also

Army; Attack; Battle; Fight; Overthrow; Strife; War.

Assembly

In the congregations will I bless the Lord. *Ps.* 26: 12.

God is greatly to be feared in the assembly of the saints. *Ps.* 89: 7.

I will praise the Lord with my whole heart in the assembly of the upright, and in the congregation. *Ps.* 111: 1.

Let all the nations be gathered together, and let the people be assembled. *Is.* 43: 9.

They shall keep my laws and my statutes in all mine assemblies. *Eze.* 44: 24.

Not forsaking the assembling of ourselves together, as the manner of some is. *He.* 10: 25.

But ye are come unto mount Sion, . . . to an innumerable company of angels. *He.* 12: 22.

See also

Association; Audience; Church; Collection; Company; Congregation; Congress; Meeting.

Assent

And all the people shall say, Amen. *De.* 27: 16.

If sinners entice thee, consent thou not. *Pr.* 1: 10.

Can two walk together, except they be agreed? *Am.* 3: 3.

That they may all call upon the name of the Lord, to serve him with one consent. *Zph.* 3: 9.

They all with one consent began to make excuse. *Lu.* 14: 18.

Saul was consenting unto his death. *Ac.* 8: 1.

The Jews also assented, saying that these things were so. *Ac.* 24: 9.

If then I do that which I would not, I consent unto the law that it is good. *Ro.* 7: 16.

The Son of God, Jesus Christ, . . . was not yea and nay, but in him was yea. *2 Co.* 1: 19.

Let your yea be yea. *Ja.* 5: 12.

See also

Acclamation; Acquiescence; Affirmation; Agreement; Approval; Consent.

Assistance

If thou meet thine enemy's ox or his ass going astray, thou shalt surely bring it back to him again. *Ex.* 23: 4.

He raiseth up the poor out of the dust. *1 S.* 2: 8.

Hitherto hath the Lord helped us. *1 S.* 7: 12.

The mountain was full of horses and chariots of fire round about Elisha. *2 K.* 6: 17.

Is not my help in me? *Jb.* 6: 13.

God is our refuge and strength, a very present help in trouble. *Ps.* 46: 1.

Thou hast lifted me up. *Ps.* 102: 10.

The Spirit also helpeth our infirmities. *Ro.* 8: 26.

Assist her in whatsoever business she hath need of you. *Ro.* 16: 2.

He is able to succour them that are tempted. *He.* 2: 18.

See also

Aid; Collaboration; Help; Service; Succor; Support.

Association

I will make a league with thee. *2 S.* 3: 13.

Gather my saints together unto me. *Ps.* 50: 5.

Behold, how good and how pleasant it is for brethren, to dwell together in unity! *Ps.* 133: 1.

Associate yourselves, O ye people, and ye shall be broken in pieces. *Is.* 8: 9.

Let all the nations be gathered together, and let the people be assembled. *Is.* 43: 9.

Can two walk together, except they be agreed? *Am.* 3: 3.

Where two or three are gathered together in my name, there am I in the midst of them. *Mat.* 18: 20.

They shall gather together his elect from the four winds. *Mat.* 24: 31.

The apostles gathered themselves together unto Jesus. *Mk.* 6: 30.

There shall be one fold, and one shepherd. *Jn.* 10: 16.

That also he should gather together in one the children of God that were scattered abroad. *Jn.* 11: 52.

And hath made of one blood all nations of men for to dwell on all the face of the earth. *Ac.* 17: 26.

We are members one of another. *Ep.* 4: 25.

Mortify therefore your members which are upon the earth. *Col.* 3: 5.

Not forsaking the assembling of ourselves together. *He.* 10: 25.

He gathered them together into a place called in the Hebrew tongue Armageddon. *Re.* 16: 16.

Come and gather yourselves together unto the supper of the great God. *Re.* 19: 17.

See also

Accomplice; Alliance; Ally; Collaboration; Colleague; Community; Company; League; Society; Union.

Assurance

Though he slay me, yet will I trust in him. *Jb.* 13: 15.

O God of our salvation; who art the confidence of all the ends of the earth. *Ps.* 65: 5.

His heart is fixed, trusting in the Lord. *Ps.* 112: 7.

It is better to trust in the Lord than to put confidence in man. *Ps.* 118: 8.

In quietness and in confidence shall be your strength. *Is.* 30: 15.

The effect of righteousness quietness and assurance for ever. *Is.* 32: 17.

I will give you assured peace in this place. *Je.* 14: 13.

That their hearts might be comforted, being knit together in love, and unto all riches of the full assurance of understanding. *Col.* 2: 2.

Our gospel came not unto you in word only but also in power, . . . and in much assurance. *1 Th.* 1: 5.

If we hold fast the confidence and the rejoicing of the hope firm unto the end. *He.* 3: 6.

To the full assurance of hope unto the end *He.* 6: 11.

Let us draw near with a true heart in full assurance of faith. *He.* 10: 22.

Cast not away therefore your confidence. *He.* 10: 35.

We . . . shall assure our hearts. *1 Jn.* 3: 19.

This is the confidence that we have in him, that, if we ask any thing according to his will, he heareth us. *1 Jn.* 5: 14.

See also

Belief; Christ, Belief in; Christ, Faith in; Confidence; Dependence; God, Confidence in; God, Faith in; God, Reliance on; God, Trust in; Self-Confidence; Trust.

Astonishment

Your enemies which dwell therein shall be astonished at it. *Le.* 26: 32.

They that come after him shall be astonied at his day, as they that went before were affrighted. *Jb.* 18: 20.

Mark me, and be astonished, and lay your hand upon your mouth. *Jb.* 21: 5.

I am as a wonder unto many; but thou art my strong refuge. *Ps.* 71: 7.

I will praise thee; for I am fearfully and wonderfully made. *Ps.* 139: 14.

All the inhabitants of the isles shall be astonished at thee. *Eze.* 27: 35.

The people were astonished at his doctrine. *Mat.* 7: 28.

The multitude wondered, when they saw the dumb to speak, the maimed to be whole, the lame to walk, and the blind to see. *Mat.* 15: 31.

They were sore amazed in themselves beyond measure, and wondered. *Mk.* 6: 51.

The disciples were astonished at his words. *Mk.* 10: 24.

They were all amazed at the mighty power of God. *Lu.* 9: 43.

They were all amazed and marvelled, saying one to another, Behold, are not all these which speak Galilæans? *Ac.* 2: 7.

They that dwell on the earth shall wonder. *Re.* 17: 8.

See also

Admiration; Amazement; Marvel; Surprise; Wonder.

Asylum

There shall be six cities for refuge. *Nu.* 35: 6.

They shall be your refuge from the avenger of blood. *Jos.* 20: 3.

The people did hide themselves in caves. *1 S.* 13: 6.

Thou shalt dig about thee, and thou shalt take thy rest in safety. *Jb.* 11: 18.

They embrace the rock for want of a shelter. *Jb.* 24: 8.

How say ye to my soul, Flee as a bird to your mountain? *Ps.* 11: 1.

Thou hast been my defence and refuge in the day of my trouble. *Ps.* 59: 16.

Thou hast been a shelter for me, and a strong tower from the enemy. *Ps.* 61: 3.

The high hills are a refuge for the wild goats. *Ps.* 104: 18.

A covert from storm and from rain. *Is.* 4: 6.

The needy shall lie down in safety. *Is.* 14: 30.

See also

God, the Refuge; Protection; Refuge; Retreat; Safety; Sanctuary; Security; Shelter.

Atheism

Curse God, and die. *Jb.* 2: 9.

That thou turnest thy spirit against God. *Jb.* 15: 13.

God is not in all his thoughts. *Ps.* 10: 4.

The fool hath said in his heart, There is no God. *Ps.* 14: 1.

She hath rebelled against her God. *Ho.* 13: 16.

Lest haply ye be found even to fight against God. *Ac.* 5: 39.

The carnal mind is enmity against God. *Ro.* 8: 7.

Even denying the Lord that bought them. *2 Pe.* 2: 1.

Ungodly men, . . . denying the only Lord God, and our Lord Jesus Christ. *Jude* 1: 4.

See also

Christ, Denial of; Christ, Doubt of; Denial; Doubt; Faithlessness; God, Denial of; Godlessness; Heresy; Unbelief.

Athlete

There were giants in the earth in those days. *Ge.* 6: 4.

With great wrestlings have I wrestled with my sister, and I have prevailed. *Ge.* 30: 8.

Jacob was left alone; and there wrestled a man with him until the breaking of the day. *Ge.* 32: 24.

A young lion roared against him. And the Spirit of the Lord came mightily upon him, and he rent him as he would have rent a kid. *Ju.* 14: 5, 6.

Tell me, I pray thee, wherein thy great strength lieth. *Ju.* 16: 6.

By strength shall no man prevail. *1 S.* 2: 9.

He runneth upon me like a giant. *Jb.* 16: 14.

Rejoiceth as a strong man to run a race. *Ps.* 19: 5.

The race is not to the swift, nor the battle to the strong. *Ec.* 9: 11.

Thy neck is an iron sinew. *Is.* 48: 4.

Know ye not that they which run in a race run all, but one receiveth the prize? *1 Co.* 9: 24.

We wrestle not against flesh and blood. *Ep.* 6: 12.

I press toward the mark for the prize of the high calling of God in Christ Jesus. *Ph.* 3: 14.

If a man also strive for masteries, yet is he not crowned, except he strive lawfully. *2 Ti.* 2: 5.

See also

Game; Race; Sport.

Atmosphere

One is so near to another, that no air can come between them. *Jb.* 41: 16.

The ungodly are not so: but are like the chaff which the wind driveth away. *Ps.* 1: 4.

The way of an eagle in the air. *Pr.* 30: 19.

A bird of the air shall carry the voice, and that which hath wings shall tell the matter. *Ec.* 10: 20.

The birds of the air come and lodge in the branches. *Mat.* 13: 32.

The wind bloweth where it listeth, and thou hearest the sound thereof, but canst not tell whence it cometh, and whither it goeth: so is every one that is born of the Spirit. *Jn.* 3: 8.

So fight I, not as one that beateth the air. *1 Co.* 9: 26.

Except ye utter by the tongue words easy to be understood, how shall it be known what is spoken? for ye shall speak into the air. *1 Co.* 14: 9.

Then we which are alive and remain shall be caught up together with them in the clouds, to meet the Lord in the air: and so shall we ever be with the Lord. *1 Th.* 4: 17.

Clouds they are without water, carried about of winds. *Jude* 12.

The sun and the air were darkened. *Re.* 9: 2.

See also

Breath; Air.

Atonement

What shall I do for you? and wherewith shall I make the atonement, that ye may bless the inheritance of the Lord? *2 S.* 21: 3.

With him is plenteous redemption. *Ps.* 130: 7.

He was wounded for our transgressions, he was bruised for our iniquities: the chastisement of our peace was upon him; and with his stripes we are healed. *Is.* 53: 5.

Behold the Lamb of God, which taketh away the sin of the world. *Jn.* 1: 29.

We also joy in God through our Lord Jesus Christ, by whom we have now received the atonement. *Ro.* 5: 11.

By the righteousness of one the free gift came upon all men unto justification of life. *Ro.* 5: 18.

Where sin abounded, grace did much more abound. *Ro.* 5: 20.

Christ died for our sins according to the scriptures. *1 Co.* 15: 3.

For as in Adam all die, even so in Christ shall all be made alive. *1 Co.* 15: 22.

All things are of God, who hath reconciled us to himself by Jesus Christ. *2 Co.* 5: 18.

For he hath made him to be sin for us, who knew no sin. *2 Co.* 5: 21.

If we believe that Jesus died and rose again, even so them also which sleep in Jesus will God bring with him. *1 Th.* 4: 14.

That he might be a merciful and faithful high priest in things pertaining to God, to make reconciliation for the sins of the people. *He.* 2: 17.

The blood of Jesus Christ his Son cleanseth us from all sin. *1 Jn.* 1: 7.

See also

Agreement; Concord; Oneness; Propitiation.

Atrophy

Man dieth, and wasteth away. *Jb.* 14: 10.

They shall soon be cut down as the grass, and wither as the green herb. *Ps.* 37: 2.

In the evening it is cut down, and withereth. *Ps.* 90: 6.

Let them be as the grass upon the housetops, which withereth afore it groweth up. *Ps.* 129: 6.

He hath made me to dwell in darkness, as those that have been long dead. *Ps.* 143: 3.

The grass withereth, the flower fadeth: but the word of our God shall stand for ever. *Is.* 40: 8.

They shall wither, and the whirlwind shall take them away as stubble. *Is.* 40: 24.

It withered away, because it lacked moisture. *Lu.* 8: 6.

See also

Death; Withering.

Attachment

The Lord thy God is with thee. *De.* 20: 1.

Intreat me not to leave thee, or to return from following after thee. *Ru.* 1: 16.

The Lord do so to me, and more also, if ought but death part thee and me. *Ru.* 1: 17.

The soul of Jonathan was knit with the soul of David, and Jonathan loved him as his own soul. *1 S.* 18: 1.

Surely in what place my lord the king shall be, whether in death or life, even there also will thy servant be. *2 S.* 15: 21.

There is a friend that sticketh closer than a brother. *Pr.* 18: 24.

Come, and let us join ourselves to the Lord in a perpetual covenant. *Je.* 50: 5.

I drew them with cords of a man, with bands of love. *Ho.* 11: 4.

What therefore God hath joined together, let not man put asunder. *Mat.* 19: 6.

Lord, I am ready to go with thee, both into prison, and to death. *Lu.* 22: 33.

Greater love hath no man than this, that a man lay down his life for his friends. *Jn.* 15: 13.

I beseech you, . . . that ye be perfectly joined together in the same mind and in the same judgment. *1 Co.* **1: 10.**

He that is joined unto the Lord is one spirit. *1 Co.* **6: 17.**

Endeavouring to keep the unity of the Spirit in the bond of peace. *Ep.* **4: 3.**

My bonds in Christ are manifest in all the palace, and in all other places. *Ph.* **1: 13.**

Put on charity, which is the bond of perfectness. *Col.* **3: 14.**

The mystery of Christ, for which I am also in bonds. *Col.* **4: 3.**

Paul, a prisoner of Jesus Christ. *Phm.* **1: 1.**

Be thou faithful unto death, and I will give thee a crown of life. *Re.* **2: 10.**

See also

Affection; Bond; Caress; Christ, Love of; Christ, Loyalty to; Coherence; Devotion; Faithfulness; God, Faithfulness of; God, Love of; God, Love to; God, Loyalty to; Love; Loyalty; Regard.

Attack

Be strong, and quit yourselves like men. *1 S.* **4: 9.**

The Lord saveth not with sword and spear: for the battle is the Lord's, and he will give you into our hands. *1 S.* **17: 47.**

Be thou valiant for me, and fight the Lord's battles. *1 S.* **18: 17.**

How are the mighty fallen in the midst of the battle! *2 S.* **1: 25.**

Who is this King of glory? The Lord strong and mighty, the Lord mighty in battle. *Ps.* **24: 8.**

They shall fall by the sword. *Ps.* **63: 10.**

A thousand shall fall at thy side, and ten thousand at thy right hand; but it shall not come nigh thee. *Ps.* **91: 7.**

Thou hast covered my head in the day of battle. *Ps.* **140: 7.**

The race is not to the swift, nor the battle to the strong. *Ec.* **9: 11.**

I will cause him to fall by the sword in his own land. *Is.* **37: 7.**

The young men . . . shall fall by the sword. *Eze.* **30: 17.**

By the swords of the mighty will I cause thy multitude to fall. *Eze.* **32: 12.**

If my kingdom were of this world, then would my servants fight. *Jn.* **18: 36.**

If the trumpet give an uncertain sound, who shall prepare himself to the battle? *1 Co.* **14: 8.**

Fight the good fight of faith. *1 Ti.* **6: 12.**

No man that warreth entangleth himself with the affairs of this life. *2 Ti.* **2: 4.**

I have fought a good fight. *2 Ti.* **4: 7.**

Waxed valiant in fight, turned to flight the armies of the aliens. *He.* **11: 34.**

See also

Assault; Battle; Enemy; Fight; Soldier; Strife; War.

Attainment

Let us build us a city, and a tower, whose top may reach unto heaven. *Ge.* **11: 4.**

Thy faithfulness reacheth unto the clouds. *Ps.* **36: 5.**

Through thy precepts I get understanding. *Ps.* **119: 104.**

Such knowledge is too wonderful for me; it is high, I cannot attain unto it. *Ps.* **139: 6.**

A man of understanding shall attain unto wise counsels. *Pr.* **1: 5.**

How long will it be ere they attain to innocency. *Ho.* **8: 5.**

What is a man profited, if he shall gain the whole world, and lose his own soul? *Mat.* **16: 26.**

Lord, thy pound hath gained ten pounds. *Lu.* **19: 16.**

If by any means I might attain unto the resurrection of the dead. *Ph.* **3: 11.**

Whereto we have already attained, let us walk by the same rule. *Ph.* **3: 16.**

Godliness with contentment is great gain. *1 Ti.* **6: 6.**

See also

Accomplishment; Achievement; Completion; Fulfilment; Success.

Attendance

If the Lord be God, follow him. *1 K.* **18: 21.**

Now, my God, let, I beseech thee, thine eyes be open, and let thine ears be attent unto the prayer that is made in this place. *2 Ch.* **6: 40.**

Hear the right, O Lord, attend unto my cry, give ear unto my prayer. *Ps.* **17: 1.**

God is our refuge and strength, a very present help in trouble. *Ps.* **46: 1.**

Hear, ye children, the instruction of a father, and attend to know understanding. *Pr.* **4: 1.**

Angels came and ministered unto him. *Mat.* **4: 11.**

Whether is greater, he that sitteth at meat, or he that serveth? is not he that sitteth at meat? but I am among you as he that serveth. *Lu.* **22: 27.**

If any man serve me, let him follow me. *Jn.* **12: 26.**

Now therefore are we all here present before God. *Ac.* **10: 33.**

Let us wait on our ministering. *Ro.* **12: 7.**

They are God's ministers, attending continually upon this very thing. *Ro.* **13: 6.**

That ye may attend upon the Lord without distraction. *1 Co.* **7: 35.**

If the ministration of condemnation be glory, much more doth the ministration of righteousness exceed in glory. *2 Co.* **3: 9.**

He therefore that ministereth to you the Spirit, and worketh miracles among you, doeth he it by the works of the law, or by the hearing of faith? *Ga.* **3: 5.**

Are not even ye in the presence of our Lord Jesus Christ? *1 Th.* **2: 19.**

Are they not all ministering spirits? *He.* **1: 14.**

See also

Attention; Christ Presence of; Presence.

Attention

Speak, Lord; for thy servant heareth. *1 S.* **3: 9.**

Now, my God, let, I beseech thee, thine eyes be open, and let thine ears be attent unto the prayer that is made in this place. *2 Ch.* **6: 40.**

The ears of all the people were attentive unto the book of the law. *Ne.* **8: 3.**

Attend unto my cry, give ear unto my prayer. *Ps.* 17: 1.

Wherewithal shall a young man cleanse his way? by taking heed thereto according to thy word. *Ps.* 119: 9.

Attend to know understanding. *Pr.* 4: 1.

Incline thine ear unto my sayings. *Pr.* 4: 20.

Hear, O heavens, and give ear, O earth: for the Lord hath spoken. *Is.* 1: 2.

I set watchmen over you, saying, Hearken to the sound of the trumpet. But they said, We will not hearken. *Je.* 6: 17.

Hear, all ye people; hearken, O earth, and all that therein is. *Mi.* 1: 2.

They are God's ministers, attending continually upon this very thing. *Ro.* 13: 6.

That ye may attend upon the Lord without distraction. *1 Co.* 7: 35.

Till I come, give attendance to reading, to exhortation, to doctrine. *1 Ti.* 4: 13.

See also

Attendance; Care; Consideration; Heed; Regard; Respect; Study.

Attire

I put on righteousness, and it clothed me. *Jb.* 29: 14.

Violence covereth them as a garment. *Ps.* 73: 6.

All of them shall wax old like a garment. *Ps.* 102: 26.

Thou art clothed with honour and majesty. *Ps.* 104: 1.

His enemies will I clothe with shame. *Ps.* 132: 18.

The moth shall eat them up like a garment, and the worm shall eat them like wool. *Is.* 51: 8.

John had his raiment of camel's hair, and a leathern girdle about his loins. *Mat.* 3: 4.

No man putteth a piece of new cloth unto an old garment. *Mat.* 9: 16.

His countenance was like lightning, and his raiment white as snow. *Mat.* 28: 3.

What went ye out for to see? A man clothed in soft raiment? *Lu.* 7: 25.

They which are gorgeously apparelled, and live delicately, are in kings' courts. *Lu.* 7: 25.

I have coveted no man's silver, or gold, or apparel. *Ac.* 20: 33.

I will therefore that . . . women adorn themselves in modest apparel, with shamefacedness and sobriety; not with braided hair, or gold, or pearls, or costly array. *1 Ti.* 2: 8, 9.

See also

Apparel; Clothes; Coat; Garment; Raiment; Robe.

Attitude

Behold every one that is proud, and abase him. *Jb.* 40: 11.

Thou wilt save the afflicted people; but wilt bring down high looks. *Ps.* 18: 27.

Him that hath an high look and a proud heart will not I suffer. *Ps.* 101: 5.

A man that hath friends must shew himself friendly. *Pr.* 18: 24.

An high look, and a proud heart . . . is sin. *Pr.* 21: 4.

An angry man stirreth up strife. *Pr.* 29: 22.

Then said the Lord, Doest thou well to be angry? *Jon.* 4: 4.

What doth the Lord require of thee, but . . to walk humbly with thy God? *Mi.* 6: 8.

Blessed are the poor in spirit. *Mat.* 5: 3.

Blessed are the meek. *Mat.* 5: 5.

Blessed are the merciful. *Mat.* 5: 7.

Whosoever is angry with his brother without a cause shall be in danger of the judgment. *Mat.* 5: 22.

He that is not with me is against me. *Mat.* 12: 30.

Ye are my friends, if ye do whatsoever I command you. *Jn.* 15: 14.

Serving the Lord with all humility of mind. *Ac.* 20: 19.

Put on therefore, as the elect of God, holy and beloved, bowels of mercies, kindness, humbleness of mind, meekness, longsuffering. *Col.* 3: 12.

Be clothed with humility. *1 Pe.* 5: 5.

See also

Feeling; Humility; Pride.

Attraction

How goodly are thy tents, O Jacob. *Nu.* 24: 5.

If thine heart turn away, so that thou wilt not hear, but shalt be drawn away, and worship other gods, and serve them; I denounce unto you this day, that ye shall surely perish. *De.* 30: 17, 18.

He drew me out of many waters. *2 S.* 22: 17.

Thou art fairer than the children of men: grace is poured into thy lips. *Ps.* 45: 2.

Beautiful for situation, the joy of the whole earth, is mount Zion, . . . the city of the great King. *Ps.* 48: 2.

He hath made every thing beautiful in his time. *Ec.* 3: 11.

Draw me, we will run after thee. *S. of S.* 1: 4.

How beautiful upon the mountains are the feet of him that bringeth good tidings! *Is.* 52: 7.

With lovingkindness have I drawn thee. *Je.* 31: 3.

I drew them . . . with bands of love. *Ho.* 11: 4.

There followed him great multitudes of people. *Mat.* 4: 25.

Peter followed afar off. *Lu.* 22: 54.

No man can come to me, except the Father which hath sent me draw him. *Jn.* 6: 44.

I, if I be lifted up from the earth, will draw all men unto me. *Jn.* 12: 32.

Also of your own selves shall men arise, . . . to draw away disciples after them. *Ac.* 20: 30.

The armies which were in heaven followed him. *Re.* 19: 14.

See also

Allurement; Charm; Enticement.

Audacity

Ye shall not be afraid of the face of man. *De.* 1: 17.

Be courageous, and be valiant. *2 S.* 13: 28.

I will not be afraid of ten thousands of people, that have set themselves against me round about. *Ps.* 3: 6.

The righteous are bold as a lion. *Pr.* 28: 1.

Fear ye not the reproach of men, neither be

ye afraid of their revilings. *Is.* 51: 7.

Grant unto thy servants, that with all boldness they may speak thy word. *Ac.* 4: 29.

Peradventure for a good man some would even dare to die. *Ro.* 5: 7.

Howbeit whereinsoever any is bold, . . . I am bold also. *2 Co.* 11: 21.

We were bold in our God to speak unto you the gospel of God with much contention. *1 Th.* 2: 2.

Let us therefore come boldly unto the throne of grace, that we may obtain mercy. *He.* 4: 16.

Herein is our love made perfect, that we may have boldness in the day of judgment. *1 Jn.* 4: 17.

See also

Arrogance; Assurance; Boldness; Confidence; Courage; Presumption; Self-Satisfaction.

Audience

Speak now in the ears of the people. *Ex.* 11: 2.

He took the book of the covenant, and read in the audience of the people. *Ex.* 24: 7.

These words the Lord spake unto all your assembly. *De.* 5: 22.

In the audience of our God, keep and seek for all the commandments of the Lord your God. *1 Ch.* 28: 8.

O Lord, I beseech thee, let now thine ear be attentive to the prayer of thy servant. *Ne.* 1: 11.

I stood up, and I cried in the congregation. *Jb.* 30: 28.

Hearken unto me, ye men of understanding. *Jb.* 34: 10.

Hear attentively the noise of his voice, and the sound that goeth out of his mouth. *Jb.* 37: 2.

I will praise the Lord with my whole heart, in the assembly of the upright, and in the congregation. *Ps.* 111: 1.

Give ear, all ye of far countries. *Is.* 8: 9.

The ears of them that hear shall hearken. *Is.* 32: 3.

Listen, O isles, unto me; and hearken, ye people, from far. *Is.* 49: 1.

O earth, earth, earth, hear the words of the Lord. *Je.* 22: 29.

Hearken, O earth, and all that therein is. *Mi.* 1: 2.

Men of Israel, and ye that fear God, give audience. *Ac.* 13: 16.

See also

Assembly; Congregation; Meeting.

Auspices

The Lord . . . will send his angel with thee, and prosper thy way. *Ge.* 24: 40.

My presence shall go with thee, and I will give thee rest. *Ex.* 33: 14.

The Lord . . . guided them on every side. *2 Ch.* 32: 22.

Let all those that put their trust in thee rejoice: let them ever shout for joy, because thou defendest them. *Ps.* 5: 11.

In the name of our God we will set up our banners. *Ps.* 20: 5.

For this God is our God for ever and ever: he will be our guide even unto death. *Ps.* 48: 14.

Thou hast given a banner to them that fear thee. *Ps.* 60: 4.

His banner over me was love. *S. of S.* 2: 4.

Lift ye up a banner upon the high mountain. *Is.* 13: 2.

My father, thou art the guide of my youth. *Je.* 3: 4.

We will walk in the name of the Lord our God for ever and ever. *Mi.* 4: 5.

The works that I do in my Father's name, they bear witness of me. *Jn.* 10: 25.

By what power, or by what name, have ye done this? *Ac.* 4: 7.

See also

Guidance; Name; Protection.

Austerity

Lord, I knew thee that thou art an hard man. *Mat.* 25: 24.

God, I thank thee, that I am not as other men are. *Lu.* 18: 11.

I feared thee, because thou art an austere man. *Lu.* 19: 21.

Behold therefore the goodness and severity of God. *Ro.* 11: 22.

Think soberly, according as God hath dealt to every man the measure of faith. *Ro.* 12: 3.

Let us, who are of the day, be sober. *1 Th.* 5: 8.

Likewise must the deacons be grave. *1 Ti.* 3: 8.

That the aged men be sober, grave. *Tit.* 2: 2.

Gird up the loins of your mind, be sober. *1 Pe.* 1: 13.

Be sober, be vigilant. *1 Pe.* 5: 8.

See also

Asceticism; Hardness; Harshness; Severity.

Authenticity

It was a true report that I heard in mine own land of thy acts and of thy wisdom. *1 K.* 10: 6.

Esther the queen . . . wrote with all authority. *Es.* 9: 29.

Shall a man be more pure than his maker? *Jb.* 4: 17.

For thou hast said, My doctrine is pure. *Jb.* 11: 4.

The words of the Lord are pure words: as silver tried in a furnace of earth, purified seven times. *Ps.* 12: 6.

Trust in him at all times. *Ps.* 62: 8.

Thy word is true from the beginning. *Ps.* 119: 160.

Every word of God is pure. *Pr.* 30: 5.

The Lord hath not sent thee; but thou makest this people to trust in a lie. *Je.* 28: 15.

By what authority doest thou these things? and who gave thee this authority? *Mat.* 21: 23.

Master, we know that thou art true. *Mat.* 22: 16.

Many false prophets shall rise, and shall deceive many. *Mat.* 24: 11.

The Father . . . hath given him authority to execute judgment also, because he is the Son of man. *Jn.* 5: 26, 27.

The witness which he witnesseth of me is true. *Jn.* 5: 32.

I trust that ye shall know that we are not reprobates. *2 Co.* 13: 6.

We know that the Son of God is come, and hath given us an understanding, that we may know him that is true, and we are in him that is true, even in his Son Jesus Christ. *1 Jn.* 5: 20.

These are the true sayings of God. *Re.* 19: 9.
See also
Authority; Truth; Validity.

Author

They that handle the pen of the writer. *Ju.* 5: 14.

It was written in the book. *Es.* 9: 32.

Oh that my words were now written! oh that they were printed in a book! *Jb.* 19: 23.

My desire is, . . . that mine adversary had written a book. *Jb.* 31: 35.

My tongue is the pen of a ready writer. *Ps.* 45: 1.

Of making many books there is no end. *Ec.* 12: 12.

In that day shall the deaf hear the words of the book. *Is.* 29: 18.

Seek ye out of the book of the Lord, and read. *Is.* 34: 16.

There are also many other things which Jesus did, the which, if they should be written every one, I suppose that even the world itself could not contain the books that should be written. Amen. *Jn.* 21: 25.

God is not the author of confusion, but of peace. *1 Co.* 14: 33.

He became the author of eternal salvation. *He.* 5: 9.

Looking unto Jesus the author and finisher of our faith. *He.* 12: 2.

What thou seest, write in a book. *Re.* 1: 11.

Who is worthy to open the book? *Re.* 5: 2.
See also
Book; Epistle; Letter; Scribe; Scripture; Writing.

Authority

The Lord our God will we serve, and his voice will we obey. *Jos.* 24: 24.

When the righteous are in authority, the people rejoice. *Pr.* 29: 2.

He taught them as one having authority, and not as the scribes. *Mat.* 7: 29.

I am a man under authority, having soldiers under me. *Mat.* 8: 9.

They that are great exercise authority upon them. *Mat.* 20: 25.

With authority commandeth he even the unclean spirits, and they do obey him. *Mk.* 1: 27.

By what authority doest thou these things? and who gave thee this authority to do these things? *Mk.* 11: 28.

He called his twelve disciples together, and gave them power and authority. *Lu.* 9: 1.

Because thou hast been faithful in a very little, have thou authority over ten cities. *Lu.* 19: 17.

It is not for you to know the times or the seasons, which the Father hath put in his own power. *Ac.* 1: 7.

Children, obey your parents in the Lord: for this is right. *Ep.* 6: 1.

Servants, obey in all things your masters according to the flesh. *Col.* 3: 22.

I exhort therefore, that, first of all, supplications, prayers, intercessions, and giving of thanks, be made for all men; For kings, and for all that are in authority. *1 Ti.* 2: 1, 2.

Obey them that have the rule over you, and submit yourselves. *He.* 13: 17.

And he that overcometh, and keepeth my works unto the end, to him will I give power over the nations. *Re.* 2: 26.
See also
Christ, Authority of; Christ, Obedience to; Christ, Power of; Commandment; Domain; Dominion; God, Dominion of; God, Law of; God, Power of; Influence; Law; Obedience; Reign; Rule; Submission.

Autocrat

Thine, O Lord, is the greatness, and the power, and the glory, and the victory, and the majesty: for all that is in the heaven and in the earth is thine; thine is the kingdom, O Lord, and thou art exalted as head above all. *1 Ch.* 29: 11.

He shall have dominion also from sea to sea. *Ps.* 72: 8.

Thou, O king, art a king of kings: for the God of heaven hath given thee a kingdom, power, and strength, and glory. *Da.* 2: 37.

I am a man under authority, having soldiers under me: and I say to this man, Go, and he goeth; and to another, Come, and he cometh; and to my servant, Do this, and he doeth it. *Mat.* 8: 9.

Ye know that the princes of the Gentiles exercise dominion over them, and they that are great exercise authority upon them. *Mat.* 20: 25.

Because thou hast been faithful in a very little, have thou authority over ten cities. *Lu.* 19: 17.

He hath put all things under his feet. *1 Co.* 15: 27.

When all things shall be subdued unto him, then shall the Son also himself be subject unto him that put all things under him, that God may be all in all. *1 Co.* 15: 28.
See also
Bondage; Despot; Oppression; Tyranny; Yoke.

Autumn

He shall be like a tree planted by the rivers of water, that bringeth forth his fruit in his season; his leaf also shall not wither. *Ps.* 1: 3.

Thou crownest the year with thy goodness; and thy paths drop fatness. *Ps.* 65: 11.

They that sow in tears shall reap in joy. *Ps.* 126: 5.

Honour the Lord with thy substance, and with the firstfruits of all thine increase. *Pr.* 3: 9.

Ye shall be as an oak whose leaf fadeth. *Is.* 1: 30.

They joy before thee according to the joy in harvest. *Is.* 9: 3.

The harvest is past, the summer is ended, and we are not saved. *Je.* 8: 20.

The harvest is the end of the world; and the reapers are the angels. *Mat.* 13: 39.

Nevertheless he left not himself without witness, in that he did good, and gave us rain from heaven, and fruitful seasons, filling our hearts with food and gladness. *Ac.* 14: 17.

He which soweth sparingly shall reap also

sparingly; and he which soweth bountifully shall reap also bountifully. *2 Co.* 9: 6.

In due season we shall reap, if we faint not. *Ga.* 6: 9.

Trees whose fruit withereth, without fruit, twice dead. *Jude* 1: 12.

Thrust in thy sickle, and reap: for the time has come for thee to reap. *Re.* 14: 15.

See also
Fruit; Fruitfulness; Harvest; Reaping; Yield.

Avarice

So are the ways of every one that is greedy of gain. *Pr.* 1: 19.

He that is greedy of gain troubleth his own house. *Pr.* 15: 27.

Yea, they are greedy dogs which can never have enough. *Is.* 56: 11.

Seek ye first the kingdom of God, and his righteousness; and all these things shall be added unto you. *Mat.* 6: 33.

Make not my Father's house an house of merchandise. *Jn.* 2: 16.

Not greedy of filthy lucre. *1 Ti.* 3: 3.

The love of money is the root of all evil. *1 Ti.* 6: 10.

See also
Acquisition; Covetousness; Cupidity; Greed.

Aversion

The Lord your God is gracious and merciful, and will not turn away his face from you, if ye return unto him. *2 Ch.* 30: 9.

I hate the work of them that turn aside. *Ps.* 101: 3.

Turn away thine eyes from me, for they have overcome me. *S. of S.* 6: 5.

To turn aside the needy from judgment. *Is.* 10: 2.

Thou shalt call me, My father; and shalt not turn away from me. *Je.* 3: 19.

Turn ye again now every one from his evil way. *Je.* 25: 5.

Repent, and turn yourselves from your idols; and turn away your faces from all your abominations. *Eze.* 14: 6.

I will not turn away the punishment thereof. *Am.* 1: 3.

They did not like to retain God in their knowledge. *Ro.* 1: 28.

They shall turn away their ears from the truth. *2 Ti.* 4: 4.

See also
Hatred.

Avoidance

Job . . . feared God, and eschewed evil. *Jb.* 1: 1.

Keep thy tongue from evil, and thy lips from speaking guile. *Ps.* 34: 13.

I have refrained my feet from every evil way. *Ps.* 119: 101.

If sinners entice thee, consent thou not. *Pr.* 1: 10.

Enter not into the path of the wicked, and go not in the way of evil men. Avoid it, pass not by it, turn from it, and pass away. *Pr.* 4: 14, 15.

I have not shunned to declare unto you all the counsel of God. *Ac.* 20: 27.

Mark them which cause divisions and offences contrary to the doctrine which ye have learned; and avoid them. *Ro.* 16: 17.

Abstain from all appearance of evil. *1 Th.* 5: 22.

Keep that which is committed to thy trust, avoiding profane and vain babblings. *1 Ti.* 6: 20.

Foolish and unlearned questions avoid, knowing that they do gender strifes. *2 Ti.* 2: 23.

Avoid foolish questions, and genealogies, and contentions, and strivings about the law. *Tit.* 3: 9.

Abstain from fleshly lusts, which war against the soul. *1 Pe.* 2: 11.

He that will love life, and see good days, let him refrain his tongue from evil, and his lips that they speak no guile. *1 Pe.* 3: 10.

Let him eschew evil, and do good; let him seek peace, and ensue it. *1 Pe.* 3: 11.

See also
Abstinence; Escape.

Avowal

O Lord, thou art our God; let not man prevail against thee. *2 Ch.* 14: 11.

I will confess my transgressions unto the Lord. *Ps.* 32: 5.

Thou art my King, O God. *Ps.* 44: 4.

Whosoever therefore shall confess me before men, him will I confess also before my Father which is in heaven. *Mat.* 10: 32.

Thou art Peter, and upon this rock I will build my church. *Mat.* 16: 18.

Peter answereth and saith unto him, Thou art the Christ. *Mk.* 8: 29.

This I confess unto thee, that after the way which they call heresy, so worship I the God of my fathers. *Ac.* 24: 14.

Thou shalt confess with thy mouth the Lord Jesus. *Ro.* 10: 9.

With the mouth confession is made unto salvation. *Ro.* 10: 10.

Christ Jesus . . . witnessed a good confession. *1 Ti.* 6: 13.

If we confess our sins, he is faithful and just to forgive us our sins. *1 Jn.* 1: 9.

Every spirit that confesseth that Jesus Christ is come in the flesh is of God. *1 Jn.* 4: 2.

See also
Admission; Confession; Declaration.

Awakening

I laid me down and slept; I awaked; for the Lord sustained me. *Ps.* 3: 5.

I shall be satisfied, when I awake, with thy likeness. *Ps.* 17: 15.

Weeping may endure for a night, but joy cometh in the morning. *Ps.* 30: 5.

I prevented the dawning of the morning. *Ps.* 119: 147.

My soul waiteth for the Lord more than they that watch for the morning. *Ps.* 130: 6.

When I awake, I am still with thee. *Ps.* 139: 18.

How long wilt thou sleep, O sluggard? when wilt thou arise out of thy sleep? *Pr.* 6: 9.

Yet a little sleep, a little slumber, a little folding of the hands to sleep: So shall thy poverty come as one that travelleth. *Pr.* 6: 10, 11.

Awake, awake, put on strength, O arm of the Lord. *Is.* 51: 9.

What meanest thou, O sleeper? arise, call upon thy God. *Jon.* 1: 6.

The angel that talked with me came again, and waked me, as a man that is wakened out of his sleep. *Zch.* 4: 1.

When they were awake, they saw his glory. *Lu.* 9: 32.

Now it is high time to awake out of sleep. *Ro.* 13: 11.

Awake to righteousness, and sin not. *1 Co.* 15: 34.

Awake thou that sleepest, and arise from the dead, and Christ shall give thee light. *Ep.* 5: 14.

See also

Birth, New; Dawn; Day, the Coming; Morning; Renewal; Revival; Spring.

Award

Verily there is a reward for the righteous. *Ps.* 58: 11.

To him that soweth righteousness shall be a sure reward. *Pr.* 11: 18.

The crown of the wise is their riches. *Pr.* 14: 24.

Great is your reward in heaven. *Mat.* 5: 12.

He shall reward every man according to his works. *Mat.* 16: 27.

When they had platted a crown of thorns, they put it upon his head. *Mat.* 27: 29.

If any man's work abide which he hath built thereupon, he shall receive a reward. *1 Co.* 3: 14.

Know ye not that they which run in a race run all, but one receiveth the prize? *1 Co.* 9: 24.

So run, that ye may obtain. *1 Co.* 9: 24.

They do it to obtain a corruptible crown; but we an incorruptible. *1 Co.* 9: 25.

I press toward the mark for the prize of the high calling of God in Christ Jesus. *Ph.* 3: 14.

We see Jesus . . . crowned with glory and honour. *He.* 2: 9.

After he had patiently endured, he obtained the promise. *He.* 6: 15.

He shall receive the crown of life, which the Lord hath promised to them that love him. *Ja.* 1: 12.

When the chief Shepherd shall appear, ye shall receive a crown of glory that fadeth not away. *1 Pe.* 5: 4.

Be thou faithful unto death, and I will give thee a crown of life. *Re.* 2: 10.

See also

Crown; Prize; Reward.

Awareness

Doth not he see my ways, and count all my steps? *Jb.* 31: 4.

Or ever I was aware. *S. of S.* 6: 12.

The earth shall be full of the knowledge of the Lord, as the waters cover the sea. *Is.* 11: 9.

Thou art also taken, O Babylon, and thou wast not aware. *Je.* 50: 24.

The lord of that servant shall come in a day when he looketh not for him, and in an hour that he is not aware of. *Mat.* 24: 50.

When they were awake, they saw his glory. *Lu.* 9: 32.

Ye are as graves which appear not, and the men that walk over them are not aware of them. *Lu.* 11: 44.

Except a man be born again, he cannot see the kingdom of God. *Jn.* 3: 3.

They were all filled with the Holy Ghost, and began to speak with other tongues. *Ac.* 2: 4.

Suddenly there shined round about him a light from heaven: And he fell to the earth, and heard a voice. *Ac.* 9: 3, 4.

When his eyes were opened, he saw no man. *Ac.* 9: 8.

In a trance I saw a vision. *Ac.* 11: 5.

God . . . hath shined in our hearts, to give the light of the knowledge of the glory of God in the face of Jesus Christ. *2 Co.* 4: 6.

Increasing in the knowledge of God. *Col.* 1: 10.

See also

God, Consciousness of; God, Knowledge of; God, Omniscience of; God, Providence of; Heed; Knowledge; Watch.

Awe

Thou shalt fear the Lord thy God, and serve him. *De.* 6: 13.

With God is terrible majesty. *Jb.* 37: 22.

Stand in awe; and sin not. *Ps.* 4: 4.

The fear of the Lord is clean, enduring for ever. *Ps.* 19: 9.

Let all the earth fear the Lord: let all the inhabitants of the world stand in awe of him. *Ps.* 33: 8.

O fear the Lord, ye his saints. *Ps.* 34: 9.

O come, let us worship and bow down: let us kneel before the Lord our maker. *Ps.* 95: 6.

Holy and reverend is his name. *Ps.* 111: 9.

The fear of the Lord is the beginning of wisdom. *Ps.* 111: 10.

My heart standeth in awe of thy word. *Ps.* 119: 161.

Fear the Lord, and depart from evil. *Pr.* 3: 7.

Holy, holy, holy, is the Lord of hosts: the whole earth is full of his glory. *Is.* 6: 3.

That at the name of Jesus every knee should bow. *Ph.* 2: 10.

Let us have grace, whereby we may serve God acceptably with reverence and godly fear. *He.* 12: 28.

Holy, holy, holy, Lord God Almighty, which was, and is, and is to come. *Re.* 4: 8.

See also

Adoration; Amazement; Astonishment; Fear; God, Adoration of; Marvel; Reverence; Wonder; Worship.

Axe

When thou shalt besiege a city a long time, . . . thou shalt not destroy the trees thereof by forcing an axe against them: for thou mayest eat of them, and thou shalt not cut them down (for the tree of the field is man's life). *De.* 20: 19.

Only the trees which thou knowest that they be not trees for meat, thou shalt destroy. *De.* 20: 20.

There is hope of a tree, if it be cut down, that it will sprout again. *Jb.* 14: 7.

A man was famous according as he had lifted up axes upon the thick trees. *Ps.* **74: 5.**

Wisdom hath builded her house, she hath hewn out her seven pillars. *Pr.* **9: 1.**

Shall the axe boast itself against him that heweth therewith? *Is.* **10: 15.**

Behold, the Lord, the Lord of hosts, shall lop the bough with terror: and the high ones of stature shall be hewn down. *Is.* **10: 33.**

One cutteth a tree out of the forest . . . with the axe. *Je.* **10: 3.**

They shall cut down thy choice cedars, and cast them into the fire. *Je.* **22: 7.**

With his axes he shall break down thy towers. *Eze.* **26: 9.**

Every tree which bringeth not forth good fruit is hewn down. *Mat.* **3: 10.**

Behold, these three years I come seeking fruit on this fig tree, and find none: cut it down; why cumbereth it the ground? *Lu.* **13: 7.**

B

Babble

Who hath babbling? . . . They that tarry long at the wine. *Pr.* **23: 29, 30.**

Surely the serpent will bite without enchantment; and a babbler is no better. *Ec.* **10: 11.**

Like a crane or a swallow, so did I chatter. *Is.* **38: 14.**

They think that they shall be heard for their much speaking. *Mat.* **6: 7.**

I say unto you, That every idle word that men shall speak, they shall give account thereof in the day of judgment. *Mat.* **12: 36.**

Their words seemed to them as idle tales. *Lu.* **24: 11.**

What will this babbler say? *Ac.* **17: 18.**

They learn to be idle, wandering about from house to house; and not only idle, but tattlers also and busybodies, speaking things which they ought not. *1 Ti.* **5: 13.**

Keep that which is committed to thy trust, avoiding profane and vain babblings. *1 Ti.* **6: 20.**

See also

Bedlam; Gossip.

Babe

As an . . . untimely birth I had not been; as infants which never saw light. *Jb.* **3: 16.**

Out of the mouth of babes and sucklings hast thou ordained strength because of thine enemies. *Ps.* **8: 2.**

I will give children to be their princes, and babes shall rule over them. *Is.* **3: 4.**

A little child shall lead them. *Is.* **11: 6.**

Can a woman forget her sucking child? *Is.* **49: 15.**

There shall be no more thence an infant of days. *Is.* **65: 20.**

The child shall die an hundred years old. *Is.* **65: 20.**

Thou hast hid these things from the wise and prudent, and hast revealed them unto babes. *Mat.* **11: 25.**

Jesus called a little child unto him, and set him in the midst of them. *Mat.* **18: 2.**

It came to pass that, when Elizabeth heard the salutation of Mary, the babe leaped in her womb. *Lu.* **1: 41.**

Ye shall find the babe wrapped in swaddling clothes. *Lu.* **2: 12.**

They brought unto him also infants, that he would touch them. *Lu.* **18: 15.**

I . . . could not speak unto you as unto spiritual, but as unto carnal, even as unto babes in Christ. *1 Co.* **3: 1.**

When I was a child, I spake as a child, I understood as a child, I thought as a child. *1 Co.* **13: 11.**

When I became a man, I put away childish things. *1 Co.* **13: 11.**

Every one that useth milk is unskilful in the word of righteousness: for he is a babe. *He.* **5: 13.**

As newborn babes, desire the sincere milk of the word, that ye may grow thereby. *1 Pe.* **2: 2.**

See also

Birth; Child; Christ, Birth of; Infant.

Babel

Let us build us a city and a tower, whose top may reach unto heaven. *Ge.* **11: 4.**

Therefore is the name of it called Babel; because the Lord did there confound the language of all the earth. *Ge.* **11: 9.**

The whole city was filled with confusion. *Ac.* **19: 29.**

God is not the author of confusion, but of peace. *1 Co.* **14: 33.**

See also

Accent; Anarchy; Chaos; Confusion; Language; Tongue.

Babylon

By the rivers of Babylon, there we sat down, yea, we wept, when we remembered Zion. *Ps.* **137: 1.**

Babylon, the glory of kingdoms, the beauty of the Chaldees' excellency, shall be as when God overthrew Sodom and Gomorrah. *Is.* **13: 19.**

Babylon is fallen, is fallen; and all the graven images of her gods he hath broken unto the ground. *Is.* **21: 9.**

The Lord hath raised us up prophets in Babylon. *Je.* **29: 15.**

Put yourselves in array against Babylon round about. *Je.* **50: 14.**

I have laid a snare for thee, and thou art also taken, O Babylon, . . . because thou hast striven against the Lord. *Je.* **50: 24.**

Babylon is suddenly fallen and destroyed: howl for her; take balm for her pain, if so be she may be healed. *Je.* **51: 8.**

Her cities are a desolation, a dry land, and a wilderness, a land wherein no man dwelleth, neither doth any son of man pass thereby. *Je.* **51: 43.**

Babylon is fallen, is fallen, that great city. *Re.* **14: 8.**

Babylon the great, the mother of harlots and abominations of the earth. *Re.* 17: 5.

Alas, alas that great city Babylon, that mighty city! for in one hour is thy judgment come. *Re.* 18: 10.

See also

Captivity; Corruption.

Back

He led the flock to the backside of the desert, and came to the mountain of God. *Ex.* 3: 1.

I will make all thine enemies turn their backs unto thee. *Ex.* 23: 27.

Thou . . . hast cast me behind thy back. *1 K.* 14: 9.

The plowers plowed upon my back: they made long their furrows. *Ps.* 129: 3.

Thou hast beset me behind and before. *Ps.* 139: 5.

A rod is for the back of him that is void of understanding. *Pr.* 10: 13.

Thou hast cast all my sins behind thy back. *Is.* 38: 17.

They have turned unto me the back, and not the face: though I taught them. *Je.* 32: 33.

See also

Background: Backsliding; Retreat.

Backbiting

Is there iniquity in my tongue? *Jb.* 6: 30.

Who shall dwell in thy holy hill? . . . He that backbiteth not with his tongue. *Ps.* 15: 1, 3.

They have spoken against me with a lying tongue. *Ps.* 109: 2.

The north wind driveth away rain: so doth an angry countenance a backbiting tongue. *Pr.* 25: 23.

Backbiters, haters of God, despiteful, proud, boasters, inventors of evil things. *Ro.* 1: 30.

I fear, lest, when I come, . . . there be debates, envyings, wraths, strifes, backbitings. *2 Co.* 12: 20.

If any man among you seem to be religious, and bridleth not his tongue, . . . this man's religion is vain. *Ja.* 1: 26.

Behold, how great a matter a little fire kindleth! And the tongue is a fire, a world of iniquity. *Ja.* 3: 5, 6.

Out of the same mouth proceedeth blessing and cursing. My brethren, these things ought not so to be. *Ja.* 3: 10.

He that will love life, and see good days, let him refrain his tongue from evil, and his lips that they speak no guile. *1 Pe.* 3: 10.

I will remember his deeds which he doeth, prating against us with malicious words. *3 Jn.* 1: 10.

See also

Calumny; Gossip; Slander; Talebearing.

Backfire

He that smiteth a man, so that he die, shall be surely put to death. *Ex.* 21: 12.

Eye for eye, tooth for tooth, hand for hand, foot for foot, Burning for burning, wound for wound, stripe for stripe. *Ex.* 21: 24, 25.

He that kindleth the fire shall surely make restitution. *Ex.* 22: 6.

Let his net that he hath hid catch himself. *Ps.* 35: 8.

He that troubleth his own house shall inherit the wind. *Pr.* 11: 29.

The wicked is snared by the transgression of his lips. *Pr.* 12: 13.

The backslider in heart shall be filled with his own ways. *Pr.* 14: 14.

Whoso causeth the righteous to go astray in an evil way, he shall fall himself into his own pit. *Pr.* 28: 10.

Background

Moses . . . led the flock to the backside of the desert, and came to the mountain of God. *Ex.* 3: 11.

The pillar of the cloud went from before their face, and stood behind them. *Ex.* 14: 19.

Underneath are the everlasting arms. *De.* 33: 27.

The Lord opened the eyes of the young man; and he saw: and, behold, the mountain was full of horses and chariots of fire round about Elisha. *2 K.* 6: 17.

Behold, God is great, and we know him not. *Jb.* 36: 26.

The angel of the Lord encampeth round about them that fear him, and delivereth them. *Ps.* 34: 7.

I will lift up mine eyes unto the hills, from whence cometh my help. *Ps.* 121: 1.

As the mountains are round about Jerusalem, so the Lord is round about his people from henceforth even for ever. *Ps.* 125: 2.

Blessed are they that have not seen, and yet have believed. *Jn.* 20: 29.

Forgetting those things which are behind, and reaching forth unto those things which are before, I press toward the mark. *Ph.* 3: 13, 14.

See also

Back.

Backsliding

As for this Moses, the man that brought us up out of the land of Egypt, we wot not what is become of him. *Ex.* 32: 1.

They have turned aside quickly out of the way which I commanded them. *Ex.* 32: 8.

Lest when thou hast eaten and art full, and hast built goodly houses, and dwelt therein; . . . Then thine heart be lifted up, and thou forget the Lord thy God. *De.* 8: 12, 14.

Surely they will turn away your heart after their gods. *1 K.* 11: 2.

His wives turned away his heart after other gods. *1 K.* 11: 4.

Shouldest thou help the ungodly, and love them that hate the Lord? *2 Ch.* 19: 2.

They are gone away backward. *Is.* 1: 4.

Thy silver is become dross, thy wine mixed with water. *Is.* 1: 22.

Thy backslidings shall reprove thee. *Je.* 2: 19.

Backsliding Israel committed adultery. *Je.* 3: 8.

Turn, O backsliding children, saith the Lord; for I am married unto you. *Je.* 3: 14.

They did worse than their fathers. *Je.* 7: 26.

Cursed be the man . . . whose heart departeth from the Lord. *Je.* 17: 5.

Because iniquity shall abound, the love of many shall wax cold. *Mat.* 24: 12.

The last state of that man is worse than the first. *Lu.* **11: 26.**

From that time many of his disciples went back, and walked no more with him. Then said Jesus unto the twelve, Will ye also go away? *Jn.* **6: 66, 67.**

This ministry and apostleship, from which Judas by transgression fell. *Ac.* **1: 25.**

Let not then your good be evil spoken of. *Ro.* **14: 16.**

After that ye have known God, or rather are known of God, how turn ye again to the weak and beggarly elements, whereunto ye desire again to be in bondage? *Ga.* **4: 9.**

Evil men and seducers shall wax worse and worse, deceiving, and being deceived. *2 Ti.* **3: 13.**

Demas hath forsaken me, having loved this present world. *2 Ti.* **4: 10.**

If any man draw back, my soul shall have no pleasure in him. *He.* **10: 38.**

If after they have escaped the pollutions of the world through the knowledge of the Lord and Saviour Jesus Christ, they are again entangled therein, and overcome, the latter end is worse with them than the beginning. *2 Pe.* **2: 20.**

Thou hast left thy first love. *Re.* **2: 4.**

See also

Apostasy; Back; Christ, Denial of; Denial; Departure; Estrangement; God, Denial of; Rejection; Retreat; Treachery.

Badness

The imagination of man's heart is evil from his youth. *Ge.* **8: 21.**

Thou . . . didst evil in the sight of the Lord. *1 S.* **15: 19.**

An evil spirit from the Lord troubled him. *1 S.* **16: 14.**

They are corrupt. *Ps.* **14: 1.**

I was shapen in iniquity. *Ps.* **51: 5.**

Treasures of wickedness profit nothing. *Pr.* **10: 2.**

Wickedness overthroweth the sinner. *Pr.* **13: 6.**

The heart of the sons of men is full of evil. *Ec.* **9: 3.**

Wherefore think ye evil in your hearts? *Mat.* **9: 4.**

He that is without sin among you, let him first cast a stone at her. *Jn.* **8: 7.**

Repent therefore of this thy wickedness. *Ac.* **8: 22.**

All have sinned. *Ro.* **5: 12.**

The Lord . . . shall stablish you, and keep you from evil. *2 Th.* **3: 3.**

Men of corrupt minds. *2 Ti.* **3: 8.**

See also

Corruption; Crime; Depravity; Evil; Fault; Guile; Iniquity; Lust; Sin; Sinner; Ungodliness; Unrighteousness; Wickedness; Wrong.

Balance

Just balances, just weights, . . . shall ye have. *Le.* **19: 36.**

He weigheth the waters by measure. *Jb.* **28: 25.**

Let me be weighed in an even balance, that God may know mine integrity. *Jb.* **31: 6.**

A false balance is abomination to the Lord:

but a just weight is his delight. *Pr.* **11: 1.**

The Lord weigheth the spirits. *Pr.* **16: 2.**

Divers weights, and divers measures, both of them are alike abomination to the Lord. *Pr.* **20: 10.**

Thou, most upright, dost weigh the path of the just. *Is.* **26: 7.**

Who hath . . . weighed . . . the hills in a balance? *Is.* **40: 12.**

Behold, the nations are as a drop of a bucket, and are counted as the small dust of the balance. *Is.* **40: 15.**

Thou art weighed in the balances, and art found wanting. *Da.* **5: 27.**

Shall I count them pure with the wicked balances, and with the bag of deceitful weights? *Mi.* **6: 11.**

See also

Accuracy; Confidence; Judgment; Measure; Poise; Serenity; Symmetry; Weight.

Balm

With my holy oil have I anointed him. *Ps.* **89: 20.**

To give unto them . . . the oil of joy for mourning. *Is.* **61: 3.**

Is there no balm in Gilead? *Je.* **8: 22.**

They . . . anointed with oil many that were sick, and healed them. *Mk.* **6: 13.**

Anoint thine eyes with eyesalve, that thou mayest see. *Re.* **3: 18.**

See also

Cure; Healing; Ointment.

Ban

The Lord sent him forth from the garden of Eden. *Ge.* **3: 23.**

Thou hast driven me out this day from the face of the earth; and from thy face shall I be hid; and I shall be a fugitive and a vagabond in the earth. *Ge.* **4: 14.**

How shall I curse, whom God hath not cursed? *Nu.* **23: 8.**

Thou art a stranger, and also an exile. *2 S.* **15: 19.**

The prophets have seen . . . for thee false burdens and causes of banishment. *La.* **2: 14.**

He shall turn the heart of the fathers to the children, and the heart of the children to their fathers, lest I come and smite the earth with a curse. *Mal.* **4: 6.**

Depart from me, ye cursed. *Mat.* **25: 41.**

The fig tree which thou cursedst is withered away. *Mk.* **11: 21.**

As many as are of the works of the law are under the curse. *Ga.* **3: 10.**

Christ hath redeemed us from the curse of the law, being made a curse for us. *Ga.* **3: 13.**

There shall be no more curse. *Re.* **22: 3.**

See also

Curse; Excommunication; Prohibition.

Band

What man is like Job? . . . Which goeth in company with the workers of iniquity, and walketh with wicked men. *Jb.* **34: 7, 8.**

Who hath loosed the bands of the wild ass? *Jb.* **39: 5.**

Is not this the fast that I have chosen? to loose the bands of wickedness. *Is.* **58: 6.**

I drew them with . . . bands of love. *Ho.* **11: 4.**

Now will I break this yoke from off thee, and will burst thy bonds in sunder. *Na.* 1: 13.

Others had trial of cruel mockings and scourgings, yea, moreover, of bonds and imprisonment. *He.* 11: 36.

See also

Alliance; Bond; Bondage; Companionship; Companionship, Evil; Company; Society; Union.

Bane

I will send the teeth of beasts upon them, with the poison of serpents of the dust. *De.* 32: 24.

The arrows of the Almighty are within me, the poison whereof drinketh up my spirit. *Jb.* 6: 4.

He shall suck the poison of asps. *Jb.* 20: 16.

Their poison is like the poison of a serpent. *Ps.* 58: 4.

The tongue . . . is an unruly evil, full of deadly poison. *Ja.* 3: 8.

See also

Curse; Injury; Pestilence; Poison.

Banishment

I have been a stranger in a strange land. *Ex.* 2: 22.

The Lord thy God . . . will return and gather thee from all the nations, whither the Lord thy God hath scattered thee. *De.* 30: 3.

We must needs die, and are as water spilt on the ground, which cannot be gathered up again; neither doth God respect any person: yet doth he devise means, that his banished be not expelled from him. *2 S.* 14: 14.

How shall we sing the Lord's song in a strange land? *Ps.* 137: 4.

My people are gone into captivity, because they have no knowledge. *Is.* 5: 13.

I have lost my children, and am desolate, a captive, and removing to and fro. *Is.* 49: 21.

The captive exile hasteneth that he may be loosed. *Is.* 51: 14.

He hath sent me . . . to proclaim liberty to the captives. *Is.* 61: 1.

I will bring you again into the place whence I caused you to be carried away captive. *Je.* 29: 14.

I was among the captives by the river of Chebar. *Eze.* 1: 1.

Therefore will I cause you to go into captivity beyond Damascus. *Am.* 5: 27.

Depart from me, ye cursed, into everlasting fire. *Mat.* 25: 41.

See also

Captivity; Condemnation; Exile; Expatriation; Judgment; Outcast; Stranger.

Bank

At the bank of the river were very many trees on the one side and on the other. *Eze.* 47: 7.

Then cometh Jesus from Galilee to Jordan unto John, to be baptized of him. *Mat.* 3: 13.

Wherefore then gavest not thou my money into the bank, that at my coming I might have required mine own with usury? *Lu.* 19: 23.

On either side of the river, was there the tree of life. *Re.* 22: 2.

See also

Money; Shore.

Banner

The Lord went before them by day in a pillar of cloud. *Ex.* 13: 21.

Every man by his own standard. *Nu.* 1: 52.

In the name of our God we will set up our banners. *Ps.* 20: 5.

Thou hast given a banner to them that fear thee. *Ps.* 60: 4.

His banner over me was love. *S. of S.* 2: 4.

Terrible as an army with banners. *S. of S.* 6: 4.

They shall be as when a standardbearer fainteth. *Is.* 10: 18.

Lift ye up a banner upon the high mountain. *Is.* 13: 2.

I will . . . set up my standard to the people. *Is.* 49: 22.

Lift up a standard for the people. *Is.* 62: 10.

See also

Standard; Symbol.

Banquet

It is better to go to the house of mourning, than to go to the house of feasting. *Ec.* 7: 2.

He brought me to the banqueting house, and his banner over me was love. *S. of S.* 2: 4.

In this mountain shall the Lord of hosts make unto all people a feast of fat things. *Is.* 25: 6.

I will turn your feasts into mourning, and all your songs into lamentation. *Am.* 8: 10.

When thou makest a feast, call the poor, the maimed, the lame, the blind. *Lu.* 14: 13.

What think ye, that he will not come to the feast? *Jn.* 11: 56.

When we walked in . . . excess of wine, revellings, banquetings. *1 Pe.* 4: 3.

See also

Feast; Festival.

Baptism

The Lord God shall . . . call his servants by another name. *Is.* 65: 15.

I indeed baptize you with water unto repentance: but he that cometh after me is mightier than I, whose shoes I am not worthy to bear: he shall baptize you with the Holy Ghost, and with fire. *Mat.* 3: 11.

I have need to be baptized of thee, and comest thou to me? *Mat.* 3: 14.

Jesus, when he was baptized, went up straightway out of the water: and, lo, the heavens were opened unto him, and he saw the Spirit of God descending like a dove, and lighting upon him. *Mat.* 3: 16.

Go ye therefore, and teach all nations, baptizing them in the name of the Father, and of the Son, and of the Holy Ghost. *Mat.* 28: 19.

I have a baptism to be baptized with; and how am I straitened till it be accomplished! *Lu.* 12: 50.

Except a man be born of water and of the Spirit, he cannot enter into the kingdom of God. *Jn.* 3: 5.

Whosoever drinketh of the water that I shall give him shall never thirst. *Jn.* 4: 14.

What doth hinder me to be baptized? *Ac.* 8: 36.

John . . . preached . . . the baptism of repentance. *Ac.* 13: 24.

Why tarriest thou? arise, and be baptized,
and wash away thy sins. *Ac.* **22: 16.**

Know ye not, that so many of us as were
baptized into Jesus Christ were baptized into
his death? *Ro.* **6: 3.**

By one Spirit are we all baptized into one
body. *1 Co.* **12: 13.**

We . . . have been all made to drink into
one Spirit. *1 Co.* **12: 13.**

One Lord, one faith, one baptism. *Ep.* **4: 5.**

See also

Immersion.

Bar

Hinder me not, seeing the Lord hath prospered my way. *Ge.* **24: 56.**

If he cut off, and shut up, or gather together, then who can hinder him? *Jb.* **11: 10.**

Contentions are like the bars of a castle.
Pr. **18: 19.**

Her bars are broken. *Je.* **51: 30.**

He hath destroyed and broken her bars.
La. **2: 9.**

I will go up to the land of unwalled villages; I will go to them that are at rest, that
dwell safely, all of them dwelling without
walls, and having neither bars nor gates. *Eze.*
38: 11.

See also

Difficulty; Door; Hindrance; Key; Obstacle;
Stumbling-block.

Barbarian

They that dwell in mine house . . . count
me for a stranger: I am an alien in their sight.
Jb. **19: 15.**

Our inheritance is turned to strangers, our
houses to aliens. *La.* **5: 2.**

From henceforth I will go unto the Gentiles.
Ac. **18: 6.**

I am debtor both to the Greeks, and to the
Barbarians. *Ro.* **1: 14.**

Is he the God of the Jews only? is he not
also of the Gentiles? *Ro.* **3: 29.**

Ye are no more strangers and foreigners, but
fellowcitizens with the saints, and of the
household of God. *Ep.* **2: 19.**

That the Gentiles should be fellowheirs,
and of the same body, and partakers of his
promise. *Ep.* **3: 6.**

Where there is neither Greek nor Jew, . . .
Barbarian, Scythian, bond nor free: but
Christ is all and in all. *Col.* **3: 11.**

See also

Alien; Gentile; Stranger.

Bargain

Joseph gave them bread in exchange for
horses, and for the flocks, and for the cattle
of the herds, and for the asses. *Ge.* **47: 17.**

The gold and the crystal cannot equal it:
and the exchange of it shall not be for jewels
of fine gold. *Jb.* **28: 17.**

Thou sellest thy people for nought. *Ps.* **44:
12.**

Come, buy wine and milk without money
and without price. *Is.* **55: 1.**

They have . . . sold a girl for wine. *Jo.* **3: 3.**

They sold the righteous for silver, and the
poor for a pair of shoes. *Am.* **2: 6.**

The kingdom of heaven is like unto a merchant man, seeking goodly pearls: Who, when

he had found one pearl of great price, went
and sold all that he had, and bought it. *Mat.*
13: 45, 46.

What is a man profited, if he shall gain the
whole world, and lose his own soul? *Mat.* **16:
26.**

What shall a man give in exchange for his
soul? *Mat.* **16: 26.**

Go and sell that thou hast, and give to the
poor, and thou shalt have treasure in heaven.
Mat. **19: 21.**

Didst not thou agree with me for a penny?
Mat. **20: 13.**

Thou hast been faithful over a few things,
I will make thee ruler over many things. *Mat.*
25: 21.

Inasmuch as ye have done it unto one of
the least of these my brethren, ye have done it
unto me. *Mat.* **25: 40.**

Give, and it shall be given unto you. *Lu.* **6:
38.**

With the same measure that ye mete withal
it shall be measured to you again. *Lu.* **6: 38.**

Yet have I made myself servant unto all,
that I might gain the more. *1 Co.* **9: 19.**

God loveth a cheerful giver. *2 Co.* **9: 7.**

Esau . . . for one morsel of meat sold his
birthright. *He.* **12: 16.**

See also

Agreement; Compact; Contract.

Barrenness

God blessed them, saying, Be fruitful, and
multiply. *Ge.* **1: 22.**

Isaac intreated the Lord for his wife, because she was barren. *Ge.* **25: 21.**

Then said the Lord unto Moses, Behold, I
will rain bread from heaven for you. *Ex.*
16: 4.

Whose house I have made the wilderness,
and the barren land his dwelling. *Jb.* **39: 6.**

They wandered in the wilderness in a
solitary way; they found no city to dwell in.
Ps. **107: 4.**

He turneth . . . A fruitful land into barrenness, for the wickedness of them that dwell
therein. *Ps.* **107: 33, 34.**

I will also command the clouds that they
rain no rain upon it. *Is.* **5: 6.**

I will make the wilderness a pool of water,
and the dry land springs of water. *Is.* **41: 18.**

Sing, O barren, thou that didst not bear;
break forth into singing. *Is.* **54: 1.**

I beheld, and, lo, the fruitful place was a
wilderness. *Je.* **4: 26.**

Behold, the hindermost of the nations shall
be a wilderness, a dry land, and a desert. *Je.*
50: 12.

Blessed are the barren. *Lu.* **23: 29.**

It is written, Rejoice, thou barren. *Ga.*
4: 27.

That they be not unfruitful. *Tit.* **3: 14.**

If these things be in you, and abound, they
make you that ye shall neither be barren nor
unfruitful in the knowledge of our Lord
Jesus Christ. *2 Pe.* **1: 8.**

See also

Aridity; Desert; Drought; Dryness; Emptiness; Fruitlessness; Waste; Wilderness.

Battle

Quit yourselves like men, and fight. *1 S.*
4: 9.

How are the mighty fallen in the midst of the battle! *2 S.* 1: 25.

The battle is not yours, but God's. *2 Ch.* 20: 15.

Who is this King of glory? . . . the Lord mighty in battle. *Ps* 24: 8.

He maketh wars to cease unto the end of the earth. *Ps.* 46: 9.

Thou hast covered my head in the day of battle. *Ps.* 140: 7.

The race is not to the swift, or the battle to the strong. *Ec.* 9: 11.

Nation shall not lift up sword against nation, neither shall they learn war any more. *Is.* 2: 4.

Cry unto her, that her warfare is accomplished. *Is.* 40: 2.

A sound of battle is in the land. *Je.* 50: 22.

The people that do know their God shall be strong, and do exploits. *Da.* 11: 32.

I see another law in my members, warring against the law of my mind. *Ro.* 7: 23.

So fight I, not as one that beateth the air. *1 Co.* 9: 26.

The weapons of our warfare are not carnal, but mighty through God to the pulling down of strong holds. *2 Co.* 10: 4.

For we wrestle not against flesh and blood, but against principalities, against powers, against the rulers of the darkness of this world, against spiritual wickedness in high places. *Ep.* 6: 12.

This charge I commit unto thee, . . . that thou by them mightest war a good warfare. *1 Ti.* 1: 18.

Fight the good fight of faith. *1 Ti.* 6: 12.

No man that warreth entangleth himself with the affairs of this life; that he may please him who hath chosen him to be a soldier. *2 Ti.* 2: 4.

I have fought a good fight, I have finished my course, I have kept the faith: Henceforth there is laid up for me a crown of righteousness. *2 Ti.* 4: 7, 8.

Waxed valiant in fight. *He.* 11: 34.

See also
Army; Conflict; Contention; Enemy; Fight; Soldier; Strife; Struggle; War; Weapon.

Beacon

Thou art my lamp, O Lord: and the Lord will lighten my darkness. *2 S.* 22: 29.

O send out thy light and thy truth: let them lead me. *Ps.* 43: 3.

He spread a cloud for a covering; and fire to give light in the night. *Ps.* 105: 39.

Thy word is a lamp unto my feet, and a light unto my path. *Ps.* 119: 105.

The commandment is a lamp; and the law is light. *Pr.* 6: 23.

The people that walked in darkness have seen a great light: they that dwell in the land of the shadow of death, upon them hath the light shined. *Is.* 9: 2.

The Lord shall be thine everlasting light. *Is.* 60: 20.

Ye are the light of the world. A city that is set on an hill cannot be hid. *Mat.* 5: 14.

Let your light so shine before men, that they may see your good works, and glorify your Father which is in heaven. *Mat.* 5: 16.

That was the true Light which lighteth every man that cometh into the world. *Jn.* 1: 9.

He was a burning and a shining light. *Jn.* 5: 35.

God, who commanded the light to shine out of darkness, hath shined in our hearts. *2 Co.* 4: 6.

Ye do well that ye take heed, as unto a light that shineth in a dark place. *2 Pe.* 1: 19.

See also
Lamp; Light; Sign.

Beast

God created . . . every living creature that moveth. *Ge.* 1: 21.

God made the beast of the earth after his kind, . . . and God saw that it was good. *Ge.* 1: 25.

Wherefore are we counted as beasts, and reputed vile in your sight? *Jb.* 18: 3.

The young lions roar after their prey, and seek their meat from God. *Ps.* 104: 21.

A righteous man regardeth the life of his beast. *Pr.* 12: 10.

He . . . was with the wild beasts. *Mk.* 1: 13.

If after the manner of men I have fought with beasts at Ephesus, what advantageth it me, if the dead rise not? *1 Co.* 15: 32.

Every creature of God is good. *1 Ti.* 4: 4.

If any man worship the beast and his image, . . . The same shall drink of the wine of the wrath of God. *Re.* 14: 9, 10.

See also
Animal; Bestiality; Brute; Creature.

Beatitude

Blessed is the man that walketh not in the counsel of the ungodly. *Ps.* 1: 1.

Blessed is the nation whose God is the Lord. *Ps.* 33: 12.

Blessed is the man that trusteth in him. *Ps.* 34: 8.

O Lord of hosts, blessed is the man that trusteth in thee. *Ps.* 84: 12.

Blessed be he that cometh in the name of the Lord. *Ps.* 118: 26.

Blessed are ye that sow beside all waters. *Is.* 32: 20.

He opened his mouth, and taught them, saying, Blessed. *Mat.* 5: 2, 3.

Blessed are the poor in spirit: for theirs is the kingdom of heaven. *Mat.* 5: 3.

Blessed are they that mourn: for they shall be comforted. *Mat.* 5: 4.

Blessed are the meek: for they shall inherit the earth. *Mat.* 5: 5.

Blessed are they which do hunger and thirst after righteousness: for they shall be filled. *Mat.* 5: 6.

Blessed are the merciful: for they shall obtain mercy. *Mat.* 5: 7.

Blessed are the pure in heart: for they shall see God. *Mat.* 5: 8.

Blessed are the peacemakers: for they shall be called the children of God. *Mat.* 5: 9.

Blessed are they which are persecuted for righteousness' sake: for theirs is the kingdom of heaven. *Mat* 5: 10.

Blessed are ye, when men shall revile you, and persecute you, and say all manner of evil

against you falsely, for my sake. *Mat.* 5: 11.
See also
Benediction; Blessedness; Blessing; God,
Blessing of; Happiness; Joy.

Beauty

One thing have I desired of the Lord, that
will I seek after, . . . to behold the beauty
of the Lord. *Ps.* 27: 4.
Thou art fairer than the children of men:
grace is poured into thy lips. *Ps.* 45: 2.
Beautiful for situation, the joy of the whole
earth, is Mount Zion. *Ps.* 48: 2.
Out of Zion, the perfection of beauty, God
hath shined. *Ps.* 50: 2.
Let the beauty of the Lord our God be
upon us. *Ps.* 90: 17.
He will beautify the meek with salvation.
Ps. 149: 4.
As a jewel of gold in a swine's snout, so is a
fair woman which is without discretion. *Pr.*
11: 22.
Favour is deceitful, and beauty is vain. *Pr.*
31: 30.
He hath made every thing beautiful in his
time. *Ec.* 3: 11.
In that day shall the branch of the Lord be
beautiful and glorious. *Is.* 4: 2.
How beautiful upon the mountains are the
feet of him that bringeth good tidings. *Is.* 52:
7.
I will lay thy stones with fair colours. *Is.*
54: 11.
To appoint unto them that mourn in Zion,
to give unto them beauty for ashes. *Is.* 61: 3.
Thou wast exceeding beautiful. *Eze.* 16: 13.
Thou didst trust in thine own beauty. *Eze.*
16: 15.
Thou art unto them as a very lovely song of
one that hath a pleasant voice. *Eze.* 33: 32.
Consider the lilies of the field, how they
grow; they toil not, neither do they spin: And
yet I say unto you, That even Solomon in all
his glory was not arrayed like one of these.
Mat. 6: 28, 29.
The beautiful gate of the temple. *Ac.* 3: 10.
That he might present it to himself a glorious church, not having spot, or wrinkle, or any
such thing; but that it should be holy and
without blemish. *Ep.* 5: 27.
Whatsoever things are lovely, . . . think on
these things. *Ph.* 4: 8.
The ornament of a meek and quiet spirit,
which is in the sight of God of great price.
1 Pe. 3: 4.
I John saw the holy city, new Jerusalem,
coming down from God out of heaven, prepared as a bride adorned for her husband. *Re.*
21: 2.
See also
Adornment; Architecture; Art; Christ, Grace
of; Excellence; God, Grace of; Grace; Loveliness; Ornament.

Bed

He took of the stones of that place, and
put them for his pillows, and lay down in
that place to sleep. *Ge.* 28: 11.
I have made my bed in the darkness. *Jb.*
17: 13.
Commune with your own heart upon your
bed, and be still. *Ps.* 4: 4.

I will both lay me down in peace, and
sleep: for thou, Lord, only makest me dwell
in safety. *Ps.* 4: 8.
I am weary with my groanings; all the night
make I my bed to swim; I water my couch
with my tears. *Ps.* 6: 6.
The Lord will . . . make all his bed in his
sickness. *Ps.* 41: 3.
Then the Lord awaked as one out of sleep.
Ps. 78: 65.
It is vain for you to rise up early, to sit up
late, to eat the bread of sorrows: for so he
giveth his beloved sleep. *Ps.* 127: 2.
If I make my bed in hell, behold, thou art
there. *Ps.* 139: 8.
Let the saints . . . sing aloud upon their
beds. *Ps.* 149: 5.
When thou liest down, thou shalt not be
afraid: yea, thou shalt lie down, and thy sleep
shall be sweet. *Pr.* 3: 24.
Love not sleep, lest thou come to poverty.
Pr. 20: 13.
The thoughts upon my bed and the visions
of my head troubled me. *Da.* 4: 5.
Take up thy bed, and go unto thine house.
Mat. 9: 6.
Is a candle brought to be put under a
bushel, or under a bed? *Mk.* 4: 21.
Why sleep ye? rise and pray, lest ye enter
into temptation. *Lu.* 22: 46.
Awake thou that sleepest, and arise from
the dead, and Christ shall bring thee light.
Ep. 5: 14.
Them also which sleep in Jesus will God
bring with him. *1 Th.* 4: 14.
See also
Repose; Rest; Sleep.

Bedlam

Therefore is the name of it called Babel.
Ge. 11: 9.
Their inhabitants were . . . confounded.
2 K. 19: 26.
Why do the heathen rage, and the people
imagine a vain thing? *Ps.* 2: 1.
Madness is in their heart while they live.
Ec. 9: 3.
The city of confusion is broken down: every
house is shut up, that no man may come in.
Is. 24: 10.
Her whole land shall be confounded, and all
her slain shall fall in the midst of her. *Je.* 51:
47.
The whole city was filled with confusion.
Ac. 19: 29.
God is not the author of confusion. *1 Co.*
14: 33.
See also
Babble; Babel; Bewilderment; Confusion;
Insanity; Madness; Tumult; Turmoil.

Beggar

Let them seek their bread also out of their
desolate places. *Ps.* 109: 10.
The sluggard will not plow by reason of
the cold; therefore shall he beg in harvest, and
have nothing. *Pr.* 20: 4.
What shall I do? for my lord taketh away
from me the stewardship: I cannot dig; to beg
I am ashamed. *Lu.* 16: 3.
It came to pass, that the beggar died, and

was carried by the angels into Abraham's bosom. *Lu.* 16: 22.

A certain man lame from his mother's womb, . . . seeing Peter and John about to go into the temple asked an alms. *Ac.* 3: 2, 3.

See also
Entreaty; Petition; Poor; Poverty; Request; Supplication.

Beginning

In the beginning God created the heaven and the earth. *Ge.* 1: 1.

O Lord God, thou hast begun. *De.* 3: 24.

The eyes of the Lord thy God are always upon it, from the beginning of the year even unto the end of the year. *De.* 11: 12.

When I begin, I will also make an end. *1 S.* 3: 12.

Though thy beginning was small, yet thy latter end should greatly increase. *Jb.* 8: 7.

The fear of the Lord is the beginning of wisdom. *Ps.* 111: 10.

Thy word is true from the beginning. *Ps.* 119: 160.

No man can find out the work that God maketh from the beginning to the end. *Ec.* 3: 11.

I . . . will build them, as at the first. *Je.* 33: 7.

The beginning of the gospel of Jesus Christ, the Son of God. *Mk.* 1: 1.

This man began to build, and was not able to finish. *Lu.* 14: 30.

That repentance and remission of sins should be preached in his name among all nations, beginning at Jerusalem. *Lu.* 24: 47.

In the beginning was the Word, and the Word was with God, and the Word was God. *Jn.* 1: 1.

Ye have been with me from the beginning. *Jn.* 15: 27.

The former treatise have I made, O Theophilus, of all that Jesus began both to do and teach. *Ac.* 1: 1.

The Holy Ghost fell on them, as on us at the beginning. *Ac.* 11: 15.

He is the head of the body, the church: who is the beginning, the firstborn from the dead. *Col.* 1: 18.

Thou, Lord, in the beginning hast laid the foundation of the earth. *He.* 1: 10.

Without father, without mother, without descent, having neither beginning of days, nor end of life. *He.* 7: 3.

Behold, · how great a matter a little fire kindleth! *Ja.* 3: 5.

This is the message that ye heard from the beginning, that we should love one another. *1 Jn.* 3: 11.

I am Alpha and Omega, the beginning and the ending, saith the Lord, which is, and which was, and which is to come. *Re.* 1: 8.

See also
Alpha; Christ, the Creator; Commencement; Creation; Creator; First; Foundation; Genesis; God, the Creator; Graduation; Inauguration; Origin.

Behavior

Ye shall not walk in the manners of the nation, which I cast out before thee. *Le.* 20: 23.

The children of Israel did evil in the sight of the Lord. *Ju.* 2: 11.

It was a true report that I heard in mine own land of thy acts and of thy wisdom. *1 K.* 10: 6.

Let us behave ourselves valiantly. *1 Ch.* 19: 13.

It is not good that ye do: ought ye not 'to walk in the fear of our God? *Ne.* 5: 9.

Depart from evil, and do good. *Ps.* 34: 14.

I will behave myself wisely in a perfect way. *Ps.* 101: 2.

Ye did not hear; but did evil before mine eyes. *Is.* 65: 12.

They have behaved themselves ill in their doings. *Mi.* 3: 4.

Charity . . . doth not behave itself unseemly. *1 Co.* 13: 4, 5.

Evil communications corrupt good manners. *1 Co.* 15: 33.

We behaved not ourselves disorderly among you. *2 Th.* 3: 7.

See also
Character; Conduct; Manners.

Being

God said, Let there be light: and there was light. *Ge.* 1: 3.

The Lord God formed man of the dust of the ground, and breathed into his nostrils the breath of life. *Ge.* 2: 7.

Enoch walked with God: and he was not; for God took him. *Ge.* 5: 24.

God said unto Moses, I AM THAT I AM. *Ex.* 3: 14.

I will sing praises unto my God while I have any being. *Ps.* 146: 2.

In him we live, and move, and have our being. *Ac.* 17: 28.

The letter killeth, but the spirit giveth life. *2 Co.* 3: 6.

What is your life? It is even a vapour, that appeareth for a little time, and then vanisheth away. *Ja.* 4: 14.

To him that overcometh will I give to eat of the tree of life. *Re.* 2: 7.

See also
Existence; Life.

Belief

Believe in the Lord your God, so shall ye be established; believe his prophets, so shall ye prosper. *2 Ch.* 20: 20.

When Jesus heard it, he marvelled, and said to them that followed, Verily I say unto you, I have not found so great faith, no, not in Israel. *Mat.* 8: 10.

Be of good comfort; thy faith hath made thee whole. *Mat.* 9: 22.

According to your faith be it unto you. *Mat.* 9: 29.

Repent ye, and believe the gospel. *Mk.* 1: 15.

Be not afraid, only believe. *Mk.* 5: 36.

If thou canst believe, all things are possible to him that believeth. *Mk.* 9: 23.

Lord, I believe; help thou mine unbelief. *Mk.* 9: 24.

When the Son of man cometh, shall he find faith on the earth? *Lu.* 18: 8.

Who against hope believed in hope. *Ro.* 4: 18.

Now the God of hope fill you with all joy

and peace in believing. *Ro.* 15: 13.

Examine yourselves, whether ye be in the faith; prove your own selves. *2 Co.* 13: 5.

The household of faith. *Ga.* 6: 10.

Above all, taking the shield of faith. *Ep.* 6: 16.

Be thou an example of the believers, in word, in conversation, in charity, in spirit, in faith, in purity. *1 Ti.* 4: 12.

Now faith is the substance of things hoped for, the evidence of things not seen. For by it the elders obtained a good report. *He.* 11: 1, 2.

See also

Assurance; Christ, Belief in; Christ, Faith in; Confidence; Conviction; Dogma; Faith; God, Confidence in; God, Faith in; Persuasion; Reliance; Trust.

Belligerent

The Lord your God, he it is that fighteth for you, as he hath promised you. *Jos.* 23: 10.

Quit yourselves like men, and fight. *1 S.* 4: 9.

Be thou valiant for me, and fight the Lord's battles. *1 S.* 18: 17.

See how he seeketh a quarrel against me. *2 K.* 5: 7.

Blessed be the Lord my strength, which teacheth my hands to war, and my fingers to fight. *Ps.* 144: 1.

With good advice make war. *Pr.* 20: 18.

7 By wise counsel thou shalt make thy war. *Pr.* 24: 6.

Every battle of the warrior is with confused noise, and garments rolled in blood. *Is.* 9: 5.

Prepare war, wake up the mighty men, let all the men of war draw near. *Jo.* 3: 9.

Beat your plowshares into swords, and your pruninghooks into spears: let the weak say, I am strong. *Jo.* 3: 10.

If the trumpet give an uncertain sound, who shall prepare himself to the battle. *1 Co.* 14: 8.

The weapons of our warfare are not carnal, but mighty through God to the pulling down of strong holds. *2 Co.* 10: 4.

Fight the good fight of faith. *1 Ti.* 6: 12.

No man that warreth entangleth himself with the affairs of this life. *2 Ti.* 2: 4.

From whence come wars and fightings among you? *Ja.* 4: 1.

Ye fight and war, yet ye have not, because ye ask not. *Ja.* 4: 2.

See also

Army; Battle; Enemy; Fight; Soldier; War.

Belongings

Dwell and trade ye therein, and get you possessions therein. *Ge.* 34: 10.

Do not interpretations belong to God? *Ge.* 40: 8.

The secret things belong unto the Lord our God. *De.* 29: 29.

Salvation belongeth unto the Lord. *Ps.* 3: 8.

The shields of the earth belong unto God. *Ps.* 47: 9.

Unto God the Lord belong the issues from death. *Ps.* 68: 20.

He went away sorrowful: for he had great possessions. *Mat.* 19: 22.

He shall make him ruler over all his goods. *Mat.* 24: 47.

Ye belong to Christ. *Mk.* 9: 41.

When a strong man armed keepeth his palace, his goods are at peace. *Lu.* 11: 21.

The half of my goods I give to the poor. *Lu.* 19: 8.

Though I bestow all my goods to feed the poor, . . . it profiteth me nothing. *1 Co.* 13: 3.

See also

Goods; Mammon; Ownership; Possessions; Wealth.

Benediction

The Lord watch between me and thee, when we are absent one from another. *Ge.* 31: 49.

The Lord bless thee, and keep thee: The Lord make his face shine upon thee, and be gracious unto thee: The Lord lift up his countenance upon thee, and give thee peace. *Nu.* 6: 24–26.

God be merciful unto us, and bless us; and cause his face to shine upon us. *Ps.* 67: 1.

The blessing of the Lord be upon you: we bless you in the name of the Lord. *Ps.* 129: 8.

Peace be unto you. *Lu.* 24: 36.

He lifted up his hands, and blessed them. *Lu.* 24: 50.

To God only wise, be glory through Jesus Christ for ever. *Ro.* 16: 27.

The grace of the Lord Jesus Christ, and the love of God, and the communion of the Holy Ghost, be with you all. Amen. *2 Co.* 13: 14.

Peace be to the brethren, and love with faith, from God the Father and the Lord Jesus Christ. *Ep.* 6: 23.

Grace be with all them that love our Lord Jesus Christ in sincerity. Amen. *Ep.* 6: 24.

Peace be with you all that are in Christ Jesus. Amen. *1 Pe.* 5: 14.

To him be glory both now and for ever. *2 Pe.* 3: 18.

Peace be to thee. *3 Jn.* 1: 14.

Now unto him that is able to keep you from falling, and to present you faultless before the presence of his glory with exceeding joy, To the only wise God our Saviour, be glory and majesty, dominion and power, both now and ever. Amen. *Jude* 1: 24, 25.

Blessing and honour, and glory, and power, be unto him that sitteth upon the throne, and unto the Lamb for ever and ever. *Re.* 5: 13.

Blessing, and glory, and wisdom, and thanksgiving, and honour, and power, and might, be unto our God for ever and ever. Amen. *Re.* 7: 12.

The grace of our Lord Jesus Christ be with you all. Amen. *Re.* 22: 21.

See also

Blessing; Christ, Grace of; God, Blessing of; God, Grace of.

Beneficence

According to the kindness that I have done unto thee, thou shalt do unto me. *Ge.* 21: 23.

I will make all my goodness pass before thee. *Ex.* 33: 19.

Is this thy kindness to thy friend? *2 S.* 16: 17.

Surely goodness and mercy shall follow me all the days of my life. *Ps.* 23: 6.

Blessed be the Lord: for he hath shewed me his marvellous kindness. *Ps.* 31: 21.

The Lord shall make bright clouds, and give

them showers of rain, to every one grass in the field. *Zch.* **10: 1.**

Give to him that asketh thee, and from him that would borrow of thee turn not thou away. *Mat.* **5: 42.**

They that exercise authority upon them are called benefactors. *Lu.* **22: 25.**

See also

Almsgiving; Benevolence; Brotherhood; Charity; Clemency; Generosity; God, Beneficence of; Liberality; Philanthropy; Unselfishness; Will, Good.

Benefit

Blessed be the Lord, who daily loadeth us with benefits. *Ps.* **68: 19.**

Bless the Lord, O my soul, and forget not all his benefits. *Ps.* **103: 2.**

Who crowneth thee with lovingkindness and tender mercies. *Ps.* **103: 4.**

Oh that men would praise the Lord for his goodness, and for his wonderful works to the children of men! *Ps.* **107: 8.**

What shall I render unto the Lord for all his benefits toward me? *Ps.* **116: 12.**

His merciful kindness is great toward us. *Ps.* **117: 2.**

It is your Father's good pleasure to give you the kingdom. *Lu.* **12: 32.**

I was minded to come unto you before, that ye might have a second benefit. *2 Co.* **1: 15.**

Partakers of the benefit. *1 Ti.* **6: 2.**

Every good gift and every perfect gift is from above, and cometh down from the Father of lights. *Ja.* **1: 17.**

See also

Gain; Gift; Good; Profit; Service; Usefulness.

Benevolence

The Lord, the Lord God, merciful and gracious, longsuffering, and abundant in goodness and truth. *Ex.* **34: 6.**

Thou art a God ready to pardon, gracious and merciful, slow to anger, and of great kindness. *Ne.* **9: 17.**

I had fainted, unless I had believed to see the goodness of the Lord in the land of the living. *Ps.* **27: 13.**

Let thy lovingkindness and thy truth continually preserve me. *Ps.* **40: 11.**

So he giveth his beloved sleep. *Ps.* **127: 2.**

The liberal soul shall be made fat: and he that watereth shall be watered also himself. *Pr.* **11: 25.**

He that hath a bountiful eye shall be blessed; for he giveth of his bread to the poor. *Pr.* **22: 9.**

With everlasting kindness will I have mercy on thee. *Is.* **54: 8.**

Is it not to deal thy bread to the hungry, and that thou bring the poor that are cast out to thy house? when thou seest the naked, that thou cover him; and that thou hide not thyself from thine own flesh? *Is.* **58: 7.**

If thou draw out thy soul to the hungry, and satisfy the afflicted soul; then shall thy light rise in obscurity, and thy darkness be as the noonday. *Is.* **58: 10.**

Sell that ye have, and give alms. *Lu.* **12: 33.**

Be kindly affectioned one to another with brotherly love. *Ro.* **12: 10.**

Let the husband render unto the wife due benevolence. *1 Co.* **7: 3.**

He which soweth bountifully shall reap also bountifully. *2 Co.* **9: 6.**

According to the good pleasure of his will. *Ep.* **1: 5.**

The kindness and love of God our Saviour toward man appeared. *Tit.* **3: 4.**

See also

Beneficence; Boon; Bounty; Brotherhood; Charity; Clemency; Generosity; Gift; Kindness; Liberality; Love; Lovingkindness; Unselfishness; Will, Good.

Benignity

The man Moses was very meek, above all the men which were upon the face of the earth. *Nu.* **12: 3.**

Because thine heart was tender, . . . I have even heard thee also, saith the Lord. *2 Ch.* **34: 27.**

Thou art a God ready to pardon, gracious and merciful, slow to anger, and of great kindness. *Ne.* **9: 17.**

Forty years didst thou sustain them in the wilderness, so that they lacked nothing; their clothes waxed not old, and their feet swelled not. *Ne.* **9: 21.**

Thy gentleness hath made me great. *Ps.* **18: 35.**

Deal bountifully with thy servant, that I may live. *Ps.* **119: 17.**

Let, I pray thee, thy merciful kindness be for my comfort. *Ps.* **119: 76.**

A bruised reed shall he not break. *Is.* **42: 3.**

My kindness shall not depart from thee. *Is.* **54: 10.**

It is of the Lord's mercies that we are not consumed. *La.* **3: 22.**

The Lord's mercies . . . are new every morning: great is thy faithfulness. *La.* **3: 22, 23.**

I will make a covenant of peace with them; it shall be an everlasting covenant with them: and I will place them, and multiply them, and will set my sanctuary in the midst of them for evermore. *Eze.* **37: 26.**

Now, I pray you, beseech God that he will be gracious unto us. *Mal.* **1: 9.**

He is kind unto the unthankful and to the evil. *Lu.* **6: 35.**

Charity suffereth long, and is kind. *1 Co.* **13: 4.**

The fruit of the Spirit is . . . gentleness. *Ga.* **5: 22.**

Be ye kind one to another, tenderhearted, forgiving one another. *Eph.* **4: 32.**

Put on therefore, . . . bowels of mercies, kindness. *Col.* **3: 12.**

The servant of the Lord must not strive; but be gentle unto all men. *2 Ti.* **2: 24.**

See also

Christ, Gentleness of; Gentleness; God, Gentleness of; Goodness; Kindness; Tenderness.

Bequest

I will give it you for an heritage: I am the Lord. *Ex.* **6: 8.**

That thou mayest live, and inherit the land which the Lord thy God giveth thee. *De.* **16: 20.**

The Lord is their inheritance. *De.* **18: 2.**

I have given you a land for which ye did not labour. *Jos.* 24: 13.

Let a double portion of thy spirit be upon me. 2 *K.* 2: 9.

The Lord is the portion of mine inheritance and of my cup. *Ps.* 16: 5.

I have a goodly heritage. *Ps.* 16: 6.

Those that wait upon the Lord, they shall inherit the earth. *Ps.* 37: 9.

The meek shall inherit the earth. *Ps.* 37: 11.

Children are an heritage of the Lord. *Ps.* 127: 3.

He that troubleth his own house shall inherit the wind. *Pr.* 11: 29.

A good man leaveth an inheritance to his children's children. *Pr.* 13: 22.

Houses and riches are the inheritance of fathers. *Pr.* 19: 14.

Wisdom is good with an inheritance. *Ec.* 7: 11.

No weapon that is formed against thee shall prosper; and every tongue that shall rise against thee in judgment thou shalt condemn. This is the heritage of the servants of the Lord. *Is.* 54: 17.

I have forsaken mine house, I have left mine heritage. *Je.* 12: 7.

Come, ye blessed of my Father, inherit the kingdom prepared for you from the foundation of the world. *Mat.* 25: 34.

What shall I do that I may inherit eternal life? *Mk.* 10: 17.

Master, speak to my brother, that he divide the inheritance with me. *Lu.* 12: 13.

Peace I leave with you, my peace I give unto you. *Jn.* 14: 27.

The unrighteous shall not inherit the kingdom of God. *1 Co.* 6: 9.

He hath by inheritance obtained a more excellent name than they. *He.* 1: 4.

Heirs with him of the same promise. *He.* 11: 9.

See also

Birthright; Heir; Heritage; Inheritance; Legacy.

Bereavement

He made a mourning for his father seven days. *Ge.* 50: 10.

Now he is dead, wherefore should I fast? can I bring him back again? I shall go to him, but he shall not return to me. 2 *S.* 12: 23.

O my son Absalom, my son, my son Absalom! would God I had died for thee, O Absalom, my son, my son! 2 *S.* 18: 33.

The Lord gave, and the Lord hath taken away; blessed be the name of the Lord. *Jb.* 1: 21.

Mine eye also is dim by reason of sorrow, and all my members are as a shadow. *Jb.* 17: 7.

Sorrow is turned into joy before him. *Jb.* 41: 22.

Thou hast laid me in the lowest pit, in darkness, in the deeps. *Ps.* 88: 6.

Wilt thou shew wonders to the dead? shall the dead arise and praise thee? *Ps.* 88: 10.

Shall thy lovingkindness be declared in the grave? *Ps.* 88: 11.

Lover and friend hast thou put far from me, and mine acquaintance into darkness. *Ps.* 88: 18.

By sorrow of the heart the spirit is broken. *Pr.* 15: 13.

They shall obtain joy and gladness, and sorrow and sighing shall flee away. *Is.* 35: 10.

A man of sorrows, and acquainted with grief. *Is.* 53: 3.

Weep ye not for the dead, neither bemoan him. *Je.* 22: 10.

Is it nothing to you, all ye that pass by? Behold, and see if there be any sorrow like unto my sorrow. *La.* 1: 12.

I am the man that hath seen affliction by the rod of his wrath. *La.* 3: 1.

Behold, O my people, I will open your graves, and cause you to come up out of your graves, and bring you into the land of Israel. *Eze.* 37: 12.

The people which sat in darkness saw great light. *Mat.* 4: 16.

There shall be weeping and gnashing of teeth. *Mat.* 8: 12.

Blessed are ye that weep now: for ye shall laugh. *Lu.* 6: 21.

Ye shall be sorrowful, but your sorrow shall be turned into joy. *Jn.* 16: 20.

O death, where is thy sting? O grave, where is thy victory? *1 Co.* 15: 55.

God shall wipe away all tears from their eyes; and there shall be no more death, neither sorrow, nor crying, neither shall there be any more pain. *Re.* 21: 4.

See also

Death; Grave; Grief; Mourning; Sorrow; Weeping.

Best

Take of the best fruits in the land in your vessels, and carry down the man a present. *Ge.* 43: 11.

Verily every man at his best state is altogether vanity. *Ps.* 39: 5.

Wisdom is better than rubies. *Pr.* 8: 11.

How much better is it to get wisdom than gold! *Pr.* 16: 16.

The best of them is as a brier. *Mi.* 7: 4.

Whosoever will be chief among you, let him be your servant. *Mat.* 20: 27.

Bring forth the best robe, and put it on him. *Lu.* 15: 22.

Thou hast kept the good wine until now. *Jn.* 2: 10.

Covet earnestly the best gifts. *1 Co.* 12: 31.

Finally, brethren, whatsoever things are true, whatsoever things are honest, whatsoever things are just, whatsoever things are pure, whatsoever things are lovely, whatsoever things are of good report: . . . think on these things. *Ph.* 4: 8.

Henceforth there is laid up for me a crown of righteousness. *2 Ti.* 4: 8.

When the chief Shepherd shall appear, ye shall receive a crown of glory that fadeth not away. *1 Pe.* 5: 4.

Be thou faithful unto death, and I will give thee a crown of life. *Re.* 2: 10.

See also

Aristocracy; Chief; Excellence; Greatness.

Bestiality

The men of Sodom were wicked and sinners before the Lord exceedingly. *Ge.* 13: 13.

Whosoever lieth with a beast shall surely be put to death. *Ex.* 22: 19.

How much more abominable and filthy is man? *Jb.* 15: 16.

They are altogether brutish. *Je.* 10: 8.

To be carnally minded is death. *Ro.* 8: 6.

Let us cleanse ourselves from all filthiness of the flesh. *2 Co.* 7: 1.

These filthy dreamers defile the flesh. *Jude* 8.
See also

Beast; Brutality; Brute; Defilement; Depravity; Vileness.

Bestowal

That he may bestow upon you a blessing this day. *Ex.* 32: 29.

I will give thee riches, and wealth, and honour, such as none of the kings have had that have been before thee. *2 Ch.* 1: 12.

Thou hast granted me life and favour. *Jb.* 10: 12.

Let all that be round about him bring presents unto him that ought to be feared. *Ps.* 76: 11.

The Lord will give grace and glory: no good thing will he withhold from them that walk uprightly. *Ps.* 84: 11.

Even unto them will I give in mine house and within my walls a place and a name better than of sons and of daughters. *Is.* 56: 5.

When they had opened their treasures, they presented unto him gifts. *Mat.* 2: 11.

Ask of me whatsoever thou wilt, and I will give it thee. *Mk.* 6: 22.

God so loved the world, that he gave his only begotten Son, that whosoever believeth in him should not perish. *Jn.* 3: 16.

Those members of the body, which we think to be less honourable, upon these we bestow more abundant honour. *1 Co.* 12: 23.

Though I bestow all my goods to feed the poor, ... it profiteth me nothing. *1 Co.* 13: 3.

His grace which was bestowed upon me was not in vain. *1 Co.* 15: 10.

I am afraid of you, lest I have bestowed upon you labour in vain. *Ga.* 4: 11.

He gave some, apostles; and some, prophets; and some, evangelists; and some, pastors and teachers. *Ep.* 4: 11.

Finding fault with them, he saith, Behold, the days come, saith the Lord, when I will make a new covenant with the house of Israel and with the house of Judah. *He.* 8: 8.

Behold, what manner of love the Father hath bestowed upon us, that we should be called the sons of God. *1 Jn.* 3: 1.

Be thou faithful unto death, and I will give thee a crown of life. *Re.* 2: 10.

I will give him the morning star. *Re.* 2: 28.
See also

Gift; Present; Presentation.

Bethel

How dreadful is this place! this is none other but the house of God, and this is the gate of heaven. *Ge.* 28: 17.

He called the name of that place Beth-el. *Ge.* 28: 19.

I am like a green olive tree in the house of God. *Ps.* 52: 8.

I had rather be a doorkeeper in the house of my God, than to dwell in the tents of wickedness. *Ps.* 84: 10.

Prophesy not again any more at Beth-el. *Am.* 7: 13.
See also

Church; God, House of; Temple.

Betrayal

The children of Ephraim . . . turned back in the day of battle. *Ps.* 78: 9.

Then shall many be offended, and shall betray one another, and shall hate one another. *Mat.* 24: 10.

If it were possible, they shall deceive the very elect. *Mat.* 24: 24.

From that time he sought opportunity to betray him. *Mat.* 26: 16.

Woe unto that man by whom the Son of man is betrayed! *Mat.* 26: 24.

Now the brother shall betray the brother to death, and the father the son. *Mk.* 13: 12.

One of you which eateth with me shall betray me. *Mk.* 14: 18.

The hand of him that betrayeth me is with me on the table. *Lu.* 22: 21.

Judas, betrayest thou the Son of man with a kiss? *Lu.* 22: 48.

They have slain them which shewed before of the coming of the Just One; of whom ye have been now the betrayers and murderers. *Ac.* 7: 52.

They lie in wait to deceive. *Ep.* 4: 14.

If any man among you seem to be religious, and bridleth not his tongue, but deceiveth his own heart, this man's religion is vain. *Ja.* 1: 26.
See also

Deceit; Faithlessness; Treachery; Treason.

Betrothal

I will betroth thee unto me for ever; yea, I will betroth thee unto me in righteousness. *Ho.* 2: 19.

The kingdom of heaven is like unto a certain king, which made a marriage for his son. *Mat.* 22: 2.

Betterment

These are the ungodly who prosper in the world; they increase in riches. *Ps.* 73: 12.

The Lord shall increase you more and more, you and your children. *Ps.* 115: 14.

They shall prosper that love thee. *Ps.* 122: 6.

Of the increase of his government and peace there shall be no end. *Is.* 9: 7.

The child grew, and waxed strong in spirit. *Lu.* 1: 80.

Jesus increased in wisdom and stature, and in favour with God and man. *Lu.* 2: 52.

So were the churches established in the faith, and increased in number daily. *Ac.* 16: 5.

I have planted, Apollos watered; but God gave the increase. *1 Co.* 3: 6.

In whom all the building fitly framed together groweth unto an holy temple in the Lord. *Ep.* 2: 21.

Many of the brethren in the Lord, waxing confident by my bonds, are much more bold to speak the word without fear. *Ph.* 1: 14.

The Lord make you to increase. *1 Th.* 3: 12.

We beseech you, brethren, that you increase more and more. *1 Th.* 4: 10.

Your faith groweth exceedingly. *2 Th.* 1: 3.

Waxed valiant in fight. *He.* 11: 34.

As newborn babes, desire the sincere milk of

the word, that ye may grow thereby. *1 Pe.* **2: 2.**

Grow in grace, and in the knowledge of our Lord. *2 Pe.* **3: 18.**

I wish above all things that thou mayest prosper. *3 Jn.* **1: 2.**

See also

Advance; Amendment; Evolution; Growth; Improvement; Increase; Progress.

Bewilderment

Let them be ashamed and confounded together that seek after my soul to destroy it. *Ps.* **40: 14.**

My confusion is continually before me. *Ps.* **44: 15.**

Let not those that seek thee be confounded. *Ps.* **69: 6.**

Let them be confounded and troubled for ever. *Ps.* **83: 17.**

Let them cover themselves with their own confusion, as with a mantle. *Ps.* **109: 29.**

To you who are troubled rest with us. *2 Th.* **1: 7.**

Be not afraid of their terror, neither be troubled. *1 Pe.* **3: 14.**

See also

Bedlam; Confusion; Perplexity.

Bias

Thou shalt take no gift: for the gift blindeth the wise. *Ex.* **23: 8.**

Neither doth God respect any person. *2 S.* **14: 14.**

Many seek the ruler's favour. *Pr.* **29: 26.**

Favour is deceitful. *Pr.* **31: 30.**

Partial in the law. *Mal.* **2: 9.**

Observe these things without preferring one before another, doing nothing by partiality. *1 Ti.* **5: 21.**

Are ye not then partial in yourselves, and are become judges of evil thoughts? *Ja.* **2: 4.**

The wisdom that is from above is . . . without partiality, and without hypocrisy. *Ja.* **3: 17.**

See also

Impartiality; Inequality; Partiality; Persons, Respect of; Prejudice.

Bible

The writing was the writing of God. *Ex.* **32: 16.**

The ears of all the people were attentive unto the book of the law. *Ne.* **8: 3.**

Ezra opened the book in the sight of all the people. *Ne.* **8: 5.**

The words of the Lord are pure words: as silver tried in a furnace of earth, purified seven times. *Ps.* **12: 6.**

For ever, O Lord, thy word is settled in heaven. *Ps.* **119: 89.**

Thy word is a lamp unto my feet, and a light unto my path. *Ps.* **119: 105.**

In that day shall the deaf hear the words of the book, and the eyes of the blind shall see out of obscurity, and out of darkness. *Is.* **29: 18.**

They also that erred in spirit shall come to understanding, and they that murmured shall learn doctrine. *Is.* **29: 24.**

Is not my word like as a fire? saith the Lord; and like a hammer that breaketh the rock in pieces? *Je.* **23: 29.**

Take thee a roll of a book, and write therein all the words that I have spoken unto thee. *Je.* **36: 2.**

Ye do err, not knowing the scriptures, nor the power of God. *Mat.* **22: 29.**

This day is this scripture fulfilled in your ears. *Lu.* **4: 21.**

Ye have taken away the key of knowledge. *Lu.* **11: 52.**

He expounded unto them in all the scriptures the things concerning himself. *Lu.* **24: 27.**

Did not our heart burn within us, . . . while he opened to us the scriptures? *Lu.* **24: 32.**

When therefore he was risen from the dead, his disciples remembered that he had said this unto them; and they believed the scripture, and the word which Jesus had said. *Jn.* **2: 22.**

Search the scriptures; for in them ye think ye have eternal life: and they are they which testify of me. *Jn.* **5: 39.**

The scripture cannot be broken. *Jn.* **10: 35.**

These are written, that ye might believe that Jesus is the Christ, the Son of God; and that believing ye might have life through his name. *Jn.* **20: 31.**

There are also many other things which Jesus did, the which, if they should be written every one, I suppose that even the world itself could not contain the books that should be written. *Jn.* **21: 25.**

This scripture must needs have been fulfilled. *Ac.* **1: 16.**

They . . . searched the scriptures daily, whether those things were so. *Ac.* **17: 11.**

Whatsoever things were written aforetime were written for our learning, that we through patience and comfort of the Scriptures might have hope. *Ro.* **15: 4.**

All scripture is given by inspiration of God, and is profitable for doctrine, for reproof, for correction, for instruction in righteousness. *2 Ti.* **3: 16.**

The grass withereth, and the flower thereof falleth away: But the word of the Lord endureth for ever. *1 Pe.* **1: 24, 25.**

No prophecy of the scripture is of any private interpretation. *2 Pe.* **1: 20.**

The prophecy came not in old time by the will of man: but holy men of God spake as they were moved by the Holy Ghost. *2 Pe.* **1: 21.**

Seal not the sayings of the prophecy of this book. *Re.* **22: 10.**

See also

God, Word of; Scripture; Testament, New; Testament, Old; Text.

Bigness

Let us build us a city and a tower, whose top may reach unto heaven. *Ge.* **11: 4.**

I will make of thee a great nation. *Ge.* **12: 2.**

I will multiply thy seed as the stars of the heaven, and as the sand which is upon the sea shore. *Ge.* **22: 17.**

Behold a ladder set up on the earth, and the top of it reached to heaven. *Ge.* **28: 12.**

I am come down . . . to bring them . . . unto a good land and a large, unto a land flowing with milk and honey. *Ex.* **3: 8.**

The staff of his spear was like a weaver's beam. *1 S.* 17: 7.

The house which I build is great: for great is our God above all gods. *2 Ch.* 2: 5.

His going forth is from the end of the heaven, and his circuit unto the ends of it. *Ps.* 19: 6.

Oh how great is thy goodness! *Ps.* 31: 19.

If I should count them they are more in number than the sand. *Ps.* 139: 18.

Now shall he be great unto the ends of the earth. *Mi.* 5: 4.

He . . . shewed me that great city, the holy Jerusalem, descending out of heaven from God. *Re.* 21: 10.

See also

Greatness; Immensity; Importance.

Bigotry

The Egyptians might not eat bread with the Hebrews; for that is an abomination unto the Egyptians. *Ge.* 43: 32.

Why eateth your Master with publicans and sinners? *Mat.* 9: 11.

The scribes and the Pharisees sit in Moses' seat. *Mat.* 23: 2.

Woe unto you, scribes and Pharisees, hypocrites! *Mat.* 23: 13.

Ye blind guides, which strain at a gnat, and swallow a camel. *Mat.* 23: 24.

The Pharisees said unto him, Behold, why do they on the sabbath day that which is not lawful? *Mk.* 2: 24.

The sabbath was made for man, and not man for the sabbath. *Mk.* 2: 27.

We saw one casting out devils in thy name, and he followeth not us: and we forbade him, because he followeth not us. *Mk.* 9: 38.

They brought young children to him, that he should touch them: and his disciples rebuked those that brought them. *Mk.* 10: 13.

They did not receive him, because his face was as though he would go to Jerusalem. *Lu.* 9: 53.

Now do ye Pharisees make clean the outside of the cup and the platter; but your inward part is full of ravening and wickedness. *Lu.* 11: 39.

The Pharisee stood and prayed thus with himself, God, I thank thee, that I am not as other men are. *Lu.* 18: 11.

They all murmured, saying, That he was gone to be guest with a man that is a sinner. *Lu.* 19: 7.

The Jews have no dealings with the Samaritans. *Jn.* 4: 9.

God hath shewed me that I should not call any man common or unclean. *Ac.* 10: 28.

I am a Pharisee, the son of a Pharisee. *Ac.* 23: 6.

After the most straitest sect of our religion I lived a Pharisee. *Ac.* 26: 5.

I punished them oft in every synagogue, and compelled them to blaspheme. *Ac.* 26: 11.

See also

Fanaticism; Hypocrisy; Pharisee; Strait; Strictness.

Biography

The days of the years of my pilgrimage are an hundred and thirty years: few and evil have the days of the years of my life been. *Ge.* 47: 9.

He is thy life, and the length of thy days. *De.* 30: 20.

The Lord is the strength of my life; of whom shall I be afraid? *Ps.* 27: 1.

We spend our years as a tale that is told. *Ps.* 90: 9.

The days of our years are threescore years and ten; and if by reason of strength they be fourscore years, yet is their strength labour and sorrow. *Ps.* 90: 10.

The years of thy life shall be many. *Pr.* 4: 10.

For me to live is Christ. *Ph.* 1: 21.

All their lifetime subject to bondage. *He.* 2: 15.

See also

Life.

Bird

There is a path which no fowl knoweth, and which the vulture's eye hath not seen. *Jb.* 28: 7.

Gavest thou the goodly wings unto the peacocks? or wings and feathers unto the ostrich? *Jb.* 39: 13.

In the Lord put I my trust: how say ye to my soul, Flee as a bird to your mountain? *Ps.* 11: 1.

I know all the fowls of the mountains. *Ps.* 50: 11.

Though ye have lain among the pots, yet shall ye be as the wings of a dove covered with silver, and her feathers with yellow gold. *Ps.* 68: 13.

Yea, the sparrow hath found an house, and the swallow a nest for herself, where she may lay her young, even thine altars. *Ps.* 84: 3.

He shall cover thee with his feathers. *Ps.* 91: 4.

Thy youth is renewed like the eagle's. *Ps.* 103: 5.

Our soul is escaped as a bird out of the snare of the fowlers. *Ps.* 124: 7.

Praise the Lord . . . creeping things, and flying fowl. *Ps.* 148: 7, 10.

He shall rise up at the voice of the bird. *Ec.* 12: 4.

The time of the singing of birds is come. *S. of S.* 2: 12.

Though thou exalt thyself as the eagle, and though thou set thy nest among the stars, thence will I bring thee down. *Ob.* 1: 4.

He saw the Spirit of God descending like a dove, and lighting upon him. *Mat.* 3: 16.

Behold the fowls of the air: for they sow not, neither do they reap, nor gather into barns; yet your heavenly Father feedeth them. *Mat.* 6: 26.

The birds of the air have nests; but the Son of man hath not where to lay his head. *Mat.* 8: 20.

Be ye therefore . . . harmless as doves. *Mat.* 10: 16.

Ye are of more value than many sparrows. *Mat.* 10: 31.

How often would I have gathered thy children together, even as a hen gathereth her chickens under her wings, and ye would not! *Mat.* 23: 37.

Except a man be born again, he cannot see the kingdom of God. *Jn.* 3: 3.

See also

Eagle; Flight; Fowl; Wing.

Birth

The Lord God . . . breathed into his nostrils the breath of life. *Ge.* **2: 7.**

Sell me this day thy birthright. *Ge.* **25: 31.**

How old art thou? *Ge.* **47: 8.**

Let the day perish wherein I was born, and the night in which it was said, There is a man child conceived. *Jb.* **3: 3.**

Art thou the first man that was born? *Jb.* **15: 7.**

A time to be born, and a time to die. *Ec.* **3:2.**

A good name is better than precious ointment; and the day of death than the day of one's birth. *Ec.* **7: 1.**

Unto us a child is born, unto us a son is given. *Is.* **9: 6.**

Now the birth of Jesus Christ was on this wise. *Mat.* **1: 18.**

Many shall rejoice at his birth. *Lu.* **1: 14.**

She brought forth her firstborn son. *Lu.* **2: 7.**

She remembereth no more the anguish, for joy that a man is born into the world. *Jn.* **16: 21.**

To this end was I born, and for this cause came I into the world. *Jn.* **18: 37.**

Seeing he giveth to all life, and breath, and all things. *Ac.* **17: 25.**

Last of all he was seen of me also, as of one born out of due time. *1 Co.* **15: 8.**

Who for one morsel of meat sold his birthright. *He.* **12: 16.**

See also

Birth, New; Christ, Birth of; Descent; Family; Nativity; Race.

Birth, New

If thou wilt enter into life, keep the commandments. *Mat.* **19: 17.**

Which were born, not of blood, nor of the will of the flesh, nor of the will of man, but of God. *Jn.* **1: 13.**

Except a man be born again, he cannot see the kingdom of God. *Jn.* **3: 3.**

Except a man be born of water and of the Spirit, he cannot enter into the kingdom of God. *Jn.* **3: 5.**

That which is born of the flesh is flesh; and that which is born of the Spirit is spirit. *Jn.* **3: 6.**

Marvel not that I said unto thee, Ye must be born again. *Jn.* **3: 7.**

The wind bloweth where it listeth, . . . so is every one that is born of the Spirit. *Jn.* **3: 8.**

He that heareth my word, and believeth on him that sent me, . . . is passed from death unto life. *Jn.* **5: 24.**

The bread of God is he which cometh down from heaven, and giveth life unto the world. *Jn.* **6: 33.**

Like as Christ was raised up from the dead by the glory of the Father, even so we also should walk in newness of life. *Ro.* **6: 4.**

Being born again, not of corruptible seed, but of incorruptible. *1 Pe.* **1: 23.**

Whosoever is born of God doth not commit sin. *1 Jn.* **3: 9.**

Whatsoever is born of God overcometh the world. *1 Jn.* **5: 4.**

See also

Conversion; Life, the New.

Birthplace

Of Zion it shall be said, This and that man was born in her. *Ps.* **87: 5.**

When Jesus was born in Bethlehem of Judaea. *Mat.* **2: 1.**

Unto you is born this day in the city of David a Saviour. *Lu.* **2: 11.**

I am verily a man which am a Jew, born in Tarsus, a city in Cilicia. *Ac.* **22: 3.**

Birthright

Jacob said, Sell me this day thy birthright. *Ge.* **25: 31.**

What profit shall this birthright do to me? *Ge.* **25: 32.**

Thus Esau despised his birthright. *Ge.* **25: 34.**

They sat before him, the firstborn according to his birthright, and the youngest according to his youth. *Ge.* **43: 33.**

The right of the firstborn is his. *De.* **21: 17.**

Esau . . . for one morsel of meat sold his birthright. *He.* **12: 16.**

See also

Heritage; Inheritance.

Bishop

Let his habitation be desolate, and let no man dwell therein: and his bishoprick let another take. *Ac.* **1: 20.**

If a man desire the office of a bishop, he desireth a good work. *1 Ti.* **3: 1.**

A bishop then must be blameless, the husband of one wife, vigilant, sober, of good behaviour, given to hospitality, apt to teach. *1 Ti.* **3: 2.**

A bishop then must be . . . Not given to wine, no striker, not greedy of filthy lucre; but patient, not a brawler, not covetous. *1 Ti.* **3: 2, 3.**

A bishop then must be . . . One that ruleth well his own house, having his children in subjection with all gravity. *1 Ti.* **3: 2. 4.**

If a man know not how to rule his own house, how shall he take care of the church of God? *1 Ti.* **3: 5.**

Bitterness

Shall the sword devour for ever? knowest thou not that it will be bitterness in the latter end? *2 S.* **2: 26.**

Thy tongue deviseth mischief; like a sharp razor, working deceitfully. *Ps.* **52: 2.**

They gave me also gall for my meat; and in my thirst they gave me vinegar to drink. *Ps.* **69: 21.**

Adder's poison is under their lips. *Ps.* **140: 3.**

The heart knoweth his own bitterness. *Pr.* **14: 10.**

He hath filled me with bitterness, he hath made me drunken with wormwood. *La.* **3: 15.**

They gave him vinegar to drink mingled with gall. *Mat.* **27: 34.**

The contention was so sharp between them, that they departed asunder one from the other. *Ac.* **15: 39.**

Whose mouth is full of cursing and bitterness. *Ro.* **3: 14.**

Let all bitterness, and wrath, and anger, and clamour, and evil speaking, be put away from you, with all malice. *Ep.* **4: 31.**

Lest any root of bitterness springing up trouble you. *He.* 12: 15.

See also
Severity; Sharpness.

Black

Let that day be darknesss; let not God regard it from above, neither let the light shine upon it. . . . Let the blackness of the day terrify it. *Jb.* 3: 4.

My skin is black upon me, and my bones are burned with heat. *Jb.* 30: 30.

I clothe the heavens with b'ackness, and I make sackcloth their covering. *Is.* 50: 3.

All faces shall gather blackness. *Jo.* 2: 6.

Thou canst not make one hair white or black. *Mat.* 5: 36.

Ye are not come . . . unto blackness and darkness, and tempest. *He.* 12: 18.

To whom is reserved the blackness of darkness for ever. *Jude* 13.

Blacksmith

He carried away all Jerusalem, . . . even ten thousand captives, and all the craftsmen and smiths. 2 *K.* 24: 14.

Behold, I have created the smith that bloweth the coals in the fire, and that bringeth forth an instrument for his work. *Is.* 54: 16.

See also
Anvil.

Blame

I do remember my faults this day. *Ge.* 41: 9.

I am a worm, and no man; a reproach of men, and despised of the people. *Ps.* 22: 6.

Make me not the reproach of the foolish. *Ps.* 39: 8.

He shall send from heaven, and save me from the reproach of him that would swallow me up. *Ps.* 57: 3.

He that regardeth reproof is prudent. *Pr.* 15: 5.

Now shall they be found faulty. *Ho.* 10: 2.

I will no more make you a reproach among the heathen. *Jo.* 2: 19.

Why doth he yet find fault? *Ro.* 9: 19.

I take pleasure in infirmities, in reproaches. 2 *Co.* 12: 10.

I withstood him to the face, because he was to be blamed. *Ga.* 2: 11.

All scripture . . . is profitable for doctrine, for reproof, for correction. 2 *Ti.* 3: 16.

Confess your faults one to another, and pray one for another. *Ja.* 5: 16.

If ye be reproached for the name of Christ, happy are ye. *1 Pe.* 4: 14.

See also
Condemnation; Rebuke; Reprimand; Reproach; Reproof.

Blamelessness

Then shall I be upright, and I shall be innocent from the great transgression. *Ps.* 19: 13.

Who shall ascend into the hill of the Lord? . . . He that hath clean hands, and a pure heart. *Ps.* 24: 3, 4.

I will wash mine hands in innocency. *Ps.* 26: 6.

Wash me, and I shall be whiter than snow. *Ps.* 51: 7.

Create in me a clean heart, O God. *Ps.* 51: 10.

Before him innocency was found in me. *Da.* 6: 22.

How long will it be ere they attain to innocency? *Ho.* 8: 5.

Who shall also confirm you unto the end, that ye may be blameless in the day of our Lord Jesus Christ. *1 Co.* 1: 8.

Giving no offence in any thing, that the ministry be not blamed. 2 *Co.* 6: 3.

That he might present it to himself a glorious church, not having spot, or wrinkle, or any such thing; but that it should be holy and without blemish. *Ep.* 5: 27.

I pray God your whole spirit and soul and body be preserved blameless unto the coming of our Lord Jesus Christ. *1 Th.* 5: 23.

These things give in charge, that they may be blameless. *1 Ti.* 5: 7.

See also
Christ, Holiness of; God, Righteousness of; Godliness; Goodness; Guilelessness; Innocence; Integrity; Purity; Righteousness; Uprightness; Virtue.

Blasphemy

He that blasphemeth the name of the Lord, he shall surely be put to death. *Le.* 24: 16.

Thou didst blaspheme God and the king. *1 K.* 21: 10.

The foolish people have blasphemed thy name. *Ps.* 74: 18.

He clothed himself with cursing. *Ps.* 109: 18.

My name continually every day is blasphemed. *Is.* 52: 5.

Certain of the scribes said within themselves, This man blasphemeth. *Mat.* 9: 3.

Out of the heart proceed evil thoughts, . . . blasphemies. *Mat.* 15: 19.

He that shall blaspheme against the Holy Ghost hath never forgiveness. *Mk.* 3: 29.

The name of God is blasphemed among the Gentiles through you. *Ro.* 2: 24.

In the last days perilous times shall come. For men shall be . . . blasphemers. 2 *Ti.* 3: 1, 2.

That the word of God be not blasphemed. *Tit.* 2: 5.

Do not they blaspheme that worthy name by which ye are called? *Ja.* 2: 7.

Out of the same mouth proceedeth blessing and cursing. *Ja.* 3: 10.

See also
Anathema; Curse; Profanity; Sacrilege.

Blemish

Whatsoever hath a blemish, that shall ye not offer. *Le.* 22: 20.

I am clean without transgression, I am innocent. *Jb.* 33: 9.

Cleanse thou me from secret faults. *Ps.* 19: 12.

The pride of Jordan is spoiled. *Zch.* 11: 3.

If thy brother shall trespass against thee, go and tell him his fault between thee and him alone. *Mat.* 18: 15.

Then said Pilate to the chief priests and to the people, I find no fault in this man. *Lu.* 23: 4.

There was given to me a thorn in the flesh, . . . lest I should be exalted above measure. 2 *Co.* 12: 7.

If a man be overtaken in a fault, . . . restore such an one in the spirit of meekness. *Ga. 6: 1.*

That ye may be blameless and harmless, the sons of God, without rebuke, in the midst of a crooked and perverse nation, among whom ye shine as lights in the world. *Ph. 2: 15.*

As of a lamb without blemish and without spot. *1 Pe. 1: 19.*

Be diligent that ye may be found of him in peace, without spot, and blameless. *2 Pe. 3: 14.*

Now unto him that is able to keep you from falling, and to present you faultless before the presence of his glory. *Jude 1: 24.*

See also

Blot; Defect; Failure; Fault; Imperfection; Lack; Spot; Taint; Want.

Blessedness

Thou shalt be a blessing. *Ge. 12: 2.*

I will bless them that bless thee, and curse him that curseth thee. *Ge. 12: 3.*

In thee shall all families of the earth be blessed. *Ge. 12: 3.*

I will not let thee go, except thou bless me. *Ge. 32: 26.*

Also they saw God, and did eat and drink. *Ex. 24: 11.*

Blessed shalt thou be in the city, and blessed shalt thou be in the field. Blessed shall be the fruit of thy body, and the fruit of thy ground, and the fruit of thy cattle, the increase of thy kine, and the flocks of thy sheep. . . . Blessed shalt thou be when thou comest in, and blessed shalt thou be when thou goest out. *De. 28: 3, 4, 6.*

Blessings are upon the head of the just. *Pr. 10: 6.*

Blessed are ye. *Mat. 5: 11.*

Come, ye blessed of my Father, inherit the kingdom prepared for you from the foundation of the world. *Mat. 25: 34.*

Where is then the blessedness ye spake of? *Ga. 4: 15.*

See also

Beatitude; Benediction; Blessing; God, Blessing of; Happiness; Joy.

Blessing

I will bless thee, and make thy name great. *Ge. 12: 2.*

I will not let thee go, except thou bless me. *Ge. 32: 26.*

The blessing of the Lord was upon all that he had in the house, and in the field. *Ge. 39: 5.*

The Almighty . . . shall bless thee with blessings of heaven above, blessings of the deep that lieth under. *Ge. 49: 25.*

The Lord thy God turned the curse into a blessing unto thee, because the Lord thy God loved thee. *De. 23: 5.*

I have set before you life and death, blessing and cursing: therefore choose life, that both thou and thy seed may live. *De. 30: 19.*

I have also given thee that which thou hast not asked, both riches, and honour: so that there shall not be any among the kings like unto thee all thy days. *1 K. 3: 13.*

Stand up and bless the Lord your God for ever and ever. *Ne. 9: 5.*

He will be favourable unto him. *Jb. 33: 26.*

He that hath clean hands, and a pure heart . . . shall receive the blessing from the Lord, and righteousness from the God of his salvation. *Ps. 24: 4, 5.*

He should have fed them also with the finest of the wheat: and with honey out of the rock should I have satisfied thee. *Ps. 81: 16.*

Bless the Lord, O my soul: and all that is within me, bless his holy name. Bless the Lord, O my soul, and forget not all his benefits. *Ps. 103: 1, 2.*

Seek ye first the kingdom of God, and his righteousness; and all these things shall be added unto you. *Mat. 6: 33.*

Bless them which persecute you: bless, and curse not. *Ro. 12: 14.*

I shall come in the fulness of the blessing of the gospel of Christ. *Ro. 15: 29.*

Being reviled, we bless; being persecuted, we suffer it. *1 Co. 4: 12.*

The earth which drinketh in the rain that cometh oft upon it . . . receiveth blessing from God. *He. 6: 7.*

Blessing I will bless thee, and multiplying I will multiply thee. *He. 6: 14.*

Now are we the sons of God, and it doth not yet appear what we shall be. *1 Jn. 3: 2.*

See also

Benediction; Blessedness; God, Blessing of.

Blight

The Lord shall smite thee . . . with mildew. *De. 28: 22.*

If there be in the land famine, if there be pestilence, blasting, mildew, locust, or if there be caterpiller; . . What prayer and supplication soever be made by any man, . . . Then hear thou in heaven thy dwelling place. *1 K. 8: 37-39.*

The seed is rotten under their clods, . . . the corn is withered. *Jo. 1: 17.*

I smote you with blasting and with mildew and with hail in all the labours of your hands; yet ye turned not to me, saith the Lord. *Hag. 2: 17.*

When the blade was sprung up, and brought forth fruit, then appeared the tares also. *Mat. 13: 26.*

See also

Contagion; Plague.

Blindness

He hideth himself . . . that I cannot see him. *Jb. 23: 9.*

I was eyes to the blind, and feet was I to the lame. *Jb. 29: 15.*

The Lord openeth the eyes of the blind. *Ps. 146: 8.*

I will bring the blind by a way that they knew not; I will lead them in paths that they have not known. *Is. 42: 16.*

We stumble at noonday as in the night; we are in desolate places as dead men. *Is. 59: 10.*

They have wandered as blind men in the streets. *La. 4: 14.*

The blind receive their sight. *Mat. 11: 5.*

If the blind lead the blind, both shall fall into the ditch. *Mat. 15: 14.*

The Spirit of the Lord is upon me, because he hath anointed me to preach . . . recovering of sight to the blind. *Lu. 4: 18.*

Unto many that were blind he gave sight. *Lu.* 7: 21.

And the men that journeyed with him stood speechless, hearing a voice, but seeing no man. *Ac.* 9: 7.

When his eyes were opened, he saw no man. *Ac.* 9: 8.

Having the understanding darkened, being alienated from the life of God through the ignorance that is in them. *Ep.* 4: 18.

See also

Eye; Sight.

Blindness, Moral

Eyes have they, but they see not. *Ps.* 115: 5.

Woe unto them that call evil good, and good evil; that put darkness for light, and light for darkness. *Is.* 5: 20.

His watchmen are blind: they are all ignorant. *Is.* 56: 10.

They be blind leaders of the blind. And if the blind lead the blind, both shall fall into the ditch. *Mat.* 15: 14.

Woe unto you, ye blind guides. *Mat.* 23: 16.

He hath blinded their eyes, and hardened their hearts; that they should not see with their eyes, nor understand with their hearts. *Jn.* 12: 40.

Thou thyself art a guide of the blind, a light of them which are in darkness. *Ro.* 2: 19.

Let their eyes be darkened, that they may not see. *Ro.* 11: 10.

Their minds were blinded. *2 Co.* 3: 14.

In whom the god of this world hath blinded the minds of them which believe not, lest the light of the glorious gospel of Christ, who is the image of God, should shine unto them. *2 Co.* 4: 4.

Being alienated from the life of God through the ignorance that is in them, because of the blindness of their hearts. *Ep.* 4: 18.

He that lacketh these things is blind, and cannot see afar off. *2 Pe.* 1: 9.

He that hateth his brother is in darkness. *1 Jn.* 2: 11.

These things saith the Amen, the faithful and true witness; . . . anoint thine eyes with eyesalve, that thou mayest see. *Re.* 3: 14, 18.

Thou art . . . poor, and blind, and naked. *Re.* 3: 17.

See also

Corruption; Immorality; Perversion.

Bliss

I have learned by experience that the Lord hath blessed me. *Ge.* 30: 27.

The Almighty . . . shall bless thee with blessings of heaven above, blessings of the deep that lieth under. *Ge.* 49: 25.

He whom thou blessest is blessed. *Nu.* 22: 6.

Till he fill thy mouth with laughing, and thy lips with rejoicing. *Jb.* 8: 21.

Thou hast made him most blessed for ever. *Ps.* 21: 6.

Thou hast . . . girded me with blessing. *Ps.* 30: 11.

The memory of the just is blessed. *Pr.* 10: 7.

The blessing of the Lord, it maketh rich. *Pr.* 10: 22.

Blessed are ye that sow beside all waters. *Is.* 32: 20.

There shall be showers of blessing. *Eze.* 34: 26.

Prove me now herewith, saith the Lord of hosts, if I will not open you the windows of heaven, and pour you out a blessing, that there shall not be room enough to receive it. *Mal.* 3: 10.

Blessed are the pure in heart. *Mat.* 5: 8.

Blessed is he that cometh in the name of the Lord. *Mat.* 21: 9.

Thou shalt have joy and gladness. *Lu.* 1: 14.

I knew a man in Christ . . . caught up to the third heaven. *2 Co.* 12; 2.

Where is then the blessedness ye spake of? *Ga.* 4: 15.

Ye rejoice with joy unspeakable and full of glory. *1 Pe.* 1: 8.

I was in the Spirit on the Lord's day. *Re.* 1: 10.

See also

Blessedness; Felicity; Gladness; Happiness; Joy; Rapture.

Blood

The voice of thy brother's blood crieth unto me from the ground. *Ge.* 4: 10.

Behold the blood of the covenant, which the Lord hath made with you concerning all these words. *Ex.* 24: 8.

It is the blood that maketh an atonement for the soul. *Le.* 17: 11.

Deliver me from bloodguiltiness, O God. *Ps.* 51: 14.

Your hands are full of blood. *Is.* 1: 15.

Woe to the bloody city! *Eze.* 24: 6.

This is my blood of the new testament, which is shed for many. *Mk.* 14: 24.

This cup is the new testament in my blood, which is shed for you. *Lu.* 22: 20.

Which were born, not of blood, . . . but of God. *Jn.* 1: 13.

My flesh is meat indeed, and my blood is drink indeed. *Jn.* 6: 55.

I will lay down my life for thy sake. *Jn.* 13: 37.

And hath made of one blood all nations of men for to dwell on all the face of the earth. *Ac.* 17: 26.

Your blood be upon your own heads. *Ac.* 18: 6.

Neither count I my life dear unto myself. *Ac.* 20: 24.

Being now justified by his blood, we shall be saved from wrath through him. *Ro.* 5: 9.

Having made peace through the blood of his cross. *Col.* 1: 20.

Without shedding of blood is no remission. *He.* 9: 22.

Ye have not yet resisted unto blood, striving against sin. *He.* 12: 4.

The blood of Jesus Christ his Son cleanseth us from all sin. *1 Jn.* 1: 7.

Unto him that loved us, and washed us from our sins in his own blood. *Re.* 1: 5.

Thou wast slain, and hast redeemed us to God by thy blood. *Re.* 5: 9.

They have shed the blood of saints and prophets, and thou hast given them blood to drink; for they are worthy. *Re.* 16: 6.

See also

Assassin; Christ, Blood of; Christ, Sacrifice of; Murder; Sacrifice; Slaughter.

Blossom

Behold, the rod of Aaron . . . was budded, and brought forth buds, and bloomed blossoms. *Nu.* 17: 8.

As a flower of the field, so he flourisheth. *Ps.* 103: 15.

The flowers appear on the earth; the time of the singing of birds is come, and the voice of the turtle is heard in our land. *S. of S.* 2: 12.

Israel shall blossom and bud. *Is.* 27: 6.

Whose glorious beauty is a fading flower. *Is.* 28: 1.

The desert shall rejoice, and blossom as the rose. *Is.* 35: 1.

All flesh is grass, and all the goodliness thereof is as the flower of the field. *Is.* 40: 6.

As the earth bringeth forth her bud, and as the garden causeth the things that are sown in it to spring forth; so the Lord God will cause righteousness and praise to spring forth before all the nations. *Is.* 61: 11.

Although the fig tree shall not blossom, neither shall fruit be in the vine; . . . Yet I will rejoice in the Lord. *Hab.* 3: 17, 18.

See also
Bud; Flower.

Blot

If any blot hath cleaved to mine hands; Then let me sow, and let another eat. *Jb.* 31: 7, 8.

According unto the multitude of thy tender mercies blot out my transgressions. *Ps.* 51: 1.

Let them be blotted out of the book of the living. *Ps.* 69: 28.

He that rebuketh a wicked man getteth himself a blot. *Pr.* 9: 7.

See also
Blemish; Spot; Taint.

Blue

Thou shalt make an hanging for the door of the tent, of blue, and purple, and scarlet. *Ex.* 26: 36.

Upon the table of shewbread they shall spread a cloth of blue. *Nu.* 4: 7.

Upon the golden altar they shall spread a cloth of blue. *Nu.* 4: 11.

The blueness of a wound cleanseth away evil. *Pr.* 20: 30.

I will lay thy stones with fair colours, and lay thy foundations with sapphires. *Is.* 54: 11.

Above the firmament that was over their heads was the likeness of a throne, as the appearance of a sapphire stone. *Eze.* 1: 26.

The Assyrians . . . were clothed with blue. *Eze.* 23: 5, 6.

See also
Color.

Blunder

I have played the fool, and have erred exceedingly. *1 S.* 26: 21.

Be it indeed that I have erred, mine error remaineth with myself. *Jb.* 19: 4.

Who can understand his errors? *Ps.* 19: 12.

The proud . . . err from thy commandments. *Ps.* 119: 21.

They are vanity, and the work of errors. *Je.* 10: 15.

If a man be overtaken in a fault, ye which are spiritual, restore such an one in the spirit of meekness. *Ga.* 6: 1.

He which converteth the sinner from the error of his way shall save a soul from death. *Ja.* 5: 20.

Ye were as sheep going astray. *1 Pe.* 2: 25.

Hereby know we the spirit of truth, and the spirit of error. *1 Jn.* 4: 6.

See also
Error; Fault; Mistake.

Boasting

And thou say in thine heart. My power and the might of mine hand hath gotten me this wealth. *De.* 8: 17.

Lest they should say, Our hand is high, and the Lord hath not done all this. *De.* 32: 27.

The wicked boasteth of his heart's desire. *Ps.* 10: 3.

The Lord shall cut off all flattering lips, and the tongue that speaketh proud things. *Ps.* 12: 3.

They are inclosed in their own fat: with their mouth they speak proudly. *Ps.* 17: 10.

My soul shall make her boast in the Lord. *Ps.* 34: 2.

In God we boast all the day long. *Ps.* 44: 8.

They that . . . boast themselves in the multitude of their riches; None of them can by any means redeem his brother, nor give to God a ransom for him. *Ps.* 49: 6, 7.

How long shall . . . all the workers of iniquity boast themselves? *Ps.* 94: 4.

Boast not thyself of to morrow: for thou knowest not what a day may bring forth. *Pr.* 27: 1.

They trust in vanity, and speak lies. *Is.* 59: 4.

The king . . . shall exalt himself, and magnify himself above every god. *Da.* 11: 36.

Though thou exalt thyself as the eagle, and though thou set thy nest among the stars, thence will I bring thee down. *Ob.* 1: 4.

Take heed, that ye do not your alms before men, to be seen of them. *Mat.* 6: 1.

If we had been in the days of our fathers, we would not have been partakers with them in the blood of the prophets. *Mat.* 23: 30.

Whosoever exalteth himself shall be abased. *Lu.* 14: 11.

Behold, thou art called a Jew, . . . and makest thy boast of God. *Ro.* 2: 17.

Even so our boasting . . . is found a truth. *2 Co.* 7: 14.

Casting down imaginations, and every high thing that exalteth itself against the knowledge of God. *2 Co.* 10: 5.

We will not boast of things without our measure, but according to the measure of the rule which God hath distributed to us. *2 Co.* 10: 13.

As the truth of Christ is in me, no man shall stop me of this boasting. *2 Co.* 11: 10.

For by grace are ye saved through faith; and that not of yourselves: it is the gift of God: Not of works, lest any man should boast. *Ep.* 2: 8, 9.

The son of perdition; Who opposeth and exalteth himself above all that is called God. *2 Th.* 2: 3, 4.

Men shall be lovers of their own selves, covetous, boasters, proud. *2 Ti.* 3: 2.

The tongue is a little member, and boasteth great things. *Ja.* 3: 5.

See also
Arrogance;   Braggart;   Conceit;   Disdain;

Haughtiness; Ostentation; Presumption; Pride;
Vanity.

Body

Fear not them which kill the body, but are
not able to kill the soul. *Mat.* 10: 28.

The spirit indeed is willing, but the flesh is
weak. *Mat.* 26: 41.

I beseech you therefore, brethren, by the
mercies of God, that ye present your bodies a
living sacrifice. *Ro.* 12: 1.

The natural man receiveth not the things of
the Spirit of God. *1 Co.* 2: 14.

Know ye not that your bodies are the members of Christ? *1 Co.* 6: 15.

Know ye not that your body is the temple
of the Holy Ghost? *1 Co.* 6: 19.

By one Spirit are we all baptized into one
body. *1 Co.* 12: 13.

The body is not one member, but many.
1 Co. 12: 14.

God hath tempered the body together. *1 Co.*
12: 24.

Now ye are the body of Christ. *1 Co.* 12: 27.

Though I give my body to be burned, and
have not charity, it profiteth me nothing. *1 Co.*
13: 3.

There are also celestial bodies, and bodies
terrestrial. *1 Co.* 15: 40.

We are . . . willing rather to be absent
from the body, and to be present with the
Lord. *2 Co.* 5: 8.

For the flesh lusteth against the Spirit, and
the Spirit against the flesh. *Ga.* 5: 17.

I bear in my body the marks of the Lord
Jesus. *Ga.* 6: 17.

There is one body, and one Spirit. *Ep.* 4: 4.

We are members of his body, of his flesh, and
of his bones. *Ep.* 5: 30.

Christ shall be magnified in my body,
whether it be by life, or by death. *Ph.* 1: 20.

In him dwelleth all the fulness of the Godhead bodily. *Col.* 2: 9.

The body without the spirit is dead. *Ja.* 2:
26.

Who his own self bare our sins in his own
body on the tree. *1 Pe.* 2: 24.

See also

Christ, Body of; Flesh.

Boldness

Deal courageously, and the Lord shall be
with the good. *2 Ch.* 19: 11.

Now shall mine head be lifted up above
mine enemies round about me. *Ps.* 27: 6.

Thou shalt not be afraid for the terror by
night; nor for the arrow that flieth by day.
Ps. 91: 5.

If it be so, our God whom we serve is able
to deliver us from the burning fiery furnace,
and he will deliver us out of thine hand, O
king. But if not, be it known unto thee, O
king, that we will not serve thy gods, nor
worship the golden image which thou hast
set up. *Da.* 3: 17, 18.

Now when they saw the boldness of Peter
and John, and perceived that they were unlearned and ignorant men, they marvelled;
and they took knowledge of them, that they
had been with Jesus. *Ac.* 4: 13.

They spake the word of God with boldness.
Ac. 4: 31.

Great is my boldness of speech toward you,
great is my glorying of you. *2 Co.* 7: 4.

In whom we have boldness and access with
confidence by the faith of him. *Ep.* 3: 12.

Therein I may speak boldly, as I ought to
speak. *Ep.* 6: 20.

Let us therefore come boldly unto the throne
of grace, that we may obtain mercy, and find
grace to help in time of need. *He.* 4: 16.

Having therefore, brethren, boldness to enter
into the holiest by the blood of Jesus. *He.* 10:
19.

See also

Assurance; Audacity; Bravery; Confidence;
Courage; Self-Confidence.

Bond

If a man vow a vow unto the Lord, . . . he
shall not break his word. *Nu.* 30: 2.

The small and great are there; and the
servant is free from his master. *Jb.* 3: 19.

Canst thou . . . loose the bands of Orion?
Jb. 38: 31.

The yoke of my transgressions is bound by
his hand. *La.* 1: 14.

My yoke is easy, and my burden is light.
Mat. 11: 30.

Whosoever committeth sin is the servant of
sin. *Jn.* 8: 34.

I see another law in my members, . . .
bringing me into captivity. *Ro.* 7: 23.

Ye have not received the spirit of bondage.
Ro. 8: 15.

So we, being many, are one body in Christ.
Ro. 12: 5.

Even so we, when we were children, were in
bondage under the elements of the world. *Ga.*
4: 3.

I am an ambassador in bonds. *Ep.* 6: 20.

And deliver them who through fear of
death were all their lifetime subject to bondage. *He.* 2: 15.

Remember them that are in bonds, as bound
with them. *He.* 13: 3.

See also

Band; Bondage; Captivity; Chain; Coherence; Imprisonment; Prison; Yoke.

Bondage

They made their lives bitter with hard
bondage. *Ex.* 1: 14.

Thou shalt remember that thou wast a
bondman in the land of Egypt. *De.* 15: 15.

Therefore shalt thou serve thine enemies
which the Lord shall send against thee. *De.*
28: 48.

The Lord thy God will turn thy captivity,
and have compassion upon thee. *De.* 30: 3.

Thou hast loosed my bonds. *Ps.* 116: 16.

His own iniquities shall take the wicked
himself, and he shall be holden with the
cords of his sins. *Pr.* 5: 22.

So shall ye serve strangers in a land that
is not yours. *Je.* 5: 19.

The Lord's flock is carried away captive.
Je. 13: 17.

Therefore will I cause you to go into captivity. *Am.* 5: 27.

Whosoever committeth sin is the servant of
sin. *Jn.* 8: 34.

I perceive that thou art in the gall of

bitterness, and in the bond of iniquity. *Ac.* **8: 23.**

Know ye not, that to whom ye yield yourselves servants to obey, his servants ye are to whom ye obey; whether of sin unto death, or of obedience unto righteousness? *Ro.* **6: 16.**

I see another law in my members, warring against the law of my mind, and bringing me into captivity to the law of sin which is in my members. *Ro.* **7: 23.**

The creature itself also shall be delivered from the bondage of corruption into the glorious liberty of the children of God. *Ro.* **8: 21.**

Stand fast therefore in the liberty wherewith Christ hath made us free, and be not entangled again with the yoke of bondage. *Ga.* **5: 1.**

That they may recover themselves out of the snare of the devil, who are taken captive by him at his will. **2** *Ti.* **2: 26.**

See also

Autocrat; Band; Bond; Captivity; Chain; Imprisonment; Oppression; Prison; Suppression; Yoke.

Bone

This is now bone of my bones, and flesh of my flesh. *Ge.* **2: 23.**

The Lord shall guide thee continually, and satisfy thy soul in drought, and make fat thy bones. *Is.* **58: 11.**

Prophesy upon these bones, and say unto them. O ye dry bones, hear the word of the Lord. *Eze.* **37: 4.**

Behold, I will cause breath to enter into you, and ye shall live. *Eze.* **37: 5.**

Ye are like unto whited sepulchres, . . . full of dead men's bones. *Mat.* **23: 27.**

A bone of him shall not be broken. *Jn.* **19: 36.**

We are members of his body, of his flesh, and of his bones. *Ep.* **5: 30.**

Book

The Lord said unto Moses, Write this for a memorial in a book. *Ex.* **17: 14.**

The Lord said, . . . Whosoever hath sinned against me, him will I blot out of my book. *Ex.* **32: 33.**

I have found the book of the law in the house of the Lord. **2** *K.* **22: 8.**

Oh . . . that mine adversary had written a book. *Jb.* **31: 35.**

My tongue is the pen of a ready writer. *Ps.* **45: 1.**

Of making many books there is no end; and much study is a weariness of the flesh. *Ec.* **12: 12.**

Search the scriptures; for in them ye think ye have eternal life: and they are they which testify of me. *Jn.* **5: 39.**

Other . . . fellowlabourers, whose names are in the book of life. *Ph.* **4: 3.**

What thou seest, write in a book. *Re.* **1: 11.**

I saw the dead, small and great, stand before God; and the books were opened: and another book was opened, which is the book of life. *Re.* **20: 12.**

See also

Author; God, Word of; Life, Book of; Scripture; Scroll; Testament, New; Testament, Old; Writing.

Boon

Thou shalt take no gift: for the gift blindeth the wise, and perverteth the words of the righteous. *Ex.* **23: 8.**

All things come of thee, and of thine own have we given thee. **1** *Ch.* **29: 14.**

A gift is as a precious stone in the eyes of him that hath it. *Pr.* **17: 8.**

A man's gift maketh room for him, and bringeth him before great men. *Pr.* **18: 16.**

Every man should eat and drink, and enjoy the good of all his labour, it is the gift of God. *Ec.* **3: 13.**

A gift destroyeth the heart. *Ec.* **7: 7.**

I was . . . Naked, and ye clothed me. *Mat.* **25: 35, 36.**

Thanks be unto God for his unspeakable gift. **2** *Co.* **9: 15.**

Every good gift and every perfect gift is from above. *Ja.* **1: 17.**

See also

Beneficence; Benevolence; Generosity; Gift; Present.

Booth

Ye shall dwell in booths seven days. *Le.* **23: 42.**

I made the children of Israel to dwell in booths. *Le.* **23: 43.**

Go forth unto the mount, and fetch olive branches, and pine branches, and myrtle branches, and palm branches, and branches of thick trees, to make booths. *Ne.* **8: 15.**

Jonah went out of the city, and sat on the east side of the city, and there made him a booth, and sat under it in the shadow, till he might see what would become of the city. *Jon.* **4: 5.**

See also

Shelter.

Booty

A wolf of the evenings shall spoil them. *Je.* **5: 6.**

The spoiler shall suddenly come upon us. *Je.* **6: 26.**

Remove violence and spoil, and execute judgment and justice. *Eze.* **45: 9.**

Thou shalt be for booties unto them. *Hab.* **2: 7.**

When a stronger than he shall come upon him, and overcome him, he taketh from him all his armour wherein he trusted, and divideth his spoils. *Lu.* **11: 22.**

See also

Plunder; Spoil.

Border

When the Most High divided to the nations their inheritance, . . . he set the bounds of the people according to the number of the children of Israel. *De.* **32: 8.**

Thou hast set a bound that they may not pass over; that they turn not again to cover the earth. *Ps.* **104: 9.**

Violence shall no more be heard in thy land, wasting nor destruction within thy borders. *Is.* **60: 18.**

Thy borders are in the midst of the seas, thy builders have perfected thy beauty. *Eze.* **27: 4.**

This shall be holy in all the borders thereof round about. *Eze.* **45: 1.**

A woman, . . . which had spent all her living upon physicians, . . . Came behind him, and touched the border of his garment. *Lu.* 8: 43, 44.
See also
Bound; Frontier; Landmark; Limitation; Margin.

Boredom

I am weary of my life. *Ge.* 27: 46.
Withdraw thy foot from thy neighbour's house; lest he be weary of thee, and so hate thee. *Pr.* 25: 17.
Much study is a weariness of the flesh. *Ec.* 12: 12.
It is a small thing for you to weary men, but will ye weary my God also? *Is.* 7: 13.
I have not caused thee to serve with an offering, nor wearied thee with incense. *Is.* 43: 23.
Thou hast wearied me with thine iniquities. *Is.* 43: 24
Thou art wearied in the multitude of thy counsels. *Is.* 47: 13.
O my people, what have I done unto thee? and wherein have I wearied thee? *Mi.* 6: 3.
Ye have wearied the Lord with your words. Yet ye say, Wherein have we wearied him? *Mal.* 2: 17.
Lest by her continual coming she weary me. *Lu.* 18: 5.
See also
Weariness.

Borrower

If a man borrow aught of his neighbour, and it be hurt, or die, the owner thereof being not with it, he shall surely make it good. *Ex.* 22: 14.
Thou shalt lend unto many nations, but thou shalt not borrow. *De.* 15: 6.
The wicked borroweth, and payeth not again. *Ps.* 37: 21.
The borrower is servant to the lender. *Pr.* 22: 7.
It shall be, . . . as with the lender, so with the borrower. *Is.* 24: 2.
From him that would borrow of thee, turn not thou away. *Mat.* 5: 42.
See also
Loan; Usury.

Bosom

One little ewe lamb . . . lay in his bosom, and was unto him a daughter. *2 S.* 12: 3.
Hiding mine iniquity in my bosom. *Jb.* 31: 33.
The inward thought of every one of them, and the heart, is deep. *Ps.* 64: 6.
I do bear in my bosom the reproach of all the mighty people. *Ps.* 89: 50.
Anger resteth in the bosom of fools. *Ec.* 7: 9.
He shall gather the lambs with his arm, and carry them in his bosom. *Is.* 40: 11.
The beggar died, and was carried by the angels into Abraham's bosom. *Lu.* 16: 22.
The publican, standing afar off, would not lift up so much as his eyes unto heaven, but smote upon his breast. *Lu.* 18: 13.
The only begotten Son, which is in the bosom of the Father, he hath declared him. *Jn.* 1: 18.

There was leaning on Jesus' bosom one of his disciples, whom Jesus loved. *Jn.* 13: 23.
See also
Breast; Heart.

Bottom

The depths have covered them: they sank into the bottom as a stone. *Ex.* 15: 5.
He spreadeth his light upon it, and covereth the bottom of the sea. *Jb.* 36; 30.
I went down to the bottoms of the mountains. *Jon.* 2: 6.
The veil of the temple was rent in twain from the top to the bottom. *Mk.* 15: 38.
See also
Ground; Root.

Bound

Thou shalt set bounds unto the people round about. *Ex.* 19: 12.
Thou hast appointed his bounds that he cannot pass. *Jb.* 14: 5.
He hath compassed the waters with bounds. *Jb.* 26: 10.
God . . . hath made of one blood all nations of men for to dwell on all the face of the earth, and hath determined the times before appointed, and the bounds of their habitations. *Ac.* 17: 24, 26.
See also
Border; Frontier; Landmark; Limit; Limitation; Margin.

Bounty

When ye reap the harvest of your land, thou shalt not wholly reap the corners of thy field. *Le.* 19: 9.
Thou shalt not glean thy vineyard, neither shalt thou gather every grape of thy vineyard; thou shalt leave them for the poor and stranger. *Le.* 19: 10.
If there be among you a poor man, . . . thou shalt open thine hand wide unto him, and shalt surely lend him sufficient for his need. *De.* 15: 7, 8.
When thou beatest thine olive tree, thou shalt not go over the boughs again: it shall be for the stranger, for the fatherless, for the widow. *De.* 24: 20.
When thou gatherest the grapes of thy vineyard, thou shalt not glean it afterward: it shall be for the stranger, for the fatherless, for the widow. *De.* 24: 21.
I have given you a land for which ye did not labour, and cities which ye built not, and ye dwell in them; of the vineyards and the oliveyards which ye planted not do ye eat. *Jos.* 24: 13.
I have commanded the ravens to feed thee there. *1 K.* 17: 4.
He hath dealt bountifully with me. *Ps.* 13: 6.
Thou preventest him with the blessings of goodness. *Ps.* 21: 3.
The earth is full of the goodness of the Lord. *Ps.* 33: 5.
Can God furnish a table in the wilderness? *Ps.* 78: 19.
Man did eat angels' food. *Ps.* 78: 25.
Forget not all his benefits. *Ps.* 103: 2.
He that hath a bountiful eye shall be blessed. *Pr.* 22: 9.
Every one loveth gifts. *Is.* 1: 23.
I will feed them in a good pasture, and

upon the high mountains of Israel shall their fold be: there shall they lie in a good fold. *Eze.* 34: 14.

He which soweth bountifully shall reap also bountifully. *2 Co.* 9: 6.

Enriched in everything to all bountifulness. *2 Co.* 9: 11.

See also

Beneficence; Benevolence; Generosity.

Boyhood

God heard the voice of the lad. *Ge.* 21: 17.

God was with the lad, and he grew. *Ge.* 21: 20.

Behold, I will send a lad. *1 S.* 20: 21.

Thou hast the dew of thy youth. *Ps.* 110: 3.

That our sons may be as plants grown up in their youth. *Ps.* 144: 12.

Train up a child in the way he should go: and when he is old, he will not depart from it. *Pr.* 22: 6.

Remember now thy Creator in the days of thy youth. *Ec.* 12: 1.

Unto us a child is born, unto us a son is given. *Is.* 9: 6.

A little child shall lead them. *Is.* 11: 6.

When Israel was a child, then I loved him. *Ho.* 11: 1.

The streets of the city shall be full of boys and girls playing in the streets thereof. *Zch.* 8: 5.

All these things have I kept from my youth up. *Mat.* 19: 20.

Jesus increased in wisdom and stature, and in favor with God and man. *Lu.* 2: 52.

There is a lad here. *Jn.* 6: 9.

When I was a child, I spake as a child, I understood as a child, I thought as a child: but when I became a man, I put away childish things. *1 Co.* 13: 11.

She brought forth a man child, who was to rule all nations with a rod of iron. *Re.* 12: 5.

See also

Child; Youth.

Braggart

Talk no more so exceeding proudly; let not arrogancy come out of your mouth. *1 S.* 2: 3.

The wicked boasteth of his heart's desire. *Ps.* 10: 3.

Speak not with a stiff neck. *Ps.* 75: 5.

Most men will proclaim every one his own goodness. *Pr.* 20: 6.

Boast not thyself of to morrow; for thou knowest not what a day may bring forth. *Pr.* 27: 1.

The haughtiness of men shall be bowed down. *Is.* 2: 11.

He saith, By the strength of my hand I have done it, and by my wisdom. *Is.* 10: 13.

Shall the saw magnify itself against him that shaketh it? *Is.* 10: 15.

My river is mine own, and I have made it for myself. *Eze.* 29: 3.

Where is boasting then? It is excluded. *Ro.* 3: 27.

He that glorieth, let him glory in the Lord. *2 Co.* 10: 17.

The tongue is a little member, and boasteth great things. *Ja.* 3: 5.

See also

Arrogance; Boasting; Conceit; Ostentation; Vanity.

Brain

Serve him . . . with a willing mind. *1 Ch.* 28: 9.

Thy thoughts are very deep. *Ps.* 92: 5.

Though a wise man think to know it, yet shall he not be able to find it. *Ec.* 8: 17.

Come now, and let us reason together. *Is.* 1: 18.

Bring forth your strong reasons. *Is.* 41: 21.

I know the thoughts that I think towards you, saith the Lord, thoughts of peace, and not of evil. *Je.* 29: 11.

The Son of man cometh at an hour when ye think not. *Lu.* 12: 40.

Why even of yourselves judge ye not what is right? *Lu.* 12: 57.

Whom think ye that I am? *Ac.* 13: 25.

Let every man be fully persuaded in his own mind. *Ro.* 14: 5.

Prove all things; hold fast that which is good. *1 Th.* 5: 21.

See also

Intelligence; Mind; Knowledge; Reason; Study; Thought; Wisdom.

Branch

Joseph is a fruitful bough, even a fruitful bough by a well; whose branches run over the wall. *Ge.* 49: 22.

Ye shall take you on the first day the boughs of goodly trees, branches of palm trees, and the boughs of thick trees, and willows of the brook; and ye shall rejoice before the Lord your God. *Le.* 23: 40.

Thou hast brought a vine out of Egypt. . . . She sent out her boughs unto the sea, and her branches unto the river. *Ps.* 80: 8, 11.

The righteous shall flourish as a branch. *Pr.* 11: 28.

In that day shall the branch of the Lord be beautiful and glorious. *Is.* 4: 2.

There shall come forth a rod out of the stem of Jesse, and a Branch shall grow out of his roots. *Is.* 11: 1.

In that day shall his strong cities be as a forsaken bough. *Is.* 17: 9.

O mountains of Israel, ye shall shoot forth your branches, and yield your fruit to my people. *Eze.* 36: 8.

Every branch that beareth fruit, he purgeth it, that it may bring forth more fruit. *Jn.* 15: 2.

I am the vine, ye are the branches. *Jn.* 15: 5.

If the root be holy, so are the branches. *Ro.* 11: 16.

See also

Arm; Member; Outgrowth; Tree.

Bravery

Be ye of good courage, and bring of the fruit of the land. *Nu.* 13: 20.

The Lord is with us: fear them not. *Nu.* 14: 9.

Israel shall do valiantly. *Nu.* 24: 18.

The Lord, he it is that doth go before thee; he will be with thee, he will not fail thee, neither forsake thee: fear not; neither be dismayed. *De.* 31: 8.

Be strong and of good courage: for thou shalt bring the children of Israel into the land which I sware unto them. *De.* 31: 23.

Our hearts did melt, neither did there remain any more courage in any man. *Jos.* 2: 11.

Only be thou valiant for me, and fight the Lord's battles. *1 S.* 18: 17.

Let your hands be strengthened, and be ye valiant. *2 S.* 2: 7.

Be of good courage, and let us play the men for our people, and for the cities of our God. *2 S.* 10: 12.

Come in; for thou art a valiant man, and bringest good tidings. *1 K.* 1: 42.

Fear not: for they that be with us are more than they that be with them. *2 K.* 6: 16.

Be of good courage, and let us behave ourselves valiantly for our people. *1 Ch.* 19: 13.

Wait on the Lord: be of good courage, and he shall strengthen thine heart. *Ps.* 27: 14.

Through God we shall do valiantly; for he it is that shall tread down our enemies. *Ps.* 60: 12.

The right hand of the Lord doeth valiantly. *Ps.* 118: 15.

Fear thou not; for I am with thee. *Is.* 41: 10.

They are not valiant for the truth upon the earth; for they proceed from evil to evil. *Je.* 9: 3.

He that is courageous among the mighty shall flee away naked in that day. *Am.* 2: 16.

Fear not them which kill the body, but are not able to kill the soul: but rather fear him which is able to destroy both soul and body in hell. *Mat.* 10: 28.

Fear not, little flock; for it is your Father's good pleasure to give you the kingdom. *Lu.* 12: 32.

Whom when Paul saw, he thanked God, and took courage. *Ac.* 28: 15.

Waxed valiant in fight. *He.* 11: 34.

Fear not; I am the first and the last. *Re.* 1: 17.

See also

Boldness; Courage; Fearlessness; Fortitude; Heroism; Valor.

Bread

He shall bless thy bread, and thy water. *Ex.* 23: 25.

Comfort thine heart with a morsel of bread. *Ju.* 19: 5.

And gavest them bread from heaven for their hunger. *Ne.* 9: 15.

As for the earth, out of it cometh bread. *Jb.* 28: 5.

Who provideth for the raven his food? when his young ones cry unto God, they wander for lack of meat. *Jb.* 38: 41.

He . . . rained down manna upon them to eat, and had given them of the corn of heaven. *Ps.* 78: 23, 24.

Man did eat angels' food: he sent them meat to the full. *Ps.* 78: 25.

Who giveth food to all flesh: for his mercy endureth for ever. *Ps.* 136: 25.

Cast thy bread upon the waters: for thou shalt find it after many days. *Ec.* 11: 1.

When the tempter came to him, he said, If thou be the Son of God, command that these stones be made bread. *Mat.* 4: 3.

Man shall not live by bread alone, but by every word that proceedeth out of the mouth of God. *Mat.* 4: 4.

It is not meet to take the children's bread, and to cast it to dogs. *Mat.* 15: 26.

Give ye them to eat. *Mk.* 6: 37.

Give us day by day our daily bread. *Lu.* 11: 3.

It came to pass, as he sat at meat with them, he took bread, and blessed it, and brake, and gave to them. *Lu.* 24: 30.

He was known of them in breaking of bread. *Lu.* 24: 35.

My Father giveth you the true bread from heaven. *Jn.* 6: 32.

The bread of God is he which cometh down from heaven, and giveth life unto the world. *Jn.* 6: 33.

He that eateth of this bread shall live for ever. *Jn.* 6: 58.

The bread which we break, is it not the communion of the body of Christ? *1 Co.* 10: 16.

We being many are one bread. *1 Co.* 10: 17.

See also

Christ, Bread of Life; Food; Hunger; Life, Bread of; Loaf; Manna; Stomach.

Breadth

Is there room in thy father's house for us to lodge in? *Ge.* 24: 23.

Now the Lord hath made room for us. *Ge.* 26: 22.

The land was wide, and quiet, and peaceable. *1 Ch.* 4: 40.

The measure thereof is longer than the earth, and broader than the sea. *Jb.* 11: 9.

Even so would he have removed thee out of the strait into a broad place. *Jb.* 36: 16.

Hast thou perceived the breadth of the earth? declare if thou knowest it all. *Jb.* 38: 18.

He brought me forth also into a large place. *Ps.* 18: 19.

Thou hast set my feet in a large room. *Ps.* 31: 8.

So is this great and wide sea, wherein are things creeping innumerable. *Ps.* 104: 25.

Thy commandment is exceeding broad. *Ps.* 119: 96.

In the broad ways I will seek him whom my soul loveth. *S. of S.* 3: 2.

The stretching out of his wings shall fill the breadth of thy land. *Is.* 8: 8.

There the glorious Lord will be unto us a place of broad rivers and streams. *Is.* 33: 21.

I will build me a wide house, and large chambers. *Je.* 22: 14.

The gates of thy land shall be set wide open unto thine enemies. *Na.* 3: 13.

Prove me now herewith, saith the Lord of hosts, if I will not open you the windows of heaven, and pour you out a blessing, that there shall not be room enough to receive it. *Mal.* 3: 10.

Wide is the gate, and broad is the way, that leadeth to destruction. *Mat.* 7: 13.

That ye, being rooted and grounded in love, May be able to comprehend with all saints what is the breadth, and length, and depth, and height. *Ep.* 3: 17, 18.

The city lieth foursquare, and the length is as large as the breadth. *Re.* 21: 16.

See also

Greatness; Liberality; Room; Strait; Tolerance.

Breast

The Almighty . . . shall bless thee with . . . blessings of the breasts, and of the womb. *Ge.* 49: 25.

They pluck the fatherless from the breast. *Jb.* 24: 9.

Thou didst make me hope when I was upon my mother's breasts. *Ps.* 22: 9.

I humbled my soul with fasting; and my prayer returned into mine own bosom. *Ps.* 35: 13.

In heart ye work wickedness. *Ps.* 58: 2.

Can a man take fire in his bosom, and his clothes not be burned? *Pr.* 6: 27.

There are many devices in a man's heart. *Pr.* 19: 21.

A gift in secret pacifieth anger: and a reward in the bosom strong wrath. *Pr.* 21: 14.

This thy stature is like to a palm tree, and thy breasts to clusters of grapes. *S. of S.* 7: 7.

Thy breasts shall be as clusters of the vine, and the smell of thy nose like apples. *S. of S.* 7: 8.

We have a little sister, and she hath no breasts. *S of S.* 8: 8.

I am a wall, and my breasts like towers. *S. of S.* 8: 10.

A good man out of the good treasure of the heart bringeth forth good things. *Mat.* 12: 35.

Out of the heart proceed evil thoughts. *Mat.* 15: 19.
See also
Bosom; Heart.

Breastplate

He put on righteousness as a breastplate. *Is.* 59: 17.

Take unto you the whole armour of God. *Ep.* 6: 13.

Stand therefore, . . . having on the breastplate of righteousness. *Ep.* 6: 14.

Let us, who are of the day, be sober, putting on the breastplate of faith and love. *1 Th.* 5: 8.
See also
Armor; Defence; Protection; Shield.

Breath

The Lord God . . . breathed into his nostrils the breath of life. *Ge.* 2: 7.

In whose hand is the soul of every living thing, and the breath of all mankind. *Jb.* 12: 10.

My breath is strange to my wife. *Jb.* 19: 17.

The breath of the Almighty hath given me life. *Jb.* 33: 4.

Thou takest away their breath, they die. *Ps.* 104: 29.

They have all one breath. *Ec.* 3: 19.

Come from the four winds, O breath, and breathe upon these slain, that they may live. *Eze.* 37: 9.

He giveth to all life, and breath, and all things. *Ac.* 17: 25.
See also
Air; Atmosphere.

Brevity

They seemed unto him but a few days, for the love he had to her. *Ge.* 29: 20.

Few and evil have the days of the years of my life been. *Ge.* 47: 9.

Are not my days few? *Jb.* 10: 20.

Man that is born of a woman is of few days, and full of trouble. *Jb.* 14: 1.

Knowest thou not this of old, . . . That the triumphing of the wicked is short, and the joy of the hypocrite but for a moment? *Jb.* 20: 4, 5.

The number of his months is cut off in the midst. *Jb.* 21: 21.

The days of his youth hast thou shortened. *Ps.* 89: 45.

Remember how short my time is. *Ps.* 89: 47.

A thousand years in thy sight are but as yesterday when it is past, and as a watch in the night. *Ps.* 90: 4.

The days of our years are threescore years and ten; and if by reason of strength they be fourscore years, yet is their strength labour and sorrow; for it is soon cut off and we fly away. *Ps.* 90: 10.

Let his days be few; and let another take his office. *Ps.* 109: 8.

The years of the wicked shall be shortened. *Pr.* 10: 27.

A little while, and ye shall not see me: and again, a little while, and ye shall see me. *Jn.* 16: 16.

Brethren, the time is short. *1 Co.* 7: 29.

For yet a little while, and he that shall come will come, and will not tarry. *He.* 10: 37.
See also
Abbreviation; Life, the Short; Shortness.

Bribe

Thou shalt take no gift: for the gift blindeth the wise, and perverteth the words of the righteous. *Ex.* 23: 8.

Thou shalt not defraud thy neighbour. *Le.* 19: 13.

A gift doth blind the eyes of the wise, and pervert the words of the righteous. *De.* 16: 19.

The Lords of the Philistines came up unto her, and brought money in their hand. *Ju.* 16: 18.

His sons walked not in his ways, but turned aside after lucre, and took bribes, and perverted judgment. *1 S.* 8: 3.

Whom have I defrauded? whom have I oppressed? or of whose hand have I received any bribe to blind mine eyes therewith? *1 S.* 12: 3.

Make an agreement with me by a present. *2 K.* 18: 31.

Fire shall consume the tabernacles of bribery. *Jb.* 15: 34.

Their right hand is full of bribes. *Ps.* 26: 10.

Every one loveth gifts, and followeth after rewards. *Is.* 1: 23.

Which justify the wicked for reward, and take away the righteousness of the righteous from him! *Is.* 5: 23.

He that despiseth the gain of oppressions, that shaketh his hands from holding of bribes, . . . He shall dwell on high. *Is.* 33: 15, 16.

They take a bribe, and they turn aside the poor in the gate from their right. *Am.* 5: 12.

They covenanted with him for thirty pieces of silver. *Mat.* 26: 15.

They gave large money unto the soldiers, Saying, Say ye, His disciples came by night, and stole him away while we slept. *Mat.* 28: 12, 13.

They . . . promised to give him money. And he sought how he might conveniently betray him. *Mk.* 14: 11.

Thy money perish with thee, because thou hast thought that the gift of God may be purchased with money. *Ac.* 8: 20.

The love of money is the root of all evil. *1 Ti.* 6: 10.

See also

Allurement; Enticement; Gift; Present.

Bride

He hath clothed me with the garments of salvation, . . . as a bride adorneth herself with her jewels. *Is.* 61: 10.

As the bridegroom rejoiceth over the bride, so shall thy God rejoice over thee. *Is.* 62: 5.

Another said, I have married a wife, and therefore I cannot come. *Lu.* 14: 20.

He that hath the bride is the bridegroom: but the friend of the bridegroom, which standeth and heareth him, rejoiceth greatly because of the bridegroom's voice. *Jn.* 3: 29.

I John saw the holy city, new Jerusalem, coming down from God out of heaven, prepared as a bride adorned for her husband. *Re.* 21: 2.

The Spirit and the bride say, Come. *Re.* 22: 17.

See also

Bridegroom; Husband; Marriage; Wedding; Wife.

Bridegroom

The sun . . . is as a bridegroom coming out of his chamber, and rejoiceth as a strong man to run a race. *Ps.* 19: 4, 5.

Can the children of the bridechamber mourn as long as the bridegroom is with them? *Mat.* 9: 15.

The days will come, when the bridegroom shall be taken from them, and then shall they fast. *Mat.* 9: 15.

Ten virgins . . . went forth to meet the bridegroom. *Mat.* 25: 1.

See also

Bride; Husband; Marriage; Wedding; Wife.

Bridle

Be ye not as the horse, or as the mule, which have no understanding: whose mouth must be held in with bit and bridle. *Ps.* 32: 9.

I will take heed to my ways, that I sin not with my tongue: I will keep my mouth with a bridle. *Ps.* 39: 1.

Harness the horses; and get up, ye horsemen, and stand forth. *Je.* 46: 4.

If any man among you . . . bridleth not his tongue, . . . this man's religion is vain. *Ja.* 1: 26.

If any man offend not in word, the same is a perfect man, and able also to bridle the whole body. *Ja.* 3: 2.

Behold, we put bits in the horses' mouths, that they may obey us. *Ja.* 3: 3.

See also

Horse; Restraint.

Brier

The way of the slothful man is as an hedge of thorns. *Pr.* 15: 19.

As a thorn goeth up into the hand of a drunkard, so is a parable in the mouth of fools. *Pr.* 26: 9.

There shall come up briers and thorns: I will also command the clouds that they rain no rain upon it. *Is.* 5: 6.

All the land shall become briers and thorns. *Is.* 7: 24.

Instead of the brier shall come up the myrtle tree. *Is.* 55: 13.

The best of them is as a brier: the most upright is sharper than a thorn hedge. *Mi.* 7: 4.

Do men gather grapes of thorns, or figs of thistles? *Mat.* 7: 16.

See also

Thorn.

Brightness

Let there be light. *Ge.* 1: 3.

The light shall shine upon thy ways. *Jb.* 22: 28.

He shall bring forth thy righteousness as the light. *Ps.* 37: 6.

The law is light. *Pr.* 6: 23.

Woe unto them . . . that put darkness for light, and light for darkness. *Is.* 5: 20.

The light of the moon shall be as the light of the sun, and the light of the sun shall be sevenfold, as the light of seven days. *Is.* 30: 26.

The Gentiles shall come to thy light, and kings to the brightness of thy rising. *Is.* 60: 3.

When I sit in darkness, the Lord shall be a light unto me. *Mi.* 7: 8.

His brightness was as the light. *Hab.* 3: 4.

At evening time it shall be light. *Zch.* 14: 7.

The light of the body is the eye. *Mat.* 6: 22.

Then all those virgins arose, and trimmed their lamps. *Mat.* 25: 7.

If thy whole body therefore be full of light, having no part dark, the whole shall be full of light, as when the bright shining of a candle doth give thee light. *Lu.* 11: 36.

I could not see for the glory of that light. *Ac.* 22: 11.

Him who hath called you out of darkness into his marvellous light. *1 Pe.* 2: 9.

They need no candle, neither light of the sun; for the Lord God giveth them light. *Re.* 22: 5.

See also

Christ, Glory of; Christ, the Light; Gleam; Glory; God, Glory of; God, the Light; Illumination; Light; Radiance; Ray; Splendor.

Brimstone

Then the Lord rained upon Sodom and upon Gomorrah brimstone and fire. *Ge.* 19: 24.

A fire is kindled in mine anger, and shall burn unto the lowest hell, and shall consume the earth with her increase. *De.* 32: 22.

Upon the wicked he shall rain snares, fire and brimstone. *Ps.* 11: 6.

Whosoever shall say, Thou fool, shall be in danger of hell fire. *Mat.* 5: 22.

The Son of man shall send forth his angels, and they shall gather out of his kingdom all things that offend, and them which do iniquity; And shall cast them into a furnace of fire. *Mat.* 13: 41, 42.

It is better for thee to enter into life with one eye, rather than having two eyes to be cast into hell fire. *Mat.* 18: 9.

Depart from me, ye cursed, into everlasting fire, prepared for the devil and his angels. *Mat.* 25: 41.

Their worm dieth not, and the fire is not quenched. *Mk.* 9: 44.

The tongue . . . is set on fire of hell. *Ja.* 3: 6.

Death and hell were cast into the lake of fire. This is the second death. *Re.* 20: 14.

The fearful, and unbelieving, and the abominable, and murderers, . . . shall have their part in the lake which burneth with fire and brimstone. *Re.* 21: 8.

See also
Damnation; Hell.

Brood

If a bird's nest chance to be before thee in the way in any tree, or on the ground, whether they be young ones, or eggs, and the dam sitting upon the young, or upon the eggs, thou shalt not take the dam with the young. *De.* 22: 6.

As an eagle stirreth up her nest, fluttereth over her young, spreadeth abroad her wings, taketh them, beareth them on her wings. *De.* 32: 11.

Under whose wings thou art come to trust. *Ru.* 2: 12.

Hide me under the shadow of thy wings. *Ps.* 17: 8.

In the shadow of thy wings will I rejoice. *Ps.* 63: 7.

The sparrow hath found an house, and the swallow a nest for herself, where she may lay her young, even thine altars. *Ps.* 84: 3.

As a bird that wandereth from her nest, so is a man that wandereth from his place. *Pr.* 27: 8.

There shall the great owl make her nest, and lay, and hatch, and gather under her shadow. *Is.* 34: 15.

As the partridge sitteth on eggs, and hatcheth them not. *Je.* 17: 11.

How often would I have gathered thy children together, even as a hen gathereth her chickens under her wings, and ye would not! *Mat.* 23: 37.

See also
Bird; Nest.

Brothel

He went the way to her house, In the twilight, in the evening, in the black and dark night. *Pr.* 7: 8, 9.

Her house is the way to hell, going down to the chambers of death. *Pr.* 7: 27.

The mouth of strange women is a deep pit. *Pr.* 22: 14.

Thou hast played the harlot with many lovers. *Je.* 3: 1.

What hath my beloved to do in mine house, seeing she hath wrought lewdness with many. *Je.* 11: 15.

The Babylonians came to her into the bed of love. *Eze.* 23: 17.

She multiplied her whoredoms. *Eze.* 23: 19.

They went in unto her, as they go in unto a woman that playeth the harlot. *Eze.* 23: 44.

Thus will I cause lewdness to cease out of the land. *Eze.* 23: 48.

Woe to them that devise iniquity, and work evil upon their beds! *Mi.* 2: 1.

Behold, I will cast her into a bed, and them that commit adultery with her into great tribulation. *Re.* 2: 22.

See also
Carnality; Debauchery; Flesh; Fornication; Harlot; Lust; Prostitute.

Brotherhood

The Lord said unto Cain, Where is Abel thy brother? *Ge.* 4: 9.

The voice of thy brother's blood crieth unto me from the ground. *Ge.* 4: 10.

Let there be no strife, I pray thee, between me and thee, . . . for we be brethren. *Ge.* 13: 8.

Thou shalt open thy hand wide unto thy brother. *De.* 15: 11.

Behold, how good and how pleasant it is for brethren to dwell together in unity. *Ps.* 133: 1.

A friend loveth at all times, and a brother is born for adversity. *Pr.* 17: 17.

They . . . remembered not the brotherly covenant. *Am.* 1: 9.

Let none of you imagine evil against his brother in your heart. *Zch.* 7: 10.

If ye salute your brethren only, what do ye more than others? do not even the publicans so? *Mat.* 5: 47.

He stretched forth his hand toward his disciples, and said, Behold my mother and my brethren! *Mat.* 12: 49.

One is your Master, even Christ; and all ye are brethren. *Mat.* 23: 8.

Sirs, ye are brethren. *Ac.* 7: 26.

Be kindly affectioned one to another with brotherly love. *Ro.* 12: 10.

Why dost thou judge thy brother? . . . for we shall all stand before the judgment seat of Christ. *Ro.* 14: 10.

It is good neither to eat flesh, nor to drink wine, nor any thing whereby thy brother stumbleth. *Ro.* 14: 21.

Through thy knowledge shall the weak brother perish, for whom Christ died? *1 Co.* 8: 11.

Bear ye one another's burdens, and so fulfil the law of Christ. *Ga.* 6: 2.

Ye yourselves are taught of God to love one another. *1 Th.* 4: 9.

We command you, . . . that ye withdraw yourselves from every brother that walketh disorderly. *2 Th.* 3: 6.

If a brother or sister be naked, and destitute of daily food, And one of you say unto them, Depart in peace, be ye warmed and filled; notwithstanding ye give them not those things which are needful to the body; what doth it profit? *Ja.* 2: 15, 16.

Be ye all of one mind, having compassion one of another, love as brethren. *1 Pe.* 3: 8.

Add . . . to godliness brotherly kindness. *2 Pe.* 1: 5, 7.

He that saith he is in the light, and hateth his brother, is in darkness even until now. *1 Jn.* 2: 9.

We know that we have passed from death unto life, because we love the brethren. *1 Jn.* 3: 14.

If a man say, I love God, and hateth his brother, he is a liar: for he that loveth not his brother whom he hath seen, how can he

love God whom he hath not seen? *1 Jn.* 4:
20.

See also

Alliance; Association; Family; Fellowship;
Fraternity; Integration; Socialism.

Bruise

A bruised reed shall he not break, and the
smoking flax shall he not quench. *Is.* 42: 3.

He was wounded for our transgressions, he
was bruised for our iniquities. *Is.* 53: 5.

It pleased the Lord to bruise him. *Is.* 53: 10.

Thy bruise is incurable, and thy wound is
grievous. *Je.* 30: 12.

He hath sent me to . . . set at liberty
them that are bruised. *Lu.* 4: 18.

See also

Harm; Hurt; Injury; Wound.

Brute

They hate me with cruel hatred. *Ps.* 25: 19.

The fool and the brutish person perish.
Ps. 49: 10.

Deliver me, O my God, out of the hand of
the wicked, out of the hand of the unrighteous
and cruel man. *Ps.* 71: 4.

A brutish man knoweth not; neither doth
a fool understand this. *Ps.* 92: 6.

He that hateth reproof is brutish. *Pr.* 12: 1.

Every man is brutish in his knowledge. *Je.*
10: 14.

I will . . . deliver thee into the hand of
brutish men. *Eze.* 21: 31.

With force and with cruelty have ye ruled
them. *Eze.* 34: 4.

See also

Animal; Beast; Creature.

Buckler

I am thy shield, and thy exceeding great
reward. *Ge.* 15: 1.

He is my shield, and the horn of my salvation. *2 S.* 22: 3.

God . . . is a buckler to all those who trust
in him. *Ps.* 18: 30.

Take hold of shield and buckler, and stand
up for mine help. *Ps.* 35: 2.

His truth shall be thy shield and buckler.
Ps. 91: 4.

He is a buckler to them that walk uprightly.
Pr. 2: 7.

See also

Armor; Defence; Protection; Shield.

Bud

Let the earth bring forth grass, the herb
yielding seed, and the fruit tree yielding fruit
after his kind. *Ge.* 1: 11.

Behold, the rod of Aaron . . . was budded,
and brought forth buds, and bloomed blossoms, and yielded almonds. *Nu.* 17: 8.

To cause the bud of the tender herb to
spring forth. *Jb.* 38: 27.

Let us get up early to the vineyards; let us
see . . . whether the tender grape appear, and
the pomegranates bud forth. *S. of S.* 7: 12.

As the rain cometh down, and the snow
from heaven, and returneth not thither, but
watereth the earth, and maketh it bring forth
and bud. *Is.* 55: 10.

As the earth bringeth forth her bud, and as
the garden causeth the things that are sown in

it to spring forth; so the Lord God will cause
righteousness and praise to spring forth before
all nations. *Is.* 61: 11.

The rod hath blossomed, pride hath budded.
Eze. 7: 10.

I have caused thee to multiply as the bud of
the field. *Eze.* 16: 7.

First the blade, then the ear, after that the
full corn in the ear. *Mk.* 4: 28.

See also

Blossom.

Builder

Go to, let us build us a city and a tower,
whose top may reach unto heaven. *Ge.* 11: 4.

Thou shalt build the altar of the Lord thy
God of whole stones. *De.* 27: 6.

Let us now prepare to build us an altar.
Jos. 22: 26.

It was in the heart of David my father to
build an house for the name of the Lord
God of Israel. *1 K.* 8: 17.

Thus saith the Lord, Thou shalt not build
me an house. . . . Furthermore I tell thee
that the Lord will build thee an house. *1 Ch.*
17: 4, 10.

The workmen wrought, and the work was
perfected by them, and they set the house of
God in his state, and strengthened it. *2 Ch.*
24: 13.

He built his sanctuary like high palaces.
Ps. 78: 69.

Except the Lord build the house, they
labour in vain that build it: except the Lord
keep the city, the watchman waketh but in
vain. *Ps.* 127: 1.

Through wisdom is an house builded; and
by understanding it is established. *Pr.* 24: 3.

A time to break down, and a time to build
up. *Ec.* 3: 3.

They shall not build, and another inhabit.
Is. 65: 22.

Thy builders have perfected thy beauty.
Eze. 27: 4.

Woe to him that buildeth a town with
blood, and stablisheth a city by iniquity!
Hab. 2: 12.

Which of you, intending to build a tower,
sitteth not down first and counteth the cost,
whether he have sufficient to finish it? *Lu.*
14: 28.

Lest I should build upon another man's
foundation. *Ro.* 15: 20.

Ye are God's building. *1 Co.* 3: 9.

But let every man take heed how he
buildeth. *1 Co.* 3: 10.

Other foundation can no man lay than that
is laid, which is Jesus Christ. *1 Co.* 3: 11.

He looked for a city which hath foundations, whose builder and maker is God. *He.*
11: 10.

See also

Architecture; Carpenter; Christ, the Creator;
Creator; God, the Creator; God, House of;
House; Maker.

Bulwark

Our little ones shall dwell in the fenced
cities because of the inhabitants of the land.
Nu. 32: 17.

God of my rock; in him will I trust: he
is my shield, and the horn of my salvation,

my high tower, and my refuge. *2 S.* **22: 3.**
Yea, the Almighty shall be thy defence.
Jb. **22: 25.**
Mark ye well her bulwarks, consider her
palaces; that ye may tell it to the generation
following. *Ps.* **48: 13.**
God is the strength of my heart. *Ps.* **73: 26.**
Peace be within thy walls, and prosperity
within thy palaces. *Ps.* **122: 7.**
As the mountains are round about Jeru-
salem, so the Lord is round about his people
from henceforth even for ever. *Ps.* **125: 2.**
We have a strong city, salvation will God
appoint for walls and bulwarks. *Is.* **26: 1.**
The defenced city shall be desolate. *Is.* **27:
10.**
I have set watchmen upon thy walls, O
Jerusalem. *Is.* **62: 6.**
The Lord is good, a strong hold in the day
of trouble. *Na.* **1: 7.**
I have cut off the nations: their towers are
desolate. *Zph.* **3: 6.**
I, saith the Lord, will be unto her a wall of
fire round about, and will be a glory in the
midst of her. *Zch.* **2: 5.**
Turn you to the strong hold, ye prisoners
of hope. *Zch.* **9: 12.**
The wall of the city had twelve founda-
tions. *Re.* **21: 14.**
See also
Defence;   Fortress;   Protection;   Shield;
Tower; Wall.

Buoyancy

Light of foot as a wild roe. *2 S.* **2: 18.**
The iron did swim. *2 K.* **6: 6.**
He maketh my feet like hinds' feet, and
setteth me upon my high places. *Ps.* **18: 33.**
Oh that I had wings like a dove! *Ps.* **55: 6.**
Though ye have lain among the pots, yet
shall ye be as the wings of a dove. *Ps.* **68: 13.**
He that is of a merry heart hath a continual
feast. *Pr.* **15: 15.**
A merry heart doeth good like a medicine.
Pr. **17: 22.**
A time to mourn, and a time to dance. *Ec.*
3: 4.
Be thou like to a roe or to a young hart
upon the mountains of spices. *S. of S.* **8: 14.**
Then shall the lame man leap as an hart.
Is. **35: 6.**
All the hills moved lightly. *Je.* **4: 24.**
Is any merry? let him sing psalms. *Ja.* **5: 13.**
See also
Cheerfulness; Gaiety.

Burden

How can I myself alone bear your cum-
brance, and your burden. *De.* **1: 12.**
Make the yoke . . . upon us lighter. *1 K.*
12: 9.
I am a burden to myself. *Jb.* **7: 20.**
Cast thy burden upon the Lord, and he
shall sustain thee. *Ps.* **55: 22.**
My soul melteth for heaviness. *Ps.* **119: 28.**
The grasshopper shall be a burden. *Ec.*
12: 5.
To give unto them . . . the garment of
praise for the spirit of heaviness. *Is.* **61: 3.**
When this people, or the prophet, or a
priest, shall ask thee, saying, What is the
burden of the Lord? thou shalt then say unto

them, What burden? *Je.* **23: 33.**
Come unto me, all ye that labour and are
heavy laden, and I will give you rest. *Mat.*
11: 28.
Take my yoke upon you. *Mat.* **11: 29.**
My yoke is easy, and my burden is light.
Mat. **11: 30.**
Thou hast made them equal unto us,
which have borne the burden and heat of the
day. *Mat.* **20: 12.**
They bind heavy burdens and grievous to
be borne, and lay them on men's shoulders.
Mat. **23: 4.**
Martha was cumbered about much serving.
Lu. **10: 40.**
They laid hold upon one Simon, a Cyrenian,
coming out of the country, and on him they
laid the cross. *Lu.* **23: 26.**
Bear ye one another's burdens, and so fulfil
the law of Christ. *Ga.* **6: 2.**
For every man shall bear his own burden.
Ga. **6: 5.**
Let us lay aside every weight. *He.* **12: 1.**
See also
Care; Concern; Duty; Handicap; Heaviness;
Load; Responsibility; Weight; Yoke.

Burglar

The murderer rising with the light killeth
the poor and needy, and in the night is as a
thief. *Jb.* **24: 14.**
Men do not despise a thief, if he steal to
satisfy his soul when he is hungry. *Pr.* **6: 30.**
The robbery of the wicked shall destroy
them. *Pr.* **21: 7.**
Who gave Jacob for a spoil, and Israel to
the robbers? *Is.* **42: 24.**
The thief cometh in, and the troop of
robbers spoileth without. *Ho.* **7: 1.**
They shall enter in at the windows like a
thief. *Jo.* **2: 9.**
If the goodman of the house had known in
what watch the thief would come, he would
have watched, and would not have suffered his
house to be broken up. *Mat.* **24: 43.**
He that entereth not by the door into the
sheepfold, but climbeth up some other way,
the same is a thief and a robber. *Jn.* **10: 1.**
The day of the Lord so cometh as a thief in
the night. *1 Th.* **5: 2.**
See also
Robbery; Theft.

Burial

No man knoweth of his sepulchre unto this
day. *De.* **34: 6.**
Thou shalt come to thy grave in full age.
Jb. **5: 26.**
O that thou wouldest hide me in the grave!
Jb. **14: 13.**
If I wait, the grave is mine house: I have
made my bed in the darkness. *Jb.* **17: 13.**
So I saw the wicked buried. *Ec.* **8: 10.**
I shall go to the gates of the grave. *Is.* **38:
10.**
He shall be buried with the burial of an
ass. *Je.* **22: 19.**
I will open your graves, and cause you to
come up out of your graves. *Eze.* **37: 12.**
In that she hath poured this ointment on
my body, she did it for my burial. *Mat.* **26: 12.**
He . . . laid him in a sepulchre which was

hewn out of a rock. *Mk.* 15: 46.

Ye are as graves which appear not. *Lu.* 11: 44.

Now in the place where he was crucified there was a garden; and in the garden a new sepulchre, wherein was never man yet laid. There laid they Jesus. *Jn.* 19: 41, 42.

He was buried, and . . . rose again the third day according to the scriptures. *1 Co.* 15: 4.

O grave, where is thy victory? *1 Co.* 15: 55.

Buried with him in baptism. *Col.* 2: 12.

See also

Death; Grave.

Burn

Let not thine anger burn against thy servant. *Ge.* 44: 18.

The bush burned with fire, and the bush was not consumed. *Ex.* 3: 2.

The mount burned with fire. *De.* 9: 15.

Can one go upon hot coals, and his feet not be burned? *Pr.* 6: 28.

An ungodly man diggeth up evil: and in his lips there is as a burning fire. *Pr.* 16: 27.

Thou shalt heap coals of fire upon his head. *Pr.* 25: 22.

Where no wood is, there the fire goeth out. *Pr.* 26: 20.

As coals are to burning coals, and wood to fire; so is a contentious man to kindle strife. *Pr.* 26: 21.

Burning instead of beauty. *Is.* 3: 24.

Behold, I will kindle a fire in thee, and it shall devour every green tree in thee, and every dry tree: the flaming flame shall not be quenched. *Eze.* 20: 47.

The chaff he will burn with fire unquenchable. *Lu.* 3: 17.

It is better to marry than to burn. *1 Co.* 7: 9.

Who through faith . . . Quenched the violence of fire. *He.* 11: 33, 34.

See also

Fire; Flame; Heat.

Burnt-Offering

God will provide himself a lamb for a burnt offering. *Ge.* 22: 8.

Let us now prepare to build us an altar, not for burnt offering, nor for a sacrifice: But that it may be a witness between us, and you. *Jos.* 22: 26, 27.

Offer up for yourselves a burnt offering. *Jb.* 42: 8.

Remember all thy offerings, and accept thy burnt sacrifices. *Ps.* 20: 3.

Burnt offering and sin offering hast thou not required. *Ps.* 40: 6.

Thou delightest not in burnt offering. *Ps.* 51: 16.

Your burnt offerings are not acceptable, nor your sacrifices sweet unto me. *Je.* 6: 20.

I desired mercy, and not sacrifice; and the knowledge of God more than burnt offerings. *Ho.* 6: 6.

Shall I come before him with burnt offerings, with calves of a year old? *Mi.* 6: 6.

To love him with all the heart, and with all the understanding, and with all the soul, and with all the strength, and to love his neighbour as himself, is more than all whole burnt offerings and sacrifices. *Mk.* 12: 33.

See also

Sacrifice.

Bush

She cast the child under one of the shrubs. *Ge.* 21: 15.

The angel of the Lord appeared unto him in a flame of fire out of the midst of a bush. *Ex.* 3: 2.

God called unto him out of the midst of the bush. *Ex.* 3: 4.

The good will of him that dwelt in the bush. *De.* 33: 16.

Of thorns men do not gather figs, nor of a bramble bush gather they grapes. *Lu.* 6: 44.

Business

The king's business required haste. *1 S.* 21: 8.

Surely every man walketh in a vain shew: surely they are disquieted in vain: he heapeth up riches, and knoweth not who shall gather them. *Ps.* 39: 6.

They that go down to the sea in ships, that do business in great waters. *Ps.* 107: 23.

The merchandise of it is better than the merchandise of silver. *Pr.* 3: 14.

Seest thou a man diligent in his business? He shall stand before kings. *Pr.* 22: 29.

Her merchandise and her hire shall be holiness to the Lord. *Is.* 23: 18.

The kingdom of heaven is like unto a merchantman, seeking goodly pearls. *Mat.* 13: 45.

Wist ye not that I must be about my Father's business? *Lu.* 2: 49.

Then came also publicans to be baptized, and said unto him, Master, what shall we do? And he said unto them, Exact no more than that which is appointed you. *Lu.* 3: 12, 13.

That he might know how much every man had gained by trading. *Lu.* 19: 15.

Not slothful in business. *Ro.* 12: 11.

Study to be quiet, and to do your own business. *1 Th.* 4: 11.

Go to now, ye that say, To day or to morrow we will go into such a city, and continue there a year, and buy and sell, and get gain: Whereas ye know not what shall be on the morrow. *Ja.* 4: 13, 14.

The merchants of the earth shall weep and mourn over her; for no man buyeth their merchandise any more. *Re.* 18: 11.

See also

Employee; Employer; Industry; Occupation; Profession; Trade.

Busybody

As thy servant was busy here and there, he was gone. *1 K.* 20: 40.

Why shouldest thou meddle to thy hurt? *2 K.* 14: 10.

Forbear thee from meddling with God. *2 Ch.* 35: 21.

Leave off contention, before it be meddled with. *Pr.* 17: 14.

Every fool will be meddling. *Pr.* 20: 3.

Meddle not with him that flattereth with his lips. *Pr.* 20: 19.

Meddle not with them that are given to change. *Pr.* 24: 21.

He that passeth by, and meddleth with

strife belonging not to him, is like one that taketh a dog by the ears. *Pr.* **26: 17.**

We hear that there are some which walk among you disorderly, working not at all, but are busybodies. *2 Th.* **3: 11.**

Let none of you suffer . . . as a busybody in other men's matters. *1 Pe.* **4: 15.**

See also
Meddling.

Byword

Thou shalt become an astonishment, a proverb, and a byword. *De.* **28: 37.**

Israel shall be a proverb and a byword among all people. *1 K.* **9: 7.**

He hath made me also a byword of the people. *Jb.* **17: 6.**

Now am I their song, yea, I am their byword. *Jb.* **30: 9.**

Thou makest us a byword among the heathen, a shaking of the head among the people. *Ps.* **44: 14.**

See also
Proverb; Saying.

C

Calamity

The flood was forty days upon the earth. *Ge.* **7: 17.**

The day of their calamity is at hand. *De.* **32: 35.**

They prevented me in the day of my calamity: but the Lord was my stay. *2 S.* **22: 19.**

He that is glad at calamities shall not be unpunished. *Pr.* **17: 5.**

The indignation of the Lord is upon all nations, and his fury upon all their armies. *Is.* **34: 2.**

I have caused him to fall upon it suddenly, and terrors upon the city. *Je.* **15: 8.**

The sword is without, and the pestilence and the famine within: he that is in the field shall die with the sword; and he that is in the city, famine and pestilence shall devour him. *Eze.* **7: 15.**

Terrors by reason of the sword shall be upon my people. *Eze.* **21: 12.**

Therefore shall her plagues come in one day, death, and mourning, and famine; and she shall be utterly burned with fire: for strong is the Lord God who judgeth her. *Re.* **18: 8.**

God shall wipe away all tears from their eyes; and there shall be no more death. *Re.* **21: 4.**

See also
Accident; Cataclysm; Catastrophe; Distress; Earthquake; Evil; Famine; Flood; Misery.

Calculation

In blessing I will bless thee, and in multiplying I will multiply thy seed as the stars of the heaven, and as the sand which is upon the sea shore. *Ge.* **22: 17.**

According to the multitude of the years thou shalt increase the price thereof, and according to the fewness of the years thou shalt diminish the price of it. *Le.* **25: 16.**

Howbeit there was no reckoning made with them of the money that was delivered into their hand, because they dealt faithfully. *2 K.* **22: 7.**

Many, O Lord my God, are thy wonderful works which thou hast done, . . . they can not be reckoned up in order unto thee. *Ps.* **40: 5.**

Counting one by one, to find out the account. *Ec.* **7: 27.**

One man among a thousand have I found; but a woman among all those have I not found. *Ec.* **7: 28.**

Therefore will I divide him a portion with the great, and he shall divide the spoil with the strong. *Is.* **53: 12.**

When he had begun to reckon, one was brought unto him, which owed him ten thousand talents. *Mat.* **18: 24.**

Man, who made me a judge or a divider over you? *Lu.* **12: 14.**

Which of you, intending to build a tower, sitteth not down first, and counteth the cost? *Lu.* **14: 28.**

How much owest thou unto my lord? *Lu.* **16: 5.**

How was it then reckoned? *Ro.* **4: 10.**

See also
Count; Division; Multiplication; Prudence.

Calf

Moses . . . took the calf which they had made, and burnt it in the fire, and strawed it upon the water. *Ex.* **32: 19, 20.**

Their cow calveth, and casteth not her calf. *Jb.* **21: 10.**

He maketh them also to skip like a calf. *Ps.* **29: 6.**

The calf and the young lion and the fatling together. *Is.* **11: 6.**

Bring hither the fatted calf, and kill it; and let us eat, and be merry. *Lu.* **15: 23.**

Calf, Golden

He that sacrificeth unto any god, save unto the Lord only, he shall be utterly destroyed. *Ex.* **22: 20.**

All the people brake off the golden earrings which were in their ears, and brought them unto Aaron. And he . . . made it a molten calf. *Ex.* **32: 3, 4.**

These be thy gods, O Israel, which brought thee up out of the land of Egypt. *Ex.* **32: 4.**

He saw the calf, and the dancing: and Moses' anger waxed hot. *Ex.* **32: 19.**

I cast it into the fire, and there came out this calf. *Ex.* **32: 24.**

This people have sinned a great sin, and have made them gods of gold. *Ex.* **32: 31.**

The Lord plagued the people, because they made the calf, which Aaron made. *Ex.* **32: 35.**

Turn ye not unto idols, nor make to yourselves molten gods: I am the Lord your God. *Le.* 19: 4.

Ye had sinned against the Lord your God, and had made you a molten calf. *De.* 9: 16.

Their idols are silver and gold, the work of men's hands. . . . They that make them are like unto them; so is every one that trusteth in them. . . . O Israel, trust thou in the Lord. *Ps.* 115: 4, 8, 9.

They say of them, let the men that sacrifice kiss the calves. *Ho.* 13: 2.

They made a calf in those days, and offered sacrifice unto the idol, and rejoiced in the works of their own hands. *Ac.* 7: 41.

Call

Go in this thy might, and thou shalt save Israel from the hand of the Midianites: have not I sent thee? *Ju.* 6: 14.

The Lord called yet again, Samuel. And Samuel arose and went to Eli, and said, Here am I; for thou didst call me. *1 S.* 3: 6.

Call ye on the name of your gods, and I will call on the name of the Lord. *1 K.* 18: 24.

Hear me when I call, O God of my righteousness. *Ps.* 4: 1.

His ears are open unto their cry. *Ps.* 34: 15.

He shall call upon me, and I will answer him: I will be with him in trouble. *Ps.* 91: 15.

Cry unto her, that her warfare is accomplished, that her iniquity is pardoned. *Is.* 40: 2.

The voice said, Cry. And he said, What shall I cry? *Is.* 40: 6.

Thou shalt call thy walls Salvation, and thy gates Praise. *Is.* 60: 18.

When I called, none did answer. *Is.* 66: 4.

Ye call me Master and Lord: and ye say well; for so I am. *Jn.* 13: 13.

Henceforth I call you not servants; for the servant knoweth not what his lord doeth: but I have called you friends. *Jn.* 15: 15.

God hath shewed me that I should not call any man common or unclean. *Ac.* 10: 28.

There stood a man of Macedonia, and prayed him, saying, Come over into Macedonia, and help us. *Ac.* 16: 9.

Ye have been called unto liberty. *Ga.* 5: 13.

See also

Christ, Call of; Cry; God, Call of; Invitation; Shout; Summons.

Calling

I heard the voice of the Lord, saying, Whom shall I send, and who will go for us? Then said I, Here am I; send me. *Is.* 6: 8.

The promise is unto you, and to your children, and to all that are afar off, even as many as the Lord our God shall call. *Ac.* 2: 39.

Go thy way: for he is a chosen vessel unto me. *Ac.* 9: 15.

Not many wise men after the flesh, not many mighty, not many noble, are called. *1 Co.* 1: 26.

He that is called in the Lord, being a servant, is the Lord's freeman. *1 Co.* 7: 22.

Brethren, let every man, wherein he is called, therein abide with God. *1 Co.* 7: 24.

I therefore, the prisoner of the Lord, beseech you that ye walk worthy of the vocation wherewith ye are called. *Ep.* 4: 1.

Ye are called in one hope of your calling. *Ep.* 4: 4.

I press toward the mark for the prize of the high calling of God in Christ Jesus. *Ph.* 3: 14.

We pray always for you, that our God would count you worthy of this calling. *2 Th.* 1: 11.

Who hath saved us, and called us with an holy calling. *2 Ti.* 1: 9.

See also

Occupation; Profession; Vocation.

Callousness

Thou hast not given water to the weary to drink, and thou hast withholden bread from the hungry. *Jb.* 22: 7.

The poor is hated even of his own neighbour. *Pr.* 14: 20.

Is it nothing to you, all ye that pass by? behold, and see if there be any sorrow like unto my sorrow. *La.* 1: 12.

All the house of Israel are impudent and hardhearted. *Eze.* 3: 7.

When his heart was lifted up, and his mind hardened in pride, he was deposed from his kingly throne. *Da.* 5: 20.

They sold the righteous for silver, and the poor for a pair of shoes. *Am.* 2: 6.

Ye were as a firebrand plucked out of the burning: yet have ye not returned unto me. *Am.* 4: 11.

They made light of it, and went their ways. *Mat.* 22: 5.

Inasmuch as ye did it not to one of the least of these, ye did it not to me. *Mat.* 25: 45.

Being grieved for the hardness of their hearts. *Mk.* 3: 5.

He . . . upbraided them with their unbelief and hardness of heart. *Mk.* 16: 14.

By chance there came down a certain priest that way: and when he saw him, he passed by on the other side. *Lu.* 10: 31.

Sir, I have no man, when the water is troubled, to put me into the pool. *Jn.* 5: 7.

And Gallio cared for none of those things. *Ac.* 18: 17.

See also

Apathy; Cruelty; Hardness; Harshness; Indifference.

Calm

Acquaint now thyself with him, and be at peace. *Jb.* 22: 21.

Commune with your own heart upon your bed, and be still. *Ps.* 4: 4.

Be still, and know that I am God. *Ps.* 46: 10.

Thou rulest the raging of the sea: when the waves thereof arise, thou stillest them. *Ps.* 89: 9.

He maketh the storm a calm, so that the waves thereof are still. *Ps.* 107: 29.

Great peace have they which love thy law. *Ps.* 119: 165.

Then he arose, and rebuked the winds and the sea; and there was a great calm. *Mat.* 8: 26.

Let us therefore follow after the things which make for peace. *Ro.* 14: 19.

The fruit of the Spirit is love, joy, peace. *Ga.* 5: 22.

Let us labour therefore to enter into that rest. *He.* 4: 11.

See also
Ease; Peace; Quiet; Repose; Rest; Stillness; Tranquillity.

Calumny

Thou shalt not bear false witness against thy neighbour. *Ex.* 20: 16.
False witnesses are risen up against me. *Ps.* 27: 12.
The words of his mouth were smoother than butter, but war was in his heart. *Ps.* 55: 21.
His words were softer than oil, yet were they drawn swords. *Ps.* 55: 21.
Let the mischief of their own lips cover them. *Ps.* 140: 9.
Thou are snared with the words of thy mouth, thou art taken with the words of thy mouth. *Pr.* 6: 2.
He that refraineth his lips is wise. *Pr.* 10: 19.
He that keepeth his mouth keepeth his life. *Pr.* 13: 3.
A wholesome tongue is a tree of life: but perverseness therein is a breach in the spirit. *Pr.* 15: 4.
An ungodly man diggeth up evil. *Pr.* 16: 27.
Seest thou a man that is hasty in his words? there is more hope of a fool than of him. *Pr.* 29: 20.
Blessed are ye, when men shall revile you. *Mat.* 5: 11.
They that passed by reviled him. *Mat.* 27: 39.
They that were crucified with him reviled him. *Mk.* 15: 32.
Do violence to no man, neither accuse any falsely. *Lu.* 3: 14.
Being reviled, we bless. *1 Co.* 4: 12.
Who, when he was reviled, reviled not again. *1 Pe.* 2: 23.
Presumptuous are they, selfwilled, they are not afraid to speak evil of dignities. *2 Pe.* 2: 10.
See also
Backbiting; Falsehood; Gossip; Lie; Scandal; Slander; Talebearing.

Calvary

With him they crucify two thieves; the one on his right hand, and the other on his left. *Mk.* 15: 27.
When they were come to the place, which is called Calvary, there they crucified him. *Lu.* 23: 33.
Now there stood by the cross of Jesus his mother, and his mother's sister, Mary the wife of Cleophas, and Mary Magdalene. *Jn.* 19: 25.
Even Christ our passover is sacrificed for us. *1 Co.* 5: 7.
But God forbid that I should glory, save in the cross of our Lord Jesus Christ, by whom the world is crucified unto me, and I unto the world. *Ga.* 6: 14.
He humbled himself, and became obedient unto death, even the death of the cross. *Ph.* 2: 8.
Having made peace through the blood of his cross. *Col.* 1: 20.
Who for the joy that was set before him endured the cross, despising the shame. *He.* 12: 2.

See also
Christ, Cross of; Christ, Crucifixion of; Christ, Death of; Christ, Sacrifice of; Christ, Suffering of; Cross; Friday, Good; Golgotha.

Camel

Behold, the hand of the Lord is upon thy cattle which is in the field, upon the horses, upon the asses, upon the camels. *Ex.* 9: 3.
The multitude of camels shall cover thee. *Is.* 60: 6.
Thou art a swift dromedary traversing her ways. *Je.* 2: 23.
John had his raiment of camel's hair. *Mat.* 3: 4.
It is easier for a camel to go through the eye of a needle, than for a rich man to enter into the kingdom of God. *Mat.* 19: 24.
Ye blind guides, which strain at a gnat, and swallow a camel. *Mat.* 23: 24.

Camp

The angel of god . . . went before the camp of Israel. *Ex.* 14: 19.
Israel camped before the mount. *Ex.* 19: 2.
The Lord thy God walketh in the midst of thy camp. *De.* 23: 14.
Though an host should encamp against me, my heart shall not fear. *Ps.* 27: 3.
The angel of the Lord encampeth round about them that fear him, and delivereth them. *Ps.* 34: 7.
I will camp against thee round about. *Is.* 29: 3.
Thy crowned are as the locusts, and thy captains as the great grasshoppers, which camp in the hedges in the cold day. *Na.* 3: 17.
I will encamp about mine house because of the army: . . . and no oppressor shall pass through them any more. *Zch.* 9: 8.
Let us go forth therefore unto him without the camp, bearing his reproach. *He.* 13: 13.
They went up on the breadth of the earth, and compassed the camp of the saints about. *Re.* 20: 9.

Cancellation

Blot me, I pray thee, out of thy book which thou hast written. *Ex.* 32: 32.
Let me alone, that I may destroy them, and blot out their name from under heaven. *De.* 9: 14.
According unto the multitude of thy tender mercies blot out my transgressions. *Ps.* 51: 1.
They have made void thy law. *Ps.* 119: 126.
Though your sins be as scarlet, they shall be as white as snow. *Is.* 1: 18.
The idols he shall utterly abolish. *Is.* 2: 18.
My righteousness shall not be abolished. *Is.* 51: 6.
Forgive us our debts. *Mat.* 6: 12.
The lord . . . was moved with compassion, and loosed him, and forgave him the debt. *Mat.* 18: 27.
When they had nothing to pay, he frankly forgave them both. *Lu.* 7: 42.
Whosoever believeth in him shall receive remission of sins. *Ac.* 10: 43.
Arise, and be baptized, and wash away thy sins. *Ac.* 22: 16.
Blotting out the handwriting of ordinances that was against us, which was contrary to us,

and took it out of the way, nailing it to his cross. *Col.* **2: 14.**

Jesus Christ . . . hath abolished death. *2 Ti.* **1: 10.**

He that overcometh, the same shall be clothed in white raiment; and I will not blot out his name out of the book of life. *Re.* **3: 5.**

See also
Abolition; Annulment.

Candle

The light shall be dark in his tabernacle, and his candle shall be put out with him. *Jb.* **18: 6.**

Oh that I were as in months past, as in the days when God preserved me; When his candle shined upon my head. *Jb.* **29: 2, 3.**

Thou wilt light my candle. *Ps.* **18: 28.**

The spirit of man is the candle of the Lord. *Pr.* **20: 27.**

Her candle goeth not out by night. *Pr.* **31: 18.**

I will take from them . . . the light of the candle. *Je.* **25: 10.**

I will search Jerusalem with candles. *Zph.* **1: 12.**

Neither do men light a candle, and put it under a bushel. *Mat.* **5: 15.**

If thy whole body therefore be full of light, having no part dark, the whole shall be full of light, as when the bright shining of a candle doth give thee light. *Lu.* **11: 36.**

Take heed, as unto a light that shineth in a dark place. *2 Pe.* **1: 19.**

Remember therefore from whence thou art fallen, and repent, . . . or else I . . . will remove thy candlestick out of his place. *Re.* **2: 5.**

These are . . . the two candlesticks standing before the God of the earth. *Re.* **11: 4.**

The light of a candle shall shine no more in thee. *Re.* **18: 23.**

There shall be no night there; and they shall need no candle, neither light of the sun. *Re.* **22: 5.**

See also
Gleam; Ray.

Candor

As for such as turn aside unto their crooked ways, the Lord shall lead them forth with the workers of iniquity. *Ps.* **125: 5.**

Trust ye not in lying words, saying, The temple of the Lord, The temple of the Lord, The temple of the Lord, are these. *Je.* **7: 4.**

If thou be the Christ, tell us plainly. *Jn.* **10: 24.**

If it were not so, I would have told you. *Jn.* **14: 2.**

These things have I spoken unto you in proverbs: but the time cometh, when I shall no more speak unto you in proverbs, but I shall shew you plainly of the Father. *Jn.* **16: 25.**

Let love be without dissimulation. *Ro.* **12: 9.**

So likewise ye, except ye utter by the tongue words easy to be understood, how shall it be known what is spoken? *1 Co.* **14: 9.**

Seeing then that we have such hope, we use great plainness of speech. *2 Co.* **3: 12.**

See also
Frankness.

Cant

An hypocrite shall not come before him. *Jb.* **13: 16.**

Give ear unto my prayer, that goeth not out of feigned lips. *Ps.* **17: 1.**

Who shall ascend into the hill of the Lord? . . . He that . . . hath not lifted up his soul unto vanity, nor sworn deceitfully. *Ps.* **24: 3, 4.**

When thou doest thine alms, do not sound a trumpet before thee, as the hypocrites do. *Mat.* **6: 2.**

When thou prayest, thou shalt not be as the hypocrites are. *Mat.* **6: 5.**

O ye hypocrites, ye can discern the face of the sky; but can ye not discern the signs of the times? *Mat.* **16: 3.**

Thou hypocrite, cast out first the beam out of thine own eye, and then shalt thou see clearly to pull out the mote that is in thy brother's eye. *Lu.* **6: 42.**

Why call ye me Lord, Lord, and do not the things which I say? *Lu.* **6: 46.**

See also
Bigotry; Hypocrisy.

Capacity

This thing is too heavy for thee; thou art not able to perform it thyself alone. *Ex.* **18: 18.**

If so be the Lord will be with me, then I shall be able to drive them out. *Jos.* **14: 12.**

Fear not them which kill the body, but are not able to kill the soul. *Mat.* **10: 28.**

Nothing shall be impossible unto you. *Mat.* **17: 20.**

Can ye drink of the cup that I drink of? . . . And they said unto him, We can. *Mk.* **10: 38, 39.**

Many . . . will seek to enter in, and shall not be able. *Lu.* **13: 24.**

Lest haply, after he hath laid the foundation, and is not able to finish it, all that behold it begin to mock him. *Lu.* **14: 29.**

Tarry ye in the city of Jerusalem, until ye be endued with power from on high. *Lu.* **24: 49.**

They were not able to draw it for the multitude of fishes. *Jn.* **21: 6.**

I have fed you with milk, and not with meat: for hitherto ye were not able to bear it, neither yet now are ye able. *1 Co.* **3: 2.**

My grace is sufficient for thee: for my strength is made perfect in weakness. *2 Co.* **12: 9.**

That ye, being rooted and grounded in love, May be able to comprehend with all saints what is the breadth, and length, and depth, and height. *Ep.* **3: 17, 18.**

I can do all things through Christ which strengtheneth me. *Ph.* **4: 13.**

See also
Ability; Aptitude; Endowment; Gift; Skill; Talent.

Capital

Thou shalt remember the Lord thy God: for it is he that giveth thee power to get wealth. *De.* **8: 18.**

I pray you, let us leave off this usury. *Ne.* **5: 10.**

Thou hast blessed the work of his hands,

and his substance is increased in the land. *Jb.* 1: 10.

Lord, who shall abide in thy tabernacle? . . . He that putteth not out his money to usury. *Ps.* 15: 1, 5.

Thou sellest thy people for nought, and dost not increase thy wealth by their price. *Ps.* 44: 12.

If ricnes increase, set not your heart upon them. *Ps.* 62: 10.

The rich man's wealth is his strong city: the destruction of the poor is their poverty. *Pr.* 10: 15.

By thy great wisdom and by thy traffick hast thou increased thy riches, and thine heart is lifted up because of thy riches. *Eze.* 28: 5.

The kingdom of heaven is like unto treasure hid in the field; the which when a man hath found, he hideth, and for joy thereof goeth and selleth all that he hath, and buyeth that field. *Mat.* 13: 44.

Unto whomsoever much is given, of him shall be much required: and to whom men have committed much, of him they will ask more. *Lu.* 12: 48.

A certain nobleman . . . called his ten servants, and delivered them ten pounds, and said unto them, Occupy till I come. *Lu.* 19: 12, 13.

Bringing into captivity every thought to the obedience of Christ. *2 Co.* 10: 5.

Captain

The Lord hath commanded him to be captain over his people. *1 S.* 13: 14.

God himself is with us for our captain. *2 Ch.* 13: 12.

Thou hast led captivity captive. *Ps.* 68: 18.

When the centurion saw what was done, he glorified God, saying, Certainly this was a righteous man. *Lu.* 23: 47.

It became him . . . to make the captain of their salvation perfect through sufferings. *He.* 2: 10.

Come and gather yourselves together unto the supper of the great God; That ye may eat the flesh of kings, and the flesh of captains. *Re.* 19: 17, 18.

See also
Christ, the Captain.

Captivity

Remember this day, in which ye came out from Egypt. *Ex.* 13: 3.

We were bondmen; yet our God hath not forsaken us in our bondage. *Ezr.* 9: 9.

He looseth the bond of kings. *Jb.* 12: 18.

My people are gone into captivity, because they have no knowledge. *Is.* 5: 13.

The Lord hath . . . sent me to . . . proclaim liberty to the captives, and the opening of the prison to them that are bound. *Is.* 61: 1.

I have caused you to be carried away captives. *Je.* 29: 7.

Hear ye therefore the word of the Lord, all ye of the captivity. *Je.* 29: 20.

I will break his yoke from off thy neck, and will burst thy bonds. *Je.* 30: 8.

Then will I bring again the captivity of thy captives in the midst of them. *Eze.* 16: 53.

Bringing into captivity every thought to the obedience of Christ. *2 Co.* 10: 5.

Remember my bonds. *Col.* 4: 18.

I John, . . . was in the isle that is called Patmos, for the word of God, and for the testimony of Jesus Christ. I was in the Spirit on the Lord's day, and heard behind me a great voice, as of a trumpet. *Re.* 1: 9, 10.

See also
Bondage; Imprisonment; Prison; Slavery; Subjection.

Capture

God hath overthrown me, and hath compassed me with his net. *Jb.* 19: 6.

In the net which they hid is their own foot taken. *Ps.* 9: 15.

The wicked . . . doth catch the poor, when he draweth him into his net. *Ps.* 10: 4, 9.

When the Lord bringeth back the captivity of his people, Jacob shall rejoice, and Israel shall be glad. *Ps.* 14: 7.

Whoso causeth the righteous to go astray in an evil way, he shall fall himself into his own pit. *Pr.* 28: 10.

The Lord hath anointed me . . . to proclaim liberty to the captives. *Is.* 61: 1.

Though thou shouldest make thy nest as high as the eagle, I will bring thee down from thence. *Je.* 49: 16.

Many of the saints did I shut up in prison. *Ac.* 26: 10.

Who shall deliver me from the body of this death? *Ro.* 7: 24.

Bringing into captivity every thought to the obedience of Christ. *2 Co.* 10: 5.

See also
Arrest; Captivity; Imprisonment; Prison; Slavery.

Care

He heapeth up riches, and knoweth not who shall gather them. *Ps.* 39: 6.

Cast thy burden upon the Lord, and he shall sustain thee. *Ps.* 55: 22.

In the multitude of my thoughts within me thy comforts delight my soul. *Ps.* 94: 19.

It is vain for you to rise up early, to sit up late, to eat the bread of sorrows. *Ps.* 127: 2.

Fret not thyself because of evil men. *Pr.* 24: 19.

To the sinner he giveth travail. *Ec.* 2: 26.

Watch and pray, that ye enter not into temptation. *Mat.* 26: 41.

Master, carest thou not that we perish? *Mk.* 4: 38.

They . . . are choked with cares and riches and pleasures of this life, and bring no fruit to perfection. *Lu.* 8: 14.

Take heed to yourselves, lest at any time your hearts be overcharged with surfeiting. *Lu.* 21: 34.

The hireling . . . careth not for the sheep. *Jn.* 10: 13.

Bear ye one another's burdens, and so fulfil the law of Christ. *Ga.* 6: 2.

See then that ye walk circumspectly. *Ep.* 5: 15.

Be careful for nothing. *Ph.* 4: 6.

Casting all your care upon him; for he careth for you. *1 Pe.* 5: 7.

See also
Anxiety; Burden; Charge; Cherishment; Concern; Duty; Fretfulness; God, the Keeper; God, Protection of; God, Providence of;

Preservation; Responsibility; Solicitude; Trial; Trouble; Vexation; Weight; Worry; Yoke.

Career

I will run the way of thy commandments, when thou shalt enlarge my heart. *Ps.* 119: 32.

Their feet run to evil. *Pr.* 1: 16.

Their course is evil. *Je.* 23: 10.

Neither count I my life dear unto myself, so that I might finish my course with joy, and the ministry, which I have received of the Lord Jesus. *Ac.* 20: 24.

As the Lord hath called every one, so let him walk. *1 Co.* 7: 17.

Brethren, let every man, wherein he is called, therein abide with God. *1 Co.* 7: 24.

Know ye not that they which run in a race run all, but one receiveth the prize? *1 Co.* 9: 24.

He gave some, apostles; and some, prophets; and some, evangelists; and some, pastors and teachers. *Ep.* 4: 11.

I have not run in vain, neither laboured in vain. *Ph.* 2: 16.

I have fought a good fight, I have finished my course, I have kept the faith. *2 Ti.* 4: 7.

Let us run with patience the race that is set before us. *He.* 12: 1.

See also

Calling; Occupation; Profession; Vocation.

Carelessness

Hear now this, thou that art given to pleasures, that dwellest carelessly, that sayest in thine heart, I am, and none else beside me. *Is.* 47: 8.

They hear thy words, but they do them not. *Eze.* 33: 32.

I will send a fire . . . among them that dwell carelessly in the isles: and they shall know that I am the Lord. *Eze.* 39: 6.

This is the rejoicing city that dwelt carelessly. *Zph.* 2: 15.

Strait is the gate, and narrow is the way, which leadeth unto life, and few there be that find it. *Mat.* 7: 14.

While men slept, his enemy came and sowed tares. *Mat.* 13: 25.

We ought to give the more earnest heed to the things which we have heard, lest at any time we should let them slip. *He.* 2: 1.

See also

Heedlessness; Indifference; Worldliness.

Caress

Come near now, and kiss me, my son. *Ge.* 27: 26.

Kiss the Son, lest he be angry, and ye perish from the way. *Ps.* 2: 12.

Righteousness and peace have kissed each other. *Ps.* 85: 10.

Be thou ravished always with her love. *Pr.* 5: 19.

She caught him, and kissed him. *Pr.* 7: 13.

Every man shall kiss his lips that giveth a right answer. *Pr.* 24: 26.

A time to embrace, and a time to refrain from embracing. *Ec.* 3: 5.

Let him kiss me with the kisses of his mouth. *S. of S.* 1: 2.

Thy lips, O my spouse, drop as the honeycomb. *S. of S.* 4: 11.

His mouth is most sweet. *S. of S.* 5: 16.

Thou gavest me no kiss: but this woman since the time I came in hath not ceased to kiss my feet. *Lu.* 7: 45.

The dogs came and licked his sores. *Lu.* 16: 21.

They brought unto him also infants, that he would touch them. *Lu.* 18: 15.

Judas . . . drew near unto Jesus to kiss him. *Lu.* 22: 47.

Be kindly affectioned one to another. *Ro.* 12: 10.

See also

Affection; Attachment; Cherishment; Kiss; Love; Tenderness.

Carnality

Thou shalt not commit adultery. *Ex.* 20: 14.

I will make thy lewdness to cease from thee. *Eze.* 23: 27.

The lusts of other things entering in, choke the word. *Mk.* 4: 19.

He that is of the earth is earthly. *Jn.* 3: 31.

Ye judge after the flesh; I judge no man. *Jn.* 8: 15.

The men, leaving the natural use of the woman, burned in their lust one toward another. *Ro.* 1: 27.

I am carnal, sold under sin. *Ro.* 7: 14.

They that are after the flesh do mind the things of the flesh; but they that are after the Spirit the things of the Spirit. *Ro.* 8: 5.

To be carnally minded is death. *Ro.* 8: 6.

The carnal mind is enmity against God. *Ro.* 8: 7.

The body is not for fornication, but for the Lord. *1 Co.* 6: 13.

We should not lust after evil things. *1 Co.* 10: 6.

Whilst we are at home in the body, we are absent from the Lord. *2 Co.* 5: 6.

The weapons of our warfare are not carnal. *2 Co.* 10: 4.

Having begun in the Spirit, are ye now made perfect by the flesh? *Ga.* 3: 3.

Use not liberty for an occasion to the flesh, but by love serve one another. *Ga.* 5: 13.

If any other man thinketh that he hath whereof he might trust in the flesh, I more. *Ph.* 3: 4.

God is their belly. *Ph.* 3: 19.

Not in the lust of concupiscence. *1 Th.* 4: 5.

This wisdom descendeth not from above, but is earthly, sensual, devilish. *Ja.* 3: 15.

See also

Adultery; Brothel; Debauchery; Flesh; Fornication; Lust; Prostitute; Sinfulness.

Carol

Then shall the trees of the wood sing out at the presence of the Lord. *1 Ch.* 16: 33.

Sing unto him a new song. *Ps.* 33: 3.

The fowls of the heaven . . . sing among the branches. *Ps.* 104: 12.

Their voice shall sing in the windows. *Zph.* 2: 14.

Unto you is born this day in the city of David a Saviour, which is Christ the Lord. *Lu.* 2: 11.

Suddenly there was with the angel a multitude of the heavenly host praising God, and saying, Glory to God in the highest. *Lu.* 2: 13, 14.

See also

Christ, Birth of; Christmas; Nativity.

Carpenter

The king . . . hired masons and carpenters to repair the house of the Lord. *2 Ch.* **24:** 12.

Wisdom hath builded her house, she hath hewn out her seven pillars. *Pr.* 9: 1.

Woe unto him that buildeth his house by unrighteousness, and his chambers by wrong. *Je.* 22: 13.

Go up to the mountain, and bring wood, and build the house; and I will take pleasure in it, and I will be glorified, saith the Lord. *Hag.* 1: 8.

He is like a man which built an house. *Lu.* 6: 48.

This will I do: I will pull down my barns, and build greater. *Lu.* 12: 18.

As a wise masterbuilder, I have laid the foundation, and another buildeth thereon. *1 Co.* 3: 10.

Every house is builded by some man; but he that built all things is God. *He.* 3: 4.
See also
Builder; Christ, the Carpenter.

Caste

Who remembered us in our low estate. *Ps.* 136: 23.

Lo, I am come to great estate. *Ec.* 1: 16.

Is Israel a servant? is he a homeborn slave? *Je.* 2: 14.

Of a truth I perceive that God is no respector of persons. *Ac.* 10: 34.

Condescend to men of low estate. *Ro.* 12: 16.

There is neither bond nor free, . . . for ye are all one in Christ Jesus. *Ga.* 3: 28.

If ye have respect to persons, ye commit sin. *Ja.* 2: 9.
See also
Class; Equality; Inequality; Persons, Respect for; Respect.

Castle

David took the castle of Zion, which is the city of David. *1 Ch.* 11: 5.

The Lord is my rock, and my fortress. *Ps.* 18: 2.

They shall enter into the king's palace. *Ps.* 45: 15.

Their contentions are like the bars of a castle. *Pr.* 18: 19.

If she be a wall, we will build upon her a palace of silver. *S. of S.* 8: 9.

Thorns shall come up in her palaces. *Is.* 34: 13.

I have set thee for a tower and a fortress among my people. *Je.* 6: 27.
See also
Fortress; Palace; Tower.

Cataclysm

Behold, I, even I, do bring a flood of waters upon the earth, to destroy all flesh. *Ge.* 6: 17.

I will establish my covenant with you; neither shall all flesh be cut off any more by the waters of a flood; neither shall there any more be a flood to destroy the earth. *Ge.* 9: 11.

Then the Lord rained upon Sodom and Gomorrah brimstone and fire from the Lord out of heaven. *Ge.* 19: 24.

The day of their calamity is at hand. *De.* 32: 35.

Behold, the Lord passed by, and a great and strong wind rent the mountains, and brake to pieces the rocks before the Lord: but the Lord was not in the wind: and after the wind an earthquake; but the Lord was not in the earthquake: and after the earthquake a fire; but the Lord was not in the fire. *1 K.* 19: 11, 12.

The fire of God came down from heaven, and consumed him. *2 K.* 1: 12.

The fire of God is fallen from heaven, and hath burned up the sheep, and the servants, and consumed them. *Jb.* 1: 16.

Which shaketh the earth out of her place, and the pillars thereof tremble. *Jb.* 9: 6.

In the shadow of thy wings will I make my refuge, until these calamities be overpast. *Ps.* 57: 1.

When thou passest through the waters, I will be with thee; and through the rivers, they shall not overflow thee: when thou walkest through the fire, thou shalt not be burned. *Is.* 43: 2.

The Lord will come with fire, and with his chariots like a whirlwind, to render his anger with fury, and his rebuke with flames of fire. *Is.* 66: 15.

There shall be famines, and pestilences, and earthquakes. *Mat.* 24: 7.

There was a great earthquake; such as was not since men were upon the earth, so mighty an earthquake, and so great. *Re.* 16: 18.
See also
Calamity; Catastrophe; Disaster; Earthquake; Famine; Flood.

Catastrophe

I will destroy man whom I have created from the face of the earth. *Ge.* 6: 7.

Behold, I, even I, do bring a flood of waters upon the earth. *Ge.* 6: 17.

Oh that my grief were throughly weighed, and my calamity laid in the balances together! *Jb.* 6: 2.

They shall not be ashamed in the evil time: and in the days of famine they shall be satisfied. *Ps.* 37: 19.

Let not the waterflood overflow me, neither let the deep swallow me up. *Ps.* 69: 15.

Surely he shall deliver thee from the . . . noisome pestilence. *Ps.* 91: 3.

I also will laugh at your calamity; I will mock when your fear cometh. *Pr.* 1: 26.

They did not stand, because the day of their calamity was come upon them, and the time of their visitation. *Je.* 46: 21.

As in the days that were before the flood they were eating and drinking, marrying and giving in marriage, until the day that Noe entered into the ark, And knew not until the flood came, . . . so shall also the coming of the Son of man be. *Mat* 24: 38, 39.

I am come to send fire on the earth; and what will I, if it be already kindled? *Lu.* 12: 49.
See also
Calamity; Cataclysm; Disaster; Earthquake; Famine; Flood.

Catholicity

Look unto me, and be ye saved, all the ends of the earth: for I am God, and there is none else. *Is.* 45: 22.

Unto me every knee shall bow, every tongue shall swear. *Is.* 45: 23.

This gospel of the kingdom shall be preached

in all the world for a witness unto all nations; and then shall the end come. *Mat.* **24: 14.**

Ye shall be witnesses unto me both in Jerusalem, and in all Judæa, and in Samaria, and unto the uttermost part of the earth. *Ac.* **1: 8.**

When the apostles which were at Jerusalem heard that Samaria had received the word of God, they sent unto them Peter and John. *Ac.* **8: 14.**

Can any man forbid water, that these should not be baptized, which have received the Holy Ghost as well as we? *Ac.* **10: 47.**

They . . . glorified God, saying, Then hath God also to the Gentiles granted repentance unto life. *Ac.* **11: 18.**

My sentence is, that we trouble not them, which from among the Gentiles are turned to God. *Ac.* **15: 19.**

They gave to me and Barnabas the right hands of fellowship; that we should go unto the heathen, and they unto the circumcision. *Ga.* **2: 9.**

There is neither Jew nor Greek, there is neither bond nor free, there is neither male nor female: for ye are all one in Christ Jesus. *Ga.* **3: 28.**

At the name of Jesus every knee should bow, of things in heaven, and things in earth, and things under the earth. *Ph.* **2: 10.**

All nations shall come and worship before thee. *Re.* **15: 4.**

See also

Oneness; Unity; Universality; Universe.

Cattle

God made the beast of the earth after his kind, and cattle after their kind. *Ge.* **1: 25.**

Every beast of the forest is mine, and the cattle upon a thousand hills. *Ps.* **50: 10.**

He causeth the grass to grow for the cattle. *Ps.* **104: 14.**

Beasts, and all cattle; . . . Let them praise the name of the Lord. *Ps.* **148: 10, 13.**

The ox knoweth his owner, and the ass his master's crib: but Israel doth not know, my people doth not consider. *Is.* **1: 3.**

The cow and the bear shall feed; their young ones shall lie down together: and the lion shall eat straw like the ox. *Is.* **11: 7.**

Neither can men hear the voice of the cattle; both the fowl of the heavens and the beast are fled; they are gone. *Je.* **9: 10.**

The herds of cattle are perplexed, because they have no pasture. *Jo.* **1: 18.**

See also

Herd; Ox; Pasture.

Cause

The Lord therefore be judge, and judge between me and thee, and see, and plead my cause, and deliver me out of thine hand. *1 S.* **24: 15.**

Blessed be the Lord, that hath pleaded the cause of my reproach. *1 S.* **25: 39.**

Unto God would I commit my cause. *Jb.* **5: 8.**

I know that the Lord will maintain the cause of the afflicted, and the right of the poor. *Ps.* **140: 12.**

Plead the cause of the poor and needy. *Pr.* **31: 9.**

To every thing there is a season, and a time to every purpose under the heaven. *Ec.* **3: 1.**

Produce your cause, saith the Lord; bring forth your strong reasons. *Is.* **41: 21.**

To subvert a man in his cause, the Lord approveth not. *La.* **3: 36.**

Whosoever is angry with his brother without a cause shall be in danger of the judgment. *Mat.* **5: 22.**

To this end was I born, and for this cause came I into the world, that I should bear witness unto the truth. *Jn.* **18: 37.**

The same time there arose no small stir about that way. *Ac.* **19: 23.**

After the way which they call heresy, so worship I the God of my fathers. *Ac.* **24: 14.**

One thing I do. *Ph.* **3: 13.**

See also

Argument; Motive; Purpose; Reason.

Caution

Ye shall even warn them that they trespass not against the Lord. *2 Ch.* **19: 10.**

A good man . . . will guide his affairs with discretion. *Ps.* **112: 5.**

Keep sound wisdom and discretion. *Pr.* **3: 21.**

A prudent man foreseeth the evil, and hideth himself. *Pr.* **22: 3.**

He that observeth the wind shall not sow; and he that regardeth the clouds shall not reap. *Ec.* **11: 4.**

Watchman, what of the night? The watchman said, The morning cometh, and also the night. *Is.* **21: 11, 12.**

If the watchman see the sword come, and blow not the trumpet, and the people be not warned; if the sword come, and take any person from among them, . . . his blood will I require at the watchman's hand. *Eze.* **33: 6.**

The prudent shall keep silence in that time; for it is an evil time. *Am.* **5: 13.**

Being warned of God in a dream, . . . they departed into their own country another way. *Mat.* **2: 12.**

O generation of vipers, who hath warned you to flee from the wrath to come? *Mat.* **3: 7.**

As my beloved sons I warn you. *1 Co.* **4: 14.**

Watch ye, stand fast in the faith, quit you like men, be strong. *1 Co.* **16: 13.**

By faith Noah being warned of God of things not seen as yet, moved with fear, prepared an ark to the saving of his house. *He.* **11: 7.**

Be watchful, and strengthen the things which remain. *Re.* **3: 2.**

See also

Admonition; Anxiety; Care; Prudence; Warning.

Cedar

The thistle that was in Lebanon sent to the cedar that was in Lebanon, saying, Give thy daughter to my son to wife. *2 K.* **14: 9.**

The voice of the Lord breaketh the cedars; yea, the Lord breaketh the cedars of Lebanon. *Ps.* **29: 5.**

The boughs thereof were like the goodly cedars. *Ps.* **80: 10.**

The righteous . . . shall grow like a cedar in Lebanon. *Ps.* **92: 12.**

I will plant in the wilderness the cedar. *Is.* 41: 19.

Open thy doors, O Lebanon, that the fire may devour thy cedars. *Zch.* 11: 1.

Howl, fir tree; for the cedar is fallen. *Zch.* 11: 2.

Celebration

From even unto even, shall ye celebrate your sabbath. *Le.* 23: 32.

In the day of your gladness, and in your solemn days, and in the beginnings of your months, ye shall blow with the trumpets. *Nu.* 10: 10.

Death cannot celebrate thee. *Is.* 38: 18.

What will ye do in the solemn day, and in the day of the feast of the Lord? *Ho.* 9: 5.

I hate, I despise your feast days, and I will not smell in your solemn assemblies. *Am.* 5: 21.

Where wilt thou that we prepare for thee to eat the passover? *Mat.* 26: 17.

Christ our passover is sacrificed for us. *1 Co.* 5: 7.

This do ye, as oft as ye drink it, in remembrance of me. *1 Co.* 11: 25.

See also

Anniversary; Ceremony; Commemoration; Festival; Holiday; Observance; Ritual; Sacrament.

Celebrity

The same became mighty men which were of old, men of renown. *Ge.* 6: 4.

The Lord was with Joshua; and his fame was noised throughout all the country. *Jos.* 6: 27.

Blessed be the Lord, which hath not left thee this day without a kinsman, that his name may be famous in Israel. *Ru.* 4: 14.

There is none like thee, neither is there any God beside thee, according to all that we have heard with our ears. *2 S.* 7: 22.

The queen of Sheba heard of the fame of Solomon. *1 K.* 10: 1.

Thy wisdom and thy prosperity exceedeth the fame which I heard. *1 K.* 10: 7.

David . . . died in a good old age, full of days, riches, and honour. *1 Ch.* 29: 26, 28.

His fame went throughout all Syria. *Mat.* 4: 24.

A prophet is not without honour, save in his own country. *Mat.* 13: 57.

Christ Jesus . . . made himself of no reputation, and took upon him the form of a servant. *Ph.* 2: 5, 7.

God also hath highly exalted him, and given him a name which is above every name. *Ph.* 2: 9.

See also

Distinction; Fame; Honor; Name; Renown; Reputation.

Celibacy

In the resurrection they neither marry, nor are given in marriage, but are as the angels of God in heaven. *Mat.* 22: 30.

I say therefore to the unmarried and widows, It is good for them if they abide even as I. *1 Co.* 7: 8.

He that is unmarried careth for the things that belong to the Lord. *1 Co.* 7: 32.

See also

Marriage.

Censoriousness

Judge not, that ye be not judged. *Mat.* 7: 1.

With what judgment ye judge, ye shall be judged: and with what measure ye mete, it shall be measured to you again. *Mat.* 7: 2.

Why beholdest thou the mote that is in thy brother's eye, but considerest not the beam that is in thine own eye? *Mat.* 7: 3.

Condemn not, and ye shall not be condemned. *Lu.* 6: 37.

He that is without sin among you, let him first cast a stone at her. *Jn.* 8: 7.

Why doth he yet find fault? *Ro.* 9: 19.

Let us not therefore judge one another any more. *Ro.* 14: 13.

Speak not evil one of another. *Ja.* 4: 11.

See also

Criticism; Disapproval; Harshness; Judgment; Severity.

Center

The tree of life also in the midst of the garden. *Ge.* 2: 9.

The Lord thy God will raise up unto thee a Prophet from the midst of thee. *De.* 18: 15.

Great is the Holy One of Israel in the midst of thee. *Is.* 12: 6.

Mine house shall be called an house of prayer for all people. *Is.* 56: 7.

They shall call Jerusalem the throne of the Lord; and all the nations shall be gathered unto it. *Je.* 3: 17.

The glory of the Lord went up from the midst of the city. *Eze.* 11: 23.

I . . . will set my sanctuary in the midst of them for evermore. *Eze.* 37: 26.

When Daniel knew that the writing was signed, he went into his house; and his windows being open in his chamber toward Jerusalem, he kneeled upon his knees three times a day, and prayed. *Da.* 6: 10.

I, saith the Lord, will be unto her a wall of fire round about, and will be the glory in the midst of her. *Zch.* 2: 5.

Seek ye first the kingdom of God, and his righteousness; and all these things shall be added unto you. *Mat.* 6: 33.

Jesus called a little child unto him, and set him in the midst of them. *Mat.* 18: 2.

Ye say, that in Jerusalem is the place where men ought to worship. *Jn.* 4: 20.

I, if I be lifted up from the earth, will draw all men unto me. *Jn.* 12: 32.

See also

Middle.

Ceremony

Remember the sabbath day, to keep it holy. *Ex.* 20: 8.

Ye shall keep it in his appointed season: according to all the rites of it, and according to all the ceremonies thereof, shall ye keep it. *Nu.* 9: 3.

To do justice and judgment is more acceptable to the Lord than sacrifice. *Pr.* 21: 3.

Bring no more vain oblations; incense is an abomination unto me; the new moons and sabbaths, the calling of assemblies, I cannot away with. *Is.* 1: 13.

Is not this the fast that I have chosen? to loose the bands of wickedness, to undo the heavy burdens, and to let the oppressed go free? *Is.* 58: 6.

I desired mercy, and not sacrifice; and the knowledge of God more than burnt offerings. *Ho.* 6: 6.

I hate, I despise your feast days, and I will not smell in your solemn assemblies. *Am.* 5: 21.

The fast . . . shall be . . . joy and gladness, and cheerful feasts. *Zch.* 8: 19.

Now do ye Pharisees make clean the outside of the cup and the platter; but your inward part is full of ravening and wickedness. *Lu.* 11: 39.

Circumcision is that of the heart, in the spirit, and not in the letter. *Ro.* 2: 29.

See also

Formalism; Observance; Ordinance; Ritual.

Certainty

Be sure your sin will find you out. *Nu.* 32: 23.

There hath not failed one word of all his good promise. *1 K.* 8: 56.

To him that soweth righteousness shall be a sure reward. *Pr.* 11: 18.

The certainty of the words of truth. *Pr.* 22: 21.

That thou mightest know the certainty of those things, wherein thou hast been instructed. *Lu.* 1: 4.

All that the Father giveth me shall come to me. *Jn.* 6: 37.

We believe and are sure that thou art that Christ, the Son of the living God. *Jn.* 6: 69.

Full assurance of understanding. *Col.* 2: 2.

We brought nothing into this world, and it is certain we can carry nothing out. *1 Ti.* 6: 7.

Full assurance of hope. *He.* 6: 11.

Full assurance of faith. *He.* 10: 22.

Give diligence to make your calling and election sure. *2 Pe.* 1: 10.

See also

Assurance; Conviction; Firmness; God, Certainty of; Truth.

Chaff

The angel of the Lord was by the threshingplace. *2 S.* 24: 16.

The ungodly are not so: but are like the chaff which the wind driveth away. *Ps.* 1: 4.

Let them be as chaff before the wind: and let the angel of the Lord chase them. *Ps.* 35: 5.

As the fire devoureth the stubble, and the flame consumeth the chaff, so their root shall be as rottenness, and their blossom shall go up as dust. *Is.* 5: 24.

The multitude of the terrible ones shall be as chaff that passeth away. *Is.* 29: 5.

The oxen likewise and the young asses that ear the ground shall eat clean provender, which hath been winnowed with the shovel and with the fan. *Is.* 30: 24.

Thou shalt thresh the mountains, and beat them small, and shalt make the hills as chaff. *Is.* 41: 15.

He that hath my word, let him speak my word faithfully. What is the chaff to the wheat? saith the Lord. *Je.* 23: 28.

He will burn up the chaff with unquenchable fire. *Mat.* 3: 12.

Chagrin

In those times there was no peace to him that went out, nor. to him that came in, but great vexations were upon all the inhabitants of the countries. *2 Ch.* 15: 5.

I am ashamed and blush to lift up my face to thee, my God. *Ezr.* 9: 6.

O Lord, heal me; for my bones are vexed. *Ps.* 6: 2.

Thou hast cast off, and put us to shame. *Ps.* 44: 9.

When pride cometh, then cometh shame. *Pr.* 11: 2.

Pride goeth before destruction, and an haughty spirit before a fall. *Pr.* 16: 18.

Ye shall cry for sorrow of heart, and shall howl for vexation of spirit. *Is.* 65: 14.

We lie down in our shame, and our confusion covereth us. *Je.* 3: 25.

They were not at all ashamed, neither could they blush: therefore they shall fall among them that fall. *Je.* 6: 15.

Shall they not rise up suddenly that shall bite thee, and awake that shall vex thee, and thou shalt be for booties unto them? *Hab.* 2: 7.

See also

Affliction; Trouble; Vexation; Worry.

Chain

He looseth the bond of kings. *Jb.* 12: 18.

Pride compasseth them about as a chain. *Ps.* 73: 6.

They shall be an ornament of grace unto thy head, and chains about thy neck. *Pr.* 1: 9.

I will break his yoke from off thy neck, and will burst thy bonds. *Je.* 30: 8.

Now, behold, I loose thee this day from the chains which were upon thine hand. *Je.* 40: 4.

He hath hedged me about, that I cannot get out: he hath made my chain heavy. *La.* 3: 7.

For the hope of Israel I am bound with this chain. *Ac.* 28: 20.

Remember my bonds. *Col.* 4: 18.

He oft refreshed me, and was not ashamed of my chain. *2 Ti.* 1: 16.

The angels which kept not their first estate, but left their own habitation, he hath reserved in everlasting chains under darkness unto the judgment of the great day. *Jude* 1: 6.

See also

Band; Bond; Bondage; Captivity; Imprisonment; Prison; Subjection.

Chalice

Can ye drink of the cup that I drink of? *Mk.* 10: 38.

The cup of blessing which we bless, is it not the communion of the blood of Christ? *1 Co.* 10: 16.

This cup is the new testament in my blood. *1 Co.* 11: 25.

See also

Christ, Blood of; Christ, Cup of; Christ, Sacrifice of; Communion, Service of; Cup.

Challenge

How shall I defy, whom the Lord hath not defied? *Nu.* 23: 8.

The Philistine said, I defy the armies of Israel this day; give me a man, that we may fight together. *1 S.* 17: 10.

The battle is the Lord's, and he will give you into our hands. *1 S.* 17: 47.

Come out, come out, thou bloody man, and thou man of Belial. *2 S.* 16: 7.

When he defied Israel, Jonathan . . . slew him. *2 S.* 21: 21.

The three mighty men with David . . . defied the Philistines that were there gathered together to battle. *2 S.* 23: 9.

Gird up thy loins now like a man: I will demand of thee, and declare thou unto me. *Jb.* 40: 7.

Deck thyself now with majesty and excellency; and array thyself with glory and beauty. . . . Then will I also confess unto thee that thine own right hand can save thee. *Jb.* 40: 10, 14.

Who then is able to stand before me? *Jb.* 41: 10.

See also
Accusation; Defiance.

Chamber

Thou hast set my feet in a large room. *Ps.* 31: 8.

Who layeth the beams of his chambers in the waters. *Ps.* 104: 3.

He watereth the hills from his chambers. *Ps.* 104: 13.

Her house is the way to hell, going down to the chambers of death. *Pr.* 7: 27.

Come, my people, enter thou into thy chambers, and shut thy doors about thee: hide thyself as it were for a little moment, until the indignation be overpast. *Is.* 26: 20.

Woe unto him that buildeth his house by unrighteousness, and his chambers by wrong. *Je.* 22: 13.

Hast thou seen what the ancients of the house of Israel do in the dark, every man in the chambers of his imagery? *Eze.* 8: 12.

Many were gathered together, insomuch that there was no room to receive them, no, not so much as about the door: and he preached the word unto them. *Mk.* 2: 2.

He marked how they chose out the chief rooms. *Lu.* 14: 7.

When thou art bidden of any man to a wedding, sit not down in the highest room. *Lu.* 14: 8.

When they were come in, they went up into an upper room. *Ac.* 1: 13.

See also
Room.

Champion

The Lord your God which goeth before you, he shall fight for you. *De.* 1: 30.

The Lord is with thee, thou mighty man of valour. *Ju.* 6: 12.

There went out a champion out of the camp of the Philistines, named Goliath. *1 S.* 17: 4.

Choose you a man for you. *1 S.* 17: 8.

When the Philistines saw their champion was dead, they fled. *1 S.* 17: 51.

Look even out the best and meetest of your master's sons, and . . . fight for your master's house. *2 K.* 10: 3.

Mighty men of valour, famous men, and heads of the house of their fathers. *1 Ch.* 5: 24.

Be not ye afraid of them: remember the Lord, which is great and terrible, and fight for your brethren, your sons, and your daughters, your wives, and your houses. *Ne.* 4: 14.

He will not be afraid of their voice, nor abase himself for the noise of them. *Is.* 31: 4.

Who is that shepherd that will stand before me? *Je.* 49: 19.

See also
Advocate; Challenge; Defiance; Valor.

Chance

It was a chance that happened to us. *1 S.* 6: 9.

As I happened by chance upon mount Gilboa, behold, Saul leaned upon his spear. *2 S.* 1: 6.

There shall no evil happen to the just. *Pr.* 12: 21.

Time and chance happeneth to them all. *Ec.* 9: 11.

From that time he sought opportunity to betray him. *Mat.* 26: 16.

By chance there came down a certain priest that way. *Lu.* 10: 31.

They talked together of all these things which had happened. *Lu.* 24: 14.

They appointed two, Joseph called Barsabas, . . . and Matthias. . . . And they gave forth their lots; and the lot fell upon Matthias; and he was numbered with the eleven Apostles. *Ac.* 1: 23, 26.

Lest haply ye be found even to fight against God. *Ac.* 5: 39.

If haply they might feel after him, and find him, though he be not far from every one of us. *Ac.* 17: 27.

All these things happened unto them for ensamples. *1 Co.* 10: 11.

As we have therefore opportunity, let us do good unto all men. *Ga.* 6: 10.

Ye lacked opportunity. *Ph.* 4: 10.

If they had been mindful of that country from whence they came out, they might have had opportunity to have returned. *He.* 11: 15.

Think it not strange concerning the fiery trial which is to try you, as though some strange thing happened unto you. *1 Pe.* 4: 12.

See also
Accident; Fate; Fortune; Gambling; Lot; Luck; Opportunity.

Chance, Second

The angel of the Lord called unto Abraham out of heaven the second time. *Ge.* 22: 15.

God appeared unto Jacob again. *Ge.* 35: 9.

Howbeit the hair of his head began to grow again. *Ju.* 16: 22.

The Lord called yet again, Samuel. *1 S.* 3: 6.

The Lord was angry with Solomon, because his heart was turned from the Lord God of Israel, which had appeared unto him twice. *1 K.* 11: 9.

God speaketh once, yea twice, yet man perceiveth it not. *Jb.* 33: 14.

The Lord turned the captivity of Job: . . . also the Lord gave Job twice as much as he had before. *Jb.* 42: 10.

Return unto me; for I have redeemed thee. *Is.* 44: 22.

For a small moment have I forsaken thee; but with great mercies will I gather thee. *Is.* 54: 7.

The word of the Lord came unto me the second time. *Je.* 1: 13.

I will bring them again into their land that I gave unto their fathers. *Je.* 16: 15.

Then shall she say, I will go and return to my first husband; for then was it better with me than now. *Ho.* 2: 7.

I will restore to you the years that the locust hath eaten. *Jo.* 2: 25.

The word of the Lord came unto Jonah the second time. *Jon.* 3: 1.

Go and shew John again those things which ye do hear and see. *Mat.* 11: 4.

A man that is a heretick after the first and second admonition reject. *Tit.* 3: 10.

Ye have need that one teach you again which be the first principles of the oracles of God. *He.* 5: 12.

This second epistle, beloved, I now write unto you. *2 Pe.* 3: 1.

See also

God, Patience of; Long-Suffering; Opportunity; Patience; Perseverance; Persistence.

Change

The wilderness and the solitary place shall be glad for them; and the desert shall rejoice, and blossom as the rose. *Is.* 35: 1.

Can the Ethiopian change his skin, or the leopard his spots? *Je.* 13: 23.

I have caused thine iniquity to pass from thee, and I will clothe thee with change of raiment. *Zch.* 3: 4.

Except ye be converted, and become as little children, ye shall not enter into the kingdom of heaven. *Mat.* 18: 3.

Jesus went into the temple of God, and cast out all them that sold and bought in the temple, and overthrew the tables of the money-changers. *Mat.* 21: 12.

No man putteth new wine into old bottles: else the new wine doth burst the bottles. and the wine is spilled, and the bottles will be marred: but new wine must be put into new bottles. *Mk.* 2: 22.

Jesus, being full of the Holy Ghost returned from Jordan, and was led by the Spirit into the wilderness. *Lu.* 4: 1.

As he prayed, the fashion of his countenance was altered. *Lu.* 9: 29.

Repent ye therefore, and be converted, that your sins may be blotted out. *Ac.* 3: 19.

They became fools, And changed the glory of the uncorruptible God into an image made like to corruptible man. *Ro.* 1: 22, 23.

Behold, I shew you a mystery; We shall not all sleep, but we shall all be changed. *1 Co.* 15: 51.

We all, with open face beholding as in a glass the glory of the Lord, are changed into the same image from glory to glory. *2 Co.* 3: 18.

Who shall change our vile body, that it may be fashioned like unto his glorious body. *Ph.* 3: 21.

See also

Alteration; Amendment; Conversion; Mutability; Substitution; Transformation.

Chaos

The earth was without form, and void. *Ge.* 1: 2.

The Lord God formed man of the dust of the ground. *Ge.* 2: 7.

Or ever thou hadst formed the earth and the world. *Ps.* 90: 2.

Then the waters had overwhelmed us, the stream had gone over our soul. *Ps.* 124: 4.

I beheld the earth, and, lo, it was without form, and void; and the heavens, and they had no light. *Je.* 4: 23.

I beheld, and, lo, the fruitful place was a wilderness, and all the cities thereof were broken down. *Je.* 4: 26.

Every city shall be forsaken, and not a man dwell therein. *Je.* 4: 29.

God is not the author of confusion. *1 Co.* 14: 33.

See also

Anarchy; Babel; Confusion.

Character

My righteousness I hold fast, and will not let it go. *Jb.* 27: 6.

A good name is better than precious ointment. *Ec.* 7: 1.

He hath clothed me with the garments of salvation, he hath covered me with the robe of righteousness, as a bridegroom decketh himself with ornaments, and as a bride adorneth herself with her jewels. *Is.* 61: 10.

Let your light so shine before men, that they may see your good works, and glorify your Father which is in heaven. *Mat.* 5: 16.

Whosoever shall compel thee to go a mile, go with him twain. *Mat.* 5: 41.

Unto every one which hath shall be given; and from him that hath not, even that he hath shall be taken away from him. *Lu.* 19: 26.

A good man, and a just: . . . who also himself waited for the kingdom of God. *Lu.* 23: 50, 51.

Brethren, let every man, wherein he is called, therein abide with God. *1 Co.* 7: 24.

Wherefore take unto you the whole armor of God, that ye may be able to withstand in the evil day, and having done all, to stand. *Ep.* 6: 13.

God hath not given us the spirit of fear; but of power, and of love, and of a sound mind. *2 Ti.* 1: 7.

Follow righteousness, faith, charity, peace, with them that call on the Lord out of a pure heart. *2 Ti.* 2: 22.

See, saith he, that thou make all things according to the pattern shewed to thee in the mount. *He.* 8: 5.

Honour all men. Love the brotherhood. Fear God. Honour the king. *1 Pe.* 2: 17.

Add to your faith virtue. *2 Pe.* 1: 5.

If we say that we have no sin, we deceive ourselves, and the truth is not in us. *1 Jn.* 1: 8.

See also

Christ, Goodness of; Christ, Holiness of; God, Righteousness of; Goodness; Holiness; Honor; Integrity; Justice; Purity; Quality; Rectitude; Righteousness; Trait.

Charge

Go down, charge the people. *Ex.* 19: 21.

Now therefore come, let me, I pray thee, give thee counsel, that thou mayest save thine own life, and the life of thy son. *1 K.* 1: 12.

My sons, be not now negligent: for the Lord hath chosen you to stand before him, to serve him. *2 Ch.* 29: 11.

Be wise now therefore, O ye kings: be instructed, ye judges of the earth. *Ps. 2: 10.*

They would none of my counsel: they despised all my reproof. *Pr. 1: 30.*

Receive my instruction, and not silver; and knowledge rather than choice gold. *Pr. 8: 10.*

Buy the truth, and sell it not; also wisdom, and instruction, and understanding. *Pr. 23: 23.*

I counsel thee to keep the king's commandment. *Ec. 8: 2.*

Jesus charged them, saying, Tell the vision to no man. *Mat. 17: 9.*

I charge thee before God, and the Lord Jesus Christ, . . . that thou observe these things without preferring one before another. *1 Ti. 5: 21.*

Charge them that are rich in this world, that they be not highminded, nor trust in uncertain riches, but in the living God. *1 Ti. 6: 17.*

Of these things put them in remembrance, charging them before the Lord that they strive not about words to no profit. *2 Ti. 2: 14.*

All scripture is given by inspiration of God, and is profitable for doctrine, for reproof, for correction, for instruction in righteousness. *2 Ti. 3: 16.*

I charge thee therefore before God, and the Lord Jesus Christ, . . . Preach the word. *2 Ti. 4: 1, 2.*

I counsel thee to buy of me gold tried in the fire, that thou mayest be rich. *Re. 3: 18.*

See also
Burden; Care; Commandment; Duty; Instruction; Load; Order; Responsibility; Trust; Weight; Yoke.

Chariot

Pharaoh's chariots and his host hath he cast into the sea. *Ex. 15: 4.*

Why is his chariot so long in coming? why tarry the wheels of his chariots? *Ju. 5: 28.*

Elisha saw it, and he cried, My father, my father, the chariot of Israel, and the horsemen thereof. *2 K. 2: 12.*

The Lord opened the eyes of the young man; and he saw: and, behold, the mountain was full of horses and chariots of fire round about Elisha. *2 K. 6: 17.*

Some trust in chariots, and some in horses: but we will remember the name of the Lord our God. *Ps. 20: 7.*

The chariots of God are twenty thousand, even thousands of angels: the Lord is among them. *Ps. 68: 17.*

Who maketh the clouds his chariot: who walketh upon the wings of the wind. *Ps. 104: 3.*

With thee will I break in pieces the chariot and his rider. *Je. 51: 21.*

Thy chariots of salvation. *Hab. 3: 8.*

I will overthrow the chariots, and those that ride in them; and the horses and their riders shall come down, every one by the sword of his brother. *Hag. 2: 22.*

Charity

He hath dispersed, he hath given to the poor; his righteousness endureth for ever. *Ps. 112: 9.*

Say not unto thy neighbour, Go, and come

again, and to morrow I will give; when thou hast it by thee. *Pr. 3: 28.*

He that covereth a transgression seeketh love; but he that repeateth a matter separateth very friends. *Pr. 17: 9.*

He that hath a bountiful eye shall be blessed; for he giveth of his bread to the poor. *Pr. 22: 9.*

All that watch for iniquity are cut off. *Is. 29: 20.*

Whosoever shall give to drink unto one of these little ones a cup of cold water only in the name of a disciple, verily I say unto you, he shall in no wise lose his reward. *Mat. 10: 42.*

Go and sell that thou hast, and give to the poor, and thou shalt have treasure in heaven: and come and follow me. *Mat. 19: 21.*

Give, and it shall be given unto you. *Lu. 6: 38.*

The poor always ye have with you. *Jn. 12: 8.*

We then that are strong ought to bear the infirmities of the weak, and not to please ourselves. *Ro. 15: 1.*

Though I speak with the tongues of men and of angels, and have not charity, I am become as sounding brass, or a tinkling cymbal. *1 Co. 13: 1.*

Though I bestow all my goods to feed the poor, and though I give my body to be burned, and have not charity, it profiteth me nothing. *1 Co. 13: 3.*

Charity suffereth long and is kind. *1 Co. 13: 4.*

The greatest of these is charity. *1 Co. 13: 13.*

Follow after charity. *1 Co. 14: 1.*

That now at this time your abundance may be a supply for their want. *2 Co. 8: 14.*

We should remember the poor. *Ga. 2: 10.*

Charity shall cover the multitude of sins. *1 Pe. 4: 8.*

Strangers . . . have borne witness of thy charity. *3 Jn. 5, 6.*

See also
Almsgiving; Beneficence; Benevolence; Christ, Compassion of; Clemency; Contribution; God, Compassion of; God, Mercy of; Mercy; Philanthropy; Tenderness; Unselfishness; Will, Good.

Charm

Neither shall ye use enchantment. *Le. 19: 26.*

There shall not be found among you any one that . . . useth divination, or an observer of times, or an enchanter, or a witch, Or a charmer. *De. 18: 10, 11.*

Saul and Jonathan were lovely and pleasant in their lives. *2 S. 1: 23.*

Ye daughters of Israel, weep over Saul, who clothed you in scarlet, with other delights, who put on ornaments of gold upon your apparel. *2 S. 1: 24.*

If it please the king, and if I have found favour in his sight, . . . and I be pleasing in his eyes, let it be written to reverse the letters. *Es. 8: 5.*

Thou art fairer than the children of men. *Ps. 45: 2.*

Bring hither the timbrel, the pleasant harp with the psaltery. *Ps. 81: 2.*

Thou hast ravished my heart. *S. of S. 4: 9.*

How fair and how pleasant art thou, O love!
S. of S. 7: 6.
They shall seek to the idols, and to the
charmers, and to them that have familiar
spirits, and to the wizards. *Is.* 19: 3.
Thou art unto them as a very lovely song
of one that hath a pleasant voice. *Eze.* 33: 32.
Ye shall be a delightsome land, saith the
Lord of hosts. *Mal.* 3: 12.
There was a certain man, called Simon,
which beforetime in the same city used
sorcery, and bewitched the people of Samaria.
Ac. 8: 9.
O foolish Galatians, who hath bewitched
you? *Ga.* 3: 1.
See also
Allurement; Attraction; Beauty; Enticement;
Loveliness; Magic.

Chastisement

She said unto them, Call me not Naomi, call
me Mara: for the Almighty hath dealt very
bitterly with me. *Ru.* 1: 20.
He knoweth the way that I take: when he
has tried me, I shall come forth as gold. *Jb.*
23: 10.
I have borne chastisement, I will not offend
any more. *Jb.* 34: 31.
I wept, and chastened my soul with fasting.
Ps. 69: 10.
O my people that dwellest in Zion, be not
afraid of the Assyrian: he shall smite thee with
a rod, and shall lift up his staff against thee.
Is. 10: 24.
The chastisement of our peace was upon
him; and with his stripes we are healed. *Is.*
53: 5.
From the first day that thou didst set thine
heart to understand, and to chasten thyself before thy God, thy words were heard. *Da.* 10: 12.
They have beaten us openly uncondemned,
being Romans, and have cast us into prison.
Ac. 16: 37.
Approving ourselves as the ministers of
God, . . . In stripes, in imprisonments, in
tumults. *2 Co.* 6: 4, 5.
My son, despise not thou the chastening of
the Lord, nor faint when thou art rebuked
of him. *He.* 12: 5.
If ye endure chastening, God dealeth with
you as with sons. *He.* 12: 7.
Afterward it yieldeth the peaceable fruit of
righteousness. *He.* 12: 11.
See also
Discipline; God, Chastisement of; God, Pun-
ishment of; Punishment; Rebuke; Reproach;
Reproof; Rod; Scourge; Stripe; Trial.

Chastity

Neither shalt thou commit adultery. *De.* 5:
18.
How can he be clean that is born of a
woman? . . . yea, the stars are not pure in
his sight. *Jb.* 25: 4, 5.
A virtuous woman is a crown to her husband. *Pr.* 12: 4.
We be not born of fornication. *Jn.* 8: 41.
All things indeed are pure. *Ro.* 14: 20.
If a virgin marry, she hath not sinned. *1 Co.*
7: 28.
Let us cleanse ourselves from all filthiness
of the flesh and spirit. *2 Co.* 7: 1.

I have espoused you to one husband, that I
may present you as a chaste virgin to Christ.
2 Co. 11: 2.
To be discreet, chaste, keepers at home,
good, obedient to their own husbands. *Tit.*
2: 5.
They behold your chaste conversation
coupled with fear. *1 Pe.* 3: 2.
See also
Innocence; Purity; Virgin.

Cheat

Wherefore then hast thou beguiled me? *Ge.*
29: 25.
His mouth is full of . . . deceit and fraud.
Ps. 10: 7.
Keep thy tongue from evil, and thy lips
from speaking guile. *Ps.* 34: 13.
A false balance is abomination to the Lord.
Pr. 11: 1.
The wicked worketh a deceitful work. *Pr.*
11: 18.
The treacherous dealer dealeth treacherously.
Is. 21: 2.
He is a merchant, the balances of deceit are
in his hand. *Ho.* 12: 7.
Shall I count them pure with the wicked
balances, and with the bag of deceitful weights?
Mi. 6: 11.
The hire of the labourers who have reaped
down your fields, which is of you kept back by
fraud, crieth. *Ja.* 5: 4.
In their mouth was found no guile: for they
are without fault before the throne of God.
Re. 14: 5.
See also
Craftiness; Deceit; Duplicity; Fraud; Guile.

Cheer

A merry heart doeth good like a medicine:
but a broken spirit drieth the bones. *Pr.* 17: 22.
Let thy heart cheer thee in the days of thy
youth. *Ec.* 11: 9.
The Lord hath comforted his people, and
will have mercy upon his afflicted. *Is.* 49: 13.
Break forth into joy, sing together, ye waste
places of Jerusalem: for the Lord hath com-
forted his people. *Is.* 52: 9.
Son, be of good cheer; thy sins be forgiven
thee. *Mat.* 9: 2.
Straightway Jesus spake unto them, saying,
Be of good cheer; it is I; be not afraid. *Mat.*
14: 27.
These things have I spoken unto you, that
my joy might remain in you, and that your
joy might be full. *Jn.* 15: 11.
I exhort you to be of good cheer. . . .
Wherefore, sirs, be of good cheer: for I believe
God. . . . Then were they all of good cheer.
Ac. 27: 22, 25, 36.
He that sheweth mercy, with cheerfulness.
Ro. 12: 8.
God loveth a cheerful giver. *2 Co.* 9: 7.
Rejoice evermore. *1 Th.* 5: 16.
Yea, brother, let me have joy of thee in the
Lord: refresh my bowels in the Lord. *Phm.*
1: 20.
See also
Christ, the Comforter; Comfort; Consolation;
Encouragement; Gaiety; God, Comfort of;
Laughter; Merriment; Mirth.

Cherishment

There will I nourish thee. *Ge.* 45: 11.

He shall be . . . a nourisher of thine old age. *Ru.* 4: 15.

The poor man had nothing, save one little ewe lamb, which he had bought and nourished up. *2 S.* 12: 3.

Thou art a God ready to pardon, gracious and merciful, slow to anger, and of great kindness. *Ne.* 9: 17.

Thy right hand shall hold me. *Ps.* 139: 10.

Why wilt thou . . . embrace the bosom of a stranger? *Pr.* 5: 20.

She looketh well to the ways of her household. *Pr.* 31: 27.

A time to embrace, and a time to refrain from embracing. *Ec.* 3: 5.

Feed thy kids beside the shepherds' tents. *S. of S.* 1: 8.

His left hand is under my head, and his right hand doth embrace me. *S. of S.* 2: 6.

I held him, and would not let him go. *S. of S.* 3: 4.

I . . . will hold thine hand, and will keep thee. *Is.* 42: 6.

They may forget, yet will I not forget thee. *Is.* 49: 15.

I will betroth thee unto me for ever; yea, I will betroth thee unto me in righteousness, and in judgment, and in lovingkindness, and in mercies. *Ho.* 2: 19.

I will have mercy upon her that had not obtained mercy; and I will say to them which were not my people, Thou art my people; and they shall say, Thou art my God. *Ho.* 2: 23.

When Israel was a child, then I loved him. *Ho.* 11: 1.

I drew them with cords of a man, with bands of love. *Ho.* 11: 4.

Then were there brought unto him little children, that he should put his hands on them. *Mat.* 19: 13.

How often would I have gathered thy children together, even as a hen gathereth her chickens under her wings, and ye would not! *Mat.* 23: 37.

He loveth our nation. *Lu.* 7: 5.

Master, I beseech thee, look upon my son: for he is mine only child. *Lu.* 9: 38.

The good shepherd giveth his life for the sheep. *Jn.* 10: 11.

Therefore doth my Father love me, because I lay down my life. *Jn.* 10: 17.

A new commandment I give unto you, That ye love one another. *Jn.* 13: 34.

No man ever yet hated his own flesh; but nourisheth and cherisheth it, even as the Lord the church. *Ep.* 5: 29.

We were gentle among you, even as a nurse cherisheth her children. *1 Th.* 2: 7.

That they may teach the young women to be sober, to love their husbands, to love their children. *Tit.* 2: 4.

See also

Affection; Care; Caress; Love.

Chief

The Lord shall make thee the head, and not the tail. *De.* 28: 13.

Thou shalt be above only, and thou shalt not be beneath. *De.* 28: 13.

Wisdom is the principal thing; therefore get wisdom. *Pr.* 4: 7.

The chiefest among ten thousand. *S. of S.* 5: 10.

The scribes and the Pharisees . . . love the uppermost rooms at feasts, and the chief seats in the synagogues. *Mat.* 23: 2, 6.

By the way they had disputed among themselves, who should be the greatest. *Mk.* 9: 34.

Whosoever of you will be the chiefest, shall be the servant of all. *Mk.* 10: 44.

Thou, child, shalt be called the prophet of the Highest. *Lu.* 1: 76.

The greatest of these is charity. *1 Co.* 13: 13.

I was not a whit behind the very chiefest apostles. *2 Co.* 11: 5.

Christ Jesus came into the world to save sinners; of whom I am chief. *1 Ti.* 1: 15.

Diotrephes, who loveth to have the preeminence among them. *3 Jn.* 1: 9.

See also

Christ, the Leader; Commander; First; Head; Leadership; Prominence; Senior, Uniqueness.

Child

Give me children, or else I die. *Ge.* 30: 1.

Spake I not against you, saying, Do not sin against the child? *Ge.* 42: 22.

Cursed be he that setteth light by his father or his mother. *De.* 27: 16.

The child grew, and the Lord blessed him. *Ju.* 13: 24.

Out of the mouth of babes and sucklings hast thou ordained strength. *Ps.* 8: 2.

He shall save the children of the needy. *Ps.* 72: 4.

Let thy work appear unto thy servants, and thy glory unto their children. *Ps.* 90: 16.

Train up a child in the way he should go: and when he is old, he will not depart from it. *Pr.* 22: 6.

Better is a poor and a wise child than an old and foolish king. *Ec.* 4: 13.

Woe to thee, O land, when thy king is a child! *Ec.* 10: 16.

Babes shall rule over them. *Is.* 3: 4.

A little child shall lead them. *Is.* 11: 6.

Except ye be converted, and become as little children, ye shall not enter into the kingdom of heaven. *Mat.* 18: 3.

Take heed that ye despise not one of these little ones. *Mat.* 18: 10.

It is not the will of your Father which is in heaven, that one of these little ones should perish. *Mat.* 18: 14.

Then were there brought unto him little children, that he should put his hands on them, and pray. *Mat.* 19: 13.

They are like unto children sitting in the marketplace, and calling one to another, and saying, We have piped unto you, and ye have not danced; we have mourned to you, and ye have not wept. *Lu.* 7: 32.

See also

Babe; Childhood; Infant.

Childhood

I have walked before you from my childhood unto this day. *1 S.* 12: 2.

Their children dance. *Jb.* 21: 11.

O God, thou hast taught me from my youth. *Ps.* 71: 17.

Better is a poor and a wise child than an old and foolish king. *Ec.* 4: 13.

Childhood and youth are vanity. *Ec.* 11: 10.

A little child shall lead them. *Is.* 11: 6.

The suckling child shall play on the hole of the asp. *Is.* 11: 8.

A little one shall become a thousand, and a small one a strong nation. *Is.* 60: 22.

When Israel was a child, then I loved him. *Ho.* 11: 1.

Take heed that ye despise not one of these little ones; for I say unto you, That in heaven their angels do always behold the face of my Father which is in heaven. *Mat.* 18: 10.

Of such is the kingdom of God. *Mk.* 10: 14.

Whosoever shall not receive the kingdom of God as a little child, he shall not enter therein. *Mk.* 10: 15.

And the child grew, and waxed strong in spirit, filled with wisdom: and the grace of God was upon him. *Lu.* 2: 40.

When I was a child, I spake as a child, I understood as a child, I thought as a child: but when I became a man, I put away childish things. *1 Co.* 13: 11.

See also

Babe; Child; Infant; Innocence; Youth.

Childlikeness

Lord, my heart is not haughty, nor mine eyes lofty: neither do I exercise myself in great matters, or in things too high for me. Surely I have behaved and quieted myself, as a child that is weaned of his mother: my soul is even as a weaned child. *Ps.* 131: 1, 2.

Whosoever shall give to drink unto one of these little ones a cup of cold water only in the name of a disciple, verily I say unto you, he shall in no wise lose his reward. *Mat.* 10: 42.

Except ye be converted, and become as little children, ye shall not enter into the kingdom of heaven. *Mat.* 18: 3.

He took a child, and set him in the midst of them. *Mk.* 9: 36.

Whosoever shall receive one of such children in my name, receiveth me: and whosoever shall receive me, receiveth not me, but him that sent me. *Mk.* 9: 37.

Suffer the little children to come unto me, and forbid them not: for of such is the kingdom of God. *Mk.* 10: 14.

When I was a child, I spake as a child, I understood as a child, I thought as a child: but when I became a man, I put away childish things. *1 Co.* 13: 11.

Be ye therefore followers of God, as dear children. *Ep.* 5: 1.

Now are ye light in the Lord: walk as children of light. *Ep.* 5: 8.

As obedient children. *1 Pe.* 1: 14.

I write unto you, little children, because ye have known the Father. *1 Jn.* 2: 13.

See also

Child; Childhood; Guilelessness; Infant; Innocence.

Choice

Who is on the Lord's side? let him come unto me. *Ex.* 32: 26.

I have set before you life and death, blessing and cursing: therefore choose life, that both thou and thy seed may live. *De.* 30: 19.

Choose you this day whom ye will serve. *Jos.* 24: 15.

Give therefore thy servant an understanding heart to judge thy people, that I may discern between good and bad. *1 K.* 3: 9.

How long halt ye between two opinions? *1 K.* 18: 21.

Blessed is the man whom thou choosest, and causest to approach unto thee. *Ps.* 65: 4.

I thought on my ways, and turned my feet unto thy testimonies. *Ps.* 119: 59.

A man's heart deviseth his way: but the Lord directeth his steps. *Pr.* 16: 9.

Ye are my witnesses, saith the Lord, and my servant whom I have chosen. *Is.* 43: 10.

Mine elect shall long enjoy the work of their hands. *Is.* 65: 22.

The Lord took me as I followed the flock. *Am.* 7: 15.

Many be called, but few chosen. *Mat.* 20: 16.

Whether of the twain will ye that I release unto you? They said, Barabbas. *Mat.* 27: 21.

Thou, Lord, which knowest the hearts of all men, shew whether of these two thou hast chosen. *Ac.* 1: 24.

Ye know how that a good while ago God made choice among us, that the Gentiles by my mouth should hear the word of the gospel, and believe. *Ac.* 15: 7.

The God of our fathers hath chosen thee, that thou shouldest know his will. *Ac.* 22: 14.

God hath chosen the foolish things of the world to confound the wise. *1 Co.* 1: 27.

The elect of God. *Col.* 3: 12.

God hath from the beginning chosen you to salvation. *2 Th.* 2: 13.

Choosing rather to suffer affliction with the people of God, than to enjoy the pleasures of sin for a season. *He.* 11: 25.

Hath not God chosen the poor of this world rich in faith, and heirs of the kingdom? *Ja.* 2: 5.

See also

Appointment; Election; Foreordination; Option; Predestination; Preference; Selection.

Chore

They rolled the stone from the well's mouth, and watered the sheep. *Ge.* 29: 3.

Thus have I been twenty years in thy house; I served thee fourteen years for thy two daughters, and six years for thy cattle: and thou hast changed my wages ten times. *Ge.* 31: 41.

Fulfil your works, your daily tasks. *Ex.* 5: 13.

Six days shalt thou labour, and do all thy work. *Ex.* 20: 9.

He will take your daughters to be confectionaries, and to be cooks, and to be bakers. *1 S.* 8: 13.

Thou shalt eat the labour of thine hands. *Ps.* 128: 2.

Whatsoever thy hand findeth to do, do it with thy might. *Ec.* 9: 10.

Martha was cumbered about much serving. *Lu.* 10: 40.

They made him a supper; and Martha served. *Jn.* 12: 2.

See also

Task; Work.

Chorus

The women came out of all the cities of Israel, singing and dancing, to meet king Saul. *1 S.* 18: 6.

They ministered . . . with singing. *1 Ch.* 6: 22.

The singers had builded them villages round about Jerusalem. *Ne.* 12: 29.

Come before his presence with singing. *Ps.* 100: 2.

I gat me men singers and women singers. *Ec.* 2: 8.

The redeemed of the Lord shall return, and come with singing unto Zion. *Is.* 51: 11.

Singing with grace in your hearts to the Lord. *Col.* 3: 16.

See also

Anthem; Hymn; Psalm; Song.

Christ

This is my beloved Son, in whom I am well pleased. *Mat.* 17: 5.

I adjure thee by the living God, that thou tell us whether thou be the Christ, the Son of God. *Mat.* 26: 63.

Peter answereth and saith unto him, Thou art the Christ. *Mk.* 8: 29.

What will ye then that I should do unto him whom ye call the King of the Jews? *Mk.* 15: 12.

Unto you is born this day in the city of David a Saviour, which is Christ the Lord. *Lu.* 2: 11.

They knew that he was Christ. *Lu.* 4: 41.

He confessed, and denied not; but confessed, I am not the Christ. *Jn.* 1: 20.

Christ also suffered for us, leaving us an example, that ye should follow his steps. *1 Pe.* 2: 21.

See also

Messiah.

Christ, Abiding in

They constrained him, saying, Abide with us. *Lu.* 24: 29.

He that eateth my flesh, and drinketh my blood, dwelleth in me, and I in him. *Jn.* 6: 56.

Then said Jesus, . . . If ye continue in my word, then are ye my disciples indeed. *Jn.* 8: 31.

Yet a little while, and the world seeth me no more; but ye see me. *Jn.* 14: 19.

Abide in me, and I in you. As the branch cannot bear fruit of itself, except it abide in the vine; no more can ye, except ye abide in me. I am the vine, ye are the branches. *Jn.* 15: 4, 5.

If any man be in Christ, he is a new creature. *2 Co.* 5: 17.

The life which I now live in the flesh I live by the faith of the Son of God. *Ga.* 2: 20.

And be found in him. *Ph.* 3: 9.

Ye are dead, and your life is hid with Christ in God. *Col.* 3: 3.

If we be dead with him, we shall also live with him. *2 Ti.* 2: 11.

Let therefore abide in you, which ye have heard from the beginning. *1 Jn.* 2: 24.

We dwell in him, and he in us, because he hath given us of his Spirit. *1 Jn.* 4: 13.

See also

Christ, Communion with; Christ, Fellowship with; Christ, the Indwelling; Christ, Life in;

Christ, Nearness of; Christ, Partnership with; Christ, Union with.

Christ, Acceptance of

Take my yoke upon you, and learn of me. *Mat.* 11: 29.

Take, eat; this is my body. *Mat.* 26: 26.

Whosoever shall receive one of such children in my name, receiveth me. *Mk.* 9: 37.

Mine eyes have seen thy salvation. *Lu.* 2: 30.

To preach the acceptable year of the Lord. *Lu.* 4: 19.

No prophet is accepted in his own country. *Lu.* 4: 24.

I am the good shepherd, and know my sheep, and am known of mine. *Jn.* 10: 14.

Take the helmet of salvation. *Ep.* 6: 17.

This is a faithful saying, and worthy of all acceptation, that Christ Jesus came into the world to save sinners. *1 Ti.* 1: 15.

See also

Christ, Appeal of; Christ, Call of; Christ, Coming to.

Christ, the Accusing

With what judgment ye judge, ye shall be judged. *Mat.* 7: 2.

Woe unto the world because of offences! for it must needs be that offences come; but woe to that man by whom the offence cometh! *Mat.* 18: 7.

Ye serpents, ye generation of vipers, how can ye escape the damnation of hell? *Mat.* 23: 33.

Depart from me, ye cursed, into everlasting fire, prepared for the devil and his angels. *Mat.* 25: 41.

Condemn not, and ye shall not be condemned. *Lu.* 6: 37.

The Father judgeth no man, but hath committed all judgment unto the Son. *Jn.* 5: 22.

Do not think that I will accuse you to the Father: there is one that accuseth you, even Moses, in whom ye trust. *Jn.* 5: 45.

Jesus said unto her, Neither do I condemn thee: go, and sin no more. *Jn.* 8: 11.

Ye judge after the flesh; I judge no man. *Jn.* 8: 15.

If I judge, my judgment is true: for I am not alone, but I and the Father that sent me. *Jn.* 8: 16.

He that rejecteth me, and receiveth not my words, hath one that judgeth him: the word that I have spoken, the same shall judge him in the last day. *Jn.* 12: 48.

There is therefore now no condemnation to them which are in Christ Jesus. *Ro.* 8: 1.

See also

Christ, Condemnation of; Christ, the Judge.

Christ, Adoration of

We have seen his star in the east, and are come to worship him. *Mat.* 2: 2.

When ye have found him, bring me word again, that I may come and worship him also. *Mat.* 2: 8.

There came a leper and worshipped him. *Mat.* 8: 2.

There came a certain ruler, and worshipped him. *Mat.* 9: 18.

They that were in the ship came and worshipped him. *Mat.* 14: 33.

Thou art the Christ, the Son of the living God. *Mat.* 16: 16.

When they saw him, they worshipped him. *Mat.* 28: 17.

Unclean spirits, when they saw him, fell down before him, and cried, saying, Thou art the Son of God. *Mk.* 3: 11.

Truly this man was the Son of God. *Mk.* 15: 39.

When Simon Peter saw it, he fell down at Jesus' knees. *Lu.* 5: 8.

At the name of Jesus every knee should bow, of things in heaven, and things in earth, and things under the earth. *Ph.* 2: 10.

Worthy is the Lamb that was slain to receive power, and riches, and wisdom, and strength, and honour, and glory, and blessing. *Re.* 5: 12.

Blessing and honour, and glory, and power, be unto him that sitteth upon the throne, and unto the Lamb for ever and ever. *Re.* 5: 13.

See also

Christ, Devotion to; Christ, Exaltation of; Christ, Praise of; Christ, Worship of.

Christ, the Advocate

He bare the sin of many, and made intercession for the transgressors. *Is.* 53: 12.

I have prayed for thee. *Lu.* 22: 32.

A mediator is not a mediator of one. *Ga.* 3: 20.

He ever liveth to make intercession for them. *He.* 7: 25.

He is the mediator of a better covenant, which was established on better promises. *He.* 8: 6.

Now to appear in the presence of God for us. *He.* 9: 24.

If any man sin, we have an advocate with the Father, Jesus Christ the righteous. *1 Jn.* 2: 1.

See also

Christ, the Mediator.

Christ, Agony of

He is despised and rejected of men; a man of sorrows, and acquainted with grief. *Is.* 53: 3.

Surely he hath borne our griefs, and carried our sorrows. *Is.* 53: 4.

He was wounded for our transgressions, he was bruised for our iniquities: the chastisement of our peace was upon him. *Is.* 53: 5.

He is brought as a lamb to the slaughter. *Is.* 53: 7.

Pilate . . . delivered Jesus, when he had scourged him, to be crucified. *Mk.* 15: 15.

They smote him on the head with a reed, and did spit upon him. *Mk.* 15: 19.

It was the third hour, and they crucified him. *Mk.* 15: 25.

My God, my God, why hast thou forsaken me? *Mk.* 15: 34.

Jesus cried with a loud voice, and gave up the ghost. *Mk.* 15: 37.

Being in an agony he prayed more earnestly: and his sweat was as it were great drops of blood falling down to the ground. *Lu.* 22: 44.

You . . . hath he quickened together with him, having forgiven you all trespasses; Blotting out the handwriting of ordinances that was against us, which was contrary to us, and took it out of the way, nailing it to his cross. *Col.* 2: 13, 14.

See also

Christ, Blood of; Christ, Body of; Christ, Cross of; Christ, Crucifixion of; Christ, Cup of; Christ, Death of; Christ, Grief of; Christ, Passion of; Christ, Sacrifice of; Christ, Suffering of.

Christ, Antagonism to

What have we to do with thee, Jesus, thou Son of God? *Mat.* 8: 29.

This night, before the cock crow, thou shalt deny me thrice. *Mat.* 26: 34.

The Jews had agreed already, that if any man did confess that he was Christ, he should be put out of the synagogue. *Jn.* 9: 22.

The cock shall not crow, till thou hast denied me thrice. *Jn.* 13: 38.

I verily thought with myself, that I ought to do many things contrary to the name of Jesus of Nazareth. *Ac.* 26: 9.

What concord hath Christ with Belial? *2 Co.* 6: 15.

At that time ye were without Christ, being aliens from the commonwealth of Israel, and strangers from the covenants of promise. *Ep.* 2: 12.

The enemies of the cross of Christ. *Ph.* 3: 18.

As ye have heard that antichrist shall come, even now are there many antichrists. *1 Jn.* 2: 18.

See also

Christ, Betrayal of; Christ, Defiance of; Christ, Denial of; Christ, Doubt of; Christ, Enemy of; Christ, Hatred of; Christ, Rejection of.

Christ, Appeal of

Follow me, and I will make you fishers of men. *Mat.* 4: 19.

Come unto me, all ye that labour and are heavy laden, and I will give you rest. *Mat.* 11: 28.

Wilt thou be made whole? *Jn.* 5: 6.

If any man thirst, let him come unto me, and drink. *Jn.* 7: 37.

When he had spoken this, he saith unto him, Follow me. *Jn.* 21: 19.

Called unto the fellowship of his Son Jesus Christ our Lord. *1 Co.* 1: 9.

Awake thou that sleepest, and arise from the dead, and Christ shall give thee light. *Ep.* 5: 14.

The Spirit and the bride say, Come. And let him that heareth say, Come. And let him that is athirst come. And whosoever will, let him take the water of life freely. *Re.* 22: 17.

See also

Christ, Acceptance of; Christ, Call of.

Christ, Appearance of

He appeared first to Mary Magdalene, out of whom he had cast seven devils. *Mk.* 16: 9.

After that he appeared in another form unto two of them, as they walked, and went into the country. *Mk.* 16: 12.

Afterward he appeared unto the eleven as they sat at meat. *Mk.* 16: 14.

The dayspring from on high hath visited us. *Lu.* 1: 78.

This beginning of miracles did Jesus in Cana of Galilee, and manifested forth his glory. *Jn.* 2: 11.

Lord, how is it that thou wilt manifest thyself unto us, and not unto the world? *Jn.* 14: 22.

After these things Jesus shewed himself again to the disciples at the sea of Tiberias. *Jn.* 21: 1.

After that, he was seen of James; then of all the apostles. *1 Co.* 15: 7.

Christ . . . hath brought life and immortality to light through the gospel. *2 Ti.* 1: 10.

The Lord Jesus Christ . . . shall judge the quick and the dead at his appearing and his kingdom. *2 Ti.* 4: 1.

Henceforth there is laid up for me a crown of righteousness, which the Lord, the righteous judge, shall give me at that day: and not to me only, but unto all them also that love his appearing. *2 Ti.* 4: 8.

Looking for that blessed hope, and the glorious appearing of the great God and our Saviour Jesus Christ. *Tit.* 2: 13.

Made like unto the Son of God. *He.* 7: 3.

Now once in the end of the world hath he appeared. *He.* 9: 26.

That the trial of your faith, being much more precious than of gold that perisheth, though it be tried with fire, might be found unto praise and honour and glory at the appearing of Jesus Christ. *1 Pe.* 1: 7.

When the chief Shepherd shall appear, ye shall receive a crown of glory that fadeth not away. *1 Pe.* 5: 4.

The life was manifested, and we have seen it, and bear witness, and shew unto you that eternal life. *1 Jn.* 1: 2.

For this purpose the Son of God was manifested, that he might destroy the works of the devil. *1 Jn.* 3: 8.

In the midst of the seven candlesticks one like unto the Son of man. *Re.* 1: 13.

See also
Christ, Face of; Christ, Manliness of; Christ, Revelation of; Christ, Second Coming of; Christ, Vision of.

Christ, Ascension of
Thou hast ascended on high, thou hast led captivity captive. *Ps.* 68: 18.

After the Lord had spoken unto them, he was received up into heaven, and sat on the right hand of God. *Mk.* 16: 19.

While he blessed them, he was parted from them, and carried up into heaven. *Lu.* 24: 51.

No man hath ascended up to heaven, but he that came down from heaven, even the Son of man which is in heaven. *Jn.* 3: 13.

It is expedient for you that I go away. *Jn.* 16: 7.

Touch me not; for I am not yet ascended to my Father. *Jn.* 20: 17.

Ye men of Galilee, why stand ye gazing up into heaven? this same Jesus, which is taken up from you into heaven, shall so come in like manner as ye have seen him go into heaven. *Ac.* 1: 11.

Seeing then that we have a great high priest, that is passed into the heavens, Jesus the Son of God, let us hold fast our profession. *He.* 4: 14.

Christ, Attitude towards
Whosoever therefore shall confess me be-fore men, him will I confess also before my Father which is in heaven. *Mat.* 10: 32.

Whom do men say that I the Son of man am? *Mat.* 16: 13.

Master, we know that thou art true, and teachest the way of God in truth. *Mat.* 22: 16.

What think ye of Christ? *Mat.* 22: 42.

Have thou nothing to do with that just man. *Mat.* 27: 19.

Pilate saith unto them, What shall I do then with Jesus, which is called Christ? *Mat.* 27: 22.

Verily I say unto you, No prophet is accepted in his own country. *Lu.* 4: 24.

If thou shalt confess with thy mouth the Lord Jesus, . . . thou shalt be saved. *Ro.* 10: 9.

Whosoever shall confess that Jesus is the Son of God, God dwelleth in him, and he in God. *1 Jn.* 4: 15.

See also
Christ, Antagonism to; Christ, Belief in; Christ, Challenge of; Christ, Denial of; Christ, Devotion to; Christ, Doubt of; Christ, Faith in; Christ, Gratitude to; Christ, Hope in; Christ, Joy in; Christ, Love of; Christ, Loyalty to; Christ, Obedience to; Christ, Rejection of.

Christ, Authority of
What manner of man is this, that even the winds and the sea obey him! *Mat.* 8: 27.

Hereafter shall ye see the Son of man sitting on the right hand of power, and coming in the clouds of heaven. *Mat.* 26: 64.

He spake unto them, saying, All power is given unto me. *Mat.* 28: 18.

He taught them as one that had authority. *Mk.* 1: 22.

With authority commandeth he even the unclean spirits, and they do obey him. *Mk.* 1: 27.

The Son of man hath power on earth to forgive sins. *Mk.* 2: 10.

I will also ask of you one question, and answer me, and I will tell you by what authority I do these things. *Mk.* 11: 29.

Tell us, by what authority doest thou these things? or who is he that gave thee this authority? *Lu.* 20: 2.

Art thou then the Son of God? And he said unto them, Ye say that I am. *Lu.* 22: 70.

The Father . . . hath given him authority to execute judgment also, because he is the Son of man. *Jn.* 5: 26, 27.

Thou hast given him power over all flesh, that he should give eternal life to as many as thou hast given him. *Jn.* 17: 2.

Let all the house of Israel know assuredly, that God hath made that same Jesus, whom ye have crucified, both Lord and Christ. *Ac.* 2: 36.

Wherefore God also hath highly exalted him, and given him a name which is above every name. *Ph.* 2: 9.

Angels and authorities and powers being made subject unto him. *1 Pe.* 3: 22.

See also
Christ, Influence of; Christ, Obedience of; Christ, Power of; Christ, Reign of; Christ, Supremacy of.

Christ, Beauty of
Thou art fairer than the children of men:

grace is poured into thy lips. *Ps.* 45: 2.

He hath no form nor comeliness; and when we shall see him, there is no beauty that we should desire him. *Is.* 53: 2.

The child grew, . . . and the grace of God was upon him. *Lu.* 2: 40.

The Word was made flesh, and dwelt among us, . . . full of grace and truth. *Jn.* 1: 14.

The grace of our Lord Jesus Christ be with you. *Ro.* 16: 20.

I count all things but loss for the excellency of the knowledge of Christ Jesus my Lord. *Ph.* 3: 8.

Unto you therefore which believe he is precious. *1 Pe.* 2: 7.

See also

Christ, Grace of; Christ, Innocence of.

Christ, Belief in

Let Christ the King of Israel descend now from the cross, that we may see and believe. *Mk.* 15: 32.

He that believeth and is baptized shall be saved. *Mk.* 16: 16.

He that believeth on the Son hath everlasting life. *Jn.* 3: 36.

We believe and are sure that thou art that Christ, the Son of the living God. *Jn.* 6: 69.

He that believeth on me, as the scripture hath said, out of his belly shall flow rivers of living water. *Jn.* 7: 38.

He said, Lord, I believe. And he worshipped him. *Jn.* 9: 38.

Whosoever liveth and believeth in me shall never die. *Jn.* 11: 26.

I believe that thou art the Christ, the Son of God, which should come into the world. *Jn.* 11: 27.

Let not your heart be troubled: ye believe in God, believe also in me. *Jn.* 14: 1.

He that believeth on me, the works that I do shall he do also; and greater works than these shall he do. *Jn.* 14: 12.

These are written, that ye might believe that Jesus is the Christ, the Son of God; and that believing ye might have life through his name. *Jn.* 20: 31.

I believe that Jesus Christ is the Son of God. *Ac.* 8: 37.

Whosoever believeth in him shall receive remission of sins. *Ac.* 10: 43.

Believe on the Lord Jesus Christ, and thou shalt be saved, and thy house. *Ac.* 16: 31.

I am not ashamed of the gospel of Christ: for it is the power of God unto salvation to every one that believeth. *Ro.* 1: 16.

Christ is the end of the law for righteousness to every one that believeth. *Ro.* 10: 4.

If we believe that Jesus died and rose again, even so them also which sleep in Jesus will God bring with him. *1 Th.* 4: 14.

Whom having not seen, ye love; in whom, though now ye see him not, yet believing, ye rejoice with joy unspeakable and full of glory. *1 Pe.* 1: 8.

See also

Christ, Faith in; Christ, Trust in.

Christ, Betrayal of

The Son of man shall be betrayed into the hands of men. *Mat.* 17: 22.

Lord, is it I? *Mat.* 26: 22.

Woe unto that man by whom the Son of man is betrayed! *Mat.* 26: 24.

Betrayest thou the Son of man with a kiss? *Lu.* 22: 48.

The devil having now put into the heart of Judas Iscariot, Simon's son, to betray him. *Jn.* 13: 2.

Lord, which is he that betrayeth thee? *Jn.* 21: 20.

See also

Christ, Denial of; Christ, Rejection of.

Christ, Birth of

Behold, a virgin shall conceive, and bear a son, and shall call his name Immanuel. *Is.* 7: 14.

Unto us a child is born, . . . and his name shall be called Wonderful. *Is.* 9: 6.

Fear not, Mary: for thou hast found favour with God. And, behold, thou shalt conceive in thy womb, and bring forth a son, and shalt call his name Jesus. *Lu.* 1: 30, 31.

She brought forth her firstborn son, and wrapped him in swaddling clothes, and laid him in a manger. *Lu.* 2: 7.

Behold, I bring you good tidings of great joy. *Lu.* 2: 10.

Unto you is born this day in the city of David a Saviour, which is Christ the Lord. *Lu.* 2: 11.

Let us now go even unto Bethlehem, and see this thing which is come to pass. *Lu.* 2: 15.

The Word was made flesh, and dwelt among us, (and we beheld his glory). *Jn.* 1: 14.

Thanks be unto God for his unspeakable gift. *2 Co.* 9: 15.

See also

Carol; Christmas.

Christ, Blood of

That field was called, The field of blood, unto this day. *Mat.* 27: 8.

I am innocent of the blood of this just person: see ye to it. *Mat.* 27: 24.

Except ye eat the flesh of the Son·of man, and drink his blood, ye have no life in you. *Jn.* 6: 53.

Ye seek to kill me, because my word hath no place in you. *Jn.* 8: 37.

Ye denied the Holy One and the Just, . . . And killed the Prince of life. *Ac.* 3: 14, 15.

To be a propitiation through faith in his blood. *Ro.* 3: 25.

Christ our passover is sacrificed for us. *1 Co.* 5: 7.

How much more shall the blood of Christ, who through the eternal Spirit offered himself without spot to God, purge your conscience from dead works to serve the living God? *He.* 9: 14.

Ye are come . . . to the blood of sprinkling. *He.* 12: 22, 24.

The blood of the everlasting covenant. *He.* 13: 20.

The precious blood of Christ. *1 Pe.* 1: 19.

The blood of Jesus Christ his Son cleanseth us from all sin. *1 Jn.* 1: 7.

This is he that came by water and blood, even Jesus Christ; not by water only, but by water and by blood. *1 Jn.* 5: 6.

These . . . have washed their robes, and made them white in the blood of the Lamb. *Re.* 7: 14.

See also

Christ, Agony of; Christ, Cross of; Christ, Cup of; Christ, Death of; Christ, Passion of; Christ, Sacrifice of; Christ, Suffering of.

Christ, Body of

Jesus took bread, and blessed it, and brake it, . . . and said, Take, eat; this is my body. *Mat.* 26: 26.

They entered in, and found not the body of the Lord Jesus. *Lu.* 24: 3.

In the beginning was the Word, . . . And the Word was made flesh. *Jn.* 1: 1, 14.

He spake of the temple of his body. *Jn.* 2: 21.

The bread that I will give is my flesh, which I will give for the life of the world. *Jn.* 6: 51.

My flesh is meat indeed, and my blood is drink indeed. *Jn.* 6: 55.

Ye also are become dead to the law by the body of Christ. *Ro.* 7: 4.

God sending his own Son in the likeness of sinful flesh. *Ro.* 8: 3.

The bread which we break, is it not the communion of the body of Christ? *1 Co.* 10: 16.

This is my body, which is broken for you. *1 Co.* 11: 24.

Not discerning the Lord's body. *1 Co.* 11: 29.

Now ye are the body of Christ, and members in particular. *1 Co.* 12: 27.

Though we have known Christ after the flesh, yet now henceforth know we him no more. *2 Co.* 5: 16.

We are members of his body, of his flesh, and of his bones. *Ep.* 5: 30.

We are sanctified through the offering of the body of Jesus Christ once for all. *He.* 10: 10.

Christ hath suffered for us in the flesh. *1 Pe.* 4: 1.

See also

Christ, Agony of; Christ, the Bread of Life; Christ, Cross of; Christ, Death of; Christ, Passion of; Christ, Sacrifice of; Christ, Suffering of.

Christ, the Bread of Life

He was known of them in breaking of bread. *Lu.* 24: 35.

Labour not for the meat which perisheth, but for that meat which endureth unto everlasting life, which the Son of man shall give unto you. *Jn.* 6: 27.

Evermore give us this bread. *Jn.* 6: 34.

Jesus said unto them, I am the bread of life: he that cometh to me shall never hunger; and he that believeth on me shall never thirst. *Jn.* 6: 35.

I am the living bread which came down from heaven: if any man eat of this bread, he shall live for ever. *Jn.* 6: 51.

See also

Christ, Body of.

Christ, Call of

He saith unto them, Follow me, and I will make you fishers of men. *Mat.* 4: 18, 19.

Come unto me, all ye that labour and are heavy laden, and I will give you rest. *Mat.* 11: 28.

Jesus called his disciples unto him. *Mat.* 15: 32.

Jesus called a little child unto him. *Mat.* 18: 2.

So the last shall be first, and the first last: for many be called, but few chosen. *Mat.* 20: 16.

Come. *Mat.* 25: 34.

Come ye after me, and I will make you to become fishers of men. *Mk.* 1: 17.

When Jesus came to the place, he looked up, and saw him, and said unto him, Zacchaeus, make haste, and come down. *Lu.* 19: 5.

Every one that is of the truth heareth my voice. *Jn.* 18: 37.

Faithful is he that calleth you. *1 Th.* 5: 24.

Who hath called you out of darkness into his marvellous light. *1 Pe.* 2: 9.

Through the knowledge of him that hath called us to glory and virtue. *2 Pe.* 1: 3.

The Spirit and the bride say, Come. And let him that heareth say, Come. And let him that is athirst come. And whosoever will, let him take the water of life freely. *Re.* 22: 17.

See also

Christ, Acceptance of; Christ, Appeal of.

Christ, the Captain

Ye . . . killed the Prince of life, whom God hath raised from the dead. *Ac.* 3: 14, 15.

Him hath God exalted with his right hand to be a Prince and a Saviour. *Ac.* 5: 31.

Our Lord Jesus Christ: . . . who is the blessed and only Potentate, the King of kings, and Lord of lords. *1 Ti.* 6: 14, 15.

It became him, for whom are all things, and by whom are all things, in bringing many sons unto glory, to make the captain of their salvation perfect through sufferings. *He.* 2: 10.

See also

Christ, Authority of; Christ, the Guide; Christ, the King; Christ, the Leader; Christ, Power of; Christ, Reign of; Christ, Supremacy of.

Christ, the Carpenter

Is not this the carpenter's son? *Mat.* 13: 55.

Is not this the carpenter, the son of Mary, the brother of James, and Joses, and of Juda, and Simon? *Mk.* 6: 3.

See also

Christ, Family of.

Christ, Centrality of

Where two or three are gathered together in my name, there am I in the midst of them. *Mat.* 18: 20.

He was transfigured before them. *Mk.* 9: 2.

After three days they found him in the temple, sitting in the midst of the doctors. *Lu.* 2: 46.

The Holy Ghost descended in a bodily shape like a dove upon him, and a voice came from heaven, which said, Thou art my beloved Son. *Lu.* 3: 22.

Jesus himself stood in the midst of them, and saith unto them, Peace be unto you. *Lu.* 24: 36.

As Moses lifted up the serpent in the wilderness, even so must the Son of man be lifted up. *Jn.* 3: 14.

I, if I be lifted up from the earth, will draw all men unto me. *Jn.* 12: 32.

That where I am, there ye may be also. *Jn.* 14: 3.

They crucified him, and two other with him, on either side one, and Jesus in the midst. *Jn.* 19: 18.

Jesus of Nazareth, a man approved of God among you by miracles and wonders and signs, which God did by him in the midst of you. *Ac.* 2: 22.

There is none other name under heaven given among men, whereby we must be saved. *Ac.* 4: 12.

In the midst of the throne . . . a Lamb as it had been slain. *Re.* 5: 6.

See also

Christ, Finality of; Christ, Pre-eminence of; Christ, Supremacy of.

Christ, Challenge of

Follow me, and I will make you fishers of men. *Mat.* 4: 19.

He saith unto them, But whom say ye that I am? *Mat.* 16: 15.

If any man will come after me, let him deny himself, and take up his cross, and follow me. *Mat.* 16: 24.

If thou wilt be perfect, go and sell that thou hast, and give to the poor, and thou shalt have treasure in heaven. *Mat.* 19: 21.

Wilt thou lay down thy life for my sake? *Jn.* 13: 38.

In Christ Jesus neither circumcision availeth any thing, nor uncircumcision, but a new creature. *Ga.* 6: 15.

See also

Christ, Hatred toward.

Christ, the Changeless

Lo, I am with you alway, even unto the end of the world. *Mat.* 28: 20.

We have heard out of the law that Christ abideth for ever. *Jn.* 12: 34.

There are differences of administrations, but the same Lord. *I Co.* 12: 5.

All the promises of God in him are yea, and in him Amen. *2 Co.* 1: 20.

Jesus, made an high priest for ever after the order of Melchisedec. *He.* 6: 20.

This man, because he continueth ever, hath an unchangeable priesthood. *He.* 7: 24.

Jesus Christ the same yesterday, and today, and for ever. *He.* 13: 8.

Jesus Christ, who is the faithful witness. *Re.* 1: 5.

I am Alpha and Omega, the beginning and the ending, saith the Lord, which is, and which was, and which is to come. *Re.* 1: 8.

Behold, I am alive for evermore. *Re.* 1: 18.

See also

Christ, the Contemporary; Christ, Finality of; Christ, Permanence of; Christ, the Rock.

Christ, the Chosen of

He stretched forth his hand toward his disciples, and said, Behold my mother and my brethren! *Mat.* 12: 49.

Whosoever shall do the will of my Father which is in heaven, the same is my brother, and sister, and mother. *Mat.* 12: 50.

Many are called, but few are chosen. *Mat.* 22: 14.

For the elect's sake, whom he hath chosen, he hath shortened the days. *Mk.* 13: 20.

After these things the Lord appointed other seventy also. *Lu.* 10: 1.

Rejoice, because your names are written in heaven. *Lu.* 10: 20.

Have I not chosen you twelve, and one of you is a devil? *Jn.* 6: 70.

I speak not of you all: I know whom I have chosen. *Jn.* 13: 18.

Ye are my friends, if ye do whatsoever I command you. *Jn.* 15: 14.

Ye have not chosen me, but I have chosen you, and ordained you. *Jn.* 15: 16.

Because ye are not of the world, but I have chosen you out of the world, therefore the world hateth you. *Jn.* 15: 19.

I pray not for the world, but for them which thou hast given me; for they are thine. *Jn.* 17: 9.

See also

Christ, Disciple of; Christ, Follower of.

Christ, the Comforter

Jesus . . . said, Daughter, be of good comfort; thy faith hath made thee whole. *Mat.* 9: 22.

And when the Lord saw her, he had compassion on her, and said unto her, Weep not. *Lu.* 7: 13.

Let not your heart be troubled: . . . I will not leave you comfortless: I will come to you. *Jn.* 14: 1, 18.

As the sufferings of Christ abound in us, so our consolation also aboundeth by Christ. *2 Co.* 1: 5.

If there be therefore any consolation in Christ, if any comfort of love, . . . Fulfil ye my joy. *Ph.* 2: 1, 2.

See also

Christ, Compassion of; Christ, Encouragement of; Christ, the Healing; Christ, Help of; Christ, the Physician; Christ, Sympathy of; Christ, Touch of.

Christ, Coming of

The Redeemer shall come to Zion. *Is.* 59: 20.

Jesus was born in Bethlehem of Judaea. *Mat.* 2: 1.

Thou Bethlehem, in the land of Juda, art not the least among the princes of Juda: for out of thee shall come a Governor, that shall rule my people Israel. *Mat.* 2: 6.

I am not come to destroy, but to fulfil. *Mat.* 5: 17.

Jesus saith unto him, I will come and heal him. *Mat.* 8: 7.

I am not come to call the righteous, but sinners to repentance. *Mat.* 9: 13.

The Son of man shall come in the glory of his Father with his angels. *Mat.* 16: 27.

The Son of man is come to save that which was lost. *Mat.* 18: 11.

Light is come into the world, and men loved darkness rather than light. *Jn.* 3: 19.

I know whence I came, and whither I go;

but ye cannot tell whence I come, and whither I go. *Jn.* 8: 14.

I am come that they might have life, and that they might have it more abundantly. *Jn.* 10: 10.

I am come a light into the world. *Jn.* 12: 46.

I will not leave you comfortless: I will come to you. *Jn.* 14: 18.

This same Jesus, which is taken up from you into heaven, shall so come in like manner as ye have seen him go into heaven. *Ac.* 1: 11.

Judge nothing before the time, until the Lord come. *1 Co.* 4: 5.

As often as ye eat this bread, and drink this cup, ye do shew the Lord's death till he come. *1 Co.* 11: 26.

When the fulness of the time was come, God sent forth his Son. *Ga.* 4: 4.

Christ being come an high priest of good things to come. *He.* 9: 11.

Every spirit that confesseth that Jesus Christ is come in the flesh is of God. *1 Jn.* 4: 2.

See also
Christ, Second Coming of.

Christ, Coming to

Come unto me, all ye that labour and are heavy laden, and I will give you rest. *Mat.* 11: 28.

Tell them which are bidden, Behold, I have prepared my dinner: . . . come unto the marriage. *Mat.* 22: 4.

Suffer the little children to come unto me, and forbid them not. *Mk.* 10: 14.

Him that cometh to me I will in no wise cast out. *Jn.* 6: 37.

In Christ Jesus I have begotten you through the gospel. *1 Co.* 4: 15.

Having a desire to depart, and to be with Christ. *Ph.* 1: 23.

To whom coming. *1 Pe.* 2: 4.

Behold, I stand at the door, and knock. *Re.* 3: 20.

See also
Christ, Acceptance of; Christ, Call of; Christ, the Door; Christ, the Way.

Christ, Commandments of

Whosoever therefore shall break one of these least commandments, and shall teach men so, he shall be called the least in the kingdom of heaven: but whosoever shall do and teach them, the same shall be called great in the kingdom of heaven. *Mat.* 5: 19.

Go ye therefore, and teach all nations, . . . Teaching them to observe all things whatsoever I have commanded you. *Mat.* 28: 19, 20.

With authority commandeth he even the unclean spirits, and they do obey him. *Mk.* 1: 27.

He . . . commanded them that they should take . . . no money in their purse. *Mk.* 6: 7, 8.

What manner of man is this! for he commandeth even the winds and water, and they obey him. *Lu.* 8: 25.

A new commandment I give unto you, That ye love one another. *Jn.* 13: 34.

He that hath my commandments, and keepeth them, he it is that loveth me. *Jn.* 14: 21.

If ye keep my commandments, ye shall abide in my love. *Jn.* 15: 10.

He that keepeth his commandments dwelleth in him, and he in him. *1 Jn.* 3: 24.

See also
Christ, Devotion to; Christ, Disciple of; Christ, Obedience to.

Christ, Communion with

Come unto me, all ye that labour and are heavy laden, and I will give you rest. *Mat.* 11: 28.

Did not our hearts burn within us, while he talked with us by the way, and while he opened to us the scriptures? *Lu.* 24: 32.

Who shall separate us from the love of Christ? *Ro.* 8: 35.

The cup of blessing which we bless, is it not the communion of the blood of Christ? The bread which we break, is it not the communion of the body of Christ? *1 Co.* 10: 16.

- As the sufferings of Christ abound in us, so our consolation also aboundeth by Christ. *2 Co.* 1: 5.

Always bearing about in the body the dying of the Lord Jesus. *2 Co.* 4: 10.

We are confident, I say, and willing rather to be absent from the body, and present with the Lord. *2 Co.* 5: 8.

That I may know him, and the power of his resurrection, and the fellowship of his sufferings. *Ph.* 3: 10.

As ye have therefore received Christ Jesus the Lord, so walk ye in him. *Col.* 2: 6.

And you, being dead in your sins, . . . hath he quickened together with him. *Col.* 2: 13.

So shall we ever be with the Lord. Wherefore comfort one another with these words. *1 Th.* 4: 17, 18.

See also
Christ, Abiding in; Christ, Companionship of; Christ, Fellowship with; Christ, Life in; Christ, Nearness of; Christ, Partnership with; Christ, Union with.

Christ, Companionship of

Ye shall indeed drink of the cup that I drink of; and with the baptism that I am baptized withal shall ye be baptized. *Mk.* 10: 39.

Joint-heirs with Christ. *Ro.* 8: 17.

Ye are the body of Christ. *1 Co.* 12: 27.

I take pleasure in infirmities . . . for Christ's sake. *2 Co.* 12: 10.

If ye then be risen with Christ, seek those things which are above. *Col.* 3: 1.

If we believe that Jesus died and rose again, even so them also which sleep in Jesus will God bring with him. *1 Th.* 4: 14.

Fellowprisoner in Christ Jesus. *Phm.* 1: 23.

Rejoice, inasmuch as ye are partakers of Christ's sufferings; that, when his glory shall be revealed, ye may be glad also with exceeding joy. *1 Pe.* 4: 13.

Companion in tribulation, and in the kingdom and patience of Jesus Christ. *Re.* 1: 9.

See also
Christ, Abiding in; Christ, Communion with; Christ, Fellowship with; Christ, the Friend; Christ, Life in; Christ, Nearness of; Christ, Partnership with; Christ, Union with.

Christ, Compassion of

Jesus . . . said, I have compassion on the multitude. *Mat.* 15: 32.

Two blind men, . . . when they heard that Jesus passed by, cried out, saying, Have mercy on us, O Lord. *Mat.* 20: 30.

Jesus had compassion on them, and touched their eyes. *Mat.* 20: 34.

Jesus, moved with compassion, put forth his hand, and touched him. *Mk.* 1: 41.

She . . . stood at his feet behind him weeping. *Lu.* 7: 37, 38.

Her sins, which are many, are forgiven; for she loved much. *Lu.* 7: 47.

And when he was come near, he beheld the city, and wept over it. *Lu.* 19: 41.

Jesus wept. *Jn.* 11: 35.

Looking for the mercy of our Lord Jesus Christ unto eternal life. *Jude* 1: 21.

See also

Christ, the Comforter; Christ, Gentleness of; Christ, Grief of; Christ, Help of; Christ, Sympathy of; Christ, Touch of.

Christ, Compulsion of

He taught them as one having authority. *Mat.* 7: 29.

Jesus constrained his disciples. *Mat.* 14: 22.

With authority commandeth he even the unclean spirits, and they do obey him. *Mk.* 1: 27.

Whether it be right in the sight of God to hearken unto you more than unto God, judge ye. For we cannot but speak the things which we have seen and heard. *Ac.* 4: 19, 20.

Paul was pressed in the spirit, and testified to the Jews that Jesus was Christ. *Ac.* 18: 5.

I go bound in the spirit unto Jerusalem. *Ac.* 20: 22.

The power of our Lord Jesus Christ. *1 Co.* 5: 4.

Though I preach the gospel, I have nothing to glory of: for necessity is laid upon me; yea, woe is unto me, if I preach not the gospel! *1 Co.* 9: 16.

The love of Christ constraineth us. *2 Co.* 5: 14.

Most gladly therefore will I rather glory in my infirmities, that the power of Christ may rest upon me. *2 Co.* 12: 9.

According to the power that worketh in us. *Ep.* 3: 20.

See also

Christ, Authority of; Christ, Influence of; Christ, Power of.

Christ, Condemnation of

Judge not, that ye be not judged. *Mat.* 7: 1.

The men of Nineveh shall rise in judgment with this generation, and shall condemn it: because they repented at the preaching of Jonas; and behold, a greater than Jonas is here. *Mat.* 12: 41.

Woe unto you, scribes and Pharisees, hypocrites! *Mat.* 23: 13.

Cast ye the unprofitable servant into outer darkness. *Mat.* 25: 30.

He shall set the sheep on his right hand, but the goats on the left. *Mat.* 25: 33.

Woe unto that man by whom the Son of man is betrayed! *Mat.* 26: 24.

What think ye? They answered and said, He is guilty of death. *Mat.* 26: 66.

Who made me a judge or a divider over you? *Lu.* 12: 14.

God sent not his Son into the world to condemn the world; but that the world through him might be saved. *Jn.* 3: 17.

As I hear, I judge: and my judgment is just. *Jn.* 5: 30.

Neither do I condemn thee: go, and sin no more. *Jn.* 8: 11.

Jesus said, For judgment I am come into this world. *Jn.* 9: 39.

If any man hear my words, and believe not, I judge him not: for I came not to judge the world, but to save the world. *Jn.* 12: 47.

See also

Christ, the Accusing; Christ, the Judge.

Christ, the Contemporary

Lo, I am with you alway, even unto the end of the world. *Mat.* 28: 20.

Why seek ye the living among the dead? *Lu.* 24: 5.

In him we live, and move, and have our being. *Ac.* 17: 28.

Now if we be dead with Christ, we believe that we shall also live with him. *Ro.* 6: 8.

Whether we live, we live unto the Lord; and whether we die, we die unto the Lord. *Ro.* 14: 8.

We are . . . willing rather to be absent from the body, and to be present with the Lord. *2 Co.* 5: 8.

I am crucified with Christ: nevertheless I live; yet not I, but Christ liveth in me. *Ga.* 2: 20.

For to me to live is Christ. *Ph.* 1: 21.

It is a faithful saying: For if we be dead with him, we shall also live with him. *2 Ti.* 2: 11.

This man, because he continueth ever, hath an unchangeable priesthood. *He.* 7: 24.

He ever liveth to make intercession for them. *He.* 7: 25.

I am he that liveth, and was dead; and, behold, I am alive for evermore. *Re.* 1: 18.

Written in the Lamb's book of life. *Re.* 21: 27.

See also

Christ, the Changeless; Christ, the Eternal; Christ, the Indwelling; Christ, Life in; Christ, the Living; Christ, Nearness of; Christ, Permanence of; Christ, Presence of.

Christ, Courage of

Behold, we go up to Jerusalem; and the Son of man shall be betrayed unto the chief priests and unto the scribes, and they shall condemn him to death. *Mat.* 20: 18.

Let this cup pass from me: nevertheless not as I will, but as thou wilt. *Mat.* 26: 39.

Then said Jesus unto him, Put up again thy sword into his place. *Mat.* 26: 52.

Are ye come out as against a thief with swords and staves for to take me? I sat daily with you teaching in the temple, and ye laid no hold on me. *Mat.* 26: 55.

Then did they spit in his face, and buffeted him; and others smote him with the palms of their hands. *Mat.* 26: 67.

I have a baptism to be baptized with; and how am I straitened till it be accomplished! *Lu.* 12: 50.

He speaketh boldly, and they say nothing unto him. *Jn.* 7: 26.

Looking unto Jesus the author and finisher of our faith; who for the joy that was set

before him endured the cross. *He.* **12: 2.**
See also
Christ, Cross of; Christ, Manliness of; Christ, Sacrifice of; Christ, Strength of.

Christ, the Creator

Without him was not any thing made that was made. *Jn.* **1: 3.**

God, who created all things by Jesus Christ. *Ep.* **3: 9.**

By him were all things created, that are in heaven, and that are in earth, visible and invisible, whether they be thrones or dominions, or principalities, or powers. *Col.* **1: 16.**

All things were created by him, and for him. *Col.* **1: 16.**

By him all things consist. *Col.* **1: 17.**

By whom also he made the worlds. *He.* **1: 2.**
See also
Alpha.

Christ, Cross of

It was the third hour, and they crucified him. *Mk.* **15: 25.**

Our old man is crucified with him. *Ro.* **6: 6.**

Unto us which are saved it is the power of God. *1 Co.* **1: 18.**

We preach Christ crucified, unto the Jews a stumblingblock, and unto the Greeks foolishness. *1 Co.* **1: 23.**

I determined not to know any thing among you, save Jesus Christ, and him crucified. *1 Co.* **2: 2.**

God forbid that I should glory, save in the cross of our Lord Jesus Christ, by whom the world is crucified unto me, and I unto the world. *Ga.* **6: 14.**

They are enemies of the cross of Christ. *Ph.* **3: 18.**

They crucify to themselves the Son of God afresh. *He.* **6: 6.**

Who for the joy that was set before him endured the cross, despising the shame. *He.* **12: 2.**
See also
Christ, Agony of; Christ, Blood of; Christ, Body of; Christ, Crucifixion of; Christ, Cup of; Christ, Death of; Christ Passion of; Christ, Sacrifice of; Christ, Suffering of.

Christ, Crown of

When they had platted a crown of thorns, they put it upon his head. *Mat.* **27: 29.**

Art thou the King of the Jews? And he answered him and said, Thou sayest it. *Lu.* **23: 3.**

My kingdom is not of this world. *Jn.* **18: 36.**

Then came Jesus forth, wearing the crown of thorns, and the purple robe. *Jn.* **19: 5.**

These all do contrary to the decrees of Caesar, saying that there is another king, one Jesus. *Ac.* **17: 7.**

We see Jesus, who was made a little lower than the angels for the suffering of death, crowned with glory and honour. *He.* **2: 9.**

When he is tried, he shall receive the crown of life, which the Lord hath promised to them that love him. *Ja.* **1: 12.**
See also
Christ, the King; Christ, Reign of; Christ, Supremacy of; Christ, Triumph of.

Christ, Crucifixion of

Surely he hath borne our griefs, and carried our sorrows. *Is.* **53: 4.**

As Moses lifted up the serpent in the wilderness, even so must the Son of man be lifted up. *Jn.* **3: 14.**

When ye have lifted up the Son of man, then shall ye know that I am he. *Jn.* **8: 28.**

Was Paul crucified for you? *1 Co.* **1: 13.**

For the Jews require a sign, and the Greeks seek after wisdom: But we preach Christ crucified, unto the Jews a stumblingblock, and unto the Greeks foolishness; But unto them which are called, both Jews and Greeks, Christ the power of God, and the wisdom of God. *1 Co.* **1: 22–24.**

I determined not to know any thing among you, save Jesus Christ, and him crucified. *1 Co.* **2: 2.**

I am crucified with Christ: nevertheless I live. *Ga.* **2: 20.**

They that are Christ's have crucified the flesh with the affections and lusts. *Ga.* **5: 24.**

Seeing they crucify to themselves the Son of God afresh. *He.* **6: 6.**
See also
Christ, Agony of; Christ, Blood of; Christ, Body of; Christ, Cross of; Christ, Cup of; Christ, Death of; Christ, Passion of; Christ, Sacrifice of; Christ, Suffering of.

Christ, Cup of

Are ye able to drink of the cup that I shall drink of? *Mat.* **20: 22.**

O my Father, if it be possible, let this cup pass from me. *Mat.* **26: 39.**

O my Father, if this cup may not pass away from me, except I drink it, thy will be done. *Mat.* **26: 42.**

Ye shall indeed drink of the cup that I drink of; and with the baptism that I am baptized withal shall ye be baptized. *Mk.* **10: 39.**

He took the cup, and gave thanks, and said, Take this, and divide it among yourselves. *Lu.* **22: 17.**

This cup is the new testament in my blood, which is shed for you. *Lu.* **22: 20.**

The cup which my Father hath given me, shall I not drink it? *Jn.* **18: 11.**

The cup of blessing which we bless, is it not the communion of the blood of Christ? *1 Co.* **10: 16.**

Ye cannot drink the cup of the Lord, and the cup of devils. *1 Co.* **10: 21.**

As often as ye . . . drink this cup, ye do shew the Lord's death till he come. *1 Co.* **11: 26.**
See also
Christ, Agony of; Christ, Blood of; Christ, Cross of; Christ, Death of; Christ, Passion of; Christ, Sacrifice of; Christ, Suffering of.

Christ, Day of

Ye know neither the day nor the hour wherein the Son of man cometh. *Mat.* **25: 13.**

In that day. *Jn.* **16: 23.**

We shall all stand before the judgment seat of Christ. *Ro.* **14: 10.**

To deliver such an one unto Satan for the destruction of the flesh, that the spirit may be saved in the day of the Lord Jesus. *1 Co.* 5: 5.

We are your rejoicing, even as ye also are ours in the day of the Lord Jesus. *2 Co.* 1: 14.

He which hath begun a good work in you will perform it until the day of Jesus Christ. *Ph.* 1: 6.

The day of the Lord so cometh as a thief in the night. *1 Th.* 5: 2.

The day of Christ is at hand. *2 Th.* 2: 2.

I know whom I have believed, and am persuaded that he is able to keep that which I have committed unto him against that day. *2 Ti.* 1: 12.

Henceforth there is laid up for me a crown of righteousness, which the Lord, the righteous judge, shall give me at that day. *2 Ti.* 4: 8.

See also

Christ, Hour of; Christ, the Judge; Christ, Second Coming of.

Christ, Death of

So shall the Son of man be three days and three nights in the heart of the earth. *Mat.* 12: 40.

There talked with him two men, which were Moses and Elias: Who appeared in glory, and spake of his decease. *Lu.* 9: 30, 31.

This spake he, signifying by what death he should glorify God. *Jn.* 21: 19.

We were reconciled to God by the death of his Son. *Ro.* 5: 10.

So many of us as were baptized into Jesus Christ were baptized into his death. *Ro.* 6: 3.

Death hath no more dominion over him. *Ro.* 6: 9.

As often as ye eat this bread, and drink this cup, ye do shew the Lord's death till he come. *1 Co.* 11: 26.

Christ died for our sins according to the scriptures. *1 Co.* 15: 3.

Since by man came death, by man came also the resurrection of the dead. *1 Co.* 15: 21.

Who . . . endured the cross, despising the shame. *He.* 12: 2.

See also

Christ, Agony of; Christ, Blood of; Christ, Body of; Christ, Cross of; Christ, Cup of; Christ, Passion of; Christ, Sacrifice of; Christ, Suffering of.

Christ, Defiance of

Jesus held his peace. *Mat.* 26: 63.

He is guilty of death. *Mat.* 26: 66.

Then did they spit in his face, and buffeted him. *Mat.* 26: 67.

Then answered all the people, and said, His blood be on us, and on our children. *Mat.* 27: 25.

Are ye come out as against a thief, with swords and with staves to take me? *Mk.* 14: 48.

Ye shall see the Son of man sitting on the right hand of power, and coming in the clouds of heaven. *Mk.* 14: 62.

What have I to do with thee, Jesus, thou Son of God most high? *Lu.* 8: 28.

Many of them said, He hath a devil, and is mad; why hear ye him? *Jn.* 10: 20.

Ye denied the Holy One and the Just. *Ac.* 3: 14.

If we deny him: he also will deny us. *2 Ti.* 2: 12.

Of how much sorer punishment, suppose ye, shall he be thought worthy, who hath trodden under foot the Son of God. *He.* 10: 29.

Even denying the Lord that bought them. *2 Pe.* 2: 1.

Who is a liar but he that denieth Jesus is the Christ? He is antichrist, that denieth the Father and the Son. *1 Jn.* 2: 22.

See also

Christ, Antagonism to; Christ, Denial of; Christ, Enemy of; Christ, Rejection of.

Christ, the Deliverer

Jesus rebuked the devil; and he departed out of him. *Mat.* 17: 18.

The Son of man came not to be ministered unto, but to minister, and to give his life a ransom for many. *Mat.* 20: 28.

He hath sent me to heal the broken-hearted, to preach deliverance to the captives. *Lu.* 4: 18.

He hath anointed me . . . to set at liberty them that are bruised. *Lu.* 4: 18.

The Son of man is not come to destroy men's lives, but to save them. *Lu.* 9: 56.

There is none other name under heaven given among men, whereby we must be saved. *Ac.* 4: 12.

Him hath God exalted with his right hand to be a Prince and a Saviour. *Ac.* 5: 31.

Sirs, what must I do to be saved? And they said, Believe on the Lord Jesus Christ, and thou shalt be saved. *Ac.* 16: 30, 31.

God commendeth his love toward us, in that, while we were yet sinners, Christ died for us. *Ro.* 5: 8.

If we be dead with Christ, we believe that we shall also live with him. *Ro.* 6: 8.

Where the Spirit of the Lord is, there is liberty. *2 Co.* 3: 17.

He became the author of eternal salvation unto all them that obey him. *He.* 5: 9.

See also

Christ, the Liberator; Christ, the Redeemer; Christ, the Saviour.

Christ, Denial of

What have we to do with thee, Jesus, thou Son of God? *Mat.* 8: 29.

Whosoever shall deny me before men, him will I also deny before my Father which is in heaven. *Mat.* 10: 33.

He denied with an oath, I do not know the man. *Mat.* 26: 72.

He trusted in God; let him deliver him now, if he will have him: for he said, I am the Son of God. *Mat.* 27: 43.

Whosoever therefore shall be ashamed of me and of my words in this adulterous and sinful generation; of him also shall the Son of man be ashamed, when he cometh in the glory of his Father with the holy angels. *Mk.* 8: 38.

Say ye of him, whom the Father hath sanctified, and sent into the world, Thou blasphemest; because I said, I am the Son of God? *Jn.* 10: 36.

Jesus answered him, Wilt thou lay down thy life for my sake? Verily, verily, I say unto thee, The cock shall not crow, till thou hast denied me thrice. *Jn.* 13: 38.

Jesus also . . . suffered without the gate. *He.* 13: 12.

Who is a liar but he that denieth that Jesus is the Christ? *1 Jn.* 2: 22.

Whosoever denieth the Son, the same hath not the Father. *1 Jn.* 2: 23.

Denying the only Lord God, and our Lord Jesus Christ. *Jude* 1: 4.

See also

Christ, Antagonism to; Christ, Betrayal of; Christ, Defiance of; Christ, Hatred of; Christ. Rejection of.

Christ, Dependence on

He shall save his people from their sins. *Mat.* 1: 21.

I ord, save me. *Mat.* 14: 30.

All power is given unto me in heaven and in earth. *Mat.* 28: 18.

The Son of man hath power on earth to forgive sins. *Mk.* 2: 10.

Whv are ye so fearful? how is it that ye have no faith? *Mk.* 4: 40.

Without me ye can do nothing. *Jn.* 15: 5.

Neither is there salvation in any other: for there is none other name under heaven given among men, whereby we must be saved. *Ac.* 4: 12.

Most gladly therefore will I rather glory in my infirmities, that the power of Christ may rest upon me. *2 Co.* 12: 9.

We can do nothing against the truth, but for the truth. *2 Co.* 13: 8.

Christ as a son over his own house; whose house are we, if we hold fast the confidence and the rejoicing of the hope firm unto the end. *He.* 3: 6.

He is able also to save them to the uttermost that come unto God by him. *He.* 7: 25.

See also

Christ, Need of; Christ, Trust in.

Christ, Destiny of

Behold upon the mountains the feet of him that bringeth good tidings, that publisheth peace! *Na.* 1: 15.

Out of thee shall come a Governor, that shall rule my people Israel. *Mat.* 2: 6.

Thus it must be. *Mat.* 26: 54.

Wist ye not that I must be about my Father's business? *Lu.* 2: 49.

All things must be fufilled, which were written in the law of Moses, and in the prophets, and in the psalms, concerning me. *Lu.* 24: 44.

God hath made that same Jesus, whom ye have crucified, both Lord and Christ. *Ac.* 2: 36.

He hath appointed a day, in the which he will judge the world in righteousness by that man whom he hath ordained. *Ac.* 17: 31.

In due time Christ died for the ungodly. *Ro.* 5: 6.

He must reign, till he hath put all enemies under his feet. *1 Co.* 15: 25.

Christ . . . was foreordained before the foundation of the world, but was manifest in these last times for you. *1 Pe.* 1: 19, 20.

See also

Christ. Fate of.

Christ, Devotion to

Master, we know that thou art true, and teachest the way of God in truth. *Mat.* 22: 16.

They forsook all, and followed him. *Lu.* 5: 11.

Let not your heart be troubled: ye believe in God, believe also in me. *Jn.* 14: 1.

Nor height, nor depth, nor any other creature, shall be able to separate us from the love of God, which is in Christ Jesus our Lord. *Ro.* 8: 39.

Put ye on the Lord Jesus Christ, and make not provision for the flesh. *Ro.* 13: 14.

That Christ may dwell in your hearts by faith. *Ep.* 3: 17.

I know whom I have believed, and am persuaded that he is able to keep that which I have committed unto him against that day. *2 Ti.* 1: 12.

Let us draw near with a true heart. *He.* 10: 22.

See also

Christ, Adoration of; Christ, Belief in; Christ, Commandments of; Christ, Faith in; Christ, Love of; Christ, Loyalty to; Christ, Obedience to; Christ, Praise of; Christ, Suffering for.

Christ, Dignity of

Whose shoes I am not worthy to bear. *Mat.* 3: 11.

He that honoureth not the Son honoureth not the Father. *Jn.* 5: 23.

I receive not honour from men. *Jn.* 5: 41.

It is my Father that honoureth me. *Jn.* 8: 54.

I have power to lay it down. *Jn.* 10: 18.

If any man serve me, him will my Father honour. *Jn.* 12: 26.

To whom be honour and power everlasting. *1 Ti.* 6: 16.

This man was counted worthy of more glory than Moses. *He.* 3: 3.

He received from God the Father honour and glory, when there came such a voice to him from the excellent glory, This is my beloved Son. *2 Pe.* 1: 17.

Worthy is the Lamb that was slain to receive power, and riches, and wisdom, and strength, and honour, and glory, and blessing. *Re.* 5: 12.

See also

Christ, Exaltation of; Christ, Glory of; Christ, Greatness of; Christ, Majesty of; Christ, Nature of; Christ, Supremacy of; Christ, Triumph of.

Christ, Disciple of

Follow me, and I will make you fishers of men. *Mat.* 4: 19.

Surely thou also art one of them; for thy speech bewrayeth thee. *Mat.* 26: 73.

Whosoever will come after me, let him deny himself, and take up the cross, and follow me. *Mk.* 8: 34.

And he said unto another, Follow me. But he said, Lord, suffer me first to go and bury my father. Jesus said unto him, Let the dead bury their dead: but go thou and preach the kingdom of God. *Lu.* 9: 59, 60.

After these things the Lord appointed other seventy also, and sent them. *Lu.* 10: 1.

Whosoever he be of you that forsaketh not

all that he hath, he cannot be my disciple. *Lu.* 14: 33.

Herein is my Father glorified, that ye bear much fruit; so shall ye be my disciples. *Jn.* 15: 8.

Peter . . . saith to Jesus, Lord, and what shall this man do? Jesus saith unto him, If I will that he tarry till I come, what is that to thee? follow thou me. *Jn.* 21: 21, 22.

The disciples were called Christians first in Antioch. *Ac.* 11: 26.

He that is called, being free, is Christ's servant. *1 Co.* 7: 22.

See also

Christ, the Captain; Christ, the Chosen of; Christ, Commandments of; Christ, Follower of; Christ, the Leader; Christ, the Lord; Christ, the Master.

Christ, Divinity of

They shall call his name Emmanuel, which being interpreted is, God with us. *Mat.* 1: 23.

Why callest thou me good? there is none good but one, that is, God. *Mat.* 19: 17.

Well, Master, thou hast said the truth: for there is one God; and there is none other but he. *Mk.* 12: 32.

In the beginning was the Word, and the Word was with God, and the Word was God. *Jn.* 1: 1.

The Word was made flesh, and dwelt among us. *Jn.* 1: 14.

The Jews sought the more to kill him, because he . . . said . . . that God was his Father, making himself equal with God. *Jn.* 5: 18.

The Son can do nothing of himself, but what he seeth the Father do. *Jn.* 5: 19.

Jesus knowing that the Father had given all things unto his hands, and that he was come from God, and went to God; . . . began to wash the disciples' feet. *Jn.* 13: 3, 5.

This is life eternal, that they might know thee the only true God, and Jesus Christ whom thou hast sent. *Jn.* 17: 3.

I ascend unto my Father, and your Father; and to my God, and your God. *Jn.* 20: 17.

Thomas answered and said unto him, My Lord and my God. *Jn.* 20: 28.

God is one. *Ga.* 3: 20.

Christ Jesus, . . . being in the form of God, thought it not robbery to be equal with God. *Ph.* 2: 5, 6.

For in him dwelleth all the fulness of the Godhead bodily. *Col.* 2: 9.

God was manifest in the flesh, justified in the Spirit, seen of angels, preached unto the Gentiles, believed on in the world, received up into glory. *1 Ti.* 3: 16.

Who being the brightness of his glory, and the express image of his person, and upholding all things by the word of his power, when he had by himself purged our sins, sat down on the right hand of the Majesty on high. *He.* 1: 3.

No man hath seen God at any time. *1 Jn.* 4: 12.

We are in him that is true, even in his Son Jesus Christ. This is the true God, and eternal life. *1 Jn.* 5: 20.

See also

Christ, God in; Christ, Incarnation of; Christ, the Lord; Christ, the Messiah; Christ, Oneness with God; Christ, the Son of God.

Christ, the Door

Not every one that saith unto me, Lord, Lord, shall enter into the kingdom of heaven. *Mat.* 7: 21.

Enter thou into the joy of thy lord. *Mat.* 25: 21.

Knock, and it shall be opened unto you. *Lu.* 11: 9.

Except a man be born of water and of the Spirit, he cannot enter into the kingdom of God. *Jn.* 3: 5.

I am the door: by me if any man enter in, he shall be saved. *Jn.* 10: 9.

A great door and effectual is opened unto me, and there are many adversaries. *1 Co.* 16: 9.

Having therefore, brethren, boldness to enter into the holiest by the blood of Jesus, . . . Let us draw near with a true heart. *He.* 10: 19, 22.

For so an entrance shall be ministered unto you abundantly into the everlasting kingdom of our Lord and Saviour Jesus Christ. *2 Pe.* 1: 11.

Behold, I have set before thee an open door, and no man can shut it. *Re.* 3: 8.

Behold, I stand at the door, and knock: if any man hear my voice, and open the door, I will come in to him, and will sup with him, and he with me. *Re.* 3: 20.

See also

Christ, Coming to; Christ, the Way.

Christ, Doubt of

O thou of little faith, wherefore didst thou doubt? *Mat.* 14: 31.

When they saw him, they worshipped him: but some doubted. *Mat.* 28: 17.

Lord, I believe; help thou mine unbelief. *Mk.* 9: 24.

How long dost thou make us to doubt? If thou be the Christ, tell us plainly. *Jn.* 10: 24.

How sayest thou, The Son of man must be lifted up? who is this Son of man? *Jn.* 12: 34.

Except I shall see in his hands the print of the nails, and put my finger into the print of the nails, and thrust my hand into his side, I will not believe. *Jn.* 20: 25.

If Christ be not raised. *1 Co.* 15: 17.

See also

Christ, Antagonism towards; Christ, Attitude towards; Christ, Denial of.

Christ, Encouragement of

Blessed are they which are persecuted for righteousness' sake: for their's is the kingdom of heaven. *Mat.* 5: 10.

Blessed are ye, when men shall revile you, and persecute you, and shall say all manner of evil against you falsely, for my sake. *Mat.* 5: 11.

Son, be of good cheer; thy sins be forgiven thee. *Mat.* 9: 2.

Be of good cheer; it is I; be not afraid. *Mat.* 14: 27.

O thou of little faith, wherefore didst thou doubt? *Mat.* 14: 31.

Arise, and be not afraid. *Mat.* 17: 7.

Said Jesus unto them, Be not afraid go tell my brethren that they go into Galilee, and there shall they see me. *Mat. 28: 10.*

Be not afraid, only believe. *Mk. 5: 36.*

Be not afraid of them that kill the body, and after that have no more that they can do. *Lu. 12: 4.*

Fear not therefore: ye are of more value than many sparrows. *Lu. 12: 7.*

Fear not, little flock; for it is your Father's good pleasure to give you the kingdom. *Lu. 12: 32.*

Let not your heart be troubled: ye believe in God, believe also in me. *Jn. 14: 1.*

I will not leave you comfortless: I will come to you. *Jn. 14: 18.*

Peace I leave with you, my peace I give unto you: not as the world giveth, give I unto you. *Jn. 14: 27.*

Let not your heart be troubled, neither let it be afraid. *Jn. 14: 27.*

In the world ye shall have tribulation: but be of good cheer; I have overcome the world. *Jn. 16: 33.*

He laid his right hand upon me, saying unto me, Fear not; I am the first and the last. *Re. 1: 17.*

See also

Christ, the Comforter; Christ, Help of; Christ, Ministry of.

Christ, Enemy of

The Lord said unto my Lord, Sit thou at my right hand, until I make thine enemies thy footstool. *Ps. 110: 1.*

And he denied him, saying, Woman, I know him not. *Lu. 22: 57.*

I am Jesus whom thou persecutest: it is hard for thee to kick against the pricks. *Ac. 9: 5.*

No man speaking by the Spirit of God calleth Jesus accursed. *1 Co. 12: 3.*

He must reign, till he hath put all enemies under his feet. *1 Co. 15: 25.*

Some indeed preach Christ even of envy and strife. *Ph. 1: 15.*

He is antichrist that denieth the Father and the Son. *1 Jn. 2: 22.*

See also

Christ, Antagonism to; Christ, Betrayal of; Christ, Defiance of; Christ, Denial of; Christ, Hatred of; Christ, Rejection of.

Christ, the Eternal

He that believeth on the Son hath everlasting life. *Jn. 3: 36.*

Whoso eateth my flesh, and drinketh my blood, hath eternal life. *Jn. 6: 54.*

Lord, to whom shall we go? thou hast the words of eternal life. *Jn. 6: 68.*

Before Abraham was, I am. *Jn. 8: 58.*

Christ abideth for ever. *Jn. 12: 34.*

This is life eternal, that they might know thee the only true God, and Jesus Christ whom thou hast sent. *Jn. 17: 3.*

The gift of God is eternal life through Jesus Christ our Lord. *Ro. 6: 23.*

If in this life only we have hope in Christ, we are of all men most miserable. *1 Co. 15: 19.*

According to the eternal purpose which he purposed in Christ Jesus our Lord. *Ep. 3: 11.*

Unto him be glory in the church by Christ Jesus throughout all ages world without end. *Ep. 3: 21.*

By him were all things created, that are in heaven, and that are in earth, visible and invisible. *Col. 1: 16.*

Our Lord Jesus Christ: . . . Who only hath immortality, dwelling in the light which no man can approach unto. *1 Ti. 6: 14, 16.*

That they may also obtain the salvation which is in Christ Jesus with eternal glory. *2 Ti. 2: 10.*

He became the author of eternal salvation unto all them that obey him. *He. 5: 9.*

He ever liveth to make intercession for them. *He. 7: 25.*

Jesus Christ the same yesterday, and to day, and for ever. *He. 13: 8.*

The God of all grace . . . hath called us unto his eternal glory by Christ Jesus. *1 Pe. 5: 10.*

God hath given to us eternal life, and this life is in his Son. *1 Jn. 5: 11.*

I am he that liveth, and was dead; and, behold, I am alive for evermore. *Re. 1: 18.*

See also

Christ, the Changeless; Christ, the Contemporary; Christ, the Creator; Christ, Permanence of.

Christ, Evidence of

Go and shew John again those things which ye do hear and see. *Mat. 11: 4.*

Master, we would see a sign from thee. *Mat. 12: 38.*

Then shall appear the sign of the Son of man in heaven. *Mat. 24: 30.*

Why doth this generation seek after a sign? verily I say unto you, There shall no sign be given unto this generation. *Mk. 8: 12.*

Jesus answering said unto them, Go your way, and tell John what things ye have seen and heard; how that the blind see, the lame walk, the lepers are cleansed, the deaf hear, the dead are raised, to the poor the gospel is preached. *Lu. 7: 22.*

We know that thou art a teacher come from God: for no man can do these miracles that thou doest, except God be with him. *Jn. 3: 2.*

Because thou hast seen me, thou hast believed: blessed are they that have not seen, and yet have believed. *Jn. 20: 29.*

Many other signs truly did Jesus in the presence of his disciples, which are not written in this book. *Jn. 20: 30.*

He shewed himself alive after his passion by many infallible proofs. *Ac. 1: 3.*

Jesus of Nazareth, a man approved of God among you by miracles and wonders and signs, which God did by him in the midst of you. *Ac. 2: 22.*

Ye seek a proof of Christ speaking in me, which to you-ward is not weak, but is mighty in you. *2 Co. 13: 3.*

He that believeth on the Son of God hath the witness in himself. *1 Jn. 5: 10.*

See also

Christ, Witness of.

Christ, Exaltation of

He was received up into heaven, and sat on the right hand of God. *Mk. 16: 19.*

As Moses lifted up the serpent in the wilderness, even so must the Son of man be lifted up. *Jn.* 3: 14.

When ye have lifted up the Son of man, then shall ye know that I am he, and that I do nothing of myself. *Jn.* 8: 28.

I, if I be lifted up from the earth, will draw all men unto me. *Jn.* 12: 32.

Him hath God exalted with his right hand to be a Prince and a Saviour. *Ac.* 5: 31.

Fear fell on them all, and the name of the Lord Jesus was magnified. *Ac.* 19: 17.

God also hath highly exalted him. *Ep.* 2: 9.

When he ascended up on high, he led captivity captive. *Ep.* 4: 8.

Christ shall be magnified in my body, whether it be by life, or by death. *Ph.* 1: 20.

At the name of Jesus every knee should bow. *Ph.* 2: 10.

God . . . hath . . . spoken unto us by his Son, . . . Who . . . sat down on the right hand of the Majesty on high. *He.* 1: 1–3.

See also

Christ, Adoration of; Christ, Dignity of; Christ, Glory of; Christ, Greatness of; Christ, Majesty of; Christ, Nature of; Christ, Praise of; Christ, Supremacy of; Christ, Triumph of.

Christ, Example of

Master, I will follow thee whithersoever thou goest. *Mat.* 8: 19.

The law was given by Moses, but grace and truth came by Jesus Christ. *Jn.* 1: 17.

Because of the people which stand by I said it, that they may believe that thou hast sent me. *Jn.* 11: 42.

I have given you an example, that ye should do as I have done to you. *Jn.* 13: 15.

I am the way, the truth, and the life. *Jn.* 14: 6.

As the truth is in Jesus. *Ep.* 4: 21.

Walk in love, as Christ also hath loved us. *Ep.* 5: 2.

As ye have therefore received Christ Jesus the Lord, so walk ye in him. *Col.* 2: 6.

A pattern to them which should hereafter believe. *1 Ti.* 1: 16.

Looking unto Jesus. *He.* 12: 2.

Christ also suffered for us, leaving us an example, that ye should follow his steps. *1 Pe.* 2: 21.

See also

Christ, Authority of; Christ, Compulsion of; Christ, Imitation of; Christ, Influence of; Christ, the Inimitable.

Christ, Eyes of

Seeing the multitude, he went up into a mountain. *Mat.* 5: 1.

His face did shine as the sun. *Mat.* 17: 2.

He lifted up his eyes on his disciples, and said, Blessed be ye poor: for your's is the kingdom of God. *Lu.* 6: 20.

When the Lord saw her, he had compassion on her. *Lu.* 7: 13.

I beheld Satan as lightning fall from heaven. *Lu.* 10: 18.

When he was come near, he beheld the city, and wept over it. *Lu.* 19: 41.

When Jesus beheld him, he said, Thou art Simon the son of Jona: thou shalt be called

Cephas, which is by interpretation, A stone. *Jn.* 1: 42.

I speak that which I have seen with my Father. *Jn.* 8: 38.

Jesus lifted up his eyes, and said, Father, I thank thee that thou hast heard me. *Jn.* 11: 41.

I will see you again, and your heart shall rejoice, and your joy no man taketh from you. *Jn.* 16: 22.

These words spake Jesus, and lifted up his eyes to heaven. *Jn.* 17: 1.

All things are naked and opened unto the eyes of him with whom we have to do. *He.* 4: 13.

His eyes were as a flame of fire. *Re.* 1: 14.

See also

Christ, Face of; Christ, Vision of.

Christ, Face of

His face did shine as the sun. *Mat.* 17: 2.

Then did they spit in his face. *Mat.* 26: 67.

The eyes of all them that were in the synagogue were fastened on him. *Lu.* 4: 20.

Master, I beseech thee, look upon my son. *Lu.* 9: 38.

The Lord turned, and looked upon Peter. *Lu.* 22: 61.

The light of the knowledge of the glory of God in the face of Jesus Christ. *2 Co.* 4: 6.

His countenance was as the sun shineth in his strength. *Re.* 1: 16.

See also

Christ, Appearance of; Christ, Eyes of; Christ, Presence of; Christ, Vision of.

Christ, Faith in

He that believeth on the Son hath everlasting life. *Jn.* 3: 36.

Dost thou believe on the Son of God? *Jn.* 9: 35.

Though ye believe not me, believe the works: that ye may know, and believe, that the Father is in me, and I in him. *Jn.* 10: 38.

Whosoever liveth and believeth in me shall never die. *Jn.* 11: 26.

Believe me that I am in the Father, and the Father in me. *Jn.* 14: 11.

We believe that thou camest from God. *Jn.* 16: 30.

Jesus saith unto her, Mary. She turned herself, and saith unto him, Rabboni; which is to say, Master. *Jn.* 20: 16.

Jesus saith unto him, Thomas, because thou hast seen me, thou hast believed: blessed are they that have not seen, and yet have believed. *Jn.* 20: 29.

I believe that Jesus Christ is the Son of God. *Ac.* 8: 37.

We believe that through the grace of the Lord Jesus Christ we shall be saved. *Ac.* 15: 11.

Believe on the Lord Jesus Christ, and thou shalt be saved. *Ac.* 16: 31.

One Lord, one faith, one baptism. *Ep.* 4: 5.

We give thanks to God . . . Since we heard of your faith in Christ Jesus, and of the love which ye have to all the saints, For the hope which is laid up for you in heaven. *Col.* 1: 3–5.

I know whom I have believed, and am persuaded that he is able to keep that which I have committed unto him against that day. *2 Ti.* 1: 12.

Looking unto Jesus the author and finisher of our faith. *He.* 12: 2.

Whosoever shall confess that Jesus is the Son of God, God dwelleth in him. *1 Jn.* 4: 15.

See also

Christ, Belief in; Christ, Devotion to; Christ, Loyalty to; Christ, Obedience to; Christ, Trust in.

Christ, Faith of

Father, into thy hands I commend my spirit. *Lu.* 23: 46.

My Father worketh hitherto. *Jn.* 5: 17.

The Son can do nothing of himself, but what he seeth the Father do. *Jn.* 5: 19.

All things that the Father hath are mine. *Jn.* 16: 15.

I came forth from the Father, and am come into the world: again, I leave the world, and go to the Father. *Jn.* 16: 28.

This is life eternal, that they might know thee the only true God, and Jesus Christ whom thou hast sent. *Jn.* 17: 3.

O righteous Father, the world hath not known thee: but I have known thee. *Jn.* 17: 25.

The life which I now live in the flesh I live by the faith of the Son of God. *Ga.* 2: 20.

Jesus the author and finisher of our faith. *He.* 12: 2.

Here are they that keep the commandments of God, and the faith of Jesus. *Re.* 14: 12.

See also

Christ, God in; Christ, Gospel of; Christ, the Son of God; Christ, the Word; Christ, Word of.

Christ, Faithfulness of

Lo, I am with you alway, even unto the end of the world. *Mat.* 28: 20.

He loved them unto the end. *Jn.* 13: 1.

Let not your heart be troubled: ye believe in God, believe also in me. *Jn.* 14: 1.

If ye shall ask anything in my name, I will do it. *Jn:* 14: 14.

I will not leave you comfortless: I will come to you. *Jn.* 14: 18.

Because I live, ye shall live also. *Jn.* 14: 19.

The Son of God . . . was not yea and nay, but in him was yea. *2 Co.* 1: 19.

Consider the Apostle and High Priest of our profession, Christ Jesus; Who was faithful to him that appointed him. *He.* 3: 1, 2.

Jesus Christ the same . . . to day. *He.* 13: 8.

Jesus Christ . . . is the faithful witness. *Re.* 1: 5.

See also

Christ, Finality of; Christ, Obedience of; Christ, Permanence of; Christ, Suffering of; Christ, Trustworthiness of.

Christ, Family of

Behold, a virgin shall conceive, and bear a son. *Is.* 7: 14.

Joseph, thou son of David, fear not to take unto thee Mary thy wife: for that which is conceived in her is of the Holy Ghost. *Mat.* 1: 20.

His mother and his brethren stood without, desiring to speak with him. *Mat.* 12: 46.

He stretched forth his hand toward his disciples, and said, Behold my mother and my brethren! *Mat.* 12: 49.

Is not this the carpenter's son? is not his mother called Mary? and his brethren, James, and Joses, and Simon, and Judas? And his sisters, are they not all with us? *Mat.* 13: 55, 56.

Wist ye not that I must be about my Father's business? *Lu.* 2: 49.

My mother and my brethren are these which hear the word of God, and do it. *Lu.* 8: 21.

I and my Father are one. *Jn.* 10: 30.

I am the vine, ye are the branches. *Jn.* 15: 5.

When Jesus therefore saw his mother, and the disciple standing by, whom he loved, he saith unto his mother, Woman, behold thy son! Then saith he to the disciple, Behold, thy mother! *Jn.* 19: 26, 27.

So we, being many, are one body in Christ. *Ro.* 12: 5.

See also

Christ, the Carpenter.

Christ, Fate of

It pleased the Lord to bruise him. *Is.* 53: 10.

From that day forth began Jesus to shew unto his disciples, how that he must go unto Jerusalem, and suffer many things. *Mat.* 16: 21.

I must walk to day, and to morrow, and the day following: for it cannot be that a prophet perish out of Jerusalem. *Lu.* 13: 33.

As Moses lifted up the serpent in the wilderness, even so must the Son of man be lifted up. *Jn.* 3: 14.

Therefore doth my Father love me, because I lay down my life, that I might take it again. *Jn.* 10: 17.

He shewed himself alive after his passion by many infallible proofs. *Ac.* 1: 3.

Whom God hath set forth to be a propitiation through faith in his blood, to declare his righteousness for the remission of sins that are past. *Ro.* 3: 25.

While we were yet sinners, Christ died for us. *Ro.* 5: 8.

Jesus also, that he might sanctify the people with his own blood, suffered without the gate. *He.* 13: 12.

See also

Christ, Destiny of.

Christ, Fellowship with

It is enough for the disciple that he be as his master, and the servant as his Lord. *Mat.* 10: 25.

Whosoever therefore shall confess me before men, him will I confess also before my Father. *Mat.* 10: 32.

Lo, I am with you alway, even unto the end of the world. *Mat.* 28: 20.

Whosoever shall do the will of God, the same is my brother, and my sister, and my mother. *Mk.* 3: 35.

Ye are they which have continued with me in my temptations. *Lu.* 22: 28.

If any man have not the Spirit of Christ, he is none of his. *Ro.* 8: 9.

Whether we live, we live unto the Lord; and whether we die, we die unto the Lord: whether we live therefore, or die, we are the Lord's. *Ro.* 14: 8.

God is faithful, by whom ye were called unto the fellowship of his Son Jesus Christ our Lord. *1 Co.* 1: 9.

The cup of blessing which we bless, is it not the communion of the blood of Christ?

The bread which we break, is it not the communion of the body of Christ? *1 Co.* **10: 16.**

God . . . hath . . . made us sit together in heavenly places in Christ Jesus. *Ep.* **2: 4, 6.**

That I may know him, and the power of his resurrection, and the fellowship of his sufferings *Ph.* **3: 10.**

He is not ashamed to call them brethren. *He.* **2: 11.**

See also

Christ, Abiding in; Christ, Communion with; Christ, Companionship with; Christ, Life in; Christ, Nearness of; Christ, Partnership with; Christ, Union with.

Christ, Fidelity to

Master, I will follow thee whithersoever thou goest. *Mat.* **8: 19.**

Blessed is he, whosoever shall not be offended in me. *Lu.* **7: 23.**

Lord, not my feet only, but also my hands and my head. *Jn.* **13: 9.**

Lord, why cannot I follow thee now? I will lay down my life for thy sake. *Jn.* **13: 37.**

I believe that Jesus Christ is the Son of God. *Ac.* **8: 37.**

Unto you it is given in the behalf of Christ, not only to believe on him, but also to suffer for his sake. *Ph.* **1: 29.**

A faithful minister of Christ. *Col.* **1: 7.**

The stedfastness of your faith in Christ. *Col.* **2: 5.**

Do all in the name of the Lord Jesus. *Col.* **3: 17.**

See also

Christ, Devotion to; Christ, Faith in; Christ, Love of; Christ, Loyalty to; Christ, Obedience to.

Christ, Finality of

Of the increase of his government and peace there shall be no end. *Is.* **9: 7.**

As many as touched were made perfectly whole. *Mat.* **14: 36.**

Heaven and earth shall pass away: but my words shall not pass away. *Mk.* **13: 31.**

Of his kingdom there shall be no end. *Lu.* **1: 33.**

Christ is the end of the law for righteousness to every one that believeth. *Ro.* **10: 4.**

My strength is made perfect in weakness. *2 Co.* **12: 9.**

Christ . . . the head over all things to the church. *Ep.* **1: 20, 22.**

Grow up into him in all things, which is the head, even Christ. *Ep.* **4: 15.**

That we may present every man perfect in Christ Jesus. *Col.* **1: 28.**

Christ is all, and in all. *Col.* **3: 11.**

Ye have . . . seen the end of the Lord. *Ja.* **5: 11.**

I am Alpha and Omega, the beginning and the end. *Re.* **21: 6.**

See also

Christ, Centrality of; Christ, the Changeless; Christ, the Eternal; Christ, the Goal; Christ, Permanence of; Christ, the Rock.

Christ, Follower of

If any man will come after me, let him deny himself, and take up his cross daily, and follow me. *Lu.* **9: 23.**

Again the next day after John stood, and two of his disciples; And looking upon Jesus as he walked, he saith, Behold the Lamb of God! And the two disciples heard him speak, and they followed Jesus. *Jn.* **1: 35–37.**

Be ye followers of me, even as I also am of Christ. *1 Co.* **11: 1.**

I follow after, if that I may apprehend that for which also I am apprehended of Christ Jesus. *Ph.* **3: 12.**

Ye serve the Lord Christ. *Col.* **3: 24.**

See also

Christ, the Captain; Christ, the Chosen of; Christ, Disciple of; Christ, the Guide; Christ, the Leader; Christ, the Lord; Christ, the Master.

Christ, Foreknowledge of

He began to teach them, that the Son of man must suffer many things, and be rejected of the elders, and of the chief priests, and scribes, and be killed, and after three days rise again. *Mk.* **8: 31.**

I have a baptism to be baptized with; and how am I straitened till it be accomplished. *Lu.* **12: 50.**

Jesus knew from the beginning who they were that believed not, and who should betray him. *Jn.* **6: 64.**

Yet a little while am I with you, and then I go unto him that sent me. *Jn.* **7: 33.**

Jesus knew that his hour was come that he should depart out of this world unto the Father. *Jn.* **13: 1.**

He knew who should betray him. *Jn.* **13: 11.**

Jesus therefore, knowing all things that should come upon him, went forth, and said unto them, Whom seek ye? *Jn.* **18: 4.**

See also

Christ the Creator; Christ, the Eternal; Christ, Knowledge of; Christ, Pre-existence of.

Christ, Forgiveness of

The Son of man hath power on earth to forgive sins. *Mat.* **9: 6.**

Whosoever speaketh a word against the Son of man, it shall be forgiven him. *Mat.* **12: 32.**

When Jesus saw their faith, he said unto the sick, . . . Son, thy sins be forgiven thee. *Mk.* **2: 5.**

Why doth this man thus speak blasphemies? who can forgive sins but God only? *Mk.* **2: 7.**

And Peter. *Mk.* **16: 7.**

They that sat at meat with him began to say within themselves, Who is this that forgiveth sins also? *Lu.* **7: 49.**

Father, forgive them; for they know not what they do. *Lu.* **23: 34.**

Repent, and be baptized every one of you in the name of Jesus Christ for the remission of sins. *Ac.* **2: 38.**

In whom we have . . . the forgiveness of sins, according to the riches of his grace. *Ep.* **1: 7.**

Even as Christ forgave you, so also do ye. *Col.* **3: 13.**

See also

Christ, the Comforter; Christ, Compassion of; Christ, the Healing; Christ, Sympathy of.

Christ, the Foundation

The stone which the builders refused is

become the head stone of the corner. *Ps.* 118: 22.

Other foundation can no man lay than that is laid, which is Jesus Christ. *1 Co.* 3: 11.

Jesus Christ himself being the chief corner stone. *Ep.* 2: 20.

Rooted and built up in him, and stablished in the faith. *Col.* 2: 7.

Who verily was foreordained before the foundation of the world. *1 Pe.* 1: 20.

Behold, I lay in Sion a chief corner stone, elect, precious: and he that believeth on him shall not be confounded. *1 Pe.* 2: 6.

The Lamb slain from the foundation of the world. *Re.* 13: 8.

See also
Christ, the Rock.

Christ, the Friend

He knew their thoughts. *Lu.* 6: 8.

A friend of publicans and sinners. *Lu.* 7: 34.

He calleth his own sheep by name. *Jn.* 10: 3.

I will not leave you comfortless: I will come to you. *Jn.* 14: 18.

Ye are my friends, if ye do whatsoever I command you. *Jn.* 15: 14.

Henceforth I call you not servants; for the servant knoweth not what his lord doeth: but I have called you friends. *Jn.* 15: 15.

Ye were called unto the fellowship of his Son Jesus Christ our Lord. *1 Co.* 1: 9.

See also
Christ, Communion with; Christ, Companionship of; Christ, Fellowship with; Christ, Life in; Christ, Partnership with; Christ, Union with.

Christ, Fulfilment in

So we, being many, are one body in Christ. *Ro.* 12: 5.

We are fools for Christ's sake, but ye are wise in Christ. *1 Co.* 4: 10.

In Christ shall all be made alive. *1 Co.* 15: 22.

God . . . causeth us to triumph in Christ. *2 Co.* 2: 14.

If any man be in Christ, he is a new creature. *2 Co.* 5: 17.

There is neither Jew nor Greek, there is neither bond nor free, . . . for ye are all one in Christ Jesus. *Ga.* 3: 28.

Bear ye one another's burdens, and so fulfil the law of Christ. *Ga.* 6: 2.

The dead in Christ shall rise first. *1 Th.* 4: 16.

That the communication of thy faith may become effectual by the acknowledgment of every good thing which is in you in Christ Jesus. *Phm.* 6.

If these things be in you, and abound, they make you that ye shall neither be barren nor unfruitful in the knowledge of our Lord Jesus Christ. *2 Pe.* 1: 8.

The life was manifested, and we have seen it, and bear witness, and shew unto you that eternal life, which was with the Father, and was manifested unto us. *1 Jn.* 1: 2.

See also
Christ, Growth in.

Christ, Fullness of

It becometh us to fulfil all righteousness. *Mat.* 3: 15.

The Word was made flesh, and dwelt among us, . . . full of grace and truth. *Jn.* 1: 14.

Of his fulness have all we received, and grace for grace. *Jn.* 1: 16.

This my joy therefore is fulfilled. *Jn.* 3: 29.

I am sure that, when I come unto you, I shall come in the fulness of the blessing of the gospel of Christ. *Ro.* 15: 29.

The church, Which is his body, the fulness of him that filleth all in all. *Ep.* 1: 22, 23.

The measure of the stature of the fulness of Christ. *Ep.* 4: 13.

For it pleased the Father that in him should all fulness dwell. *Col.* 1: 19.

In him dwelleth all the fulness of the Godhead bodily. *Col.* 2: 9.

The grace of our Lord was exceeding abundant. *1 Ti.* 1: 14.

See also
Christ, Finality of; Christ, Riches of.

Christ, Gentleness of

A bruised reed shall he not break, and the smoking flax shall he not quench. *Is.* 42: 3.

Jesus called a little child unto him, and set him in the midst of them. *Mat.* 18: 2.

Behold, thy King cometh unto thee, meek, and sitting upon an ass. *Mat.* 21: 5.

He loved them unto the end. *Jn.* 13: 1.

Now there was leaning on Jesus' bosom one of his disciples, whom Jesus loved. *Jn.* 13: 23.

As the Father hath loved me, so have I loved you: continue ye in my love. *Jn.* 15: 9.

Gentleness of Christ. *2 Co.* 10: 1.

To know the love of Christ, which passeth knowledge. *Ep.* 3: 19.

See also
Christ, Compassion of; Christ, Goodness of; Christ, Humility of; Christ, Meekness of; Christ, the Shepherd; Christ, Touch of;

Christ, Gift of

The Son of man came not to be ministered unto, but to minister, and to give his life a ransom for many. *Mat.* 20: 28.

Suppose ye that I am come to give peace on earth? *Lu.* 12: 51.

This is my body which is given for you. *Lu.* 22: 19.

If thou knewest the gift of God, and who it is that saith to thee, Give me to drink; thou wouldest have asked of him, and he would have given thee living water. *Jn.* 4: 10.

I give unto them eternal life. *Jn.* 10: 28.

Not as the world giveth, give I unto you. *Jn.* 14: 27.

Unto every one of us is given grace according to the measure of the gift of Christ. *Ep.* 4: 7.

When he ascended up on high, he . . . gave gifts unto men. *Ep.* 4: 8.

Awake thou that sleepest, and arise from the dead, and Christ shall give thee light. *Ep.* 5: 14.

The supply of the Spirit of Jesus Christ. *Ph.* 1: 19.

See also
Christ, Help of; Christ, Promise of.

Christ, Glory of

And, lo, the angel of the Lord came upon them, and the glory of the Lord shone round about them. *Lu.* 2: 9.

When they were awake, they saw his glory. *Lu.* 9: 32.

Now is the Son of man glorified, and God is glorified in him. *Jn.* 13: 31.

Father, the hour is come; glorify thy Son, that thy Son also may glorify thee. *Jn.* 17: 1.

He that glorieth, let him glory in the Lord. *1 Co.* 1: 31.

The light of the knowledge of the glory of God in the face of Jesus Christ. *2 Co.* 4: 6.

God forbid that I should glory, save in the cross of our Lord Jesus Christ. *Ga.* 6: 14.

Looking for . . . the glorious appearing of the great God and our Saviour Jesus Christ. *Tit.* 2: 13.

This man was counted worthy of more glory than Moses. *He.* 3: 3.

Jesus Christ, the Lord of glory. *Ja.* 2: 1.

See also

Christ, Dignity of; Christ, Exaltation of; Christ, Greatness of; Christ, Majesty of; Christ, Nature of; Christ, Supremacy of; Christ, Triumph of.

Christ, the Goal

Lo, I am with you alway, even unto the end of the world. *Mat.* 28: 20.

Then said Jesus unto the twelve, Will ye also go away? Then Simon Peter answered him, Lord, to whom shall we go? thou hast the words of eternal life. *Jn.* 6: 67, 68.

Lord Jesus, receive my spirit. *Ac.* 7: 59.

Christ is the end of the law for righteousness to every one that believeth. *Ro.* 10: 4.

Looking unto Jesus the author and finisher of our faith. *He.* 12: 2.

See also

Christ, Finality of.

Christ, God in

Hereafter ye shall see heaven open, and the angels of God ascending and descending upon the Son of man. *Jn.* 1: 51.

The Son can do nothing of himself, but what he seeth the Father do. *Jn.* 5: 19.

I am come in my Father's name, and ye receive me not. *Jn.* 5: 43.

Jesus answered them, and said, My doctrine is not mine, but his that sent me. *Jn.* 7: 16.

Now is the Son of man glorified, and God is glorified in him. *Jn.* 13: 31.

He that hath seen me hath seen the Father. *Jn.* 14: 9.

The Father that dwelleth in me, he doeth the works. *Jn.* 14: 10.

Now, O Father, glorify thou me with thine own self with the glory which I had with thee before the world was. *Jn.* 17: 5.

I in them, and thou in me, that they may be made perfect in one. *Jn.* 17: 23.

God anointed Jesus of Nazareth with the Holy Ghost and with power. *Ac.* 10: 38.

God was with him. *Ac.* 10: 38.

We speak before God in Christ. *2 Co.* 12: 19.

See also

Christ, Divinity of; Christ, Incarnation of;

Christ, the Lord; Christ, the Messiah· Christ, Oneness with God; Christ, the Son of God.

Christ, Goodness of

Why callest thou me good? there is none good but one, that is, God. *Mat.* 19: 17.

Jesus, immediately knowing in himself that virtue had gone out of him, . . . said, Who touched my clothes? *Mk.* 5: 30.

Jesus beholding him loved him. *Mk.* 10: 21.

I am the good shepherd. *Jn.* 10: 11.

Jesus of Nazareth . . . who went about doing good. *Ac.* 10: 38.

My grace is sufficient for thee. *2 Co.* 12: 9.

The exceeding riches of his grace. *Ep.* 2: 7.

To know the love of Christ. *Ep.* 3: 19.

He . . . gave gifts unto men. *Ep.* 4: 8.

Filled with the fruits of righteousness, which are by Jesus Christ. *Ph.* 1: 11.

See also

Christ, Beauty of; Christ, Compassion of; Christ, Example of; Christ, the Friend; Christ, Gentleness of; Christ, Grace of; Christ, Holiness of; Christ, Innocence of; Christ, Love of; Christ, Perfection of; Christ, Sinlessness of; Christ, Strength of.

Christ, Gospel of

Behold upon the mountains the feet of him that bringeth good tidings, that publisheth peace! *Na.* 1: 15.

This gospel of the kingdom shall be preached in all the world for a witness unto all nations. *Mat.* 24: 14.

The beginning of the gospel of Jesus Christ, the Son of God. *Mk.* 1: 1.

Fear not: for, behold, I bring you good tidings of great joy. *Lu.* 2: 10.

I am not ashamed of the gospel of Christ. *Ro.* 1: 16.

That I should be the minister of Jesus Christ to the Gentiles, ministering the gospel of God. *Ro.* 15: 16.

I have fully preached the gospel of Christ *Ro.* 15: 19.

When I come unto you, I shall come in the fulness of the blessing of the gospel of Christ. *Ro.* 15: 29.

Christ sent me not to baptize, but to preach the gospel: not with wisdom of words, lest the cross of Christ should be made of none effect. *1 Co.* 1: 17.

See also

Christ, Message of; Christ, Preaching of; Christ, Promise of; Christ, the Teacher; Christ, the Word; Christ, Word of.

Christ, Grace of

Grace is poured into thy lips. *Ps.* 45: 2.

All bare him witness, and wondered at the gracious words which proceeded out of his mouth. *Lu.* 4: 22.

For the law was given by Moses, but grace and truth came by Jesus Christ. *Jn.* 1: 17.

We believe that through the grace of Jesus Christ we shall be saved. *Ac.* 15: 11.

The grace of God, and the gift by grace, which is by one man, Jesus Christ, hath abounded unto many. *Ro.* 5: 15.

By grace are ye saved. *Ep.* 2: 8.

Be strong in the grace that is in Christ Jesus. *2 Ti.* 2: 1.

Grow in grace, and in the knowledge of our Lord and Saviour Jesus Christ. *2 Pe.* **3: 18.**

See also

Christ, Beauty of; Christ, Gentleness of; Christ, Holiness of; Christ, Innocence of; Christ, Love of; Christ, Perfection of.

Christ, Gratitude to

They that were in the ship came and worshipped him, saying, Of a truth thou art the Son of God. *Mat.* **14: 33.**

Then came she and worshipped him. *Mat.* **15: 25.**

Immediately their eyes received sight, and they followed him. *Mat.* **20: 34.**

He went out, and began to publish it much, and to blaze abroad the matter. *Mk.* **1: 45.**

And, behold, a woman in the city, which was a sinner, when she knew that Jesus sat at meat in the Pharisee's house, brought an alabaster box of ointment, And stood at his feet behind him weeping, and began to wash his feet with tears, and did wipe them with the hairs of her head, and kissed his feet, and anointed them with the ointment. *Lu.* **7: 37, 38.**

One of them . . . fell down on his face at his feet, giving him thanks: and he was a Samaritan. *Lu.* **17: 15, 16.**

I thank Christ Jesus our Lord, who hath enabled me. *1 Ti.* **1: 12.**

See also

Christ, Attitude towards.

Christ, Greatness of

In this place is one greater than the temple. *Mat.* **12: 6.**

Behold, a greater than Solomon is here. *Mat.* **12: 42.**

He shall be great, and shall be called the Son of the Highest. *Lu.* **1: 32.**

Making himself equal with God. *Jn.* **5: 18.**

The name of the Lord Jesus was magnified. *Ac.* **19: 17.**

Christ shall be magnified in my body, whether it be by life, or by death. *Ph.* **1: 20.**

Wherefore God also hath highly exalted him, and given him a name which is above every name. *Ph.* **2: 9.**

That in all things he might have the preeminence. *Col.* **1: 18.**

We have a great high priest, that is passed into the heavens, Jesus the Son of God. *He.* **4: 14.**

Jesus, that great shepherd of the sheep. *He.* **13: 20.**

See also

Christ,. Dignity of; Christ, Exaltation of; Christ, Majesty of; Christ, Nature of; Christ, Supremacy of; Christ, Triumph of.

Christ, Grief of

He is . . . a man of sorrows, and acquainted with grief. *Is.* **53: 3.**

Surely he hath borne our griefs, and carried our sorrows. *Is.* **53: 4.**

How often would I have gathered thy children together, even as a hen gathereth her chickens under her wings, and ye would not! *Mat.* **23: 37.**

He . . . began to be sorrowful and very heavy. *Mat.* **26: 37.**

My soul is exceeding sorrowful, even unto death. *Mat.* **26: 38.**

O my Father, if it be possible, let this cup pass from me. *Mat.* **26: 39.**

My God, my God, why hast thou forsaken me? *Mat.* **27: 46.**

Being grieved for the hardness of their hearts. *Mk.* **3: 5.**

He beheld the city, and wept over it. *Lu.* **19: 41.**

Jesus wept. *Jn.* **11: 35.**

See also

Christ, Agony of; Christ, Compassion of; Christ, Passion of; Christ, Sorrow of; Christ, Suffering of.

Christ, Growth in

The apostles said unto the Lord, Increase our faith. *Lu.* **17: 5.**

But speaking the truth in love, may grow up into him in all things, which is the head, even Christ. *Ep.* **4: 15.**

The Lord make you increase and abound in love one toward another, and toward all men. *1 Th.* **3: 12.**

Your faith groweth exceedingly. *2 Th.* **1: 3.**

As newborn babes, desire the sincere milk of the word, that ye may grow thereby. *1 Pe.* **2: 2.**

Grow in grace, and in the knowledge of our Lord and Saviour Jesus Christ. *2 Pe.* **3: 18.**

See also

Christ, Fulfilment in.

Christ, the Guide

Follow me, and I will make you fishers of men. *Mat.* **4: 19.**

Master, we know that thou art true, and teachest the way of God in truth. *Mat.* **22: 16.**

Jesus . . . leadeth them up into an high mountain. *Mk.* **9: 2.**

To guide our feet into the way of peace. *Lu.* **1: 79.**

Lord, I will follow thee whithersoever thou goest. *Lu.* **9: 57.**

He calleth his own sheep by name, and leadeth them out. *Jn.* **10: 3.**

He goeth before them, and the sheep follow him. *Jn.* **10: 4.**

My sheep hear my voice, and I know them, and they follow me. *Jn.* **10: 27.**

If any man serve me, let him follow me. *Jn.* **12: 26.**

Lord, why cannot I follow thee now? *Jn.* **13: 37.**

I go to prepare a place for you. *Jn.* **14: 2.**

I am the way, the truth, and the life: no man cometh unto the Father, but by me. *Jn.* **14: 6.**

A new and living way, which he hath consecrated for us. *He.* **10: 20.**

The Lamb which is in the midst of the throne shall feed them, and shall lead them unto living fountains of water. *Re.* **7: 17.**

These are they which follow the Lamb whithersoever he goeth. *Re.* **14: 4.**

See also

Christ, the Captain; Christ, Follower of; Christ, the Leader; Christ, the Lord; Christ, the Master; Christ, the Way.

Christ, Hand of

They beseech him to put his hand upon him. *Mk.* **7: 32.**

Jesus took him by the hand, and lifted him up. *Mk.* 9: 27.

Behold my hands. *Lu.* 24: 39.

He lifted up his hands, and blessed them. *Lu.* 24: 50.

My Father worketh hitherto, and I work. *Jn.* 5: 17.

Jesus stooped down, and with his finger wrote on the ground. *Jn.* 8: 6.

Except I shall see in his hands the print of the nails, and put my finger into the print of the nails, and thrust my hand into his side, I will not believe. *Jn.* 20: 25.

Reach hither thy finger, and behold my hands; and reach hither thy hand, and thrust it into my side. *Jn.* 20: 27.

See also

Christ, Gentleness of; Christ, the Healing; Christ, Help of; Christ, Touch of; Christ, Work of.

Christ, Hatred of

Ye shall be hated of all men for my name's sake. *Mat.* 10: 22.

The world cannot hate you; but me it hateth, because I testify of it, that the works thereof are evil. *Jn.* 7: 7.

If the world hate you, ye know that it hated me before it hated you. *Jn.* 15: 18.

He that hateth me hateth my Father also. *Jn.* 15: 23.

Now have they both seen and hated both me and my Father. *Jn.* 15: 24.

They hated me without a cause. *Jn.* 15: 25.

Ye denied the Holy One and the Just, and desired a murderer to be granted unto you. *Ac.* 3: 14.

If any man love not the Lord Jesus Christ, let him be Anathema Maran-atha. *1 Co.* 16: 22.

They crucify to themselves the Son of God afresh, and put him to an open shame. *He.* 6: 6.

See also

Christ, Antagonism to; Christ, Defiance of; Christ, Denial of; Christ, Enemy of; Christ, Indifference to; Christ, Rejection of.

Christ, the Healing

At even, when the sun did set, they brought unto him all that were diseased, and them that were possessed with devils. *Mk.* 1: 32.

If thou wilt, thou canst make me clean. *Mk.* 1: 40.

What wilt thou that I should do unto thee? The blind man said unto him, Lord, that I might receive my sight. *Mk.* 10: 51.

The power of the Lord was present to heal them. *Lu.* 5: 17.

So Jesus came again into Cana of Galilee, where he made the water wine. And there was a certain nobleman, whose son was sick at Capernaum. *Jn.* 4: 46.

In the name of Jesus Christ of Nazareth rise up and walk. *Ac.* 3: 6.

Jesus Christ maketh thee whole. *Ac.* 9: 34.

You hath he quickened, who were dead in trespasses and sins. *Ep.* 2: 1.

By whose stripes ye were healed. *1 Pe.* 2: 24.

See also

Christ, the Comforter; Christ, the Physician.

Christ, Help of

He departed, and began to publish in Decapolis how great things Jesus had done for him. *Mk.* 5: 20.

He maketh both the deaf to hear, and the dumb to speak. *Mk.* 7: 37.

If thou canst do any thing, have compassion on us, and help us. *Mk.* 9: 22.

The Lord working with them. *Mk.* 16: 20.

Jesus said unto them, I am the bread of life: he that cometh to me shall never hunger. *Jn.* 6: 35.

I know whom I have believed, and am persuaded that he is able to keep that which I have committed unto him against that day. *2 Ti.* 1: 12.

In that he himself hath suffered being tempted, he is able to succour them that are tempted. *He.* 2: 18.

Jesus Christ the same . . . to day. *He.* 13: 8.

See also

Christ, the Comforter; Christ, Compassion of; Christ, Encouragement of; Christ, Hand of; Christ, the Healing; Christ, Ministry of; Christ, the Physician; Christ, Power of; Christ, the Servant; Christ, Strength of; Christ, Touch of; Christ, Work of.

Christ, the Hidden

Jesus withdrew himself with his disciples to the sea. *Mk.* 3: 7.

While he thus spake, there came a cloud, and overshadowed them. *Lu.* 9: 34.

But their eyes were holden that they should not know him. *Lu.* 24: 16.

There standeth one among you, whom ye know not. *Jn.* 1: 26.

Jesus hid himself, and went out of the temple. *Jn.* 8: 59.

She turned herself back, and saw Jesus standing, and knew not that it was Jesus. *Jn.* 20: 14.

Supposing him to be the gardener. *Jn.* 20: 15.

While they beheld, he was taken up; and a cloud received him out of their sight. *Ac.* 1: 9.

Christ; In whom are hid all the treasures of wisdom and knowledge. *Col.* 2: 2, 3.

Ye are dead, and your life is hid with Christ in God. *Col.* 3: 3.

Whom having not seen, ye love; in whom, though now ye see him not, yet believing, ye rejoice with joy unspeakable and full of glory. *1 Pe.* 1: 8.

See also

Christ, Isolation of; Christ, Loneliness of; Christ, Mystery of; Christ, Silence of.

Christ, Holiness of

Depart from me; for I am a sinful man, O Lord. *Lu.* 5: 8.

They are not of the world, even as I am not of the world. *Jn.* 17: 16.

For their sakes I sanctify myself. *Jn.* 17: 19.

To them that are sanctified in Christ Jesus, called to be saints. *1 Co.* 1: 2.

Boldness to enter into the holiest by the blood of Jesus. *He.* 10: 19.

See also

Christ, Goodness of; Christ, Grace of; Christ,

Innocence of; Christ, Perfection of; Christ, Sinlessness of.

Christ, Hope in

We have seen his star in the east. *Mat.* 2: 2.

If in this life only we have hope in Christ, we are of all men most miserable. *1 Co.* 15: 19.

Be not moved away from the hope of the gospel, which ye have heard. *Col.* 1: 23.

Christ in you, the hope of glory. *Col.* 1: 27.

Remembering without ceasing your . . . patience of hope in our Lord Jesus Christ. *1 Th.* 1: 3.

Jesus Christ, which is our hope. *1 Ti.* 1: 1.

Hope to the end for the grace that is to be brought unto you at the revelation of Jesus Christ. *1 Pe.* 1: 13.

See also

Christ, Faith in; Christ, Trust in.

Christ, Hour of

Take ye heed, watch and pray: for ye know not when the time is. *Mk.* 13: 33.

Ye know not when the master of the house cometh, at even, or at midnight, or at the cockcrowing, or in the morning. *Mk.* 13: 35.

He . . . prayed that, if it were possible, the hour might pass from him. *Mk.* 14: 35.

The days will come, when ye shall desire to see one of the days of the Son of man, and ye shall not see it. *Lu.* 17: 22.

Thus shall it be in the day when the Son of man is revealed. *Lu.* 17: 30.

Many shall come in my name, saying, I am Christ; and the time draweth near: go ye not therefore after them. *Lu.* 21: 8.

Woman, what have I to do with thee? mine hour is not yet come. *Jn.* 2: 4.

The hour cometh, and now is, when the true worshippers shall worship the Father in spirit and in truth. *Jn.* 4: 23.

The hour is coming, and now is, when the dead shall hear the voice of the Son of God: and they that hear shall live. *Jn.* 5: 25.

The hour is coming, in the which all that are in the graves shall hear his voice. *Jn.* 5: 28.

No man laid hands on him, because his hour was not yet come. *Jn.* 7: 30 .

The hour is come, that the Son of man should be glorified. *Jn.* 12: 23.

Father, save me from this hour: but for this cause came I unto this hour. *Jn.* 12: 27.

When Jesus knew that his hour was come that he should depart out of this world unto the Father, having loved his own which were in the world, he loved them unto the end. *Jn.* 13: 1.

The time cometh, when I shall no more speak unto you in proverbs. *Jn.* 16: 25.

Behold; the hour cometh, yea, is now come, that ye shall be scattered, every man to his own, and shall leave me alone: and yet I am not alone, because the Father is with me. *Jn.* 16: 32.

Father, the hour is come. *Jn.* 17: 1.

The cup which my Father hath given me, shall I not drink it? *Jn.* 18: 11.

See also

Christ, day of.

Christ, Humanity of

Jesus Christ, the son of David, the son of Abraham. *Mat.* 1: 1.

Is not this the carpenter's son? *Mat.* 13: 55.

Shouldest not thou also have had compassion on thy fellowservant, even as I had pity on thee? *Mat.* 18: 33.

Thou shalt love thy neighbour as thyself. *Mat.* 19: 19.

Inasmuch as ye have done it unto one of the least of these my brethren, ye have done it unto me. *Mat.* 25: 40.

Daughters of Jerusalem, weep not for me, but weep for yourselves, and for your children. *Lu.* 23: 28.

The Word was made flesh, and dwelt among us. *Jn.* 1: 14.

I am the good shepherd: the good shepherd giveth his life for the sheep. *Jn.* 10: 11.

There is therefore now no condemnation to them which are in Christ Jesus. *Ro.* 8: 1.

God sending his own Son in the likeness of sinful flesh, and for sin, condemned sin in the flesh. *Ro.* 8: 3.

God sent forth his Son, made of a woman, made under the law. *Ga.* 4: 4.

Being found in fashion as a man, he humbled himself, and became obedient unto death, even the death of the cross. *Ph.* 2: 8.

There is one God, and one mediator between God and men, the man Christ Jesus. *1 Ti.* 2: 5.

Forasmuch then as the children are partakers of flesh and blood, he also himself likewise took part of the same. *He.* 2: 14.

In all things it behoved him to be made like unto his brethren. *He.* 2: 17.

Touched with the feeling of our infirmities. *He.* 4: 15.

Tempted like as we are. *He.* 4: 15.

See also

Christ, Compassion of; Christ, Gentleness of; Christ, Goodness of; Christ, Grace of; Christ, Manliness of; Christ, the Son of Man.

Christ, Humiliation of

He made his grave with the wicked. *Is.* 53: 9.

He was numbered with the transgressors. *Is.* 53: 12.

She brought forth her firstborn son, and wrapped him in swaddling clothes, and laid him in a manger. *Lu.* 2: 7.

He was reckoned among the transgressors. *Lu.* 22: 37.

In his humiliation his judgment was taken away. *Ac.* 8: 33.

Christ hath redeemed us from the curse of the law, being made a curse for us. *Ga.* 3: 13.

Christ Jesus . . . thought it not robbery to be equal with God: But made himself of no reputation, and took upon him the form of a servant, and was made in the likeness of man. *Ph.* 2: 5–7.

He . . . became obedient unto death, even the death of the cross. *Ph.* 2: 8.

See also

Christ, Betrayal of; Christ, Blood of; Christ, Cross of; Christ, Crucifixion of; Christ, Death of; Christ, Obedience of; Christ, the Passover; Christ, Rejection of; Christ, Sacrifice of; Christ, Suffering of.

Christ, Humility of

He hath no form nor comeliness; and when

we shall see him, there is no beauty that we should desire him. *Is.* **53: 2.**

John forbad him, saying, I have need to be baptized of thee, and comest thou to me? *Mat.* **3: 14.**

Blessed are the meek: for they shall inherit the earth. *Mat.* **5: 5.**

I say unto you, That ye resist not evil: but whosoever shall smite thee on thy right cheek, turn to him the other also. *Mat.* **5: 39.**

I am meek and lowly in heart. *Mat.* **11: 29.**

Every one that exalteth himself shall be abased. *Lu.* **18: 14.**

I do nothing of myself; but as my Father hath taught me, I speak these things. *Jn.* **8: 28.**

Now Jesus loved Martha, and her sister, and Lazarus. *Jn.* **11: 5.**

Walk in love, as Christ also hath loved us, and hath given himself for us an offering and a sacrifice to God. *Ep.* **5: 2.**

Verily he took not on him the nature of angels; but he took on him the seed of Abraham. *He.* **2: 16.**

See also

Christ, Humiliation of; Christ, Impotence of; Christ, Meekness of; Christ, Obedience of.

Christ, Imitation of

Simon and they that were with him followed after him. *Mk.* **1: 36.**

We have left all, and have followed thee. *Mk.* **10: 28.**

There followed him a certain young man. *Mk.* **14: 51.**

Jesus turned, and saw them following. *Jn.* **1: 38.**

If any man serve me, let him follow me. *Jn.* **12: 26.**

I have given you an example, that ye should do as I have done to you. *Jn.* **13: 15.**

Be ye followers of me, even as I also am of Christ. *1 Co.* **11: 1.**

That in me first Jesus Christ might shew forth . . . a pattern to them which should hereafter believe on him. *1 Ti.* **1: 16.**

Looking unto Jesus. *He.* **12: 2.**

Christ also suffered for us, leaving us an example, that ye should follow his steps. *1 Pe.* **2: 21.**

See also

Christ, Example of; Christ, Influence of; Christ, the Inimitable.

Christ, Impotence of

To sit on my right hand, and on my left, is not mine to give. *Mat.* **20: 23.**

Jesus said unto him, Why callest thou me good? none is good, save one, that is, God. *Lu.* **18: 19.**

I can of mine own self do nothing. *Jn.* **5: 30.**

Even Christ pleased not himself. *Ro.* **15: 3.**

God hath chosen the weak things of the world to confound the things which are mighty. *1 Co.* **1: 27.**

He was crucified through weakness, yet he liveth by the power of God. *2 Co.* **13: 4.**

Put to death in the flesh, but quickened by the Spirit. *1 Pe.* **3: 18.**

See also

Christ, Humility of; Christ, Meekness of.

Christ, Incarnation of

She brought forth her firstborn son. *Lu.* **2: 7.**

Unto you is born this day in the city of David a Saviour, which is Christ the Lord. *Lu.* **2: 11.**

He was in the world, and the world was made by him, and the world knew him not. *Jn.* **1: 10.**

The Word was made flesh, and dwelt among us. *Jn.* **1: 14.**

I saw, and bare record that this is the Son of God. *Jn.* **1: 34.**

Looking upon Jesus as he walked, he saith, Behold the Lamb of God! *Jn.* **1: 36.**

Rabbi, thou art the Son of God; thou art the King of Israel. *Jn.* **1: 49.**

The Father that dwelleth in me, he doeth the works. *Jn.* **14: 10.**

I have manifested thy name. *Jn.* **17: 6.**

If Christ be in you, the body is dead because of sin. *Ro.* **8: 10.**

Being found in fashion as a man, he humbled himself, and became obedient unto death. *Ph.* **2: 8.**

It pleased the Father that in him should all fulness dwell. *Col.* **1: 19.**

God was manifest in the flesh, justified in the Spirit, seen of angels, preached unto the Gentiles, believed on in the world, received up into glory. *1 Ti.* **3: 16.**

Christ glorified not himself to be made an high priest; but he that said unto him, Thou art my Son, to day have I begotten thee. *He.* **5: 5.**

In the days of his flesh. *He.* **5: 7.**

Christ hath suffered for us in the flesh. *1 Pe.* **4: 1.**

Every spirit that confesseth not that Jesus Christ is come in the flesh is not of God. *1 Jn.* **4: 3.**

See also

Christ, Divinity of; Christ, God in; Christ, Oneness with God; Christ, the Son of God; God, Eminence of; God, Incarnation of; Incarnation.

Christ, Indifference toward

When we shall see him, there is no beauty that we should desire him. *Is.* **53: 2.**

We hid as it were our faces from him. *Is.* **53: 3.**

We have turned every one to his own way. *Is.* **53: 6.**

How often would I have gathered thy children together, even as a hen gathereth her chickens under her wings, and ye would not! *Mat.* **23: 37.**

Because iniquity shall abound, the love of many shall wax cold. *Mat.* **24: 12.**

What, could ye not watch with me one hour? *Mat.* **26: 40.**

Their heart was hardened. *Mk.* **6: 52.**

The stone which the builders rejected is become the head of the corner. *Mk.* **12: 10.**

Lest coming suddenly he find you sleeping. *Mk.* **13: 36.**

I marvel that ye are so soon removed from him that called you into the grace of Christ unto another gospel. *Ga.* **1: 6.**

All seek their own, not the things which are Jesus Christ's. *Ph.* **2: 21.**

Whosoever denieth the Son, the same hath not the Father. *1 Jn.* **2: 23.**

Every spirit that confesseth not that Jesus

Christ is come in the flesh is not of God. *1 Jn.* *4: 3.*
See also
Christ, Hatred of.

Christ, the Indwelling

In him was life; and the life was the light of men. *Jn.* 1: 4.

If Christ be in you, the body is dead because of sin; but the Spirit is life because of righteousness. *Ro.* 8: 10.

Know ye not your own selves, how that Jesus Christ is in you, except ye be reprobates? *2 Co.* 13: 5.

I am crucified with Christ: nevertheless I live; yet not I, but Christ liveth in me. *Ga.* 2: 20.

That Christ may dwell in your hearts by faith. *Ep.* 3: 17.

Christ in you, the hope of glory. *Col.* 1: 27.
See also
Christ, Abiding in; Christ, Communion with; Christ, the Contemporary; Christ, Fellowship with; Christ, Life in; Christ, Nearness of; Christ, Union with.

Christ, Influence of

Master, I will follow thee whithersoever thou goest. *Mat.* 8: 19.

The disciples went, and did as Jesus commanded them. *Mat.* 21: 6.

There went out a fame of him through all the region round about. *Lu.* 4: 14.

They took knowledge of them, that they had been with Jesus. *Ac.* 4: 13.

The name of the Lord Jesus was magnified. *Ac.* 19: 17.

I obtained mercy, that in me first Jesus Christ might shew forth . . . a pattern to them which should hereafter believe on him to life everlasting. *1 Ti.* 1: 16.

An example. *1 Pe.* 2: 21.
See also
Christ, Authority of; Christ, Compulsion of; Christ, Imitation of; Christ, the Inimitable.

Christ, the Inimitable

Sit ye here, while I go and pray yonder. *Mat.* 26: 36.

He was withdrawn from them about a stone's cast. *Lu.* 22: 41.

And Peter followed afar off. *Lu.* 22: 54.

Never man spake like this man. *Jn.* 7: 46.
See also
Christ, Authority of; Christ, Compulsion of; Christ, Imitation of; Christ, Supremacy of; Christ, Uniqueness of.

Christ, Innocence of

He had done no violence, neither was any deceit in his mouth. *Is.* 53: 9.

If ye had known what this meaneth, I will have mercy, and not sacrifice, ye would not have condemned the guiltless. *Mat.* 12: 7.

I have sinned in that I have betrayed the innocent blood. *Mat.* 27: 4.

Behold the Lamb of God, which taketh away the sin of the world. *Jn.* 1: 29.

Which of you convinceth me of sin? *Jn.* 8: 46.

I find in him no fault at all. *Jn.* 18: 38.

He was led as a sheep to the slaughter. *Ac.* 8: 32.

Is therefore Christ the minister of sin? God forbid. *Ga.* 2: 17.

Christ . . . offered himself without spot to God. *He.* 9: 14.

Christ, . . . a lamb without blemish and without spot. *1 Pe.* 1: 19.

Christ also suffered for us, leaving us an example, that ye should follow his steps: Who did no sin, neither was guile found in his mouth. *1 Pe.* 2: 21, 22.

Worthy is the Lamb that was slain. *Re.* 5: 12.
See also
Christ, Beauty of; Christ, Goodness of; Christ, Grace of; Christ, Holiness of; Christ, Perfection of; Christ, Sinlessness of.

Christ, Isolation of

Perceive ye not yet, neither understand? *Mk.* 8: 17.

Jesus was left alone, and the woman standing in the midst. *Jn.* 8: 9.

I am not alone, but I and the Father that sent me. *Jn.* 8: 16.

The Father hath not left me alone. *Jn.* 8: 29.

These things spake Jesus, and departed, and did hide himself from them. *Jn.* 12: 36.

The hour cometh, yea, is now come, that ye shall be scattered, every man to his own, and shall leave me alone: and yet I am not alone, because the Father is with me. *Jn.* 16: 32.
See also
Christ, the Hidden; Christ, Loneliness of; Christ, Mystery of; Christ, Silence of.

Christ, Joy in

The kingdom of heaven is like unto treasure hid in a field; the which when a man hath found, he hideth, and for joy thereof goeth and selleth all that he hath, and buyeth that field. *Mat.* 13: 44.

The common people heard him gladly. *Mk.* 12: 37.

It came to pass, that, when Jesus was returned, the people gladly received him. *Lu.* 8: 40.

While they yet believed not for joy, and wondered, he said unto them, Have ye here any meat? *Lu.* 24: 41.

I will see you again, and your heart shall rejoice, and your joy no man taketh from you. *Jn.* 16: 22.

Then were the disciples glad, when they saw the Lord. *Jn.* 20: 20.

We also joy in God through our Lord Jesus Christ. *Ro.* 5: 11.

Finally, my brethren, rejoice in the Lord. *Ph.* 3: 1.

For what is our hope, or joy, or crown of rejoicing? Are not even ye in the presence of our Lord Jesus Christ at his coming? *1 Th.* 2: 19.

Jesus Christ: Whom having not seen, ye love; in whom, though now ye see him not, yet believing, ye rejoice with joy unspeakable and full of glory. *1 Pe.* 1: 7, 8.

Unto you therefore which believe he is precious. *1 Pe.* 2: 7.

Christ, Joy of

Enter thou into the joy of thy lord. *Mat.* 25: 21.

Jesus rejoiced in spirit. *Lu.* 10: 21.

These things have I spoken unto you, that

my joy might remain in you, and that your joy might be full. *Jn.* 15: 11.

Who for the joy that was set before him endured the cross. *He.* 12: 2.

Christ, the Judge

When the Son of man shall sit in the throne of his glory, ye also shall sit upon twelve thrones, judging the twelve tribes of Israel. *Mat.* 19: 28.

They shall see the Son of man coming in the clouds of heaven with power and great glory. *Mat.* 24: 30.

Whosoever shall confess me before men, him shall the Son of man also confess before the angels of God. *Lu.* 12: 8.

Man, who made me a judge or a divider over you? *Lu.* 12: 14.

Watch ye therefore, and pray always, that ye may be accounted worthy . . . to stand before the Son of man. *Lu.* 21: 36.

God sent not his Son into the world to condemn the world; but that the world through him might be saved. *Jn.* 3: 17.

The Father judgeth no man, but hath committed all judgment unto the Son. *Jn.* 5: 22.

The Father . . . hath given him authority to execute judgment also, because he is the Son of man. *Jn.* 5: 26, 27.

My judgment is just. *Jn.* 5: 30.

Jesus said unto her, Neither do I condemn thee: go, and sin no more. *Jn.* 8: 11.

Ye judge after the flesh; I judge no man. *Jn.* 8: 15.

Jesus said, For judgment I am come into this world. *Jn.* 9: 39.

I came not to judge the world, but to save the world. *Jn.* 12: 47.

The word that I have spoken, the same shall judge him in the last day. *Jn.* 12: 48.

God shall judge the secrets of men by Jesus Christ. *Ro.* 2: 16.

We shall all stand before the judgment seat of Christ. *Ro.* 14: 10.

We must all appear before the judgment seat of Christ; that every one may receive the things done in his body, according to that he hath done, whether it be good or bad. *2 Co.* 5: 10.

See also

Christ, the Accusing; Christ, Condemnation of; Christ, Day of; Christ, Second Coming of.

Christ, the King

Behold, thy King cometh unto thee: he is just, and having salvation; lowly, and riding upon an ass. *Zch.* 9: 9.

Jesus answered, My kingdom is not of this world. *Jn.* 18: 36.

Jesus answered, Thou sayest that I am a king. *Jn.* 18: 37.

Pilate . . . saith unto the Jews, Behold your King! *Jn.* 19: 13, 14.

These all do contrary to the decrees of Cæsar, saying that there is another king, one Jesus. *Ac.* 17: 7.

The Father . . . hath translated us into the kingdom of his dear Son. *Col.* 1: 12, 13.

So an entrance shall be ministered unto you abundantly into the everlasting kingdom of our Lord and Saviour Jesus Christ. *2 Pe.* 1: 11.

Jesus Christ, who is . . . the prince of the kings of the earth. *Re.* 1: 5.

In the kingdom and patience of Jesus Christ. *Re.* 1: 9.

The kingdoms of this world are become the kingdoms of our Lord, and of his Christ; and he shall reign for ever and ever. *Re.* 11: 15.

The Lamb . . . is Lord of lords, and King of kings. *Re.* 17: 14.

See also

Christ, Crown of; Christ, Reign of; Christ, Supremacy of; Christ, Triumphal Entry of.

Christ, Knowledge of

Jesus did not commit himself unto them, because he knew all men. *Jn.* 2: 24.

This is life eternal, that they might know thee the only true God, and Jesus Christ whom thou hast sent. *Jn.* 17: 3.

Thou, Lord, . . . knowest the hearts of all men. *Ac.* 1: 24.

Who art thou, Lord? *Ac.* 9: 5.

I determined not to know any thing among you, save Jesus Christ, and him crucified. *1 Co.* 2: 2.

Yea doubtless, and I count all things but loss for the excellency of the knowledge of Christ Jesus my Lord. *Ph.* 3: 8.

Filled with the knowledge of his will. *Col.* 1: 9.

In whom are hid all the treasures of wisdom and knowledge. *Col.* 2: 3.

They make you that ye shall neither be barren nor unfruitful in the knowledge of our Lord Jesus Christ. *2 Pe.* 1: 8.

Grow in grace, and in the knowledge of our Lord and Saviour Jesus Christ. *2 Pe.* 3: 18.

If we keep his commandments. *1 Jn.* 2: 3.

See also

Christ, Mind of; Christ, Wisdom of.

Christ, the Lamb of God

As a sheep before her shearers is dumb, so he openeth not his mouth. *Is.* 53: 7.

Behold the Lamb of God, which taketh away the sin of the world! *Jn.* 1: 29.

Christ our passover is sacrificed for us. *1 Co:* 5: 7.

With the precious blood of Christ, as of a lamb without blemish and without spot. *1 Pe.* 1: 19.

The blood of Jesus Christ his Son cleanseth us from all sin. *1 Jn.* 1: 7.

Worthy is the Lamb. *Re.* 5: 12.

Blessing, and honour, and glory, and power, be unto him that sitteth upon the throne, and unto the Lamb for ever and ever. *Re.* 5: 13.

A great multitude, which no man could number, . . . stood before the throne, and before the Lamb. *Re.* 7: 9.

These are they which came out of great tribulation, and have washed their robes, and made them white in the blood of the Lamb. *Re.* 7: 14.

For the Lamb which is in the midst of the throne shall feed them, and shall lead them unto living fountains of water. *Re.* 7: 17.

The Lamb slain from the foundation of the world. *Re.* 13: 8.

The Lord God Almighty and the Lamb are the temple of it. *Re.* 21: 22.

See also

Christ, Blood of; Christ, Cross of; Christ, Crucifixion of; Christ, Cup of; Christ, Death of; Christ, the Passover; Christ, Sacrifice of; Christ, Suffering of.

Christ, the Leader

One is your Master, even Christ. *Mat.* **23: 8.**
Jesus . . . leadeth them up into an high mountain. *Mk.* **9: 2.**
Jesus went before them: and they were amazed; and as they followed, they were afraid. *Mk.* **10: 32.**
Pilate therefore said unto him, Art thou a king then? Jesus answered, Thou sayest that I am a king. *Jn.* **18: 37.**
The head of every man is Christ. *1 Co.* **11: 3.**
Christ is the head of the church. *Ep.* **5: 23.**
Our Lord Jesus Christ, direct our way unto you. *1 Th.* **3: 11.**
The Lamb which is in the midst of the throne . . . shall lead them unto living fountains of waters. *Re.* **7: 17.**
See also
Christ, the Captain; Christ, Disciple of; Christ, Follower of; Christ, the Guide; Christ, the Lord; Christ, the Master.

Christ, the Liberator

He hath sent me . . . to proclaim liberty to the captives, and the opening of the prison to them that are bound. *Is.* **61: 1.**
Ye shall know the truth, and the truth shall make you free. *Jn.* **8: 32.**
If the Son therefore shall make you free, ye shall be free indeed. *Jn.* **8: 36.**
There is therefore now no condemnation to them which are in Christ Jesus. *Ro.* **8: 1.**
The law of the Spirit of life in Christ Jesus hath made me free from the law of sin and death. *Ro.* **8: 2.**
He that is called in tne Lord, being a servant, is the Lord's freeman: likewise also he that is called, being free, is Christ's servant. *1 Co.* **7: 22.**
There is neither bond nor free, . . . for ye are all one in Christ Jesus. *Ga.* **3: 28.**
Stand fast therefore in the liberty wherewith Christ hath made us free. *Ga.* **5: 1.**
So an entrance shall be ministered unto you abundantly into the everlasting kingdom of our Lord and Saviour Jesus Christ. *2 Pe.* **1: 11.**
See also
Christ, the Deliverer; Christ, the Redeemer; Christ, the Saviour.

Christ, Life in

In him was life; and the life was the light of men. *Jn.* **1: 4.**
The Son quickeneth whom he will. *Jn.* **5: 21.**
Because I live, ye shall live also. *Jn.* **14: 19.**
Abide in me, and I in you. *Jn.* **15: 4.**
If we be dead with Christ, we believe that we shall also live with him. *Ro.* **6: 8.**
Alive unto God through Jesus Christ our Lord. *Ro.* **6: 11.**
As in Adam all die, even so in Christ shall all be made alive. *1 Co.* **15: 22.**
Always bearing about in the body the dying of the Lord Jesus, that the life also of Jesus

might be made manifest in our body. *2 Co.* **4: 10.**
For we which live are always delivered unto death for Jesus' sake, that the life also of Jesus might be made manifest in our mortal flesh. *2 Co.* **4: 11.**
I am crucified with Christ: nevertheless I live; yet not I, but Christ liveth in me. *Ga.* **2: 20.**
God . . . hath quickened us together with Christ. *Ep.* **2: 4, 5.**
For to me to live is Christ. *Ph.* **1: 21.**
He that hath the Son hath life. *1 Jn.* **5: 12.**
See also
Christ, Abiding in; Christ, Communion with; Christ, Companionship with; Christ, the Contemporary; Christ, Fellowship with; Christ, the Indwelling; Christ, Nearness of; Christ, Partnership with; Christ, Presence of; Christ, Union with.

Christ, the Light

The people that walked in darkness have seen a great light: they that dwell in the land of the shadow of death, upon them hath the light shined. *Is.* **9: 2.**
His face did shine as the sun, and his raiment was white as the light. *Mat.* **17: 2.**
In him was life; and the life was the light of men. *Jn.* **1: 4.**
The light shineth in darkness. *Jn.* **1: 5.**
That was the true light, which lighteth every man. *Jn.* **1: 9.**
I am the light of the world: he that followeth me shall not walk in darkness, but shall have the light of life. *Jn.* **8: 12.**
I am come a light into the world. *Jn.* **12: 46.**
Awake thou that sleepest, and arise from the dead, and Christ shall give thee light. *Ep.* **5: 14.**
The darkness is past, and the true light now shineth. *1 Jn.* **2: 8.**
The glory of God did lighten it, and the Lamb is the light thereof. *Re.* **21: 23.**

Christ, the Living

As the Father hath life in himself; so hath he given to the Son to have life in himself. *Jn.* **5: 26.**
Because I live, ye shall live also. *Jn.* **14: 19.**
As Christ was raised up from the dead by the glory of the Father, even so we also should walk in newness of life. *Ro.* **6: 4.**
If we be dead with Christ, we believe that we shall also live with him. *Ro.* **6: 8.**
Christ being raised from the dead dieth no more; death hath no more dominion over him. *Ro.* **6: 9.**
Alive unto God through Jesus Christ our Lord. *Ro.* **6: 11.**
In Christ shall all be made alive. *1 Co.* **15: 22.**
We shall live with him by the power of God toward you. *2 Co.* **13: 4.**
Jesus Christ the same yesterday, and to day, and for ever. *He.* **13: 8.**
God . . . hath begotten us again unto a lively hope by the resurrection of Jesus Christ from the dead. *1 Pe.* **1: 3.**
God sent his only begotten Son into the world, that we might live through him. *1 Jn.* **4: 9.**
I am he that liveth, and was dead; and, be-

hold, I am alive for evermore. *Re.* 1: 18.

I am he that liveth. *Re.* 1: 28.

See also

Christ, Abiding in; Christ, the Changeless; Christ, Communion with; Christ, Companionship of; Christ, the Contemporary; Christ, the Eternal; Christ, the Indwelling; Christ, Permanence of; Christ, Presence of.

Christ, Loneliness of

My God,, my God, why hast thou forsaken me? *Ps.* 22: 1.

The foxes have holes, and the birds of the air have nests; but the Son of man hath not where to lay his head. *Mat.* 8: 20.

When the evening was come, he was there alone. *Mat.* 14: 23.

The ship was in the midst of the sea, and he alone on the land. *Mk.* 6: 47.

He was alone praying. *Lu.* 9: 18.

He departed again into a mountain himself alone. *Jn.* 6: 15.

He that sent me is with me: the Father hath not left me alone. *Jn.* 8: 29.

Behold, the hour cometh, yea, is now come, that ye shall be scattered, every man to his own, and shall leave me alone. *Jn.* 16: 32.

Yet I am not alone, because the Father is with me. *Jn.* 16: 32.

See also

Christ, the Hidden; Christ, Isolation of; Christ, Mystery of; Christ, Silence of.

Christ, the Lord

The spirit of the Lord shall rest upon him, the spirit of wisdom and understanding. the spirit of counsel and might, the spirit of knowledge and of the fear of the Lord. *Is.* 11: 2.

Not every one that saith unto me, Lord, Lord, shall enter into the kingdom of heaven. *Mat.* 7: 21.

The Son of man is Lord even of the sabbath day. *Mat.* 12: 8.

Unto you is born this day in the city of David a Saviour, which is Christ the Lord. *Lu.* 2: 11.

Why call ye me, Lord, Lord, and do not the things which I say? *Lu.* 6: 46.

Lord, to whom shall we go? thou hast the words of eternal life. *Jn.* 6: 68.

Ye call me Master and Lord: and ye say well; for so I am. *Jn.* 13: 13.

We have seen the Lord. *Jn.* 20: 25.

He . . . set him at his own right hand in the heavenly places, Far above all principality, and power, and might, and dominion. *Ep.* 1: 20, 21.

One Lord, one faith, one baptism, One God and Father of all. *Ep.* 4: 5, 6.

That every tongue should confess that Jesus Christ is Lord, to the glory of God the Father. *Ph.* 2: 11.

Whatsoever ye do in word or deed, do all in the name of the Lord Jesus. *Col.* 3: 17.

Jesus Christ: . . . who is the blessed and only Potentate, the King of kings, and Lord of lords. *1 Ti.* 6: 14, 15.

See also

Christ, the Captain; Christ, God in; Christ, the Guide; Christ, the Leader; Christ, the Master; Christ, the Messiah; Christ, the Son of God.

Christ, Love of

He that loveth father or mother more than me is not worthy of me: and he that loveth son or daughter more than me is not worthy of me. *Mat.* 10: 37.

Jesus beholding him loved him. *Mk.* 10: 21.

Neither do I condemn thee. *Jn.* 8: 11.

Jesus loved Martha, and her sister, and Lazarus. *Jn.* 11: 5.

Having loved his own which were in the world, he loved them unto the end. *Jn.* 13: 1.

If ye love me, keep my commandments. *Jn.* 14: 15.

If a man love me, he will keep my words: and my Father will love him. *Jn.* 14: 23.

The Father himself loveth you, because ye have loved me. *Jn.* 16: 27.

Thou lovedst me before the foundation of the world. *Jn.* 17: 24.

Simon son of Jonas, lovest thou me more than these? *Jn.* 21: 15.

Yea, Lord; thou knowest that I love thee. *Jn.* 21: 15.

Who shall separate us from the love of Christ? *Ro.* 8: 35.

If any man love not the Lord Jesus Christ, let him be Anathema Maranatha. *1 Co.* 16: 22.

The love of Christ constraineth us. *2 Co.* 5: 14.

To know the love of Christ, which passeth knowledge. *Ep.* 3: 19.

Walk in love, as Christ also hath loved us. *Ep.* 5: 2.

Grace be with all them that love our Lord Jesus Christ in sincerity. *Ep.* 6: 24.

We love him, because he first loved us. *1 Jn.* 4: 19.

See also

Christ, Attitude towards; Christ, the Comforter; Christ, Compassion of; Christ, Devotion to; Christ, Faith in; Christ, Faithfulness of; Christ, Gentleness of; Christ, Goodness of; Christ, Loyalty to; Christ, Sympathy of.

Christ, Loyalty to

Whose I am, and whom I serve. *Ac.* 27: 23.

We are buried with him by baptism into. death. *Ro.* 6: 4.

Whosoever believeth on him shall not be ashamed. *Ro.* 9: 33.

Ye were called unto the fellowship of his Son Jesus Christ our Lord. *1 Co.* 1: 9.

I determined not to know any thing among you, save Jesus Christ, and him crucified. *1 Co.* 2: 2.

This they did, not as we hoped, but first gave their own selves to the Lord, and unto us by the will of God. *2 Co.* 8: 5.

The church is subject unto Christ. *Ep.* 5: 24.

To me to live is Christ. *Ph.* 1: 21.

Rooted . . . in him. *Col.* 2: 7.

Whatsoever ye do in word or deed, do all in the name of the Lord Jesus, giving thanks to God and the Father by him. *Col.* 3: 17.

See also

Christ, Belief in; Christ, Devotion to; Christ, Faith in; Christ, Love of; Christ, Obedience to.

Christ, Majesty of

The Son of man shall come in the glory of his Father with his angels. *Mat.* 16: 27.

When the Son of man shall come in his glory, and all the holy angels with him, then shall he sit upon the throne of his glory. *Mat.* **25: 31.**

And he saith unto him, Verily, verily, I say unto you, Hereafter ye shall see heaven open, and the angels of God ascending and descending upon the Son of man. *Jn.* **1: 51.**

The hour is come, that the Son of man should be glorified. *Jn.* **12: 23.**

O Father, glorify thou me with thine own self with the glory which I had with thee before the world was. *Jn.* **17: 5.**

He saith unto the Jews, Behold your King! *Jn.* **19: 14.**

The God of our fathers hath glorified his Son Jesus. *Ac.* **3: 13.**

He, being full of the Holy Ghost, looked up stedfastly into heaven, and saw the glory of God, and Jesus standing on the right hand of God. *Ac.* **7: 55.**

That the name of our Lord Jesus Christ may be glorified in you, and ye in him. *2 Th.* **1: 12.**

We see Jesus, who was made a little lower than the angels for the suffering of death, crowned with glory and honour. *He.* **2: 9.**

The everlasting kingdom of our Lord and Saviour Jesus Christ. *2 Pe.* **1: 11.**

See also

Christ, Dignity of; Christ, Exaltation of; Christ, Greatness of; Christ, Nature of; Christ, Supremacy of; Christ, Triumph of.

Christ, Manliness of

The Son of man came eating and drinking. *Mat.* **11: 19.**

The common people heard him gladly. *Mk.* **12: 37.**

They said, Is not this Joseph's son? *Lu.* **4: 22.**

He knew what was in man. *Jn.* **2: 25.**

As soon then as he had said unto them, I am he, they went backward, and fell to the ground. *Jn.* **18: 6.**

In all points tempted like as we are. *He.* **4: 15.**

See also

Christ, Courage of; Christ, Humanity of; Christ, the Son of Man.

Christ, the Master

One is your Master, even Christ; and all ye are brethren. *Mat.* **23: 8.**

Ye belong to Christ. *Mk.* **9: 41.**

Good Master, what shall I do that I may inherit eternal life? *Mk.* **10: 17.**

The disciple is not above his master: but every one that is perfect shall be as his master. *Lu.* **6: 40.**

The Father . . . hath given him authority to execute judgment, because he is the Son of man. *Jn.* **5: 26, 27.**

The Master is come, and calleth for thee. *Jn.* **11: 28.**

To us there is but . . . one Lord Jesus Christ, by whom are all things, and we by him. *1 Co.* **8: 6.**

Thanks be to God, which giveth us the victory through our Lord Jesus Christ. *1 Co.* **15: 57.**

The head, even Christ. *Ep.* **4: 15.**

Having spoiled principalities and powers, he made a shew of them openly, triumphing over them. *Col.* **2: 15.**

A prisoner of Jesus Christ. *Phm.* **1: 1.**

See also

Christ, the Captain; Christ, Disciple of; Christ, Follower of; Christ, the Guide; Christ, the Leader; Christ, the Lord.

Christ, the Mediator

He saw that there was no man, and wondered that there was no intercessor: therefore his arm brought salvation unto him. *Is.* **59: 16.**

I pray . . . for them which thou hast given me; for they are thine. *Jn.* **17: 9.**

Christ . . . is even at the right hand of God, who also maketh intercession for us. *Ro.* **8: 34.**

The head of every man is Christ; . . . and the head of Christ is God. *1 Co.* **11: 3.**

God was in Christ, reconciling the world unto himself. *2 Co.* **5: 19.**

There is . . . one mediator between God and men, the man Christ Jesus. *1 Ti.* **2: 5.**

He is able also to save them to the uttermost that come unto God by him, seeing he ever liveth to make intercession for them. *He.* **7: 25.**

He is the mediator of the new testament. *He.* **9: 15.**

Christ is not entered into the holy places made with hands, . . . but into heaven itself, now to appear in the presence of God for us. *He.* **9: 24.**

Ye are come . . . to Jesus the mediator of the new covenant. *He.* **12: 22, 24.**

He is the propitiation for our sins: and not for ours only, but also for the sins of the whole world. *1 Jn.* **2: 2.**

Christ, Meekness of

Behold, thy King cometh unto thee: he is just, and having salvation; lowly, and riding upon an ass, and upon a colt the foal of an ass. *Zch.* **9: 9.**

I am meek and lowly in heart. *Mat.* **11: 29.**

I . . . beseech you by the meekness and gentleness of Christ. *2 Co.* **10: 1.**

He humbled himself, and became obedient unto death. *Ph.* **2: 8.**

Who, when he was reviled, reviled not again; when he suffered, he threatened not; but committed himself to him that judgeth righteously. *1 Pe.* **2: 23.**

See also

Christ, Gentleness of; Christ, Humility of; Christ, Impotence of; Christ, Obedience to.

Christ, Message of

Preach, saying, The kingdom of heaven is at hand. *Mat.* **10: 7.**

The people pressed upon him to hear the word of God. *Lu.* **5: 1.**

He . . . sent messengers before his face. *Lu.* **9: 51, 52.**

He that heareth my word, and believeth on him that sent me, hath everlasting life. *Jn.* **5: 24.**

I am one that bear witness of myself. *Jn.* **8: 18.**

We preach Christ crucified. *1 Co.* **1: 23.**

Ye are manifestly declared to be the epistle of Christ ministered by us. *2 Co.* **3: 3.**

Unto me, who am less than the least of all saints, is this grace given, that I should preach among the Gentiles the unsearchable riches of Christ. *Ep.* 3: 8.

This then is the message which we have heard of him, and declare unto you, that God is light. *1 Jn.* 1: 5.

See also

Christ, Gospel of; Christ, Preaching of; Christ, Promise of; Christ, the Teacher; Christ, the Word; Christ, Word of.

Christ, the Messiah

This man shall be the peace. *Mi.* 5: 5.

They shall call his name Emmanuel. *Mat.* 1: 23.

Thou art the Christ, the Son of the living God. *Mat.* 16: 16.

Art thou the Christ, the Son of the Blessed? *Mk.* 14: 61.

We have found the Messias, which is, being interpreted, the Christ. *Jn.* 1: 41.

I know that Messias cometh, which is called Christ: when he is come, he will tell us all things. *Jn.* 4: 25.

We believe and are sure that thou art that Christ, the Son of the living God. *Jn.* 6: 69.

Others said, This is the Christ. *Jn.* 7: 41.

This Jesus, whom I preach unto you, is Christ. *Ac.* 17: 3.

He mightily convinced the Jews, and that publickly, shewing by the scriptures that Jesus was Christ. *Ac.* 18: 28.

See also

Christ, God in; Christ, the Lord; Christ, the Son of God.

Christ, Mind of

Jesus knew their thoughts. *Mat.* 12: 25.

We have the mind of Christ. *1 Co.* 2: 16.

Let this mind be in you, which was also in Christ Jesus. *Ph.* 2: 5.

I count all things but loss for the excellency of the knowledge of Christ Jesus my Lord. *Ph.* 3: 8.

In whom are hid all the treasures of wisdom and of knowledge. *Col.* 2: 3.

As Christ hath suffered for us in the flesh, arm yourselves likewise with the same mind. *1 Pe.* 4: 1.

See also

Christ, Knowledge of; Christ, Wisdom of.

Christ, Ministry of

Even . . . the Son of man came not to be ministered unto, but to minister. *Mat.* 20: 28.

Jesus Christ was a minister . . . for the truth of God. *Ro.* 15: 8.

Let a man so account of us, as of the ministers of Christ. *1 Co.* 4: 1.

Are they ministers of Christ? . . . I am more. *2 Co.* 11: 23.

Bear ye one another's burdens, and so fulfil the law of Christ. *Ga.* 6: 2.

Consider the Apostle and High Priest of our profession, Christ Jesus. *He.* 3: 1.

We have a great high priest, that is passed into the heavens. *He.* 4: 14.

This man . . . hath an unchangeable priesthood. *He.* 7: 24.

See also

Christ, the Comforter; Christ, Compassion of; Christ, Encouragement of; Christ, the Healing; Christ, Mission of; Christ, the Physi-

cian; Christ, Power of; Christ, Priesthood of; Christ, Purpose of; Christ, the Servant; Christ, Touch of; Christ, Work of

Christ, Miracles of

Then began he to upbraid the cities wherein most of his mighty works were done, because they repented not. *Mat.* 11: 20.

An evil and adulterous generation seeketh after a sign; and there shall no sign be given to it, but the sign of the prophet Jonas. *Mat.* 12: 39.

Whence hath this man this wisdom, and these mighty works? *Mat.* 13: 54.

He did not many mighty works there because of their unbelief. *Mat.* 13: 58.

What wisdom is this which is given unto him, that even such mighty works are wrought by his hands? *Mk.* 6: 2.

There is no man which shall do a miracle in my name, that can lightly speak evil of me. *Mk.* 9: 39.

The whole multitude of the disciples began to rejoice and praise God with a loud voice for all the mighty works that they had seen. *Lu.* 19: 37.

He hoped to have seen some miracle done by him. *Lu.* 23: 8.

This beginning of miracles did Jesus in Cana of Galilee, and manifested forth his glory. *Jn.* 2: 11.

Many believed in his name, when they saw the miracles which he did. *Jn.* 2: 23.

No man can do these miracles that thou doest, except God be with him. *Jn.* 3: 2.

Except ye see signs and wonders, ye will not believe. *Jn.* 4: 48.

A great multitude followed him, because they saw his miracles. *Jn.* 6: 2.

Then those men, when they had seen the miracle that Jesus did, said, This is of a truth that prophet that should come into the world. *Jn.* 6: 14.

John did no miracle: but all things that John spake of this man were true. *Jn.* 10: 41.

The Father that dwelleth in me, he doeth the works. *Jn.* 14: 10.

Verily, verily, I say unto you, He that believeth on me, the works that I do shall he do also; and greater works than these shall he do. *Jn.* 14: 12.

Many other signs truly did Jesus in the presence of his disciples, which are not written in this book. *Jn.* 20: 30.

Jesus of Nazareth, a man approved of God among you by miracles and wonders and signs, which God did by him in the midst of you. *Ac.* 2: 22.

Christ, Mission of

He that receiveth me receiveth him that sent me. *Mat.* 10: 40.

The Son of man came not to be ministered unto, but to minister, and to give his life a ransom for many. *Mk.* 10: 45.

To give light to them that sit in darkness and in the shadow of death, to guide our feet into the way of peace. *Lu.* 1: 79.

He hath anointed me to preach the gospel to the poor; he hath sent me to heal the brokenhearted, to preach deliverance to the captives, and recovering of sight to the blind, to set at liberty them that are bruised. *Lu. 4: 18.*

He stedfastly set his face to go to Jerusalem. *Lu. 9: 51.*

The Son of man is not come to destroy men's lives, but to save them. *Lu. 9: 56.*

The Son of man is come to seek and to save that which was lost. *Lu. 19: 10.*

I seek not mine own will, but the will of the Father which hath sent me. *Jn. 5: 30.*

He that seeketh his glory that sent him, the same is true, and no unrighteousness is in him. *Jn. 7: 18.*

Though he was rich, yet for your sakes he became poor, that ye through his poverty might be rich. *2 Co. 8: 9.*

According to the eternal purpose which he purposed in Christ Jesus our Lord. *Ep. 3: 11.*

Christ Jesus came into the world to save sinners. *1 Ti. 1: 15.*

He is able also to save them to the uttermost that come unto God by him. *He. 7: 25.*

He laid down his life for us. *1 Jn. 3: 16.*

See also

Christ, the Comforter; Christ, the Healing; Christ, the Physician; Christ, Purpose of; Christ, the Servant; Christ, Work of.

Christ, Mystery of

Unto you it is given to know the mysteries of the kingdom of God. *Lu. 8: 10.*

In that hour Jesus rejoiced in spirit, and said, I thank thee, O Father, Lord of heaven and earth, that thou hast hid these things from the wise and prudent, and hast revealed them unto babes. *Lu. 10: 21.*

The mystery, which from the beginning of the world hath been hid in God. *Ep. 3: 9.*

To comprehend . . . what is the breadth, and length, and depth, and height; And to know the love of Christ, which passeth knowledge. *Ep. 3: 18, 19.*

This is a great mystery: but I speak concerning Christ and the church. *Ep. 5: 32.*

To the acknowledgement of the mystery of God and of the Father, and of the Christ. *Col. 2: 2.*

Praying also for us, that God would open unto us a door of utterance, to speak the mystery of Christ, for which I am also in bonds. *Col. 4: 3.*

See also

Christ, the Hidden; Christ, Isolation of; Christ, Loneliness of; Christ, Silence of.

Christ, Name of

A virgin shall conceive, and bear a son, and shall call his name Immanuel. *Is. 7: 14.*

His name shall be called Wonderful, Counsellor, The mighty God, The everlasting Father, The Prince of Peace. *Is. 9: 6.*

Thou shalt call his name JESUS: for he shall save his people from their sins. *Mat. 1: 21.*

He called his name JESUS. *Mat. 1: 25.*

His fame went throughout all Syria. *Mat. 4: 24.*

Where two or three are gathered together in my name, there am I in the midst of them. *Mat. 18: 20.*

Baptizing them in the name of the Father, and of the Son, and of the Holy Ghost. *Mat. 28: 19.*

Whatsoever ye shall ask in my name, that will I do, that the Father may be glorified in the Son. *Jn. 14: 13.*

That believing ye might have life through his name. *Jn. 20: 31.*

Repent, and be baptized every one of you in the name of Jesus Christ. *Ac. 2: 38.*

There is none other name under heaven given among men, whereby we must be saved. *Ac. 4: 12.*

That signs and wonders may be done by the name of thy holy child Jesus. *Ac. 4: 30.*

They were baptized in the name of the Lord Jesus. *Ac. 8: 16.*

Wherefore God also hath highly exalted him, and given him a name which is above every name. *Ph. 2: 9.*

At the name of Jesus every knee should bow. *Ph. 2: 10.*

Let every one that nameth the name of Christ depart from iniquity. *2 Ti. 2: 19.*

He hath by inheritance obtained a more excellent name than they. *He. 1: 4.*

His name is called The Word of God. *Re. 19: 13.*

His name shall be in their foreheads. *Re. 22: 4.*

See also

Christ; Christ, the Lamb of God; Christ, the Lord; Christ, the Messiah; Christ, Nature of; Christ, the Son of God; Christ, the Son of Man.

Christ, Nature of

Of a truth thou art the Son of God. *Mat. 14: 33.*

This is my beloved Son, in whom I am well pleased. *Mat. 17: 5.*

What think ye of Christ? whose son is he? *Mat. 22: 42.*

He asked his disciples, saying unto them, Whom do men say that I am? And they answered, John the Baptist: but some say, Elias; and others, One of the prophets. *Mk. 8: 27, 28.*

Is not this Jesus, the son of Joseph, whose father and mother we know? *Jn. 6: 42.*

If thou be the Christ, tell us plainly. *Jn. 10: 24.*

Jesus saith unto him, Have I been so long time with you, and yet hast thou not known me, Philip? *Jn. 14: 9.*

He that hath seen me hath seen the Father. *Jn. 14: 9.*

Whence art thou? *Jn. 19: 9.*

Behold, I see the heavens opened, and the Son of man standing on the right hand of God. *Ac. 7: 56.*

This Jesus, whom I preach unto you, is Christ. *Ac. 17: 3.*

Who art thou, Lord? *Ac. 22: 8.*

Thou art my Son, this day have I begotten thee. *He. 1: 5.*

He took not on him the nature of angels; but he took on him the seed of Abraham. *He. 2: 16.*

See also

Christ, Divinity of; Christ, the Lamb of God; Christ, the Lord; Christ, the Messiah; Christ, Name of; Christ, Recognition of; Christ, the Son of God; Christ, the Son of Man.

Christ, Nearness of

Where two or three are gathered together in my name, there am I in the midst of them. *Mat.* 18: 20.

This generation shall not pass, till all these things be fulfilled. *Mat.* 24: 34.

He went in to tarry with them. *Lu.* 24: 29.

Where they crucified him, and two others with him, on either side one, and Jesus in the midst. *Jn.* 19: 18.

Ye are Christ's; and Christ is God's. *1 Co.* 3: 23.

Christ liveth in me. *Ga.* 2: 20.

Now in Christ Jesus ye who sometimes were far off are made nigh. *Ep.* 2: 13.

That Christ may dwell in your hearts by faith. *Ep.* 3: 17.

Are not even ye in the presence of our Lord Jesus Christ at his coming? *1 Th.* 2: 19.

See also

Christ, Abiding in; Christ, Communion with; Christ, Companionship of; Christ, the Contemporary; Christ, Fellowship with; Christ, the Indwelling; Christ, Life in; Christ, Partnership with; Christ, Presence of; Christ, Union with.

Christ, Need of

I have need to be baptized of thee. *Mat.* 3: 14.

The Lord hath need of them. *Mat.* 21: 3.

Ye have the poor with you always, and whensoever ye will ye may do them good: but me ye have not always. *Mk.* 14: 7.

Mine eyes have seen thy salvation. *Lu.* 2: 30.

They that are whole need not a physician; but they that are sick. *Lu.* 5: 31.

He . . . healed them that had need of healing. *Lu.* 9: 11.

Foxes have holes, and birds of the air have nests; but the Son of man hath not where to lay his head. *Lu.* 9: 58.

I am the door: by me if any man enter in, he shall be saved, and shall go in and out, and find pasture. *Jn.* 10: 9.

There is none other name under heaven given among men, whereby we must be saved. *Ac.* 4: 12.

How shall we escape, if we neglect so great salvation. *He.* 2: 3.

Let us therefore come boldly unto the throne of grace, that we may obtain mercy, and find grace to help in time of need. *He.* 4: 16.

See also

Christ, Dependence on.

Christ, Obedience of

The Son can do nothing of himself, but what he seeth the Father do. *Jn.* 5: 19.

I am not come of myself, but he that sent me is true. *Jn.* 7: 28.

I proceeded forth and came from God; neither came I of myself, but he sent me. *Jn.* 8: 42.

This commandment have I received of my Father. *Jn.* 10: 18.

As the Father gave me commandment, even so I do. *Jn.* 14: 31.

By the obedience of one shall many be made righteous. *Ro.* 5: 19.

When all things shall be subdued unto him, then shall the Son also himself be subject unto him that put all things under him, that God may be all in all. *1 Co.* 15: 28.

He humbled himself, and became obedient unto death. *Ph.* 2: 8.

Though he were a Son, yet learned he obedience by the things which he suffered. *He.* 5: 8.

See also

Christ, Faithfulness of; Christ, Humiliation of; Christ, Humility of; Christ, Meekness of; Christ, Sacrifice of.

Christ, Obedience to

What manner of man is this, that even the winds and the sea obey him! *Mat.* 8: 27.

These twelve Jesus sent forth, and commanded them. *Mat.* 10: 5.

Even the unclean spirits . . . obey him. *Mk.* 1: 27.

Ye call me Master and Lord: and ye say well; for so I am. *Jn.* 13: 13.

If a man love me, he will keep my words. *Jn.* 14: 23.

Whether we live therefore, or die, we are the Lord's. *Ro.* 14: 8.

Bringing into captivity every thought to the obedience of Christ. *2 Co.* 10: 5.

See also

Christ, the Captain; Christ, Devotion to; Christ, Disciple of; Christ, Follower of; Christ, the Leader; Christ, the Lord; Christ, Loyalty to; Christ, the Master.

Christ, Oneness with God

No man knoweth the Son, but the Father; neither knoweth any man the Father, save the Son, and he to whomsoever the Son will reveal him. *Mat.* 11: 27.

No man hath seen God at any time; the only begotten Son, which is in the bosom of the Father, he hath declared him. *Jn.* 1: 18.

I am not alone, but I and the Father that sent me. *Jn.* 8: 16.

I proceeded forth and came from God: neither came I of myself, but he sent me. *Jn.* 8: 42.

I and my Father are one. *Jn.* 10: 30.

The Father is in me, and I in him. *Jn.* 10: 38.

Holy Father, keep through thine own name those whom thou hast given me, that they may be one, as we are. *Jn.* 17: 11.

That they all may be one; as thou, Father, art in me, and I in thee, that they also may be one in us. *Jn.* 17: 21.

All things are your's; . . . And ye are Christ's; and Christ is God's. *1 Co.* 3: 21, 23.

See also

Christ, Divinity of; Christ, God in; Christ, Incarnation of; Christ, the Son of God.

Christ, Partnership with

The Lord working with them. *Mk.* 16: 20.

Workers together with him. *2 Co.* 6: 1.

In whom ye also are builded together. *Ep.* 2: 22.

That the Gentiles should be fellowheirs, and of the same body, and partakers of his promise in Christ. *Ep.* 3: 6.

A faithful minister and fellowservant in the Lord. *Col.* 4: 7.

We . . . live together with him. *1 Th.* 5: 10.

Be thou partaker of the afflictions of the gospel according to the power of God. *2 Ti.* **1: 8.**

We are made partakers of Christ, if we hold the beginning of our confidence stedfast unto the end. *He.* **3: 14.**

See also

Christ, Communion with; Christ, Companionship with; Christ, Fellowship with; Christ, Life in; Christ, Union with.

Christ, Passion of

He began to teach them, that the Son of man must suffer many things. *Mk.* **8: 31.**

Ought not Christ to have suffered these things, and to enter into his glory? *Lu.* **24: 26.**

It behoved Christ to suffer. *Lu.* **24: 46.**

He shewed himself alive after his passion by many infallible proofs. *Ac.* **1: 3.**

Opening and alleging, that Christ must needs have suffered. *Ac.* **17: 3.**

As the sufferings of Christ abound in us, so our consolation also aboundeth by Christ. *2 Co.* **1: 5.**

Being found in fashion as a man, he humbled himself, and became obedient unto death, even the death of the cross. *Ph.* **2: 8.**

That I may know him, and the power of his resurrection, and the fellowship of his sufferings, being made conformable unto his death. *Ph.* **3: 10.**

We see Jesus, who was made a little lower than the angels for the suffering of death, crowned with glory and honour; that he by the grace of God should taste death for every man. *He.* **2: 9.**

Looking unto Jesus the author and finisher of our faith; who for the joy that was set before him endured the cross, despising the shame. *He.* **12: 2.**

Jesus . . . suffered without the gate. *He.* **13: 12.**

Rejoice, inasmuch as ye are partakers of Christ's sufferings. *1 Pe.* **4: 13.**

I . . . am . . . a witness of the sufferings of Christ. *1 Pe.* **5: 1.**

See also

Christ, Agony of; Christ, Blood of; Christ, Body of; Christ, Cross of; Christ, Crucifixion of; Christ, Cup of; Christ, Death of; Christ, Grief of; Christ, Sacrifice of; Christ, Suffering of.

Christ, the Passover

With desire have I desired to eat this passover with you before I suffer. *Lu.* **22: 15.**

Christ our passover is sacrificed for us. *1 Co.* **5: 7.**

See also

Christ, the Lamb of God; Christ, Sacrifice of.

Christ, Patience of

He was oppressed, and he was afflicted, yet he opened not his mouth: he is brought as a lamb to the slaughter, and as a sheep before her shearers is dumb, so he openeth not his mouth. *Is.* **53: 7.**

Jesus answering said unto him, Suffer it to be so now: for thus it becometh us to fulfil all righteousness. *Mat.* **3: 15.**

What, could ye not watch with me one hour? *Mat.* **26: 40.**

Then said Jesus unto him? Put up again thy sword into his place. *Mat.* **26: 52.**

Thinkest thou that I cannot now pray to my Father, and he shall presently give me more than twelve legions of angels? *Mat.* **26: 53.**

When ye shall hear of wars and rumours of wars, be ye not troubled: for such things must needs be; but the end shall not be yet. *Mk.* **13: 7.**

What I say unto you I say unto all, Watch. *Mk.* **13: 37.**

He held his peace, and answered nothing. *Mk.* **14: 61.**

Father, forgive them; for they know not what they do. *Lu.* **23: 34.**

My time is not yet come. *Jn.* **7: 6.**

The Lord direct your hearts . . . into the patient waiting for Christ. *2 Th.* **3: 5.**

Companion in tribulation, and in the kingdom and patience of Jesus Christ. *Re.* **1: 9.**

Behold, I come as a thief. Blessed is he that watcheth. *Re.* **16: 15.**

See also

Christ, the Servant.

Christ, Peace of

The Prince of Peace. *Is.* **9: 6.**

Come unto me, all ye that labour and are heavy laden, and I will give you rest. *Mat.* **11: 28.**

He arose, and rebuked the wind, and said unto the sea, Peace, be still. *Mk.* **4: 39.**

Suppose ye that I am come to give peace on earth? I tell you, Nay; but rather division. *Lu.* **12: 51.**

Peace I leave with you, my peace I give unto you. *Jn.* **14: 27.**

These things I have spoken unto you, that in me ye might have peace. *Jn.* **16: 33.**

Then came Jesus, the doors being shut, and stood in the midst, and said, Peace be unto you. *Jn.* **20: 26.**

He is our peace. *Ep.* **2: 14.**

Christ . . . came and preached peace to you. *Ep.* **2: 13, 17.**

Peace be with you all that are in Christ Jesus. *1 Pe.* **5: 14.**

Christ, Perfection of

He had done no violence, neither was any deceit in his mouth. *Is.* **53: 9.**

The Word was made flesh, and dwelt among us, . . . full of grace and truth. *Jn.* **1: 14.**

Which of you convinceth me of sin? *Jn.* **8: 46.**

I in them, and thou in me, that they may be made perfect in one. *Jn.* **17: 23.**

I find no fault in him. *Jn.* **19: 4.**

He hath made him to be sin for us, who knew no sin. *2 Co.* **5: 21.**

Till we all come in the unity of the faith, and of the knowledge of the Son of God, unto a perfect man. *Ep.* **4: 13.**

Ye are complete in him. *Col.* **2: 10.**

It became him, for whom are all things, and by whom are all things, in bringing many sons unto glory, to make the captain of their salvation perfect through sufferings. *He.* **2: 10.**

Being made perfect, he became the author of eternal salvation. *He.* **5: 9.**

Therefore leaving the principles of the doctrine of Christ, let us go on unto perfection. *He.* 6: 1.

For such a high priest became us, who is holy, harmless, undefiled, separate from sinners, and made higher than the heavens. *He.* 7: 26.

By one offering he hath perfected for ever them that are sanctified. *He.* 10: 14.

See also

Christ, Beauty of; Christ, Example of; Christ, Finality of; Christ, the Goal; Christ, Goodness of; Christ, Grace of; Christ, Holiness of; Christ, Innocence of; Christ, Sinlessness of.

Christ, Permanence of

My words shall not pass away. *Mat.* 24: 35.

Heaven and earth shall pass away; but my words shall not pass away. *Lu.* 21: 33.

Before Abraham was, I am. *Jn.* 8: 58.

Christ abideth for ever. *Jn.* 12: 34.

Jesus Christ the same . . . for ever. *He.* 13: 8.

Behold, I am alive for evermore. *Re.* 1: 18.

See also

Christ, the Changeless; Christ, the Contemporary; Christ, the Creator; Christ, the Eternal; Christ, Preëxistence of; Christ, the Rock.

Christ, the Physician

Jesus went about, . . . healing all manner of sickness and all manner of disease among the people. *Mat.* 4: 23.

As many as touched were made perfectly whole. *Mat.* 14: 36.

They that were vexed with unclean spirits: and they were healed. *Lu.* 6: 18.

In that same hour he cured many of their infirmities. *Lu.* 7: 21.

He touched his ear, and healed him. *Lu.* 22: 51.

A great multitude followed him, because they saw his miracles which he did on them that were diseased. *Jn.* 6: 2.

Jesus of Nazareth . . . who went about doing good. *Ac.* 10: 38.

In Christ shall all be made alive. *1 Co.* 15: 22.

See also

Christ, the Comforter; Christ, the Healing.

Christ, Power of

Lord, if thou wilt, thou canst make me clean. And Jesus put forth his hand, and touched him, saying, I will; be thou clean. *Mat.* 8: 2, 3.

The Son of man hath power on earth to forgive sins. *Mat.* 9: 6.

Believe ye that I am able to do this? *Mat.* 9: 28.

There cometh one mightier than I after me. *Mk.* 1: 7.

Jesus returned in the power of the Spirit into Galilee. *Lu.* 4: 14.

They were astonished at his doctrine: for his word was with power. *Lu.* 4: 32.

No man can do these miracles that thou doest, except God be with him. *Jn.* 3: 2.

I have power to lay it down, and I have power to take it again. *Jn.* 10: 18.

God anointed Jesus of Nazareth with the Holy Ghost and with power. *Ac.* 10: 38.

Christ the power of God. *1 Co.* 1: 24.

Most gladly therefore will I rather glory in my infirmities, that the power of Christ may rest upon me. *2 Co.* 12: 9.

Now unto him that is able to do exceeding abundantly above all that we ask or think. *Ep.* 3: 20.

He is able also to save them to the uttermost. *He.* 7: 25.

That God in all things may be glorified through Jesus Christ, to whom be praise and dominion for ever and ever. *1 Pe.* 4: 11.

See also

Christ, Authority of; Christ, Compulsion of; Christ, Greatness of; Christ, Preëminence of; Christ, Strength of; Christ, Supremacy of.

Christ, Praise of

Thou art Peter, and upon this rock I will build my church. *Mat.* 16: 18.

Children crying in the temple, and saying, Hosanna to the son of David. *Mat.* 21: 15.

Jesus saith unto them, Yea; have ye never read, Out of the mouth of babes and sucklings thou hast perfected praise? *Mat.* 21: 16.

Well done, thou good and faithful servant. *Mat.* 25: 21.

She hath wrought a good work upon me. *Mat.* 26: 10.

Wheresoever this gospel shall be preached in the whole world, there shall also this, that this woman hath done, be told for a memorial of her. *Mat.* 26: 13.

There came a voice from heaven, saying, Thou art my beloved Son, in whom I am well pleased. *Mk.* 1: 11.

He hath done all things well. *Mk.* 7: 37.

Jesus beholding him loved him. *Mk.* 10: 21.

The shepherds returned, glorifying and praising God for all the things that they had heard and seen. *Lu.* 2: 20.

I have not found so great faith, no, not in Israel. *Lu.* 7: 9.

One thing is needful: and Mary hath chosen that good part. *Lu.* 10: 42.

I tell you, this man went down to his house justified rather than the other. *Lu.* 18: 14.

All the people, when they saw it, gave praise to God. *Lu.* 18: 43.

I receive not honour from men. *Jn.* 5: 41.

Whether he be a sinner or no, I know not: one thing I know, that, whereas I was blind, now I see. *Jn.* 9: 25.

Ye call me Master and Lord: and ye say well; for so I am. *Jn.* 13: 13.

Praise the Lord, all ye Gentiles. *Ro.* 15: 11.

To whom be honour and power everlasting. Amen. *1 Ti.* 6: 16.

Shew forth the praises of him who hath called you out of darkness into his marvellous light. *1 Pe.* 2: 9.

That God in all things may be glorified through Jesus Christ, to whom be praise and dominion for ever and ever. Amen. *1 Pe.* 4: 11.

Worthy is the Lamb that was slain to receive power, and riches, and wisdom, and strength, and honour, and glory, and blessing. *Re.* 5: 12.

Blessing, and honour, and glory, and power, be unto him that sitteth upon the throne, and unto the Lamb for ever and ever. *Re.* 5: 13.

See also

Christ, Adoration of; Christ, Devotion to; Christ, Exaltation of; Christ, Worship of.

Christ, Preaching of

The Spirit of the Lord God is upon me; because the Lord hath anointed me to preach good tidings unto the meek. *Is.* 61: 1.

This gospel of the kingdom shall be preached in all the world for a witness unto all nations. *Mat.* 24: 14.

Go ye therefore, and teach all nations, baptizing them in the name of the Father, and of the Son, and of the Holy Ghost. *Mat.* 28: 19.

He departed, and began to publish in Decapolis how great things Jesus had done for him. *Mk.* 5: 20.

I saw, and bare record that this is the Son of God. *Jn.* 1: 34.

They ceased not to teach and preach Jesus Christ. *Ac.* 5: 42.

He preached Christ in the synagogues, that he is the Son of God. *Ac.* 9: 20.

He preached unto them Jesus, and the resurrection. *Ac.* 17: 18.

The preaching of the cross. *1 Co.* 1: 18.

If Christ be not risen, then is our preaching vain. *1 Co.* 15: 14.

Your feet shod with the preparation of the gospel of peace. *Ep.* 6: 15.

Some indeed preach Christ even of envy and strife; and some also of good will. *Ph.* 1: 15.

Whom we preach, warning every man, and teaching every man in all wisdom; that we may present every man perfect in Christ Jesus. *Col.* 1: 28.

See also

Christ, Gospel of; Christ, Message of; Christ, Promise of; Christ, the Teacher; Christ, the Word; Christ, Word of.

Christ, Preëminence of

He that loveth father or mother more than me is not worthy of me. *Mat.* 10: 37.

The stone which the builders rejected, the same is become the head of the corner. *Mat.* 21: 42.

He came unto his own, and his own received him not. *Jn.* 1: 11.

He that cometh from heaven is above all. *Jn.* 3: 31.

God hath made that same Jesus, whom ye have crucified, both Lord and Christ. *Ac.* 2: 36.

And hath put all things under his feet, and gave him to be the head over all things to the church. *Ep.* 1: 22.

Jesus Christ himself being the chief corner stone. *Ep.* 2: 20.

For to me to live is Christ, and to die is gain. *Ph.* 1: 21.

God also hath highly exalted him, and given him a name which is above every name. *Ph.* 2: 9.

That in all things he might have preeminence. *Col.* 1: 18.

In him dwelleth all the fulness of the Godhead bodily. *Col.* 2: 9.

Ye are complete in him, which is the head of all principality and power. *Col.* 2: 10.

Being made so much better than the angels, as he hath by inheritance obtained a more excellent name than they. *He.* 1: 4.

Let all the angels of God worship him. *He.* 1: 6.

For this man was counted worthy of more glory than Moses, inasmuch as he who hath builded the house hath more honour than the house. *He.* 3: 3.

He became the author of eternal salvation unto all them that obey him. *He.* 5: 9.

Jesus Christ . . . is gone into heaven, and is on the right hand of God; angels and authorities and powers being made subject unto him. *1 Pe.* 3: 21, 22.

Jesus Christ, who is the faithful witness, and the first begotten of the dead. *Re.* 1: 5.

I am Alpha and Omega, the first and the last. *Re.* 1: 11.

See also

Christ, Centrality of; Christ, Crown of; Christ, Exaltation of; Christ, Glory of; Christ, Majesty of; Christ, Supremacy of; Christ, Triumph of.

Christ, Preëxistence of

Whose goings forth have been from of old, from everlasting. *Mi.* 5: 2.

Verily, verily, I say unto you, Before Abraham was, I am. *Jn.* 8: 58.

Now, O Father, glorify thou me with thine own self with the glory which I had with thee before the world was. *Jn.* 17: 5.

Thou lovedst me before the foundation of the world. *Jn.* 17: 24.

Without father, without mother, without descent, having neither beginning of days, nor end of life; but made like unto the Son of God; abideth a priest continually. *He.* 7: 3.

I am Alpha and Omega, the beginning and the end, the first and the last. *Re.* 22: 13.

See also

Christ, the Changeless; Christ, the Creator; Christ, the Eternal; Christ, Foreknowledge of; Christ, Knowledge of; Christ, Permanence of.

Christ, Presence of

Lo, I am with you alway, even unto the end of the world. *Mat.* 28: 20.

Their eyes were opened, and they knew him. *Lu.* 24: 31.

Did not our hearts burn within us, while he talked with us by the way? *Lu.* 24: 32.

Little children, yet a little while I am with you. *Jn.* 13: 33.

Then came Jesus, the doors being shut, and stood in the midst. *Jn.* 20: 26.

We are . . . willing rather to be absent from the body, and to be present with the Lord. *2 Co.* 5: 8.

We must all appear before the judgment seat of Christ. *2 Co.* 5: 10.

I am crucified with Christ: nevertheless I live; yet not I, but Christ liveth in me. *Ga.* 2: 20.

That Christ may dwell in your hearts by faith. *Ep.* 3: 17.

Are not even ye in the presence of our Lord Jesus Christ at his coming? *1 Th.* 2: 19.

So shall we ever be with the Lord. *1 Th.* 4: 17.

See also

Christ, Abiding in; Christ, Communion with; Christ, Companionship of; Christ, the Contemporary; Christ, Fellowship with; Christ, the Indwelling; Christ, Life in; Christ, Nearness of; Christ, Partnership with; Christ, Union with.

Christ, Priesthood of

Consider the Apostle and High Priest of our profession, Christ Jesus. *He.* 3: 1.

We have a great high priest, that is passed into the heavens, Jesus the Son of God. *He.* 4: 14.

So also Christ glorified not himself to be made an high priest. *He.* 5: 5.

Thou art a priest for ever after the order of Melchisedec. *He.* 7: 17.

We have such an high priest. *He.* 8: 1.

Christ being come an high priest of good things to come. *He.* 9: 11.

Having an high priest over the house of God; Let us draw near. *He.* 10: 21, 22.

See also

Christ, the Comforter; Christ, Compassion of; Christ, the Healing; Christ, Ministry of; Christ, Mission of; Christ, the Physician; Christ, Purpose of; Christ, the Servant; Christ, Work of.

Christ, Promise of

I will pray the Father, and he shall give you another Comforter, that he may abide with you for ever; Even the Spirit of truth. *Jn.* 14: 16, 17.

Ye shall receive power, after that the Holy Ghost is come upon you. *Ac.* 1: 8.

This cup is the new testament in my blood. *1 Co.* 11: 25.

All the promises of God in him are yea, and in him Amen, unto the glory of God by us. *2 Co.* 1: 20.

The promise of life which is in Christ Jesus. *2 Ti.* 1: 1.

He is the mediator of a better covenant. *He.* 8: 6.

The blood of the everlasting covenant. *He.* 13: 20.

See also

Christ, the Comforter; Christ, Gospel of; Christ, Message of; Christ, Preaching of; Christ, the Word; Christ, Word of.

Christ, Purpose of

I am not sent but unto the lost sheep of the house of Israel. *Mat.* 15: 24.

The Son of man came not to be ministered unto, but to minister, and to give his life a ransom for many. *Mat.* 20: 28.

I must preach the kingdom of God to other cities also: for therefore am I sent. *Lu.* 4: 43.

The Son of man is not come to destroy men's lives, but to save them. *Lu.* 9: 56.

My meat is to do the will of him that sent me, and to finish his work. *Jn.* 4: 34.

I must work the works of him that sent me, while it is day. *Jn.* 9: 4.

I am come that they might have life, and that they might have it more abundantly. *Jn.* 10: 10.

Father, save me from this hour: but for this cause came I unto this hour. *Jn.* 12: 27.

To this end was I born, and for this cause came I into the world, that I should bear witness unto the truth. *Jn.* 18: 37.

Christ died for our sins according to the scriptures. *1 Co.* 15: 3.

He died for all, that they which live should

not henceforth live unto themselves, but unto him which died for them. *2 Co.* 5: 15.

According to the eternal purpose, which he purposed in Christ Jesus our Lord. *Ep.* 3: 11.

Jesus Christ . . . hath brought life and immortality to light through the gospel. *2 Ti.* 1: 10:

See also

Christ, Ministry of; Christ, Mission of; Christ, the Physician; Christ, Priesthood of; Christ, Purpose of; Christ, Work of.

Christ, Quest for

Where is he that is born King of the Jews? *Mat.* 2: 2.

Behold, the whole city came out to meet Jesus. *Mat.* 8: 34.

Fear not ye: for I know that ye seek Jesus. *Mat.* 28: 5.

All men seek for thee. *Mk.* 1: 37.

Thy mother and thy brethren without seek for thee. *Mk.* 3: 32.

Ye seek me, . . . because ye did eat of the loaves. *Jn.* 6: 26.

Ye shall seek me, and shall not find me. *Jn.* 7: 34.

Sir, we would see Jesus. *Jn.* 12: 21.

See also

Christ, Coming to; Christ, Follower of.

Christ, Recognition of

Lo a voice from heaven, saying, This is my beloved Son, in whom I am well pleased. *Mat.* 3: 17.

He saith unto them, But whom say ye that I am? And Simon Peter answered and said, Thou art the Christ, the Son of the living God. *Mat.* 16: 15, 16.

Whomsoever I shall kiss, that same is he: hold him fast. *Mat.* 26: 48.

He denied with an oath, I do not know the man. *Mat.* 26: 72.

I know thee who thou art, the Holy One of God. *Mk.* 1: 24.

He . . . suffered not the devils to speak, because they knew him. *Mk.* 1: 34.

When they were come out of the ship, straightway they knew him. *Mk.* 6: 54.

If any man shall say unto you, Lo, here is Christ; or, lo, he is there; believe him not. *Mk.* 13: 21.

Their eyes were opened, and they knew him. *Lu.* 24: 31.

He was in the world, and the world was made by him, and the world knew him not. *Jn.* 1: 10.

He was before me. And I knew him not. *Jn.* 1: 30, 31.

When he putteth forth his own sheep, he goeth before them, and the sheep follow him: for they know his voice. *Jn.* 10: 4.

I am the good shepherd, and know my sheep, and am known of mine. *Jn.* 10: 14.

Mary . . . turned herself back, and saw Jesus standing, and knew not that it was Jesus. *Jn.* 20: 11. 14.

Thomas answered and said unto him, My Lord and my God. *Jn.* 20: 28.

Blessed are they that have not seen, and yet have believed. *Jn.* 20: 29.

Jesus stood on the shore: but the disciples knew not that it was Jesus. *Jn.* 21: 4.

None of the disciples durst ask him, Who art thou? knowing that it was the Lord. *Jn.* 21: 12.

I know whom I have believed. *2 Ti.* 1: 12.

He that saith, I know him, and keepeth not his commandments, is a liar, and the truth is not in him. *1 Jn.* 2: 4.

See also
Christ, Nature of.

Christ, the Redeemer

Thou shalt call his name JESUS: for he shall save his people from their sins. *Mat.* 1: 21.

The Son of man came not to be ministered unto, but to minister, and to give his life a ransom for many. *Mat.* 20: 28.

An horn of salvation for us. *Lu.* 1: 69.

Jesus, Master, have mercy on us. *Lu.* 17: 13.

It shall come to pass, that whosoever shall call on the name of the Lord shall be saved. *Ac.* 2: 21.

When we were yet without strength, in due time Christ died for the ungodly. *Ro.* 5: 6.

Of him are ye in Christ Jesus, who of God is made unto us wisdom, and righteousness, and sanctification, and redemption. *1 Co.* 1: 30.

He hath made him to be sin for us, who knew no sin; that we might be made the righteousness of God in him. *2 Co.* 5: 21.

Blotting out the handwriting of ordinances that was against us, which was contrary to us, and took it out of the way, nailing it to his cross. *Col.* 2: 14.

Christ Jesus came into the world to save sinners. *1 Ti.* 1: 15.

Ye were not redeemed with corruptible things, as silver and gold, . . . But with the precious blood of Christ. *1 Pe.* 1: 18, 19.

See also
Christ, the Deliverer; Christ, the Liberator; Christ, the Saviour.

Christ, Reign of

The government shall be upon his shoulder. *Is.* 9: 6.

My yoke is easy, and my burden is light. *Mat.* 11: 30.

They shall see the Son of man coming in the clouds of heaven with power and great glory. *Mat.* 24: 30.

Jesus came and spake unto them, saying, All power is given unto me in heaven and in earth. *Mat.* 28: 18.

A superscription also was written over him in letters of Greek, and Latin, and Hebrew, THIS IS THE KING OF THE JEWS. *Lu.* 23: 38.

The Father loveth the Son, and hath given all things into his hand. *Jn.* 3: 35.

This man is the great power of God. *Ac.* 8: 10.

Christ came, who is over all, God blessed for ever. *Ro.* 9: 5.

To this end Christ both died, and rose, and revived, that he might be Lord both of the dead and living. *Ro.* 14: 9.

Ye are Christ's. *1 Co.* 3: 23.

Then cometh the end, when he shall have delivered up the kingdom to God, even the Father; when he shall have put down all rule and all authority and power. For he must reign, till he hath put all enemies under his feet. *1 Co.* 15: 24, 25.

Thanks be unto God, which always causeth us to triumph in Christ. *2 Co.* 2: 14.

Christ . . . shall reign for ever and ever. *Re.* 11: 15.

See also
Christ, Crown of; Christ, the King; Christ, Supremacy of.

Christ, Rejection of

He is despised and rejected of men. *Is.* 53: 3.

The stone which the builders rejected, the same is become the head of the corner. *Mat.* 21: 42.

They began to pray him to depart out of their coasts. *Mk.* 5: 17.

The Son of man must suffer many things, and be rejected. *Mk.* 8: 31.

Whosoever therefore shall be ashamed of me and of my words in this adulterous and sinful generation; of him also shall the Son of man be ashamed, when he cometh in the glory of his Father. *Mk.* 8: 38.

The Son of man is delivered into the hands of men, and they shall kill him; and after that he is killed, he shall rise the third day. *Mk.* 9: 31.

There was no room for them in the inn. *Lu.* 2: 7.

We know this man whence he is: but when Christ cometh, no man knoweth whence he is. *Jn.* 7: 27.

Some said, Shall Christ come out of Galilee? *Jn.* 7: 41.

Saul, Saul, why persecutest thou me? *Ac.* 9: 4.

I heard a voice speaking unto me, and saying in the Hebrew tongue, Saul, Saul, why persecutest thou me? *Ac.* 26: 14.

We preach Christ crucified, unto the Jews a stumblingblock, and unto the Greeks foolishness. *1 Co.* 1: 23.

See also
Christ, Antagonism to; Christ, Betrayal of; Christ, Defiance of; Christ, Denial of; Christ, Enemy of; Christ, Hatred of.

Christ, Resurrection of

He is risen; he is not here. *Mk.* 16: 6.

The Lord is risen indeed, and hath appeared to Simon. *Lu.* 24: 34.

I am the resurrection, and the life: he that believeth in me, though he were dead, yet shall he live: And whosoever liveth and believeth in me shall never die. *Jn.* 11: 25, 26.

Verily, verily, I say unto you, Except a corn of wheat fall into the ground and die, it abideth alone: but if it die, it bringeth forth much fruit. *Jn.* 12: 24.

They have taken away my Lord, and I know not where they have laid him. *Jn.* 20: 13.

He shewed himself alive after his passion by many infallible proofs. *Ac.* 1: 3.

Whom God hath raised up, having loosed the pains of death: because it was not possible that he should be holden of it. *Ac.* 2: 24.

This Jesus hath God raised up, whereof we all are witnesses. *Ac.* 2: 32.

With great power gave the apostles witness

of the resurrection of the Lord Jesus. *Ac.* 4: 33.

He preached unto them Jesus, and the resurrection. *Ac.* 17: 18.

One Jesus, which was dead, whom Paul affirmed to be alive. *Ac.* 25: 19.

Why should it be thought a thing incredible with you, that God should raise the dead? *Ac.* 26: 8.

Declared to be the Son of God with power, according to the spirit of holiness, by the resurrection from the dead. *Ro.* 1: 4.

We shall be also in the likeness of his resurrection. *Ro.* 6: 5.

He that raised up Christ from the dead shall also quicken your mortal bodies by his Spirit. *Ro.* 8: 11.

If Christ be not risen, then is our preaching vain, and your faith is also vain. *1 Co.* 15: 14.

Now is Christ risen from the dead. *1 Co.* 15: 20.

The first fruits of them that slept. *1 Co.* 15: 20.

The resurrection of the dead . . . is sown in weakness; it is raised in power. *1 Co.* 15: 42, 43.

He which raised up the Lord Jesus shall raise up us also by Jesus. *2 Co.* 4: 14.

He raised him from the dead, and set him at his own right hand in the heavenly places. *Ep.* 1: 20.

When he ascended up on high, he led captivity captive. *Ep.* 4: 8.

That I may know him, and the power of his resurrection. *Ph.* 3: 10.

Jesus Christ . . . hath abolished death, and hath brought life and immortality to light through the gospel. *2 Ti.* 1: 10.

Which according to his abundant mercy hath begotten us again unto a lively hope by the resurrection of Jesus Christ from the dead. *1 Pe.* 1: 3.

See also
Christ, the Eternal.

Christ, Revelation of

He could not be hid. *Mk.* 7: 24.

Thus shall it be in the day when the Son of man is revealed. *Lu.* 17: 30.

He that hath seen me hath seen the Father. *Jn.* 14: 9.

How is it that thou wilt manifest thyself unto us, and not unto the world? *Jn.* 14: 22.

All things that I have heard of my Father I have made known unto you. *Jn.* 15: 15.

Until this day remaineth the same vail untaken away in the reading of the old testament; which vail is done away in Christ. *2 Co.* 3: 14.

When the Lord Jesus shall be revealed from heaven with his mighty angels. *2 Th.* 1: 7.

By his Son. *He.* 1: 2.

That, when his glory shall be revealed, ye may be glad also with exceeding joy. *1 Pe.* 4: 13.

See also
Christ, Appearance of; Christ, Second Coming of; Christ, Vision of.

Christ, Riches of

The riches of his grace. *Ep.* 1: 7.

The riches of the glory of his inheritance in the saints. *Ep.* 1: 18.

The unsearchable riches of Christ. *Ep.* 3: 8.

According to the measure of the gift of Christ. *Ep.* 4: 7.

Christ; In whom are hid all the treasures of wisdom and knowledge. *Col.* 2: 2, 3.

Worthy is the Lamb that was slain to receive power, and riches. *Re.* 5: 12.

See also
Christ, Fullness of.

Christ, the Rock

The stone which the builders refused is become the head stone of the corner. *Ps.* 118: 22.

I lay in Zion for a foundation a stone, a tried stone, a precious corner stone, a sure foundation. *Is.* 28: 16.

Whosoever shall fall upon that stone shall be broken; but on whomsoever it shall fall, it will grind him to powder. *Lu.* 20: 18.

Other foundation can no man lay than that is laid, which is Jesus Christ. *1 Co.* 3: 11.

They drank of that spiritual Rock that followed them: and that Rock was Christ. *1 Co.* 10: 4.

See also
Christ, the Changeless; Christ, the Eternal; Christ, Finality of; Christ, the Foundation; Christ, Permanence of.

Christ, Sacrifice of

Are ye able to drink of the cup that I shall drink of? *Mat.* 20: 22.

Had they known it, they would not have crucified the Lord of glory. *1 Co.* 2: 8.

Christ died for our sins according to the scriptures. *1 Co.* 15: 3.

He died for all, that they which live should not henceforth live unto themselves, but unto him which died for them. *2 Co.* 5: 15.

Though he was rich, yet for your sakes he became poor, that ye through his poverty might be rich. *2 Co.* 8: 9.

God forbid that I should glory, save in the cross of our Lord Jesus Christ. *Ga.* 6: 14.

Christ also hath . . . given himself for us an offering. *Ep.* 5: 2.

This man, after he had offered one sacrifice for sins for ever, sat down on the right hand of God. *He.* 10: 12.

Forasmuch then as Christ hath suffered for us in the flesh, arm yourselves likewise with the same mind. *1 Pe.* 4: 1.

He laid down his life for us. *1 Jn.* 3: 16.

Worthy is the Lamb that was slain to receive power, and riches, and wisdom, and strength, and honour, and glory, and blessing. *Re.* 5: 12.

See also
Christ, Agony of; Christ, Blood of; Christ, Cross of; Christ, Crucifixion of; Christ, Cup of; Christ, Death of; Christ, the Lamb of God; Christ, Passion of; Christ, the Passover; Christ, Suffering of.

Christ, the Saviour

Thou shalt call his name JESUS: for he shall save his people from their sins. *Mat.* 1: 21.

He saved others; himself he cannot save. *Mat.* 27: 42.

Unto you is born this day in the city of David a Saviour. *Lu.* 2: 11.

This day is salvation come to this house. *Lu.* 19: 9.

Behold the Lamb of God, which taketh away the sin of the world! *Jn.* 1: 29.

We have heard him ourselves, and know that this is indeed the Christ, the Saviour of the world. *Jn.* 4: 42.

Neither is there salvation in any other. *Ac.* 4: 12.

Jesus Christ maketh thee whole. *Ac.* 9: 34.

Sirs, what must I do to be saved? And they said, Believe on the Lord Jesus Christ, and thou shalt be saved, and thy house. *Ac.* 16: 30, 31.

The gospel of Christ . . . is the power of God unto salvation to every one that believeth. *Ro.* 1: 16.

The preaching of the cross is to them that perish foolishness; but unto us which are saved it is the power of God. *1 Co.* 1: 18.

If Christ be not raised, your faith is vain. *1 Co.* 15: 17.

In whom we have redemption, through his blood, even the forgiveness of sins. *Col.* 1: 14.

God hath not appointed us to wrath, but to obtain salvation by our Lord Jesus Christ. *1 Th.* 5: 9.

The washing of regeneration, and renewing of the Holy Ghost; Which he shed on us abundantly through Jesus Christ our Saviour. *Tit.* 3: 5, 6.

The captain of their salvation. *He.* 2: 10.

They sing the song of Moses the servant of God, and the song of the Lamb. *Re.* 15: 3.

See also

Christ, the Deliverer; Christ, the Liberator; Christ, the Redeemer.

Christ, Second Coming of

Ye shall not have gone over the cities of Israel, till the Son of man be come. *Mat.* 10: 23.

There be some standing here, which shall not taste of death, till they see the Son of man coming in his kingdom. *Mat.* 16: 28.

As the lightning cometh out of the east, and shineth even unto the west; so shall also the coming of the Son of man be. *Mat.* 24: 27.

Ye know not what hour your Lord doth come. *Mat.* 24: 42.

At even, or at midnight, or at the cockcrowing, or in the morning. *Mk.* 13: 35.

Be ye therefore ready also: for the Son of man cometh at an hour when ye think not. *Lu.* 12: 40.

Occupy till I come. *Lu.* 19: 13.

Then shall they see the Son of man coming in a cloud with power and great glory. *Lu.* 21: 27.

I will not leave you comfortless: I will come to you. *Jn.* 14: 18.

And ye now therefore have sorrow: but I will see you again, and your heart shall rejoice, and your joy no man taketh from you. *Jn.* 16: 22.

This same Jesus, which is taken up from you into heaven, shall so come in like manner as ye have seen him go into heaven. *Ac.* 1: 11.

So that ye come behind in no gift; waiting for the coming of our Lord Jesus Christ. *1 Co.* 1: 7.

Judge nothing before the time, until the Lord come, who both will bring to light the hidden things of darkness, and will make manifest the counsels of the hearts: and then

shall every man have praise of God. *1 Co.* 4: 5.

Our conversation is in heaven; from whence also we look for the Saviour, the Lord Jesus Christ. *Ph.* 3: 20.

When Christ, who is our life, shall appear, then shall ye also appear with him in glory. *Col.* 3: 4.

Yet a little while, and he that shall come will come, and will not tarry. *He.* 10: 37.

The coming of the Lord draweth nigh. *Ja.* 5: 8.

When the chief Shepherd shall appear, ye shall receive a crown of glory that fadeth not away. *1 Pe.* 5: 4.

Where is the promise of his coming? *2 Pe.* 3: 4.

Behold, the Lord cometh with ten thousands of his saints. *Jude* 1: 14.

Behold, he cometh with clouds; and every eye shall see him. *Re.* 1: 7.

He which testifieth these things saith, Surely I come quickly. Amen. Even so, come, Lord Jesus. *Re.* 22: 20.

See also

Christ, Coming of; Christ, Day of; Christ, the Judge.

Christ, the Servant

Behold my servant, whom I uphold. *Is.* 42: 1.

By his knowledge shall my righteous servant justify many. *Is.* 53: 11.

Jesus knowing that the Father had given all things into his hands, and that he was come from God, and went to God; . . . began to wash the disciples' feet. *Jn.* 13: 3, 5.

Even Christ pleased not himself. *Ro.* 15: 3.

Then shall the Son also himself be subject unto him that put all things under him, that God may be all in all. *1 Co.* 15: 28.

Christ Jesus . . . took upon him the form of a servant, and was made in the likeness of men. *Ph.* 2: 5, 7.

See also

Christ, the Comforter; Christ, Hand of; Christ, Help of; Christ, Ministry of; Christ, Mission of: Christ, Patience of; Christ, Priesthood of; Christ, Work of.

Christ, the Shepherd

He calleth his own sheep by name. *Jn.* 10: 3.

Verily, verily, I say unto you, I am the door of the sheep. *Jn.* 10: 7.

I am the door: by me if any man enter in, he shall be saved, and shall go in and out, and find pasture. *Jn.* 10: 9.

I am the good shepherd, and know my sheep, and am known of mine. As the Father knoweth me, even so know I the Father: and I lay down my life for the sheep. *Jn.* 10: 14, 15.

Other sheep I have, which are not of this fold: them also I must bring, and they shall hear my voice; and there shall be one fold, and one shepherd. *Jn.* 10: 16.

My sheep hear my voice, and I know them, and they follow me. *Jn.* 10: 27.

He saith unto him, Feed my sheep. *Jn.* 21: 16.

That great shepherd of the sheep. *He.* 13: 20.

When the chief Shepherd shall appear. *1 Pe.* 5: 4.

See also

Christ, Compassion of; Christ, Faithfulness

of; Christ, Gentleness of; Christ, Goodness of; Christ, Love of; Christ, Sympathy of; Christ, Watchfulness of.

Christ, Silence of

As a sheep before her shearers is dumb, so he openeth not his mouth. *Is.* 53: 7.

He answered her not a word. *Mat.* 15: 23.

Then charged he his disciples that they should tell no man that he was Jesus the Christ. *Mat.* 16: 20.

Jesus charged them, saying, Tell the vision to no man, until the Son of man be risen again from the dead. *Mat.* 17: 9.

Jesus held his peace. *Mat.* 26: 63.

The kingdom of God cometh not with observation. *Lu.* 17: 20.

He questioned with him in many words; but he answered him nothing. *Lu.* 23: 9.

Jesus stooped down, and with his finger wrote on the ground. *Jn.* 8: 6.

Like a lamb dumb before his shearer, so opened he not his mouth. *Ac.* 8: 32.

See also

Christ, the Hidden; Christ, Isolation of; Christ, Loneliness of; Christ, Mystery of.

Christ, Simplicity of

Take no thought, saying, What shall we eat? or, What shall we drink? or, Wherewithal shall we be clothed? . . . for your heavenly Father knoweth that ye have need of all these things. *Mat.* 6: 31, 32.

Thou hast hid these things from the wise and prudent, and hast revealed them unto babes. *Mat.* 11: 25.

The Lord hath need of him. *Lu.* 19: 34.

Christ sent me not to baptize, but to preach the gospel: not with wisdom of words, lest the cross of Christ should be made of none effect. *I Co.* 1: 17.

Babes in Christ. *I Co.* 3: 1.

We are fools for Christ's sake. *I Co.* 4: 10.

I fear, lest by any means . . . your minds should be corrupted from the simplicity that is in Christ. *2 Co.* 11: 3.

In singleness of your heart, as unto Christ. *Ep.* 6: 5.

See also

Christ, Humility of; Christ, Meekness of.

Christ, Sinlessness of

Pilate . . . washed his hands before the multitude, saying, I am innocent of the blood of this just person. *Mat.* 27: 24.

Which of you convinceth me of sin? *Jn.* 8: 46.

Now are ye clean through the word which I have spoken unto you. *Jn.* 15: 3.

What concord hath Christ with Belial? *2 Co.* 6: 15.

We have not an high priest which cannot be touched with the feeling of our infirmities; but was in all points tempted like as we are, yet without sin. *He.* 4: 15.

Unto them that look for him shall he appear the second time without sin unto salvation. *He.* 9: 28.

In him is no sin. *I Jn.* 3: 5.

See also

Christ, Finality of; Christ, Holiness of; Christ, Perfection of; Christ, Sinlessness of.

Christ, the Son of God

Thou art my Son; this day have I begotten thee. *Ps.* 2: 7.

No man knoweth the Son, but the Father; neither knoweth any man the Father, save the Son. *Mat.* 11: 27.

Truly this was the Son of God. *Mat.* 27: 54.

Art thou the Christ, the Son of the Blessed? *Mk.* 14: 61.

God so loved the world, that he gave his only begotten Son. *Jn.* 3: 16.

Because ye are sons, God hath sent forth the Spirit of his Son into your hearts, crying, Abba, Father. *Ga.* 4: 6.

God . . . hath in these last days spoken unto us by his Son. *He.* 1: 1, 2.

I will be to him a Father, and he shall be to me a Son? *He.* 1: 5.

God sent his only begotten Son into the world, that we might live through him. *I Jn.* 4: 9.

Whosoever shall confess that Jesus is the Son of God, God dwelleth in him, and he in God. *I Jn.* 4: 15.

The Lord Jesus Christ, the Son of the Father. *2 Jn.* 1: 3.

See also

Christ, Divinity of; Christ, God in; Christ, Incarnation of; Christ, the Lord; Christ, the Messiah; Christ, Oneness with God.

Christ, the Son of Man

Behold, a virgin shall conceive, and bear a son. *Is.* 7: 14.

Unto us a child is born, unto us a son is given. *Is.* 9: 6.

The Son of man came eating and drinking. *Mat.* 11: 19.

Is not this the carpenter's son? *Mat.* 13: 55.

Whom do men say that I the Son of man am? *Mat.* 16: 13.

The Son of man shall come in the glory of his Father with his angels; and then he shall reward every man according to his works. *Mat.* 16: 27.

What think ye of Christ? whose son is he? *Mat.* 22: 42.

They said, Is not this Joseph's son? *Lu.* 4: 22.

We have not an high priest which can not be touched with the feeling of our infirmities. *He.* 4: 15.

See also

Christ, Humanity of; Christ, Manliness of; Christ, Nature of.

Christ, Sorrow of

A man of sorrows, and acquainted with grief. *Is.* 53: 3.

Surely he hath borne our griefs, and carried our sorrows. *Is.* 53: 4.

Likewise shall also the Son of man suffer of them. *Mat.* 17: 12.

Are ye able to drink of the cup that I shall drink of, and to be baptized with the baptism that I am baptized with? *Mat.* 20: 22.

How often would I have gathered thy children together, even as a hen gathereth her chickens under her wings, and ye would not! *Mat.* 23: 37.

My soul is exceeding sorrowful, even unto death. *Mat.* 26: 38.

He beheld the city, and wept over it. *Lu.* 19: 41.

Ought not Christ to have suffered these things, and to enter into his glory? *Lu.* 24: 26.

It behoved Christ to suffer, and to rise from the dead the third day. *Lu.* 24: 46.

Jesus wept. *Jn.* 11: 35.

Now is my soul troubled. *Jn.* 12: 27.

The cup which my Father hath given me, shall I not drink it? *Jn.* 18: 11.

When he had offered up prayers and supplications with strong crying and tears. *He.* 5: 7.

Jesus also, that he might sanctify the people with his own blood, suffered without the gate. *He.* 13: 12.

Rejoice, inasmuch as ye are partakers of Christ's sufferings. *1 Pe.* 4: 13.

See also

Christ, Agony of; Christ, Compassion of; Christ, Cross of; Christ, Cup of; Christ, Death of; Christ, Grief of; Christ, Suffering of; Christ, Sympathy of.

Christ, Spirit of

Jesus returned in the power of the Spirit. *Lu.* 4: 14.

If any man have not the Spirit of Christ, he is none of his. *Ro.* 8: 9.

Where the Spirit of the Lord is, there is liberty. *2 Co.* 3: 17.

God hath sent forth the Spirit of his Son into your hearts, crying, Abba, Father. *Ga.* 4: 6.

Strengthened with might by his Spirit. *Ep.* 3: 16.

The supply of the Spirit of Jesus Christ. *Ph.* 1: 19.

Let this mind be in you, which was also in Christ Jesus. *Ph.* 2: 5.

See also

Christ, Courage of; Christ, Faith of; Christ, Gentleness of; Christ, Goodness of; Christ, Humility of; Christ, Joy of; Christ, Love of; Christ, Manliness of; Christ, Peace of; Christ, Simplicity of; Christ, Sinlessness of; Christ, Sympathy of.

Christ, Strength of

He that cometh after me is mightier than I. *Mat.* 3: 11.

Whosoever shall fall on this stone shall be broken. *Mat.* 21: 44.

Ye shall see the Son of man sitting on the right hand of power. *Mk.* 14: 62.

The child grew, and waxed strong in spirit. *Lu.* 1: 80.

I give unto you power to tread on serpents and scorpions, and over all the power of the enemy: and nothing shall by any means hurt you. *Lu.* 10: 19.

Jesus of Nazareth . . . was a prophet mighty in deed and word before God and all the people. *Lu.* 24: 19.

As many as received him, to them gave he power to become the sons of God, even to them that believe on his name. *Jn.* 1: 12.

They drank of that spiritual Rock that followed them: and that Rock was Christ. *1 Co.* 10: 4.

Thanks be to God, which giveth us the victory through our Lord Jesus Christ. *1 Co.* 15: 57.

He said unto me, My grace is sufficient for thee: for my strength is made perfect in weakness. *2 Co.* 12: 9.

I can do all things through Christ which strengtheneth me. *Ph.* 4: 13.

Strengthened with all might, according to his glorious power. *Col.* 1: 11.

His working . . . worketh in me mightily. *Col.* 1: 29.

I thank Christ Jesus our Lord, who hath enabled me. *1 Ti.* 1: 12.

See also

Christ, Compulsion of; Christ, Greatness of; Christ, Power of; Christ, Preëminence of; Christ, Supremacy of.

Christ, Suffering for

Pray for them which despitefully use you, and persecute you. *Mat.* 5: 44.

Ye shall be hated of all men for my name's sake. *Lu.* 21: 17.

The time cometh, that whosoever killeth you will think that he doeth God service. *Jn.* 16: 2.

When thou shalt be old, thou shalt stretch forth thy hands, and another shall gird thee, and carry thee whither thou wouldest not. *Jn.* 21: 18.

Rejoicing that they were counted worthy to suffer shame for his name. *Ac.* 5: 41.

Joint-heirs with Christ; if so be that we suffer with him, that we may be also glorified together. *Ro.* 8: 17.

As the sufferings of Christ abound in us, so our consolation also aboundeth by Christ. *2 Co.* 1: 5.

Lest they should suffer persecution for the cross of Christ. *Ga.* 6: 12.

For the work of Christ he was nigh unto death, not regarding his life. *Ph.* 2: 30.

I count all things but loss for the excellency of the knowledge of Christ Jesus my Lord: for whom I have suffered the loss of all things, and do count them but dung, that I may win Christ. *Ph.* 3: 8.

Ye are partakers of Christ's sufferings. *1 Pe.* 4: 13.

If any man suffer as a Christian, let him not be ashamed. *1 Pe.* 4: 16.

See also

Christ, Devotion to.

Christ, Suffering of

He is despised and rejected of men; a man of sorrows, and acquainted with grief. *Is.* 53: 3.

In all their affliction he was afflicted. *Is.* 63: 9.

Foxes have holes, and the birds of the air have nests; but the Son of man hath not where to lay his head. *Mat.* 8: 20.

Let this cup pass from me: nevertheless not as I will, but as thou wilt. *Mat.* 26: 39.

And being in an agony he prayed more earnestly: and his sweat was as it were great drops of blood falling down to the ground. *Lu.* 22: 44.

Ought not Christ to have suffered these things, and to enter into his glory? *Lu.* 24: 26.

The good shepherd giveth his life for the sheep. *Jn.* 10: 11.

And the soldiers platted a crown of thorns, and put it on his head. *Jn.* 19: 2.

I thirst. *Jn.* 19: 28.

For as the sufferings of Christ abound in us, so our consolation also aboundeth by Christ. *2 Co.* 1: 5.

That I may know . . . the fellowship of his sufferings. *Ph.* 3: 10.

Though he were a Son, yet learned he obedience by the things which he suffered. *He.* 5: 8.

Without shedding of blood is no remission. *He.* 9: 22.

For Christ also hath once suffered for sins, the just for the unjust, that he might bring us to God. *1 Pe.* 3: 18.

Rejoice, inasmuch as ye are partakers of Christ's suffering; that, when his glory shall be revealed, ye may be glad also with exceeding joy. *1 Pe.* 4: 13.

See also

Christ, Agony of; Christ, Blood of; Christ, Cross of; Christ, Crucifixion of; Christ, Cup of; Christ, Death of; Christ, Grief of; Christ, Humiliation of; Christ, the Lamb of God; Christ, Passion of; Christ, Sacrifice of; Christ, Sorrow of.

Christ, Supremacy of

The Lord said unto my Lord, Sit thou at my right hand, until I make thine enemies thy footstool. *Ps.* 110: 1.

And lo a voice from heaven, saying, This is my beloved Son. *Mat.* 3: 17.

The Son of man is Lord also of the sabbath. *Mk.* 2: 28.

And suddenly, when they had looked round about, they saw no man any more, save Jesus only with them. *Mk.* 9: 8.

Neither is there salvation in any other. *Ac.* 4: 12.

Whether we live therefore, or die, we are the Lord's. *Ro.* 14: 8.

He is before all things, and by him all things consist. *Col.* 1: 17.

See also

Christ, Centrality of; Christ, Dignity of; Christ, Exaltation of; Christ, Glory of; Christ, Greatness of; Christ, Majesty of; Christ, Nature of; Christ, Triumph of.

Christ, Sympathy of

Shouldest not thou have had compassion on thy fellowservant, even as I had pity on thee? *Mat.* 18: 33.

How often would I have gathered thy children together, even as a hen gathereth her chickens under her wings, and ye would not! *Mat.* 23: 37.

Weep not for me, but weep for yourselves, and for your children. *Lu.* 23: 28.

All that the Father giveth me shall come to me; and him that cometh to me I will in no wise cast out. *Jn.* 6: 37.

If there be any consolation in Christ, . . . Fulfil ye my joy. *Ph.* 2: 1, 2.

For we have not an high priest which can not be touched with the feeling of our infirmities. *He.* 4: 15.

See also

Christ, the Comforter; Christ, Compassion of; Christ, Forgiveness of; Christ, the Healing.

Christ, Table of

He took bread, and gave thanks, and brake it. *Lu.* 22: 19.

He was known of them in breaking of bread. *Lu.* 24: 35.

Jesus said unto them, I am the bread of life. *Jn.* 6: 35.

They made him a supper; and Martha served. *Jn.* 12: 2.

Therefore let us keep the feast. *1 Co.* 5: 8.

We being many are one bread, and one body: for we are all partakers of that one bread. *1 Co.* 10: 17.

Ye cannot be partakers of the Lord's table, and of the table of devils. *1 Co.* 10: 21.

I will come in to him, and will sup with him, and he with me. *Re.* 3: 20.

Blessed are they which are called unto the marriage supper of the Lamb. *Re.* 19: 9.

See also

Christ, Blood of; Christ, Body of; Christ, the Bread of Life; Christ, Communion with.

Christ, the Teacher

Jesus went about all Galilee, teaching in their synagogues, and preaching the gospel of the kingdom. *Mat.* 4: 23.

He opened his mouth, and taught them. *Mat.* 5: 2.

He taught them as one having authority. *Mat.* 7: 29.

Master, we know that thou art true, and teachest the way of God in truth. *Mat.* 22: 16.

Teaching them to observe all things whatsoever I have commanded you. *Mat.* 28: 20.

He taught them many things by parables. *Mk.* 4: 2.

Lord, teach us to pray. *Lu.* 11: 1.

Master, we know that thou sayest and teachest rightly, neither acceptest thou the person of any, but teachest the way of God truly. *Lu.* 20: 21.

We know that thou art a teacher come from God. *Jn.* 3: 2.

It is written in the prophets, And they shall be all taught of God. *Jn.* 6: 45.

Jesus answered and said unto him, What I do thou knowest not now; but thou shalt know hereafter. *Jn.* 13: 7.

All things that I have heard of my Father I have made known unto you. *Jn.* 15: 15.

Ye have not so learned Christ; If so be that ye have heard him, and have been taught by him. *Ep.* 4: 20, 21.

The Lord give thee understanding in all things. *2 Ti.* 2: 7.

He went and preached unto the spirits in prison. *1 Pe.* 3: 19.

See also

Christ, Gospel of; Christ, Message of; Christ, Preaching of; Christ, the Word; Christ, Word of.

Christ, Temptation of

When the tempter came to him, he said, If thou be the Son of God, command that these stones be made bread. *Mat.* 4: 3.

The devil taketh him up into an exceeding high mountain, and sheweth him all the kingdoms of the world, and the glory of them; And saith unto him, All these things will I give thee, if thou wilt fall down and worship me. *Mat.* 4: 8, 9.

Immediately the Spirit driveth him into the wilderness. *Mk.* 1: 12.

He was there in the wilderness forty days, tempted of Satan. *Mk.* 1: 13.

Jesus returned in the power of the Spirit into Galilee. *Lu.* 4: 14.

In that he himself hath suffered being tempted, he is able to succour them that are tempted. *He.* 2: 18.

In all points tempted like as we are, yet without sin. *He.* 4: 15.

Christ, Touch of

He touched her hand, and the fever left her. *Mat.* 8: 15.

Jesus came and touched them, and said, Arise, and be not afraid. *Mat.* 17: 7.

Jesus had compassion on them, and touched their eyes. *Mat.* 20: 34.

Jesus, immediately knowing in himself that virtue had gone out of him, turned him about in the press, and said, Who touched my clothes? *Mk.* 5: 30.

They beseech him to put his hand upon him. *Mk.* 7: 32.

They bring a blind man unto him, and besought him to touch him. *Mk.* 8: 22.

They brought young children to him, that he should touch them. *Mk.* 10: 13.

See also

Christ, Gentleness of; Christ, Hand of; Christ, the Healing.

Christ, Transfiguration of

Jesus taketh Peter, James, and John his brother, and bringeth them up into an high mountain apart. *Mat.* 17: 1.

Jesus . . . was transfigured before them: and his face did shine as the sun. *Mat.* 17: 1, 2.

Lord, it is good for us to be here. *Mat.* 17: 4.

Behold, a bright cloud overshadowed them: and behold a voice out of the cloud, which said, This is my beloved Son, in whom I am well pleased. *Mat.* 17: 5.

Jesus charged them, saying, Tell the vision to no man. *Mat.* 17: 9.

His raiment became shining, exceeding white as snow; so as no fuller on earth can white them. *Mk.* 9: 3.

There appeared unto him Elias with Moses. *Mk.* 9: 4.

As he prayed, the fashion of his countenance was altered, and his raiment was white and glistering. *Lu.* 9: 29.

When they were awake, they saw his glory, and the two men that stood with him. *Lu.* 9: 32.

See also

Christ, Exaltation of; Christ, Glory of.

Christ, Triumph of

The stone which the builders rejected, the same is become the head of the corner. *Mat.* 21: 42.

In the world ye shall have tribulation: but be of good cheer; I have overcome the world. *Jn.* 16: 33.

Thanks be to God, which giveth us the victory through our Lord Jesus Christ. *1 Co.* 15: 57.

Thanks be unto God, which always causeth

us to triumph in Christ. *2 Co.* 2: 14.

Having spoiled principalities and powers, he made a shew of them openly, triumphing over them in it. *Col.* 2: 15.

Jesus Christ . . . is gone into heaven, and is on the right hand of God. *1 Pe.* 3: 21, 22.

Behold, I am alive for evermore. *Re.* 1: 18.

See also

Christ, Crown of; Christ, Exaltation of; Christ, Glory of; Christ, Majesty of; Christ, Preëminence of; Christ, Supremacy of; Christ, Triumphal Entry of.

Christ, Triumphal Entry of

Tell ye the daughter of Sion, Behold, thy King cometh unto thee, meek, and sitting upon an ass, and a colt the foal of an ass. *Mat.* 21: 5.

A very great multitude spread their garments in the way; others cut down branches from the trees, and strawed them in the way. *Mat.* 21: 8.

The multitudes that went before, and that followed, cried, saying, Hosanna to the son of David: Blessed is he that cometh in the name of the Lord; Hosanna in the highest. *Mat.* 21: 9.

When he was come into Jerusalem, all the city was moved, saying, Who is this? *Mat.* 21: 10.

Blessed be the kingdom of our father David, that cometh in the name of the Lord: Hosanna in the highest. *Mk.* 11: 10.

Jesus went into the temple, and began to cast out them that sold and bought in the temple, and overthrew the tables of the money-changers, and the seats of them that sold doves. *Mk.* 11: 15.

My house shall be called of all nations the house of prayer? but ye have made it a den of thieves. *Mk.* 11: 17.

Fear not, daughter of Sion: behold, thy King cometh, sitting on an ass's colt. *Jn.* 12: 15.

See also

Christ, the King; Palm Sunday.

Christ, Trust in

Jesus saith unto them, Believe ye that I am able to do this? They said unto him, Yea, Lord. *Mat.* 9: 28.

I have not found so great faith, no, not in Israel. *Lu.* 7: 9.

Lord, increase our faith. *Lu.* 17: 5.

When the Son of man cometh, shall he find faith on the earth? *Lu.* 18: 8.

Ye believe in God, believe also in me. *Jn.* 14: 1.

Whosoever shall call on the name of the Lord shall be saved. *Ac.* 2: 21.

Testifying . . . repentance toward God, and faith toward our Lord Jesus Christ. *Ac.* 20: 21.

In him shall the Gentiles trust. *Ro.* 15: 12.

Such trust have we through Christ to God-ward. *2 Co.* 3: 4.

If any man trust to himself that he is Christ's, let him of himself think this again, that, as he is Christ's, even so are we Christ's. *2 Co.* 10: 7.

We . . . first trusted in Christ. *Ep.* 1: 12.

Ye also trusted, after that ye heard the word of truth, the gospel of your salvation. *Ep.* 1: 13.

That Christ may dwell in your hearts by faith. *Ep.* 3: 17.

I trust in the Lord. *Ph.* **2: 24.**
I will put my trust in him. *He.* **2: 13.**
See also
Christ, Belief in; Christ, Dependence on; Christ, Faith in; Christ, Hope in.

Christ, Trustworthiness of

That thou mightest know the certainty of those things, wherein thou hast been instructed. *Lu.* **1: 4.**
We believe and are sure that thou art that Christ, the Son of the living God. *Jn.* **6: 69.**
Let not your heart be troubled: ye believe in God, believe also in me. *Jn.* **14: 1.**
Teaching those things which concern the Lord Jesus, with all confidence. *Ac.* **28: 31.**
I certify you, brethren, that the gospel which was preached of me is not after man. *Ga.* **1: 11.**
In whom we have boldness and access with confidence by the faith of him. *Ep.* **3: 12.**
This is a faithful saying, and worthy of all acceptation, that Christ Jesus came into the world to save sinners. *1 Ti.* **1: 15.**
I know whom I have believed, and am persuaded that he is able to keep that which I have committed unto him against that day. *2 Ti.* **1: 12.**
Worthy is the Lamb that was slain. *Re.* **5: 12.**
He which testifieth these things saith, Surely I come quickly. Amen. Even so, come, Lord Jesus. *Re.* **22: 20.**
See also
Christ, Faithfulness of.

Christ, the Truth

Master, we know that thou art true, and teachest the way of God in truth. *Mat.* **22: 16.**
The same came for a witness, to bear witness of the Light. *Jn.* **1: 7.**
The law was given by Moses, but grace and truth came by Jesus Christ. *Jn.* **1: 17.**
Ye sent unto John, and he bare witness unto the truth. *Jn.* **5: 33.**
Because I tell you the truth, ye believe me not. *Jn.* **8: 45.**
Jesus saith unto him, I am . . . the truth. *Jn.* **14: 6.**
To this end was I born, and for this cause came I into the world, that I should bear witness unto the truth. *Jn.* **18: 37.**
Every one that is of the truth heareth my voice. *Jn.* **18: 37.**
He that saw it bare record, and his record is true. *Jn.* **19: 35.**
I say the truth in Christ. *Ro.* **9: 1.**
The truth of Christ is in me. *2 Co.* **11: 10.**
As the truth is in Jesus. *Ep.* **4: 21.**
Faithful is he that calleth you, who also will do it. *1 Th.* **5: 24.**
I speak the truth in Christ, and lie not. *1 Ti.* **2: 7.**
See also
Christ, Gospel of; Christ, the Light; Christ, Message of; Christ, Preaching of; Christ, the Teacher; Christ, the Word; Christ, Word of.

Christ, Union with

I know that ye seek Jesus. *Mat.* **28: 5.**
Joint-heirs with Christ. *Ro.* **8: 17.**
Who shall separate us from the love of Christ? *Ro.* **8: 35.**
Know ye not that your bodies are the members of Christ? *1 Co.* **6: 15.**

I knew a man in Christ. *2 Co.* **12: 2.**
Ye are all one in Christ Jesus. *Ga.* **3: 28.**
God . . . hath blessed us with all spiritual blessings in heavenly places in Christ. *Ep.* **1: 3.**
That in the dispensation of the fulness of times he might gather together in one all things in Christ, both which are in heaven, and which are on earth. *Ep.* **1: 10.**
To me to live is Christ. *Ph.* **1: 21.**
That I may know . . . the fellowship of his sufferings. *Ph.* **3: 10.**
So shall we ever be with the Lord. *1 Th.* **4: 17.**
The Lord Jesus Christ be with thy spirit. *2 Ti.* **4: 22.**
Ye are partakers of Christ's sufferings. *1 Pe.* **4: 13.**
See also
Christ, Abiding in; Christ, Communion with; Christ, Companionship with; Christ, Fellowship with; Christ, Life in; Christ, Nearness of; Christ, Partnership with; Christ, Presence of.

Christ, Uniqueness of

They saw no man, save Jesus only. *Mat.* **17: 8.**
One is your Master, even Christ; and all ye are brethren. *Mat.* **23: 8.**
Neither is there salvation in any other: for there is none other name under heaven given among men, whereby we must be saved. *Ac.* **4: 12.**
One Jesus. *Ac.* **25: 19.**
To us there is but . . . one Lord Jesus Christ, by whom are all things. *1 Co.* **8: 6.**
One Lord. *Ep.* **4: 5.**
God also hath highly exalted him, and given him a name which is above every name. *Ph.* **2: 9.**
Christ . . . is before all things, and by him all things consist. *Col.* **1: 7, 17.**
Being made perfect, he became the author of eternal salvation unto all them that obey him. *He.* **5: 9.**
See also
Christ, Authority of; Christ, Exaltation of; Christ, Finality of; Christ, the Inimitable; Christ, Preëminence of; Christ, the Son of God; Christ, Supremacy of.

Christ, Unity of

I and my Father are one. *Jn.* **10: 30.**
Is Christ divided? *1 Co.* **1: 13.**
As the body is one, and hath many members: . . . so also is Christ. *1 Co.* **12: 12.**
By one Spirit we are all baptized into one body. *1 Co.* **12: 13.**
There are three that bear record in heaven, the Father, the Word, and the Holy Ghost: and these are one. *1 Jn.* **5: 7.**
See also
Christ, Divinity of; Christ, Nature of.

Christ, Universality of

The field is the world. *Mat.* **13: 38.**
A superscription also was written over him, in letters of Greek, and Latin, and Hebrew. *Lu.* **23: 38.**
That was the true Light, which lighteth every man that cometh into the world. *Jn.* **1: 9.**
He was in the world, and the world was made by him, and the world knew him not. *Jn.* **1: 10.**

Behold the Lamb of God, which taketh away the sin of the world! *Jn. 1: 29.*

This is indeed the Christ, the Saviour of the world. *Jn. 4: 42.*

The bread that I will give is my flesh, which I will give for the life of the world. *Jn. 6: 51.*

I am the light of the world. *Jn. 8: 12.*

Many of the Jews went away, and believed on Jesus. *Jn. 12: 11.*

All things in Christ, both which are in heaven and which are on earth; even in him. *Ep. 1: 10.*

That the Gentiles should be fellowheirs, and of the same body, and partakers of his promise in Christ by the gospel. *Ep. 3: 6.*

Whom we preach, warning every man, and teaching every man in all wisdom; that we may present every man perfect in Christ Jesus. *Col. 1: 28.*

Christ is all, and in all. *Col. 3: 11.*

Christ, the Vine

I will not drink henceforth of this fruit of the vine, until that day when I drink it new with you in my Father's kingdom. *Mat. 26: 29.*

I am the true vine, and my Father is the husbandman. *Jn. 15: 1.*

The branch cannot bear fruit of itself, except it abide in the vine: no more can ye, except ye abide in me. *Jn. 15: 4.*

I am the vine, ye are the branches: He that abideth in me, and I in him, the same bringeth forth much fruit: for without me ye can do nothing. *Jn. 15: 5.*

If a man abide not in me, he is cast forth as a branch, and is withered. *Jn. 15: 6.*

Christ, Vision of

Their eyes were opened, and they knew him. *Lu. 24: 31.*

Certain Greeks . . . came therefore to Philip, . . . and desired him, saying, Sir, we would see Jesus. *Jn. 12: 20, 21.*

Have I not seen Jesus Christ our Lord. *1 Co. 9: 1.*

He was seen of Cephas. *1 Co. 15: 5.*

But we see Jesus. *He. 2: 9.*

Unto them that look for him shall he appear. *He. 9: 28.*

See also
Christ, Appearance of; Christ, Eyes of; Christ, Revelation of; Christ, Second Coming of.

Christ, Voice of

He was oppressed, and he was afflicted, yet he opened not his mouth. *Is. 53: 7.*

He opened his mouth, and taught them. *Mat. 5: 2.*

I will open my mouth in parables. *Mat. 13: 35.*

The disciples were astonished at his words. *Mk. 10: 24.*

They remembered his words. *Lu. 24: 8.*

These are the words which I spake unto you, while I was yet with you. *Lu. 24: 44.*

The sheep follow him: for they know his voice. *Jn. 10: 4.*

Every one that is of the truth heareth my voice. *Jn. 18: 37.*

Like a lamb dumb before his shearer, so opened he not his mouth. *Ac. 8: 22.*

The Lord himself shall descend from heaven with a shout, with the voice of the archangel, and with the trump of God. *1 Th. 4: 16.*

See also
Christ, Word of.

Christ, Washing Disciples' Feet

He riseth from supper, and laid aside his garments; and took a towel, and girded himself. After that he poured water into a bason, and began to wash the disciples' feet. *Jn. 13: 4, 5.*

If I wash thee not, thou hast no part with me. *Jn. 13: 8.*

Lord, not my feet only, but also my hands and my head. *Jn. 13: 9.*

Jesus saith to him, He that is washed needeth not save to wash his feet, but is clean every whit. *Jn. 13: 10.*

If I then, your Lord and Master, have washed your feet; ye also ought to wash one another's feet. *Jn. 13: 14.*

I have given you an example, that ye should do as I have done to you. *Jn. 13: 15.*

Christ, Watchfulness of

How often would I have gathered thy children together, even as a hen gathereth her chickens under her wings, and ye would not! *Mat. 23: 37.*

Watch therefore: for ye know not what hour your Lord doth come. *Mat. 24: 42.*

Tarry ye here, and watch with me. *Mat. 26: 38.*

What, could ye not watch with me one hour? *Mat. 26: 40.*

What I say unto you I say unto all, Watch. *Mk. 13: 37.*

I am the good shepherd: the good shepherd giveth his life for the sheep. *Jn. 10: 11.*

He that is an hireling, and not the shepherd, whose own the sheep are not, seeth the wolf coming, and leaveth the sheep, and fleeth: and the wolf catcheth them, and scattereth the sheep. *Jn. 10: 12.*

Of them which thou gavest me have I lost none. *Jn. 18: 9.*

Christ, the Way

Whither I go ye know, and the way ye know. *Jn. 14: 4.*

I am the way, the truth, and the life: no man cometh unto the Father, but by me. *Jn. 14: 6.*

There arose no small stir about that way. *Ac. 19: 23.*

Walk in love, as Christ also hath loved us. *Ep. 5: 2.*

As ye have therefore received Christ Jesus the Lord, so walk ye in him. *Col. 2: 6.*

God . . . hath called us unto his eternal glory by Christ Jesus. *1 Pe. 5: 10.*

See also
Christ, Coming to; Christ, the Door; Christ, the Guide; Christ, the Leader.

Christ, Will of

Not my will, but thine, be done. *Lu. 22: 42.*

As the Father raiseth up the dead, and quickeneth them; even so the Son quickeneth whom he will. *Jn. 5: 21.*

I seek not mine own will, but the will of the Father which hath sent me. *Jn. 5: 30.*

I came down from heaven, not to do mine own will, but the will of him that sent me. *Jn.* 6: 38.

Father, I will that they also, whom thou hast given me. be with me where I am. *Jn.* 17: 24.

The will of the Lord be done. *Ac.* 21: 14.

Wherefore be ye not unwise, but understanding what the will of the Lord is. *Ep.* 5: 17.

We . . . desire that ye might be filled with the knowledge of his will in all wisdom and spiritual understanding. *Col.* 1: 9.

Christ, Wisdom of

All that heard him were astonished at his understanding and answers. *Lu.* 2: 47.

Jesus increased in wisdom and stature, and in favour with God and man. *Lu.* 2: 52.

They were all amazed, and spake among themselves, saying, What a word is this! *Lu.* 4: 36.

The words that I speak unto you, they are spirit, and they are life. *Jn.* 6: 63.

Now are we sure that thou knowest all things, and needest not that any man should ask thee. *Jn.* 16: 30.

Christ the power of God, and the wisdom of God. *1 Co.* 1: 24.

But we have the mind of Christ. *1 Co.* 2: 16.

Let this mind be in you, which was also in Christ Jesus. *Ph.* 2: 5.

See also

Christ, Knowledge of; Christ, Mind of.

Christ, Witness of

We speak that we do know, and testify that we have seen. *Jn.* 3: 11.

Now we believe, not because of thy saying: for we have heard him ourselves, and know that this is indeed the Christ, the Saviour of the world. *Jn.* 4: 42.

If I bear witness of myself, my witness is not true. *Jn.* 5: 31.

There is another that beareth witness of me; and I know that the witness which he witnesseth of me is true. *Jn.* 5: 32.

I have greater witness than that of John. *Jn.* 5: 36.

The Father himself, which hath sent me, hath borne witness of me. *Jn.* 5: 37.

The scriptures . . . are they which testify of me. *Jn.* 5: 39.

The Comforter . . . shall testify of me. *Jn.* 15: 26.

This Jesus hath God raised up, whereof we all are witnesses. *Ac.* 2: 32.

To him give all the prophets witness. *Ac.* 10: 43.

The testimony of Christ was confirmed in you. *1 Co.* 1: 6.

Christ Jesus . . . before Pontius Pilate witnessed a good confession. *1 Ti.* 6: 13.

Be not thou therefore ashamed of the testimony of our Lord. *2 Ti.* 1: 8.

Christ . . . was manifest in these last times for you, Who by him do believe in God, that raised him up from the dead, and gave him glory; that your faith and hope might be in God. *1 Pe.* 1: 19–21.

A witness of the sufferings of Christ. *1 Pe.* 5: 1.

We . . . were eyewitnesses of his majesty. *2 Pe.* 1: 16.

Jesus Christ . . . is the faithful witness. *Re.* 1: 5.

The testimony of Jesus is the spirit of prophecy. *Re.* 19: 10.

I Jesus have sent mine angel to testify unto you these things in the churches. *Re.* 22: 16.

See also

Christ, Evidence of.

Christ, the Word

Beginning at Moses and all the prophets, he expounded unto them in all the Scriptures the things concerning himself. *Lu.* 24: 27.

In the beginning was the Word, and the Word was with God, and the Word was God. *Jn.* 1: 1.

The Word was . . . full of grace and truth. *Jn.* 1: 14.

There are three that bear record in heaven, the Father, the Word, and the Holy Ghost. *1 Jn.* 5: 7.

His name is called The Word of God. *Re.* 19: 13.

See also

Christ, Gospel of; Christ, Message of; Christ, Preaching of; Christ, the Teacher; Christ, Word of.

Christ, Word of

Speak the word only, and my servant shall be healed. *Mat.* 8: 8.

Heaven and earth shall pass away, but my words shall not pass away. *Mat.* 24: 35.

He preached the word unto them. *Mk.* 2: 2.

Whosoever therefore shall be ashamed of me and of my words; . . . of him also shall the Son of man be ashamed. *Mk.* 8: 38.

All bear him witness, and wondered at the gracious words which proceeded out of his mouth. *Lu.* 4: 22.

His word was with power. *Lu.* 4: 32.

They remembered his words. *Lu.* 24: 8.

Jesus of Nazareth, which was a prophet mighty in deed and word before God and all the people. *Lu.* 24: 19.

Lord, to whom shall we go? thou hast the words of eternal life. *Jn.* 6: 68.

As he spake these words, many believed on him. *Jn.* 8: 30.

If a man love me, he will keep my words. *Jn.* 14: 23.

He that loveth me not keepeth not my sayings. *Jn.* 14: 24.

The word which ye hear is not mine, but the Father's which sent me. *Jn.* 14: 24.

Sanctify them through thy truth: thy word is truth. *Jn.* 17: 17.

Let the word of Christ dwell in you richly in all wisdom. *Col.* 3: 16.

These things saith the Amen, the faithful and true witness. *Re.* 3: 14.

See also

Christ, Gospel of; Christ, Message of; Christ, Preaching of; Christ, Promise of; Christ, the Teacher; Christ, the Word.

Christ, Work of

The Lord hath anointed me to preach good tidings unto the meek; he hath sent me to bind up the brokenhearted, to proclaim liberty to the captives, and the opening of the prison to them that are bound. *Is.* 61: 1.

The Son of man hath power on earth to forgive sins. *Mat.* 9: 6.

Wist ye not that I must be about my Father's business? *Lu.* 2: 49.

My meat is to do the will of him that sent me, and to finish his work. *Jn.* 4: 34.

My Father worketh hitherto, and I work. *Jn.* 5: 17.

The works which the Father hath given me to finish, the same works that I do, bear witness of me, that the Father hath sent me. *Jn.* 5: 36.

I must work the works of him that sent me, while it is day. *Jn.* 9: 4.

I have finished the work which thou gavest me to do. *Jn.* 17: 4.

It is finished. *Jn.* 19: 30.

See also

Christ, the Comforter; Christ, Compassion of; Christ, Hand of; Christ, the Healing; Christ, Help of; Christ, Ministry of; Christ, Mission of; Christ, the Physician; Christ, Power of; Christ, Priesthood of; Christ, Strength of.

Christ, Worship of

There came a leper and worshipped him. *Mat.* 8: 2.

There came a certain ruler, and worshipped him. *Mat.* 9: 18.

They that were in the ship came and worshipped him. *Mat.* 14: 33.

The servant therefore fell down, and worshipped him. *Mat.* 18: 26.

Then the eleven disciples, . . . when they saw him, . . . worshipped him. *Mat.* 28: 16, 17.

When he saw Jesus afar off, he ran and worshipped him. *Mk.* 5: 6.

At the name of Jesus every knee should bow, of things in heaven, and things in earth, and things under the earth. *Ph.* 2: 10.

Let all the angels of God worship him. *He.* 1: 6.

See also

Christ, Adoration of; Christ, Devotion to; Christ, Exaltation of; Christ, Praise of.

Christ, Wrath of

He . . . looked round about on them with anger, being grieved for the hardness of their hearts. *Mk.* 3: 5.

When Jesus saw it, he was much displeased. *Mk.* 10: 14.

The wrath of the Lamb. *Re.* 6: 16.

Christian

The disciples were called Christians first in Antioch. *Ac.* 11: 26.

Then Agrippa said unto Paul, Almost thou persuadest me to be a Christian. *Ac.* 26: 28.

Walk not as other Gentiles walk. *Ep.* 4: 17.

That worthy name by the which ye are called. *Ja.* 2: 7.

If any man suffer as a Christian, let him not be ashamed; but let him glorify God on this behalf. *1 Pe.* 4: 16.

See also

Christ, Disciple of; Christ, Follower of.

Christianity

Upon this rock I will build my church. *Mat.* 16: 18.

The same time there arose no small stir about that way. *Ac.* 19: 23.

With all that in every place call upon the name of Jesus Christ our Lord. *1 Co.* 1: 2.

Gods many, and lords many, But to us there is but one God. *1 Co.* 8: 5, 6.

God . . . hath blessed us with all spiritual blessings in heavenly places in Christ. *Ep.* 1: 3.

There is one body, and one Spirit. *Ep.* 4: 4.

Christ . . . loved the church, and gave himself for it. *Ep.* 5: 25.

A glorious church, not having spot, or wrinkle, or any such thing. *Ep.* 5: 27.

Love the brotherhood. *1 Pe.* 2: 17.

See also

Christian; Church.

Christmas

The government shall be upon his shoulder. *Is.* 9: 6.

Where is he? *Mat.* 2: 2.

We have seen his star in the east. *Mat.* 2: 2.

They presented unto him gifts. *Mat.* 2: 11.

The people which sat in darkness saw great light; and to them which sat in the region and shadow of death light is sprung up. *Mat.* 4: 16.

Let us now go even unto Bethlehem. *Lu.* 2: 15.

Lord, now lettest thou thy servant depart in peace. *Lu.* 2: 29.

God hath chosen the weak things of the world to confound the things which are mighty. *1 Co.* 1: 27.

Of these things put them in remembrance. *2 Ti.* 2: 14.

God . . . Hath in these last days spoken unto us by his Son. *He.* 1: 1, 2.

Beloved, if God so loved us, we ought also to love one another. *1 Jn.* 4: 11.

See also

Carol; Christ, Birth of; Nativity.

Church

Thou shalt also be a crown of glory in the hand of the Lord, and a royal diadem in the hand of thy God. *Is.* 62: 3.

There shall be, like people, like priest. *Ho.* 4: 9.

Blow the trumpet . . . , sanctify a fast, call a solemn assembly. *Jo.* 2: 15.

He that toucheth you, toucheth the apple of his eye. *Zch.* 2: 8.

The Lord their God shall save them in that day as the flock of his people. *Zch.* 9: 16.

They shall be mine, saith the Lord of hosts, in that day when I make up my jewels. *Mal.* 3: 17.

Upon this rock I will build my church; and the gates of hell shall not prevail against it. *Mat.* 16: 18.

As his custom was, he went into the synagogue on the sabbath day, and stood up for to read. *Lu.* 4: 16.

Whose soever sins ye remit, they are remitted unto them; and whose soever sins ye retain, they are retained. *Jn.* 20: 23.

Many of them which heard the word believed. *Ac.* 4: 4.

The temple of God is holy, which temple ye are. *1 Co.* 3: 17.

I persecuted the church of God. *1 Co.* **15: 9.**

The church, Which is his body, the fulness of him that filleth all in all. *Ep.* **1: 22, 23.**

Unto him be the glory in the church. *Ep.* **3: 21.**

The church is subject unto Christ. *Ep.* **5: 24.**

Christ also loved the church, and gave himself for it. *Ep.* **5: 25.**

That he might present it to himself a glorious church. *Ep.* **5: 27.**

He is the head of the body, the church. *Col.* **1: 18.**

Let the word of Christ dwell in you richly in all wisdom; teaching and admonishing one another in psalms and hymns and spiritual songs, singing with grace in your hearts to the Lord. *Col.* **3: 16.**

Love the brotherhood. *1 Pe.* **2: 17.**

Feed the flock of God which is among you, taking the oversight thereof, not by constraint, but willingly. *1 Pe.* **5: 2.**

He that hath an ear, let him hear what the Spirit saith unto the churches. *Re.* **2: 7.**

See also

Congregation; Meeting.

Church, Absence from

The Lord watch between me and thee, when we are absent one from another. *Ge.* **31: 49.**

God forbid that we should forsake the Lord, to serve other gods. *Jos.* **24: 16.**

Who is there among all the tribes of Israel that came not up with the congregation unto the Lord? *Ju.* **21: 5.**

What doest thou here, Elijah? *1 K.* **19: 9.**

Why is the house of God forsaken? *Ne.* **13: 11.**

The man that wandereth out of the way of understanding shall remain in the congregation of the dead. *Pr.* **21: 16.**

I marvel that ye are so soon removed from him that called you into the grace of Christ. *Ga.* **1: 6.**

Though I be absent in the flesh, yet am I with you in the spirit, joying and beholding your order, and the stedfastness of your faith in Christ. *Col.* **2: 5.**

That day shall not come, except there come a falling away first. *2 Th.* **2: 3.**

I have somewhat against thee, because thou hast left thy first love. *Re.* **2: 4.**

Because thou art lukewarm, and neither cold not hot, I will spue thee out of my mouth. *Re.* **3: 16.**

See also

Church, Attendance at; Church, Neglect of.

Church, Attendance at

The Lord blessed the sabbath day, and hallowed it. *Ex.* **20: 11.**

Ye shall keep the sabbath therefore; for it is holy unto you. *Ex.* **31: 14.**

Let us meet together in the house of God. *Ne.* **6: 10.**

As the hart panteth after the water brooks, so panteth my soul after thee, O God. *Ps.* **42: 1.**

We took sweet counsel together, and walked into the house of God in company. *Ps.* **55: 14.**

Blessed is the man whom thou choosest, and

causest to approach unto thee, that he may dwell in thy courts. *Ps.* **65: 4.**

Open to me the gates of righteousness: I will go into them, and I will praise the Lord. *Ps.* **118: 19.**

It is time to seek the Lord. *Ho.* **10: 12.**

He went into their synagogues. *Mat.* **12: 9.**

Where two or three are gathered together in my name, there am I in the midst of them. *Mat.* **18: 20.**

The blind and the lame came to him in the temple. *Mat.* **21: 14.**

Children crying in the temple, and saying, Hosanna to the son of David. *Mat.* **21: 15.**

They found him in the temple. *Lu.* **2: 46.**

They . . . were continually in the temple, praising and blessing God. *Lu.* **24: 52, 53.**

I ever taught in the synagogue, and in the temple. *Jn.* **18: 20.**

Not forsaking the assembling of ourselves together, as the manner of some is. *He.* **10: 25.**

See also

Church, Absence from; Sabbath; Sunday.

Church, Building the

The house which I build is great: for great is our God above all gods. *2 Ch.* **2: 5.**

The children of the captivity builded the temple unto the Lord God of Israel. *Ezr.* **4: 1.**

Israel hath forgotten his Maker, and buildeth temples. *Ho.* **8: 14.**

He loveth our nation, and he hath built us a synagogue. *Lu.* **7: 5.**

Our fathers had the tabernacle of witness in the wilderness. *Ac.* **7: 44.**

David . . . found favour before God, and desired to find a tabernacle for the God of Jacob. *Ac.* **7: 45, 46.**

Solomon built him an house. *Ac.* **7: 47.**

The most High dwelleth not in temples made with hands. *Ac.* **7: 48.**

Heaven is my throne, and earth is my footstool: what house will ye build me? saith the Lord: or what is the place of my rest? *Ac.* **7: 49.**

Every house is builded by some man; but he that built all things is God. *He.* **3: 4.**

See also

Church, Dedication of; God, House of; Shrine; Synagogue; Tabernacle; Temple.

Church, Closing of

The Lord God sent him forth from the garden of Eden. *Ge.* **3: 23.**

They have burned up all the synagogues of God in the land. *Ps.* **74: 8.**

Then said the Lord unto me; This gate shall be shut, it shall not be opened, and no man shall enter in by it. *Eze.* **44: 2.**

For the wickedness of their doings I will drive them out of mine house, I will love them no more. *Ho.* **9: 15.**

They were all scattered abroad. *Ac.* **8: 1.**

Despise ye the church of God? *1 Co.* **11: 22.**

That day shall not come, except there come a falling away first. *2 Th.* **2: 3.**

Church, Criticism of

They hate me with a cruel hatred. *Ps.* **25: 19.**

Thine enemies roar in the midst of thy congregations. *Ps.* **74: 4.**

They have burned up all the synagogues of God in the land. *Ps.* **74: 8.**

Blessed are ye, when men shall hate you. *Lu.* **6: 22.**

Every one that doeth evil hateth the light. *Jn.* **3: 20.**

The priests, and the captain of the temple, and the Sadducees, came upon them, Being grieved that they taught the people, and preached through Jesus the resurrection from the dead. *Ac.* **4: 1, 2.**

They suborned men, which said, We have heard him speak blasphemous words against Moses, and against God. *Ac.* **6: 11.**

At that time there was a great persecution against the church. *Ac.* **8: 1.**

As for Saul, he made havock of the church. *Ac.* **8: 3.**

Now about this time Herod the king stretched forth his hands to vex certain of the church. And he killed James the brother of John with the sword. *Ac.* **12: 1, 2.**

When the Jews saw the multitudes, they were filled with envy, and spake against those things which were spoken by Paul, contradicting and blaspheming. *Ac.* **13: 45.**

Give none offence, neither to the Jews, nor to the Gentiles, nor to the church of God. *1 Co.* **10: 32.**

Despise ye the church of God? *1 Co.* **11: 22.**

If any man love not the Lord Jesus Christ, let him be Anathema Maran-atha. *1 Co.* **16: 22.**

Ye have heard of my conversation in time past in the Jews' religion, how that beyond measure I persecuted the church of God, and wasted it. *Ga.* **1: 13.**

Concerning zeal, persecuting the church. *Ph.* **3: 6.**

See also
Church, Failure of.

Church, Dedication of

I will sanctify the tabernacle of the congregation, and the altar. *Ex.* **29: 44.**

This was the dedication of the altar, in the day when it was anointed. *Nu.* **7: 84.**

What man is there that hath built a new house, and hath not dedicated it? let him go and return to his house, lest he die in battle, and another man dedicate it. *De.* **20: 5.**

Behold, I build an house to the name of the Lord my God, to dedicate it to him. *2 Ch.* **2: 4.**

Forasmuch as it was in thine heart to build an house for my name, thou didst well. *2 Ch.* **6: 8.**

Behold, heaven and the heaven of heavens cannot contain thee; how much less this house which I have built! *2 Ch.* **6: 18.**

Hearken unto the cry and the prayer which thy servant prayeth before thee: That thine eyes may be open upon this house day and night, upon the place whereof thou hast said that thou wouldest put thy name there. *2 Ch.* **6: 19, 20.**

Now therefore arise, O Lord God, into thy resting place, thou, and the ark of thy strength: let thy priests, O Lord God, be clothed with salvation, and let thy saints rejoice in goodness. *2 Ch.* **6: 41.**

Solomon finished the house of the Lord, and the king's house: and all that came into Solomon's heart to make in the house of the Lord, and in his own house, he prosperously effected. *2 Ch.* **7: 11.**

The Lord appeared to Solomon by night, and said unto him, I have heard thy prayer, and have chosen this place to myself for an house of sacrifice. *2 Ch.* **7: 12.**

Now have I chosen and sanctified this house, that my name may be there for ever: and mine eyes and mine heart shall be there perpetually. *2 Ch.* **7: 16.**

This house, which is high, shall be an astonishment to everyone that passeth by it; so that he shall say, Why hath the Lord done thus unto this land, and unto this house? *2 Ch.* **7: 21.**

It was at Jerusalem the feast of the dedication, and it was winter. And Jesus walked in the temple in Solomon's porch. *Jn.* **10: 22, 23.**

Howbeit the most High dwelleth not in temples made with hands. *Ac.* **7: 48.**

See also
Church, Building the; Church, the House of God.

Church, Divisions of

Their heart is divided. *Ho.* **10: 2.**

Every city or house divided against itself shall not stand. *Mat.* **12: 25.**

Is Christ divided? was Paul crucified for you? or were ye baptized in the name of Paul? *1 Co.* **1: 13.**

If any man seem to be contentious, we have no such custom, neither the churches of God. *1 Co.* **11: 16.**

I hear that there be divisions among you. *1 Co.* **11: 18.**

There are diversities of gifts, but the same Spirit. *1 Co.* **12: 4.**

There should be no schism in the body. *1 Co.* **12: 25.**

God is not the author of confusion, but of peace, as in all churches of the saints. *1 Co.* **14: 33.**

Let all things be done decently and in order. *1 Co.* **14: 40.**

See also
Church, Failure of; Division; Heresy; Sect.

Church, Failure of

How long shall I bear with this evil congregation, which murmur against me? *Nu.* **14: 27.**

I am ashamed and blush to lift up my face to thee, my God: for our iniquities are increased over our head. *Ezr.* **9: 8.**

The ungodly shall not stand in the judgment, nor sinners in the congregation of the righteous. *Ps.* **1: 5.**

I have hated the congregation of evil doers. *Ps.* **26: 5.**

She hath seen that the heathen entered into her sanctuary. *La.* **1: 10.**

Do not sound a trumpet before thee, as the hypocrites do in the synagogues. *Mat.* **6: 2.**

They . . . love the uppermost rooms at feasts, and the chief seats in the synagogues. *Mat.* **23: 56.**

Behold, the veil of the temple was rent in twain from the top to the bottom. *Mat.* **27: 51.**

There be some that trouble you, and would pervert the gospel of Christ. *Ga.* **1: 7.**

That day shall not come, except there come a falling away first. *2 Th.* **2: 3.**

That man of sin . . . opposeth and exalteth himself above all that is called God, or that is worshipped; so that he as God sitteth in the temple of God, shewing himself that he is God. *2 Th.* **2: 3, 4.**

There are many unruly and vain talkers, . . . whose mouths must be stopped. *Tit.* **1: 10, 11.**

Nevertheless, I have somewhat against thee, because thou hast left thy first love. *Re.* **2: 4.**

I know the blasphemy of them which say they are Jews, and are not, but are the synagogue of Satan. *Re.* **2: 9.**

I know thy works, that thou hast a name that thou livest, and art dead. *Re.* **3: 1.**

I have not found thy works perfect before God. *Re.* **3: 2.**

Remember therefore how thou hast received and heard, and hold fast, and repent. *Re.* **3: 3.**

If therefore thou shalt not watch, I will come on thee as a thief, and thou shalt not know what hour I will come upon thee. *Re.* **3: 3.**

I know thy works, that thou art neither cold nor hot: I would thou wert cold or hot. *Re.* **3: 15.**

Because thou sayest, I am rich, and increased with goods, and have need of nothing; and knowest not that thou art wretched, and miserable, and poor, and blind, and naked: I counsel thee to buy of me gold tried in the fire, that thou mayest be rich; and white raiment, that thou mayest be clothed, and that the shame of thy nakedness do not appear; and anoint thine eyes with eyesalve, that thou mayest see. *Re.* **3: 17, 18.**

See also
Church, Criticism of; Church, Divisions of; Church, Neglect of.

Church, Fellowship of

If two or three shall agree on earth as touching any thing that they shall ask, it shall be done for them of my Father which is in heaven. *Mat.* **18: 19.**

They continued stedfastly in the apostles' doctrine and fellowship, and in breaking of bread, and in prayers. *Ac.* **2: 42.**

God is faithful, by whom ye were called unto the fellowship of his Son Jesus Christ our Lord. *1 Co.* **1: 9.**

What fellowship hath righteousness with unrighteousness? and what communion hath light with darkness? *2 Co.* **6: 14.**

Praying us with much intreaty that we would receive the gift, and take upon us the fellowship of the ministering to the saints. *2 Co.* **8: 4.**

When James, Cephas, and John, who seemed to be pillars, perceived the grace that was given unto me, they gave to me and Barnabas the right hand of fellowship. *Ga.* **2: 9.**

Ye are no more strangers and foreigners, but fellowcitizens with the saints, and of the household of God. *Ep.* **2: 19.**

Let us do good unto all men, especially unto them that are of the household of faith. *Ga.* **6: 10.**

I thank my God upon every remembrance of you, . . . For your fellowship in the gospel from the first day until now. *Ph.* **1: 3, 5.**

If there be therefore . . . any fellowship of the Spirit, . . . Fulfil ye my joy. *Ph.* **2: 1, 2.**

Let brotherly love continue. *He.* **13: 1.**

Love the brotherhood. *1 Pe.* **2: 17.**

Truly our fellowship is with the Father, and with his Son Jesus Christ. *1 Jn.* **1: 3.**

See also
Church, Membership of.

Church, Glory of

The glory of the Lord appeared in the tabernacle of the congregation. *Nu.* **14: 10.**

How goodly are thy tents, O Jacob, and thy tabernacles, O Israel! *Nu.* **24: 5.**

The glory of the Lord had filled the house of God. *2 Ch.* **5: 14.**

The priests could not enter into the house of the Lord, because the glory of the Lord had filled the Lord's house. *2 Ch.* **7: 2.**

One thing have I desired of the Lord, that will I seek after; that I may dwell in the house of the Lord all the days of my life, to behold the beauty of the Lord, and to enquire in his temple. *Ps.* **27: 4.**

In his temple doth every one speak of his glory. *Ps.* **29: 9.**

How amiable are thy tabernacles, O Lord of hosts! *Ps.* **84: 1.**

It shall come to pass in the last days, that the mountain of the Lord's house shall be established in the top of the mountains, and shall be exalted above the hills; and all nations shall flow unto it. *Is.* **2: 2.**

I saw also the Lord sitting upon a throne, high and lifted up, and his train filled the temple. *Is.* **6: 1.**

He had seen a vision in the temple. *Lu.* **1: 22.**

Unto him be glory in the church by Jesus Christ, throughout all ages, world without end. Amen. *Ep.* **3: 21.**

That he might present it to himself a glorious church, nor having spot, or wrinkle, or any such thing; but that it should be holy and without blemish. *Ep.* **5: 27.**

Ye are come unto mount Sion, and unto the city of the living God, the heavenly Jerusalem, and to an innumerable company of angels. *He.* **12: 22.**

Ye are come . . . To the general assembly and church of the firstborn, which are written in heaven. *He.* **12: 22, 23.**

I heard a great voice out of the temple. *Re.* **16: 1.**

Church, Growth of

The Lord added to the church daily such as should be saved. *Ac.* **2: 47.**

The word of God increased; and the number of the disciples multiplied in Jerusalem greatly. *Ac.* **6: 7.**

The churches, . . . walking in the fear of the Lord, and in the comfort of the Holy Ghost, were multiplied. *Ac.* **9: 31.**

So were the churches established in the faith, and increased in number daily. *Ac.* **16: 5.**

All the building fitly framed together groweth unto an holy temple in the Lord. *Ep.* **2: 21.**

Church, Head of

In this place is one greater than the temple. *Mat.* **12: 6.**

He spake of the temple of his body. *Jn.* **2: 21.**

God . . . hath put all things under his feet, and gave him to be the head over all things to the church, Which is his body, the fulness of him that filleth all in all. *Ep.* **1: 17, 22, 23.**

Christ is the head of the church. *Ep.* **5: 23.**

The church is subject unto Christ. *Ep.* **5: 24.**

This is a great mystery: but I speak concerning Christ and the church. *Ep.* **5: 32.**

He is the head of the body, the church. *Col.* **1: 18.**

For his body's sake, which is the church. *Col.* **1: 24.**

Christ is not entered into the holy places made with hands, which are the figures of the true; but into heaven itself. *He.* **9: 24.**

All the churches shall know that I am he which searcheth the reins and hearts. *Re.* **2: 23.**

I Jesus have sent mine angel to testify unto you these things in the churches. *Re.* **22: 16.**

Church, the House of God

Surely the Lord is in this place; and I knew it not. *Ge.* **28: 16.**

How dreadful is this place! this is none other but the house of God, and this is the gate of heaven. *Ge.* **28: 17.**

The glory of the Lord had filled the house of God. *2 Ch.* **5: 14.**

The Lord is in his holy temple. *Ps.* **11: 4.**

God standeth in the congregation of the mighty. *Ps.* **82: 1.**

God is greatly to be feared in the assembly of the saints. *Ps.* **89: 7.**

I dwell in the high and holy place, with him also that is of a contrite and humble spirit. *Is.* **57: 15.**

The Lord is in his holy temple: let all the earth keep silence before him. *Hab.* **2: 20.**

He . . . was in the church in the wilderness. *Ac.* **7: 38.**

Know ye not that ye are the temple of God, and that the Spirit of God dwelleth in you? *1 Co.* **3: 16.**

The house of God, which is the church of the living God, the pillar and ground of the truth. *1 Ti.* **3: 15.**

I saw no temple therein: for the Lord God Almighty and the Lamb are the temple of it. *Re.* **21: 22.**

See also

Church, Dedication of; Shrine; Synagogue; Tabernacle; Temple.

Church, Love toward

We shall be satisfied with the goodness of thy house, even of thy holy temple. *Ps.* **65: 4.**

How amiable are thy tabernacles, O Lord of hosts! *Ps.* **84: 1.**

My soul longeth, yea, even fainteth for the courts of the Lord: my heart and my flesh crieth out for the living God. *Ps.* **84: 2.**

Those that be planted in the house of the Lord shall flourish in the courts of our God. *Ps.* **92: 13.**

They, continuing daily with one accord in the temple, and breaking bread from house to house, did eat their meat with gladness and singleness of heart. *Ac.* **2: 46.**

Phebe our sister, which is a servant of the church. *Ro.* **16: 1.**

Christ also loved the church, and gave himself for it. *Ep.* **5: 25.**

No man ever yet hated his own flesh; but nourisheth and cherisheth it, even as the Lord the church. *Ep.* **5: 29.**

See that ye love one another with a pure heart fervently. *1 Pe.* **1: 22.**

Love the brotherhood. *1 Pe.* **2: 17.**

Love not the world, neither the things that are in the world. *1 Jn.* **2: 15.**

This commandment have we from him, That he who loveth God love his brother also. *1 Jn.* **4: 21.**

We love the children of God, when we love God, and keep his commandments. *1 Jn.* **5: 2.**

Thou holdest fast my name, and hast not denied my faith. *Re.* **2: 13.**

See also

Church, Loyalty to.

Church, Loyalty to

The seventh day is the sabbath of the Lord thy God. *Ex.* **20: 10.**

In the midst of the congregation will I praise thee. *Ps.* **22: 22.**

Blessed is the man that . . . keepeth the sabbath. *Is.* **56: 2.**

As his custom was, he went into the synagogue on the sabbath day. *Lu.* **4: 16.**

Whereupon, O king Agrippa, I was not disobedient unto the heavenly vision. *Ac.* **26: 19.**

Be ye therefore followers of God, as dear children. *Ep.* **5: 1.**

The church is subject unto Christ. *Ep.* **5: 24.**

Let your conversation be as it becometh the gospel of Christ: that whether I come and see you, or else be absent, I may hear of your affairs, that ye stand fast in one spirit. *Ph.* **1: 27.**

Ye, brethren, became followers of the churches of God. *1 Th.* **2: 14.**

I know thy works, and thy labour, and thy patience, and how thou canst not bear them which are evil: and thou hast tried them which say they are apostles, and are not, and hast found them liars: And hast borne, and hast patience, and for my name's sake hast laboured, and hast not fainted. *Re.* **2: 2, 3.**

Fear none of those things which thou shalt suffer. *Re.* **2: 10.**

Be thou faithful unto death, and I will give thee a crown of life. *Re.* **2: 10.**

To him that overcometh will I give to eat of the hidden manna. *Re.* **2: 17.**

I know thy works, and charity, and service, and faith, and thy patience, and thy works; and the last to be more than the first. *Re.* **2: 19.**

That which ye have already hold fast till I come. *Re.* **2: 25.**

He that overcometh, and keepeth my works unto the end, to him will I give power over the nations. *Re.* **2: 26.**

I will give him the morning star. *Re.* **2: 28.**

He that overcometh, the same shall be clothed in white raiment; and I will not blot out his name out of the book of life, but I will confess his name before my Father, and before his angels. *Re.* **3: 5.**

Because thou hast kept the word of my patience, I also will keep thee from the hour of temptation, which shall come upon all the world, to try them that dwell upon the earth. *Re.* **3: 10.**

Hold thou fast that which thou hast, that no man take thy crown. *Re.* **3: 11.**

Him that overcometh will I make a pillar in the temple of my God, and he shall go no more out: and I will write upon him the name of my God, and the name of the city of my God, which is new Jerusalem, which cometh down out of heaven from my God: and I will write upon him my new name. *Re.* **3: 12.**

To him that overcometh will I grant to sit with me in my throne, even as I also overcame, and am set down with my Father in his throne. *Re.* **3: 22.**

See also
Church, Love toward.

Church, Membership of

That I may dwell in the house of the Lord all the days of my life. *Ps.* **27: 4.**

O magnify the Lord with me, and let us exalt his name together. *Ps.* **34: 3.**

Those that be planted in the house of the Lord shall flourish in the courts of our God. *Ps.* **92: 13.**

They brought him to Jerusalem, to present him to the Lord. *Lu.* **2: 22.**

Ye also are become dead to the law by the body of Christ; that ye should be married to another, even to him who is raised from the dead, that we should bring forth fruit unto God. *Ro.* **7: 4.**

The eye cannot say unto the hand, I have no need of thee: nor again the head to the feet, I have no need of you. *1 Co.* **12: 21.**

I am jealous over you with godly jealousy: for I have espoused you to one husband, that I may present you as a chaste virgin to Christ. *2 Co.* **11: 2.**

There is one body, and one Spirit, even as ye are called in one hope of your calling; one Lord, one faith, one baptism. *Ep.* **4: 4, 5.**

We are members of his body. *Ep.* **5: 30.**

Ye are come . . . to an innumerable company of angels. *He.* **12: 22.**

Ye are come . . . to the spirits of just men. *He.* **12: 22, 23.**

See also
Christianity; Church; Church, Fellowship of; Member.

Church, Message of

The just shall live by his faith. *Hab.* **2: 4.**

The Spirit of the Lord is upon me, because he hath anointed me to preach the gospel to the poor; he hath sent me to heal the brokenhearted, to preach deliverance to the captives, and recovering of sight to the blind, to set at liberty them that are bruised, To preach the acceptable year of the Lord. *Lu.* **4: 18, 19.**

Go thou and preach the kingdom of God. *Lu.* **9: 60.**

Daily in the temple, . . . they ceased not to teach and preach Jesus Christ. *Ac.* **5: 42.**

Opening and alleging, that Christ must needs have suffered. *Ac.* **17: 3.**

We preach Christ crucified. *1 Co.* **1: 23.**

He that speaketh in an unknown tongue edifieth himself; but he that prophesieth edifieth the church. *1 Co.* **14: 4.**

Greater is he that prophesieth than he that speaketh with tongues, except he interpret, that the church may receive edifying. *1 Co.* **14: 5.**

In the church I had rather speak five words with my understanding, that by my voice I might teach others also, than ten thousand words in an unknown tongue. *1 Co.* **14: 19.**

If therefore the whole church be come together into one place, and all speak with tongues, and there come in those that are unlearned, or unbelievers, will they not say that ye are mad? *1 Co.* **14: 23.**

When ye come together, every one of you hath a psalm, hath a doctrine, hath a tongue, hath a revelation, hath an interpretation. Let all things be done unto edifying. *1 Co.* **14: 26.**

If there be no interpreter, let him keep silence in the church; and let him speak to himself, and to God. *1 Co.* **14: 28.**

If any man preach any other gospel unto you than that ye have received, let him be accursed. *Ga.* **1: 9.**

The gospel of the uncircumcision was committed unto me, as the gospel of the circumcision was unto Peter. *Ga.* **2: 7.**

That which was from the beginning, which we have heard, which we have seen with our eyes, which we have looked upon, and our hands have handled, of the Word of life. *1 Jn.* **1: 1.**

That which we have seen and heard declare we unto you. *1 Jn.* **1: 3.**

He that hath an ear, let him hear what the Spirit saith unto the churches. *Re.* **2: 7.**

See also
Church, Mission of; Church, Ministry of.

Church, Ministry of

Seemeth it but a small thing unto you, that the God of Israel hath separated you from the congregation of Israel, to bring you near to himself to do the service of the tabernacle of the Lord, and to stand before the congregation to minister unto them? *Nu.* **16: 9.**

That the congregation of the Lord be not as sheep which have no shepherd. *Nu.* **27: 17.**

He stood before the altar of the Lord in the presence of all the congregation of Israel, and spread forth his hands. *2 Ch.* **6: 12.**

I have preached righteousness in the great congregation. *Ps.* **40: 9.**

The eyes of all them that were in the synagogue were fastened on him. *Lu.* **4: 20.**

He preached in the synagogues of Galilee. *Lu.* **4: 44.**

They were not able to resist the wisdom and the spirit by which he spake. *Ac.* **6: 10.**

He preached Christ in the synagogues, that he is the Son of God. *Ac.* **9: 20.**

It came to pass, that a whole year they assembled themselves with the church, and taught much people. *Ac.* **11: 26.**

There were in the church that was at Antioch certain prophets and teachers. *Ac.* **13: 1.**

When they had ordained them elders in every church, and had prayed with fasting, they commended them to the Lord, on whom they believed. *Ac.* **14: 23.**

He reasoned in the synagogue every sabbath. *Ac.* **18: 4.**

Take heed therefore unto yourselves, and to all the flock, over the which the Holy Ghost hath made you overseers, to feed the church of God, which he hath purchased with his own blood. *Ac.* **20: 28.**

I teach every where in every church. *1 Co. 4: 17.*

If all prophesy, and there come in one that believeth not, or one unlearned, he is convinced of all, he is judged of all: And thus are the secrets of his heart made manifest; and so falling down on his face he will worship God, and report that God is in you in truth. *1 Co. 14: 24, 25.*

They are the messengers of the churches, and the glory of Christ. *2 Co. 8: 23.*

That he might sanctify and cleanse it with the washing of water by the word. *Ep. 5: 26.*

Praying always . . . that utterance may be given unto me, that I may open my mouth boldly, to make known the mystery of the gospel. *Ep. 6: 18, 19.*

Do the work of an evangelist, make full proof of thy ministry. *2 Ti. 4: 5.*

He went and preached unto the spirits in prison. *1 Pe. 3: 19.*

See also

Church, Message of; Church, Mission of.

Church, Mission of

He shall feed his flock like a shepherd. *Is. 40: 11.*

If he shall neglect to hear them, tell it unto the church. *Mat. 18: 17.*

Confirming the souls of the disciples, and exhorting them to continue in the faith, and that we must through much tribulation enter into the kingdom of God. *Ac. 14: 22.*

When they were come, and had gathered the church together, they rehearsed all that God had done with them, and how he had opened the door of faith unto the Gentiles. *Ac. 14: 27.*

Being brought on their way by the church. *Ac. 15: 3.*

Then pleased it the apostles and elders, with the whole church, to send chosen men of their own company to Antioch. *Ac. 15: 22.*

God hath set some in the church, first apostles, secondarily prophets, thirdly teachers, after that miracles, then gifts of healing, helps, governments, diversities of tongues. *1 Co. 12: 28.*

To the intent that now unto the principalities and powers in heavenly places might be known by the church the manifold wisdom of God. *Ep. 3: 10.*

Teaching and admonishing one another in psalms and hymns and spiritual songs, singing with grace in your hearts to the Lord. *Col. 3: 16.*

Is any sick among you? let him call for the elders of the church. *Ja. 5: 14.*

See also

Church, Message of; Church, Ministry of.

Church, Neglect of

It will be, seeing ye rebel to day against the Lord, that to morrow he will be wroth with the whole congregation of Israel. *Jos. 22: 18.*

The man that wandereth out of the way of understanding shall remain in the congregation of the dead. *Pr. 21: 16.*

If any man defile the temple of God, him shall God destroy; for the temple of God is holy, which temple ye are. *1 Co. 3: 17.*

Despise ye the church of God? *1 Co. 11: 22.*

That day shall not come, except there come a falling away first. *2 Th. 2: 3.*

If a man know not how to rule his own house, how shall he take care of the church of God? *1 Ti. 3: 5.*

How shall we escape, if we neglect so great salvation. *He. 2: 3.*

Nevertheless, I have somewhat against thee, because thou hast left thy first love. *Re. 2: 4.*

I know thy works, that thou hast a name that thou livest, and art dead. *Re. 3: 1.*

Remember therefore how thou hast received and heard, and hold fast, and repent. *Re. 3: 3.*

I know thy works, that thou art neither cold nor hot: I would thou wert cold or hot. *Re. 3: 15.*

Because thou art lukewarm, and neither cold nor hot, I will spue thee out of my mouth. *Re. 3: 16.*

As many as I love, I rebuke and chasten: be zealous therefore, and repent. *Re. 3: 19.*

See also

Church, Absence from; Church, Failure of.

Church, Praise of

I will give thee thanks in the great congregation. *Ps. 35: 18.*

I had gone with the multitude, I went with them to the house of God, with the voice of joy and praise. *Ps. 42: 4.*

Yea, the sparrow hath found an house, and the swallow a nest for herself, where she may lay her young, even thine altars, O Lord of hosts, my King, and my God. *Ps. 84: 3.*

Blessed are they that dwell in thy house: they will be still praising thee. *Ps. 84: 4.*

A day in thy courts is better than a thousand. *Ps. 84: 10.*

I had rather be a doorkeeper in the house of my God, than to dwell in the tents of wickedness. *Ps. 84: 10.*

The heavens shall praise thy wonders, O Lord: thy faithfulness also in the congregation of the saints. *Ps. 89: 5.*

Let them exalt him also in the congregation of the people, and praise him in the assembly of the elders. *Ps. 107: 32.*

I will praise the Lord with my whole heart, in the assembly of the upright, and in the congregation. *Ps. 111: 1.*

He . . . saluted the Church. *Ac. 18: 22.*

Greet the church that is in their house. *Ro. 16: 5.*

The churches of Christ salute you. *Ro. 16: 16.*

We have sent with him the brother, whose praise is in the gospel throughout all the churches. *2 Co. 8: 18.*

Church, Strength of

Thou art Peter, and upon this rock I will build my church. *Mat. 16: 18.*

The gates of hell shall not prevail against it *Mat. 16: 18.*

Thou hast a little strength, and hast kept my word, and hast not denied my name. *Re. 3: 8.*

Church, Support of

Of all that thou shalt give me I will surely give the tenth unto thee. *Ge. 28: 22.*

He went through Syria and Cilicia, confirming the churches. *Ac. 15: 41.*

Forasmuch as ye are zealous of spiritual gifts,

seek that ye may excel to the edifying of the church. *1 Co.* 14: 12.

In a great trial of affliction the abundance of their joy and their deep poverty abounded unto the riches of their liberality. *2 Co.* 8: 2.

The care of all the churches. *2 Co.* 11: 28.

Church, Worship in

All the congregation blessed the Lord God of their fathers, and bowed down their heads, and worshipped the Lord, and the king. *1 Ch.* 29: 20.

All the congregation said, Amen, and praised the Lord. *Ne.* 5: 13.

My praise shall be of thee in the great congregation. *Ps.* 22: 25.

We have thought of thy lovingkindness, O God, in the midst of thy temple. *Ps.* 48: 9.

We thy people and sheep of thy pasture will give thee thanks for ever. *Ps.* 79: 13.

Let them exalt him also in the congregation of the people, and praise him in the assembly of the elders. *Ps.* 107: 32.

Lord, teach us to pray, as John also taught his disciples. *Lu.* 11: 1.

Two men went up into the temple to pray. *Lu.* 18: 10.

Ye worship ye know not what: we know what we worship. *Jn.* 4: 22.

Praising God, and having favour with all the people. *Ac.* 2: 47.

Peter therefore was kept in prison: but prayer was made without ceasing of the church unto God for him. *Ac.* 12: 5.

Every man praying or prophesying, having his head covered, dishonoureth his head. *1 Co.* 11: 4.

Every woman that prayeth or prophesieth with her head uncovered dishonoureth her head. *1 Co.* 11: 5.

Falling down on his face he will worship God. *1 Co.* 14: 25.

Speaking to yourselves in psalms and hymns and spiritual songs, singing and making melody in your heart to the Lord. *Ep.* 5: 19.

I exhort therefore, that, first of all, supplications, prayers, intercessions, and giving of thanks, be made for all men; For kings, and for all that are in authority. *1 Ti.* 2: 1, 2.

I will therefore that men pray every where, lifting up holy hands. *1 Ti.* 2: 8.

I will declare thy name unto my brethren, in the midst of the church will I sing praise unto thee. *He.* 2: 12.

Circle

The waves of death compassed me. *2 S.* 22: 5.

He walketh in the circuit of heaven. *Jb.* 22: 14.

His going forth is from the end of the heaven, and his circuit unto the ends of it. *Ps.* 19: 6.

Innumerable evils have compassed me about. *Ps.* 40: 12.

Walk about Zion, and go round about her. *Ps.* 48: 12.

All nations compassed me about. *Ps.* 118: 10.

As the mountains are round about Jerusalem, so the Lord is round about his people from henceforth even for ever. *Ps.* 125: 2.

When he prepared the heavens, I was there: when he set a compass upon the face of the depth. *Pr.* 8: 27.

Righteousness shall be the girdle of his loins, and faithfulness the girdle of his reins. *Is.* 11: 5.

It is he that sitteth upon the circle of the earth. *Is.* 40: 22.

We . . . are compassed about with so great a cloud of witnesses. *He.* 12: 1.

See also
Girdle.

Circumcision

Ye shall circumcise the flesh of your foreskin; and it shall be a token of the covenant betwixt me and you. *Ge.* 17: 11.

Circumcise therefore the foreskin of your heart. *De.* 10: 16.

The Lord thy God will circumcise thine heart, and the heart of thy seed. *De.* 30: 6.

Circumcise yourselves to the Lord. *Je.* 4: 4.

If thou be a breaker of the law, thy circumcision is made uncircumcision. *Ro.* 2: 25.

Circumcision is that of the heart, in the spirit, and not in the letter. *Ro.* 2: 29.

What profit is there of circumcision? Much every way. *Ro.* 3: 1, 2.

Circumcision is nothing, and uncircumcision is nothing, but the keeping of the commandments of God. *1 Co.* 7: 19.

For in Jesus Christ neither circumcision availeth any thing, nor uncircumcision; but faith which worketh by love. *Ga.* 5: 6.

In Christ Jesus neither circumcision availeth any thing, nor uncircumcision, but a new creature. *Ga.* 6: 15.

Citizenship

Let us play the men for our people, and for the cities of our God. *2 S.* 10: 12.

Lord, who shall abide in thy tabernacle? who shall dwell in thy holy hill? *Ps.* 15: 1.

Blessed is the nation whose God is the Lord. *Ps.* 33: 12.

Of Zion it shall be said, This and that man was born in her: and the highest himself shall establish her. *Ps.* 87: 5.

Jerusalem is builded as a city that is compact together. *Ps.* 122: 3.

When it goeth well with the righteous, the city rejoiceth. *Pr.* 11: 10.

By the blessing of the upright the city is exalted. *Pr.* 11: 11.

They shall repair the waste cities. *Is.* 61: 4.

A citizen of no mean city. *Ac.* 21: 39.

Ye are . . . fellowcitizens with the saints, and of the household of God. *Ep.* 2: 19.

See also
City; Nation.

City

Blessed shalt thou be in the city. . . . Cursed shalt thou be in the city. *De.* 28: 3, 16.

The cry of the city went up to heaven. *1 S.* 5: 12.

God . . . will build the cities of Judah. *Ps.* 69: 35..

They found no city to dwell in. *Ps.* 107: 4.

Except the Lord keep the city, the watchman waketh but in vain. *Ps.* 127: 1.

Seek the peace of the city whither I have caused you to be carried away captives, and pray unto the Lord for it: for in the peace thereof shall ye have peace. *Je.* 29: 7.

The city . . . weepeth sore in the night, and

her tears are on her cheeks. *La.* 1: 2.

Now, thou son of man, wilt thou judge, wilt thou judge the bloody city? *Eze.* 22: 2.

Thus saith the Lord God, The city sheddeth blood in the midst of it. *Eze.* 22: 3.

A city that is set on an hill cannot be hid. *Mat.* 5: 14.

Jesus went about all the cities and villages. *Mat.* 9: 35.

Unto you is born this day in the city of David a Saviour. *Lu.* 2: 11.

They . . . rose up, and thrust him out of the city. *Lu.* 4: 28, 29.

He beheld the city, and wept over it. *Lu.* 19: 41.

The place where Jesus was crucified was nigh to the city. *Jn.* 19: 20.

Arise, and go into the city, and it shall be told thee what thou must do. *Ac.* 9: 6.

The Holy Ghost witnesseth in every city. *Ac.* 20: 23.

In perils in the city. *2 Co.* 11: 26.

Here we have no continuing city. *He.* 13: 14.
See also
Citizenship; Civilization; Town.

City, the Holy
Glorious things are spoken of thee, O city of God. *Ps.* 87: 3.

They shall call thee, The city of the Lord, The Zion of the Holy One of Israel. *Is.* 60: 14.

A city which hath foundations, whose builder and maker is God. *He.* 11: 10.

Ye are come unto mount Sion, and unto the city of the living God, the heavenly Jerusalem. *He.* 12: 22.

I John saw the holy city, new Jerusalem, coming down from God out of heaven, prepared as a bride adorned for her husband. *Re.* 21: 2.
See also
Civilization; Jerusalem; Zion.

City, the Ideal
Let us build us a city and a tower, whose top may reach unto heaven. *Ge.* 11: 4.

We have a strong city, salvation will God appoint for walls and bulwarks. *Is.* 26: 1.

I will also make thy officers peace, and thine exactors righteousness. . . . Thou shalt call thy walls Salvation, and thy gates Praise. *Is.* 60: 17, 18.

Is this the city that men call The perfection of beauty, The joy of the whole earth? *La.* 2: 15.

I . . . will dwell in the midst of Jerusalem: and Jerusalem shall be called a city of truth. *Zch.* 8: 3.

The streets of the city shall be full of boys and girls playing in the streets thereof. *Zch.* 8: 5.

He carried me away in the spirit to a great and high mountain, and shewed me that great city, the holy Jerusalem, descending out of heaven from God. *Re.* 21: 10.
See also
City, the Holy; Civilization; Jerusalem; Zion.

Civilization
I will make of thee a great nation. *Ge.* 12: 2.

Ye shall be unto me a kingdom of priests, and an holy nation. *Ex.* 19: 6.

Blessed is the nation whose God is the Lord. *Ps.* 33: 12.

As we have heard, so have we seen in the city of the Lord of hosts, in the city of our God: God will establish it for ever. *Ps.* 48: 8.

Glorious things are spoken of thee, O city of God. *Ps.* 87: 3.

Happy is that people, that is in such a case: yea, happy is that people, whose God is the Lord. *Ps.* 144: 15.

Righteousness exalteth a nation. *Pr.* 14: 34.

Nation shall not lift up sword against nation, neither shall they learn war any more. *Is.* 2: 4.

Is this the city that men call The perfection of beauty, The joy of the whole earth? *La.* 2: 15.

I . . . will save them by the Lord their God, and will not save them by bow, nor by sword, nor by battle, by horses, nor by horsemen. *Ho.* 1: 7.

Many nations shall come, and say, Come, and let us go up to the mountain of the Lord; . . . and he will teach us of his ways, and we will walk in his paths. *Mi.* 4: 2.

The streets of the city shall be full of boys and girls playing in the streets thereof. *Zch.* 8: 5.

The kingdom of God shall be taken from you, and given to a nation bringing forth the fruits thereof. *Mat.* 21: 43.

I am . . . a citizen of no mean city. *Ac.* 21: 39.

I am debtor both to the Greeks, and to the Barbarians; both to the wise, and to the unwise. *Ro.* 1: 14.

Jerusalem which is above is free, which is the mother of us all. *Ga.* 4: 26.

He looked for a city which hath foundations, whose builder and maker is God. *He.* 11: 10.

Ye are come unto mount Sion, and unto the city of the living God, the heavenly Jerusalem. *He.* 12: 22.

The city had no need of the sun, neither of the moon, to shine in it: for the glory of God did lighten it. *Re.* 21: 23.
See also
Age, the Coming; Age, the Golden; City; City, the Holy; City, the Ideal; Jerusalem; Land, the Promised; Millenium; Nation; Nation, the Greatness of; Nations, League of; Nations, United; Progress; Refinement; Zion.

Clamor
There is a noise of war in the camp. *Ex.* 32: 17.

Wherefore is this noise of the city being in an uproar? *1 K.* 1: 41.

Which stilleth the noise of the seas, the noise of their waves, and the tumult of the people. *Ps.* 65: 7.

The tumult of those that rise up against thee increaseth continually. *Ps.* 74: 23.

A foolish woman is clamorous. *Pr.* 9: 13.

Thou hast heard, O my soul, the sound of the trumpet, the alarm of war. *Je.* 4: 19.

They shall make great noise by reason of the multitude of men. *Mi.* 2: 12.

They shall . . . make a noise as through wine. *Zch.* 9: 15.

All Jerusalem was in an uproar. *Ac.* 21: 31.

God is not the author of confusion. *1 Co.* 14: 33.

See also

Confusion; Din; Disorder; Hue; Noise; Tumult; Turmoil.

Class

Wealth maketh many friends. *Pr.* 19: 4.

How hardly shall they that have riches enter into the kingdom of God! *Mk.* 10: 23.

So is he that layeth up treasure for himself, and is not rich toward God. *Lu.* 12: 21.

He is our peace, who . . . hath broken down the middle wall of partition between us. *Ep.* 2: 14.

Be kindly affectioned one to another with brotherly love. *Ro.* 12: 10.

Whatsoever good thing any man doeth, the same shall he receive of the Lord, whether he be bond or free. *Ep.* 6: 8.

Are ye not then partial in yourselves, and are become judges of evil thoughts? *Ja.* 2: 4.

Hath not God chosen the poor of this world rich in faith, and heirs of the kingdom? *Ja.* 2: 5.

Ye have despised the poor. *Ja.* 2: 6.

Do not rich men oppress you, and draw you before the judgment seats? *Ja.* 2: 6.

If ye have respect to persons, ye commit sin. *Ja.* 2: 9.

Go to now, ye rich men, weep and howl for your miseries that shall come upon you. *Ja.* 5: 1.

See also

Caste; Equality; Equality, Racial; Persons, Respect of; Society; Wealth; Worldliness.

Clay

The Lord God formed man of the dust of the ground. *Ge.* 2: 7.

Behold, I am according to thy wish in God's stead: I also am formed out of the clay. *Jb.* 33: 6.

He brought me up also out of an horrible pit, out of the miry clay, and set my feet upon a rock. *Ps.* 40: 2.

Surely your turning of things upside down shall be esteemed as the potter's clay: for shall the work say of him that made it, He made me not? *Is.* 29: 16.

Shall the clay say to him that fashioneth it, What makest thou? or thy work, He hath no hands? *Is.* 45: 9.

We are the clay, and thou our potter; and we all are the work of thy hand. *Is.* 64: 8.

Behold, as the clay is in the potter's hand, so are ye in mine hand, O house of Israel. *Je.* 18: 6.

Hath not the potter power over the clay, of the same lump to make one vessel unto honour, and another unto dishonour? *Ro.* 9: 21.

We have this treasure in earthen vessels. 2 *Co.* 4: 7.

See also

Earth; Potter.

Cleanness

With the pure thou wilt shew thyself pure. 2 *S.* 22: 27.

The commandment of the Lord is pure. *Ps.* 19: 8.

The fear of the Lord is clean, enduring for ever. *Ps.* 19: 9.

Who shall ascend into the hill of the Lord? or who shall stand in his holy place? He that hath clean hands, and a pure heart. *Ps.* 24: 3, 4.

Truly God is good to Israel, even to such as are of a clean heart. *Ps.* 73: 1.

Shall I count them pure with the wicked balances? *Mi.* 6: 11.

Behold, all things are clean unto you. *Lu.* 11: 41.

Keep thyself pure. 1 *Ti.* 5: 22.

I stir up your pure minds by way of remembrance. 2 *Pe.* 3: 1.

See also

Chastity; Clearness; Innocence; Purity.

Cleansing

Who can understand his errors? cleanse thou me from secret faults. *Ps.* 19: 12.

Wash me, and I shall be whiter than snow. *Ps.* 51: 7.

As for our transgressions, thou shalt purge them away. *Ps.* 65: 3.

Wherewithal shall a young man cleanse his way? by taking heed thereto according to thy word. *Ps.* 119: 9.

Let thy garments be always white. *Ec.* 9: 8.

Wash you, make you clean; put away the evil of your doings from before mine eyes. *Is.* 1: 16.

I will turn my hand upon thee, and purely purge away thy dross. *Is.* 1: 25.

Thine iniquity is taken away, and thy sin purged. *Is.* 6: 7.

Wash thine heart from wickedness, that thou mayest be saved. *Je.* 4: 14.

Then will I sprinkle clean water upon you, and ye shall be clean. *Eze.* 36: 25.

In that day there shall be a fountain opened to the house of David. *Zch.* 13: 1.

He shall . . . purge them as gold and silver, that they may offer unto the Lord an offering in righteousness. *Mal.* 3: 3.

Lord, if thou wilt, thou canst make me clean. *Mat.* 8: 2.

Ye make clean the outside of the cup and of the platter, but within they are full of extortion and excess. *Mat.* 23: 25.

Many lepers were in Israel in the time of Eliseus the prophet; and none of them was cleansed, saving Naaman the Syrian. *Lu.* 4: 27.

And when he had made a scourge of small cords, he drove them all out of the temple, and the sheep, and the oxen; and poured out the changers' money, and overthrew the tables. *Jn.* 2: 15.

Jesus saith to him, He that is washed needeth not save to wash his feet. *Jn.* 13: 10.

What God hath cleansed, that call not thou common. *Ac.* 10: 15.

If a man therefore purge himself from these, he shall be a vessel unto honour, sanctified, and meet for the master's use. 2 *Ti.* 2: 21.

How much more shall the blood of Christ, who through the eternal Spirit offered himself without spot to God, purge your conscience from dead works to serve the living God? *He.* 9: 14.

Our hearts sprinkled from an evil conscience, and our bodies washed with pure water. *He.* 10: 22.

Cleanse your hands, ye sinners. *Ja.* 4: 8.

If we confess our sins, he is faithful and just

to forgive us our sins, and to cleanse us from all unrighteousness. *1 Jn.* 1: 9.

Every man that hath this hope in him purifieth himself, even as he is pure. *1 Jn.* 3: 3.
See also
Purification.

Clearness

As the tender grass springing out of the earth by clear shining after rain. *2 S.* 23: 4.

Thine age shall be clearer than the noonday. *Jb.* 11: 17.

The way of the righteous is made plain. *Pr.* 15: 19.

Fair as the moon, clear as the sun. *S. of S.* 6: 10.

It shall come to pass in that day, that the light shall not be clear, nor dark. *Zch.* 14: 6.

The string of his tongue was loosed, and he spake plain. *Mk.* 7: 35.

If I pray in an unknown tongue, my spirit prayeth, but my understanding is unfruitful. *1 Co.* 14: 14.

Having the glory of God: and her light was like unto a stone most precious, even like a jasper stone, clear as crystal. *Re.* 21: 11.
See also
Light.

Clear-Sightedness

Lead me in a plain path. *Ps.* 27: 11.

They are all plain to him that understandeth, and right to them that find knowledge. *Pr.* 8: 9.

Woe unto them that call evil good, and good evil! *Is.* 5: 20.

Then shalt thou see clearly to cast out the mote out of thy brother's eye. *Mat.* 7: 5.

He was restored, and saw every man clearly. *Mk.* 8: 25.
See also
Discernment; Eye; Sight; Vision.

Clemency

I am not worthy of the least of all the mercies, and of all the truth, which thou hast shewed unto thy servant. *Ge.* 32: 10.

Surely goodness and mercy shall follow me all the days of my life. *Ps.* 23: 6.

Blessed are the merciful: for they shall obtain mercy. *Mat.* 5: 7.

Be ye therefore merciful, as your Father also is merciful. *Lu.* 6: 36.

By kindness. *2 Co.* 6: 6.

Put on therefore, as the elect of God, holy and beloved, bowels of mercies. *Col.* 3: 12.

Let us therefore come boldly unto the throne of grace, that we may obtain mercy, and find grace to help in time of need. *He.* 4: 16.

The Lord is very pitiful, and of tender mercy. *Ja.* 5: 11.
See also
Charity; Christ, Compassion of; Gentleness; God, Compassion of; God, Mercy of; Indulgence; Kindness; Lovingkindness; Mercy; Pity; Tenderness.

Clergy

Because the preacher was wise, he still taught the people knowledge. *Ec.* 12: 9.

The preacher sought to find out acceptable words. *Ec.* 12: 10.

He shall feed his flock like a shepherd. *Is.* 40: 11.

I have put my words in thy mouth. *Is.* 51: 16.

The priests said not, Where is the Lord? *Je.* 2: 8.

The pastors also transgressed against me, and the prophets prophesied by Baal, and walked after things that do not profit. *Je.* 2: 8.

I will give you pastors according to mine heart, which shall feed you with knowledge and understanding. *Je.* 3: 15.

Many pastors have destroyed my vineyard. *Je.* 12: 10.

Woe be unto the pastors that destroy and scatter the sheep of my pasture! *Je.* 23: 1.

There shall be, like people, like priest. *Ho.* 4: 9.

How shall they hear without a preacher? *Ro.* 10: 14.

He gave some, apostles; and some, prophets; and some, evangelists; and some, pastors and teachers. *Ep.* 4: 11.

I am ordained a preacher. *1 Ti.* 2: 7.

Do the work of an evangelist. *2 Ti.* 4: 5.
See also
Ministry; Missionary; Pastor; Preaching; Priesthood; Sermon; Shepherd; Teaching.

Climax

In the vine there were three branches; and it was as though it budded, and her blossoms shot forth; and the clusters thereof brought forth ripe grapes. *Ge.* 40: 10.

Repent ye: for the kingdom of heaven is at hand. *Mat.* 3: 2.

He that endureth to the end shall be saved. *Mat.* 10: 22.

The harvest is the end of the world; and the reapers are the angels. *Mat.* 13: 39.

First the blade, then the ear, after that the full corn in the ear. *Mk.* 4: 28.

The kingdom of God . . . is like a grain of mustard seed, 'which, when it is sown in the earth, is less than all the seeds that be in the earth: But when it is sown, it groweth up, and becometh greater than all herbs, and shooteth out great branches. *Mk.* 4: 30-32.

There be some standing here, which shall not taste of death, till they see the kingdom of God. *Lu.* 9: 27.

Lift up your eyes, and look on the fields; for they are white already to harvest. *Jn.* 4: 35.

Eye hath not seen, nor ear heard, neither have entered into the heart of man, the things which God hath prepared for them that love him. *1 Co.* 2: 9.

I am Alpha and Omega, the beginning and the end. *Re.* 21: 6.
See also
Age, the Golden; End; Fruit; Fulfilment; God, Kingdom of; Harvest; Heaven, Kingdom of; Kingdom, the Coming; Millenium; Reaping; Termination.

Climbing

Behold a ladder set up on the earth, and the top of it reached to heaven: and behold the angels of God ascending and descending on it. *Ge.* 28: 12.

Who shall ascend into the hill of the Lord? *Ps.* 24: 3.

Though they climb up to heaven, thence will I bring them down. *Am.* 9: 2.

He ran before, and climbed up into a sycomore tree to see him. *Lu.* 19: 4.

Hereafter ye shall see heaven open, and the angels of God ascending and descending upon the Son of man. *Jn.* 1: 51.

He that entereth not by the door into the sheepfold, but climbeth up some other way, the same is a thief and a robber. *Jn.* 10: 1.

See also

Ascension; Hill; Mountain.

Clothes

Who coverest thyself with light as with a garment. *Ps.* 104: 2.

She maketh herself coverings of tapestry; her clothing is silk and purple. *Pr.* 31: 22.

Can a maid forget her ornaments, or a bride her attire? yet my people have forgotten me days without number. *Je.* 2: 32.

Even Solomon in all his glory was not arrayed like one of these. *Mat.* 6: 29.

If God so clothe the grass of the field, which to day is, and to morrow is cast into the oven, shall he not much more clothe you, O ye of little faith. *Mat.* 6: 30.

Wherewithal shall we be clothed? *Mat.* 6: 31.

If I may but touch his garment, I shall be made whole. *Mat.* 9: 21.

Naked, and ye clothed me. *Mat.* 25: 36.

Beware of the scribes, which love to go in long clothing. *Mk.* 12: 38.

As he went, they spread their clothes in the way. *Lu.* 19: 36.

Now they have no cloke for their sin. *Jn.* 15: 22.

The soldiers, when they had crucified Jesus, took his garments, and made four parts, to every soldier a part; and also his coat. *Jn.* 19: 23.

I will . . . that women adorn themselves in modest apparel, with shamefacedness and sobriety; not with broided hair, or gold, or pearls, or costly array. *1 Ti.* 2: 8, 9.

Be clothed with humility. *1 Pe.* 5: 5.

See also

Apparel; Attire; Coat; Garment; Raiment; Robe.

Cloud

Clouds and darkness are round about him. *Ps.* 97: 2.

I do set my bow in the cloud. *Ge.* 9: 13.

The Lord went before them by day in a pillar of cloud. *Ex.* 13: 21.

It was a cloud and darkness to them, but it gave light by night to these. *Ex.* 14: 20.

The glory of the Lord appeared in the cloud. *Ex.* 16: 10.

It came to pass in the mean while, that the heaven was black with clouds and wind, and there was a great rain. *1 K.* 18: 45.

He bindeth up the waters in his thick clouds. *Jb.* 26: 8.

With clouds he covereth the light; and commandeth it not to shine by the cloud that cometh betwixt. *Jb.* 36: 32.

Who can number the clouds in wisdom? *Jb.* 38: 37.

Thy faithfulness reacheth unto the clouds. *Ps.* 36: 5.

Who maketh the clouds his chariot. *Ps.* 104: 3.

He spread a cloud for a covering; and fire to give light in the night. *Ps.* 105: 39.

The clouds drop down the dew. *Pr.* 3: 20.

Behold, the Lord rideth upon a swift cloud. *Is.* 19: 1.

I have blotted out, as a thick cloud, thy transgressions, and, as a cloud, thy sins. *Is.* 44: 22.

The day of the Lord is near, a cloudy day. *Eze.* 30: 3.

Your goodness is as a morning cloud, and as the early dew it goeth away. *Ho.* 6: 4.

When ye see a cloud rise out of the west, straightway ye say, There cometh a shower; and so it is. *Lu.* 12: 54.

Then shall they see the Son of man coming in a cloud with power and great glory. *Lu.* 21: 27.

Clouds they are without water. *Jude* 1: 12.

Coat

Unto Adam also and to his wife did the Lord God make coats of skins, and clothed them. *Ge.* 3: 21.

He made him a coat of many colours. *Ge.* 37: 3.

If any man will . . . take away thy coat, let him have thy cloke also. *Mat.* 5: 40.

Provide . . . neither two coats, neither shoes, nor yet staves. *Mat.* 10: 9, 10.

He that hath two coats, let him impart to him that hath none. *Lu.* 3: 11.

Now they have no cloke for their sin. *Jn.* 15: 22.

Now the coat was without seam, woven from the top throughout. *Jn.* 19: 23.

Not using your liberty for a cloke of maliciousness, but as the servants of God. *1 Pe.* 2: 16.

Come up hither, and I will shew thee things which must be hereafter. *Re.* 4: 1.

See also

Apparel; Attire; Clothes, Garment.

Coercion

Thou shalt give it me now: and if not, I will take it by force. *1 S.* 2: 16.

Behold, he taketh away, who can hinder him? *Jb.* 9: 12.

Thy hand presseth me sore. *Ps.* 38: 2.

Do no violence to the stranger, the fatherless, nor the widow, neither shed innocent blood in this place. *Je.* 22: 3.

Behold, I am pressed under you, as a cart is pressed that is full of sheaves. *Am.* 2: 13.

For thy violence against thy brother Jacob shame shall cover thee. *Ob.* 10.

Do violence to no man. *Lu.* 3: 14.

See also

Compulsion; Constraint; Enforcement; Force; Might; Power; Restraint; Strength; Violence.

Coherence

Thou shalt fear the Lord thy God; him shalt thou serve, and to him shalt thou cleave. *De.* 10: 20.

The soul of Jonathan was knit with the soul of David. *1 S.* 18: 1.

When the dust groweth into hardness, and the clods cleave fast together. *Jb.* 38: 38.

There is a friend that sticketh closer than a brother. *Pr.* 18: 24.

Woe unto them that join house to house, that lay field to field. *Is.* 5: 8.

Many nations shall be joined to the Lord in that day, and shall be my people. *Zch.* 2: 11.

What therefore God hath joined together, let not man put asunder. *Mk.* 10: 9.

He . . . exhorted them all, that with purpose of heart they should cleave unto the Lord. *Ac.* 11: 23.

Cleave to that which is good. *Ro.* 12: 9.

He that is joined unto the Lord is one spirit. *1 Co.* 6: 17.

The whole body fitly joined together and compacted by that which every joint supplieth, according to the effectual working in the measure of every part. *Ep.* 4: 16.

See also

Adhesion; Attachment; Bond.

Cold

They cause the naked to lodge without clothing, that they have no covering in the cold. *Jb.* 24: 7.

Out of the south cometh the whirlwind: and cold out of the north. *Jb.* 37: 9.

The face of the deep is frozen. *Jb.* 38: 30.

He casteth forth his ice like morsels: who can stand before his cold? *Ps.* 147: 17.

The sluggard will not plow by reason of the cold. *Pr.* 20: 4.

As the cold of snow in the time of harvest, so is a faithful messenger to them that send him. *Pr.* 25: 13.

As cold waters to a thirsty soul, so is good news from a far country. *Pr.* 25: 25.

Thy crowned are as the locusts, and thy captains as the great grasshoppers, which camp in the hedges in the cold day. *Na.* 3: 17.

Whosoever shall give to drink unto one of these little ones a cup of cold water only in the name of a disciple, verily I say unto you, he shall in no wise lose his reward. *Mat.* 10: 42.

The love of many shall wax cold. *Mat.* 24: 12.

In cold and nakedness. *2 Co.* 11: 27.

I know thy works, that thou art neither hot nor cold: I would thou wert cold or hot. *Re.* 3: 15.

See also

Frost; Snow; Weather; Winter.

Collaboration

Fear not: for they that be with us are more than they that be with them. *2 K.* 6: 16.

I . . . will not sit with the wicked. *Ps.* 26: 5.

Two are better than one. *Ec.* 4: 9.

Praying us with much intreaty that we would . . . take upon us the fellowship of the ministering to the saints. *2 Co.* 8: 4.

They gave . . . the right hands of fellowship. *Ga.* 2: 9.

Bear ye one another's burdens. *Ga.* 6: 2.

These only are my fellowworkers unto the kingdom of God, which have been a comfort unto me. *Col.* 4: 11.

That we might be fellowhelpers to the truth. *3 Jn.* 8.

See also

Assistance; Association; Christ, Partnership with; Companionship; Comradeship; Cooperation; Fellowship; Fellow-Worker; God, Partnership with.

Collapse

The wicked shall fall by his own wickedness. *Pr.* 11: 5.

Where no counsel is, the people fall. *Pr.* 11: 14.

Whoso diggeth a pit shall fall therein: and he that rolleth a stone it will return upon him. *Pr.* 26: 27.

How art thou fallen from heaven, O Lucifer, son of the morning! *Is.* 14: 12.

I will overturn, overturn, overturn, it: and it shall be no more. *Eze.* 21: 27.

They shall say to the mountains, Cover us; and to the hills, Fall on us. *Ho.* 10: 8.

And great was the fall of it. *Mat.* 7: 27.

A house divided against a house falleth. *Lu.* 11: 17.

Let him that thinketh he standeth take heed lest he fall. *1 Co.* 10: 12.

God . . . condemned them with an overthrow. *2 Pe.* 2: 4, 6.

I saw a star fall from heaven unto the earth. *Re.* 9: 1.

See also

Defeat; Destruction; Failure; Fall; Overthrow; Ruin; Wreck.

Colleague

We be come from a far country: now therefore make ye a league with us. *Jos.* 9: 6.

A man after his own heart. *1 S.* 13: 14.

Make thy league with me, and, behold, my hand shall be with thee. *2 S.* 3: 12.

Sit thou at my right hand, until I make thine enemies thy footstool. *Ps.* 110: 1.

I am a companion of all them that fear thee. *Ps.* 119: 63.

Where two or three are gathered together in my name, there am I in the midst of them. *Mat.* 18: 20.

My Father worketh hitherto, and I work. *Jn.* 5: 17.

He is my partner and fellowhelper concerning you. *2 Co.* 8: 23.

Ye are . . . fellowcitizens with the saints, and of the household of God. *Ep.* 2: 19.

My fellowprisoner in Christ Jesus. *Phn.* 1: 23.

Abraham . . . was called the Friend of God. *Ja.* 2: 23.

The four and twenty elders . . . sat before God on their seats. *Re.* 11: 16.

I am thy fellowservant. *Re.* 19: 10.

See also

Association; Companionship; Comradeship; Fellow-Worker; Partnership.

Collection

Cain brought of the fruit of the ground an offering unto the Lord. *Ge.* 4: 3.

The Lord had respect unto Abel and to his offering. *Ge.* 4: 4.

Take ye from among you an offering unto the Lord: whosoever is of a willing heart, let him bring it, an offering of the Lord. *Ex.* 35: 5.

The people willingly offered themselves. *Ju.* 5: 2.

Give unto the Lord the glory due unto his name: bring an offering, and come before him. *1 Ch.* 16: 29.

All things come of thee, and of thine own have we given thee. *1 Ch.* 29: 14.

Gather of all Israel money to repair the house of your God from year to year. *2 Ch.* 24: 5.

They made a proclamation through Judah and Jerusalem, to bring in to the Lord the collection. *2 Ch.* 24: 9.

Bring an offering, and come into his courts. *Ps.* 96: 8.

There is that maketh himself rich, yet hath nothing: there is that maketh himself poor, yet hath great riches. *Pr.* 13: 7.

Bring ye all the tithes into the storehouse, that there may be meat in mine house, and prove me now herewith, saith the Lord of hosts, if I will not open you the windows of heaven, and pour you out a blessing, that there shall not be room enough to receive it. *Mal.* 3: 10.

Let your light so shine before men, that they may see your good works, and glorify your Father which is in heaven. *Mat.* 5: 16.

First be reconciled to thy brother, and then come and offer thy gift. *Mat.* 5: 24.

Lay up for yourselves treasures in heaven, where neither moth nor rust doth corrupt, and where thieves do not break through nor steal. *Mat.* 6: 20.

All things whatsoever ye would that men should do to you, do ye even so to them. *Mat.* 7: 12.

Shew thyself to the priest, and offer the gift that Moses commanded. *Mat.* 8: 4.

Freely ye have received, freely give. *Mat.* 10: 8.

Give, and it shall be given unto you. *Lu.* 6: 38.

Ye tithe mint and rue and all manner of herbs, and pass over judgment and the love of God. *Lu.* 11: 42.

Of a truth I say unto you, that this poor widow hath cast in more than they all. *Lu.* 21: 3.

Remember the words of the Lord Jesus, how he said, It is more blessed to give than to receive. *Ac.* 20: 35.

Now concerning the collection. *1 Co.* 16: 1.

Bear ye one another's burdens, and so fulfil the law of Christ. *Ga.* 6: 2.

To do good and to communicate forget not: for with such sacrifices God is well pleased. *He.* 13: 16.

See also

Assembly; Gift; Offering.

Color

He made him a coat of many colours. *Ge.* 37: 3.

This is the offering which ye shall take of them; gold, and silver, and brass, And blue, and purple, and scarlet. *Ex.* 25: 3, 4.

He made the ephod of gold, blue, and purple, and scarlet, and fine twined linen. *Ex.* 39: 2.

In the court of the garden of the king's palace; Where were white, green, and blue, hangings, fastened with cords of fine linen and purple to silver rings and pillars of marble: the beds were of gold and silver, upon a pavement of red, and blue, and white, and black, marble. *Es.* 1: 5, 6.

I am like a green olive tree in the house of God. *Ps.* 52: 8.

Yet shall ye be as the wings of a dove covered with silver, and her feathers with yellow gold. *Ps.* 68: 13.

Look not thou upon the wine when it is red, when it giveth his colour in the cup. *Pr.* 23: 31.

I will lay thy stones with fair colours, and lay thy foundations with sapphires. *Is.* 54: 11.

See also

Blue; Green; Hue; Red; Scarlet; White; Yellow.

Comfort

To set up on high those that be low; that those which mourn may be exalted to safety. *Jb.* 5: 11.

Miserable comforters are ye all. *Jb.* 16: 2.

Where is God my maker, who giveth songs in the night. *Jb.* 35: 10.

Thy rod and thy staff they comfort me. *Ps.* 23: 4.

Shew me a token for good; that they which hate me may see it, and be ashamed. *Ps.* 86: 17.

Comfort ye, comfort ye my people, saith your God. *Is.* 40: 1.

The Lord hath anointed me . . . to comfort all that mourn. *Is.* 61: 1, 2.

Rachel weeping for her children refused to be comforted for her children, because they were not. *Je.* 31: 15.

Blessed are they that mourn: for they shall be comforted. *Mat.* 5: 4.

These things I have spoken unto you, that in me ye might have peace. *Jn.* 16: 33.

Be of good cheer. *Jn.* 16: 33.

As the sufferings of Christ abound in us, so our consolation also aboundeth by Christ. *2 Co.* 1: 5.

Comfort one another with these words. *1 Th.* 4: 18.

The God of all grace, . . . after that ye have suffered a while, make you perfect, stablish, strengthen, settle you. *1 Pe.* 5: 10.

See also

Christ, the Comforter; Christ, Sympathy of; Comforter; Consolation; Ease; Relief; Solace; Well-Being.

Comforter

The Holy Ghost shall teach you in the same hour what ye ought to say. *Lu.* 12: 12.

I will pray the Father, and he shall give you another Comforter, that he may abide with you for ever. *Jn.* 14: 16.

The Comforter, which is the Holy Ghost, whom the Father will send in my name, he shall teach you all things. *Jn.* 14: 26.

When the Comforter is come, whom I will send unto you from the Father, even the Spirit of truth, which proceedeth from the Father, he shall testify of me. *Jn.* 15: 26.

It is expedient for you that I go away: for if I go not away, the Comforter will not come unto you; but if I depart, I will send him unto you. *Jn.* 16: 7.

When he is come, he will reprove the world of sin, and of righteousness, and of judgment. *Jn.* 16: 8.

When he, the Spirit of truth, is come, he will guide you into all truth. *Jn.* 16: 13.

The comfort of the Holy Ghost. *Ac.* 9: 31.

See also
Ghost, Holy; Spirit, Holy.

Coming, Second

Of that day and hour knoweth no man, no, not the angels of heaven, but my Father only. *Mat.* **24: 36.**

In such an hour as ye think not the Son of man cometh. *Mat.* **24: 44.**

Watch therefore, for ye know neither the day nor the hour wherein the Son of man cometh. *Mat.* **25: 13.**

As the lightning, that lighteneth out of the one part under heaven, shineth unto the other part under heaven; so shall also the Son of man be in his day. *Lu.* **17: 24.**

When Christ, who is our life, shall appear, then shall ye also appear with him in glory. *Col.* **3: 4.**

The day of the Lord so cometh as a thief in the night. *1 Th.* **5: 2.**

Keep this commandment without spot, unrebukeable, until the appearing of our Lord Jesus Christ. *1 Ti.* **6: 14.**

Unto them that look for him shall he appear the second time without sin unto salvation. *He.* **9: 28.**

The coming of the Lord draweth nigh. *Ja.* **5: 8.**

The power and coming of our Lord Jesus Christ. *2 Pe.* **1: 16.**

Behold, the Lord cometh with ten thousands of his saints. *Jude* **1: 14.**

If therefore thou shalt not watch, I will come on thee as a thief, and thou shalt not know what hour I will come upon thee. *Re.* **3: 3.**

See also
Advent; Christ, Second Coming of.

Commander

They shall make captains of the armies to lead the people. *De.* **20: 9.**

As captain of the host of the Lord am I now come. *Jos.* **5: 14.**

The Lord said to thee, Thou shalt feed my people Israel, and thou shalt be captain over Israel. *2 S.* **5: 2.**

I have given him for a witness to the people, a leader and commander to the people. *Is.* **55: 4.**

I am a man under authority, having soldiers under me; and I say to this man, Go, and he goeth; and to another, Come, and he cometh; and to my servant, Do this, and he doeth it. *Mat.* **8: 9.**

See also
Chief; Christ, Authority of; Christ, the Captain; Christ, the King; Christ, the Leader; Head; Leadership; Rule.

Commandment

He wrote upon the tables the words of the covenant, the ten commandments. *Ex.* **34: 28.**

Thou shalt keep therefore his statutes. *De.* **4: 40.**

The Lord thy God commanded thee to keep the sabbath day. *De.* **5: 15.**

The law of the Lord is perfect, converting the soul. *Ps.* **19: 7.**

Thy God hath commanded thy strength. *Ps.* **68: 28.**

He hath commanded his covenant for ever. *Ps.* **111: 9.**

There the Lord commanded the blessing, even life for evermore. *Ps.* **133: 3.**

Jesus said unto him. Thou shalt love the Lord thy God. . . . This is the first and great commandment. And the second is like unto it, Thou shalt love thy neighbour as thyself. *Mat.* **22: 37-39.**

I know that his commandment is life everlasting. *Jn.* **12: 50.**

This is my commandment, That ye love one another, as I have loved you. *Jn.* **15: 12.**

Ye are my friends, if ye do whatsoever I command you. *Jn.* **15: 14.**

He commanded them to be baptized in the name of the Lord. *Ac.* **10: 48.**

The law is holy, and the commandment holy, and just, and good. *Ro.* **7: 12.**

Honour thy father and mother; which is the first commandment with promise. *Ep.* **6: 2.**

The commandment of God our Saviour. *1 Ti.* **1: 1.**

The end of the commandment is charity out of a pure heart. *1 Ti.* **1: 5.**

I write no new commandment unto you, but an old commandment which ye had from the beginning. The old commandment is the word which ye have heard from the beginning. *1 Jn.* **2: 7.**

Again, a new commandment I write unto you, which thing is true in him and in you: because the darkness is past, and the true light now shineth. *1 Jn.* **2: 8.**

This commandment have we from him, That he who loveth God love his brother also. *1 Jn.* **4: 21.**

See also
Decree; God, Commandment of; God, Law of; Law; Order; Ordinance; Precept; Statute.

Commemoration

There were giants in the earth in those days. *Ge.* **6: 4.**

This is my memorial unto all generations. *Ex.* **3: 15.**

These stones shall be for a memorial. *Jos.* **4: 7.**

Their memorial is perished with them. *Ps.* **9: 6.**

Their posterity approve their sayings. *Ps.* **49: 13.**

Thy name, O Lord, endureth for ever. *Ps.* **135: 13.**

The memory of the just is blessed: but the name of the wicked shall rot. *Pr.* **10: 7.**

The living know that they shall die: but the dead know not any thing, neither have they any more a reward; for the memory of them is forgotten. *Ec.* **9: 5.**

Wheresoever this gospel shall be preached in the whole world, there shall also this, that this woman hath done, be told for a memorial of her. *Mat.* **26: 13.**

Call to remembrance the former days. *He.* **10: 32.**

See also
Anniversary; Celebration; History; Memorial; Memory; Remembrance.

Commencement

In the beginning God created the heaven and the earth. *Ge.* **1: 1.**

` The fear of the Lord is the beginning of knowledge. *Pr.* 1: 7.

Honour the Lord . . . with the firstfruits of all thine increase. *Pr.* 3: 9.

The fear of the Lord is a fountain of life. *Pr.* 14: 27.

Better is the end of a thing than the beginning thereof. *Ec.* 7: 8.

I have even from the beginning declared it to thee. *Is.* 48: 5.

Shall I give my firstborn for my transgression? *Mi.* 6: 7.

The kingdom of God . . . is like a grain of mustard seed. *Lu.* 13: 18, 19.

Beginning at Moses and all the prophets, he expounded unto them in all the scriptures the things concerning himself. *Lu.* 24: 27.

In the beginning was the Word. *Jn.* 1: 1.

God hath from the beginning chosen you to salvation. *2 Th.* 2: 13.

The latter end is worse with them than the beginning. *2 Pe.* 2: 20.

I am Alpha and Omega. *Re.* 22: 13.

See also
Alpha Beginning; Christ the Creator; Creation; Creator; First; Foundation; Genesis; God, the Creator; Graduation; Inauguration.

Commendation

Jesus answered and said unto her, O woman, great is thy faith: be it unto thee even as thou wilt. *Mat.* 15: 28.

Jesus said, Let her alone; why trouble ye her? she hath wrought a good work on me. *Mk.* 14: 6.

I say unto you, I have not found so great faith, no, not in Israel. *Lu.* 7: 9.

Of a truth I say unto you, that this poor widow hath cast in more than they all. *Lu.* 21: 3.

See also
Adulation; Eulogy; Honor; Praise; Renown; Reputation.

Commerce

The men are shepherds, for their trade hath been to feed cattle. *Ge.* 46: 32.

Buy the truth, and sell it not. *Pr.* 23: 23.

She perceiveth that her merchandise is good. *Pr.* 31: 18.

In that day there shall be a highway out of Egypt to Assyria, and the Assyrian shall come to Egypt, and the Egyptian into Assyria. *Is.* 19: 23.

Whose merchants are princes, whose traffickers are the honourable of the earth. *Is.* 23: 8.

The highways lie waste, the wayfaring man ceaseth. *Is.* 33: 8.

Syria was thy merchant by reason of the multitude of the wares of thy·making: they occupied in thy fairs with emeralds, purple, and broidered work, and fine linen, and coral, and agate. *Eze.* 27: 16.

Arabia, and all the princes of Kedar, they occupied with thee in lambs, and rams, and goats: in these were they thy merchants. *Eze.* 27: 21.

In that day shall there be upon the bells of the horses, HOLINESS UNTO THE LORD. *Zch.* 14: 20.

See also
Business; Industry; Merchant; Trade.

Commercialism

His sons walked not in his ways, but turned aside after lucre, and took bribes, and perverted judgment. *1 S.* 8: 3.

Is it a time to receive money? *2 K.* 5: 26.

He that by usury and unjust gain increaseth his substance, he shall gather it for him that will pity the poor. *Pr.* 28: 8.

The crowning city, whose merchants are princes, whose traffickers are the honourable of the earth? *Is.* 23: 8.

Her princes in the midst thereof are like wolves ravening the prey, to shed blood, and to destroy souls, to get dishonest gain. *Eze.* 22: 27.

Thy riches, and thy fairs, thy merchandise, thy mariners, and thy pilots, thy calkers, and the occupiers of thy merchandise, . . . shall fall into the midst of the seas in the day of thy ruin. *Eze.* 27: 27.

Thy merchandise and all thy company in the midst of thee shall fall. *Eze.* 27: 34.

By thy great wisdom and by thy traffick hast thou increased thy riches, and thine heart is lifted up because of thy riches. *Eze.* 28: 5.

Thou hast defiled thy sanctuaries . . . by the iniquity of thy traffick. *Eze.* 28: 18.

He is a merchant, the balances of deceit are in his hand. *Ho.* 12: 7.

The heads thereof judge for reward, and the priests thereof teach for hire, and the prophets thereof divine for money. *Mi.* 3: 11.

Therefore they sacrifice unto their net, and burn incense unto their drag. *Hab.* 1: 16.

Jesus went into the temple of God, and cast out all them that sold and bought in the temple. *Mat.* 21: 12.

These things shall be added unto you. *Lu.* 12: 31.

My house is the house of prayer: but ye have made it a den of thieves. *Lu.* 19: 46.

Make not my Father's house an house of merchandise. *Jn.* 2: 16.

Thy money perish with thee, because thou hast thought that the gift of God may be purchased with money. *Ac.* 8: 20.

The merchants of the earth are waxed rich through the abundance of her delicacies. *Re.* 18: 3.

Thy merchants were the great men of the earth. *Re.* 18: 23.

See also
Gain; Profit; Worldliness.

Commission

I will not eat, until I have told my errand. *Ge.* 24: 33.

I have a secret errand unto thee, O king. *Ju.* 3: 19.

I have an errand to thee, O captain. *2 K.* 9: 5.

They delivered the king's commissions unto the king's lieutenants. *Ezr.* 8: 36.

The Lord said unto me, Go, prophesy unto my people Israel. *Am.* 7: 15.

Arise, go to Nineveh, that great city, and cry against it. *Jon.* 1: 2.

After these things the Lord appointed other seventy also, and sent them two and two before his face into every city and place, whither he himself would come. *Lu.* 10: 1.

Ye shall be witnesses unto me. *Ac.* 1: 8.

Lord, what wilt thou have me to do? *Ac.* 9: 6.

The angel said unto him, Gird thyself, and bind on thy sandals. *Ac.* 12: 8.

I went to Damascus with authority and commission from the chief priests. *Ac.* 26: 12.

See also
Ambassador; Authority; Charge; Forerunner; Messenger; Mission; Office; Trust.

Commonplace

As the angels were gone away from them into heaven. *Lu.* 2: 15.

I have never eaten any thing that is common or unclean. *Ac.* 10: 14.

What God hath cleansed, that call not thou common. *Ac.* 10: 15.

God hath shewed me that I should not call any man common or unclean. *Ac.* 10: 28.

There hath no temptation taken you but such as is common to man. *1 Co.* 10: 13.

We have this treasure in earthen vessels, that the excellency of the power may be of God, and not of us. *2 Co.* 4: 7.

In a great house there are not only vessels of gold and of silver, but also of wood and of earth. *2 Ti.* 2: 20.

I gave all diligence to write unto you of the common salvation. *Jude* 1: 3.

See also
Little; Pettiness; Thing, Common; Thing, Little; Trifle.

Communion

Commune with your own heart upon your bed, and be still. *Ps.* 4: 4.

That they all may be one; as thou, Father, art in me, and I in thee, that they also may be one in us. *Jn.* 17: 21.

They continued stedfastly in the apostles' doctrine and fellowship. *Ac.* 2: 42.

And when he had thus spoken, he kneeled down, and prayed with them all. *Ac.* 20: 36.

The cup of blessing which we bless, is it not the communion of the blood of Christ? *1 Co.* 10: 16.

Many members, yet but one body. *1 Co.* 12: 20.

What communion hath light with darkness? *2 Co.* 6: 14.

All the saints salute you. *2 Co.* 13: 13.

The communion of the Holy Ghost, be with you all. *2 Co.* 13: 14.

Fellowcitizens with the saints. *Ep.* 2: 19.

For we are members one of another. *Ep.* 4: 25.

If there be . . . any fellowship of the Spirit, . . . Fulfil ye my joy. *Ph.* 2: 1, 2.

Pray one for another. *Ja.* 5: 16.

That which we have seen and heard declare we unto you, that ye also may have fellowship with us: and truly our fellowship is with the Father, and with his Son Jesus Christ. *1 Jn.* 1: 3.

See also
Agreement; Christ, Abiding in; Christ, Companionship of; Christ, Fellowship with; Christ, Life in; Christ, Partnership with; Christ, Union with; Communion, Service of; Companionship; Concord; Fellowship; God, Communion with; God, Companionship with; God, Fellowship with; God, Partnership with; Unity.

Communion, Service of

It is good for me to draw near to God. *Ps.* 73: 28.

This is my body. *Mat.* 26: 26.

He took bread, and gave thanks, and brake it, and gave unto them, saying, This is my body which is given for you. *Lu.* 22: 19.

This do in remembrance of me. *Lu.* 22: 19.

This cup is the new testament in my blood, which is shed for you. *Lu.* 22: 20.

The bread of God is he which cometh down from heaven, and giveth life unto the world. *Jn.* 6: 33.

He that eateth me, even he shall live by me. *Jn.* 6: 57.

Therefore let us keep the feast. *1 Co.* 5: 8.

The cup of blessing which we bless, is it not the communion of the blood of Christ? The bread which we break, is it not the communion of the body of Christ? *1 Co.* 10: 16.

Let a man examine himself, and so let him eat of that bread, and drink of that cup. *1 Co.* 11: 28.

We are made partakers of Christ, if we hold the beginning of our confidence stedfast unto the end. *He.* 3: 14.

See also
Chalice; Christ, Blood of; Christ, Body of; Eucharist; Mass; Supper, the Last; Supper, the Lord's.

Communism, Christian

The rich and poor meet together: the Lord is the maker of them all. *Pr.* 22: 2.

The profit of the earth is for all. *Ec.* 5: 9.

All things come alike to all. *Ec.* 9: 2.

Thou hast made them equal unto us, which have borne the burden and heat of the day. *Mat.* 20: 12.

I will give unto this last, even as unto thee. *Mat.* 20: 14.

He hath filled the hungry with good things. *Lu.* 1: 53.

The multitude of them that believed were of one heart and of one soul: neither said any of them that aught of the things which he possessed was his own; but they had all things common. *Ac.* 4: 32.

Neither was there any among them that lacked. *Ac.* 4: 34.

As many as were possessors of lands or houses sold them, and brought the prices of the things that were sold, And laid them down at the apostles' feet. *Ac.* 4: 34, 35.

Distribution was made unto every man according as he had need. *Ac.* 4: 35.

Let no man seek his own, but every man another's wealth. *1 Co.* 10: 24.

Whether one member suffer, all the members suffer with it. *1 Co.* 12: 26.

That now at this time your abundance may be a supply for their want, that their abundance also may be a supply for your want; that there may be equality. *2 Co.* 8: 14.

Let the brother of low degree rejoice in that he is exalted: but the rich, in that he is made low. *Ja.* 1: 9, 10.

See also
Brotherhood; Equality; Fairness; Socialism.

Community

Go to, let us build us a city. *Ge.* 11: 4.

Their substance was great, so that they could
not dwell together. *Ge.* 13: 6.

I am the Lord your God, which have
separated you from other people. *Le.* 20: 24.

There shall be a place which the Lord your
God shall choose to cause his name to dwell
there. *De.* 12: 11.

I dwell among my own people. 2 *K.* 4: 13.

Both low and high, rich and poor, together.
Ps. 49: 2.

Jerusalem is builded as a city that is compact together. *Ps.* 122: 3.

Behold, how good and how pleasant it is for
brethren to dwell together in unity! *Ps.* 133: 1.

The ants are a people not strong, yet they
prepare their meat in the summer. *Pr.* 30: 25.

The locusts have no king, yet go they forth
all of them by bands. *Pr.* 30: 27.

To him that is joined to all the living there
is hope. *Ec.* 9: 4.

A little one shall become a thousand, and a
small one a strong nation. *Is.* 60: 22.

Ye are . . . fellowcitizens with the saints. *Ep.*
2: 19.

I will be to them a God, and they shall be
to me a people. *He.* 8: 10.

See also
Association; Communism, Christian; Fellowship; Nation; People; Society; State.

Compact

With thee will I establish my covenant. *Ge.*
6: 18.

Their heart was not right with him, neither
were they stedfast in his covenant. *Ps.* 78: 37.

My covenant will I not break, nor alter the
thing that is gone out of my lips. *Ps.* 89: 34.

Jerusalem is builded as a city that is compact together. *Ps.* 122: 3.

Many nations shall be joined to the Lord in
that day. *Zch.* 2: 11.

I beseech you, brethren, . . . that there be
no divisions among you; but that ye be perfectly joined together. *1 Co.* 1: 10.

There should be no schism in the body.
1 Co. 12: 25.

The whole body fitly joined together and
compacted. *Ep.* 4: 16.

See also
Accord; Agreement; Bargain; Contract;
Covenant; Treaty.

Companionship

I am a brother to dragons, and a companion to owls. *Jb.* 30: 29.

I am a companion of all them that fear
thee, and of them that keep thy precepts. *Ps.*
119: 63.

That thou mayest walk in the way of good
men, and keep the paths of the righteous. *Pr.*
2: 20.

He that walketh with wise men shall be
wise. *Pr.* 13: 20.

Two are better than one. *Ec.* 4: 9.

Woe to him that is alone when he falleth;
for he hath not another to help him up. *Ec.*
4: 10.

If two lie together, then they have heat: but
how can one be warm alone? *Ec.* 4: 11.

There were also with them other little ships.
Mk. 4: 36.

The right hands of fellowship. *Ga.* 2: 9.

Our conversation is in heaven; from whence
also we look for the Saviour, the Lord Jesus
Christ. *Ph.* 3: 20.

Ye are come unto . . . the city of the living
God, the heavenly Jerusalem, and to an innumerable company of angels. *He.* 12: 22.

See also
Association; Christ, Companionship of;
Christ, Fellowship with; Christ, Partnership
with; Collaboration; Colleague; Companionship, Evil; Company; Concord; Fellowship;
God, Communion with; God, Companionship
with; God, Fellowship with; God, Partnership
with.

Companionship, Evil

Ye shall not walk in the manners of the
nation, which I cast out before you. *Le.* 20: 23.

If ye will not drive out the inhabitants of
the land from before you; then it shall come
to pass, that those which ye let remain of
them shall be pricks in your eyes, and thorns
in your sides, and shall vex you in the land
wherein ye dwell. *Nu.* 33: 55.

Jehu the son of Hanani the seer . . . said
to King Jehoshaphat, Shouldest thou help the
ungodly? 2 *Ch.* 19: 2.

Which goeth in company with the workers
of iniquity, and walketh with wicked men. *Jb.*
34: 8.

Depart from me, ye evil doers: for I will
keep the commandments of my God. *Ps.* 119:
115.

If they say, Come with us, . . . We shall
find all precious substance, we shall fill our
houses with spoil: . . . walk not thou in the
way with them. *Pr.* 1: 11, 13, 15.

If they say, Come with us, . . . Cast in thy
lot among us; let us all have one purse: . . .
walk not thou in the way with them. *Pr.* 1: 11,
14, 15.

A companion of fools shall be destroyed. *Pr.*
13: 20.

Go from the presence of a foolish man. *Pr.*
14: 7.

Make no friendship with an angry man. *Pr.*
22: 24.

Be not thou envious against evil men,
neither desire to be with them. *Pr.* 24: 1.

He that is a companion of riotous men
shameth his father. *Pr.* 28: 7.

He that keepeth company with harlots
spendeth his substance. *Pr.* 29: 3.

Whoso is partner with a thief hateth his
own soul. *Pr.* 29: 24.

Evil communications corrupt good manners.
1 Co. 15: 33.

Be ye not unequally yoked together with
unbelievers. 2 *Co.* 6: 14.

Have no fellowship with the unfruitful
works of darkness, but rather reprove them.
Ep. 5: 11.

We command you, brethren, in the name of
our Lord Jesus Christ, that ye withdraw yourselves from every brother that walketh disorderly. 2 *Th.* 3: 6.

If any man obey not our word by this

epistle, note that man, and have no company with him, that he may be ashamed. *2 Th.* 3: 14.

Company

Accompanying the ark of God. *2 S.* 6: 4.

I am . . . a companion to owls. *Jb.* 30: 29.

The Lord gave the word: great was the company of those that published it. *Ps.* 68: 11.

A companion of fools shall be destroyed. *Pr.* 13: 20.

I have compared thee, O my love, to a company of horses. *S. of S.* 1: 9.

We will go with you: for we have heard that God is with you. *Zch.* 8: 23.

Jesus . . . saw a great company come unto him. *Jn.* 6: 5.

God . . . hath raised us up together, and made us sit together in heavenly places in Christ Jesus. *Ep.* 2: 4, 6.

We are members one of another. *Ep.* 4: 25.

If any man obey not our word, . . . have no company with him. *2 Th.* 3: 14.

Things that accompany salvation. *He.* 6: 9.

Ye are come unto . . . the city of the living God, the heavenly Jerusalem, and to an innumerable company of angels. *He.* 12: 22.

See also

Association; Companionship; Comradeship; Cooperation; Fellowship; Fellow-Worker.

Compassion

Take up thy son. *2 K.* 4: 36.

His mercy endureth for ever. *Ps.* 106: 1.

If thine enemy be hungry, give him bread to eat; and if he be thirsty, give him water to drink. *Pr.* 25: 21.

It is of the Lord's mercies that we are not consumed, because his compassions fail not. *La.* 3: 22.

Shew mercy and compassions every man to his brother. *Zch.* 7: 9.

He was moved with compassion on them, because they fainted, and were scattered abroad, as sheep having no shepherd. *Mat.* 9: 36.

I have compassion on the multitude. *Mat.* 15: 32.

Inasmuch as ye have done it unto one of the least of these my brethren, ye have done it unto me. *Mat.* 25: 40.

When the Lord saw her, he had compassion on her, and said unto her, Weep not. *Lu.* 7: 13.

When he was yet a great way off, his father saw him, and had compassion, and ran, and fell on his neck, and kissed him. *Lu.* 15: 20.

Put on therefore, as the elect of God, . . . bowels of mercies. *Col.* 3: 12.

Finally, be ye all of one mind, having compassion one of another, love as brethren, be pitiful, be courteous. *1 Pe.* 3: 8.

See also

Christ, Compassion of; Christ, the Comforter; Christ, Sympathy of; God, Compassion of; God, Sympathy of; Mercy; Pity; Sympathy; Tenderness.

Compatibility

Can two walk together, except they be agreed? *Am.* 3: 3.

Thou art a Galilæan, and thy speech agreeth thereto. *Mk.* 14: 70.

No man putteth a piece of a new garment upon an old. *Lu.* 5: 36.

Now the God of patience and consolation grant you to be likeminded one toward another. *Ro.* 15: 5.

What concord hath Christ with Belial? *2 Co.* 6: 15.

What part hath he that believeth with an infidel? *2 Co.* 6: 15.

Fulfil ye my joy, that ye be likeminded, having the same love, being of one accord, of one mind. *Ph.* 2: 2.

See also

Accord; Agreement; Concord; Fellowship; Harmony; Peace.

Compensation

As I have done, so God hath requited me. *Ju.* 1: 7.

Thou art more righteous than I: for thou hast rewarded me good, whereas I have rewarded thee evil. *1 S.* 24: 17.

He hath requited me evil for good. *1 S.* 25:21.

To make the weight for the winds. *Jb.* 28: 25.

Verily there is a reward for the righteous: verily he is a God that judgeth in the earth. *Ps.* 58: 11.

With thine eyes shalt thou behold and see the reward of the wicked. *Ps.* 91: 8.

The righteous shall be recompensed in the earth: much more the wicked and the sinner. *Pr.* 11: 31.

He that tilleth his land shall be satisfied with bread. *Pr.* 12: 11.

To the righteous good shall be repayed. *Pr.* 13: 21.

Every valley shall be exalted, and every mountain and hill shall be made low: and the crooked shall be made straight, and the rough places plain. *Is.* 40: 4.

Shall evil be recompensed for good? *Je.* 18: 20.

As I was among the captives, . . . the heavens were opened, and I saw visions of God. *Eze.* 1: 1.

He that receiveth a righteous man in the name of a righteous man shall receive a righteous man's reward. *Mat.* 10: 41.

He that is called in the Lord, being a servant, is the Lord's freeman: likewise also he that is called, being free, is Christ's servant. *1 Co.* 7: 22.

Without were fightings, within were fears. Nevertheless God, that comforteth those that are cast down, comforted us. *2 Co.* 7: 5, 6.

Whatsoever a man soweth, that shall he also reap. *Ga.* 6: 7.

Not rendering evil for evil, or railing for railing: but contrariwise blessing. *1 Pe.* 3: 9.

He that overcometh, and keepeth my works unto the end, to him will I give power over the nations. *Re.* 2: 26.

See also

Amends; God, Reward of; Payment; Recompense; Reparation; Restitution;, Restoration; Reward.

Competition

Let there be no strife, I pray thee, between me and thee; . . . for we be brethren. *Ge.* 13: 8.

There was also a strife among them, which

of them should be accounted the greatest. *Lu.* **22: 24.**

If by any means I may provoke to emulation them which are my flesh, and might save some of them. *Ro.* **11: 14.**

There are contentions among you. *1 Co.* **1: 11.**

Whereas there is among you envying, and strife, and divisions, are ye not carnal, and walk as men? *1 Co.* **3: 3.**

I know the forwardness of your mind, for which I boast of you to them of Macedonia; . . . and your zeal hath provoked very many. *2 Co.* **9: 2.**

Now the works of the flesh are manifest, which are these; . . . emulations, . . . strife. *Ga.* **5: 19, 20.**

If ye have bitter envying and strife in your hearts, glory not. *Ja.* **3: 14.**

See also
Contest; Emulation; Envy; Jealousy; Rivalry.

Complacency

He hath said in his heart, I shall not be moved: for I shall never be in adversity. *Ps.* **10: 6.**

The lines are fallen unto me in pleasant places. *Ps.* **16: 6.**

Seest thou a man wise in his own conceit? there is more hope of a fool than of him. *Pr.* **26: 12.**

Boast not thyself of to morrow; for thou knowest not what a day may bring forth. *Pr.* **27: 1.**

I made me great works; I builded me houses; . . . and, behold, all was vanity. *Ec.* **2: 4, 11.**

Who is blind as he that is perfect? *Is.* **42: 19.**

Woe to them that are at ease in Zion. *Am.* **6: 1.**

I will search Jerusalem with candles, and punish the men that are settled on their lees. *Zph.* **1: 12.**

Think not to say within yourselves, We have Abraham to our father. *Mat.* **3: 9.**

Not every one that saith unto me, Lord, Lord, shall enter into the kingdom of heaven. *Mat.* **7: 21.**

Why beholdest thou the mote that is in thy brother's eye, but perceivest not the beam that is in thine own eye? *Lu.* **6: 41.**

God, I thank thee, that I am not as other men are. *Lu.* **18: 11.**

They, measuring themselves by themselves, and comparing themselves among themselves, are not wise. *2 Co.* **10: 12.**

See also
Contentment; Ease; Pleasure; Satisfaction; Self-Satisfaction.

Complaint

Your murmurings are not against us, but against the Lord. *Ex.* **16: 8.**

Even to day is my complaint bitter. *Jb.* **23: 2.**

I am feeble and sore broken: I have roared by reason of the disquietness of my heart. *Ps.* **38: 8.**

I complained, and my spirit was overwhelmed. *Ps.* **77: 3.**

The foolishness of man perverteth his way: and his heart fretteth against the Lord. *Pr.* **19: 3.**

The eyes of man are never satisfied. *Pr.* **27: 20.**

Murmur not among yourselves. *Jn.* **6: 43.**

Neither murmur ye, as some of them also murmured, and were destroyed of the destroyer. *1 Co.* **10: 10.**

Do all things without murmurings and disputings. *Ph.* **2: 14.**

These are murmurers, complainers. *Jude* **1: 16.**

See also
Disease; Disorder; Grief; Illness; Murmur; Rebuke; Reproach; Reproof.

Completion

The heavens and the earth were finished. *Ge.* **2: 1.**

Put ye in the sickle, for the harvest is ripe. *Jo.* **3: 13.**

Till heaven and earth pass, one jot or one tittle shall in no wise pass from the law, till all be fulfilled. *Mat.* **5: 18.**

He closed the book, and he gave it again to the minister. *Lu.* **4: 20.**

My meat is to do the will of him that sent me, and to finish his work. *Jn.* **4: 34.**

I am come that they might have life, and that they might have it more abundantly. *Jn.* **10: 10.**

I have glorified thee on the earth: I have finished the work which thou gavest me to do. *Jn.* **17: 4.**

He said, It is finished: and he bowed his head, and gave up the ghost. *Jn.* **19: 30.**

That I might finish my course with joy. *Ac.* **20: 24.**

That the righteousness of the law might be fulfilled in us. *Ro.* **8: 4.**

He will finish the work, and cut it short in righteousness: because a short work will the Lord make upon the earth. *Ro.* **9: 28.**

He that loveth another hath fulfilled the law. *Ro.* **13: 8.**

When I became a man, I put away childish things. *1 Co.* **13: 11.**

A perfect man. *Ep.* **4: 13.**

Ye are complete in him. *Col.* **2: 10.**

I have fought a good fight, I have finished my course. *2 Ti.* **4: 7.**

Looking unto Jesus, the author and finisher of our faith. *He.* **12: 2.**

See also
Christ, Fullness of; Christ, the Goal; Christ, Perfection of; End; Fulfilment; Harvest; Perfection; Realization.

Comprehension

They are a nation void of counsel, neither is there any understanding in them. *De.* **32: 28.**

Thou only knowest the hearts of the children of men. *2 Ch.* **6: 30.**

With the ancient is wisdom; and in length of days understanding. *Jb.* **12: 12.**

He . . . taketh away the understanding of the aged. *Jb.* **12: 20.**

Where shall wisdom be found? and where is the place of understanding? *Jb.* **28: 12.**

There is a spirit in man: and the inspiration of the Almighty giveth them understanding. *Jb.* **32: 8.**

He knoweth our frame. *Ps.* **103: 14.**

Give me understanding, and I shall keep thy law. *Ps.* **119: 34.**

Then shalt thou . . . find the knowledge of God. *Pr.* 2: 5.

Lean not unto thine own understanding. *Pr.* 3: 5.

See ye indeed, but perceive not. *Is.* 6: 9.

See also

Christ, Knowledge of; God, Knowledge of; Intelligence; Knowledge; Understanding.

Compromise

How long halt ye between two opinions? *1 K.* 18: 21.

So these nations feared the Lord, and served their graven images, both their children, and their children's children. *2 K.* 17: 41.

He hath left off to be wise, and to do good. *Ps.* 36: 3.

God hath made man upright; but they have sought out many inventions. *Ec.* 7: 29.

Shall I give . . . the fruit of my body for the sin of my soul? *Mi.* 6: 7.

Agree with thine adversary quickly. *Mat.* 5: 25.

I am in a strait betwixt two. *Ph.* 1: 23.

See also

Expediency; Loyalty, Divided.

Compulsion

The spirit within me constraineth me. *Jb.* 32: 18.

I have seen violence and strife in the city. *Ps.* 55: 9.

Evil shall hunt the violent man to overthrow him. *Ps.* 140: 11.

He made his grave with the wicked, and with the rich in his death; because he had done no violence. *Is.* 53: 9.

The land is full of bloody crimes, and the city is full of violence. *Eze.* 7: 23.

The kingdom of heaven suffereth violence. *Mat.* 11: 12.

Paul was pressed in the spirit. *Ac.* 18: 5.

See also

Coercion; Constraint; Enforcement; Force; Power; Restraint; Violence.

Comradeship

Whither thou goest, I will go; and where thou lodgest, I will lodge: thy people shall be my people, and thy God my God. *Ru.* 1: 16.

A man after his own heart. *1 S.* 13: 14.

Saul and Jonathan were lovely and pleasant in their lives, and in their death they were not divided. *2 S.* 1: 23.

It was thou, a man my equal, my guide, and mine acquaintance. *Ps.* 55: 13.

A man that hath friends must shew himself friendly: and there is a friend that sticketh closer than a brother. *Pr.* 18: 24.

Iron sharpeneth iron; so a man sharpeneth the countenance of his friend. *Pr.* 27: 17.

Freely ye have received, freely give. *Mat.* 10: 8.

My Father worketh hitherto, and I work. *Jn.* 5: 17.

Then said Jesus, . . . I do nothing of myself; but as my Father hath taught me, I speak these things. *Jn.* 8: 28.

My fellowprisoner in Christ Jesus. *Phm.* 1: 23.

See also

Association; Christ, Companionship of; Christ, Fellowship with; Christ, Partnership with; Collaboration; Colleague; Companionship; Companionship, Evil; Company; Fellowship; God, Companionship with; God, Fellowship with; God, Partnership with; Partner.

Concealment

From thy face shall I be hid. *Ge.* 4: 14.

Is there any secret thing with thee? *Jb.* 15: 11.

Hide me under the shadow of thy wings. *Ps.* 17: 8.

Cleanse thou me from secret faults. *Ps.* 19: 12.

In the time of trouble he shall hide me in his pavilion. *Ps.* 27: 5.

Thou art my hiding place; thou shalt preserve me from trouble. *Ps.* 32: 7.

I have not concealed thy lovingkindness and thy truth from the great congregation. *Ps.* 40: 10.

In the hidden part thou shalt make me to know wisdom. *Ps.* 51: 6.

Thou hast covered all their sin. *Ps.* 85: 2.

Stolen waters are sweet, and bread eaten in secret is pleasant. *Pr.* 9: 17.

A talebearer revealeth secrets: but he that is of a faithful spirit concealeth the matter. *Pr.* 11: 13.

A prudent man concealeth knowledge. *Pr.* 12: 23.

A prudent man foreseeth the evil, and hideth himself. *Pr.* 22: 3.

It is the glory of God to conceal a thing. *Pr.* 25: 2.

He that covereth his sins shall not prosper: but whoso confesseth and forsaketh them shall have mercy. *Pr.* 28: 13.

Why sayest thou, . . . My way is hid from the Lord? *Is.* 40: 27.

They shall say to the mountains, Cover us; and to the hills, Fall on us. *Ho.* 10: 8.

A city that is set on a hill cannot be hid. *Mat.* 5: 14.

The kingdom of heaven is like unto treasure hid in a field. *Mat.* 13: 44.

Charity shall cover the multitude of sins. *1 Pe.* 4: 8.

Hide us from the face of him that sitteth on the throne, and from the wrath of the Lamb. *Re.* 6: 16.

See also

Christ, the Hidden; Christ, Mystery of; Cloud; Cover; God, the Hiding; Mystery; Secrecy; Veil.

Conceit

Be not wise in thine own eyes: fear the Lord, and depart from evil. *Pr.* 3: 7.

He that exalteth his gate seeketh destruction. *Pr.* 17: 19.

The rich man's wealth is his strong city, and as a high wall in his own conceit. *Pr.* 18: 11.

Put not forth thyself in the presence of the king, and stand not in the place of great men. *Pr.* 25: 6.

Better it is that it be said unto thee, Come up hither; than that thou shouldest be put lower in the presence of the prince whom thine eyes have seen. *Pr.* 25: 7.

Seest thou a man wise in his own conceit?

there is more hope of a fool than of him. *Pr.* 26: 12.

The sluggard is wiser in his own conceit than seven men that can render a reason. *Pr.* 26: 16.

Woe unto them that are wise in their own eyes, and prudent in their own sight! *Is.* 5: 21.

The pride of thine heart hath deceived thee. *Ob.* 1: 3.

Though thou exalt thyself as the eagle, and though thou set thy nest among the stars, thence will I bring thee down. *Ob.* 1: 4.

He spake this parable unto certain which trusted in themselves that they were righteous, and despised others. *Lu.* 18: 9.

Be not wise in your own conceits. *Ro.* 12: 16.

If any man among you seemeth to be wise in this world, let him become a fool, that he may be wise. *1 Co.* 3: 18.

If any man think . that he knoweth any thing, he knoweth nothing yet as he ought to know. *1 Co.* 8: 2.

Let him that thinketh he standeth take heed lest he fall. *1 Co.* 10: 12.

God resisteth the proud. *Ja.* 4: 6.

See also

Arrogance; Boasting; Braggart; Complacency; Egotism; Haughtiness; Pride; Selfishness; Self-Satisfaction.

Conception

They conceive mischief, and bring forth vanity, and their belly prepareth deceit. *Jb.* 15: 35.

In sin did my mother conceive me. *Ps.* 51: 5.

Behold, a virgin shall conceive, and bear a son, and shall call his name Immanuel. *Is.* 7: 14.

Conceiving and uttering from the heart words of falsehood. *Is.* 59: 13.

Behold, thou shalt conceive in thy womb, and bring forth a son, and shalt call his name JESUS. *Lu.* 1: 31.

Concern

Thou hast been careful for us with all this care. *2 K.* 4: 13.

I am troubled; I am bowed down greatly. *Ps.* 38: 6.

Cast thy burden upon the Lord. *Ps.* 55: 22.

The Lord will perfect that which concerneth me. *Ps.* 138: 8.

Fret not thyself because of evil men. *Pr.* 24: 19.

Behold, my servant shall deal prudently. *Is.* 52: 13.

Get you up unto the wealthy nation, that dwelleth without care. *Je.* 49: 31.

Why take ye thought for raiment? *Mat.* 6: 28.

The care of this world, and the deceitfulness of riches, choke the word. *Mat.* 13: 22.

Martha, Martha, thou art careful and troubled about many things. *Lu.* 10: 41.

Take heed to yourselves, lest at any time your hearts be overcharged with . . . cares of this life. *Lu.* 21: 34.

Teaching those things which concern the Lord Jesus Christ. *Ac.* 28: 31.

Doth God take care for oxen? *1 Co.* 9: 9.

I will glory of the things which concern mine infirmities. *2 Co.* 11: 30.

Be careful for nothing. *Ph.* 4: 6.

Casting all your care upon him; for he careth for you. *1 Pe.* 5: 7.

See also

Anxiety; Burden; Care; Solicitude; Trouble; Worry; Yoke.

Conciliation

Yielding pacifieth great offences. *Ec.* 10: 4.

There shall be peace and truth in my days. *Is.* 39: 8.

He shall turn the heart of the fathers to the children, and the heart of the children to their fathers. *Mal.* 4: 6.

First be reconciled to thy brother, and then come and offer thy gift. *Mat.* 5: 24.

On earth peace, good will toward men. *Lu.* 2: 14.

Christ . . . maketh intercession for us. *Ro.* 8: 34.

You, that were sometime alienated and enemies in your mind by wicked works, yet now hath he reconciled. *Col.* 1: 21.

There is . . . one mediator between God and men, the man Christ Jesus. *1 Ti.* 2: 5.

He is the propitiation for our sins. *1 Jn.* 2: 2.

See also

Christ, the Mediator; Peace; Reconciliation.

Conclusion

How long will it be ere ye make an end of words? *Jb.* 18: 2.

The end of his talk is mischievous madness. *Ec.* 10: 13.

Of making many books there is no end. *Ec.* 12: 12.

Let us hear the conclusion of the whole matter: Fear God, and keep his commandments. *Ec.* 12: 13.

Shut up the words, and seal the book, even to the time of the end. *Da.* 12: 4.

Multitudes, multitudes in the valley of decision. *Jo.* 3: 14.

The harvest is the end of the world. *Mat.* 13: 39.

We conclude that a man is justified by faith without the deeds of the law. *Ro.* 3: 28.

God hath concluded them all in unbelief, that he might have mercy upon all. *Ro.* 11: 32.

Then cometh the end. *1 Co.* 15: 24.

The scripture hath concluded all under sin. *Ga.* 3: 22.

See also

Decision; End; Finality; Finish; Termination.

Concord

Behold, how good and how pleasant it is for brethren to dwell together in unity! *Ps.* 133: 1.

The wolf also shall dwell with the lamb, and the leopard shall lie down with the kid; and the calf and the young lion and the fatling together; and a little child shall lead them. *Is.* 11: 6.

Can two walk together, except they be agreed? *Am.* 3: 3.

Nation shall not lift up a sword against nation, neither shall they learn war any more. *Mi.* 4: 3.

Have peace one with another. *Mk.* 9: 50.

Being assembled with one accord. *Ac.* 15: 25.

Now there are diversities of gifts, but the same Spirit. *1 Co.* **12: 4.**

Be of one mind, live in peace. *2 Co.* **13: 11.**

There is neither Jew nor Greek, there is neither bond nor free, there is neither male nor female: for ye are all one in Christ Jesus. *Ga.* **3: 28.**

He is our peace, who hath made both one. *Ep.* **2: 14.**

Endeavouring to keep the unity of the Spirit in the bond of peace. *Ep.* **4: 3.**

See also

Accord; Agreement; Compatibility; Harmony; Oneness; Peace; Unanimity; Unity.

Condemnation

Fear not: for am I in the place of God? *Ge.* **50: 19.**

Nathan said to David, Thou art the man. *2 S.* **12: 7.**

I have found thee: because thou hast sold thyself to work evil in the sight of the Lord. *1 K.* **21: 20.**

Because ye have forsaken the Lord, he hath also forsaken you. *2 Ch.* **24: 20.**

If I justify myself, mine own mouth shall condemn me. *Jb.* **9: 20.**

The Lord God will help me; who is he that shall condemn me? *Is.* **50: 9.**

Every tongue that shall rise against thee in judgment thou shalt condemn. *Is.* **54: 17.**

The queen of the south shall rise up in the judgment with this generation, and shall condemn it. *Mat.* **12: 42.**

Jesus answered and said unto it, No man eat fruit of thee hereafter for ever. *Mk.* **11: 14.**

Judge not, and ye shall not be judged. *Lu.* **6: 37.**

Those eighteen, upon whom the tower in Siloam fell, and slew them, think ye that they were sinners above all men that dwelt in Jerusalem? *Lu..* **13: 4.**

Out of thine own mouth will I judge thee. *Lu.* **19: 22.**

This is the condemnation, that light is come into the world, and men loved darkness rather than light, because their deeds were evil. *Jn.* **3: 19.**

They which heard it, being convicted by their own conscience, went out one by one. *Jn.* **8: 9.**

Wherein thou judgest another, thou condemnest thyself; for thou that judgest doest the same things. *Ro.* **2: 1.**

There is therefore now no condemnation to them which are in Christ Jesus. *Ro.* **8: 1.**

That ye come not together unto condemnation. *1 Co.* **11: 34.**

We shall receive the greater condemnation. For in many things we offend all. *Ja.* **3: 1, 2.**

Ye have condemned and killed the just. *Ja.* **5: 6.**

For if our heart condemn us, God is greater than our heart, and knoweth all things. *1 Jn.* **3: 20.**

See also

Blame; Censoriousness; Criticism; Denunciation; Disapproval; Harshness; Judgment; Rebuke; Reproach; Reproof.

Conduct

In the way of righteousness is life. *Pr.* **12: 28.**

This is the way, walk ye in it. *Is.* **30: 21.**

Except your righteousness shall exceed the righteousness of the scribes and Pharisees, ye shall in no case enter into the kingdom of heaven. *Mat.* **5: 20.**

Whatsoever ye would that men should do to you, do ye even so to them: for this is the law and the prophets. *Mat.* **7: 12.**

Whatsoever ye do, do all to the glory of God. *1 Co.* **10: 31.**

Be ye stedfast, unmoveable, always abounding in the work of the Lord. *1 Co.* **15: 58.**

Strengthened with might by his Spirit in the inner man. *Ep.* **3: 16.**

Put on the whole armour of God, that ye may be able to stand against the wiles of the devil. *Ep.* **6: 11.**

Let your conversation be as it becometh the gospel of Christ. *Ph.* **1: 27.**

That ye might walk worthy of the Lord unto all pleasing, being fruitful in every good work, and increasing in the knowledge of God. *Col.* **1: 10.**

Finally, be ye all of one mind, having compassion one of another; love as brethren, be pitiful, be courteous. *1 Pe.* **3: 8.**

He that doeth the will of God abideth for ever. *1 Jn.* **2: 17.**

See also

Behavior; Character; Goodness; Honor; Integrity; Manners; Quality; Rectitude; Trait.

Confession

Then they shall confess their sin which they have done. *Nu.* **5: 7.**

I have sinned; for I knew not that thou stoodest in the way against me: now therefore, if it displease thee, I will get me back again. *Nu.* **22: 34.**

I have sinned against the Lord God of Israel, and thus and thus have I done. *Jos.* **7: 20.**

I have transgressed the commandment of the Lord, and thy words: because I feared the people, and obeyed their voice. *1 S.* **15: 24.**

Making confession to the Lord God of their fathers. *2 Ch.* **30: 22.**

I said, I will confess my transgressions unto the Lord. *Ps.* **32: 5.**

The rich man's wealth is his strong city, and as a high wall in his own conceit. *Pr.* **18: 11.**

Only acknowledge thine iniquity, that thou hast transgressed against the Lord thy God, and hast scattered thy ways to the strangers under every green tree, and ye have not obeyed my voice, saith the Lord. *Je.* **3: 13.**

I prayed unto the Lord my God, and made my confession. *Da.* **9: 4.**

Baptized of him in Jordan, confessing their sins. *Mat.* **3: 6.**

Simon Peter answered and said, Thou art the Christ, the Son of the living God. *Mat.* **16: 16.**

Depart from me; for I am a sinful man, O Lord. *Lu.* **5: 8.**

Father, I have sinned against heaven, and before thee. *Lu.* **15: 18.**

Nathanael answered and saith unto him,

Rabbi, thou art the Son of God; thou art the King of Israel. *Jn.* 1: 49.

Come, see a man, which told me all things that ever I did: is not this the Christ? *Jn.* 4: 29.

We believe and are sure that thou art that Christ, the Son of the living God. *Jn.* 6: 69.

Thomas answered and said unto him, My Lord and my God. *Jn.* 20: 28.

No man can say that Jesus is the Lord, but by the Holy Ghost. *1 Co.* 12: 3.

Every tongue should confess that Jesus Christ is Lord. *Ph.* 2: 11.

Christ Jesus . . . witnessed a good confession. *1 Ti.* 6: 13.

Confess your faults one to another. *Ja.* 5: 16.

If we confess our sins, he is faithful and just to forgive us our sins. *1 Jn.* 1: 9.

Whosoever shall confess that Jesus is the Son of God, God dwelleth in him, and he in God. *1 Jn.* 4: 15.

See also

Contrition; Creed; Penitence; Remorse.

Confidence

Fear not: for they that be with us are more than they that be with them. *2 K.* 6: 16.

It is better to trust in the Lord than to put confidence in man. *Ps.* 118: 8.

They shall dwell safely, . . . and shall build houses, and plant vineyards; yea, they shall dwell with confidence. *Eze.* 28: 26.

Trust ye not in a friend, put ye not confidence in a guide. *Mi.* 7: 5.

If ye have faith as a grain of mustard seed, ye shall say unto this mountain, Remove hence to yonder place; and it shall remove. *Mat.* 17: 20.

So is the kingdom of God, as if a man should cast seed into the ground; And should sleep, and rise night and day, and the seed should spring and grow up, he knoweth not how. *Mk.* 4: 26, 27.

She said, If I may touch but his clothes, I shall be whole. . . . He said unto her, Daughter, thy faith hath made tnee whole. *Mk.* 5: 28, 34.

All things are possible to him that believeth. *Mk.* 9: 23.

Increase our faith. *Lu.* 17: 5.

While ye have light, believe in the light, that ye may be children of light. *Jn.* 12: 36.

Now I exhort you to be of good cheer: for there shall be no loss of any man's life among you, but of the ship. *Ac.* 27: 22.

The great confidence which I have in you. *2 Co.* 8: 22.

I have confidence in you through the Lord. *Ga.* 5: 10.

We . . . have no confidence in the flesh. *Ph.* 3: 3.

Rooted and built up in him, and stablished in the faith. *Col.* 2: 7.

We have confidence in the Lord touching you, that ye both do and will do the things which we command you. *2 Th.* 3: 4.

Having confidence in thy obedience I wrote unto thee, knowing that thou wilt also do more than I say. *Phm.* 1: 21.

See also

Assurance; Audacity; Belief; Christ, Belief in; Christ, Faith in; Dependence; God, Confidence in; God, Faith in; God, Reliance in; God, Trust in; Self-Confidence; Trust.

Confinement

The Lord shut him in. *Ge.* 7: 16.

They . . . limited the Holy One of Israel. *Ps.* 78: 41.

Thou hast loosed my bonds. *Ps.* 116: 16.

Bring my soul out of prison. *Ps.* 142: 7.

He hath sent me . . . to proclaim liberty to the captives, and the opening of the prison to them that are bound. *Is.* 61: 1.

Turn you to the strong hold, ye prisoners of hope. *Zch.* 9: 12.

The prisoner of Jesus Christ. *Ep.* 3: 1.

Others had trial . . . of bonds and imprisonment. *He.* 11: 36.

Remember them that are in bonds, as bound with them. *He.* 13: 3.

He laid hold on the dragon, that old serpent, which is the Devil, . . . And cast him into the bottomless pit, and shut him up, and set a seal upon him. *Re.* 20: 2, 3.

The gates of it shall not be shut at all by day. *Re.* 21: 25.

See also

Bound; Constraint; Imprisonment; Limitation; Prison.

Confirmation

Renew a right spirit within me. *Ps.* 51: 10.

Strengthen ye the weak hands, and confirm the feeble knees. *Is.* 35: 3.

Except a man be born again, he cannot see the kingdom of God. *Jn.* 3: 3.

Be ye tranformed by the renewing of your mind. *Ro.* 12: 2.

To confirm the promises. *Ro.* 15: 8.

Be renewed in the spirit of your mind. *Ep.* 4: 23.

See also

Acquiescence; Approval; Quickening; Renewal; Revival.

Conflict

The Lord your God is he that hath fought for us. *Jos.* 23: 3.

Though war should rise against me, in this will I be confident. *Ps.* 27: 3.

A sound of battle is in the land. *Je.* 50: 22.

The tempter came to him. *Mat.* 4: 3.

And was with the wild beasts; and the angels ministered unto him. *Mk.* 1: 13.

The wind was contrary unto them. *Mk.* 6: 48.

Fight the good fight of faith. *1 Ti.* 6: 12.

The battle of that great day of God Almighty. *Re.* 16: 14.

These shall make war with the Lamb. *Re.* 17: 14.

See also

Army; Battle; Contention; Enemy; Fight; Soldier; Strife; Struggle; War; Weapon.

Conformity

Each one resembled the children of a king. *Ju.* 8: 18.

Suffer it to be so now: for thus it becometh us to fulfil all righteousness. *Mat.* 3: 15.

Unto what is the kingdom of God like? and

whereunto shall I resemble it? *Lu.* 13: 18.

Whom he did foreknow, he also did predestinate to be conformed to the image of his Son. *Ro.* 8: 29.

Be not conformed to this world. *Ro.* 12: 2.

All things are of God, who hath reconciled us to himself by Jesus Christ. *2 Co.* 5: 18.

God was in Christ, reconciling the world unto himself. *2 Co.* 5: 19.

That I may know . . . the fellowship of his sufferings, being made conformable unto his death. *Ph.* 3: 10.

See, saith he, that thou make all things according to the pattern shewed to thee in the mount. *He.* 8: 5.

See also
Accord; Agreement; Assent; Concord; Conservatism; Custom; Harmony; Tradition.

Confusion

Go to, let us go down, and there confound their language. *Ge.* 11: 7.

They trusted in thee, and were not confounded. *Ps.* 22: 5.

Let them be confounded and put to shame that seek after my soul. *Ps.* 35: 4.

Horror hath overwhelmed me. *Ps.* 55: 5.

From the end of the earth will I cry unto thee, when my heart is overwhelmed. *Ps.* 61: 2.

Let me never be put to confusion. *Ps.* 71: 1.

They shall fight every one against his brother, and every one against his neighbour; city against city, and kingdom against kingdom. *Is.* 19: 2.

Jesus . . . overthrew the tables of the moneychangers, and the seats of them that sold doves. *Mat.* 21: 12.

God hath chosen the foolish things of the world to confound the wise. *1 Co.* 1: 27.

We behaved not ourselves disorderly among you. *2 Th.* 3: 7.

Where envying and strife is, there is confusion and every evil work. *Ja.* 3: 16.

He that believeth on him shall not be confounded. *1 Pe.* 2: 6.

See also
Anarchy; Babel; Bedlam; Bewilderment; Chaos; Clamor; Din.

Congregation

Let the Lord, the God of the spirits of all flesh, set a man over the congregation. *Nu.* 27: 16.

That the congregation of the Lord be not as sheep which have no shepherd. *Nu.* 27: 17.

All the congregation said, Amen, and praised the Lord. *Ne.* 5: 13.

Let us meet together in the house of God, within the temple. *Ne.* 6: 10.

I have not concealed thy lovingkindness and thy truth from the great congregation. *Ps.* 40: 10.

Let them exalt him also in the congregation of the people. *Ps.* 107: 32.

Where two or three are gathered together in my name, there am I in the midst of them. *Mat.* 18: 20.

See also
Assembly; Audience; Church; Crowd; Meeting.

Congress

I will make a league with thee. *2 S.* 3: 13.

The rulers take counsel together. *Ps.* 2: 2.

Let all the nations be gathered together, and let the people be assembled. *Is.* 43: 9.

I will gather all nations and tongues; and they shall come, and see my glory. *Is.* 66: 18.

Many nations shall come, and say, Come and let us go up to the mountain of the Lord . . . and he will teach us of his ways. *Mi.* 4: 2.

Before him shall be gathered all nations. *Mat.* 25: 32.

We then that are strong ought to bear the infirmities of the weak. *Ro.* 15: 1.

Bear ye one another's burdens. *Ga.* 6: 2.

See also
Assembly, Meeting.

Conquest

Arise, go over this Jordan. *Jos.* 1: 2.

Then thou shalt have good success. *Jos.* 1: 8.

Joshua said unto the people, Shout; for the Lord hath given you the city. *Jos.* 6: 16.

He that is slow to anger is better than the mighty; and he that ruleth his spirit than he that taketh a city. *Pr.* 16: 32.

In the world ye shall have tribulation: but be of good cheer; I have overcome the world. *Jn.* 16: 33.

Now thanks be unto God, which always causeth us to triumph in Christ. *2 Co.* 2: 14.

This is the victory that overcometh the world, even our faith. *1 Jn.* 5: 4.

He went forth conquering, and to conquer. *Re.* 6: 2.

See also
Christ, Triumph of; Mastery; Subjection; Success; Triumph; Victory.

Conscience

The wicked flee when no man pursueth: but the righteous are bold as a lion. *Pr.* 28: 1.

Herod . . . said, . . . This is John the Baptist; he is risen from the dead. *Mat.* 14: 1, 2.

And they which heard it, being convicted by their own conscience, went out one by one, beginning at the eldest, even unto the last: and Jesus was left alone, and the woman standing in the midst. *Jn.* 8: 9.

Paul, earnestly beholding the council, said, Men and brethren, I have lived in all good conscience before God until this day. *Ac.* 23: 1.

Herein do I exercise myself, to have always a conscience void of offence toward God, and toward men. *Ac.* 24: 16.

Take heed lest by any means this liberty of yours become a stumblingblock to them that are weak. *1 Co.* 8: 9.

When ye sin so against the brethren, and wound their weak conscience, ye sin against Christ. *1 Co.* 8: 12.

If meat make my brother to offend, I will eat no flesh while the world standeth, lest I make my brother to offend. *1 Co.* 8: 13.

Commending ourselves to every man's conscience in the sight of God. *2 Co.* 4: 2.

God, who is rich in mercy, . . . hath quickened us together with Christ. *Ep.* 2: 4, 5.

A good conscience. *1 Ti.* 1: 5.

Having their conscience seared with a hot iron. *1 Ti.* 4: 2.

As pertaining to the conscience. *He.* 9: 9.

We trust we have a good conscience, in all things willing to live honestly. *He.* 13: 18.

The answer of a good conscience toward God. *1 Pe.* 3: 21.

See also

Behavior; Character; Fairness; Godliness; Goodness; Holiness; Integrity; Light, the Inner; Rectitude; Right; Righteousness; Uprightness; Virtue.

Consecration

Consecrate yourselves to day to the Lord. *Ex.* 32: 29.

They have wholly followed the Lord. *Nu.* 32: 12.

They had sworn with all their heart, and sought him with their whole desire; and he was found of them. *2 Ch.* 15: 15.

Then said I, Here am I; send me. *Is.* 6: 8.

They shall consecrate themselves. *Eze.* 43: 26.

The Son . . . is consecrated for evermore. *He.* 7: 28.

By a new and living way, which he hath consecrated for us. *He.* 10: 20.

We ought to lay down our lives for the brethren. *1 Jn.* 3: 16.

See also

Dedication; Inauguration; Initiation; Installation; Offering; Ordination; Saint; Sanctification; Votary.

Consent

If ve will . . . walk contrary unto me; Then will I also walk contrary unto you. *Le.* 26: 23, 24.

And Ruth said, Intreat me not to leave thee, or to return from following after thee: for whither thou goest, I will go; and where thou lodgest, I will lodge: thy people shall be my people, and thy God my God. *Ru.* 1: 16.

I will walk in thy truth. *Ps.* 86: 11.

If sinners entice thee, consent thou not. *Pr.* 1: 10.

We will walk in the name of the Lord our God for ever and ever. *Mi.* 4: 5.

That they may all call upon the name of the Lord, to serve him with one consent. *Zph.* 3: 9.

Pilate gave sentence, that it should be as they required. *Lu.* 23: 24.

They were all with one accord in one place. *Ac.* 2: 1.

Continuing daily with one accord in the temple. *Ac.* 2: 46.

If then I do that which I would not, I consent unto the law that it is good. *Ro.* 7: 16.

Fulfil ve my joy, that ye be likeminded, having the same love, being of one accord, of one mind. *Ph.* 2: 2.

Consequence

Life shall go for life, eye for eye, tooth for tooth, hand for hand, foot for foot. *De.* 19: 21.

Choose life, that both thou and thy seed may live. *De.* 30: 19.

The sword shall never depart from thine house; because thou hast despised me. *2 S.* 12: 10.

They that plow iniquity, and sow wickedness, reap the same. *Jb.* 4: 8.

If I have rewarded evil unto him that was at peace with me; . . . Let the enemy persecute my soul. *Ps.* 7: 4, 5.

His mischief shall return upon his own head *Ps.* 7: 16.

I will fear no evil, for thou art with me. *Ps.* 23: 4.

Because thou hast made the Lord, which is my refuge, even the most High, thy habitation; There shall no evil befall thee. *Ps.* 91: 9, 10.

I will set him on high, because he hath known my name. *Ps.* 91: 14.

To the sinner he giveth travail, to gather and to heap up. *Ec.* 2: 26.

Cast thy bread upon the waters: for thou shalt find it after many days. *Ec.* 11: 1.

They have sown wheat, but shall reap thorns. *Je.* 12: 13.

Plant gardens, and eat the fruit of them. *Je.* 29: 5.

Yet say ye, Why? doth not the son bear the iniquity of the father? When the son hath done that which is lawful and right, and hath kept all my statutes, and hath done them, he shall surely live. *Eze.* 18: 19.

They have sown the wind, and they shall reap the whirlwind. *Ho.* 8: 7.

Sow to yourselves in righteousness, reap in mercy. *Ho.* 10: 12.

Ye have plowed wickedness, ye have reaped iniquity. *Ho.* 10: 13.

As thou hast done, it shall be done unto thee: thy reward shall return upon thine own head. *Ob.* 1: 15.

If ye have faith as a grain of mustard seed, ye shall say unto this mountain, Remove hence to yonder place; and it shall remove. *Mat.* 17: 20.

This do, and thou shalt live. *Lu.* 10: 28.

He that reapeth receiveth wages, and gathereth fruit unto life eternal. *Jn.* 4: 36.

If it be of God, ye cannot overthrow it. *Ac.* 5: 39.

Be not deceived; God is not mocked: for whatsover a man soweth, that shall he also reap. *Ga.* 6: 7.

Unto the pure all things are pure. *Tit.* 1: 15.

He that leadeth into captivity shall go into captivity: he that killeth with the sword must be killed with the sword. Here is the patience and the faith of the saints. *Re.* 13: 10.

See also

Aftermath; Fruit; Harvest; Reaping; Result.

Conservatism

Ask for the old paths, where is the good way, and walk therein. *Je.* 6: 16.

Can the Ethiopian change his skin, or the leopard his spots? *Je.* 13: 23.

Thus have ye made the commandment of God of none effect by your tradition. *Mat.* 15: 6.

No man putteth new wine into old bottles. *Mk.* 2: 22.

Ye reject the commandment of God, that ye may keep your own tradition. *Mk.* 7: 9.

As his custom was, he went into the synagogue on the sabbath day. *Lu.* 4: 16.

Our fathers worshiped in this mountain; and ye say, that in Jerusalem is the place where men ought to worship. *Jn.* 4: 20.

Zealous of the traditions of my fathers. *Ga.* 1: 14.

Since the fathers fell asleep, all things con-

tinue as they were from the beginning of the creation. *2 Pe. 3: 4.*
See also
Conformity; Custom; Tradition.

Consideration

O that they were wise, that they understood this, that they would consider their latter end! *De. 32: 29.*
Stand still, and consider the wondrous works of God. *Jb. 37: 14.*
When I consider thy heavens, the work of thy fingers. *Ps. 8: 3.*
Blessed is he that considereth the poor. *Ps. 41: 1.*
I have considered the days of old, the years of ancient times. *Ps. 77: 5.*
Go to the ant, thou sluggard; consider her ways, and be wise. *Pr. 6: 6.*
The ox knoweth his owner, and the ass his master's crib: but Israel doth not know, my people doth not consider. *Is. 1: 3.*
Come now, and let us reason together, saith the Lord. *Is. 1: 18.*
That they may see, and know, and consider, and understand together, that the hand of the Lord hath done this. *Is. 41: 20.*
Consider the lilies of the field how they grow. *Mat. 6: 28.*
Consider him that endured such contradiction of sinners against himself, lest ye be wearied and faint in your minds. *He. 12: 3.*
See also
Attention; Contemplation; Deliberation; Examination; God, Thought of; Meditation; Reflection; Regard; Reputation; Study; Thought.

Consolation

Miserable comforters are ye all. *Jb. 16: 2.*
I looked for some to take pity, but there was none; and for comforters, but I found none. *Ps. 69: 20.*
Let, I pray thee, thy merciful kindness be for my comfort. *Ps. 119: 76.*
Comfort ye, comfort ye my people, saith your God. *Is. 40: 1.*
That ye may . . . be satisfied with the breasts of her consolations. *Is. 66: 11.*
As one whom his mother comforteth, so will I comfort you. *Is. 66: 13.*
Woe unto you that are rich! for ye have received your consolation. *Lu. 6: 24.*
And now I exhort you to be of good cheer. *Ac. 27: 22.*
Whether we be afflicted, it is for your consolation and salvation: . . . or whether we be comforted, it is for your consolation and salvation. *2 Co. 1: 6.*
There shall be no more curse. *Re. 22: 3.*
See also
Christ, the Comforter; Christ, Sympathy of; Comforter; Ease; Relief; Solace.

Conspiracy

Blessed is the man that walketh not in the counsel of the ungodly. *Ps. 1: 1.*
They intended evil against thee: they imagined a mischievous device. *Ps. 21: 11.*
Hide me from the secret counsel of the wicked. *Ps. 64: 2.*
They encourage themselves in an evil matter. *Ps. 64: 5.*

The counsels of the wicked are deceit. *Pr. 12: 5.*
An evil man seeketh only rebellion. *Pr. 17: 11.*
These are the men that devise mischief, and give wicked counsel in this city. *Eze. 11: 2.*
Though I have bound and strengthened their arms, yet do they imagine mischief against me. *Ho. 7: 15.*
See also
Intrigue; Plot.

Constancy

He shall not alter it, nor change it, a good for a bad, or a bad for a good. *Le. 27: 10.*
I will establish his kingdom for ever, if he be constant to do my commandments and my judgments, as at this day. *1 Ch. 28: 7.*
A false witness shall perish: but the man that heareth speaketh constantly. *Pr. 21: 28.*
They continued stedfastly in the apostles' doctrine and fellowship. *Ac. 2: 42.*
Be ye stedfast, unmoveable, always abounding in the work of the Lord. *1 Co. 15: 58.*
Do all in the name of the Lord Jesus. *Col. 3: 17.*
These things I will that thou affirm constantly. *Tit. 3: 8.*
We are made partakers of Christ, if we hold the beginning of our confidence stedfast unto the end. *He. 3: 14.*
See also
Allegiance; Attachment; Christ, Faithfulness of; Devotion; Fidelity; Firmness; God, Faithfulness of; Loyalty; Security; Stability; Stedfastness.

Constellation

God said, Let there be a firmament in the midst of the waters. *Ge. 1: 6.*
God said, Let there be lights in the firmament of the heaven. *Ge. 1: 14.*
Which maketh Arcturus, Orion, and Pleiades. *Jb. 9: 9.*
Behold the height of the stars, how high they are. *Jb. 22: 12.*
Canst thou bind the sweet influences of Pleiades? *Jb. 38: 31.*
Canst thou guide Arcturus with his sons? *Jb. 38: 32.*
The sun to rule by day: . . . The moon and stars to rule by night. *Ps. 136: 8, 9.*
He telleth the number of the stars; he calleth them all by their names. *Ps. 147: 4.*
I will cover the heaven, and make the stars thereof dark; I will cover the sun with a cloud, and the moon shall not give her light. All the bright lights of heaven will I make dark over thee. *Eze. 32: 7, 8.*
There shall be signs in the sun, and in the moon, and in the stars. *Lu. 21: 25.*
There are also celestial bodies. *1 Co. 15: 40.*
There is one glory of the sun, and another glory of the moon, and another glory of the stars: for one star differeth from another star in glory. *1 Co. 15: 41.*
Wandering stars. *Jude 13.*
See also
Firmament; Heaven; Sky; Star.

Constraint

He enlargeth the nations, and straiteneth them again. *Jb. 12: 23.*

The spirit within me constraineth me. *Jb.* 32: 18.

He shall redeem their soul from deceit and violence. *Ps.* 72: 14.

Preserve me from the violent man. *Ps.* 140: 1.

They . . . drink the wine of violence. *Pr.* 4: 17.

Not by might, nor by power, but by my spirit, saith the Lord of hosts. *Zch.* 4: 6.

The truth shall make you free. *Jn.* 8: 32.

He that. is called, being free, is Christ's servant. *1 Co.* 7: 22.

We were pressed out of measure, above strength. *2 Co.* 1: 8.

The love of Christ constraineth us. *2 Co.* 5: 14.

Why compellest thou the Gentiles to live as do the Jews? *Ga.* 2: 14.

Not by constraint, but willingly. *1 Pe.* 5: 2.

See also

Coercion; Compulsion; Confinement; Force; Might; Restraint; Violence.

Contagion

He put his hand into his bosom: and when he took it out, behold, his hand was leprous as snow. *Ex.* 4: 6.

Thou shalt burn that wherein the plague is with fire. *Le.* 13: 57.

What man is there that is fearful and faint-hearted? let him go and return unto his house, lest his brethren's heart faint as well as his heart. *De.* 20: 8.

Surely he shall deliver thee from . . . the noisome pestilence. *Ps.* 91: 3.

Thou shalt not be afraid . . . for the pestilence that walketh in darkness. *Ps.* 91: 5, 6.

A merry heart doeth good like a medicine. *Pr.* 17: 22.

As coals are to burning coals, and wood to fire; so is a contentious man to kindle strife. *Pr.* 26: 21.

Behold a man full of leprosy: who seeing Jesus fell on his face, and besought him, saying, Lord, if thou wilt, thou canst make me clean. *Lu.* 5: 12.

Ye are manifestly declared to be the epistle of Christ. *2 Co.* 3: 3.

Be thou an example of the believers, in word, in conversation, in charity, in spirit, in faith, in purity. *1 Ti.* 4: 12.

See also

Blight; Defilement; Disease; Pestilence; Plague.

Contemplation

Mine eyes prevent the night watches, that I might meditate in thy word. *Ps.* 119: 148.

How precious also are thy thoughts unto me, O God! how great is the sum of them! *Ps.* 139: 17.

The ways of man are before the eyes of the Lord, and he pondereth all his goings. *Pr.* 5: 21.

Every way of a man is right in his own eyes: but the Lord pondereth the hearts. *Pr.* 21: 2.

I know the thoughts that I think toward you, saith the Lord, thoughts of peace, and not of evil. *Je.* 29: 11.

Mary kept all these things, and pondered them in her heart. *Lu.* 2: 19.

Finally, brethren, whatsoever things are true, whatsoever things are honest, whatsoever things are just, whatsoever things are pure, whatsoever things are lovely, whatsoever things are of good report: if there be any virtue, and if there be any praise, think on these things. *Ph.* 4: 8.

See also

Attention; Consideration; Deliberation; Examination; God, Thought of; Meditation; Reflection; Regard; Study; Thought.

Contempt

Them that honour me I will honour, and they that despise me shall be lightly esteemed. *1 S.* 2: 30.

The seat of the scornful. *Ps.* 1: 1.

A broken and a contrite heart, O God, thou wilt not despise. *Ps.* 51: 17.

We are exceedingly filled with contempt. *Ps.* 123: 3.

They have cast away the law of the Lord of hosts, and despised the word of the Holy One of Israel. *Is.* 5: 24.

Hear the word of the Lord, ye scornful men. *Is.* 28: 14.

Ye say, The table of the Lord is contemptible. *Mal.* 1: 7.

Whosoever shall say, Thou fool, shall be in danger of hell fire. *Mat.* 5: 22.

They laughed him to scorn. *Lu.* 8: 53.

Let no man despise thee. *Tit.* 2: 15.

Jesus . . . endured the cross, despising the shame. *He.* 12: 2.

See also

Disdain; Dishonor; Scorn.

Contention

Will ye contend for God? *Jb.* 13: 8.

I am for peace: but when I speak, they are for war. *Ps.* 120: 7.

A brother offended is harder to be won than a strong city: and their contentions are like the bars of a castle. *Pr.* 18: 19.

The contentions of a wife are a continual dropping. *Pr.* 19: 13.

It is an honour for a man to cease from strife. *Pr.* 20: 3.

It is better to dwell in a corner of the housetop, than with a brawling woman in a wide house. *Pr.* 21: 9.

They shall fight every one against his brother, and every one against his neighbour; city against city, and kingdom against kingdom. *Is.* 19: 2.

There are that raise up strife and contention. *Hab.* 1: 3.

We were bold in our God to speak unto you the gospel of God with much contention. *1 Th.* 2: 2.

Avoid . . . contentions. *Tit.* 3: 9.

See also

Battle; Conflict; Contest; Controversy; Fight; Quarrel; Strife; War.

Contentment

Ye shall eat, and not be satisfied. *Le.* 26: 26.

The lines are fallen unto me in pleasant places. *Ps.* 16: 6.

Rest in the Lord, and wait patiently for him. *Ps.* 37: 7.

Satisfy us early with thy mercy. *Ps.* 90: 14.

He . . . satisfied them with the bread of heaven. *Ps.* 105: 40.

He satisfieth the longing soul, and filleth the hungry soul with goodness. *Ps.* 107: 9.

Great peace have they which love thy law: and nothing shall offend them. *Ps.* 119: 165.

Better is little with the fear of the Lord, than great treasure and trouble therewith. *Pr.* 15: 16.

Better is a dinner of herbs where love is, than a stalled ox and hatred therewith. *Pr.* 15: 17.

Better is a little with righteousness, than great revenues without right. *Pr.* 16: 8.

Better is a handful with quietness, than both the hands full with travail and vexation of spirit. *Ec.* 4: 6.

To be spiritually minded is life and peace. *Ro.* 8: 6.

I have learned, in whatsoever state I am, therewith to be content. *Ph.* 4: 11.

Godliness with contentment is great gain. *1 Ti.* 6: 6.

Having food and raiment let us be therewith content. *1 Ti.* 6: 8.

Be content with such things as ye have. *He.* 13: 5.

See also

Christ, the Comforter; Comfort; Comforter; Ease; Happiness; Pleasure; Relief; Satiety.

Contest

Send me good speed this day. *Ge.* 24: 12.

Jacob was left alone; and there wrestled a man with him until the breaking of the day. *Ge.* 32: 24.

Rejoiceth as a strong man to run a race. *Ps.* 19: 5.

They shall run, and not be weary. *Is.* 40: 31.

Their horses also are swifter than the leopards. *Hab.* 1: 8.

The kingdom of heaven suffereth violence and the violent take it by force. *Mat.* 11: 12.

Suppose ye·that I am come to give peace on earth? I tell you, Nay; but rather division. *Lu.* 12: 51.

What king, going to make war against another king, sitteth not down first, and consulteth whether he be able with ten thousand to meet him that cometh against him with twenty thousand? *Lu.* 14: 31.

The one preach Christ of contention, not sincerely, supposing to add affliction to my bonds. *Ph.* 1: 16.

Fight the good fight of faith. *1 Ti.* 6: 12.

If a man also strive for masteries, yet is he not crowned, except he strive lawfully. *2 Ti.* 2: 5.

I will give unto every one of you according to your works. *Re.* 2: 23.

See also

Athlete; Competition; Contention; Game; Race; Rivalry.

Continence

Keep thee from every wicked thing. *De.* 23: 9.

Write unto them, that they abstain from pollutions of idols. *Ac.* 15: 20.

Abstain from meats offered to idols. *Ac.* 15: 29.

After long abstinence Paul stood forth in the midst of them. *Ac.* 27: 21.

Every man that striveth for the mastery is temperate in all things. *1 Co.* 9: 25.

We should not lust after evil things. *1 Co.* 10: 6.

Flee also youthful lusts. *2 T.* 2: 22.

Abstain from fleshy lusts, which war against the soul. *1 Pe.* 2: 11.

Add . . . to knowledge temperance. *2 Pe.* 1: 5, 6.

The world passeth away, and the lust thereof: but he that doeth the will of God abideth for ever. *1 Jn.* 2: 17.

See also

Abstinence; Control; Mastery; Self-Control; Temperance.

Continuity

Speak unto the children of Israel, that they go forward. *Ex.* 14: 15.

Seek the Lord and his strength, seek his face continually. *1 Ch.* 16: 11.

Thy God whom thou servest continually, he will deliver thee. *Da.* 6: 16.

Think not that I am come to destroy the law, or the prophets: I am not come to destroy, but to fulfill. *Mat.* 5: 17.

Continually in the temple, praising and blessing God. *Lu.* 24: 53.

In my Father's house are many mansions: if it were not so, I would have told you. I go to prepare a place for you. *Jn.* 14: 2.

Continue ye in my love. *Jn.* 15: 9.

Patient continuance in well doing. *Ro.* 2: 7.

Continuing instant in prayer. *Ro.* 12: 12.

I have planted, Apollos watered; but God gave the increase. . . . We are labourers together with God. *1 Co.* 3: 6, 9.

That the truth of the gospel might continue with you. *Ga.* 2: 5.

Being confident of this very thing, that he which hath begun a good work in you will perform it until the day of Jesus Christ. *Ph.* 1: 6.

Continue in the faith grounded and settled. *Col.* 1: 23.

Let us go on unto perfection. *He.* 6: 1.

Jesus Christ the same yesterday, and to day, and for ever. *He.* 13: 8.

If that which ye have heard from the beginning shall remain in you, ye also shall continue in the Son, and in the Father. *1 Jn.* 2: 24.

See also

Constancy; Immortality; Life, Eternal; Progress.

Contract

Therefore shall a man leave his father and his mother, and shall cleave unto his wife. *Ge.* 2: 24.

I will remember my covenant, which is between me and you and every living creature of all flesh; and the waters shall no more become a flood to destroy all flesh. *Ge.* 9: 15.

Let there be now an oath betwixt us, even betwixt us and thee. *Ge.* 26: 28.

The Lord made not this covenant with our fathers, but with us, even us. *De.* 5: 3.

Ye shall walk in all the ways which the Lord your God hath commanded you, that ye may live. *De.* 5: 33.

They are joined one to another, they stick together, that they cannot be sundered. *Jb.* 41: 17.

Come, and let us join ourselves to the Lord in a perpetual covenant. *Je.* 50: 5.

They . . . remembered not the brotherly covenant. *Am.* 1: 9.

What therefore God hath joined together, let not man put asunder. *Mat.* 19: 6.

At that time ye were . . . strangers from the covenants of promise. *Ep.* 2: 12.

Knit together in love. *Col.* 2: 2.

See also

Accord; Agreement; Bargain; Compact; Covenant; Treaty.

Contradiction

I will give you a mouth and wisdom, which all your adversaries shall not be able to gainsay nor resist. *Lu.* 21: 15.

The Jews . . . spake against those things which were spoken by Paul, contradicting and blaspheming. *Ac.* 13: 45.

Mark them which cause divisions and offences contrary to the doctrine which ye have learned; and avoid them. *Ro.* 16: 17.

That he may be able by sound doctrine both to exhort and to convince the gainsayers. *Tit.* 1: 9.

Consider him that endured such contradiction of sinners against himself. *He.* 12: 3.

See also

Argument; Christ, Denial of; Controversy; Denial; God, Denial of; Opposition.

Contribution

I will appease him with the present that goeth before me, and afterward I will see his face; peradventure he will accept of me. *Ge.* 32: 20.

Thou shalt take no gift: for the gift blindeth the wise. *Ex.* 23: 8.

Out of all your gifts ye shall offer every heave offering of the Lord, of all the best thereof, even the hallowed part thereof out of it. *Nu.* 18: 29.

The people willingly offered themselves. *Ju.* 5: 2.

Eli called Samuel, and said, Samuel, my son. And he answered, Here am I. *1 S.* 3: 16.

Let a double portion of thy spirit be upon me. *2 K.* 2: 9.

Is it a time to receive money? *2 K.* 5: 26.

A gift in secret pacifieth anger. *Pr.* 21: 14.

Whoso boasteth himself of a false gift is like clouds and wind without rain. *Pr.* 25: 14.

Give me neither poverty nor riches; feed me with food convenient for me. *Pr.* 30: 8.

First be reconciled to thy brother, and then come and offer thy gift. *Mat.* 5: 24.

Father, give me the portion of goods that falleth to me. And he divided unto them his living. *Lu.* 15: 12.

Thou never gavest me a kid, that I might make merry with my friends. *Lu.* 15: 29.

Silver and gold have I none; but such as I have give I thee. *Ac.* 3: 6.

God gave them the like gift as he did unto us. *Ac.* 11: 17.

Remember the words of the Lord Jesus, how he said, It is more blessed to give than to receive. *Ac.* 20: 35.

It hath pleased them of Macedonia and Achaia to make a certain contribution for the poor saints which are at Jerusalem. *Ro.* 15: 26.

So that ye come behind in no gift. *1 Co.* 1: 7.

Every man hath his proper gift of God, one after this manner, and another after that. *1 Co.* 7: 7.

My God shall supply all your need. *Ph.* 4: 19.

That they be rich in good works, ready to distribute, willing to communicate. *1 Ti.* 6: 18.

I am now ready to be offered. *2 Ti.* 4: 6.

See also

Almsgiving; Charity; Donation; Generosity; Gift; Present.

Contrition

The Lord hath heard the voice of my weeping. *Ps.* 6: 8.

The Lord is nigh unto them that are of a broken heart. *Ps.* 34: 18.

A broken and a contrite heart, O God, thou wilt not despise. *Ps.* 51: 17.

I dwell . . . with him also that is of a contrite and humble spirit, to revive the spirit of the humble, and to revive the heart of the contrite ones. *Is.* 57: 15.

Return unto me, and I will return unto you, saith the Lord of hosts. *Mal.* 3: 7.

Father, I have sinned against heaven, and before thee. *Lu.* 15: 18.

God . . . now commandeth all men every where to repent. *Ac.* 17: 30.

Repent and turn to God, and do works meet for repentance. *Ac.* 26: 20.

If they shall fall away, to renew them again unto repentance. *He.* 6: 6.

See also

Ash Wednesday; Grief; Lent; Penitence; Regret; Remorse; Repentance; Sorrow.

Control

They grope in the dark without light, and he maketh them to stagger like a drunken man. *Jb.* 12: 25.

Canst thou bind the sweet influences of Pleiades, or loose the bands of Orion? *Jb.* 38: 31.

When I consider thy heavens, the work of thy fingers, the moon and the stars, which thou hast ordained. *Ps.* 8: 3.

Thou hast put all things under his feet. *Ps.* 8: 6.

The steps of a good man are ordered by the Lord. *Ps.* 37: 23.

They reel to and fro, and stagger like a drunken man, and are at their wit's end. *Ps.* 107: 27.

He that is slow to anger is better than the mighty; and he that ruleth his spirit than he that taketh a city. *Pr.* 16: 32.

He that hath no rule over his own spirit is like a city that is broken down, and without walls. *Pr.* 25: 28.

They stagger, but not with strong drink. *Is.* 29: 9.

Abstain from fleshly lusts, which war against the soul. *1 Pe.* 2: 11.

See also

Abstinence; Continence; Mastery; Self-Control; Temperance.

Controversy

Debate thy cause with thy neighbour himself. *Pr.* 25: 9.

The Lord hath a controversy with the nations, he will plead with all flesh. *Je.* 25: 31.

The Lord hath a controversy with the inhabitants of the land, because there is no truth, nor mercy, nor knowledge of God in the land. *Ho.* 4: 1.

Hear ye, O mountains, the Lord's controversy. *Mi.* 6: 2.

By the way they had disputed among themselves, who should be the greatest. *Mk.* 9: 34.

There arose no small stir about that way. *Ac.* 19: 23.

Him that is weak in the faith receive ye, but not to doubtful disputations. *Ro.* 14: 1.

See also

Argument; Conflict; Contention; Debate; Dispute; Fight; Quarrel; Strife.

Conversation

Should a man full of talk be justified? *Jb.* 11: 2.

Should he reason with unprofitable talk? or with speeches wherewith he can do no good? *Jb.* 15: 3.

Hereafter I will not talk much with you. *Jn.* 14: 30.

Be not deceived: evil communications corrupt good manners. *1 Co.* 15: 33.

Let no corrupt communication proceed out of your mouth, but that which is good to the use of edifying, that it may minister grace unto the hearers. *Ep.* 4: 29.

Our conversation is in heaven. *Ph.* 3: 20.

Let your speech be alway with grace, seasoned with salt, that ye may know how ye ought to answer every man. *Col.* 4: 6.

Be thou an example of the believers, in word, in conversation, in charity. *1 Ti.* 4: 12.

Be ye holy in all manner of conversation. *1 Pe.* 1: 15.

Redeemed . . . from your vain conversation received by tradition from your fathers. *1 Pe.* 1: 18.

Having your conversation honest among the Gentiles. *1 Pe.* 2: 12.

Vexed with the filthy conversation of the wicked. *2 Pe.* 2: 7.

See also

Communion; Gossip; Lip; Mouth; Speech; Talk; Tongue.

Conversion

The law of the Lord is perfect, converting the soul. *Ps.* 19: 7.

Restore unto me the joy of thy salvation. *Ps.* 51: 12.

Sinners shall be converted unto thee. *Ps.* 51: 13.

I thought on my ways, and turned my feet unto thy testimonies. *Ps.* 119: 59.

Wash you, make you clean; put away the evil of your doings from before mine eyes; cease to do evil; Learn to do well. *Is.* 1: 16, 17.

Zion shall be redeemed with judgment, and her converts with righteousness. *Is.* 1: 27.

Let the wicked forsake his way, and the unrighteous man his thoughts: and let him return unto the Lord, and he will have mercy upon him; and to our God, for he will abundantly pardon. *Is.* 55: 7.

The Spirit of the Lord God is upon me;

. . . to give unto them beauty for ashes, the oil of joy for mourning, the garment of praise for the spirit of heaviness. *Is.* 61: 1, 3.

It is time to seek the Lord, till he come and rain righteousness upon you. *Ho.* 10: 12.

Turn thou to thy God: keep mercy and judgment, and wait on thy God continually. *Ho.* 12: 6.

Except ye be converted, and become as little children, ye shall not enter into the kingdom of heaven. *Mat.* 18: 3.

When thou art converted, strengthen thy brethren. *Lu.* 22: 32.

Marvel not that I said unto thee, Ye must be born again. *Jn.* 3: 7.

Repent ye therefore, and be converted, that your sins may be blotted out. *Ac.* 3: 19.

They passed through Phenice and Samaria, declaring the conversion of the Gentiles. *Ac.* 15: 3.

I am not ashamed of the gospel of Christ: for it is the power of God unto salvation to every one that believeth. *Ro.* 1: 16.

If all prophesy, and there come in one that believeth not, or one unlearned, he is convinced of all, he is judged of all: And thus are the secrets of his heart made manifest; and so falling down on his face he will worship God, and report that God is in you of a truth. *1 Co.* 14: 24, 25.

That ye put off . . . the old man, . . . And that ye put on the new man. *Ep.* 4: 22, 24.

He which converteth the sinner from the error of his way shall save a soul from death, and shall hide a multitude of sins. *Ja.* 5: 20.

See also

Amendment; Change; Contrition; Lent; Life, the New; Penitence; Proselyte; Purification; Renascence, Repentance; Turn.

Conviction

That thou mightest know the certainty of those things, wherein thou hast been instructed. *Lu.* 1: 4.

When the centurion saw what was done, he glorified God, saying, Certainly this was a righteous man. *Lu.* 23: 47.

Many more believed because of his own word. *Jn.* 4: 41.

Convicted by their own conscience. *Jn.* 8: 9.

Which of you convinceth me of sin? *Jn.* 8: 46.

Whether he be a sinner or no, I know not: one thing I know, that, whereas I was blind, now I see. *Jn.* 9: 25.

While ye have light, believe in the light, that ye may be the children of light. *Jn.* 12: 36.

He mightily convinced the Jews, and that publickly, shewing by the scriptures that Jesus was Christ. *Ac.* 18: 28.

We are sure that the judgment of God is according to truth. *Ro.* 2: 2.

Let every man be fully persuaded in his own mind. *Ro.* 14: 5.

Charity . . . believeth all things. *1 Co.* 13: 4, 7.

That he may be able by sound doctrine both to exhort and to convince the gainsayers. *Tit.* 1: 9.

The Lord cometh . . . to convince all that are ungodly among them of all their ungodly deeds which they have ungodly committed. *Jude* 1: 14, 15.

See also

Assurance; Belief; Certainty; Christ, Belief in; Christ, Faith in; Confidence; Faith; God, Faith in; Persuasion.

Cooperation

Aaron and Hur stayed up his hands, the one on the one side, and the other on the other side. *Ex.* 17: 12.

The sword of the Lord, and of Gideon. *Ju.* 7: 20.

All the men of Israel were gathered against the city, knit together as one man. *Ju.* 20: 11.

Behold, I am with thee according to thy heart. *1 S.* 14: 7.

Arise; for this matter belongeth unto thee: we also will be with thee: be of good courage, and do it. *Ezr.* 10: 4.

They helped every one his neighbour; and every one said to his brother, Be of good courage. *Is.* 41: 6.

So the carpenter encouraged the goldsmith, and he that smootheth with the hammer him that smote the anvil. *Is.* 41: 7.

If two of you shall agree on earth as touching any thing that they shall ask, it shall be done for them of my Father which is in heaven. *Mat.* 18: 19.

The Lord working with them. *Mk.* 16: 20.

They beckoned unto their partners, . . . that they should come and help them. *Lu.* 5: 7.

All that believed were together, and had all things common. *Ac.* 2: 44.

God . . . provided some better thing for us, that they without us should not be made perfect. *He.* 11: 40.

See also

Association; Christ, Fellowship with; Christ, Partnership with; Collaboration; Company; Fellowship; Fellow-Worker; God, Fellowship with; God, Partnership with; Partner.

Cordiality

Turn in, I pray you, into your servant's house, and tarry all night, and wash your feet, and ye shall rise up early, and go on your ways. *Ge.* 19: 2.

Love ye therefore the stranger: for ye were strangers. *De.* 10: 19.

Why have I found grace in thine eyes that thou shouldest take knowledge of me, seeing I am a stranger? *Ru.* 2: 10.

The stranger did not lodge in the street: but I opened my doors to the traveller. *Jb.* 31: 32.

A friend loveth at all times. *Pr.* 17: 17.

A man that hath friends must show himself friendly. *Pr.* 18: 24.

There is a friend that sticketh closer than a brother. *Pr.* 18: 24.

How can one be warm alone? *Ec.* 4: 11.

I was an hungred, and ye gave me meat: I was thirsty, and ye gave me drink: I was a stranger, and ye took me in. *Mat.* 25: 35.

When he was yet a great way off, his father saw him, and had compassion, and ran and fell on his neck, and kissed him. *Lu.* 15: 20.

They constrained him, saying, Abide with us: for it is toward evening, and the day is far spent. *Lu.* 24: 29.

Be kindly affectioned one to another with brotherly love. *Ro.* 12: 10.

Whatsoever ye do, do it heartily, as to the Lord. *Col.* 3: 23.

Greet all the brethren with an holy kiss. *1 Th.* 5: 26.

If a brother or sister be naked, and destitute of daily food, And one of you say unto them, Depart in peace, be ye warmed and filled; notwithstanding ye give them not those things which are needful to the body; what doth it profit? *Ja.* 2: 15, 16.

See also

Hospitality; Welcome.

Cornerstone

The stone which the builders rejected is become the head of the corner. *Mk.* 12: 10.

Other foundation can no man lay than that is laid, which is Jesus Christ. *1 Co.* 3: 11.

Jesus Christ himself being the chief corner stone. *Ep.* 2: 20.

Behold, I lay in Sion a chief corner stone, elect, precious: and he that believeth on him shall not be confounded. *1 Pe.* 2: 6.

See also

Christ, the Foundation; Foundation.

Coronation

Thou . . . hast crowned him with glory and honour. *Ps.* 8: 5.

The Lord . . . crowneth thee with lovingkindness and tender mercies. *Ps.* 103: 2, 4.

I put a jewel on thy forehead, and earrings in thine ears, and a beautiful crown upon thine head. *Eze.* 16: 12.

They do it to obtain a corruptible crown; but we an incorruptible. *1 Co.* 9: 25.

I have kept the faith: Henceforth there is laid up for me a crown of righteousness, which the Lord, the righteous judge, shall give me at that day. *2 Ti.* 4: 7, 8.

Thou madest him a little lower than the angels; thou crownedst him with glory and honour. *He.* 2: 7.

Upon the cloud one sat like unto the Son of man, having on his head a golden crown. *Re.* 14: 14.

See also

Christ, Crown of; Crown; Diadem.

Correction

My punishment is greater than I can bear. *Ge.* 4: 13.

When thou with rebukes dost correct man for iniquity, thou makest his beauty to consume away like a moth. *Ps.* 39: 11.

He that spareth his rod hateth his son. *Pr.* 13: 24.

The rod and reproof give wisdom: but a child left to himself bringeth his mother to shame. *Pr.* 29: 15.

Thine own wickedness shall correct thee. *Je.* 2: 19.

When Aquila and Priscilla had heard, they took him unto them, and expounded unto him the way of God more perfectly. *Ac.* 18: 26.

In stripes above measure, in prisons more frequent, in deaths oft. *2 Co.* 11: 23.

Thrice was I beaten with rods, once was I stoned. *2 Co.* 11: 25.

All Scripture is . . . profitable for doctrine, for reproof, for correction. *2 Ti.* 3: 16.

No chastening for the present seemeth to be joyous, but grievous. *He.* 12: 11.

Governors, . . . sent by him for the punishment of evil doers, and for the praise of them that do well. *1 Pe.* 2: 14.

See also

Amendment; Amends; Chastisement; Discipline; God, Chastisement of; God, Punishment of; Punishment; Rebuke; Reproach; Reproof; Rod; Scourge; Stripe.

Corruption

Help, Lord; for the godly man ceaseth; for the faithful fail from among the children of men. *Ps.* 12: 1.

Ye . . . trust in oppression and perverseness. *Is.* 30: 12.

Your hands are defiled with blood, and your fingers with iniquity; your lips have spoken lies, your tongue hath muttered perverseness. *Is.* 59: 3.

Judgment is turned away backward, and justice standeth afar off: for truth is fallen in the street, and equity cannot enter. *Is.* 59: 14.

Ye have perverted the words of the living God. *Je.* 23: 36.

They have even defiled my holy name by their abominations. *Eze.* 43: 8.

Princes . . . that abhor judgment, and pervert all equity. *Mi.* 3: 9.

The good man is perished out of the earth: and there is none upright among men. *Mi.* 7: 2.

Deliver us from evil. *Mat.* 6: 13.

Lay not up for yourselves treasures upon earth, where moth and rust doth corrupt. *Mat.* 6: 19.

O faithless and perverse generation, . . . how long shall I suffer you? *Mat.* 17: 17.

Jesus went into the temple, and began to cast out them that sold and bought in the temple. *Mk.* 11: 15.

Wheresoever the body is, thither will the eagles be gathered together. *Lu.* 17: 37.

His soul was not left in hell, neither his flesh did see corruption. *Ac.* 2: 31.

The creature itself also shall be delivered from the bondage of corruption into the glorious liberty of the children of God. *Ro.* 8: 21.

This corruptible must put on incorruption. *1 Co.* 15: 53.

Looking diligently lest any man fail of the grace of God. *He.* 12: 15.

See also

Adulteration; Crime; Defilement; Degeneration; Depravity; Evil; Impurity; Iniquity; Lust; Sin; Sinner; Stain; Ungodliness; Unrighteousness; Vileness; Wickedness.

Cost

The price of wisdom is above rubies. *Jb.* 28: 18.

Ye shall seek me, and find me, when ye shall search for me with all your heart. *Je.* 29: 13.

Good master, what good thing shall I do, that I may have eternal life? *Mat.* 19: 16.

Which of you, intending to build a tower, sitteth not down first, and counteth the cost? *Lu.* 14: 28.

Know ye not that . . . ye are not your own? For ye are bought with a price. *1 Co.* 6: 19, 20.

I count all things but loss for the excellency of the knowledge of Christ Jesus. *Ph.* 3: 8.

Not with broided hair, or gold, or pearls, or costly array. *1 Ti.* 2: 9.

Look to yourselves, that we lose not those things which we have wrought, but that we receive a full reward. *2 Jn.* 1: 8.

See also

Price; Sacrifice; Suffering.

Counsel

Come now therefore, and let us take counsel together. *Ne.* 6: 7.

Thou gavest also thy good spirit to instruct them. *Ne.* 9: 20.

Thy testimonies also are my delight and my counsellors. *Ps.* 119: 24.

Counsel is mine, and sound wisdom: I am understanding. *Pr.* 8: 14.

Give instruction to a wise man, and he will be yet wiser. *Pr.* 9: 9.

In the multitude of counsellors there is safety. *Pr.* 11: 14.

The way of a fool is right in his own eyes: but he that hearkeneth unto counsel is wise. *Pr.* 12: 15.

With the well advised is wisdom. *Pr.* 13: 10.

His name shall be called Wonderful, Counsellor. *Is.* 9: 6.

The Lord of hosts, which is wonderful in counsel, and excellent in working. *Is.* 28: 29.

Woe to the rebellious children, saith the Lord, that take counsel, but not of me! *Is.* 30: 1.

Take heed therefore how ye hear. *Lu.* 8: 18.

Herein I give my advice: for this is expedient for you. *2 Co.* 8: 10.

See also

Admonition; Advice; Charge; Exhortation; Instruction.

Count

Look now toward heaven, and tell the stars, if thou be able to number them. *Ge.* 15: 5.

The Lord your God hath multiplied you, and, behold, ye are this day as the stars of heaven for multitude. *De.* 1: 10.

Canst thou number the months that they fulfil? *Jb.* 39: 2.

If I should count them, they are more in number than the sand. *Ps.* 139: 18.

He telleth the number of the stars. *Ps.* 147: 4.

As the host of heaven cannot be numbered, neither the sand of the sea measured: so will I multiply the seed of David my servant. *Je.* 33: 22.

But the very hairs of your head are all numbered. *Mat.* 10: 30.

I count all things but loss for the excellency of the knowledge of Christ Jesus my Lord. *Ph.* 3: 8.

The number of them was ten thousand times ten thousand, and thousands of thousands. *Re.* 5: 11.

See also

Account; Calculation; Division; Multiplication.

Countenance

A man of God came unto me, and his

countenance was like the countenance of an angel of God. *Ju.* 13: 6.

Then shalt thou lift up thy face without spot. *Jb.* 11: 15.

A merry heart maketh a cheerful countenance. *Pr.* 15: 13.

The Lord God will wipe away tears from off all faces. *Is.* 25: 8.

Whosoever shall smite thee on thy right cheek, turn to him the other also. *Mat.* 5: 39.

All . . . saw his face as it had been the face of an angel. *Ac.* 6: 15.

See also

Christ, Face of; Encouragement; Face; Favor; God, Face of.

Counterfeit

The people gathered themselves together unto Aaron, and said unto him, Up, make us gods, which shall go before us. *Ex.* 32: 1.

He set a carved image, the idol which he had made, in the house of God. *2 Ch.* 33: 7.

Ye are forgers of lies. *Jb.* 13: 4.

The proud have forged a lie. *Ps.* 119: 69.

His molten image is falsehood, and there is no breath in them. *Je.* 10: 14.

Woe unto him that saith to the wood, Awake; to the dumb stone, Arise, it shall teach! Behold, it is laid over with gold and silver, and there is no breath at all in the midst of it. *Hab.* 2: 19.

Ye devour widows' houses, and for a pretence make long prayer. *Mat.* 23: 14.

We know that an idol is nothing in the world, and that there is none other God but one. *1 Co.* 8: 4.

As we have borne the image of the earthy, we shall also bear the image of the heavenly. *1 Co.* 15: 49.

See also

Adulteration; Fraud; Sham.

Country

He . . . will be merciful unto his land, and. to his people. *De.* 32: 43.

Blessed of the Lord be his land. *De.* 33: 13.

The Lord will give strength unto his people; the Lord will bless his people with peace. *Ps.* 29: 11.

Lord, thou hast been favourable unto thy land. *Ps.* 85: 1.

Open ye the gates, that the righteous nation which keepeth the truth may enter in. *Is.* 26: 2.

I will gather the remnant of my flock out of all countries whither I have driven them, and will bring them again to their folds. *Je.* 23: 3.

A prophet hath no honour in his own country. *Jn.* 4: 44.

In perils by mine own countrymen. *2 Co.* 11: 26.

See also

Land; Nation; Nation, Decadence of; Nation, Greatness of; Nation, Prosperity of; Nations, League of; People; Race; State.

Country, the Better

I will give unto thee, and to thy seed after thee, the land wherein thou art a stranger. *Ge.* 17: 8.

Unto a good land and a large, unto a land flowing with milk and honey. *Ex.* 3: 8.

Go up and view the country. *Jos.* 7: 2.

I will make the wilderness a pool of water, and the dry land springs of water. *Is.* 41: 18.

The kingdom of heaven is as a man travelling into a far country. *Mat.* 25: 14.

He went out from thence, and came into his own country. *Mk.* 6: 1.

They . . . declare plainly that they seek a country. *He.* 11: 14.

Now they desire a better country, that is, an heavenly. *He.* 11: 16.

See also

Age, the Golden; Day, the Coming; Future; Land, the Promised; Millennium; Pilgrim.

Courage

After these things the word of the Lord came unto Abram in a vision, saying, Fear not, Abram: I am thy shield, and thy exceeding great reward. *Ge.* 15: 1.

Ye shall not be afraid of the face of man; for the judgment is God's. *De.* 1: 17.

When thou goest out to battle against thine enemies, and seest horses, and chariots, and a people more than thou, be not afraid of them. *De.* 20: 1.

Be strong and of good courage. *De.* 31: 6.

Only be thou strong and very courageous. *Jos.* 1: 7.

As captain of the host of the Lord am I now come. *Jos.* 5: 14.

If so be the Lord will be with me, then I shall be able to drive them out. *Jos.* 14: 12.

There is no restraint to the Lord to save by many or by few. *1 S.* 14: 6.

Let no man's heart fail because of him; thy servant will go and fight with this Philistine. *1 S.* 17: 32.

Fear not: for they that be with us are more than they that be with them. *2 K.* 6: 16.

These were . . . men of valour, famous men. *1 Ch.* 5: 24.

Should such a man as I flee? *Ne.* 6: 11.

Whoso putteth his trust in the Lord shall be safe. *Pr.* 29: 25.

Fear thou not; for I am with thee: be not dismayed; for I am thy God: I will strengthen thee; yea, I will help thee; yea, I will uphold thee with the right hand of my righteousness. *Is.* 41: 10.

Who art thou, that thou shouldest be afraid of a man that shall die, and of the son of man which shall be made as grass. *Is.* 51: 12.

When Daniel knew that the writing was signed, he went into his house; and his windows being open in his chamber toward Jerusalem, he kneeled upon his knees three times a day, and prayed, and gave thanks before his God, as he did aforetime. *Da.* 6: 10.

They were all filled with the Holy Ghost, and they spake the word of God with boldness. *Ac.* 4: 31.

He spake boldly in the name of the Lord Jesus. *Ac.* 9: 29.

There stood by me this night the angel of God, whose I am, and whom I serve, saying, Fear not, Paul; thou must be brought before Caesar. *Ac.* 27: 23, 24.

In nothing terrified by your adversaries. *Ph.* 1: 28.

I can do all things through Christ that strengtheneth me. *Ph.* 4: 13.

So that we may boldly say, The Lord is my helper, and I will not fear what man shall do unto me. *He.* 13: 6.

See also
Audacity; Boldness; Bravery; Decision; Fearlessness; Fortitude; Heroism; Valor.

Court

The palace is not for man, but for the Lord God. *1 Ch.* 29: 1.
God is known in her palaces for a refuge. *Ps.* 48: 3.
He built his sanctuary like high palaces. *Ps.* 78: 69.
My soul longeth, yea, even fainteth for the courts of the Lord. *Ps.* 84: 2.
A day in thy courts is better than a thousand. *Ps.* 84: 10.
Those that be planted in the house of the Lord shall flourish in the courts of our God. *Ps.* 92: 13.
Bring an offering, and come into his courts. *Ps.* 96: 8.
Enter into his gates with thanksgiving, and into his courts with praise. *Ps.* 100: 4.
Ye that stand in the house of the Lord, in the courts of the house of our God, Praise the Lord. *Ps.* 135: 2, 3.

See also
God, House of; King; Palace.

Courtesy

Thou hast spoken friendly unto thine handmaid. *Ru.* 2: 13.
A gracious woman retaineth honour: . . . The merciful man doeth good to his own soul. *Pr.* 11: 16, 17.
A soft answer turneth away wrath: but grievous words stir up anger. *Pr.* 15: 1.
He that giveth, let him do it with simplicity; he that ruleth, with diligence; he that sheweth mercy, with cheerfulness. *Ro.* 12: 8.
In honour preferring one another. *Ro.* 12: 10.
Evil communications corrupt good manners. *1 Co.* 15: 33.
Gentle, showing all meekness unto all men. *Tit.* 3: 2.
Though I might be much bold in Christ to enjoin thee, . . . Yet . . . I rather beseech thee. *Phm.* 1: 8, 9.
Who, when he was reviled, reviled not again. *1 Pe.* 2: 23.
Be courteous. *1 Pe.* 3: 8.

See also
Behavior; Character; Conduct; Kindness; Manners.

Covenant

With thee will I establish my covenant. *Ge.* 6: 18.
I do set my bow in the cloud, and it shall be for a token of a covenant between me and the earth. *Ge.* 9: 13.
My covenant shall be in your flesh for an everlasting covenant. *Ge.* 17: 13.
I will never break my covenant with you. *Ju.* 2: 1.
They entered into a covenant to seek the Lord God of their fathers with all their heart and with all their soul. *2 Ch.* 15: 12.

We have made a covenant with death, and with hell are we at agreement. *Is.* 28: 15.
He hath broken the covenant. *Is.* 33: 8.
Come, and let us join ourselves to the Lord in a perpetual covenant. *Je.* 50: 5.
If that first covenant had been faultless, then should no place have been sought for the second. *He.* 8: 7.
The days come, saith the Lord, when I will make a new covenant with the house of Israel. *He.* 8: 8.
This is the covenant that I will make; . . . I will put my laws into their mind, and write them in their hearts: and I will be to them a God, and they shall be to me a people. *He.* 8: 10.
In that he saith, A new covenant, he hath made the first old. *He.* 8: 13.

See also
Compact; Contract; Oath; Promise; Testament, New; Testament, Old; Treaty; Vow.

Cover

Moses went up into the mount, and a cloud covered the mount. *Ex.* 24: 15.
I . . . will cover thee with my hand while I pass by. *Ex.* 33: 22.
With favour wilt thou compass him as with a shield. *Ps.* 5: 12.
Hide me under the shadow of thy wings. *Ps.* 17: 8.
Thou hast forgiven the iniquity of thy people, thou hast covered all their sin. *Ps.* 85: 2.
If I say, Surely the darkness shall cover me; even the night shall be light about me. *Ps.* 139: 11.
Above it stood the seraphims: each one had six wings; with twain he covered his face. *Is.* 6: 2.
A man shall be as an hiding place from the wind, and a covert from the tempest. *Is.* 32: 2.
I have put my words in thy mouth, and I have covered thee in the shadow of mine hand, that I may plant the heavens. *Is.* 51: 16.
Darkness shall cover the earth, and gross darkness the people. *Is.* 60: 2.
They shall say to the mountains, Cover us; and to the hills, Fall on us. *Ho.* 10: 8.
There is nothing covered, that shall not be revealed; and hid, that shall not be known. *Mat.* 10: 26.
Charity shall cover the multitude of sins. *1 Pe.* 4: 8.

See also
Cloud; Concealment; Mystery; Secrecy; Shield; Veil.

Covetousness

Thou shalt not covet. *Ex.* 20: 17.
Thou shalt not desire the silver or gold that is on them. *De.* 7: 25.
The wicked . . . blesseth the covetous, whom the Lord abhorreth. *Ps.* 10: 3.
Like as a lion that is greedy of his prey. *Ps.* 17: 12.
Incline my heart unto thy testimonies, and not to covetousness. *Ps.* 119: 36.
He coveteth greedily all the day long. *Pr.* 21: 26.
They are greedy dogs which can never have enough. *Is.* 56: 11.

Take heed, and beware of covetousness: for a man's life consisteth not in the abundance of the things which he possesseth. *Lu.* 12: 15.

Covet earnestly the best gifts. *1 Co.* 12: 31.

Covet to prophesy. *1 Co.* 14: 39.

Covetousness, which is idolatry. *Col.* 3: 5.

An heart they have exercised with covetous practices. *2 Pe.* 2: 14.

See also

Acquisition; Avarice; Cupidity; Greed.

Cowardice

I will send a faintness into their hearts in the lands of their enemies; and the sound of a shaken leaf shall chase them; and they shall flee, as fleeing from a sword; and they shall fall when none pursueth. *Le.* 26: 36.

We were in our own sight as grasshoppers. *Nu.* 13: 33.

Wherefore hath the Lord brought us unto this land, to fall by the sword, that our wives and our children should be a prey? were it not better for us to return into Egypt? *Nu.* 14: 3.

What man is there that is fearful and fainthearted? let him go and return unto his house, lest his brethren's heart faint as well as his heart. *De.* 20: 8.

The children of Israel made them the dens which are in the mountains, and caves, and strong holds. *Ju.* 6: 2.

Whosoever is fearful and afraid, let him return and depart early from mount Gilead. And there returned of the people twenty and two thousand; and there remained ten thousand. *Ju.* 7: 3.

All the men of Israel, when they saw the man, fled from him, and were sore afraid. *1 S.* 17: 24.

Arise, and let us flee. *2 S.* 15: 14.

As people being ashamed steal away when they flee in battle. *2 S.* 19: 3.

There were they in great fear, where no fear was. *Ps.* 53: 5.

Fearfulness and trembling are come upon me, and horror hath overwhelmed me. *Ps.* 55: 5.

Oh that I had wings like a dove! for then would I fly away, and be at rest. *Ps.* 55: 6.

The children of Ephraim, being armed, and carrying bows, turned back in the day of battle. *Ps.* 78: 9.

The wicked flee when no man pursueth: but the righteous are bold as a lion. *Pr.* 28: 1.

One thousand shall flee at the rebuke of one; at the rebuke of five shall ye flee: till ye be left as a beacon upon the top of a mountain, and as an ensign on an hill. *Is.* 30: 17.

All the disciples forsook him, and fled. *Mat.* 26: 56.

Peter followed him afar off. *Mk.* 14: 54.

No man, having put his hand to the plow, and looking back, is fit for the kingdom of God. *Lu.* 9: 62.

No man spake openly of him for fear of the Jews. *Jn.* 7: 13.

Because of the Pharisees they did not confess him, lest they should be put out of the synagogue. *Jn.* 12: 42.

Peter then denied again: and immediately the cock crew. *Jn.* 18: 27

A disciple of Jesus, but secretly for fear of the Jews. *Jn.* 19: 38.

Before that certain came from James, he did eat with the Gentiles: but when they were come, he withdrew and separated himself, fearing them which were of the circumcision. *Ga.* 2: 12.

See also

Caution; Fear; Terror; Timidity; Trembling.

Craftiness

He disappointeth the devices of the crafty. *Jb.* 5: 12.

Thou choosest the tongue of the crafty. *Jb.* 15: 5.

The words of his mouth were smoother than butter, but war was in his heart. *Ps.* 55: 21.

The kisses of an enemy are deceitful. *Pr.* 27: 6.

Though they say, The Lord liveth; surely they swear falsely. *Je.* 5: 2.

Go ye, and tell that fox, Behold, I cast out devils. *Lu.* 13: 32.

He perceived their craftiness. *Lu.* 20: 23.

Not walking in craftiness, nor handling the word of God deceitfully. *2 Co.* 4: 2.

Such are false apostles, deceitful workers, transforming themselves into the apostles of Christ. *2 Co.* 11: 13.

That we henceforth be no more children, . . . carried about with every wind of doctrine, . . . by the sleight of man, and cunning craftiness, whereby they lie in wait to deceive. *Ep.* 4: 14.

See also

Cheat; Deceit; Falsehood; Hypocrisy; Skill.

Creation

In the beginning God created the heaven and the earth. *Ge.* 1: 1.

The earth was without form, and void. *Ge.* 1: 2.

Let the dry land appear. *Ge.* 1: 9.

God saw every thing that he had made, and, behold, it was very good. *Ge.* 1: 31.

When I consider thy heavens, the work of thy fingers, the moon and the stars, which thou hast ordained; What is man, that thou art mindful of him? *Ps.* 8: 3, 4.

Thou hast made summer and winter. *Ps.* 74: 17.

The sea is his, and he made it: and his hands formed the dry land. *Ps.* 95: 5.

It is he that hath made us, and not we ourselves. *Ps.* 100: 3.

O Lord, how manifold are thy works! in wisdom hast thou made them all. *Ps.* 104: 24.

This is the day which the Lord hath made. *Ps.* 118: 24.

We are his workmanship. *Ep.* 2: 10.

See also

Christ, the Creator; Commencement; Creator: Creature; Genesis; God, the Creator.

Creator

Many, O Lord my God, are thy wonderful works which thou hast done. *Ps.* 40: 5.

Create in me a clean heart, O God. *Ps.* 51: 10.

All men shall fear, and shall declare the work of God. *Ps.* 64: 9.

O Lord, how manifold are thy works! in wisdom hast thou made them all. *Ps.* 104: 24.

Thou renewest the face of the earth. *Ps.* 104: 30.

Remember now thy Creator in the days of thy youth, while the evil days come not, nor the years draw nigh, when thou shalt say, I have no pleasure in them. *Ec.* 12: 1.

Hath not one God created us? *Mal.* 2: 10.

Thou hast created all things, and for thy pleasure they are and were created. *Re.* 4: 11.

See also

Christ, the Creator; Creation; Creature; Genesis; God, the Creator.

Creature

God created . . . every living creature that moveth. *Ge.* 1: 21.

God created man in his own image. *Ge.* 1: 27.

The spirit of the living creature was in the wheels. *Eze.* 1: 20.

If any man be in Christ, he is a new creature. *2 Co.* 5: 17.

We are his workmanship. *Ep.* 2: 10.

See also

Animal; Christ, the Creator; Creation; Creator; God, the Creator.

Creed

When the Son of man cometh, shall he find faith on the earth? *Lu.* 18: 8.

Therein is the righteousness of God revealed from faith to faith. *Ro.* 1: 17.

Charity . . . believeth all things. *1 Co.* 13: 4, 7.

The fruit of the Spirit is . . . faith. *Ga.* 5: 22.

One Lord, one faith, one baptism. *Ep.* 4: 5.

He that cometh to God must believe that he is. *He.* 11: 6.

Whosoever believeth that Jesus is the Christ is born of God. *1 Jn.* 5: 1.

This is the victory that overcometh the world, even our faith. *1 Jn.* 5: 4.

I . . . exhort you that ye should earnestly contend for the faith which was once delivered unto the saints. *Jude* 1: 3.

Thou holdest fast my name, and hast not denied my faith. *Re.* 2: 13.

See also

Belief; Christ, Belief in; Christ, Faith in; Confession; Conviction; Dogma; Faith; God, Faith in; Persuasion.

Crime

Whoso sheddeth man's blood, by man shall his blood be shed. *Ge.* 9: 6.

They search out iniquities. *Ps.* 64: 6.

If they say, Come with us, let us lay wait for blood, let us lurk privily for the innocent: . . . walk not thou in the way with them. *Pr.* 1: 11, 15.

They lay wait for their own blood; they lurk privily for their own lives. *Pr.* 1: 18.

Put away the evil of your doings from before mine eyes; cease to do evil; learn to do well. *Is.* 1: 16, 17.

They lay wait, as he that setteth snares; they set a trap, they catch men. *Je.* 5: 26.

Will ye steal, murder, and commit adultery, and swear falsely? *Je.* 7: 9.

The land is full of bloody crimes, and the city is full of violence. *Eze.* 7: 23.

Let them turn every one from his evil way, and from the violence that is in their hands. *Jon.* 3: 8.

Out of the heart proceed evil thoughts, murders, adulteries, fornications, thefts, false witness, blasphemies: These are the things which defile a man. *Mat.* 15: 19, 20.

Men loved darkness rather than light, because their deeds were evil. *Jn.* 3: 19.

Inventors of evil things. *Ro.* 1: 30.

Nor thieves, nor covetous, nor drunkards, nor revilers, nor extortioners, shall inherit the kingdom of God. *1 Co.* 6: 10.

See also

Badness; Corruption; Depravity; Evil; Fault; Iniquity; Murder; Robbery; Sin; Theft; Transgression; Trespass; Vice; Wickedness; Wrong.

Cripple

I was the eyes to the blind, and feet was I to the lame. *Jb.* 29: 15.

The legs of the lame are not equal: so is a parable in the mouth of fools. *Pr.* 26: 7.

If ye offer the lame and sick, is it not evil? *Mal.* 1: 8.

Jesus seeing their faith said unto the sick of the palsy; Son, be of good cheer; thy sins be forgiven thee. *Mat.* 9: 2.

It is better to enter into life halt or maimed, rather than having two hands or two feet to be cast into everlasting fire. *Mat.* 18: 8.

When thou makest a feast, call the poor, the maimed, the lame, the blind. *Lu.* 14: 13.

Bring in hither the poor, and the maimed, and the halt, and the blind. *Lu.* 14: 21.

In these lay a great multitude of impotent folk, of blind, halt, withered, waiting for the moving of the water. *Jn.* 5: 3.

Many taken with palsies, and that were lame, were healed. *Ac.* 8: 7.

There sat a certain man at Lystra, impotent in his feet, being a cripple from his mother's womb. *Ac.* 14: 8.

See also

Foot; Halt; Lame.

Crisis

We came to Kadesh-Barnea. *De.* 1: 19.

Howl ye; for the day of the Lord is at hand. *Is.* 13: 6.

The indignation of the Lord is upon all nations, and his fury upon all their armies. *Is.* 34: 2.

An end, the end is come upon the four corners of the land. *Eze.* 7: 2.

At the time appointed the end shall be. *Da.* 8: 19.

Multitudes, multitudes in the valley of decision: for the day of the Lord is near. *Jo.* 3: 14.

Repent ye: for the kingdom of heaven is at hand. *Mat.* 3: 2.

My servant lieth at home sick of the palsy, grievously tormented. *Mat.* 8: 6.

As the lightning cometh out of the east, and shineth even unto the west; so shall also the coming of the Son of man be. *Mat.* 24: 27.

When ye shall see all these things, know that it is near, even at the doors. *Mat.* 24: 33.

While they went to buy, . . . the door was shut. *Mat.* 25: 10.

Watch therefore, for ye know neither the

day nor the hour wherein the Son of man cometh. *Mat.* 25: 13.

Lo, he that betrayeth me is at hand. *Mk.* 14: 42.

It was about the tenth hour. *Jn.* 1: 39.

The day of the Lord so cometh as a thief in the night. *1 Th.* 5: 2.

The time of my departure is at hand. *2 Ti.* 4: 6.

The end of all things is at hand: be ye therefore sober, and watch unto prayer. *1 Pe.* 4: 7.

See also

Calamity; Catastrophe; Decision; God, Day of.

Criticism

Behold a man with a measuring line in his hand. Then said I, Whither goest thou? And he said unto me, To measure Jerusalem, to see what is the breadth thereof, and what is the length thereof. *Zch.* 2: 1, 2.

Before him shall be gathered all nations; and he shall separate them one from another, as a shepherd divideth his sheep from the goats. *Mat.* 25: 32.

Ye have heard the blasphemy: what think ye? And they all condemned him to be guilty of death. *Mk.* 14: 64.

Judge not. *Lu.* 6: 37.

If it bear fruit, well: and if not, then after that thou shalt cut it down. *Lu.* 13: 9.

I say, through the grace given unto me, to every man that is among you, not to think of himself more highly than he ought to think; but to think soberly. *Ro.* 12: 3.

Who art thou that judgest another man's servant? to his own master he standeth or falleth. *Ro.* 14: 4.

That ye might learn in us not to think of men above that which is written, that no one of you be puffed up for one against another. *1 Co.* 4: 6.

Who maketh thee to differ from another? and what hast thou that thou didst not receive? *1 Co.* 4: 7.

If we would judge ourselves, we should not be judged. *1 Co.* 11: 31.

Not that we are sufficient of ourselves to think any thing as of ourselves; but our sufficiency is of God. *2 Co.* 3: 5.

That no man should blame us in this abundance which is administered by us. *2 Co.* 8: 20.

The angel stood, saying, Rise, and measure the temple of God, and the altar, and them that worship therein. *Re.* 11: 1.

See also

Censoriousness:Harshness; Judgment;Severity.

Cross

His accusation written. THIS IS JESUS THE KING OF THE JEWS. *Mat.* 27: 37.

Now when the centurion, and they that were with him, watching Jesus, saw the earthquake, and those things that were done, they feared greatly, saying, Truly this was the Son of God. *Mat.* 27: 54.

Let Christ the King of Israel descend now from the cross, that we may see and believe. *Mk.* 15: 32.

On him they laid the cross, that he might bear it after Jesus. *Lu.* 23: 26.

And he bearing his cross went forth. *Jn.* 19: 17.

The place where Jesus was crucified was nigh to the city. *Jn.* 19: 20.

I am crucified with Christ. *Ga.* 2: 20.

God forbid that I should glory, save in the cross of our Lord Jesus Christ. *Ga.* 6: 14.

Rejoice, inasmuch as ye are partakers of Christ's sufferings; that, when his glory shall be revealed, ye may be glad also with exceeding joy. *1 Pe.* 4: 13.

See also

Christ, Cross of; Christ, Crucifixion of; Christ, Death of; Christ, Sacrifice of; Christ, Suffering of; Offering; Sacrifice; Self-Forgetfulness; Self-Sacrifice.

Crowd

He scorneth the multitude of the city. *Jb.* 39: 7.

I will not be afraid of ten thousands of people. *Ps.* 3: 6.

There is no king saved by the multitude of an host. *Ps.* 33: 16.

He feared the multitude. *Mat.* 14: 5.

The multitudes . . . cried, . . . Hosanna in the highest. *Mat.* 21: 9.

The chief priests and elders persuaded the multitude that they should ask Barabbas, and destroy Jesus. *Mat.* 27: 20.

All the city was gathered together at the door. *Mk.* 1: 33.

There was no room for them in the inn. *Lu.* 2: 7.

They were instant with loud voices, requiring that he might be crucified. *Lu.* 23: 23.

See also

Host; Multitude; Rabble.

Crown

My judgment was as a robe and a diadem. *Jb.* 29: 14.

Thou settest a crown of pure gold on his head. *Ps.* 21: 3.

Thou crownest the year with thy goodness. *Ps.* 65: 11.

Thou shalt also be a crown of glory in the hand of the Lord, and a royal diadem in the hand of thy God. *Is.* 62: 3.

Great is your reward in heaven. *Mat.* 5: 12.

Every man shall receive his own reward according to his own labour. *1 Co.* 3: 8.

They do it to obtain a corruptible crown; but we an incorruptible. *1 Co.* 9: 25.

What is our hope, or joy, or crown of rejoicing? . . . Ye are our glory and joy. *1 Th.* 2: 19, 20.

If a man also strive for masteries, yet is he not crowned, except he strive lawfully. *2 Ti.* 2: 5.

I have fought a good fight, I have finished my course, I have kept the faith: Henceforth there is laid up for me a crown of righteousness. *2 Ti.* 4: 7, 8.

Be thou faithful unto death, and I will give thee a crown of life. *Re.* 2: 10.

Behold, I come quickly; and my reward is with me. *Re.* 22: 12.

See also

Award; Christ, Crown of; Christ, the King;

Coronation; Diadem; God, the King; God, the Kingdom of; King; Kingdom; Prize.

Crucifixion

I send unto you prophets, and wise men, and scribes: and some of them ye shall kill and crucify. *Mat.* 23: 34.

After that they had mocked him, they . . . led him away to crucify him. *Mat.* 27: 31.

He saved others; himself he cannot save. *Mat.* 27: 42.

They compel one Simon a Cyrenian, who passed by, coming out of the country, the father of Alexander and Rufus, to bear his cross. *Mk.* 15: 21.

The scripture was fulfilled, which saith, And he was numbered with the transgressors. *Mk.* 15: 28.

They cried, saying, Crucify him, crucify him. *Lu.* 23: 21.

Then said Jesus, Father, forgive them; for they know not what they do. *Lu.* 23: 34.

I, if I be lifted up from the earth, will draw all men unto me. *Jn.* 12: 32.

Crucify him, . . . I find no fault in him. *Jn.* 19: 6.

I determined not to know any thing among you, save Jesus Christ, and him crucified. *1 Co.* 2: 2.

They that are Christ's have crucified the flesh with the affections and lusts. *Ga.* 5: 24.

See also
Christ, Cross of; Christ, Crucifixion of; Christ, Death of; Christ, Sacrifice of; Christ, Suffering of; Cross; Friday, Good.

Cruelty

I will harden his heart, that he shall not let the people go. *Ex.* 4: 21.

Thou shalt not seethe a kid in his mother's milk. *De.* 14: 21.

Thou art become cruel to me: with thy strong hand thou opposest thyself against me. *Jb.* 30: 21.

False witnesses are risen up against me, and such as breathe out cruelty. *Ps.* 27: 12.

A righteous man regardeth the life of his beast: but the tender mercies of the wicked are cruel. *Pr.* 12: 10.

What mean ye that ye beat my people to pieces, and grind the faces of the poor? *Is.* 3: 15.

Because he cruelly oppressed, . . . even he shall die in his iniquity. *Eze.* 18: 18.

His lord was wroth, and delivered him to the tormentors. *Mat.* 18: 34.

Others had trial of cruel mockings and scourgings. *He.* 11: 36.

See also
Ferocity; Hardness; Harshness; Inhumanity; Oppression; Persecution; Rod; Scourge; Severity; Stripe; Trial; Unkindness; Unmercifulness.

Crusade

Speak unto the children of Israel, that they go forward. *Ex.* 14: 15.

Behold, I have set the land before you: go in and possess the land. *De.* 1: 8.

When ye had girded on every man his weapons of war, ye were ready to go up into the hill. *De.* 1: 41.

Be strong and of good courage: be not afraid, neither be thou dismayed: for the Lord thy God is with thee whithersoever thou goest. *Jos.* 1: 9.

All that thou commandest us we will do, and whithersoever thou sendest us, we will go. *Jos.* 1: 16.

The Lord said, Judah shall go up: behold, I have delivered the land into his hand. *Ju.* 1: 2.

The Spirit of the Lord came upon Gideon, and he blew a trumpet. *Ju.* 6: 34.

Prepare ye the way of the Lord, make straight in the desert a highway for our God. *Is.* 40: 3.

Thus saith the Lord; Say, A sword, a sword is sharpened. *Eze.* 21: 9.

I am ready not to be bound only, but also to die at Jerusalem for the name of the Lord Jesus. *Ac.* 21: 13.

The will of the Lord be done. *Ac.* 21: 14.

They are the enemies of the cross of Christ. *Ph.* 3: 18.

Fight the good fight of faith. *1 Ti.* 6: 12.

Cry

I have heard their cry; . . . I know their sorrows. *Ex.* 3: 7.

The people shall shout with a great shout. *Jos.* 6: 5.

He heareth the cry of the afflicted. *Jb.* 34: 28.

Awake, why sleepest thou, O Lord? arise, cast us not off for ever. *Ps.* 44: 23.

Doth not wisdom cry? and understanding put forth her voice? *Pr.* 8: 1.

Whoso stoppeth his ears at the cry of the poor, he also shall cry himself, but shall not be heard. *Pr.* 21: 13.

Awake and sing, ye that dwell in dust. *Is.* 26: 19.

Ho, ho, come forth, and flee from the land of the north. *Zch.* 2: 6.

The voice of one crying in the wilderness. *Mat.* 3: 3.

He shall not strive, nor cry; neither shall any man hear his voice in the streets. *Mat.* 12: 19.

I tell you that, if these should hold their peace, the stones would immediately cry out. *Lu.* 19: 40.

The Lord himself shall descend from heaven with a shout, with the voice of the archangel. *1 Th.* 4: 16.

See also
Call; Christ, Call of; Entreaty; God, Call of; Weeping.

Cultivation

There was not a man to till the ground. *Ge.* 2: 5.

He causeth the grass to grow for the cattle. *Ps.* 104: 14.

A time to plant, and a time to pluck up that which is planted. *Ec.* 3: 2.

I will plant in the wilderness the cedar. *Is.* 41: 19.

I will set in the desert the fir tree, and the pine, and the box tree together. *Is.* 41: 19.

I have refined thee, but not with silver. *Is.* 48: 10.

Plant gardens, and eat the fruit of them. *Je.* 29: 5.

So will I watch over them, to build, and to plant, saith the Lord. *Je.* 31: 28.

The kingdom of heaven is likened unto a man which sowed good seed in his field. *Mat.* 13: 24.

The kingdom of heaven is like to a grain of mustard seed, which a man took, and sowed in his field. *Mat.* 13: 31.

I have planted, Apollos watered: but God gave the increase. *1 Co.* 3: 6.

He that planteth and he that watereth are one. *1 Co.* 3: 8.

See also
Culture; Harvest; Plant; Plow; Reaping; Refinement; Seed.

Culture
Joseph is a fruitful bough, even a fruitful bough by a well; whose branches run over the wall. *Ge.* 49: 22.

He shall be like a tree planted by the rivers of water, that bringeth forth his fruit in his season; his leaf also shall not wither; and whatsoever he doeth shall prosper. *Ps.* 1: 3.

Thy wife shall be as a fruitful vine by the sides of thine house: thy children like olive plants round about thy table. *Ps.* 128: 3.

He shall grow up before him as a tender plant, and as a root out of a dry ground. *Is.* 53: 2.

It was planted in a good soil by great waters, that it might bring forth branches, and that it might bear fruit, that it might be a goodly vine. *Eze.* 17: 8.

Every plant, which my heavenly Father hath not planted, shall be rooted up. *Mat.* 15: 13.

If the root be holy, so are the branches. *Ro.* 11: 16.

If thou wert cut out of the olive tree which is wild by nature, and wert graffed contrary to nature into a good olive tree: how much more shall these, which be the natural branches, be graffed into their own olive tree? *Ro.* 11: 24.

Ye are God's husbandry. *1 Co.* 3: 9.

Can the fig tree, my brethren, bear olive berries? *Ja.* 3: 12.

See also
Civilization; Cultivation: Enlightenment; Refinement.

Cunning
The boys grew: and Esau was a cunning hunter. *Ge.* 25: 27.

The voice is Jacob's voice, but the hands are the hands of Esau. *Ge.* 27: 22.

Thy brother came with subtilty, and hath taken away thy blessing. *Ge.* 27: 35.

Saul sent the messengers again to see David, saying, Bring him up to me in the bed, that I may slay him. And when the messengers were come in, behold, there was an image in the bed, with a pillow of goat's hair for his bolster. *1 S.* 19: 15, 16.

He taketh the wise in their own craftiness. *Jb.* 5: 13.

If I forget thee, O Jerusalem, let my right hand forget her cunning. *Ps.* 137: 5.

Thou art able; for the spirit of the holy gods is in thee. *Da.* 4: 18.

He perceived their craftiness, and said unto them, Why tempt ye me? *Lu.* 20: 23.

Not walking in craftiness, nor handling the word of God deceitfully. *2 Co.* 4: 2.

By the sleight of men, and cunning craftiness, whereby they lie in wait to deceive. *Eph.* 4: 14.

We have not followed cunningly devised fables. *2 Pe.* 1: 16.

See also
Deceit; Skill.

Cup
My cup runneth over. *Ps.* 23: 5.

In the hand of the Lord there is a cup, and the wine is red; it is full of mixture; and he poureth out of the same. *Ps.* 75: 8.

I will take the cup of salvation, and call upon the name of the Lord. *Ps.* 116: 13.

Thou . . . hast drunk at the hand of the Lord the cup of his fury; thou hast drunken the dregs of the cup of trembling. *Is.* 51: 17.

Cleanse first that which is within the cup and platter, that the outside of them may be clean also. *Mat.* 23: 26.

He took the cup, and gave thanks, and gave it to them. *Mat.* 26: 27.

This cup is the new testament in my blood. *1 Co.* 11: 25.

See also
Christ, Blood of; Christ, Crucifixion of; Christ, Cup of; Christ, Death of; Christ, Sacrifice of; Christ, Suffering of; Drink.

Cupidity
Neither shalt thou desire thy neighbour's wife, neither shalt thou covet thy neighbour's house. *De.* 5: 21.

The wicked boasteth of his heart's desire, and blesseth the covetous, whom the Lord abhorreth. *Ps.* 10: 3.

Like as a lion that is greedy of his prey. *Ps.* 17: 12.

He heapeth up riches, and knoweth not who shall gather them. *Ps.* 39: 6.

Be not thou afraid when one is made rich, when the glory of his house is increased. *Ps.* 49: 16.

If riches increase, set not your heart upon them. *Ps.* 62: 10.

So are the ways of every one that is greedy of gain. *Pr.* 1: 19.

He that is greedy of gain troubleth his own house. *Pr.* 15: 27.

He coveteth greedily all the day long. *Pr.* 21: 26.

He that hateth covetousness shall prolong his days. *Pr.* 28: 16.

They are greedy dogs which can never have enough. *Is.* 56: 11.

They all look to their own way, every one for his gain. *Is.* 56: 11.

Thou hast greedily gained of thy neighbours by extortion, and hast forgotten me, saith the Lord God. *Eze.* 22: 12.

They covet fields, and take them by violence; and houses, and take them away. *Mi.* 2: 2.

Jesus . . . overthrew the tables of the money-changers, and the seats of them that sold doves. *Mat.* 21: 12.

Ye devour widow's houses, and for a pretence make long prayer. *Mat.* 23: 14.

Ye love the uppermost seats in the synagogues. *Lu.* 11: 43.

Covet earnestly the best gifts. *1 Co.* 12: 31.

Supposing that gain is godliness. *1 Ti.* 6: 5.

They . . . ran greedily after the error of Balaam for reward. *Jude* 11.
See also
Avarice; Covetousness; Greed.

Cure

He healeth the broken in heart, and bindeth up their wounds. *Ps.* 147: 3.

A time to kill, and a time to heal. *Ec.* 3: 3.

Thus saith the Lord, Thy bruise is incurable, and thy wound is grievous. *Je.* 30: 12.

I brought him to thy disciples, and they could not cure him. *Mat.* 17: 16.

The power of the Lord was present to heal them. *Lu.* 5: 17.

In that same hour he cured many of their infirmities. *Lu.* 7: 21.

He . . . gave them power and authority over all devils, and to cure diseases. *Lu.* 9: 1.

Whosoever then first after the troubling of the water stepped in was made whole of whatsoever disease he had. *Jn.* 5: 4.

Jesus Christ maketh thee whole. *Ac.* 9: 34.
See also
Doctor; Healing; Medicine; Physician; Remedy.

Curiosity

He smote the men of Beth-Shemesh, because they had looked into the ark of the Lord. *1 S.* 6: 19.

Master, we would see a sign from thee. *Mat.* 12: 38.

John have I beheaded; but who is this, of whom I hear such things? *Lu.* 9: 9.

Likewise a Levite, when he was at the place, came and looked on him, and passed by on the other side. *Lu.* 10: 32.

Then said Jesus unto him, Except ye see signs and wonders, ye will not believe. *Jn.* 4: 48.

They came not for Jesus' sake only, but that they might see Lazarus also, whom he had raised from the dead. *Jn.* 12: 9.

All the Athenians . . . spent their time in nothing else, but either to tell or to hear some new thing. *Ac.* 17: 21.

The Jews require a sign, and the Greeks seek after wisdom. *1 Co.* 1: 22.

Foolish and unlearned questions avoid. *2 Ti.* 2: 23.
See also
Inquiry; Question.

Curse

The Lord said in his heart, I will not again curse the ground any more for man's sake. *Ge.* 8: 21.

I will bless them that bless thee, and curse him that curseth thee. *Ge.* 12: 3.

How shall I curse, whom God hath not cursed? *Nu.* 23: 8.

Behold, I set before you this day a blessing and a curse. *De.* 11: 26.

The Lord thy God turned the curse into a blessing unto thee. *De.* 23: 5.

Curse God, and die. *Jb.* 2: 9.

As he loved cursing, so let it come unto him: as he delighted not in blessing, so let it be far from him. *Ps.* 109: 17.

Therefore hath the curse devoured the earth. *Is.* 24: 6.

Cursed be the day wherein I was born. *Je.* 20: 14.

I will curse your blessings: yea, I have cursed them already. *Mal.* 2: 2.

Ye are cursed with a curse: for ye have robbed me. *Mal.* 3: 9.

Bless them that curse you. *Mat.* 5: 44.

The fig tree which thou cursedst is withered away. *Mk.* 11: 21.

If any man love not the Lord Jesus Christ, let him be Anathema. *1 Co.* 16: 22.

Christ hath redeemed us from the curse of the law. *Ga.* 3: 13.

Out of the same mouth proceedeth blessing and cursing. My brethren, these things ought not to be. *Ja.* 3: 10.

There shall be no more curse. *Re.* 22: 3.
See also
Anathema; Ban; Bane; Blasphemy; Excommunication; Oath; Profanity.

Custom

He shall not alter it, nor change it, a good for a bad, or a bad for a good. *Le.* 27: 10.

Hast thou marked the old way which wicked men have trodden? *Jb.* 22: 15.

Ask for the old paths, where is the good way, and walk therein, and ye shall find rest for your souls. *Je.* 6: 16.

They have caused them to stumble in their ways from the ancient paths. *Je.* 18: 15.

Laying aside the commandment of God, ye hold the tradition of men. *Mk.* 7: 8.

We have heard him say, that this Jesus of Nazareth shall destroy this place, and shall change the customs which Moses delivered us. *Ac.* 6: 14.

But Peter said, Not so, Lord; for I have never eaten any thing that is common or unclean. *Ac.* 10: 14.
See also
Conservatism; Fashion; Habit; Tradition.

Cycle

The eyes of the Lord thy God are always upon it, from the beginning of the year even unto the end of the year. *De.* 11: 12.

He went from year to year in circuit to Beth-el, and Gilgal, and Mizpeh. *1 S.* 7: 16.

He walketh in the circuit of heaven. *Jb.* 22: 14.

His going forth is from the end of the heaven, and his circuit unto the ends of it. *Ps.* 19: 6.

One generation passeth away, and another generation cometh. *Ec.* 1: 4.

The sun also ariseth, and the sun goeth down, and hasteth to his place where he arose. *Ec.* 1: 5.

The wind goeth toward the south, and turneth about unto the north: it whirleth about continually, and the wind returneth again according to his circuits. *Ec.* 1: 6.

All the rivers run into the sea; yet the sea is not full; unto the place from whence the rivers come, thither they return again. *Ec.* 1: 7.

The thing that hath been, it is that which shall be; and that which is done is that which shall be done. *Ec.* 1: 9.

There is no new thing under the sun. *Ec.* 1: 9.

To every thing there is a season. *Ec.* 3: 1.

That which hath been is now; and that which is to be hath already been. *Ec.* 3: 15.

God requireth that which is past. *Ec.* **3: 15.**
All are of the dust, and all turn to dust again. *Ec.* **3: 20.**
It is he that sitteth upon the circle of the earth. *Is.* **40: 22.**
First the blade, then the ear, after that the full corn in the ear. *Mk.* **4: 28.**
See also
Season.

Cynicism

Doth Job fear God for naught? *Jb.* **1: 9.**
Now men see not the bright light which is in the clouds: but the wind passeth, and cleanseth them. *Jb.* **37: 21.**
Nor sitteth in the seat of the scornful. *Ps.* **1: 1.**
What profit hath a man of all his labour which he taketh under the sun? *Ec.* **1: 3.**
In much wisdom is much grief. *Ec.* **1: 18.**

I looked on all the works that my hands had wrought, and on the labour that I had laboured to do: and, behold, all was vanity and vexation of spirit, and there was no profit under the sun. *Ec.* **2: 11.**
There is nothing better for a man, than that he should eat and drink, and that he should make his soul enjoy good in his labour. *Ec.* **2: 24.**
I praised the dead which are already dead more than the living which are yet alive. *Ec.* **4: 2.**
It is better to go to the house of mourning, than to go to the house of feasting. *Ec.* **7: 2.**
Sorrow is better than laughter. *Ec.* **7: 3.**
There is not a just man upon earth, that doeth good, and sinneth not. *Ec.* **7: 20.**
See also
Depression; Despair; Gloom; Hopelessness; Melancholy; Pessimism.

D

Damnation

The sorrows of hell compassed me about. *2 S.* **22: 6.**
Thou wilt not leave my soul in hell. *Ps.* **16: 10.**
It shall come to pass in that day, that the Lord shall punish the host of the high ones that are on high, and the kings of the earth upon the earth. *Is.* **24: 21.**
Ye shall receive the greater damnation. *Mat.* **23: 14.**
Ye generation of vipers, how can ye escape the damnation of hell? *Mat.* **23: 33.**
He that believeth not shall be damned. *Mk.* **16: 16.**
That they all might be damned who believed not the truth, but had pleasure in unrighteousness. *2 Th.* **2: 12.**
Having damnation, because they have cast off their first faith. *1 Ti.* **5: 12.**
Their damnation slumbereth not. *2 Pe.* **2: 3.**
The vengeance of eternal fire. *Jude* **1: 7.**
See also
Brimstone; Hell; Judgment, the Last.

Dance

David danced before the Lord with all his might. *2 S.* **6: 14.**
Thou hast turned for me my mourning into dancing. *Ps.* **30: 11.**
Praise him with the timbrel and dance. *Ps.* **150: 4.**
A time to mourn, and a time to dance. *Ec.* **3: 4.**
Then shall the virgin rejoice in the dance, both young men and old together. *Je.* **31: 13.**
Our dance is turned into mourning. *La.* **5: 15.**

We have piped unto you, and ye have not danced; we have mourned unto you, and ye have not lamented. *Mat.* **11: 17.**
As he came and drew nigh to the house, he heard musick and dancing. *Lu.* **15: 25.**

Danger

A people that jeoparded their lives unto the death in the high places of the field. *Ju.* **5: 18.**
Thou shalt go no more out with us to battle, that thou quench not the light of Israel. *2 S.* **21: 17.**
Let a bear robbed of her whelps meet a man, rather than a fool in his folly. *Pr.* **17: 12.**
We gat our bread with the peril of our lives because of the sword of the wilderness. *La.* **5: 9.**
They were filled with water, and were in jeopardy. *Lu.* **8: 23.**
Men that have hazarded their lives. *Ac.* **15: 26.**
When sailing was now dangerous. *Ac.* **27: 9.**
Who shall separate us from the love of Christ? shall tribulation, or distress, or persecution, or famine, or nakedness, or peril, or sword? *Ro.* **8: 35.**
In perils of waters, in perils of robbers, in perils by mine own countrymen, in perils by the heathen, in perils in the city, in perils in the wilderness, in perils in the sea, in perils among false brethren. *2 Co.* **11: 26.**
Thou therefore endure hardness as a good soldier of Jesus Christ. *2 Ti.* **2: 3.**
Perilous times shall come. For men shall be lovers of their own selves. *2 Ti.* **3: 1, 2.**
See also
Hardship; Hazard; Insecurity; Peril; Trial; Urgency.

Darkness

Thou shalt grope at noonday, as the blind gropeth in darkness. *De.* 28: 29.

He made darkness his secret place. *Ps.* 18: 11.

The Lord my God will enlighten my darkness. *Ps.* 18: 28.

Shall thy wonders be known in the dark? *Ps.* 88: 12.

If I say, Surely the darkness shall cover me; even the night shall be light about me. *Ps.* 139: 11.

The fool walketh in darkness. *Ec.* 2: 14.

The house was filled with smoke. *Is.* 6: 4.

We wait for light, but behold obscurity; for brightness, but we walk in darkness. *Is.* 59: 9.

Their ways shall be unto them as slippery ways in the darkness. *Je.* 23: 12.

I will cover the heaven, and make the stars thereof dark. *Eze.* 32: 7.

Therefore night shall be unto you, that ye shall not have a vision; and it shall be dark unto you. *Mi.* 3: 6.

The sun shall go down over the prophets, and the day shall be dark over them. *Mi.* 3: 6.

If the blind lead the blind, both shall fall into the ditch. *Mat.* 15: 14.

There was a darkness over all the earth. *Lu.* 23: 44.

Then spake Jesus again unto them, saying, I am the light of the world: he that followeth me shall not walk in darkness, but shall have the light of life. *Jn.* 8: 12.

Have no fellowship with the unfruitful works of darkness. *Ep.* 5: 11.

Against the rulers of the darkness of this world. *Ep.* 6: 12.

Who hath delivered us from the power of darkness, and hath translated us into the kingdom of his dear Son. *Col.* 1: 13.

Ye, brethren, are not in darkness. *1 Th.* 5: 4.

He that saith he is in the light, and hateth his brother, is in darkness even until now. *1 Jn.* 2: 9.

See also

Blindness; Darkness; Delusion; Gloom; Midnight; Night; Obscurity.

Daughter

The sons of God saw the daughters of men that they were fair; and they took them wives of all which they chose. *Ge.* 6: 2.

Let the daughters of Judah be glad, because of thy judgments. *Ps.* 48: 11.

Many daughters have done virtuously, but thou excellest them all. *Pr.* 31: 29.

Hear my voice, ye careless daughters. *Is.* 32: 9.

Thy sons shall come from far, and thy daughters shall be nursed at thy side. *Is.* 60: 4.

The daughter riseth up against her mother. *Mi.* 7: 6.

Be glad and rejoice with all the heart, O daughter of Jerusalem. *Zph.* 3: 14.

Daughter, be of good comfort; thy faith hath made thee whole. *Mat.* 9: 22.

Tell ye the daughter of Sion, Behold, thy King cometh unto thee. *Mat.* 21: 5.

Daughters of Jerusalem, weep not for me, but weep for yourselves, and for your children. *Lu.* 23: 28.

Your daughters shall prophesy. *Ac.* 2: 17.

See also

Girl; Maiden; Virgin.

Dawn

He shall be as the light of the morning, when the sun riseth. *2 S.* 23: 4.

Thou shalt shine forth, thou shalt be as the morning. *Jb.* 11: 17.

His eyes are like the eyelids of the morning. *Jb.* 41: 18.

My soul waiteth for the Lord more than they that watch for the morning. *Ps.* 130: 6.

The watchman said, The morning cometh, and also the night. *Is.* 21: 12.

Arise, shine; for thy light is come, and the glory of the Lord is risen upon thee. *Is.* 60: 1.

The glory of the God of Israel came from the way of the east. *Eze.* 43: 2.

They shall be as the morning cloud, and as the early dew that passeth away. *Ho.* 13: 3.

He maketh the sun to rise on the evil and on the good. *Mat.* 5: 45.

As it began to dawn toward the first day of the week. *Mat.* 28: 1.

He went out into the porch; and the cock crew. *Mk.* 14: 68.

The night is far spent, the day is at hand: let us therefore cast off the works of darkness, and let us put on the armour of light. *Ro.* 13: 12.

We have also a more sure word of prophecy; whereunto ye do well that ye take heed, as unto a light that shineth in a dark place, until the day dawn, and the day star arise in your hearts. *2 Pe.* 1: 19.

See also

Beginning; Day; Day, the Coming; Freshness; Morning; Sunrise.

Day

God called the light Day. *Ge.* 1: 5.

Day and night shall not cease. *Ge.* 8: 22.

The Lord went before them by day. *Ex.* 13: 21.

The cloud of the Lord was upon the tabernacle by day. *Ex.* 40: 38.

There was no day like that before it or after it. *Jos.* 10: 14.

Day unto day uttereth speech. *Ps.* 19: 2.

On thee do I wait all the day. *Ps.* 25: 5.

The Lord will command his lovingkindness in the daytime. *Ps.* 42: 8.

The day is thine, the night also is thine. *Ps.* 74: 16.

A day in thy courts is better than a thousand. *Ps.* 84: 10.

The night shineth as the day. *Ps.* 139: 12.

Every day will I bless thee. *Ps.* 145: 2.

Thou knowest not what a day may bring forth. *Pr.* 27: 1.

Sufficient unto the day is the evil thereof. *Mat.* 6: 34.

I must work the works of him that sent me, while it is day. *Jn.* 9: 4.

Jesus answered, Are there not twelve hours in the day? If any man walk in the day, he stumbleth not, because he seeth the light of this world. *Jn.* 11: 9.

Every man's work shall be made manifest: for the day shall declare it, because it shall be revealed by fire. *1 Co.* 3: 13.

One day is with the Lord as a thousand years. *2 Pe. 3: 8.*
See also
Day, the Coming; God, Day of; Light.

Day, the Coming

He shall be as the light of the morning, when the sun riseth, even a morning without clouds. *2 S. 23: 4.*
Thine eyes shall see the King in his beauty: they shall behold the land that is very far off. *Is. 33: 17.*
The parched ground shall become a pool. *Is. 35: 7.*
The great day of the Lord is near, it is near, and hasteth greatly, even the voice of the day of the Lord. *Zph. 1: 14.*
They shall be mine, saith the Lord of hosts, in that day when I make up my jewels. *Mal. 3: 17.*
I will send you Elijah the prophet before the coming of the great and dreadful day of the Lord. *Mal. 4: 5.*
The night is far spent, the day is at hand. *Ro. 13: 12.*
When that which is perfect is come, then that which is in part shall be done away. *1 Co. 13: 10.*
That I may rejoice in the day of Christ. *Ph. 2: 16.*
Be patient therefore, brethren, unto the coming of the Lord. *Ja. 5: 7.*
Until the day dawn. *2 Pe. 1: 19.*
See also
Age, the Golden; Civilization; Future; God, Day of; Land, the Promised; Millenium.

Deacon

God hath set some in the Church, first apostles, secondarily prophets, thirdly teachers. *1 Co. 12: 28.*
If a man know not how to rule his own house, how shall he take care of the church of God? *1 Ti. 3: 5.*
Likewise must the deacons be grave, not doubletongued, not given to much wine, not greedy of filthy lucre; Holding the mystery of the faith in a pure conscience. *1 Ti. 3: 8, 9.*
Let the deacons be the husbands of one wife, ruling their children and their own houses well. *1 Ti. 3: 12.*
They that have used the office of a deacon well purchase to themselves a good degree, and great boldness in the faith which is in Christ Jesus. *1 Ti. 3: 13.*

Deafness

Who maketh the . . . deaf? . . . have not I the Lord? *Ex. 4: 11.*
In that day shall the deaf hear the words of the book. *Is. 29: 18.*
Then the eyes of the blind shall be opened, and the ears of the deaf shall be unstopped. *Is. 35: 5.*
Hear, ye deaf. *Is. 42: 18.*
Who is . . . deaf, as my messenger that I sent? *Is. 42: 19.*
Their ear is uncircumcised, and they cannot hearken. *Je. 6: 10.*
They refused to hearken, and pulled away the shoulder, and stopped their ears, that they should not hear. *Zch. 7: 11.*

The deaf hear. *Mat. 11: 5.*
He maketh both the deaf to hear and the dumb to speak. *Mk. 7: 37.*
Thou dumb and deaf spirit, I charge thee, come out of him. *Mk. 9: 25.*
They that were with me saw indeed the light, and were afraid; but they heard not the voice of him that spake to me. *Ac. 22: 9.*
They shall turn away their ears from the truth, and shall be turned unto fables. *2 Ti. 4: 4.*
See also
Dullness; Ear; Handicap; Hearing.

Death

I have set before thee this day life and good, and death and evil. *De. 30: 15.*
O that they were wise, that they understood this, that they would consider their latter end! *De. 32: 29.*
Can I bring him back again? I shall go to him, but he shall not return to me. *2 S. 12: 23.*
We must needs die, and are as water spilt on the ground, which cannot be gathered up again. *2 S. 14: 14.*
I go the way of all the earth. *1 K. 2: 2.*
The Lord gave, and the Lord hath taken away; blessed be the name of the Lord. *Jb. 1: 21.*
I shall go the way whence I shall not return. *Jb. 16: 22.*
Yea, though I walk through the valley of the shadow of death, I will fear no evil: for thou art with me. *Ps. 23: 4.*
The righteous hath hope in his death. *Pr. 14: 32.*
The man that wandereth out of the way of understanding shall remain in the congregation of the dead. *Pr. 21: 16.*
A time to be born, and a time to die. *Ec. 3: 2.*
There is no man that hath power over the spirit to retain the spirit. *Ec. 8: 8.*
Love is strong as death. *S. of S. 8: 6.*
To them which sat in the region and shadow of death light is sprung up. *Mat. 4: 16.*
There be some standing here which shall not taste of death, till they see the Son of man coming in his kingdom. *Mat. 16: 28.*
She is not dead, but sleepeth. *Lu. 8: 52.*
If a man keep my saying, he shall never see death. *Jn. 8: 51.*
But he, being full of the Holy Ghost, looked up stedfastly into heaven, and saw the glory of God. *Ac. 7: 55.*
Wherefore, as by one man sin entered into the world, and death by sin; and so death passed upon all men, for that all have sinned. *Ro. 5: 12.*
The wages of sin is death. *Ro. 6: 23.*
All things are yours; . . . death. *1 Co. 3: 21, 22.*
The last enemy that shall be destroyed is death. *1 Co. 15: 26.*
The sting of death is sin. *1 Co. 15: 56.*
She that liveth in pleasure is dead while she liveth. *1 Ti. 5: 6.*
By faith Enoch was translated that he should not see death. *He. 11: 5.*
Behold a pale horse: and his name that sat on him was Death. *Re. 6: 8.*
Blessed are the dead which die in the Lord

from henceforth: Yea, saith the Spirit, that they may rest from their labours. *Re.* 14: 13.

There shall be no more death. *Re.* 21: 4.

See also

Burial; Christ, Death of; Decease; Disappearance; Expiration; Funeral; Grave; Immortality; Life, the Eternal; Tomb.

Debate

Surely I would speak to the Almighty, and I desire to reason with God. *Jb.* 13: 3.

I could heap up words against you. *Jb.* 16: 4.

Debate thy cause with thy neighbour himself; and discover not a secret to another. *Pr.* 25: 9.

Come now, and let us reason together, saith the Lord. *Is.* 1: 18.

Behold, ye fast for strife and debate, and to smite with the fist of wickedness. *Is.* 58: 4.

He went into the synagogue, and spake boldly for the space of three months, disputing and persuading the things concerning the kingdom of God. *Ac.* 19: 8.

Nay but, O man, who art thou that repliest against God? *Ro.* 9: 20.

Where is the disputer of this world? hath not God made foolish the wisdom of this world? *1 Co.* 1: 20.

Perverse disputings of men of corrupt minds. *1 Ti.* 6: 5.

Shun profane and vain babblings. *2 Ti.* 2: 16.

See also

Argument; Controversy; Dispute.

Debauchery

He remembered that they were but flesh. *Ps.* 78: 39.

They have begotten strange children. *Ho.* 5: 7.

Who being past feeling have given themselves over unto lasciviousness, to work all uncleanness with greediness. *Eph.* 4: 19.

Put off concerning the former conversation the old man, which is corrupt according to the deceitful lusts. *Ep.* 4: 22.

Every one of you should know how to possess his vessel in sanctification and honour; Not in the lust of concupiscence. *1 Th.* 4: 4, 5.

Of this sort are they which creep into houses, and lead captive silly women laden with sins, led away with divers lusts. *2 Ti.* 3: 6.

From whence come wars and fightings among you? come they not hence, even of your lusts that war in your members? *Ja.* 4: 1.

Having escaped the corruption that is in the world through lust. *2 Pe.* 1: 4.

Giving themselves over to fornication, and going after strange flesh. *Jude* 7.

Filthy dreamers defile the flesh. *Jude* 8.

See also

Adultery; Brothel; Carnality; Dissipation; Flesh; Fornication; Lust; Prostitute; Sensuality.

Debt

Withhold not good from them to whom it is due. *Pr.* 3: 27.

Be not one of them that . . . are sureties for debts. *Pr.* 22: 26.

Forgive us our debts, as we forgive our debtors. *Mat.* 6: 12.

The lord of that servant was moved with compassion, and . . . forgave him the debt. *Mat.* 18: 27.

How much owest thou? *Lu.* 16: 5.

I am debtor both to the Greeks, and to the Barbarians; both to the wise, and to the unwise. So, as much as in me is, I am ready to preach the gospel to you that are at Rome also. *Ro.* 1: 14, 15.

We are debtors, not to the flesh, to live after the flesh. *Ro.* 8: 12.

Owe no man any thing, but to love one another. *Ro.* 13: 8.

Thou owest unto me even thine own self besides. *Phm.* 1: 19.

See also

Loan; Obligation; Trespass.

Decay

Dust thou art, and unto dust shalt thou return. *Ge.* 3: 19.

After I am waxed old, shall I have pleasure? *Ge.* 18: 12.

If thy brother be waxen poor, and fallen in decay with thee; then thou shalt relieve him. *Le.* 25: 35.

Thou shalt come to thy grave in a full age, like as a shock of corn cometh in in his season. *Jb.* 5: 26.

Man that is born of woman is of few days, and full of trouble. He cometh forth like a flower, and is cut down: he fleeth also as a shadow, and continueth not. *Jb.* 14: 1, 2.

Yea, his soul draweth near unto the grave. *Jb.* 33: 22.

In the morning it flourisheth, and groweth up; in the evening it is cut down, and withereth. *Ps.* 90: 6.

By much slothfulness the building decayeth; and through idleness of the hands the house droppeth through. *Ec.* 10: 18.

Thy pomp is brought down to the grave. *Is.* 14: 11.

Woe to the rebellious children, . . . that take counsel, but not of me; . . . that they may add sin to sin. *Is.* 30: 1.

We all do fade as a leaf. *Is.* 64: 6.

Gray hairs are here and there upon him, yet he knoweth not. *Ho.* 7: 9.

Thou fool, that which thou sowest is not quickened, except it die. *1 Co.* 15: 36.

Seeing then that all these things shall be dissolved, what manner of persons ought ye to be. *2 Pe.* 3: 11.

See also

Atrophy; Corruption; Ruin; Waste; Withering.

Decease

When the waves of death compassed me, the floods of ungodly men made me afraid. *2 S.* 22: 5.

Is it well with the child? And she answered, It is well. *2 K.* 4: 26.

O Lord, thou hast brought up my soul from the grave. *Ps.* 30: 3.

God will redeem my soul from the power of the grave. *Ps.* 49: 15.

Thou hast delivered my soul from death. *Ps.* 56: 13.

Shall thy lovingkindness be declared in the grave? *Ps.* 88: 11.

He hath not given me over unto death. *Ps.* 118: 18.

Better . . . the day of death than the day of one's birth. *Ec.* 7: 1.

I have no pleasure in the death of the wicked. *Eze.* 33: 11.

They shall be as . . . the chaff that is driven with the whirlwind out of the floor. *Ho.* 13: 3.

I will ransom them from the power of the grave. *Ho:* 13: 14.

This night thy soul shall be required of thee. *Lu.* 12: 20.

He fell asleep. *Ac.* 7: 60.

I am persuaded, that neither death, nor life, . . . shall be able to separate us from the love of God. *Ro.* 8: 38, 39.

Some man will say, How are the dead raised up? and with what body do they come? *1 Co.* 15: 35.

Death is swallowed up in victory. *1 Co.* 15: 54.

Deliver them who through fear of death were all their lifetime subject to bondage. *He.* 2: 15.

It is appointed unto men once to die. *He.* 9: 27.

See also
Burial; Christ, Death of; Disappearance; Expiration; Funeral; Grave; Immortality; Life, the Eternal; Tomb.

Deceit

There is treachery. *2 K.* 9: 23.

Who shall ascend into the hill of the Lord? or who shall stand in his holy place? He that hath clean hands, and a pure heart; who hath not lifted up his soul unto vanity, nor sworn deceitfully. *Ps.* 24: 3, 4.

He flattereth himself in his own eyes. *Ps.* 36: 2.

They did flatter him with their mouth, and they lied unto him with their tongues. *Ps.* 78: 36.

There is a way that seemeth right unto a man; but the end thereof are the ways of death. *Pr.* 16: 25.

Bread of deceit is sweet to a man; but afterwards his mouth shall be filled with gravel. *Pr.* 20: 17.

As a mad man who casteth firebrands, arrows, and death, So is the man that deceiveth his neighbour, and saith, Am not I in sport? *Pr.* 26: 18, 19.

Faithful are the wounds of a friend; but the kisses of an enemy are deceitful. *Pr.* 27: 6.

A deceived heart hath turned him aside. *Is.* 44: 20.

Their tongue . . . speaketh deceit. *Je.* 9: 8.

With their mouth they shew much love, but their heart goeth after their covetousness. *Eze.* 33: 31.

They hear thy words, but they do them not. *Eze.* 33: 32.

Falsifying the balances by deceit. *Am.* 8: 5.

The care of this world, and the deceitfulness of riches, choke the word. *Mat.* 13: 22.

Many shall come in my name, saying, I am Christ; and shall deceive many. *Mat.* 24: 5.

This people honoureth me with their lips. but their heart is far from me. *Mk.* 7: 6.

Out of the heart of men, proceed evil thoughts, . . . deceit. *Mk.* 7: 21, 22.

They . . . by good words and fair speeches deceive the hearts of the simple. *Ro.* 16: 18.

If a man think himself to be something, when he is nothing, he deceiveth himself. *Ga.* 6: 3.

For this cause God shall send them strong delusion, that they should believe a lie. *2 Th.* 2: 11.

They profess that they know God; but in works they deny him, being abominable, and disobedient, and unto every good work reprobate. *Tit.* 1: 16.

There were false prophets also among the people, even as there shall be false teachers among you. *2 Pe.* 2: 1.

Little children, let no man deceive you. *1 Jn.* 3: 7.

See also
Betrayal; Cheat; Craftiness; Cunning; Duplicity; Faithlessness; Falsehood; Fraud; Hypocrisy; Lie; Perfidy; Treachery.

Decision

We will hear it and do it. *De.* 5: 27.

All that thou commandest us we will do, and whithersoever thou sendest us, we will go. *Jos.* 1: 16.

One thing have I desired of the Lord, that will I seek after. *Ps.* 27: 4.

My counsel shall stand, and I will do all my pleasure. *Is.* 46: 10.

I have spoken it, I will also bring it to pass; I have purposed it, I will also do it. *Is.* 46: 11.

Multitudes, multitudes in the valley of decision: for the day of the Lord is near in the valley of decision. *Jo.* 3: 14.

I am resolved what to do. *Lu.* 16: 4.

Whatsoever ye shall ask in my name, that will I do. *Jn.* 14: 13.

I determined not to know any thing among you, save Jesus Christ, and him crucified. *1 Co.* 2: 2.

This one thing I do, forgetting those things which are behind, and reaching forth unto those things which are before, I press toward the mark for the prize of the high calling of God in Christ Jesus. *Ph.* 3: 13, 14.

See also
Conclusion; Determination; Firmness; Judgment, Resolution.

Declaration

Declare his glory among the heathen; his marvellous works among all nations. *1 Ch.* 16: 24.

Where wast thou when I laid the foundations of the earth? Declare, if thou hast understanding. *Jb.* 38: 4.

The heavens declare the glory of God. *Ps.* 19: 1.

That I may publish with the voice of thanksgiving, and tell of all thy wondrous works. *Ps.* 26: 7.

Shall the dust praise thee? shall it declare thy truth? *Ps.* 30: 9.

One generation shall praise thy works to another, and shall declare thy mighty acts. *Ps.* 145: 4.

The Lord hath anointed me . . . to proclaim liberty to the captives. *Is.* 61: 1.

Declare ye in Judah, and publish in Jerusalem; and say, Blow ye the trumpet in the land. *Je.* 4: 5.

Whom therefore ye ignorantly worship, him declare I unto you. *Ac.* 17: 23.

Declared to be the Son of God with power. *Ro.* 1: 4.

See also

Affirmation; Announcement; Annunciation; Avowal; Proclamation; Publicity.

Decline

He cometh forth like a flower, and is cut down. *Jb.* 14: 2.

My foot hath held his steps, his way have I kept, and not declined. *Jb.* 23: 11.

My days are like a shadow that declineth. *Ps.* 102: 11.

I was brought low, and he helped me. *Ps.* 116: 6.

Many are my persecutors and mine enemies; yet do I not decline from thy testimonies. *Ps.* 119: 157.

Get wisdom, get understanding: forget it not; neither decline from the words of my mouth. *Pr.* 4: 5.

Art thou also become weak as we? *Is.* 14: 10.

When the boughs thereof are withered, they shall be broken off. *Is.* 27: 11.

The grass withereth, the flower fadeth: because the spirit of the Lord bloweth upon it. *Is.* 40: 7.

Even to your old age I am he; and even to hoar hairs will I carry you: I have made, and I will bear; even I will carry, and will deliver you. *Is.* 46: 4.

He must increase, but I must decrease. *Jn.* 3: 30.

See also

Degeneration, Worsening.

Decree

Thou shalt teach them ordinances and laws. *Ex.* 18: 20.

Proclaim liberty throughout all the land unto all the inhabitants thereof. *Le.* 25: 10.

He made a decree for the rain. *Jb.* 28: 26.

They kept his testimonies, and the ordinance that he gave them. *Ps.* 99: 7.

By me kings reign, and princes decree justice. *Pr.* 8: 15.

He gave to the sea his decree, that the waters should not pass his commandment. *Pr.* 8: 29.

Woe unto them that decree unrighteous decrees. *Is.* 10: 1.

They ask of me the ordinances of justice; they take delight in approaching to God. *Is.* 58: 2.

Then an herald cried aloud, To you it is commanded, O people. *Da.* 3: 4.

Whosoever therefore resisteth the power, resisteth the ordinance of God. *Ro.* 13: 2.

Submit yourselves to every ordinance of man for the Lord's sake. *1 Pe.* 2: 13.

See also

Commandment; God, Commandment of; God, Law of; Law; Ordinance; Statute.

Dedication

This was the dedication of the altar, in the day when it was anointed. *Nu.* 7: 84.

What man is there that hath built a new house, and hath not dedicated it? let him go and return to his house, lest he die in the battle, and another man dedicate it. *De.* 20: 5.

Praise ye the Lord for the avenging of Israel, when the people willingly offered themselves. *Ju.* 5: 2.

The child shall be a Nazarite to God from the womb to the day of his death. *Ju.* 13: 7.

Behold, I build an house to the name of the Lord my God, to dedicate it to him. *2 Ch.* 2: 4.

All the people dedicated the house of God. *2 Ch.* 7: 5.

It was at Jerusalem the feast of the dedication, and it was winter. *Jn.* 10: 22.

I beseech you therefore, brethren, by the mercies of God, that ye present your bodies a living sacrifice, holy, acceptable unto God, which is your reasonable service. *Ro.* 12: 1.

A new and living way, which he hath consecrated for us. *He.* 10: 20.

See also

Consecration; Devotion; Installation; Offering; Ordination; Sanctification; Votary.

Deed

Even a child is known by his doings, whether his work be pure, and whether it be right. *Pr.* 20: 11.

He is strong that executeth his word. *Jo.* 2: 11.

Why call ye me, Lord, Lord, and do not the things which I say? *Lu.* 6: 46.

Jesus of Nazareth, which was a prophet mighty in deed and word. *Lu.* 24: 19.

Men loved darkness rather than light, because their deeds were evil. *Jn.* 3: 19.

Why stand ye gazing up into heaven? *Ac.* 1: 11.

God . . . will render to every man according to his deeds. *Ro.* 2: 5, 6.

To will is present with me; but how to perform that which is good I find not. *Ro.* 7: 18.

Ye have put off the old man with his deeds. *Col.* 3: 9.

Whatsoever ye do in word or deed, do all in the name of the Lord Jesus. *Col.* 3: 17.

A doer of the work . . . shall be blessed in his deed. *Ja.* 1: 25.

Let us not love in word, neither in tongue; but in deed and in truth. *1 Jn.* 3: 18.

The dead were judged out of those things which were written in the books, according to their works. *Re.* 20: 12.

See also

Achievement; Action; Happening; Operation; Performance.

Deep

The Almighty . . . shall bless thee with blessings of heaven above, blessings of the deep that lieth under. *Ge.* 49: 25.

The Lord made . . . the sea. *Ex.* 20: 11.

He discovereth deep things out of darkness. *Jb.* 12: 22.

He hath founded it upon the seas, and established it upon the floods. *Ps.* 24: 2.

Thy judgments are a great deep. *Ps.* 36: 6.

Deep calleth unto deep at the noise of thy waterspouts. *Ps.* 42: 7.

Let me be delivered . . . out of the deep waters. *Ps.* 69: 14.

He gave them drink as out of the great depths. *Ps.* 78: 15.

Thy thoughts are very deep. *Ps. 92: 5.*

Who hath measured the waters in the hollow of his hand. *Is. 40: 12.*

What manner of man is this, that even the winds and the sea obey him? *Mat. 8: 27.*

Immediately it sprang up, because it had no depth of earth. *Mk. 4: 5.*

Launch out into the deep. *Lu. 5: 4.*

God hath revealed them unto us by his Spirit: for the Spirit searcheth all things, yea, the deep things of God. *1 Co. 2: 10.*

Worship him that made . . . the sea, and the fountain of waters. *Re. 14: 7.*

See also

Abyss; Depth; Flood; Ocean; Sea; Water; Wave.

Defeat

Wherefore hath the Lord smitten us to day? *1 S. 4: 3.*

The people are fled from the battle, and many of the people also are fallen and dead. *2 S. 1: 4.*

How are the mighty fallen! *2 S. 1: 19.*

My God, my God, why hast thou forsaken me? *Ps. 22: 1.*

He hath stretched forth his hand against them, and hath smitten them. *Is. 5: 25.*

The children are come to the birth, and there is not strength to bring forth. *Is. 37: 3.*

Then I said, I have laboured in vain, I have spent my strength for nought, and in vain: yet surely my judgment is with the Lord, and my work with my God. *Is. 49: 4.*

Asshur shall not save us; we will not ride upon horses. *Ho. 14: 3.*

This man began to build, and was not able to finish. *Lu. 14: 30.*

Thou therefore endure hardness as a good soldier of Jesus Christ. *2 Ti. 2: 3.*

Let us therefore fear, lest, a promise being left us of entering into his rest, any of you should seem to come short of it. *He. 4: 1.*

See also

Failure; Fall; Frustration; Overthrow; Ruin.

Defect

But he was a leper. *2 K. 5: 1.*

Cleanse thou me from secret faults. *Ps. 19: 12.*

He was faithful, neither was there any error or fault found in him. *Da. 6: 4.*

If thy hand or thy foot offend thee, cut them off, and cast them from thee. *Mat. 18: 8.*

That he might present it to himself a glorious church, not having spot, or wrinkle, or any such thing; but that it should be holy and without blemish. *Ep. 5: 27.*

Whosoever shall keep the whole law, and yet offend in one point, he is guilty of all. *Ja. 2: 10.*

Confess your faults one to another. *Ja. 5: 16.*

What glory is it, if, when ye be buffeted for your faults, ye shall take it patiently? *1 Pe. 2: 20.*

See also

Blemish; Failure; Fault; Imperfection; Lack; Spot; Taint; Want.

Defence

The Lord, the shield of thy help. *De. 33: 29.*

Suffer me a little, and I will shew thee that I have yet to speak on God's behalf. *Jb. 36: 2.*

Thou, O Lord, art a shield for me; my glory, and the lifter up of mine head. *Ps. 3: 3.*

The name of the God of Jacob defend thee. *Ps. 20: 1.*

As birds flying, so will the Lord of Hosts defend Jerusalem. *Is. 31: 5.*

In that day shall the Lord defend the inhabitants of Jerusalem. *Zch. 12: 8.*

Hear ye my defence which I make now unto you. *Ac. 22: 1.*

Above all, taking the shield of faith, wherewith ye shall be able to quench all the fiery darts of the wicked. *Ep. 6: 16.*

In the defence and confirmation of the gospel. *Ph. 1: 7.*

See also

Buckler; Fortress; Protection; Tower; Wall.

Defiance

How shall I defy, whom the Lord hath not defied? *Nu. 23: 8.*

The Philistine said, I defy the armies of Israel this day; give me a man, that we may fight together. *1 S. 17: 10.*

He hath defied the armies of the living God. *1 S. 17: 36.*

Come out, come out, thou bloody man, and thou man of Belial. *2 S. 16: 7.*

The three mighty men with David . . . defied the Philistines that were there gathered together to battle. *2 S. 23: 9.*

Thou hast reproached the Lord, and hast said, With the multitude of my chariots I am come up to the height of the mountains. *2 K. 19: 23.*

If thou canst answer me, set thy words in order before me, stand up. *Jb. 33: 5.*

Woe to them that . . . trust in chariots, because they are many; and in horsemen, because they are very strong; but they look not unto the Holy One of Israel, neither seek the Lord! *Is. 31: 1.*

Thus saith the Lord God; Behold, I am against thee, O Tyrus, and I will cause many nations to come up against thee, as the sea causeth his waves to come up. *Eze. 26: 3.*

See also

Challenge; Champion.

Defilement

Neither wilt thou suffer thine Holy One to see corruption. *Ps. 16: 10.*

Perverse lips put far from thee. *Pr. 4: 24.*

Thou . . . didst debase thyself even unto hell. *Is. 57: 9.*

They have even defiled my holy name by their abominations. *Eze. 43: 8.*

Not that which goeth into the mouth defileth a man; but that which cometh out of the mouth, this defileth a man. *Mat. 15: 11.*

Whatsoever thing from without entereth into the man, it cannot defile him. *Mk. 7: 18.*

We have wronged no man, we have corrupted no man, we have defrauded no man. *2 Co. 7: 2.*

Filthy dreamers defile the flesh. *Jude 1: 8.*

He which is filthy, let him be filthy still. *Re. 22: 11.*

See also

Adulteration; Contagion; Corruption; Defilement; Degeneration; Depravity; Evil; Impurity; Iniquity; Lust; Pollution; Sin; Sinner; Taint; Uncleanness; Ungodliness; Unrighteousness; Vileness; Wickedness.

Degeneration

His wife . . . became a pillar of salt. *Ge.* 19: 26.

I sink in deep mire. *Ps.* 69: 2.

Folly is set in great dignity, and the rich sit in low place. *Ec.* 10: 6.

Thou . . . didst debase thyself even unto hell. *Is.* 57: 9.

Thine own wickedness shall correct thee, and thy backslidings shall reprove thee. *Je.* 2: 19.

I had planted thee a noble vine, wholly a right seed: how then art thou turned into the degenerate plant of a strange vine unto me? *Je.* 2: 21.

The last state of that man is worse than the first. *Lu.* 11: 26.

Evil men and seducers shall wax worse and worse. *2 Ti.* 3: 13.

If after they have escaped the pollutions of the world through the knowledge of the Lord and Saviour Jesus Christ, they are again entangled therein, and overcome, the latter end is worse with them than the beginning. *2 Pe.* 2: 20.

Deity

I am the Almighty God; walk before me, and be thou perfect. *Ge.* 17: 1.

God said unto Moses, I AM THAT I AM. *Ex.* 3: 14.

The Lord is a God of knowledge, and by him actions are weighed. *1 S.* 2: 3.

I am God, even thy God. *Ps.* 50: 7.

Before the mountains were brought forth, or ever thou hadst formed the earth and the world, even from everlasting to everlasting, thou art God. *Ps.* 90: 2.

Who can utter the mighty acts of the Lord? *Ps.* 106: 2.

How precious also are thy thoughts unto me, O God! how great is the sum of them! *Ps.* 139: 17.

Before me there was no God formed, neither shall there be after me. I, even I, am the Lord. *Is.* 43: 10, 11.

Before the day was I am he. *Is.* 43: 13.

I am the first, and I am the last; and beside me there is no God. *Is.* 44: 6.

I have made the earth, and created man upon it. *Is.* 45: 12.

I am God, and not man; the Holy One in the midst of thee. *Ho.* 11: 9.

All people will walk every one in the name of his god, and we will walk in the name of the Lord our God for ever and ever. *Mic.* 4: 5.

I am Alpha and Omega, the beginning and the ending, saith the Lord, which is, and which was, and which is to come, the Almighty. *Re.* 1: 8.
See also
Almighty; God; Lord.

Dejection

In the morning thou shalt say, Would God it were even! and at even thou shalt say, Would God it were morning! *De.* 28: 67.

The bitter in soul . . . long for death, but it cometh not. *Jb.* 3: 20, 21.

Lover and friend hast thou put far from me, and mine acquaintance into darkness. *Ps.* 88: 18.

I have lost my children, and am desolate. *Is.* 49: 21.

The mighty man shall cry there bitterly. *Zph.* 1: 14.

That day is a day of wrath, a day of trouble and distress, a day of wasteness and desolation, a day of darkness and gloominess, a day of clouds and thick darkness. *Zph.* 1: 15.

He cast down the pieces of silver in the temple, and departed, and went and hanged himself. *Mat.* 27: 5.

Even unto this present hour we both hunger, and thirst, and are naked, and are buffeted, and have no certain dwellingplace. *1 Co.* 4: 11.

We are perplexed, but not in despair. *2 Co.* 4: 8.

Cast down, but not destroyed. *2 Co.* 4: 9.

In those days shall men seek death and shall not find it; and shall desire to die, and death shall flee from them. *Re.* 9: 6.
See also
Depression; Despair; Despondency; Dismay; Gloom; Melancholy; Sadness; Sorrow; Unhappiness.

Delay

How long wilt thou forget me, O Lord? *Ps.* 13: 1.

Make no tarrying, O my God. *Ps.* 40: 17.

I made haste, and delayed not to keep thy commandments. *Ps.* 119: 60.

My salvation shall not tarry. *Is.* 46: 13.

The harvest is past, the summer is ended, and we are not saved. *Je.* 8: 20.

The vision is yet for an appointed time, . . . though it tarry, wait for it; because it will surely come, it will not tarry. *Hab.* 2: 3.

While the bridegroom tarried, they all slumbered and slept. *Mat.* 25: 5.

Afterward came also the other virgins. *Mat.* 25: 11.

Tarry ye here, and watch with me. *Mat.* 26: 38.

When once the master of the house is risen up, and hath shut to the door, and ye begin to stand without, and to knock at the door, saying, Lord, Lord, open unto us; and he shall answer and say unto you, I know you not whence ye are. *Lu.* 13: 25.

Tarry ye in the city of Jerusalem, until ye be endued with power from on high. *Lu.* 24: 49.

If I will that he tarry till I come, what is that to thee? follow thou me. *Jn.* 21: 22.

When I have a convenient season, I will call for thee. *Ac.* 24: 25.

Without any delay . . . I sat on the judgment seat. *Ac.* 25: 17.

When ye come together to eat, tarry one for another. *1 Co.* 11: 33.

Yet a little while, and he that shall come will come, and will not tarry. *He.* 10: 37.

Afterward, when he would have inherited the blessing, he was rejected: for he found no place of repentance, though he sought it carefully with tears. *He.* 12: 17.

Be patient therefore, brethren, unto the coming of the Lord. *Ja.* 5: 7.

See also
Abeyance; Arrest; Patience; Procrastination; Wait.

Deliberation

Hear the causes between your brethren, and judge righteously between every man and his brother. *De.* 1: 16.

Give therefore thy servant an understanding heart to judge thy people. *1 K.* 3: 9.

Ezra the priest with certain chief of the fathers, . . . sat down . . . to examine the matter. *Ezr.* 10: 16.

I thought on my ways, and turned my feet unto thy testimonies. *Ps.* 119: 59.

He that answereth a matter before he heareth it, it is folly and shame unto him. *Pr.* 18: 13.

He that hasteth with his feet sinneth. *Pr.* 19: 2.

A wise man's heart discerneth both time and judgment. *Ec.* 8: 5.

He that believeth shall not make haste. *Is.* 28: 16.

Go thy way for this time; when I have a convenient season, I will call for thee. *Ac.* 24: 25.

Let a man examine himself. *1 Co.* 11: 28.

Examine yourselves, whether ye be in the faith; prove your own selves. *2 Co.* 13: 5.
See also
Consideration; Contemplation; Delay; Examination; God, Thought of; Meditation; Reflection; Study; Thought.

Delight

Blessed be the Lord thy God, which delighted in thee. *1 K.* 10: 9.

He hath said, It profiteth a man nothing that he should delight himself with God. *Jb.* 34: 9.

My heart is glad, and my glory rejoiceth: my flesh also shall rest in hope. *Ps.* 16: 9.

My soul shall make her boast in the Lord: the humble shall hear thereof, and be glad. *Ps.* 34: 2.

I delight to do thy will, O my God. *Ps.* 40: 8.

God hath spoken in his holiness; I will rejoice. *Ps.* 60: 6.

Because thou hast been my help, therefore in the shadow of thy wings will I rejoice. *Ps.* 63: 7.

The Lord reigneth; let the earth rejoice. *Ps.* 97: 1.

Let the floods clap their hands: let the hills be joyful together. *Ps.* 98: 8.

Blessed is the man that . . . delighteth greatly in his commandments. *Ps.* 112: 1.

Thy testimonies also are my delight and my counsellors. *Ps.* 119: 24.

Let thy saints shout for joy. *Ps.* 132: 9.

His mouth is most sweet: yea, he is altogether lovely. *S. of S.* 5: 16.

Sing, O heavens; and be joyful, O earth; and break forth into singing, O mountains. *Is.* 49: 13.

They seek me daily, and delight to know my ways, as a nation that did righteousness. *Is.* 58: 2.

The word of the Lord is unto them a reproach; they have no delight in it. *Je.* 6: 10.

Is this the city that men call The perfection of beauty, The joy of the whole earth? *La.* 2: 15.

He retaineth not his anger for ever, because he delighteth in mercy. *Mi.* 7: 18.

Rejoice ye in that day, and leap for joy: for, behold, your reward is great in heaven. *Lu.* 6: 23.

Glad tidings of good things. *Ro.* 10: 15.

The God of hope fill you with all joy and peace in believing. *Ro.* 15: 13.
See also
Charm; Christ, Joy in; Christ, Joy of; Contentment; Gladness; God, Joy in; Happiness; Joy; Pleasure; Rapture; Rejoicing; Satisfaction.

Deliverance

Blessed is he whose transgression is forgiven, whose sin is covered. *Ps.* 32: 1.

Thou shalt compass me about with songs of deliverance. *Ps.* 32: 7.

I was brought low, and he helped me. *Ps.* 116: 6.

In returning and rest shall ye be saved; in quietness and in confidence shall be your strength. *Is.* 30: 15.

Thou hast in love to my soul delivered it from the pit. *Is.* 38: 17.

The princes . . . saw these men, upon whose bodies the fire had no power, nor was an hair of their head singed, neither were their coats changed, nor the smell of fire had passed on them. *Da.* 3: 27.

My God hath sent his angel, and hath shut the lions' mouths, that they have not hurt me. *Da.* 6: 22.

I was to them as they that take off the yoke on their jaws, and I laid meat unto them. *Ho.* 11: 4.

He that endureth to the end shall be saved. *Mat.* 10: 22.

Deliver us from evil. *Lu.* 11: 4.

The angel of the Lord by night opened the prison doors, and brought them forth. *Ac.* 5: 19.

His chains fell off from his hands. *Ac.* 12: 7.

Immediately all the doors were opened, and every one's bands were loosed. *Ac.* 16: 26.

The prayer of faith shall save the sick. *Ja.* 5: 15.
See also
Christ, the Redeemer; Christ, the Saviour; Emancipation; God, Deliverance of; God, the Redeemer; God, Salvation of; Ransom; Redemption; Rescue; Restoration; Salvation; Succor.

Deluge

I, even I, do bring a flood of waters upon the earth. *Ge.* 6: 17.

I will cause it to rain upon the earth forty days and forty nights; and every living substance that I have made will I destroy from off the face of the earth. *Ge.* 7: 4.

The waters were on the face of the whole earth. *Ge.* 8: 9.

I will establish my covenant with you; neither shall all flesh be cut off any more by the waters of a flood. *Ge.* 9: 11.

The Lord sitteth upon the flood. *Ps.* 29: 10.

Thou carriest them away as with a flood. *Ps.* 90: 5.

The floods have lifted up, O Lord, the floods

have lifted up their voice. *Ps.* 93: 3.

It shall rise up wholly as a flood; and it shall be cast out and drowned, as by the flood of Egypt. *Am.* 8: 8.

God . . . spared not the old world, but saved Noah the eighth person, a preacher of righteousness, bringing in the flood upon the world of the ungodly. *2 Pe.* 2: 4, 5.

The world that then was, being overflowed with water, perished. *2 Pe.* 3: 6.
See also
Flood.

Delusion

An horror of great darkness fell upon him. *Ge.* 15: 12.

We cannot order our speech by reason of darkness. *Jb.* 37: 19.

Who is this that darkeneth counsel by words without knowledge? *Jb.* 38: 2.

They err in vision, they stumble in judgment. *Is.* 28: 7.

We wait for light, but behold obscurity. *Is.* 59: 9.

I also will choose their delusions, and will bring their fears upon them. *Is.* 66: 4.

They prophesy unto you a false vision and divination, and a thing of nought, and the deceit of their heart. *Je.* 14: 14.

Their foolish heart was darkened. *Ro.* 1: 21.

Professing themselves to be wise, they became fools. *Ro.* 1: 22.

Their minds were blinded. *2 Co.* 3: 14.

Having the understanding darkened. *Ep.* 4: 18.

God shall send them strong delusion, that they should believe a lie. *2 Th.* 2: 11.
See also
Darkness; Error; Insanity.

Democracy

Proclaim liberty throughout all the land unto all the inhabitants thereof. *Le.* 25: 10.

Hearken unto the voice of the people in all that they say unto thee. *1 S.* 8: 7.

He looseth the bond of kings. *Jb.* 12: 18.

I will walk at liberty. *Ps.* 119: 45.

The rich and poor meet together: the Lord is the maker of them all. *Pr.* 22: 2.

Prepare ye the way of the people. *Is.* 62: 10.

With a great sum obtained I this freedom. *Ac.* 22: 28.

I was free born. *Ac.* 22: 28.

Whether one member suffer, all the members suffer with it. *1 Co.* 12: 26.

Where there is neither Greek nor Jew, circumcision nor uncircumcision, Barbarian, Scythian, bond nor free. *Col.* 3: 11.

The perfect law of liberty. *Ja.* 1: 25.

So speak ye, and so do, as they that shall be judged by the law of liberty. *Ja.* 2: 12.
See also
Equality; Freedom; Independence; Liberty.

Denial

Before the cock crow twice, thou shalt deny me thrice. *Mk.* 14: 72.

And he said to them all, If any man will come after me, let him deny himself. *Lu.* 9: 23.

He that denieth me before men shall be denied before the angels of God. *Lu.* 12: 9.

Then came to him certain of the Sadducees, which deny that there is any resurrection. *Lu.* 20: 27.

How say some among you that there is no resurrection of the dead? *1 Co.* 15: 12.

Who is a liar but he that denieth that Jesus is the Christ? *1 Jn.* 2: 22.

Thou holdest fast my name, and hast not denied my faith. *Re.* 2: 13.
See also
Christ, Denial of; Cross; God, Denial of; Hindrance; Opposition; Sacrifice; Self-Sacrifice.

Denomination

In all thy ways acknowledge him, and he shall direct thy paths. *Pr.* 3: 6.

My thoughts are not your thoughts, neither are your ways my ways, saith the Lord. *Is.* 55: 8.

Unto one he gave five talents, to another two, and to another one; to every man according to his several ability. *Mat.* 25: 15.

In my Father's house are many mansions. *Jn.* 14: 2.

That they may be one, as we are. *Jn.* 17: 11.

One man esteemeth one day above another: another esteemeth every day alike. Let every man be fully persuaded in his own mind. *Ro.* 14: 5.

Let us not therefore judge one another any more. *Ro.* 14: 13.

Mark them which cause divisions and offences contrary to the doctrine which ye have learned. *Ro.* 16: 17.

Now I beseech you, brethren, by the name of our Lord Jesus Christ, that ye all speak the same thing, and that there be no divisions among you. *1 Co.* 1: 10.

I beseech you . . . that ye be perfectly joined together in the same mind and in the same judgment. *1 Co.* 1: 10.

Every one of you saith, I am of Paul; and I of Apollos; and I of Cephas; and I of Christ. *1 Co.* 1: 12.

Is Christ divided? *1 Co.* 1: 13.

We being many are one bread, and one body: for we are all partakers of that one bread. *1 Co.* 10: 17.

The body is not one member, but many. *1 Co.* 12: 14.

There should be no schism in the body. *1 Co.* 12: 25.

Ye are all one in Christ Jesus. *Ga.* 3: 28.
See also
Church; Division; Heresy; Orthodoxy; Schism; Sect.

Denunciation

Thou shalt not raise a false report. *Ex.* 23: 1.

I denounce unto you this day, that ye shall surely perish. *De.* 30: 18.

They gather themselves together against the soul of the righteous, and condemn the innocent blood. *Ps.* 94: 21.

Accuse not a servant unto his master. *Pr.* 30: 10.

They hearkened not unto me, nor inclined their ear, but hardened their neck: they did worse than their fathers. *Je.* 7: 26.

Blessed are ye, when men shall revile you. *Mat.* 5: 11.

And set up over his head his accusation. *Mat.* 27: 37.

Condemn not, and ye shall not be condemned. *Lu.* 6: 37.

When the people were gathered thick together, he began to say, This is an evil generation. *Lu.* 11: 29.

Of a truth this fellow also was with him. *Lu.* 22: 59.

Against an elder brother receive not an accusation. *1 Ti.* 5: 19.

See also

Accusation; Condemnation.

Departure

He wist not that the Lord was departed from him. *Ju.* 16: 20.

There is but a step between me and death. *1 S.* 20: 3.

I shall go to him, but he shall not return to me. *2 S.* 12: 23.

On my eyelids is the shadow of death. *Jb.* 16: 16.

Into thine hand I commit my spirit. *Ps.* 31: 5.

Depart from evil, and do good. *Ps.* 34: 14.

The end of that man is peace. *Ps.* 37: 37.

A wise man feareth, and departeth from evil. *Pr.* 14: 16.

Man goeth to his long home. *Ec.* 12: 5.

Then shall the dust return to the earth as it was: and the spirit shall return unto God who gave it. *Ec.* 12: 7.

Lord, now lettest thou thy servant depart in peace. *Lu.* 2: 29.

Their eyes were opened, and they knew him; and he vanished out of their sight. *Lu.* 24: 31.

The time of my departure is at hand. *2 Ti.* 4: 6.

See also

Absence; Parting; Removal; Withdrawal.

Dependence

The Lord recompense thy work, and a full reward be given thee of the Lord God of Israel, under whose wings thou art come to trust. *Ru.* 2: 12.

Blessed are all they that put their trust in him. *Ps.* 2: 12.

Some trust in chariots, and some in horses: but we will remember the name of the Lord our God. *Ps.* 20: 7.

The Lord shall be thy confidence, and shall keep thy foot from being taken. *Pr.* 3: 26.

Thou wilt keep him in perfect peace, whose mind is stayed on thee. *Is.* 26: 3.

When he saw the wind boisterous, he was afraid; and beginning to sink, he cried, Lord, save me. *Mat.* 14: 30.

How hard is it for them that trust in riches to enter into the kingdom of God! *Mk.* 10: 24.

The Son can do nothing of himself. *Jn.* 5: 19.

I know nothing by myself. *1 Co.* 4: 4.

We can do nothing against the truth, but for the truth. *2 Co.* 13: 8.

Without thy mind would I do nothing. *Phm.* 1: 14.

See also

Confidence; God, Confidence in; God, Reliance on; God, Trust in; Reliance; Trust.

Depravity

The earth also was corrupt before God, and the earth was filled with violence. *Ge.* 6: 11.

We have sinned, and have done perversely, we have committed wickedness. *1 K.* 8: 47.

A corrupt tree bringeth forth evil fruit. *Mat.* 7: 17.

An evil man out of the evil treasure bringeth forth evil things. *Mat.* 12: 35.

Those things which proceed out of the mouth come forth from the heart; and they defile the man. *Mat.* 15: 18.

From within, out of the heart of men, proceed evil thoughts, adulteries, fornications, murders, Thefts, covetousness, wickedness, deceit, lasciviousness, an evil eye, blasphemy, pride, foolishness. *Mk.* 7: 21, 22.

Ye are of your father the devil. *Jn.* 8: 44.

Being filled with . . . maliciousness. *Ro.* 1: 29.

All have sinned, and come short of the glory of God. *Ro.* 3: 23.

By one man sin entered into the world. *Ro.* 5: 12.

Who shall deliver me from the body of this death? *Ro.* 7: 24.

If any man defile the temple of God, him shall God destroy. *1 Co.* 3: 17.

So also is the resurrection of the dead. It is sown in corruption; it is raised in incorruption. *1 Co.* 15: 42.

They themselves are the servants of corruption. *2 Pe.* 2: 19.

The whole world lieth in wickedness. *1 Jn.* 5: 19.

See also

Bestiality; Corruption; Crime; Defilement; Degeneration; Evil; Impurity; Iniquity; Lust; Sin; Sinner; Ungodliness; Unrighteousness; Vileness; Wickedness.

Depression

The soul of the people was much discouraged because of the way. *Nu.* 21: 4.

Fear not, neither be discouraged. *De.* 1: 21.

Then the angel of the Lord departed out of his sight. *Ju.* 6: 21.

He requested for himself that he might die; and said, It is enough; now, O Lord, take away my life; for I am not better than my fathers. *1 K.* 19: 4.

Oh that I were as in months past, as in the days when God preserved me; . . . When the Almighty was yet with me, when my children were about me. *Jb.* 29: 2, 5.

Why art thou cast down, O my soul? and why art thou disquieted within me? *Ps.* 43: 5.

By the rivers of Babylon, there we sat down, yea, we wept, when we remembered Zion. *Ps.* 137: 1.

I have cut off like a weaver my life: he will cut me off with pining sickness: from day even to night wilt thou make an end of me. *Is.* 38: 12.

He shall not fail nor be discouraged, till he have set judgment in the earth. *Is.* 42: 4.

See also

Abasement; Depression; Despondency; Dismay; Fall; Gloom; Melancholy; Mourning; Sadness; Sorrow; Unhappiness.

Depth

The depth saith, It is not in me. *Jb.* 28: 14.

He keepeth back his soul from the pit. *Jb.* **33: 18.**

The heathen are sunk down in the pit that they made. *Ps.* **9: 15.**

He layeth up the depth in storehouses. *Ps.* **33: 7.**

I will bring my people again from the depths of the sea. *Ps.* **68: 22.**

Out of the depths have I cried unto thee, O Lord. *Ps.* **130: 1.**

Let them be cast into the fire; into deep pits, that they rise not up again. *Ps.* **140: 10.**

The depth closed me round about. *Jon.* **2: 5.**

O the depth of the riches both of the wisdom and knowledge of God! *Ro.* **11: 33.**

The breadth, and length, and depth, and height. *Ep.* **3: 18.**

He . . . cast him into the bottomless pit. *Re.* **20: 2, 3.**

See also

Abyss; Deep; Hell; Pit.

Descent

Behold a ladder set up on the earth, . . . and behold the angels of God ascending and descending on it. *Ge.* **28: 12.**

The Lord descended upon it in fire. *Ex.* **19: 18.**

The Lord descended in the cloud, and stood with him there. *Ex.* **34: 5.**

As the dew that descended upon the mountains of Zion. *Ps.* **133: 3.**

Who hath ascended up into heaven, or descended? *Pr.* **30: 4.**

Who knoweth . . . the spirit of the beast that goeth downward to the earth? *Ec.* **3: 21.**

When he was come down from the mountain. *Mat.* **8: 1.**

The angel of the Lord descended from heaven. *Mat.* **28: 2.**

Let Christ the King of Israel descend now from the cross, that we may see and believe. *Mk.* **15: 32.**

Because he was of the house and lineage of David. *Lu.* **2: 4.**

The Holy Ghost descended in a bodily shape like a dove upon him. *Lu.* **3: 22.**

Who shall descend into the deep? *Ro.* **10: 7.**

He that descended is the same also that ascended up far above all heavens, that he might fill all things. *Ep.* **4: 10.**

The Lord himself shall descend from heaven with a shout. *1 Th.* **4: 16.**

Without father, without mother, without descent, having neither beginning of days, nor end of life. *He.* **7: 3.**

This wisdom descendeth not from above. *Ja.* **3: 15.**

He . . . shewed me that great city, the holy Jerusalem, descending out of heaven from God. *Re.* **21: 10.**

See also

Ancestor; Father; Genealogy; Generation; Heritage.

Desert

He knoweth thy walking through this great wilderness. *De.* **2: 7.**

I am like an owl of the desert. *Ps.* **102: 6.**

The wilderness and the solitary place shall be glad for them; and the desert shall rejoice and blossom as the rose. *Is.* **35: 1.**

I will plant in the wilderness the cedar. *Is.* **41: 19.**

I will even make a way in the wilderness, and rivers in the desert. *Is.* **43: 19.**

They thirsted not when he led them through the deserts. *Is.* **48: 21.**

Thy holy cities are a wilderness. *Is.* **64: 10.**

Oh that I had in the wilderness a lodging place of wayfaring men! *Je.* **9: 2.**

Thy prophets are like the foxes in the deserts. *Eze.* **13: 4.**

I found Israel like grapes in the wilderness. *Ho.* **9: 10.**

Come ye yourselves apart into a desert place, and rest a while. *Mk.* **6: 31.**

The child . . . was in the deserts till the day of his shewing unto Israel. *Lu.* **1: 80.**

Our fathers did eat manna in the desert. *Jn.* **6: 31.**

He carried me away in the spirit into the wilderness. *Re.* **17: 3.**

See also

Aridity; Desolation; Dryness; Solitude; Waste; Wilderness.

Desertion

I will not leave thee, until I have done that which I have spoken to thee of. *Ge.* **28: 15.**

Intreat me not to leave thee, or to return from following after thee. *Ru.* **1: 16.**

Thou wilt not leave my soul in hell. *Ps.* **16: 10.**

I am desolate and afflicted. *Ps.* **25: 16.**

My lovers and my friends stand aloof from my sore. *Ps.* **38: 11.**

Leave not my soul destitute. *Ps.* **141: 8.**

Thou hast forgotten me, and trusted in falsehood. *Je.* **13: 25.**

They have dealt treacherously against the Lord. *Ho.* **5: 7.**

They like men have transgressed the covenant: there have they dealt treacherously against me. *Ho.* **6: 7.**

One shall say unto him, What are these wounds in thine hands? Then he shall answer, Those with which I was wounded in the house of my friend. *Zch.* **13: 6.**

Whomsoever I shall kiss, that same is he; take him, and lead him away. *Mk.* **14: 44.**

Then said Jesus unto the twelve, Will ye also go away? *Jn.* **6: 67.**

I will not leave you comfortless. *Jn.* **14: 18.**

The hour cometh, yea, is now come, that ye shall be scattered, every man to his own, and shall leave me alone. *Jn.* **16: 32.**

He hath said, I will never leave thee, nor forsake thee. *He.* **13: 5.**

See also

Abandonment; Cowardice; Departure; Desolation; Destitution; Parting; Surrender; Treachery.

Desire

What man is he that desireth life, and loveth many days, that he may see good? *Ps.* **34: 12.**

Thou desirest not sacrifice; else would I give it. *Ps.* **51: 16.**

Thou openest thine hand, and satisfiest the desire of every living thing. *Ps.* **145: 16.**

When the desire cometh, it is a tree of life. *Pr.* **13: 12.**

The desire accomplished is sweet to the soul. *Pr.* 13: 19.

Better is the sight of the eyes than the wandering of the desire. *Ec.* 6: 9.

I desired mercy, and not sacrifice. *Ho.* 6: 6.

Desire spiritual gifts. *1 Co.* 14: 1.

Now they desire a better country. *He.* 11: 16.

Which things the angels desire to look into. *1 Pe.* 1: 12.

See also

Aspiration; Hope; Inclination; Longing; Request; Yearning.

Desolation

The land is defiled. *Le.* 18: 25.

None of them that trust in him shall be desolate. *Ps.* 34: 22.

All the land shall become briers and thorns. *Is.* 7: 24.

The indignation of the Lord is upon all nations, and his fury upon all their armies: he hath utterly destroyed them. *Is.* 34: 2.

Thorns shall be in their tabernacles. *Ho.* 9: 6.

That which the palmerworm hath left hath the locust eaten; and that which the locust hath left hath the cankerworm eaten; and that which the cankerworm hath left hath the caterpiller eaten. *Jo.* 1: 4.

The field is wasted, the land mourneth; for the corn is wasted: the new wine is dried up, the oil languisheth. *Jo.* 1: 10.

The land is as the garden of Eden before them, and behind them a desolate wilderness. *Jo.* 2: 3.

Every kingdom divided against itself is brought to desolation. *Mat.* 12: 25.

See also

Desert; Destruction; Devastation; Gloom; Melancholy; Ruin; Sadness; Solitude; Waste.

Despair

Let me not see my wretchedness. *Nu.* 11: 15.

Would to God we had been content, and dwelt on the other side Jordan! *Jos.* 7: 7.

Ye have taken away my gods, . . . and what have I more? *Ju.* 18: 24.

Now, O Lord, take away my life; for I am not better than my fathers. *1 K.* 19: 4.

The speeches of one that is desperate, which are as wind. *Jb.* 6: 26.

My soul is weary of my life; I will leave my complaint upon myself; I will speak in the bitterness of my soul. *Jb.* 10: 1.

Many sorrows shall be to the wicked. *Ps.* 32: 10.

O my God, my soul is cast down within me: therefore will I remember thee from the land of Jordan. *Ps.* 42: 6.

Thy holy cities are a wilderness. *Is.* 64: 10.

Woe is me, my mother, that thou hast borne me a man of strife and a man of contention to the whole earth! *Je.* 15: 10.

O Lord, how long shall I cry, and thou wilt not hear! even cry out unto thee of violence, and thou wilt not save! *Hab.* 1: 2.

And the door was shut. *Mat.* 25: 10.

My God, my God, why hast thou forsaken me? *Mk.* 15: 34.

What manner of communications are these that ye have one to another, as ye walk, and are sad? *Lu.* 24: 17.

We are perplexed, but not in despair. *2 Co.* 4: 8.

See also

Desolation; Gloom; Hopelessness; Melancholy; Sadness.

Despondency

Can I hear any more the voice of singing men and singing women? *2 S.* 19: 35.

Naked came I out of my mother's womb, and naked shall I return thither. *Jb.* 1: 21.

Desire not the night. *Jb.* 36: 20.

Why art thou cast down, O my soul? and why art thou disquieted in me? *Ps.* 42: 5.

Put thou my tears into thy bottle: are they not in thy book? *Ps.* 56: 8.

Leave not my soul destitute. *Ps.* 141: 8.

He hath smitten my life down to the ground. *Ps.* 143: 3.

My heart within me is desolate. *Ps.* 143: 4.

As he that taketh away a garment in cold weather, . . . so is he that singeth songs to an heavy heart. *Pr.* 25: 20.

As a wandering bird cast out of the nest. *Is.* 16: 2.

The harvest shall be a heap in the day of grief and of desperate sorrow. *Is.* 17: 11.

Strip you, and make you bare, and gird sackcloth upon your loins. *Is.* 32: 11.

Ye shall pine away for your iniquities. *Eze.* 24: 23.

He hath laid my vine waste, and barked my fig tree. *Jo.* 1: 7.

Desolation shall be in the thresholds. *Zph.* 2: 14.

We were pressed out of measure, above strength, insomuch that we despaired even of life. *2 Co.* 1: 8.

The blackness of darkness. *Jude* 1: 13.

See also

Dejection; Depression; Despair; Gloom; Melancholy; Unhappiness.

Despot

They did set over them taskmasters to afflict them with their burdens. *Ex.* 1: 11.

They made their lives bitter with hard bondage. *Ex.* 1: 14.

And Pharaoh said, Who is the Lord, that I should obey his voice to let Israel go? I know not the Lord, neither will I let Israel go. *Ex.* 5: 2.

And Pharaoh hardened his heart at this time also, neither would he let the people go. *Ex.* 8: 32.

I delivered you out of the hand of the Egyptians, and out of the hand of all that oppressed you. *Ju.* 6: 9.

My little finger shall be thicker than my father's loins. *1 K.* 12: 10.

My father made your yoke heavy, and I will add to your yoke: my father also chastised you with whips, but I will chastise you with scorpions. *1 K.* 12: 14.

Deliver me from the oppression of man. *Ps.* 119: 134.

A a roaring lion, and a ranging bear; so is a wicked ruler over the poor people. *Pr.* 28: 15.

The prince that wanteth understanding is also a great oppressor. *Pr.* 28: 16.

He . . . gathereth unto him all nations, and heapeth unto him all people. *Hab.* 2: 5.

Woe . . . to the oppressing city. *Zph.* 3: 1.

See also

Autocrat; Harshness; Oppression; Persecution; Tyranny; Yoke.

Destiny

Who knoweth whether thou art come to the kingdom for such a time as this? *Es. 4: 14.*

All the rivers run into the sea. *Ec. 1: 7.*

Mine elect shall inherit it, and my servants shall dwell there. *Is. 65: 9.*

If they say unto thee, Whither shall we go forth? then thou shalt tell them, Thus saith the Lord; Such as are for death, to death; and such as are for the sword, to the sword; and such as are for the famine, to the famine; and such as are for the captivity, to the captivity. *Je. 15: 2.*

Christ, the chosen of God. *Lu. 23: 35.*

Then shall I know even as also I am known. *1 Co. 13: 12.*

Chosen of God, and precious. *1 Pe. 2: 4.*

Ye are a chosen generation, a royal priesthood, an holy nation, a peculiar people. *1 Pe. 2: 9.*

Give diligence to make your calling and election sure. *2 Pe. 1: 10.*

See also

Calling; Doom; Election; Fate; Fortune; Lot; Predestination.

Destitution

Therefore shalt thou serve thine enemies which the Lord shall send against thee, in hunger, and in thirst, and in nakedness, and in want of all things. *De. 28: 48.*

Now for a long season Israel hath been without the true God, and without a teaching priest, and without law. *2 Ch. 15: 3.*

Did not I weep for him that was in trouble? was not my soul grieved for the poor? *Jb. 30: 25.*

He delivereth the poor in his affliction. *Jb. 36: 15.*

This poor man cried, and the Lord heard him, and saved him out of all his troubles. *Ps. 34: 6.*

Blessed is he that considereth the poor. *Ps. 41: 1.*

There is no more any prophet. *Ps. 74: 9.*

In thee is my trust; leave not my soul destitute. *Ps. 141: 8.*

There is that maketh himself rich, yet hath nothing. *Pr. 13: 7.*

A poor man that oppresseth the poor is like a sweeping rain which leaveth no food. *Pr. 28: 3.*

What mean ye that ye beat my people to pieces, and grind the faces of the poor? saith the Lord God of hosts. *Is. 3: 15.*

The law is no more; her prophets also find no vision from the Lord. *La. 2: 9.*

The law shall perish from the priest, and counsel from the ancients. *Eze. 7: 26.*

I will send a famine in the land, not a famine of bread, nor a thirst for water, but of hearing the words of the Lord. *Am. 8: 11.*

Ye have the poor always with you; but me ye have not always. *Mat. 26: 11.*

I have shewed you all things, how that so labouring ye ought to support the weak. *Ac. 20: 35.*

At that time ye were without Christ, being aliens from the commonwealth of Israel, and strangers from the covenants of promise, having no hope and without God in the world. *Ep. 2: 12.*

Destitute of the truth. *1 Ti. 6: 5.*

If a brother or sister be naked, and destitute of daily food, And one of you say unto them, Depart in peace, be ye warmed and filled; notwithstanding ye give them not those things which are needful to the body; what doth it profit? *Ja. 2: 15, 16.*

Thou . . . knowest not that thou art wretched, and miserable, and poor, and blind, and naked. *Re. 3: 17.*

See also

Charity; Lack; Need; Philanthropy; Poor; Poverty; Want.

Destruction

Wilt thou also destroy the righteous with the wicked? *Ge. 18: 23.*

It shall come to pass, that as the Lord rejoiced over you to do you good, and to multiply you; so the Lord will rejoice over you to destroy you. *De. 28: 63.*

The wicked is reserved to the day of destruction. *Jb. 21: 30.*

I have kept me from the paths of the destroyer. *Ps. 17: 4.*

But now they break down the carved work thereof at once with axes and hammers. *Ps. 74: 6.*

The destruction that wasteth at noonday. *Ps. 91: 6.*

I will early destroy all the wicked of the land. *Ps. 101: 8.*

Who redeemeth thy life from destruction. *Ps. 103: 4.*

The Lord will destroy the house of the proud. *Pr. 15: 25.*

They shall not hurt nor destroy in all my holy mountain. *Is. 11: 9.*

O grave, I will be thy destruction. *Ho. 13: 14.*

I destroyed his fruit from above, and his roots from beneath. *Am. 2: 9.*

Herod will seek the young child to destroy him. *Mat. 2: 13.*

I am not come to destroy, but to fulfil. *Mat. 5: 17.*

Enter ye in at the strait gate: for wide is the gate, and broad is the way, that leadeth to destruction. *Mat. 7: 13.*

Fear him which is able to destroy both soul and body in hell. *Mat. 10: 28.*

Thou that destroyest the temple, and buildest it in three days, save thyself. *Mat. 27: 40.*

The Son of man is not come to destroy men's lives, but to save them. *Lu. 9: 56.*

The last enemy that shall be destroyed is death. *1 Co. 15: 26.*

The Lord, having saved the people out of the land of Egypt, afterward destroyed them that believed not. *Jude 1: 5.*

See also

Collapse; Defeat; Desolation; Fall; Overthrow; Ruin.

Determination

As for me and my house, we will serve the Lord. *Jos. 24: 15.*

Solomon determined to build an house for the name of the Lord. *2 Ch. 2: 1.*

His days are determined, the number of his months are with thee. *Jb. 14: 5.*

I am purposed. *Ps.* 17: 3.

I will speak of thy testimonies also before kings, and will not be ashamed. I will delight myself in thy commandments. *Ps.* 119: 46, 47.

To every purpose there is time and judgment. *Ec.* 8: 6.

Thine ears shall hear a word behind thee, saying, This is the way, walk ye in it, when ye turn to the right hand, and when ye turn to the left. *Is.* 30: 21.

Whither the spirit was to go, they went; and they turned not when they went. *Eze.* 1: 12.

The light of the body is the eye: if therefore thine eye be single, thy whole body shall be full of light. *Mat.* 6: 22.

I will arise and go to my father. *Lu.* 15: 18.

Truly the Son of man goeth, as it was determined. *Lu.* 22: 22.

God . . . hath determined the times before appointed. *Ac.* 17: 24, 26.

None of these things move me. *Ac.* 20: 24.

I determined this with myself. *2 Co.* 2: 1.

Having done all, to stand. *Ep.* 6: 13.

This one thing I do, forgetting those things which are behind, . . . I press toward the mark. *Ph.* 3: 13, 14.

See also

Decision; Firmness; Fortitude; Judgment; Purpose; Resolution; Steadfastness.

Devastation

I will sweep it with the besom of destruction. *Is.* 14: 23.

It shall be an habitation of dragons, and a court for owls. *Is.* 34: 13.

He hath utterly destroyed them, he hath delivered them to the slaughter. *Is.* 34: 2.

Thy sons have fainted, they lie at the head of all the streets, as a wild bull in a net. *Is.* 51: 20.

Our skin was black like an oven because of the terrible famine. *La.* 5: 10.

I will give thee unto the ravenous birds of every sort, and to the beasts of the field to be devoured. *Eze.* 39: 4.

He hath . . . barked my fig tree: he hath made it clean bare, and cast it away. *Jo.* 1: 7.

The seed is rotten under their clods, the garners are laid desolate, the barns are broken down. *Jo.* 1: 17.

Who shall separate us from the love of Christ? shall tribulation, or distress, or persecution, or famine, or nakedness, or peril, or sword? *Ro.* 8: 35.

Rejoice, thou barren that bearest not; break forth and cry, thou that travailest not: for the desolate hath many more children than she which hath an husband. *Ga.* 4: 27.

Babylon the great is fallen, is fallen, and is become . . . a cage of every unclean and hateful bird. *Re.* 18: 2.

See also

Desolation; Waste.

Development

A man of knowledge increaseth strength. *Pr.* 24: 5.

Behold the man whose name is The BRANCH; and he shall grow up out of his place. *Zch.* 6: 12.

Consider the lilies of the field, how they grow. *Mat.* 6: 28.

The seed should spring and grow up, he knoweth not how. *Mk.* 4: 27.

The child grew, and waxed strong in spirit, filled with wisdom. *Lu.* 2: 40.

In whom all the building fitly framed together groweth unto an holy temple in the Lord. *Ep.* 2: 21.

That we henceforth be no more children, . . . But . . . may grow up into him in all things, which is the head, even Christ. *Ep.* 4: 14, 15.

Bring them up in the nurture and admonition of the Lord. *Ep.* 6: 4.

We beseech you, brethren, that ye increase more and more. *1 Th.* 4: 10.

Grow in grace, and in the knowledge of our Lord and Saviour Jesus Christ. *2 Pe.* 3: 18.

See also

Education; Evolution; Growth; Increase; Progress; Unfolding.

Devil

Get thee hence, Satan. *Mat.* 4: 10.

If they have called the master of the house Beelzebub, how much more shall they call them of his household? *Mat.* 10: 25.

If I by Beelzebub cast out devils, by whom do your children cast them out? *Mat.* 12: 27.

Jesus rebuked the devil; and he departed out of him. *Mat.* 17: 18.

There met him out of the city a certain man, which had devils. *Lu.* 8: 27.

He called his twelve disciples together, and gave them power and authority over all devils. *Lu.* 9: 1.

Lord, even the devils are subject unto us through thy name. *Lu.* 10: 17.

He casteth out devils through Beelzebub the chief of the devils. *Lu.* 11: 15.

One of you is a devil. *Jn.* 6: 70.

These are not the words of him that hath a devil. *Jn.* 10: 21.

Can a devil open the eyes of the blind? *Jn.* 10: 21.

The God of peace shall bruise Satan under your heel shortly. *Ro.* 16: 20.

Ye cannot drink the cup of the Lord, and the cup of devils. *1 Co.* 10: 21.

Satan himself is transformed into an angel of light. *2 Co.* 11: 14.

There was given to me a thorn in the flesh, the messenger of Satan to buffet me. *2 Co.* 12: 7.

We wrestle . . . against the rulers of the darkness of this world, against spiritual wickedness in high places. *Ep.* 6: 12.

Giving heed to . . . doctrines of devils. *1 Ti.* 4: 1.

Some are already turned aside after Satan. *1 Ti.* 5: 15.

Resist the devil, and he will flee from you. *Ja.* 4: 7.

Babylon . . . is become the habitation of devils, and the hold of every foul spirit. *Re.* 18: 2.

See also

Exorcism; Fiend; Insanity; Lucifer; Satan.

Devotion

I wholly followed the Lord my God. *Jos.* 14: 8.

The soul of Jonathan was knit with the soul of David. *1 S.* 18: 1.

Thy love to me was wonderful, passing the love of women. *2 S.* 1: 26.

Not every one that saith unto me, Lord, Lord, shall enter into the kingdom of heaven; but he that doeth the will of my Father which is in heaven. *Mat.* 7: 21.

There came a woman having an alabaster box of ointment of spikenard very precious; and she brake the box, and poured it on his head. *Mk.* 14: 3.

Thou gavest me no kiss. *Lu.* 7: 45.

I say unto thee, Her sins, which are many, are forgiven; for she loved much: but to whom little is forgiven, the same loveth little. *Lu.* 7: 47.

Then said Thomas, which is called Didymus, unto his fellowdisciples, Let us also go, that we may die with him. *Jn.* 11: 16.

Behold how he loved him! *Jn.* 11: 36.

To prove the sincerity of your love. *2 Co.* 8: 8.

That their hearts might be comforted, being knit together in love. *Col.* 2: 2.

See also

Affection; Allegiance; Ardor; Attachment; Christ, Crown of; Christ, Loyalty to; Consecration; Constancy; Earnestness; Faithfulness; Fidelity; God, Faithfulness of; God, Love of; God, Love to; God, Loyalty to; Love; Loyalty; Piety; Regard.

Devoutness

Seven times a day do I praise thee. *Ps.* 119: 164.

There were dwelling at Jerusalem Jews, devout men, out of every nation under heaven. *Ac.* 2: 5.

Great is the mystery of godliness. *1 Ti.* 3: 16.

Follow after righteousness, godliness, faith, love, patience, meekness. *1 Ti.* 6: 11.

Let us have grace, whereby we may serve God acceptably with reverence and godly fear. *He.* 12: 28.

We have an altar. *He.* 13: 10.

Spiritual sacrifices, acceptable to God by Jesus Christ. *1 Pe.* 2: 5.

And to patience godliness. *2 Pe.* 1: 6.

I fell at his feet to worship him. *Re.* 19: 10.

See also

Consecration; Dedication; Godliness; Holiness; Piety; Righteousness; Saint.

Diadem

I put on righteousness, and it clothed me: my judgment was as a robe and a diadem. *Jb.* 29: 14.

Children's children are the crown of old men; and the glory of children are their fathers. *Pr.* 17: 6.

Riches are not for ever: and doth the crown endure to every generation? *Pr.* 27: 24.

In that day shall the Lord of hosts be for a crown of glory, and for a diadem of beauty. *Is.* 28: 5.

Thou shalt also be . . . a royal diadem in the hand of thy God. *Is.* 62: 3.

Thus saith the Lord God; Remove the diadem, and take off the crown: . . . exalt him that is low, and abase him that is high. *Eze.* 21: 26.

Hold that fast which thou hast, that no man take thy crown. *Re.* 3: 11.

Upon her head a crown of twelve stars. *Re.* 12: 1.

See also

Christ, Crown of; Christ, the King; Coronation; Crown; God, the King; Throne.

Difficulty

Is any thing too hard for the Lord? *Ge.* 18: 14.

But none saith, Where is God my maker, who giveth songs in the night? *Jb.* 35: 10.

How shall we sing the Lord's song in a strange land? *Ps.* 137: 4.

The way of transgressors is hard. *Pr.* 13: 15.

The lame take the prey. *Is.* 33: 23.

There is nothing too hard for thee. *Je.* 32: 17.

Narrow is the way, which leadeth unto life, and few there be that find it. *Mat.* 7: 14.

Some fell among thorns. *Lu.* 8: 7.

They found the stone rolled away from the sepulchre. *Lu.* 24: 2.

It is hard for thee to kick against the pricks. *Ac.* 9: 5.

I know that this shall turn to my salvation through your prayer, and the supply of the Spirit of Jesus Christ. *Ph.* 1: 19.

We have many things to say, and hard to be uttered. *He.* 5: 11.

In which are some things hard to be understood. *2 Pe.* 3: 16.

See also

Bar; Hindrance; Obstacle; Obstruction; Stumbling-block.

Dignity

The excellency of dignity. *Ge.* 49: 3.

The Lord hath avouched thee this day . . . to make thee high above all nations. *De.* 26: 18, 19.

Deck thyself now with majesty and excellency; and array thyself with glory and beauty. *Jb.* 40: 10.

Thou hast made him a little lower than the angels, and hast crowned him with glory and honour. *Ps.* 8: 5.

Thou madest him to have dominion over the works of thy hands. *Ps.* 8: 6.

The king's daughter is all glorious within: her clothing is of wrought gold. *Ps.* 45: 13.

Man being in honour abideth not. *Ps.* 49: 12.

Honour and majesty are before him: strength and beauty are in his sanctuary. *Ps.* 96: 6.

Wisdom is the principal thing; . . . Exalt her, and she shall promote thee: she shall bring thee to honour, when thou dost embrace her. *Pr.* 4: 7, 8.

Before honour is humility. *Pr.* 15: 33.

Folly is set in great dignity. *Ec.* 10: 6.

He hath clothed me with the garments of salvation, he hath covered me with the robe of righteousness, as a bridegroom decketh himself with ornaments, and as a bride adorneth herself with her jewels. *Is.* 61: 10.

Let the elders that rule well be counted worthy of double honour. *1 Ti.* 5: 17.

He who hath builded the house hath more honour than the house. *He.* 3: 3.

See also

Excellence; Gravity; Honor; Majesty; Nobility; Solemnity.

Diligence

Keep thy heart with all diligence; for out of it are the issues of life. *Pr. 4: 23.*

She looketh well to the ways of her household, and eateth not the bread of idleness. *Pr. 31: 27.*

This shall come to pass, if ye will diligently obey the voice of the Lord your God. *Zch. 6: 15.*

Go and search diligently for the young child. *Mat. 2: 8.*

Take heed therefore unto yourselves. *Ac. 20: 28.*

We desire that every one of you do shew the same diligence. *He. 6: 11.*

He that cometh to God must believe that he is, and that he is the rewarder of them that diligently seek him. *He. 11: 6.*

Of which salvation the prophets have enquired and searched diligently. *1 Pe. 1: 10.*

Giving all diligence, add to your faith. *2 Pe. 1: 5.*

Give diligence to make your calling and election sure. *2 Pe. 1: 10.*

Wherefore, beloved, seeing that ye look for such things, be diligent that ye may be found of him in peace. *2 Pe. 3: 14.*

See also

Attention; Care; Constancy; Earnestness; Heed; Industry; Zeal.

Dimness

Moses was an hundred and twenty years old when he died: his eye was not dim, nor his natural force abated. *De. 34: 7.*

Mine eye also is dim by reason of sorrow. *Jb. 17: 7.*

His lamp shall be put out in obscure darkness. *Pr. 20: 20.*

In that day shall the deaf hear the words of the book, and the eyes of the blind shall see out of obscurity, and out of darkness. *Is. 29: 18.*

The eyes of them that see shall not be dim, and the ears of them that hear shall hearken. *Is. 32: 3.*

If thou draw out thy soul to the hungry, and satisfy the afflicted soul; then shall thy light rise in obscurity, and thy darkness be as the noon day. *Is. 58: 10.*

We grope for the wall like the blind, and we grope as if we had no eyes. *Is. 59: 10.*

We stumble at noon day as in the night. *Is. 59: 10.*

How is the gold become dim! how is the most fine gold changed! *La. 4: 1.*

For this our heart is faint; for these things our eyes are dim. *La. 5: 17.*

See also

Darkness; Dullness; Gloom; Obscurity.

Din

Deep calleth unto deep at the noise of thy waterspouts. *Ps. 42: 7.*

The heathen raged. *Ps. 46: 6.*

The tumult of those that rise up against thee increaseth continually. *Ps. 74: 23.*

The contentions of a wife are a continual dropping. *Pr. 19: 13.*

Every battle of the warrior is with confused noise. *Is. 9: 5.*

Thou that art full of stirs, a tumultuous city, a joyous city. *Is. 22: 2.*

My heart maketh a noise in me. *Je. 4: 19.*

Let all . . . clamour . . . be put away from you. *Ep. 4: 31.*

The heavens shall pass away with a great noise. *2 Pe. 3: 10.*

I heard, as it were the noise of thunder. *Re. 6: 1.*

See also

Clamor; Confusion; Disorder; Noise; Tumult; Turmoil.

Direction

The Lord went before them . . . by night in a pillar of fire. *Ex. 13: 21.*

He knoweth the way that I take. *Jb. 23: 10.*

Blessed is the man that walketh not in the counsel of the ungodly. *Ps. 1: 1.*

In all thy ways acknowledge him, and he shall direct thy paths. *Pr. 3: 6.*

Let thine eyes look right on, and let thine eyelids look straight before thee. *Pr. 4: 25.*

Wisdom is profitable to direct. *Ec. 10: 10.*

Thine ears shall hear a word behind thee, saying, This is the way, walk ye in it, when ye turn to the right hand, and when ye turn to the left. *Is. 30: 21.*

Who hath directed the Spirit of the Lord? *Is. 40: 13.*

They shall ask the way to Zion with their faces thitherward. *Je. 50: 5.*

Strait is the gate, and narrow is the way, which leadeth unto life, and few there be that find it. *Mat. 7: 14.*

Now God himself and our Father, and our Lord Jesus Christ, direct our way unto you. *1 Th. 3: 11.*

The Lord direct your hearts into the love of God, and into the patient waiting for Christ. *2 Th. 3: 5.*

See also

Administration; Commandment; Execution; Government; Guidance; Leadership; Order; Supervision.

Dirt

Dust shalt thou eat all the days of thy life. *Ge. 3: 14.*

Dust thou art, and unto dust shalt thou return. *Ge. 3: 19.*

Wash thyself therefore, and anoint thee. *Ru. 3: 3.*

If I wash myself with snow water, and make my hands never so clean; Yet shalt thou plunge me in the ditch. *Jb. 9: 30, 31.*

My face is foul with weeping. *Jb. 16: 16.*

He that hath clean hands shall be stronger and stronger. *Jb. 17: 9.*

Then did I beat them small as the dust before the wind: I did cast them out as the dirt in the streets. *Ps. 18: 42.*

Shall the dust praise thee? Shall it declare thy truth? *Ps. 30: 9.*

Create in me a clean heart, O God. *Ps. 51: 10.*

He remembereth that we are dust. *Ps. 103: 14.*

The wicked are like the troubled sea, when it cannot rest, whose waters cast up mire and dirt. *Is. 57: 20.*

He that is washed needeth not save to wash his feet, but is clean every whit. *Jn.* 13: 10.

What God hath cleansed, that call not thou common. *Ac.* 10: 15.

We have this treasure in earthen vessels. *2 Co.* 4: 7.

Let us cleanse ourselves from all filthiness of the flesh and spirit. *2 Co.* 7: 1.

Cleanse your hands, ye sinners; and purify your hearts, ye double minded. *Ja.* 4: 8.

Filthy dreamers defile the flesh. *Jude* 8.

See also

Dust; Earth.

Disappearance

Moses the servant of the Lord died there in the land of Moab. *De.* 34: 5.

Elijah went up by a whirlwind into heaven. *2 K.* 2: 11.

There the wicked cease from troubling. *Jb.* 3: 17.

As the cloud is consumed and vanisheth away: so he that goeth down to the grave shall come up no more. *Jb.* 7: 9.

They shall perish, but thou shalt endure. *Ps.* 102: 26.

Man goeth to his long home. *Ec.* 12: 5.

Then shall the dust return to the earth as it was: and the spirit shall return unto God who gave it. *Ec.* 12: 7.

The heavens shall vanish away like smoke, and the earth shall wax old like a garment, and they that dwell therein shall die in like manner: but my salvation shall be for ever. *Is.* 51: 6.

Is counsel perished from the prudent? is their wisdom vanished? *Je.* 49: 7.

Their eyes were opened, and they knew him; and he vanished out of their sight. *Lu.* 24: 31.

Charity never faileth: but whether there be prophecies, they shall fail; whether there be tongues, they shall cease; whether there be knowledge, it shall vanish away. *1 Co.* 13: 8.

In that he saith, A new covenant, he hath made the first old. Now that which decayeth and waxeth old is ready to vanish away. *He.* 8: 13.

What is your life? It is even a vapour, that appeareth for a little time, and then vanisheth away. *Ja.* 4: 14.

They ascended up to heaven in a cloud. *Re.* 11: 12.

See also

Ascension; Death; Expiration.

Disappointment

Ye shall sow your seed in vain, for your enemies shall eat it. *Le.* 26: 16.

Thou shalt plant vineyards, and dress them, but shalt neither drink of the wine, nor gather the grapes: for the worms shall eat them. *De.* 28: 39.

Thou shalt see the land before thee; but thou shalt not go thither unto the land which I gave the children of Israel. *De.* 32: 52.

And David said to Solomon, My son, as for me, it was in my mind to build an house unto the name of the Lord my God. *1 Ch.* 22: 7.

He disappointeth the devices of the crafty. *Jb.* 5: 12.

Their hope shall be as the giving up of the ghost. *Jb.* 11: 20.

Arise, O Lord, disappoint him, cast him down. *Ps.* 17: 13.

Put not your trust in princes, nor in the son of man, in whom there is no help. *Ps.* 146: 3.

Without counsel purposes are disappointed. *Pr.* 15: 22.

He looked that it should bring forth grapes, and it brought forth wild grapes. *Is.* 5: 2.

He looked for judgment, but behold oppression; for righteousness, but behold a cry. *Is.* 5: 7.

In the year that King Uzziah died I saw also the Lord. *Is.* 6: 1.

The harvest shall be a heap in the day of grief and of desperate sorrow. *Is.* 17: 11.

Woe to them that . . . trust in chariots, because they are many; and in horsemen, because they are very strong. *Is.* 31: 1.

Wherefore do ye spend money for that which is not bread? and your labour for that which satisfieth not? *Is.* 55: 2.

We looked for peace, and there is no good; and for the time of healing, and behold trouble! *Je.* 14: 19.

Ye have built houses of hewn stone, but ye shall not dwell in them. *Am.* 5: 11.

Thou shalt tread the olives, but thou shalt not anoint thee with oil. *Mi.* 6: 15.

Their goods shall become a booty, and their houses a desolation. *Zph.* 1: 13.

Ye have sown much, and bring in little; ye eat, but ye have not enough; ye drink, but ye are not filled with drink; ye clothe you, but there is none warm; and he that earneth wages earneth wages to put it into a bag with holes. *Hag.* 1: 6.

O Jerusalem, Jerusalem, . . . how often would I have gathered thy children together, as a hen doth gather her brood under her wings, and ye would not! *Lu.* 13: 34.

The days will come, when ye shall desire to see one of the days of the Son of man, and ye shall not see it. *Lu.* 17: 22.

We trusted that it had been he which should have redeemed Israel. *Lu.* 24: 21.

They essayed to go into Bithynia: but the Spirit suffered them not. *Ac.* 16: 7.

See also

Defeat; Failure; Fall; Frustration; Overthrow; Ruin.

Disapproval

For all this they sinned still, and believed not for his wondrous works. *Ps.* 78: 32.

I hate the work of them that turn aside. *Ps.* 101: 3.

Him that hath an high look and a proud heart will not I suffer. *Ps.* 101: 5.

He that worketh deceit shall not dwell within my house: he that telleth lies shall not tarry in my sight. *Ps.* 101: 7.

Pride, and arrogancy, and the evil way, and the froward mouth, do I hate. *Pr.* 8: 13.

Behold, I am against them that . . . cause my people to err by their lies. *Je.* 23: 32.

To subvert a man in his cause, the Lord approveth not. *La.* 3: 36.

I sought for a man among them, that should make up the hedge, and stand in the gap before me for the land, that I should not destroy it; but I found none. *Eze.* 22: 30.

I hate, I despise your feast days, and I will not smell in your solemn assemblies. *Am.* **5: 21.**

Let none of you imagine evil in your heart against his neighbours; and love no false oath: for all these are things that I hate, saith the Lord. *Zch.* **8: 17.**

I tell you, this man went down to his house justified rather than the other. *Lu.* **18: 14.**

Sirs, ye are brethren; why do ye wrong one to another? *Ac.* **7: 26.**

Wherein thou judgest another, thou condemnest thyself. *Ro.* **2: 1.**

See also

Censoriousness; Condemnation; Judgment; Rebuke; Reproach; Reproof.

Disarmament

The Lord saveth not with sword and spear. *1 S.* **17: 47.**

In famine he shall redeem thee from death: and in war from the power of the sword. *Jb.* **5: 20.**

He maketh wars to cease unto the end of the earth. *Ps.* **46: 9.**

He shall deliver thee from the snare of the fowler. *Ps.* **91: 3.**

They shall beat their swords into plowshares, and their spears into pruninghooks. *Is.* **2: 4.**

Neither shall they learn war any more. *Is.* **2: 4.**

I will break the bow and the sword and the battle out of the earth, and will make them to lie down safely. *Ho.* **2: 18.**

Beat your plowshares into swords, and your pruninghooks into spears. *Jo.* **3: 10.**

Nation shall not lift up a sword against nation. *Mi.* **4: 3.**

Think not that I am come to send peace on earth: I came not to send peace, but a sword. *Mat.* **10: 34.**

Then said Jesus unto him, Put up again thy sword into his place: for all they that take the sword shall perish with the sword. *Mat.* **26: 52.**

He taketh from him all his armour wherein he trusted. *Lu.* **11: 22.**

See also

Concord; Nations, League of; Peace; War; Weapon.

Disaster

I, even I, do bring a flood of waters upon the earth, to destroy all flesh. *Ge.* **6: 17.**

Their calamity shall rise suddenly; and who knoweth the ruin of them both? *Pr.* **24: 22.**

The harvest shall be a heap in the day of grief and of desperate sorrow. *Is.* **17: 11.**

Who shall be sorry for thee? desolation, and destruction, and the famine, and the sword: by whom shall I comfort thee? *Is.* **51: 19.**

I will go up, and will cover the earth; I will destroy the city and the inhabitants thereof. *Je.* **46: 8.**

How doth the city sit solitary, that was full of people! *La.* **1: 1.**

I will cause thee to perish out of the countries. *Eze.* **25: 7.**

Thou hadst cast me into the deep, in the midst of the seas; and the floods compassed me about. *Jon.* **2: 3.**

Nation shall rise against nation, and king-dom against kingdom: and there shall be famines, and pestilences, and earthquakes, in divers places. *Mat.* **24: 7.**

See also

Accident; Calamity; Cataclysm; Catastrophe; Distress; Evil; Misery; Misfortune; Ruin.

Disbelief

Then came the disciples to Jesus apart, and said, Why could not we cast him out? And Jesus said unto them, Because of your unbelief. *Mat.* **17: 19, 20.**

Why did ye not then believe him? *Mat.* **21: 25.**

John came unto you in the way of righteousness, and ye believed him not. *Mat.* **21: 32.**

Lord, I believe; help thou mine unbelief. *Mk.* **9: 24.**

Their words seemed to them as idle tales, and they believed them not. *Lu.* **24: 11.**

They yet believed not for joy. *Lu.* **24: 41.**

Whom he hath sent, him ye believe not. *Jn.* **5: 38.**

Had ye believed Moses, ye would have believed me: for he wrote of me. *Jn.* **5: 46.**

If ye believe not that I am he, ye shall die in your sins. *Jn.* **8: 24.**

We have not so much as heard whether there be any Holy Ghost. *Ac.* **19: 2.**

The unbelieving husband is sanctified by the wife, and the unbelieving wife is sanctified by the husband. *1 Co.* **7: 14.**

If we believe not, yet he abideth faithful. *2 Ti.* **2: 13.**

I will therefore put you in remembrance, though ye once knew this, how that the Lord, having saved the people out of the land of Egypt, afterward destroyed them that believed not. *Jude 5.*

See also

Christ, Denial of; Christ, Doubt of; Dissent; Doubt; Faithlessness; God, Denial of; Suspicion; Unbelief.

Discernment

Can I discern between good and evil? *2 S.* **19: 35.**

I have given thee a wise and an understanding heart. *1 K.* **3: 12.**

Behold now, I perceive that this is an holy man of God, which passeth by us continually. *2 K.* **4: 9.**

The wise man's eyes are in his head; but the fool walketh in darkness. *Ec.* **2: 14.**

Persons that cannot discern between their right hand and their left hand. *Jon.* **4: 11.**

Sir, I perceive that thou art a prophet. *Jn.* **4: 19.**

Of a truth I perceive that God is no respecter of persons. *Ac.* **10: 34.**

The natural man receiveth not the things of the spirit of God: for they are foolishness unto him: neither can he know them, because they are spiritually discerned. *1 Co.* **2: 14.**

To another discerning of spirits. *1 Co.* **12: 10.**

Wherefore henceforth know we no man after the flesh: yea, though we have known Christ after the flesh, yet now henceforth know we him no more. *2 Co.* **5: 16.**

The word of God . . . is a discerner of the thoughts and intents of the heart. *He.* **4: 12.**

See also
Discrimination; Insight; Judgment; Perception; Understanding; Wisdom.

Disciple

There followed him great multitudes of people from Galilee. *Mat.* 4: 25.

His disciples followed him. *Mat.* 8: 23.

The disciple is not above his master, nor the servant above his lord. *Mat.* 10: 24.

He suffered no man to follow him, save Peter, and James, and John the brother of James. *Mk.* 5: 37.

She had a sister called Mary, which also sat at Jesus' feet, and heard his word. *Lu.* 10: 39.

If any man serve me, let him follow me. *Jn.* 12: 26.

By this shall all men know that ye are my disciples, if ye have love one to another. *Jn.* 13: 35.

Lord, why cannot I follow thee now? *Jn.* 13: 37.

Father, I will that they also, whom thou hast given me, be with me where I am. *Jn.* 17: 24.

Be followers together of me. *Ph.* 3: 17.

These are they which follow the Lamb whithersoever he goeth. *Re.* 14: 4.

See also
Apostle; Christ, Disciple of; Christ, Follower of; Follower; Messenger; Missionary.

Discipline

He humbled thee, and suffered thee to hunger. *De.* 8: 3.

From his right hand went a fiery law for them. Yea, he loved the people. *De.* 33: 2, 3.

Shall we receive good at the hand of God, and shall we not receive evil? *Jb.* 2: 10.

He openeth also their ear to discipline, and commandeth that they return from iniquity. *Jb.* 36: 10.

Because they have no changes, therefore they fear not God. *Ps.* 55: 19.

It is good for me that I have been afflicted; that I might learn thy statutes. *Ps.* 119: 71.

Behold, I have refined thee, but not with silver; I have chosen thee in the furnace of affliction. *Is.* 48: 10.

Behold, I have taken out of thine hand the cup of trembling, even the dregs of the cup of my fury; thou shalt no more drink it again. *Is.* 51: 22.

For a small moment have I forsaken thee; but with great mercies will I gather thee. In a little wrath I hid my face from thee for a moment; but with everlasting kindness will I have mercy on thee. *Is.* 54: 7, 8.

Therefore, behold, I will allure her, and bring her into the wilderness. *Ho.* 2: 14.

He shall sit as a refiner and purifier of silver. *Mal.* 3: 3.

Whose fan is in his hand, and he will throughly purge his floor. *Mat.* 3: 12.

This kind goeth not out but by prayer and fasting. *Mat.* 17: 21.

Every one shall be salted with fire, and every sacrifice shall be salted with salt. *Mk.* 9: 49.

Whom the Lord loveth he chasteneth, and scourgeth every son whom he receiveth. *He.* 12: 6.

If ye be without chastisement, whereof all are partakers, then are ye bastards and not sons. *He.* 12: 8.

The God of all grace, . . . after that ye have suffered a while, make you perfect. *1 Pe.* 5: 10.

See also
Chastisement; Correction; Culture; Education; God, Chastisement of; God, Punishment of; Instruction; Punishment; Rod; Scourge; Stripe; Training; Trial.

Disclosure

Then was the secret revealed unto Daniel in a night vision. *Da.* 2: 19.

There is a God in heaven that revealeth secrets. *Da.* 2: 28.

The vision is yet for an appointed time, but at the end it shall speak, and not lie. *Hab.* 2: 3.

He could not be hid. *Mk.* 7: 24.

See also
Manifestation; Revelation.

Discontent

The Lord heareth your murmurings which ye murmur against him. *Ex.* 16: 8.

Every one that was in distress, and every one that was in debt, and every one that was discontented, gathered themselves unto him. *1 S.* 22: 2.

I poured out my complaint before him. *Ps.* 142: 2.

That there be no complaining in our streets. *Ps.* 144: 14.

For three things the earth is disquieted. *Pr.* 30: 21.

He shall snatch on the right hand, and be hungry; and he shall eat on the left hand, and they shall not be satisfied: they shall eat every man the flesh of his own arm. *Is.* 9: 20.

It displeased Jonah exceedingly. *Jon.* 4: 1.

Murmur not among yourselves. *Jn.* 6: 43.

There was much murmuring among the people concerning him. *Jn.* 7: 12.

See also
Complaint; Dissatisfaction; Tension.

Discord

They devise deceitful matters against them that are quiet in the land. *Ps.* 35: 20.

He soweth discord. *Pr.* 6: 14.

It is better to dwell in the wilderness, than with a contentious and an angry woman. *Pr.* 21: 19.

If a wise man contendeth with a foolish man, whether he rage or laugh, there is no rest. *Pr.* 29: 9.

I am come to set a man at variance against his father, and the daughter against her mother, and the daughter in law against her mother in law. *Mat.* 10: 35.

A man's foes shall be they of his own household. *Mat.* 10: 36.

The works of the flesh are . . . these; . . . hatred, variance, emulations, wrath, strife. *Ga.* 5: 19, 20.

See also
Argument; Conflict; Contention; Controversy; Fight; Quarrel; Strife; Struggle; War.

Discouragement

The soul of the people was much discouraged because of the way. *Nu.* 21: 4.

Wherefore discourage ye the heart of the children of Israel from going over into the land which the Lord hath given them? *Nu.* **32: 7.**

It is enough; now, O Lord, take away my life. *1 K.* **19: 4.**

The strength of the bearers of burdens is decayed and there is much rubbish; so that we are not able to build the wall. *Ne.* **4: 10.**

My tears have been my meat day and night, while they continually say unto me, Where is thy God? *Ps.* **42: 3.**

Why art thou cast down, O my soul? *Ps.* **42: 5.**

As for me, my feet were almost gone; my steps had well nigh slipped. *Ps.* **73: 2.**

I said in my haste, All men are liars. *Ps.* **116: 11.**

Hope deferred maketh the heart sick. *Pr.* **13: 12.**

He shall not fail nor be discouraged. *Is.* **42: 4.**

The Lord hath forsaken me, and my Lord hath forgotten me. *Is.* **49: 14.**

Master, we have toiled all the night, and have taken nothing. *Lu.* **5: 5.**

Fathers, provoke not your children to anger, lest they be discouraged. *Col.* **3: 21.**

Quench not the Spirit. *1 Th.* **5: 19.**

See also

Abasement; Defeat; Depression; Disappointment; Dismay; Failure; Frustration; Gloom; Melancholy; Pessimism.

Discovery

Let me go over, and see the good land that is beyond Jordan. *De.* **3: 25.**

Go up and possess the land which I have given you. *De.* **9: 23.**

Canst thou by searching find out God? *Jb.* **11: 7.**

They that go down to the sea in ships, that do business in great waters; These see the works of the Lord, and his wonders in the deep. *Ps.* **107: 23, 24.**

I rejoice in thy word, as one that findeth great spoil. *Ps.* **119: 162.**

I brought you into a plentiful country. *Je.* **2: 7.**

Ye shall seek me, and find me, when ye shall search for me with all your heart. *Je.* **29: 13.**

He that findeth his life shall lose it: and he that loseth his life for my sake shall find it. *Mat.* **10: 39.**

They went out to see what it was that was done. And they come to Jesus. *Mk.* **5: 14, 15.**

Launch out into the deep. *Lu.* **5: 4.**

I have found my sheep which was lost. *Lu.* **15: 6.**

When the Son of man cometh, shall he find faith on the earth? *Lu.* **18: 8.**

Wherefore, beloved, seeing that ye look for such things, be diligent that ye may be found of him in peace, without spot, and blameless. *2 Pe.* **3: 14.**

See also

Country, the Better; Land, the Promised; Pilgrim; Pioneer; Revelation.

Discretion

Forasmuch as God hath shewed thee all this, there is none so discreet and wise as thou art. *Ge.* **41: 39.**

To give . . . to the young man knowledge and discretion. *Pr.* **1: 4.**

Discretion shall preserve thee. *Pr.* **2: 11.**

As a jewel of gold in a swine's snout, so is a fair woman which is without discretion. *Pr.* **11: 22.**

The prudent man looketh well to his going. *Pr.* **14: 15.**

The discretion of a man deferreth his anger. *Pr.* **19: 11.**

My servant shall deal prudently. *Is.* **52: 13.**

Who is wise, and he shall understand these things? prudent, and he shall know them? *Ho.* **14: 9.**

Teach the young women . . . To be discreet. *Tit.* **2: 4, 5.**

See also

Care; Caution; Discernment; Discrimination; Heed; Judgment; Prudence.

Discrimination

That ye may put difference between holy and unholy, and between unclean and clean. *Le.* **10: 10.**

He that justifieth the wicked, and he that condemneth the just, even they both are abomination to the Lord. *Pr.* **17: 15.**

That he may know to refuse the evil, and choose the good. *Is.* **7: 15.**

They shall teach my people the difference between the holy and profane. *Eze.* **44: 23.**

Then shall ye return, and discern between the righteous and the wicked. *Mal.* **3: 18.**

Render therefore unto Cæsar the things which be Cæsar's, and unto God the things that be God's. *Lu.* **20: 25.**

One star differeth from another in glory. *1 Co.* **15: 41.**

Those who by reason of use have their senses exercised to discern both good and evil. *He.* **5: 14.**

See also

Discernment; Insight; Judgment; Perception; Understanding; Wisdom.

Disdain

Because he hath despised the word of the Lord, and hath broken his commandment, that soul shall utterly be cut off. *Nu.* **15: 31.**

When the Philistine looked about, and saw David, he disdained him. *1 S.* **17: 42.**

My friends scorn me. *Jb* **16: 20.**

Blessed is the man that . . . sitteth not in the seat of the scornful. *Ps.* **1: 1.**

Remove from me reproach and contempt. *Ps.* **119: 22.**

How long . . . will . . . the scorners delight in their scorning? *Pr.* **1: 22.**

My son, despise not the chastening of the Lord. *Pr.* **3: 11.**

He is despised and rejected of men. *Is.* **53: 3.**

He that despiseth you despiseth me; and he that despiseth me despiseth him that sent me. *Lu.* **10: 16.**

When they heard of the resurrection of the dead, some mocked: and others said, We will hear thee again of this matter. *Ac.* **17: 32.**

His bodily presence is weak, and his speech contemptible. *2 Co.* **10: 10.**

Ye have despised the poor. *Ja.* **2: 6.**

See also
Arrogance; Contempt; Haughtiness; Pride; Scorn.

Disease

Who forgiveth all thine iniquities; who healeth all thy diseases. *Ps.* 103: 3.

The spirit of a man will sustain his infirmity. *Pr.* 18: 14.

I shall go to the gates of the grave. *Is.* 38: 10.

Heal the sick, cleanse the lepers, raise the dead, cast out devils: freely ye have received, freely give. *Mat.* 10: 8.

He . . . healed them that had need of healing. *Lu.* 9: 11.

We then that are strong ought to bear the infirmities of the weak. *Ro.* 15: 1.

There was given to me a thorn in the flesh. 2 *Co.* 12: 7.

The prayer of faith shall save the sick. *Ja.* 5: 15.

See also
Ailment; Contagion; Disorder; Faith-Healing; Healing; Illness; Immunity; Infirmity; Sickness.

Disfigurement

The Philistines took him, and put out his eyes. *Ju.* 16: 21.

They cried aloud, and cut themselves after their manner with knives and lancets till the blood gushed out upon them. *1 K.* 18: 28.

A wound and dishonor shall he get; and his reproach shall not be wiped away. *Pr.* 6: 33.

A wicked man hardeneth his face. *Pr.* 21: 29.

Who hath wounds without cause? who hath redness of eyes? *Pr.* 23: 29.

From the sole of the foot even unto the head there is no soundness in it; but wounds, and bruises, and putrifying sores. *Is.* 1: 6.

Thy bruise is incurable, and thy wound is grievous. *Je.* 30: 12.

There fell a noisome and grievous sore upon the men which had the mark of the beast, and upon them which worshipped his image. *Re.* 16: 2.

Disgrace

God hath taken away my reproach. *Ge.* 30: 23.

For thy sake I have borne reproach. *Ps.* 69: 7.

O Lord, put me not to shame. *Ps.* 119: 31.

Do not disgrace the throne of thy glory. *Je.* 14: 21.

They departed, . . . rejoicing that they were counted worthy to suffer shame for his name. *Ac.* 5: 41.

They crucify to themselves the Son of God afresh, and put him to an open shame. *He.* 6: 6.

Esteeming the reproach of Christ greater riches than the treasures of Egypt. *He.* 11: 26.

See also
Christ, Humiliation of; Dishonor; Ignominy; Reproach; Shame.

Disguise

They . . . have also stolen, and dissembled also. *Jos.* 7: 11.

Why feignest thou thyself to be another? *1 K.* 14: 6.

Now there was a day when the sons of God

came to present themselves before the Lord, and Satan came also among them. *Jb.* 1: 6.

Give ear unto my prayer, that goeth not out of feigned lips. *Ps.* 17: 1.

I have not sat with vain persons, neither will I go in with dissemblers. *Ps.* 26: 4.

How long, Lord? wilt thou hide thyself for ever? *Ps.* 89: 46.

It is the glory of God to conceal a thing. *Pr.* 25: 2.

He that hateth dissembleth with his lips, and layeth up deceit within him. *Pr.* 26: 24.

Her treacherous sister Judah hath not turned unto me with her whole heart, but feignedly, saith the Lord. *Je.* 3: 10.

Through covetousness shall they with feigned lips make merchandise of you. 2 *Pe.* 2: 3.

See also
Christ, the Hidden; Christ, Mystery of; Cover; God, the Hiding; Mystery; Secrecy; Veil.

Dishonesty

They . . . have also stolen, and dissembled also. *Jos.* 7: 11.

Truly my words shall not be false. *Jb.* 36: 4.

He travaileth with iniquity, and hath conceived mischief, and brought forth falsehood. *Ps.* 7: 14.

Put away from thee a froward mouth, and perverse lips put far from thee. *Pr.* 4: 24.

A faithful witness will not lie: but a false witness will utter lies. *Pr.* 14: 5.

He that speaketh lies shall perish. *Pr.* 19: 9.

It is naught, it is naught, saith the buyer: but when he is gone his way, then he boasteth. *Pr.* 20: 14.

The getting of treasures by a lying tongue is a vanity tossed to and fro of them that seek death. *Pr.* 21: 6.

We have made lies our refuge, and under falsehood have we hid ourselves. *Is.* 28: 15.

As the partridge sitteth on eggs, and hatcheth them not; so he that getteth riches, and not by right, shall leave them in the midst of his days, and at his end shall be a fool. *Je.* 17: 11.

Woe unto him that . . . useth his neighbour's service without wages, and giveth him not for his work. *Je.* 22: 13.

Thou hast greedily gained of thy neighbours by extortion, and hast forgotten me, saith the Lord God. *Eze.* 22: 12.

They commit falsehood. *Ho.* 7: 1.

Ye have eaten the fruit of lies. *Ho.* 10: 13.

He is a merchant, the balances of deceit are in his hand: he loveth to oppress. *Ho.* 12: 7.

Thou speakest lies in the name of the Lord. *Zch.* 13: 3.

Exact no more than that which is appointed you. *Lu.* 3: 13.

We . . . have renounced the hidden things of dishonesty. 2 *Co.* 4: 1, 2.

Putting away lying, speak every man truth with his neighbour. *Ep.* 4: 25.

Behold, the hire of the labourers who have reaped down your fields, which is of you kept back by fraud, crieth. *Ja.* 5: 4.

See also
Faithlessness; Falsehood; Lie; Untruthfulness.

Dishonor

Men shall clap their hands at him, and shall hiss him out of his place. *Jb.* 27: 23.

Let the enemy . . . lay mine honour in the dust. *Ps.* 7: 5.

Let them be ashamed and brought to confusion together that rejoice at mine hurt. *Ps.* 35: 26.

He that is of a perverse heart shall be despised. *Pr.* 12: 8.

He that saith unto the wicked, Thou art righteous; him shall the people curse, nations shall abhor him. *Pr.* 24: 24.

They shall be an abhorring unto all flesh. *Is.* 66: 24.

In vain shalt thou make thyself fair; thy lovers will despise thee, they will seek thy life. *Je.* 4: 30.

Many of them that sleep in the dust of the earth shall awake, some to everlasting life, and some to shame and everlasting contempt. *Da.* 12: 2.

Blessed are ye, when men . . . shall reproach you, and cast out your name as evil. *Lu.* 6: 22.

I honour my Father, and ye do dishonour me. *Jn.* 8: 49.

Thou that makest thy boast of the law, through breaking the law dishonourest thou God? *Ro.* 2: 23.

Hath not the potter power over the clay, of the same lump to make one vessel unto honour, and another unto dishonour? *Ro.* 9: 21.

In a great house there are not only vessels of gold and of silver, but also of wood and of earth; and some to honour, and some to dishonour. *2 Ti.* 2: 20.

See also

Christ, Humiliation of; Disgrace; Ignominy; Reproach; Shame.

Dismay

Fear and dread shall fall upon them. *Ex.* 15: 16.

Fear not, neither be dismayed. *De.* 31: 8.

The thing which I greatly feared is come upon me, and that which I was afraid of is come unto me. *Jb.* 3: 25.

They meet with darkness in the daytime, and grope in the noonday as in the night. *Jb.* 5: 14.

His archers compass me round about. *Jb.* 16: 13.

Snares are round about thee, and sudden fear troubleth thee. *Jb.* 22: 10.

I am . . . a companion to owls. *Jb.* 30: 29.

I am come into deep waters, where the floods overflow me. *Ps.* 69: 2.

My flesh trembleth for fear of thee. *Ps.* 119: 120.

Trouble and anguish have taken hold on me. *Ps.* 119: 143.

Be not afraid of sudden fear. *Pr.* 3: 25.

Thus saith the Lord, Learn not the way of the heathen, and be not dismayed at the signs of heaven; for the heathen are dismayed at them. *Je.* 10: 2.

There shall be signs in the sun, and in the moon, and in the stars; and upon the earth distress of nations, with perplexity; the sea and the waves roaring; Men's hearts failing them for fear. *Lk.* 21: 25, 26.

Great fear came upon all the church, and upon as many as heard these things. *Ac.* 5: 11.

See also

Alarm; Dejection; Depression; Despair; Discouragement; Fear.

Dismissal

The Lord watch between me and thee, when we are absent one from another. *Ge.* 31: 49.

The people that are with thee are too many. *Ju.* 7: 2.

Samuel called Saul to the top of the house, saying, Up, that I may send thee away. *1 S.* 9: 26.

Go in peace, forasmuch as we have sworn both of us in the name of the Lord, saying, The Lord be between me and thee, and between my seed and thy seed for ever. *1 S.* 20: 42.

O God, thou hast cast us off, thou hast scattered us. *Ps.* 60: 1.

Go thy way, sell whatsoever thou hast, and give to the poor, and thou shalt have treasure in heaven. *Mk.* 10: 21.

Go your ways: behold, I send you forth as lambs among the wolves. *Lu.* 10: 3.

Peace I leave with you, my peace I give unto you. *Jn.* 14: 27.

Fare ye well. *Ac.* 15: 29.

Finally, brethren, farewell. Be perfect, be of good comfort, be of one mind, live in peace; and the God of love and peace shall be with you. *2 Co.* 13: 11.

Disobedience

Who is the Lord, that I should obey his voice? *Ex.* 5: 2.

Thou hast done foolishly: thou hast not kept the commandment of the Lord thy God. *1 S.* 13: 13.

Thou hast disobeyed the mouth of the Lord. *1 K.* 13: 21.

This is a nation that obeyeth not the voice of the Lord their God. *Je.* 7: 28.

Cursed be the man that obeyeth not the words of this covenant. *Je.* 11: 3.

Why do ye also transgress the commandment of God by your tradition? *Mat.* 15: 3.

I was not disobedient unto the heavenly vision. *Ac.* 26: 19.

O foolish Galatians, who hath bewitched you, that ye should not obey the truth? *Ga.* 3: 1.

Because of these things cometh the wrath of God upon the children of disobedience. *Ep.* 5: 6.

In flaming fire taking vengeance on them that know not God, and that obey not the gospel of our Lord Jesus Christ. *2 Th.* 1: 8.

If any man obey not our word, . . . note that man, and have no company with him. *2 Th.* 3: 14.

The law is not made for the righteous man, but for the lawless and disobedient. *1 Ti.* 1: 9.

We ourselves also were sometimes foolish, disobedient, deceived. *Tit.* 3: 3.

Every transgression and disobedience received a just recompense of reward. *He.* 2: 2.

How shall we escape, if we neglect so great salvation? *He.* 2: 3.

See also

Christ, Denial of; Denial; Faithlessness; God, Denial of; Heedlessness; Refusal; Rejection; Transgression.

Disorder

The Lord discomfited them before Israel. *Jos.* 10: 10.

I am full of confusion; therefore see thou mine affliction. *Jb.* 10: 15.

The sea overwhelmed their enemies. *Ps.* 78: 53.

A sound of battle is in the land. *Je.* 50: 22.

There are that raise up strife and contention. *Hab.* 1: 3.

The riders on horses shall be confounded. *Zch.* 10: 5.

The whole city was filled with confusion. *Ac.* 19: 29.

The assembly was confused. *Ac.* 19: 32.

Without were fightings, within were fears. *2 Co.* 7: 5.

Withdraw yourselves from every brother that walketh disorderly. *2 Th.* 3: 6.

See also

Agitation; Chaos; Clamor; Confusion; Din; Disease; Disturbance; Infirmity; Sickness; Tumult; Turmoil.

Dispensation

Thou shalt rejoice in every good thing which the Lord thy God hath given unto thee. *De.* 26: 11.

I have set before thee this day life and good, and death and evil. *De.* 30: 15.

Ye are not under the law, but under grace. *Ro.* 6: 14.

If I do this thing willingly, I have a reward: but if against my will, a dispensation of the gospel is committed unto me. *1 Co.* 9: 17.

His grace which was bestowed upon me was not in vain. *1 Co.* 15: 10.

That in the dispensation of the fulness of times he might gather together in one all things in Christ. *Ep.* 1: 10.

By grace are ye saved through faith; and that not of yourselves: it is the gift of God: Not of works, lest any man should boast. *Ep.* 2: 8, 9.

Ye have heard of the dispensation of the grace of God which is given me to you-ward. *Ep.* 3: 2.

I am made a minister, according to the dispensation of God which is given to me for you. *Col.* 1: 25.

The manifold grace of God. *1 Pe.* 4: 10.

See also

Bestowal; Distribution; Justice; Remission.

Dispersion

Rise up, Lord, and let thine enemies be scattered. *Nu.* 10: 35.

The Lord shall scatter you among the nations. *De.* 4: 27.

The lips of the wise disperse knowledge. *Pr.* 15: 7.

He shall . . . assemble the outcasts of Israel, and gather together the dispersed of Judah from the four corners of the earth. *Is.* 11: 12.

The days . . . of your dispersions are accomplished. *Je.* 25: 34.

I will scatter into all winds them that are in the utmost corners. *Je.* 49: 32.

I will even gather you from the people, and assemble you out of the countries where ye have been scattered, and I will give you

the land of Israel. *Eze.* 11: 17.

I will scatter thee among the heathen, and disperse thee in the countries. *Eze.* 22: 15.

Thy people is scattered upon the mountains. *Na.* 3: 18.

Smite the shepherd, and the sheep shall be scattered. *Zch.* 13: 7.

He was moved with compassion on them, because they fainted, and were scattered abroad, as sheep having no shepherd. *Mat.* 9: 36.

That also he should gather together in one the children of God that were scattered abroad. *Jn.* 11: 52.

The hour cometh, yea, is now come, that ye shall be scattered, every man to his own. *Jn.* 16: 32.

To the twelve tribes which are scattered abroad. *Ja.* 1: 1.

See also

Banishment; Captivity; Exile.

Display

Thou hast given a banner to them that fear thee, that it may be displayed because of the truth. *Ps.* 60: 4.

Hezekiah . . . shewed them the house of his precious things, the silver, and the gold, and the spices, and the precious ointment, and all the house of his armour, and all that was found in his treasures. *Is.* 39: 2.

Take heed that ye do not your alms before men, to be seen of them. *Mat.* 6: 1.

When thou doest thine alms, do not sound a trumpet before thee. *Mat.* 6: 2.

They love to pray standing in the synagogues and in the corners of the streets, that they may be seen of men. *Mat.* 6: 5.

The hypocrites . . . disfigure their faces, that they may appear unto men to fast. *Mat.* 6: 16.

They make broad their phylacteries, and enlarge the borders of their garments. *Mat.* 23: 5.

Nothing is secret, that shall not be made manifest. *Lu.* 8: 17.

Beware of the scribes, which desire to walk in long robes, and love greetings in the markets, and the highest seats in the synagogues, and the chief rooms at feasts. *Lu.* 20: 46.

God . . . hath in due time manifested his word through preaching. *Tit.* 1: 2, 3.

See also

Haughtiness; Manifestation; Pomp; Pride.

Displeasure

O Lord God, turn not away the face of thine anointed. *2 Ch.* 6: 42.

The arrows of the Almighty are within me. *Jb.* 6: 4.

Thou . . . increasest thine indignation upon me. *Jb.* 10: 17.

The Lord shall have them in derision. *Ps.* 2: 4.

Then shall he speak unto them in his wrath, and vex them in his sore displeasure. *Ps.* 2: 5.

O Lord rebuke me not in thy wrath: neither chasten me in thy hot displeasure. *Ps.* 38: 1.

O God, . . . thou hast been displeased; O turn thyself to us again. *Ps.* 60: 1.

It is a people of no understanding: therefore he that made them will not have mercy on them, and he that formed them will shew them no favour. *Is.* 27: 11.

In a little wrath I hid my face from thee for a moment; but with everlasting kindness will I have mercy on thee. *Is.* 54: 8.

His watchmen are blind: they are all ignorant, they are all dumb dogs, they cannot bark. *Is.* 56: 10.

Turn ye now from your evil ways and from your evil doings. *Zch.* 1: 4.

See also

Anger; Christ, Wrath of; Dislike; Distaste; God, Anger of; Indignation; Vexation.

Dispute

By pride cometh contention. *Pr.* 13: 10.

By the way they had disputed among themselves, who should be the greatest. *Mk.* 9: 34.

He . . . spake boldly for the space of three months, disputing and persuading the things concerning the kingdom of God. *Ac.* 19: 8.

Where is the disputer of this world? hath not God made foolish the wisdom of this world? *1 Co.* 1: 20.

Do all things without murmurings and disputings. *Ph.* 2: 14.

Forbearing one another, and forgiving one another, if any man have a quarrel against any: even as Christ forgave you, so also do ye. *Col.* 3: 13.

Perverse disputings of men of corrupt minds, and destitute of the truth: . . . from such withdraw thyself. *1 Ti.* 6: 5.

See also

Argument; Contention; Controversy; Debate; Quarrel; Struggle.

Dissatisfaction

Their vine is of the vine of Sodom, and of the fields of Gomorrah: their grapes are grapes of gall, their clusters are bitter. *De.* 32: 32.

God was displeased with this thing; therefore he smote Israel. *1 Ch.* 21: 7.

I will complain in the bitterness of my soul. *Jb.* 7: 11.

As for me, is my complaint to man? and if it were so, why should not my spirit be troubled. *Jb.* 21: 4.

Surely they are disquieted in vain. *Ps.* 39: 6.

Why art thou cast down, O my soul? and why art thou disquieted in me? *Ps.* 42: 5.

Lest the Lord see it, and it displease him. *Pr.* 24: 18.

The eye is not satisfied with seeing. *Ec.* 1: 8.

Then I looked on all the works that my hands had wrought, and on the labour that I had laboured to do: and, behold, all was vanity and vexation of spirit, and there was no profit under the sun. *Ec.* 2: 11.

For whom do I labour, and bereave my soul of good? *Ec.* 4: 8.

He that loveth silver shall not be satisfied with silver; nor he that loveth abundance with increase. *Ec.* 5: 10.

All the labour of man is for his mouth, and yet the appetite is not filled. *Ec.* 6: 7.

He feedeth on ashes. *Is.* 44: 20.

Murmur not among yourselves. *Jn.* 6: 43.

Do all things without murmurings and disputings. *Ph.* 2: 14.

See also

Discontent.

Dissent

Ye have heard that it was said by them of old time, . . . But I say unto you. *Mat.* 5: 21, 22.

Beware of false prophets. *Mat.* 7: 15.

Many will say to me in that day, Lord, Lord, have we not prophesied in thy name? . . . And then will I profess unto them, I never knew you. *Mat.* 7: 22, 23.

Think not that I am come to send peace on earth: I came not to send peace, but a sword. *Mat.* 10: 34.

The new agreeth not with the old. *Lu.* 5: 36.

I am not the Christ. *Jn.* 1: 20.

After the way which they call heresy, so worship I the God of my fathers. *Ac.* 24: 14.

They agreed not among themselves. *Ac.* 28: 25.

Who maketh thee to differ from another? *1 Co.* 4: 7.

See also

Christ, Denial of; Denial; Disbelief; God, Denial of; Heresy; Protest; Unbelief.

Dissipation

He is a glutton, and a drunkard. *De.* 21: 20.

To add drunkenness to thirst. *De.* 29: 19.

I was the song of the drunkards. *Ps.* 69: 12.

Incline not my heart to any evil thing, to practise wicked works with men that work iniquity: and let me not eat of their dainties. *Ps.* 141: 4.

The drunkard and the glutton shall come to poverty. *Pr.* 23: 21.

Whoso causeth the righteous to go astray in an evil way, he shall fall himself into his own pit. *Pr.* 28: 10.

Awake, ye drunkards, and weep; and howl, all ye drinkers of wine. *Jo.* 1: 5.

While they are drunken as drunkards, they shall be devoured as stubble fully dry. *Na.* 1: 10.

Turn ye now from your evil ways, and from your evil doings. *Zch.* 1: 4.

Ye have yielded your members servants to uncleanness and to iniquity unto iniquity. *Ro.* 6: 19.

Know ye not that the unrighteous shall not inherit the kingdom of God? Nor drunkards. *1 Co.* 6: 9, 10.

Be not drunk with wine, wherein is excess. *Ep.* 5: 18.

These are murmurers, complainers, walking after their own lusts. *Jude* 16.

The fruits that thy soul lusteth after are departed from thee. *Re.* 18: 14.

See also

Debauchery; Drunkenness; Flesh; Indulgence; Intoxication; Lust.

Distance

My father fought for you, and adventured his life far. *Ju.* 9: 17.

If iniquity be in thine hand, put it far away. *Jb.* 11: 14.

As far as the east is from the west, so far hath he removed our transgressions from us. *Ps.* 103: 12.

The Lord is far from the wicked. *Pr.* 15: 29.

As cold waters to a thirsty soul, so is good news from a far country. *Pr.* 25: 25.

They come from a far country, from the end of heaven. *Is.* 13: 5.

Behold, the name of the Lord cometh from far. *Is.* 30: 27.

Thine eyes shall see the king in his beauty: they shall behold the land that is very far off. *Is.* 33: 17.

Lift up thine eyes round about, and see: all they gather themselves together, they come to thee: thy sons shall come from far, and thy daughters shall be nursed at thy side. *Is.* 60: 4.

The kingdom of heaven is as a man travelling into a far country. *Mat.* 25: 14.

Thou art not far from the kingdom of God. *Mk.* 12: 34.

The Son of man is as a man taking a far journey. *Mk.* 13: 34.

I have set thee to be a light of the Gentiles, that thou shouldest be for salvation unto the ends of the earth. *Ac.* 13: 47.

In journeyings often. *2 Co.* 11: 26.

Now in Christ Jesus ye who sometimes were far off are made nigh by the blood of Christ. *Ep.* 2: 13.

Distinction

What one nation in the earth is like thy people Israel? *1 Ch.* 17: 21.

He poureth contempt upon princes, and weakeneth the strength of the mighty. *Jb.* 12: 21.

Whosoever shall do and teach them, the same shall be called great in the kingdom of heaven. *Mat.* 5: 19.

What do ye more than others? *Mat.* 5: 47.

The princes of the Gentiles exercise dominion over them, and they that are great exercise authority upon them. *Mat.* 20: 25.

Whosoever will be chief among you, let him be your servant. *Mat.* 20: 27.

He shall be great in the sight of the Lord. *Lu.* 1: 15.

Whosoever exalteth himself shall be abased. *Lu.* 14: 11.

Now consider how great this man was. *He.* 7: 4.

See also

Celebrity; Discrimination; Diversity; Eminence; Excellence; Fame; Preference, Renown; Reputation; Superiority; Variety.

Distress

Why are ye come unto me now when ye are in distress? *Ju.* 11: 7.

In my distress I called upon the Lord, and cried to my God: and he did hear my voice out of his temple. *2 S.* 22: 7.

Why should not my countenance be sad, when the city, the place of my fathers' sepulchres, lieth waste? *Ne.* 2: 3.

Have mercy upon me, O Lord, for I am in trouble. *Ps.* 31: 9.

This poor man cried, and the Lord heard him, and saved him out of all his troubles. *Ps* 34: 6.

Thine arrows stick fast in me. *Ps.* 38: 2.

Thou hast been my defence and refuge in the day of my trouble. *Ps.* 59: 16.

The fig tree languisheth; the pomegranate tree, the palm tree also, and the apple tree, even all the trees of the field, are withered: because joy is withered away from the sons of men. *Jo.* 1: 12.

He was sad at that saying, and went away grieved. *Mk.* 10: 22.

The God of all comfort; Who comforteth us in all our tribulation, that we may be able to comfort them which are in any trouble. *2 Co.* 1: 3, 4.

I take pleasure in infirmities, in reproaches, in necessities, in persecutions, in distresses for Christ's sake. *2 Co.* 12: 10.

See also

Adversity; Affliction; Anguish; Calamity; Disaster; Evil; Grief; Hardship; Misery; Misfortune; Torment; Trial; Tribulation; Trouble.

Distribution

God distributeth sorrows in his anger. *Jb.* 21: 17.

Sell all that thou hast, and distribute unto the poor, and thou shalt have treasure in heaven. *Lu.* 18: 22.

Jesus took the loaves; and when he had given thanks, he distributed to the disciples. *Jn.* 6: 11.

Distribution was made unto every man according as he had need. *Ac.* 4: 35.

Distributing to the necessity of saints. *Ro.* 12: 13.

As God hath distributed to every man, as the Lord hath called every one, so let him walk. *1 Co.* 7: 17.

The administration of this service not only supplieth the want of the saints, but is abundant also by many thanksgivings unto God. *2 Co.* 9: 12.

Charge them that are rich in this world, . . . that they be rich in good works, ready to distribute, willing to communicate. *1 Ti.* 6: 17, 18.

See also

Dispensation; Dispersion.

Distrust

He put no trust in his servants; and his angels he charged with folly. *Jb.* 4: 18.

Behold, he putteth no trust in his saints. *Jb.* 15: 15.

They believed not in God, and trusted not in his salvation. *Ps.* 78: 22.

Put not your trust in princes, nor in the son of man, in whom there is no help. *Ps.* 146: 3.

Trust ye not in lying words. *Je.* 7: 4.

Trust ye not in a friend, put ye not confidence in a guide. *Mi.* 7: 5.

She trusted not in the Lord. *Zph.* 3: 2.

Be not faithless, but believing. *Jn.* 20: 27.

We had the sentence of death in ourselves, that we should not trust in ourselves, but in God which raiseth the dead. *2 Co.* 1: 9.

Charge them that are rich in this world, that they be not highminded, nor trust in uncertain riches, but in the living God. *1 Ti.* 6: 17.

See also

Doubt; Suspicion.

Disturbance

Every man's sword was against his fellow, and there was a very great discomfiture. *1 S.* 14: 20.

Lo, thine enemies make a tumult. *Ps.* 83: 2.

While I suffer thy terrors I am distracted. *Ps.* 88: 15.

Great peace have they which love thy law: and nothing shall offend them., *Ps.* 119: 165.

There were many coming and going, and they had no leisure so much as to eat. *Mk.* 6: 31.

That ye may attend upon the Lord without distraction. *1 Co.* 7: 35.

We hear that there are some which walk among you disorderly. *2 Th.* 3: 11.

See also

Agitation; Annoyance; Confusion; Disorder; Noise; Storm; Tumult; Turmoil.

Diversity

Thou shalt not have in thy bag divers weights, a great and a small. *De.* 25: 13.

The kingdom of heaven is like unto a net, that was cast into the sea, and gathered of every kind. *Mat.* 13: 47.

There are diversities of operations, but it is the same God which worketh all in all. *1 Co.* 12: 6.

To another divers kinds of tongues. *1 Co.* 12: 10.

There are, it may be, so many kinds of voices in the world, and none of them is without signification. *1 Co.* 14: 10.

Do ye look on things after the outward appearance? If any man trust himself that he is Christ's, let him of himself think this again, that, as he is Christ's, even so are we Christ's. *2 Co.* 10: 7.

Count it all joy when ye fall into divers temptations. *Ja.* 1: 2.

See also

Variety.

Divinity

Worship him, all ye gods. *Ps.* 97: 7.

Where are thy gods that thou hast made thee? Let them arise, if they can save thee. *Je.* 2: 28.

The gods are come down to us in the likeness of men. *Ac.* 14: 11.

Forasmuch then as we are the offspring of God, we ought not to think that the Godhead is like unto gold, or silver, or stone, graven by art and man's device. *Ac.* 17: 29.

His eternal power and Godhead. *Ro.* 1: 20.

God sending his own Son in the likeness of sinful flesh. *Ro.* 8: 3.

There is but one God, the Father, of whom are all things, and we in him; and one Lord Jesus Christ, by whom are all things, and we by him. *1 Co.* 8: 6.

When the fulness of the time was come, God sent forth his Son. *Ga.* 4: 4.

In him dwelleth all the fulness of the Godhead bodily. *Col.* 2: 9.

His divine power hath given unto us all things that pertain unto life and godliness. *2 Pe.* 1: 3.

He that doeth good is of God. *3 Jn.* 1: 11.

See also

Christ, Divinity of; Godliness; Gods.

Division

By these were the nations divided in the earth after the flood. *Ge.* 10: 32.

Their heart is divided. *Ho.* 10: 2.

No man can serve two masters. *Mat.* 6: 24.

Every city or house divided against itself shall not stand. *Mat.* 12: 25.

If Satan cast out Satan, he is divided against himself; how shall then his kingdom stand? *Mat.* 12: 26.

He shall separate them one from another, as a shepherd divideth his sheep from the goats. *Mat.* 25: 32.

They crucified him, and parted his garments, casting lots. *Mat.* 27: 35.

Suppose ye that I am come to give peace on earth? I tell you, Nay; but rather division. *Lu.* 12: 51.

From henceforth there shall be five in one house divided, three against two, and two against three. *Lu.* 12: 52.

They . . . sold their possessions and goods, and parted them to all men, as every man had need. *Ac.* 2: 42, 45.

The multitude of the city was divided. *Ac.* 14: 4.

I beseech you, brethren, . . . that there be no divisions among you. *1 Co.* 1: 10.

Is Christ divided? *1 Co.* 1: 13.

All these worketh that one and the selfsame Spirit, dividing to every man severally as he will. *1 Co.* 12: 11.

The great city was divided. *Re.* 16: 19.

See also

Church, Divisions of; Denomination; Discord; Distribution; Part; Partition; Portion; Schism; Sect; Separation; Share.

Divorce

Whosoever shall put away his wife, saving for the cause of fornication, causeth her to commit adultery: and whosoever shall marry her that is divorced committeth adultery. *Mat.* 5: 32.

What therefore God hath joined together, let not man put asunder. *Mat.* 19: 6.

Moses because of the hardness of your hearts suffered you to put away your wives: but from the beginning it was not so. *Mat.* 19: 8.

Is it lawful for a man to put away his wife? *Mk.* 10: 2.

Moses suffered to write a bill of divorcement. . . . For the hardness of your heart he wrote you this precept. *Mk.* 10: 4, 5.

Let not the wife depart from her husband: But and if she depart, let her remain unmarried, or be reconciled to her husband: and let not the husband put away his wife. *1 Co.* 7: 10, 11.

Art thou bound to a wife? seek not to be loosed. *1 Co.* 7: 27.

See also

Parting; Separation.

Doctor

Solomon's wisdom excelled the wisdom of all the children of the east country, and all the wisdom of Egypt. *1 K.* 4: 30.

In his disease he sought not to the Lord, but to the physicians. *2 Ch.* 16: 12.

A wise man will hear, and will increase learning. *Pr.* 1: 5.

The Lord God hath given me the tongue of the learned. *Is.* 50: 4.

Is there no balm in Gilead? *Je.* 8: 22.

Thou hast no healing medicines. *Je.* 30: 13.

In vain shalt thou use many medicines; for thou shalt not be cured. *Je.* 46: 11.

As for these four children, God gave them

knowledge and skill in all learning and wisdom: and Daniel had understanding in all visions and dreams. *Da.* 1: 17.

They that are whole have no need of the physician, but they that are sick. *Mk.* 2: 17.

After three days they found him in the temple, sitting in the midst of the doctors, both hearing them, and asking them questions. *Lu.* 2: 46.

Physician, heal thyself. *Lu.* 4: 23.

It came to pass on a certain day, as he was teaching, that there were Pharisees and doctors of the law sitting by. *Lu.* 5: 17.

A woman . . . had spent all her living upon physicians, neither could be healed of any. *Lu.* 8: 43.

The Jews marvelled, saying, How knoweth this man letters, having never learned? *Jn.* 7: 15.

Then stood there up one in the council, a Pharisee, named Gamaliel, a doctor of the law *Ac.* 5: 34.

Moses was learned in all the wisdom of the Egyptians, and was mighty in words and in deeds. *Ac.* 7: 22.

See also

Cure; Healing; Knowledge; Medicine; Physician; Remedy; Wisdom.

Doctrine

My doctrine shall drop as the rain. *De.* 32: 2.

I will meditate in thy precepts. *Ps.* 119: 15.

The people were astonished at his doctrine. *Mat.* 7: 28.

Jesus . . . said, My doctrine is not mine, but his that sent me. *Jn.* 7: 16.

If any man will do his will, he shall know of the doctrine. *Jn.* 7: 17.

The high priest then asked Jesus . . . of his doctrine. *Jn.* 18: 19.

After the way which they call heresy, so worship I the God of my fathers. *Ac.* 24: 14.

What shall I profit you, except I shall speak to you either by revelation, or by knowledge, or by prophesying, or by doctrine. *1 Co.* 14: 6.

Every·one of you hath a psalm, hath a doctrine, hath a tongue, hath a revelation. *1 Co.* 14: 26.

All scripture is given by inspiration of God, and is profitable for doctrine. *2 Ti.* 3: 16.

See also

Belief; Creed; Dogma; Faith; Heresy; Orthodoxy; Principle; Rule; Tenet; Unorthodoxy.

Dogma

My doctrine shall drop as the rain, my speech shall distil as the dew, as the small rain upon the tender herb, and as the showers upon the grass. *De.* 32: 2.

The law of the Lord is perfect, converting the soul. *Ps.* 19: 7.

These signs shall follow them that believe; In my name shall they cast out devils. *Mk.* 16: 17.

If any man will do his will, he shall know of the doctrine. *Jn.* 7: 17.

Believe on the Lord Jesus Christ, and thou shalt be saved, and thy house. *Ac.* 16: 31.

May we know what this new doctrine, whereof thou speakest, is? *Ac.* 17: 19.

Nourished up in the words of faith and of good doctrine, whereunto thou hast attained. *1 Ti.* 4: 6.

The doctrine which is according to godliness. *1 Ti.* 6: 3.

He that abideth in the doctrine of Christ, he hath both the Father and the Son. *2 Jn.* 9.

See also

Belief; Creed; Doctrine; Heresy; Orthodoxy; Tenet.

Domain

Let them have dominion. *Ge.* 1: 26.

Gideon said unto them, I will not rule over you, neither shall my son rule over you: the Lord shall rule over you. *Ju.* 8: 23.

Thou madest him to have dominion over the works of thy hands. *Ps.* 8: 6.

The God of heaven hath given thee a kingdom, power, and strength, and glory. *Da.* 2: 37.

The kingdom shall be the Lord's. *Ob.* 21.

His dominion shall be from sea even to sea, and from the river even to the ends of the earth. *Zch.* 9: 10.

See also

Authority; Christ, the King; Christ, Reign of; Dominion; God, the King; God, Kingdom of; Kingdom.

Dominion

Yet have I set my king upon my holy hill of Zion. *Ps.* 2: 6.

All the kings of the earth shall praise thee. *Ps.* 138: 4.

The Gentiles shall come to thy light, and kings to the brightness of thy rising. *Is.* 60: 3.

Of a truth it is, that your God is a God of gods, and a Lord of kings. *Da.* 2: 47.

Thy greatness is grown, and reacheth unto heaven, and thy dominion to the end of the earth. *Da.* 4: 22.

The most High, whose kingdom is an everlasting kingdom, and all dominions shall serve and obey him. *Da.* 7: 27.

Blessed be the King that cometh in the name of the Lord. *Lu.* 19: 38.

Death hath no more dominion over him. *Ro.* 6: 9.

Sin shall not have dominion over you. *Ro.* 6: 14.

Let every soul be subject unto the higher powers. *Ro.* 13: 1.

We shall reign on the earth. *Re.* 5: 10.

They shall reign for ever and ever. *Re.* 22: 5.

See also

Authority; Christ, the King; Christ, Reign of; Christ, Supremacy of; Domain; God, the King; God, Kingdom of; God, Sovereignty of; God, Supremacy of; King; Kingdom; Power; Realm; Reign; Rule; Theocracy; Throne.

Donation

Because of thy temple at Jerusalem shall kings bring presents unto thee. *Ps.* 68: 29.

Yea, the Lord shall give that which is good. *Ps.* 85: 12.

Honour the Lord with thy substance, and with the firstfruits of all thine increase. *Pr.* 3: 9.

Silver and gold have I none; but such as I have give I thee. *Ac.* 3: 6.

It is more blessed to give than to receive. *Ac.* 20: 35.

See also

Almsgiving; Beneficence; Benevolence; Charity: Christ, Gift of; Contribution; Generosity; Gift; God, Gift of; Grant; Philanthropy; Present; Unselfishness.

Doom

The ungodly shall not stand in the judgment. *Ps.* 1: 5.

God shall likewise destroy thee for ever. *Ps.* 52: 5.

He that is courageous among the mighty shall flee away naked in that day. *Am.* 2: 16.

Behold, I will set a plumbline in the midst of my people Israel: I will not pass again by them any more. *Am.* 7: 8.

Depart. *Mat.* 25: 41.

These shall go away into everlasting punishment. *Mat.* 25: 46.

This night thy soul shall be required of thee. *Lu.* 12: 20.

Punished with everlasting destruction from the presence of the Lord. 2 *Th.* 1: 9.

The angels which kept not their first estate, but left their own habitation, he hath reserved in everlasting chains under darkness unto the judgment of the great day. *Jude* 1: 6.

The great day of his wrath is come; and who shall be able to stand? *Re.* 6: 17.

See also

Damnation; Decree; Destruction; Destiny; Fate; Fortune; Judgment; Judgment, Last; Lot; Predestination; Ruin.

Door

Be ye lift up, ye everlasting doors; and the King of glory shall come in. *Ps.* 24: 7.

For a day in thy courts is better than a thousand. I had rather be a doorkeeper in the house of my God, than to dwell in the tents of wickedness. *Ps.* 84: 10.

Enter not into the path of the wicked. *Pr.* 4: 14.

When thou hast shut thy door, pray to thy Father which is in secret. *Mat.* 6: 6.

It is easier for a camel to go through the eye of a needle, than for a rich man to enter into the kingdom of God. *Mat.* 19: 24.

They that were ready went in: . . . and the door was shut. *Mat.* 25: 10.

The angel of the Lord descended from heaven, and came and rolled back the stone from the door. *Mat.* 28: 2.

Lord, trouble not thyself: for I am not worthy that thou shouldest enter under my roof. *Lu.* 7: 6.

He that entereth in by the door is the shepherd of the sheep. *Lu.* 10: 2.

Trouble me not: the door is now shut, and my children are with me in bed; I cannot rise and give thee. *Lu.* 11: 7.

I am the door: by me if any man enter in, he shall be saved, and shall go in and out, and find pasture. *Jn.* 10: 9.

Whose heart the Lord opened. *Ac.* 16: 14.

They shall not enter into my rest. *He.* 3: 11.

The judge standeth before the door. *Ja.* 5: 9.

Behold, I stand at the door, and knock. *Re.* 3: 20.

See also

Admission; Christ, the Door; Christ, the Way; Entrance; Gate; Key; Opening.

Double

If the thief be found, let him pay double. *Ex.* 22: 7.

Elisha said, I pray thee, let a double portion of thy spirit be upon me. 2 *K.* 2: 9.

The Lord gave Job twice as much as he had before. *Jb.* 42: 10.

With flattering lips and with a double heart do they speak. *Ps.* 12: 2.

She hath received of the Lord's hand double for all her sins. *Is.* 40: 2.

Ye compass sea and land to make one proselyte, and when he is made, ye make him twofold more the child of hell than yourselves. *Mat.* 23: 15.

Purify your hearts, ye double minded. *Ja.* 4: 8.

Reward her even as she rewarded you, and double unto her double according to her works. *Re.* 18: 6.

See also

Twin; Two.

Doubt

Shall a child be born unto him that is an hundred years old? *Ge.* 17: 17.

Who is the Lord, that I should obey his voice? *Ex.* 5: 2.

The people, among whom I am, are six hundred thousand footmen; and thou hast said, I will give them flesh, that they may eat a whole month. *Nu.* 11: 21.

Thy life shall hang in doubt before thee. *De.* 28: 66.

If the Lord be with us, why then is all this befallen us? *Ju.* 6: 13.

No man is sure of life. *Jb.* 24: 22.

If ye have faith, and doubt not, . . . ye shall say unto this mountain, Be thou removed, and be thou cast into the sea; it shall be done. *Mat.* 21: 21.

Why are ye so fearful? how is it that ye have no faith? *Mk.* 4: 40.

Neither be ye of doubtful mind. *Lu.* 12: 29.

Increase our faith. *Lu.* 17: 5.

O fools, and slow of heart to believe all that the prophets have spoken. *Lu.* 24: 25.

Some of them said, Could not this man, which opened the eyes of the blind, have caused that even this man should not have died? *Jn.* 11: 37.

Be not faithless, but believing. *Jn.* 20: 27.

While Peter thought on the vision, the Spirit said unto him, Behold, three men seek thee. Arise therefore, and get thee down, and go with them, doubting nothing. *Ac.* 10: 19, 20.

TO THE UNKNOWN GOD. *Ac.* 17: 23.

Now we see through a glass, darkly. *1 Co.* 13: 12.

I stand in doubt of you. *Ga.* 4: 20.

I will therefore that men pray every where, lifting up holy hands, without wrath and doubting. *1 Ti.* 2: 8.

Take heed, brethren, lest there be in any of you an evil heart of unbelief. *He.* 3: 12.

See also

Christ, Doubt of; Disbelief; Distrust; Loyalty, Divided; Scepticism; Suspicion; Uncertainty.

Doxology

Glory ye in his holy name. *1 Ch.* 16: 10.

I will extol thee, O Lord. *Ps.* 30: 1.

In God we boast all the day long, and praise thy name for ever. *Ps.* 44: 8.

Because thy lovingkindness is better than life, my lips shall praise thee. *Ps.* 63: 3.

Let the people praise thee, O God, let all the people praise thee. *Ps.* 67: 3.

Let them exalt him also in the congregation of the people, and praise him in the assembly of the elders. *Ps.* 107: 32.

Praise God in his sanctuary. *Ps.* 150: 1.

Let everything that hath breath praise the Lord. Praise ye the Lord. *Ps.* 150: 6.

And suddenly there was with the angel a multitude of the heavenly host praising God, and saying, Glory to God in the highest. *Lu.* 2: 13, 14.

See also

Extol; God, Praise of; Praise.

Dread

How dreadful is this place! this is none other but the house of God. *Ge.* 28: 17.

Be strong, and of good courage; dread not, nor be dismayed. *1 Ch.* 22: 13.

Canst thou make him afraid as a grasshopper? *Jb.* 39: 20.

Thou shalt not be afraid for the terror by night. *Ps.* 91: 5.

Be not afraid of sudden fear. *Pr.* 3: 25.

Sanctify the Lord of hosts himself; and let him be your fear, and let him be your dread. *Is.* 8: 13.

My heart panted, fearfulness affrighted me. *Is.* 21: 4.

Be astonished, O ye heavens, at this, and be horribly afraid, be ye very desolate, saith the Lord. *Je.* 2: 12.

I will send you Elijah the prophet before the coming of the great and dreadful day of the Lord. *Mal.* 4: 5.

They fell on their face, and were sore afraid. *Mat.* 17: 6.

The glory of the Lord shone round about them: and they were sore afraid. *Lu.* 2: 9.

God hath not given us the spirit of fear; but of power, and of love, and of a sound mind. *2 Ti.* 1: 7.

Be not afraid of their terror, neither be troubled. *1 Pe.* 3: 14.

See also

Alarm; Fear; Terror.

Dream

He dreamed, and behold a ladder set up on the earth, and the top of it reached to heaven. *Ge.* 28: 12.

Behold, this dreamer cometh. *Ge.* 37: 19.

If there be a prophet among you, I the Lord will make myself known unto him in a vision, and will speak unto him in a dream. *Nu.* 12: 6.

Thou scarest me with dreams, and terrifiest me through visions. *Jb.* 7: 14.

In a dream, in a vision of the night, when deep sleep falleth upon men, in slumberings upon the bed; Then he openeth the ears of men. *Jb.* 33: 15, 16.

As a dream when one awaketh; so, O Lord, when thou awakest, thou shalt despise their image. *Ps.* 73: 20.

We were like them that dream. *Ps.* 126: 1.

Where there is no vision, the people perish. *Pr.* 29: 18.

In the multitude of dreams and many words there are also divers vanities. *Ec.* 5: 7.

It shall even be as when an hungry man dreameth, and, behold, he eateth; but he awaketh, and his soul is empty: or as when a thirsty man dreameth, and, behold, he drinketh; but he awaketh, and, behold, he is faint, and his soul hath appetite. *Is.* 29: 8.

Neither hearken to your dreams which ye cause to be dreamed. *Je.* 29: 8.

Your old men shall dream dreams, your young men shall see visions. *Jo.* 2: 28.

The angel of the Lord appeared unto him in a dream. *Mat.* 1: 20.

I have suffered many things this day in a dream because of him. *Mat.* 27: 19.

Then spake the Lord to Paul in the night by a vision. *Ac.* 18: 9.

Eye hath not seen, nor ear heard, neither have entered into the heart of man, the things which God hath prepared for them that love him. *1 Co.* 2: 9.

Filthy dreamers defile the flesh. *Jude* 1: 8.

See also

Christ, Vision of; God, Vision of; Vision.

Drink

Wine that maketh glad the heart of man. *Ps.* 104: 15.

Come ye to the waters; . . . come, buy wine and milk. *Is.* 55: 1.

I was thirsty, and ye gave me drink. *Mat.* 25: 35.

He shall be great in the sight of the Lord, and shall drink neither wine nor strong drink. *Lu.* 1: 15.

If any man thirst, let him come unto me, and drink. *Jn.* 7: 37.

They drank of that spiritual Rock that followed them: and that Rock was Christ. *1 Co.* 10: 4.

Whether therefore ye eat, or drink, or whatsoever ye do, do all to the glory of God. *1 Co.* 10: 31.

We . . . have been all made to drink into one Spirit. *1 Co.* 12: 13.

Drink no longer water but use a little wine for thy stomach's sake. *1 Ti.* 5: 23.

See also

Drunkenness; God, Thirst for; Intoxication; Milk; Thirst; Water; Wine.

Drought

My soul thirsteth for thee, my flesh longeth for thee in a dry and thirsty land, where no water is. *Ps.* 63: 1.

The rebellious dwell in a dry land. *Ps.* 68: 6.

He turneth rivers into a wilderness, and the watersprings into dry ground. *Ps.* 107: 33.

Ye shall be as an oak whose leaf fadeth, and as a garden that hath no water. *Is.* 1: 30.

The parched ground shall become a pool, and the thirsty land springs of water. *Is.* 35: 7.

When the poor and needy seek water, and there is none, and their tongue faileth for thirst, I the Lord will hear them. *Is.* 41: 17.

I will pour water upon him that is thirsty, and floods upon the dry ground. *Is.* 44: 3.

He shall grow . . . as a root out of a dry ground. *Is.* 53: 2.

The Lord shall . . . satisfy thy soul in drought. *Is.* 58: 11.

Thou shalt be like a watered garden, and like a spring of water. *Is.* 58: 11.

He . . . shall inhabit the parched places in the wilderness. *Je.* 17: 6.

I called for a drought upon the land, and upon the mountains, and upon the corn, and upon the new wine, and upon the oil, and upon that which the ground bringeth forth. *Hag.* 1: 11.
See also
Desert; Dryness; Wilderness; Withering.

Drudgery

Moses kept the flock of Jethro. . . . And the Angel of the Lord appeared unto him in a flame of fire. *Ex.* 3: 1, 2.
Fulfil your works, your daily tasks, as when there was straw. *Ex.* 5: 13.
As his part is that goeth down to the battle, so shall his part be that tarrieth by the stuff. *1 S.* 30: 24.
All things are full of labour; man cannot utter it. *Ec.* 1: 8.
I hated all my labour which I had taken under the sun. *Ec.* 2: 18.
What hath man of all his labour, and of the vexation of his heart, wherein he hath laboured under the sun? *Ec.* 2: 22.
Yet is there no end of all his labour. *Ec.* 4: 8.
For whom do I labour, and bereave my soul of good? This is also vanity, yea, it is a sore travail. *Ec.* 4: 8.
They shall walk, and not faint. *Is.* 40: 31.
Come unto me, all ye that labour and are heavy laden. *Mat.* 11: 23.
Martha was cumbered about much serving. *Lu.* 10: 40.
Labouring night and day. *1 Th.* 2: 9.
See also
Burden; Heaviness; Labor; Toil; Travail.

Drunkenness

Wine is a mocker, strong drink is raging. *Pr.* 20: 1.
The drunkard and the glutton shall come to poverty. *Pr.* 23: 21.
The priest and the prophet have erred through strong drink, they are swallowed up of wine. *Is.* 28: 7.
We will fill ourselves with strong drink; and to morrow shall be as this day. *Is.* 56: 12.
Take heed to yourselves, lest at any time your hearts be overcharged with surfeiting, and drunkenness, and cares of this life, and so that day come upon you unawares. *Lu.* 21: 34.
These are not drunken, as ye suppose. *Ac.* 2: 15.
Nor drunkards . . . shall inherit the kingdom of God. *1 Co.* 6: 10.
Be not drunk with wine, wherein is excess; but be filled with the spirit. *Ep.* 5: 18.
See also
Dissipation; Grape; Intoxication; Wine.

Dryness

Dust thou art, and unto dust shalt thou return. *Ge.* 3: 19.
He found him in a desert land. *De.* 32: 10.
We have heard how the Lord dried up the water of the Red sea. *Jos.* 2: 10.
In a dry and thirsty land, where no water is. *Ps.* 63: 1.
I am like an owl of the desert. *Ps.* 102: 6.
He turneth . . . A fruitful land into barrenness. *Ps.* 107: 33, 34.
He turneth the wilderness into a standing water, and dry ground into watersprings. *Ps.* 107: 35.
A man shall be . . . as rivers of water in a dry place. *Is.* 32: 2.
I will even make a way in the wilderness, and rivers in the desert. *Is.* 43: 19.
I will dry up her sea, and make her springs dry. *Je.* 51: 36.
O ye dry bones, hear the word of the Lord. *Eze.* 37: 4.
Come ye yourselves apart into a desert place, and rest a while. *Mk.* 6: 31.

Dullness

They know not, neither will they understand; they walk on in darkness. *Ps.* 82: 5.
A brutish man knoweth not; neither doth a fool understand this. *Ps.* 92: 6.
They are altogether brutish. *Je.* 10: 8.
Let his heart be changed from man's, and let a beast's heart be given unto him. *Da.* 4: 16.
They know not the thoughts of the Lord, neither understand they his counsel. *Mi.* 4: 12.
And Jesus said, Are ye also yet without understanding? *Mat.* 15: 16.
How is it that ye do not discern this time? *Lu.* 12: 56.
They understood none of these things: and this saying was hid from them, neither knew they the things which were spoken. *Lu.* 18: 34.
O fools, and slow of heart to believe all that the prophets have spoken. *Lu.* 24: 25.
Have I been so long time with you, and yet hast thou not known me, Philip? *Jn.* 14: 9.
There is none that understandeth, there is none that seeketh after God. *Ro.* 3: 11.
Ever learning, and never able to come to the knowledge of the truth. *2 Ti.* 3: 7.
See also
Apathy; Blindness; Deafness; Dimness; Ignorance; Insensibility.

Dumbness

Who hath made man's mouth? or who maketh the dumb? . . . have not I the Lord? *Ex.* 4: 11.
Then shall . . . the tongue of the dumb sing. *Is.* 35: 6.
As a sheep before her shearers is dumb, so he openeth not his mouth. *Is.* 53: 7.
In that day . . . thou shalt speak, and be no more dumb. *Eze.* 24: 27.
When the devil was cast out, the dumb spake. *Mat.* 9: 33.
There was brought unto him one possessed of a devil, blind, and dumb: and he healed him. *Mat.* 12: 22.
He maketh both the deaf to hear, and the dumb to speak. *Mk.* 7: 37.
Thou dumb and deaf spirit, I charge thee, come out of him. *Mk.* 9: 25.
Thou shalt be dumb, and not able to speak, until the day that these things shall be performed. *Lu.* 1: 20.
The dumb ass speaking with man's voice forbad the madness of the prophet. *2 Pe.* 2: 16.
See also
Lip; Mouth; Speech; Tongue.

Duplicity

So these nations feared the Lord, and served their graven images. 2 K. 17: 41.

They change the night into day. Jb. 17: 12.

The counsels of the wicked are deceit. Pr. 12: 5.

Lying lips are abomination to the Lord. Pr. 12: 22.

The folly of fools is deceit. Pr. 14: 8.

Blind guides, which strain at a gnat, and swallow a camel. Mat. 23: 24.

Speaking lies in hypocrisy; having their conscience seared with a hot iron. 1 Ti. 4: 2.

The wisdom that is from above is . . . without hypocrisy. Ja. 3: 17.

See also

Betrayal; Cheat; Craftiness; Deceit; Faithlessness; Falsehood; Fraud; Hypocrisy; Inconsistency; Lie; Treachery.

Duration

Blessed of the Lord be his land, . . . for the precious things of the lasting hills. De. 33: 13, 15.

Canst thou number the months? Jb. 39: 2.

His anger endureth but a moment. Ps. 30: 5.

Weeping may endure for a night, but joy cometh in the morning. Ps. 30: 5.

The goodness of God endureth continually. Ps. 52: 1.

In his days shall the righteous flourish; and abundance of peace so long as the moon endureth. Ps. 72: 7.

His name shall be continued as long as the sun. Ps. 72: 17.

His mercy is everlasting. Ps. 100: 5.

His truth endureth to all generations. Ps. 100: 5.

Thou, O Lord, shalt endure for ever. Ps. 102: 12.

His mercy endureth for ever. Ps. 136: 1.

Riches are not for ever: and doth the crown endure to every generation? Pr. 27: 24.

Why is my pain perpetual? Je. 15: 18.

Go thou thy way till the end be. Da. 12: 13.

He that shall endure unto the end, the same shall be saved. Mat. 24: 13.

It is easier for heaven and earth to pass, than one tittle of the law to fail. Lu. 16: 17.

As many as were ordained to eternal life believed. Ac. 13: 48.

Now abideth faith, hope, charity, these three; but the greatest of these is charity. 1 Co. 13: 13.

See also

Time.

Dust

The Lord God formed man of the dust of the ground. Ge. 2: 7.

Dust shalt thou eat all the days of thy life. Ge. 3: 14.

Dust thou art, and unto dust shalt thou return. Ge. 3: 19.

As for the earth, . . . it hath dust of gold. Jb. 28: 5, 6.

I am become like dust and ashes. Jb. 30: 19.

Thou hast brought me into the dust of death. Ps. 22: 15.

He remembereth that we are dust. Ps. 103: 14.

Then shall the dust return to the earth as it was: and the spirit shall return unto God who gave it. Ec. 12: 7.

The lofty city, he layeth it low; he layeth it low, even to the ground. Is. 26: 5.

The clouds are the dust of his feet. Na. 1: 3.

See also

Dirt; Earth; Ground; Mortality; Soil.

Duty

That I may prove them, whether they will walk in my law, or no. Ex. 16: 4.

Ye have dwelt long enough in this mount. De. 1: 6.

Turn you, and take your journey, and go. De. 1: 7.

Thou shalt do that which is right and good in the sight of the Lord: that it may be well with thee. De. 6: 18.

Give unto the Lord the glory due unto his name. 1 Ch. 16: 29.

So will I sing praise unto thy name for ever, that I may daily perform my vows. Ps. 61: 8.

Withhold not good from them to whom it is due. Pr. 3: 27.

Take fast hold of instruction; let her not go: keep her; for she is thy life. Pr. 4: 13.

Let us hear the conclusion of the whole matter: Fear God, and keep his commandments: for this is the whole duty of man. Ec. 12: 13.

The word of the Lord came unto Jonah, . . . saying, Arise, go to Nineveh, . . . but Jonah rose up to flee unto Tarshish. Jon. 1: 1–3.

Wist ye not that I must be about my Father's business? Lu. 2: 49.

He stood over her, and rebuked the fever; and it left her: and immediately she arose and ministered unto them. Lu. 4: 39.

I have a baptism to be baptized with; and how am I straitened till it be accomplished! Lu. 12: 50.

How much owest thou? Lu. 16: 5.

We have done that which was our duty to do. Lu. 17: 10.

Is it lawful for us to give tribute unto Caesar, or no? . . . And he said unto them, Render therefore unto Caesar the things which be Caesar's, and unto God the things which be God's. Lu. 20: 22, 25.

I must work the works of him that sent me, while it is day. Jn. 9: 4.

Render therefore to all their dues: tribute to whom tribute is due; custom to whom custom; fear to whom fear; honor to whom honor. Ro. 13: 7.

Owe no man any thing, but to love one another. Ro. 13: 8.

I will tarry at Ephesus. . . . For a great door and effectual is opened unto me, and there are many adversaries. 1 Co. 16: 8, 9.

Now we exhort you, brethren, warn them that are unruly, comfort the feebleminded, support the weak, be patient toward all men. 1 Th. 5: 14.

Honour all men. Love the brotherhood. Fear God. Honour the king. 1 Pe. 2: 17.

See also

Debt; Indebtedness; Obligation; Requirement; Respect; Responsibility; Reverence; Task; Tribute.

Dwelling

Their houses are safe from fear. *Jb.* **21: 9.**
Lord, who shall abide in thy tabernacle? who shall dwell in thy holy hill? *Ps.* **15: 1.**
Why leap ye, ye high hills? this is the hill which God desireth to dwell in. *Ps.* **68: 16.**
Lord, thou hast been our dwelling place in all generations. *Ps.* **90: 1.**
He that dwelleth in the secret place of the most High shall abide under the shadow of the Almighty. *Ps.* **91: 1.**
We shall live with him by the power of God toward you. *2 Co.* **13: 4.**
That Christ may dwell in your hearts by faith. *Ep.* **3: 17.**
Your life is hid with Christ in God. *Col.* **3: 3.**
To whom coming, as unto a living stone, . . . Ye also, as lively stones, . . . built up a spiritual house. *1 Pe.* **2: 4, 5.**
See also
Abode; God, House of; Habitation; Home; House; Lodge; Residence; Roof; Shelter; Tenant.

E

Eagerness

Come with me, and see my zeal for the Lord. *2 K.* **10: 16.**
So we laboured in the work: and half of them held the spears from the rising of the morning till the stars appeared. *Ne.* **4: 21.**
My zeal hath consumed me. *Ps.* **119: 139.**
Whatsoever thy hand findeth to do, do it with thy might. *Ec.* **9: 10.**
For Zion's sake will I not hold my peace, and for Jerusalem's sake I will not rest, until the righteousness thereof go forth as brightness, and the salvation thereof as a lamp that burneth. *Is.* **62: 1.**
His word was in mine heart as a burning fire shut up in my bones. *Je.* **20: 9.**
Ye shall seek me, and find me, when ye shall search for me with all your heart. *Je.* **29: 13.**
The zeal of thine house hath eaten me up. *Jn.* **2: 17.**
My heart's desire and prayer to God for Israel is, that they might be saved. *Ro.* **10: 1.**
If by any means I may provoke to emulation them which are my flesh, and might save some of them. *Ro.* **11: 14.**
Striving according to his working, which worketh in me mightily. *Col.* **1: 29.**
See also
Ardor; Earnestness; Enthusiasm; Fervor; Zeal; Zest.

Eagle

The Lord shall bring a nation against thee from far, from the end of the earth, as swift as the eagle flieth. *De.* **28: 49.**
As an eagle stirreth up her nest, fluttereth over her young, spreadeth abroad her wings, taketh them, beareth them on her wings: So the Lord alone did lead him. *De.* **32: 11, 12.**
My days are swifter than a post. . . . They are passed away as the swift ships: as the eagle that hasteth to the prey. *Jb.* **9: 26.**
Doth the eagle mount up at thy command, and make her nest on high? *Jb.* **39: 27.**
Thy youth is renewed like the eagle's. *Ps.* **103: 5.**
Riches certainly make themselves wings; they fly away as an eagle toward heaven. *Pr.* **23: 5.**
They that wait upon the Lord shall renew their strength; they shall mount up with wings as eagles. *Is.* **40: 31.**
Though thou shouldest make thy nest as high as the eagle, I will bring thee down from thence, saith the Lord. *Je.* **49: 16.**
Wheresoever the carcass is there will the eagles be gathered together. *Mat.* **24: 28.**

Ear

Who maketh the dumb, or deaf, or the seeing, or the blind? have not I the Lord? *Ex.* **4: 11.**
The ear of the wise seeketh knowledge. *Pr.* **18: 15.**
The hearing ear, and the seeing eye, the Lord hath made even both of them. *Pr.* **20: 12.**
Whoso stoppeth his ears at the cry of the poor, he also shall cry himself, but shall not be heard. *Pr.* **21: 13.**
The ears of them that hear shall hearken. *Is.* **32: 3.**
The Lord God hath opened mine ear. *Is.* **50: 5.**
Neither his ear heavy, that it cannot hear. *Is.* **59: 1.**
Their ears shall be deaf. *Mi.* **7: 16.**
Blessed are . . . your ears, for they hear. *Mat.* **13: 16.**
If the ear shall say, Because I am not the eye, I am not of the body; is it therefore not of the body? *1 Co.* **12: 16.**
To day if ye will hear his voice. *He.* **3: 7.**
See also
Deafness; Hearing; Listening.

Earnestness

Take diligent heed to do the commandment and the law. *Jos.* **22: 5.**
Turn ye even to me with all your heart. *Jo.* **2: 12.**
With both hands earnestly. *Mi.* **7: 3.**
The earnest expectation of the creature waiteth. *Ro.* **8: 19.**
Covet earnestly the best gifts. *1 Co.* **12: 31.**
In this we groan, earnestly desiring to be clothed upon with our house which is from heaven. *2 Co.* **5: 2.**
He told us your earnest desire. *2 Co.* **7: 7.**
As ye abound in every thing, in faith, and utterance, and knowledge, and in all diligence. *2 Co.* **8: 7.**
As the servants of Christ, doing the will of God from the heart. *Ep.* **6: 6.**
Whatsoever ye do, do it heartily, as to the Lord. *Col.* **3: 23.**

We ought to give the more earnest heed to the things which we have heard. *He.* **2: 1.**

Looking diligently lest any man fail of the grace of God. *He.* **12: 15.**

See also

Ardor: Eagerness; Enthusiasm; Fervor; Gravity; Zeal.

Earth

All the earth shall be filled with the glory of the Lord. *Nu.* **14: 21.**

The pillars of the earth are the Lord's. *1 S.* **2: 8.**

The earth is the Lord's, and the fulness thereof. *Ps.* **24: 1.**

Thou visitest the earth, and waterest it. *Ps.* **65: 9.**

And blessed be his glorious name for ever: and let the whole earth be filled with his glory. *Ps.* **72: 19.**

In his hand are the deep places of the earth. *Ps.* **95: 4.**

One generation passeth away, and another generation cometh: but the earth abideth for ever. *Ec.* **1: 4.**

The earth shall be full of the knowledge of the Lord, as the waters cover the sea. *Is.* **11: 9.**

Do not I fill heaven and earth? saith the Lord. *Je.* **23: 24.**

Thy will be done in earth, as it is in heaven. *Mat.* **6: 10.**

We have this treasure in earthen vessels, that the excellency of the power may be of God, and not of us. *2 Co.* **4: 7.**

See also

Dirt; Globe; Ground; Land; Soil; World.

Earthquake

Then the earth shook and trembled; the foundations of heaven moved and shook, because he was wroth. *2 S.* **22: 8.**

After the wind an earthquake; but the Lord was not in the earthquake. *1 K.* **19: 11.**

Which shaketh the earth out of her place, and the pillars thereof tremble. *Jb.* **9: 6.**

Then the earth shook and trembled; the foundations also of the hills moved and were shaken. *Ps.* **18: 7.**

Therefore will not we fear, though the earth be removed, and though the mountains be carried into the midst of the sea. *Ps.* **46: 2.**

Tremble, thou earth, at the presence of the Lord. *Ps.* **114: 7.**

They shall go into the holes of the rocks, and into the caves of the earth, for fear of the Lord, and for the glory of his majesty, when he ariseth to shake terribly the earth. *Is.* **2: 19.**

The earth shall reel to and fro like a drunkard. *Is.* **24: 20.**

Thou shalt be visited of the Lord of hosts with thunder, and with earthquake, and great noise, with storm and tempest, and the flame of devouring fire. *Is.* **29: 6.**

The earth shall quake before them; the heavens shall tremble. *Jo.* **2: 10.**

There shall be famines, and pestilences, and earthquakes, in divers places. *Mat.* **24: 7.**

Behold, there was a great earthquake: for the angel of the Lord descended from heaven. *Mat.* **28: 2.**

Whose voice then shook the earth. *He.* **12: 26.**

There were voices, and thunderings, and lightnings, and an earthquake. *Re.* **8: 5.**

There was a great earthquake; such as was not since men were upon the earth, so mighty an earthquake, and so great. *Re.* **16: 18.**

Ease

I was at ease, but he hath broken me asunder. *Jb.* **16: 12.**

One dieth in his full strength, being wholly at ease and quiet. *Jb.* **21: 23.**

When he giveth quietness, who then can make trouble? *Jb.* **34: 29.**

The lines are fallen unto me in pleasant places; yea, I have a goodly heritage. *Ps.* **16: 6.**

Thy comforts delight my soul. *Ps.* **94: 19.**

Ye shall eat in plenty, and be satisfied. *Jo.* **2: 26.**

Woe to them that are at ease in Zion. *Am.* **6: 1.**

It shall come to pass at that time, that I will search Jerusalem with candles, and punish the men that are settled on their lees: that say in their heart, The Lord will not do good, neither will he do evil. *Zph.* **1: 12.**

I will say to my soul, Soul, thou hast much goods laid up for many years; take thine ease, eat, drink, and be merry. *Lu.* **12: 19.**

See also

Christ, the Comforter; Comfort; Comforter; Consolation; Contentment; Enjoyment; Quiet; Relief; Repose; Rest; Satisfaction; Solace.

East

The Lord God planted a garden eastward in Eden. *Ge.* **2: 8.**

Lift up now thine eyes, and look from the place where thou art northward, and southward, and eastward, and westward: For all the land which thou seest, to thee will I give it. *Ge.* **13: 14, 15.**

As far as the east is from the west, so far hath he removed our transgressions from us. *Ps.* **103: 12.**

He . . . gathered them out of the lands, from the east, and from the west, from the north, and from the south. *Ps.* **107: 2, 3.**

Who raised up the righteous man from the east? *Is.* **41: 2.**

They worshipped the sun toward the east. *Eze.* **8: 16.**

The glory of the God of Israel came from the way of the east. *Eze.* **43: 2.**

Behold, there came wise men from the east to Jerusalem. *Mat.* **2: 1.**

We have seen his star in the east, and are come to worship him. *Mat.* **2: 2.**

Many shall come from the east and west, and shall sit down with Abraham, and Isaac, and Jacob, in the kingdom of heaven. *Mat.* **8: 11.**

As the lightning cometh out of the east, and shineth even unto the west; so shall also the coming of the Son of man be. *Mat.* **24: 27.**

Easter

Underneath are the everlasting arms. *De.* **33: 27.**

If a man die, shall he live again? *Jb.* **14: 14.**

O death, I will be thy plagues; O grave, I will be thy destruction. *Ho.* **13: 14.**

As it began to dawn toward the first day of the week, came Mary Magdalene and the other Mary to see the sepulchre. *Mat.* 28: 1.

Fear not ye: . . . He is not here: for he is risen, . . . Come, see the place where the Lord lay. *Mat.* 28: 5, 6.

Go quickly, and tell his disciples that he is risen from the dead. *Mat.* 28: 7.

They departed quickly from the sepulchre with fear and great joy. *Mat.* 28: 8.

When they looked, they saw that the stone was rolled away. *Mk.* 16: 4.

Behold the place where they laid him. *Mk.* 16: 6.

Now when Jesus was risen early the first day of the week, he appeared first to Mary Magdalene. *Mk.* 16: 9.

The Son of man must be delivered into the hands of sinful men, and be crucified, and the third day rise again. *Lu.* 24: 7.

I am the resurrection, and the life: he that believeth in me, though he were dead, yet shall he live. *Jn.* 11: 25.

If Christ be not risen, then is our preaching vain, and your faith is also vain. *1 Co.* 15: 14.

In Christ shall all be made alive. *1 Co.* 15: 22.

By faith . . . he being dead yet speaketh. *He.* 11: 4.

Be thou faithful unto death, and I will give thee a crown of life. *Re.* 2: 10.

See also
Christ, Resurrection of; Eternity; Immortality; Life, the Eternal; Resurrection.

Ecstasy

This is none other but the house of God. *Ge.* 28: 17.

I saw the Lord sitting on his throne, and all the host of heaven standing by him. *1 K.* 22: 19.

In thy presence is fulness of joy. *Ps.* 16: 11.

There is a river, the streams whereof shall make glad the city of God. *Ps.* 46: 4.

There shall be showers of blessing. *Eze.* 34: 26.

I bring you good tidings of great joy. *Lu.* 2: 10.

Hereafter ye shall see heaven open, and the angels of God ascending and descending upon the Son of man. *Jn.* 1: 51.

We all, with open face beholding as in a glass the glory of the Lord, are changed into the same image from glory to glory. *2 Co.* 3:18.

Our light affliction . . . worketh for us a far more exceeding and eternal weight of glory. *2 Co.* 4: 17.

He was caught up into paradise, and heard unspeakable words, which it is not lawful for a man to utter. *2 Co.* 12: 4.

The Lamb which is in the midst of the throne shall feed them, and shall lead them unto living fountains of waters: and God shall wipe away all tears from their eyes. *Re.* 7: 17.

I saw a new heaven and a new earth. *Re.* 21: 1.

God shall wipe away all tears from their eyes; and there shall be no more death, neither sorrow, nor crying, neither shall there be any more pain. *Re.* 21: 4.

See also
Christ, Joy in; Delight; Exaltation; Exultation; Joy; Rapture.

Eden

The Lord God planted a garden eastward in Eden. *Ge.* 2: 8.

The Lord God took the man, and put him into the garden of Eden. *Ge.* 2: 15.

The Lord God sent him forth from the garden of Eden. *Ge.* 3: 23.

He placed at the east of the garden of Eden Cherubims, and a flaming sword which turned every way, to keep the way of the tree of life. *Ge.* 3: 24.

He will comfort all her waste places; and he will make her wilderness like Eden, and her desert like the garden of the Lord. *Is.* 51: 3.

Thou hast been in Eden the garden of God. *Eze.* 28: 13.

All the trees of Eden, that were in the garden of God, envied him. *Eze.* 31: 9.

This land that was desolate has become like the garden of Eden. *Eze.* 36: 35.

The land is as the garden of Eden before them, and behind them a desolate wilderness. *Jo.* 2: 3.

See also
Paradise.

Edification

Then had the churches rest, . . . and were edified. *Ac.* 9: 31.

Instructed out of the law. *Ro.* 2: 18.

Who hath known the mind of the Lord, that he may instruct him? But we have the mind of Christ. *1 Co.* 2: 16.

Knowledge puffeth up, but charity edifieth. *1 Co.* 8: 1.

All things are lawful for me, but all things edify not. *1 Co.* 10: 23.

He that prophesieth speaketh unto men to edification, and exhortation, and comfort. *1 Co.* 14: 3.

He that speaketh in an unknown tongue edifieth himself. *1 Co.* 14: 4.

We do all things, dearly beloved, for your edifying. *2 Co.* 12: 19.

See also
Admonition; Advice; Builder; Christ, the Teacher; Counsel; Education; Instruction; Knowledge; Teaching; Training.

Education

Thou shalt teach them diligently unto thy children. *De.* 6: 7.

Train up a child in the way he should go: and when he is old, he will not depart from it. *Pr.* 22: 6.

In the morning sow thy seed, and in the evening withhold not thine hand: for thou knowest not whether shall prosper, either this or that, or whether they both shall be alike good. *Ec.* 11: 6.

For precept must be upon precept, precept upon precept; line upon line, line upon line; here a little, and there a little. *Is.* 28: 10.

Ephraim is a cake not turned. *Ho.* 7: 8.

Learn of me. *Mat.* 11: 29.

Whoso shall offend one of these little ones which believe in me, it were better for him that a millstone were hanged about his neck, and that he were drowned in the depth of the sea. *Mat.* 18: 6.

Go ye therefore, and teach all nations. *Mat.* 28: 19.

What manner of child shall this be! *Lu.* 1: 66.

Jesus increased in wisdom and stature, and in favor with God and man. *Lu.* 2: 52.

Canst thou speak Greek? *Ac.* 21: 37.

Let every one of us please his neighbour for his good to edification. *Ro.* 15: 2.

The heir, as long as he is a child, . . . is under tutors and governors until the time appointed of the father. *Ga.* 4: 1, 2.

That we . . . may grow up into him in all things, which is the head, even Christ. *Ep.* 4: 14, 15.

Ye fathers, provoke not your children to wrath: but bring them up in the nurture and admonition of the Lord. *Ep.* 6: 4.

These things command and teach. *1 Ti.* 4: 11.

For it became him . . . to make the captain of their salvation perfect through sufferings. *He.* 2: 10.

See also

Admonition; Christ, the Teacher; Education; Graduation; Instruction; Knowledge; Pupil; School; Study; Teaching; Teaching, False; Training.

Effort

Except the Lord build the house, they labour in vain that build it. *Ps.* 127: 7.

Labour not to be rich. *Pr.* 23: 4.

Prepare thy work without, and make it fit for thyself in the field. *Pr.* 24: 27.

The sleep of a labouring man is sweet. *Ec.* 5: 12.

Be strong, all ye people of the land, saith the Lord, and work. *Hag.* 2: 4.

Strive to enter in at the strait gate. *Lu.* 13: 24.

Every man shall receive his own reward according to his own labour. *1 Co.* 3: 8.

I laboured more abundantly than they all: yet not I, but the grace of God which was with me. *1 Co.* 15: 10.

We labour, that, whether present or absent, we may be accepted of him. *2 Co.* 5: 9.

Endeavouring to keep the unity of the Spirit in the bond of peace. *Ep.* 4: 3.

Stand fast in one spirit, with one mind striving together for the faith of the gospel. *Ph.* 1: 27.

.I also labour, striving according to his working, which worketh in me mightily. *Col.* 1: 29.

Study to be quiet, and to do your own business, and to work with your own hands. *1 Th.* 4: 11.

Let us labour therefore to enter into that rest. *He.* 4: 11.

See also

Endeavor, Labor; Trial.

Egotism

Verily every man at his best state is altogether vanity. *Ps.* 39: 5.

Surely every man walketh in a vain shew. *Ps.* 39: 6.

Lord, my heart is not haughty, nor mine eyes lofty. *Ps.* 131: 1.

A man's pride shall bring him low. *Pr.* 29: 23.

Vanity of vanities; all is vanity. *Ec.* 1: 2.

He saith, By the strength of my hand I have done it. *Is.* 10: 13.

Thou hast said in thine heart, . . . I will ascend above the heights of the clouds; I will be like the most High. *Is.* 14: 13, 14.

I will exalt my throne above the stars of God. *Is.* 14: 13.

Walk not as other Gentiles walk, in the vanity of their mind. *Ep.* 4: 17.

Let nothing be done through strife or vainglory. *Ph.* 2: 3.

See also

Arrogance; Boasting; Complacency; Conceit; Haughtiness; Pride; Selfishness; Self-Satisfaction.

Egypt

I will go down with thee into Egypt. *Ge.* 46: 4.

There arose up a new king over Egypt, which knew not Joseph. *Ex.* 1: 8.

I have surely seen the affliction of my people which are in Egypt. *Ex.* 3: 7.

The Egyptians shall know that I am the Lord. *Ex.* 7: 5.

By strength of hand the Lord brought us out from Egypt, from the house of bondage. *Ex.* 13: 14.

Would to God we had died by the hand of the Lord in the land of Egypt. *Ex.* 16: 3.

I am the Lord thy God, which have brought thee out of the land of Egypt. *Ex.* 20: 2.

They said one to another, Let us make a captain, and let us return unto Egypt. *Nu.* 14: 4.

We were Pharaoh's bondmen in Egypt; and the Lord brought us out of Egypt with a mighty hand. *De.* 6: 21.

Did not the Lord bring us up from Egypt? but now the Lord hath forsaken us. *Ju.* 6: 13.

In that day shall there be an altar to the Lord in the midst of the land of Egypt. *Is.* 19: 19.

Woe to them that go down to Egypt for help. *Is.* 31: 1.

The Egyptians are men, and not God; and their horses flesh, and not spirit. *Is.* 31: 3.

All the inhabitants of Egypt shall know that I am the Lord. *Eze.* 29: 6.

They shall tremble as a bird out of Egypt. *Ho.* 11: 11.

Out of Egypt have I called my son. *Mat.* 2: 15.

Esteeming the reproach of Christ greater riches than the treasures in Egypt. *He.* 11: 26.

By faith he forsook Egypt, not fearing the wrath of the king. *He.* 11: 27.

See also

Bondage; Captivity; Exile; Slavery.

Elder

Moses with the elders of Israel commanded the people, saying, keep all the commandments which I command you this day. *De.* 27: 1.

Why do thy disciples transgress the tradition of the elders? *Mat.* 15: 2.

When they had ordained them elders in every church, and had prayed with fasting, they commended them to the Lord. *Ac.* 14: 23.

Rebuke not an elder, but entreat him as a father. *1 Ti.* 5: 1.

Let the elders that rule well be counted worthy of double honour, especially they who labour in the word and doctrine. *1 Ti.* 5: 17.

Against an elder receive not an accusation, but before two or three witnesses. *1 Ti.* **5: 19.**

Ordain elders in every city. *Tit.* **1: 5.**

By it the elders obtained a good report. *He.* **11: 2.**

Is any sick among you? let him call for the elders of the church; and let them pray over him, anointing him with oil in the name of the Lord. *Ja.* **5: 14.**

The elders which are among you I exhort, who am also an elder. *1 Pe.* **5: 1.**

Round about the throne were four and twenty seats: and upon the seats I saw four and twenty elders sitting, clothed in white raiment; and they had on their heads crowns of gold. *Re.* **4: 4.**

In the midst of the elders stood a Lamb as it had been slain. *Re.* **5: 6.**

See also

Age; Honor; Oldness; Respect; Senior.

Election

It shall be that the man whom the Lord doth choose, he shall be holy. *Nu.* **16: 7.**

The Lord did not set his love upon you, nor choose you, because ye were more in number than any people; for ye were the fewest of all people. *De.* **7: 7.**

The Lord shall yet comfort Zion, and shall yet choose Jerusalem. *Zch.* **1: 17.**

Many be called, but few chosen. *Mat.* **20: 16.**

Christ, the chosen of God. *Lu.* **23: 35.**

I know whom I have chosen. *Jn.* **13: 18.**

Ye have not chosen me, but I have chosen you. *Jn.* **15: 16.**

The called of Jesus Christ. *Ro.* **1: 6.**

That the purpose of God according to election might stand. *Ro.* **9: 11.**

Paul, an apostle, (not of men, neither by man, but by Jesus Christ, and God the Father). *Ga.* **1: 1.**

Peter, an apostle of Jesus Christ, to the . . . elect. *1 Pe.* **1: 2.**

Elect according to the foreknowledge of God the Father, through sanctification of the Spirit. *1 Pe.* **1: 2.**

Chosen of God, and precious. *1 Pe.* **2: 4.**

Ye are a chosen generation, a royal priesthood, a holy nation, a peculiar people. *1 Pe.* **2: 9.**

See also

Appointment; Choice; Foreordination; Predestination.

Elevation

The trees went forth on a time to anoint a king over them. *Ju.* **9: 8.**

Thou also hast lifted me up on high. *2 S.* **22: 49.**

Lift up your heads, O ye gates; and be ye lift up, ye everlasting doors. *Ps.* **24: 7.**

His foundation is in the holy mountains. *Ps.* **87: 1.**

As the heaven is high above the earth, so great is his mercy toward them that fear him. *Ps.* **103: 11.**

The mountains skipped like rams, and the little hills like lambs. *Ps.* **114: 4.**

The mountain of the Lord's house shall be established in the top of the mountains, and shall be exalted above the hills. *Is.* **2: 2.**

Jesus taketh Peter, James, and John his

brother, and bringeth them up into an high mountain apart. *Mat.* **17: 1.**

He departed again into a mountain himself alone. *Jn.* **6: 15.**

I, if I be lifted up from the earth, will draw all men unto me. *Jn.* **12: 32.**

God . . . hath raised us up together, and made us sit together in heavenly places in Christ Jesus. *Ep.* **2: 4, 6.**

Set your affection on things above, not on things on the earth. *Col.* **3: 2.**

See also

Eminence; Exaltation; Height; Mountain; Summit; Top.

Eloquence

O my Lord, I am not eloquent, neither heretofore, nor since thou hast spoken to thy servant: but I am slow of speech, and of a slow tongue. *Ex.* **4: 10.**

The tongue of the just is as choice silver. *Pr.* **10: 20.**

A word fitly spoken is like apples of gold in pictures of silver. *Pr.* **25: 11.**

The Lord . . . doth take away . . . the eloquent orator. *Is.* **3: 1, 3.**

Then flew one of the seraphims unto me, having a live coal in his hand, which he had taken with the tongs from off the altar: And he laid it upon my mouth, and said, Lo, this hath touched thy lips. *Is.* **6: 6, 7.**

And touched his tongue. *Mk.* **7: 33.**

Upon a set day Herod, arrayed in royal apparel, sat upon his throne, and made an oration unto them. *Ac.* **12: 21.**

The people gave a shout, saying, It is the voice of a god, and not of a man. *Ac.* **12: 22.**

A certain Jew named Apollos, born at Alexandria, an eloquent man. *Ac.* **18: 24.**

Being fervent in the spirit, he spake and taught diligently the things of the Lord. *Ac.* **18: 25.**

I . . . came not with excellency of speech. *1 Co.* **2: 1.**

My speech and my preaching was not with enticing words of man's wisdom. *1 Co.* **2: 4.**

The word of God is quick, and powerful, and sharper than any twoedged sword. *He.* **4: 12.**

See also

Argument; God, Voice of; God, Word of; Mouth; Speech; Tongue; Utterance; Word.

Emancipation

Let my people go. *Ex.* **5: 1.**

Proclaim liberty throughout all the land unto all the inhabitants thereof. *Le.* **25: 10.**

Because the Lord loved you, . . . hath the Lord brought you out with a mighty hand. *De.* **7: 8.**

Out of prison he cometh to reign. *Ec.* **4: 14.**

That thou mayest say to the prisoners, Go forth. *Is.* **49: 9.**

Kings shall be thy nursing fathers, and their queens thy nursing mothers: they shall bow down to thee. *Is.* **49: 23.**

I will be found of you, saith the Lord: and I will turn away your captivity. *Je.* **29: 14.**

Ye shall find the babe wrapped in swaddling clothes. *Lu.* **2: 12.**

Behold, the men whom ye put in prison are standing in the temple. *Ac.* **5: 25.**

The same did God send to be a ruler and a deliverer. *Ac.* 7: 35.

He . . . declared unto them how the Lord had brought him out of the prison. *Ac.* 12: 17.

Immediately all the doors were opened, and every one's bands were loosed. *Ac.* 16: 26.

See also

Christ, the Redeemer; Christ, the Saviour; Democracy; Freedom; God, Deliverance of; God, the Redeemer; God, Salvation of; Independence; Liberty; Ransom; Redemption; Release; Rescue; Salvation.

Emigration

I have been a stranger in a strange land. *Ex.* 2: 22.

Love ye therefore the stranger: for ye were strangers in the land of Egypt. *De.* 10: 19.

The Lord also will be a refuge for the oppressed. *Ps.* 9: 9.

As a bird that wandereth from her nest, so is a man that wandereth from his place. *Pr.* 27: 8.

Weep sore for him that goeth away: for he shall return no more, nor see his native country. *Je.* 22: 10.

Moses . . . was a stranger in the land of Madian. *Ac.* 7: 29.

See also

Exile; Expatriation; Migration; Refugee; Stranger.

Eminence

The bramble said unto the trees, If in truth ye anoint me king over you, then come and put your trust in my shadow. *Ju.* 9: 15.

Deck thyself now with majesty and excellency. *Jb.* 40: 10.

Thy judgments are far above out of his sight. *Ps.* 10: 5.

I will extol thee, O Lord; for thou hast lifted me up. *Ps.* 30: 1.

God, thy God, hath anointed thee with the oil of gladness above thy fellows. *Ps.* 45: 7.

In Judah is God known: his name is great in Israel. *Ps.* 76: 1.

Seest thou a man diligent in his business? he shall stand before kings. *Pr.* 22: 29.

He shall not stand before mean men. *Pr.* 22: 29.

The mean man boweth down, and the great man humbleth himself. *Is.* 2: 9.

I saw also the Lord sitting upon a throne, high and lifted up. *Is.* 6: 1.

Grant that these my two sons may sit, the one on thy right hand, and the other on thy left, in thy kingdom. *Mat.* 20: 21.

Whosoever will be great among you, let him be your minister. *Mat.* 20: 26.

If then God so clothe the grass, which is to day in the field, and to morrow is cast into the oven; how much more will he clothe you, O ye of little faith? *Lu.* 12: 28.

In all these things we are more than conquerors through him that loved us. *Ro.* 8: 37.

If I must needs glory, I will glory of the things which concern mine infirmities. *2 Co.* 11: 30.

God . . . hath highly exalted him, and given him a name which is above every name. *Ph.* 2: 9.

See also

Distinction; Elevation; Exaltation; Importance; Mountain; Pinnacle; Prominence; Superiority.

Emotion

Then David and the people that were with him lifted up their voice and wept, until they had no more power to weep. *1 S.* 30: 4.

When the morning stars sang together, and all the sons of God shouted for joy. *Jb.* 38: 7.

He maketh my feet like hinds' feet, and setteth me upon my high places. *Ps.* 18: 33.

My flesh trembleth for fear of thee. *Ps.* 119: 120.

When he was yet a great way off, his father saw him, and had compassion, and ran, and fell on his neck, and kissed him. *Lu.* 15: 20.

Being in an agony he prayed more earnestly. *Lu.* 22: 44.

Being past feeling. *Ep.* 4: 19.

We have not an high priest which cannot be touched with the feeling of our infirmities. *He.* 4: 15.

Seeing ye have purified your souls in obeying the truth through the Spirit unto unfeigned love of the brethren, see that ye love one another with a pure heart fervently. *1 Pe.* 1: 22.

Unto him that is able . . . to present you faultless before the presence of his glory with exceeding joy. *Jude* 1: 24.

I have somewhat against thee, because thou hast left thy first love. *Re.* 2: 4.

See also

Feeling; Sentiment.

Empire

I will . . . enlarge thy borders. *Ex.* 34: 24.

His kingdom shall be exalted. *Nu.* 24: 7.

The Lord sent me to anoint thee to be king over his people. *1 S.* 15: 1.

There have been mighty kings also over Jerusalem, which have ruled over all countries beyond the river; and toll, tribute, and custom, was paid unto them. *Ezr.* 4: 20.

Thou rulest the raging of the sea. *Ps.* 89: 9.

Creator of the ends of the earth. *Is.* 40: 28.

He changeth the times and the seasons: he removeth kings, and setteth up kings. *Da.* 2: 21.

His dominion shall be from sea even to sea, and from the river even to the ends of the earth. *Zch.* 9: 10.

Because thou hast been faithful in a very little, have thou authority over ten cities. *Lu.* 19: 17.

Sin shall not have dominion over you. *Ro.* 6: 14.

Far above all principality, and power, and might, and dominion, and every name that is named, not only in this world, but also in that which is to come. *Ep.* 1: 21.

Christ . . . is the head of all principality and power. *Col.* 2: 8, 10.

See also

Christ, the King; Christ, Reign of; Christ, Supremacy of; Dominion; God, the King; God, Kingdom of; God, Sovereignty of; King; Reign; Rule; Sovereignty; State.

Employee

Six days shalt thou labour, and do all thy work. *Ex.* 20: 9.

These are the singers: . . . they were em-

ployed in that work day and night. *1 Ch.* **9:**
33.

Are not his days also like the days of an
hireling? *Jb.* **7: 1.**

Turn from him, that he may rest, till he
shall accomplish, as an hireling, his day. *Jb.*
14: 6.

Man goeth forth unto his work and to his
labour until the evening. *Ps.* **104: 23.**

The sleep of a labouring man is sweet. *Ec.*
5: 12.

The priests . . . teach for hire. *Mi.* **3: 11.**

Before these days there was no hire for man,
nor any hire for beast. *Zch.* **8: 10.**

The harvest truly is plenteous, but the
labourers are few; Pray ye therefore the Lord
of the harvest, that he will send forth labourers
into his harvest. *Mat.* **9: 37, 38.**

The workman is worthy of his meat. *Mat.* **10:**
10.

No man hath hired us. *Mat.* **20: 7.**

The labourer is worthy of his hire. *Lu.* **10:**
7.

He that is an hireling, and not the shepherd, . . . leaveth the sheep, and fleeth. *Jn.*
10: 12.

Every man shall receive his own reward according to his own labour. *1 Co.* **3: 8.**

Servants, be obedient to them that are your
masters according to the flesh. *Ep.* **6: 5.**

Masters, give unto your servants that which
is just and equal. *Col.* **4: 1.**

Work with your own hands, as we commanded you. *1 Th.* **4: 11.**

We command and exhort, . . . that with
quietness they work, and eat their own bread.
2 Th. **3: 12.**

See also

Employer; Labor; Master; Toil; Wage;
Work.

Employer

The wages of him that is hired shall not
abide with thee all night until the morning.
Le. **19: 13.**

At his day thou shalt give him his hire,
neither shall the sun go down upon it; for he
is poor, and setteth his heart upon it. *De.*
24: 15.

The king and Jehoiada . . . hired masons
and carpenters to repair the house of the Lord.
2 Ch. **24: 12.**

It shall be, . . . as with the servant, so with
his master. *Is.* **24: 2.**

They lavish gold out of the bag, and weigh
silver in the balance, and hire a goldsmith. *Is.*
46: 6.

I will be a swift witness . . . against those
that oppress the hireling in his wages. *Mal.* **3:**
5.

The kingdom of heaven is like unto a man
that is an householder, which went out early
in the morning to hire labourers into his vineyard. *Mat.* **20: 1.**

Call the labourers, and give them their hire,
beginning from the last unto the first. *Mat.* **20:**
8.

Other men laboured, and ye are entered
into their labours. *Jn.* **4: 38.**

Ye know that by this craft we have our
wealth. *Ac.* **19: 25.**

As a wise masterbuilder, I have laid the

foundation, and another buildeth thereon. *1*
Co. **3: 10.**

The labourer is worthy of his reward. *1 Ti.*
5: 18.

The hire of the labourers who have reaped
down your fields, which is of you kept back
by fraud, crieth. *Ja.* **5: 4.**

See also

Employee; Labor; Servant; Toil; Wage;
Work.

Emptiness

In the days of Shamgar, . . . the highways
were unoccupied, and the travellers walked
through byways. *Ju.* **5: 6.**

Thou hast sent widows away empty. *Jb.* **22:**
9.

He that followeth vain persons is void of
understanding. *Pr.* **12: 11.**

If the clouds be full of rain, they empty
themselves upon the earth. *Ec.* **11: 3.**

He shall stretch out upon it the line of confusion, and the stones of emptiness. *Is.* **34:**
11.

Israel is an empty vine, he bringeth forth
fruit unto himself. *Ho.* **10: 1.**

He hath filled the hungry with good things:
and the rich he hath sent empty away. *Lu.* **1:**
53.

Then goeth he, and taketh to himself seven
other spirits more wicked than himself; and
they enter in, and dwell there: and the last
state of that man is worse than the first. *Lu.*
11: 26.

I exercise myself, to have always a conscience
void of offence toward God, and toward men.
Ac. **24: 16.**

Though I speak with the tongues of men
and of angels, and have not charity, I am become as sounding brass, or a tinkling cymbal.
1 Co. **13: 1.**

If after the manner of men I have fought
with beasts at Ephesus, what advantageth it
me, if the dead rise not? let us eat and drink;
for to morrow we die. *1 Co.* **15: 32.**

See also

Destitution; Fruitlessness; Hunger; Nothing;
Space; Vanity; Void; Zero.

Emulation

Unstable as water, thou shalt not excel. *Ge.*
49: 4.

I magnify my office: If by any means I may
provoke to emulation them which are my
flesh, and might save some of them. *Ro.* **11:**
13, 14.

The eye cannot say unto the hand, I have no
need of thee. *1 Co.* **12: 21.**

Seek that ye may excel to the edifying of the
church. *1 Co.* **14: 12.**

They measuring themselves by themselves,
and comparing themselves among themselves,
are not wise. *2 Co.* **10: 12.**

I suppose I was not a whit behind the very
chiefest apostles. *2 Co.* **11: 5.**

Seeing that many glory after the flesh, I will
glory also. *2 Co.* **11: 18.**

Are they Hebrews? so am I. Are they
Israelites? so am I. Are they the seed of Abraham? so am I. *2 Co.* **11: 22.**

Are they ministers of Christ? . . . I am more.
2 Co. **11: 23.**

Can the fig tree, my brethren, bear olive berries? *Ja.* 3: 12.
See also
Competition; Rivalry.

Encouragement

Fear not, for I am with thee, and will bless thee. *Ge.* 26: 24.
Stand still, and see the salvation of the Lord, which he will shew to you to-day. *Ex.* 14: 13.
Only be thou strong and very courageous. *Jos.* 1: 7.
David encouraged himself in the Lord his God. *1 S.* 30: 6.
Fear not: for they that be with us are more than they that be with them. *2 K.* 6: 16.
Speak ye comfortably to Jerusalem, and cry unto her, that her warfare is accomplished, that her iniquity is pardoned. *Is.* 40: 2.
The carpenter encouraged the goldsmith. *Is.* 41: 7.
Fear thou not; for I am with thee: be not dismayed; for I am thy God: I will strengthen thee; yea, I will help thee; yea, I will uphold thee with the right hand of my righteousness. *Is.* 41: 10.
Fear not; I will help thee. *Is.* 41: 13.
Fear not: for I have redeemed thee, I have called thee by thy name; thou art mine. *Is.* 43: 1.
The very hairs of your head are all numbered. *Mat.* 10: 30.
Ye are of more value than many sparrows. *Mat.* 10: 31.
Be of good cheer; it is I; be not afraid. *Mat.* 14: 27.
I exhort you to be of good cheer. *Ac.* 27: 22.
He thanked God, and took courage. *Ac.* 28: 15.
Comfort the feebleminded, support the weak. *1 Th.* 5: 14.
Exhort one another daily, while it is called To day; lest any of you be hardened through the deceitfulness of sin. *He.* 3: 13.
For even hereunto were ye called: because Christ also suffered for us, leaving us an example, that ye should follow his steps. *1 Pe.* 2: 21.
See also
Admonition; Charge; Christ, the Comforter; Comfort; Counsel; Courage; Exhortation; Fearlessness.

End

The people went up into the city, every man straight before him. *Jos.* 6: 20.
All the ends of the world shall remember and turn unto the Lord. *Ps.* 22: 27.
The end of the wicked shall be cut off. *Ps.* 37: 38.
Lord, make me to know mine end. *Ps.* 39: 4.
Teach me, O Lord, the way of thy statutes; and I shall keep it unto the end. *Ps.* 119: 33.
I have seen an end of all perfection. *Ps.* 119: 96.
There is a way which seemeth right unto a man, but the end thereof are the ways of death. *Pr.* 14: 12.
Better is the end of a thing than the beginning thereof. *Ec.* 7: 8.

At the end it shall speak, and not lie. *Hab.* 2: 3.
His dominion shall be from sea even to sea, and from the river even to the ends of the earth. *Zch.* 9: 10.
He that shall endure unto the end, the same shall be saved. *Mat.* 24: 13.
Of his kingdom there shall be no end. *Lu.* 1: 33.
We know that all things work together for good to them that love God, to them who are the called according to his purpose. *Ro.* 8: 28.
So run, that ye may obtain. *1 Co.* 9: 24.
To this end also did I write, that I might know the proof of you, whether ye be obedient in all things. *2 Co.* 2: 9.
See also
Ambition; Aspiration; Christ, Purpose of; Climax; Conclusion; Death; Destruction; Expiration; Finality; Finish; Goal; Intention; Omega; Purpose; Termination.

Endeavor

Give them according to their deeds, and according to the wickedness of their endeavours. *Ps.* 28: 4.
Strive to enter in at the strait gate. *Lu.* 13: 24.
After he had seen the vision, immediately we endeavoured to go into Macedonia. *Ac.* 16: 10.
Herein do I exercise myself, to have always a conscience void of offence toward God, and toward men. *Ac.* 24: 16.
So have I strived to preach the gospel. *Ro.* 15: 20.
Endeavouring to keep the unity of the Spirit in the bond of peace. *Ep.* 4: 3.
We . . . endeavoured the more abundantly to see your face with great desire. *1 Th.* 2: 17.
Exercise thyself rather unto godliness. *1 Ti.* 4: 7.
See also
Deed; Effort; Exertion; Task; Trial.

Endowment

The king will enrich him with great riches. *1 S.* 17: 25.
Blessed be the Lord God, . . . who hath given to David the king a wise son, endued with prudence and understanding. *2 Ch.* 2: 12.
Thou visitest the earth, and waterest it: thou greatly enrichest it with the river of God. *Ps.* 65: 9.
Tarry ye in the city of Jerusalem until ye be endued with power from on high. *Lu.* 24: 49.
Ye shall receive power, after that the Holy Ghost is come upon you. *Ac.* 1: 8.
On the Gentiles also was poured out the gift of the Holy Ghost. *Ac.* 10: 45.
I long to see you, that I may impart unto you some spiritual gift, to the end ye may be established. *Ro.* 1: 11.
In every thing we are enriched by him, in all utterance, and in all knowledge. *1 Co.* 1: 5.
Now there are diversities of gifts, but the same Spirit. *1 Co.* 12: 4.
Being enriched in every thing to all bountifulness. *2 Co.* 9: 11.
Stir up the gift of God, which is in thee. *2 Ti.* 1: 6.
That the man of God may be perfect,

throughly furnished unto all good works. *2 Ti. 3: 17.*

Who is a wise man and endued with knowledge among you? *Ja. 3: 13.*

See also

Ability; Aptitude; Capacity; Gift; Grant; Skill; Talent.

Endurance

If thou shalt do this thing, and God command thee so, then thou shalt be able to endure. *Ex. 18: 23.*

The fear of the Lord is clean, enduring for ever. *Ps. 19: 9.*

The goodness of God endureth continually. *Ps. 52: 1.*

God is the strength of my heart, and my portion for ever. *Ps. 73: 26.*

In your patience possess ye your souls. *Lu. 21: 19.*

He that reapeth receiveth wages, and gathereth fruit unto life eternal. *Jn. 4: 36.*

God . . . will render . . . To them who by patient continuance in well doing seek for glory and honour and immortality, eternal life. *Ro. 2: 5–7.*

Ye were not able to bear it, neither yet now are ye able. *1 Co. 3: 2.*

Charity . . . beareth all things, believeth all things, hopeth all things, endureth all things. Charity never faileth. *1 Co. 13: 4, 7, 8.*

If ye continue in the faith grounded and settled, and be not moved away from the hope of the gospel, which ye have heard. *Col. 1: 23.*

Thou therefore endure hardness as a good soldier of Jesus Christ. *2 Ti. 2: 3.*

If we hold fast the confidence and the rejoicing of the hope firm unto the end. *He. 3: 6.*

After he had patiently endured he obtained the promise. *He. 6: 15.*

He endured, as seeing him who is invisible. *He. 11: 27.*

That those things which cannot be shaken may remain. *He. 12: 27.*

We count them happy which endure. *Ja. 5: 11.*

See also

Courage; Firmness; Fortitude; Patience; Resignation; Suffering.

Enemy

If thou see the ass of him that hateth thee lying under his burden, and wouldest forbear to help him, thou shalt surely help with him. *Ex. 23: 5.*

The Lord your God is he that goeth with you, to fight for you against your enemies, to save you. *De. 20: 4.*

Art thou for us, or for our adversaries? *Jos. 5: 13.*

Stay ye not, but pursue after your enemies. *Jos. 10: 19.*

Let us fetch the ark of the covenant of the Lord, . . . that, when it cometh among us, it may save us out of the hand of our enemies. *1 S. 4: 3.*

And he prepared great provision for them: and when they had eaten and drunk, he sent them away. *2 K. 6: 23.*

Thou preparest a table before me in the presence of mine enemies. *Ps. 23: 5.*

Mine enemies speak evil of me. *Ps. 41: 5.*

Deliver me from mine enemies, O my God: defend me from them that rise up against me. *Ps. 59: 1.*

Let them be confounded and consumed that are adversaries to my soul. *Ps. 71: 13.*

O God, the proud are risen against me, and the assemblies of violent men have sought after my soul; and have not set thee before them. *Ps. 86: 14.*

Rejoice not when thine enemy falleth, and let not thine heart be glad when he stumbleth. *Pr. 24: 17.*

The kisses of an enemy are deceitful. *Pr. 27: 6.*

They have digged a pit for my soul. *Je. 18: 20.*

Will ye hunt the souls of my people? *Eze. 13: 18.*

They have devoured souls; they have taken the treasure and precious things; they have made her many widows in the midst thereof. *Eze. 22: 25.*

A man's enemies are the men of his own house. *Mi. 7: 6.*

Are ye come out, as against a thief, with swords and with staves to take me? *Mk. 14: 48.*

Love ye your enemies, and do good, and lend hoping for nothing again; and your reward shall be great, and ye shall be the children of the Highest. *Lu. 6: 35.*

All his adversaries were ashamed. *Lu. 13: 17.*

Avenge me of mine adversary. *Lu. 18: 3.*

Satan hath desired to have you, that he may sift you as wheat. *Lu. 22: 31.*

If thine enemy hunger, feed him; if he thirst, give him drink: for in so doing thou shalt heap coals of fire on his head. *Ro. 12: 20.*

The last enemy that shall be destroyed is death. *1 Co. 15: 26.*

There are many adversaries. *1 Co. 16: 9.*

See that none render evil for evil unto any man; but ever follow that which is good, both among yourselves, and to all men. *1 Th. 5: 15.*

Count him not as an enemy, but admonish him as a brother. *1 Ti. 3: 15.*

See also

Adversary; Animosity; Antagonism; Antichrist; Antipathy; Attack; Belligerent; Foe; Hostility; Opponent; Opposition; Satan.

Energy

Be strong, and quit yourselves like men. *1 S. 4: 9.*

Ascribe ye strength unto God. *Ps. 68: 34.*

The Lord on high is mightier than the noise of many waters. *Ps. 93: 4.*

Like the rushing of mighty waters! *Is. 17: 12.*

Have salt in yourselves. *Mk. 9: 50.*

Rise and pray. *Lu. 22: 46.*

I must work the works of him that sent me, while it is day. *Jn. 9: 4.*

Always abounding in the work of the Lord. *1 Co. 15: 58.*

See also

Christ, Power of; Christ, Strength of; Energy, Creative; Firmness; Force; God, Omnipotence of; God, Power of; God, Strength of; Might; Omnipotence; Power; Strength; Vigor; Vitality.

Energy, Creative

Behold, I create new heavens and a new

earth. *Is.* 65: 17.

Lo, he that formeth the mountains, and createth the wind, and declareth unto man what is his thought, . . . The Lord, The God of hosts, is his name. *Am.* 4: 13.

We know that the whole creation groaneth and travaileth in pain together until now. *Ro.* 8: 22.

Workers together with him. 2 *Co.* 6: 1.

According to the gift of the grace of God given unto me by the effectual working of his power. *Ep.* 3: 7.

According to the eternal purpose which he purposed in Christ Jesus our Lord. *Ep.* 3: 11.

It is God which worketh in you both to will and to do of his good pleasure. *Ph.* 2: 13.

Behold, I make all things new. *Re.* 21: 5.

See also

Christ, the Creator; Creation; Creator; Creature; God, the Creator; God, Omnipotence of; God, Power of; God, Strength of; Omnipotence.

Enforcement

Whosoever will not do the law of thy God and the law of the king, let judgment be executed speedily upon him. *Ezr.* 7: 26.

How forcible are right words! *Jb.* 6: 25.

When wilt thou execute judgment on them that persecute me? *Ps.* 119: 84.

Take counsel, execute judgment. *Is.* 16: 3.

With force and with cruelty have ye ruled. *Eze.* 34: 4.

Whosoever shall compel thee to go a mile, go with him twain. *Mat.* 5: 41.

Him they compelled to bear his cross. *Mat.* 27: 32.

The love of Christ constraineth us. 2 *Co.* 5: 14.

See also

Coercion; Compulsion; Constraint; Force; Power; Violence.

Enigma

With him will I speak mouth to mouth, even apparently, and not in dark speeches. *Nu.* 12: 8.

I will now put forth a riddle unto you. *Ju.* 14: 12.

Out of the eater came forth meat, and out of the strong came forth sweetness. *Ju.* 14: 14.

The queen of Sheba . . . came to prove him with hard questions. *1 K.* 10: 1.

I will open my mouth in a parable: I will utter dark sayings of old. *Ps.* 78: 2.

I will utter things which have been kept secret from the foundation of the world. *Mat.* 13: 35.

Thou hast made known to me the ways of life. *Ac.* 2: 28.

According to the revelation of the mystery, which was kept secret since the world began. *Ro.* 16: 25.

The bread which we break, is it not the communion of the body of Christ? *1 Co.* 10: 16.

Which things are an allegory. *Ga.* 4: 24.

Having made known unto us the mystery of his will. *Ep.* 1: 9.

To make all men see what is the fellowship of the mystery, which from the beginning of the world hath been hid in God. *Ep.* 3: 9.

Praying always . . . that utterance may be given unto me, that I may open my mouth boldly, to make known the mystery of the gospel. *Ep.* 6: 18, 19.

In the days of the voice of the seventh angel, when he shall begin to sound, the mystery of God should be finished. *Re.* 10: 7.

Let him that hath understanding count the number of the beast: for it is the number of a man. *Re.* 13: 18.

See also

Riddle.

Enjoyment

That the children of Israel may enjoy every man the inheritance of his fathers. *Nu.* 36: 8.

The Lord thy God shall bless thee in all thine increase, and in all the works of thine hands, therefore thou shalt surely rejoice. *De.* 16: 15.

His soul shall dwell at ease; and his seed shall inherit the earth. *Ps.* 25: 13.

We shall be satisfied with the goodness of thy house. *Ps.* 65: 4.

The voice of rejoicing and salvation is in the tabernacles of the righteous. *Ps.* 118: 15.

This is the day which the Lord hath made; we will rejoice and be glad in it. *Ps.* 118: 24.

I was glad when they said unto me, Let us go into the house of the Lord. *Ps.* 122: 1.

God giveth to a man that is good in his sight wisdom, and knowledge, and joy. *Ec.* 2: 26.

A man hath no better thing under the sun, than to eat, and to drink, and to be merry. *Ec.* 8: 15.

Be ye glad and rejoice for ever in that which I create: for, behold, I create Jerusalem a rejoicing, and her people a joy. *Is.* 65: 18.

Mine elect shall long enjoy the work of their hands. *Is.* 65: 22.

Rejoice in the Lord alway: and again I say, Rejoice. *Ph.* 4: 4.

Trust . . . in the living God, who giveth us richly all things to enjoy. *1 Ti.* 6: 17.

He that will love life, and see good days, let him refrain his tongue from evil, and his lips that they speak no guile: Let him eschew evil, and do good; let him seek peace, and ensue it. *1 Pe.* 3: 10, 11.

See also

Christ, Joy in; Christ, Joy of; Contentment; Delight; Gladness; God, Joy in; Happiness; Joy; Pleasure; Rejoicing; Satisfaction; Zest.

Enlargement

The Lord thy God shall bless thee in all thine increase. *De.* 16: 15.

He increaseth the nations, . . . he enlargeth the nations. *Jb.* 12: 23.

Thou hast enlarged me when I was in distress. *Ps.* 4: 1.

The troubles of my heart are enlarged. *Ps.* 25: 17.

They shall still bring forth fruit in old age; they shall be fat and flourishing. *Ps.* 92: 14.

The Lord shall increase you more and more. *Ps.* 115: 14.

I will run the way of thy commandments, when thou shalt enlarge my heart. *Ps.* 119: 32.

A wise man will hear, and will increase learning. *Pr.* 1: 5.

Thine heart shall fear, and be enlarged. *Is.* **60: 5.**

Increase our faith. *Lu.* **17: 5.**

Having hope, when your faith is increased, that we shall be enlarged by you according to our rule abundantly. *2 Co.* **10: 15.**

See also

Development; Education; Evolution; Expansion; Growth; Increase; Room; Stature.

Enlightenment

I have given thee a wise and an understanding heart; so that there was none like thee before thee, neither after thee shall any arise like unto thee. *1 K.* **3: 12.**

There came of all people to hear the wisdom of Solomon, from all kings of the earth, which had heard of his wisdom. *1 K.* **4: 34.**

Give me now wisdom and knowledge, that I may go out and come in before this people. *2 Ch.* **1: 10.**

Because . . . thou hast not asked riches, wealth, or honour, nor the life of thine enemies, neither yet hast asked long life; but hast asked wisdom and knowledge for thyself, that thou mayest judge my people, over whom I have made thee king: Wisdom and knowledge is granted unto thee; and I will give thee riches, and wealth, and honour. *2 Ch.* **1: 11, 12.**

All the kings of the earth sought the presence of Solomon, to hear his wisdom, that God had put in his heart. *2 Ch.* **9: 23.**

Speak to the earth, and it shall teach thee. *Jb.* **12: 8.**

Declare among the people his doings. *Ps.* **9: 11.**

Teach me thy way, O Lord. *Ps.* **27: 11.**

So teach us to number our days, that we may apply our hearts unto wisdom. *Ps.* **90: 12.**

He that teacheth man knowledge, shall not he know? *Ps.* **94: 10.**

All the things thou canst desire are not to be compared unto her. *Pr.* **3: 15.**

Wisdom . . . shall bring thee to honour, when thou dost embrace her. *Pr.* **4: 7, 8.**

Bow thine ear to mine understanding. *Pr.* **5: 1.**

Wisdom . . . hath hewn out her seven pillars. *Pr.* **9: 1.**

He that walketh with wise men shall be wise. *Pr.* **13: 20.**

The words of a man's mouth are as deep waters, and the wellspring of wisdom as a flowing brook. *Pr.* **18: 4.**

Apply thine heart unto instruction, and thine ears to the words of knowledge. *Pr.* **23: 12.**

The spirit of the Lord . . . shall make him of quick understanding in the fear of the Lord. *Is.* **11: 2, 3.**

Whom therefore ye ignorantly worship, him declare I unto you. *Ac.* **17: 23.**

I will destroy the wisdom of the wise. *1 Co.* **1: 19.**

The wisdom of this world is foolishness with God. *1 Co.* **3: 19.**

Be ye not unwise, but understanding what the will of the Lord is. *Ep.* **5: 17.**

Ever learning, and never able to come to the knowledge of the truth. *2 Ti.* **3: 7.**

If any of you do err from the truth, and one convert him; Let him know, that he which converteth the sinner from the error of his way shall save a soul from death, and shall hide a multitude of sins. *Ja.* **5: 19. 20.**

See also

Christ, Knowledge of; Christ, Mind of; Christ, Wisdom of; Culture; God, Knowledge of; God, Wisdom of; Learning; Understanding; Wisdom.

Enrichment

Though he heap up silver as the dust. *Jb.* **27: 16.**

He heapeth up riches. *Ps.* **39: 6.**

If riches increase, set not your heart upon them. *Ps.* **62: 10.**

Then shall the earth yield her increase. *Ps.* **67: 6.**

Wealth maketh many friends. *Pr.* **19: 4.**

When goods increase, they are increased that eat them: and what good is there to the owners thereof, saving the beholding of them with their eyes? *Ec.* **5: 11.**

I will set in the desert the fir tree, and the pine, and the box tree together. *Is.* **41: 19.**

It shall bring forth boughs, and bear fruit, and be a goodly cedar. *Eze.* **17: 23.**

That we may buy the poor for silver. *Am.* **8: 6.**

All these things shall be added unto you. *Mat.* **6: 33.**

Soul, thou hast much goods laid up for many years. *Lu.* **12: 19.**

So is he that layeth up treasure for himself, and is not rich toward God. *Lu.* **12: 21.**

Peter said unto him, Thy money perish with thee, because thou hast thought that the gift of God may be purchased with money. *Ac.* **8: 20.**

I have planted, Apollos watered; but God gave the increase. *1 Co.* **3: 6.**

Increase the fruits of your righteousness. *2 Co.* **9: 10.**

The fruit of the Spirit is love, joy, peace, longsuffering, gentleness, goodness, faith, Meekness, temperance. *Ga.* **5: 22, 23.**

Christ: From whom the whole body fitly joined together and compacted by that which every joint supplieth, according to the effectual working in the measure of every part, maketh increase of the body unto the edifying of itself in love. *Ep.* **4: 15, 16.**

Supposing that gain is godliness. *1 Ti.* **6: 5.**

Ye have heaped treasure together for the last days. *Ja.* **5: 3.**

Add to your faith virtue; and to virtue knowledge; And to knowledge temperance; and to temperance patience; and to patience godliness; and to godliness brotherly kindness; and to brotherly kindness charity. *2 Pe.* **1: 5-7.**

Grow in grace. *2 Pe.* **3: 18.**

See also

Gold; Mammon; Riches; Wealth.

Enthusiasm

He was zealous for his God. *Nu.* **25: 13.**

Come with me, and see my zeal for the Lord. *2 K.* **10: 16.**

The people had a mind to work. *Ne.* **4: 6.**

My zeal hath consumed me. *Ps.* **119: 139.**

Whatsoever thy hand findeth to do, do it with thy might. *Ec.* **9: 10.**

I . . . was zealous toward God, as ye all are this day. *Ac.* 22: 3.

Fervent in spirit. *Ro.* 12: 11.

It is good to be zealously affected always in a good thing. *Ga.* 4: 18.

I press toward the mark for the prize of the high calling of God in Christ Jesus. *Ph.* 3: 14.

Whatsoever ye do, do it heartily, as to the Lord, and not unto men. *Col.* 3: 23.

See also

Ardor; Eagerness; Earnestness; Fervor; Zeal; Zest.

Enticement

My heart hath been secretly enticed. *Jb.* 31: 27.

To deliver thee from the strange woman, even from the stranger which flattereth with her words. *Pr.* 2: 16.

Why wilt thou, my son, be ravished with a strange woman, and embrace the bosom of a stranger? *Pr.* 5: 20.

He that winketh with the eye causeth sorrow. *Pr.* 10: 10.

A violent man enticeth his neighbour. *Pr.* 16: 29.

His mouth is most sweet: yea, he is altogether lovely. *S. of S.* 5: 16.

My speech and my preaching was not with enticing words of man's wisdom, but in demonstration of the Spirit and of power. *1 Co.* 2: 4.

Every man is tempted, when he is drawn away of his own lust, and enticed. *Ja.* 1: 14.

See also

Allurement; Attraction; Temptation.

Entrance

Yield yourselves unto the Lord, and enter into his sanctuary. *2 Ch.* 30: 8.

Lift up your heads, O ye gates; . . . and the King of glory shall come in. *Ps.* 24: 7.

Enter into his gates with thanksgiving, and into his courts with praise. *Ps.* 100: 4.

Open to me the gates of righteousness. *Ps.* 118: 19.

Go through, go through the gates. *Is.* 62: 10.

They shall enter in at the windows like a thief. *Jo.* 2: 9.

Strait is the gate, and narrow is the way, which leadeth unto life. *Mat.* 7: 14.

It is better for thee to enter into life halt or maimed, rather than having two hands or two feet to be cast into everlasting fire. *Mat.* 18: 8.

If thou wilt enter into life, keep the commandments. *Mat.* 19: 17.

Watch and pray, that ye enter not into temptation. *Mat.* 26: 41.

I entered into thine house, thou gavest me no water for my feet. *Lu.* 7: 44.

He entered into a certain village. *Lu.* 10: 38.

Many . . . will seek to enter in, and shall not be able. *Lu.* 13: 24.

He . . . sat for alms at the Beautiful gate of the temple. *Ac.* 3: 10.

By one man sin entered into the world, and death by sin. *Ro.* 5: 12.

They could not enter in because of unbelief. *He.* 3: 19.

Let us labor therefore to enter into that rest. *He.* 4: 11.

After this I looked, and, behold, a door was opened in heaven. *Re.* 4: 1.

The Spirit of life from God entered into them. *Re.* 11: 11.

Blessed are they that do his commandments, that they may have right to the tree of life, and may enter in through the gates into the city. *Re.* 22: 14.

See also

Admission; Christ, the Door; Christ, the Way; Door; Introduction; Opening.

Entreaty

Intreat me not to leave thee, or to return from following after thee. *Ru.* 1: 16.

Hear me, O Lord, hear me, that this people may know that thou art the Lord God. *1 K.* 18: 37.

Blessed be the Lord, because he hath heard the voice of my supplications. *Ps.* 28: 6.

Lord, all my desire is before thee. *Ps.* 38: 9.

Out of the depths have I cried unto thee, O Lord. *Ps.* 130: 1.

The poor useth intreaties. *Pr.* 18: 23.

Praying always with all prayer and supplication in the Spirit. *Ep.* 6: 18.

Let your requests be made known unto God. *Ph.* 4: 6.

We pray always for you. *2 Th.* 1: 11.

The wisdom that is from above is first pure, then peaceable, gentle, and easy to be intreated. *Ja.* 3: 17.

Is any among you afflicted? let him pray. *Ja.* 5: 13.

See also

Appeal; God, Prayer to; Petition; Plea; Prayer; Request; Supplication.

Environment

He made darkness pavilions round about him. *2 S.* 22: 12.

The angel of the Lord encampeth round about them that fear him. *Ps.* 34: 7.

As the mountains are round about Jerusalem, so the Lord is round about his people from henceforth even for ever. *Ps.* 125: 2.

According to their pasture, so were they filled. *Ho.* 13: 6.

I, saith the Lord, will be unto her a wall of fire round about, and will be the glory in the midst of her. *Zch.* 2: 5.

I tell you, in that night there shall be two men in one bed; the one shall be taken, and the other shall be left. Two women shall be grinding together; the one shall be taken, and the other left. *Lu.* 17: 34, 35.

The days shall come upon thee, that thine enemies shall cast a trench about thee, and compass thee round, and keep thee in on every side. *Lu.* 19: 43.

Be not conformed to this world. *Ro.* 12: 2.

Paul, . . . to the saints which are at Ephesus. *Ep.* 1: 1.

Seeing we also are compassed about with so great a cloud of witnesses. *He.* 12: 1.

Thou hast a few names even in Sardis which have not defiled their garments; and they shall walk with me in white, for they are worthy. *Re.* 3: 4.

See also

Surroundings.

Envy

Moses said unto him, Enviest thou for my sake? would God that all the Lord's people were prophets, that the Lord would put his spirit upon them! *Nu.* 11: 29.

Wrath killeth the foolish man, and envy slayeth the silly one. *Jb.* 5: 2.

Let them wander up and down for meat, and grudge if they be not satisfied. *Ps.* 59: 15.

Envy thou not the oppressor, and choose none of his ways. *Pr.* 3: 31.

Jealousy is the rage of a man: therefore he will not spare in the day of vengeance. *Pr.* 6: 34.

Fret not thyself because of evil men, neither be thou envious at the wicked. *Pr.* 24: 19.

Who is able to stand before envy? *Pr.* 27: 4.

Curse not the rich in thy bedchamber. *Ec.* 10: 20.

I have made him fair by the multitude of his branches: so that all the trees of Eden, that were in the garden of God, envied him. *Eze.* 31: 9.

The chief priests had delivered him for envy. *Mk.* 15: 10.

And he was angry, and would not go in. *Lu.* 15: 28.

Let us walk honestly, as in the day; . . . not in strife and envying. *Ro.* 13: 13.

Whereas there is among you envying, and strife, and divisions, are ye not carnal, and walk as men? *1 Co.* 3: 3.

Some indeed preach Christ even of envy and strife. *Ph.* 1: 15.

If ye have bitter envying and strife in your hearts, glory not. *Ja.* 3: 14.

The spirit that dwelleth in us lusteth to envy. *Ja.* 4: 5.

Grudge not one against another, brethren, lest ye be condemned. *Ja.* 5: 9.

Laying aside all . . . envies, and all evil speakings. *1 Pe.* 2: 1.

See also
Avarice; Covetousness; Greed; Jealousy.

Epistle

Need we, as some others, epistles of commendation to you, or letters of commendation from you? *2 Co.* 3: 1.

Ye are our epistle written in our hearts, known and read of all men. *2 Co.* 3: 2.

Ye are manifestly declared to be the epistle of Christ ministered by us, written not with ink, but with the Spirit of the living God; not in tables of stone, but in fleshy tables of the heart. *2 Co.* 3: 3.

Such as we are in word by letters when we are absent, such will we be also in deed when we are present. *2 Co.* 10: 11.

Hold the traditions which ye have been taught, whether by word or our epistle. *2 Th.* 2: 15.

Having many things to write unto you, I would not write with paper and ink: but I trust to come unto you. *2 Jn.* 1: 12.

See also
Author; Letter; Scripture; Writing.

Epitaph

He did that which was right in the sight of the Lord. *2 K.* 15: 3.

His remembrance shall perish from the earth, and he shall have no name in the street. *Jb.* 18: 17.

In death there is no remembrance of thee. *Ps.* 6: 5.

Their memorial is perished with them. *Ps.* 9: 6.

I will make thy name to be remembered in all generations. *Ps.* 45: 17.

The righteous shall be in everlasting remembrance. *Ps.* 112: 6.

He hath dispersed, he hath given to the poor: his righteousness endureth for ever. *Ps.* 112: 9.

They shall abundantly utter the memory of thy great goodness. *Ps.* 145: 7.

The memory of the just is blessed. *Pr.* 10: 7.

Her children arise up, and call her blessed. *Pr.* 31: 28.

Verily I say unto you, Wheresoever this gospel shall be preached in the whole world, there shall also this that this woman hath done, be told for a memorial of her. *Mat.* 26: 13.

Truly this was the Son of God. *Mat.* 27: 54.

These all died in faith, not having received the promises, but having seen them afar off, and were persuaded of them, and embraced them. *He.* 11: 13.

See also
Memorial; Monument; Remembrance.

Epoch

Enquire, I pray thee, of the former age. *Jb.* 8: 8.

Thy kingdom is an everlasting kingdom, and thy dominion endureth throughout all generations. *Ps.* 145: 13.

To every thing there is a season, and a time to every purpose under the heaven. *Ec.* 3: 1.

He hath made everything beautiful in his time. *Ec.* 3: 11.

To every purpose there is time and judgment. *Ec.* 8: 6.

Awake, awake, put on strength, O arm of the Lord; awake, as in the ancient days, in the generations of old. *Is.* 51: 9.

Hath this been in your days, or even in the days of your fathers? *Jo.* 1: 2.

Tell ye your children of it, and let your children tell their children, and their children another generation. *Jo.* 1: 3.

He shall turn the heart of the fathers to the children, and the heart of the children to their fathers. *Mal.* 4: 6.

Whereunto shall I liken this generation? *Mat.* 11: 16.

The fashion of this world passeth away. *1 Co.* 7: 31.

Beloved, be not ignorant of this one thing, that one day is with the Lord as a thousand years, and a thousand years as one day. *2 Pe.* 3: 8.

The time is at hand. *Re.* 1: 3.

See also
Era, Genealogy; Generation; Time.

Equality

Let there be no strife, I pray thee, between me and thee, and between my herdmen and thy herdmen; for we be brethren. *Ge.* 13: 8.

The rich and the poor meet together: the Lord is the maker of them all. *Pr.* 22: 2.

It is not good to have respect of persons in judgment. *Pr.* 24: 23.

It is good and comely for one to eat and to drink, and to enjoy the good of all his labour that he taketh under the sun all the days of his life, which God giveth him: for it is his portion. *Ec.* 5: 18.

Every valley shall be exalted, and every mountain and hill shall be made low: and the crooked shall be made straight. *Is.* 40: 4.

Ye have not kept my ways, but have been partial in the law. *Mal.* 2: 9.

These last have wrought but one hour, and thou hast made them equal unto us, which have borne the burden and heat of the day. *Mat.* 20: 12.

I will give unto this last, even as unto thee. *Mat.* 20: 14.

Whosoever will be great among you, let him be your minister. *Mat.* 20: 26.

One is your Master, even Christ; and all ye are brethren. *Mat.* 23: 8.

They are equal unto the angels. *Lu.* 20: 36.

The same Lord over all is rich unto all that call upon him. *Ro.* 10: 12.

Having then gifts differing according to the grace that is given to us. *Ro.* 12: 6.

The fire shall try every man's work of what sort it is. *1 Co.* 3: 13.

That now at this time your abundance may be a supply for their want, that their abundance also may be a supply for your want: that there may be equality. *2 Co.* 8: 14.

There is neither male nor female: for ye are all one in Christ Jesus. *Ga.* 3: 28.

Who . . . thought it not robbery to be equal with God. *Ph.* 2: 6.

Let the brother of low degree rejoice in that he is exalted: But the rich, in that he is made low: because as the flower of the grass he shall pass away. *Ja.* 1: 9, 10.

The length and the breadth and the height of it are equal. *Re.* 21: 16.

See also
Brotherhood; Caste; Class; Impartiality; Inequality; Partner; Persons, Respect of; Socialism.

Equality, Racial

The profit of the earth is for all. *Ec.* 5: 9.

I will gather all nations and tongues; and they shall come, and see my glory. *Is.* 66: 18.

Are ye not as children of the Ethiopians unto me, O children of Israel? saith the Lord. *Am.* 9: 7.

In Jerusalem, and in all Judaea, and in Samaria, and unto the uttermost part of the earth. *Ac.* 1: 8.

God . . . hath made of one blood all nations of men for to dwell on all the face of the earth. *Ac.* 17: 24, 26.

Where there is neither Greek nor Jew, circumcision nor uncircumcision, Barbarian, Scythian, bond nor free: but Christ is all, and in all. *Col.* 3: 11.

I saw another angel fly in the midst of heaven, having the everlasting gospel to preach unto them that dwell on the earth, and to every nation, and kindred, and tongue, and people. *Re.* 14: 6.

The leaves of the tree were for the healing of the nations. *Re.* 22: 2.

See also
Nations, League of; Race.

Era

Instead of thy fathers shall be thy children. *Ps.* 45: 16.

He appointed the moon for seasons. *Ps.* 104: 19.

One generation passeth away, and another generation cometh: but the earth abideth for ever. *Ec.* 1: 4.

A wise man's heart discerneth both time and judgment. *Ec.* 8: 5.

Remember ye not the former things, neither consider the things of old. *Is.* 43: 18.

I the Lord will hasten it in his time. *Is.* 60: 22.

There shall be no more thence an infant of days, nor an old man that hath not filled his days. *Is.* 65: 20.

He changeth the times and the seasons. *Da.* 2: 21.

The children of this world are in their generation wiser than the children of light. *Lu.* 16: 8.

It is not for you to know the times or the seasons, which the Father hath put in his own power. *Ac.* 1: 7.

David, after he had served his own generation by the will of God, fell on sleep. *Ac.* 13: 36.

Ye observe days, and months, and times, and years. *Ga.* 4: 10.

The mystery . . . Which in other ages was not made known unto the sons of men. *Ep.* 3: 3, 5.

See also
Epoch; Genealogy; Generation; Period; Time.

Errand

He shall send his angel before thee. *Ge.* 24: 7.

God did send me before you to preserve life. *Ge.* 45: 5.

Come now therefore, and I will send thee unto Pharaoh. *Ex.* 3: 10.

Send thou men, that they may search the land of Canaan. *Nu.* 13: 2.

Up, that I may send thee away. *1 S.* 9: 26.

A wicked messenger falleth into mischief. *Pr.* 13: 17.

As the cold of snow in the time of harvest, so is a faithful messenger to them that send him: for he refresheth the soul of his masters. *Pr.* 25: 13.

He that sendeth a message by the hand of a fool cutteth off the feet. *Pr.* 26: 6.

I heard the voice of the Lord, saying, Whom shall I send, and who will go for us? Then said I, Here am I; send me. *Is.* 6: 8.

The Lord . . . hath sent me . . . to proclaim liberty to the captives. *Is.* 61: 1.

Behold, I will send my messenger, and he shall prepare the way before me. *Mal.* 3: 1.

Behold, I send my messenger before thy face. *Mat.* 11: 10.

He hath sent me . . . to set at liberty them that are bruised. *Lu.* 4: 18.

I will send my beloved son. *Lu.* 20: 13.

Gird thyself, and bind on thy sandals. *Ac.* 12: 8.

See also
Ambassador; God, Messenger of.

Error

It is a people that do err in their heart. *Ps. 95: 10.*

He that refuseth reproof erreth. *Pr. 10: 17.*

Cease, my son, to hear the instruction that causeth to err from the words of knowledge. *Pr. 19: 27.*

They err in vision, they stumble in judgment. *Is. 28: 7.*

The wayfaring men, though fools, shall not err therein. *Is. 35: 8.*

Neither was there any error or fault found in him. *Da. 6: 4.*

They shall run to and fro to seek the word of the Lord, and shall not find it. *Am. 8: 12.*

Ye do err, not knowing the scriptures, nor the power of God. *Mat. 22: 29.*

If a man be overtaken in a fault, ye which are spiritual, restore such an one in the spirit of meekness. *Ga. 6: 1.*

See also

Blunder; Defect; Delusion; Fault; Imperfection; Mistake.

Escape

They have slain the servants with the edge of the sword; and I only am escaped alone to tell thee. *Jb. 1: 15.*

The eyes of the wicked shall fail, and they shall not escape. *Jb. 11: 20.*

He looseth the bond of kings, and girdeth their loins with a girdle. *Jb. 12: 18.*

Oh that I had wings like a dove! *Ps. 55: 6.*

Shall they escape by iniquity? in thine anger cast down the people, O God. *Ps. 56: 7.*

Deliver me in thy righteousness, and cause me to escape. *Ps. 71: 2.*

Our soul is escaped as a bird out of the snare of the fowlers: the snare is broken, and we are escaped. *Ps. 124: 7.*

He that speaketh lies shall not escape. *Pr. 19: 5.*

Therefore I fled before unto Tarshish: for I knew that thou art a gracious God, and merciful, slow to anger, and of great kindness, and repentest thee of the evil. *Jon. 4: 2.*

How can ye escape the damnation of hell? *Mat. 23: 33.*

The younger son gathered all together, and took his journey into a far country. *Lu. 15: 13.*

Pray always, that ye may be accounted worthy to escape all these things that shall come to pass. *Lu. 21: 36.*

His chains fell off from his hands. *Ac. 12: 7.*

Thinkest thou this, O man, that judgest them which do such things, and doest the same, that thou shalt escape the judgment of God? *Ro. 2: 3.*

God . . . will with the temptation also make a way of escape. *1 Co. 10: 13.*

How shall we escape, if we neglect so great salvation? *He. 2: 3.*

Through faith . . . escaped the edge of the sword. *He. 11: 33, 34.*

Having escaped the corruption that is in the world through lust. *2 Pe. 1: 4.*

See also

Avoidance; Flight.

Establishment

With thee will I establish my covenant. *Ge. 6: 18.*

The Lord shall establish thee an holy people unto himself. *De. 28: 9.*

He hath founded it upon the seas, and established it upon the floods. *Ps. 24: 2.*

He built his sanctuary like high palaces, like the earth which he hath established for ever. *Ps. 78: 69.*

Establish thou the work of our hands upon us. *Ps. 90: 17.*

Thy throne is established of old: thou art from everlasting. *Ps. 93: 2.*

Through wisdom is an house builded; and by understanding it is established. *Pr. 24: 3.*

It shall come to pass in the last days, that the mountain of the Lord's house shall be established in the top of the mountains. *Is. 2: 2.*

In mercy shall the throne be established. *Is. 16: 5.*

In-righteousness shalt thou be established: thou shalt be far from oppression; for thou shalt not fear. *Is. 54: 14.*

Hate the evil, and love the good, and establish judgment in the gate. *Am. 5: 15.*

So were the churches established in the faith, and increased in number daily. *Ac. 16: 5.*

Comfort your hearts, and stablish you in every good word and work. *2 Th. 2: 17.*

Be ye also patient; stablish your hearts: for the coming of the Lord draweth nigh. *Ja. 5: 8.*

See also

Certainty; Foundation.

Esteem

The Lord hath avouched thee this day to be his peculiar people. *De. 26: 18.*

Will he esteem thy riches? no, nor gold, nor all the forces of strength. *Jb. 36: 19.*

Thou . . . hast crowned him with glory and honour. *Ps. 8: 5.*

Nevertheless man being in honour abideth not. *Ps. 49: 12.*

I esteem all thy precepts concerning all things to be right. *Ps. 119: 128.*

Before honour is humility. *Pr. 15: 33.*

We esteemed him not. *Is. 53: 3.*

A prophet is not without honour, save in his own country, and in his own house. *Mat. 13: 57.*

I am . . . a citizen of no mean city. *Ac. 21: 39.*

Glory, honour, and peace, to every man that worketh good. *Ro. 2: 10.*

Render therefore to all their dues: . . . honour to whom honour. *Ro. 13: 7.*

One man esteemeth one day above another: another esteemeth every day alike. Let every man be fully persuaded in his own mind. *Ro. 14: 5.*

In lowliness of mind let each esteem other better than themselves. *Ph. 2: 3.*

Esteeming the reproach of Christ greater riches than the treasures in Egypt. *He. 11: 26.*

Honour all men. Love the brotherhood. Fear God. Honour the king. *1 Pe. 2: 17.*

See also

Admiration; Honor; Regard; Respect.

Estrangement

The wicked are estranged from the womb: they go astray as soon as they be born, speaking lies. *Ps. 58: 3.*

What iniquity have your fathers found in

me, that they are gone far from me, and have walked after vanity? *Je.* **2: 5.**

They are all estranged from me through their idols. *Eze.* **14: 5.**

Their heart is far from me. *Mat.* **15: 8.**

Having no hope, and without God in the world. *Ep.* **2: 12.**

See also

Apostasy; Backsliding; Christ, Denial of; God, Denial of; God, Estrangement from; God, Rejection of.

Eternity

The Lord shall reign for ever and ever. *Ex.* **15: 18.**

O that there were such an heart in them, that they would fear me, and keep all my commandments always, that it might be well with them, and with their children for ever! *De.* **5: 29.**

I will dwell in the house of the Lord for ever. *Ps.* **23: 6.**

My times are in thy hand. *Ps.* **31: 15.**

Before the mountains were brought forth, . . . even from everlasting to everlasting, thou art God. *Ps.* **90: 2.**

Thy years are throughout all generations. *Ps.* **102: 24.**

The mercy of the Lord is from everlasting to everlasting upon them that fear him. *Ps.* **103: 17.**

Lead me in the way everlasting. *Ps.* **139: 24.**

Thy kingdom is an everlasting kingdom, and thy dominion endureth throughout all generations. *Ps.* **145: 13.**

They that be wise shall shine as the brightness of the firmament; and they that turn many to righteousness as the stars for ever and ever. *Da.* **12: 3.**

Good Master, what shall I do that I may inherit eternal life? *Mk.* **10: 17.**

Lord, evermore give us this bread. *Jn.* **6: 34.**

This is life eternal, that they might know thee the only true God, and Jesus Christ whom thou hast sent. *Jn.* **17: 3.**

The things which are not seen are eternal. *2 Co.* **4: 18.**

According to the eternal purpose. *Ep.* **3: 11.**

Lay hold on eternal life. *1 Ti.* **6: 12.**

Thou art the same, and thy years shall not fail. *He.* **1: 12.**

Beloved, be not ignorant of this one thing, that one day is with the Lord as a thousand years, and a thousand years as one day. *2 Pe.* **3: 8.**

Dominion and power, both now and ever. *Jude* **1: 25.**

See also

Christ, Resurrection of; Easter; Immortality; Life, the Eternal; Resurrection.

Eucharist

It is good for me to draw near to God. *Ps.* **73: 28.**

This is my body. *Mat.* **26: 26.**

This is my blood of the new testament, which is shed for many for the remission of sins. *Mat.* **26: 28.**

With desire I have desired to eat this passover with you before I suffer. *Lu.* **22: 15.**

This cup is the new testament in my blood, which is shed for you. *Lu.* **22: 20.**

Except ye eat the flesh of the Son of man, and drink his blood, ye have no life in you. *Jn.* **6: 53.**

He that eateth me, even he shall live by me. *Jn.* **6: 57.**

The cup of blessing which we bless, is it not the communion of the blood of Christ? The bread which we break, is it not the communion of the body of Christ? *1 Co.* **10: 16.**

As often as ye eat this bread, and drink this cup, ye do shew the Lord's death till he come. *1 Co.* **11: 26.**

Whosoever shall eat this bread, and drink this cup of the Lord, unworthily, shall be guilty of the body and blood of the Lord. *1 Co.* **11: 27.**

We are made partakers of Christ. *He.* **3: 14.**

See also

Christ, Blood of; Christ, Body of; Communion, Service of; Supper, the Last; Supper, the Lord's.

Eulogy

Enoch walked with God: and he was not; for God took him. *Ge.* **5: 24.**

His name shall be continued as long as the sun. *Ps.* **72: 17.**

Precious in the sight of the Lord is the death of his saints. *Ps.* **116: 15.**

The path of the just is as the shining light, that shineth more and more unto the perfect day. *Pr.* **4: 18.**

The memory of the just is blessed. *Pr.* **10: 7.**

The fruit of the righteous is a tree of life; and he that winneth souls is wise. *Pr.* **11: 30.**

The hoary head is a crown of glory, if it be found in the way of righteousness. *Pr.* **16: 31.**

A good name is rather to be chosen than great riches. *Pr.* **22: 1.**

Let another man praise thee, and not thine own mouth; a stranger, and not thine own lips. *Pr.* **27: 2.**

Favour is deceitful, and beauty is vain: but a woman that feareth the Lord, she shall be praised. *Pr.* **31: 30.**

A good name is better than precious ointment; and the day of death than the day of one's birth. *Ec.* **7: 1.**

Inasmuch as ye have done it unto one of the least of these my brethren, ye have done it unto me. *Mat.* **25: 40.**

Wheresoever this gospel shall be preached in the whole world, there shall also this, that this woman hath done, be told for a memorial of her. *Mat.* **26: 13.**

Truly this was the Son of God. *Mat.* **27: 54.**

Woe unto you! for ye build the sepulchres of the prophets, and your fathers killed them. *Lu.* **11: 47.**

He being dead yet speaketh. *He.* **11: 4.**

Jesus the author and finisher of our faith . . . endured the cross, despising the shame, and is set down at the right hand of the throne of God. *He.* **12: 2.**

Ye are come . . . to the spirits of just men made perfect. *He.* **12: 22, 23.**

These are they which came out of great tribulation, and have washed their robes, and made them white in the blood of the Lamb. *Re.* **7: 14.**

Blessed are the dead which die in the Lord from henceforth: Yea, saith the Spirit, that they may rest from their labours; and their works do follow them. *Re.* 14: 13.

See also

Adulation; Commendation; Fame; Praise; Renown· Reputation.

Evangelism

He that winneth souls is wise. *Pr.* 11: 30.

A true witness delivereth souls. *Pr.* 14: 25.

How beautiful upon the mountains are the feet of him that bringeth good tidings, that publisheth peace. *Is.* 52: 7.

They that be wise shall shine as the brightness of the firmament; and they that turn many to righteousness as the stars for ever and ever. *Da.* 12: 3.

Follow me, and I will make you fishers of men. *Mat.* 4: 19.

Go ye therefore, and teach all nations. *Mat.* 28: 19.

The gospel must first be published among all nations. *Mk.* 13: 10.

Go ye into all the world, and preach the gospel to every creature. *Mk.* 16: 15.

I am the voice of one crying in the wilderness, Make straight the way of the Lord. *Jn.* 1: 23.

I am not ashamed of the gospel of Christ. *Ro.* 1: 16.

I declare unto you the gospel which I preached unto you, which also ye have received, and wherein ye stand. *1 Co.* 15: 1.

He gave some, . . . evangelists. *Ep.* 4: 11.

Do the work of an evangelist, make full proof of thy ministry. *2 Ti.* 4: 5.

See also

Gospel; News, Good; Proselyte; Tidings.

Evening

They heard the voice of the Lord God walking in the garden in the cool of the day. *Ge.* 3: 8.

At even thou shalt say, Would God it were morning! *De.* 28: 67.

Let the stars of the twilight thereof be dark. *Jb.* 3: 9.

Evening, and morning, and at noon, will I pray. *Ps.* 55: 17.

In the evening it is cut down, and withereth. *Ps.* 90: 6.

Man goeth forth unto his work and to his labour until the evening. *Ps.* 104: 23.

In the evening withhold not thine hand. *Ec.* 11: 6.

The shadows of evening are stretched out. *Je.* 6: 4.

When it is evening ye say, It will be fair weather: for the sky is red. *Mat.* 16: 2.

Ye know not when the master of the house cometh, at even, or at midnight, or at the cockcrowing, or in the morning. *Mk.* 13: 35.

Abide with us: for it is toward evening. *Lu.* 24: 29.

See also

Night; Twilight.

Evidence

This sign shalt thou have of the Lord, that the Lord will do the thing that he hath spoken. *2 K.* 20: 9.

It shall be to the Lord for a name, for an everlasting sign that shall not be cut off. *Is.* 55: 13.

Philip saith unto him, Come and see. *Jn.* 1: 46.

They took knowledge of them, that they had been with Jesus. *Ac.* 4: 13.

That signs and wonders may be done by the name of thy holy child Jesus. *Ac.* 4: 30.

Simon . . . continued with Philip, and wondered, beholding the miracles and signs which were done. *Ac.* 8: 13.

Last of all he was seen of me also, as of one born out of due time. *1 Co.* 15: 8.

Shew ye to them, and before the churches, the proof of your love. *2 Co.* 8: 24.

The signs of an apostle were wrought among you in all patience, in signs, and wonders, and mighty deeds. *2 Co.* 12: 12.

Ye seek a proof of Christ speaking in me. *2 Co.* 13: 3.

Make full proof of thy ministry. *2 Ti.* 4: 5.

It is evident that our Lord sprang out of Juda. *He.* 7: 14.

Now faith is the substance of things hoped for, the evidence of things not seen. *He.* 11: 1.

See also

Christ, Witness of; God, Evidence of; God, Witness of; Proof; Testimony; Witness.

Evil

The Lord said unto Satan, Behold, all that he hath is in thy power. *Jb.* 1: 12.

Wickedness shall be broken as a tree. *Jb.* 24: 20.

Yea, though I walk through the valley of the shadow of death, I will fear no evil. *Ps.* 23: 4.

I had rather be a doorkeeper in the house of my God, than to dwell in the tents of wickedness. *Ps.* 84: 10.

Ye that love the Lord, hate evil. *Ps.* 97: 10.

He shall not be afraid of evil tidings. *Ps.* 112: 7.

Woe unto them that call evil good, ana good evil. *Is.* 5: 20.

Their works are in the dark. *Is.* 29: 15.

Wherefore doth the way of the wicked prosper? wherefore are all they happy that deal very treacherously? *Je.* 12: 1.

Shall there be evil in a city, and the Lord hath not done it? *Am.* 3: 6.

Then was Jesus led up of the spirit into the wilderness to be tempted of the devil. *Mat.* 4: 1.

I say unto you, That ye resist not evil. *Mat.* 5: 39.

If thine eye be evil, thy whole body shall be full of darkness. *Mat.* 6: 23.

They . . . gathered the good into vessels, but cast the bad away. *Mat.* 13: 48.

Then entered Satan into Judas surnamed Iscariot, being of the number of the twelve. *Lu.* 22: 3.

Abhor that which is evil; cleave to that which is good. *Ro.* 12: 9.

Be not overcome of evil, but overcome evil with good. *Ro.* 12: 21.

Redeeming the time, because the days are evil. *Ep.* 5: 16.

Take unto you the whole armour of God, that ye may be able to withstand in the evil day. *Ep.* 6: 13.

Abstain from all appearance of evil. *1 Th.* 5: 22.

See also

Affliction; Crime; Error; Fault; Guile; Iniquity; Injury; Injustice; Malevolence; Misfortune; Sin; Sinner; Transgression; Trespass; Unrighteousness; Wickedness; Wrong.

Evolution

The righteous shall flourish like the palm tree: he shall grow like a cedar in Lebanon. *Ps.* 92: 12.

Who knoweth the spirit of man that goeth upward? *Ec.* 3: 21.

Instead of the thorn shall come up the fir tree, and instead of the brier shall come up the myrtle tree. *Is.* 55: 13.

He shall grow as the lily, and cast forth his roots as Lebanon. *Ho.* 14: 5.

The kingdom of heaven is like to a grain of mustard seed, which a man took, and sowed in his field: Which indeed is the least of all seeds: but when it is grown, it is the greatest among herbs. *Mat.* 13: 31, 32.

First the blade, then the ear, after that the full corn in the ear. *Mk.* 4: 28.

Thou shalt see greater things than these. *Jn.* 1: 50.

I have yet many things to say unto you, but ye cannot bear them now. *Jn.* 16: 12.

I have planted, Apollos watered; but God gave the increase. *1 Co.* 3: 6.

Now I know in part; but then shall I know even as also I am known. *1 Co.* 13: 12.

Let us go on unto perfection. *He.* 6: 1.

Which in time past were not a people, but are now the people of God. *1 Pe.* 2: 10.

Beloved, now are we the sons of God, and it doth not yet appear what we shall be. *1 Jn.* 3: 2.

See also

Development; Education; Growth; Increase; Progress; Unfolding.

Exaltation

The Lord thy God will set thee on high above all nations of the earth. *De.* 28: 1.

The Lord . . . bringeth low, and lifteth up. *1 S.* 2: 7.

I took thee from the sheepcote, from following the sheep, to be ruler over my people, over Israel. *2 S.* 7: 8.

Thou also hast lifted me up on high above them that rose up against me. *2 S.* 22: 49.

Thou, O Lord, art . . . the lifter up of mine head. *Ps.* 3: 3.

Thou . . . liftest me up from the gates of death. *Ps.* 9: 13.

Let thy salvation, O God, set me up on high. *Ps.* 69: 29.

God is the judge: he putteth down one, and setteth up another. *Ps.* 75: 7.

I will set him on high, because he hath known my name. *Ps.* 91: 14.

Thou, Lord, art high above all the earth: thou art exalted far above all gods. *Ps.* 97: 9.

Thou art my God, I will exalt thee. *Ps.* 118: 28.

It shall come to pass in the last days, that the mountain of the Lord's house shall be established in the top of the mountains. *Is.* 2: 2.

Behold, my servant shall deal prudently, he shall be exalted and extolled, and be very high. *Is.* 52: 13.

I will cause thee to ride upon the high places of the earth. *Is.* 58: 14.

They that be wise shall shine as the brightness of the firmament. *Da.* 12: 3.

He shall be great in the sight of the Lord. *Lu.* 1: 15.

The dayspring from on high hath visited us. *Lu.* 1: 78.

Because thou hast been faithful in a very little, have thou authority over ten cities. *Lu.* 19: 17.

I appoint unto you a kingdom. *Lu.* 22: 29.

Tarry ye, . . . until ye be endued with power from on high. *Lu.* 24: 49.

Do ye not know that the saints shall judge the world? *1 Co.* 6: 2.

Caught up to the third heaven. *2 Co.* 12: 2.

And hath made us kings and priests unto God and his Father. *Re.* 1: 6.

See also

Ecstasy; Elevation; Exultation; Rapture.

Examination

Examine me, O Lord, and prove me; try my reins and my heart. *Ps.* 26: 2.

Search me, O God, and know my heart: try me, and know my thoughts: And see if there be any wicked way in me, and lead me in the way everlasting. *Ps.* 139: 23, 24.

For God shall bring every work into judgment. *Ec.* 12: 14.

They . . . searched the scriptures daily, whether those things were so. *Ac.* 17: 11.

I have brought him forth before you, . . . O king Agrippa, that, after examination had, I might have somewhat to write. *Ac.* 25: 26.

Let a man examine himself, and so let him eat of that bread, and drink of that cup. *1 Co.* 11: 28.

We dare not make ourselves of the number, or compare ourselves with some that commend themselves; but they measuring themselves by themselves, and comparing themselves among themselves, are not wise. *2 Co.* 10: 12.

See also

Consideration; Inquiry; Study.

Example

Thou shalt not follow a multitude to do evil. *Ex.* 23: 2.

Take heed to thyself . . . that thou enquire not after their gods, saying, How did these nations serve their gods? even so will I do likewise. *De.* 12: 30.

What man is there that is fearful and fainthearted? let him go and return unto his house, lest his brethren's heart faint as well as his heart. *De.* 20: 8.

His sons walked not in his ways, but turned aside after lucre, and took bribes, and perverted judgment. *1 S.* 8: 3.

Nay; but we will have a king over us; That we also may be like all the nations. *1 S.* 8: 19, 20.

If a ruler hearken to lies, all his servants are wicked. *Pr.* 29: 12.

Ye are the light of the world. *Mat.* 5: 14.

Neither do men light a candle, and put it under a bushel, but on a candlestick; and it giveth light unto all that are in the house. *Mat.* 5: 15.

Take my yoke upon you, and learn of me. *Mat.* 11: 29.

We are made a spectacle unto the world, and to angels, and to men. *1 Co.* 4: 9.

These things were our examples, to the intent we should not lust after evil things. *1 Co.* 10: 6.

Brethren, be followers together of me. *Ph.* 3: 17.

Ye know what manner of men we were among you for your sake. *1 Th.* 1: 5.

Ye were ensamples to all that believe. *1 Th.* 1: 7.

Be thou an example of the believers, in word, in conversation, . . . in faith, in purity. *1 Ti.* 4: 12.

Consider the Apostle and High Priest of our profession, Christ Jesus. *He.* 3: 1.

Looking unto Jesus the author and finisher of our faith. *He.* 12: 2.

So is the will of God, that with well doing ye may put to silence the ignorance of foolish men. *1 Pe.* 2: 15.

Neither as being lords over God's heritage, but being ensamples to the flock. *1 Pe.* 5: 3.

Sodom and Gomorrah . . . are set forth for an example, suffering the vengeance of eternal fire. *Jude* 1: 7.

See also

Ideal; Influence; Leaven; Model; Pattern; Standard.

Excellence

O Lord our Lord, how excellent is thy name in all the earth! *Ps.* 8: 1.

The excellent, in whom is all my delight. *Ps.* 16: 3.

How excellent is thy lovingkindness, O God! *Ps.* 36: 7.

Thou art more glorious and excellent than the mountains of prey. *Ps.* 76: 4.

His name alone is excellent. *Ps.* 148: 13.

I saw that wisdom excelleth folly, as far as light excelleth darkness. *Ec.* 2: 13.

Sing unto the Lord; for he hath done excellent things. *Is.* 12: 5.

I will make thee an eternal excellency, a joy of many generations. *Is.* 60: 15.

Is this the city that men call The perfection of beauty, The joy of the whole earth? *La.* 2: 15.

Thy borders are in the midst of the seas, thy builders have perfected thy beauty. *Eze.* 27: 4.

Thou wast perfect in thy ways from the day that thou wast created, till iniquity was found in thee. *Eze.* 28: 15.

I . . . came not with excellency of speech or of wisdom. *1 Co.* 2: 1.

Yet shew I unto you a more excellent way. *1 Co.* 12: 31.

We have this treasure in earthen vessels, that the excellency of the power may be of God, and not of us. *2 Co.* 4: 7.

That ye may approve things that are excellent. *Ph.* 1: 10.

Whatsoever things are lovely, . . . think on these things. *Ph.* 4: 8.

Now hath he obtained a more excellent ministry. *He.* 8: 6.

See also

Christ, Preëminence of; Dignity; God, Primacy of; Goodness; Greatness; Perfection; Pre-

eminence; Superiority; Supremacy; Value; Worth.

Excess

The stuff they had was sufficient for all the work to make it, and too much. *Ex.* 36: 7.

Ye take too much upon you, seeing all the congregation are holy. *Nu.* 16: 3.

If riches increase, set not your heart upon them. *Ps.* 62: 10.

Be not righteous over much; neither make thyself overwise. *Ec.* 7: 16.

Be not over much wicked, neither be thou foolish. *Ec.* 7: 17.

Except your righteousness shall exceed the righteousness of the scribes and Pharisees, ye shall in no case enter into the kingdom of heaven. *Mat.* 5: 20.

If ye salute your brethren only, what do ye more than others? *Mat.* 5: 47.

Within they are full of extortion and excess. *Mat.* 23: 25.

Gather up the fragments that remain. *Jn.* 6: 12.

At midday, O king, I saw in the way a light from heaven, above the brightness of the sun, shining round about me. *Ac.* 26: 13.

In all these things we are more than conquerors through him that loved us. *Ro.* 8: 37.

We were pressed out of measure, above strength, insomuch that we despaired even of life. *2 Co.* 1: 8.

If the ministration of condemnation be glory, much more doth the ministration of righteousness exceed in glory. *2 Co.* 3: 9.

We stretch not ourselves beyond our measure. *2 Co.* 10: 14.

In labours more abundant, in stripes above measure, in prisons more frequent, in deaths oft. *2 Co.* 11: 23.

Be not drunk with wine, wherein is excess; but be filled with the Spirit. *Ep.* 5: 18.

Having confidence in thy obedience, . . . knowing that thou wilt also do more than I say. *Phm.* 21.

See also

Superfluity.

Excommunication

Whosoever hath sinned against me, him will I blot out of my book. *Ex.* 32: 33.

Let me alone, that I may destroy them, and blot out their name from under heaven. *De.* 9: 14.

All the curses that are written in this book shall lie upon him. *De.* 29: 20.

I have set before you life and death, blessing and cursing: therefore choose life that both thou and thy seed may live. *De.* 30: 19.

The Lord said not that he would blot out the name of Israel from under heaven. *2 K.* 14: 27.

I did cast them out as the dirt in the streets. *Ps.* 18: 42.

Though he fall, he shall not be utterly cast down. *Ps.* 37: 24.

Let them be blotted out of the book of the living, and not be written with the righteous. *Ps.* 69: 28.

As he loved cursing, so let it come unto him: as he delighted not in blessing, so let it be far from him. *Ps.* 109: 17.

I will cast you out of my sight. *Je.* 7: 15.

I will give unto thee the keys of the kingdom of heaven: and whatsoever thou shalt bind on earth shall be bound in heaven: and whatsoever thou shalt loose on earth shall be loosed in heaven. *Mat.* 16: 19.

Depart from me, ye cursed, into everlasting fire, prepared for the devil and his angels. *Mat.* 25: 41.

These shall go away into everlasting punishment. *Mat.* 25: 46.

I . . . have the keys of hell and of death. *Re.* 1: 18.

See also

Anathema; Ban; Curse.

Excuse

Ah, Lord God! behold, I cannot speak: for I am a child. *Je.* 1: 6.

When the young man heard that saying he went away sorrowful: for he had great possessions. *Mat.* 19: 22.

They all with one consent began to make excuse. *Lu.* 14: 18.

I have bought a piece of ground, and I must needs go and see it: I pray thee have me excused. *Lu.* 14: 18.

I have bought five yoke of oxen, and I go to prove them: I pray thee have me excused. *Lu.* 14: 19.

I have married a wife, and therefore I cannot come. *Lu.* 14: 20.

Go thy way for this time; when I have a convenient season, I will call for thee. *Ac.* 24: 25.

The invisible things of him from the creation of the world are clearly seen, being understood by the things that are made; . . . so that they are without excuse. *Ro.* 1: 20.

Their conscience also bearing witness, and their thoughts the mean while accusing or else excusing one another. *Ro.* 2: 15.

Think ye that we excuse ourselves unto you? 2 *Co.* 12: 19.

See also

Cowardice; Palliation; Pardon; Timidity.

Execution

Thou hast done well in executing that which is right in mine eyes. 2 *K.* 10: 30.

Whosoever will not do the law of thy God, and the law of the king, let judgment be executed speedily upon him. *Ezr.* 7: 26.

He performeth the thing that is appointed for me. *Jb.* 23: 14.

The Lord is known by the judgment which he executeth. *Ps.* 9: 16.

The Lord executeth righteousness and judgment for all that are oppressed. *Ps.* 103: 6.

I have sworn, and I will perform it. *Ps.* 119: 106.

Being fully persuaded that, what he had promised, he was able also to perform. *Ro.* 4: 21.

See also

Accomplishment; Achievement; Administration; Completion; Fulfilment; Operation; Performance; Slaughter.

Exercise

Saul secretly practised mischief against him. *1 S.* 23: 9.

Incline not my heart to any evil thing, to practise wicked works with men that work iniquity. *Ps.* 141: 4.

The vile person will speak villany, and his heart will work iniquity, to practise hypocrisy, and to utter error against the Lord. *Is.* 32: 6.

I am the Lord which exercise lovingkindness, judgment, and righteousness, in the earth. *Je.* 9: 24.

Herein do I exercise myself, to have always a conscience void of offence toward God, and toward men. *Ac.* 24: 16.

Exercise thyself rather unto godliness. *1 Ti.* 4: 7.

Bodily exercise profiteth little: but godliness is profitable unto all things. *1 Ti.* 4: 8.

See also

Custom; Discipline; Habit; Manners; Practice.

Exertion

My spirit shall not always strive with man, for that he also is flesh. *Ge.* 6: 3.

There is no straw given unto thy servants, and they say to us, Make brick. *Ex.* 5: 16.

Go therefore now, and work. *Ex.* 5: 18.

The people had a mind to work. *Ne.* 4: 6.

Go to the ant, thou sluggard; consider her ways, and be wise. *Pr.* 6: 6.

I gave my heart to seek and search out by wisdom concerning all things that are done under heaven: this sore travail hath God given to the sons of man to be exercised therewith. *Ec.* 1: 13.

Strive to enter in at the strait gate. *Lu.* 13: 24.

My Father worketh hitherto, and I work. *Jn.* 5: 17.

I must work the works of him that sent me, while it is day: the night cometh, when no man can work. *Jn.* 9: 4.

Not slothful in business. *Ro.* 12: 11.

I strived to preach the gospel. *Ro.* 15: 20.

Work out your own salvation with fear and trembling. *Ph.* 2: 12.

If any would not work, neither should he eat. 2 *Th.* 3: 10.

Exercise thyself rather unto godliness. *1 Ti.* 4: 7.

Senses exercised to discern both good and evil. *He.* 5: 14.

That ye be not slothful, but followers of them who through faith and patience inherit the promises. *He.* 6: 12.

See also

Effort; Endeavor; Labor; Trial.

Exhaustion

They made their lives bitter with hard bondage, in morter, and in brick. *Ex.* 1: 14.

This thing is too heavy for thee. *Ex.* 18: 18.

Your strength shall be spent in vain. *Le.* 26: 20.

There the weary be at rest. *Jb.* 3: 17.

My days are swifter than a weaver's shuttle, and are spent without hope. *Jb.* 7: 6.

There is treasure to be desired and oil in the dwelling of the wise; but a foolish man spendeth it up. *Pr.* 21: 20.

He that keepeth company with harlots spendeth his substance. *Pr.* 29: 3.

Who knoweth what is good for a man in this life, all the days of his vain life which he spendeth as a shadow? *Ec.* 6: 12.

There is no healing of thy bruise. *Na.* 3: 19.

When he saw the multitudes, he was moved with compassion on them, because they fainted. *Mat.* 9: 36.

They bind heavy burdens and grievous to be borne, and lay them on men's shoulders. *Mat.* 23: 4.

Jesus therefore, being wearied with his journey, sat thus on the well. *Jn.* 4: 6.

The hour cometh, yea, is now come, that ye shall be scattered, every man to his own, and shall leave me alone. *Jn.* 16: 32.

The night is far spent, the day is at hand. *Ro.* 13: 12.

We then that are strong ought to bear the infirmities of the weak. *Ro.* 15: 1.

The weakness of God is stronger than men. *1 Co.* 1: 25.

My strength is made perfect in weakness. *2 Co.* 12: 9.

I will very gladly spend and be spent for you. *2 Co.* 12: 15.

See also

Faintness; Weariness; Work.

Exhortation

Fear thou not; for I am with thee: be not dismayed; for I am thy God. *Is.* 41: 10.

The Lord God hath given me the tongue of the learned, that I should know how to speak a word in season to him that is weary. *Is.* 50: 4.

Confirming the souls of the disciples, and exhorting them to continue in the faith. *Ac.* 14: 22.

I exhort you to be of good cheer. *Ac.* 27: 22.

Till I come, give attendance to reading, to exhortation, to doctrine. *1 Ti.* 4: 13.

These things teach and exhort. *1 Ti.* 6: 2.

Exhort one another daily, while it is called To day. *He.* 3: 13.

Exhorting one another: and so much the more, as ye see the day approaching. *He.* 10: 25.

Ye have forgotten the exhortation which speaketh unto you as unto children. *He.* 12: 5.

See also

Admonition; Advice; Charge; Counsel; Instruction; Persuasion.

Exile

Thou art a stranger, and also an exile. *2 S.* 15: 19.

So was Israel carried away out of their own land. *2 K.* 17: 23.

The children of the captivity kept the passover. *Ezr.* 6: 19.

I am a stranger in the earth: hide not thy commandments from me. *Ps.* 119: 19.

By the rivers of Babylon, there we sat down, yea, we wept, when we remembered Zion. *Ps.* 137: 1.

There they that carried us away captive required of us a song. *Ps.* 137: 3.

How shall we sing the Lord's song in a strange land? *Ps.* 137: 4.

The captive exile hasteneth that he may be loosed. *Is.* 51: 14.

Weep sore for him that goeth away: for he shall return no more, nor see his native country. *Je.* 22: 10.

They called thee an Outcast, saying, This is Zion, whom no man seeketh after. *Je.* 30: 17.

Arise, and let us go again to our own people, and to the land of our nativity, from the oppressing sword. *Je.* 46: 16.

I scattered them among the heathen, and they were dispersed through the countries. *Eze.* 36: 19.

These are the people of the Lord, and are gone forth out of his land. *Eze.* 36: 20.

They shall not dwell in the Lord's land. *Ho.* 9: 3.

In that day . . . will I assemble her that halteth, and I will gather her that is driven out, and her that I have afflicted. *Mi.* 4: 6.

Blessed are ye, when men shall hate you, and when they shall separate you from their company. *Lu.* 6: 22.

He that leadeth into captivity shall go into captivity. *Re.* 13: 10.

See also

Banishment; Captivity; Dispersion; Emigration; Expatriation; Fugitive; Migration; Outcast: Refugee.

Existence

God said, Let the waters bring forth abundantly the moving creature that hath life. *Ge.* 1: 20.

Man became a living soul. *Ge.* 2: 7.

Enoch walked with God: and he was not; for God took him. *Ge.* 5: 24.

I AM THAT I AM. *Ex.* 3: 14.

In whose hand is the soul of every living thing, and the breath of all mankind. *Jb.* 12: 10.

I shall not die, but live, and declare the works of the Lord. *Ps.* 118: 17.

Son of man, can these bones live? *Eze.* 37: 3.

Behold, I will cause breath to enter into you, and ye shall live. *Eze.* 37: 6.

This do, and thou shalt live. *Lu.* 10: 28.

The life is more than meat. *Lu.* 12: 23.

In him we live, and move, and have our being. *Ac.* 17: 28.

One Jesus, which was dead, whom Paul affirmed to be alive. *Ac.* 25: 19.

Whether we live therefore, or die, we are the Lord's. *Ro.* 14: 8.

As dying, and, behold, we live. *2 Co.* 6: 9.

For me to live is Christ. *Ph.* 1: 21.

I am he that liveth, and was dead; and, behold, I am alive for evermore. *Re.* 1: 18.

Thou hast a name that thou livest, and art dead. *Re.* 3: 1.

See also

Being; Life.

Exit

Depart ye, depart ye, go ye out from thence. *Is.* 52: 11.

Ye shall go out with joy, and be led forth with peace. *Is.* 55: 12.

When ye depart out of that house or city, shake off the dust of your feet. *Mat.* 10: 14.

Lord, now lettest thou thy servant depart in peace, according to thy word. *Lu.* 2: 29.

I go away, and come again unto you. *Jn.* 14: 28.

Depart, and go in peace. *Ac.* 16: 36.

I am in a strait betwixt the two, having a desire to depart, and to be with Christ. *Ph.* 1: 23.

He went out, not knowing whither he went. *He.* 11: 8.

See also

Departure; Parting.

Exorcism

I will cause . . . the unclean spirit to pass out of the land. *Zch.* **13: 2.**

He gave them power against unclean spirits, to cast them out. *Mat.* **10: 1.**

Gather ye together first the tares, and bind them in bundles to burn them. *Mat.* **13: 30.**

Jesus rebuked the devil; and he departed out of the man. *Mat.* **17: 18.**

Come out of the man, thou unclean spirit. *Mk.* **5: 8.**

He had commanded the unclean spirit to come out of the man. For oftentimes it had caught him: and he was kept bound with chains and in fetters; and he brake the bands, and was driven of the devil into the wilderness. *Lu.* **8: 29.**

Then went the devils out of the man, and entered into the swine. *Lu.* **8: 33.**

Jesus rebuked the unclean spirit, and healed the child, and delivered him again to his father. *Lu.* **9: 42.**

The evil spirits went out of them. *Ac.* **19: 12.**

The God of peace shall bruise Satan under your feet shortly. *Ro.* **16: 20.**

See also

Devil.

Expansion

I will . . . enlarge thy borders. *Ex.* **34: 24.**

I will run the way of thy commandments, when thou shalt enlarge my heart. *Ps.* **119: 32.**

By me thy days shall be multiplied, and the years of thy life shall be increased. *Pr.* **9: 11.**

Thou hast multiplied the nation, and not increased the joy. *Is.* **9: 3.**

Of the increase of his government and peace there shall be no end. *Is.* **9: 7.**

Thou hast increased the nation, O Lord, thou hast increased the nation. *Is.* **26: 15.**

Enlarge the place of thy tent, and let them stretch forth the curtains of thine habitations. *Is.* **54: 2.**

Many shall run to and fro, and knowledge shall be increased. *Da.* **12: 4.**

I will be as the dew unto Israel: he shall grow as the lily, and cast forth his roots as Lebanon. *Ho.* **14: 5.**

See also

Development; Enlargement; Evolution; Growth; Increase; Room; Stature.

Expatriation

Art not thou our God, who didst drive out the inhabitants of this land before thy people Israel? *2 Ch.* **20: 7.**

We have heard with our ears, O God, . . . How thou didst drive out the heathen with thy hand. *Ps.* **44: 1, 2.**

Hide the outcasts; bewray not him that wandereth. *Is.* **16: 3.**

Let mine outcasts dwell with thee. *Is.* **16: 4.**

I will restore health unto thee, and I will heal thee of thy wounds, saith the Lord; because they called thee an Outcast. *Je.* **30: 17.**

For the wickedness of their doings I will drive them out of mine house, I will love them no more. *Ho.* **9: 15.**

See also

Banishment; Emigration; Exile; Migration; Outcast; Refugee; Repatriation.

Expectancy

All the days of my appointed time will I wait, till my change come. *Jb.* **14: 14.**

On thee do I wait all the day. *Ps.* **25: 5.**

My soul, wait thou only upon God; for my expectation is from him. He only is my rock and my salvation: he is my defence; I shall not be moved. *Ps.* **62: 5, 6.**

The eyes of all wait upon thee. *Ps.* **145: 15.**

Hope deferred maketh the heart sick. *Pr.* **13: 12.**

Lo, this is our God; we have waited for him, and he will save us. *Is.* **25: 9.**

The Lord is a God of judgment: blessed are all they that wait for him. *Is.* **30: 18.**

Thine eyes shall see the king in his beauty. *Is.* **33: 17.**

It is good that a man should both hope and quietly wait for the salvation of the Lord. *La.* **3: 26.**

The vision is yet for an appointed time: . . . though it tarry, wait for it; because it will surely come, it will not tarry. *Hab.* **2: 3.**

They were all waiting for him. *Lu.* **8: 40.**

Blessed are those servants, whom the lord when he cometh shall find watching. *Lu.* **12: 37.**

Thou shalt see greater things than these. *Jn.* **1: 50.**

He gave heed unto them, expecting to receive something of them. *Ac.* **3: 5.**

The earnest expectation of the creature waiteth. *Ro.* **8: 19.**

The God of hope. *Ro.* **15: 13.**

Waiting for the coming of our Lord Jesus Christ. *1 Co.* **1: 7.**

As often as ye eat this bread, and drink this cup, ye do shew the Lord's death till he come. *1 Co.* **11: 26.**

Our hope of you is stedfast. *2 Co.* **1: 7.**

According to my earnest expectation and my hope. *Ph.* **1: 20.**

Which hope we have as an anchor of the soul. *He.* **6: 19.**

He looked for a city which hath foundations, whose builder and maker is God. *He.* **11: 10.**

They desire a better country, that is, an heavenly. *He.* **11: 16.**

Looking for and hasting unto the coming of the day of God. *2 Pe.* **3: 12.**

See also

Anticipation; Christ, Hope in; Future; God, Hope in; Hope; Progress; Wait.

Expediency

Be not righteous over much; neither make thyself over wise: why shouldest thou destroy thyself? *Ec.* **7: 16.**

It is expedient for us, that one man should die for the people, and that the whole nation perish not. *Jn.* **11: 50.**

It is expedient for you that I go away: for if I go not away, the Comforter will not come unto you. *Jn.* **16: 7.**

I would that all men were even as I myself. But every man hath his proper gift of God, one after this manner, and another after that. *1 Co.* **7: 7.**

To the weak became I as weak, that I might gain the weak: I am made all things to all men, that I might by all means save some. *1 Co.* 9: 22.

All things are lawful for me, but all things are not expedient: all things are lawful for me, but all things edify not. *1 Co.* 10: 23.

It is not expedient for me doubtless to glory. *2 Co.* 12: 1.

Not with eyeservice, as menpleasers; but as the servants of Christ. *Ep.* 6: 6.

See also

Compromise; Fitness; Loyalty, Divided.

Experience

I have learned by experience that the Lord hath blessed me for thy sake. *Ge.* 30: 27.

Ye know the heart of a stranger, seeing ye were strangers in the land of Egypt. *Ex.* 23: 9.

Thou shalt remember all the way which the Lord thy God led thee these forty years in the wilderness, to humble thee, and to prove thee. *De.* 8: 2.

Whence then cometh wisdom? and where is the place of understanding? *Jb.* 28: 20.

I have heard of thee by the hearing of the ear: but now mine eye seeth thee. *Jb.* 42: 5.

If I forget thee, O Jerusalem. *Ps.* 137: 5.

Though thou shouldest bray a fool in a mortar among wheat with a pestle, yet will not his foolishness depart from him. *Pr.* 27: 22.

My heart had great experience of wisdom and knowledge. *Ec* 1: 16.

Go home to thy friends, and tell them how great things the Lord hath done for thee, and hath had compassion on thee. *Mk.* 5: 19.

Even as they delivered them unto us, which from the beginning were eyewitnesses.*Lu.*1:2.

We have seen strange things to day. *Lu.* 5: 26.

Art thou a master of Israel, and knowest not these things? *Jn.* 3: 10.

We speak that we do know, and testify that we have seen; and ye receive not our witness. *Jn.* 3: 11.

Now we believe, not because of thy saying: for we have heard him ourselves, and know that this is indeed the Christ. *Jn.* 4: 42.

One thing I know, that, whereas I was blind, now I see. *Jn.* 9: 25.

He shall receive of mine, and shall shew it unto you. *Jn.* 16: 14.

Except I shall see in his hands the print of the nails, and put my finger into the print of the nails, and thrust my hand into his side, I will not believe. *Jn.* 20: 25.

Because thou hast seen me, thou hast believed: blessed are they that have not seen, and yet have believed. *Jn.* 20: 29.

When they were come, and had gathered the church together, they rehearsed all that God had done with them. *Ac.* 14: 27.

Tribulation worketh patience; And patience, experience; and experience, hope. *Ro.* 5: 3, 4.

Eye hath not seen, nor ear heard, neither have entered into the heart of man, the things which God hath prepared for them that love him. *1 Co.* 2: 9.

The natural man receiveth not the things of the Spirit of God: for they are foolishness unto him: neither can he know them, because they are spiritually discerned. *1 Co.* 2: 14.

Have I not seen Jesus Christ our Lord? *1 Co.* 9: 1.

That we may be able to comfort them which are in any trouble, by the comfort wherewith we ourselves are comforted of God. *2 Co.* 1: 4.

I would ye should understand, brethren, that the things which happened unto me have fallen out rather unto the furtherance of the gospel. *Ph.* 1: 12.

For we have not followed cunningly devised fables, when we made known unto you the power and coming of our Lord Jesus Christ, but were eyewitnesses of his majesty. *2 Pe.* 1: 16.

That which was from the beginning, which we have heard, which we have seen with our eyes, which we have looked upon, and our hands have handled, of the Word of life; . . . That which we have seen and heard declare we unto you. *1 Jn.* 1: 1, 3.

The life was manifested, and we have seen it, and bear witness, and shew unto you that eternal life, which was with the Father, and was manifested unto us. *1 Jn.* 1: 2.

We have known and believed the love that God hath to us. *1 Jn.* 4: 16.

See also

Custom; Discipline; Knowledge; Memory; Test; Trial: Wisdom.

Experiment

Call ye on the name of your gods, and I will call on the name of the Lord: and the God that answereth by fire, let him be God.*1 K.*18:24.

Doth not the ear try words? and the mouth taste his meat? *Jb.* 12: 11.

Thou, O God, hast proved us: thou hast tried us, as silver is tried. *Ps.* 66: 10.

I will walk at liberty: for I seek thy precepts. *Ps.* 119: 45.

Take away the dross from the silver, and there shall come forth a vessel for the finer. *Pr.* 25: 4.

All this have I proved by wisdom. *Ec.* 7: 23.

Let us search and try our ways, and turn again to the Lord. *La.* 3: 40.

And I will bring the third part through the fire, and will refine them as silver is refined, and will try them as gold is tried. *Zch.* 13: 9.

Whose fan is in his hand, and he will throughly purge his floor. *Mat.* 3: 12.

Be ye transformed by the renewing of your mind, that ye may prove what is that good, and acceptable, and perfect will of God. *Ro.* 12: 2.

The fire shall try every man's work of what sort it is. *1 Co.* 3: 13.

If any man's work abide which he hath built thereupon, he shall receive a reward. If any man's work shall be burned, he shall suffer loss: but he himself shall be saved; yet so as by fire. *1 Co.* 3: 14, 15.

By the experiment of this ministration they glorify God for your professed subjection unto the gospel of Christ, and for your liberal distribution unto them. *2 Co.* 9: 13.

Let every man prove his own work. *Ga.* 6: 4.

Prove all things; hold fast that which is good. *1 Th.* 5: 21.

Harden not your hearts, as in the provocation, in the day of temptation in the wilderness. *He.* 3: 8.

Beloved, believe not every spirit, but try

the spirits whether they are of God. *1 Jn.* 4: 1.
See also
Fire; Furnace; Proof; Test; Trial.

Expert

They are craftsmen. *1 Ch.* 4: 14.
These were the potters: . . . they dwelt with the king for his work. *1 Ch.* 4: 23.
The way of a fool is right in his own eyes: but he that hearkeneth unto counsel is wise. *Pr.* 12: 15.
They all hold swords, being expert in war. *S. of S.* 3: 8.
Their arrows shall be as of a mighty expert man. *Je.* 50: 9.
Well favoured, and skilful in all wisdom, and cunning in knowledge, and understanding science. *Da.* 1: 4.
God gave them knowledge and skill in all learning and wisdom. *Da.* 1: 17.
Have any of the rulers or of the Pharisees believed on him? *Jn.* 7: 48.
I know thee to be expert in all customs and questions which are among the Jews. *Ac.* 26: 3.
As a wise masterbuilder, I have laid the foundation, and another buildeth thereon. *1 Co.* 3: 10.
See also
Ability; Adept; Aptitude; Capacity; Handiwork; Knowledge; Mastery; Skill; Workmanship.

Expiation

The land cannot be cleansed of the blood that is shed therein, but by the blood of him that shed it. *Nu.* 35: 33.
Every man shall die for his own sin. *2 Ch.* 25: 4.
Whosoever will not do the law of thy God, and the law of the king, let judgment be executed speedily upon him, whether it be unto death, or to banishment, or to confiscation of goods, or to imprisonment. *Ezr.* 7: 26.
If that nation, against whom I have pronounced, turn from their evil, I will repent of the evil that I thought to do unto them. *Je.* 18: 8.
Therefore now amend your ways and your doings, and obey the voice of the Lord your God. *Je.* 26: 13.
Thus saith the Lord God; Repent, and turn yourselves from your idols. *Eze.* 14: 6.
The people of Nineveh believed God, and proclaimed a fast, and put on sackcloth, from the greatest of them even to the least of them. *Jon.* 3: 5.
Bring forth therefore fruits meet for repentance. *Mat.* 3: 8.
If thou bring thy gift to the altar, and there rememberest that thy brother hath ought against thee; Leave there thy gift before the altar, and go thy way; first be reconciled to thy brother, and then come and offer thy gift. *Mat.* 5: 23, 24.
The children of the kingdom shall be cast out into outer darkness. *Mat.* 8: 12.
If the mighty works, which have been done in you, had been done in Tyre and Sidon, they would have repented long ago in sackcloth and ashes. *Mat.* 11: 21.
He cast down the pieces of silver in the temple, and departed, and went and hanged himself. *Mat.* 27: 5.

Father, I have sinned against heaven, and before thee, And am no more worthy to be called thy son: make me as one of thy hired servants. *Lu.* 15: 18, 19.
This thy brother was dead, and is alive again; and was lost, and is found. *Lu.* 15: 32.
See also
Atonement; Fault; Guilt, Propitiation; Reparation; Satisfaction.

Expiration

Every thing that is in the earth shall die. *Ge.* 6: 17.
Let me die the death of the righteous, and let my last end be like his! *Nu.* 23: 10.
This day I am going the way of all the earth. *Jos.* 23: 14.
Let the day perish wherein I was born. *Jb.* 3: 3.
There the wicked cease from troubling; and there the weary be at rest. *Jb.* 3: 17.
The bitter in soul . . . long for death, . . . and dig for it more than for hid treasures. *Jb.* 3: 20, 21.
Are not my days few? cease then, and let me alone, that I may take comfort a little, Before I go whence I shall not return, even to the land of darkness and the shadow of death. *Jb.* 10: 20, 21.
He maketh wars to cease unto the end of the earth. *Ps.* 46: 9.
Wise men die, likewise the fool and the brutish person perish. *Ps.* 49: 10.
Thou takest away their breath, they die, and return to their dust. *Ps.* 104: 29.
His breath goeth forth, he returneth to his earth. *Ps.* 146: 4.
Man goeth to his long home. *Ec.* 12: 5.
The spirit shall return unto God who gave it. *Ec.* 12: 7.
Lo, I am with you alway, even unto the end of the world. *Mat.* 28: 20.
Whosoever liveth and believeth in me shall never die. *Jn.* 11: 26.
He giveth to all life, and breath, and all things. *Ac.* 17: 25.
I die daily. *1 Co.* 15: 31.
Blessed are the dead which die in the Lord. *Re.* 14: 13.
When the thousand years are expired, Satan shall be loosed out of his prison. *Re.* 20: 7.
See also
Death; Decease; Disappearance; End; Grave.

Exploration

Send thou men, that they may search the land of Canaan. *Nu.* 13: 2.
Get you up . . . And see the land, what it is; and the people that dwelleth therein, whether they be strong or weak, few or many. *Nu.* 13: 17, 18.
Get you up . . . And see . . . what the land is, whether it be fat or lean, whether there be wood therein, or not. And be ye of good courage, and bring of the fruit of the land. *Nu.* 13: 20.
The land, which we passed through to search it, is an exceeding good land. *Nu.* 14: 7.
We will send men before us, and they shall search us out the land, and bring us word again by what way we must go up. *De.* 1: 22.
Joshua the son of Nun sent out of Shittim two men to spy secretly, saying, Go view the

land, even Jericho. *Jos.* **2: 1.**

Go and walk through the land, and describe it, and come again to me. *Jos.* **18: 8.**

They that go down to the sea in ships, that do business in great waters; these see the works of the Lord, and his wonders in the deep. *Ps.* **107: 23: 24.**

The kingdom of heaven is as a man travelling into a far country. *Mat.* **25: 14.**

See also

Quest; Scout; Search; Survey.

Exposure

Be sure your sin will find you out. *Nu.* **32: 23.**

The heaven shall reveal his iniquity; and the earth shall rise up against him. *Jb.* **20: 27.**

Whose hatred is covered by deceit, his wickedness shall be shewed before the whole congregation. *Pr.* **26: 26.**

God shall bring every work into judgment, with every secret thing, whether it be good, or whether it be evil. *Ec.* **12: 14.**

I have shewed thee new things from this time, even hidden things. *Is.* **48: 6.**

I know the things that come into your mind, every one of them. *Eze.* **11: 5.**

He revealeth the deep and secret things: he knoweth what is in the darkness. *Da.* **2: 22.**

Their own doings have beset them about; they are before my face. *Ho.* **7: 2.**

Jesus knew their thoughts. *Mat.* **12: 25.**

There is nothing covered, that shall not be revealed; neither hid, that shall not be known. *Lu.* **12: 2.**

The Lord . . . will bring to light the hidden things of darkness, and will make manifest the counsels of the hearts. *1 Co.* **4: 5.**

See also

Manifestation; **Revelation.**

Exterior

Man looketh on the outward appearance. but the Lord looketh on the heart. *1 S.* **16: 7.**

When ye fast, be not, as the hypocrites, of a sad countenance. *Mat.* **6: 16.**

Ye make clean the outside of the cup and of the platter, but within they are full of extortion and excess. *Mat.* **23: 25.**

Beware of the scribes, which love to go in long clothing. *Mk.* **12: 38.**

I fast twice in the week. *Lu.* **18: 12.**

Judge not according to the appearance. *Jn.* **7: 24.**

That ye may have somewhat to answer them which glory in appearance, and not in heart. *2 Co.* **5: 12.**

Do ye look on things after the outward appearance? *2 Co.* **10: 7.**

Let it not be that outward adorning of plaiting the hair, and of wearing of gold, or of putting on of apparel: But let it be the hidden man of the heart. *1 Pe.* **3: 3, 4.**

See also

Appearance; Inside; Interior; Outside.

Extreme

The Lord God formed man of the dust of the ground. *Ge.* **2: 7.**

From Dan even to Beer-sheba. *Ju.* **20: 1.**

His going forth is from the end of the heaven, and his circuit unto the ends of it. *Ps.* **19: 6.**

According to thy name, O God, so is thy praise unto the ends of the earth. *Ps.* **48: 10.**

As far as the east is from the west. *Ps.* **103: 12.**

The heaven for height, and the earth for depth. *Pr.* **25: 3.**

Who hath established all the ends of the earth? *Pr.* **30: 4.**

Thy pomp is brought down to the grave. *Is.* **14: 11.**

How art thou fallen from heaven, O Lucifer. son of the morning! *Is.* **14: 12.**

Thou hast said in thine heart, I will ascend into heaven. . . . Yet thou shalt be brought down to hell. *Is.* **14: 13, 15.**

Every valley shall be exalted, and every mountain and hill shall be made low. *Is.* **40: 4.**

Upon Elam will I bring the four winds from the four quarters of heaven. *Je.* **49: 36.**

Thou, Capernaum, which art exalted to heaven, shalt be thrust down to hell. *Lu.* **10: 15.**

The kingdom of God . . . is like a grain of mustard seed. *Lu.* **13: 18, 19.**

I saw a star fall from heaven unto the earth *Re.* **9: 1.**

See also

Antithesis; End.

Exultation

God saw everything that he had made, and, behold, it was very good. *Ge.* **1: 31.**

It is a day of blowing the trumpets unto you. *Nu.* **29: 1.**

Shout; for the Lord hath given you the city. *Jos.* **6: 16.**

The morning stars sang together, and all the sons of God shouted for joy. *Jb.* **38: 7.**

Let all those that put their trust in thee rejoice: let them ever shout for joy. *Ps.* **5: 11.**

Rejoice in the Lord, O ye righteous. *Ps.* **33: 1.**

O clap your hands, all ye people; shout unto God with the voice of triumph. *Ps.* **47: 1.**

The singers went before, the players on instruments followed after. *Ps.* **68: 25.**

Let the floods clap their hands: let the hills be joyful together. *Ps.* **98: 8.**

Come before his presence with singing. *Ps.* **100: 2.**

Let the saints be joyful in glory. *Ps.* **149: 5.**

Rejoice ye in that day, and leap for joy. *Lu.* **6: 23.**

My joy is the joy of you all. *2 Co.* **2: 3.**

Rejoice in the Lord alway: and again I say, Rejoice. *Ph.* **4: 4.**

See also

Christ, Joy in; Ecstasy; Exaltation; Gladness; Glory; God, Joy in; Happiness; Joy; Jubilee; Rapture; Rejoicing.

Eye

Eye for eye. *Ex.* **21: 24.**

Lighten mine eyes, lest I sleep the sleep of death. *Ps.* **13: 3.**

Keep me as the apple of the eye. *Ps.* **17: 8.**

The eyes of all wait upon thee. *Ps.* **145: 15.**

The eye is not satisfied with seeing. *Ec.* **1: 8.**

Mine eyes have seen the King, the Lord of hosts. *Is.* **6: 5.**

In that day . . . the eyes of the blind shall see out of obscurity, and out of darkness. *Is.* **29: 18.**

Hear, ye deaf; and look, ye blind, that ye may see. *Is.* 42: 18.

Who is blind, but my servant? *Is.* 42: 19.

Who is blind as he that is perfect? *Is.* 42: 19.

If therefore thine eye be single, thy whole body shall be full of light. *Mat.* 6: 22.

Cast out the beam out of thine own eye; and then shalt thou see clearly to cast out the mote out of thy brother's eye. *Mat.* 7: 5.

The blind receive their sight. *Mat.* 11: 5.

Blessed are your eyes, for they see. *Mat.* 13: 16.

If thine eye offend thee, pluck it out, and cast it from thee. *Mat.* 18: 9.

It is better for thee to enter into the kingdom of God with one eye, than having two eyes to be cast into hell fire. *Mk.* 9: 47.

Mine eyes have seen thy salvation. *Lu.* 2: 30.

Blessed are the eyes which see the things that ye see. *Lu.* 10: 23.

The light of the body is the eye. *Lu.* 11: 34.

If the whole body were an eye, where were the hearing? *1 Co.* 12: 17.

We shall all be changed, In a moment, in the twinkling of an eye. *1 Co.* 15: 51, 52.

Not with eyeservice, as menpleasers. *Ep.* 6: 6.

Round about the throne, were four beasts full of eyes before and behind. *Re.* 4: 6.

God shall wipe away all tears from their eyes. *Re.* 7: 17.

See also

Blindness; God, Eye of; Sight.

F

Fable

Every idle word that men shall speak, they shall give account thereof in the day of judgment. *Mat.* 12: 36.

All these things spake Jesus unto the multitude in parables. *Mat.* 13: 34.

Lo, now speakest thou plainly, and speakest no proverb. *Jn.* 16: 29.

Neither give heed to fables. *1 Ti.* 1: 4.

Refuse profane and old wives' fables. *1 Ti.* 4: 7.

They shall turn away their ears from the truth, and shall be turned unto fables. *2 Ti.* 4: 4.

Not giving heed to Jewish fables. *Tit.* 1: 14.

We have not followed cunningly devised fables. *2 Pe.* 1: 16.

See also

Allegory; Parable.

Face

In the sweat of thy face shalt thou eat bread. *Ge.* 3: 19.

Moses wist not that the skin of his face shone. *Ex.* 34: 29.

O Lord God, turn not away the face of thine anointed. *2 Ch.* 6: 42.

Lord, lift thou up the light of thy countenance upon us. *Ps.* 4: 6.

I gave my back to the smiters, and my cheeks to them that plucked off the hair. *Is.* 50: 6.

He giveth his cheek to him that smiteth him. *La.* 3: 30.

I put a jewel on thy forehead. *Eze.* 16: 12.

We all, with open face beholding as in a glass the glory of the Lord, are changed into the same image from glory to glory. *2 Co* 3: 18.

See also

Christ, Face of; Christ, Vision of; Countenance; God, Face of; God, Vision of.

Failure

He hath left off to be wise, and to do good. *Ps.* 36: 3.

My heart faileth me. *Ps.* 40: 12.

The labour of the foolish wearieth every one of them, because he knoweth not how to go to the city. *Ec.* 10: 15.

We have not wrought any deliverance in the earth; neither have the inhabitants of the world fallen. *Is.* 26: 18.

He shall not fail nor be discouraged, till he have set judgment in the earth. *Is.* 42: 4.

Consider your ways. Ye have sown much, and bring in little. *Hag.* 1: 5, 6.

Inasmuch as ye did it not. *Mat.* 25: 45.

He cometh, and findeth them sleeping, and saith unto Peter, Simon, sleepest thou? Couldest thou not watch one hour? *Mk.* 14: 37.

Master, we have toiled all the night, and have taken nothing. *Lu.* 5: 5.

I have prayed for thee, that thy faith fail not. *Lu.* 22: 32.

Though I . . . understand . . . all knowledge; . . . and have not charity, I am nothing. *1 Co.* 13: 2.

If Christ be not risen, then is our preaching vain. *1 Co.* 15: 14.

If we sin wilfully after that we have received the knowledge of the truth, there remaineth no more sacrifice for sins. *He.* 10: 26.

Of whom the world was not worthy. *He.* 11: 38.

Lest any man fail of the grace of God. *He.* 12: 15.

See also

Collapse; Defeat; Fall; Overthrow; Ruin.

Faintness

What man is there that is fearful and fainthearted? let him go and return unto his house, lest his brethren's heart faint as well as his heart. *De.* 20: 8.

I had fainted, unless I had believed to see the goodness of the Lord in the land of the living. *Ps.* 27: 13.

My soul longeth, yea, even fainteth for the courts of the Lord. *Ps.* 84: 2.

If thou faint in the day of adversity thy strength is small. *Pr.* 24: 10.

They shall be as when a standardbearer fainteth. *Is.* 10: 18.

The everlasting God, the Lord, the Creator of the ends of the earth, fainteth not, neither is weary. *Is.* **40: 28.**

He giveth power to the faint; and to them that have no might he increaseth strength. *Is.* **40: 29.**

They shall run, and not be weary; and they shall walk, and not faint. *Is.* **40: 31.**

He spake a parable unto them to this end, that men ought always to pray, and not to faint. *Lu.* **18: 1.**

For which cause we faint not; but though our outward man perish, yet the inward man is renewed day by day. *2 Co.* **4: 16.**

Let us not be weary in well doing: for in due season we shall reap, if we faint not. *Ga.* **6: 9.**

Thou . . . hast borne, and hast patience, and for my name's sake hast laboured, and hast not fainted. *Re.* **2: 2, 3.**

See also

Feebleness; Infirmity; Unconsciousness; Weakness.

Fairness

Ye shall hear the small as well as the great. *De.* **1: 17.**

A just weight is his delight. *Pr.* **11: 1.**

It is joy to the just to do judgment. *Pr.* **21: 15.**

There is nothing better, than that a man should rejoice in his own works; for that is his portion. *Ec.* **3: 22.**

Thou hast made them equal unto us, which have borne the burden and heat of the day. *Mat.* **20: 12.**

Then came also publicans to be baptized, and said unto him, Master, what shall we do? And he said unto them, Exact no more than that which is appointed you. *Lu.* **3: 12, 13.**

The labourer is worthy of his hire. *Lu.* **10: 7.**

Beware of covetousness. *Lu.* **12: 15.**

Observe these things without preferring one another. *1 Ti.* **5: 21.**

Are ye not then partial in yourselves, and are become judges of evil thoughts? *Ja.* **2: 4.**

See also

Candor; Clearness; Equality; Equality, Racial; God, Fairness of; God, Impartiality of; Honesty; Impartiality; Judgment; Justice; Justice, Social.

Faith

O our God, wilt thou not judge them? for we have no might against this great company that cometh against us; neither know we what to do: but our eyes are upon thee. *2 Ch.* **20: 12.**

Commit thy way unto the Lord; trust also in him; and he shall bring it to pass. *Ps.* **37: 5.**

I have not found so great faith, no, not in Israel. *Mat.* **8: 10.**

According to your faith be it unto you. *Mat.* **9: 29.**

Lord, I believe; help thou mine unbelief. *Mk.* **9: 24.**

Thy faith hath saved thee; go in peace. *Lu.* **7: 50.**

He said unto them, Where is your faith? *Lu.* **8: 25.**

The apostles said unto the Lord, Increase our faith. *Lu.* **17: 5.**

Blessed are they that have not seen, and yet have believed. *Jn.* **20: 29.**

I know that thou believest. *Ac.* **26: 27.**

I believe God, that it shall be even as it was told me. *Ac.* **27: 25.**

The just shall live by faith. *Ro.* **1: 17.**

The word is nigh thee, even in thy mouth, and in thy heart: that is, the word of faith. *Ro.* **10: 8.**

Faith cometh by hearing, and hearing by the word of God. *Ro.* **10: 17.**

Hast thou faith? have it to thyself before God. *Ro.* **14: 22.**

Though I have all faith, so that I could remove mountains, and have not charity, I am nothing. *1 Co.* **13: 2.**

Now abideth faith. *1 Co.* **13: 13.**

Faith which worketh by love. *Ga.* **5: 6.**

Till we all come in the unity of the faith. *Ep.* **4: 13.**

Putting on the breastplate of faith and love. *1 Th.* **5: 8.**

We are bound to thank God always for you, brethren, as it is meet, because that your faith groweth exceedingly. *2 Th.* **1: 3.**

Fight the good fight of faith, lay hold on eternal life. *1 Ti.* **6: 12.**

The word preached did not profit them, not being mixed with faith in them that heard it. *He.* **4: 2.**

Let us draw near with a true heart in full assurance of faith. *He.* **10: 22.**

Now faith is the substance of things hoped for, the evidence of things not seen. *He.* **11: 1.**

Without faith it is impossible to please him. *He.* **11: 6.**

He went out, not knowing whither he went. *He.* **11: 8.**

By faith he sojourned in the land of promise, as in a strange country. *He.* **11: 9.**

Hath not God chosen the poor of this world rich in faith? *Ja.* **2: 5.**

Faith, if it hath not works, is dead. *Ja.* **2: 17.**

By works was faith made perfect. *Ja.* **2: 22.**

Ye see then how that by works a man is justified, and not by faith only. *Ja.* **2: 24.**

The prayer of faith shall save the sick. *Ja.* **5: 15.**

Add to your faith. *2 Pe.* **1: 5.**

See also

Assurance; Belief; Christ, Belief in; Christ, Faith in; Confidence; Conviction; God, Confidence in; God, Faith in; Persuasion; Reliance; Trust.

Faith, Justification by

The just shall live by his faith. *Hab.* **2: 4.**

The just shall live by faith. *Ro.* **1: 17.**

We conclude that a man is justified by faith without the deeds of the law. *Ro.* **3: 28.**

To him that worketh not, but believeth on him that justifieth the ungodly, his faith is counted for righteousness. *Ro.* **4: 5.**

Being justified by faith, we have peace with God through our Lord Jesus Christ. *Ro.* **5: 1.**

We walk by faith, not by sight. *2 Co.* **5: 7.**

By grace are ye saved through faith. *Ep.* **2: 8.**

Faith-Healing

Thy faith hath made thee whole. *Mat.* **9: 22.**

They shall lay hands on the sick, and they shall recover. *Mk.* **16: 18.**

Woman, thou art loosed from thine infirmity. *Lu.* 13: 12.

Jesus said unto him, Receive thy sight: thy faith hath saved thee. *Lu.* 18: 42.

He had faith to be healed. *Ac.* 14: 9.

From his body were brought unto the sick handkerchiefs or aprons, and the diseases departed from them. *Ac.* 19: 12.

The prayer of faith shall save the sick, and the Lord shall raise him up. *Ja.* 5: 15.

Faithfulness

He left all that he had in Joseph's hand. *Ge.* 39: 6.

We are true men; thy servants are no spies. *Ge.* 42: 11.

If ye will . . . keep my covenant, then ye shall be a peculiar treasure unto me above all people. *Ex.* 19: 5.

But Ruth clave unto her. *Ru.* 1: 14.

Whither thou goest, I will go; and where thou lodgest, I will lodge: thy people shall be my people, and thy God my God. *Ru.* 1: 16.

As the Lord liveth, and as thy soul liveth, I will not leave thee. *2 K.* 2: 2.

They dealt faithfully. *2 K.* 12: 15.

The men did the work faithfully. *2 Ch.* 34: 12.

They were counted faithful, and their office was to distribute unto their brethren. *Ne.* 13: 13.

Rejoice with the wife of thy youth. . . . And be thou ravished always with her love. *Pr.* 5: 18, 19.

Thou hast been faithful over a few things, I will make thee ruler over many things. *Mat.* 25: 21.

Many women . . . followed Jesus from Galilee, ministering unto him. *Mat.* 27: 55.

Who then is that faithful and wise steward? *Lu.* 12: 42.

He that is faithful in that which is least is faithful also in much. *Lu.* 16: 10.

Having loved his own which were in the world, he loved them unto the end. *Jn.* 13: 1.

I was not disobedient unto the heavenly vision. *Ac.* 26: 19.

It is required in stewards, that a man be found faithful. *1 Co.* 4: 2.

Therefore, my beloved brethren, be ye stedfast, unmoveable, always abounding in the work of the Lord, forasmuch as ye know that your labour is not in vain in the Lord. *1 Co.* 15: 58.

Watch ye, stand fast in the faith, quit you like men, be strong. *1 Co.* 16: 13.

He oft refreshed me, and was not ashamed of my chain. *2 Ti.* 1: 16.

Holding fast the faithful word. *Tit.* 1: 9.

Shewing all good fidelity. *Tit.* 2: 10.

Thou doest faithfully whatsoever thou doest to the brethren, and to strangers. *3 Jn.* 1: 5.

Be thou faithful unto death, and I will give thee a crown of life. *Re.* 2: 10.

These words are true and faithful. *Re.* 21: 5.

See also

Allegiance; Attachment; Christ, Loyalty to; Consecration; Constancy; Devotion; Fidelity; God, Faithfulness of; God, Love to; God, Loyalty to; Loyalty.

Faithlessness

Because ye believed me not, to sanctify me in the eyes of the children of Israel, therefore ye shall not bring this congregation into the land which I have given them. *Nu.* 20: 12.

They are a very froward generation, children in whom is no faith. *De.* 32: 20.

Who said unto his father and to his mother, I have not seen him; neither did he acknowledge his brethren, nor knew his own children. *De.* 33: 9.

Woe to thee that spoilest, and thou wast not spoiled; and dealest treacherously, and they dealt not treacherously with thee! *Is.* 33: 1.

All her friends have dealt treacherously with her. *Lam.* 1: 2.

O faithless and perverse generation, how long shall I be with you? *Mat.* 17: 17.

Art thou the Christ? Tell us. And he said unto them, If I tell you, ye will not believe. *Lu.* 22: 67.

I know you, that ye have not the love of God in you. *Jn.* 5: 42.

Ye also have seen me, and believe not. *Jn.* 6: 36.

Be not faithless, but believing. *Jn.* 20: 27.

Except these abide in the ship, ye cannot be saved. *Ac.* 27: 31.

For what if some did not believe? shall their unbelief make the faith of God without effect? *Ro.* 3: 3.

The god of this world hath blinded the minds of them which believe not. *2 Co.* 4: 4.

Having begun in the Spirit, are ye now made perfect by the flesh? *Ga.* 3: 3.

In the last days . . . men shall be . . . trucebreakers. *2 Ti.* 3: 1–3.

Take heed, brethren, lest there be in any of you an evil heart of unbelief. *He.* 3: 12.

See also

Christ, Denial of; Christ, Doubt of; Deceit; Denial; Disbelief; Doubt; God, Denial of; Perfidy; Scepticism; Treachery; Unbelief; Unfaithfulness.

Fall

See that ye fall not out by the way. *Ge.* 45: 24.

As the Lord liveth, there shall not one hair of his head fall to the ground. *1 S.* 14: 45.

Let us fall now into the hand of the Lord; for his mercies are great: and let me not fall into the hand of man. *2 S.* 24: 14.

After they had rest, they did evil again before thee. *Ne.* 9: 28.

The lines are fallen unto me in pleasant places. *Ps.* 16: 6.

The terrors of death are fallen upon me. *Ps.* 55: 4.

A just man falleth seven times, and riseth up again: but the wicked shall fall into mischief. *Pr.* 24: 16.

The stars shall fall from heaven. *Mat.* 24: 29.

Except a corn of wheat fall into the ground and die, it abideth alone: but if it die, it bringeth forth much fruit. *Jn.* 12: 24.

Judge this rather, that no man put a stumblingblock or an occasion to fall in his brother's way. *Ro.* 14: 13.

Some are fallen asleep. *1 Co.* 15: 6.

It is a fearful thing to fall into the hands of the living God. *He.* 10: 31.

Count it all joy when ye fall into divers temptations. *Ja.* 1: 2.

The flower thereof falleth, and the grace of the fashion of it perisheth. *Ja.* 1: 11.

Beware lest ye also . . . fall from your own stedfastness. 2 *Pe.* 3: 17.

I have somewhat against thee, because thou hast left thy first love. *Re.* 2: 4.

Remember therefore from whence thou art fallen, and repent. *Re.* 2: 5.

See also
Autumn; Collapse; Defeat; Descent; Desolation; Destruction; Failure; Overthrow; Ruin.

Falsehood

Thou shalt not raise a false report. *Ex.* 23: 1.

He that speaketh truth sheweth forth righteousness: but a false witness deceit. *Pr.* 12: 17.

A righteous man hateth lying. *Pr.* 13: 5.

Remove far from me vanity and lies. *Pr.* 30: 8.

The prophet that teacheth lies, he is the tail. *Is.* 9: 15.

Ye trust in lying words, that cannot profit. *Je.* 7: 8.

They are not valiant for the truth upon the earth. *Je.* 9: 3.

They have taught their tongue to speak lies. *Je.* 9: 5.

Blessed are ye, when men shall . . . say all manner of evil against you falsely, for my sake. *Mat.* 5: 11.

Speak every man truth. *Ep.* 4: 25.

Lie not one to another, seeing that ye have put off the old man with his deeds. *Col.* 3: 9.

See also
Calumny; Dishonesty; Fraud; Lie; Untruthfulness.

Fame

A good name is rather to be chosen than great riches, and loving favour rather than silver and gold. *Pr.* 22: 1.

For men to search their own glory is not glory. *Pr.* 25: 27.

A living dog is better than a dead lion. *Ec.* 9: 4.

All the inhabitants of the earth are reputed as nothing: . . . none can stay his hand. *Da.* 4: 35.

They shall be . . . as the smoke out of the chimney. *Ho.* 13: 3.

Your faith is spoken of throughout the whole world. *Ro.* 1: 8.

Let not then your good be evil spoken of. *Ro.* 14: 16.

Hold such in reputation. *Ph.* 2: 29.

See also
Celebrity; Distinction; Glory; Honor; Name; Renown; Report; Reputation.

Family

In thee shall all families of the earth be blessed. *Ge.* 12: 3.

Thou art an holy people unto the Lord thy God, and the Lord hath chosen thee to be a peculiar people unto himself. *De.* 14: 2.

God setteth the solitary in families. *Ps.* 68: 6.

Yet setteth he the poor on high from affliction, and maketh him families like a flock. *Ps.* 107: 41.

Behold, how good and how pleasant it is for brethren to dwell together in unity! *Ps.* 133: 1.

Doubtless thou art our Father, though Abraham be ignorant of us, and Israel acknowledge us not. *Is.* 63: 16.

When Israel was a child, then I loved him, and called my son out of Egypt. *Ho.* 11: 1.

You only have I known of all the families of the earth: therefore I will punish you for all your iniquities. *Am.* 3: 2.

He shall turn the heart of the fathers to the children, and the heart of the children to their fathers, lest I come and smite the earth with a curse. *Mal.* 4: 6.

A man's foes shall be they of his own household. *Mat.* 10: 36.

He stretched forth his hand toward his disciples, and said, Behold my mother and my brethren! *Mat.* 12: 49.

A prophet is not without honour, save in his own country, and in his own house. *Mat.* 13: 57.

He first findeth his own brother Simon. *Jn.* 1: 41.

Love worketh no ill to his neighbour: therefore love is the fulfilling of the law. *Ro.* 13: 10.

Greet the church that is in their house. *Ro.* 16: 5.

I . . . will be a Father unto you, and ye shall be my sons and daughters, saith the Lord Almighty. 2 *Co.* 6: 17, 18.

Let us do good unto all men, especially unto them who are of the household of faith. *Ga.* 6: 10.

Ye are no more strangers and foreigners, but fellowcitizens with the saints, and of the household of God. *Ep.* 2: 19.

Our Lord Jesus Christ, Of whom the whole family in heaven and earth is named. *Ep.* 3: 14, 15.

If any provide not for his own, and specially for those of his own house, he hath denied the faith. *1 Ti.* 5: 8.

Both he that sanctifieth and they who are sanctified are all of one: for which cause he is not ashamed to call them brethren. *He.* 2: 11.

This is the message that ye heard from the beginning, that we should love one another. *1 Jn.* 3: 11.

See also
Brotherhood; Fraternity; Home; House; Kinship.

Famine

The famine was over all the face of the earth. *Ge.* 41: 56.

There was a dearth in the land. 2 *K.* 4: 38.

At destruction and famine thou shalt laugh. *Jb.* 5: 22.

He called for a famine upon the land: he brake the whole staff of bread. *Ps.* 105: 16.

The Lord will not suffer the soul of the righteous to famish. *Pr.* 10: 3.

I shall send upon them the evil arrows of famine. *Eze.* 5: 16.

The sword is without, and the pestilence and the famine within. *Eze.* 7: 15.

I will send a famine in the land, not a

famine of bread, nor a thirst for water, but
of hearing the words of the Lord. *Am.* 8: 11.

There shall be famines. *Mat.* 24: 7.

They shall hunger no more, neither thirst
any more. *Re.* 7: 16.

See also

Destitution; Drought; Hunger; Starvation.

Fanaticism

They cried aloud, and cut themselves after
their manner with knives and lancets, till the
blood gushed out upon them. *1 K.* 18: 28.

They cried out, Away with him, away with
him, crucify him. *Jn.* 19: 15.

Saul, yet breathing out threatenings and
slaughter against the disciples of the Lord,
went unto the high priest. *Ac.* 9: 1.

They cried out, and cast off their clothes,
and threw dust into the air. *Ac.* 22: 23.

I punished them oft in every synagogue, and
compelled them to blaspheme; and being exceedingly mad against them, I persecuted them
even unto strange cities. *Ac.* 26: 11.

See also

Bigotry; Pharisee; Strictness.

Farewell

The Lord bless thee, and keep thee: The
Lord make his face shine upon thee, and be
gracious unto thee: The Lord lift up his countenance upon thee, and give thee peace. *Nu.*
6: 24-26.

Go in peace: before the Lord is your way
wherein ye go. *Ju.* 18: 6.

Go in peace: and the God of Israel grant
thee thy petition that thou hast asked of him.
1 S. 1: 17.

The Lord be between me and thee, and
between my seed and thy seed for ever. *1 S.*
20: 42.

Peace be both to thee, and peace be to thine
house, and peace be unto all that thou hast.
1 S. 25: 6.

Leave me not, neither forsake me, O God of
my salvation. *Ps.* 27: 9.

Lord, I will follow thee; but let me first go
bid them farewell, which are at home at my
house. *Lu.* 9: 61.

I go to prepare a place for you. *Jn.* 14: 2.

I will not leave you comfortless: I will come
to you. *Jn.* 14: 18.

Yet a little while, and the world seeth me no
more. *Jn.* 14: 19.

Peace I leave with you, my peace I give unto
you. *Jn.* 14: 27.

I came forth from the Father, and am come
into the world: again, I leave the world, and
go to the Father. *Jn.* 16: 28.

Now therefore depart, and go in peace. *Ac.*
16: 36.

Finally, brethren, farewell. Be perfect, be of
good comfort, be of one mind, live in peace;
and the God of love and peace shall be with
you. *2 Co.* 13: 11.

I will never leave thee, nor forsake thee. *He.*
13: 5.

See also

Departure; Exit; Parting.

Fashion

He fashioneth their hearts alike. *Ps.* 33: 15.

They have sought out many inventions. *Ec.*
7: 29.

He hath no form nor comeliness. *Is.* 53: 2.

As he prayed, the fashion of his countenance
was altered. *Lu.* 9: 29.

The fashion of this world passeth away.
1 Co. 7: 31.

Being found in fashion as a man, he
humbled himself, and became obedient unto
death. *Ph.* 2: 8.

Christ . . . shall change our vile body, that
it may be fashioned like unto his glorious
body. *Ph.* 3: 20, 21.

The sun . . . withereth the grass, and the
flower therof falleth, and the grace of the
fashion of it perisheth. *Ja.* 1: 11.

See also

Custom; Form; Habit; Manners; Shape;
Tradition.

Fast

He was there with the Lord forty days and
forty nights; he did neither eat bread, nor
drink water. *Ex.* 34: 28.

Thou didst fast and weep for the child,
while it was alive; but when the child was
dead, thou didst rise and eat bread. *2 S.* 12: 21.

He arose, and did eat and drink, and went
in the strength of that meat forty days and
forty nights. *1 K.* 19: 8.

He did eat no bread, nor drink water: for
he mourned because of the transgression of
them that had been carried away. *Ezr.* 10: 6.

I humbled my soul with fasting. *Ps.* 35: 13.

My knees are weak through fasting; and my
flesh faileth of fatness. *Ps.* 109: 24.

Behold, ye fast for strife and debate, and
to smite with the fist of wickedness. *Is.* 58: 4.

Is it such a fast that I have chosen? a day
for a man to afflict his soul? is it to bow down
his head as a bulrush, and to spread sackcloth and ashes under him? wilt thou call this
a fast, and an acceptable day to the Lord? *Is.*
58: 5.

Is not this the fast that I have chosen? to
loose the bands of wickedness, to undo the
heavy burdens, and to let the oppressed go
free, and that ye break every yoke? Is it not
to deal thy bread to the hungry, and that thou
bring the poor that are cast out to thy house?
Is. 58: 6, 7.

When they fast, I will not hear their cry.
Je. 14: 12.

I ate no pleasant bread, neither came flesh
nor wine in my mouth, neither did I anoint
myself at all, till three whole weeks were
fulfilled. *Da.* 10: 3.

Turn ye even to me with all your heart,
and with fasting, and with weeping, and with
mourning. *Jo.* 2: 12.

When he had fasted forty days and forty
nights, he was afterward an hungred. *Mat.*
4: 2.

When ye fast, be not, as the hypocrites, of a
sad countenance: for they disfigure their faces,
that they may appear unto men to fast. *Mat.*
6: 16.

Thou, when thou fastest, anoint thine head,
and wash thy face; That thou appear not
unto men to fast, but unto thy Father which
is in secret. *Mat.* 6: 17, 18.

Why do we and the Pharisees fast oft, but thy
disciples fast not? *Mat.* 9: 14.

Can the children of the bridechamber fast,

while the bridegroom is with them? *Mk.* **2: 19.**

I fast twice in the week, I give tithes of all that I possess. *Lu.* **18: 12.**

He was three days without sight, and neither did eat nor drink. *Ac.* **9: 9.**

Approving ourselves as the ministers of God, . . . in fastings. *2 Co.* **6: 4, 5.**

In fastings often. *2 Co.* **11: 27.**

See also

Abstinence; Formalism; Hunger; Ritual; Starvation.

Fat

God give thee of the dew of heaven, and the fatness of the earth, and plenty of corn and wine. *Ge.* **27: 28.**

Ye shall eat the fat of the land. *Ge.* **45: 18.**

Jeshurun waxed fat, and kicked. *De.* **32: 15.**

Should I leave my fatness, wherewith by me they honour God and man, and go to be promoted over the trees? *Ju.* **9: 9.**

To obey is better than sacrifice, and to hearken than the fat of rams. *1 S.* **15: 22.**

Thy paths drop fatness. *Ps.* **65: 11.**

They shall still bring forth fruit in old age; they shall be fat and flourishing. *Ps.* **92: 14.**

Their heart is as fat as grease. *Ps.* **119: 70.**

The liberal soul shall be made fat. *Pr.* **11: 25.**

A good report maketh the bones fat. *Pr.* **15: 30.**

He that putteth his trust in the Lord shall be made fat. *Pr.* **28: 25.**

In that day it shall come to pass, that the glory of Jacob shall be made thin, and the fatness of his flesh shall wax lean. *Is.* **17: 4.**

See also

Prosperity.

Fate

The Lord did not set his love upon you, nor choose you, because you were more in number than any people; for ye were the fewest of all people. *De.* **7: 7.**

God shall likewise destroy thee for ever. *Ps.* **52: 5.**

There shall no evil happen to the just. *Pr.* **12: 21.**

As it happeneth to the fool, so it happeneth even to me; and why was I then more wise? *Ec.* **2: 15.**

All go unto one place; all are of the dust, and all turn to dust again. *Ec.* **3: 20.**

Truly the Son of man goeth, as it was determined. *Lu.* **22: 22.**

God . . . hath determined the times before appointed. *Ac.* **17: 24, 26.**

Grieve not the holy Spirit of God, whereby ye are sealed unto the day of redemption. *Ep.* **4: 30.**

See also

Calling; Chance; Destiny; Doom; Fortune; Lot; Predestination.

Father

I am the Lord God of Abraham thy father. *Ge.* **28: 13.**

The Lord our God be with us, as he was with our fathers. *1 K.* **8: 57.**

I have chosen him to be my son, and I will be his father. *1 Ch.* **28: 6.**

Blessed be the Lord God of our fathers. *Ezr.* **7: 27.**

I was a father to the poor. *Jb.* **29: 16.**

Hath the rain a father? *Jb.* **38: 28.**

Hear, ye children, the instruction of a father. *Pr.* **4: 1.**

A wise son maketh a glad father. *Pr.* **10: 1.**

A fool despiseth his father's instruction. *Pr.* **15: 5.**

The glory of children are their fathers. *Pr.* **17: 6.**

Whoso curseth his father or his mother, his lamp shall be put out in obscure darkness. *Pr.* **20: 20.**

His name shall be called . . . The everlasting Father. *Is.* **9: 6.**

He shall turn the heart of the fathers to the children, and the heart of the children to their fathers. *Mal.* **4: 6.**

Call no man your father upon the earth: for one is your Father, which is in heaven. *Mat.* **23: 9.**

Honour thy father and mother; which is the first commandment with promise. *Ep.* **6: 2.**

Ye fathers, provoke not your children to wrath. *Ep.* **6: 4.**

See also

Ancestor; Descent; Father's Day; Genealogy; Generation; Parent.

Father's Day

Honour thy father and thy mother: that thy days may be long upon the land which the Lord thy God giveth thee. *Ex.* **20: 12.**

A father of the fatherless . . . is God in his holy habitation. *Ps.* **68: 5.**

Like as a father pitieth his children, so the Lord pitieth them that fear him. *Ps.* **103: 13.**

My son, hear the instruction of thy father. *Pr.* **1: 8.**

Whom the Lord loveth he correcteth; even as a father the son in whom he delighteth. *Pr.* **3: 12.**

A foolish son is the calamity of his father. *Pr.* **19: 13.**

Whoso curseth his father or his mother, his lamp shall be put out in obscure darkness. *Pr.* **20: 20.**

The father of the righteous shall greatly rejoice: and he that begetteth a wise child shall have joy of him. *Pr.* **23: 24.**

Whoso loveth wisdom rejoiceth his father. *Pr.* **29: 3.**

A son honoureth his father. *Mal.* **1: 6.**

He shall turn the heart of the father to the children, and the heart of the children to their fathers, lest I come and smite the earth with a curse. *Mal.* **4: 6.**

God commanded, saying, Honour thy father and mother. *Mat.* **15: 4.**

If a son shall ask bread of any of you that is a father, will he give him a stone? *Lu.* **11: 11.**

What son is he whom the father chasteneth not? *He.* **12: 7.**

See also

Father.

Fault

Who can understand his errors? cleanse thou me from secret faults. *Ps.* **19: 12.**

Their heart is divided; now shall they be found faulty. *Ho.* **10: 2.**

Forgive, and ye shall be forgiven. *Lu.* 6: 37.

Thou wilt say then unto me, Why doth he yet find fault? For who hath resisted his will? *Ro.* 9: 19.

That ye may be sincere and without offence till the day of Christ. *Ph.* 1: 10.

They do alway err in their heart: and they have not known my ways. *He.* 3: 10.

Do not err, my beloved brethren. *Ja.* 1: 16.

In many things we offend all. If any man offend not in word, the same is a perfect man. *Ja.* 3: 2.

Who art thou that judgest another? *Ja.* 4: 12.

Confess your faults one to another, and pray one for another, that ye may be healed. *Ja.* 5: 16.

See also

Blemish; Defect; Error; Failure; Imperfection; Infirmity; Lack; Spot; Want; Weakness.

Favor

A good man sheweth favour, and lendeth. *Ps.* 112: 5.

In the light of the king's countenance is life; and his favour is as a cloud of the latter rain. *Pr.* 16: 15.

Let favour be shewed to the wicked. *Is.* 26: 10.

Blessed art thou among women. *Lu.* 1: 28.

Jesus increased in wisdom and stature, and in favour with God and man. *Lu.* 2: 52.

They . . . did eat their meat with gladness and singleness of heart, Praising God, and having favour with all the people. *Ac.* 2: 46, 47.

See also

Benefit; Benevolence; Countenance; Encouragement; Gift; Grace; Kindness.

Favoritism

Isaac loved Esau, . . . but Rebekah loved Jacob. *Ge.* 25: 28.

Art thou my very son Esau? *Ge.* 27: 24.

Esau hated Jacob because of the blessing. *Ge.* 27: 41.

Now Israel loved Joseph more than all his children. *Ge.* 37: 3.

When his brethren saw that their father loved him more than all his brethren, they hated him. *Ge.* 37: 4.

The lad cannot leave his father: for if he should leave his father, his father would die. *Ge.* 44: 22.

Would God I had died for thee, O Absalom, my son, my son! *2 S.* 18: 33.

Whither is thy beloved gone, O thou fairest among women? *S. of S.* 1: 8.

I am my beloved's. *S. of S.* 6: 3.

I will make a man more precious than fine gold. *Is.* 13: 12.

Thou wast precious in my sight, . . . and I have loved thee. *Is.* 43: 4.

The precious sons of Zion, comparable to fine gold. *La.* 4: 2.

See also

Favor; Pet.

Fear

I sought the Lord, and he heard me, and delivered me from all my fears. *Ps.* 34: 4.

Whoso hearkeneth unto me shall dwell safely, and shall be quiet from fear of evil. *Pr.* 1: 33.

I will trust, and not be afraid: for the Lord Jehovah is my strength and my song. *Is.* 12: 2.

They . . . were afraid to ask him. *Mk.* 9: 32.

I was with you in weakness, and in fear, and in much trembling. *1 Co.* 2: 3.

God hath not given us the spirit of fear; but of power, and of love, and of a sound mind. *2 Ti.* 1: 7.

That through death he might . . . deliver them who through fear of death were all their lifetime subject to bondage. *He.* 2: 14, 15.

He that feareth is not made perfect in love. *1 Jn.* 4: 18.

There is no fear in love; but perfect love casteth out fear. *1 Jn.* 4: 18.

Fear hath torment. *1 Jn.* 4: 18.

Pass the time of your sojourning here in fear. *1 Pe.* 1: 17.

See also

Alarm; Caution; Cowardice; Dismay; Dread; Terror; Timidity; Trembling.

Fearlessness

Though an host should encamp against me, my heart shall not fear. *Ps.* 27: 3.

Therefore will not we fear, though the earth be removed, and though the mountains be carried into the midst of the sea. *Ps.* 46: 2.

I will not fear what flesh can do unto me. *Ps.* 56: 4.

The wicked flee when no man pursueth: but the righteous are bold as a lion. *Pr.* 28: 1.

Be not dismayed; for I am thy God. *Is.* 41: 10.

Fear not: for I have redeemed thee, I have called thee by thy name; thou art mine. *Is.* 43: 1.

Hearken unto me, ye stouthearted. *Is.* 46: 12.

That we being delivered out of the hand of our enemies might serve him without fear. *Lu.* 1: 74.

Fear not, Paul; thou must be brought before Caesar. *Ac.* 27: 24.

In nothing terrified by your adversaries. *Ph.* 1: 28.

The Lord is my helper, and I will not fear what man shall do unto me. *He.* 13: 6.

Be not afraid of their terror, neither be troubled; But sanctify the Lord God in your hearts. *1 Pe.* 3: 14, 15.

See also

Audacity; Boldness; Bravery; Courage; Fortitude; Heroism; Valor.

Feast

Better is a dinner of herbs where love is, than a stalled ox and hatred therewith. *Pr.* 15: 17.

It is better to go to the house of mourning, than to go to the house of feasting. *Ec.* 7: 2.

A feast is made for laughter, and wine maketh merry. *Ec.* 10: 19.

Behold joy and gladness, slaying oxen, and killing sheep, eating flesh, and drinking wine. *Is.* 22: 13.

Let us eat and drink; for to morrow we shall die. *Is.* 22: 13.

A feast of fat things. *Is.* 25: 6.

What will ye do in the solemn day, and in the day of the feast of the Lord? *Ho.* 9: 5.

When thou makest a feast, call the poor, the maimed, the lame, the blind. *Lu.* 14: 13.

Jesus saith unto them, Come and dine. *Jn.* **21: 12.**

If any of them that believe not bid you to a feast, and ye be disposed to go; whatsoever is set before you, eat, asking no questions for conscience' sake. *1 Co.* **10: 27.**

See also

Banquet; Festival; Holiday.

Feebleness

Upon them that are left alive of you I will send a faintness into their hearts in the lands of their enemies. *Le.* **26: 36.**

His strength shall be hungerbitten. *Jb.* **18: 12.**

My soul fainteth for thy salvation. *Ps.* **119: 81.**

Strengthen ye the weak hands, and confirm the feeble knees. *Is.* **35: 3.**

Even the youths shall faint and be weary, and the young men shall utterly fall. *Is.* **40: 30.**

When my soul fainted within me I remembered the Lord. *Jon.* **2: 7.**

The spirit indeed is willing, but the flesh is weak. *Mat.* **26: 41.**

The impotent man answered him, Sir, I have no man, when the water is troubled, to put me into the pool: but while I am coming, another steppeth down before me. *Jn.* **5: 7.**

We then that are strong ought to bear the infirmities of the weak, and not to please ourselves. *Ro.* **15: 1.**

The foolishness of God is wiser than men. *1 Co.* **1: 25.**

The weakness of God is stronger than men. *1 Co.* **1: 25.**

I was with you in weakness, and in fear, and in much trembling. *1 Co.* **2: 3.**

To the weak became I as weak, that I might gain the weak: I am made all things to all men, that I might by all means save some. *1 Co.* **9: 22.**

His bodily presence is weak, and his speech contemptible. *2 Co.* **10: 10.**

When I am weak, then am I strong. *2 Co.* **12: 10.**

Though he was crucified through weakness, yet he liveth by the power of God. *2 Co.* **13: 4.**

Consider him that endured such contradiction of sinners against himself, lest ye be wearied and faint in your minds. *He.* **12: 3.**

See also

Faintness; Frailty; Impotence; Inability; Infirmity; Weakness.

Feeling

Come near, I pray thee, that I may feel thee, my son. *Ge.* **27: 21.**

Darkness which may be felt. *Ex.* **10: 21.**

Suffer me that I may feel the pillars whereupon the house standeth, that I may lean upon them. *Ju.* **16: 26.**

Surely he shall not feel quietness. *Jb.* **20: 20.**

They have beaten me, and I felt it not. *Pr.* **23: 35.**

Whoso keepeth the commandment shall feel no evil thing. *Ec.* **8: 5.**

That they should seek the Lord, if haply they might feel after him, and find him. *Ac.* **17: 27.**

He shook off the beast into the fire, and felt no harm. *Ac.* **28: 5.**

See also

Attitude; Emotion; Passion; Sensitivity; Sentiment.

Felicity

He that goeth forth and weepeth, bearing precious seed, shall doubtless come again with rejoicing, bringing his sheaves with him. *Ps.* **126: 6.**

Happy is the man that findeth wisdom. *Pr.* **3: 13.**

Thy word was unto me the joy and rejoicing of mine heart, for I am called by thy name. *Je.* **15: 16.**

There shall be showers of blessing. *Eze.* **34: 26.**

The cup of blessing which we bless, is it not the communion of the blood of Christ? *1 Co.* **10: 16.**

Death is swallowed up in victory. *1 Co.* **15: 54.**

The God and Father of our Lord Jesus Christ . . . hath blessed us with all spiritual blessings in heavenly places in Christ. *Ep.* **1: 3.**

Surely blessing I will bless thee, and multiplying I will multiply thee. *He.* **6: 14.**

If ye suffer for righteousness' sake, happy are ye. *1 Pe.* **3: 14.**

There shall be no more death, neither sorrow, nor crying. *Re.* **21: 4.**

Neither shall there be any more pain. *Re.* **21: 4.**

See also

Blessedness; Bliss; Christ, Joy in; Christ, Joy of; Gladness; God, Joy in; Happiness; Rejoicing.

Fellowship

Commune with your own heart upon your bed, and be still. *Ps.* **4: 4.**

I am a companion of all them that fear thee, and of them that keep thy precepts. *Ps.* **119: 63.**

He that walketh with wise men shall be wise: but a companion of fools shall be destroyed. *Pr.* **13: 20.**

My beloved is mine, and I am his. *S. of S.* **2: 16.**

Where two or three are gathered together in my name, there am I in the midst of them. *Mat.* **18: 20.**

While they communed together and reasoned, Jesus himself drew near, and went with them. *Lu.* **24: 15.**

They took knowledge of them, that they had been with Jesus. *Ac.* **4: 13.**

If so be that we suffer with him, that we may be also glorified together. *Ro.* **8: 17.**

What fellowship hath righteousness with unrighteousness? *2 Co.* **6: 14.**

The fellowship of the ministering to the saints. *2 Co.* **8: 4.**

The communion of the Holy Ghost. *2 Co.* **13: 14.**

They gave to me and Barnabas the right hands of fellowship. *Ga.* **2: 9.**

Ye are all one in Christ Jesus. *Ga.* **3: 28.**

Bear ye one another's burdens. *Ga.* **6: 2.**

For your fellowship in the gospel from the first day until now. *Ph.* **1: 5.**

That which we have seen and heard declare we unto you, that ye also may have fellowship with us. *1 Jn.* **1: 3.**

If any man hear my voice, and open the door, I will come in to him, and will sup with him, and he with me. *Re.* 3: 20.

See also

Alliance; Association; Christ, Collaboration with; Christ, Companionship of; Christ, Fellowship with; Christ, Partnership with; Collaboration; Community; Companionship; Companionship, Evil; Company; Compatibility; Comradeship; God, Companionship with; God, Fellowship with; God, Partnership with; Partner.

Fellow-Worker

Wist ye not that I must be about my Father's business? *Lu.* 2: 49.

My Father worketh hitherto, and I work. *Jn.* 5: 17.

Workers together with him. *2 Co.* 6: 1.

I thank my God . . . For your fellowship in the gospel from the first day until now. *Ph.* 1: 3, 5.

I intreat thee also, true yokefellow, help those women which laboured with me in the gospel, with Clement also, and with other my fellowlabourers, whose names are in the book of life. *Ph.* 4: 3.

These only are my fellowworkers unto the kingdom of God, which have been a comfort unto me. *Col.* 4: 11.

Our fellowsoldier. *Phm.* 1: 2.

Fellowhelpers to the truth. *3 Jn.* 1: 8.

I am thy fellowservant, and of thy brethren that have the testimony of Jesus. *Re.* 19: 10.

See also

Alliance; Association; Christ, Collaboration with; Christ, Fellowship with; Christ, Partnership with; Collaboration; Colleague; Company; Cooperation; Fellowship; God, Cooperation of; God, Fellowship with; God, Partnership with; Partner.

Female

The rib, which the Lord God had taken from man, made he a woman. *Ge.* 2: 22.

Adam said, This is now bone of my bones, and flesh of my flesh: she shall be called Woman, because she was taken out of Man. *Ge.* 2: 23.

The woman whom thou gavest to be with me, she gave me of the tree, and I did eat. *Ge.* 3: 12.

Blessings of the breasts, and of the womb. *Ge.* 49: 25.

He will love thee, and bless thee, and multiply thee: he will also bless the fruit of thy womb. *De.* 7: 13.

That our daughters may be as corner stones, polished after the similitude of a palace. *Ps.* 144: 12.

A foolish woman is clamorous. *Pr.* 9: 13.

A gracious woman retaineth honour. *Pr.* 11: 16.

Every wise woman buildeth her house. *Pr.* 14: 1.

Give not thy strength unto women. *Pr.* 31: 3.

Behold, thy people in the midst of thee are women. *Na.* 3: 13.

Blessed art thou among women. *Lu.* 1: 28.

Blessed is the womb that bare thee. *Lu.* 11: 27.

The days are coming, in which they shall say, Blessed are the barren, and the wombs that never bare. *Lu.* 23: 29.

The man is not of the woman; but the woman of the man. *1 Co.* 11: 8.

See also

Daughter; Girl; Maiden; Male; Woman.

Ferocity

He will be a wild man; his hand will be against every man, and every man's hand against him. *Ge.* 16: 12.

Cursed be their anger, for it was fierce; and their wrath, for it was cruel. *Ge.* 49: 7.

I will also send wild beasts among you, which shall rob you of your children. *Le.* 26: 22.

The roaring of the lion, and the voice of the fierce lion, and the teeth of the young lions, are broken. *Jb.* 4: 10.

Thou huntest me as a fierce lion. *Jb.* 10: 16.

The wild beast may break them. *Jb.* 39: 15.

He swalloweth the ground with fierceness and rage. *Jb.* 39: 24.

He cast upon them the fierceness of his anger, wrath, and indignation. *Ps.* 78: 49.

The boar out of the wood doth waste it, and the wild beast of the field doth devour it. *Ps.* 80: 13.

Wrath is cruel, and anger is outrageous. *Pr.* 27: 4.

The Egyptians will I give over into the hand of a cruel lord; and a fierce king shall rule over them. *Is.* 19: 4.

The daughter of my people is become cruel, like the ostriches in the wilderness. *La.* 4: 3.

I will meet them as a bear that is bereaved of her whelps. *Ho.* 13: 8.

There will I devour them like a lion: the wild beast shall tear them. *Ho.* 13: 8.

Their horses also are swifter than the leopards, and are more fierce than the evening wolves. *Hab.* 1: 8.

See also

Brute; Cruelty; Inhumanity; Savage; Slaughter; Violence.

Fertility

The Lord God took the man, and put him into the garden of Eden to dress it and to keep it. *Ge.* 2: 15.

I will multiply thy seed as the stars of the heaven, and as the sand which is upon the sea shore. *Ge.* 22: 17.

God hath caused me to be fruitful in the land of my affliction. *Ge.* 41: 52.

Ye shall eat the fat of the land. *Ge.* 45: 18.

The God of thy father . . . shall bless thee with blessings of heaven above, blessings of the deep that lieth under, blessings of the breast, and of the womb. *Ge.* 49: 25.

I am come down . . . to bring them up out of that land unto a good land and a large, unto a land flowing with milk and honey. *Ex.* 3: 8.

The Lord thy God bringeth thee into a good land, a land of brooks of water, of fountains and depths that spring out of valleys and hills; A land of wheat, and barley, and vines, and fig trees, and pomegranates; a land of oil olive, and honey. *De.* 8: 7, 8.

When thou hast eaten and art full, then thou shalt bless the Lord thy God for the good land which he hath given thee. *De.* 8: 10.

The Lord thy God shall bless thee in all thine increase. *De.* 16: 15.

Blessed of the Lord be his land, for the precious things of heaven, for the dew, and for the deep that coucheth beneath. *De.* 33: 13.

Blessed of the Lord be his land, . . . for the precious fruits brought forth by the sun, and for the precious things put forth by the moon. *De.* 33: 13, 14.

Jordan overfloweth all his banks all the time of harvest. *Jos.* 3: 15.

The wilderness yieldeth food for them and for their children. *Jb.* 24: 5.

He turneth the wilderness into a standing water. *Ps.* 107: 35.

He blesseth them also, so that they are multiplied greatly. *Ps.* 107: 38.

In the wilderness shall waters break out, and streams in the desert. *Is.* 35: 6.

The earth bringeth forth fruit of herself; first the blade, then the ear, after that the full corn in the ear. *Mk.* 4: 28.

That ye might walk worthy of the Lord unto all pleasing, being fruitful in every good work. *Col.* 1: 10.

See also

Abundance; Fruit; Fruitfulness; Harvest; Plenty; Productivity; Yield.

Fervor

Whatsoever thy hand findeth to do, do it with thy might. *Ec.* 9: 10.

He . . . was clad with zeal as a cloke. *Is.* 59: 17.

I the Lord have spoken it in my zeal. *Eze.* 5: 13.

Although the fig tree shall not blossom, neither shall fruit be in the vine; the labour of the olive shall fail, and the fields shall yield no meat; the flock shall be cut off from the fold, and there shall be no herd in the stalls: Yet I will rejoice in the Lord, I will joy in the God of my salvation. *Hab.* 3: 17, 18.

He shall baptize you with the Holy Ghost and with fire. *Lu.* 3: 16.

She runneth. *Jn.* 20: 2.

Fervent in spirit. *Ro.* 12: 11.

Ye are zealous of spiritual gifts. *1 Co.* 14: 12.

Your zeal hath provoked very many. *2 Co.* 9: 2.

According to my earnest expectation and my hope. *Ph.* 1: 20.

Labouring fervently for you in prayers. *Col.* 4: 12.

Above all things have fervent charity among yourselves. *1 Pe.* 4: 8.

See also

Ardor; Eagerness; Earnestness; Enthusiasm; Passion; Zeal; Zest.

Festival

Ye shall hallow the fiftieth year, and proclaim liberty throughout all the land unto all the inhabitants thereof: it shall be a jubilee unto you. *Le.* 25: 10.

Thou hast turned for me my mourning into dancing: thou hast put off my sackcloth, and girded me with gladness. *Ps.* 30: 11.

He that is of a merry heart hath a continual feast. *Pr.* 15: 15.

He brought me to the banqueting house. *S. of S.* 2: 4.

In this mountain shall the Lord of hosts make unto all people a feast of fat things. *Is.* 25: 6.

I will turn your feasts into mourning, and all your songs into lamentation. *Am.* 8: 10.

I have prepared my dinner: my oxen and my fatlings are killed, and all things are ready. *Mat.* 22: 4.

Take thine ease, eat, drink, and be merry. *Lu.* 12: 19.

I must by all means keep this feast that cometh in Jerusalem. *Ac.* 18: 21.

See also

Banquet; Celebration; Feast; Holiday; Revel.

Fickleness

They change the night into day. *Jb.* 17: 12.

Their heart was not right with him, neither were they stedfast in his covenant. *Ps.* 78: 37.

Her ways are moveable, that thou canst not know them. *Pr.* 5: 6.

Meddle not with them that are given to change. *Pr.* 24: 21.

Your goodness is as a morning cloud, and as the early dew it goeth away. *Ho.* 6: 4.

All bear him witness, and wondered at the gracious words which proceeded out of his mouth. . . . All they in the synagogue, when they heard these things, were filled with wrath. *Lu.* 4: 22, 28.

They said among themselves, No doubt this man is a murderer. . . . They changed their minds, and said that he was a god. *Ac.* 28: 4, 6.

Having begun in the Spirit, are ye now made perfect by the flesh? *Ga.* 3: 3.

Carried about with every wind. *Ep.* 4: 14.

A double minded man is unstable in all his ways. *Ja.* 1: 8.

See also

Alteration; Change; Loyalty, Divided.

Fidelity

While the earth remaineth, seedtime and harvest, and cold and heat, and summer and winter, and day and night shall not cease. *Ge.* 8: 22.

I love my master, my wife, and my children. *Ex.* 21: 5.

Who is on the Lord's side? *Ex.* 32: 26.

Him shalt thou serve, and to him shalt thou cleave. *De.* 10: 20.

Cleave unto the Lord your God. *Jos.* 23: 8.

I will never break my covenant with you. *Ju.* 2: 1.

Where thou lodgest, I will lodge. *Ru.* 1: 16.

Thine are we, David, and on thy side. *1 Ch.* 12: 18.

When thou goest, it shall lead thee; when thou sleepest, it shall keep thee; and when thou awakest, it shall talk with thee. *Pr.* 6: 22.

Faithful are the wounds of a friend. *Pr.* 27: 6.

Well done, thou good and faithful servant. *Mat.* 25: 21.

Greater love hath no man than this, that a man lay down his life for his friends. *Jn.* 15: 13.

We ought to obey God rather than men. *Ac.* 5: 29.

He . . . exhorted them all, that with purpose of heart they would cleave unto the Lord. *Ac.* 11: 23.

Cleave to that which is good. *Ro.* **12: 9.**

He that is joined unto the Lord is one spirit. *1 Co.* **6: 17.**

He that is called in the Lord, being a servant, is the Lord's freeman. *1 Co.* **7: 22.**

He that is called, being free, is Christ's servant. *1 Co.* **7: 22.**

By faith ye stand. *2 Co.* **1: 24.**

The love of Christ constraineth us. *2 Co.* **5: 14.**

It is good to be zealously affected always in a good thing. *Ga.* **4: 18.**

If any provide not for his own, and specially for those of his own house, he hath denied the faith, and is worse than an infidel. *1 Ti.* **5: 8.**

Follow after righteousness, godliness, faith, love, patience, meekness. *1 Ti.* **6: 11.**

Teach the young women to be sober, to love their husbands, to love their children. *Tit.* **2: 4.**

These things I will that thou affirm constantly. *Tit.* **3: 8.**

Lo, I come to do thy will, O God. *He.* **10: 9.**

See also

Allegiance; Constancy; Devotion; Faithfulness; Loyalty; Servant.

Field

A man shall sanctify unto the Lord some part of a field of his possession. *Le.* **27: 16.**

Neither shalt thou covet thy neighbor's . . . field. *De.* **5: 21.**

Let the field be joyful, and all that is therein. *Ps.* **96: 12.**

As a flower of the field, so he flourisheth. *Ps.* **103: 15.**

I went by the field of the slothful, . . . And, lo, it was all grown over with thorns. *Pr.* **24: 30, 31.**

Woe unto them that join house to house, that lay field to field. *Is.* **5: 8.**

Zion shall be plowed like a field. *Je.* **26: 18.**

The field is wasted, the land mourneth. *Jo.* **1: 10.**

The kingdom of heaven is like unto treasure hid in a field. *Mat.* **13: 44.**

That field was called, The field of blood, unto this day. *Mat.* **27: 8.**

Fiend

The Lord said unto Satan, The Lord rebuke thee, O Satan. *Zch.* **3: 2.**

Then the devil taketh him up into the holy city. *Mat.* **4: 5.**

The devil taketh him up into an exceeding high mountain, and sheweth him all the kingdoms of the world, and the glory of them. *Mat.* **4: 8.**

Then the devil leaveth him, and, behold, angels came and ministered unto him. *Mat.* **4: 11.**

The Pharisees said, He casteth out devils through the prince of the devils. *Mat.* **9: 34.**

If they have called the master of the house Beelzebub, how much more shall they call them of his household? *Mat.* **10: 25.**

Get thee behind me, Satan. *Mat.* **16: 23.**

Neither give place to the devil. *Ep.* **4: 27.**

The children of God are manifest, and the children of the devil: whosoever doeth not righteousness is not of God. *1 Jn.* **3: 10.**

The great dragon was cast out, that old serpent, called the Devil, and Satan, which deceiveth the whole world: he was cast out into the earth, and his angels were cast out with him. *Re.* **12: 9.**

See also

Devil; Lucifer; Satan.

Fig

They sewed fig leaves together, and made themselves aprons. *Ge.* **3: 7.**

The trees said to the fig tree, Come thou, and reign over us. *Ju.* **9: 10.**

Judah and Israel dwelt safely, every man under his vine and under his fig tree. *1 K.* **4: 25.**

Eat ye every man of his own vine, and every one of his fig tree. *2 K.* **18: 31.**

Whoso keepeth the fig tree shall eat the fruit thereof. *Pr.* **27: 18.**

The fig tree putteth forth her green figs. *S. of S.* **2: 13.**

There shall be no grapes on the vine, nor figs on the fig tree. *Je.* **8: 13.**

I . . . will make them like vile figs, that cannot be eaten. *Je.* **29: 17.**

The fig tree and the vine do yield their strength. *Jo.* **2: 22.**

Do men gather grapes of thorns, or figs of thistles? *Mat.* **7: 16.**

Can the fig tree, my brethren, bear olive berries? *Ja.* **3: 12.**

Fight

One man of you shall chase a thousand: for the Lord your God, he it is that fighteth for you. *Jos.* **23: 10.**

The battle is the Lord's. *1 S.* **17: 47.**

The Lord will certainly make my Lord a sure house; because my lord fighteth the battles of the Lord. *1 S.* **25: 28.**

Fight for your master's house. *2 K.* **10: 3.**

Remember the Lord, which is great and terrible, and fight for your brethren. *Ne.* **4: 14.**

He that soweth discord among brethren. *Pr.* **6: 19.**

The Lord Jehovah is my strength and my song; he also is become my salvation. *Is.* **12: 2.**

If it be of God, ye cannot overthrow it; lest haply ye be found even to fight against God. *Ac.* **5: 39.**

We wrestle not against flesh and blood. *Ep.* **6: 12.**

That thou by them mightest war a good warfare. *1 Ti.* **1: 18.**

I have fought a good fight. *2 Ti.* **4: 7.**

Repent; or else I will come unto thee quickly, and will fight against them with the sword of my mouth. *Re.* **2: 16.**

See also

Attack; Battle; Belligerent; Conflict; Contention; Discord; Quarrel; Strife; Struggle; War; Weapon.

Finality

Thus the heavens and the earth were finished. *Ge.* **2: 1.**

I have finished the work which thou gavest me to do. *Jn.* **17: 4.**

When Jesus therefore had received the vinegar, he said, It is finished. *Jn.* **19: 30.**

Finally, brethren, farewell. *2 Co.* **13: 11.**

He which hath begun a good work in you
will perform it. *Ph.* 1: 6.

I have finished my course. 2 *Ti.* 4: 7.

When the thousand years are expired, Satan
shall be loosed out of his prison. *Re.* 20: 7.

See also

Christ, Finality of; Conclusion; End; Finish;
Last; Omega; Termination.

Finger

The voice is Jacob's voice, but the hands
are the hands of Esau. *Ge.* 27: 22.

This is the finger of God. *Ex.* 8: 19.

He gave unto Moses . . . two tables of testimony, tables of stone, written with the finger
of God. *Ex.* 31: 18.

When I consider thy heavens, the work of
thy fingers. *Ps.* 8: 3.

Keep my commandments . . . Bind them
upon thy fingers. *Pr.* 7: 2, 3.

Jesus stooped down, and with his finger
wrote on the ground. *Jn.* 8: 6.

Reach hither thy finger, and behold my
hands. *Jn.* 20: 27.

See also

Christ, Hand of; Hand.

Finish

He is the Rock, his work is perfect. *De.* 32:
4.

This man began to build and was not able
to finish. *Lu.* 14: 30.

The works which the Father hath given me
to finish, the same works that I do, bear witness of me. *Jn.* 5: 36.

Let us cleanse ourselves from all filthiness of
the flesh and spirit, perfecting holiness in the
fear of God. 2 *Co.* 7: 1.

Ye are complete in him. *Col.* 2: 10.

That ye may stand perfect and complete
in all the will of God. *Col.* 4: 12.

Looking unto Jesus the author and finisher
of our faith. *He.* 12: 2.

Sin, when it is finished, bringeth forth death.
Ja. 1: 15.

See also

Christ, Finality of; Christ, the Goal; Conclusion; End; Finality; Last; Termination.

Fir

The fir trees rejoice at thee. *Is.* 14: 8.

I will set in the desert the fir tree. *Is.* 41: 19.

Instead of the thorn shall come up the fir
tree. *Is.* 55: 13.

The glory of Lebanon shall come unto thee,
the fir tree, the pine tree, and the box together, to beautify the place of my sanctuary.
Is. 60: 13.

I am like a green fir tree. *Ho.* 14: 8.

Howl, fir tree; for the cedar is fallen. *Zch.*
11: 2.

Fire

The bush burned with fire, and the bush
was not consumed. *Ex.* 3: 2.

The Lord was not in the fire. 1 *K.* 19: 12.

My heart was hot within me; while I was
musing the fire burned. *Ps.* 39: 3.

Wherefore glorify ye the Lord in the fires.
Is. 24: 15.

He shall baptize you with the Holy Ghost,
and with fire. *Mat.* 3: 11.

I am come to send fire on the earth; and
what will I, if it be already kindled? *Lu.* 12:
49.

The fire shall try every man's work of what
sort it is. 1 *Co.* 3: 13.

If any man's work shall be burned, he shall
suffer loss: but he himself shall be saved; yet
so as by fire. 1 *Co.* 3: 15.

How great a matter a little fire kindleth!
Ja. 3: 5.

The tongue is a fire, a world of iniquity.
Ja. 3: 6.

See also

Burn; Flame; Furnace; Heat.

Firmament

Let there be a firmament in the midst of the
waters, and let it divide the waters from the
waters. *Ge.* 1: 6.

God called the firmament Heaven. *Ge.* 1: 8.

He made the stars also. *Ge.* 1: 17.

I saw the Lord sitting on his throne, and
all the host of heaven standing by him on his
right hand and on his left. 1 *K.* 22: 19.

The heavens declare the glory of God. *Ps.*
19: 1.

God . . . covereth the heaven with clouds.
Ps. 147: 7, 8.

His glory is above the earth and heaven. *Ps.*
148: 13.

Praise him in the firmament of his power.
Ps. 150: 1.

Thus saith the Lord, The heaven is my
throne, and the earth is my footstool. *Is.* 66: 1.

Swear not at all; neither by heaven; for it
is God's throne: Nor by the earth; for it is
his footstool. *Mat.* 5: 34, 35.

I saw a star fall from heaven unto the
earth. *Re.* 9: 1.

See also

Constellation; Heaven; Sky; Star.

Firmness

Thou shalt be stedfast, and shalt not fear.
Jb. 11: 15.

The Lord reigneth, he is clothed with
majesty; . . . the world also is stablished, that
it cannot be moved. *Ps.* 93: 1.

If thou faint in the day of adversity, thy
strength is small. *Pr.* 24: 10.

In quietness and in confidence shall be your
strength. *Is.* 30: 15.

Enlarge the place of thy tent: . . . lengthen
thy cords, and strengthen thy stakes. *Is.* 54: 2.

Son of man, stand upon thy feet, and I will
speak unto thee. *Eze.* 2: 1.

My spirit remaineth among you: fear ye
not. *Hag.* 2: 5.

None of these things move me. *Ac.* 20: 24.

My strength is made perfect in weakness.
2 *Co.* 12: 9.

Having done all, to stand. *Ep.* 6: 13.

Rooted and built up in him, and stablished
in the faith, as ye have been taught. *Col.*
2: 7.

The Lord is faithful, who shall stablish you,
and keep you from evil. 2 *Th.* 3: 3.

If we hold fast the confidence and the rejoicing of the hope firm unto the end. *He.* 3: 6.

See also

Constancy; Decision; Faithfulness; Hardness;
Security; Stability; Steadfastness.

First

In the beginning God created the heaven
and the earth. *Ge.* 1: 1.

Art thou the first man that was born? *Jb.* 15: 7.

I will make him my firstborn, higher than the kings of the earth. *Ps.* 89: 27.

Seek ye first the kingdom of God, and his righteousness. *Mat.* 6: 33.

Many that are first shall be last; and the last shall be first. *Mat.* 19: 30.

He marked how they chose out the chief rooms. *Lu.* 14: 7.

In the beginning was the Word, and the Word was with God, and the Word was God. *Jn.* 1: 1.

This beginning of miracles did Jesus in Cana of Galilee. *Jn.* 2: 11.

The image of the invisible God, the first-born of every creature. *Col.* 1: 15.

The dead in Christ shall rise first. *1 Th.* 4: 16.

Adam was first formed, then Eve. *1 Ti.* 2: 13.

Ye are come . . . To the general assembly and church of the firstborn. *He.* 12: 22, 23.

I am Alpha and Omega, the beginning and the ending, saith the Lord. *Re.* 1: 8.

These things saith the Amen, the faithful and true witness, the beginning of the creation of God. *Re.* 3: 14.

See also

Alpha; Beginning; Christ, the Creator; Commencement; Creation; Creator; Foundation; Genesis; God, the Creator; Origin; Priority; Preëminence; Senior; Uniqueness.

Fisher

Let them have dominion over the fish of the sea. *Ge.* 1: 26.

Thou madest him to have dominion over the works of thy hands; . . . the fish of the sea, and whatsoever passeth through the paths of the seas. *Ps.* 8: 6, 8.

I will send for many fishers, saith the Lord, and they shall fish them. *Je.* 16: 16.

Follow me, and I will make you fishers of men. *Mat.* 4: 19.

Simon Peter saith unto them, I go a fishing. *Jn.* 21: 3.

Cast the net on the right side of the ship, and ye shall find. They cast therefore, and now they were not able to draw it for the multitude of fishes. *Jn.* 21: 6.

Jesus saith unto them, Bring of the fish which ye have now caught. *Jn.* 21: 10.

See also

Sport.

Fitness

Soldiers, fit to go out for war and battle. *1 Ch.* 7: 11.

Holiness becometh thine house, O Lord, for ever. *Ps.* 93: 5.

Delight is not seemly for a fool. *Pr.* 19: 10.

Prepare thy work without, and make it fit for thyself in the field; and afterwards build thine house. *Pr.* 24: 27.

A word fitly spoken is like apples of gold in pictures of silver. *Pr.* 25: 11.

As snow in summer, and as rain in harvest, so honour is not seemly for a fool. *Pr.* 26: 1.

Suffer it to be so now: for thus it becometh us to fulfil all righteousness. *Mat.* 3: 15.

No man, having put his hand to the plow,

and looking back, is fit for the kingdom of God. *Lu.* 9: 62.

In whom all the building fitly framed together groweth unto an holy temple of the Lord. *Ep.* 2: 21.

The whole body fitly joined together and compacted by that which every joint supplieth. *Ep.* 4: 16.

Let your conversation be as it becometh the gospel of Christ. *Ph.* 1: 27.

Wives, submit yourselves unto your own husbands, as it is fit in the Lord. *Col.* 3: 18.

See also

Expediency; Right.

Flag Day

Every man by his own standard. *Nu.* 1: 52.

In the name of our God we will set up our banners. *Ps.* 20: 5.

Thou hast given a banner to them that fear thee. *Ps.* 60: 4.

Terrible as an army with banners. *S. of S.* 6: 4.

Lift ye up a banner upon the high mountain. *Is.* 13: 2.

I will . . . set up my standard to the people. *Is.* 49: 22.

When the enemy shall come in like a flood, the Spirit of the Lord shall lift up a standard against him. *Is.* 59: 19.

Lift up a standard for the people. *Is.* 62: 10.

Flame

The angel of the Lord appeared unto him in a flame of fire out of the midst of a bush. *Ex.* 3: 2.

The Lord went before them . . . by night in a pillar of fire, to give them light. *Ex.* 13: 21.

The Lord descended upon it in fire. *Ex.* 19: 18.

His breath kindleth coals, and a flame goeth out of his mouth. *Jb.* 41: 21.

We went through fire and through water. *Ps.* 66: 12.

A fire goeth before him, and burneth up his enemies round about. *Ps.* 97: 3.

A fire was kindled in their company; the flame burned up the wicked. *Ps.* 106: 18.

Can a man take fire in his bosom, and his clothes not be burned? *Pr.* 6: 27.

When thou walkest through the fire, thou shalt not be burned; neither shall the flame kindle upon thee. *Is.* 43: 2.

Ye were as a firebrand plucked out of the burning. *Am.* 4: 11.

I am come to send fire on the earth. *Lu.* 12: 49.

There appeared unto them cloven tongues like as of fire, and it sat upon each of them. *Ac.* 2: 3.

See also

Burn; Fire; Furnace; Heat.

Flattery

They said unto him, From a very far country thy servants are come because of the name of the Lord thy God. *Jos.* 9: 9.

As an angel of God, so is my lord the king to discern good and bad: therefore the Lord thy God will be with thee. *2 S.* 14: 17.

He that speaketh flattery to his friends, even the eyes of his children shall fail. *Jb.* 17: 5.

I know not to give flattering titles. *Jb.* **32: 22.**

With flattering lips and with a double heart do they speak. *Ps.* **12: 2.**

He flattereth himself in his own eyes. *Ps.* **36: 2.**

They did flatter him with their mouth, and they lied unto him with their tongues. *Ps.* **78: 36.**

With her much fair speech she caused him to yield. *Pr.. 7: 21.*

Many will intreat the favour of the prince. *Pr.* **19: 6.**

Every man is a friend to him that giveth gifts. *Pr.* **19: 6.**

Meddle not with him that flattereth with his lips. *Pr.* **20: 19.**

He that saith unto the wicked, Thou art righteous; him shall the people curse, nations shall abhor him. *Pr.* **24: 24.**

It is not good to eat much honey. *Pr.* **25: 27.**

A flattering mouth worketh ruin. *Pr.* **26: 28.**

A man that flattereth his neighbour spreadeth a net for his feet. *Pr.* **29: 5.**

He shall come in peaceably, and obtain the kingdom by flatteries. *Da.* **11: 21.**

Many shall cleave to them with flatteries. *Da.* **11: 34.**

The people gave a shout, saying, It is the voice of a god, and not of a man. *Ac.* **12: 22.**

Not with eyeservice, as menpleasers. *Ep.* **6: 6.**

Even so we speak; not as pleasing men, but God, which trieth our hearts. *1 Th.* **2: 4.**

Neither at any time used we flattering words. *1 Th.* **2: 5.**

See also

Eulogy; Hypocrisy; Insincerity; Praise.

Flesh

All flesh is grass. *Is.* **40: 6.**

Shall I give . . . the fruit of my body for the sin of my soul? *Mi.* **6: 7.**

Take no thought . . . for your body. *Mat.* **6: 25.**

It is the spirit that quickeneth; the flesh profiteth nothing. *Jn.* **6: 63.**

With the mind I myself serve the law of God; but with the flesh the law of sin. *Ro.* **7: 25.**

The carnal mind is enmity against God. *Ro.* **8: 7.**

Ye are not in the flesh, but in the Spirit, if so be that the Spirit of God dwell in you. *Ro.* **8: 9.**

If ye through the Spirit do mortify the deeds of the body, ye shall live. *Ro.* **8: 13.**

Know ye not that your bodies are the members of Christ? *1 Co.* **6: 15.**

Know ye not that your body is the temple of the Holy Ghost? *1 Co.* **6: 19.**

The flesh lusteth against the Spirit, and the Spirit against the flesh. *Ga.* **5: 17.**

He is the saviour of the body. *Ep.* **5: 23.**

No man ever yet hated his own flesh. *Ep.* **5: 29.**

Vainly puffed up by his fleshly mind. *Col.* **2: 18.**

A body hast thou prepared me. *He.* **10: 5.**

See also

Body; Christ, Body of; Debauchery; Dissipation; Fornication; Lust; Prostitute; Sensuality.

Flight

An hundred of you shall put ten thousand to flight. *Le.* **26: 8.**

As swift as the eagle flieth. *De.* **28: 49.**

In the Lord put I my trust: how say ye to my soul, Flee as a bird to your mountain? *Ps.* **11: 1.**

Thou shalt not be afraid . . . for the arrow that flieth by day. *Ps.* **91: 5.**

Whither shall I flee from thy presence? *Ps.* **139: 7.**

Deliver me, O Lord, from mine enemies: I flee unto thee to hide me. *Ps.* **143: 9.**

The wicked flee when no man pursueth. *Pr.* **28: 1.**

Until the day break, and the shadows flee away. *S. of S.* **2: 17.**

They shall obtain joy and gladness, and sorrow and sighing shall flee away. *Is.* **35: 10.**

Ye shall not go out with haste, nor go by flight: for the Lord will go before you. *Is.* **52: 12.**

Arise, and take the young child and his mother, and flee into Egypt. *Mat.* **2: 13.**

Pray ye that your flight be not in the winter, neither on the sabbath day. *Mat.* **24: 20.**

All the disciples forsook him, and fled. *Mat.* **26: 56.**

Turned to flight the armies of the aliens. *He.* **11: 34.**

Resist the devil, and he will flee from you. *Ja.* **4: 7.**

See also

Escape.

Flock

I took thee from the sheepcote, from following the sheep, to be ruler over my people. *2 S.* **7: 8.**

The pastures are clothed with flocks. *Ps.* **65: 13.**

I will gather the remnant of my flock out of all countries whither I have driven them, and will bring them again to their folds. *Je.* **23: 3.**

My people hath been lost sheep: their shepherds have caused them to go astray. *Je.* **50: 6.**

He saith unto him, Feed my lambs. *Jn.* **21: 15.**

After my departing shall grievous wolves enter in among you, not sparing the flock. *Ac.* **20: 29.**

Feed the flock of God which is among you. *1 Pe.* **5: 2.**

See also

Collection; Crowd; Herd; Multitude; Sheep.

Flood

Neither shall there any more be a flood to destroy the earth. *Ge.* **9: 11.**

They went through the flood on foot. *Ps.* **66: 6.**

Let not the waterflood overflow me, neither let the deep swallow me up. *Ps.* **69: 15.**

Thou carriest them away as with a flood. *Ps.* **90: 5.**

The waters stood above the mountains. *Ps.* **104: 6.**

Then the proud waters had gone over our soul. *Ps.* **124: 5.**

Many waters cannot quench love, neither can the floods drown it. *S. of S.* **8: 7.**

When thou passest through the waters, I
will be with thee. *Is.* 43: 2.

All thy billows and thy waves passed over
me. *Jon.* 2: 3.

The rain descended, and the floods came,
and the winds blew, and beat upon that house;
and it fell: and great was the fall of it. *Mat.*
7: 27.
See also
Deep; Deluge; Ocean; River; Sea; Stream;
Water; Wave.

Flower
All the increase of thine house shall die in
the flower of their age. *1 S.* 2: 33.

I am the rose of Sharon, and the lily of the
valleys. *S. of S.* 2: 1.

The flowers appear on the earth; the time
of the singing of birds is come. *S. of S.* 2: 12.

My beloved . . . feedeth among the lilies.
S. of S. 2: 16.

His cheeks are as a bed of spices, as sweet
flowers: his lips like lilies, dropping sweet
smelling myrrh. *S. of S.* 5: 13.

Woe to the crown of pride, to the drunkards
of Ephraim, whose glorious beauty is a
fading flower. *Is.* 28: 1.

The desert shall rejoice, and blossom as the
rose. *Is.* 35: 1.

All flesh is as grass, and all the goodliness
thereof is as the flower of the field. *Is.* 40: 6.

I will be as the dew unto Israel: he shall
grow as the lily. *Ho.* 14: 5.

Consider the lilies of the field. *Mat.* 6: 28.
See also
Garden.

Foe
Thou hast smitten all mine enemies. *Ps.* 3: 7.

Lead me, O Lord, in thy righteousness because of mine enemies. *Ps.* 5: 8.

I have delivered him that without cause is
mine enemy. *Ps.* 7: 4.

Hide me . . . from my deadly enemies, who
compass me about. *Ps.* 17: 8, 9.

They also that render evil for good are
mine adversaries; because I follow the thing
that good is. *Ps.* 38: 20.

Thou hast been a shelter for me, and a
strong tower from the enemy. *Ps.* 61: 3.

When a man's ways please the Lord, he
maketh even his enemies to be at peace with
him. *Pr.* 16: 7.

Thine hand shall be lifted up upon thine
adversaries, and all thine enemies shall be cut
off. *Mi.* 5: 9.

The gates of thy land shall be set wide open
unto thine enemies. *Na.* 3: 13.

Love your enemies, do good to them which
hate you, Bless them that curse you, and pray
for them which despitefully use you. *Lu.* 6:
27, 28.

I will give you a mouth and wisdom, which
all your adversaries shall not be able to gainsay nor resist. *Lu.* 21: 15.

In nothing terrified by your adversaries. *Ph.*
1: 28.
See also
Adversary; Antagonism; Antichrist; Antipathy; Enemy; Opponent; Opposition.

Fold
Build you cities for your little ones, and

folds for your sheep. *Nu.* 32: 24.

It shall never be inhabited; . . . neither
shall the shepherds make their fold there. *Is.*
13: 20.

Sharon shall be a fold of flocks, and the
valley of Achor a place for the herds to lie
down in. *Is.* 65: 10.

I will gather the remnant of my flock out
of all countries whither I have driven them,
and will bring them again to their folds. *Je.*
23: 3.

I will feed them in a good pasture, and
upon the high mountains of Israel shall their
fold be: there shall they lie in a good fold,
and in a fat pasture shall they feed. *Eze.* 34: 14.

The flock shall be cut off from the fold, and
there shall be no herd in the stalls. *Hab.* 3:
17.

Other sheep I have, which are not of this
fold; . . . there shall be one fold, and one
shepherd. *Jn.* 10: 16.
See also
Flock; Herd; Pasture; Sheep; Shepherd.

Follower
Thou shalt not follow a multitude to do
evil. *Ex.* 23: 2.

That which is altogether just shalt thou
follow, that thou mayest live. *De.* 16: 20.

If the Lord be God, follow him. *1 K.* 18: 21.

My soul followeth hard after thee. *Ps.* 63: 8.

Hearken to me, ye that follow after righteousness, ye that seek the Lord. *Is.* 51: 1.

Then shall we know, if we follow on to
know the Lord. *Ho.* 6: 3.

I will follow thee whithersoever thou goest.
Mat. 8: 19.

He that followeth me shall not walk in
darkness. *Jn.* 8: 12.

Whither I go, thou canst not follow me
now. *Jn.* 13: 36.

Let us therefore follow after the things
which make for peace. *Ro.* 14: 19.

Thou, O man of God, . . . follow after
righteousness. *1 Ti.* 6: 11.
See also
Apostle; Attachment; Christ, Disciple of;
Christ, Follower of; Christ, the Leader; De-
votion; Disciple; Faithfulness; God, Loyalty to;
Loyalty; Successor.

Folly
Let a bear robbed of her whelps meet a
man, rather than a fool in his folly. *Pr.* 17: 12.

Answer a fool according to his folly. *Pr.* 26:
5.

As a dog returneth to his vomit, so a fool
returneth to his folly. *Pr.* 26: 11.

Though thou shouldest bray a fool in a
mortar among wheat with a pestle, yet will
not his foolishness depart from him. *Pr.* 27: 22.

Wisdom excelleth folly, as far as light excelleth darkness. *Ec.* 2: 13.

The foolishness of God is wiser than men.
1 Co. 1: 25.
See also
Fool; Ignorance; Nonsense; Stupidity.

Food
Dust shalt thou eat all the days of thy life.
Ge. 3: 14.

The wilderness yieldeth food for them. *Jb.*
24: 5.

I have been young, and now am old; yet have I not seen the righteous forsaken, nor his seed begging bread. *Ps.* 37: 25.

Bread which strengtheneth man's heart. *Ps.* 104: 15.

The young lions roar after their prey, and seek their meat from God. *Ps.* 104: 21.

Stolen waters are sweet, and bread eaten in secret is pleasant. *Pr.* 9: 17.

In this mountain shall the Lord of hosts make unto all people a feast of fat things, a feast of wines on the lees, of fat things full of marrow, of wines on the lees well refined. *Is.* 25: 6.

Wherefore do ye spend money for that which is not bread? *Is.* 55: 2.

Man shall not live by bread alone, but by every word that proceedeth out of the mouth of God. *Mat.* 4: 4.

What man is there of you, whom if his son ask bread, will he give him a stone? *Mat.* 7: 9.

I was an hungred, and ye gave me meat. *Mat.* 25: 35.

Give us day by day our daily bread. *Lu.* 11: 3.

I have fed you with milk, and not with meat. *1 Co.* 3: 2.

Blessed are they which are called unto the marriage supper of the Lamb. *Re.* 19: 9.
See also
Bread; Christ, the Bread of Life; Hunger; Manna; Meat; Nourishment; Stomach.

Fool

The fool hath said in his heart, There is no God. *Ps.* 14: 1.

A foolish woman is clamorous: she is simple, and knoweth nothing. *Pr.* 9: 13.

A fool despiseth his father's instruction. *Pr.* 15: 5.

A whip for the horse, a bridle for the ass, and a rod for the fool's back. *Pr.* 26: 3.

The legs of the lame are not equal: so is a parable in the mouth of fools. *Pr.* 26: 7.

How dieth the wise man? as the fool. *Ec.* 2: 16.

As the crackling of thorns under a pot, so is the laughter of the fool. *Ec.* 7: 6.

Whosoever shall say, Thou fool, shall be in danger of hell fire. *Mat.* 5: 22.

Every one that heareth these sayings of mine, and doeth them not, shall be likened unto a foolish man, which built his house upon the sand. *Mat.* 7: 26.

Ye suffer fools gladly, seeing ye yourselves are wise. *2 Co.* 11: 19.

See then that ye walk circumspectly, not as fools, but as wise. *Ep.* 5: 15.
See also
Folly; Ignorance; Nonsense; Stupidity.

Foot

He maketh my feet like hinds' feet: and setteth me upon my high places. *2 S.* 22: 34.

Thou hast put all things under his feet. *Ps.* 8: 6.

Thou hast set my feet in a large room. *Ps.* 31: 8.

He . . . set my feet upon a rock, and established my goings. *Ps.* 40: 2.

Feet have they, but they walk not. *Ps.* 115: 7.

Thou hast delivered . . . my feet from falling. *Ps.* 116: 8.

Thy word is a lamp unto my feet. *Ps.* 119: 105.

He will not suffer thy foot to be moved. *Ps.* 121: 3.

Ponder the path of thy feet. *Pr.* 4: 26.

Then shall the lame man leap as an hart. *Is.* 35: 6.

How beautiful upon the mountains are the feet of him that bringeth good tidings. *Is.* 52: 7.

Son of man, stand upon thy feet, and I will speak unto thee. *Eze.* 2: 1.

If thy hand or thy foot offend thee, cut them off, and cast them from thee. *Mat.* 18: 8.

Mary . . . sat at Jesus' feet. *Lu.* 10: 39.

He shewed them his hands and his feet. *Lu.* 24: 40.

If the foot shall say, Because I am not the hand, I am not of the body; is it therefore not of the body? *1 Co.* 12: 15.

Your feet shod with the preparation of the gospel of peace. *Ep.* 6: 15.
See also
Footstep; Footstool; Shoe; Step; Walk.

Footstep

Enoch walked with God. *Ge.* 5: 24.

Hold up my goings in thy paths, that my footsteps slip not. *Ps.* 17: 5.

Thy footsteps are not known. *Ps.* 77: 19.

From that time many of his disciples went back, and walked no more with him. *Jn.* 6: 66.

Walked we not in the same spirit? walked we not in the same steps? *2 Co.* 12: 18.

Walk in love, as Christ also hath loved us. *Ep.* 5: 2.

As ye have therefore received Christ Jesus the Lord, so walk ye in him. *Col.* 2: 6.

He that saith he abideth in him ought himself also so to walk, even as he walked. *1 Jn.* 2: 6.
See also
Apostle; Christ, Disciple of; Christ, Follower of; Disciple; Follower; Foot; Shoe; Step; Walk.

Footstool

I had in mine heart to build an house of rest for the ark of the covenant of the Lord, and for the footstool of our God. *1 Ch.* 28: 2.

Exalt ye the Lord our God, and worship at his footstool. *Ps.* 99: 5.

The earth is my footstool. *Is.* 66: 1.

He must reign, till he hath put all enemies under his feet. *1 Co.* 15: 25.

Till his enemies be made his footstool. *He.* 10: 13.
See also
Earth; Foot.

Forbearance

Therefore I will not refrain my mouth. *Jb.* 7: 11.

I have refrained my feet from every evil way. *Ps.* 119: 101.

He that refraineth his lips is wise. *Pr.* 10: 19.

Wilt thou refrain thyself for these things, O Lord? wilt thou hold thy peace, and afflict us very sore? *Is.* 64: 12.

He that forbeareth, let him forbear. *Eze.* **3: 27.**

In your patience possess ye your souls. *Lu.* **21: 19.**

Despisest thou the riches of his goodness and forbearance and longsuffering? *Ro.* **2: 4.**

Through the forbearance of God. *Ro.* **3: 25.**

With longsuffering, forbearing one another in love. *Ep.* **4: 2.**

Be ye kind one to another, tenderhearted, forgiving one another. *Ep.* **4: 32.**

Be patient toward all men. *1 Th.* **5: 14.**

He that will love life, and see good days, let him refrain his tongue from evil, and his lips that they speak no guile. *1 Pe.* **3: 10.**

See also

Abstinence; Endurance; Fortitude; Long-Suffering; Patience; Resignation; Restraint; Tolerance.

Force

How forcible are right words! *Jb.* **6: 25.**

The spirit within me constraineth me. *Jb.* **32: 18.**

Violence covereth the mouth of the wicked. *Pr.* **10: 6.**

Whosoever shall compel thee to go a mile, go with him twain. *Mat.* **5: 41.**

Until now the kingdom of heaven suffereth violence, and the violent take it by force. *Mat.* **11: 12.**

They compel one Simon . . . to bear his cross. *Mk.* **15: 21.**

Go out into the highways and hedges, and compel them to come in, that my house may be filled. *Lu.* **14: 23.**

The kingdom of God is preached, and every man presseth into it. *Lu.* **16: 16.**

The love of Christ constraineth us. *2 Co.* **5: 14.**

This I say therefore. *Ep.* **4: 17.**

See also

Christ, Power of; Christ, Strength of; Coercion; Compulsion; Constraint; Energy; Energy, Creative; Enforcement; God, Omnipotence of; God, Power of; God, Strength of; Might; Omnipotence; Power; Restraint; Strength; Vigor; Violence; Vitality.

Foreigner

Thou art a stranger, and also an exile. *2 S.* **15: 19.**

We are strangers before thee, and sojourners, as were all our fathers. *1 Ch.* **29: 15.**

Even them will I bring to my holy mountain, and make them joyful in my house of prayer. *Is.* **56: 7.**

I will make them one nation. *Eze.* **37: 22.**

I will pour out my spirit upon all flesh. *Jo.* **2: 28.**

Are ye not as children of the Ethiopians unto me, O children of Israel? saith the Lord. *Am.* **9: 7.**

Other sheep I have, which are not of this fold. *Jn.* **10: 16.**

God . . . hath made of one blood all nations of men for to dwell on all the face of the earth. *Ac.* **17: 24, 26.**

There is neither Jew nor Greek, there is neither bond nor free, there is neither male nor female: for ye are all one in Christ Jesus. *Ga.* **3: 28.**

Aliens from the commonwealth of Israel. *Ep.* **2: 12.**

Now in Christ Jesus ye who sometimes were afar off are made nigh by the blood of Christ. *Ep.* **2: 13.**

Now therefore ye are no more strangers and foreigners, but fellowcitizens with the saints, and of the household of God. *Ep.* **2: 19.**

See also

Alien; Immigration; Stranger.

Foreknowledge

Ye shall be as gods, knowing good and evil. *Ge.* **3: 5.**

A prudent man foreseeth the evil, and hideth himself. *Pr.* **22: 3.**

Before I formed thee in the belly I knew thee. *Je.* **1: 5.**

Among the tribes of Israel have I made known that which shall surely be. *Ho* **5: 9.**

Take ye heed: behold, I have foretold you all things. *Mk.* **13: 23.**

He knew what was in man. *Jn.* **2: 25.**

Jesus knew from the beginning who they were that believed not, and who should betray him. *Jn.* **6: 64.**

David speaketh concerning him, I foresaw the Lord always before my face. *Ac.* **2: 25.**

All the prophets from Samuel and those that follow after, as many as have spoken, have likewise foretold of these days. *Ac.* **3: 24.**

He that searcheth the hearts knoweth what is the mind of the Spirit. *Ro.* **8: 27.**

I told you before, and foretell you, as if I were present, the second time. *2 Co.* **13: 2.**

The scripture, foreseeing that God would justify the heathen through faith, preached before the gospel unto Abraham, saying, In thee shall all nations be blessed. *Ga.* **3: 8.**

See also

Christ, Foreknowledge of; Foreordination; God, Foreknowledge of; God, Omniscience of; Preordination.

Foreordination

Inherit the kingdom prepared for you from the foundation of the world. *Mat.* **25: 34.**

Whom he did foreknow, he also did predestinate to be conformed to the image of his Son. *Ro.* **8: 29.**

Whom he did predestinate, them he also called: and whom he called, them he also justified: and whom he justified, them he also glorified. *Ro.* **8: 30.**

God hath not cast away his people which he foreknew. *Ro.* **11: 2.**

He hath chosen us in him before the foundation of the world. *Ep.* **1: 4.**

Having predestinated us unto the adoption of children by Jesus Christ to himself, according to the good pleasure of his will. *Ep.* **1: 5.**

Elect according to the foreknowledge of God the Father, through sanctification of the Spirit. *1 Pe.* **1: 2.**

Who verily was foreordained before the foundation of the world. *1 Pe.* **1: 20.**

See also

Election; God, Foreknowledge of; Predestination; Preordination.

Forerunner

He shall send his angel before thee. *Ge.* **24: 7.**

Make straight in the desert a highway for our God. *Is.* 40: 3.

Behold, I send my messenger before thy face, which shall prepare thy way before thee. *Mat.* 11: 10.

Jesus constrained his disciples . . . to go before him unto the other side. *Mat.* 14: 22.

I send unto you prophets, and wise men, and scribes. *Mat.* 23: 34.

Thou shalt go before the face of the Lord to prepare his ways. *Lu.* 1: 76.

He was not that Light, but was sent to bear witness of that Light. *Jn.* 1: 8.

I am the voice of one crying in the wilderness, Make straight the way of the Lord. *Jn.* 1: 23.

All that ever came before me are thieves and robbers. *Jn.* 10: 8.

Many resorted unto him, and said, John did no miracle: but all things that John spake of this man were true. *Jn.* 10: 41.

These going before tarried for us. *Ac.* 20: 5.

Whither the forerunner is for us entered. *He.* 6: 20.

See also

Ambassador; God, Messenger of; Harbinger; Herald; Messenger; Missionary; Predecessor; Prophet; Sign; Vanguard.

Forest

The voice of the Lord . . . discovereth the forests. *Ps.* 29: 9.

Every beast of the forest is mine. *Ps.* 50: 10.

Then shall all the trees of the wood rejoice. *Ps.* 96: 12.

The trees of the Lord are full of sap. *Ps.* 104: 16.

Under his glory he shall kindle a burning like the burning of a fire. . . . And shall consume the glory of his forest. *Is.* 10: 16, 18.

Break forth into singing, ye mountains, O forest, and every tree therein. *Is.* 44: 23.

All the trees of the field shall clap their hands. *Is.* 55: 12.

I will kindle a fire in the forest thereof, and it shall devour all things round about it. *Je.* 21: 14.

As the vine tree among the trees of the forest, which I have given to the fire for fuel, so will I give the inhabitants of Jerusalem. *Eze.* 15: 6.

They shall dwell safely in the wilderness, and sleep in the woods. *Eze.* 34: 25.

I will destroy her vines and her fig trees: . . . and I will make them a forest, and the beasts of the field shall eat them. *Ho.* 2: 12.

They sacrifice . . . under oaks and poplars and elms, because the shadow thereof is good. *Ho.* 4: 13.

See also

Tree; Verdure; Wood.

Foretaste

He shall send his angel before thee. *Ge.* 24: 7.

They came unto the brook of Eshcol, and cut down from thence a branch with one cluster of grapes, and they bare it between two upon a staff. *Nu.* 13: 23.

Thou preventest him with the blessings of goodness. *Ps.* 21: 3.

O taste and see that the Lord is good. *Ps.* 34: 8.

Mercy and truth shall go before thy face. *Ps.* 89: 14.

It shall come to pass, that before they call, I will answer. *Is.* 65: 24.

The fathers have eaten a sour grape, and the children's teeth are set on edge. *Je.* 31: 29.

Thou lovedst me before the foundation of the world. *Jn.* 17: 24.

It is impossible for those who . . . have tasted of the heavenly gift, And were made partakers of the Holy Ghost, and have tasted the good word of God, . . . If they shall fall away, to renew them again unto repentance. *He.* 6: 4-6.

Forethought

Set thine house in order; for thou shalt die, and not live. *2 K.* 20: 1.

The ant . . . Provideth her meat in the summer, and gathereth her food in the harvest. *Pr.* 6: 6, 8.

A prudent man foreseeth the evil, and hideth himself: but the simple pass on, and are punished. *Pr.* 22: 3.

Prepare thy work without, and make it fit for thyself in the field; and afterwards build thine house. *Pr.* 24: 27.

Therefore be ye also ready: for in such an hour as ye think not the Son of man cometh. *Mat.* 24: 44.

Provide yourselves bags which wax not old, a treasure in the heavens that faileth not, where no thief approacheth, neither moth corrupteth. *Lu.* 12: 33.

See also

Preparation; Readiness.

Forgetfulness

Yet did not the chief butler remember Joseph, but forgat him. *Ge.* 40: 23.

God . . . hath made me forget all my toil. *Ge.* 41: 51.

It shall be, when the Lord thy God shall have brought thee into the land which he sware unto thy fathers, . . . to give thee great and goodly cities, which thou buildest not, And houses full of all good things, which thou filledst not, . . . Then beware lest thou forget the Lord. *De.* 6: 10–12.

Of the Rock that begat thee thou art unmindful, and hast forgotten God that formed thee. *De.* 32: 18.

The children of Israel did evil in the sight of the Lord, and forgat the Lord their God, and served Baalim and the groves. *Ju.* 3: 7.

Bless the Lord, O my soul, and forget not all his benefits. *Ps.* 103: 2.

If I forget thee, O Jerusalem, let my right hand forget her cunning. *Ps.* 137: 5.

Lest they drink, and forget the law, and pervert the judgment. *Pr.* 31: 5.

The dead know not any thing. *Ec.* 9: 5.

Thou shalt forget the shame of thy youth. *Is.* 54: 4.

They . . . remembered not the brotherly covenant. *Am.* 1: 9.

Shouldest not thou also have had compassion on thy fellowservant, even as I had pity on thee? *Mat.* 18: 33.

This one thing I do, forgetting those things

which are behind, and reaching forth unto those things which are before. *Ph.* 3: 13.

Be not forgetful to entertain strangers: for thereby some have entertained angels unawares. *He.* 13: 2.

If any be a hearer of the word, and not a doer, he is like unto a man beholding his natural face in a glass: For he beholdeth himself, and goeth his way, and straightway forgetteth what manner of man he was. *Ja.* 1: 23, 24.

He that lacketh these things is blind, and cannot see afar off, and hath forgotten that he was purged from his old sins. *2 Pe.* 1: 9.

See also
Amnesty; Oblivion; Thankfulness.

Forgiveness

Forgive, I pray thee now, the trespass of thy brethren, and their sin. *Ge.* 50: 17.

Speak ye comfortably to Jerusalem, and cry unto her, that her warfare is accomplished, that her iniquity is pardoned. *Is.* 40: 2.

Come, and let us return unto the Lord. *Ho.* 6: 1.

Leave there thy gift before the altar, and go thy way; first be reconciled to thy brother, and then come and offer thy gift. *Mat.* 5: 24.

Forgive us our debts, as we forgive our debtors. *Mat.* 6: 12.

All manner of sin and blasphemy shall be forgiven unto men: but the blasphemy against the Holy Ghost, it shall not be forgiven him. *Mat.* 12: 31.

Then came Peter to him, and said, Lord, how oft shall my brother sin against me, and I forgive him? till seven times? Jesus saith unto him, I say not unto thee, Until seven times: but, Until seventy times seven. *Mat.* 18: 21, 22.

When ye stand praying, forgive, if ye have aught against any. *Mk.* 11: 25.

Wherefore I say unto thee, Her sins, which are many, are forgiven; for she loved much: but to whom little is forgiven, the same loveth little. *Lu.* 7: 47.

Forgive us our sins; for we also forgive every one that is indebted to us. *Lu.* 11: 4.

If thy brother trespass against thee, rebuke him; and if he repent, forgive him. *Lu.* 17: 3.

Brethren, if a man be overtaken in a fault, ye which are spiritual, restore such a one in the spirit of meekness; considering thyself, lest thou also be tempted. *Ga.* 6: 1.

See also
Christ, Forgiveness of; Deliverance; God, Forgiveness of; Pardon; Remission; Reprieve.

Form

He that formed the eye, shall he not see? *Ps.* 94: 9.

He knoweth our frame. *Ps.* 103: 14.

The great God that formed all things, both rewardeth the fool, and rewardeth transgressors. *Pr.* 26: 10.

Shall the clay say to him that fashioneth it, What makest thou? *Is.* 45: 9.

No weapon that is formed against thee shall prosper. *Is.* 54: 17.

My little children, of whom I travail in birth again until Christ be formed in you. *Ga.* 4: 19.

Adam was first formed, then Eve. *1 Ti.* 2: 13.

Not fashioning yourselves according to the former lusts in your ignorance. *1 Pe.* 1: 14.

See also
Fashion; Formalism; Shape.

Formalism

Man looketh on the outward appearance, but the Lord looketh on the heart. *1 S.* 16: 7.

Your burnt offerings are not acceptable, nor your sacrifices sweet unto me. *Je.* 6: 20.

Shall I give my firstborn for my transgression, the fruit of my body for the sin of my soul? *Mi.* 6: 7.

Ye devour widows' houses, and for a pretence make long prayer. *Mat.* 23: 14.

Ye make clean the outside of the cup and of the platter, but within they are full of extortion and excess. *Mat.* 23: 25.

Cleanse first that which is within the cup and platter, that the outside of them may be clean also. *Mat.* 23: 26.

Ye are like unto whited sepulchres, which indeed appear beautiful outward, but are within full of dead men's bones, and of all uncleanness. *Mat.* 23: 27.

Ye also outwardly appear righteous unto men, but within ye are full of hypocrisy and iniquity. *Mat.* 23: 28.

John truly baptized with water; but ye shall be baptized with the Holy Ghost. *Ac.* 1: 5.

Thou therefore which teachest another, teachest thou not thyself? *Ro.* 2: 21.

Thou that preachest a man should not steal, dost thou steal? *Ro.* 2: 21.

Thou that makest thy boast of the law, through breaking the law dishonourest thou God? *Ro.* 2: 23.

Circumcision is nothing, and uncircumcision is nothing, but the keeping of the commandments of God. *1 Co.* 7: 19.

Do ye look on things after the outward appearance? *2 Co.* 10: 7.

In Jesus Christ neither circumcision availeth any thing, nor uncircumcision; but faith which worketh in love. *Ga.* 5: 6.

Having a form of godliness, but denying the power thereof. *2 Ti.* 3: 5.

See also
Ceremony; Form; Hypocrisy; Observance; Ritual.

Fornication

Out of the heart proceed . . . adulteries, fornications. *Mat.* 15: 19.

We be not born of fornication; we have one Father, even God. *Jn.* 8: 41.

We write unto them, that they abstain from pollutions of idols, and from fornication. *Ac.* 15: 20.

Filled with all unrighteousness, fornication, wickedness. *Ro.* 1: 29.

The body is not for fornication, but for the Lord; and the Lord for the body. *1 Co.* 6: 13.

Lest, when I come again, . . . I shall bewail many which have sinned already, and have not repented of the uncleanness and fornication and lasciviousness which they have committed. *2 Co.* 12: 21.

Walk in the Spirit, and ye shall not fulfil the lust of the flesh. *Ga.* 5: 16.

The works of the flesh are manifest, which

are these; Adultery, fornication, uncleanness, lasciviousness. *Ga.* 5: 19.

They that are Christ's have crucified the flesh with the affections and lusts. *Ga.* 5: 24.

All that is in the world, the lust of the flesh, and the lust of the eyes, and the pride of life, is not of the Father, but is of the world. *1 Jn.* 2: 16.

See also

Brothel; Carnality; Debauchery; Flesh; Lust; Prostitute; Sensuality.

Fortitude

I was strengthened as the hand of the Lord my God was upon me. *Ezr.* 7: 28.

Be of good courage. *Ps.* 27: 14.

The Lord will give strength unto his people. *Ps.* 29: 11.

Say to them that are of a fearful heart, Be strong, fear not. *Is.* 35: 4.

Not by might, nor by power, but by my spirit, saith the Lord of hosts. *Zch.* 4: 6.

He that shall endure unto the end, the same shall be saved. *Mat.* 24: 13.

Let us not be weary in well doing: for in due season we shall reap, if we faint not. *Ga.* 6: 9.

I can do all things through Christ which strengtheneth me. *Ph.* 4: 13.

We were bold in our God to speak unto you the gospel of God. *1 Th.* 2: 2.

Thou therefore endure hardness as a good soldier of Jesus Christ. *2 Ti.* 2: 3.

After he had patiently endured, he obtained the promise. *He.* 6: 15.

Let us run with patience. *He.* 12: 1.

We count them happy which endure. *Ja.* 5: 11.

See also

Audacity; Boldness; Bravery; Courage; Fearlessness; Firmness; Heroism; Resolution; Valor.

Fortress

The Lord is my fortress. *2 S.* 22: 2.

The God of my rock; in him will I trust: he is my shield, and the horn of my salvation, my high tower, and my refuge. *2 S.* 22: 3.

I have set thee for a tower and a fortress among my people. *Je.* 6: 27.

O Lord, my strength, and my fortress, and my refuge in the day of affliction. *Je.* 16: 19.

All thy fortresses shall be spoiled. *Ho.* 10: 14.

The Lord is good, a strong hold in the day of trouble. *Na.* 1: 7.

Turn you to the strong hold, ye prisoners of hope. *Zch.* 9: 12.

The weapons of our warfare are not carnal, but mighty through God to the pulling down of strong holds. *2 Co.* 10: 4.

See also

Castle; Defence; Protection; Tower; Wall.

Fortune

They are thy people and thine inheritance. *De.* 9: 29.

Many evils and troubles shall befall them. *De.* 31: 17.

If the Lord be with us, why then is all this befallen us? *Ju.* 6: 13.

It was a chance that happened to us. *1 S.* 6: 9.

His days are determined, the number of his months are with me. *Jb.* 14: 5.

Thou maintainest my lot. *Ps.* 16: 5.

My flesh and my heart faileth: but God is the strength of my heart, and my portion for ever. *Ps.* 73: 26.

There shall no evil befall thee. *Ps.* 91: 10.

Time and chance happeneth to them all. *Ec.* 9: 11.

I have called thee by thy name; thou art mine. *Is.* 43: 1.

Ye have not chosen me, but I have chosen you. *Jn.* 15: 16.

Now are we the sons of God, and it doth not yet appear what we shall be. *1 Jn.* 3: 2.

See also

Chance; Destiny; Doom; Fate; Lot; Luck; Predestination.

Foundation

All the people shouted with a great shout, when they praised the Lord, because the foundation of the house of the Lord was laid. *Ezr.* 3: 11.

Whereupon are the foundations thereof fastened? or who laid the corner stone thereof? *Jb.* 38: 6.

Concerning thy testimonies, I have known of old that thou hast founded them for ever. *Ps.* 119: 152.

The righteous is an everlasting foundation. *Pr.* 10: 25.

Therefore thus saith the Lord God, Behold, I lay in Zion for a foundation a stone, a tried stone, a precious corner stone, a sure foundation. *Is.* 28: 16.

Mine hand also hath laid the foundation of the earth. *Is.* 48: 13.

I will lay thy stones with fair colours, and lay thy foundations with sapphires. *Is.* 54: 11.

Thou art Peter, and upon this rock I will build my church. *Mat.* 16: 16.

He is like a man which built an house, and digged deep, and laid the foundation on a rock. *Lu.* 6: 48.

I have laid the foundation, and another buildeth thereon. *1 Co.* 3: 10.

Other foundation can no man lay than that is laid, which is Jesus Christ. *1 Co.* 3: 11.

Built upon the foundation of the apostles and prophets. *Ep.* 2: 20.

Laying up in store for themselves a good foundation against the time to come. *1 Ti.* 6: 19.

Behold, I lay in Sion a chief corner stone. *1 Pe.* 2: 6.

The wall of the city had twelve foundations, and in them the names of the twelve apostles of the Lamb. *Re.* 21: 14.

See also

Christ, the Foundation; Commencement; Cornerstone.

Fowl

Let them have dominion over the fish of the sea, and over the fowl of the air. *Ge.* 1: 26.

Out of the ground the Lord God formed every beast of the field, and every fowl of the air; and brought them unto Adam to see what he would call them. *Ge.* 2: 19.

Ask now the beasts, and they shall teach

thee; and the fowls of the air, and they shall tell thee. *Jb.* 12: 7.

There is a path which no fowl knoweth. *Jb* 28: 7.

Surely he shall deliver thee from the snare of the fowler. *Ps.* 91: 3.

By them shall the fowls of the heaven have their habitation, which sing among the branches. *Ps.* 104: 12.

Creeping things, and flying fowl: . . . Let them praise the name of the Lord. *Ps.* 148: 10, 13.

As birds flying, so will the Lord of hosts defend Jerusalem. *Is.* 31: 5.

Behold the fowls of the air: for they sow not, neither do they reap, nor gather into barns; yet your heavenly Father feedeth them. *Mat.* 6: 26.

The foxes have holes, and the birds of the air have nests; but the Son of man hath not where to lay his head. *Mat.* 8: 20.

See also
Bird; Eagle; Flight; Wing.

Fragrance

The Lord smelled a sweet savour. *Ge.* 8: 21.

All thy garments smell of myrrh, and aloes, and cassia. *Ps.* 45: 8.

Let my prayer be set forth before thee as incense. *Ps.* 141: 2.

Ointment and perfume rejoice the heart. *Pr.* 27: 9.

Incense is an abomination unto me. *Is.* 1: 13.

The house was filled with the odour of the ointment. *Jn.* 12: 3.

We are unto God a sweet savour of Christ. 2 *Co.* 2: 15.

Christ . . . hath given himself for us an offering and a sacrifice to God for a sweet-smelling savour. *Ep.* 5: 2.

An odour of a sweet smell, a sacrifice acceptable, well pleasing to God. *Ph.* 4: 18.

The smoke of the incense, which came with the prayers of the saints, ascended up before God out of the angel's hand. *Re.* 8: 4.

See also
Flower; Incense; Perfume; Savor; Scent; Smell.

Frailty

Faint, yet pursuing. *Ju.* 8: 4.

Be ye strong therefore, and let not your hands be weak. 2 *Ch.* 15: 7.

Thou hast strengthened the feeble knees. *Jb.* 4: 4.

Houses of clay, whose foundation is in the dust. *Jb.* 4: 19.

Is my strength the strength of stones? or is my flesh of brass? *Jb.* 6: 12.

He . . . weakeneth the strength of the mighty. *Jb.* 12: 21.

Cleanse thou me from secret faults. *Ps.* 19: 12.

Make me to know mine end, and the measure of my days, what it is; that I may know how frail I am. *Ps.* 39: 4.

The strong men shall bow themselves. *Ec.* 12: 3.

Strengthen ye the weak hands, and confirm the feeble knees. *Is.* 35: 3.

A bruised reed shall he not break. *Is.* 42: 3.

We acknowledge, O Lord, our wickedness. *Je.* 14: 20.

The flight shall perish from the swift, and the strong shall not strengthen his force, neither shall the mighty deliver himself. *Am.* 2: 14.

Men ought always to pray, and not to faint. *Lu.* 18: 1.

Let him that thinketh he standeth take heed lest he fall. *1 Co.* 10: 12.

God . . . will not suffer you to be tempted above that ye are able. *1 Co.* 10: 13.

Those members of the body, which seem to be more feeble, are necessary. *1 Co.* 12: 22.

We also are weak in him, but we shall live with him by the power of God toward you. 2 *Co.* 13: 4.

We are glad when we are weak, and ye are strong. 2 *Co.* 13: 9.

See also
Feebleness; Inability; Infirmity; Weakness.

Frankness

My words shall be of the uprightness of my heart: and my lips shall utter knowledge clearly. *Jb.* 33: 3.

Write the vision, and make it plain upon tables, that he may run that readeth it. *Hab.* 2: 2.

When they had nothing to pay, he frankly forgave them both. *Lu.* 7: 42.

Lo, now speakest thou plainly, and speakest no proverb. *Jn.* 16: 29.

They . . . by good words and fair speeches deceive the hearts of the simple. *Ro.* 16: 18.

So likewise ye, except ye utter by the tongue words easy to be understood, how shall it be known what is spoken? *1 Co.* 14: 9.

Grace be with all them that love our Lord Jesus Christ in sincerity. *Ep.* 6: 24.

Our exhortation was not of deceit, nor of uncleanness, nor in guile. *1 Th.* 2: 3.

They that say such things declare plainly that they seek a country. *He.* 11: 14.

See also
Candor.

Fraternity

Thy brother's blood crieth unto me from the ground. *Ge.* 4: 10.

Let there be no strife, I pray thee, between me and thee; . . . for we be brethren. *Ge.* 13: 8.

Is not the whole land before thee? separate thyself, I pray thee, from me: if thou wilt take the left hand, then I will go to the right; or if thou depart to the right hand, then I will go to the left. *Ge.* 13: 9.

Let us make a covenant with thee; That thou wilt do us no hurt, as we have not touched thee, and as we have done unto thee nothing but good, and have sent thee away in peace. *Ge.* 26: 28, 29.

What profit is it if we slay our brother? *Ge.* 37: 26.

Ye shall not see my face, except your brother be with you. *Ge.* 43: 3.

Thou shalt not hate thy brother in thine heart. *Le.* 19: 17.

Behold, how good and how pleasant it is for brethren to dwell together in unity! *Ps.* 133: 1.

There is a friend that sticketh closer than a brother. *Pr.* 18: 24.

Two are better than one. *Ec.* 4: 9.

Can two walk together, except they be agreed? *Am.* 3: 3.

They hunt every man his brother with a net. *Mi.* 7: 2.

Why beholdest thou the mote that is in thy brother's eye, but considerest not the beam that is in thine own eye? *Mat.* 7: 3.

Whosoever shall do the will of my Father which is in heaven, the same is my brother, and sister, and mother. *Mat.* 12: 50.

My mother and my brethren are these which hear the word of God, and do it. *Lu.* 8: 21.

Ye are my friends, if ye do whatsoever I command you. *Jn.* 15: 14.

Know ye not that the friendship of the world is enmity with God? *Ja.* 4: 4.

See also

Brotherhood; Family.

Fraud

Swear unto me here by God that thou wilt not deal falsely with me. *Ge.* 21: 23.

Ye shall not steal, neither deal falsely, neither lie one to another. *Le.* 19: 11.

His mouth is full of cursing and deceit and fraud. *Ps.* 10: 7.

The treacherous dealer dealeth treacherously. *Is.* 21: 2.

The prophets prophesy lies in my name. *Je.* 14: 14.

Woe to the bloody city! it is all full of lies and robbery. *Na.* 3: 1.

Out of the heart proceed evil thoughts, . . . false witness. *Mat.* 15: 19.

If I have taken any thing from any man by false accusation, I restore him fourfold. *Lu.* 19: 8.

If Christ be not risen, . . . we are found false witnesses of God. *1 Co.* 15: 14, 15.

Behold, the hire of the labourers, . . . which is of you kept back by fraud, crieth. *Ja.* 5: 4.

See also

Betrayal; Cheat; Counterfeit; Craftiness; Deceit; Dishonesty; Duplicity; Falsehood; Guile; Hypocrisy; Lie; Perfidy; Sham; Treachery; Untruthfulness.

Freedom

He looseth the bond of kings. *Jb.* 12: 18.

Uphold me with thy free spirit. *Ps.* 51: 12.

Ho, every one that thirsteth, come ye to the waters, and he that hath no money; come ye, buy, and eat; yea, come, buy wine and milk without money and without price. *Is.* 55: 1.

Freely ye have received, freely give. *Mat.* 10: 8.

If the Son therefore shall make you free, ye shall be free indeed. *Jn.* 8: 36.

Paul said, But I was free born. *Ac.* 22: 28.

He that is called in the Lord, being a servant, is the Lord's freeman: likewise also he that is called, being free, is Christ's servant. *1 Co.* 7: 22.

Am I not free? *1 Co.* 9: 1.

As without law, . . . but under the law to Christ. *1 Co.* 9: 21.

By one Spirit are we all baptized into one body, . . . whether we be bond or free. *1 Co.* 12: 13.

Stand fast therefore in the liberty wherewith Christ hath made us free. *Ga.* 5: 1.

As the servants of Christ, doing the will of God from the heart. *Ep.* 6: 6.

The perfect law of liberty. *Ja.* 1: 25.

As free, and not using your liberty for a cloke of maliciousness, but as the servants of God. *1 Pe.* 2: 16.

See also

Democracy; Emancipation; Independence; Liberty; Licence; Release.

Freshness

His heavens shall drop down dew. *De.* 33: 28.

Who hath begotten the drops of dew? *Jb.* 38: 28.

Thou hast the dew of thy youth. *Ps.* 110: 3.

The clouds drop down the dew. *Pr.* 3: 20.

Your goodness is as a morning cloud, and as the early dew it goeth away. *Ho.* 6: 4.

No man putteth a piece of a new garment upon an old; if otherwise, then both the new maketh a rent, and the piece that was taken out of the new agreeth not with the old. *Lu.* 5: 36.

We also should walk in newness of life. *Ro.* 6: 4.

We should serve in newness of spirit. *Ro.* 7: 6.

As newborn babes, desire the sincere milk of the word. *1 Pe.* 2: 2.

Until the day dawn, and the day star arise in your hearts. *2 Pe.* 1: 19.

See also

Dawn; Life, the New; Noon.

Fretfulness

Fret not thyself because of evil doers. *Ps.* 37: 1.

Fret not thyself in any wise to do evil. *Ps.* 37: 8.

Why art thou cast down, O my soul? and why art thou disquieted within me? hope in God. *Ps.* 43: 5.

Take no thought. *Mat.* 6: 25.

Which of you with taking thought can add to his stature one cubit? *Lu.* 12: 25.

Let not your heart be troubled: ye believe in God, believe also in me. *Jn.* 14: 1.

Casting all your care upon him. *1 Pe.* 5: 7.

See also

Anxiety; Tribulation; Vexation; Worry.

Friday, Good

A man of sorrows, and acquainted with grief. *Is.* 53: 3.

They crucified him, and parted his garments, casting lots. *Mat.* 27: 35.

Now from the sixth hour there was darkness over all the land unto the ninth hour. *Mat.* 27: 45.

My God, my God, why hast thou forsaken me? *Mat.* 27: 46.

The vail of the temple was rent in twain from the top to the bottom. *Mat.* 27: 51.

The earth did quake, and the rocks rent; And the graves were opened; and many bodies of the saints which slept arose. *Mat.* 27: 51, 52.

They bring him unto the place Golgotha, which is, being interpreted, The place of a skull. *Mk.* 15: 22.

It was the third hour, and they crucified him. *Mk.* 15: 25.

Father, forgive them; for they know not what they do. *Lu.* 23: 34.

And the people stood beholding. *Lu.* **23: 35.**
To day shalt thou be with me in paradise.
Lu. **23: 43.**
Father, into thy hands I commend my spirit.
Lu. **23: 46.**
It was the preparation of the passover. *Jn.*
19: 14.
Woman, behold thy son! . . . Behold thy
mother! *Jn.* **19: 26, 27.**
I thirst. *Jn.* **19: 28.**
It is finished. *Jn.* **19: 30.**
Ye have condemned and killed the just; and
he doth not resist you. *Ja.* **5: 6.**
See also
Christ, Cross of; Christ, Crucifixion of;
Christ, Death of; Christ, Sacrifice of; Christ,
Suffering of; Cross.

Friendship

The soul of Jonathan was knit with the
soul of David, and Jonathan loved him as his
own soul. *1 S.* **18: 1.**
The Lord turned the captivity of Job, when
he prayed for his friends. *Jb.* **42: 10.**
I am a companion of all them that fear thee.
Ps. **119: 63.**
The rich hath many friends. *Pr.* **14: 20.**
A friend loveth at all times, and a brother
is born for adversity. *Pr.* **17: 17.**
There is a friend that sticketh closer than
a brother. *Pr.* **18: 24.**
Faithful are the wounds of a friend. *Pr.*
27: 6.
Two are better than one; because they have
a good reward for their labour. *Ec.* **4: 9.**
Woe to him that is alone when he falleth;
for he hath not another to help him up. *Ec.*
4: 10.
This is my beloved, and this is my friend.
S. of S. **5: 16.**
Trust ye not in a friend. *Mi.* **7: 5.**
I was wounded in the house of my friends.
Zch. **13: 6.**
Have salt in yourselves, and have peace
one with another. *Mk.* **9: 50.**
Make to yourselves friends. *Lu.* **16: 9.**
He that hath the bride is the bridegroom:
but the friend of the bridegroom, which stand-
eth and heareth him, rejoiceth greatly because
of the bridegroom's voice. *Jn.* **3: 29.**
Greater love hath no man than this, that a
man lay down his life for his friends. *Jn.*
15: 13.
Whom when Paul saw, he thanked God, and
took courage. *Ac.* **28: 15.**
I had no rest in my spirit, because I found
not Titus my brother. *2 Co.* **2: 13.**
See also
Christ, the Friend; God, the Friend.

Frontier

Thou shalt stand by the river's brink. *Ex.*
7: 15.
I will cast out the nations before thee, and
enlarge thy borders. *Ex.* **34: 24.**
The Lord hath made Jordan a border. *Jos.*
22: 25.
Thou hast set all the borders of the earth.
Ps. **74: 17.**
He maketh peace in thy borders. *Ps.* **147: 14.**
See also
Border; Bound.

Frost

In the day the drought consumed me, and
the frost by night. *Ge.* **31: 40.**
By the breath of God frost is given. *Jb.* **37:
10.**
Out of whose womb came the ice? and the
hoary frost of heaven, who hath gendered it?
Jb. **38: 29.**
He giveth snow like wool: he scattereth the
hoarfrost like ashes. *Ps.* **147: 16.**
See also
Cold; Snow; Weather.

Fruit

God said, Let the earth bring forth. *Ge.* **1: 11.**
Like a tree . . . that bringeth forth his
fruit in his season. *Ps.* **1: 3.**
They shall still bring forth fruit in old age;
they shall be fat and flourishing. *Ps.* **92: 14.**
Let us destroy the tree with the fruit thereof.
Je. **11: 19.**
Put ye in the sickle, for the harvest is ripe.
Jo. **3: 13.**
Shall I give . . . the fruit of my body for
the sin of my soul? *Mi.* **6: 7.**
Bring forth therefore fruits meet for re-
pentance. *Mat.* **3: 8.**
Ye shall know them by their fruits. Do men
gather grapes of thorns, or figs of thistles? *Mat.*
7: 16.
Every good tree bringeth forth good fruit;
but a corrupt tree bringeth forth evil fruit.
Mat. **7: 17.**
By their fruits ye shall know them. *Mat.*
7: 20.
Other fell into good ground, and brought
forth fruit, some an hundredfold, some sixty-
fold, some thirtyfold. *Mat.* **13: 8.**
First the blade, then the ear, after that the
full corn in the ear. *Mk.* **4: 28.**
As the branch cannot bear fruit of itself,
except it abide in the vine; no more can ye,
except ye abide in me. *Jn.* **15: 4.**
I have chosen you, and ordained you, that
ye should go and bring forth fruit. *Jn.* **15: 16.**
Chastening . . . yieldeth the peaceable fruit
of righteousness unto them which are exercised thereby. *He.* **12: 11.**
The wisdom that is from above is . . . full
of mercy and good fruits. *Ja.* **3: 17.**
The husbandman waiteth for the precious
fruit of the earth, and hath long patience for
it. *Ja.* **5: 7.**
The tree of life . . . bare twelve manner of
fruits, and yielded her fruit every month. *Re.*
22: 2.
See also
Abundance; Climax; Consequence; Fertility;
Fruitfulness; Fruitlessness; Fruits, First; Harvest; Orchard; Productivity; Reaping; Result;
Yield.

Fruitfulness

Be fruitful, and multiply. *Ge.* **1: 22.**
Those that be planted in the house of the
Lord shall flourish in the courts of our God.
Ps. **92: 13.**
They shall still bring forth fruit in old age.
Ps. **92: 14.**
Thy wife shall be as a fruitful vine by the
sides of thine house. *Ps.* **128: 3.**

Other fell into good ground, and brought forth fruit, some an hundredfold, some sixty-fold, some thirtyfold. *Mat.* 13: 8.

Blessed art thou among women, and blessed is the fruit of thy womb. *Lu.* 1: 42.

He that reapeth receiveth wages, and gathereth fruit unto life eternal. *Jn.* 4: 36.

Every branch that beareth fruit, he purgeth it, that it may bring forth more fruit. *Jn.* 15: 2.

Herein is my Father glorified, that ye bear much fruit. *Jn.* 15: 8.

The fruit of the Spirit is love, joy, peace, longsuffering, gentleness, goodness, faith, Meekness, temperance. *Ga.* 5: 22, 23.

That ye might walk worthy of the Lord unto all pleasing, being fruitful in every good work, and increasing in the knowledge of God. *Col* 1: 10.

That they be not unfruitful. *Tit.* 3: 14.

If these things be in you, and abound, they make you that ye shall neither be barren nor unfruitful in the knowledge of our Lord Jesus Christ. *2 Pe.* 1: 8.

See also

Abundance; Fertility; Fruit; Fruits, First; Harvest; Reaping; Result; Yield.

Fruitlessness

Their grapes are grapes of gall, their clusters are bitter. *De.* 32: 32.

He looked that it should bring forth grapes, and it brought forth wild grapes. *Is.* 5: 2.

Their root is dried up, they shall bear no fruit. *Ho.* 9: 16.

Israel is an empty vine, he bringeth forth fruit unto himself. *Ho.* 10: 1.

Ye have plowed wickedness, ye have reaped iniquity. *Ho.* 10: 13.

The harvest of the field is perished. *Jo.* 1: 11.

Every tree which bringeth not forth good fruit is hewn down, and cast into the fire. *Mat.* 3: 10.

The care of this world, and the deceitfulness of riches, choke the word, and he becometh unfruitful. *Mat.* 13: 22.

If it bear fruit, well: and if not, then after that thou shalt cut it down. *Lu.* 13: 9.

Lord, behold, here is thy pound, which I have kept laid up in a napkin. *Lu.* 19: 20.

Every branch in me that beareth not fruit he taketh away. *Jn.* 15: 2.

If I pray in an unknown tongue, my spirit prayeth, but my understanding is unfruitful. *1 Co.* 14: 14.

Have no fellowship with the unfruitful works of darkness. *Ep.* 5: 11.

That which beareth thorns and briers is rejected, and is nigh unto cursing. *He.* 6: 8.

See also

Barrenness; Desert; Drought; Emptiness; Waste; Wilderness; Worthlessness.

Fruits, First

Honour the Lord with thy substance, and with the firstfruits of all thine increase. *Pr.* 3: 9.

Not only they, but ourselves also, which have the firstfruits of the Spirit, even we ourselves groan within ourselves. *Ro.* 8: 23.

If the firstfruit be holy, the lump is also holy. *Ro.* 11: 16.

The firstfruits of Achaia unto Christ. *Ro.* 16: 5.

Now is Christ risen from the dead, and become the firstfruits of them that slept. *1 Co.* 15: 20.

Of his own will begat he us with the word of truth, that we should be a kind of firstfruits of his creatures. *Ja.* 1: 18.

These were redeemed from among men, being the firstfruits unto God and to the Lamb. *Re.* 14: 4.

Frustration

Oh that I were made judge in the land, that every man which hath any suit or cause might come unto me, and I would do him justice. *2 S.* 15: 4.

The people of the land . . . hired counsellors against them, to frustrate their purpose. *Ezr.* 4: 4, 5.

My purposes are broken off. *Jb.* 17: 11.

The children are come to the birth, and there is not strength to bring forth. *Is.* 37: 3.

I am the Lord . . . That frustrateth the tokens of the liars. *Is.* 44: 24, 25.

She shall follow after her lovers, but she shall not overtake them; and she shall seek them, but shall not find them. *Ho.* 2: 7.

Master, we have toiled all the night, and have taken nothing. *Lu.* 5: 5.

Ye entered not in yourselves, and them that were entering in ye hindered. *Lu.* 11: 52.

Behold, these three years I come seeking fruit on this fig tree, and find none. *Lu.* 13: 7.

This man began to build, and was not able to finish. *Lu.* 14: 30.

I do not frustrate the grace of God. *Ga.* 2: 21.

Satan hindered us. *1 Th.* 2: 18.

See also

Defeat; Disappointment; Failure; Fall; Overthrow; Ruin.

Fugitive

Ye shall flee when none pursueth you. *Le.* 26: 17.

He shall fly away as a dream, and shall not be found. *Jb.* 20: 8.

Terrors are turned upon me: they pursue my soul as the wind. *Jb.* 30: 15.

Oh that I had wings like a dove! for then would I fly away, and be at rest. *Ps.* 55: 6.

I am like a pelican of the wilderness. *Ps.* 102: 6.

Riches certainly make themselves wings; they fly away as an eagle toward heaven. *Pr.* 23: 5.

Who are these that fly as a cloud, and as the doves to their windows? *Is.* 60: 8.

Israel is . . . a wild ass alone by himself *Ho.* 8: 8, 9.

Their glory shall fly away like a bird. *Ho.* 9: 11.

As if a man did flee from a lion, and a bear met him. *Am.* 5: 19.

Jesus withdrew himself with his disciples to the sea. *Mk.* 3: 7.

Thinkest thou this, O man, . . . that thou shalt escape the judgment of God? *Ro.* 2: 3.

We . . . have fled for refuge to lay hold upon the hope set before us. *He.* 6: 18.

Much more shall not we escape, if we turn

away from him that speaketh from heaven.
He. 12: 25.
See also
Exile; Refugee.

Fulfilment

The Lord fulfil all thy petitions. *Ps.* 20: 5.
I am not come to destroy, but to fulfil. *Mat.*
5: 17.
The time is fulfilled, and the kingdom of
God is at hand. *Mk.* 1: 15.
What shall be the sign when all these things
shall be fulfilled? *Mk.* 13: 4.
They came with haste, and found Mary, and
Joseph, and the babe lying in a manger. *Lu.*
2: 16.
This man began to build, and was not able
to finish. *Lu.* 14: 30.
I have finished the work which thou gavest
me to do. *Jn.* 17: 4.
All the law is fulfilled in one word, even in
this; Thou shalt love thy neighbour as thyself.
Ga. 5: 14.
Bear ye one another's burdens, and so fulfil
the law of Christ. *Ga.* 6: 2.
Fulfil ye my joy. *Ph.* 2: 2.
See also
Accomplishment; Achievement; Christ, Full-
ness of; Christ, the Goal; Christ, Perfection of;
Climax; Completion; End; Execution; Harvest;
Life, the Full; Perfection; Performance; Reali-
zation.

Fullness

Joshua the son of Nun was full of the spirit
of wisdom. *De.* 34: 9.
Behold, the mountain was full of horses and
chariots of fire round about Elisha. *2 K.* 6: 17.
Thou preparest a table before me. *Ps.* 23: 5.
Man did eat angels' food: he sent them meat
to the full. *Ps.* 78: 25.
The earth shall be full of the knowledge of
the Lord, as the waters cover the sea. *Is.* 11: 9.
If therefore thine eye be single, thy whole
body shall be full of light. *Mat.* 6: 22.
The harvest truly is plenteous, but the
labourers are few. *Mat.* 9: 37.
The full corn in the ear. *Mk.* 4: 28.
He shall be filled with the Holy Ghost. *Lu.*
1: 15.
Woe unto you that are full! for ye shall
hunger. *Lu.* 6: 25.
I am come that they might have life, and
that they might have it more abundantly. *Jn.*
10: 10.
They chose Stephen, a man full of faith and
of the Holy Ghost. *Ac.* 6: 5.
Love is the fulfilling of the law. *Ro.* 13: 10.
That ye may be perfect and entire, wanting
nothing. *Ja.* 1: 4.
That your joy may be full. *1 Jn.* 1: 4.
See also
Accomplishment; Achievement; Adequacy;
Ampleness; Christ, Fullness of; Christ, the
Goal; Christ, Perfection of; Completion; End;
Fulfilment; Life, the Full; Perfection; Realiza-
tion; Sufficiency

Funeral

Isaac was comforted after his mother's death.
Ge. 24: 67.
Joseph commanded his servants the physi-

cians to embalm his father: and the physicians
embalmed Israel. *Ge.* 50: 2.
Where thou diest, will I die, and there will
I be buried. *Ru.* 1: 17.
Naked came I out of my mother's womb,
and naked shall I return thither: the Lord
gave, and the Lord hath taken away; blessed
be the name of the Lord. *Jb.* 1: 21.
There the wicked cease from troubling; and
there the weary be at rest. *Jb.* 3: 17.
The small and the great are there; and the
servant is free from his master. *Jb.* 3: 19.
Thou shalt come to thy grave in a full age,
like as a shock of corn cometh in in his season.
Jb. 5: 26.
Precious in the sight of the Lord is the
death of his saints. *Ps.* 116: 15.
Boast not thyself of to morrow. *Pr.* 27: 1.
A time to be born, and a time to die; a
time to plant, and a time to pluck up that
which is planted. *Ec.* 3: 2.
That which befalleth the sons of men befalleth beasts; even one thing befalleth them:
as the one dieth, so dieth the other; yea, they
have all one breath; so that a man hath no
preëminence above a beast. *Ec.* 3: 19.
Until the day break, and the shadows flee
away. *S. of S.* 2: 17.
When thou passest through the waters, . . .
they shall not overflow thee. *Is.* 43: 2.
They shall die of grievous deaths; they shall
not be lamented; neither shall they be buried.
Je. 16: 4.
Weep ye not for the dead, neither bemoan
him. *Je.* 22: 10.
He shall be buried with the burial of an ass.
Je. 22: 19.
The joy of our heart is ceased; our dance is
turned into mourning. *La.* 5: 15.
Woe unto you, scribes and Pharisees, hypo-
crites! because ye build the tombs of the
prophets, and garnish the sepulchres of the
righteous. *Mat.* 23: 29.
In that she hath poured this ointment on
my body, she did it for my burial. *Mat.* 26: 12.
When Joseph had taken the body, he
wrapped it in a clean linen cloth, And laid it
in his own new tomb. *Mat.* 27: 59, 60.
When the sabbath was past, Mary Magdalene, and Mary the mother of James, and
Salome, had brought sweet spices, that they
might come and anoint him. *Mk.* 16: 1.
See also
Burial; Death; Grave; Tomb.

Furnace

The Lord hath taken you, and brought you
forth out of the iron furnace, even out of
Egypt. *De.* 4: 20.
The words of the Lord are pure words: as
silver tried in a furnace of earth, purified
seven times. *Ps.* 12: 6.
The fining pot is for silver, and the furnace
for gold: but the Lord trieth the hearts. *Pr.*
17: 3.
The Lord, whose fire is in Zion, and his
furnace in Jerusalem. *Is.* 31: 9.
I have refined thee, but not with silver; I
have chosen thee in the furnace of affliction.
Is. 48: 10.
Son of man, the house of Israel is to me be-

come dross: . . . they are even the dross of silver. *Eze.* 22: 18.

As silver is melted in the midst of the furnace, so shall ye be melted in the midst thereof. *Eze.* 22: 22.

God whom we serve is able to deliver us from the burning fiery furnace. *Da.* 3: 17.

His angels . . . shall gather out of his kingdom all things that offend, . . . And shall cast them into a furnace of fire. *Mat.* 13: 41, 42.
See also
Burn; Fire; Flame; Heat; Test.

Fury

If ye will not for all this hearken unto me, but walk contrary unto me; Then I will walk contrary unto you also in fury. *Le.* 26: 27, 28.

God shall cast the fury of his wrath upon him. *Jb.* 20: 23.

He swalloweth the ground with fierceness and rage. *Jb.* 39: 24.

Thy wrath lieth hard upon me, and thou hast afflicted me with all thy waves. *Ps.* 88: 7.

Riches profit not in the day of wrath. *Pr.* 11: 4.

He that is slow to anger appeaseth strife. *Pr.* 15: 18.

The wrath of a king is as messengers of death: but a wise man will pacify it. *Pr.* 16: 14.

Leave off contention, before it be meddled with. *Pr.* 17: 14.

Make no friendship with an angry man. *Pr.* 22: 24.

In a little wrath I hid my face from thee for a moment; but with everlasting kindness will I have mercy on thee. *Is.* 54: 8.

Deliver ye every man his soul from the fierce anger of the Lord. *Je.* 51: 45.

As I live, saith the Lord God, surely with a mighty hand, and with a stretched out arm, and with fury poured out, will I rule over you. *Eze.* 20: 33.

Who can tell if God will turn and repent, and turn away from his fierce anger? *Jon.* 3: 9.

Then said the Lord, Doest thou well to be angry? *Jon.* 4: 4.

I will execute vengeance in anger and fury upon the heathen. *Mi.* 5: 15.

The Lord is slow to anger. *Na.* 1: 3.

Because of these things cometh the wrath of God upon the children of disobedience. *Ep.* 5: 6.

Provoke not your children to wrath. *Ep.* 6: 4.

A bishop then must be . . . patient, not a brawler. *1 Ti.* 3: 2, 3.

To be no brawlers, but gentle. *Tit.* 3: 2.

The great day of his wrath is come. *Re.* 6: 17.
See also
Anger; God, Anger of; God, Wrath of; Passion; Rage; Wrath.

Futility

The bows of the mighty men are broken. *1 S.* 2: 4.

Will he esteem thy riches? no, not gold, nor all the forces of strength. *Jb.* 36: 19.

I will not trust in my bow. *Ps.* 44: 6.

He that soweth iniquity shall reap vanity. *Pr.* 22: 8.

A poor man that oppresseth the poor is like a sweeping rain which leaveth no food. *Pr.* 28: 3.

Ye shall conceive chaff, ye shall bring forth stubble. *Is.* 33: 11.

They have sown the wind, and they shall reap the whirlwind. *Ho.* 8: 7.

It is not possible that the blood of bulls and of goats should take away sins. *He.* 10: 4.

Future

We know not with what we must serve the Lord, until we come thither. *Ex.* 10: 26.

Speak unto the children of Israel, that they go forward. *Ex.* 14: 15.

Possess thou the west. *De.* 33: 23.

Moses my servant is dead; now therefore arise. *Jos.* 1: 2.

The place where we dwell with thee is too strait for us. Let us go, we pray thee, unto Jordan. *2 K.* 6: 1, 2.

Thou shalt guide me with thy counsel. *Ps.* 73: 24.

Boast not thyself of to morrow; for thou knowest not what a day may bring forth. *Pr.* 27: 1.

Thine eyes shall see the king in his beauty: they shall behold the land that is very far off. *Is.* 33: 17.

The great day of the Lord is near, it is near, and hasteth greatly, even the voice of the day of the Lord. *Zph.* 1: 14.

Greater works than these shall he do; because I go unto my Father. *Jn.* 14: 12.

Now I know in part; but then shall I know even as also I am known. *1 Co.* 13: 12.

Let us go on unto perfection. *He.* 6: 1.

Now faith is the substance of things hoped for, the evidence of things not seen. *He.* 11: 1.

Here we have no continuing city, but we seek one to come. *He.* 13: 14.
See also
Age, the Golden; Day, the Coming; Land, the Promised; Millennium.

G

Gaiety

God hath made me to laugh. *Ge.* 21: 6.

Let all those that put their trust in thee rejoice: let them ever shout for joy. *Ps.* 5: 11.

Make a joyful noise unto God, all ye lands.

Ps. 66: 1.

Blessed is the people that know the joyful sound. *Ps.* 89: 15.

Let us come before his presence with thanksgiving, and make a joyful noise unto him with psalms. *Ps.* 95: 2.

He that loveth pleasure shall be a poor man. *Pr.* 21: 17.

My servants shall sing for joy of heart.*Is.*65:14.

And Levi made him a great feast in his own house. *Lu.* 5: 29.

It was meet that we should make merry, and be glad. *Lu.* 15: 32.

Rejoice with them that do rejoice, and weep with them that weep. *Ro.* 12: 15.

I would have you without carefulness. *1 Co.* 7: 32.

See also

Cheer; Laughter; Merriment; Mirth; Smile.

Gain

They took no gain of money. *Ju.* 5: 19.

Doth Job fear God for nought? *Jb.* 1: 9.

So are the ways of every one that is greedy of gain. *Pr.* 1: 19.

The merchandise of it is better than the merchandise of silver, and the gain thereof than fine gold. *Pr.* 3: 14.

In the revenues of the wicked is trouble. *Pr.* 15: 6.

He that is greedy of gain troubleth his own house. *Pr.* 15: 27.

The priests thereof teach for hire. *Mi.* 3: 11.

The prophets thereof divine for money. *Mi.* 3: 11.

What is a man profited, if he shall gain the whole world, and lose his own soul? *Mat.* 16: 26.

To die is gain. *Ph.* 1: 21.

What things were gain to me, those I counted loss for Christ. *Ph.* 3: 7.

See also

Abundance; Acquisition; Addition; **Goods**; Growth; Harvest; Increase; Plenty; Profit; **Progress**; Riches; Spoil; Yield.

Galilee

After I am risen again, I will go before you into Galilee. *Mat.* 26: 32.

Thou also wast with Jesus of Galilee. *Mat.* 26: 69.

His fame spread abroad throughout all the region round about Galilee. *Mk.* 1: 28.

Remember how he spake unto you when he was yet in Galilee. *Lu.* 24: 6.

Some said, Shall Christ come out of Galilee? *Jn.* 7: 41.

Search, and look: for out of Galilee ariseth no prophet. *Jn.* 7: 52.

The word which God sent unto the children of Israel . . . began from Galilee. *Ac.* 10: 36, 37.

Gambling

They cast lots, ward against ward, as well the small as the great, the teacher as the scholar. *1 Ch.* 25: 8.

The lot is cast into the lap; but the whole disposing thereof is of the Lord. *Pr.* 16: 33.

He hath cast the lot for them, and his hand hath divided it unto them by line. *Is.* 35: 17.

They have cast lots for my people; and have given a boy for an harlot, and sold a girl for wine, that they might drink. *Jo.* 3: 3.

Foreigners entered into his gates, and cast lots upon Jerusalem. *Ob.* 1: 11.

They cast lots for her honourable men, and

all her great men were bound in chains. *Na.* 3: 10.

He that earneth wages earneth wages to put it into a bag with holes. *Hag.* 1: 6.

They crucified him, and parted his garments, casting lots: that it might be fulfilled which was spoken by the prophet, They parted my garments among them, and upon my vesture did they cast lots. *Mat.* 27: 35.

They gave forth their lots; and the lot fell upon Matthias; and he was numbered with the eleven apostles. *Ac.* 1: 26.

Men that have hazarded their lives for the name of our Lord Jesus Christ. *Ac.* 15: 26.

See also

Chance; Fortune; Lot; Luck.

Game

The people sat down to eat and to drink, and rose up to play. *Ex.* 32: 6.

All the beasts of the field play. *Jb.* 40: 20.

Wilt thou play with him as with a bird? *Jb.* 41: 5.

There is that leviathan, whom thou hast made to play therein. *Ps.* 104: 26.

The sucking child shall play on the hole of the asp. *Is.* 11: 8.

The streets of the city shall be full of boys and girls, playing in the streets thereof. *Zch.* 8: 5.

See also

Athlete; Competition; Contest; Play; Race.

Garden

The Lord God planted a garden eastward in Eden. *Ge.* 2: 8.

God took the man, and put him into the garden. *Ge.* 2: 15.

They heard the voice of the Lord God walking in the garden in the cool of the day. *Ge.* 3: 8.

As gardens by the river's side, as the trees of lign aloes which the Lord hath planted, and as cedar trees beside the waters. *Nu.* 24: 6.

I made me gardens and orchards, and I planted trees in them of all kind of fruits. *Ec.* 2: 5.

Ye shall be as an oak whose leaf fadeth, and as a garden that hath no water. *Is.* 1: 30.

He will make her wilderness like Eden, and her desert like the garden of the Lord. *Is.* 51: 3.

Thou shalt be like a watered garden, *Is.* 58: 11.

As the earth bringeth forth her bud, and as the garden causeth the things that are sown in it to spring forth; so the Lord God will cause righteousness and praise to spring forth before all the nations. *Is.* 61: 11.

Thou hast been in Eden the garden of God. *Eze.* 28: 13.

In the garden a new sepulchre. *Jn.* 19: 41.

She, supposing him to be the gardener. *Jn.* 20: 15.

See also

Flower; Orchard; Tree; Wood.

Garment

All of them shall wax old like a garment; as a vesture shalt thou change them, and they shall be changed. *Ps.* 102: 26.

He hath clothed me with the garments of salvation, he hath covered me with the robe of righteousness. *Is.* 61: 10.

Rend your heart, and not your garments. *Jo.* 2: 13.

If any man will sue thee at the law, and take away thy coat, let him have thy cloke also. *Mat.* 5: 40.

I say unto you, That even Solomon in all his glory was not arrayed like one of these. *Mat.* 6: 29.

Provide . . . neither two coats, neither shoes, nor yet staves: for the workman is worthy of his meat. *Mat.* 10: 9, 10.

A very great multitude spread their garments in the way. *Mat.* 21: 8.

What went ye out for to see? A man clothed in soft raiment? *Lu.* 7: 25.

Now the coat was without seam, woven from the top throughout. *Jn.* 19: 23.

See also

Apparel; Attire; Clothes; Coat; Raiment; Robe.

Gate

This is the gate of heaven. *Ge.* 28: 17.

God hath delivered him into mine hand; for he is shut in, by entering into a town that hath gates and bars. *1 S.* 23: 7.

Lift up your heads, O ye gates; and be ye lift up, ye everlasting doors; and the King of glory shall come in. *Ps.* 24: 7.

The Lord loveth the gates of Zion. *Ps.* 87: 2.

This gate of the Lord, into which the righteous shall enter. *Ps.* 118: 20.

Wisdom . . . crieth at the gates, at the entry of the city, at the coming in at the doors. *Pr.* 8: 1, 3.

Thou shalt call thy walls Salvation, and thy gates Praise. *Is.* 60: 18.

Stand in the gate of the Lord's house, and proclaim there this word. *Je.* 7: 2.

Her gates are sunk into the ground; he hath destroyed and broken her bars. *La.* 2: 9.

The glory of the Lord came into the house by the way of the gate. *Eze.* 43: 4.

I will break also the bar of Damascus. *Am.* 1: 5.

Establish judgment in the gate. *Am.* 5: 15.

Strive to enter in at the strait gate. *Lu.* 13: 24.

A certain man lame from his mother's womb was carried, whom they laid daily at the gate of the temple which is called Beautiful. *Ac.* 3: 2.

Jesus . . . suffered without the gate. *He.* 13: 12.

Every several gate was of one pearl. *Re.* 21: 21.

The gates of it shall not be shut at all by day. *Re.* 21: 25.

See also

Christ, the Door; Christ, the Way; Door; Entrance; Opening.

Genealogy

These are the generations of the heavens and of the earth when they were created. *Ge.* 2: 4.

They declared their pedigrees after their families. *Nu.* 1: 18.

All Israel were reckoned by genealogies. *1 Ch.* 9: 1.

Enquire, I pray thee, of the former age, and

prepare thyself to the search of their fathers. *Jb.* 8: 8.

One generation passeth away, and another generation cometh. *Ec.* 1: 4.

Because he was of the house and lineage of David. *Lu.* 2: 4.

Neither give heed to fables and endless genealogies. *1 Ti.* 1: 4.

Avoid foolish questions, and genealogies. *Tit.* 3: 9.

Without father, without mother, without descent, having neither beginning of days, nor end of life. *He.* 7: 3.

See also

Ancestor; Descent; Father; Generation; Heritage.

Generation

Know therefore that the Lord thy God, he is God, the faithful God, which keepeth covenant and mercy with them that love him and keep his commandments to a thousand generations. *De.* 7: 9.

God is in the generation of the righteous. *Ps.* 14: 5.

This is the generation of them that seek him, that seek thy face, O Jacob. *Ps.* 24: 6.

Mark ye well her bulwarks, consider her palaces; that ye may tell it to the generation following. *Ps.* 48: 13.

Shewing to the generations to come the praises of the Lord, and his strength, and his wonderful works that he hath done. *Ps.* 78: 4.

Lord, thou hast been our dwelling place in all generations. *Ps.* 90: 1.

The generation of the upright shall be blessed. *Ps.* 112: 2.

Thy name, O Lord, endureth for ever; and thy memorial, O Lord, throughout all generations. *Ps.* 135: 13.

One generation shall praise thy works to another, and shall declare thy mighty acts. *Ps.* 145: 4.

There is a generation that are pure in their own eyes, and yet is not washed from their filthiness. *Pr.* 30: 12.

Who hath wrought and done it, calling the generations from the beginning? I the Lord, the first, and with the last; I am he. *Is.* 41: 4.

My righteousness shall be for ever, and my salvation from generation to generation. *Is.* 51: 8.

I will make thee an eternal excellency, a joy of many generations. *Is.* 60: 15.

His dominion is from generation to generation. *Da.* 4: 3.

From henceforth all generations shall call me blessed. *Lu.* 1: 48.

Ye are a chosen generation. *1 Pe.* 2: 9.

See also

Age; Ancestor; Descent; Epoch; Era; Father; Genealogy; Heritage.

Generosity

Of all that thou shalt give me I will surely give the tenth unto thee. *Ge.* 28: 22.

Every man shall give as he is able, according to the blessing of the Lord thy God which he hath given thee. *De.* 16: 17.

He asked water, and she gave him milk. *Ju.* 5: 25.

Let her glean even among the sheaves, and reproach her not. *Ru.* **2: 15.**

Wouldest thou smite those whom thou hast taken captive with thy sword and with thy bow? set bread and water before them, that they may eat and drink, and go to their master. *2 K.* **6: 22.**

All things come of thee, and of thine own have we given thee. *1 Ch.* **29: 14.**

He . . . filleth the hungry soul with goodness. *Ps.* **107: 9.**

He that hath pity upon the poor lendeth unto the Lord and that which he hath given will he pay him again. *Pr.* **19: 17.**

He that hath a bountiful eye shall be blessed; for he giveth of his bread to the poor. *Pr.* **22: 9.**

He that giveth unto the poor shall not lack. *Pr.* **28: 27.**

Cast thy bread upon the waters: for thou shalt find it after many days. *Ec.* **11: 1.**

In the morning sow thy seed, and in the evening withhold not thine hand. *Ec.* **11: 6.**

Give to every man that asketh thee. *Lu.* **6: 30.**

And many others, which ministered unto him of their substance. *Lu.* **8: 3.**

Give alms of such things as ye have. *Lu.* **11: 41.**

She of her penury hath cast in all the living that she had. *Lu.* **21: 4.**

Remember the words of the Lord Jesus, how he said, It is more blessed to give than to receive. *Ac.* **20: 35.**

He that spared not his own Son, . . . how shall he not with him also freely give us all things? *Ro.* **8: 32.**

So that ye come behind in no gift. *1 Co.* **1: 7.**

Therefore, as ye abound in everything, in faith, in utterance, in knowledge, and in all diligence, and in your love to us, see that ye abound in this grace also. *2 Co.* **8: 7.**

Every man according as he purposeth in his heart, so let him give; not grudgingly, nor of necessity: for God loveth a cheerful giver. *2 Co.* **9: 7.**

God . . . giveth to all men liberally. *Ja.* **1: 5.**
See also
Almsgiving; Beneficence; Benevolence; Boon; Bounty; Charity; Christ, Gift of; Contribution; Gift; God, Gift of; Liberality; Philanthropy; Present; Unselfishness.

Genesis

In the beginning God created the heaven and the earth. *Ge.* **1: 1.**

God said, Let there be light: and there was light. *Ge.* **1: 3.**

God said, Let us make man in our image, after our likeness. *Ge.* **1: 26.**

Thus the heavens and the earth were finished, and all the host of them. *Ge.* **2: 1.**

These are the generations of the heavens and of the earth when they were created. *Ge.* **2: 4.**

Jabal . . . was the father of such as dwell in tents, and of such as have cattle. *Ge.* **4: 20.**

Jubal . . . was the father of all such as handle the harp and organ. *Ge.* **4: 21.**

Then began men to call upon the name of the Lord. *Ge.* **4: 26.**

This is the book of the generations of Adam. *Ge.* **5: 1.**

The Lord said unto him, Who hath made man's mouth? or who maketh the dumb, or deaf, or the seeing, or the blind? have not I the Lord? *Ex.* **4: 11.**

The pillars of the earth are the Lord's, and he hath set the world upon them. *1 S.* **2: 8.**

Before the mountains were brought forth, or ever thou hadst formed the earth and the world, even from everlasting to everlasting, thou art God. *Ps.* **90: 2.**

Who laid the foundations of the earth, that it should not be removed for ever. *Ps.* **104: 5.**

Thou sendest forth thy spirit, they are created. *Ps.* **104: 30.**

He hath made the earth by his power, he hath established the world by his wisdom. *Je.* **10: 12.**

Jesus began to preach, and to say, Repent. *Mat.* **4: 17.**

This day is this scripture fulfilled in your ears. *Lu.* **4: 21.**

In the beginning was the Word. *Jn.* **1: 1.**

All things were made by him; and without him was not any thing made that was made. *Jn.* **1: 3.**
See also
Alpha; Beginning; Christ, the Creator; Commencement; Creation; Creator; First; God, the Creator; Origin; Source.

Gentile

Behold my servant, whom I uphold; . . . he shall bring forth judgment to the Gentiles. *Is.* **42: 1.**

I the Lord . . . will . . . give thee for a covenant of the people, for a light of the Gentiles. *Is.* **42: 6.**

The Gentiles shall come unto thee from the ends of the earth. *Je.* **16: 19.**

From the rising of the sun even unto the going down of the same my name shall be great among the Gentiles. *Mal.* **1: 11.**

Go not into the way of the Gentiles. *Mat.* **10: 5.**

They rehearsed all that God had done with them, and how he had opened the door of faith unto the Gentiles. *Ac.* **14: 27.**

Glory, honour, and peace, to every man that worketh good, to the Jew first, and also to the Gentile: For there is no respect of persons with God. *Ro.* **2: 10, 11.**

Rejoice, ye Gentiles, with his people. *Ro.* **15: 10.**

That I should be the minister of Jesus Christ to the Gentiles, ministering the gospel of God, that the offering up of the Gentiles might be acceptable, being sanctified by the Holy Ghost. *Ro.* **15: 16.**

That the Gentiles should be fellowheirs, and of the same body, and partakers of his promise in Christ. *Ep.* **3: 6.**

Unto me . . . is this grace given, that I should preach among the Gentiles the unsearchable riches of Christ. *Ep.* **3: 8.**
See also
Alien; Foreigner; Stranger.

Gentleman

Seemeth it to you a light thing to be a king's son in law? *1 S.* **18: 23.**

Both riches and honour come of thee. *1 Ch.* **29: 12.**

They are exalted for a little while. *Jb.* **24: 24.**

Verily every man at his best state is altogether vanity. *Ps.* **39: 5.**

There is a generation, O how lofty are their eyes! *Pr.* **30: 13.**

Blessed art thou, O land, when thy king is the son of nobles. *Ec.* **10: 17.**

The ancient and honourable, he is the head. *Is.* **9: 15.**

From thy state shall he pull thee down. *Is.* **22: 19.**

Think not to say within yourselves, We have Abraham to our father. *Mat.* **3: 9.**

Go and sit down in the lowest room. *Lu.* **14: 10.**

I am not as other men are. *Lu.* **18: 11.**

A good man, and a just: . . . who also himself waited for the kingdom of God. *Lu.* **23: 50, 51.**

Render therefore to all their dues: . . . honour to whom honour. *Ro.* **13: 7.**

Put on therefore, as the elect of God, holy and beloved, bowels of mercies, kindness, humbleness of mind, meekness. *Col.* **3: 12.**

We were gentle among you. *1 Th.* **2: 7.**

The servant of the Lord must not strive; but be gentle unto all men, apt to teach, patient, In meekness instructing those that oppose them. *2 Ti.* **2: 24, 25.**

To speak evil of no man, to be no brawlers, but gentle, shewing all meekness unto all men. *Tit.* **3: 2.**

Honour all men. *1 Pe.* **2: 17.**

See also
Character; Honor; Manners; Nobility.

Gentleness

The meek shall inherit the earth. *Ps.* **37: 11.**

He shall feed his flock like a shepherd: . . . and shall gently lead those that are with young. *Is.* **40: 11.**

A bruised reed shall he not break, and the smoking flax shall he not quench. *Is.* **42: 3.**

Walk humbly with thy God. *Mi.* **6: 8.**

I . . . beseech you by the meekness and gentleness of Christ. *2 Co.* **10: 1.**

The fruit of the Spirit is . . . gentleness. *Ga.* **5: 22.**

Be ye kind one to another, tenderhearted, forgiving one another. *Ep.* **4: 32.**

The wisdom that is from above is first pure, then peaceable, gentle, and easy to be intreated, full of mercy. *Ja.* **3: 17.**

Love as brethren, be pitiful, be courteous. *1 Pe.* **3: 8.**

Be clothed with humility. *1 Pe.* **5: 5.**

See also
Benignity; Christ, Compassion of; Christ, Gentleness of; Clemency; Compassion; Favor; God, Compassion of; God, Gentleness of; Goodness; Grace; Humanity; Kindness; Lovingkindness; Tenderness.

Gethsemane

Then cometh Jesus with them unto a place called Gethsemane. *Mat.* **26: 36.**

Tarry ye here, and watch with me. *Mat.* **26: 38.**

O my Father, if it be possible, let this cup pass from me: nevertheless not as I will, but as thou wilt. *Mat.* **26: 39.**

Watch and pray, that ye enter not into temptation: the spirit indeed is willing, but the flesh is weak. *Mat.* **26: 41.**

The hour is at hand, and the Son of man is betrayed into the hands of sinners. *Mat.* **26: 45.**

Rise up, let us go; lo, he that betrayeth me is at hand. *Mk.* **14: 42.**

He came out, and went, as he was wont, to the mount of Olives. *Lu.* **22: 39.**

There appeared an angel unto him from heaven, strengthening him. *Lu.* **22: 43.**

Judas, betrayest thou the Son of man with a kiss? *Lu.* **22: 48.**

He went forth with his disciples over the brook Cedron, where was a garden, into the which he entered, and his disciples. *Jn.* **18: 1.**

Put up thy sword into the sheath: the cup which my Father hath given me, shall I not drink it? *Jn.* **18: 11.**

Ghost

Oh that I had given up the ghost, and no eye had seen me. *Jb.* **10: 18.**

The eyes of the wicked shall fail, . . . and their hope shall be as the giving up of the ghost. *Jb.* **11: 20.**

Man dieth, and wasteth away: yea, man giveth up the ghost, and where is he? *Jb.* **14: 10.**

Into thine hand I commit my spirit. *Ps.* **31: 5.**

Jesus, when he had cried again with a loud voice, yielded up the ghost. *Mat.* **27: 50.**

A spirit hath not flesh and bones. *Lu.* **24: 39.**

They stoned Stephen, calling upon God, and saying, Lord Jesus, receive my spirit. *Ac.* **7: 59.**

See also
Ghost, Holy; Soul; Spirit; Spirit, Holy.

Ghost, Holy

The blasphemy against the Holy Ghost shall not be forgiven unto men. *Mat.* **12: 31.**

He shall baptize you with the Holy Ghost and with fire. *Lu.* **3: 16.**

The Holy Ghost descended in a bodily shape like a dove upon him. *Lu.* **3: 22.**

They were all filled with the Holy Ghost. *Ac.* **2: 4.**

Ye shall receive the gift of the Holy Ghost. *Ac.* **2: 38.**

We have not so much as heard whether there be any Holy Ghost. *Ac.* **19: 2.**

The Holy Ghost witnesseth in every city. *Ac.* **20: 23.**

The love of God is shed abroad in our hearts by the Holy Ghost which is given unto us. *Ro.* **5: 5.**

If any man have not the Spirit of Christ, he is none of his. *Ro.* **8: 9.**

The Spirit also helpeth our infirmities. *Ro.* **8: 26.**

The Spirit searcheth all things, yea, the deep things of God. *1 Co.* **2: 10.**

Which things also we speak, not in the words which man's wisdom teacheth, but which the Holy Ghost teacheth. *1 Co.* **2: 13.**

Know ye not that your body is the temple of the Holy Ghost. *1 Co.* **6: 19.**

With joy of the Holy Ghost. *1 Th.* **1: 6.**

The Holy Ghost also is a witness to us. *He.* **10: 15.**

See also
Comforter; Spirit, Holy.

Giant

There were giants in the earth in those days. *Ge.* 6: 4.

All the people that we saw in it are men of a great stature. *Nu.* 13: 32.

There we saw the giants: . . . and we were in our own sight as grasshoppers, and so we were in their sight. *Nu.* 13: 33.

If thou be a great people, then get thee up to . . . the land . . . of the giants. *Jos.* 17: 15.

Look not on his countenance, or on the height of his stature; . . . for man looketh on the outward appearance, but the Lord looketh on the heart. *1 S.* 16: 7.

There went out a champion out of the camp of the Philistines, named Goliath, of Gath, whose height was six cubits and a span. *1 S.* 17: 4.

He runneth upon me like a giant. *Jb.* 16: 14.

This thy stature is like to a palm tree. *S. of S.* 7: 7.

The high ones of stature shall be hewn down. *Is.* 10: 33.

See also
Height; Stature.

Gift

I will appease him with the present that goeth before me. *Ge.* 32: 20.

All that a man hath will he give for his life. *Jb.* 2: 4.

They presented unto him gifts; gold, and frankincense, and myrrh. *Mat.* 2: 11.

Give us this day our daily bread. *Mat.* 6: 11.

Ask, and it shall be given you. *Mat.* 7: 7.

What man is there of you, whom if his son ask bread, will he give him a stone? *Mat.* 7: 9.

If ye then, being evil, know how to give good gifts unto your children, how much more shall your Father which is in heaven give good things to them that ask him? *Mat.* 7: 11.

It might have been sold. *Mk.* 14: 5.

For she loved much. *Lu.* 7: 47.

Remember the words of the Lord Jesus, how he said, It is more blessed to give than to receive. *Ac.* 20: 35.

Present your bodies a living sacrifice, holy, acceptable unto God. *Ro.* 12: 1.

As every man hath received the gift, even so minister the same one to another. *1 Pe.* 4: 10.

See also
Ability; Almsgiving; Aptitude; Beneficence; Benevolence; Boon; Capacity; Charity; Christ, Gift of; Contribution; Donation; Endowment; Generosity; God, Gift of; Grant; Philanthropy; Present; Talent; Unselfishness.

Girdle

Thou hast girded me with strength to battle. *2 S.* 22: 40.

It is God that girdeth me with strength. *Ps.* 18: 32.

Thou hast . . . girded me with gladness. *Ps.* 30: 11.

Gird yourselves, and ye shall be broken in pieces. *Is.* 8: 9.

Righteousness shall be the girdle of his loins. *Is.* 11: 5.

I am the Lord, and there is none else, there is no God beside me: I girded thee, though thou hast not known me. *Is.* 45: 5.

When thou wast young, thou girdedst thyself, and walkedst whither thou wouldest: but when thou shalt be old, thou shalt stretch forth thy hands, and another shall gird thee, and carry thee whither thou wouldest not. *Jn.* 21: 18.

See also
Circle.

Girl

Behold, as the eyes of servants look unto the hand of their masters, and as the eyes of a maiden unto the hand of her mistress; so our eyes wait upon the Lord our God. *Ps.* 123: 2.

Young men, and maidens; . . . Let them praise the name of the Lord. *Ps.* 148: 12, 13.

The way of a man with a maid. *Pr.* 30: 19.

She shall sing there, as in the days of her youth, and as in the day when she came up out of the land of Egypt. *Ho.* 2: 15.

They have . . . sold a girl for wine. *Jo.* 3: 3.

And the streets of the city shall be full of boys and girls playing in the streets thereof. *Zch.* 8: 5.

Ye shall be my sons and daughters, saith the Lord Almighty. *2 Co.* 6: 18.

See also
Daughter; Maiden.

Gladness

Let the fields rejoice, and all that is therein. *1 Ch.* 16: 32.

Neither be ye sorry; for the joy of the Lord is your strength. *Ne.* 8: 10.

Thou hast put gladness in my heart. *Ps.* 4: 7.

Thou wilt shew me the path of life: in thy presence is fulness of joy; at thy right hand there are pleasures for evermore. *Ps.* 16: 11.

Thou hast turned for me my mourning into dancing: thou hast put off my sackcloth, and girded me with gladness. *Ps.* 30: 11.

God, thy God, hath anointed thee with the oil of gladness above thy fellows. *Ps.* 45: 7.

There is a river, the streams whereof shall make glad the city of God. *Ps.* 46: 4.

Make us glad according to the days wherein thou hast afflicted us. *Ps.* 90: 15.

He maketh the storm a calm, so that the waves thereof are still. Then are they glad because they be quiet. *Ps.* 107: 29, 30.

The ransomed of the Lord shall return, and come to Zion with songs and everlasting joy upon their heads: they shall obtain joy and gladness, and sorrow and sighing shall flee away. *Is.* 35: 10.

Again there shall be heard in this place. . . . The voice of joy, and the voice of gladness. *Je.* 33: 10, 11.

Rejoice, and be exceeding glad: for great is your reward in heaven. *Mat.* 5: 12.

I bring you good tidings of great joy, which shall be to all people. *Lu.* 2: 10.

Rejoice, ye heavens, and ye that dwell in them. *Re.* 12: 12.

Let us be glad and rejoice, and give honour to him. *Re.* 19: 7.

See also
Bliss; Christ, Joy in; Christ, Joy of; Con-

tentment; Delight; Ecstasy; Exultation; God, Joy in; Happiness; Joy; Pleasure; Rejoicing; Satisfaction.

Glass

Now we see through a glass, darkly; but then face to face. *1 Co.* 13: 12.

We all, with open face beholding as in a glass the glory of the Lord, are changed into the same image from glory to glory. *2 Co.* 3: 18.

If any be a hearer of the word, and not a doer, he is like unto a man beholding his natural face in a glass. *Ja.* 1: 23.

Before the throne there was a sea of glass like unto crystal. *Re.* 4: 6.

The city was pure gold, like unto clear glass. *Re.* 21: 18.

Gleam

Let them that love him be as the sun when he goeth forth in his might. *Ju.* 5: 31.

He shall be as the light of the morning, when the sun riseth, even a morning without clouds. *2 S.* 23: 4.

As the tender grass springing out of the earth by clear shining after rain. *2 S.* 23: 4.

Thine age shall be clearer than the noonday; thou shalt shine forth, thou shalt be as the morning. *Jb.* 11: 17.

If I beheld the sun when it shined, or the moon walking in brightness. *Jb.* 31: 26.

The spirit of man is the candle of the Lord. *Pr.* 20: 27.

Fair as the moon, clear as the sun. *S. of S.* 6: 10.

Like a clear heat upon herbs. *Is.* 18: 4.

The sun shall be no more thy light by day; neither for brightness shall the moon give light unto thee: but the Lord shall be unto thee an everlasting light, and thy God thy glory. *Is.* 60: 19.

I will darken the earth in the clear day. *Am.* 8: 9.

If thy whole body therefore be full of light, having no part dark, the whole shall be full of light, as when the bright shining of a candle doth give thee light. *Lu.* 11: 36.

Her light was like unto a stone most precious, even like a jasper stone, clear as crystal. *Re.* 21: 11.

The city was pure gold, like unto clear glass. *Re.* 21: 18.

I am . . . the bright and morning star. *Re.* 22: 16.

See also
Brightness; Candle; Light; Radiance; Ray.

Globe

The earth was without form, and void. *Ge.* 1: 2.

The whole earth was of one language, and of one speech. *Ge.* 11: 1.

That thou mayest know that the earth is the Lord's. *Ex.* 9: 29.

All the earth is mine. *Ex.* 19: 5.

Thou, even thou, art Lord alone; thou hast made heaven, the heaven of heavens, with all their host, the earth, and all things that are therein, the seas, and all that is therein, and thou preservest them all. *Ne.* 9: 6.

Where wast thou when I laid the foundations of the earth? *Jb.* 38: 4.

Let the whole earth be filled with his glory. *Ps.* 72: 19.

The heaven, even the heavens, are the Lord's: but the earth hath he given to the children of men. *Ps.* 115: 16.

The Lord by wisdom hath founded the earth. *Pr.* 3: 19.

See also
Creation; Earth; Universe; World.

Gloom

That those which mourn may be exalted to safety. *Jb.* 5: 11.

My harp also is turned to mourning. *Jb.* 30: 31.

My sorrow is continually before me. *Ps.* 38: 17.

Thou feedest them with the bread of tears; and givest them tears to drink in great measure. *Ps.* 80: 5.

The bread of sorrows. *Ps.* 127: 2.

Therefore is my spirit overwhelmed within me; my heart within me is desolate. *Ps.* 143: 4.

The earth mourneth and fadeth away, the world languisheth and fadeth away. *Is.* 24: 4.

The country shall be destitute of that whereof it was full. *Eze.* 32: 15.

When my soul fainted within me I remembered the Lord. *Jon.* 2: 7.

Ye shall weep and lament, but the world shall rejoice. *Jn.* 16: 20.

We are troubled on every side, yet not distressed; we are perplexed, but not in despair; Persecuted, but not forsaken; cast down, but not destroyed. *2 Co.* 4: 8, 9.

See also
Dejection; Depression; Despondency; Dimness; Melancholy; Mourning; Obscurity; Sadness; Sorrow.

Glory

The glory is departed from Israel. *1 S.* 4: 21.

I will extol thee, O Lord; for thou hast lifted me up. *Ps.* 30: 1.

The path of the just is as the shining light, that shineth more and more unto the perfect day. *Pr.* 4: 18.

The glory of children are their fathers. *Pr.* 17: 6.

The Lord hath . . . glorified himself in Israel. *Is.* 44: 23.

Let not the wise man glory in his wisdom, neither let the mighty man glory in his might, let not the rich man glory in his riches: But let him that glorieth glory in this, that he understandeth and knoweth me. *Je.* 9: 23, 24.

Their glory shall fly away like a bird. *Ho.* 9: 11.

Even Solomon in all his glory was not arrayed like one of these. *Mat.* 6: 29.

All have sinned, and come short of the glory of God. *Ro.* 3: 23.

Wherefore receive ye one another, as Christ also received us to the glory of God. *Ro.* 15: 7.

Glorify God in your body, and in your spirit, which are God's. *1 Co.* 6: 20.

A man indeed ought not to cover his head, forasmuch as he is the image and glory of God. *1 Co.* 11: 7.

We all, with open face beholding as in a glass the glory of the Lord, are changed into the same image from glory to glory, even as by the Spirit of the Lord. *2 Co.* 3: 18.

He that glorieth, let him glory in the Lord. *2 Co.* 10: 17.

Seeing that many glory after the flesh, I will glory also. *2 Co.* 11: 18.

They glorified God in me. *Ga.* 1: 24.

As always, so now also Christ shall be magnified in my body, whether it be by life, or by death. *Ph.* 1: 20.

Who shall change our vile body, that it may be fashioned like unto his glorious body. *Ph.* 3: 21.

Ye are our glory and joy. *1 Th.* 2: 20.

Pray for us, that the word of the Lord may have free course, and be glorified. *2 Th.* 3: 1.

All flesh is as grass, and all the glory of man as the flower of grass. *1 Pe.* 1: 24.

The spirit of glory and of God resteth upon you. *1 Pe.* 4: 14.

See also

Brightness; Christ, Glory of; Display; Distinction; Fame; God, Glory of; God, Majesty of; Grandeur; Honor; Magnificence; Majesty; Renown; Reputation; Splendor; Sublimity.

Gluttony

We sat by the flesh pots, and . . . we did eat bread to the full. *Ex.* 16: 3.

We remember the fish, which we did eat in Egypt freely; the cucumbers, and the melons, and the leeks, and the onions, and the garlick. *Nu.* 11: 5.

This our son is . . . a glutton, and a drunkard. *De.* 21: 20.

Put a knife to thy throat, if thou be a man given to appetite. *Pr.* 23: 2.

Be not desirous of his dainties: for they are deceitful meat. *Pr.* 23: 3.

The drunkard and the glutton shall come to poverty. *Pr.* 23: 21.

He hath filled his belly with my delicates. *Je.* 51: 34.

The Son of man came eating and drinking, and they say, Behold a man gluttonous, and a winebibber. *Mat.* 11: 19.

Wheresoever the carcass is, there will the eagles be gathered together. *Mat.* 24: 28.

Then certain philosophers of the Epicureans . . . encountered him. *Ac.* 17: 18.

They that are such serve not our Lord Jesus Christ, but their own belly. *Ro.* 16: 18.

Whether therefore ye eat, or drink, or whatsoever ye do, do all to the glory of God. *1 Co.* 10: 31.

Whose God is their belly, and whose glory is in their shame. *Ph.* 3: 19.

Excess of wine, revellings, banquetings. *1 Pe.* 4: 3.

See also

Appetite; Dissipation; Greed.

Goal

I have set the Lord always before me. *Ps.* 16: 8.

The path of the just is as the shining light, that shineth more and more unto the perfect day. *Pr.* 4: 18.

Better is the end of a thing than the beginning thereof. *Ec.* 7: 8.

He that endureth to the end shall be saved. *Mat.* 10: 22.

Neither count I my life dear unto myself, so that I might finish my course with joy. *Ac.* 20: 24.

Ye have your fruit unto holiness, and the end everlasting life. *Ro.* 6: 22.

Called to be saints. *1 Co.* 1: 2.

Till we all come in the unity of the faith, and of the knowledge of the Son of God, unto a perfect man, unto the measure of the stature of the fulness of Christ. *Ep.* 4: 13.

This one thing I do, forgetting those things which are behind, and reaching forth unto those things which are before, I press toward the mark for the prize of the high calling of God in Christ Jesus. *Ph.* 3: 13, 14.

Leaving the principles of the doctrine of Christ, let us go on unto perfection. *He.* 6: 1.

Hope to the end for the grace that is to be brought unto you at the revelation of Jesus Christ. *1 Pe.* 1: 13.

The end of all things is at hand. *1 Pe.* 4: 7.

See also

Aim; Ambition; Aspiration; Christ, Purpose of; End; Intention; Purpose.

Goat

The goat shall bear upon him all their iniquities unto a land not inhabited: and he shall let go the goat in the wilderness. *Le.* 16: 22.

Knowest thou the time when the wild goats of the rock bring forth? *Jb.* 39: 1.

The high hills are a refuge for the wild goats. *Ps.* 104: 18.

Thy hair is as a flock of goats. *S. of S.* 4: 1.

I delight not in the blood of bullocks, or of lambs, or of he goats. *Is.* 1: 11.

He shall set the sheep on his right hand, but the goats on the left. *Mat.* 25: 33.

It is not possible that the blood of bulls and of goats should take away sins. *He.* 10: 4.

God, Access to

Acquaint now thyself with him, and be at peace. *Jb.* 22: 21.

They take delight in approaching to God. *Is.* 58: 2.

When ye pray. *Mat.* 6: 7.

The vail of the temple was rent in twain from the top to the bottom. *Mk.* 15: 38.

By whom also we have access by faith into this grace wherein we stand, and rejoice in hope of the glory of God. *Ro.* 5: 2.

Through him we both have access by one Spirit unto the Father. *Ep.* 2: 18.

In whom we have boldness and access with confidence by the faith of him. *Ep.* 3: 12.

Draw nigh to God, and he will draw nigh to you. *Ja.* 4: 8.

See also

God, Finding.

God, Adoration of

Who is like unto thee, O Lord, among the gods? *Ex.* 15: 11.

There shall no man be able to stand before thee. *De.* 7: 24.

The Lord your God is God of gods, and Lord of lords. *De.* 10: 17.

All the gods of the people are idols: but the Lord made the heavens. *1 Ch.* 16: 26.

Let us kneel before the Lord our maker. *Ps.* 95: 6.

It shall come to pass, that from one new moon to another, and from one sabbath to another, shall all flesh come to worship before me, saith the Lord. *Is.* **66: 23.**

The four beasts fell down and worshipped God that sat on the throne, saying, Amen; Alleluja. *Re.* **19: 4.**

See also

God, Praise to; God, Prayer to; God, Worship of.

God, the Almighty

I am the Almighty God; walk before me, and be thou perfect. *Ge.* **17: 1.**

I am God Almighty: be fruitful and multiply. *Ge.* **35: 11.**

I will cast out the nations before thee, and enlarge thy borders. *Ex.* **34: 24.**

Behold, the heaven and the heaven of heavens is the Lord's thy God, the earth also, with all that therein is. *De.* **10: 14.**

See now that I, even I, am he, and there is no god with me: I kill, and I make alive; I wound, and I heal. *De.* **32: 39.**

The Lord killeth, and maketh alive: he bringeth down to the grave, and bringeth up. *1 S.* **2: 6.**

The Lord maketh poor, and maketh rich: he bringeth low, and lifteth up. *1 S.* **2: 7.**

The arrows of the Almighty are within me. *Jb.* **6: 4.**

Canst thou find out the Almighty unto perfection? *Jb.* **11: 7.**

He enlargeth the nations. *Jb.* **12: 23.**

The Almighty shall be thy defence. *Jb.* **22: 25.**

The breath of the Almighty hath given me life. *Jb.* **33: 4.**

Touching the Almighty, we cannot find him out. *Jb.* **37: 23.**

Where wast thou when I laid the foundations of the earth? declare, if thou hast understanding. *Jb.* **38: 4.**

The day is thine, the night also is thine. *Ps.* **74: 16.**

He that dwelleth in the secret place of the most High shall abide under the shadow of the Almighty. *Ps.* **91: 1.**

Who laid the foundations of the earth, that it should not be removed for ever. *Ps.* **104: 5.**

Praise him for his mighty acts. *Ps.* **150: 2.**

I have made the earth, and created man upon it. *Is.* **45: 12.**

The Lord hath made bare his holy arm in the eyes of all the nations. *Is.* **52: 10.**

He removeth kings, and setteth up kings. *Da.* **2: 21.**

The Lord . . . layeth the foundation of the earth. *Zch.* **12: 1.**

With God all things are possible. *Mk.* **10: 27.**

Holy, holy, holy, Lord God Almighty, which was, and is, and is to come. *Re.* **4: 8.**

Even so, Lord God Almighty, true and righteous are thy judgments. *Re.* **16: 7.**

The Lord God Almighty and the Lamb are the temple of it. *Re.* **21: 22.**

See also

Almighty; God, Power of; God, Omnipotence of; God, Strength of; God, Supremacy of.

God, Anger of

The anger of the Lord was kindled against Israel. *Nu.* **25: 3.**

Great is the wrath of the Lord that is kindled against us, because our fathers have not hearkened unto the words of this book. *2 K.* **22: 13.**

Then shall he speak unto them in his wrath, and vex them in his sore displeasure. *Ps.* **2: 5.**

God is angry with the wicked every day. *Ps.* **7: 11.**

O God, thou hast cast us off, thou hast scattered us, thou hast been displeased; O turn thyself to us again. *Ps.* **60: 1.**

The Lord is merciful and gracious, slow to anger, and plenteous in mercy. *Ps.* **103: 8.**

Will he reserve his anger for ever? will he keep it to the end? *Je.* **3: 5.**

Why have they provoked me to anger with their graven images, and with strange vanities? *Je.* **8: 19.**

Great is the anger and the fury that the Lord hath pronounced against this people. *Je.* **36: 7.**

He retaineth not his anger for ever, because he delighteth in mercy. *Mi.* **7: 18.**

He that believeth not the Son shall not see life; but the wrath of God abideth on him. *Jn.* **3: 36.**

He treadeth the winepress of the fierceness and wrath of Almighty God. *Re.* **19: 15.**

See also

God, Wrath of.

God, Antagonism to

Shall he that contendeth with the Almighty instruct him? *Jb.* **40: 2.**

Let God arise, let his enemies be scattered. *Ps.* **68: 1.**

Rule thou in the midst of thine enemies. *Ps.* **110: 2.**

They speak against thee wickedly, and thine enemies take thy name in vain. *Ps.* **139: 20.**

Woe unto him that striveth with his Maker! *Is.* **45: 9.**

What was I, that I could withstand God? *Ac.* **11: 17.**

Thou child of the devil, thou enemy of all righteousness, wilt thou not cease to pervert the right ways of the Lord? *Ac.* **13: 10.**

The carnal mind is enmity against God. *Ro.* **8: 7.**

Know ye not that the friendship of the world is enmity with God? *Ja.* **4: 4.**

See also

Atheism; God, Denial of; God, Rebellion against; God, Rejection of; Godlessness.

God, Aspiration for

The cry of the city went up to heaven. *1 S.* **5: 12.**

Unto thee, O Lord, do I lift up my soul. *Ps.* **25: 1.**

Hear my prayer, O Lord, and give ear unto my cry. *Ps.* **39: 12.**

As the hart panteth after the water brooks, so panteth my soul after thee, O God. *Ps.* **42: 1.**

Pour out your heart before him. *Ps.* **62: 8.**

My flesh longeth for thee in a dry and thirsty land, where no water is. *Ps.* **63: 1.**

My soul followeth hard after thee. *Ps.* **63: 8.**

Whom have I in heaven but thee? and there is none upon earth that I desire beside thee. *Ps.* **73: 25.**

My soul longeth, yea, even fainteth for the courts of the Lord. *Ps.* **84: 2.**

With my whole heart have I sought thee. *Ps.* **119: 10.**

I have longed for thy salvation, O Lord. *Ps.* **119: 174.**

I will lift up mine eyes unto the hills, from whence cometh my help. *Ps.* **121: 1.**

Let us lift up our heart with our hands unto God in the heavens. *La.* **3: 41.**

We would see Jesus. *Jn.* **12: 21.**

See also

God, Cry to; God, Longing for; God, Prayer to; God, Quest for; God, Thirst for; God, Yearning for.

God, Beauty of

He thundereth with the voice of his excellency. *Jb.* **37: 4.**

One thing have I desired of the Lord, that will I seek after; that I may . . . behold the beauty of the Lord. *Ps.* **27: 4.**

Let the beauty of the Lord our God be upon us. *Ps.* **90: 17.**

In that day shall the Lord of hosts be for a crown of glory, and for a diadem of beauty, unto the residue of his people. *Is.* **28: 5.**

Thine eyes shall see the king in his beauty. *Is.* **33: 17.**

The excellency of our God. *Is.* **35: 2.**

See also

God, Grace of.

God, Belief in

He believed in the Lord; and he counted it to him for righteousness. *Ge.* **15: 6.**

Believe in the Lord your God, so shall ye be established; believe his prophets, so shall ye prosper. *2 Ch.* **20: 20.**

Though he slay me, yet will I trust in him. *Jb.* **13: 15.**

O Lord my God, in thee do I put my trust. *Ps.* **7: 1.**

Be still, and know that I am God. *Ps.* **46: 10.**

Trust ye in the Lord for ever. *Is.* **26: 4.**

No manner of hurt was found upon him, because he believed in his God. *Da.* **6: 23.**

So the people of Nineveh believed God. *Jon.* **3: 5.**

What things soever ye desire, when ye pray, believe that ye receive them, and ye shall have them. *Mk.* **11: 24.**

Now the God of hope fill you with all joy and peace in believing. *Ro.* **15: 13.**

We trust in the living God. *1 Ti.* **4: 10.**

He that cometh to God must believe that he is, and that he is the rewarder of them that diligently seek him. *He.* **11: 6.**

Thou believest that there is one God; thou doest well: the devils also believe, and tremble. *Ja.* **2: 19.**

See also

God, Confidence in; God, Faith in; God, Reliance in; God, Trust in.

God, Beneficence of

The breath of the Almighty hath given me life. *Jb.* **33: 4.**

The Lord God is a sun and shield. *Ps.* **84: 11.**

Forget not all his benefits. *Ps.* **103: 2.**

The eyes of all wait upon thee; and thou givest them their meat in due season. *Ps.* **145: 15.**

This also I saw, that it was from the hand of God. *Ec.* **2: 24.**

I will be as the dew unto Israel. *Ho.* **14: 5.**

God so loved the world that he gave his only begotten Son, that whosoever believeth in him should not perish, but have everlasting life. *Jn.* **3: 16.**

Thanks be unto God for his unspeakable gift. *2 Co.* **9: 15.**

My God shall supply all your need according to his riches in glory by Jesus Christ. *Ph.* **4: 19.**

Every good gift and every perfect gift is from above. *Ja.* **1: 17.**

See also

God, Favor of; God, Generosity of; God, Goodness of; God, Kindness of; God, Providence of.

God, the Besetting

With favour wilt thou compass him as with a shield. *Ps.* **5: 12.**

He that trusteth in the Lord, mercy shall compass him about. *Ps.* **32: 10.**

The angel of the Lord encampeth round about them that fear him, and delivereth them. *Ps.* **34: 7.**

Thou compassest my path and my lying down, and art acquainted with all my ways. *Ps.* **139: 3.**

Thou hast beset me behind and before, and laid thine hand upon me. *Ps.* **139: 5.**

In all thy ways acknowledge him. *Pr.* **3: 6.**

The word of the Lord came expressly unto Ezekiel the priest; . . . and the hand of the Lord was there upon him. *Eze.* **1: 3.**

Though they dig into hell, thence shall mine hand take them; though they climb up to heaven, thence will I bring them down. *Am.* **9: 2.**

Jonah rose up to flee unto Tarshish from the presence of the Lord, and went down to Joppa. *Jon.* **1: 3.**

The word of the Lord came unto Jonah the second time, saying, Arise, go unto Nineveh, that great city, and preach unto it the preaching that I bid thee. *Jon.* **3: 1, 2.**

I am persuaded, that neither death, nor life, nor angels, nor principalities, nor powers, nor things present, nor things to come, . . . shall be able to separate us from the love of God, which is in Christ Jesus our Lord. *Ro.* **8: 38, 39.**

For whether we live, we live unto the Lord; and whether we die, we die unto the Lord: whether we live therefore, or die, we are the Lord's. *Ro.* **14: 8.**

See also

God, the Inescapable; God, Overruling of; God, Power of; God, Primacy of; God, Sovereignty of.

God, Blessing of

The Lord bless thee, and keep thee: The Lord make his face to shine upon thee, and be gracious unto thee. *Nu.* **6: 24, 25.**

All these blessings shall come on thee, and

overtake thee, if thou shalt hearken unto the voice of the Lord thy God. *De.* 28: 2.

Blessed shalt thou be in the city, and blessed shalt thou be in the field. *De.* 28: 3.

Blessed shalt thou be when thou comest in, and blessed shalt thou be when thou goest out. *De.* 28: 6.

They saw that the Lord his God was with him. *2 Ch.* 15: 9.

Lord, lift thou up the light of thy countenance upon us. *Ps.* 4: 6.

The Lord is the portion of mine inheritance and of my cup. *Ps.* 16: 5.

At thy right hand there are pleasures for evermore. *Ps.* 16: 11.

Blessed is the nation whose God is the Lord. *Ps.* 33: 12.

God hath blessed thee for ever. *Ps.* 45: 2.

Thou hast holden me by my right hand. *Ps.* 73: 23.

Blessed is every one that feareth the Lord. *Ps.* 128: 1.

Blessed be the God and Father of our Lord Jesus Christ, who hath blessed us with all spiritual blessings. *Ep.* 1: 3.

Surely blessing I will bless thee. *He.* 6: 14.

Blessed are the dead which die in the Lord from henceforth. *Re.* 14: 13.

See also

God, Beneficence of; God, Favor of; God, Grace of; God, Providence of.

God, the Builder

His foundation is in the holy mountain. *Ps.* 87: 1.

As for the world and the fulness thereof, thou hast founded them. *Ps.* 89: 11.

Of old hast thou laid the foundation of the earth. *Ps.* 102: 25.

So shall I talk of thy wondrous works. *Ps.* 119: 27.

All thy works shall praise thee, O Lord. *Ps.* 145: 10.

God that made the world and all things therein . . . dwelleth not in temples made with hands. *Ac.* 17: 24.

The foundation of God standeth sure. *2 Ti.* 2: 19.

Thou, Lord, in the beginning hast laid the foundation of the earth. *He.* 1: 10.

He that built all things is God. *He.* 3: 4.

He looked for a city which hath foundations, whose builder and maker is God. *He.* 11: 10.

See also

God, the Creator; God, Work of.

God, Call of

The Lord God called unto Adam, and said unto him, Where art thou? *Ge.* 3: 9.

My people would not hearken to my voice; and Israel would none of me. *Ps.* 81: 11.

I heard the voice of the Lord, saying, Whom shall I send, and who will go for us? *Is.* 6: 8.

Come, my people, enter thou into thy chambers, and shut thy doors about thee. *Is.* 26: 20.

The voice of him that crieth in the wilderness. *Is.* 40: 3.

The voice said, Cry. And he said, What shall I cry? *Is.* 40: 6.

Ho, every one that thirsteth, come ye to the waters, and he that hath no money; come ye, buy, and eat; yea, come, buy wine and milk without money and without price. *Is.* 55: 1.

When I called, ye did not answer; when I spake, ye did not hear. *Is.* 65: 12.

Return ye now every man from his evil way, and amend your doings. *Je.* 35: 15.

Turn ye, turn ye from your evil ways; for why will ye die, O house of Israel? *Eze.* 33: 11.

The Lord's voice crieth unto the city. *Mi.* 6: 9.

God . . . hath called you unto his kingdom and glory. *1 Th.* 2: 12.

The Lord himself shall descend from heaven with a shout, with the voice of the archangel, and with the trump of God. *1 Th.* 4: 16.

The Spirit and the bride say, Come. *Re.* 22: 17.

See also

God, Voice of; God, Word of.

God, Care of

God will provide. *Ge.* 22: 8.

The eternal God is thy refuge, and underneath are the everlasting arms. *De.* 33: 27.

Hitherto hath the Lord helped us. *1 S.* 7: 12.

The barrel of meal shall not waste, neither shall the cruse of oil fail. *1 K.* 17: 14.

The Lord is my shepherd; I shall not want. *Ps.* 23; 1.

Thou preparest a table before me in the presence of mine enemies. *Ps.* 23: 5.

He that dwelleth in the secret place of the most High shall abide under the shadow of the Almighty. *Ps.* 91: 1.

He shall give his angels charge over thee, to keep thee in all thy ways. *Ps.* 91: 11.

They shall still bring forth fruit in old age; they shall be fat and flourishing; to shew that the Lord is upright. *Ps.* 92: 14, 15.

In the multitude of my thoughts within me thy comforts delight my soul. *Ps.* 94: 19.

I will lift up mine eyes unto the hills. *Ps.* 121: 1.

The Lord is thy keeper. *Ps.* 121: 5.

In the shadow of his hand hath he hid me. *Is.* 49: 2.

If God so clothe the grass of the field, which to day is, and to morrow is cast into the oven, shall he not much more clothe you, O ye of little faith? *Mat.* 6: 30.

Your heavenly Father knoweth that ye have need of all these things. *Mat.* 6: 32.

Are not two sparrows sold for a farthing? and one of them shall not fall on the ground without your Father. *Mat.* 10: 29.

The very hairs of your head are all numbered. *Mat.* 10: 30.

We know that all things work together for good to them that love God, to them who are the called according to his purpose. *Ro.* 8: 28.

My God shall supply all your need according to his riches in glory by Christ Jesus. *Ph.* 4: 19.

Casting all your care upon him; for he careth for you. *1 Pe.* 5: 7.

See also

God, Beneficence of; God, Comfort of; God, Compassion of; God, Favor of; God, Goodness of; God, the Keeper; God, Providence of; God, Solicitude of; God, the Sustainer; God, Sympathy of.

God, Certainty of

Certainly I will be with thee. *Ex.* 3: 12.

The testimony of the Lord is sure, making wise the simple. *Ps.* 19: 7.

My heart is fixed, O God,. my heart is fixed. *Ps.* 57: 7.

Commit thy ways unto the Lord, and thy thoughts shall be established. *Pr.* 16: 3.

I am the Lord, I change not. *Mal.* 3: 6.

Be ye sure of this, that the kingdom of God is come nigh unto you. *Lu.* 10: 11.

The foundation of God standeth sure. 2 *Ti.* 2: 19.

The immutability of his counsel. *He.* 6: 17.

Every good gift and every perfect gift is from above, and cometh down from the Father of lights, with whom is no variableness, neither shadow of turning. *Ja.* 1: 17.

See also

God, Confidence in; God, Primacy of; God, Overruling of; God, Security of; God, Supremacy of; God, Truth of.

God, Chastisement of

I, even I, will chastise you seven times for your sins. *Le.* 26: 28.

If he commit iniquity, I will chasten him with the rod of men. 2 *S.* 7: 14.

Behold, happy is the man whom God correcteth: therefore despise not thou the chastening of the Almighty. *Jb.* 5: 17.

Then will I visit their transgression with the rod, and their iniquity with stripes. *Ps.* 89: 32.

The Lord hath chastened me sore: but he hath not given me over unto death. *Ps.* 118: 18.

The Lord of hosts shall stir up a scourge for him. *Is.* 10: 26.

I will punish the world for their evil, and the wicked for their iniquity. *Is.* 13: 11.

The days of visitation are come, the days of recompense are come. *Ho.* 9: 7.

You only have I known of all the families of the earth: therefore I will punish you for all your iniquities. *Am.* 3: 2.

It is a righteous thing with God to recompense tribulation to them that trouble you. 2 *Th.* 1: 6.

Whom the Lord loveth he chasteneth. *He.* 12: 6.

The Lord knoweth how to deliver the godly out of temptation, and to reserve the unjust unto the day of judgment to be punished. 2 *Pe.* 2: 9.

As many as I love, I rebuke and chasten. *Re.* 3: 19.

See also

God, Anger of; God, Punishment of; God, Reward of; God, Wrath of.

God, Child of

Ye are the children of the Lord your God. *De.* 14: 1.

We are his people. *Ps.* 100: 3.

Like as a father pitieth his children, so the Lord pitieth them that fear him. *Ps.* 103: 13.

Lo, children are an heritage of the Lord. *Ps.* 127: 3.

All thy children shall be taught of the Lord; and great shall be the peace of thy children. *Is.* 54: 13.

God is able of these stones to raise up children unto Abraham. *Mat.* 3: 9.

Blessed are the peacemakers: for they shall be called the children of God. *Mat.* 5: 9.

Suffer little children, and forbid them not, to come unto me: for of such is the kingdom of heaven. *Mat.* 19: 14.

Thou, child, shalt be called the prophet of the Highest. *Lu.* 1: 76.

As many as received him, to them gave he power to become the sons of God, even to them that believe on his name. *Jn.* 1: 12.

We are the children of God. *Ro.* 8: 16.

The glorious liberty of the children of God. *Ro.* 8: 21.

In the place where it was said unto them, Ye are not my people; there shall they be called the children of the living God. *Ro.* 9: 26.

Now are we the sons of God, and it doth not yet appear what we shall be. *1 Jn.* 3: 2.

See also

God, People of; God, Son of.

God, City of

Glorious things are spoken of thee, O city of God. *Ps.* 87: 3.

Say unto the cities of Judah, Behold your God! *Is.* 40: 9.

He looked for a city which hath foundations. *He.* 11: 10.

Ye are come unto mount Sion, and unto the city of the living God, the heavenly Jerusalem. *He.* 12: 22.

On the east three gates; on the north three gates; on the south three gates; and on the west three gates. *Re.* 21: 13.

The city had no need of the sun, neither of the moon, to shine in it: for the glory of God did lighten it,' and the Lamb is the light thereof. *Re.* 21: 23.

See also

God, Dominion of; God, Kingdom of; God, Sovereignty of.

God, Comfort of

Are the consolations of God small with thee? *Jb.* 15: 11.

Thy rod and thy staff they comfort me. *Ps.* 23: 4.

Comfort ye, comfort ye my people, saith your God. *Is.* 40: 1.

I, even I, am he that comforteth you. *Is.* 51: 12.

O thou afflicted, tossed with tempest, and not comforted, behold, I will lay thy stones with fair colours, and lay thy foundations with sapphires. *Is.* 54: 11.

As one whom his mother comforteth, so will I comfort you; and ye shall be comforted in Jerusalem. *Is.* 66: 13.

Now the God of patience and consolation grant you to be likeminded one toward another according to Christ Jesus. *Ro.* 15: 5.

The Father of mercies, and the God of all comfort. 2 *Co.* 1: 3.

God . . . hath given us everlasting consolation and good hope through grace. 2 *Th.* 2: 16.

See also

God, Beneficence of; God, Care of; God, Compassion of; God, Goodness of; God, Providence of; God, Solicitude of; God, Sympathy of.

God, Commandment of

This is the thing which the Lord doth command. *Nu. 36: 6.*

These words, which I command thee this day, shall be in thine heart. *De. 6: 6.*

The word is very nigh unto thee, in thy mouth, and in thy heart, that thou mayest do it. *De. 30: 14.*

Keep and seek for all the commandments of the Lord your God. *1 Ch. 28: 8.*

The law of the Lord is perfect, converting the soul. *Ps. 19: 7.*

The Lord will command his lovingkindness in the daytime. *Ps. 42: 8.*

All his commandments are sure. *Ps. 111: 7.*

Thou hast commanded us to keep thy precepts diligently. *Ps. 119: 4.*

Blessed art thou, O Lord: teach me thy statutes. *Ps. 119: 12.*

Great peace have they which love thy law. *Ps. 119: 165.*

Let them praise the name of the Lord: for he commanded, and they were created. *Ps. 148: 5.*

Fear God, and keep his commandments. *Ec. 12: 13.*

Now therefore are we all here present before God, to hear all things that are commanded thee of God. *Ac. 10: 33.*

The commandment of the everlasting God. *Ro. 16: 26.*

If any man think himself to be a prophet, or spiritual, let him acknowledge that the things that I write unto you are the commandments of the Lord. *1 Co. 14: 37.*

His commandments are not grievous. *1 Jn. 5: 3.*

Blessed are they that do his commandments, that they may have right to the tree of life. *Re. 22: 14.*

See also

God, Law of; God, Voice of; God, Word of.

God, Communion with

He dreamed, and behold a ladder set up on the earth, and the top of it reached to heaven: and behold the angels of God ascending and descending on it. And, behold, the Lord stood above it. *Ge. 28: 12, 13.*

There I will meet with thee, and I will commune with thee from above the mercy seat. *Ex. 25: 22.*

There arose not a prophet since in Israel like unto Moses, whom the Lord knew face to face. *De. 34: 10.*

Let us draw near hither unto God. *1 S. 14: 36.*

My soul followeth hard after thee: thy right hand upholdeth me. *Ps. 63: 8.*

Now when all the people were baptized, it came to pass, that Jesus also being baptized, and praying, the heaven was opened. *Lu. 3: 21.*

He that is joined unto the Lord is one spirit. *1 Co. 6: 17.*

The law made nothing perfect, but the bringing in of a better hope did; by the

which we draw nigh unto God. *He. 7: 19.*

He was called the Friend of God. *Ja. 2: 23.*

Our fellowship is with the Father, and with his Son Jesus Christ. *1 Jn. 1: 3.*

If we say that we have fellowship with him, and walk in darkness, we lie. *1 Jn. 1: 6.*

If we walk in the light, as he is in the light, we have fellowship one with another. *1 Jn. 1: 7.*

See also

God, Companionship of; God, Fellowship of; God, Life in; God, Partnership with.

God, Companionship of

I am with thee, and will keep thee in all places whither thou goest. *Ge. 28: 15.*

Samuel grew, and the Lord was with him. *1 S. 3: 19.*

The Lord be with thee, as he hath been with my father. *1 S. 20: 13.*

The Lord be between thee and me for ever. *1 S. 20: 23.*

I am a companion of all them that fear thee, and of them that keep thy precepts. *Ps. 119: 63.*

Yet I am not alone, because the Father is with me. *Jn. 16: 32.*

Now the God of peace be with you all. *Ro. 15: 33.*

God is not ashamed to be called their God. *He. 11: 16.*

Partakers of his holiness. *He. 12: 10.*

Some have entertained angels unawares. *He. 13: 2.*

See also

God, Communion with; God, Cooperation of; God, Fellowship with; God, Life in; God, Nearness of; God, Partnership with.

God, Compassion of

Shewing mercy unto thousands of them that love me. *Ex. 20: 6.*

Be merciful, O Lord, unto thy people. *De. 21: 8.*

He, being full of compassion, forgave their iniquity. . . . For he remembered that they were but flesh; a wind that passeth away, and cometh not again. *Ps. 78: 38, 39.*

He knoweth our frame; he remembereth that we are dust. *Ps. 103: 14.*

Our eyes wait upon the Lord our God, until that he have mercy upon us. *Ps. 123: 2.*

It is of the Lord's mercies that we are not consumed, because his compassions fail not. *La. 3: 22.*

To the Lord our God belong mercies. *Da. 9: 9.*

I drew them with cords of a man, with bands of love. *Ho. 11: 4.*

I knew that thou art a gracious God, and merciful, slow to anger, and of great kindness. *Jon. 4: 2.*

When I sit in darkness, the Lord shall be a light unto me. *Mi. 7: 8.*

He will turn again, he will have compassion upon us; he will subdue our iniquity; and thou wilt cast all their sins into the depths of the sea. *Mi. 7: 19.*

Jesus . . . saith unto him, Go home to thy friends, and tell them how great things the

Lord hath done for thee, and hath had compassion on thee. *Mk.* **5: 19.**

Draw nigh to God, and he will draw nigh to you. *Ja.* **4: 8.**

See also

God, Comfort of; God, Gentleness of; God, Help of; God, Kindness of; God, Mercy of; God, Providence of; God, Solicitude of; God, Sympathy of.

God, Compulsion of

The Lord God hath spoken, who can but prophesy? *Am.* **3: 8.**

The Lord is slow to anger, and great in power. *Na.* **1: 3.**

Immediately the Spirit driveth him into the wilderness. *Mk.* **1: 12.**

The power of the Highest shall overshadow thee. *Lu.* **1: 35.**

Wist ye not that I must be about my Father's business? *Lu.* **2: 49.**

With the finger of God. *Lu.* **11: 20.**

I must walk to day, and to morrow, and the day following. *Lu.* **13: 33.**

We cannot but speak the things which we have seen and heard. *Ac.* **4: 20.**

In demonstration of the Spirit and of power. *1 Co.* **2: 4.**

See also

God, Dominion of; God, Overruling of; God, Power of; God, Strength of.

God, Confidence in

Though he slay me, yet will I trust in him. *Jb.* **13: 15.**

Wilt thou believe him, that he will bring home thy seed, and gather it into thy barn? *Jb.* **39: 12.**

Commit thy way unto the Lord. *Ps.* **37: 5.**

Thou art my trust from my youth. *Ps.* **71: 5.**

The Lord shall be thy confidence, and shall keep thy foot from being taken. *Pr.* **3: 26.**

Whoso trusteth in the Lord, happy is he. *Pr.* **16: 20.**

If ye had faith as a grain of mustard seed, ye might say unto this sycamine tree, Be thou plucked up by the root, and be thou planted in the sea; and it should obey you. *Lu.* **17: 6.**

Being confident of this very thing, that he which hath begun a good work in you will perform it until the day of Jesus Christ. *Ph.* **1: 6.**

The living God . . . is the Saviour of all men, especially of those that believe. *1 Ti.* **4: 10.**

If our heart condemn us not, then have we confidence toward God. *1 Jn.* **3: 21.**

See also

God, Belief in; God, Certainty of; God, Faith in; God, Hope in; God, Reliance on; God, Trust in.

God, Consciousness of

I have seen God face to face. *Ge.* **32: 30.**

He knoweth thy walking through this great wilderness. *De.* **2: 7.**

Acquaint now thyself with him, and be at peace. *Jb.* **22: 21.**

Thou art with me. *Ps.* **23: 4.**

The secret of the Lord is with them that fear him. *Ps.* **25: 14.**

When I awake, I am still with thee. *Ps.* **139: 18.**

The heavens were opened, and I saw visions of God. *Eze.* **1: 1.**

Then shall we know, if we follow on to know the Lord. *Ho.* **6: 3.**

Yet I am not alone, because the Father is with me. *Jn.* **16: 32.**

In him we live, and move, and have our being. *Ac.* **17: 28.**

He that is joined unto the Lord is one spirit. *1 Co.* **6: 17.**

That ye might be filled with the knowledge of his will. *Col.* **1: 9.**

Increasing in the knowledge of God. *Col.* **1: 10.**

Partakers of his holiness. *He.* **12: 10.**

See also

God, Communion with; God, Knowledge of; God, Presence of.

God, Cooperation of

The Lord your God is he that goeth with you, to fight for you against your enemies, to save you. *De.* **20: 4.**

The Lord is with thee, thou mighty man of valour. *Ju.* **6: 12.**

As the Lord liveth, there shall not one hair of his head fall to the ground; for he hath wrought with God this day. *1 S.* **14: 45.**

O Israel, thou hast destroyed thyself; but in me is thine help. *Ho.* **13: 9.**

They went forth, and preached every where, the Lord working with them. *Mk.* **16: 20.**

We know that all things work together for good to them that love God. *Ro.* **8: 28.**

We are labourers together with God. *1 Co.* **3: 9.**

For it is God which worketh in you both to will and to do of his good pleasure. *Ph.* **2: 13.**

See also

God, Communion with; God, Companionship of; God, Fellowship of; God, Life in; God, Partnership with.

God, the Creator

On the seventh day God ended his work which he had made. *Ge.* **2: 2.**

Thine hands have made me and fashioned me together round about. *Jb.* **10: 8.**

He stretcheth out the north over the empty place, and hangeth the earth upon nothing. *Jb.* **26: 7.**

Where wast thou when I laid the foundations of the earth? *Jb.* **38: 4.**

He hath founded it upon the seas. *Ps.* **24: 2.**

It is he that hath made us, and not we ourselves. *Ps.* **100: 3.**

Of old hast thou laid the foundation of the earth: and the heavens are the work of thy hands. *Ps.* **102: 25.**

O Lord, how manifold are thy works! in wisdom hast thou made them all. *Ps.* **104: 24.**

All thy works shall praise thee, O Lord; and thy saints shall bless thee. *Ps.* **145: 10.**

The Lord by wisdom hath founded the earth. *Pr.* **3: 19.**

The Creator of the ends of the earth. *Is.* 40:
28.

I have created him for my glory, I have
formed him; yea, I have made him. *Is.* 43:
7.

I am the Lord, your Holy One, the Creator
of Israel, your King. *Is.* 43: 15.

I form the light, and create darkness: I make
peace, and create evil: I the Lord do all these
things. *Is.* 45: 7.

Behold, I create new heavens and a new
earth. *Is.* 65: 17.

The living God, which made heaven, and
earth, and the sea, and all things that are
therein. *Ac.* 14: 15.

We are his workmanship, created in Christ
Jesus unto good works. *Ep.* 2: 10.

Through faith we understand that the
worlds were framed by the word of God. *He.*
11: 3.

A faithful Creator. *1 Pe.* 4: 19.

See also

God, the Builder; God, Work of.

God, Cry to

When we cried unto the Lord, he heard
our voice, and sent an angel. *Nu.* 20: 16.

The cry of the city went up to heaven. *1 S.*
5: 12.

The battle was before and behind: and they
cried unto the Lord. *2 Ch.* 13: 14.

My voice shalt thou hear in the morning, O
Lord. *Ps.* 5: 3.

Hear my prayer, O Lord, and give ear unto
my cry. *Ps.* 39: 12.

I waited patiently for the Lord; and he inclined unto me, and heard my cry. *Ps.* 40: 1.

As for me, I will call upon God; and the
Lord shall save me. *Ps.* 55: 16.

Then they cry unto the Lord in their
trouble, and he saveth them out of their distresses. *Ps.* 107: 19.

What meanest thou, O sleeper? arise, call
upon thy God. *Jon.* 1: 6.

Then shall they cry unto the Lord, but he
will not hear them: he will even hide his face
from them at that time, as they have behaved
themselves ill in their doings. *Mi.* 3: 4.

See also

God, Aspiration for; God, Longing for; God,
Prayer to; God, Thirst for; God, Yearning for.

God, Day of

Weeping may endure for a night, but joy
cometh in the morning. *Ps.* 30: 5.

The righteous hath hope in his death. *Pr.*
14: 32.

The day of the Lord is great and very terrible; and who can abide it? *Jo.* 2: 11.

The sun shall be turned into darkness, and
the moon into blood, before the great and
terrible day of the Lord come. *Jo.* 2: 31.

The great day of the Lord is near, it is near,
and hasteth greatly, even the voice of the day
of the Lord. *Zph.* 1: 14.

Grieve not the Holy Spirit of God, whereby
ye are sealed unto the day of redemption. *Ep.*
4: 30.

In hope of eternal life. *Tit.* 1: 2.

These all died in faith, not having received
the promises, but having seen them afar off.
He. 11: 13.

Looking for and hasting unto the coming of
the day of God. *2 Pe.* 3: 12.

See also

God, the Judge; God, the Light; God, Reward of.

God, Deliverance of

Ye shall not fear them: for the Lord your
God he shall fight for you. *De.* 3: 22.

The Lord is my rock, and my fortress, and
my deliverer. *2 S.* 22: 2.

He delivereth the poor in his affliction. *Jb.*
36: 15.

Thou hast enlarged me when I was in distress. *Ps.* 4: 1.

The Lord is my light and my salvation;
whom shall I fear? *Ps.* 27: 1.

I sought the Lord, and he heard me. *Ps.*
34: 4.

Thou hast delivered my soul from death:
wilt not thou deliver my feet from falling? *Ps.*
56: 13.

That thy way may be known upon earth,
thy saving health among all nations. *Ps.* 67: 2.

Shew us thy mercy, O Lord, and grant us
thy salvation. *Ps.* 85: 7.

I was brought low, and he helped me. *Ps.*
116: 6.

How beautiful upon the mountains are the
feet of him . . . that publisheth salvation. *Is.*
52: 7.

It is good that a man should both hope
and quietly wait for the salvation of the Lord.
La. 3: 26.

O Daniel, servant of the living God, is thy
God, whom thou servest continually, able to
deliver thee from the lions? *Da.* 6: 20.

My God hath sent his angel, and hath shut
the lions' mouths. *Da.* 6: 22.

It shall come to pass, that whosoever shall
call on the name of the Lord shall be delivered. *Jo.* 2: 32.

Giving thanks unto the Father, . . . Who
hath delivered us from the power of darkness,
and hath translated us into the kingdom of his
dear Son. *Col.* 1: 12, 13.

See also

God, the Redeemer; God, Salvation of; God,
Security of.

God, Denial of

I know not the Lord. *Ex.* 5: 2.

Depart from us: and what can the Almighty
do for them? *Jb.* 22: 17.

Wherefore doth the wicked contemn God?
Ps. 10: 13.

The fool hath said in his heart, There is no
God. *Ps.* 53: 1.

Lest I be full, and deny thee, and say, Who
is the Lord? or lest I be poor, and steal, and
take the name of my God in vain. *Pr.* 30: 9.

They have belied the Lord, and said, It is
not he; neither shall evil come upon us;
neither shall we see sword nor famine. *Je.* 5:
12.

Wherefore should they say among the
people, Where is their God? *Jo.* 2: 17.

See also

Atheism; God, Antagonism to; God, Estrangement from; God, Rebellion against; God,
Rejection of; Godlessness.

God, Dominion of

The Lord shall reign for ever and ever. *Ex.* **15: 18.**

Behold, the heaven and the heaven of heavens is the Lord's thy God, the earth also, with all that therein is. *De.* **10: 14.**

The Lord our God will we serve, and his voice will we obey. *Jos.* **24: 24.**

I will sing of thy power. *Ps.* **59: 16.**

He ruleth by his power for ever. *Ps.* **66: 7.**

He shall have dominion also from sea to sea, and from the river unto the ends of the earth. *Ps.* **72: 8.**

His kingdom ruleth over all. *Ps.* **103: 19.**

Bless the Lord, all his works in all places of his dominion: bless the Lord, O my soul. *Ps.* **103: 22.**

Thy kingdom is an everlasting kingdom, and thy dominion endureth throughout all generations. *Ps.* **145: 13.**

Holy, holy, holy, is the Lord of hosts: the whole earth is full of his glory. *Is.* **6: 3.**

I have made the earth, the man, and the beast that are upon the ground, by my great power. *Je.* **27: 5.**

The kingdom of God is not in word, but in power. *1 Co.* **4: 20.**

Be strong in the Lord, and in the power of his might. *Ep.* **6: 10.**

Kept by the power of God. *1 Pe.* **1: 5.**

Now unto him that is able to keep you from falling, and to present you faultless before the presence of his glory with exceeding joy, To the only wise God our Saviour, be glory and majesty, dominion and power, both now and ever. *Jude* **1: 24, 25.**

The Lord God omnipotent reigneth. *Re.* **19: 6.**

See also

God, the King; God, Kingdom of; God, Majesty of; God, Omnipotence of; God, Overruling of; God, Power of; God, Sovereignty of; God, Supremacy of.

God, Estrangement from

He forsook God which made him, and lightly esteemed the Rock of his salvation. *De.* **32: 15.**

Solomon did evil in the sight of the Lord, and went not fully after the Lord. *1 K.* **11: 6.**

Satan went forth from the presence of the Lord. *Jb.* **1: 12.**

Thus saith the Lord, . . . I will contend with him that contendeth with thee. *Is.* **49: 25.**

We hid as it were our faces from him. *Is.* **53: 3.**

They are all estranged from me through their idols. *Eze.* **14: 5.**

Despisest thou the riches of his goodness and forbearance and longsuffering; not knowing that the goodness of God leadeth thee to repentance? *Ro.* **2: 4.**

You, that were sometime alienated and enemies in your mind by wicked works, yet now hath he reconciled. *Col.* **1: 21.**

Whosoever therefore will be a friend of the world is the enemy of God. *Ja.* **4: 4.**

See also

Atheism; God, Antagonism to; God, Denial of; God, Loss of; God, Rebellion against; God, Rejection of; Godlessness.

God, the Eternal

I lift up my hand to heaven, and say, I live for ever. *De.* **32: 40.**

Blessed be the Lord God of Israel for ever and ever. *1 Ch.* **16: 36.**

The Lord sitteth King for ever. *Ps.* **29: 10.**

This God is our God for ever and ever. *Ps.* **48: 14.**

His righteousness endureth for ever. *Ps.* **111: 3.**

As the mountains are round about Jerusalem, so the Lord is round about his people from henceforth even for ever. *Ps.* **125: 2.**

Thy name, O Lord, endureth for ever; and thy memorial, O Lord, throughout all generations. *Ps.* **135: 13.**

The Lord shall reign for ever, even thy God, O Zion, unto all generations. *Ps.* **146: 10.**

The everlasting Father. *Is.* **9: 6.**

In the Lord Jehovah is everlasting strength. *Is.* **26: 4.**

Thus saith the high and lofty One that inhabiteth eternity. *Is.* **57: 15.**

Unto him be glory in the church by Christ Jesus throughout all ages, world without end. *Ep.* **3: 21.**

Now unto the King eternal, immortal, invisible, the only wise God, be honour and glory for ever and ever. *1 Ti.* **1: 17.**

One day is with the Lord as a thousand years, and a thousand years as one day. *2 Pe.* **3: 8.**

See also

God, the Infinite; God, the Unchanging.

God, Evidence of

How long will this people provoke me? and how long will it be ere they believe me, for all the signs which I shewed among them? *Nu.* **14: 11.**

The Lord brought us forth out of Egypt with a mighty hand, and with an outstretched arm, and with great terribleness, and with signs, and with wonders. *De.* **26: 8.**

This sign shalt thou have of the Lord, that the Lord will do the thing that he hath spoken. *2 K.* **20: 9.**

God, . . . which doeth great things past finding out; yea, and wonders without number. *Jb.* **9: 2, 10.**

Thy testimonies are wonderful. *Ps.* **119: 129.**

How great are his signs! and how mighty are his wonders! *Da.* **4: 3.**

Blessed are the pure in heart: for they shall see God. *Mat.* **5: 8.**

If any man will do his will, he shall know of the doctrine, whether it be of God. *Jn.* **7: 17.**

We walk by faith, not by sight. *2 Co.* **5: 7.**

God also bearing them witness, both with signs and wonders, and with divers miracles, and gifts of the Holy Ghost. *He.* **2: 4.**

Now faith is the substance of things hoped for, the evidence of things not seen. *He.* **11: 1.**

Hereby we know that he abideth in us, by the Spirit which he hath given us. *1 Jn.* **3: 24.**

Believe not every spirit, but try the spirits whether they are of God. *1 Jn.* **4: 1.**

No man hath seen God at any time. If we love one another, God dwelleth in us. *1 Jn.* **4: 12.**

See also
God, Truth of; God, Witness of.

God, Existence of

God said unto Moses, I AM THAT I AM. *Ex.* 3: 14.

Thus shalt thou say unto the children of Israel, I AM hath sent me. *Ex.* 3: 14.

Thou hast beset me behind and before, and laid thine hand upon me. *Ps.* 139: 5.

God is in heaven, and thou upon earth: therefore let thy words be few. *Ec.* 5: 2.

Then shalt thou call, and the Lord shall answer; thou shalt cry, and he shall say, Here I am. *Is.* 58: 9.

I am the Lord, I change not. *Mal.* 3: 6.

Whether we live, we live unto the Lord; and whether we die, we die unto the Lord: whether we live therefore, or die, we are the Lord's. *Ro.* 14: 8.

He that cometh to God must believe that he is, and that he is the rewarder of them that diligently seek him. *He.* 11: 6.

Grace be unto you, and peace, from him which is, and which was, and which is to come. *Re.* 1: 4.

See also
God, Evidence of; God, Immanence of; God, the Living; God, Presence of.

God, Eye of

That thine eyes may be open toward this house night and day. *1 K.* 8: 29.

The eyes of the Lord run to and fro throughout the whole earth. *2 Ch.* 16: 9.

His eye seeth every precious thing. *Jb.* 28: 10.

Let the words of my mouth, and the meditation of my heart, be acceptable in thy sight, O Lord, my strength, and my redeemer. *Ps.* 19: 14.

Behold, the eye of the Lord is upon them that fear him. *Ps.* 33: 18.

The eyes of the Lord are upon the righteous. *Ps.* 34: 15.

He that planted the ear, shall he not hear? he that formed the eye, shall he not see? *Ps.* 94: 9.

The eyes of the Lord are in every place, beholding the evil and the good. *Pr.* 15: 3.

See also
God, Knowledge of; God, Omnipresence of; God, Omniscience of; God, Vision of.

God, Face of

I have seen God face to face, and my life is preserved. *Ge.* 32: 30.

The Lord spake unto Moses, face to face, as a man speaketh unto his friend. *Ex.* 33: 11.

The Lord make his face shine upon thee, and be gracious unto thee. *Nu.* 6: 25.

The Lord make his face shine upon thee, and give thee peace. *Nu.* 6: 26.

The Lord talked with you face to face in the mount out of the midst of the fire. *De.* 5: 4.

Entreat now the face of the Lord thy God, and pray for me. *1 K.* 13: 6.

Seek the Lord and his strength, seek his face continually. *1 Ch.* 16: 11.

The Lord your God . . . will not turn away his face from you, if ye return unto him. *2 Ch.* 30: 9.

When thou saidst, Seek ye my face; my heart said unto thee, Thy face, Lord, will I seek. *Ps.* 27: 8.

The face of the Lord is against them that do evil. *Ps.* 34: 16.

God be merciful unto us, and bless us; and cause his face to shine upon us. *Ps.* 67: 1.

Mercy and truth shall go before thy face. *Ps.* 89: 14.

They shall walk, O Lord, in the light of thy countenance. *Ps.* 89: 15.

Thou hast set . . . our secret sins in the light of thy countenance. *Ps.* 90: 8.

Put away the evil of your doings from before mine eyes. *Is.* 1: 16.

Thine eyes shall see the king in his beauty. *Is.* 33: 17.

In heaven their angels do always behold the face of my Father. *Mat.* 18: 10.

Thy heart is not right in the sight of God. *Ac.* 8: 21.

They shall see his face; and his name shall be in their foreheads. *Re.* 22: 4.

See also
God, Revelation of; God, Vision of.

God, Fairness of

Manoah said unto his wife, We shall surely die, because we have seen God. But his wife said unto him, If the Lord were pleased to kill us, he would not have received a burnt offering . . . at our hands. *Ju.* 13: 22, 23.

There is no iniquity with the Lord our God, nor respect of persons, nor taking of gifts. *2 Ch.* 19: 7.

Let me be weighed in an even balance. *Jb.* 31: 6.

Thy word is true from the beginning: and every one of thy righteous judgments endureth for ever. *Ps.* 119: 160.

All the ways of a man are clean in his own eyes; but the Lord weigheth the spirits. *Pr.* 16: 2.

The rich and poor meet together: the Lord is the maker of them all. *Pr.* 22: 2.

They shall all know me, from the least of them unto the greatest of them, saith the Lord. *Je.* 31: 34.

Are not my ways equal? are not your ways unequal? *Eze.* 18: 29.

Also upon the servants and upon the handmaids in those days will I pour out my spirit. *Jo.* 2: 29.

Thy money perish with thee, because thou hast thought that the gift of God may be purchased with money. *Ac.* 8: 20.

Just and true are thy ways, thou King of saints. *Re.* 15: 3.

See also
God, Impartiality of; God, the Judge; God, Righteousness of.

God, Faith in

How long will this people provoke me? and how long will it be ere they believe me? *Nu.* 14: 11.

Our fathers trusted in thee: they trusted, and thou didst deliver them. *Ps.* 22: 4.

The children of men put their trust under the shadow of thy wings. *Ps.* 36: 7.

Trust in the Lord, and do good; so shalt thou dwell in the land, and verily thou shalt be fed. *Ps.* **37: 3.**

Blessed is that man that maketh the Lord his trust. *Ps.* **40: 4.**

Whoso trusteth in the Lord, happy is he. *Pr.* **16: 20.**

So Daniel was taken up out of the den, and no manner of hurt was found upon him. *Da.* **6: 23.**

When they deliver you up, take no thought how or what ye shall speak: for it shall be given you in that same hour what ye shall speak. *Mat.* **10: 19.**

Jesus answering saith unto them, Have faith in God. *Mk.* **11: 22.**

I have not found so great faith, no, not in Israel. *Lu.* **7: 9.**

He . . . rejoiced, believing in God with all his house. *Ac.* **16: 34.**

Without faith it is impossible to please him. *He.* **11: 6.**

He went out, not knowing whither he went. *He.* **11: 8.**

See also

God, Belief in; God, Certainty of; God, Confidence in; God, Reliance on; God, Trust in.

God, Faithfulness of

Know therefore that the Lord thy God, he is God, the faithful God, which keepeth covenant and mercy with them that love him and keep his commandments to a thousand generations. *De.* **7: 9.**

Yea, he loved the people; all his saints are in thy hand: and they sat down at thy feet; every one shall receive of thy words. *De.* **33: 3.**

There hath not failed one word of all his good promise. *1 K.* **8: 56.**

Thy faithfulness reacheth unto the clouds. *Ps.* **36: 5.**

I have declared thy faithfulness and thy salvation. *Ps.* **40: 10.**

O Lord God of hosts, who is a strong Lord like unto thee? or to thy faithfulness round about thee? *Ps.* **89: 8.**

The mercy of the Lord is from everlasting to everlasting upon them that fear him. *Ps.* **103: 17.**

Thy faithfulness is unto all generations. *Ps.* **119: 90.**

If thy children will keep my covenant and my testimony that I shall teach them, their children shall also sit upon thy throne for evermore. *Ps.* **132: 12.**

Thy counsels of old are faithfulness and truth. *Is.* **25: 1.**

The Lord is the true God. *Je.* **10: 10.**

This is life eternal, that they might know thee the only true God. *Jn.* **17: 3.**

God is faithful, by whom ye were called. *1 Co.* **1: 9.**

God is faithful, who will not suffer you to be tempted above that ye are able. *1 Co.* **10: 13.**

The Lord is faithful, who shall stablish you, and keep you from evil. *2 Th.* **3: 3.**

That by two immutable things, in which it was impossible for God to lie, we might have a strong consolation. *He.* **6: 18.**

He is faithful that promised. *He.* **10: 23.**

A faithful Creator. *1 Pe.* **4: 19.**

He is faithful and just to forgive us our sins. *1 Jn.* **1: 9.**

Just and true are thy ways, thou King of Saints. *Re.* **15: 3.**

See also

God, Care of; God, Confidence in; God, Goodness of; God, the Keeper; God, Reliance on; God, Righteousness of; God, Security of; God, the Shepherd; God, Solicitude of; God, the Sustainer.

God, Fatherhood of

A father of the fatherless, and a judge of the widows, is God in his holy habitation. *Ps.* **68: 5.**

Like as a father pitieth his children, so the Lord pitieth them that fear him. For . . . he remembereth that we are dust. *Ps.* **103: 13, 14.**

Now, O Lord, thou art our father; we are the clay, and thou our potter; and we all are the work of thy hand. *Is.* **64: 8.**

Have we not all one father? *Mal.* **2: 10.**

Be ye therefore perfect, even as your Father which is in heaven is perfect. *Mat.* **5: 48.**

Your Father knoweth what things ye have need of, before ye ask him. *Mat.* **6: 8.**

Our Father which art in heaven. *Mat.* **6: 9.**

Not every one that saith unto me, Lord, Lord, shall enter into the kingdom of heaven; but he that doeth the will of my Father which is in heaven. *Mat.* **7: 21.**

Are not two sparrows sold for a farthing? and one of them shall not fall on the ground without your Father. *Mat.* **10: 29.**

No man knoweth the Son, but the Father. *Mat.* **11: 27.**

It is not the will of your Father which is in heaven, that one of these little ones should perish. *Mat.* **18: 14.**

Wist ye not that I must be about my Father's business? *Lu.* **2: 49.**

No man knoweth who . . . the Father is, but the Son, and he to whom the Son will reveal him. *Lu.* **10: 22.**

When ye pray, say, Our Father. *Lu.* **11: 2.**

The Father loveth the Son, and hath given all things into his hand. *Jn.* **3: 35.**

The hour cometh, and now is, when the true worshippers shall worship the Father in spirit and in truth: for the Father seeketh such to worship him. *Jn.* **4: 23.**

My Father worketh hitherto, and I work. *Jn.* **5: 17.**

No man can come to me, except the Father which hath sent me draw him. *Jn.* **6: 44.**

Not that any man hath seen the Father, save he which is of God, he hath seen the Father. *Jn.* **6: 46.**

No man cometh unto the Father, but by me. *Jn.* **14: 6.**

Lord, shew us the Father, and it sufficeth us. *Jn.* **14: 8.**

He that hath seen me hath seen the Father. *Jn.* **14: 9.**

Believe me that I am in the Father, and the Father in me. *Jn.* **14: 11.**

My Father is greater than I. *Jn.* **14: 28.**

I am the true vine, and my Father is the husbandman. *Jn.* **15: 1.**

That ye may with one mind and one mouth glorify God, even the Father of our Lord Jesus Christ. *Ro.* **15: 6.**

To us there is but one God, the Father, of whom are all things, and we in him. *1 Co.* **8: 6.**

For this cause I bow my knees unto the Father of our Lord Jesus Christ. *Ep.* **3: 14.**

One God and Father of all, who is above all, and through all, and in you all. *Ep.* **4: 6.**

I will be to him a Father, and he shall be to me a Son. *He.* **1: 5.**

Every good gift and every perfect gift is from above, and cometh down from the Father of lights. *Ja.* **1: 17.**

Our fellowship is with the Father. *1 Jn.* **1: 3.**

God, Favor of

Wherefore have I not found favour in thy sight? *Nu.* **11: 11.**

Be favourable unto them for our sakes. *Ju.* **21: 22.**

Thou hast granted me life and favour, and thy visitation hath preserved my spirit. *Jb.* **10: 12.**

Thou, Lord, wilt bless the righteous; with favour wilt thou compass him as with a shield. *Ps.* **5: 12.**

Will the Lord cast off for ever? and will he be favourable no more? *Ps.* **77: 7.**

Remember me, O Lord, with the favour that thou bearest unto thy people. *Ps.* **106: 4.**

His tender mercies are over all his works. *Ps.* **145: 9.**

When a man's ways please the Lord, he maketh even his enemies to be at peace with him. *Pr.* **16: 7.**

In my favour have I had mercy on thee. *Is.* **60: 10.**

I have caused thine iniquity to pass from thee, and I will clothe thee with change of raiment. *Zch.* **3: 4.**

Hail, thou that art highly favoured, the Lord is with thee. *Lu.* **1: 28.**

The angel said unto her, Fear not, Mary: for thou hast found favor with God. *Lu.* **1: 30.**

They that are in the flesh cannot please God. *Ro.* **8: 8.**

It is not of him that willeth, nor of him that runneth, but of God that sheweth mercy. *Ro.* **9: 16.**

See also

God, Beneficence of; God, Goodness of; God, Grace of; God, Kindness of; God, Mercy of; God, Providence of.

God, Fear of

The fear of the Lord is clean, enduring for ever. *Ps.* **19: 9.**

The fear of the Lord is the beginning of wisdom. *Ps.* **111: 10.**

The fear of the Lord is the beginning of knowledge: but fools despise wisdom and instruction. *Pr.* **1: 7.**

If thou seekest her as silver, and searchest for her as for hid treasures; Then shalt thou understand the fear of the Lord. *Pr.* **2: 4, 5.**

The fear of the Lord is a fountain of life, to depart from the snares of death. *Pr.* **14: 27.**

Be thou in the fear of the Lord all the day long. *Pr.* **23: 17.**

Let us hear the conclusion of the whole matter: Fear God, and keep his command-ments: for this is the whole duty of man. *Ec.* **12: 13.**

I fear the Lord, the God of heaven, which hath made the sea and the dry land. *Jon.* **1: 9.**

Fear God. *1 Pe.* **2: 17.**

God, Fellowship with

Moses drew near unto the thick darkness where God was. *Ex.* **20: 21.**

I will commune with thee from above the mercy seat. *Ex.* **25: 22.**

The cloudy pillar descended, and stood at the door of the tabernacle, and the Lord talked with Moses. *Ex.* **33: 9.**

The Lord your God is he that goeth with you, to fight for you against your enemies, to save you. *De.* **20: 4.**

I will not fail thee, nor forsake thee. *Jos.* **1: 5.**

The Lord is with thee, thou mighty man of valour. *Ju.* **6: 12.**

He walked with me in peace and equity and did turn many away from iniquity. *Mal* **2: 6.**

As thou, Father, art in me, and I in thee, that they also may be one in us. *Jn.* **17: 21.**

What agreement hath the temple of God with idols? *2 Co.* **6: 16.**

Ye are no more strangers and foreigners, but fellowcitizens with the saints, and of the household of God. *Ep.* **2: 19.**

The fellowship of the mystery, which from the beginning of the world hath been hid in God. *Ep.* **3: 9.**

Truly our fellowship is with the Father, and with his Son Jesus Christ. *1 Jn.* **1: 3.**

They shall walk with me in white: for they are worthy. *Re.* **3: 4.**

See also

God, Communion with; God, Companion-ship of; God, Cooperation of; God, Life in; God, Partnership with.

God, Finding

If thou seek him, he will be found of thee. *1 Ch.* **28: 9.**

Canst thou by searching find out God? canst thou find out the Almighty unto perfection? It is as high as heaven; what canst thou do? deeper than hell; what canst thou know? *Jb.* **11: 7, 8.**

Oh that I knew where I might find him! *Jb.* **23: 3.**

There is no searching of his understanding. *Is.* **40: 28.**

Ye shall seek me, and find me, when ye shall search for me with all your heart. *Je.* **29: 13.**

If haply they might feel after him, and find him, though he be not far from every one of us. *Ac.* **17: 27.**

He is the rewarder of them that diligently seek him. *He.* **11: 6.**

See also

God, Access to; God, Quest for; God, Search for.

God, Fire of

The God that answereth by fire, let him be God. *1 K.* **18: 24.**

The mountain was full of horses and char-iots of fire round about Elisha. *2 K.* **6: 17.**

The light of Israel shall be for a fire, and his Holy One for a flame. *Is.* 10: 17.

I, saith the Lord, will be unto her a wall of fire round about. *Zch.* 2: 5.

Who maketh his angels spirits, and his ministers a flame of fire. *He.* 1: 7.

Our God is a consuming fire. *He.* 12: 29.

See also

God, the Light; God, Spirit of.

God, Foolishness of

Hath not God made foolish the wisdom of this world? *1 Co.* 1: 20.

After that in the wisdom of God the world by wisdom knew not God, it pleased God by the foolishness of preaching to save them that believe. *1 Co.* 1: 21.

We preach Christ crucified, unto the Jews a stumblingblock, and unto the Greeks foolishness. *1 Co.* 1: 23.

The foolishness of God is wiser than men. *1 Co.* 1: 25.

The wisdom of this world is foolishness with God. *1 Co.* 3: 19.

We are fools for Christ's sake. *1 Co.* 4: 10.

God, Foreknowledge of

Thine eyes did see my substance, yet being unperfect; and in thy book all my members were written, which in continuance were fashioned, when as yet there was none of them. *Ps.* 139: 16.

Your Father knoweth what things ye have need of, before ye ask him. *Mat.* 6: 8.

Thou lovedst me before the foundation of the world. *Jn.* 17: 24.

Him, being delivered by the determinate counsel and foreknowledge of God, ye have taken, and by wicked hands have crucified and slain. *Ac.* 2: 23.

Whom he did foreknow, he also did predestinate to be conformed to the image of his Son. *Ro.* 8: 29.

God hath not cast away his people which he foreknew. *Ro.* 11: 2.

Elect according to the foreknowledge of God the Father. *1 Pe.* 1: 2.

Christ . . . was foreordained before the foundation of the world, but was manifest in these last times for you. *1 Pe.* 1: 19, 20.

See also

God, Omniscience of; God, Wisdom of.

God, Forgetfulness of

Beware lest thou forget the Lord. *De.* 6: 12.

Of the Rock that begat thee thou art unmindful, and hast forgotten God that formed thee. *De.* 32: 18.

He hath said in his heart, God hath forgotten: he hideth his face; he will never see it. *Ps.* 10: 11.

If we have forgotten the name of our God, or stretched out our hands to a strange god; Shall not God search this out? *Ps.* 44: 20, 21.

Hath God forgotten to be gracious? *Ps.* 77: 9.

Thou hast forgotten the God of thy salvation, and hast not been mindful of the rock of thy strength. *Is.* 17: 10.

She went after her lovers, and forgat me, saith the Lord. *Ho.* 2: 13.

Israel slideth back as a backsliding heifer. *Ho.* 4: 16.

Your goodness is as a morning cloud, and as the early dew it goeth away. *Ho.* 6: 4.

Israel hath forgotten his Maker, and buildeth temples. *Ho.* 8: 14.

My people are bent to backsliding from me. *Ho.* 11: 7.

They were filled, and their heart was exalted; therefore have they forgotten me. *Ho.* 13: 6.

See also

God, Denial of; God, Rejection of; Godlessness.

God, Forgiveness of

Hear thou in heaven thy dwelling place: and when thou hearest, forgive. *1 K.* 8: 30.

Thou art a God ready to pardon, gracious and merciful. *Ne.* 9: 17.

For thy name's sake, O Lord, pardon mine iniquity; for it is great. *Ps.* 25: 11.

O remember not against us former iniquities. *Ps.* 79: 8.

Thou hast forgiven the iniquity of thy people, thou hast covered all their sin. *Ps.* 85: 2.

Thou, Lord, art good, and ready to forgive; and plenteous in mercy unto all them that call upon thee. *Ps.* 86: 5.

Who forgiveth all thine iniquities; who healeth all thy diseases. *Ps.* 103: 3.

But there is forgiveness with thee, that thou mayest be feared. *Ps.* 130: 4.

Though your sins be as scarlet, they shall be as white as snow; though they be red like crimson, they shall be as wool. *Is.* 1: 18.

I have blotted out, as a thick cloud, thy transgressions, and, as a cloud, thy sins. *Is.* 44: 22.

Let the wicked forsake his way, and the unrighteous man his thoughts: and let him return unto the Lord, and he will have mercy upon him; and to our God, for he will abundantly pardon. *Is.* 55: 7.

I will forgive their iniquity, and I will remember their sin no more. *Je.* 31: 34.

I will pardon all their iniquities. *Je.* 33: 8.

The Lord will not cast off for ever. *La.* 3: 31.

To the Lord our God belong mercies and forgivenesses. *Da.* 9: 9.

I will heal their backsliding, I will love them freely. *Ho.* 14: 4.

And I will restore to you the years that the locust hath eaten. *Jo.* 2: 25.

Who is a God like unto thee, that pardoneth iniquity, and passeth by the transgression of the remnant of his heritage? he retaineth not his anger for ever, because he delighteth in mercy. *Mi.* 7: 18.

God be merciful to me a sinner. *Lu.* 18: 13.

Forgiving one another, even as God for Christ's sake hath forgiven you. *Ep.* 4: 32.

See also

God, Compassion of; God, Mercy of.

God, the Friend

Enoch walked with God. *Ge.* 5: 22.

The Lord is nigh unto all them that call upon him. *Ps.* 145: 18.

Abraham my friend. *Is.* 41: 8.

I am not alone. *Jn.* 8: 16.

He was called the Friend of God. *Ja.* 2: 23.

See also
God, Communion with; God, Companionship of; God, Fellowship with; God, Love of; God, Partnership with.

God, Fulness of

The voice of the Lord is full of majesty. *Ps.* 29: 4.

The earth is full of the goodness of the Lord. *Ps.* 33: 5.

Thy right hand is full of righteousness. *Ps.* 48: 10.

The world is mine, and the fulness thereof. *Ps.* 50: 12.

The Lord is . . . plenteous in mercy. *Ps.* 103: 8.

The trees of the Lord are full of sap. *Ps.* 104: 16.

The earth, O Lord, is full of thy mercy. *Ps.* 119: 64.

With him is plenteous redemption. *Ps.* 130: 7.

The whole earth is full of his glory. *Is.* 6: 3.

Truly I am full of power by the spirit of the Lord. *Mi.* 3: 8.

That ye might be filled with all the fulness of God. *Ep.* 3: 19.

That ye may stand perfect and complete in all the will of God. *Col.* 4: 12.

According to his abundant mercy. *1 Pe.* 1: 3.

See also
God, Perfection of; God, Riches of; God, Sufficiency of; God, Wealth of.

God, Generosity of

Blessed be the Lord, who daily loadeth us with benefits. *Ps.* 68: 19.

The Lord will feed them as a lamb in a large place. *Ho.* 4: 16.

If God so clothe the grass of the field, . . . shall he not much more clothe you, O ye of little faith? *Mat.* 6: 30.

If ye then, being evil, know how to give good gifts unto your children, how much more shall your Father? *Mat.* 7: 11.

God giveth not the Spirit by measure. *Jn.* 3: 34.

He that spared not his own Son, but delivered him up for us all, how shall he not with him also freely give us all things? *Ro.* 8: 32.

Trust . . . in the living God, who giveth us richly all things to enjoy. *1 Ti.* 6: 17.

If the blood of bulls and of goats, . . . How much more shall the blood of Christ? *He.* 9: 13, 14.

If any of you lack wisdom, let him ask of God, that giveth to all men liberally, and upbraideth not. *Ja.* 1: 5.

See also
God, Beneficence of; God, Favor of; God, Gift of; God, Goodness of; God, Grace of; God, Kindness of; God, Providence of.

God, Gentleness of

The Lord deal kindly with you. *Ru.* 1: 8.

Thy gentleness hath made me great. *Ps.* 18: 35.

Remember, O Lord, thy tender mercies and thy lovingkindnesses; for they have been ever of old. *Ps.* 25: 6.

Yet the Lord will command his lovingkindness in the daytime. *Ps.* 42: 8.

He shall come down like rain upon the mown grass: as showers that water the earth. *Ps.* 72: 6.

The mercy of the Lord is from everlasting to everlasting upon them that fear him. *Ps.* 103: 17.

The Lord is good to all: and his tender mercies are over all his works. *Ps.* 145: 9.

Behold, the Lord God will come with strong hand, . . . he shall gather the lambs with his arm. *Is.* 40: 10, 11.

The Lord is very pitiful, and of tender mercy. *Ja.* 5: 11.

See also
God, Comfort of; God, Compassion of; God, Kindness of; God, Mercy of; God, Solicitude of; God, Sympathy of.

God, Gift of

When he giveth quietness, who then can make trouble? *Jb.* 34: 29.

Delight thyself also in the Lord; and he shall give thee the desires of thine heart. *Ps.* 37: 4.

The earth hath he given to the children of men. *Ps.* 115: 16.

He giveth his beloved sleep. *Ps.* 127: 2.

Give us day by day our daily bread. *Lu.* 11: 3.

If thou knewest the gift of God, and who it is that saith to thee, Give me to drink; thou wouldest have asked of him, and he would have given thee living water. *Jn.* 4: 10.

He giveth to all life, and breath, and all things. *Ac.* 17: 25.

God hath given thee all them that sail with thee. *Ac.* 27: 24.

I long to see you, that I may impart unto you some spiritual gift. *Ro.* 1: 11.

Not as the offence, so also is the free gift. *Ro.* 5: 15.

The gift of God is eternal life through Jesus Christ our Lord. *Ro.* 6: 23.

Desire spiritual gifts. *1 Co.* 14: 1.

By grace are ye saved through faith; and that not of yourselves: it is the gift of God. *Ep.* 2. 8.

God hath not given us the spirit of fear; but of power, and of love, and of a sound mind. *2 Ti.* 1: 7.

Every good gift and every perfect gift is from above, and cometh down from the Father of lights, with whom is no variableness, neither shadow of turning. *Ja.* 1: 17.

He hath given us of his Spirit. *1 Jn.* 4: 13.

To him that overcometh will I give to eat of the tree of life. *Re.* 2: 7.

See also
God, Beneficence of; God, Favor of; God, Generosity of; God, Goodness of; God, Grace of; God, Kindness of; God, Providence of.

God, Glory of

Who is able to stand before this holy Lord God? *1 S.* 6: 20.

I will call on the Lord, who is worthy to be praised. *2 S.* 22: 4.

The heavens declare the glory of God. *Ps.* 19: 1.

Lift up your heads, O ye gates; . . . and the King of glory shall come in. *Ps.* 24: 7.

Extol him that rideth upon the heavens. *Ps.* 68: 4.

Blessed be his glorious name for ever. *Ps.* 72: 19.

Exalt the Lord our God, and worship at his holy hill. *Ps.* 99: 9.

O Lord my God, thou art very great; thou art clothed with honour and majesty. *Ps.* 104: 1.

I will extol thee, my God, O king. *Ps.* 145: 1.

To make known to the sons of men his mighty acts, and the glorious majesty of his kingdom. *Ps.* 145: 12.

Holy, holy, holy, is the Lord of hosts: the whole earth is full of his glory. *Is.* 6: 3.

I dwell in the high and holy place. *Is.* 57: 15.

The Lord shall be unto thee an everlasting light, and thy God thy glory. *Is.* 60: 19.

The everlasting mountains were scattered, the perpetual hills did bow: his ways are everlasting. *Hab.* 3: 6.

I will fill this house with glory, saith the Lord of hosts. *Hag.* 2: 7.

Glory to God in the highest. *Lu.* 2: 14.

Now unto him that is able to do exceeding abundantly above all that we ask or think, . . . Unto him be glory. *Ep.* 3: 20, 21.

Blessing and honour, and glory, and power, be unto him that sitteth upon the throne. *Re.* 5: 13.

Let us be glad and rejoice, and give honour to him. *Re.* 19: 7.

See also

God, Greatness of; God, Majesty of; God, Power of; God, Sovereignty of; God, Strength of; God, Supremacy of.

God, Goodness of

I will make all my goodness pass before thee. *Ex.* 33: 19.

Shall mortal man be more just than God? shall a man be more pure than his maker? *Jb.* 4: 17.

Thou art not a God that hath pleasure in wickedness. *Ps.* 5: 4.

He shall give thee the desires of thine heart. *Ps.* 37: 4.

Thy right hand is full of righteousness. *Ps.* 48: 10.

The goodness of God endureth continually. *Ps.* 52: 1.

Who crowneth thee with lovingkindness and tender mercies. *Ps.* 103: 4.

For the mountains shall depart, and the hills be removed; but my kindness shall not depart from thee. *Is.* 54: 10.

The Lord is good, a strong hold in the day of trouble; and he knoweth them that trust in him. *Na.* 1: 7.

If ye then, being evil, know how to give good gifts unto your children, how much more shall your Father which is in heaven give good things to them that ask him? *Mat.* 7: 11.

What shall I do? I will send my beloved son: it may be they will reverence him when they see him. *Lu.* 20: 13.

He that spared not his own Son, but delivered him up for us all, how shall he not with him also freely give us all things? *Ro.* 8: 32.

See also

God, Beneficence of; God, Favor of; God, Generosity of; God, Gift of; God, Grace of;

God, Holiness of; God, Kindness of; God, Providence of; God, Righteousness of.

God, Grace of

The Lord make his face to shine upon thee: and be gracious unto thee. *Nu.* 6: 25.

I have given you a land for which ye did not labour, and cities which ye built not, and ye dwell in them; of the vineyards and olive-yards which ye planted not do ye eat. *Jos.* 24: 13.

Thou preventest him with the blessings of goodness. *Ps.* 21: 3.

Hath God forgotten to be gracious? *Ps.* 77: 9.

The Lord will give grace and glory. *Ps.* 84: 11.

If we follow on to know the Lord: his going forth is prepared as the morning. *Ho.* 6: 3.

I will be as the dew unto Israel. *Ho.* 14: 5.

I knew that thou art a gracious God, and merciful. *Jon.* 4: 2.

Justified freely by his grace through the redemption that is in Christ Jesus. *Ro.* 3: 24.

The grace of God . . . is given you by Jesus Christ. *1 Co.* 1: 4.

By the grace of God I am what I am: and his grace which was bestowed upon me was not in vain; but I laboured more abundantly than they all: yet not I, but the grace of God which was with me. *1 Co.* 15: 10.

Not with fleshly wisdom, but by the grace of God. *2 Co.* 1: 12.

The exceeding riches of his grace. *Ep.* 2: 7.

The grace of God . . . bringeth salvation. *Tit.* 2: 11.

Let us therefore come boldly unto the throne of grace, that we may obtain mercy, and find grace to help in time of need. *He.* 4: 16.

See also

God, Beauty of; God, Beneficence of; God, Favor of; God, Kindness of; God, Mercy of.

God, Gratitude to

Do ye thus requite the Lord? *De.* 32: 6.

His praise shall continually be in my mouth. *Ps.* 34: 1.

Blessed are they that dwell in thy house: they will be still praising thee. *Ps.* 84: 4.

Enter into his gates with thanksgiving. *Ps.* 100: 4.

I will offer to thee the sacrifice of thanksgiving. *Ps.* 116: 17.

Praise ye the Lord. Praise the Lord, O my soul. While I live will I praise the Lord: I will sing praises unto my God while I have any being. *Ps.* 146: 1, 2.

I thank thee, O Father, Lord of heaven and earth, because thou hast hid these things from the wise and prudent, and hast revealed them unto babes. *Mat.* 11: 25.

He thanked God, and took courage. *Ac.* 28: 15.

By the grace of God I am what I am. *1 Co.* 15: 10.

We give thanks to God and the Father of our Lord Jesus Christ. *Col.* 1: 3.

See also

God, Praise to; God, Thankfulness to.

God, Greatness of

Behold, the Lord our God hath shewed us his glory and his greatness. *De.* 5: 24.

Ascribe ye greatness unto our God. *De.* 32: 3.

Thou shalt increase my greatness, and comfort me on every side. *Ps.* 71: 21.

Great is the Lord, and greatly to be praised; and his greatness is unsearchable. *Ps.* 145: 3.

I will declare thy greatness. *Ps.* 145: 6.

He healeth the broken in heart. . . . He telleth the number of the stars. *Ps.* 147: 3, 4.

Praise him according to his excellent greatness. *Ps.* 150: 2.

I form the light, and create darkness: I make peace, and create evil: I the Lord do all these things. *Is.* 45: 7.

God, who commanded the light to shine out of darkness, hath shined in our hearts. 2 *Co.* 4: 6.

The exceeding greatness of his power to us-ward who believe. *Ep.* 1: 19.

See also

God, Glory of; God, Majesty of; God, Power of; God, Sovereignty of; God, Strength of; God, Supremacy of.

God, Guidance of

Thou in thy mercy hast led forth the people which thou hast redeemed. *Ex.* 15: 13.

He maketh me to lie down in green pastures: he leadeth me beside the still waters. *Ps.* 23: 2.

The steps of a good man are ordered by the Lord. *Ps.* 37: 23.

He will be our guide even unto death. *Ps.* 48: 14.

Lead me to the rock that is higher than I. *Ps.* 61: 2.

He rebuked the Red sea also, and it was dried up: so he led them through the depths, as through the wilderness. *Ps.* 106: 9.

He led them forth by the right way, that they might go to a city of habitation. *Ps.* 107: 7.

If I take the wings of the morning, and dwell in the uttermost parts of the sea; Even there shall thy hand lead me. *Ps.* 139: 9, 10.

Lead me in the way everlasting. *Ps.* 139: 24.

I will bring the blind by a way that they knew not; I will lead them in paths that they have not known. *Is.* 42: 16.

I girded thee, though thou hast not known me. *Is.* 45: 5.

He that hath mercy on them shall lead them, even by the springs of water shall he guide them. *Is.* 49: 10.

The Lord shall guide thee continually, and satisfy thy soul in drought. *Is.* 58: 11.

My father, thou art the guide of my youth. *Je.* 3: 4.

Lead us not into temptation. *Mat.* 6: 13.

The dayspring from on high hath visited us, . . . to guide our feet into the way of peace. *Lu.* 1: 78, 79.

The Lord direct your hearts into the love of God, and into the patient waiting for Christ. 2 *Th.* 3: 5.

See also

God, Hand of; God, Leadership of; God, Way of.

God, Hand of

The hand of God was very heavy there. *1 S.* 5: 11.

The hand of our God is upon all them for good that seek him. *Ezr.* 8: 22.

In whose hand is the soul of every living thing, and the breath of all mankind. *Jb.* 12: 10.

Into thine hand I commit my spirit. *Ps.* 31: 5.

In the hand of the Lord there is a cup, and the wine is red. *Ps.* 75: 8.

Strong is thy hand, and high is thy right hand. *Ps.* 89: 13.

His hands formed the dry land. *Ps.* 95: 5.

His right hand, and his holy arm, hath gotten him the victory. *Ps.* 98: 1.

Thou openest thine hand, they are filled with good. *Ps.* 104: 28.

He toucheth the hills, and they smoke. *Ps.* 104: 32.

The Lord will perfect that which concerneth me: thy mercy, O Lord, endureth for ever: forsake not the works of thine own hands. *Ps.* 138: 8.

If I take the wings of the morning, . . . Even there shall thy hand lead me, and thy right hand shall hold me. *Ps.* 139: 9, 10.

I, even my hands, have stretched out the heavens. *Is.* 45: 12.

I have covered thee in the shadow of mine hand. *Is.* 51: 16.

The Lord's hand is not shortened, that it cannot save. *Is.* 59: 1.

We are the clay, and thou our potter; and we are all the work of thy hand. *Is.* 64: 8.

The hand of the Lord was with him. *Lu.* 1: 66.

Father, into thy hands I commend my spirit. *Lu.* 23: 46.

It is a fearful thing to fall into the hands of the living God. *He.* 10: 31.

Humble yourselves therefore under the mighty hand of God. *1 Pe.* 5: 6.

See also

God, Guidance of; God, Help of; God, Leadership of; God, Protection of; God, Work of.

God, the Healer

I am the Lord that healeth thee. *Ex.* 15: 26.

I kill, and I make alive; I wound, and I heal. *De.* 32: 39.

He healeth the broken in heart, and bindeth up their wounds. *Ps.* 147: 3.

I will heal your backslidings. *Je.* 3: 22.

I am with thee, saith the Lord, to save thee. *Je.* 30: 11.

I will cure them, and will reveal unto them the abundance of peace and truth. *Je.* 33: 6.

Come, and let us return unto the Lord: for he hath torn, and he will heal us. *Ho.* 6: 1.

Unto you that fear my name shall the Sun of righteousness arise with healing in his wings. *Mal.* 4: 2.

God, Help of

The eternal God is thy refuge, and underneath are the everlasting arms. *De.* 33: 27.

Hitherto hath the Lord helped us. *1 S.* 7: 12.

Thou art the helper of the fatherless. *Ps.* 10: 14.

Help, Lord; for the godly man ceaseth. *Ps.* 12: 1.

The Lord . . . Send thee help from the sanctuary. *Ps.* 20: 1, 2.

Thou hast been my help. *Ps.* 27: 9.

I shall yet praise him for the help of his countenance. *Ps.* 42: 5.

He will not suffer thy foot to be moved: he that keepeth thee will not slumber. *Ps.* 121: 3.

Our help is in the name of the Lord. *Ps.* 124: 8.

The way of the righteous is made plain. *Pr.* 15: 19.

Fear not; I will help thee. *Is.* 41: 13.

These things will I do unto them, and not forsake them. *Is.* 42: 16.

O Israel, thou hast destroyed thyself; but in me is thine help. *Ho.* 13: 9.

Let us therefore come boldly unto the throne of grace, that we may obtain mercy, and find grace to help in time of need. *He.* 4: 16.

See also

God, Care of; God, Guidance of; God, Hand of; God, Protection of; God, Providence of; God, Work of.

God, the Hiding

He called unto Moses out of the midst of the cloud. *Ex.* 24: 16.

Wherefore hidest thou thy face, and holdest me for thine enemy? *Jb.* 13: 24.

Behold, I go forward, but he is not there; and backward, but I cannot perceive him: On the left hand, where he doth work, but I cannot behold him: he hideth himself on the right hand, that I cannot see him. *Jb.* 23: 8, 9.

Lo, these are parts of his ways: but how little a portion is heard of him? *Jb.* 26: 14.

When he hideth his face, who then can behold him? *Jb.* 34: 29.

Why standest thou afar off, O Lord? why hidest thou thyself in times of trouble? *Ps.* 10: 1.

He hath said in his heart, God hath forgotten: he hideth his face; he will never see it. *Ps.* 10: 11.

How long wilt thou hide thy face from me? *Ps.* 13: 1.

He made darkness his secret place; his pavilion round about him were dark waters and thick clouds of the skies. *Ps.* 18: 11.

Hide not thy face far from me. *Ps.* 27: 9.

Clouds and darkness are round about him. *Ps.* 97: 2.

No man can find out the work that God maketh from the beginning to the end. *Ec.* 3: 11.

I will hide mine eyes from you. *Is.* 1: 15.

Verily thou art a God that hidest thyself. *Is.* 45: 15.

In a little wrath I hid my face from thee for a moment. *Is.* 54: 8.

Neither will I hide my face any more from them. *Eze.* 39: 29.

Pray to thy Father which is in secret. *Mat.* 6: 6.

To him that overcometh will I give to eat of the hidden manna. *Re.* 2: 17.

See also

God, Secret of; God, Silence of; God, the Unseen.

God, Holiness of

Worship the Lord in the beauty of holiness. *1 Ch.* 16: 29.

God sitteth upon the throne of his holiness. *Ps.* 47: 8.

His right hand, and his holy arm, hath gotten him the victory. *Ps.* 98: 1.

He shall be for a sanctuary. *Is.* 8: 14.

I am the Lord thy God, the Holy One of Israel. *Is.* 43: 3.

Thus saith the high and lofty One that inhabiteth eternity, whose name is Holy; I dwell in the high and holy place, with him also that is of a contrite and humble spirit. *Is.* 57: 15.

I am God, and not man; the Holy One in the midst of thee. *Ho.* 11: 9.

Hallowed be thy name. *Mat.* 6: 9.

That we might be partakers of his holiness. *He.* 12: 10.

Be ye holy; for I am holy. *1 Pe.* 1: 16.

Thou only art holy. *Re.* 15: 4.

See also

God, Goodness of; God, Righteousness of.

God, Our Home

The beloved of the Lord shall dwell in safety by him; and the Lord shall cover him all the day long. *De.* 33: 12.

I will dwell in the house of the Lord for ever. *Ps.* 23: 6.

One thing have I desired of the Lord, that will I seek after; that I may dwell in the house of the Lord all the days of my life. *Ps.* 27: 4.

We shall be satisfied with the goodness of thy house. *Ps.* 65: 4.

Be thou my strong habitation, whereunto I may continually resort. *Ps.* 71: 3.

Lord, thou hast been our dwelling place in all generations. *Ps.* 90: 1.

He that dwelleth in the secret place of the most High shall abide under the shadow of the Almighty. *Ps.* 91: 1.

Because thou hast made the Lord, which is my refuge, even the most High, thy habitation; There shall no evil befall thee. *Ps.* 91: 9, 10.

In my Father's house are many mansions. *Jn.* 14: 2.

See also

God, House of; God, Life in.

God, Hope in

Be of good courage, . . . all ye that hope in the Lord. *Ps.* 31: 24.

In thee, O Lord, do I hope. *Ps.* 38: 15.

Why art thou cast down, O my soul? and why art thou disquieted within me? Hope thou in God. *Ps.* 42: 11.

Thou art my hope, O Lord God: thou art my trust from my youth. *Ps.* 71: 5.

That they might set their hope in God. *Ps.* 78: 7.

Happy is he . . . whose hope is in the Lord his God. *Ps.* 146: 5.

Blessed is the man that trusteth in the Lord, and whose hope the Lord is. *Je.* 17: 7.

It is good that a man should both hope and quietly wait for the salvation of the Lord. *La.* 3: 26.

The Lord will be the hope of his people. *Jo.* 3: 16.

I am cast out of thy sight; yet I will look again toward thy holy temple. *Jon.* 2: 4.

The God of hope fill you with all joy and peace in believing, that ye may abound in hope, through the power of the Holy Ghost. *Ro.* 15: 13.

Ye were without Christ, . . . having no hope and without God. *Ep.* 2: 12.

He looked for a city which hath foundations, whose builder and maker is God. *He.* 11: 10.

That your faith and hope might be in God. *1 Pe.* 1: 21.

See also

God, Confidence in; God, Faith in; God, Reliance on; God, Trust in.

God, House of

Surely the Lord is in this place; and I knew it not. *Ge.* 28: 16.

Thou shalt not build an house unto my name, because thou hast shed much blood upon the earth in my sight. *1 Ch.* 22: 8.

Let the house of God be builded in his place. *Ezr.* 5: 15.

Lord, I have loved the habitation of thy house, and the place where thine honour dwelleth. *Ps.* 26: 8.

I had gone with the multitude, I went with them to the house of God, with the voice of joy and praise, with a multitude that kept holyday. *Ps.* 42: 4.

I was glad when they said unto me, Let us go into the house of the Lord. *Ps.* 122: 1.

I will fill this house with glory, saith the Lord. *Hag.* 2: 7.

The glory of this latter house shall be greater than of the former, saith the Lord of hosts: and in this place will I give peace. *Hag.* 2: 9.

I will build my church. *Mat.* 16: 18.

Is it not written, My house shall be called of all nations the house of prayer? but ye have made it a den of thieves. *Mk.* 11: 17.

Other foundation can no man lay than that is laid, which is Jesus Christ. *1 Co.* 3: 11.

The household of God. *Ep.* 2: 19.

An habitation of God. *Ep.* 2: 22.

The house of God, which is the church of the living God, the pillar and ground of the truth. *1 Ti.* 3: 15.

The time is come that judgment must begin at the house of God. *1 Pe.* 4: 17.

See also

Bethel; Church; Church, Building the; Congregation; God, Our Home; Meeting; Temple; Synagogue.

God, Image of

God created man in his own image, in the image of God created he him. *Ge.* 1: 27.

Thou shalt not make unto thee any graven image, or any likeness of any thing that is in heaven above, or that is in the earth beneath,

or that is in the water under the earth. *Ex.* 20: 4.

The sight of the glory of the Lord was like devouring fire. *Ex.* 24: 17.

I shall be satisfied, when I awake, with thy likeness. *Ps.* 17: 15.

To whom then will ye liken me, or shall I be equal? *Is.* 40: 25.

As we have borne the image of the earthy, we shall also bear the image of the heavenly. *1 Co.* 15: 49.

Christ, who is the image of God, *2 Co.* 4: 4.

Who is the image of the invisible God. *Col.* 1: 15.

See also

God, Face of; God, Imitation of.

God, Imitation of

Let us make man in our image. *Ge.* 1: 26.

I shall be satisfied, when I awake, with thy likeness. *Ps.* 17: 15.

Who in the heaven can be compared unto the Lord? *Ps.* 89: 6.

What things soever he doeth, these also doeth the Son likewise. *Jn.* 5: 19.

Be ye therefore followers of God, as dear children. *Ep.* 5: 1.

See . . . that thou make all things according to the pattern shewed to thee in the mount. *He.* 8: 5.

See also

God, Face of; God, Image of; God, Obedience to.

God, Immanence of

I the Lord dwell among the children of Israel. *Nu.* 35: 34.

Thou visitest the earth, and waterest it. *Ps.* 65: 9.

Surely his salvation is nigh them that fear him; that glory may dwell in our land. *Ps.* 85: 9.

If I ascend up into heaven, thou art there: if I make my bed in hell, behold, thou art there. *Ps.* 139: 8.

I dwell in the high and holy place, with him also that is a contrite and humble spirit. *Is.* 57: 15.

Thus saith the Lord; I am returned unto Zion, and will dwell in the midst of Jerusalem. *Zch.* 8: 3.

Ye are the temple of the living God; as God hath said, I will dwell in them, and walk in them. *2 Co.* 6: 16.

If we love one another, God dwelleth in us. *1 Jn.* 4: 12.

See also

Christ, Incarnation of; God, Consciousness of; God, Incarnation of; God, Presence of.

God, Impartiality of

There is no iniquity with the Lord our God, nor respect of persons, nor taking of gifts. *2 Ch.* 19: 7.

The darkness and the light are both alike to thee. *Ps.* 139: 12.

The rich and poor meet together: the Lord is the maker of them all. *Pr.* 22: 2.

All things come alike to all: there is one

event to the righteous, and to the wicked. *Ec.* 9: 2.

He maketh his sun to rise on the evil and on the good. *Mat.* 5: 45.

He . . . sendeth rain on the just and on the unjust. *Mat.* 5: 45.

Where there is neither Greek nor Jew, circumcision nor uncircumcision, Barbarian, Scythian, bond nor free. *Col.* 3: 11.

The wisdom that is from above is . . . without partiality. *Ja.* 3: 17.

The Father . . . without respect of persons judgeth according to every man's work. *1 Pe.* 1: 17.

See also
God, Fairness of; God, the Judge; God, Righteousness of.

God, Incarnation of
They shall call his name Emmanuel; which being interpreted is, God with us. *Mat.* 1: 23.

In the beginning was the Word, and the Word was with God, and the Word was God. *Jn.* 1: 1.

And the Word was made flesh, and dwelt among us. *Jn.* 1: 14.

Now, O Father, glorify thou me with thine own self with the glory which I had with thee before the world was. *Jn.* 17: 5.

The gods are come down to us in the likeness of men. *Ac.* 14: 11.

God sending his own Son in the likeness of sinful flesh, and for sin, condemned sin in the flesh. *Ro.* 8: 3.

Christ Jesus . . . took upon him the form of a servant, and was made in the likeness of men. *Ph.* 2: 5, 7.

In him dwelleth all the fulness of the Godhead bodily. *Col.* 2: 9.

God was manifest in the flesh, justified in the Spirit, seen of angels, preached unto the Gentiles, believed on in the world, received up into glory. *1 Ti.* 3: 16.

See also
Christ, Divinity of; Christ, God in; Christ, the Son of God; God, Immanence of; Incarnation.

God, the Inescapable
Know now that God hath overthrown me, and hath compassed me with his net. *Jb.* 19: 6.

The angel of the Lord encampeth round about them that fear him. *Ps.* 34: 7.

Thou compassest my path and my lying down, and art acquainted with all my ways. *Ps.* 139: 3.

Thou hast beset me behind and before, and laid thine hand upon me. *Ps.* 139: 5.

Whither shall I go from thy spirit? or whither shall I flee from thy presence? *Ps.* 139: 7.

The darkness hideth not from thee. *Ps.* 139: 12.

Therefore will the Lord wait, that he may be gracious unto you. *Is.* 30: 18.

Though they dig into hell, thence shall mine hand take them; though they climb up to heaven, thence will I bring them down. *Am.* 9: 2.

How can ye escape the damnation of hell? *Mat.* 23: 33.

Thinkest thou this, O man, that judgest them which do such things, and doest the same, that thou shalt escape the judgment of God? *Ro.* 2: 3.

How shall we escape, if we neglect so great salvation? *He.* 2: 3.

Neither is there any creature that is not manifest in his sight: but all things are naked and opened unto the eyes of him with whom we have to do. *He.* 4: 13.

See also
God, the Besetting; God, Overruling of; God, Power of; God, Primacy of; God, Sovereignty of.

God, the Infinite
The Lord shall reign for ever and ever. *Ex.* 15: 18.

'Thy throne, O God, is for ever and ever. *Ps.* 45: 6.

Blessed be his glorious name for ever: and let the whole earth be filled with his glory. *Ps.* 72: 19.

The mercy of the Lord is from everlasting to everlasting upon them that fear him. *Ps.* 103: 17.

If I take the wings of the morning, and dwell in the uttermost parts of the sea; even there shall thy hand lead me. *Ps.* 139: 9, 10.

His understanding is infinite. *Ps.* 147: 5.

The eyes of the Lord are in every place, beholding the evil and the good. *Pr.* 15: 3.

There is no searching of his understanding. *Is.* 40: 28.

I praised and honoured him that liveth for ever, whose dominion is an everlasting dominion. *Da.* 4: 34.

One day is with the Lord as a thousand years, and a thousand years as one day. *2 Pe.* 3: 8.

Dominion and power, both now and ever. *Jude* 1: 25.

See also
God, the Eternal; God, the Unchanging.

God, Jealousy of
Thou shalt have no other gods before me. *Ex.* 20: 3.

I the Lord thy God am a jealous God. *Ex.* 20: 5.

The Lord thy God is a consuming fire, even a jealous God. *De.* 4: 24.

I, even I, am he, and there is no god with me. *De.* 32: 39.

How long, Lord? wilt thou be angry for ever? shall thy jealousy burn like fire? *Ps.* 79: 5.

Then will the Lord be jealous for his land, and pity his people. *Jo.* 2: 18.

The whole land shall be devoured by the fire of his jealousy. *Zph.* 1: 18.

See also
God, Anger of; God, Fire of.

God, Joy in
Ye shall rejoice before the Lord your God, ye, and your sons, and your daughters. *De.* 12: 12.

The joy of the Lord is your strength. *Ne.* 8: 10.

His delight is in the law of the Lord. *Ps.* 1: 2.

Be glad in the Lord, and rejoice, ye righteous:

and shout for joy, all ye that are upright in heart. *Ps.* 32: 11.

My soul shall be joyful in the Lord: it shall rejoice in his salvation. *Ps.* 35: 9.

Delight thyself also in the Lord; and he shall give thee the desires of thine heart. *Ps.* 37: 4.

Let all those that seek thee rejoice and be glad in thee. *Ps.* 70: 4.

I have rejoiced in the way of thy testimonies, as much as in all riches. *Ps.* 119: 14.

They joy before thee according to the joy in harvest. *Is.* 9: 3.

My spirit hath rejoiced in God my Saviour. *Lu.* 1: 47.

We also joy in God through our Lord Jesus Christ. *Ro.* 5: 11.

Rejoice in the Lord alway: and again I say, Rejoice. *Ph.* 4: 4.

God, the Judge

Shall not the Judge of all the earth do right? *Ge.* 18: 25.

I will say unto God, Do not condemn me. *Jb.* 10: 2.

Thy judgments are far above out of his sight. *Ps.* 10: 5.

The judgments of the Lord are . . . sweeter also than honey and the honeycomb. *Ps.* 19: 9, 10.

Examine me, O Lord, and prove me; try my reins and my heart. *Ps.* 26: 2.

Thy judgments are a great deep. *Ps.* 36: 6.

The end of the wicked shall be cut off. *Ps.* 37: 38.

With righteousness shall he judge the world, and the people with equity. *Ps.* 98: 9.

In thy sight shall no man living be justified. *Ps.* 143: 2.

By me princes rule, and nobles, even all the judges of the earth. *Pr.* 8: 16.

The Lord hath made all things for himself: yea, even the wicked for the day of evil. *Pr.* 16: 4.

God shall bring every work into judgment. *Ec.* 12: 14.

When thy judgments are in the earth, the inhabitants of the world will learn righteousness. *Is.* 26: 9.

The Lord is our Judge, the Lord is our lawgiver, the Lord is our king; he will save us. *Is.* 33: 22.

Thy judgments are as the light. *Ho.* 6: 5.

I caused it to rain upon one city, and caused it not to rain upon another city. *Am.* 4: 7.

All the sinners of my people shall die by the sword, which say, The evil shall not overtake nor prevent us. *Am.* 9: 10.

Who shall stand when he appeareth? *Mal.* 3: 2.

Ananias answered, Lord, I have heard by many of this man, how much evil he hath done: . . . But the Lord said unto him, Go thy way: for he is a chosen vessel unto me. *Ac.* 9: 13, 15.

How unsearchable are his judgments. *Ro.* 11: 33.

The Lord shall judge his people. *He.* 10: 30.

Ye are come . . . to God the Judge of all. *He.* 12: 22, 23.

The Father . . . without respect of persons judgeth according to every man's work. *1 Pe.* 1: 17.

God . . . condemned them with an overthrow. *2 Pe.* 2: 4, 6.

The great day of his wrath is come; and who shall be able to stand? *Re.* 6: 17.

See also

God, Chastisement of; God, Day of; God, Punishment of; God, Reward of.

God, the Keeper

My defence is of God. *Ps.* 7: 10.

He maketh me to lie down in green pastures. *Ps.* 23: 2.

Thou preparest a table before me in the presence of mine enemies. *Ps.* 23: 5.

Thou shalt hide them in the secret of thy presence from the pride of man. *Ps.* 31: 20.

The Lord will preserve him, and keep him alive. *Ps.* 41: 2.

He only is my rock and my salvation: he is my defence; I shall not be moved. *Ps.* 62: 6.

The Lord is thy keeper: the Lord is thy shade upon thy right hand. *Ps.* 121: 5.

See also

God, Beneficence of; God, Care of; God, Favor of; God, Goodness of; God, Providence of; God, the Shepherd; God, Solicitude of; God, the Sustainer.

God, Kindness of

The Lord will command his lovingkindness in the daytime. *Ps.* 42: 8.

Have mercy upon me, O God, according to thy lovingkindness. *Ps.* 51: 1.

Because thy lovingkindness is better than life, my lips shall praise thee. *Ps.* 63: 3.

The Lord shall give thee rest from thy sorrow. *Is.* 14: 3.

The mountains shall depart, and the hills be removed; but my kindness shall not depart from thee. *Is.* 54: 10.

With lovingkindness have I drawn thee. *Je.* 31: 3.

Whatsoever ye shall ask the Father in my name, he will give it you. *Jn.* 16: 23.

See also

God, Beneficence of; God, Favor of; God, Generosity of; God, Gift of; God, Goodness of; God, Grace of; God, Providence of.

God, the King

Thine, O Lord, is the greatness, and the power, and the glory, and the victory, and the majesty. *1 Ch.* 29: 11.

Thine is the kingdom, O Lord, and thou art exalted as head above all. *1 Ch.* 29: 11.

The Lord is King for ever and ever. *Ps.* 10: 16.

The kingdom is the Lord's. *Ps.* 22: 28.

Who is this King of glory? The Lord of hosts, he is the King of glory. *Ps.* 24: 10.

The Lord reigneth, he is clothed with majesty. *Ps.* 93: 1.

The Lord reigneth; let the people tremble. *Ps.* 99: 1.

The glorious majesty of his kingdom. *Ps.* 145: 12.

Woe is me! for I am undone; . . . for mine eyes have seen the King, the Lord of hosts. *Is.* 6: 5.

I am a great King, saith the Lord of hosts, and my name is dreadful among the heathen. *Mal.* 1: 14.

Now unto the King eternal, immortal, invisible, the only wise God, be honour and glory for ever and ever. *1 Ti.* 1: 17.

Thy throne, O God, is for ever and ever. *He.* 1: 8.

See also

God, City of; God, Dominion of; God, Kingdom of; God, Majesty of; God, Omnipotence of; God, Power of; God, Sovereignty of; God, Supremacy of.'

God, Kingdom of

Thy kingdom is an everlasting kingdom. *Ps.* 145: 13.

From that time Jesus began to preach, and to say, Repent: for the kingdom of heaven is at hand. *Mat.* 4: 17.

It is given unto you to know the mysteries of the kingdom of heaven. *Mat.* 13: 11.

It is easier for a camel to go through the eye of a needle, than for a rich man to enter into the kingdom of God. *Mat.* 19: 24.

The kingdom of God is at hand. *Mk.* 1: 15.

Suffer the little children to come unto me, and forbid them not: for of such is the kingdom of God. *Mk.* 10: 14.

Thou art not far from the kingdom of God. *Mk.* 12: 34.

Blessed be ye poor: for yours is the kingdom of God. *Lu.* 6: 20.

He went throughout every city and village, preaching and shewing the glad tidings of the kingdom of God. *Lu.* 8: 1.

Thy kingdom come. *Lu.* 11: 2.

Unto what is the kingdom of God like? *Lu.* 13: 18.

It is like a grain of mustard seed. *Lu.* 13: 19.

It is like leaven. *Lu.* 13: 21.

Blessed is he that shall eat bread in the kingdom of God. *Lu.* 14: 15.

Preaching the kingdom of God. *Ac.* 28: 31.

The kingdom of God is not in word, but in power. *1 Co.* 4: 20.

Thy throne, O God, is for ever and ever. *He.* 1: 8.

See also

God, City of; God, Dominion of; God, the King; God, Majesty of; God, Omnipotence of; God, Power of; God, Sovereignty of; God, Supremacy of.

God, Knowledge of

There arose not a prophet since in Israel like unto Moses, whom the Lord knew face to face. *De.* 34: 10.

Canst thou by searching find out God? *Jb.* 11: 7.

Acquaint now thyself with him, and be at peace. *Jb.* 22: 21.

The secret of the Lord is with them that fear him; and he will shew them his covenant. *Ps.* 25: 14.

The earth shall be full of the knowledge of the Lord, as the waters cover the sea. *Is.* 11: 9.

Can any hide himself in secret places that I shall not see him? *Je.* 23: 24.

Then shall we know, if we follow on to know the Lord. *Ho.* 6: 3.

Though they hide themselves in the top of

Carmel, I will search and take them out thence; and though they be hid from my sight in the bottom of the sea, thence will I command the serpent, and he shall bite them. *Am.* 9: 3.

No man hath seen God at any time; the only begotten Son, which is in the bosom of the Father, he hath declared him. *Jn.* 1: 18.

The light of the knowledge of the glory of God in the face of Jesus Christ. *2 Co.* 4: 6.

That ye might be filled with the knowledge of his will in all wisdom and spiritual understanding. *Col.* 1: 9.

Increasing in the knowledge of God. *Col.* 1: 10.

See also

God, Omniscience of; God, Wisdom of; Theology.

God, Law of

Incline your ears to the words of my mouth. *Ps.* 78: 1.

I will delight myself in thy statutes. *Ps.* 119: 16.

Open thou mine eyes, that I may behold wondrous things out of thy law. *Ps.* 119: 18.

Thy statutes have been my songs in the house of my pilgrimage. *Ps.* 119: 54.

Thy word is true from the beginning: and every one of thy righteous judgments endureth for ever. *Ps.* 119: 160.

The commandment is a lamp; and the law is light. *Pr.* 6: 23.

I know that, whatsoever God doeth, it shall be for ever. *Ec.* 3: 14.

I will put my law in their inward parts, and write it in their hearts. *Je.* 31: 33.

What doth the Lord require of thee, but to do justly, and to love mercy, and to walk humbly with thy God? *Mi.* 6: 8.

God commanded, saying, Honour thy father and mother. *Mat.* 15: 4.

Thou shalt love the Lord thy God, with all thy heart, and with all thy soul, and with all thy mind, and with all thy strength. *Mk.* 12: 30.

With the mind I myself serve the law of God; but with the flesh the law of sin. *Ro.* 7: 25.

See also

God, Commandment of; God, Dominion of; God, Voice of; God, Word of.

God, Leadership of

So that I come again to my father's house in peace; then shall the Lord be my God. *Ge.* 28: 21.

The Lord went before them. *Ex.* 13: 21.

Thou shalt remember all the way which the Lord thy God led thee these forty years in the wilderness. *De.* 8: 2.

The Lord, he it is that doth go before thee; he will be with thee, he will not fail thee, neither forsake thee. *De.* 31: 8.

As an eagle stirreth up her nest, fluttereth over her young, spreadeth abroad her wings, taketh them, beareth them on her wings: So the Lord alone did lead him. *De.* 32: 11, 12.

The Lord alone did lead him, and there was no strange god with him. *De.* 32: 12.

He leadeth me. *Ps.* 23: 2.

This God is our God for ever and ever: he will be our guide even unto death. *Ps.* 48: 14.

He . . . guided them in the wilderness like a flock. *Ps. 78: 50, 52.*

He brought them out of darkness and the shadow of death. *Ps. 107: 14.*

O that my ways were directed to keep thy statutes! *Ps. 119: 5.*

In all thy ways acknowledge him, and he shall direct thy paths. *Pr. 3: 6.*

I will bring the blind by a way that they knew not; I will lead them in paths that they have not known. *Is. 42: 16.*

I am the Lord thy God . . . which leadeth thee by the way that thou shouldest go. *Is. 48: 17.*

The Lord shall guide thee continually, and satisfy thy soul in drought. *Is. 58: 11.*

O Lord, I know that the way of man is not in himself: it is not in man that walketh to direct his steps. *Je. 10: 23.*

He calleth his own sheep by name, and leadeth them out. *Jn. 10: 3.*

See also

God, Guidance of; God, Hand of; God, Way of.

God, Life in

The spirit of God hath made me, and the breath of the Almighty hath given me life. *Jb. 33: 4.*

The Lord is the strength of my life. *Ps. 27: 1.*

Thou hast kept me alive. *Ps. 30: 3.*

With thee is the fountain of life. *Ps. 36: 9.*

Thou hast made . . . the most High thy habitation. *Ps. 91: 9.*

Whoso findeth me findeth life. *Pr. 8: 35.*

He is not a God of the dead, but of the living: for all live unto him. *Lu. 20: 38.*

For in him we live, and move, and have our being. *Ac. 17: 28.*

Ye are dead, and your life is hid with Christ in God. *Col. 3: 3.*

See also

God, Communion with; God, Companionship of; God, Cooperation of; God, Fellowship with; God, Our Home; God, Partnership with.

God, the Light

The Lord will lighten my darkness. *2 S. 22: 29.*

Lift thou up the light of thy countenance upon us. *Ps. 4: 6.*

Thou wilt light my candle: the Lord my God will enlighten my darkness. *Ps. 18: 28.*

In thy light shall we see light. *Ps. 36: 9.*

God be merciful unto us, and bless us; and cause his face to shine upon us. *Ps. 67: 1.*

The Lord God is a sun. *Ps. 84: 11.*

Who coverest thyself with light as with a garment. *Ps. 104: 2.*

Arise, shine; for thy light is come, and the glory of the Lord is risen upon thee. *Is. 60: 1.*

The Lord shall be unto thee an everlasting light. *Is. 60: 19.*

God, who commanded the light to shine out of darkness, hath shined in our hearts. *2 Co. 4: 6.*

The Father of lights. *Ja. 1: 17.*

God is light, and in him is no darkness at all. *1 Jn. 1: 5.*

See also

God, Fire of.

God, the Living

The Lord liveth; and blessed be my rock. *2 S. 22: 47.*

Who knoweth not in all these that the hand of the Lord hath wrought this? In whose hand is the soul of every living thing, and the breath of all mankind. *Jb. 12: 9, 10.*

I know that my redeemer liveth. *Jb. 19: 25.*

My people . . . have forsaken me the fountain of living waters. *Je. 2: 13.*

God is not the God of the dead, but of the living. *Mat. 22: 32.*

As the living Father hath sent me, and I live by the Father: so he that eateth me, even he shall live by me. *Jn. 6: 57.*

I am he that liveth, and was dead; and, behold, I am alive for evermore. *Re. 1: 18.*

See also

God, Existence of; God, Immanence of; God, Presence of.

God, Longing for

Oh that I knew where I might find him! *Jb. 23: 3.*

This is the generation of them that seek him. *Ps. 24: 6.*

As the hart panteth after the water brooks, so panteth my soul after thee, O God. *Ps. 42: 1.*

O God, thou art my God; early will I seek thee. *Ps. 63: 1.*

Whom have I in heaven but thee? and there is none upon earth that I desire beside thee. My flesh and my heart faileth: but God is the strength of my heart, and my portion for ever. *Ps. 73: 25, 26.*

With my whole heart have I sought thee. *Ps. 119: 10.*

They shall call upon me, but I will not answer; they shall seek me early, but they shall not find me. *Pr. 1: 28.*

There is none that understandeth, there is none that seeketh after God. *Ro. 3: 11.*

See also

God, Aspiration for; God, Prayer to; God, Quest for; God, Thirst for; God, Yearning for.

God, the Lord

Thou shalt not take the name of the Lord thy God in vain. *Ex. 20: 7.*

Thou shalt love the Lord thy God, and keep . . . his statutes. *De. 11: 1.*

This glorious and fearful name, THE LORD THY GOD. *De. 28: 58.*

Blessed be the Lord God of Israel. *1 K. 1: 48.*

The Lord our God be with us, as he was with our fathers: let him not leave us, nor forsake us. *1 K. 8: 57.*

Thine, O Lord, is the greatness, and the power, and the glory, and the victory, and the majesty. *1 Ch. 29: 11.*

The Lord is in his holy temple. *Ps. 11: 4.*

The Lord is my light and my salvation; whom shall I fear? *Ps. 27: 1.*

O taste and see that the Lord is good. *Ps. 34: 8.*

Know ye that the Lord he is God. *Ps. 100: 3.*

From the rising of the sun unto the going down of the same the Lord's name is to be praised. *Ps. 113: 3.*

I am the Lord thy God, the Holy One of Israel, thy Saviour. *Is. 43: 3.*

Seek ye the Lord while he may be found, call ye upon him while he is near. *Is.* 55: 6.

Ye shall know that I am the Lord God. *Eze.* 13: 9.

Sanctify the Lord God in your hearts. *1 Pe.* 3: 15.

Holy, holy, holy, Lord God Almighty, which was, and is, and is to come. *Re.* 4: 8.

Thou art worthy, O Lord, to receive glory and honour and power. *Re.* 4: 11.

Salvation, and glory, and honour, and power, unto the Lord our God. *Re.* 19: 1.

God, Loss of

Go not up, for the Lord is not among you. *Nu.* 14: 42.

There arose another generation after them, which knew not the Lord. *Ju.* 2: 10.

He wist not that the Lord was departed from him. *Ju.* 16: 20.

The light shall be dark in his tabernacle. *Jb.* 18: 6.

Take not thy holy spirit from me. *Ps.* 51: 11.

He gave them their request; but sent leanness into their soul. *Ps.* 106: 15.

Then said God, Call his name Lo-ammi: for ye are not my people, and I will not be your God. *Ho.* 1: 9.

Take heed, brethren, lest there be in any of you an evil heart of unbelief, in departing from the living God. *He.* 3: 12.

See also

God, Denial of; God, Estrangement from; God, Rebellion against; God, Rejection of.

God, Love of

The Lord did not set his love upon you, nor choose you, because ye were more in number than any people; for ye were the fewest of all people: But because the Lord loved you. *De.* 7: 7, 8.

The Lord had a delight in thy fathers to love them. *De.* 10: 15.

The Lord is my shepherd. *Ps.* 23: 1.

The Lord loveth the righteous. *Ps.* 146: 8.

I have loved thee with an everlasting love. *Je.* 31: 3.

When Israel was a child, then I loved him. *Ho.* 11: 1.

I drew them with cords of a man, with bands of love. *Ho.* 11: 4.

I will love them freely. *Ho.* 14: 4.

I have loved you, saith the Lord. Yet ye say, Wherein hast thou loved us? *Mal.* 1: 2.

For God so loved the world. *Jn.* 3: 16.

The Father loveth the Son. *Jn.* 3: 35.

Beloved of God. *Ro.* 1: 7.

God commandeth his love towards us. *Ro.* 5: 8.

Nor height, nor depth, nor any other creature, shall be able to separate us from the love of God. *Ro.* 8: 39.

Whom the Lord loveth he chasteneth. *He.* 12: 6.

Behold, what manner of love the Father hath bestowed upon us, that we should be called the sons of God. *1 Jn.* 3: 1.

Let us love one another: for love is of God; and every one that loveth is born of God, and knoweth God. *1 Jn.* 4: 7.

God sent his only begotten Son into the world, that we might live through him. *1 Jn.* 4: 9.

Herein is love, not that we loved God, but that he loved us, and sent his Son to be the propitiation for our sins. *1 Jn.* 4: 10.

God is love; and he that dwelleth in love dwelleth in God, and God in him. *1 Jn.* 4: 16.

Keep yourselves in the love of God. *Jude* 1: 21.

See also

God, Beneficence of; God, Communion with; God, Companionship of; God, Favor of; God, Fellowship with; God, the Friend; God, Goodness of; God, Kindness of; God, Nearness of; God, the Shepherd.

God, Love to

Thou shalt love the Lord thy God with all thine heart, and with all thy soul, and with all thy might. *De.* 6: 5.

The Lord your God proveth you, to know whether ye love the Lord your God with all your heart and with all your soul. *De.* 13: 3.

Take diligent heed . . . to love the Lord your God. *Jos.* 22: 5.

Let them also that love thy name be joyful in thee. *Ps.* 5: 11.

Lord, I have loved the habitation of thy house. *Ps.* 26: 8.

O love the Lord, all ye his saints. *Ps.* 31: 23.

Because he hath set his love upon me, therefore will I deliver him. *Ps.* 91: 14.

Ye that love the Lord, hate evil. *Ps.* 97: 10.

I love the Lord, because he hath heard my voice and my supplications. *Ps.* 116: 1.

O how love I thy law! it is my meditation all the day. *Ps.* 119: 97.

I love thy commandments above gold; yea, above fine gold. *Ps.* 119: 127.

Great peace have they which love thy law. *Ps.* 119: 165.

The Lord preserveth all them that love him. *Ps.* 145: 20.

Thou shalt love the Lord thy God with all thy heart, and with all thy soul, and with all thy strength, and with all thy mind. *Lu.* 10: 27.

We know that all things work together for good to them that love God. *Ro.* 8: 28.

We love him, because he first loved us. *1 Jn.* 4: 19.

See also

God, Confidence in; God, Faith in; God, Loyalty to; God, Reliance on.

God, Loyalty to

I have been very jealous for the Lord God of hosts. *1 K.* 19: 10.

Stablish thy word unto thy servant, who is devoted to thy fear. *Ps.* 119: 38.

I set my face unto the Lord God. *Da.* 9: 3.

Judah yet ruleth with God, and is faithful with the saints. *Ho.* 11: 12.

Paul . . . said, Men and brethren, I have lived in all good conscience before God until this day. *Ac.* 23: 1.

Be ye therefore followers of God, as dear children. *Ep.* 5: 1.

He pleased God. *He.* 11: 5.

See also

God, Faith in; God, Fellowship with; God,

Love of; God, Nearness to; God, Obedience to.

God, Majesty of

I will sing unto the Lord, for he hath triumphed gloriously. *Ex.* 15: 1.

Thy right hand, O Lord, is become glorious in power. *Ex.* 15: 6.

The glory of the Lord filled the tabernacle. *Ex.* 40: 34.

Behold, the heaven and the heaven of heavens is the Lord's thy God, the earth also, with all that therein is. *De.* 10: 14.

Glory and honour are in his presence. *1 Ch.* 16: 27.

O Lord our Lord, how excellent is thy name in all the earth: who hast set thy glory above the heavens. *Ps.* 8: 1.

He bowed the heavens also, and came down: and darkness was under his feet. And he rode upon a cherub, and did fly: yea, he did fly upon the wings of the wind. *Ps.* 18: 9, 10.

Great is the Lord, and greatly to be praised in the city of our God, in the mountain of his holiness. *Ps.* 48: 1.

I saw also the Lord sitting upon a throne, high and lifted up. *Is.* 6: 1.

Who hath . . . weighed the mountains in scales, and the hills in a balance? *Is.* 40: 12.

As the heavens are higher than the earth, so are my ways higher than your ways. *Is.* 55: 9.

Thus saith the high and lofty One that inhabiteth eternity, whose name is Holy; I dwell in the high and holy place. *Is.* 57: 15.

A glorious high throne from the beginning is the place of our sanctuary. *Je.* 17: 12.

The glory of the Lord came into the house by the way of the gate. *Eze.* 43: 4.

Now I . . . praise and extol and honour the King of heaven. *Da.* 4: 37.

Now unto the King eternal, immortal, invisible, the only wise God, be honour and glory for ever and ever. *1 Ti.* 1: 17.

Thou art worthy, O Lord, to receive glory and honour and power. *Re.* 4: 11.

See also

God, Dominion of; God, Greatness of; God, the King; God, Kingdom of; God, Omnipotence of; God, Overruling of; God, Power of; God, Sovereignty of; God, Supremacy of.

God, Memory of

Remember not the sins of my youth. *Ps.* 25: 7.

Remember thy congregation, which thou hast purchased of old. *Ps.* 74: 2.

O remember not against us former iniquities. *Ps.* 79: 8.

He remembereth that we are dust. *Ps.* 103: 14.

If I do not remember thee, let my tongue cleave to the roof of my mouth. *Ps.* 137: 6.

Remember now thy Creator in the days of thy youth. *Ec.* 12: 1.

Can a woman forget her sucking child, that she should not have compassion on the son of her womb? yea, they may forget, yet will I not forget thee. *Is.* 49: 15.

O Lord, thou knowest, remember me. *Je.* 15: 15.

I will remember their sin no more. *Je.* 31: 34.

They consider not in their hearts that I remember all their wickedness. *Ho.* 7: 2.

O Lord, . . . in wrath remember mercy. *Hab.* 3: 2.

Are not five sparrows sold for two farthings, and not one of them is forgotten before God? *Lu.* 12: 6.

God, Mercy of

I will meet with thee, and I will commune with thee from above the mercy seat. *Ex.* 25: 22.

O give thanks unto the Lord; for he is good; for his mercy endureth for ever. *1 Ch.* 16: 34.

According to thy manifold mercies thou gavest them saviours. *Ne.* 9: 27.

The earth is full of the goodness of the Lord. *Ps.* 33: 5.

Thy mercy, O Lord, is in the heavens; and thy faithfulness reacheth unto the clouds. *Ps.* 36: 5.

God hath spoken once; twice have I heard this; that power belongeth unto God. Also unto thee, O Lord, belongeth mercy: for thou renderest to every man according to his work. *Ps.* 62: 11, 12.

God be merciful unto us, and bless us; and cause his face to shine upon us. *Ps.* 67: 1.

O satisfy us early with thy mercy. *Ps.* 90: 14.

Thy mercy, O Lord, endureth for ever. *Ps.* 138: 8.

I have blotted out, as a thick cloud, thy transgressions, and, as a cloud, thy sins: return unto me; for I have redeemed thee. *Is.* 44: 22.

As one whom his mother comforteth, so will I comfort you. *Is.* 66: 13.

The Lord's mercies . . . are new every morning. *La.* 3: 22, 23.

Spare thy people, O Lord, and give not thine heritage to reproach. *Jo.* 2: 17.

I will restore to you the years that the locust hath eaten. *Jo.* 2: 25.

God repented of the evil, that he had said that he would do unto them. *Jon.* 3: 10.

Should not I spare Nineveh, that great city? *Jon.* 4: 11.

His mercy is on them that fear him from generation to generation. *Lu.* 1: 50.

Are not five sparrows sold for two farthings, and not one of them is forgotten before God? *Lu.* 12: 6.

God so loved the world, that he gave his only begotten Son, that whosoever believeth in him should not perish, but have everlasting life. *Jn.* 3: 16.

I beseech you therefore, brethren, by the mercies of God. *Ro.* 12: 1.

See also

God, Comfort of; God, Compassion of; God, Forgiveness of; God, Gentleness of; God, Kindness of; God, Solicitude of; God, Sympathy of.

God, Messenger of

I have a message from God unto thee. *Ju.* 3: 20.

Then said I, Here am I; send me. *Is.* 6: 8.

Prepare ye the way of the Lord. *Is.* 40: 3.

Who is blind, but my servant? or deaf, as my messenger that I sent? *Is.* 42: 19.

Then spake Haggai the Lord's messenger in the Lord's message unto the people, saying, I am with you. *Hag.* 1: 13.

The Lord answered the angel that talked with me with good words and comfortable words. *Zch.* 1: 13.

He is the messenger of the Lord of hosts. *Mal.* 2: 7.

Behold, I will send my messenger, and he shall prepare the way before me: . . . saith the Lord. *Mal.* 3: 1.

Thou shalt go before the face of the Lord to prepare his ways. *Lu.* 1: 76.

God sent not his Son into the world to condemn the world; but that the world through him might be saved. *Jn.* 3: 17.

God hath sent forth the Spirit of his Son into your hearts. *Ga.* 4: 6.

See also
God, Servant of.

God, Name of

The Lord is his name. *Ex.* 15: 3.

Thou shalt not take the name of the Lord thy God in vain. *Ex.* 20: 7.

The Lord, whose name is Jealous, is a jealous God. *Ex.* 34: 14.

This glorious and fearful name, THE LORD THY GOD. *De.* 28: 58.

Let them also that love thy name be joyful in thee. *Ps.* 5: 11.

Blessed be his glorious name for ever. *Ps.* 72: 19.

Let them praise thy great and terrible name; for it is holy. *Ps.* 99: 3.

Thy name, O Lord, endureth for ever. *Ps.* 135: 13.

The name of the Lord is a strong tower. *Pr.* 18: 10.

Hallowed be thy name. *Mat.* 6: 9.

I am come in my Father's name, and ye receive me not. *Jn.* 5: 43.

Father, glorify thy name. *Jn.* 12: 28.

I will write upon him my new name. *Re.* 3: 12.

Lo, a Lamb stood on the mount Sion, and with him an hundred forty and four thousand, having his Father's name written in their foreheads. *Re.* 14: 1.

God, in Nature

All the earth shall be filled with the glory of the Lord. *Nu.* 14: 21.

He did fly upon the wings of the wind. *Ps.* 18: 10.

The heavens declare the glory of God; and the firmament sheweth his handywork. *Ps.* 19: 1.

In his hand are the deep places of the earth: the strength of the hills is his also. *Ps.* 95: 4.

The earth is full of thy riches. *Ps.* 104: 24.

They that go down to the sea in ships, that do business in great waters; These see the works of the Lord, and his wonders in the deep. *Ps.* 107: 23, 24.

I will lift up mine eyes unto the hills, from whence cometh my help. *Ps.* 121: 1.

God, Who covereth the heaven with clouds, who prepareth rain for the earth, who maketh grass to grow upon the mountain. *Ps.* 147: 7, 8.

He maketh peace in thy borders, and filleth thee with the finest of the wheat. *Ps.* 147: 14.

Praise God in his sanctuary: praise him in the firmament of his power. *Ps.* 150: 1.

He hath made every thing beautiful in his time. *Ec.* 3: 11.

The earth shall be full of the knowledge of the Lord, as the waters cover the sea. *Is.* 11: 9.

Do not I fill heaven and earth? saith the Lord. *Je.* 23: 24.

See also
God, Immanence of; God, Presence of.

God, Nature of

The Lord is a God of knowledge. *1 S.* 2: 3.

The voice of the Lord is powerful. *Ps.* 29: 4.

His understanding is infinite. *Ps.* 147: 5.

The everlasting Father. *Is.* 9: 6.

The Lord is our judge, the Lord is our lawgiver, the Lord is our king. *Is.* 33: 22.

It shall be at that day, saith the Lord, that thou shalt call me Ishi; and shalt call me no more Baali. *Ho.* 2: 16.

I am the Lord, I change not. *Mal.* 3: 6.

God is a Spirit: and they that worship him must worship him in spirit and in truth. *Jn.* 4: 24.

Not that any man hath seen the Father, save he which is of God, he hath seen the Father. *Jn.* 6: 46.

We have one Father, even God. *Jn.* 8: 41.

Believe me that I am in the Father, and the Father in me. *Jn.* 14: 11.

They should seek the Lord, if haply they might feel after him, and find him, though he be not far from every one of us. *Ac.* 17: 27.

One God and Father of all, who is above all, and through all, and in you all. *Ep.* 4: 6.

God is love. *1 Jn.* 4: 8.

See also
God, Personality of.

God, Nearness of

Behold a ladder set up on the earth, and the top of it reached to heaven. *Ge.* 28: 12.

The word is very nigh unto thee. *De.* 30: 14.

But it is good for me to draw near to God. *Ps.* 73: 28.

Thou art near, O Lord. *Ps.* 119: 151.

The Lord is nigh. *Ps.* 145: 18.

He is near that justifieth me. *Is.* 50: 8.

My righteousness is near. *Is.* 51: 5.

Seek ye the Lord while he may be found, call ye upon him while he is near. *Is.* 55: 6.

My salvation is near to come. *Is.* 56: 1.

The day of the Lord is near upon all the heathen. *Ob.* 1: 15.

See also
God, Communion with; God, Companionship of; God, Fellowship with; God, the Friend; God, Immanence of; God, Presence of.

God, Obedience to

Ye shall observe to do therefore as the Lord your God hath commanded you: ye shall not turn aside to the right hand or to the left. *De.* 5: 32.

Ye shall walk in all the ways which the Lord your God hath commanded you. *De.* 5: 33.

Hath the Lord as great delight in burnt offerings and sacrifices, as in obeying the voice of the Lord? *1 S.* 15: 22.

That he may incline our hearts unto him, to walk in all his ways, and to keep his commandments. *1 K.* 8: 58.

And Naboth said to Ahab, The Lord forbid me. *1 K.* 21: 3.

Whatsoever is commanded by the God of heaven, let it be diligently done for the house of the God of heaven. *Ezr.* 7: 23.

I was dumb, I opened not my mouth; because thou didst it. *Ps.* 39: 9.

I will keep thy statutes. *Ps.* 119: 8.

As the eyes of servants look unto the hand of their masters; . . . so our eyes wait upon the Lord our God. *Ps.* 123: 2.

In the way of thy judgments, O Lord, have we waited for thee. *Is.* 26: 8.

Obey my voice, and I will be your God, and ye shall be my people. *Je.* 7: 23.

All dominions shall serve and obey him. *Da.* 7: 27.

Even so, Father: for so it seemed good in thy sight, *Mat.* 11: 26.

They were both righteous before God, walking in all the commandments and ordinances of the Lord blameless. *Lu.* 1: 6.

Ye shall be the children of the Highest. *Lu.* 6: 35.

Here are they that keep the commandments of God, and the faith of Jesus. *Re.* 14: 12.

See also

God, Loyalty to; God, Obligation to.

God, Obligation to

All that the Lord speaketh, that I must do. *Nu.* 23: 26.

Thou shalt do that which is right and good in the sight of the Lord: that it may be well with thee. *De.* 6: 18.

Give unto the Lord the glory due unto his name. *1 Ch.* 16: 29.

Let us hear the conclusion of the whole matter: Fear God, and keep his commandments: for this is the whole duty of man. *Ec.* 12: 13.

Wist ye not that I must be about my Father's business? *Lu.* 2: 49.

I must preach the kingdom of God to other cities also: for therefore am I sent. *Lu.* 4: 43.

I must work the works of him that sent me, while it is day. *Jn.* 9: 4.

We ought to obey God rather than men. *Ac.* 5: 29.

He that cometh to God must believe that he is. *He.* 11: 6.

See also

God, Loyalty to; God, Obedience to.

God, Omnipotence of

Is any thing too hard for the Lord? *Ge.* 18: 14.

In thine hand it is to make great, and to give strength unto all. *1 Ch.* 29: 12.

The thunder of his power who can understand? *Jb.* 26: 14.

God hath spoken once; twice have I heard this; that power belongeth unto God. *Ps.* 62: 11.

O Lord God of hosts, who is a strong Lord like unto thee? *Ps.* 89: 8.

In the Lord JEHOVAH is everlasting strength. *Is.* 26: 4.

As the clay is in the potter's hand, so are ye in mine hand, O house of Israel. *Je.* 18: 6.

God is able of these stones to raise up children unto Abraham. *Mat.* 3: 9.

Strengthened with all might, according to his glorious power. *Col.* 1: 11.

I heard as it were the voice of a great multitude, and as the voice of many waters, and as the voice of mighty thunderings, saying, Alleluia: for the Lord God omnipotent reigneth. *Re.* 19: 6.

See also

Almighty; God, the Almighty; God, Power of; God, Strength of.

God, Omnipresence of

Behold, I am with thee, and will keep thee in all places whither thou goest. *Ge.* 28: 15.

Nevertheless I am continually with thee. *Ps.* 73: 23.

Thou compassest my path and my lying down, and art acquainted with all my ways. *Ps.* 139: 3.

Thou hast beset me behind and before, and laid thine hand upon me. *Ps.* 139: 5.

Whither shall I go from thy spirit? or whither shall I flee from thy presence? *Ps.* 139: 7.

If I take the wings of the morning, and dwell in the uttermost parts of the sea; Even there shall thy hand lead me. *Ps.* 139: 9, 10.

The eyes of the Lord are in every place, beholding the evil and the good. *Pr.* 15: 3.

Can any hide himself in secret places that I shall not see him? *Je.* 23: 24.

Do not I fill heaven and earth? saith the Lord. *Je.* 23: 24.

Though they dig into hell, thence shall mine hand take them; though they climb up to heaven, thence will I bring them down. *Am.* 9: 2.

Though he be not far from every one of us *Ac.* 17: 27.

I am persuaded, that neither death, nor life . . . shall be able to separate us from the love of God. *Ro.* 8: 38, 39.

See also

God, Universality of.

God, Omniscience of

He looketh to the ends of the earth, and seeth under the whole heaven. *Jb.* 28: 24.

I know that thou canst do every thing, and that no thought can be withholden from thee. *Jb.* 42: 2.

He knoweth the secrets of the heart. *Ps.* 44: 21.

Thou . . . art acquainted with all my ways. *Ps.* 139: 3.

There is not a word in my tongue, but, lo, O Lord, thou knowest it altogether. *Ps.* 139: 4.

His understanding is infinite. *Ps.* 147: 5.

The eyes of the Lord are in every place, beholding the evil and the good. *Pr.* 15: 3.

There is no searching of his understanding. *Is.* 40: 28.

I will search Jerusalem with candles, and punish the men that are settled on their lees. *Zph.* 1: 12.

He that searcheth the hearts knoweth what is the mind of the Spirit. *Ro.* 8: 27.

All things are naked and opened unto the

eyes of him with whom we have to do. *He.* 4: 13.

See also

God, Knowledge of; God, Wisdom of.

God, Overruling of

As for you, ye thought evil against me; but God meant it unto good, to bring to pass, as it is this day. *Ge.* 50: 20.

Know now that God hath overthrown me, and hath compassed me with his net. *Jb.* 19: 6.

I caused the widow's heart to sing for joy. *Jb.* 29: 13.

The Lord executeth righteousness and judgment for all that are oppressed. *Ps.* 103: 6.

Thou hast beset me behind and before, and laid thine hand upon me. *Ps.* 139: 5.

Whither shall I flee from thy presence? *Ps.* 139: 7.

Then the eyes of the blind shall be opened, and the ears of the deaf shall be unstopped. *Is.* 35: 5.

The Lord God hath spoken, who can but prophesy? *Am.* 3: 8.

Though they dig into hell, thence shall mine hand take them; though they climb up to heaven, thence will I bring them down. *Am.* 9: 2.

If this counsel or this work be of men, it will come to nought: But if it be of God, ye cannot overthrow it; lest haply ye be found even to fight against God. *Ac.* 5: 38, 39.

They essayed to go into Bithynia: but the Spirit suffered them not. *Ac.* 16: 7.

See also

God, the Besetting; God, the Inescapable; God, Power of; God, Primacy of; God, Sovereignty of.

God, Partnership with

Who is on the Lord's side? *Ex.* 32: 26.

The Lord your God is he that goeth with you, to fight for you against your enemies. *De.* 20: 4.

The Lord is with thee. *Ju.* 6: 12.

I will say to them which were not my people, Thou art my people; and they shall say, Thou art my God. *Ho.* 2: 23.

For we are labourers together with God. *1 Co.* 3: 9.

It is God which worketh in you both to will and to do of his good pleasure. *Ph.* 2: 13.

Partakers of the divine nature. *2 Pe.* 1: 4.

See also

God, Communion with; God, Companionship of; God, Cooperation of; God, Fellowship with; God, Life in.

God, Patience of

The Lord, . . . longsuffering. *Ex.* 34: 6.

God speaketh once, yea twice, yet man perceiveth it not. *Jb.* 33: 14.

Take me not away in thy longsuffering. *Je.* 15: 15.

I will go and return to my place, till they acknowledge their offence, and seek my face. *Ho.* 5: 15.

The word of the Lord came unto Jonah the second time. *Jon.* 3: 1.

The God of patience and consolation grant you to be likeminded one toward another. *Ro.* 15: 5.

Once the longsuffering of God waited in the days of Noah. *1 Pe.* 3: 20.

The Lord is not slack concerning his promise, as some men count slackness; but is longsuffering to us-ward, not willing that any should perish. *2 Pe.* 3: 9.

Account that the longsuffering of our Lord is salvation. *2 Pe.* 3: 15.

Because thou hast kept the word of my patience, I also will keep thee from the hour of temptation. *Re.* 3: 10.

God, Peace of

Thou wilt keep him in perfect peace, whose mind is stayed on thee. *Is.* 26: 3.

Now the God of hope fill you with all joy and peace in believing. *Ro.* 15: 13.

Grace be unto you and peace from God our Father, and from the Lord Jesus Christ. *1 Co.* 1: 3.

God hath called us to peace. *1 Co.* 7: 15.

The peace of God, which passeth all understanding, shall keep your hearts and minds through Christ Jesus. *Ph.* 4: 7.

Let the peace of God rule in your hearts, to the which also ye are called in one body. *Col.* 3: 15.

The very God of peace sanctify you wholly. *1 Th.* 5: 23.

See also

God, Rest in; God, Security of.

God, People of

I will take you to me for a people, and I will be to you a God. *Ex.* 6: 7.

I will walk among you and will be your God. *Le.* 26: 12.

The Lord's portion is his people. *De.* 32: 9.

The Lord God of Israel hath given rest unto his people. *1 Ch.* 23: 25.

The Lord will not cast off his people, neither will he forsake his inheritance. *Ps.* 94: 14.

We are his people, and the sheep of his pasture. *Ps.* 100: 3.

As the mountains are round about Jerusalem, so the Lord is round about his people from henceforth even for ever. *Ps.* 125: 2.

The Lord taketh pleasure in his people. *Ps.* 149: 4.

The Lord hath comforted his people. *Is.* 49: 13.

I will . . . joy in my people. *Is.* 65: 19.

All souls are mine. *Eze.* 18: 4.

God hath visited his people. *Lu.* 7: 16.

I will call them my people, which were not my people. *Ro.* 9: 25.

They shall be his people, and God himself shall be with them, and be their God. *Re.* 21: 3.

See also

God, Child of; God, Son of.

God, Perfection of

He is the Rock, his work is perfect. *De.* 32: 4.

As for God, his way is perfect. *2 S.* 22: 31.

All the ends of the earth have seen the salvation of our God. *Ps.* 98: 3.

I know that, whatsoever God doeth, it shall be for ever: nothing can be put to it, nor any thing taken from it. *Ec.* 3: 14.

Be ye therefore perfect, even as your Father

which is in heaven is perfect. *Mat.* 5: 48.

That good, and acceptable, and perfect, will of God. *Ro.* 12: 2.

Our sufficiency is of God. *2 Co.* 3: 5.

Every good gift and every perfect gift is from above. *Ja.* 1: 17.

Whoso keepeth his word, in him verily is the love of God perfected. *1 Jn.* 2: 5.

If we love one another, God dwelleth in us, and his love is perfected in us. *1 Jn.* 4: 12.

See also

God, Fullness of; God, Holiness of; God, Righteousness of.

God, Personality of

God said unto Moses, I AM THAT I AM. *Ex.* 3: 14.

I am the Lord, and there is none else, there is no God beside me. *Is.* 45: 5.

There is one God; and there is none other but he. *Mk.* 12: 32.'

To us there is but one God, the Father. *1 Co.* 8: 6.

There are three that bear record in heaven, the Father, the Word, and the Holy Ghost: and these three are one. *1 Jn.* 5: 7.

See also

God, Nature of.

God, Power of

Thy right hand, O Lord, is become glorious in power. *Ex.* 15: 6.

Lord, it is nothing with thee to help. *2 Ch.* 14: 11.

Our God whom we serve is able to deliver us. *Da.* 3: 17.

The thunder of his power who can understand? *Jb.* 26: 14.

The voice of the Lord is powerful. *Ps.* 29: 4.

The God of Israel is he that giveth strength and power unto his people. *Ps.* 68: 35.

O Lord God of hosts, who is a strong Lord like unto thee? *Ps.* 89: 8.

My help cometh from the Lord, which made heaven and earth. *Ps.* 121: 2.

They shall speak of the glory of thy kingdom, and talk of thy power. *Ps.* 145: 11.

See also

Almighty; God, the Almighty; God, the Besetting; God, Compulsion of; God, Omnipotence of; God, Overruling of; God, Sovereignty of; God, Strength of; God, Supremacy of.

God, Praise to

Great is the Lord, and greatly to be praised. *1 Ch.* 16: 25.

Enter into his gates with thanksgiving, and into his courts with praise. *Ps.* 100: 4.

Praise the Lord from the earth, ye dragons, and all deeps: Fire, and hail; snow, and vapours; stormy wind fulfilling his word: Mountains, and all hills; fruitful trees, and all cedars: Beasts, and all cattle; creeping things, and flying fowl: King of the earth, and all people. *Ps.* 148: 7–11.

Both young men, and maidens; . . . Let them praise the name of the Lord. *Ps.* 148: 12, 13.

Suddenly there was with the angel a multitude of the heavenly host praising God, and saying. *Lu.* 2: 13.

If these should hold their peace, the stones would immediately cry out. *Lu.* 19: 40.

They . . . were continually in the temple, praising and blessing God. *Lu.* 24: 52, 53.

See also

God, Adoration of; God, Gratitude to; God, Thankfulness to; God, Worship of.

God, Prayer to

The Lord said unto Joshua, Get thee up; wherefore liest thou thus upon thy face? *Jos.* 7: 10.

What profit should we have, if we pray unto him? *Jb.* 21: 15.

The prayer of the upright is his delight. *Pr.* 15: 8.

Even them will I bring to my holy mountain, and make them joyful in my house of prayer. *Is.* 56: 7.

Your Father knoweth what things ye have need of before ye ask him. *Mat.* 6: 8.

He went out, and departed into a solitary place, and there prayed. *Mk.* 1: 35.

The whole multitude of the people were praying without at the time of the incense. *Lu.* 1: 10.

Continuing instant in prayer. *Ro.* 12: 12.

I will therefore that men pray every where, lifting up holy hands. *1 Ti.* 2: 8.

See also

God, Adoration of; God, Cry to; God, Gratitude to; God, Praise to; God, Thankfulness to; God, Worship of.

God, Preaching

The heavens declare the glory of God, and the firmament sheweth his handywork. *Ps.* 19: 1.

Then will I teach transgressors thy ways; and sinners shall be converted unto thee. *Ps.* 51: 13.

Say unto the cities of Judah, Behold your God! *Is.* 40: 9.

How beautiful upon the mountains are the feet of him that bringeth good tidings, that publisheth peace; that bringeth good tidings of good, that publisheth salvation; that saith unto Zion, Thy God reigneth. *Is.* 52: 7.

Go ye into all the world, and preach the gospel to every creature. *Mk.* 16: 15.

Go thou and preach the kingdom of God. *Lu.* 9: 60.

I kept back nothing that was profitable unto you, but have shewed you, and have taught you publickly, and from house to house, Testifying both to the Jews, and also to the Greeks, repentance toward God, and faith toward our Lord Jesus Christ. *Ac.* 20: 20, 21.

Preaching the kingdom of God. *Ac.* 28: 31.

If any man speak, let him speak as the oracles of God; if any man minister, let him do it as of the ability which God giveth. *1 Pe.* 4: 11.

See also

God, Revelation of; God, Word of.

God, Presence of

They heard the voice of the Lord God walking in the garden in the cool of the day. *Ge.* 3: 8.

Enoch walked with God. *Ge.* 5: 22.

Is the Lord among us, or not? *Ex.* 17: 7.

In all places where I record my name I will come unto thee, and I will bless thee. *Ex.* 20: 24.

My presence shall go with thee, and I will give thee rest. *Ex.* 33: 14.

There was upon the tabernacle as it were the appearance of fire, until the morning. *Nu.* 9: 15.

Ye stand this day all of you before the Lord your God. *De.* 29: 10.

Ye shall know that the living God is among you. *Jos.* 3: 10.

Therefore am I troubled at his presence. *Jb.* 23: 15.

In thy presence is fulness of joy. *Ps.* 16: 11.

Thou shalt hide them in the secret of thy presence from the pride of man. *Ps.* 31: 20.

God is in the midst of her; she shall not be moved: God shall help her, and that right early. *Ps.* 46: 5.

Cast me not away from thy presence. *Ps.* 51: 11.

Nevertheless I am continually with thee. *Ps.* 73: 23.

Let us come before his presence with thanksgiving. *Ps.* 95: 2.

Whither shall I go from thy spirit? or whither shall I flee from thy presence? *Ps.* 139: 7.

The upright shall dwell in thy presence. *Ps.* 140: 13.

When thou passest through the waters, I will be with thee; and through the rivers, they shall not overflow thee. *Is.* 43: 2.

Hold thy peace at the presence of the Lord God. *Zph.* 1: 7.

The Lord of hosts hath visited his flock. *Zch.* 10: 3.

I am Gabriel, that stand in the presence of the Lord. *Lu.* 1: 19.

Now therefore are we all here present before God, to hear all things that are commanded thee of God. *Ac.* 10: 33.

Though he be not far from every one of us. *Ac.* 17: 27.

No flesh should glory in his presence. *1 Co.* 1: 29.

He hath said, I will never leave thee, nor forsake thee. *He.* 13: 5.

Unto him that is able to keep you from falling, and to present you faultless before the presence of his glory with exceeding joy. *Jude* 1: 24.

See also

God, Communion with; God, Companionship of; God, Fellowship with; God, the Friend; God, Immanence of; God, Life in; God, Nearness of.

God, Primacy of

Hear, O Israel: the Lord our God is one Lord. *De.* 6: 4.

There is none holy as the Lord. *1 S.* 2: 2.

The pillars of the earth are the Lord's, and he hath set the world upon them. *1 S.* 2: 8.

I have set the Lord always before me. *Ps.* 16: 8.

I thank thee, O Father, Lord of heaven and earth. *Mat.* 11: 25.

There is no power but of God: the powers that be are ordained of God. *Ro.* 13: 1.

There be gods many, and lords many, But to us there is but one God, the Father. *1 Co.* 8: 5, 6.

See also

God, Leadership of; God, Omnipotence of; God, Overruling of; God, Sovereignty of; God, Sufficiency of; God, Supremacy of; God, Transcendence of.

God, Promise of

He declared unto you his covenant. *De.* 4: 13.

The Lord our God made a covenant with us. *De.* 5: 2.

The Lord thy God blesseth thee, as he promised thee. *De.* 15: 6.

Ye shall possess their land, as the Lord thy God hath promised unto you. *Jos.* 23: 5.

The Lord your God, he it is that fighteth for you, as he hath promised you. *Jos.* 23: 10.

All the paths of the Lord are mercy and truth unto such as keep his covenant. *Ps.* 25: 10.

He shall give thee the desires of thine heart. *Ps.* 37: 4.

The Lord shall preserve thy going out and thy coming in from this time forth, and even for evermore. *Ps.* 121: 8.

Behold, I send the promise of my Father upon you. *Lu.* 24: 49.

Behold, the days come, saith the Lord, when I will make a new covenant with the house of Israel. *He.* 8: 8.

For he is faithful that promised. *He.* 10: 23.

These all died in faith, not having received the promises, but having seen them afar off, and were persuaded of them, and embraced them. *He.* 11: 13.

We, according to his promise, look for new heavens and a new earth, wherein dwelleth righteousness. *2 Pe.* 3: 13.

This is the promise that he hath promised us, even eternal life. *1 Jn.* 2: 25.

See also

God, Word of.

God, Protection of

The terror of God was upon the cities that were round about them, and they did not pursue after the sons of Jacob. *Ge.* 35: 5.

The Lord shall fight for you, and ye shall hold your peace. *Ex.* 14: 14.

I will send my fear before thee, and will destroy all the people to whom thou shalt come, and I will make all thine enemies turn their backs unto thee. *Ex.* 23: 27.

Thou shalt bestir thyself: for then shall the Lord go out before thee, to smite the host of the Philistines. *2 S.* 5: 24.

I will defend this city, to save it. *2 K.* 19: 34.

The eyes of the Lord run to and fro throughout the whole earth, to shew himself strong in the behalf of them whose heart is perfect toward him. *2 Ch.* 16: 9.

The fear of God was on all the kingdoms of those countries, when they had heard that the Lord fought against the enemies of Israel. *2 Ch.* 20: 29.

With him is an arm of flesh; but with us is the Lord our God to help us, and to fight our battles. *2 Ch.* 32: 8.

The hand of our God was upon us, and he

delivered us from the hand of the enemy, and of such as lay in wait by the way. *Ezr.* 8: 31.

Be thou my strong rock, for an house of defence to save me. *Ps.* 31: 2.

He is my defence; I shall not be greatly moved. *Ps.* 62: 2.

Now also when I am old and greyheaded, O God, forsake me not. *Ps.* 71: 18.

According to the greatness of thy power preserve thou those that are appointed to die. *Ps.* 79: 11.

A thousand shall fall at thy side, and ten thousand at thy right hand; but it shall not come nigh thee. *Ps.* 91: 7.

My God is the rock of my refuge. *Ps.* 94: 22.

Save with thy right hand, and answer me. *Ps.* 108: 6.

As the mountains are round about Jerusalem, so the Lord is round about his people. *Ps.* 125: 2.

As birds flying, so will the Lord of hosts defend Jerusalem; defending also he will deliver it; and passing over he will preserve it. *Is.* 31: 5.

In the shadow of his hand hath he hid me, and made me a polished shaft; in his quiver hath he hid me. *Is.* 49: 2.

I will preserve thee, . . . to inherit the desolate heritages. *Is.* 49: 8.

The Lord will go before you; and the God of Israel will be your rereward. *Is.* 52: 12.

My God hath sent his angel, and hath shut the lions' mouths, that they have not hurt me. *Da.* 6: 22.

There shall not a hair of your head perish. *Lu.* 21: 18.

See also

God, Care of; God, Confidence in; God, the Keeper; God, Providence of; God, the Refuge; God, Reliance on; God, Security of; God, Solicitude of; God, the Sustainer.

God, Providence of

God will provide. *Ge.* 22: 8.

Ye have seen what I did unto the Egyptians, and how I bare you on eagles' wings, and brought you unto myself. *Ex.* 19: 4.

I will put thee in a clift of the rock, and will cover thee with my hand while I pass by. *Ex.* 33: 22.

Behold, God is mighty, and despiseth not any. *Jb.* 36: 5.

I laid me down and slept; I awaked; for the Lord sustained me. *Ps.* 3: 5.

He maketh me to lie down in green pastures: he leadeth me beside the still waters. *Ps.* 23: 2.

Oh how great is thy goodness, which thou hast laid up for them that fear thee. *Ps.* 31: 19.

I have been young, and now am old; yet have I not seen the righteous forsaken. *Ps.* 37: 25.

Thou hast delivered my soul from death. *Ps.* 56: 13.

Truly my soul waiteth upon God: from him cometh my salvation. *Ps.* 62: 1.

Forsake me not when my strength faileth. *Ps.* 71: 9.

Can God furnish a table in the wilderness? *Ps.* 78: 19.

It is vain for you to rise up early, to sit up late, to eat the bread of sorrows: for so he giveth his beloved sleep. *Ps.* 127: 2.

Lord, remember David, and all his afflictions. *Ps.* 132: 1.

Who giveth food to all flesh: for his mercy endureth for ever. *Ps.* 136: 25.

Until the spirit be poured upon us from on high, and the wilderness be a fruitful field, and the fruitful field be counted for a forest. *Is.* 32: 15.

As one whom his mother comforteth, so will I comfort you. *Is.* 66: 13.

I am with thee to deliver thee. *Je.* 1: 8.

His compassions fail not. *La.* 3: 22.

He maketh his sun to rise on the evil and on the good, and sendeth rain on the just and on the unjust. *Mat.* 5: 45.

Are not two sparrows sold for a farthing? and one of them shall not fall on the ground without your Father. *Mat.* 10: 29.

Not one of them is forgotten before God. *Lu.* 12: 6.

Consider the lilies. *Lu.* 12: 27.

How much more will he clothe you, O ye of little faith? *Lu.* 12: 28.

There shall not an hair of your head perish. *Lu.* 21: 18.

God having provided some better thing for us, that they without us should not be made perfect. *He.* 11: 40.

See also

God, Beneficence of; God, Care of; God, Comfort of; God, Compassion of; God, Favor of; God, Generosity of; God, Gift of; God, Goodness of; God, Grace of; God, the Keeper; God, Kindness of; God, the Shepherd; God, Solicitude of; God, the Sustainer; God, Sympathy of.

God, Punishment of

Blessed is the man whom thou chastenest, O Lord, and teachest him out of thy law. *Ps.* 94: 12.

Whom the Lord loveth he correcteth; even as a father the son in whom he delighteth. *Pr.* 3: 12.

I will punish the world for their evil, and the wicked for their iniquity. *Is.* 13: 11.

Behold, I have refined thee, but not with silver; I have chosen thee in the furnace of affliction. *Is.* 48: 10.

I will not turn away the punishment thereof; because they sold the righteous for silver, and the poor for a pair of shoes. *Am.* 2: 6.

You only have I known of all the families of the earth: therefore I will punish you for all your iniquities. *Am.* 3: 2.

It is a fearful thing to fall into the hands of the living God. *He.* 10: 31.

If ye endure chastening, God dealeth with you as with sons. *He.* 12: 7.

They verily for a few days chastened us after their own pleasure; but he for our profit, that we might be partakers of his holiness. *He.* 12: 10.

The Lord knoweth how to deliver the godly out of temptations, and to reserve the unjust unto the day of judgment to be punished. *2 Pe.* 2: 9.

See also

God, Anger of; God, Chastisement of; God, Reward of; God, Wrath of.

God, Purpose of

I have spoken it, I will also bring it to pass; I have purposed it, I will also do it. *Is.* 46: 11.

Hear . . . his purposes, that he hath purposed. *Je.* 49: 20.

Every purpose of the Lord shall be performed. *Je.* 51: 29.

God so loved the world, that he gave his only begotten Son, that whosoever believeth in him should not perish, but have everlasting life. *Jn.* 3: 16.

God sending his own Son in the likeness of sinful flesh, and for sin, condemned sin in the flesh. *Ro.* 8: 3.

We know that all things work together for good to them that love God, to them who are the called according to his purpose. *Ro.* 8: 28.

That the purpose of God according to election might stand, not of works, but of him that calleth. *Ro.* 9: 11.

Even for this same purpose have I raised thee up, that I might shew my power in thee, and that my name might be declared throughout all the earth. *Ro.* 9: 17.

Having made known unto us the mystery of his will, according to his good pleasure which he hath purposed in himself. *Ep.* 1: 9.

According to the purpose of him who worketh all things after the counsel of his own will. *Ep.* 1: 11.

According to the eternal purpose which he purposed in Christ Jesus our Lord. *Ep.* 3: 11.

Who hath saved us, and called us with an holy calling, not according to our works, but according to his own purpose and grace. *2 Ti.* 1: 9.

See also
God, Will of.

God, Quest for

Seek for all the commandments of the Lord your God. *1 Ch.* 28: 8.

If thou seek him, he will be found of thee. *1 Ch.* 28: 9.

The good Lord pardon every one That prepareth his heart to seek God. *2 Ch.* 30: 18, 19.

Canst thou by searching find out God? *Jb.* 11: 7.

When thou saidst, Seek ye my face; my heart said unto thee, Thy face, Lord, will I seek. *Ps.* 27: 8.

My soul followeth hard after thee: thy right hand upholdeth me. *Ps.* 63: 8.

Let all those that seek thee rejoice and be glad in thee. *Ps.* 70: 4.

They shall go with their flocks and with their herds to seek the Lord; but they shall not find him. *Ho.* 5: 6.

It is time to seek the Lord, till he come and rain righteousness upon you. *Ho.* 10: 12.

Ye who turn judgment to wormwood, and leave off righteousness in the earth, Seek him that maketh the seven stars and Orion, and turneth the shadow of death into the morning, and maketh the day dark with night. *Am.* 5: 7, 8.

Seek ye first the kingdom of God, and his righteousness; and all these things shall be added unto you. *Mat.* 6: 33.

That they should seek the Lord, if haply they might feel after him, and find him, though he be not far from every one of us. *Ac.* 17: 27.

See also
God, Longing for; God, Search for; God, Thirst for; God, Yearning for.

God, Rebellion against

I have sinned against the Lord your God, and against you. *Ex.* 10: 16.

Your murmurings are not against us, but against the Lord. *Ex.* 16: 8.

Rebel not ye against the Lord. *Nu.* 14: 9.

God forbid that we should rebel against the Lord, and turn this day from following the Lord. *Jos.* 22: 29.

He wist not that the Lord was departed from him. *Ju.* 16: 20.

Ye said unto me, Nay; but a king shall reign over us: when the Lord your God was your king. *1 S.* 12: 12.

Because thou hast rejected the word of the Lord, he hath also rejected thee from being king. *1 S.* 15: 23.

They say unto God, Depart from us; for we desire not the knowledge of thy ways. *Jb.* 21: 14.

What is the Almighty, that we should serve him? and what profit should we have, if we pray unto him? *Jb.* 21: 15.

The kings of the earth set themselves, and the rulers take counsel together, against the Lord, and against his anointed. *Ps.* 2: 2.

Cast them out in the multitude of their transgressions; for they have rebelled against thee. *Ps.* 5: 10.

Let not the rebellious exalt themselves. *Ps.* 66: 7.

They rebelled against the words of God, and contemned the counsel of the most High. *Ps.* 107: 11.

As for our iniquities, we know them; In transgressing and lying against the Lord, and departing away from our God, speaking oppression and revolt. *Is.* 59: 12, 13.

Behold, I will cast thee from off the face of the earth: this year thou shalt die, because thou hast taught rebellion against the Lord. *Je.* 28: 16.

The God in whose hand thy breath is, and whose are all thy ways, hast thou not glorified. *Da.* 5: 23.

They have dealt treacherously against the Lord. *Ho.* 5: 7.

The younger son gathered all together, and took his journey into a far country. *Lu.* 15: 13.

He is antichrist, that denieth the Father and the Son. *1 Jn.* 2: 22.

See also
Atheism; God, Antagonism to; God, Denial of; God, Estrangement from; God, Rejection of; Godlessness.

God, the Redeemer

Arise, O Lord; save me, O my God. *Ps.* 3: 7.

Salvation belongeth unto the Lord. *Ps.* 3: 8.

Return, O Lord, deliver my soul. *Ps.* 6: 4.

Preserve me, O God: for in thee do I put my trust. *Ps.* 16: 1.

O Lord, my strength, and my redeemer. *Ps.* 19: 14.

I have declared thy faithfulness and thy salvation. *Ps.* 40: 10.

They cried unto the Lord in their trouble, and he saved them out of their distresses. *Ps.* 107: 13.

With the Lord there is mercy, and with him is plenteous redemption. *Ps.* 130: 7.

Fear not: for I have redeemed thee, I have called thee by thy name; thou art mine. *Is.* 43: 1.

I am the Lord thy God, the Holy One of Israel, thy Saviour. *Is.* 43: 3.

My righteousness shall be for ever, and my salvation from generation to generation. *Is.* 51: 8.

He hath clothed me with the garments of salvation. *Is.* 61: 10.

The living God . . . is the Saviour of all men, especially of those that believe. *1 Ti.* 4: 10.

See also

God, Deliverance of; God, Salvation of; God, Security of.

God, the Refuge

The eternal God is thy refuge. *De.* 33: 27.

The Lord also will be a refuge for the oppressed, a refuge in times of trouble. *Ps.* 9: 9.

The eye of the Lord is upon them that fear him, . . . To deliver their soul from death, and to keep them alive in famine. *Ps.* 33: 18, 19.

Lead me to the rock that is higher than I. *Ps.* 61: 2.

Thou hast been a shelter for me, and a strong tower from the enemy. *Ps.* 61: 3.

Thou hast made the Lord, which is my refuge, even the most High, thy habitation. *Ps.* 91: 9.

O Lord, my strength, and my fortress, and my refuge in the day of affliction. *Je.* 16: 19.

When my soul fainted within me I remembered the Lord. *Jon.* 2: 7.

See also

God, Confidence in; God, Protection of; God, the Rock; God, Security of; God, the Unchanging.

God, Rejection of

They have not rejected thee, but they have rejected me. *1 S.* 8: 7.

Ye have this day rejected your God. *1 S.* 10: 19.

Because thou hast rejected the word of the Lord, he hath also rejected thee from being king. *1 S.* 15: 23.

They say unto God, Depart from us; for we desire not the knowledge of thy ways. *Jb.* 21: 14.

Their root shall be as rottenness, and their blossom shall go up as dust: because they have cast away the law of the Lord of hosts, and despised the word of the Holy One of Israel. *Is.* 5: 24.

They have rejected the word of the Lord; and what wisdom is in them? *Je.* 8: 9.

Because thou hast rejected knowledge, I will also reject thee. *Ho.* 4: 6.

My God will cast them away, because they did not hearken unto him: and they shall be wanderers among the nations. *Ho.* 9: 17.

They made their hearts as an adamant stone, lest they should hear the law, and the words which the Lord of hosts hath sent in his spirit by the former prophets. *Zch.* 7: 12.

Full well ye reject the commandment of God, that ye may keep your own tradition. *Mk.* 7: 9.

The Pharisees and lawyers rejected the counsel of God against themselves. *Lu.* 7: 30.

Ye will not come to me, that ye might have life. *Jn.* 5: 40.

Even as they did not like to retain God in their knowledge, God gave them over to a reprobate mind, to do those things which are not convenient. *Ro.* 1: 28.

All day long I have stretched forth my hands unto a disobedient and gainsaying people. *Ro.* 10: 21.

See also

Atheism; Estrangement; God, Antagonism to; God, Estrangement from; God, Rebellion against; Godlessness.

God, Reliance on

I will not fail thee, nor forsake thee. *Jos.* 1: 5.

Lord, it is nothing with thee to help, whether with many, or with them that have no power. *2 Ch.* 14: 11.

Because thou hast relied on the king of Syria, and not relied on the Lord thy God, therefore is the host of the king of Syria escaped out of thine hand. *2 Ch.* 16: 7.

With him is an arm of flesh; but with us is the Lord our God to help us, and to fight our battles. *2 Ch.* 32: 8.

Unto thee, O Lord, do I lift up my soul. *Ps.* 25: 1.

Thou art my help and my deliverer; make no tarrying, O my God. *Ps.* 40: 17.

God is our refuge and strength, a very present help in trouble. *Ps.* 46: 1.

Unless the Lord had been my help, my soul had almost dwelt in silence. *Ps.* 94: 17.

What will ye do in the day of visitation? . . . to whom will ye flee for help? *Is.* 10: 3.

I did know thee in the wilderness, in the land of great drought. *Ho.* 13: 5.

The Son can do nothing of himself, but what he seeth the Father do. *Jn.* 5: 19.

If any of you lack wisdom, let him ask of God. *Ja.* 1: 5.

See also

God, Belief in; God, Certainty of; God, Confidence in; God, Faith in; God, Hope in; God, Trust in.

God, Rest in

When he giveth quietness, who then can make trouble? *Jb.* 34: 29.

I laid me down and slept; I awaked; for the Lord sustained me. *Ps.* 3: 5.

He maketh me to lie down in green pastures. *Ps.* 23: 2.

They looked unto him, and were lightened: and their faces were not ashamed. *Ps.* 34: 5.

Rest in the Lord, and wait patiently for him. *Ps.* 37: 7.

My hope is in thee. *Ps.* 39: 7.

God is our refuge and strength, a very present help in trouble. *Ps.* 46: 1.

In the shadow of thy wings will I make my refuge, until these calamities be overpast. *Ps.* 57: 1.

Return unto thy rest, O my soul. *Ps.* 116: 7.

There shall be a tabernacle for a shadow in the daytime from the heat, and for a place of refuge, and for a covert from storm and from rain. *Is.* 4: 6.

It is good that a man should both hope and quietly wait for the salvation of the Lord. *Lam.* 3: 26.

There remaineth therefore a rest to the people of God. *He.* 4: 9.

See also

God, Confidence in; God, Peace of; God, the Refuge; God, Security of.

God, Return to

Thou shalt return and obey the voice of the Lord. *De.* 30: 8.

If they return to thee with all their heart and with all their soul in the land of their captivity: . . . Then hear thou from the heavens, . . . and forgive thy people which have sinned against thee. *2 Ch.* 6: 38, 39.

My son, give me thine heart. *Pr.* 23: 26.

Then shall the dust return to the earth as it was: and the spirit shall return unto God who gave it. *Ec.* 12: 7.

Return, ye backsliding children, and I will heal your backsliding. *Je.* 3: 22.

Afterward shall the children of Israel return, . . . and shall fear the Lord and his goodness in the latter days. *Ho.* 3: 5.

Come, and let us return unto the Lord. *Ho.* 6: 1.

O Israel, return unto the Lord thy God; for thou hast fallen by thine iniquity. *Ho.* 14: 1.

Return unto me, and I will return unto you, saith the Lord of hosts. *Mal.* 3: 7.

Ye were as sheep going astray; but are now returned unto the Shepherd and Bishop of your souls. *1 Pe.* 2: 25.

See also

God, Surrender to.

God, Revelation of

God Almighty appeared unto me. *Ge.* 48: 3.

Let thy work appear unto thy servants, and thy glory unto their children. *Ps.* 90: 16.

In the year that king Uzziah died I saw also the Lord. *Is.* 6: 1.

The glory of the Lord shall be revealed. *Is.* 40: 5.

To whom then will ye liken God? *Is.* 40: 18.

Blessed be the name of God for ever and ever. . . . He revealeth the deep and secret things. *Da.* 2: 20, 22.

Your God is . . . a revealer of secrets. *Da.* 2: 47.

Thou hast hid these things from the wise and prudent, and hast revealed them unto babes. *Mat.* 11: 25.

Flesh and blood hath not revealed it unto thee, but my Father which is in heaven. *Mat.* 16: 17.

Therein is the righteousness of God revealed from faith to faith. *Ro.* 1: 17.

God hath revealed them unto us by his Spirit. *1 Co.* 2: 10.

God shall reveal even this unto you. *Ph.* 3: 15.

See also

God, Face of; God, Vision of; God, Voice of; God, Word of.

God, Reward of

The Lord your God is God of gods, and Lord of lords, a great God, a mighty, and a terrible, which regardeth not persons, nor taketh reward. *De.* 10: 17.

To me belongeth vengeance, and recompense. *De.* 32: 35.

I will render vengeance to mine enemies, and will reward them that hate me. *De.* 32: 41.

As I have done, so God hath requited me. *Ju.* 1: 7.

It may be that the Lord will . . . requite me good for his cursing this day. *2 S.* 16: 12.

The Lord gave Job twice as much as he had before. *Jb.* 42: 10.

Thou shalt make them drink of the river of thy pleasures. *Ps.* 36: 8.

He hath not dealt with us after our sins; nor rewarded us according to our iniquities. *Ps.* 103: 10.

Thou shalt heap coals of fire upon his head, and the Lord shall reward thee. *Pr.* 25: 22.

Since the beginning of the world, men have not heard, nor perceived by the ear, neither hath the eye seen, O God, beside thee, what he hath prepared for him that waiteth for him. *Is.* 64: 4.

I will recompense their iniquity and their sin double. *Je.* 16: 18.

The Lord God of recompences shall surely requite. *Je.* 51: 56.

All the trees of the field shall know that I the Lord have brought down the high tree, have exalted the low tree, have dried up the green tree, and have made the dry tree to flourish. *Eze.* 17: 24.

Take heed that ye do not your alms before men, to be seen of them: otherwise ye have no reward of your Father. *Mat.* 6: 1.

Thy Father which seeth in secret himself shall reward thee openly. *Mat.* 6: 4.

Thou shalt be recompensed at the resurrection of the just. *Lu.* 14: 14.

He is a rewarder of them that diligently seek him. *He.* 11: 6.

See also

God, Chastisement of; God, Punishment of.

God, Riches of

Both riches and honour come of thee, and thou reignest over all. *1 Ch.* 29: 12.

All things come of thee, and of thine own have we given thee. *1 Ch.* 29: 14.

The earth is full of thy riches. *Ps.* 104: 24.

God hath given riches and wealth. *Ec.* 5: 19.

I will give thee the treasures of darkness, and hidden riches of secret places. *Is.* 45: 3.

The gift of God is eternal life. *Ro.* 6: 23.

O the depth of the riches both of the wisdom and knowledge of God! how unsearchable are his judgments, and his ways past finding out! *Ro.* 11: 33.

See also
God, Fullness of; God, Generosity of; God, Gift of; God, Perfection of; God, Sufficiency of; God, Wealth of.

God, Righteousness of

Shall not the Judge of all the earth do right? *Ge.* 18: 25.
The Lord is righteous, and I and my people are wicked. *Ex.* 9: 27.
The righteous Lord loveth righteousness. *Ps.* 11: 7.
The judgments of the Lord are true and righteous altogether. *Ps.* 19: 9.
Good and upright is the Lord. *Ps.* 25: 8.
The heavens shall declare his righteousness. *Ps.* 50: 6.
Thy righteousness also, O God, is very high. *Ps.* 71: 19.
My tongue also shall talk of thy righteousness all the day long. *Ps.* 71: 24.
His righteousness endureth for ever. *Ps.* 111: 3.
The Lord is righteous in all his ways, and holy in all his works. *Ps.* 145: 17.
I the Lord speak righteousness, I declare things that are right. *Is.* 45: 19.
This is his name whereby he shall be called, THE LORD OUR RIGHTEOUSNESS. *Je.* 23: 6.
O Lord, righteousness belongeth unto thee. *Da.* 9: 7.
The ways of the Lord are right, and the just shall walk in them. *Ho.* 14: 9.
Unto you that fear my name shall the Sun of righteousness arise with healing in his wings. *Mal.* 4: 2.
See also
God, Fairness of; God, Faithfulness of; God, Goodness of; God, Holiness of; God, Impartiality of; God, the Judge.

God, the Rock

The Lord is my strength and song. *Ex.* 15: 2.
He forsook the God which made him, and lightly esteemed the Rock of his salvation. *De.* 32: 15.
Of the Rock that begat thee thou art unmindful. *De.* 32: 18.
The Lord is my rock, and my fortress. *2 S.* 22: 2.
The God of my rock; in him will I trust. *2 S.* 22: 3.
Exalted be the God of the rock of my salvation. *2 S.* 22: 47.
He is wise in heart, and mighty in strength. *Jb.* 9: 4.
For who is God save the Lord? or who is a rock save our God? *Ps.* 18: 31.
Unto thee will I cry, O Lord, my rock. *Ps.* 28: 1.
Give unto the Lord, O ye mighty, give unto the Lord glory and strength. *Ps.* 29: 1.
Be thou my strong rock, for an house of defence to save me. *Ps.* 31: 2.
Lead me to the rock that is higher than I. *Ps.* 61: 2.
Be thou my strong habitation. *Ps.* 71: 3.
The Lord is clothed with strength. *Ps.* 93: 1.
Let us make a joyful noise to the rock of our salvation. *Ps.* 95: 1.

The strength of the hills is his also. *Ps.* 95: 4.
The weakness of God is stronger than men. *1 Co.* 1: 25.
Be strong in the Lord, and in the power of his might. *Ep.* 6: 10.
See also
God, Certainty of; God, Confidence in; God, the Eternal; God, Protection of; God, the Refuge; God, Security of; God, the Unchanging.

God, Salvation of

The Lord will preserve him, and keep him alive. *Ps.* 41: 2.
Surely his salvation is nigh them that fear him. *Ps.* 85: 9.
Because he hath set his love upon me, therefore will I deliver him. *Ps.* 91: 14.
Shew forth his salvation from day to day. *Ps.* 96: 2.
Plead my cause, and deliver me. *Ps.* 119: 154.
I have longed for thy salvation, O Lord. *Ps.* 119: 174.
Beside me there is no saviour. *Is.* 43: 11.
All the ends of the earth shall see the salvation of our God. *Is.* 52: 10.
Behold, thy salvation cometh. *Is.* 62: 11.
Mighty to save. *Is.* 63: 1.
My spirit hath rejoiced in God my Saviour. *Lu.* 1: 47.
Mine eyes have seen thy salvation. *Lu.* 2: 30.
The Lord knoweth how to deliver the godly out of temptations. *2 Pe.* 2: 9.
See also
God, Deliverance of; God, the Redeemer; God, Security of.

God, Scorn of

As one man mocketh another, do ye so mock him? *Jb.* 13: 9.
Why do the heathen rage, and the people imagine a vain thing? . . . He that sitteth in the heavens shall laugh: the Lord shall have them in derision. *Ps.* 2: 1, 4.
Wherefore doth the wicked contemn God? *Ps.* 10: 13.
With the froward thou wilt shew thyself froward. *Ps.* 18: 26.
Thou, O Lord, shalt laugh at them; thou shalt have all the heathen in derision. *Ps.* 59: 8.
They rebelled against the words of God, and contemned the counsel of the most High. *Ps.* 107: 11.
I also will laugh at your calamity; I will mock when your fear cometh. *Pr.* 1: 26.
Surely he scorneth the scorners. *Pr.* 3: 34.
Whoso mocketh the poor reproacheth his Maker. *Pr.* 17: 5.
Therefore have I made thee a reproach unto the heathen, and a mocking to all countries. *Eze.* 22: 4.
Be not deceived; God is not mocked. *Ga.* 6: 7.
See also
God, Antagonism to; God, Denial of; God, Estrangement from; God, Loss of; God, Rejection of.

God, Search for

Seek the Lord and his strength, seek his face continually. *1 Ch.* 16: 11.

They entered into a covenant to seek the Lord God of their fathers with all their heart and with all their soul. *2 Ch.* 15: 12.

Oh that I knew where I might find him! *Jb.* 23: 3.

They that seek the Lord shall not want any good thing. *Ps.* 34: 10.

They returned and inquired early after God. *Ps.* 78: 34.

They that seek the Lord understand all things. *Pr.* 28: 5.

Ye shall seek for me, and find me, when ye shall search for me with all your heart. *Je.* 29: 13.

Let us search and try our ways, and turn again to the Lord. *La.* 3: 40.

Thus saith the Lord unto the house of Israel, Seek ye me, and ye shall live. *Am.* 5: 4.

Seek the Lord, and ye shall live. *Am.* 5: 6.

I will cut off . . . those that have not sought the Lord. *Zph.* 1: 3, 6.

The Lord, whom ye seek, shall suddenly come to his temple. *Mal.* 3: 1.

If ye then be risen with Christ, seek those things which are above. *Col.* 3: 1.

See also

God, Longing for; God, Quest for; God, Thirst for; God, Yearning for.

God, Secret of

The secret things belong unto the Lord our God. *De.* 29: 29.

Hast thou heard the secret of God? *Jb.* 15: 8.

As I was in the days of my youth when the secret of God was upon my tabernacle. *Jb.* 29: 4.

The secret of the Lord is with them that fear him. *Ps.* 25: 14.

His secret is with the righteous. *Pr.* 3: 32.

It is the glory of God to conceal a thing. *Pr.* 25: 2.

I will give thee the treasures of darkness, and the hidden riches of secret places. *Is.* 45: 3.

Verily thou art a God that hidest thyself. *Is.* 45: 15.

He revealeth his secret unto his servants the prophets. *Am.* 3: 7.

I thank thee, O Father, Lord of heaven and earth, because thou hast hid these things from the wise and prudent, and hast revealed them unto babes. *Mat.* 11: 25.

Unto you it is given to know the mystery of the kingdom of God. *Mk.* 4: 11.

We speak the wisdom of God in a mystery, even the hidden wisdom. *1 Co.* 2: 7.

Great is the mystery of godliness. *1 Ti.* 3: 16.

See also

God, the Hiding; God, Silence of; God, the Unseen.

God, Security of

Their rock is not as our Rock, even our enemies themselves being judges. *De.* 32: 31.

Underneath are the everlasting arms. *De.* 33: 27.

His heart is fixed, trusting in the Lord. *Ps.* 112: 7.

The horse is prepared against the day of battle: but safety is of the Lord. *Pr.* 21: 31.

My people shall dwell in a peaceable habitation, and in sure dwellings, and in quiet resting places. *Is.* 32: 18.

The Lord is good, a strong hold in the day of trouble; and he knoweth them that trust in him. *Na.* 1: 7.

Whether we live therefore, or die, we are the Lord's. *Ro.* 14: 8.

See also

God, Certainty of; God, Confidence in; God, Protection of; God, the Refuge; God, the Rock; God, the Unchanging.

God, Servant of

As for me and my house, we will serve the Lord. *Jos.* 24: 15.

We are the servants of the God of heaven and earth. *Ezr.* 5: 11.

Hide not thy face from thy servant. *Ps.* 69: 17.

I have found David my servant; with my holy oil have I anointed him. *Ps.* 89: 20.

Let thy work appear unto thy servants. *Ps.* 90: 16.

Behold my servant, whom I uphold. *Is.* 42: 1.

Behold, my servant shall deal prudently, he shall be exalted and extolled, and be very high. *Is.* 52: 13.

Is thy God, whom thou servest continually, able to deliver thee? *Da.* 6: 20.

Thou shalt worship the Lord thy God, and him only shalt thou serve. *Mat.* 4: 10.

No man can serve two masters. . . . Ye cannot serve God and mammon. *Mat.* 6: 24.

Lord, now lettest thou thy servant depart in peace. *Lu.* 2: 29.

There stood by me this night the angel of God, whose I am, and whom I serve. *Ac.* 27: 23.

Being made free from sin, and become servants to God. *Ro.* 6: 22.

With good will doing service, as to the Lord, and not to men. *Ep.* 6: 7.

He pleased God. *He.* 11: 5.

See also

God, Love of; God, Loyalty to; God, Obedience to; God, Obligation to.

God, the Shepherd

The Lord is my shepherd; I shall not want. *Ps.* 23: 1.

He maketh me to lie down in green pastures. *Ps.* 23: 2.

Thou leddest thy people like a flock by the hand of Moses and Aaron. *Ps.* 77: 20.

We are the people of his pasture. *Ps.* 95: 7.

He shall feed his flock like a shepherd. *Is.* 40: 11.

The Lord hath spoiled their pasture. *Je.* 25: 36.

I will feed them in a good pasture, and upon the high mountains of Israel shall their fold be. *Eze.* 34: 14.

Fear not, little flock; for it is your Father's good pleasure to give you the kingdom. *Lu.* 12: 32.

See also

God, Beneficence of; God, Care of; God, Goodness of; God, the Keeper; God, Kindness of; God, Solicitude of; God, the Sustainer.

God, Silence of

He rested on the seventh day. *Ge.* 2: 2.

There is no speech nor language, where their voice is not heard. *Ps.* 19: 3.

Be not silent to me. *Ps.* 28: 1.

Be still, and know that I am God. *Ps.* 46: 10.

Keep not thou silence, O God: hold not thy peace, and be not still, O God. *Ps.* 83: 1.

The Lord is in his holy temple: let all the earth keep silence before him. *Hab.* 2: 20.

Be silent, O all flesh, before the Lord. *Zch.* 2: 13.

See also

God, the Hiding; God, Secret of; God, the Unseen.

God, Solicitude of

Thou preparest a table before me in the presence of mine enemies. *Ps.* 23: 5.

Can he give bread also? can he provide flesh for his people? *Ps.* 78: 20.

He shall give his angels charge over thee, to keep thee in all thy ways. *Ps.* 91: 11.

In the multitude of my thoughts within me thy comforts delight my soul. *Ps.* 94: 19.

His compassions fail not. *La.* 3: 22.

For why will ye die, O house of Israel? *Eze.* 18: 31.

How shall I give thee up, Ephraim? how shall I deliver thee, Israel? *Ho.* 11: 8.

Not one of them is forgotten before God. *Lu.* 12: 6.

Consider the ravens. *Lu.* 12: 24.

There shall not an hair of your head perish. *Lu.* 21: 18.

Blessed be God, even the Father of our Lord Jesus Christ, the Father of mercies, and the God of all comfort; Who comforteth us in all our tribulation, that we may be able to comfort them which are in any trouble, by the comfort wherewith we ourselves are comforted of God. *2 Co.* 1: 3, 4.

Casting all your care upon him; for he careth for you. *1 Pe.* 5: 7.

See also

God, Comfort of; God, Compassion of; God, Favor of; God, Goodness of; God, Grace of; God, the Keeper; God, Kindness of; God, the Shepherd; God, the Sustainer; God, Sympathy of.

God, the Son of

Thus saith the Lord, Israel is my son, even my firstborn. *Ex.* 4: 22.

Ye are gods; and all of you are children of the most High. *Ps.* 82: 6.

In the place where it was said unto them, Ye are not my people, there it shall be said unto them, Ye are the sons of the living God. *Ho.* 1: 10.

Love your enemies, . . . That ye may be the children of your Father which is in heaven. *Mat.* 5: 44, 45.

As many as are led by the Spirit of God, they are the sons of God. *Ro.* 8: 14.

Ye shall be my sons and daughters, saith the Lord Almighty. *2 Co.* 6: 18.

Ye are all the children of God by faith in Christ Jesus. *Ga.* 3: 26.

Because ye are sons, God hath sent forth the Spirit of his Son into your hearts. *Ga.* 4: 6.

Thou art no more a servant, but a son; and if a son, then an heir of God through Christ. *Ga.* 4: 7.

It became him, . . . in bringing many sons unto glory, to make the captain of their salvation perfect through sufferings. *He.* 2: 10.

God dealeth with you as with sons. *He.* 12: 7.

Beloved, now are we the sons of God, and it doth not yet appear what we shall be: but we know that, when he shall appear, we shall be like him; for we shall see him as he is. *1 Jn.* 3: 2.

He that overcometh shall inherit all things; and I will be his God, and he shall be my son. *Re.* 21: 7.

See also

God, Child of; God, People of.

God, Sovereignty of

O Lord God, thou hast begun to shew thy servant thy greatness, and thy mighty hand. *De.* 3: 24.

Behold, the heaven and the heaven of heavens is the Lord's thy God, the earth also, with all that therein is. *De.* 10: 14.

Thou reignest over all; and in thine hand is power and might. *1 Ch.* 29: 12.

God himself is with us for our captain. *2 Ch.* 13: 12.

He leadeth princes away spoiled, and overthroweth the mighty. *Jb.* 12: 19.

I will be exalted among the heathen, I will be exalted in the earth. *Ps.* 46: 10.

All kings shall fall down before him. *Ps.* 72: 11.

God is my King of old, working salvation in the midst of the earth. *Ps.* 74: 12.

The Holy One of Israel is our king. *Ps.* 89: 18.

The Lord reigneth; let the earth rejoice. *Ps.* 97: 1.

The king's heart is in the hand of the Lord as the rivers of water: he turneth it whithersoever he will. *Pr.* 21: 1.

The Lord is the true God, he is the living God, and an everlasting king. *Je.* 10: 10.

That the living may know that the most High ruleth in the kingdom of men. *Da.* 4: 17.

We ought to obey God rather than men. *Ac.* 5: 29.

He must reign, till he hath put all enemies under his feet. *1 Co.* 15: 25.

To the only wise God our Saviour, be glory and majesty, dominion and power, both now and ever. *Jude* 1: 25.

I heard as it were the voice of a great multitude, and as the voice of many waters, and as the voice of mighty thunderings, saying, Alleluia: for the Lord God omnipotent reigneth. *Re.* 19: 6.

See also

God, Compulsion of; God, Dominion of; God, the King; God, Kingdom of; God, Majesty of; God, Omnipotence of; God, Overruling of; God, Power of; God, Supremacy of.

God, Spirit of

The Spirit of God moved upon the face of the waters. *Ge.* 1: 2.

The Spirit of the Lord came upon Gideon. *Ju.* 6: 34.

The Spirit of the Lord began to move him. *Ju.* 13: 25.

The spirit of God hath made me, and the breath of the Almighty hath given me life. *Jb.* 33: 4.

Thou sendest forth thy spirit, they are created. *Ps.* 104: 30.

Whither shall I go from thy spirit? *Ps.* 139: 7.

I will pour out my spirit unto you. *Pr.* 1: 23.

Behold my servant, whom I uphold; . . . I have put my spirit upon him. *Is.* 42: 1.

The Spirit of the Lord God is upon me. *Is.* 61: 1.

I will pour out my spirit upon all flesh. *Jo.* 2: 28.

Not by might, nor by power, but by my spirit, saith the Lord of hosts. *Zch.* 4: 6.

As many as are led by the Spirit of God, they are the sons of God. *Ro.* 8: 14.

The things of God knoweth no man, but the Spirit of God. *1 Co.* 2: 11.

We have received, not the spirit of the world, but the spirit which is of God. *1 Co.* 2: 12.

The natural man receiveth not the things of the Spirit of God. *1 Co.* 2: 14.

Know ye not that ye are the temple of God, and that the Spirit of God dwelleth in you? *1 Co.* 3: 16.

Ye are sanctified . . . by the Spirit of our God. *1 Co.* 6: 11.

Strengthened with might by his Spirit in the inner man. *Ep.* 3: 16.

Grieve not the holy Spirit of God. *Ep.* 4: 30.

Hereby know ye the Spirit of God: Every spirit that confesseth that Jesus Christ is come in the flesh is of God. *1 Jn.* 4: 2.

Hereby know we that we dwell in him, and he in us, because he hath given us of his Spirit. *1 Jn.* 4: 13.

God, Strength of

In thine hand it is to make great, and to give strength unto all. *1 Ch.* 29: 12.

God hath power to help, and to cast down. *2 Ch.* 25: 8.

The joy of the Lord is your strength. *Ne.* 8: 10.

I know that thou canst do every thing. *Jb.* 42: 2.

The Lord strong and mighty, the Lord mighty in battle. *Ps.* 24: 8.

Happy is he that hath the God of Jacob for his help. *Ps.* 146: 5.

Let him take hold of my strength, that he may make peace with me; and he shall make peace with me. *Is.* 27: 5.

To them that have no might he increaseth strength. *Is.* 40: 29.

I will work, and who shall let it? *Is.* 43: 13.

Seek him . . . That strengtheneth the spoiled against the strong, so that the spoiled shall come against the fortress. *Am.* 5: 8, 9.

The Lord God is my strength. *Hab.* 3: 19.

With God all things are possible. *Mat.* 19: 26.

If it be of God, ye cannot overthrow it. *Ac.* 5: 39.

According to the working of his mighty power. *Ep.* 1: 19.

Be strong in the Lord, and in the power of his might. *Ep.* 6: 10.

See also

Almighty; God, the Almighty; God, Omnipotence of; God, Power of.

God, Sufficiency of

Forty years didst thou sustain them in the wilderness, so that they lacked nothing. *Ne.* 9: 21.

In thy presence is fulness of joy. *Ps.* 16: 11.

I will be thy king: where is any other that may save thee in all thy cities? *Ho.* 13: 10.

Prove me now herewith, saith the Lord of hosts, if I will not open you the windows of heaven, and pour you out a blessing, that there shall not be room enough to receive it. *Mal.* 3: 10.

How shall he not with him also freely give us all things? *Ro.* 8: 32.

Our sufficiency is of God. *2 Co.* 3: 5.

God is able to make all grace abound toward you. *2 Co.* 9: 8.

My grace is sufficient for thee: for my strength is made perfect in weakness. *2 Co.* 12: 9.

Unto him that is able to do exceeding abundantly above all that we ask or think. *Ep.* 3: 20.

One God and Father of all, who is above all, and through all, and in you all. *Ep.* 4: 6.

Just and true are thy ways, thou King of saints. *Re.* 15: 3.

See also

God, Confidence in; God, Fullness of; God, Perfection of; God, Primacy of.

God, Supremacy of

Let men say among the nations, The Lord reigneth. *1 Ch.* 16: 31.

All the congregation blessed the Lord God of their fathers, and bowed down their heads, and worshipped the Lord, and the king. *1 Ch.* 29: 20.

Let us exalt his name together. *Ps.* 34: 3.

Be thou exalted, O God, above the heavens; let thy glory be above all the earth. *Ps.* 57: 5.

He ruleth by his power for ever; his eyes behold the nations. *Ps.* 66: 7.

Thy kingdom is an everlasting kingdom. *Ps.* 145: 13.

The kingdoms of this world are become the kingdoms of our Lord, and of his Christ. *Re.* 11: 15.

See also

God, Dominion of; God, the King; God, Kingdom of; God, Majesty of; God, Omnipotence of; God, Overruling of; God, Power of; God, Primacy of; God, Sovereignty of.

God, Surrender to

Be ye not stiffnecked, as your fathers were, but yield yourselves unto the Lord, and enter his sanctuary. *2 Ch.* 30: 8.

My son, give me thine heart. *Pr.* 23: 26.

I will go and return to my place, till they acknowledge their offence, and seek my face. *Ho.* 5: 15.

Jesus, when he had cried again with a loud voice, yielded up the ghost. *Mat.* 27: 50.

Yield yourselves unto God, as those that are alive from the dead. *Ro.* 6: 13.

Know ye not, that to whom ye yield yourselves servants to obey, his servants ye are to whom ye obey; whether of sin unto death, or of obedience unto righteousness? *Ro.* 6: 16.

Yield your members servants to righteousness unto holiness. *Ro.* 6: 19.

We have had fathers of our flesh which corrected us, and we gave them reverence: shall we not much rather be in subjection unto the Father of spirits, and live? *He.* 12: 9.

Humble yourselves therefore under the mighty hand of God. *1 Pe.* 5: 6.

See also
God, Return to.

God, the Sustainer

I laid me down and slept; I awaked; for the Lord sustained me. *Ps.* 3: 5.

Cast thy burden upon the Lord, and he shall sustain thee. *Ps.* 55: 22.

Thou preparest them corn, when thou hast so provided for it. *Ps.* 65: 9.

Can he give bread also? can he provide flesh for his people? *Ps.* 78: 20.

Unless the Lord had been my help, my soul had almost dwelt in silence. *Ps.* 94: 17.

Hold thou me up, and I shall be safe: and I will have respect unto thy statutes continually. *Ps.* 119: 117.

Come ye, buy, and eat; come, buy wine and milk without money and without price. *Is.* 55: 1.

His arm brought salvation unto him; and his righteousness, it sustained him. *Is.* 59: 16.

He which stablisheth us with you in Christ, and hath anointed us, is God. *2 Co.* 1: 21.

Casting all your care upon him; for he careth for you. *1 Pe.* 5: 7.

See also
God, Beneficence of; God, Care of; God, Favor of; God, Goodness of; God, Grace of; God, the Keeper; God, the Shepherd; God, Solicitude of.

God, Sympathy of

He knoweth thy walking through this great wilderness. *De.* 2: 7.

I have heard thy prayer, I have seen thy tears: behold, I will heal thee. *2 K.* 20: 5.

Lord, lift thou up the light of thy countenance upon us. *Ps.* 4: 6.

According unto the multitude of thy tender mercies blot out my transgressions. *Ps.* 51: 1.

Thou, O Lord, art a God full of compassion, and gracious, longsuffering, and plenteous in mercy and truth. *Ps.* 86: 15.

He will abundantly pardon. *Is.* 55: 7.

In all their affliction he was afflicted, and the angel of his presence saved them. *Is.* 63: 9.

As one whom his mother comforteth, so will I comfort you. *Is.* 66: 13.

Then will the Lord be jealous for his land, and pity his people. *Jo.* 2: 18.

Who is a God like unto thee, that pardoneth iniquity, and passeth by the transgression of the remnant of his heritage? *Mi.* 7: 18.

See also
God, Comfort of; God, Mercy of; God, Providence of; God, Solicitude of.

God, the Teacher

Now therefore go, and I will be with thy mouth, and teach thee what thou shalt say. *Ex.* 4: 12.

Teach them the good way wherein they should walk. *1 K.* 8: 36.

That which I see not teach thou me. *Jb.* 34: 32.

The words of the Lord are pure words. *Ps.* 12: 6.

Lead me in thy truth, and teach me. *Ps.* 25: 5.

Blessed is the man whom thou chastenest, O Lord, and teachest him out of thy law. *Ps.* 94: 12.

To . . . teach his senators wisdom. *Ps.* 105: 22.

Teach me good judgment and knowledge. *Ps.* 119: 66.

Teach me to do thy will. *Ps.* 143: 10.

The hearing ear, and the seeing eye, the Lord hath made even both of them. *Pr.* 20: 12.

Thy counsels of old are faithfulness and truth. *Is.* 25: 1.

See also
God, Knowledge of; God, the Light; God, Truth of; God, Way of; God, Wisdom of; God, Word of.

God, Thankfulness to

Because thy lovingkindness is better than life, my lips shall praise thee. *Ps.* 63: 3.

Praise waiteth for thee, O God, in Sion. *Ps.* 65: 1.

It is a good thing to give thanks unto the Lord. *Ps.* 92: 1.

Enter into his gates with thanksgiving, and into his courts with praise. *Ps.* 100: 4.

From the rising of the sun unto the going down of the same the Lord's name is to be praised. *Ps.* 113: 3.

At midnight I will rise to give thanks unto thee because of thy righteous judgments. *Ps.* 119: 62.

Seven times a day do I praise thee because of thy righteous judgments. *Ps.* 119: 164.

Praise ye the Lord from the heavens: praise him in the heights. *Ps.* 148: 1.

Thanks be to God, which giveth us the victory through our Lord Jesus Christ. *1 Co.* 15: 57.

By prayer and supplication with thanksgiving let your requests be made known unto God. *Ph.* 4: 6.

See also
God, Gratitude to; God, Praise to.

God, Thirst for

One thing have I desired of the Lord, that will I seek after; that I may . . . behold the beauty of the Lord. *Ps.* 27: 4.

My soul thirsteth for God, for the living God: when shall I come and appear before God? *Ps.* 42: 2.

My soul thirsteth for thee, my flesh longeth for thee in a dry and thirsty land, where no water is. *Ps.* 63: 1.

My heart and my flesh crieth out for the living God. *Ps.* 84: 2.

I will pour water upon him that is thirsty. *Is.* 44: 3.

Ho, every one that thirsteth, come ye to the waters, and he that hath no money; come ye, buy, and eat; yea, come, buy wine and milk without money and without price. *Is.* **55: 1.**

Blessed are they which do hunger and thirst after righteousness. *Mat.* **5: 6.**

In the last day, that great day of the feast, Jesus stood and cried, saying, If any man thirst, let him come unto me, and drink. *Jn.* **7: 37.**

Let him that is athirst come. And whosoever will, let him take the water of life freely. *Re.* **22: 17.**

See also

God, Aspiration for; God, Longing for; God, Prayer to; God, Quest for; God, Yearning for.

God, Thought of

The Lord repented of the evil which he thought to do unto his people. *Ex.* **32: 14.**

Think upon me, my God, for good. *Ne.* **5: 19.**

What is man, that thou art mindful of him? *Ps.* **8: 4.**

He will ever be mindful of his covenant. *Ps.* **111: 5.**

Surely as I have thought, so shall it come to pass; and as I have purposed, so shall it stand. *Is.* **14: 24.**

My thoughts are not your thoughts, neither are your ways my ways, saith the Lord. For as the heavens are higher than the earth, so are my ways higher than your ways, and my thoughts than your thoughts. *Is.* **55: 8, 9.**

Though Moses and Samuel stood before me, yet my mind could not be toward this people: cast them out of my sight, and let them go forth. *Je.* **15: 1.**

They have built also the high places of Baal, . . . which I commanded not, nor spake it, neither came it into my mind. *Je.* **19: 5.**

I know the thoughts that I think toward you, saith the Lord, thoughts of peace, and not of evil. *Je.* **29: 11.**

Call upon thy God, if so be that God will think upon us, that we perish not. *Jon.* **1: 6.**

Like as the Lord of hosts thought to do unto us, according to our ways, and according to our doings, so hath he dealt with us. *Zch.* **1: 6.**

See also

God, Wisdom of; God, Word of.

God, Transcendence of

Will God indeed dwell on the earth? behold, the heaven and heaven of heavens cannot contain thee. *1 K.* **8: 27.**

Who is like unto the Lord our God, who dwelleth on high. *Ps.* **113: 5.**

Unto thee lift I up mine eyes, O thou that dwellest in the heavens. *Ps.* **123: 1.**

The Lord is exalted; for he dwelleth on high. *Is.* **33: 5.**

Thus saith the high and lofty One that inhabiteth eternity. *Is.* **57: 15.**

The most High dwelleth not in temples made with hands. *Ac.* **7: 48.**

Dwelling in the light which no man can approach unto. *1 Ti.* **6: 16.**

See also

God, Omnipotence of; God, Omnipresence of; God, Omniscience of; God, Overruling of; God, Sovereignty of; God, Supremacy of.

God, Trust in

Though he slay me, yet will I trust in him. *Jb.* **13: 15.**

Put your trust in the Lord. *Ps.* **4: 5.**

Thou, Lord, hast not forsaken them that seek thee. *Ps.* **9: 10.**

I had fainted, unless I had believed to see the goodness of the Lord in the land of the living. *Ps.* **27: 13.**

The Lord of hosts is with us; the God of Jacob is our refuge. *Ps.* **46: 7.**

His heart is fixed, trusting in the Lord. *Ps.* **112: 7.**

Trust in the Lord with all thine heart; and lean not unto thine own understanding. *Pr.* **3: 5.**

Although the fig tree shall not blossom, neither shall fruit be in the vines; . . . Yet I will rejoice in the Lord, I will joy in the God of my salvation. *Hab.* **3: 17, 18.**

Shall he not much more clothe you, O ye of little faith? *Mat.* **6: 30.**

Jesus answering saith unto them, Have faith in God. *Mk.* **11: 22.**

Eye hath not seen, nor ear heard, neither have entered into the heart of man, the things which God hath prepared for them that love him. *1 Co.* **2: 9.**

See also

God, Belief in; God, Certainty of; God, Confidence in; God, Faith in; God, Reliance on.

God, Truth of

God is not a man that he should lie; . . . hath he said, and shall he not do it? *Nu.* **23: 19.**

The faithful God, which keepeth covenant and mercy with them that love him. *De.* **7: 9.**

My doctrine shall drop as the rain, my speech shall distil as the dew, as the small rain upon the tender herb, and as the showers upon the grass. *De.* **32: 2.**

God shall send forth his mercy and his truth. *Ps.* **57: 3.**

With my mouth will I make known thy faithfulness to all generations. *Ps.* **89: 1.**

His truth endureth to all generations. *Ps.* **100: 5.**

All thy commandments are faithful. *Ps.* **119: 86.**

Thy word is true from the beginning. *Ps.* **119: 160.**

He that hath received his testimony hath set to his seal that God is true. *Jn.* **3: 33.**

The hour cometh, and now is, when the true worshippers shall worship the Father in spirit and in truth. *Jn.* **4: 23.**

Sanctify them through thy truth: thy word is truth. *Jn.* **17: 17.**

We are sure that the judgment of God is according to truth. *Ro.* **2: 2.**

By two immutable things, in which it was impossible for God to lie. *He.* **6: 18.**

Lord God Almighty, true and righteous are thy judgments. *Re.* **16: 7.**

Behold a white horse; and he that sat upon him was called Faithful and True. *Re.* **19: 11.**

These sayings are faithful and true. *Re.* **22: 6.**

See also

God, Knowledge of; God, the Light; God,

the Teacher; God, Way of; God, Wisdom of; God, Word of.

God, the Unchanging

My covenant will I not break, nor alter the thing that is gone out of my lips. *Ps.* **89: 34.**

The heavens are the work of thy hands. They shall perish, but thou shalt endure: yea, all of them shall wax old like a garment; as a vesture shalt thou change them, and they shall be changed. *Ps.* **102: 25, 26.**

I know that, whatsoever God doeth, it shall be for ever. *Ec.* **3: 14.**

The Creator of the ends of the earth, fainteth not, neither is weary. *Is.* **40: 28.**

His compassions fail not. They are new every morning. *La.* **3: 22, 23.**

Blessed be the name of God for ever and ever: . . . he changeth the times and seasons. *Da.* **2: 20, 21.**

He is the living God, and stedfast for ever. *Da.* **6: 26.**

I am the Lord, I change not. *Mal.* **3: 6.**

With whom is no variableness. *Ja.* **1: 17.**

See also

God, Certainty of; God, Confidence in; God, the Eternal; God, the Infinite; God, the Rock; God, Security of; God, the Unwearied.

God, Unity of

Hear, O Israel: the Lord our God is one Lord. *De.* **6: 4.**

Before me there was no God formed, neither shall there be after me. *Is.* **43: 10.**

In that day there shall be one Lord, and his name one. *Zch.* **14: 9.**

One is your Father, which is in heaven. *Mat.* **23: 9.**

I in them, and thou in me, that they may be made perfect in one. *Jn.* **17: 23.**

There is none other God but one. *1 Co.* **8: 4.**

To us there is but one God, the Father. *1 Co.* **8: 6.**

One God and Father of all. *Ep.* **4: 6.**

There are three that bear record in heaven, the Father, the Word, and the Holy Ghost: and these are one. *1 Jn.* **5: 7.**

See also

Monotheism.

God, Universality of

All the nations of the earth shall be blessed in him. *Ge.* **18: 18.**

Shall not the Judge of all the earth do right? *Ge.* **18: 25.**

I am the Lord in the midst of the earth. *Ex.* **8: 22.**

He cometh to judge the earth. *1 Ch.* **16: 33.**

He shall judge the world in righteousness. *Ps.* **9: 8.**

All the ends of the world shall remember and turn unto the Lord. *Ps.* **22: 27.**

From the place of his habitation he looketh upon all the inhabitants of the earth. *Ps.* **33: 14.**

The world is mine, and the fulness thereof. *Ps.* **50: 12.**

The Lord reigneth; let the earth rejoice. *Ps.* **97: 1.**

The everlasting God, the Lord, the Creator of the ends of the earth, fainteth not, neither is weary. *Is.* **40: 28.**

Look unto me, and be ye saved, all the ends of the earth. *Is.* **45: 22.**

The heaven is my throne, and the earth is my footstool. *Is.* **66: 1.**

He shall speak peace unto the heathen: and his dominion shall be from sea even to sea. *Zch.* **9: 10.**

God so loved the world, that he gave his only begotten Son. *Jn.* **3: 16.**

The everlasting gospel to preach unto them that dwell on the earth, and to every nation, and kindred, and tongue, and people. *Re.* **14: 6.**

See also

God, Impartiality of; God, Omnipresence of.

God, the Unseen

My face shall not be seen. *Ex.* **33: 23.**

Unto God would I commit my cause: Which doeth great things and unsearchable. *Jb.* **5: 8, 9.**

Thy way is in the sea, and thy path in the great waters, and thy footsteps are not known. *Ps.* **77: 19.**

His greatness is unsearchable. *Ps.* **145: 3.**

Ye have neither heard his voice at any time, nor seen his shape. *Jn.* **5: 37.**

Not that any man hath seen the Father, save he which is of God. *Jn.* **6: 46.**

I found an altar with this inscription, TO THE UNKNOWN GOD. *Ac.* **17: 23.**

How unsearchable are his judgments, and his ways past finding out! *Ro.* **11: 33.**

The things which are not seen are eternal. *2 Co.* **4: 18.**

Now unto the King eternal, immortal, invisible. *1 Ti.* **1: 17.**

He endured, as seeing him who is invisible. *He.* **11: 27.**

He that loveth not his brother whom he hath seen, how can he love God whom he hath not seen? *1 Jn.* **4: 20.**

See also

God, the Hiding; God, Secret of; God, Silence of.

God, the Unwearied

God, said he, hath made me forget all my toil. *Ge.* **41: 51.**

The Lord thy God, he it is that doth go with thee; he will not fail thee, nor forsake thee. *De.* **31: 6.**

Cast thy burden upon the Lord, and he shall sustain thee. *Ps.* **55: 22.**

This is the rest wherewith ye may cause the weary to rest. *Is.* **28: 12.**

The everlasting God, the Lord, the Creator of the ends of the earth, fainteth not, neither is weary. *Is.* **40: 28.**

They that wait upon the Lord shall renew their strength; . . . they shall run, and not be weary; and they shall walk, and not faint. *Is.* **40: 31.**

I have satiated the weary soul, and I have replenished every sorrowful soul. *Je.* **31: 25.**

His compassions fail not. *La.* **3: 22.**

Every morning doth he bring his judgment to light, he faileth not. *Zph.* **3: 5.**

The exceeding greatness of his power to us-ward who believe, according to the working of his mighty power. *Ep.* **1: 19.**

Being confident of this very thing, that he

which hath begun a good work in you will perform it until the day of Jesus Christ. *Ph.* **1: 6.**

He hath said, I will never leave thee, nor forsake thee. *He.* **13: 5.**

The Lord is not slack concerning his promise, as some men count slackness; but is longsuffering to us-ward. *2 Pe.* **3: 9.**

See also

God, Confidence in; God, the Eternal; God, the Infinite; God, the Rock; God, Security of; God, the Unchanging.

God, Victory of

I will sing unto the Lord, for he hath triumphed gloriously. *Ex.* **15: 1.**

The Lord wrought a great victory that day. *2 S.* **23: 10.**

Thine, O Lord, is the greatness, and the power, and the glory, and the victory. *1 Ch.* **29: 11.**

His right hand, and his holy arm, hath gotten him the victory. *Ps.* **98: 1.**

He will swallow up death in victory. *Is.* **25: 8.**

I the Lord thy God will hold thy right hand, saying unto thee, Fear not; I will help thee. *Is.* **41: 13.**

I will bring thy seed from the east, and gather thee from the west; I will say to the north, Give up; and to the south, Keep not back. *Is.* **43: 5, 6.**

Now thanks be unto God, which always causeth us to triumph in Christ. *2 Co.* **2: 14.**

He went forth conquering, and to conquer. *Re.* **6: 2.**

See also

God, Sovereignty of; God, Supremacy of.

God, Vision of

There builded he an altar unto the Lord, who appeared unto him. *Ge.* **12: 7.**

God Almighty appeared unto me at Luz in the land of Canaan, and blessed me. *Ge.* **48: 3.**

Who is like unto thee, O Lord, among the gods? who is like thee, glorious in holiness, fearful in praises, doing wonders? *Ex.* **15: 11.**

The sight of the glory of the Lord was like devouring fire on the top of the mount in the eyes of the children of Israel. *Ex.* **24: 17.**

The Lord descended in the cloud, and stood with him there, and proclaimed the name of the Lord. *Ex.* **34: 5.**

Whom I shall see for myself, and mine eyes shall behold, and not another. *Jb.* **19: 27.**

I have heard of thee by the hearing of the ear: but now mine eye seeth thee. *Job* **42: 5.**

As for me, I will behold thy face in righteousness. *Ps.* **17: 15.**

Who is like unto the Lord our God, who dwelleth on high! *Ps.* **113: 5.**

In the year that king Uzziah died I saw also the Lord. *Is.* **6: 1.**

Then said I, Woe is me! for I am undone; . . . for mine eyes have seen the King, the Lord of hosts. *Is.* **6: 5.**

The burden of the valley of vision. *Is.* **22: 1.**

O Zion, that bringest good tidings, get thee up into the high mountain; . . . say unto the cities of Judah, Behold your God! *Is.* **40: 9.**

He shall appear to your joy. *Is.* **66: 5.**

As the appearance of the bow that is in the cloud in the day of rain, so was the appearance of the brightness round about. This was the appearance of the likeness of the glory of the Lord. *Eze.* **1: 28.**

Mine eyes have seen thy salvation. *Lu.* **2: 30.**

God hath visited his people. *Lu.* **7: 16.**

We beheld his glory. *Jn.* **1: 14.**

I was not disobedient unto the heavenly vision. *Ac.* **26: 19.**

His servants shall serve him: And they shall see his face. *Re.* **22: 3, 4.**

See also

God, Eye of; God, Face of; God, Knowledge of; God, Revelation of.

God, Voice of

Thou shalt return and obey the voice of the Lord. *De.* **30: 8.**

Speak, Lord; for thy servant heareth. *1 S.* **3: 9.**

After the fire a still small voice. *1 K.* **19: 12.**

They obeyed not the voice of the Lord their God. *2 K.* **18: 12.**

The voice of the Lord is powerful; the voice of the Lord is full of majesty. *Ps.* **29: 4.**

The voice of the Lord divideth the flames of fire. *Ps.* **29: 7.**

The voice of the Lord shaketh the wilderness. *Ps.* **29: 8.**

He uttered his voice, the earth melted. *Ps.* **46: 6.**

Lo, he doth send out his voice, and that a mighty voice. *Ps.* **68: 33.**

They . . . murmured in their tents, and hearkened not unto the voice of the Lord. *Ps.* **106: 24, 25.**

The Lord spake thus to me with a strong hand. *Is.* **8: 11.**

A voice of noise from the city, a voice from the temple, a voice of the Lord that rendereth recompence to his enemies. *Is.* **66: 6.**

O earth, earth, earth, hear the word of the Lord. *Je.* **22: 29.**

We will obey the voice of the Lord our God, to whom we send thee. *Je.* **42: 6.**

His voice was like a noise of many waters. *Eze.* **43: 2.**

The voice of his words like the voice of a multitude. *Da.* **10: 6.**

Not a famine of bread, nor a thirst for water, but of hearing the words of the Lord. *Am.* **8: 11.**

This shall come to pass, if ye will diligently obey the voice of the Lord your God. *Zch.* **6: 15.**

Lo a voice from heaven, saying, This is my beloved Son, in whom I am well pleased. *Mat.* **3: 17.**

It is not ye that speak, but the Spirit of your Father which speaketh in you. *Mat.* **10: 20.**

God . . . spake in time past unto the fathers by the prophets. *He.* **1: 1.**

See also

God, Call of; God, Word of.

God, Way of

Lead me, O Lord, in thy righteousness. *Ps.* **5: 8.**

Thou wilt shew me the path of life: in thy presence is fulness of joy; at thy right hand there are pleasures for evermore. *Ps.* 16: 11.

He leadeth me in the paths of righteousness for his name's sake. *Ps.* 23: 3.

Shew me thy ways, O Lord; teach me thy paths. *Ps.* 25: 4.

The meek will he teach his way. *Ps.* 25: 9.

All the paths of the Lord are mercy and truth unto such as keep his covenant and his testimonies. *Ps.* 25: 10.

Teach me thy way, O Lord, and lead me in a plain path. *Ps.* 27: 11.

Thy paths drop fatness. *Ps.* 65: 11.

Thy way, O God, is in the sanctuary. *Ps.* 77: 13.

The Lord is righteous in all his ways, and holy in all his works. *Ps.* 145: 17.

Neither are your ways my ways, saith the Lord. *Is.* 55: 8.

The ways of the Lord are right, and the just shall walk in them. *Ho.* 14: 9.

Prepare ye the way of the Lord. *Mat.* 3: 3.

Master, we know that thou art true, and teachest the way of God in truth. *Mat.* 22: 16.

How unsearchable are his judgments, and his ways past finding out! *Ro.* 11: 33.

See also
God, Guidance of; God, Leadership of.

God, Wealth of

I will give thee riches, and wealth, and honour, such as none of the kings have had that have been before thee. *2 Ch.* 1: 12.

Delight thyself also in the Lord; and he shall give thee the desires of thine heart. *Ps.* 37: 4.

There is that maketh himself poor, yet hath great riches. *Pr.* 13: 7.

In the house of the righteous is much treasure. *Pr.* 15: 6.

The fear of the Lord is his treasure. *Is.* 33: 6.

Lay up for yourselves treasures in heaven. *Mat.* 6: 20.

If ye then, being evil, know how to give good gifts unto your children, how much more shall your Father which is in heaven. *Mat.* 7: 11.

The kingdom of heaven is like unto treasure. *Mat.* 13: 44.

Give to the poor, and thou shalt have treasure in heaven. *Mat.* 19: 21.

Not rich toward God. *Lu.* 12: 21.

The same Lord over all is rich unto all that call upon him. *Ro.* 10: 12.

O the depth of the riches both of the wisdom and knowledge of God! *Ro.* 11: 33.

See also
God, Fullness of; God, Generosity of; God, Gift of; God, Perfection of; God, Sufficiency of; God, Riches of.

God, Will of

Thy will be done on earth, as it is in heaven. *Mat.* 6: 10.

Not every one that saith unto me, Lord, Lord, shall enter into the kingdom of heaven; but he that doeth the will of my Father which is in heaven. *Mat.* 7: 21.

Not my will, but thine, be done. *Lu.* 22: 42.

Born, not of blood, nor of the will of the flesh, nor of the will of man, but of God. *Jn.* 1: 13.

When he would not be persuaded, we ceased, saying, The will of the Lord be done. *Ac.* 21: 14.

That ye may prove what is that good, and acceptable, and perfect, will of God. *Ro.* 12: 2.

Now hath God set the members every one of them in the body, as it hath pleased him. *1 Co.* 12: 18.

Wherefore be ye not unwise, but understanding what the will of the Lord is. *Ep.* 5: 17.

That ye may stand perfect and complete in all the will of God. *Col.* 4: 12.

This is the will of God, even your sanctification. *1 Th.* 4: 3.

Ye ought to say, If the Lord will, we shall live, and do this, or that. *Ja.* 4: 15.

So is the will of God, that with well doing ye may put to silence the ignorance of foolish men. *1 Pe.* 2: 15.

The prophecy came not in old time by the will of man: but holy men of God spake as they were moved by the Holy Ghost. *2 Pe.* 1: 21.

He that doeth the will of God abideth for ever. *1 Jn.* 2: 17.

See also
God, Purpose of;

God, Wisdom of

The Lord is a God of knowledge. *1 S.* 2: 3.

He looketh to the ends of the earth, and seeth under the whole heaven. *Jb.* 28: 24.

The secret of the Lord is with them that fear him; and he will shew them his covenant. *Ps.* 25: 14.

He knoweth the secrets of the heart. *Ps.* 44: 21.

The Lord hath been mindful of us. *Ps.* 115: 12.

O Lord, thou hast searched me, and known me. *Ps.* 139: 1.

Thou understandest my thought afar off. *Ps.* 139: 2.

His understanding is infinite. *Ps.* 147: 5.

By his knowledge the depths are broken up, and the clouds drop down the dew. *Pr.* 3: 20.

There is no searching of his understanding. *Is.* 40: 28.

Then shall we know, if we follow on to know the Lord. *Ho.* 6: 3.

Who hath known the mind of the Lord? *Ro.* 11: 34.

The foolishness of God is wiser than men. *1 Co.* 1: 25.

The manifold wisdom of God. *Ep.* 3: 10.

If any of you lack wisdom, let him ask of God, . . . and it shall be given him. *Ja.* 1: 5.

See also
God, Knowledge of; God, Omniscience of.

God, Witness of

The Lord be witness between us, if we do not so according to thy words. *Ju.* 11: 10.

My witness is in heaven, and my record is on high. *Jb.* 16: 19.

Thy testimonies also are my delight and my counsellors. *Ps.* 119: 24.

I will speak of thy testimonies also before kings. *Ps.* 119: 46.

Thy testimonies are wonderful. *Ps.* 119: 129.

Even I know, and am a witness, saith the Lord. *Je.* 29: 23.

God is my witness, whom I serve with my spirit in the gospel of his Son. *Ro.* 1: 9.

There are three that bear record in heaven, the Father, the Word, and the Holy Ghost: and these three are one. *1 Jn.* 5: 7.

If we receive the witness of men, the witness of God is greater. *1 Jn.* 5: 9.

See also

God, Evidence of; God, Truth of.

God, Wonder of

The sight of the glory of the Lord was like devouring fire. *Ex.* 24: 17.

Before all thy people I will do marvels, such as have not been done in all the earth, nor in any nation. *Ex.* 34: 10.

Stand still, and consider the wondrous works of God. *Jb.* 37: 14.

Surely I will remember thy wonders of old. *Ps.* 77: 11.

This is the Lord's doing; it is marvellous in our eyes. *Ps.* 118: 23.

Marvellous are thy works; and that my soul knoweth right well. *Ps.* 139: 14.

I will exalt thee, I will praise thy name; for thou hast done wonderful things. *Is.* 25: 1.

How great are his signs! and how mighty are his wonders! *Da.* 4: 3.

I will shew wonders in the heavens and in the earth, blood, and fire, and pillars of smoke. *Jo.* 2: 30.

Every good gift and every perfect gift is from above. *Ja.* 1: 17.

See also

God, Adoration of; God, Beauty of; God, Glory of; God, Majesty of; God, Worship of.

God, Word of

Man doth not live by bread only, but by every word that proceedeth out of the mouth of the Lord doth man live. *De.* 8: 3.

The words of the Lord are pure words: as silver tried in a furnace of earth, purified seven times. *Ps.* 12: 6.

I will hear what God the Lord will speak. *Ps.* 85: 8.

For ever, O Lord, thy word is settled in heaven. *Ps.* 119: 89.

The entrance of thy words giveth light. *Ps.* 119: 130.

Every word of God is pure. *Pr.* 30: 5.

The word is gone out of my mouth in righteousness, and shall not return. *Is.* 45: 23.

As the rain cometh down, and the snow from heaven, and returneth not thither, but watereth the earth, and maketh it bring forth and bud, . . . So shall my word be that goeth forth out of my mouth. *Is.* 55: 10, 11.

Speak unto all the cities of Judah, . . . all the words that I command thee to speak unto them; diminish not a word. *Je.* 26: 2.

They shall wander from sea to sea, and from the north even to the east, they shall run to and fro to seek the word of the Lord, and shall not find it. *Am.* 8: 12.

When any one heareth the word of the Kingdom, and understandeth it not, then cometh the wicked one, and catcheth away that which

was sown in his heart. This is he which received seed by the way side. *Mat.* 13: 19.

The seed is the word of God. *Lu.* 8: 11.

Mightily grew the word of God and prevailed. *Ac.* 19: 20.

The sword of the Spirit, which is the word of God. *Ep.* 6: 17.

The word of God is not bound. *2 Ti.* 2: 9.

The worlds were framed by the word of God. *He.* 11: 3.

The word of God, which liveth and abideth for ever. *1 Pe.* 1: 23.

See also

God, Call of; God, Voice of.

God, Work of

God . . . rested on the seventh day from all his work which he had made. *Ge.* 2: 2.

Thou wilt have a desire to the work of thine hands. *Jb.* 14: 15.

He sealeth up the hand of every man; that all men may know his work. *Jb.* 37: 7.

Stand still, and consider the wondrous works of God. *Jb.* 37: 14.

I will remember the works of the Lord: surely I will remember thy wonders of old. *Ps.* 77: 11.

O Lord, how manifold are thy works! *Ps.* 104: 24.

Marvellous are thy works; and that my soul knoweth right well. *Ps.* 139: 14.

All thy works shall praise thee, O Lord. *Ps.* 145: 10.

He hath made every thing beautiful in his time. *Ec.* 3: 11.

I know that, whatsoever God doeth, it shall be for ever. *Ec.* 3: 14.

Pray ye therefore the Lord of the harvest, that he will send forth labourers into his harvest. *Mat.* 9: 38.

I must work the works of him that sent me, while it is day. *Jn.* 9: 4.

It is the same God which worketh all in all. *1 Co.* 12: 6.

We are his workmanship, created in Christ Jesus unto good works. *Ep.* 2: 10.

According to the eternal purpose which he purposed in Christ Jesus our Lord. *Ep.* 3: 11.

It is God which worketh in you both to will and to do of his good pleasure. *Ph.* 2: 13.

See also

God, the Builder; God, the Creator; God, Hand of; God, Help of.

God, Worship of

Thou shalt worship no other god: for the Lord, whose name is Jealous, is a jealous God. *Ex.* 34: 14.

Wait on the Lord: be of good courage, and he shall strengthen thine heart: wait, I say, on the Lord. *Ps.* 27: 14.

Whoso offereth praise glorifieth me. *Ps.* 50: 23.

O come, let us worship and bow down: let us kneel before the Lord our maker. *Ps.* 95: 6.

I desired mercy, and not sacrifice; and the knowledge of God more than burnt offerings. *Ho.* 6: 6.

Wherewith shall I come before the Lord, and bow myself before the high God? *Mi.* 6: 6.

The inhabitants of one city shall go to another, saying, Let us go speedily to pray before the Lord, and to seek the Lord of hosts: I will go also. *Zch.* 8: 21.

The hour cometh, when ye shall neither in this mountain, not yet at Jerusalem, worship the Father. *Jn.* 4: 21.

Whom therefore ye ignorantly worship, him declare I unto you. *Ac.* 17: 23.

I bow my knees unto the Father of our Lord Jesus Christ. *Ep.* 3: 14.

Blessing and honour, and glory, and power, be unto him that sitteth upon the throne. *Re.* 5: 13.

See also

God, Adoration of; God, Praise to; God, Prayer to.

God, Wrath of

The Lord thy God is a consuming fire, even a jealous God. *De.* 4: 24.

A fire is kindled in mine anger, and shall burn unto the lowest hell, and shall consume the earth with her increase, and set on fire the foundations of the mountains. *De.* 32: 22.

Thou art a God ready to pardon, gracious and merciful, slow to anger, and of great kindness. *Ne.* 9: 17.

He shall drink of the wrath of the Almighty. *Jb.* 21: 20.

O Lord, rebuke me not in thine anger, neither chasten me in thy hot displeasure. *Ps.* 6: 1.

God is angry with the wicked every day. *Ps.* 7: 11.

Who knoweth the power of thine anger? *Ps.* 90: 11.

Ah sinful nation: . . . they have provoked the Holy One of Israel unto anger, they are gone away backward. *Is.* 1: 4.

Therefore is the anger of the Lord kindled against his people, and he hath stretched forth his hand against them. *Is.* 5: 25.

In a little wrath I hid my face from thee for a moment; but with everlasting kindness will I have mercy on thee. *Is.* 54: 8.

I will not contend for ever, neither will I be always wroth. *Is.* 57: 16.

O Lord, correct me, but with judgment; not in thine anger, lest thou bring me to nothing. *Je.* 10: 24.

In the day of the Lord's anger none escaped nor remained. *La.* 2: 22.

Their silver and their gold shall not be able to deliver them in the day of the wrath of the Lord. *Eze.* 7: 19.

I will be unto them as a lion: as a leopard by the way will I observe them. *Ho.* 13: 7.

I gave thee a king in mine anger, and took him away in my wrath. *Ho.* 13: 11.

I will execute vengeance in anger and fury upon the heathen, such as they have not heard. *Mi.* 5: 15.

Seek ye the Lord, all ye meek of the earth· . . . it may be ye shall be hid in the day of the Lord's anger. *Zph.* 2: 3.

The Lord hath been sore displeased with your fathers. *Zch.* 1: 2.

The wrath of God is revealed from heaven against all ungodliness and unrighteousness of men, who hold the truth in unrighteousness. *Ro.* 1: 18.

The same shall drink of the wine of the wrath of God. *Re.* 14: 10.

See also

God, Anger of; God, Chastisement of; God, Punishment of; God, Reward of.

God, Yearning for

Unto thee, O Lord, do I lift up my soul. *Ps.* 25: 1.

Lord, all my desire is before thee. *Ps.* 38: 9.

There is none upon earth that I desire beside thee. *Ps.* 73: 25.

My heart and my flesh crieth out for the living God. *Ps.* 84: 2.

I longed for thy commandments. *Ps.* 119: 131.

I will lift up mine eyes unto the hills, from whence cometh my help. *Ps.* 121: 1.

Let us lift up our heart with our hands unto God in the heavens. *La.* 3: 41.

See also

God, Aspiration for; God, Longing for; God, Prayer to; God, Quest for; God, Thirst for.

Godlessness

I know not the Lord. *Ex.* 5: 2.

He forsook God which made him. *De.* 32: 15.

God is not in all his thoughts. *Ps.* 10: 4.

The fool hath said in his heart, There is no God. *Ps.* 53: 1.

We hid as it were our faces from him. *Is.* 53: 3.

They are all estranged from me through their idols. *Eze.* 14: 5.

Wherefore should they say among the people, Where is their God? *Jo.* 2: 17.

Having no hope and without God in the world. *Ep.* 2: 12.

Whosoever therefore will be a friend of the world is the enemy of God. *Ja.* 4: 4.

See also

Atheism; Christ, Denial of; Christ, Doubt of; Denial; Doubt; Faithlessness; God, Denial of; Heresy; Unbelief.

Godliness

Know that the Lord hath set apart him that is godly for himself. *Ps.* 4: 3.

As for me, I will behold thy face in righteousness. *Ps.* 17: 15.

Light is sown for the righteous, and gladness for the upright in heart. *Ps.* 97: 11.

My son, forget not my law; but let thine heart keep my commandments. *Pr.* 3: 1.

The froward is abomination to the Lord: but his secret is with the righteous. *Pr.* 3: 32.

Blessed are they which do hunger and thirst after righteousness: for they shall be filled. *Mat.* 5: 6.

Christ is the end of the law for righteousness to every one that believeth. *Ro.* 10: 4.

Great is the mystery of godliness. *1 Ti.* 3: 16.

Exercise thyself . . . unto godliness. *1 Ti.* 4: 7.

Godliness is profitable unto all things, having promise of the life that now is, and of that which is to come. *1 Ti.* 4: 8.

Teaching us that . . . we should live soberly, righteously, and godly, in this present world. *Tit.* 2: 12.

Add to your faith virtue. *2 Pe.* 1: 5.

The Lord knoweth how to deliver the godly out of temptations. *2 Pe.* 2: 9.

See also
Consecration; Dedication; Devoutness; Holiness; Piety; Righteousness; Saint; Sanctification.

Gods

Thou shalt not make unto thee any graven image, or any likeness of any thing that is in heaven above, or that is in the earth beneath, or that is in the water under the earth. *Ex.* 20: 4.

If thou . . . walk after other gods, and serve them, . . . I testify against you this day that ye shall surely perish. *De.* 8: 19.

Where are their gods, their rock in whom they trusted? *De.* 32: 37.

Ye have taken away my gods which I made. *Ju.* 18: 24.

If ye do return unto the Lord with all your hearts, then put away the strange gods . . . from among you, and prepare your hearts unto the Lord, and serve him only. *1 S.* 7: 3.

Yet I have left me seven thousand in Israel, all the knees which have not bowed unto Baal. *1 K.* 19: 18.

They served idols, whereof the Lord had said unto them, Ye shall not do this thing. 2 *K.* 17: 12.

Their land also is full of idols; they worship the work of their own hands. *Is.* 2: 8.

He burneth part thereof in the fire; with part thereof he eateth flesh; he roasteth roast, and is satisfied: . . . And the residue thereof he maketh a god. *Is.* 44: 16, 17.

Ye pollute yourselves with all your idols, even unto this day. *Eze.* 20: 31.

Thou shalt know no god but me: for there is no saviour beside me. *Ho.* 13: 4.

The mariners were afraid, and cried every man unto his god. *Jon.* 1: 5.

He seemeth to be a setter forth of strange gods. *Ac.* 17: 18.

When ye knew not God, ye did service unto them which by nature are no gods. *Ga.* 4: 8.

Little children, keep yourselves from idols. *1 Jn.* 5: 21.

See also
Idol.

Gold

The earth . . . hath dust of gold. *Jb.* 28: 5, 6.

Then shalt thou lay up gold as dust. *Jb.* 22: 24.

A word fitly spoken is like apples of gold in pictures of silver. *Pr.* 25: 11.

Let not the rich man glory in his riches. *Je.* 9: 23.

I . . . will try them as gold is tried. *Zch.* 13: 9.

Provide neither gold, nor silver, nor brass in your purses. *Mat.* 10: 9.

We ought not to think that the Godhead is like unto gold, or silver, or stone. *Ac.* 17: 29.

Ye were not redeemed with corruptible things, as silver and gold. *1 Pe.* 1: 18.

I counsel thee to buy of me gold tried in the fire, that thou mayest be rich. *Re.* 3: 18.

They should not worship devils, and idols of gold, and silver. *Re.* 9: 20.

The city was pure gold, like unto clear glass. *Re.* 21: 18.

See also
Enrichment; God, Wealth of; Goods; Mammon; Money; Silver; Wealth; Worldliness.

Golgotha

He delivered him to be crucified. *Mat.* 27: 26.

When they were come unto a place called Golgotha, that is to say, a place of a skull, They gave him vinegar to drink mingled with gall. *Mat.* 27: 33, 34.

They crucified him, and parted his garments, casting lots. *Mat.* 27: 35.

If thou be the Son of God, come down from the cross. *Mat.* 27: 40.

Jesus, when he had cried again with a loud voice, yielded up the ghost. *Mat.* 27: 50.

They cried out again, Crucify him. *Mk.* 15: 13.

It was the third hour, and they crucified him. *Mk.* 15: 25.

There was a darkness over all the earth. *Lu.* 23: 44.

When Jesus had cried with a loud voice, he said, Father, into thy hands I commend my spirit: and having said thus, he gave up the ghost. *Lu.* 23: 46.

Caiaphas . . . said unto them, Ye know nothing at all, Nor consider that it is expedient for us, that one man should die for the people, and that the whole nation perish not. *Jn.* 11: 49, 50.

The cup which my Father hath given me, shall I not drink it? *Jn.* 18: 11.

These things were done, that the scripture should be fulfilled. *Jn.* 19: 36.

See also
Calvary; Christ, Cross of; Christ, Crucifixion of; Christ, Death of; Christ, Sacrifice of; Christ, Suffering of; Cross; Friday, Good.

Goodness

I was eyes to the blind, and feet was I to the lame. *Jb.* 29: 15.

Far be it from God, that he should do wickedness. *Jb.* 34: 10.

Who will shew us any good? *Ps.* 4: 6.

Surely goodness and mercy shall follow me all the days of my life. *Ps.* 23: 6.

Many are the afflictions of the righteous: but the Lord delivereth him out of them all. *Ps.* 34: 19.

The steps of a good man are ordered by the Lord. *Ps.* 37: 23.

Treasures of wickedness profit nothing: but righteousness delivereth from death. *Pr.* 10: 2.

The Lord . . . heareth the prayer of the righteous. *Pr.* 15: 29.

She will do him good and not evil all the days of her life. *Pr.* 31: 12.

Learn to do well. *Is.* 1: 17.

Let judgment run down as waters, and righteousness as a mighty stream. *Am.* 5: 24.

Therefore all things whatsoever ye would that men should do to you, do ye even so to them: for this is the law and the prophets. *Mat.* 7: 12.

Why callest thou me good? *Mk.* 10: 18.

Mary hath chosen that good part, which shall not be taken away from her. *Lu.* 10: 42.

Why callest thou me good? none is good,
save one, that is, God. *Lu.* **18: 19.**

Abhor that which is evil; cleave to that which
is good. *Ro.* **12: 9.**

Overcome evil with good. *Ro.* **12: 21.**

I would have you wise unto that which is
good, and simple concerning evil. *Ro.* **16: 19.**

As we have therefore opportunity, let us do
good unto all men. *Ga.* **6: 10.**

Stand therefore, having your loins girt about
with truth, and having on the breastplate of
righteousness. *Ep.* **6: 14.**

Prove all things; hold fast that which is
good. *1 Th.* **5: 21.**

He that is righteous, let him be righteous
still. *Re.* **22: 11.**

See also

Beneficence; Benevolence; Benignity; Christ,
Goodness of; Christ, Holiness of; Excellence;
Generosity; God, Generosity of; God, Goodness
of; God, Righteousness of; Holiness; Kindness;
Purity; Rectitude; Righteousness; Strength;
Virtue.

Goods

Ye shall dwell with us: and the land shall
be before you; dwell and trade ye therein, and
get you possessions therein. *Ge.* **34: 10.**

The Lord shall make thee plenteous in goods.
De. **28: 11.**

I got me servants and maidens and had
servants born in my house; also I had great
possessions. *Ec.* **2: 7.**

When goods increase, they are increased that
eat them: and what good is there to the owners
thereof. *Ec.* **5: 11.**

Give to every man that asketh of thee; and
of him that taketh away thy goods ask them
not again. *Lu.* **6: 30.**

Soul, thou hast much goods laid up for
many years; take thine ease, eat, drink, and
be merry. *Lu.* **12: 19.**

So is he that layeth up treasure for himself,
and is not rich toward God. *Lu.* **12: 21.**

The half of my goods I give to the poor. *Lu.*
19: 8.

Though I bestow all my goods to feed the
poor, and though I give my body to be burned,
and have not charity, it profiteth me nothing.
1 Co. **13: 3.**

See also

Abundance; Accumulation; Belongings; God,
Wealth of; Gold; Mammon; Store; Wealth;
Worldliness.

Gospel

As cold waters to a thirsty soul, so is good
news from a far country. *Pr.* **25: 25.**

O Zion, that bringest good tidings, get thee
up into the high mountain; O Jerusalem, that
bringest good tidings, lift up thy voice with
strength. *Is.* **40: 9.**

The Lord God hath given me the tongue of
the learned, that I should know how to speak a
word in season to him that is weary. *Is.* **50: 4.**

How beautiful upon the mountains are the
feet of him that bringeth good tidings, that
publisheth peace; that bringeth good tidings
of good! *Is.* **52: 7.**

According to my gospel. *Ro.* **2: 16.**

I declare unto you the gospel which I
preached unto you, which also ye have received,

and wherein ye stand; By which also ye are
saved. *1 Co.* **15: 1, 2.**

They walked not uprightly according to
the truth of the gospel. *Ga.* **2: 14.**

The hope of the gospel. *Col.* **1: 23.**

See also

Evangelism; News, Good; Tidings.

Gospel, Social

Am I my brother's keeper? *Ge.* **4: 9.**

Let there be no strife, I pray thee, between
me and thee, and between my herdmen and
thy herdmen; for we be brethren. *Ge.* **13: 8.**

That there be no complaining in our
streets. *Ps.* **144: 14.**

To do justice and judgment is more acceptable to the Lord than sacrifice. *Pr.* **21: 3.**

Every man should eat and drink, and enjoy
the good of all his labour, it is the gift of God.
Ec. **3: 13.**

The profit of the earth is for all. *Ec.* **5: 9.**

They shall not build, and another inhabit.
Is. **65: 22.**

Establish judgment in the gate. *Am.* **5: 15.**

Fear not, little flock; for it is your Father's
good pleasure to give you the kingdom. *Lu.*
12: 32.

We then that are strong ought to bear the
infirmities of the weak, and not to please ourselves. *Ro.* **15: 1.**

That now at this time your abundance may
be a supply for their want, that their abundance also may be a supply for your want: that
there may be equality. *2 Co.* **8: 14.**

We ought to lay down our lives for the
brethren. *1 Jn.* **3: 16.**

If God so loved us, we ought also to love
one another. *1 Jn.* **4: 11.**

See also

Equality; Equality, Racial; Injustice; Injustice, Social; Justice; Justice, Social; Right.

Gossip

Tell it not in Gath, publish it not in the
streets of Askelon. *2 S.* **1: 20.**

A talebearer revealeth secrets. *Pr.* **11: 13.**

The talk of the lips tendeth only to penury.
Pr. **14: 23.**

A whisperer separateth chief friends. *Pr.* **16:
28.**

Where no wood is, there the fire goeth out:
so where there is no talebearer, the strife
ceaseth. *Pr.* **26: 20.**

A bird of the air shall carry the voice, and
that which hath wings shall tell the matter.
Ec. **10: 20.**

Take ye heed every one of his neighbour,
and trust ye not in any brother: for every
brother will utterly supplant, and every
neighbour will walk with slanders. *Je.* **9: 4.**

Keep the doors of thy mouth from her that
lieth in thy bosom. *Mi.* **7: 5.**

Their words seemed to them as idle tales,
and they believed them not. *Lu.* **24: 11.**

Lest there be debates, envyings, wraths,
strifes, backbitings, whisperings, swellings,
tumults. *2 Co.* **12: 20.**

Refuse profane and old wives' fables. *1 Ti.* **4:
7.**

See also

Babble; Calumny; Scandal; Slander; Talebearing; Tongue.

Government

Look out a man discreet and wise, and set him over the land of Egypt. *Ge.* 41: 33.

Curse not the king, no not in thy thought. *Ec.* 10: 20.

Thy princes are rebellious, and companions of thieves. *Is.* 1: 23.

I will commit thy government into his hand. *Is.* 22: 21.

He that remaineth, even he, shall be for our God, and he shall be as a governor in Judah. *Zch.* 9: 7.

Out of thee shall come a Governor, that shall rule my people Israel. *Mat.* 2: 6.

Ye shall be brought before governors and kings for my sake. *Mat.* 10: 18.

Let every soul be subject unto the higher powers. For there is no power but of God: the powers that be are ordained of God. *Ro.* 13: 1.

Render therefore to all their dues: tribute to whom tribute is due; custom to whom custom; fear to whom fear; honour to whom honour. *Ro.* 13: 7.

It is required in stewards, that a man be found faithful. *1 Co.* 4: 2.

Submit yourselves to every ordinance of man for the Lord's sake: whether it be to the king, as supreme; Or unto governors, as unto them that are sent by him. *1 Pe.* 2: 13, 14.

He shall rule them with a rod of iron. *Re.* 2: 27.
See also
Christ, the King; Commandment; Dominion; God, Commandment of; God, the King; God, Kingdom of; God, Law of; Law; Order; Reign; Rule.

Grace

A gracious woman retaineth honour. *Pr.* 11: 16.

He took the five loaves and the two fishes, and looking up to heaven, he blessed them. *Lu.* 9: 16.

He took bread, and gave thanks. *Lu.* 22: 19.

Where sin abounded, grace did much more abound. *Ro.* 5: 20.

By the grace of God I am what I am. *1 Co.* 15: 10.

God is able to make all grace abound toward you. *2 Co.* 9: 8.

My grace is sufficient for thee: for my strength is made perfect in weakness. *2 Co.* 12: 9.

Grace be with all them that love our Lord Jesus Christ in sincerity. *Ep.* 6: 24.

Ye all are partakers of my grace. *Ph.* 1: 7.

Let your speech be alway with grace. *Col.* 4: 6.

Let us have grace, whereby we may serve God acceptably with reverence and godly fear. *He.* 12: 28.

Grow in grace, and in the knowledge of our Lord and Saviour Jesus Christ. *2 Pe.* 3: 18.
See also
Charm; Christ, Grace of; Elegance; Favor; God, Grace of; Kindness; Loveliness; Mercy.

Graduation

When I begin, I will also make an end. *1 S.* 3: 12.

Stand thou still a while, that I may shew

thee the word of God. *1 S.* 9: 27.

Though thy beginning was small, yet thy latter end should greatly increase. *Jb.* 8: 7.

I will instruct thee and teach thee in the way which thou shalt go. *Ps.* 32: 8.

O God, thou hast taught me from my youth. *Ps.* 71: 17.

The fear of the Lord is the beginning of knowledge. *Pr.* 1: 7.

Honour the Lord . . . with the firstfruits of all thine increase. *Pr* 3: 9.

Wisdom is the principal thing; therefore get wisdom. *Pr.* 4: 7.

In the morning sow thy seed, and in the evening withhold not thine hand. *Ec.* 11: 6.

Precept must be upon precept, precept upon precept; line upon line, line upon line: here a little, and there a little. *Is.* 28: 10.

Full of wisdom, and perfect in beauty. *Eze.* 28: 12.

Then shall we know, if we follow on to know the Lord. *Ho.* 6: 3.

Jesus increased in wisdom and stature, and in favour with God and man. *Lu.* 2: 52.

The kingdom of God . . . is like a grain of mustard seed. *Lu.* 13: 18, 19.

This man began to build, and was not able to finish. *Lu.* 14: 30.

All things are your's. *1 Co.* 3: 21.

Study to be quiet, and to do your own business, and to work with your own hands, as we commanded you. *1 Th.* 4: 11.

The Lord give thee understanding in all things. *2 Ti.* 2: 7.

Study to shew thyself approved unto God. *2 Ti.* 2: 15.
See also
Beginning; Commencement; Education.

Grain

As the Lord thy God liveth, I have not a cake, but an handful of meal in a barrel, and a little oil in a cruse. *1 K.* 17: 12.

I will break the staff of bread in Jerusalem: and they shall eat bread by weight, and with care. *Eze.* 4: 16.

The seed is rotten under their clods, the garners are laid desolate, the barns are broken down; for the corn is withered. *Jo.* 1: 17.

I will sift the house of Israel among all nations, like as corn is sifted in a sieve, yet shall not the least grain fall upon the earth. *Am.* 9: 9.

They shall . . . make gardens, and eat the fruit of them. *Am.* 9: 14.

A sower went forth to sow. *Mat.* 13: 3.

The kingdom of heaven is like to a grain of mustard seed. *Mat.* 13: 31.

If ye have faith as a grain of mustard seed, ye shall say unto this mountain. Remove hence to yonder place; and it shall remove. *Mat.* 17: 20.

So is the kingdom of God, as if a man should cast seed into the ground. *Mk.* 4: 26.

Thou sowest not that body that shall be, but bare grain, it may chance of wheat, or of some other grain: But God giveth it a body as it hath pleased him. *1 Co.* 15: 37, 38.
See also
Seed.

Grandeur

Look now toward heaven, and tell the stars,

if thou be able to number them. *Ge.* 15: 5.

The sight of the glory of the Lord was like devouring fire. *Ex.* 24: 17.

Thou canst not see my face: for there shall no man see me, and live. *Ex.* 33: 20.

As truly as I live, all the earth shall be filled with the glory of the Lord. *Nu.* 14: 21.

Alas, O Lord God! for because I have seen an angel of the Lord face to face. *Ju.* 6: 22.

The heavens declare the glory of God. *Ps.* 19: 1.

Who in the heaven can be compared unto the Lord? *Ps.* 89: 6.

I will also clothe her priests with salvation. *Ps.* 132: 16.

I am fearfully and wonderfully made. *Ps.* 139: 14.

All her household are clothed with scarlet. *Pr.* 31: 21.

She maketh herself coverings of tapestry; her clothing is silk and purple. *Pr.* 31: 22.

Put on thy beautiful garments, O Jerusalem. *Is.* 52: 1.

This was the appearance of the likeness of the glory of the Lord. *Eze.* 1: 28.

As a strong people set in battle array. *Jo.* 2: 5.

When it is grown, it is thē greatest among herbs, and becometh a tree. *Mat.* 13: 32.

His face did shine as the sun, and his raiment was white as the light. *Mat.* 17: 2.

The sufferings of this present time are not worthy to be compared with the glory which shall be revealed in us. *Ro.* 8: 18.

See also

Christ, Glory of; Glory; God, Glory of; Magnificence; Majesty; Splendor; Sublimity.

Grant

For all the land which thou seest, to thee will I give it, and to thy seed for ever. *Ge.* 13: 15.

To many thou shalt give the more inheritance, and to few thou shalt give the less inheritance. *Nu.* 26: 54.

He hath brought us into this place, and hath given us this land, even a land that floweth with milk and honey. *De.* 26: 9.

Oh that I might have my request; and that God would grant me the thing that I long for! *Jb.* 6: 8.

Grant not, O Lord, the desires of the wicked. *Ps.* 140: 8.

The desire of the righteous shall be granted. *Pr.* 10: 24.

Grant that these my two sons may sit, the one on thy right hand, and the other on the left hand, in thy kingdom. *Mat.* 20: 21.

To sit on my right hand, and on my left, is not mine to give, but it shall be given to them for whom it is prepared of my Father. *Mat.* 20: 23.

Take therefore the talent from him, and give it unto him which hath ten talents. *Mat.* 25: 28.

He . . . shall give the vineyard to others. *Lu.* 20: 16.

Distribution was made unto every man according as he had need. *Ac.* 4: 35.

As God hath distributed to every man, as the Lord hath called every one, so let him walk. *1 Co.* 7: 17.

To him that overcometh will I grant to sit with me in my throne. *Re.* 3: 21.

See also

Christ, Gift of; Donation; Endowment; Gift; God, Gift of.

Grape

Thou shalt plant a vineyard, and shalt not gather the grapes thereof. *De.* 28: 30.

Thou didst drink the pure blood of the grape. *De.* 32: 14.

The vines with the tender grape give a good smell. *S. of S.* 2: 13.

What could have been done more to my vineyard, that I have not done in it? wherefore, when I looked that it should bring forth grapes, brought it forth wild grapes? *Is.* 5: 4.

There shall be no grapes on the vine, nor figs on the fig tree. *Je.* 8: 13.

The fathers have eaten sour grapes, and the children's teeth are set on edge. *Eze.* 18: 2.

I found Israel like grapes in the wilderness. *Ho.* 9: 10.

Woe is me! for I am as when they have gathered the summer fruits, as the grapegleanings of the vintage: there is no cluster to eat. *Mi.* 7: 1.

Do men gather grapes of thorns? *Mat.* 7: 16.

Thrust in thy sharp sickle, and gather the clusters of the vine of the earth; for her grapes are fully ripe. *Re.* 14: 18.

See also

Christ, the Vine; Drunkenness; Vine; Wine.

Grass

Let the earth bring forth grass. *Ge.* 1: 11.

They shall soon be cut down as the grass. *Ps.* 37: 2.

In the morning it flourisheth, and groweth up; in the evening it is cut down, and withereth. *Ps.* 90: 6.

My heart is smitten, and withered like grass. *Ps.* 102: 4.

As for man, his days are as grass. *Ps.* 103: 15.

The hay appeareth, and the tender grass sheweth itself, and herbs of the mountains are gathered. *Pr.* 27: 25.

They shall make thee to eat grass as oxen. *Da.* 4: 25.

If God so clothe the grass of the field, which to day is, and to morrow is cast into the oven, shall he not much more clothe you, O ye of little faith? *Mat.* 6: 30.

As the flower of the grass he shall pass away. *Ja.* 1: 10.

See also

Life, the Short; Verdure; Withering.

Gratitude

Remember all the way which the Lord thy God led thee. *De.* 8: 2.

When thou hast eaten and art full, then thou shalt bless the Lord thy God for the good land which he hath given thee. *De.* 8: 10.

Why have I found grace in thine eyes, that thou shouldest take knowledge of me, seeing I am a stranger? *Ru.* 2: 10.

Is there yet any that is left of the house of Saul, that I may shew him kindness for Jonathan's sake? *2 S.* 9: 1.

Praise is comely for the upright. *Ps.* 33: 1.

Oh that men would praise the Lord for his

goodness, and for his wonderful works to the children of men! *Ps.* 107: 8.

It is good to sing praises unto our God; for it is pleasant; and praise is comely. *Ps.* 147: 1.

One of them, when he saw that he was healed, turned back, and with a loud voice glorified God, And fell down on his face at his feet, giving him thanks: and he was a Samaritan. *Lu.* 17: 15, 16.

Where are the nine? *Lu.* 17: 17.

There are not found that returned to give glory to God, save this stranger. *Lu.* 17: 18.

Thanks be unto God for his unspeakable gift. *2 Co.* 9: 15.

Giving thanks always for all things unto God and the Father in the name of our Lord Jesus Christ. *Ep.* 5: 20.

See also

Christ, Gratitude to; God, Gratitude to; God, Praise to; God, Thankfulness to; Praise; Thanksgiving.

Grave

There the wicked cease from troubling; and there the weary be at rest. *Jb.* 3: 17.

In the grave who shall give thee thanks? *Ps.* 6: 5.

Though I walk through the valley of the shadow of death, I will fear no evil. *Ps.* 23: 4.

He will be our guide even unto death. *Ps.* 48: 14.

He brought them out of darkness and the shadow of death. *Ps.* 107: 14.

Jealousy is cruel as the grave. *S. of S.* 8: 6.

Behold, O my people, I will open your graves. *Eze.* 37: 12.

I will ransom them from the power of the grave. *Ho.* 13: 14.

O grave, I will be thy destruction. *Ho.* 13: 14.

The graves were opened; and many bodies of the saints which slept arose. *Mat.* 27: 52.

Ye are as graves which appear not, and the men that walk over them are not aware of them. *Lu.* 11: 44.

After this the judgment. *He.* 9: 27.

See also

Christ, Death of; Death; Decease; Funeral; Immortality; Life, the Eternal; Tomb.

Gravity

Folly is set in great dignity. *Ec.* 10: 6.

They are terrible and dreadful: their judgment and their dignity shall proceed of themselves. *Hab.* 1: 7.

Being in an agony he prayed more earnestly. *Lu.* 22: 44.

Behold therefore the goodness and severity of God: on them which fell, severity; but toward thee, goodness, if thou continue in his goodness. *Ro.* 11: 22.

Continue in faith and charity and holiness with sobriety. *1 Ti.* 2: 15.

One that ruleth well his own house, having his children in subjection with all gravity. *1 Ti.* 3: 4.

Likewise must the deacons be grave, not doubletongued, not given to much wine, not greedy of filthy lucre. *1 Ti.* 3: 8.

That the aged men be sober, grave, temperate, sound in faith, in charity, in patience. *Tit.* 2: 2.

In all things shewing thyself a pattern of good works: in doctrine shewing uncorruptness, gravity, sincerity. *Tit.* 2: 7.

We should live soberly. *Tit.* 2: 12.

We ought to give the more earnest heed to the things which we have heard, lest at any time we should let them slip. *He.* 2: 1.

Presumptuous are they, selfwilled, they are not afraid to speak evil of dignities. *2 Pe.* 2: 10.

Ye should earnestly contend for the faith which was once delivered unto the saints. *Jude* 3.

See also

Dignity; Earnestness; Importance; Solemnity.

Greatness

He that is slow to anger is better than the mighty; and he that ruleth his spirit than he that taketh a city. *Pr.* 16: 32.

Now there was found in it a poor wise man, and he by his wisdom delivered the city. *Ec.* 9: 15.

My beloved is . . . the chiefest among ten thousand. *S. of S.* 5: 10.

Son of man, speak unto Pharaoh; . . . Whom art thou like in thy greatness? *Eze.* 31: 2.

Whosoever therefore shall humble himself as this little child, the same is greatest in the kingdom of heaven. *Mat.* 18: 4.

Whosoever will be great among you, let him be your minister. *Mat.* 20: 26.

Whosoever of you will be the chiefest, shall be servant of all. *Mk.* 10: 44.

Then there arose a reasoning among them, which of them should be greatest. *Lu.* 9: 46.

Zacchaeus . . . was chief among the publicans, and he was rich. *Lu.* 19: 2.

See also

Bigness; Christ, Finality of; Christ, Preëminence of; Excellence; God, Primacy of; Goodness; Importance; Perfection; Preëminence; Superiority; Supremacy; Worth.

Greed

The rich man . . . spared to take of his own flock; . . . but took the poor man's lamb. *2 S.* 12: 4.

So are the ways of every one that is greedy of gain; which taketh away the life of the owners thereof. *Pr.* 1: 19.

He that is greedy of gain troubleth his own house. *Pr.* 15: 27.

He that loveth silver shall not be satisfied with silver; nor he that loveth abundance with increase. *Ec.* 5: 10.

He that getteth riches, and not by right, shall leave them in the midst of his days. *Je.* 17: 11.

They covet fields, and take them by violence; and houses, and take them away. *Mi.* 2: 2.

Tyrus did build herself a strong hold, and heaped up silver as the dust, and fine gold as the mire of the streets. *Zch.* 9: 3.

What will ye give me, and I will deliver him unto you? *Mat.* 26: 15.

They covenanted with him for thirty pieces of silver. *Mat.* 26: 15.

Take heed, and beware of covetousness: for a man's life consisteth not in the abundance of the things which he possesseth. *Lu.* 12: 15.

I have coveted no man's silver, or gold, or apparel. *Ac.* **20: 33.**

He hoped also that money should have been given him of Paul, that he might loose him. *Ac.* **24: 26.**

Being filled with all unrighteousness, . . . wickedness, covetousness. *Ro.* **1: 29.**

To work all uncleanness with greediness. *Ep.* **4: 19.**

Not greedy of filthy lucre. *1 Ti.* **3: 3.**

The love of money is the root of all evil. *1 Ti.* **6: 10.**

Your gold and silver is cankered; and the rust of them shall be a witness against you. *Ja.* **5: 3.**

Ye have heaped treasure together for the last days. *Ja.* **5: 3.**

See also

Acquisition; Avarice; Covetousness; Cupidity; Desire; Longing.

Greek

A superscription also was written over him in letters of Greek, and Latin, and Hebrew. *Lu.* **23: 38.**

Testifying both to the Jews, and also to the Greeks, repentance toward God. *Ac.* **20: 21.**

I am debtor both to the Greeks, and to the Barbarians. *Ro.* **1: 14.**

The gospel of Christ . . . is the power of God unto salvation to every one that believeth; to the Jew first, and also to the Greek. *Ro.* **1: 16.**

There is no difference between the Jew and the Greek: for the same Lord over all is rich unto all that call upon him. *Ro.* **10: 12.**

The Greeks seek after wisdom. *1 Co.* **1: 22.**

We preach Christ crucified, unto the Jews a stumblingblock, and unto the Greeks foolishness. *1 Co.* **1: 23.**

Green

Can the flag grow without water? Whilst it is yet in his greenness, and not cut down, it withereth before any other herb. *Jb.* **8: 11, 12.**

His branch shall not be green. *Jb.* **15: 32.**

He shall shake off his unripe grape as the vine, and shall cast off his flower as the olive. *Jb.* **15: 33.**

The range of the mountains is his pasture, and he searcheth after every green thing. *Jb.* **39: 8.**

He maketh me to lie down in green pastures. *Ps.* **23: 2.**

They shall soon be cut down like the grass, and wither as the green herb. *Ps.* **37: 2.**

I have seen the wicked in great power, and spreading himself like a green bay tree. *Ps.* **37: 35.**

I am like a green olive tree in the house of God. *Ps.* **52: 8.**

The fig tree putteth forth her green figs, and the vines with the tender grape give a good smell. *S. of S.* **2: 13.**

The hay is withered away, the grass faileth, there is no green thing. *Is.* **15: 6.**

I am like a green fir tree. From me is thy fruit found. *Ho.* **14: 8.**

If they do these things in a green tree, what shall be done in the dry? *Lu.* **23: 31.**

See also

Grass; Life, the Short; Verdure; Withering.

Grief

The woman was left of her two sons and her husband. *Ru.* **1: 5.**

How oft did they provoke him in the wilderness, and grieve him in the desert! *Ps.* **78: 40.**

Out of the depths have I cried unto thee, O Lord. Lord, hear my voice. *Ps.* **130: 1, 2.**

In much wisdom is much grief. *Ec.* **1: 18.**

His life shall be grievous unto him. *Is.* **15: 4.**

To give unto them beauty for ashes. *Is.* **61: 3.**

They bind heavy burdens and grievous to be borne, and lay them on men's shoulders. *Mat.* **23: 4.**

Grieve not the holy Spirit of God. *Ep.* **4: 30.**

No chastening for the present seemeth to be joyous, but grievous. *He.* **12: 11.**

That they may do it with joy, and not with grief. *He.* **13: 17.**

This is thankworthy, if a man for conscience toward God endure grief, suffering wrongfully. *1 Pe.* **2: 19.**

His commandments are not grievous. *1 Jn.* **5: 3.**

See also

Affliction; Christ, Sorrow of; Depression; Gloom; Lamentation; Melancholy; Mourning; Sadness; Sorrow; Tear; Unhappiness; Weeping; Woe.

Groan

God heard their groaning. *Ex.* **2: 24.**

Men groan from out of the city, and the soul of the wounded crieth out. *Jb.* **24: 12.**

They bemoaned him, and comforted him over all the evil that the Lord had brought upon him. *Jb.* **42: 11.**

I am weary with my groaning. *Ps.* **6: 6.**

Lord, all my desire is before thee; and my groaning is not hid from thee. *Ps.* **38: 9.**

Enter not into the house of mourning, neither go to lament nor bemoan them: for I have taken away my peace from this people. *Je.* **16: 5.**

Weep ye not for the dead, neither bemoan him: but weep sore for him that goeth away: for he shall return no more, nor see his native country. *Je.* **22: 10.**

Jesus . . . groaned in the spirit, and was troubled. *Jn.* **11: 33.**

The whole creation groaneth and travaileth in pain together until now. *Ro.* **8: 22.**

Even we ourselves groan within ourselves, waiting for the adoption, to wit, the redemption of our body. *Ro.* **8: 23.**

The Spirit itself maketh intercession for us with groanings which cannot be uttered. *Ro.* **8: 26.**

In this we groan, earnestly desiring to be clothed upon with our house which is from heaven. *2 Co.* **5: 2.**

See also

Grief; Mourning; Sadness; Sorrow; Weeping; Woe.

Ground

God called the dry land Earth. *Ge.* **1: 10.**

The Lord God formed man of the dust of the ground. *Ge.* **2: 7.**

Blessed shall be . . . the fruit of thy ground. *De.* **28: 4.**

As for the earth, out of it cometh bread. *Jb.* **28: 5.**

The earth is the Lord's, and the fulness thereof. *Ps. 24: 1.*

Then shall the earth yield her increase. *Ps. 67: 6.*

He turneth the wilderness into a standing water, and dry ground into watersprings. *Ps. 107: 35.*

The earth abideth for ever. *Ec. 1: 4.*

The profit of the earth is for all: the king himself is served by the field. *Ec. 5: 9.*

The earth shall reel to and fro like a drunkard. *Is. 24: 20.*

The lofty city, he layeth it low; he layeth it low, even to the ground; he bringeth it even to the dust. *Is. 26: 5.*

Thou shalt be brought down, and shalt speak out of the ground, and thy speech shall be low out of the dust, and thy voice shall be, as of one that hath a familiar spirit, out of the ground, and thy speech shall whisper out of the dust. *Is. 29: 4.*

It was planted in a good soil by great waters, that it might bring forth branches, and that it might bear fruit. *Eze. 17: 8.*

So is the kingdom of God, as if a man should cast seed into the ground. *Mk. 4: 26.*

Jesus stooped down, and with his finger wrote on the ground. *Jn. 8: 6.*

Except a corn of wheat fall into the ground and die, it abideth alone: but if it die, it bringeth forth much fruit. *Jn. 12: 24.*

The house of God . . . is . . . the pillar and ground of the truth. *1 Ti. 3: 15.*

See also
Bottom; Earth; Foundation; Ground, Holy; Land; Soil.

Ground, Holy

This is none other but the house of God, and this is the gate of heaven. *Ge. 28: 17.*

Draw not nigh hither: put off thy shoes from off thy feet, for the place whereon thou standest is holy ground. *Ex. 3: 5.*

Loose thy shoe from off thy foot; for the place whereon thou standest is holy. *Jos. 5: 15.*

Who shall stand in his holy place? *Ps. 24: 3.*

The whole earth is full of his glory. *Is. 6: 3.*

An highway shall be there, and a way, and it shall be called The way of holiness. *Is. 35: 8.*

Jerusalem shall be called a city of truth; and the mountain of the Lord of hosts the holy mountain. *Zch. 8: 3.*

Peter answered and said to Jesus, Master, it is good for us to be here. *Mk. 9: 5.*

The temple of God is holy, which temple ye are. *1 Co. 3: 17.*

We were with him in the holy mount. *2 Pe. 1: 18.*

See also
God, House of; Holiness; Temple.

Growth

The land shall yield her increase. *Le. 26: 4.*

I am like a green olive tree in the house of God: I trust in the mercy of God for ever and ever. *Ps. 52: 8.*

In the morning they are like grass which groweth up. *Ps. 90: 5.*

The path of the just is as the shining light; that shineth more and more unto the perfect day. *Pr. 4: 18.*

He shall grow up before him as a tender plant, and as a root out of a dry ground. *Is. 53: 2.*

A little one shall become a thousand, and a small one a strong nation. *Is. 60: 22.*

The earth bringeth forth fruit of herself; first the blade, then the ear, after that the full corn in the ear. *Mk. 4: 28.*

The kingdom of God . . . is like a grain of mustard seed, which, when it is sown in the earth, is less than all the seeds that be in the earth: But when it is sown, it groweth up, and becometh greater than all herbs. *Mk. 4: 30–32.*

It grew, and waxed a great tree. *Lu. 13: 19.*

He must increase, but I must decrease. *Jn. 3: 30.*

Thou sowest not that body that shall be, but bare grain, . . . But God giveth it a body as it hath pleased him, and to every seed his own body. *1 Co. 15: 37, 38.*

No more children. *Ep. 4: 14.*

May grow up into him in all things. *Ep. 4: 15.*

All the body . . . increaseth with the increase of God. *Col. 2: 19.*

We are bound to thank God always for you, . . . because that your faith groweth exceedingly. *2 Th. 1: 3.*

As newborn babes, desire the sincere milk of the word, that ye may grow thereby. *1 Pe. 2: 2.*

Grow in grace. *2 Pe. 3: 18.*

Grow . . . in the knowledge of our Lord and Saviour Jesus Christ. *2 Pe. 3: 18.*

See also
Development; Education; Evolution; Increase; Progress; Stature; Unfolding.

Guest

Make ready quickly three measures of fine meal, knead it, and make cakes upon the hearth. *Ge. 18: 6.*

Turn in, I pray you, into your servant's house, and tarry all night, and wash your feet, and ye shall rise up early, and go your way. *Ge. 19: 2.*

They turned in unto him, and entered into his house; and he made them a feast, and did bake unleavened bread, and they did eat. *Ge. 19: 3.*

Is there room in thy father's house for us to lodge in? *Ge. 24: 23.*

He is my God, and I will prepare him a habitation. *Ex. 15: 2.*

Lodge here this night, and I will bring you word again, as the Lord shall speak unto me. *Nu. 22: 8.*

Her guests are in the depths of hell. *Pr. 9:18.*

The Lord hath prepared a sacrifice, he hath bid his guests. *Zph. 1: 7.*

The wedding was furnished with guests. *Mat. 22: 10.*

Afterward came also the other virgins, saying, Lord, Lord, open to us. *Mat. 25: 11.*

I was a stranger, and ye took me in. *Mat. 25: 35.*

They all murmured, saying, That he was gone to be guest with a man that is a sinner. *Lu. 19: 7.*

Where is the guestchamber, where I shall eat the passover with my disciples? *Lu. 22: 11.*

If I go and prepare a place for you, I will come again, and receive you unto myself. *Jn. 14: 3.*

If she have brought up children, if she have lodged strangers, if she have washed the saints' feet, if she have relieved the afflicted, if she have diligently followed every good work. *1 Ti.* 5: 10.

Withal prepare me also a lodging. *Phm.* 22.
See also

Cordiality; Hospitality; Welcome.

Guidance

The Lord alone did lead him, and there was no strange god with him. *De.* 32: 12.

Arise; for this matter belongeth unto thee: we also will be with thee: be of good courage, and do it. *Ezr.* 10: 4.

Canst thou guide Arcturus with his sons? *Jb.* 38: 32.

For thy name's sake lead me, and guide me. *Ps.* 31: 3.

I will instruct thee and teach thee in the way which thou shalt go. *Ps.* 32: 8.

O send out thy light and thy truth: let them lead me. *Ps.* 43: 3.

Put ye not confidence in a guide. *Mi.* 7: 5.

Ye are the light of the world. A city that is set on a hill cannot be hid. *Mat.* 5: 14.

He . . . leadeth them out. *Jn.* 10: 3.

Cornelius the centurion . . . was warned from God by an holy angel to send for thee. *Ac.* 10: 22.

The goodness of God leadeth thee to repentance. *Ro.* 2: 4.

See also

Administration; Auspices; Christ, the Leader; Direction; Execution; Government; Leadership; Order; Supervision.

Guile

What is the hope of the hypocrite, . . . when God taketh away his soul? *Jb.* 27: 8.

Keep thy tongue from evil, and thy lips from speaking guile. *Ps.* 34: 13.

Deceit and guile depart not from her streets. *Ps.* 55: 11.

Bread of deceit is sweet to a man; but afterwards his mouth shall be filled with gravel. *Pr.* 20: 17.

Being crafty, I caught you with guile. *2 Co.* 12: 16.

Having a form of godliness, but denying the power thereof: from such turn away. *2 Ti.* 3: 5.

Laying aside all malice, and all guile, and hypocrisies, and envies. *1 Pe.* 2: 1.

We have not followed cunningly devised fables, when we made known unto you the power and coming of our Lord Jesus Christ. *2 Pe.* 1: 16.

See also

Betrayal; Cheat; Craftiness; Deceit; Duplicity; Evil; Faithlessness; Fraud; Hypocrisy; Iniquity; Lie; Treachery; Wickedness; Wrong.

Guilelessness

I will wash mine hands in innocency. *Ps.* 26: 6.

In whose spirit there is no guile. *Ps.* 32: 2.

Blessed are the pure in heart: for they shall see God. *Mat.* 5: 8.

Except ye be converted, and become as little children, ye shall not enter into the kingdom of heaven. *Mat.* 18: 3.

In simplicity and godly sincerity, . . . we have had our conversation in the world. *2 Co.* 1: 12.

Grace be with all them that love our Lord Jesus Christ in sincerity. *Ep.* 6: 24.

Yet without sin. *He.* 4: 15.

In their mouth was found no guile. *Re.* 14: 5.
See also

Childlikeness; Holiness; Innocence; Purity; Saint; Sanctification.

Guilt

Adam and his wife hid themselves from the presence of the Lord God. *Ge.* 3: 8.

We saw the anguish of his soul, when he besought us, and we would not hear. *Ge.* 42: 21.

The Lord is righteous, and I and my people are wicked. *Ex.* 9: 27.

The Lord will not hold him guiltless that taketh his name in vain. *Ex.* 20: 7.

Thou shalt put away the guilt of innocent blood. *De.* 19: 13.

The fathers shall not be put to death for the children, neither shall the children be put to death for the fathers: every man shall be put to death for his own sin. *De.* 24: 16.

O my God, I am ashamed and blush to lift up my face to thee, my God: for our iniquities are increased over our head, and our trespass is grown up unto the heavens. *Ezr.* 9: 6.

Mine iniquities are gone over mine head: as a heavy burden they are too heavy for me. *Ps.* 38: 4.

Mine iniquities have taken hold upon me, so that I am not able to look up; they are more than the hairs of mine head: therefore my heart faileth me. *Ps.* 40: 12.

My sin is ever before me. *Ps.* 51: 3.

Deliver me from bloodguiltiness, O God, thou God of my salvation. *Ps.* 51: 14.

Though your sins be as scarlet, they shall be as white as snow. *Is.* 1: 18.

They shall go into the holes of the rocks, and into the caves of the earth, for fear of the Lord. *Is.* 2: 19.

The sinners in Zion are afraid; fearfulness hath surprised the hypocrites. *Is.* 33: 14.

Your iniquities have separated between you and your God. *Is.* 59: 2.

In thy skirts is found the blood of the souls of the poor innocents. *Je.* 2: 34.

His thoughts troubled him, so that the joints of his loins were loosed, and his knees smote one against another. *Da.* 5: 6.

Depart from me; for I am a sinful man. *Lu.* 5: 8.

They which heard it, being convicted by their own conscience, went out one by one, beginning at the eldest, even unto the last. *Jn.* 8: 9.

When they heard this, they were pricked in their heart. *Ac.* 2: 37.

We know that what things soever the law saith, it saith to them who are under the law: that every mouth may be stopped, and all the world may become guilty before God. *Ro.* 3: 19.

Whosoever shall eat this bread, and drink this cup of the Lord, unworthily, shall be guilty of the body and blood of the Lord. *1 Co.* 11: 27.

Whosoever shall keep the whole law, and yet offend in one point, he is guilty of all. *Ja.* 2: 10.

See also

Blame; Crime; Evil; Fault; Guile; Iniquity; Sin; Transgression; Trespass; Unrighteousness; Wickedness; Wrong.

H

Habit

Ask for the old paths, where is the good way, and walk therein. *Je.* 6: 16.

They shall walk every one in his path. *Jo.* 2: 8.

He went out, and departed into a solitary place, and there prayed. *Mk.* 1: 35.

As his custom was, he went into the synagogue on the sabbath day. *Lu.* 4: 16.

John the Baptist came neither eating bread nor drinking wine. . . . The Son of man is come eating and drinking. *Lu.* 7: 33, 34.

Peter continued knocking. *Ac.* 12: 16.

Walk in love, as Christ also hath loved us. *Ep.* 5: 2.

See also

Behavior; Character; Conduct; Custom; Exercise; Fashion; Manners; Practice; Rule.

Habitation

Be thou my strong habitation, whereunto I may continually resort. *Ps.* 71: 3.

The sparrow hath found an house, and the swallow a nest for herself. *Ps.* 84: 3.

Because thou hast made the Lord, which is my refuge, even the most High, thy habitation; There shall no evil befall thee. *Ps.* 91: 9, 10.

He that troubleth his own house shall inherit the wind. *Pr.* 11: 29.

Woe unto them that join house to house, that lay field to field. *Is.* 5: 8.

Thine eyes shall see Jerusalem a quiet habitation. *Is.* 33: 20.

Is it time for you, O ye, to dwell in your cieled houses, and this house lie waste? *Hag.* 1: 4.

The church that is in their house. *1 Co.* 16: 19.

In whom ye also are builded together for an habitation of God through the Spirit. *Ep.* 2: 22.

See also

Abode; Dwelling; God, House of; Home; House; Residence; Roof; Shelter; Tenant.

Hair

He shall be holy, and shall let the locks of the hair of his head grow. *Nu.* 6: 5.

If I be shaven, then my strength will go from me, and I shall become weak. *Ju.* 16: 17.

Innumerable evils have compassed me about: . . . they are more than the hairs of mine head. *Ps.* 40: 12.

Cut off thine hair, O Jerusalem, and cast it away, and take up a lamentation on high places. *Je.* 7: 29.

The same John had his raiment of camel's hair. *Mat.* 3: 4.

Neither shalt thou swear by thy head, because thou canst not make one hair white or black. *Mat.* 5: 36.

The very hairs of your head are all numbered. *Mat.* 10: 30.

A woman in the city, which was a sinner, . . . began to wash his feet with tears, and did wipe them with the hairs of her head. *Lu.* 7: 37, 38.

Mary . . . anointed the Lord with ointment, and wiped his feet with her hair. *Jn.* 11: 2.

See also

Head.

Half

Divide the living child in two, and give half to the one, and half to the other. *1 K.* 3: 25.

Bloody and deceitful men shall not live out half their days; but I will trust in thee. *Ps.* 55: 23.

Their heart is divided. *Ho.* 10: 2.

A certain man . . . fell among thieves, which stripped him of his raiment, and wounded him, and departed, leaving him half dead. *Lu.* 10: 30.

The half of my goods I give to the poor. *Lu.* 19: 8.

There was silence in heaven about the space of half an hour. *Re.* 8: 1.

See also

Division.

Half-Heartedness

Solomon . . . went not fully after the Lord. *1 K.* 11: 6.

How long halt ye between two opinions? *1 K.* 18: 21.

He did that which was right in the sight of the Lord, but not with a perfect heart. *2 Ch.* 25: 2.

Her treacherous sister Judah hath not turned unto me with her whole heart, but feignedly. *Je.* 3: 10.

Their heart is divided. *Ho.* 10: 2.

No man can serve two masters. *Mat.* 6: 24.

Almost thou persuadest me to be a Christian. *Ac.* 26: 28.

Purify your hearts, ye double minded. *Ja.* 4: 8.

Thou hast a name that thou livest, and art dead. *Re.* 3: 1.

I know thy works, that thou art neither cold nor hot: I would thou wert cold or hot. *Re.* 3: 15.

So then because thou art lukewarm, and neither cold nor hot, I will spue thee out of my mouth. *Re.* 3: 16.

See also

Indifference; Loyalty, Divided; Lukewarmness.

Hallelujah

Praise ye the Lord. *Ps.* 105: 45.

Blessed be the Lord God of Israel from everlasting to everlasting. *Ps.* 106: 48.

I will praise the Lord with my whole heart. *Ps.* 111: 1.

Praise, O ye servants of the Lord, praise the name of the Lord. *Ps.* 113: 1.

While I live will I praise the Lord. *Ps.* 146: 2.

Sing unto the Lord a new song, and his

praise in the congregation of saints. *Ps.* **149: 1.**

I heard a great voice of much people in heaven, saying, Alleluia; Salvation, and glory, and honour, and power, unto the Lord our God. *Re.* **19: 1.**

Alleluia: for the Lord God omnipotent reigneth. *Re.* **19: 6.**

See also

Alleluia; God, Praise of; Praise.

Halo

Moses wist not that the skin of his face shone. *Ex.* **34: 29.**

His countenance was like the countenance of an angel of God. *Ju.* **13: 6.**

The beauty of old men is the grey head. *Pr.* **20: 29.**

Upon them hath the light shined. *Is.* **9: 2.**

Everlasting joy shall be upon their head. *Is.* **51: 11.**

An helmet of salvation upon his head. *Is.* **59: 17.**

His brightness was as the light. *Hab.* **3: 4.**

He shall baptize you with the Holy Ghost, and with fire. *Mat.* **3: 11.**

His countenance was like lightning. *Mat.* **28: 3.**

There appeared unto them cloven tongues like as of fire, and it sat upon each of them. *Ac.* **2: 3.**

He shall receive the crown of life. *Ja.* **1: 12.**

His countenance was as the sun shineth in his strength. *Re.* **1: 16.**

A rainbow was upon his head. *Re.* **10: 1.**

On his head were many crowns. *Rev.* **19: 12.**

Halt

Stand still, and see the salvation of the Lord. *Ex.* **14: 13.**

Stand still, and I will hear what the Lord will command concerning you. *Nu.* **9: 8.**

The sun stood still in the midst of heaven. *Jos.* **10: 13.**

Stand thou still 'a while, that I may shew thee the word of God. *1 S.* **9: 27.**

Stand still, that I may reason with you before the Lord. *1 S.* **12: 7.**

The blind and the lame shall not come into the house. *2 S.* **5: 8.**

How long halt ye between two opinions? If the Lord be God, follow him: but if Baal, then follow him. *1 K.* **18: 21.**

I was eyes to the blind, and feet was I to the lame. *Jb.* **29: 15.**

Stand still, and consider the wondrous works of God. *Jb.* **37: 14.**

I am ready to halt, and my sorrow is continually before me. *Ps.* **38: 17.**

Be still, and know that I am God. *Ps.* **46: 10.**

Then shall the lame man leap as an hart. *Is.* **35: 6.**

In that day, saith the Lord, will I assemble her that halteth, and I will gather her that is driven out, and her that I have afflicted. *Mi.* **4: 6.**

I will save her that halteth, and gather her that was driven out. *Zph.* **3: 19.**

It is better for thee to enter into life halt or maimed, rather than having two hands or two feet to be cast into everlasting fire. *Mat.* **18: 8.**

Go out quickly into the streets and lanes of the city, and bring in hither the poor, and the maimed, and the halt, and the blind. *Lu.* **14: 21.**

Many taken with palsies, and that were lame, were healed. *Ac.* **8: 7.**

See also

Cripple; Foot; Lameness.

Hand

God shall bless thee in all thine increase, and in all the works of thine hands. *De.* **16: 15.**

My little finger shall be thicker than my father's loins. *1 K.* **12: 10.**

Clean hands, and a pure heart. *Ps.* **24: 4.**

Establish thou the work of our hands upon us; yea, the work of our hands establish thou it. *Ps.* **90: 17.**

They have hands, but they handle not. *Ps.* **115: 7.**

When ye spread forth your hands, I will hide mine eyes from you: yea, when ye make many prayers, I will not hear: your hands are full of blood. *Is.* **1: 15.**

Mine elect shall long enjoy the work of their hands. *Is.* **65: 22.**

The work of the workman, and of the hands of the founder. *Je.* **10: 9.**

If thy right hand offend thee, cut it off, and cast it from thee. *Mat.* **5: 30.**

The eye cannot say unto the hand, I have no need of thee. *1 Co.* **12: 21.**

Study . . . to work with your own hands, as we commanded you. *1 Th.* **4: 11.**

But be ye doers of the word, and not hearers only. *Ja.* **1: 22.**

Cleanse your hands, ye sinners. *Ja.* **4: 8.**

See also

Finger; Handiwork; Helpfulness; Labor; Occupation; Service; Task; Toil; Travail; Usefulness.

Handicap

Ye shall no more give the people straw to make brick, as heretofore: let them go and gather straw for themselves. *Ex.* **5: 7.**

Not with thy sword, nor with thy bow. *Jos.* **24: 12.**

The people that are with thee are too many. *Ju.* **7: 2.**

He was also a mighty man in valour, but he was a leper. *2 K.* **5: 1.**

If the foundations be destroyed, what can the righteous do? *Ps.* **11: 3.**

They bind heavy burdens and grievous to be borne, and lay them on men's shoulders. *Mat.* **23: 4.**

They uncovered the roof where he was: and when they had broken it up, they let down the bed wherein the sick of the palsy lay. *Mk.* **2: 4.**

There was a man there which had a withered hand. *Mk.* **3: 1.**

They bring a blind man unto him, and besought him to touch him. *Mk.* **8: 22.**

He sought to see Jesus who he was; and could not for the press, because he was little of stature. *Lu.* **19: 3.**

The impotent man answered him, Sir, I have no man, when the water is troubled, to put me into the pool. *Jn.* **5: 7.**

I mean not that other men be eased, and ye burdened. *2 Co.* **8: 13.**

Ye did run well; who did hinder you that ye

should not obey the truth? *Ga.* 5: 7.

Every man shall bear his own burden. *Ga.* 6: 5.

See also

Blindness; Burden; Cripple; Deafness; Halt; Hindrance; Lameness; Limitation.

Handiwork

He hath filled him with the spirit of God, in wisdom, in understanding, and in knowledge, and in all manner of workmanship. *Ex.* 35: 31.

He hath filled him with the spirit of God, . . . to devise curious works, to work in gold, and in silver, and in brass. *Ex.* 35: 31, 32.

He hath filled him with the spirit of God, . . . in the cutting of stones, to set them, and in carving of wood, to make any manner of cunning work. *Ex.* 35: 31. 33.

Them hath he filled with wisdom of heart, to work all manner of work, of the engraver, and of the cunning workman, and of the embroiderer, . . . and of the weaver, even of them that do any work, and of those that devise cunning work. *Ex.* 35: 35.

There shall be with thee for all manner of workmanship every willing skilful man. *1 Ch.* 28: 21.

The firmament sheweth his handywork. *Ps.* 19: 1.

He . . . guided them by the skilfulness of his hands. *Ps.* 78: 72.

Establish thou the work of our hands upon us; yea, the work of our hands establish thou it. *Ps.* 90: 17.

I will triumph in the works of thy hands. *Ps.* 92: 4.

The heavens are the work of thy hands. *Ps.* 102: 25.

Thy hands have made me and fashioned me. *Ps.* 119: 73.

Whatsoever thy hand findeth to do, do it with thy might. *Ec.* 9: 10.

The joints of thy thighs are like jewels, the work of the hands of a cunning workman. *S. of S.* 7: 1.

He seeketh unto him a cunning workman to prepare a graven image, that shall not be moved. *Is.* 40: 20.

The workman made it; therefore it is not God. *Ho.* 8: 6.

See also

Expert; Hand; Labor; Skill; Workmanship.

Happening

Your eyes have seen all the great acts of the Lord which he did. *De.* 11: 7.

There shall they rehearse the righteous acts of the Lord. *Ju.* 5: 11.

Stand and see this great thing, which the Lord will do before your eyes. *1 S.* 12: 16.

Talk ye of all his wondrous works. *1 Ch.* 16: 9.

Declare among the people his doings. *Ps.* 9: 11.

Many, O Lord my God, are thy wonderful works which thou hast done. *Ps.* 40: 5.

I shall not die, but live, and declare the works of the Lord. *Ps.* 118: 17.

Marvellous are thy works; and that my soul knoweth right well. *Ps.* 139: 14.

As it happeneth to the fool, so it happeneth even to me. *Ec.* 2: 15.

There is one event to the righteous, and to the wicked. *Ec.* 9: 2.

Time and chance happeneth to them all. *Ec.* 9: 11.

Declare his doings among the people. *Is.* 12: 4.

Then began he to upbraid the cities wherein most of his mighty works were done, because they repented not. *Mat.* 11: 20.

He . . . began to tell them what things should happen unto him. *Mk.* 10: 32.

The whole multitude of the disciples began to rejoice and praise God with a loud voice for all the mighty works that they had seen. *Lu.* 19: 37.

They were filled with wonder and amazement at that which had happened unto him. *Ac.* 3: 10.

Truly the signs of an apostle were wrought among you in all patience, in signs, and wonders, and mighty deeds. *2 Co.* 12: 12.

The things which happened unto me have fallen out rather unto the furtherance of the gospel. *Ph.* 1: 12.

Beloved, think it not strange concerning the fiery trial which is to try you, as though some strange thing happened unto you. *1 Pe.* 4: 12.

See also

Action; Deed.

Happiness

Blessed is the man that walketh not in the counsel of the ungodly, nor standeth in the way of sinners. *Ps.* 1: 1.

I will be glad and rejoice in thee. *Ps.* 9: 2.

Weeping may endure for a night, but joy cometh in the morning. *Ps.* 30: 5.

Let the nations be glad and sing for joy. *Ps.* 67: 4.

Light is sown for the righteous, and gladness for the upright in heart. *Ps.* 97: 11.

Serve the Lord with gladness: come before his presence with singing. *Ps.* 100: 2.

When the Lord turned again the captivity of Zion, we were like them that dream. *Ps.* 126: 1.

The Lord hath done great things for us; whereof we are glad. *Ps.* 126: 3.

They that sow in tears shall reap in joy. *Ps.* 126: 5.

Happy is that people, whose God is the Lord. *Ps.* 144: 15.

The poor among men shall rejoice in the Holy One of Israel. *Is.* 29: 19.

To give unto them beauty for ashes, the oil of joy for mourning, the garment of praise for the spirit of heaviness. *Is.* 61: 3.

Blessed are they which are persecuted for righteousness' sake: for theirs is the kingdom of heaven. *Mat.* 5: 10.

From henceforth all generations shall call me blessed. *Lu.* 1: 48.

My joy. *Jn.* 15: 11.

Such as I have give I thee. *Ac.* 3: 6.

He went on his way rejoicing. *Ac.* 8: 39.

The kingdom of God is . . . righteousness, and peace, and joy in the Holy Ghost. *Ro.* 14: 17.

If I be offered upon the sacrifice and service of your faith, I joy, and rejoice with you all. *Ph.* 2: 17.

We count them happy which endure. *Ja.* 5: 11.

These things write we unto you, that your joy may be full. *1 Jn.* 1: 4.

See also

Beatitude; Blessedness; Bliss; Cheerfulness; Christ, Joy in; Christ, Joy of; Contentment; Delight; Enjoyment; Gladness; God, Joy in; Joy; Pleasure; Rejoicing; Satisfaction; Well-being.

Harbinger

To morrow is the new moon. *1 S.* 20: 5.

Lo, the winter is past, the rain is over and gone; The flowers appear on the earth; the time of the singing of birds is come, and the voice of the turtle is heard in our land. *S. of S.* 2: 11, 12.

Until the day break, and the shadows flee away. *S. of S.* 2: 17.

The stork in the heaven knoweth her appointed times; and the turtle and the crane and the swallow observe the time of their coming. *Je.* 8: 7.

Behold upon the mountains the feet of him that bringeth good tidings, that publisheth peace! *Na.* 1: 15.

Lo, the star, which they saw in the east, went before them. *Mat.* 2: 9.

When it is evening, ye say, It will be fair weather: for the sky is red. *Mat.* 16: 2.

O ye hypocrites, ye can discern the face of the sky; but can ye not discern the signs of the times? *Mat.* 16: 3.

What shall be the sign of thy coming? *Mat.* 24: 3.

This shall be a sign unto you. *Lu.* 2: 12.

I am the voice of one crying in the wilderness, Make straight the way of the Lord. *Jn.* 1: 23.

God sent forth his Son . . . To redeem them that were under the law. *Ga.* 4: 4, 5.

See also

Forerunner; Herald; Messenger; Predecessor.

Hardness

I will harden the hearts of the Egyptians. *Ex.* 14: 17.

He made him to suck honey out of the rock, and oil out of the flinty rock. *De.* 32: 13.

I would harden myself in sorrow. *Jb.* 6: 10.

Which turned the rock into a standing water, the flint into a fountain of waters. *Ps.* 114: 8.

Whoso stoppeth his ears at the cry of the poor, he also shall cry himself, but shall not be heard. *Pr.* 21: 13.

Therefore have I set my face like a flint, and I know that I shall not be ashamed. *Is.* 50: 7.

O Lord, why hast thou made us to err from thy ways, and hardened our heart from thy fear? *Is.* 63: 17.

They have made their faces harder than a rock; they have refused to return. *Je.* 5: 3.

As an adamant harder than flint have I made thy forehead: fear them not. *Eze.* 3: 9.

Moses because of the hardness of your hearts suffered you to put away your wives. *Mat.* 19: 8.

If they hear not Moses and the prophets, neither will they be persuaded, though one rose from the dead. *Lu.* 16: 31.

After thy hardness and impenitent heart treasurest up unto thyself wrath against the day of wrath. *Ro.* 2: 5.

Thou therefore endure hardness as a good soldier of Jesus Christ. *2 Ti.* 2: 3.

Harden not your hearts. *He.* 3: 8.

Exhort one another daily, while it is called To day; lest any of you be hardened through the deceitfulness of sin. *He.* 3: 13.

See also

Austerity; Christ, the Rock; Cruelty; Firmness; Fortitude; Harshness; Insensibility; Rock; Severity; Stone.

Hardship

How shall we sing the Lord's song in a strange land? *Ps.* 137: 4.

The way of transgressors is hard. *Pr.* 13: 15.

Men that have hazarded their lives for the name of our Lord Jesus. *Ac.* 15: 26.

Our light affliction, which is but for a moment, worketh for us a far more exceeding and eternal weight of glory. *2 Co.* 4: 17.

In labours more abundant, in stripes above measure, in prisons more frequent, in deaths oft. *2 Co.* 11: 23.

Thrice I suffered shipwreck, a night and a day I have been in the deep. *2 Co.* 11: 25.

In journeyings often, in perils of waters, in perils of robbers, in perils by mine own countrymen, in perils by the heathen, in perils in the city, in perils in the wilderness, in perils in the sea, in perils among false brethren. *2 Co.* 11: 26.

In weariness and painfulness, in watchings often, in hunger and thirst, in fastings often, in cold and nakedness. *2 Co.* 11: 27.

Therefore I take pleasure in infirmities, in reproaches, in necessities, in persecutions, in distresses for Christ's sake: for when I am weak, then am I strong. *2 Co.* 12: 10.

Thou therefore endure hardness as a good soldier of Jesus Christ. *2 Ti* 2: 3.

See also

Austerity; Christ, the Rock; Cruelty; Disaster; Fortitude; Hardness; Severity; Trial; Tribulation; Trouble.

Harlot

A woman with the attire of a harlot, and subtil of heart. *Pr.* 7: 10.

He goeth after her straightway, . . . as a bird hasteth to the snare, and knoweth not that it is for his life. *Pr.* 7: 22, 23.

Her house is the way to hell, going down to the chambers of death. *Pr.* 7: 27.

A whore is a deep ditch; and a strange woman is a narrow pit. *Pr.* 23: 27.

He that keepeth company with harlots spendeth his substance. *Pr.* 29: 3.

The publicans and the harlots go into the kingdom of God before you. *Mat.* 21: 31.

Know ye not that your bodies are the members of Christ? shall I then take the members of Christ, and make them the members of an harlot? God forbid. *1 Co.* 6: 15.

Whoremongers and adulterers God will judge. *He.* 13: 4.

See also

Brothel; Flesh; Fornication; Lust; Prostitute.

Harm

Touch not mine anointed, and do my prophets no harm. *1 Ch. 16: 22.*

They shall not hurt nor destroy in all my holy mountain. *Is. 11: 9.*

Wounded in the house of my friends. *Zch. 13: 6.*

Be ye therefore wise as serpents, and harmless as doves. *Mat. 10: 16.*

At him they cast stones, and wounded him in the head. *Mk. 12: 4.*

Do thyself no harm. *Ac. 16: 28.*

He shook off the beast into the fire, and felt no harm. *Ac. 28: 5.*

That ye may be blameless and harmless, the sons of God, without rebuke. *Ph. 2: 15.*

Others had trial of cruel mockings and scourgings. *He. 11: 36.*

Who is he that will harm you, if ye be followers of that which is good? *1 Pe. 3: 13.*

See also

Bruise; Evil; Hurt; Iniquity; Injury; Mischief; Misfortune; Wound.

Harmlessness

This pillar be witness, that I will not pass over this heap to thee, and that thou shalt not pass over this heap and this pillar unto me, for harm. *Ge. 31: 52.*

I will no more do thee harm. *1 S. 26: 21.*

Strive not with a man without cause, if he have done thee no harm. *Pr. 3: 30.*

The calf and the young lion and the fatling together; and a little child shall lead them. *Is. 11: 6.*

The cow and the bear shall feed; their young ones shall lie down together. *Is. 11: 7.*

They shall not hurt nor destroy in all my holy mountain. *Is. 11: 9.*

The wolf and the lamb shall feed together. *Is. 65: 25.*

The lion shall eat straw like the bullock. *Is. 65: 25.*

Be ye therefore wise as serpents, and harmless as doves. *Mat. 10: 16.*

Paul cried with a loud voice, saying, Do thyself no harm: for we are all here. *Ac. 16: 28.*

Ye have not injured me at all. *Ga. 4: 12.*

Do all things without murmurings and disputings: That ye may be blameless and harmless, the sons of God. *Ph. 2: 14, 15.*

For such an high priest became us, who is holy, harmless, undefiled, separate from sinners, and made higher than the heavens. *He. 7: 26.*

Who is he that will harm you, if ye be followers of that which is good? *1 Pe. 3: 13.*

See also

Innocence.

Harmony

All the people arose as one man. *Ju. 20: 8.*

Righteousness and peace have kissed each other. *Ps. 85: 10.*

Behold, how good and how pleasant it is for brethren to dwell together in unity! *Ps. 133: 1.*

The leopard shall lie down with the kid. *Is. 11: 6.*

Can two walk together, except they be agreed? *Am. 3: 3.*

If it be possible, as much as lieth in you, live peaceably with all men. *Ro. 12: 18.*

Endeavouring to keep the unity of the Spirit in the bond of peace. *Ep. 4: 3.*

Be at peace among yourselves. *1 Th. 5: 13.*

See, saith he, that thou make all things according to the pattern shewed to thee in the mount. *He. 8: 5.*

See also

Accord; Agreement; Compatibility; Concord; Oneness; Peace; Symmetry; Unanimity; Unity.

Harp

Jubal . . . was the father of all such as handle the harp and organ. *Ge. 4: 21.*

My harp also is turned to mourning, and my organ into the voice of them that weep. *Jb. 30: 31.*

Praise the Lord with harp. *Ps. 33: 2.*

I will open my dark saying upon the harp. *Ps. 49: 4.*

Unto thee will I sing with the harp, O thou Holy One of Israel. *Ps. 71: 22.*

Take a psalm, and bring hither the timbrel, the pleasant harp with the psaltery. *Ps. 81: 2.*

We hanged our harps upon the willows. *Ps. 137: 2.*

I will cause the noise of thy songs to cease; and the sound of thy harps shall be no more heard. *Eze. 26: 13.*

I saw . . . them that had gotten the victory . . . stand on the sea of glass, having the harps of God. *Re. 15: 2.*

See also

Instrument; Melody; Music.

Harshness

The Egyptians made the children of Israel to serve with rigour. *Ex. 1: 13.*

The poor useth entreaties; but the rich answereth roughly. *Pr. 18: 23.*

A wicked man hardeneth his face. *Pr. 21: 29.*

Hear this, O ye that swallow up the needy, even to make the poor of the land to fail. *Am. 8: 4.*

God repented. . . . But it displeased Jonah exceedingly, and he was very angry. *Jon. 3: 10; 4: 1.*

I knew thee that thou art an hard man, reaping where thou hast not sown. *Mat. 25: 24.*

They that passed by reviled him. *Mat. 27: 39.*

Have ye your heart yet hardened? *Mk. 8: 17.*

Whom he will he hardeneth. *Ro. 9: 18.*

Who art thou that judgest another man's servant? To his own master he standeth or falleth. *Ro. 14: 4.*

See also

Austerity; Cruelty; Despot; Hardness; Severity; Tyranny; Unmercifulness.

Harvest

While the earth remaineth, seedtime and harvest, and cold and heat, and summer and winter, and day and night shall not cease. *Ge. 8: 22.*

Thou crownest the year with thy goodness. *Ps. 65: 11.*

He that goeth forth and weepeth, bearing precious seed, shall doubtless come again with rejoicing, bringing his sheaves with him. *Ps. 126: 6.*

So shall thy barns be filled with plenty. *Pr.* **3: 10.**

He that sleepeth in harvest is a son that causeth shame. *Pr.* **10: 5.**

Like a cloud of dew in the heat of harvest. *Is.* **18: 4.**

The harvest is past, the summer is ended, and we are not saved. *Je.* **8: 20.**

They have sown wheat, but shall reap thorns. *Je.* **12: 13.**

They have sown the wind, and they shall reap the whirlwind. *Ho.* **8: 7.**

Sow to yourselves in righteousness, reap in mercy. *Ho.* **10: 12.**

Do men gather grapes of thorns, or figs of thistles? *Mat.* **7: 16.**

Every good tree bringeth forth good fruit; but a corrupt tree bringeth forth evil fruit. *Mat.* **7: 17.**

The harvest truly is plenteous, but the labourers are few. *Mat.* **9: 37.**

Pray ye therefore the Lord of the harvest, that he will send forth labourers into his harvest. *Mat.* **9: 38.**

Let both grow together until the harvest. *Mat.* **13: 30.**

The harvest is the end of the world; and the reapers are the angels. *Mat.* **13: 39.**

Every branch that beareth fruit, he purgeth it, that it may bring forth more fruit. *Jn.* **15: 2.**

Ye are God's husbandry. *1 Co.* **3: 9.**

Whatsoever a man soweth, that shall he also reap. *Ga.* **6: 7.**

Let us not be weary in well doing: for in due season we shall reap, if we faint not. *Ga.* **6: 9.**

The fruit of the Spirit is in all goodness and righteousness and truth. *Ep.* **5: 9.**

See also

Abundance; Accumulation; Climax; Consequence; Cultivation; Fruit; Fruitfulness; Fruits, First; Fulfilment; Productivity; Reaping; Result; Yield.

Haste

Thus shall ye eat it; with your loins girded, your shoes on your feet, and your staff in your hand; and ye shall eat it in haste. *Ex.* **12: 11.**

The king's business required haste. *1 S.* **21: 8.**

His nurse took him up, and fled: and it came to pass, as she made haste to flee, that he fell, and became lame. *2 S.* **4: 4.**

Make speed to depart, lest he overtake us suddenly, and bring evil upon us. *2 S.* **15: 14.**

See that ye hasten the matter. *2 Ch.* **24: 5.**

God commanded me to make haste. *2 Ch.* **35: 21.**

O my strength, haste thee to help me. *Ps.* **22: 19.**

I am poor and needy: make haste unto me, O God. *Ps.* **70: 5.**

He that is hasty of spirit exalteth folly. *Pr.* **14: 29.**

The thoughts of the diligent tend only to plenteousness; but of every one that is hasty only to want. *Pr.* **21: 5.**

He that hasteth to be rich hath an evil eye. *Pr.* **28: 22.**

Seest thou a man that is hasty in his words?

there is more hope of a fool than of him. *Pr.* **29: 20.**

He that believeth shall not make haste. *Is.* **28: 16.**

Let us go speedily to pray before the Lord, and to seek the Lord of hosts. *Zch.* **8: 21.**

Agree with thine adversary quickly. *Mat.* **5: 25.**

Go quickly, and tell his disciples that he is risen from the dead. *Mat.* **28: 7.**

They came with haste, and found Mary, and Joseph, and the babe lying in a manger. *Lu.* **2: 16.**

After he had seen the vision, immediately we endeavoured to go into Macedonia. *Ac.* **16: 10.**

Seeing then that these things cannot be spoken against, ye ought to be quiet, and to do nothing rashly. *Ac.* **19: 36.**

See also

Hurry; Impatience; Quickness; Speed; Swiftness.

Hatred

I the Lord thy God am a jealous God, visiting the iniquity of the fathers upon the children unto the third and fourth generation of them that hate me. *Ex.* **20: 5.**

They hate me with cruel hatred. *Ps.* **25: 19.**

Ye that love the Lord, hate evil. *Ps.* **97: 10.**

I hate every false way. *Ps.* **119: 104.**

Do I not hate them, O Lord, that hate thee? *Ps.* **139: 21.**

I hate them with perfect hatred. *Ps.* **139: 22.**

Hatred stirreth up strifes. *Pr.* **10: 12.**

He that despiseth his neighbour sinneth. *Pr.* **14: 21.**

A time to love, and a time to hate. *Ec.* **3: 8.**

Do good to them that hate you. *Mat.* **5: 44.**

They were filled with madness; and communed one with another what they might do to Jesus. *Lu.* **6: 11.**

Blessed are ye, when men shall hate you. *Lu.* **6: 22.**

If the world hate you, ye know that it hated me before it hated you. *Jn.* **15: 18.**

He that hateth me hateth my Father also. *Jn.* **15: 23.**

Abhor that which is evil. *Ro.* **12: 9.**

Hateful, and hating one another. *Tit.* **3: 3.**

He that hateth his brother is in darkness. *1 Jn.* **2: 11.**

Whosoever hateth his brother is a murderer. *1 Jn.* **3: 15.**

If a man say, I love God, and hateth his brother, he is a liar. *1 Jn.* **4: 20.**

This thou hast, that thou hatest the deeds of the Nicolaitanes, which I also hate. *Re.* **2: 6.**

Babylon the great is fallen, is fallen, and is become . . . a cage of every unclean and hateful bird. *Re.* **18: 2.**

See also

Abhorrence; Adversary; Animosity; Antagonism; Antipathy; Aversion; Enemy; Foe; Hostility; Malevolence; Malice; Opposition; Resentment; Vindictiveness.

Haughtiness

They are exalted for a little while. *Jb.* **24: 24.**

Pride goeth before destruction, and an haughty spirit before a fall. *Pr.* **16: 18.**

Before destruction the heart of man is haughty; and before honour is humility. *Pr.* 18: 12.

Thorns and snares are in the way of the froward. *Pr.* 22: 5.

Because thou hast lifted up thyself in height, . . . and his heart is lifted up in his height; I have therefore delivered him into the hand of the mighty one of the heathen. *Eze.* 31: 10, 11.

Prophesy not again any more at Bethel: for it is the king's chapel, and it is the king's court. *Am.* 7: 13.

I am not as other men are. *Lu.* 18: 11.

Charity vaunteth not itself, is not puffed up. *1 Co.* 13: 4.

He is proud, knowing nothing. *1 Ti.* 6: 4.

The pride of life. *1 Jn.* 2: 16.

See also

Arrogance; Contempt; Disdain; Pomp; Pride; Scorn; Self-Satisfaction.

Hazard

Whosoever is fearful and afraid, let him return and depart early. *Ju.* 7: 3.

He . . . is fallen into the ditch which he made. *Ps.* 7: 15.

The way of the wicked is as darkness: they know not at what they stumble. *Pr.* 4: 19.

We gat our bread with the peril of our lives because of the sword of the wilderness. *La.* 5: 9.

Whosoever shall kill shall be in danger of the judgment. *Mat.* 5: 21.

Whosoever is angry with his brother without a cause shall be in danger of the judgment. *Mat.* 5: 22.

He that shall blaspheme against the Holy Ghost hath never forgiveness, but is in danger of eternal damnation. *Mk.* 3: 29.

Men that have hazarded their lives for the name of our Lord Jesus Christ. *Ac.* 15: 26.

Who shall separate us from the love of Christ? shall tribulation, or distress, or persecution, or famine, or nakedness, or peril, or sword? *Ro.* 8: 35.

Why stand we in jeopardy every hour? *1 Co.* 15: 30.

I die daily. *1 Co.* 15: 31.

Are they ministers of Christ? (I speak as a fool) I am more; in labours more abundant, in stripes above measure, in prisons more frequent, in deaths oft. *2 Co.* 11: 23.

No man that warreth entangleth himself with the affairs of this life. *2 Ti.* 2: 4.

Head

Moses chose able men out of all Israel, and made them heads over the people. *Ex.* 18: 25.

Thou anointest my head with oil. *Ps.* 23: 5.

Lift up your heads, O ye gates. *Ps.* 24: 7.

Blessings are upon the head of the just. *Pr.* 10: 6.

The beauty of old men is the grey head. *Pr.* 20: 29.

He shall be a father to the inhabitants of Jerusalem. *Is.* 22: 21.

Everlasting joy shall be upon their head. *Is.* 51: 11.

An helmet of salvation upon his head. *Is.* 59: 17.

Whosoever will be chief among you, let him be your servant. *Mat.* 20: 27.

The eye cannot say unto the hand, I have no need of thee: nor again the head to the feet, I have no need of you. *1 Co.* 12: 21.

On his head were many crowns. *Re.* 19: 12.

See also

Commander; Christ, the Leader; First; Government; Guidance; Leadership; Prominence; Rule; Senior; Uniqueness.

Healing

He healeth the broken in heart, and bindeth up their wounds. *Ps.* 147: 3.

Is it lawful to heal on the sabbath days? *Mat.* 12: 10.

He saith unto the man, Stretch forth thine hand. And he stretched it out: and his hand was restored whole as the other. *Mk.* 3: 5.

Power to heal sicknesses, and to cast out devils. *Mk.* 3: 15.

The power of the Lord was present to heal them. *Lu.* 5: 17.

There went virtue out of him, and healed them all. *Lu.* 6: 19.

In that same hour he cured many of their infirmities. *Lu.* 7: 21.

The blind see, the lame walk, the lepers are cleansed, the deaf hear, the dead are raised. *Lu.* 7: 22.

Jesus saith unto him, Rise, take up thy bed, and walk. *Jn.* 5: 8.

Jesus Christ maketh thee whole. *Ac.* 9: 34.

To another the gifts of healing. *1 Co.* 12: 9.

The leaves of the tree were for the healing of the nations. *Re.* 22: 2.

See also

Cure; Doctor; Faith-Healing; Medicine; Ointment; Physician.

Health

I will put none of these diseases upon thee, which I have brought upon the Egyptians: for I am the Lord that healeth thee. *Ex.* 15: 26.

The Lord will take away from thee all sickness. *De.* 7: 15.

Tell me, I pray thee, wherein thy great strength lieth. *Ju.* 16: 6.

The Lord is the strength of my life. *Ps.* 27: 1.

I shall yet praise him, who is the health of my countenance, and my God. *Ps.* 42: 11.

God be merciful unto us, and bless us; and cause his face to shine upon us; Selah. That thy way may be known upon earth, thy saving health among all nations. *Ps.* 67: 1, 2.

They are life unto those that find them, and health to all their flesh. *Pr.* 4: 22.

The tongue of the wise is health. *Pr.* 12: 18.

A faithful ambassador is health. *Pr.* 13: 17.

Then shall thy light break forth as the morning, and thine health shall spring forth speedily. *Is.* 58: 8.

I will restore health unto thee, and I will heal thee of thy wounds. *Je.* 30: 17.

See also

Strength; Well-being.

Hearing

They heard the voice of the Lord God walking in the garden in the cool of the day. *Ge.* 3: 8.

I have heard of thee by the hearing of the ear: but now mine eye seeth thee. *Jb.* 42: 5.

My voice shalt thou hear in the morning, O Lord; in the morning will I direct my prayer unto thee. *Ps. 5: 3.*

There is no speech nor language, where their voice is not heard. *Ps. 19: 3.*

I sought the Lord, and he heard me. *Ps. 34: 4.*

They are like the deaf adder that stoppeth her ear. *Ps. 58: 4.*

They have ears, but they hear not. *Ps. 115: 6.*

Be more ready to hear, than to give the sacrifice of fools: for they consider not that they do evil. *Ec. 5: 1.*

Hast thou not heard, that the everlasting God, the Lord, the Creator of the ends of the earth, fainteth not, neither is weary? *Is. 40: 28.*

Hear, ye deaf; and look, ye blind, that ye may see. *Is. 42: 18.*

While they are yet speaking, I will hear. *Is. 65: 24.*

O Lord, hear; O Lord, forgive; O Lord, hearken and do. *Da. 9: 19.*

Many prophets and righteous men have desired . . . to hear those things which ye hear, and have not heard them. *Mat. 13: 17.*

That on the good ground are they, which in an honest and good heart, having heard the word, keep it, and bring forth fruit with patience. *Lu. 8: 15.*

The dead shall hear the voice of the Son of God: and they that hear shall live. *Jn. 5: 25.*

The sheep hear his voice: and he calleth his own sheep by name. *Jn. 10: 3.*

So then faith cometh by hearing, and hearing by the word of God. *Ro. 10: 17.*

He was caught up into paradise, and heard unspeakable words. *2 Co. 12: 4.*

Let every man be swift to hear. *Ja. 1: 19.*

Be ye doers of the word, and not hearers only. *Ja. 1: 22.*

I was in the Spirit on the Lord's day, and heard behind me a great voice, as of a trumpet. *Re. 1: 10.*

See also

Deafness; Ear; Listening.

Hearsay

There is none like thee, neither is there any God beside thee, according to all that we have heard with our ears. *2 S. 7: 22.*

I have heard of thee by the hearing of the ear: but now mine eye seeth thee. *Jb. 42: 5.*

He shall not . . . reprove after the hearing of his ears. *Is. 11: 3.*

Take heed therefore how ye hear. *Lu. 8: 18.*

Sayest thou this thing of thyself, or did others tell it thee of me? *Jn. 18: 34.*

Tidings of these things came unto the ears of the church which was in Jerusalem. *Ac. 11: 22.*

Thou bringest certain strange things to our ears. *Ac. 17: 20.*

Teachers, having itching ears. *2 Ti. 4: 3.*

They shall turn away their ears from the truth, and shall be turned unto fables. *2 Ti. 4: 4.*

See also

Fame; Gossip; Renown; Report; Reputation; Slander; Talebearing.

Heart

Thou shalt love the Lord thy God with all thine heart. *De. 6: 5.*

These words, which I command thee this day, shall be in thine heart. *De. 6: 6.*

Man looketh on the outward appearance, but the Lord looketh on the heart. *1 S. 16: 7.*

I have given thee a wise and an understanding heart. *1 K. 3: 12.*

God gave Solomon . . . largeness of heart. *1 K. 4: 29.*

God is the strength of my heart, and my portion for ever. *Ps. 73: 26.*

Trust in the Lord with all thine heart. *Pr 3: 5.*

Keep thy heart with all diligence; for out of it are the issues of life. *Pr. 4: 23.*

A merry heart maketh a cheerful countenance. *Pr. 15: 13.*

He that is of a merry heart hath a continual feast. *Pr. 15: 15.*

The fining pot is for silver, and the furnace for gold: but the Lord trieth the hearts. *Pr. 17: 3.*

A merry heart doeth good like a medicine. *Pr. 17: 22.*

He hath set the world in their heart. *Ec. 3: 11.*

Say to them that are of a fearful heart, Be strong, fear not. *Is. 35: 4.*

The heart is deceitful above all things. *Je. 17: 9.*

Make you a new heart and a new spirit: for why will ye die? *Eze. 18: 31.*

I am meek and lowly in heart. *Mat. 11: 29.*

With the heart man believeth unto righteousness. *Ro. 10: 10.*

God . . . hath shined in our hearts. *2 Co. 4: 6.*

Let us draw near with a true heart in full assurance of faith. *He. 10: 22.*

God is love. *1 Jn. 4: 8.*

See also

Affection; Attachment; Bosom; Christ, Love of; Devotion; God, Love of; God, Love to; Love; Lovingkindness; Tenderness.

Heart, Broken

The Lord is nigh unto them that are of a broken heart. *Ps. 34: 18.*

The bread of sorrows. *Ps. 127: 2.*

When my spirit was overwhelmed within me, then thou knewest my path. *Ps. 142: 3.*

Heaviness in the heart of man maketh it stoop. *Pr. 12: 25.*

Hope deferred maketh the heart sick. *Pr. 13: 12.*

The heart knoweth his own bitterness; and a stranger doth not intermeddle with his joy. *Pr. 14: 10.*

He hath sent me to bind up the brokenhearted. *Is. 61: 1.*

Blessed are they that mourn: for they shall be comforted. *Mat. 5: 4.*

God shall wipe away all tears from their eyes. *Re. 7: 17.*

See also

Gloom; Grief; Melancholy; Mourning; Sadness; Sorrow; Tear; Weeping, Woe.

Heart, Searching of

There were great searchings of heart. *Ju. 5: 16.*

The Lord searcheth all hearts, and understandeth all the imaginations of the thoughts. *1 Ch.* 28: 9.

Shall not God search this out? for he knoweth the secrets of the heart. *Ps.* 44: 21.

Every way of a man is right in his own eyes: but the Lord pondereth the hearts. *Pr.* 21: 2.

I the Lord search the heart. *Je.* 17: 10.

They began to be sorrowful, and to say unto him one by one, Is it I? and another said, Is it I? *Mk.* 14: 19.

Mary kept these things, and pondered them in her heart. *Lu.* 2: 19.

Thou, Lord, . . . knowest the hearts of all men. *Ac.* 1: 24.

He that searcheth the hearts knoweth what is the mind of the Spirit. *Ro.* 8: 27.

See also

Contemplation; Examination; Meditation; Quest; Search; Self-Realization.

Heartlessness

A froward heart shall depart from me. *Ps.* 101: 4.

Him that hath an high look and a proud heart will not I suffer. *Ps.* 101: 5.

The heart of the wicked is little worth. *Pr.* 10: 20.

Every one that is proud in heart is an abomination to the Lord. *Pr.* 16: 5.

He that hath a froward heart findeth no good. *Pr.* 17: 20.

An high look, and a proud heart, and the plowing of the wicked, is sin. *Pr.* 21: 4.

He that hardeneth his heart shall fall into mischief. *Pr.* 28: 14.

He that is of a proud heart stirreth up strife. *Pr.* 28: 25.

All the house of Israel are impudent and hardhearted. *Eze.* 3: 7.

Ephraim also is like a silly dove without heart. *Ho.* 7: 11.

This people's heart is waxed gross. *Mat.* 13: 15.

He . . . upbraided them with their unbelief and hardness of heart. *Mk.* 16: 14.

See also

Carelessness; Cruelty; Despair; Hardness; Heedlessness; Indifference; Severity.

Heat

While the earth remaineth, seedtime and harvest, and cold and heat, and summer and winter, and day and night shall not cease. *Ge.* 8: 22.

There is nothing hid from the heat thereof. *Ps.* 19: 6.

Thou hast made summer. *Ps.* 74: 17.

Can one go upon hot coals, and his feet not be burned? *Pr.* 6: 28.

If two lie together, then they have heat. *Ec.* 4: 11.

There shall be a tabernacle for a shadow in the daytime from the heat, and for a place of refuge. *Is.* 4: 6.

Like a cloud of dew in the heat of harvest. *Is.* 18: 4.

Thou hast made them equal unto us, which have borne the burden and heat of the day. *Mat.* 20: 12.

The sun is no sooner risen with a burning heat, but it withereth the grass, and the flower thereof falleth, and the grace of the fashion of it perisheth. *Ja.* 1: 11.

I know thy works, that thou art neither cold nor hot: I would thou wert cold or hot. *Re.* 3: 15.

Neither shall the sun light on them, nor any heat. *Re.* 7: 16.

See also

Burn; Fire; Flame; Furnace; Summer; Weather.

Heathen

I will be exalted among the heathen. *Ps.* 46: 10.

The heathen are come into thine inheritance; thy holy temple have they defiled. *Ps.* 79: 1.

Wherefore should the heathen say, Where is their God? *Ps.* 79: 10.

He hath shewed his people the power of his works, that he may give them the heritage of the heathen. *Ps.* 111: 6.

The Gentiles shall see thy righteousness. *Is.* 62: 2.

I will stretch out mine hand upon thee, and will deliver thee for a spoil to the heathen. *Eze.* 25: 7.

He shall speak peace unto the heathen. *Zch.* 9: 10.

Behold, a woman of Canaan came out of the same coasts. *Mat.* 15: 22.

There is no respect of persons with God. *Ro.* 2: 11.

Rejoice, ye Gentiles, with his people. *Ro.* 15: 10.

Aliens from the commonwealth of Israel. *Ep.* 2: 12.

See also

Alien; Foreigner; Gentile; Pagan; Stranger.

Heaven

In the beginning God created the heaven and the earth. *Ge.* 1: 1.

Behold a ladder set up on the earth, and the top of it reached to heaven. *Ge.* 28: 12.

The heaven and the heaven of heavens cannot contain thee; how much less this house that I have builded? *1 K.* 8: 27.

There the wicked cease from troubling; and there the weary be at rest. *Jb.* 3: 17.

When I consider thy heavens, the work of thy fingers. *Ps.* 8: 3.

The heavens declare the glory of God; and the firmament sheweth his handywork. *Ps.* 19: 1.

Whom have I in heaven but thee? *Ps.* 73: 25.

God . . . had rained down manna upon them to eat, and had given them of the corn of heaven. *Ps.* 78: 22, 24.

If I ascend up into heaven, thou art there. *Ps.* 139: 8.

God is in heaven, and thou upon earth: therefore let thy words be few. *Ec.* 5: 2.

I will give unto thee the keys of the kingdom. *Mat.* 16: 19.

Your names are written in heaven. *Lu.* 10: 20.

To day shalt thou be with me in paradise. *Lu.* 23: 43.

I was not disobedient unto the heavenly vision. *Ac.* 26: 19.

The glory of the celestial is one, and the

glory of the terrestrial is another. *1 Co.* **15: 40.**

We shall also bear the image of the heavenly. *1 Co.* **15: 49.**

He was caught up into paradise, and heard unspeakable words, which it is not lawful for a man to utter. *2 Co.* **12: 4.**

Blessed be the God and Father of our Lord Jesus Christ, who hath blessed us with all spiritual blessings in heavenly places in Christ. *Ep.* **1: 3.**

There remaineth therefore a rest to the people of God. *He.* **4: 9.**

To him that overcometh will I give to eat of the tree of life, which is in the midst of the paradise of God. *Re.* **2: 7.**

I saw a new heaven and a new earth. *Re.* **21: 1.**

Blessed are they that do his commandments, that they may have right to the tree of life, and may enter in through the gates into the city. *Re.* **22: 14.**

See also

Altitude; Constellation; Firmament; Paradise; Sky.

Heaven, Kingdom of

Both riches and honour come of thee, and thou reignest over all; and in thine hand is power and might; and in thine hand it is to make great, and to give strength unto all. *1 Ch.* **29: 12.**

Seek ye first the kingdom of God, and his righteousness; and all these things shall be added unto you. *Mat.* **6: 33.**

From the days of John the Baptist until now the kingdom of heaven suffereth violence, and the violent take it by force. *Mat.* **11: 12.**

At the same time came the disciples unto Jesus, saying, Who is the greatest in the kingdom of heaven? *Mat.* **18: 1.**

Jesus came into Galilee, preaching the gospel of the kingdom of God. *Mk.* **1: 14.**

Unto you it is given to know the mystery of the kingdom of God. *Mk.* **4: 11.**

I must preach the kingdom of God to other cities also: for therefore am I sent. *Lu.* **4: 43.**

Blessed be ye poor: for yours is the kingdom of God. *Lu.* **6: 20.**

No man, having put his hand to the plow, and looking back, is fit for the kingdom of God. *Lu.* **9: 62.**

The kingdom of God is come upon you. *Lu.* **11: 20.**

The kingdom of God is within you. *Lu.* **17: 21.**

Except a man be born again, he cannot see the kingdom of God. *Jn.* **3: 3.**

The kingdom of God is not meat and drink; but righteousness, and peace, and joy in the Holy Ghost. *Ro.* **14: 17.**

Flesh and blood cannot inherit the kingdom of God. *1 Co.* **15: 50.**

See also

God, Kingdom of; Kingdom, the Coming.

Heaviness

Day and night thy hand was heavy upon me. *Ps.* **32: 4.**

Mine iniquities are gone over mine head: as an heavy burden they are too heavy for me. *Ps.* **38: 4.**

Heaviness in the heart of man maketh it stoop. *Pr.* **12: 25.**

A stone is heavy, and the sand weighty; but a fool's wrath is heavier than them both. *Pr.* **27: 3.**

In that day will I make Jerusalem a burdensome stone for all people. *Zch.* **12: 3.**

Come unto me, all ye that labour and are heavy laden, and I will give you rest. *Mat.* **11: 28.**

My yoke is easy, and my burden is light. *Mat.* **11: 30.**

Thou hast made them equal unto us, which have borne the burden and heat of the day. *Mat.* **20: 12.**

They bind heavy burdens and grievous to be borne. *Mat.* **23: 4.**

Every man shall bear his own burden. *Ga.* **6: 5.**

Let us lay aside every weight. *He.* **12: 1.**

Let your laughter be turned to mourning, and your joy to heaviness. *Ja.* **4: 9.**

See also

Bond; Burden; Care; Load; Oppression; Responsibility; Sadness; Sorrow; Weight; Yoke.

Hebrew

The Lord God of the Hebrews hath sent me unto thee. *Ex.* **7: 16.**

Peace shall be upon Israel. *Ps.* **125: 5.**

I am an Hebrew: and I fear the Lord. *Jon.* **1: 9.**

Behold an Israelite indeed, in whom is no guile! *Jn.* **1: 47.**

How is it that thou, being a Jew, askest drink of me, which am a woman of Samaria? *Jn.* **4: 9.**

The Jews sought the more to kill him. *Jn.* **5: 18.**

What advantage then hath the Jew? or what profit is there of circumcision? Much every way. *Ro.* **3: 1, 2.**

Is he the God of the Jews only? is he not also of the Gentiles? Yes, of the Gentiles also. *Ro.* **3: 29.**

We preach Christ crucified, unto the Jews a stumblingblock, and unto the Greeks foolishness. *1 Co.* **1: 23.**

Unto the Jews I became as a Jew, that I might gain the Jews. *1 Co.* **9: 20.**

Circumcised the eighth day, of the stock of Israel, of the tribe of Benjamin, an Hebrew of the Hebrews. *Ph.* **3: 5.**

See also

Israel; Jew; Judah.

Heed

A wicked doer giveth heed to false lips. *Pr.* **17: 4.**

Apply thine heart unto instruction, and thine ears to the words of knowledge. *Pr.* **23: 12.**

Because the preacher was wise, he still taught the people knowledge; yea, he gave good heed, and sought out, and set in order many proverbs. *Ec.* **12: 9.**

Take heed what ye hear. *Mk.* **4: 24.**

He charged them, saying, Take heed, beware of the leaven of the Pharisees, and of the leaven of Herod. *Mk.* **8: 15.**

Take ye heed, watch and pray. *Mk.* **13: 33.**

I charge thee before God, and the Lord

Jesus Christ, . . . that thou observe these things. *1 Ti.* 5: 21.

We ought to give the more earnest heed. *He.* 2: 1.

See also

Attention; Care; Consideration; Observance; Regard; Respect.

Heedlessness

Beware that thou forget not the Lord thy God. *De.* 8: 11.

Jehu took no heed to walk in the law of the Lord God of Israel with all his heart. *2 K.* 10: 31.

Whoso stoppeth his ears at the cry of the poor, he also shall cry himself, but shall not be heard. *Pr.* 21: 13.

Israel doth not know, my people doth not consider. *Is.* 1: 3.

Let us not give heed to any of his words. *Je.* 18: 18.

That drink wine in bowls, and anoint themselves with the chief ointments: but they are not grieved for the affliction of Joseph. *Am.* 6: 6.

A certain man lame from his mother's womb . . . whom they laid daily at the gate of the temple. *Ac.* 3: 2.

How shall we escape, if we neglect so great salvation? *He.* 2: 3.

See also

Carelessness; Forgetfulness; Indifference; Neglect.

Height

To morrow I will stand on the top of the hill with the rod of God in mine hand. *Ex.* 17: 9.

Look not on his countenance, or on the height of his stature; because I have refused him. *1 S.* 16: 7.

Is not God in the height of heaven ? *Jb.* 22: 12.

He hath looked down from the height of his sanctuary. *Ps.* 102: 19.

Praise him in the heights. *Ps.* 148: 1.

The mountain of the Lord's house shall be established in the top of the mountains, and shall be exalted above the hills; and all nations shall flow unto it. *Is.* 2: 2.

They sacrifice upon the tops of the mountains, and burn incense upon the hills. *Ho.* 4: 13.

Which of you by taking thought can add one cubit unto his stature? *Mat.* 6: 27.

Jesus increased in wisdom and stature. *Lu.* 2: 52.

Nor height, nor depth, nor any other creature, shall be able to separate us from the love of God. *Ro.* 8: 39.

Unto the measure of the stature of the fulness of Christ. *Ep.* 4: 13.

The length and the breadth and the height of it are equal. *Re.* 21: 16.

See also

Altitude; Climbing; Elevation; Eminence; Hill; Mountain; Stature; Summit; Top.

Heir

The Lord is the portion of mine inheritance and of my cup. *Ps.* 16: 5.

The righteous shall inherit the land, and dwell therein for ever. *Ps.* 37: 29.

An inheritance may be gotten hastily at the beginning; but the end thereof shall not be blessed. *Pr.* 20: 21.

Come, ye blessed of my Father, inherit the kingdom prepared for you from the foundation of the world. *Mat.* 25: 34.

Master, speak to my brother, that he divide the inheritance with me. *Lu.* 12: 13.

If children, then heirs; heirs of God, and joint-heirs with Christ. *Ro.* 8: 17.

Thou art no more a servant, but a son; and if a son, then an heir of God through Christ. *Ga.* 4: 7.

That the Gentiles should be fellowheirs, and of the same body. *Ep.* 3: 6.

That being justified by his grace, we should be made heirs according to the hope of eternal life. *Tit.* 3: 7.

God . . . Hath in these last days spoken unto us by his Son, whom he hath appointed heir of all things. *He.* 1: 1, 2.

He condemned the world, and became heir of the righteousness which is by faith. *He.* 11: 7.

An inheritance incorruptible, and undefiled, and that fadeth not away, reserved in heaven for you. *1 Pe.* 1: 4.

Unto him that loved us, and washed us from our sins in his own blood, And hath made us kings and priests unto God and his Father; to him be glory and dominion for ever and ever. *Re.* 1: 5, 6.

See also

Bequest; Birthright; Heritage; Inheritance; Legacy; Successor.

Hell

It is . . . deeper than hell; what canst thou know? *Jb.* 11: 8.

If I make my bed in hell, behold, thou art there. *Ps.* 139: 8.

Hell hath enlarged herself, and opened her mouth without measure: and their glory, and their multitude, and their pomp, . . . shall descend into it. *Is.* 5: 14.

Their worm shall not die, neither shall their fire be quenched. *Is.* 66: 24.

Fear not them which kill the body, but are not able to kill the soul: but rather fear him which is able to destroy both soul and body in hell. *Mat.* 10: 28.

The gates of hell shall not prevail against it. *Mat.* 16: 18.

Depart from me, ye cursed, into everlasting fire, prepared for the devil and his angels. *Mat.* 25: 41.

These shall go away into everlasting punishment: but the righteous into life eternal. *Mat.* 25: 46.

Fear him, which after he hath killed hath power to cast into hell. *Lu.* 12: 5.

In hell he lift up his eyes, being in torments. *Lu.* 16: 23.

In flaming fire taking vengeance on them that know not God, and that obey not the gospel of our Lord Jesus Christ. *2 Th.* 1: 8.

Punished with everlasting destruction from the presence of the Lord, and from the glory of his power. *2 Th.* 1: 9.

He went and preached unto the spirits in prison. *1 Pe.* 3: 19.

The vengeance of eternal fire. *Jude* 1: 7.

I . . . have the keys of hell and of death. *Re.* 1: 18.

He shall be tormented with fire and brimstone in the presence of the holy angels, and in the presence of the Lamb. *Re.* 14: 10.

Death and hell were cast into the lake of fire. This is the second death. *Re.* 20: 14.

The fearful, and unbelieving, and the abominable, and murderers, and whoremongers, and sorcerers, and idolaters, and all liars, shall have their part in the lake which burneth with fire and brimstone. *Re.* 21: 8.

See also

Abyss; Brimstone; Damnation; Deep; Depth; Judgment, the Last; Pit.

Helmet

He put on righteousness as a breastplate, and an helmet of salvation upon his head. *Is.* 59: 17.

Get up, ye horsemen, and stand forth with your helmets. *Je.* 46: 4.

All of them with shield and helmet. *Eze.* 38: 5.

Take the helmet of salvation, and the sword of the Spirit. *Ep.* 6: 17.

Let us, who are of the day, be sober, putting on the breastplate of faith and love; and for an helmet, the hope of salvation. *1 Th.* 5: 8.

See also

Armor; Defence; Protection.

Help

When Moses held up his hand, . . . Israel prevailed: . . . But Moses' hands were heavy; . . . and Aaron and Hur stayed up his hands, . . . and his hands were steady. *Ex.* 17: 11, 12.

Thou, Lord, hast holpen me, and comforted me. *Ps.* 86: 17.

I was brought low, and he helped me. *Ps.* 116: 6.

The Lord helped me. *Ps.* 118: 13.

I will lift up mine eyes unto the hills, from whence cometh my help. *Ps.* 121: 1.

Happy is he that hath the God of Jacob for his help. *Ps.* 146: 5.

They helped every one his neighbour. *Is.* 41: 6.

A cup of cold water. *Mat.* 10: 42.

One sick of the palsy, which was borne of four. *Mk.* 2: 3.

Sir, I have no man, when the water is troubled, to put me into the pool. *Jn.* 5: 7.

Come over into Macedonia, and help us. *Ac.* 16: 9.

We . . . are helpers of your joy. *2 Co.* 1: 24.

The Lord give mercy unto the house of Onesiphorus; for he oft refreshed me, and was not ashamed of my chain: But, when he was in Rome, he sought me out very diligently, and found me. *2 Ti.* 1: 16, 17.

The Lord is my helper, and I will not fear what man shall do unto me. *He.* 13: 6.

See also.

Aid; Almsgiving; Beneficence; Benevolence; Charity; Christ, Help of; God, Help of; Philanthropy; Relief; Succor; Support.

Herald

I will publish the name of the Lord. *De.* 32: 3.

And Cushi said, Tidings, my lord the king. *2 S.* 18: 31.

He shall not be afraid of evil tidings. *Ps.* 112: 7.

As cold waters to a thirsty soul, so is good news from a far country. *Pr.* 25: 25.

Prepare ye the way of the people. *Is.* 62: 10.

Blow ye the trumpet in the land: cry, gather together, and say, Assemble yourselves. *Je.* 4: 5.

Hear the word of the Lord, O ye nations, and declare it in the isles afar off. *Je.* 31: 10.

Declare ye among the nations, and publish, and set up a standard; publish, and conceal not. *Je.* 50: 2.

Then an herald cried aloud. *Da.* 3: 4.

Behold, I will send my messenger, and he shall prepare the way before me. *Mal.* 3: 1.

The voice of one crying in the wilderness, Prepare ye the way of the Lord. *Mat.* 3: 3.

He that cometh after me is mightier than I. *Mat.* 3: 11.

I am Gabriel, that stand in the presence of God; and am sent to speak unto thee, and to shew thee these glad tidings. *Lu.* 1: 19.

See also

Announcement; Forerunner; Harbinger; News, Good; Predecessor; Proclamation; Tidings.

Herb

Let the earth bring forth grass, the herb yielding seed. *Ge.* 1: 11.

As a garden of herbs. *De.* 11: 10.

They shall soon be cut down like the grass, and wither as the green herb. *Ps.* 37: 2.

He causeth the grass to grow for the cattle, and herb for the service of man. *Ps.* 104: 14.

Better is a dinner of herbs, where love is, than a stalled ox and hatred therewith. *Pr.* 15: 17.

Thy dew is as the dew of herbs, and the earth shall cast out the dead. *Is.* 26: 19.

I will make waste mountains and hills, and dry up all their herbs. *Is.* 42: 15.

A grain of mustard seed . . . is the least of all seeds: but when it is grown, it is the greatest among herbs. *Mat.* 13: 31, 32.

One believeth that he may eat all things: another, who is weak, eateth herbs. *Ro.* 14: 2.

See also

Verdure.

Herd

Let there be no strife . . . between my herdmen and thy herdmen; for we be brethren. *Ge.* 13: 8.

To make a sweet savour unto the Lord, of the herd, or of the flock. *Nu.* 15: 3.

The rich man . . . spared to take of his own flock and of his own herd, to dress for the wayfaring man that was come unto him; but took the poor man's lamb. *2 S.* 12: 4.

Be thou diligent to know the state of thy flocks, and look well to thy herds. *Pr.* 27: 23.

They shall go with their flocks and with their herds to seek the Lord; but they shall not find him. *Ho.* 5: 6.

The herds of cattle are perplexed, because they have no pasture. *Jo.* 1: 18.

Amos . . . was among the herdmen of Tekoa. *Am.* 1: 1.

I was no prophet, neither was I a prophet's son; but I was a herdman. *Am.* 7: 14.

Although . . . there shall be no herd in the

stalls: Yet I will rejoice in the Lord. *Hab.* 3: 17, 18.

See also

Cattle; Collection; Crowd; Flock; Multitude; Ox.

Heredity

I the Lord thy God am a jealous God, visiting the iniquity of the fathers upon the children unto the third and fourth generation of them that hate me. *Ex.* 20: 5.

Of the seed royal. *2 K.* 25: 25.

Behold, I was shapen in iniquity; and in sin did my mother conceive me. *Ps.* 51: 5.

The wicked are estranged from the womb: they go astray as soon as they be born, speaking lies. *Ps.* 58: 3.

The fathers have eaten a sour grape, and the children's teeth are set on edge. *Je.* 31: 29.

Our fathers have sinned, and are not: and we have borne their iniquities. *La.* 5: 7.

Every one that useth proverbs shall use this proverb against thee, saying, As is the mother, so is her daughter. *Eze.* 16: 44.

The fathers have eaten sour grapes, and the children's teeth are set on edge? *Eze.* 18: 2.

Do men gather grapes of thorns? *Mat.* 7: 16.

Of this man's seed hath God according to his promise raised unto Israel a Saviour, Jesus. *Ac.* 13: 23.

Are they the seed of Abraham? so am I. *2 Co.* 11: 22.

Know ye therefore that they which are of faith, the same are the children of Abraham. *Ga.* 3: 7.

Neither give heed to . . . endless genealogies. *1 Ti.* 1: 4.

See also

Ancestor; Descent; Father; Genealogy; Generation; Heritage; Inheritance.

Ieresy

In vain they do worship me, teaching for doctrines the commandments of men. *Mat.* 15: 9.

Ye do err, not knowing the scriptures, nor the power of God. *Mat.* 22: 29.

After the way which they call heresy, so worship I the God of my fathers. *Ac.* 24: 14.

Mark them which cause divisions and offences contrary to the doctrine which ye have learned; and avoid them. *Ro.* 16: 17.

What part hath he that believeth with an infidel? *2 Co.* 6: 15.

Now the works of the flesh are manifest, which are these; . . . Idolatry, . . . variance, . . . seditions, heresies. *Ga.* 5: 19, 20.

That we henceforth be no more children, tossed to and fro, and carried about with every wind of doctrine. *Ep.* 4: 14.

Contrary to sound doctrine. *1 Ti.* 1: 10.

He which converteth the sinner from the error of his way shall save a soul from death. *Ja.* 5: 20.

There shall be false teachers among you, who privily shall bring in damnable heresies. *2 Pe.* 2: 1.

Which they that are unlearned and unstable wrest, as they do also the other scriptures, unto their own destruction. *2 Pe.* 3: 16.

Whosoever transgresseth, and abideth not in the doctrine of Christ, hath not God. *2 Jn.* 1: 9.

See also

Atheism; Christ, Denial of; Christ, Doubt of; Church, Divisions of; Denial; Denomination; Dissent; Dogma; Doubt; Faithlessness; God, Denial of; Godlessness; Schism; Teaching, False; Unbelief; Unorthodoxy.

Heritage

The Lord is their inheritance. *De.* 18: 2.

Ask of me, and I shall give thee the heathen for thine inheritance, and the uttermost parts of the earth for thy possession. *Ps.* 2: 8.

Those that wait upon the Lord, they shall inherit the earth. *Ps.* 37: 9.

Lo, children are an heritage of the Lord. *Ps.* 127: 3.

We are the children of God: And if children, then heirs; heirs of God, and joint-heirs with Christ. *Ro.* 8: 16, 17.

Flesh and blood cannot inherit the kingdom of God. *1 Co.* 15: 50.

Thou art no more a servant, but a son; and if a son, then an heir of God through Christ. *Ga.* 4: 7.

In whom also we have obtained an inheritance. *Ep.* 1: 11.

Partakers of the inheritance of the saints in light. *Col.* 1: 12.

The promise of eternal inheritance. *He.* 9: 15.

An inheritance . . . that fadeth not away. *1 Pe.* 1: 4.

Giving honour unto the wife, as unto the weaker vessel, and as being heirs together of the grace of life. *1 Pe.* 3: 7.

Ye are thereunto called, that ye should inherit a blessing. *1 Pe.* 3: 9.

See also

Ancestor; Bequest; Birthright; Descent; Father; Genealogy; Generation; Heir; Inheritance; Legacy.

Heroism

This is nothing else save the sword of Gideon: . . . for into his hand hath God delivered Midian, and all the host. *Ju.* 7: 14.

My father fought for you, and adventured his life far, and delivered you. *Ju.* 9: 17.

There is no restraint to the Lord to save by many or by few. *1 S.* 14: 6.

I come to thee in the name of the Lord of hosts, the God of the armies of Israel, whom thou hast defied. *1 S.* 17: 45.

The mountain was full of horses and chariots of fire round about Elisha. *2 K.* 6: 17.

The way of the Lord is strength to the upright. *Pr.* 10: 29.

No man, having put his hand to the plow, and looking back, is fit for the kingdom of God. *Lu.* 9: 62.

None of these things move me, neither count I my life dear unto myself, so that I might finish my course with joy. *Ac.* 20: 24.

Peradventure for a good man some would even dare to die. *Ro.* 5: 7.

By faith the walls of Jericho fell down. *He.* 11: 30.

Waxed valiant in fight, turned to flight the armies of the aliens. *He.* 11: 34.

Let us go forth therefore unto him without the camp. *He.* 13: 13.

They loved not their lives unto the death. *Re.* 12: 11.
See also
Audacity; Boldness; Bravery; Courage; Fearlessness; Fortitude; Valor.

Hesitancy

Solomon . . . went not fully after the Lord. *1 K.* 11: 6.
How long halt ye between two opinions? *1 K.* 18: 21.
Lord, suffer me first to go and bury my father. *Mat.* 8: 21.
Lord, I will follow thee; but . . . *Lu.* 9: 61.
No man, having put his hand to the plow, and looking back, is fit for the kingdom of God. *Lu.* 9: 62.
Agrippa said unto Paul, Almost thou persuadest me to be a Christian. *Ac.* 26: 28.
He that wavereth is like a wave of the sea driven with the wind and tossed. *Ja.* 1: 6.
Purify your hearts, ye double minded. *Ja.* 4: 8.
See also
Delay; Indecision; Procrastination; Reluctance.

Highway

Thou compassest my path. *Ps.* 139: 3.
An highway shall be there, and a way, and it shall be called The way of holiness. *Is.* 35: 8.
Prepare ye the way of the Lord, make straight in the desert a highway for our God. *Is.* 40: 3.
I will make all my mountains a way, and my highways shall be exalted. *Is.* 49: 11.
Set thine heart toward the highway, even the way which thou wentest: turn again. *Je.* 31: 21.
Prepare ye the way of the Lord, make his paths straight. *Mat.* 3: 3.
Go ye therefore into the highways, and as many as ye shall find, bid to the marriage. *Mat.* 22: 9.
Go out quickly into the streets and lanes of the city, and bring in hither the poor, and the maimed, and the halt, and the blind. *Lu.* 14: 21.
See also
Christ, Way of; God, Way of; Life, Path of; Path; Road; Street; Way.

Hill

Unto the utmost bound of the everlasting hills. *Ge.* 49: 26.
Their gods are gods of the hills; therefore they were stronger than we. *1 K.* 20: 23.
Who shall ascend into the hill of the Lord? *Ps.* 24: 3.
O send out thy light and thy truth: let them lead me; let them bring me unto thy holy hill. *Ps.* 43: 3.
The little hills rejoice on every side. *Ps.* 65: 12.
The mountains shall bring peace to the people. *Ps.* 72: 3.
In his hand are the deep places of the earth: the strength of the hills is his also. *Ps.* 95: 4.
The hills melted like wax at the presence of the Lord. *Ps.* 97: 5.
Let the hills be joyful together. *Ps.* 98: 8.

I will lift up mine eyes unto the hills. *Ps.* 121: 1.
Every valley shall be exalted, and every mountain and hill shall be made low. *Is.* 40: 4.
It shall come to pass in that day, that the mountains shall drop down new wine, and the hills shall flow with milk. *Jo.* 3: 18.
A city that is set on an hill cannot be hid. *Mat.* 5: 14.
Paul stood in the midst of Mars' hill. *Ac.* 17: 22.
See also
Altitude; Ascension; Climbing; Mountain; Summit; Top.

Hindrance

How shall we sing the Lord's song in a strange land? *Ps.* 137: 4.
When thou goest, thy steps shall not be straitened; and when thou runnest, thou shalt not stumble. *Pr.* 4: 12.
They bring unto him one that was deaf, and had an impediment in his speech. *Mk.* 7: 32.
Ye have entered not in yourselves, and them that were entering in ye hindered. *Lu.* 11: 52.
They took away the stone from the place where the dead was laid. *Jn.* 11: 41.
What doth hinder me to be baptized? *Ac.* 8: 36.
We . . . suffer all things, lest we should hinder the gospel of Christ. *1 Co.* 9: 12.
Satan hindered us. *1 Th.* 2: 18.
Let us lay aside every weight. *He.* 12: 1.
That your prayers be not hindered. *1 Pe.* 3: 7.
See also
Bar; Delay; Difficulty; Handicap; Impediment; Limitation; Obstacle; Obstruction; Restraint; Stumbling-block.

History

Ask now of the days that are past. *De.* 4: 32.
There shall they rehearse the righteous acts of the Lord. *Ju.* 5: 11.
The rest of the acts of Solomon, and all that he did, and his wisdom, are they not written in the book of the acts of Solomon? *1 K.* 11: 41.
Now concerning his sons, and the greatness of the burdens laid upon him, and the repairing of the house of God, behold, they are written in the story of the book of the kings. *2 Ch.* 24: 27.
That search may be made in the book of the records of thy fathers. *Ezr.* 4: 15.
On that night could not the king sleep, and he commanded to bring the book of records of the chronicles; and they were read before the king. *Es.* 6: 1.
My witness is in heaven, and my record is on high. *Jb.* 16: 19.
Take thee a great roll, and write in it with a man's pen. *Is.* 8: 1.
Remember ye not the former things, neither consider the things of old. *Is.* 43: 18.
Remember the former things of old. *Is.* 46: 9.
This is the record of John. *Jn.* 1: 19.
See also
Annals; Anniversary; Commemoration; Memorial; Past; Remembrance; Time, Past.

Holiday

Verily my sabbaths ye shall keep: for it is a sign between me and you throughout your generations. *Ex.* 31: 13.

Six days thou shalt work, but on the seventh day thou shalt rest. *Ex.* 34: 21.

Moses declared unto the children of Israel the feasts of the Lord. *Le.* 23: 44.

I had gone with the multitude, I went with them to the house of God, with the voice of joy and praise, with a multitude that kept holyday. *Ps.* 42: 4.

He that is of a merry heart hath a continual feast. *Pr.* 15: 15.

Bring hither the fatted calf, and kill it; and let us eat, and be merry. *Lu.* 15: 23.

It was meet that we should make merry, and be glad: for this thy brother was dead, and is alive again. *Lu.* 15: 32.

Let no man therefore judge you in meat, or in drink, or in respect of an holyday. *Col.* 2: 16.

See also

Celebration; Feast; Festival.

Holiness

Remember the sabbath day, to keep it holy. *Ex.* 20: 8.

Let thy saints rejoice in goodness. *2 Ch.* 6: 41.

Offer the sacrifices of righteousness, and put your trust in the Lord. *Ps.* 4: 5.

Worship the Lord in the beauty of holiness. *Ps.* 29: 2.

What man is he that desireth life, and loveth many days, that he may see good? Keep thy tongue from evil, and thy lips from speaking guile. Depart from evil, and do good; seek peace, and pursue it. *Ps.* 34: 12–14.

Holiness becometh thine house, O Lord, for ever. *Ps.* 93: 5.

The righteous shall be in everlasting remembrance. *Ps.* 112: 6.

An highway shall be there, and a way, and it shall be called The way of holiness. *Is.* 35: 8.

Give not that which is holy unto the dogs. *Mat.* 7: 6.

Whether is greater, the gift, or the altar that sanctifieth the gift? *Mat.* 23: 19.

Hallowed be thy name. *Lu.* 11: 2.

Present your bodies a living sacrifice, holy, acceptable unto God. *Ro.* 12: 1.

The temple of God is holy, which temple ye are. *1 Co.* 3: 17.

Awake to righteousness, and sin not. *1 Co.* 15: 34.

As he which hath called you is holy, so be ye holy in all manner of conversation; Because it is written, Be ye holy; for I am holy. *1 Pe.* 1: 15, 16.

See also

Consecration; Dedication; Devoutness; Godliness; Piety; Righteousness; Saint; Sanctification.

Homage

I will praise thee, O Lord, with my whole heart; I will shew forth all thy marvellous works. *Ps.* 9: 1.

I shall yet praise him for the help of his countenance. *Ps.* 42: 5.

O come, let us worship and bow down. *Ps.* 95: 6.

All thy works shall praise thee, O Lord; and thy saints shall bless thee. *Ps.* 145: 10.

While I live will I praise the Lord. *Ps.* 146: 2.

Praise ye him, sun and moon: praise him, all ye stars of light. *Ps.* 148: 3.

Out of the mouth of babes and sucklings thou hast perfected praise. *Mat.* 21: 16.

And were continually in the temple, praising and blessing God. *Lu.* 24: 53.

See also

Adulation; God, Praise to; Honor; Loyalty; Praise; Regard; Respect; Reverence.

Home

This is none other but the house of God, and this is the gate of heaven. *Ge.* 28: 17.

I will depart to mine own land, and to my kindred. *Nu.* 10: 30.

Let thy servant, I pray thee, turn back again, that I may die in mine own city, and be buried by the grave of my father and of my mother. *2 S.* 19: 37.

Oh that one would give me drink of the water of the well of Bethlehem, which is by the gate. *2 S.* 23: 15.

The lines are fallen unto me in pleasant places. *Ps.* 16: 6.

Behold, how good and how pleasant it is for brethren to dwell together in unity! *Ps.* 133: 1.

If I do not remember thee, let my tongue cleave to the roof of my mouth; if I prefer not Jerusalem above my chief joy. *Ps.* 137: 6.

Hear the instruction of thy father, and forsake not the law of thy mother. *Pr.* 1: 8.

Drink waters out of thine own cistern, and running waters out of thine own well. *Pr.* 5: 15.

Every wise woman buildeth her house. *Pr.* 14: 1.

Better is a dry morsel, and quietness therewith, than a house full of sacrifices with strife. *Pr.* 17: 1.

Withdraw thy foot from thy neighbour's house; lest he be weary of thee, and so hate thee. *Pr.* 25: 17.

Man goeth to his long home. *Ec.* 12: 5.

They made me the keeper of the vineyards; but mine own vineyard have I not kept. *S. of S.* 1: 6.

A little child shall lead them. *Is.* 11: 6.

He is a proud man, neither keepeth at home, who enlargeth his desire as hell, and is as death, and cannot be satisfied. *Hab.* 2: 5.

Every . . . house divided against itself shall not stand. *Mat.* 12: 25.

When they were come out of the synagogue, they entered into the house. *Mk.* 1: 29.

They were both righteous before God, walking in all the commandments and ordinances of the Lord blameless. *Lu.* 1: 6.

Jesus loved Martha, and her sister, and Lazarus. *Jn.* 11: 5.

Be at peace among yourselves. *1 Th.* 5: 13.

To be discreet, chaste, keepers at home. *Tit.* 2: 5.

To the church in thy house. *Phm.* 1: 2.

See also
Abode; Dwelling; God, House of; Habitation; House; Residence; Roof; Shelter; Tenant.

Homesickness

Thou sore longedst after thy father's house. *Ge.* 31: 30.

Thy sons and thy daughters shall be given unto another people, and thine eyes shall look, and fail with longing for them all the day long. *De.* 28: 32.

He shall return no more to his house, neither shall his place know him any more. *Jb.* 7: 10.

When my children were about me. *Jb.* 29: 5.

How shall we sing the Lord's song in a strange land? *Ps.* 137: 4.

As a bird that wandereth from her nest, so is a man that wandereth from his place. *Pr.* 27: 8.

Return to thine own house, and shew how great things God hath done unto thee. *Lu.* 8: 39.

When he came to himself, he said, How many hired servants of my father's have bread enough and to spare, and I perish with hunger! *Lu.* 15: 17.

Honesty

Thou shalt not have in thy bag divers weights, a great and a small. *De.* 25: 13.

Tell me nothing but that which is true in the name of the Lord. *1 K.* 22: 16.

He that worketh deceit shall not dwell within my house: he that telleth lies shall not tarry in my sight. *Ps.* 101: 7.

They that deal truly are his delight. *Pr.* 12: 22.

Divers weights are an abomination unto the Lord. *Pr.* 20: 23.

Making the ephah small, and the shekel great, and falsifying the balances by deceit. *Am.* 8: 5.

Provide things honest in the sight of all men. *Ro.* 12: 17.

Let us walk honestly, as in the day. *Ro.* 13: 13.

Not walking in craftiness, nor handling the word of God deceitfully; but by manifestation of the truth commending ourselves to every man's conscience in the sight of God. *2 Co.* 4: 2.

Providing for honest things, not only in the sight of the Lord, but also in the sight of men. *2 Co.* 8: 21.

We can do nothing against the truth, but for the truth. *2 Co.* 13: 8.

Putting away lying, speak every man truth with his neighbour. *Ep.* 4: 25.

Whatsoever things are honest, . . . think on these things. *Ph.* 4: 8.

In all godliness and honesty. *1 Ti.* 2: 2.

Having your conversation honest among the Gentiles. *1 Pe.* 2: 12.

See also
Candor; Christ, Truth of; Clearness; Fairness; Faithfulness; Falsehood; God, Truth of; Honor; Integrity; Justice; Sincerity; Truth; Uprightness; Veracity; Verity.

Honey

What is sweeter than honey? *Ju.* 14: 18.

More to be desired are they than gold, yea, than much fine gold: sweeter also than honey and the honeycomb. *Ps.* 19: 10.

Pleasant words are as an honeycomb, sweet to the soul, and health to the bones. *Pr.* 16: 24.

It is not good to eat much honey. *Pr.* 25: 27.

The full soul loatheth an honeycomb; but to the hungry soul every bitter thing is sweet. *Pr.* 27: 7.

I have eaten my honeycomb with my honey. *S. of S.* 5: 1.

Butter and honey shall every one eat that is left in the land. *Is.* 7: 22.

His meat was locusts and wild honey. *Mat.* 3: 4.

See also
Sweetness.

Honor

Honour thy father and thy mother. *Ex.* 20: 12.

Thou shalt . . . honour the face of the old man. *Le.* 19: 32.

Seemeth it to you a light thing to be a king's son in law? *1 S.* 18: 23.

Both riches and honour come of thee, and thou reignest over all. *1 Ch.* 29: 12.

The young men saw me, and hid themselves: and the aged arose, and stood up. *Jb.* 29: 8.

Verily every man at his best state is altogether vanity. *Ps.* 39: 5.

When he dieth he shall carry nothing away: his glory shall not descend after him. *Ps.* 49: 17.

Not unto us, O Lord, not unto us, but unto thy name give glory. *Ps.* 115: 1.

He that hateth gifts shall live. *Pr.* 15: 27.

The ancient and honourable, he is the head. *Is.* 9: 15.

A prophet is not without honour, save in his own country. *Mat.* 13: 57.

Rejoicing that they were counted worthy to suffer shame for his name. *Ac.* 5: 41.

In honour preferring one another. *Ro.* 12: 10.

Render therefore to all their dues: . . . honour to whom honour. *Ro.* 13: 7.

That ye may be counted worthy of the kingdom of God, for which ye also suffer. *2 Th.* 1: 5.

Honour all men. *1 Pe.* 2: 17.

Fear God, and give glory to him. *Re.* 14: 7.

See also
Adulation; Celebrity; Dignity; Distinction; Fame; Glory; Honesty; Renown; Report; Reputation.

Hope

Lift up now thine eyes, and look from the place where thou art. *Ge.* 13: 14.

My flesh also shall rest in hope. *Ps.* 16: 9.

Hope deferred maketh the heart sick: but when the desire cometh, it is a tree of life. *Pr.* 13: 12.

Who against hope believed in hope. *Ro.* 4: 18.

Tribulation worketh patience; And patience, experience; and experience, hope: And hope maketh not ashamed. *Ro.* 5: 3–5.

We are saved by hope: but hope that is seen is not hope: for what a man seeth, why doth he yet hope for? *Ro.* 8: 24.

Rejoicing in hope. *Ro.* 12: 12.

Now the God of hope fill you with all joy and peace in believing, that ye may abound in hope. *Ro.* 15: 13.

He that ploweth should plow in hope. *1 Co.* 9: 10.

He that thresheth in hope should be partaker of his hope. *1 Co.* 9: 10.

Now abideth . . . hope. *1 Co.* 13: 13.

That ye may know what is the hope of his calling, . . . And what is the exceeding greatness of his power. *Ep.* 1: 18, 19.

For an helmet, the hope of salvation. *1 Th.* 5: 8.

Hope we have as an anchor of the soul, both sure and stedfast. *He.* 6: 19.

Now faith is the substance of things hoped for, the evidence of things not seen. *He.* 11: 1.

A lively hope. *1 Pe.* 1: 3.

The hope that is in you. *1 Pe.* 3: 15.

Every man that hath this hope in him purifieth himself, even as he is pure. *1 Jn.* 3: 3.

See also

Anticipation; Christ, Hope in; Expectancy; Future; God, Hope in; Trust; Reliance; Wait.

Hopelessness

The bread of affliction. *De.* 16: 3.

And the door was shut. *Mat.* 25: 10.

My God, my God, why hast thou forsaken me? *Mk.* 15: 34.

Ye shall weep and lament, but the world shall rejoice. *Jn.* 16: 20.

If there be no resurrection of the dead. *1 Co.* 15: 13.

We despaired even of life. *2 Co.* 1: 8.

The sorrow of the world worketh death. *2 Co.* 7: 10.

Having no hope. *Ep.* 2: 12.

Without God in the world. *Ep.* 2: 12.

See also

Desolation; Despair; Gloom; Melancholy; Sadness.

Horn

Mine horn is exalted in the Lord. *1 S.* 2: 1.

All the horns of the wicked also will I cut off; but the horns of the righteous shall be exalted. *Ps.* 75: 10.

Bind the sacrifice with cords, even unto the horns of the altar. *Ps.* 118: 27.

He also exalteth the horn of his people, the praise of all his saints. *Ps.* 148: 14.

The Lord God of Israel . . . hath raised up an horn of salvation for us in the house of his servant David. *Lu.* 1: 68, 69.

See also

Trumpet.

Horror

Lo, an horror of great darkness fell upon him. *Ge.* 15: 12.

The river shall bring forth frogs abundantly, which shall go up and come into thine house, and into thy bedchamber, and upon thy bed, and into the house of thy servants, and upon thy people, and into thine ovens, and into thy kneadingtroughs. *Ex.* 8: 3.

I will send swarms of flies upon thee. *Ex.* 8: 21.

The sword without, and terror within. *De.* 32: 25.

Terrors shall make him afraid on every side. *Jb.* 18: 11.

Behold, my terror shall not make thee afraid. *Jb.* 33: 7.

Upon the wicked he shall rain snares, fire and brimstone, and an horrible tempest: this shall be the portion of their cup. *Ps.* 11: 6.

He brought me up also out of an horrible pit. *Ps.* 40: 2.

For thy sake are we killed all the day long. *Ps.* 44: 22.

Fearfulness and trembling are come upon me, and horror hath overwhelmed me. *Ps.* 55: 5.

Thou shalt not be afraid for the terror by night. *Ps.* 91: 5.

Be astonished, O ye heavens, at this, and be horribly afraid. *Je.* 2: 12.

The young and the old lie on the ground in the streets: my virgins and my young men are fallen by the sword; thou hast slain them in the day of thine anger. *La.* 2: 21.

They shall also gird themselves with sackcloth, and horror shall cover them. *Eze.* 7: 18.

I have seen an horrible thing in the house of Israel. *Ho.* 6: 10.

See also

Terror.

Horse

Hast thou given the horse strength? *Jb.* 39: 19.

Be ye not as the horse, or as the mule, which have no understanding. *Ps.* 32: 9.

An horse is a vain thing for safety: neither shall he deliver any by his great strength. *Ps.* 33: 17.

He delighteth not in the strength of the horse. *Ps.* 147: 10.

The horse is prepared against the day of battle: but safety is of the Lord. *Pr.* 21: 31.

A whip for the horse, a bridle for the ass, and a rod for the fool's back. *Pr.* 26: 3.

Woe to them that go down to Egypt for help; and stay on horses, and trust in chariots, because they are many; and in horsemen, because they are very strong. *Is.* 31: 1.

The Egyptians are men, and not God; and their horses flesh, and not spirit. *Is.* 31: 3.

If thou hast run with the footmen, and they have wearied thee, then how canst thou contend with horses? *Je.* 12: 5.

I will . . . save them by the Lord their God, and will not save them by bow, nor by sword, nor by battle, by horses, nor by horsemen. *Ho.* 1: 7.

Hospitality

I have been a stranger in a strange land. *Ex.* 2: 22.

The Lord your God . . . loveth the stranger. *De.* 10: 17, 18.

Why have I found grace in thine eyes, that thou shouldest take knowledge of me, seeing I am a stranger? *Ru.* 2: 10.

Withdraw thy foot from thy neighbour's house; lest he be weary of thee, and so hate thee. *Pr.* 25: 17.

Thy gates shall be open continually; they shall not be shut day nor night. *Is.* 60: 11.

The Lord hath prepared a sacrifice, he hath bid his guests. *Zph.* 1: 7.

So those servants went out into the highways, and gathered together all as many as they found, both bad and good: and the wedding was furnished with guests. *Mat.* **22**: 10.

I was a stranger, and ye took me in. *Mat.* **25**: 35.

There was no room for them in the inn. *Lu.* **2**: 7.

When thou makest a dinner . . . call not thy friends. *Lu.* **14**: 12.

When thou makest a feast, call the poor, the maimed, the lame, the blind: And thou shalt be blessed. *Lu.* **14**: 13, 14.

Yet there is room. *Lu.* **14**: 22.

There shall a man meet you, bearing a pitcher of water; follow him into the house where he entereth in. *Lu.* **22**: 10.

Paul dwelt two whole years in his own hired house, and received all that came in unto him. *Ac.* **28**: 30.

Given to hospitality. *Ro.* **12**: 13.

Receive ye one another, as Christ also received us to the glory of God. *Ro.* **15**: 7.

Well reported of for good works; if she have brought up children, if she have lodged strangers. *1 Ti.* **5**: 10.

A lover of hospitality. *Tit.* **1**: 8.

Be not forgetful to entertain strangers: for thereby some have entertained angels unawares. *He.* **13**: 2.

Use hospitality one to another without grudging. *1 Pe.* **4**: 9.

See also

Christ, Call of; Christ, the Door; Cordiality; God, Call of; Guest; Invitation; Welcome.

Host

Thus the heavens and the earth were finished, and all the host of them. *Ge.* **2**: 1.

Though an host should encamp against me, my heart shall not fear. *Ps.* **27**: 3.

There is no king saved by the multitude of an host. *Ps.* **33**: 16.

Bless ye the Lord, all ye his hosts. *Ps.* **103**: 21.

Wilt not thou, O God, go forth with our hosts? *Ps.* **108**: 11.

It shall come to pass in that day, that the Lord shall punish the host of the high ones that are on high, and the kings of the earth upon the earth. *Is.* **24**: 21.

Suddenly there was with the angel a multitude of the heavenly host praising God. *Lu.* **2**: 13.

See also

Army; Crowd; Multitude; Number; Rabble.

Hostage

I will be surety for him; of my hand shalt thou require him. *Ge.* **43**: 9.

He took . . . hostages, and returned to Samaria. *2 K.* **14**: 14.

Be surety for thy servant for good. *Ps.* **119**: 122.

My son, if thou be surety for thy friend, . . . Thou art snared with the words of thy mouth. *Pr.* **6**: 1, 2.

He that is surety for a stranger shall smart for it: and he that hateth suretiship is sure. *Pr.* **11**: 15.

A man void of understanding striketh hands, and becometh surety in the presence of his friend. *Pr.* **17**: 18.

Be not thou one of them . . . that are sureties for debts. *Pr.* **22**: 26.

By so much was Jesus made surety of a better testament. *He.* **7**: 22.

Hostility

Cursed be he that smiteth his neighbour secretly. *De.* **27**: 24.

The stars in their courses fought against Sisera. *Ju.* **5**: 20.

The Lord is departed from thee, and is become thine enemy. *1 S.* **28**: 16.

Lord, how are they increased that trouble me! *Ps.* **3**: 1.

Out of the mouth of babes and sucklings hast thou ordained strength because of thine enemies. *Ps.* **8**: 2.

Mine enemies are lively, and they are strong. *Ps.* **38**: 19.

They lie in wait for my soul. *Ps.* **59**: 3.

I am for peace: but when I speak, they are for war. *Ps.* **120**: 7.

The words of the wicked are to lie in wait for blood. *Pr.* **12**: 6.

Rejoice not when thine enemy falleth, and let not thine heart be glad when he stumbleth. *Pr.* **24**: 17.

The enemy hath magnified himself. *La.* **1**: 9.

He was unto me as a bear lying in wait, and as a lion in secret places. *La.* **3**: 10.

I will meet them as a bear that is bereaved of her whelps. *Ho.* **13**: 8.

Many nations are gathered against thee. *Mi.* **4**: 11.

Agree with thine adversary quickly. *Mat.* **5**: 25.

I say unto you, Love your enemies. *Mat.* **5**: 44.

The kings of the earth stood up, and the rulers were gathered together against the Lord. *Ac.* **4**: 26.

The last enemy that shall be destroyed is death. *1 Co.* **15**: 26.

Am I therefore become your enemy, because I tell you the truth? *Ga.* **4**: 16.

The friendship of the world is enmity with God. *Ja.* **4**: 4.

See also

Animosity; Antagonism; Antipathy; Enemy; Hatred; Opposition.

Hour

Of that day and hour knoweth no man, no, not the angels of heaven, but my Father only. *Mat.* **24**: 36.

Ye know neither the day nor the hour wherein the Son of man cometh. *Mat.* **25**: 13.

Could ye not watch with me one hour? *Mat.* **26**: 40.

He . . . prayed that, if it were possible, the hour might pass from him. *Mk.* **14**: 35.

The hour cometh, when ye shall neither in this mountain, nor yet at Jerusalem, worship the Father. *Jn.* **4**: 21.

Jesus answered, Are there not twelve hours in the day? *Jn.* **11**: 9.

I will come on thee as a thief, and thou shalt not know what hour I will come upon thee. *Re.* **3**: 3.

See also

Time.

House

The Lord thy God . . . brought thee forth . . . from the house of bondage. *De.* **8**: 14.

Look down from thy holy habitation, from heaven, and bless thy people Israel. *De.* 26: 15.

I had rather be a doorkeeper in the house of my God, than to dwell in the tents of wickedness. *Ps.* 84: 10.

He blesseth the habitation of the just. *Pr.* 3: 33.

The house of the righteous shall stand. *Pr.* 12: 7.

The house of the wicked shall be overthrown. *Pr.* 14: 11.

I will liken him unto a wise man, which built his house upon a rock. *Mat.* 7: 24.

This day is salvation come to this house. *Lu.* 19: 9.

Let us do good unto all men, especially unto them who are of the household of faith. *Ga.* 6: 10.

Ye also, as lively stones, are built up a spiritual house. *1 Pe.* 2: 5.

See also

Abode; Dwelling; God, House of; Habitation; Home; Residence; Roof; Shelter; Tenant.

Hue

He made him a coat of many colours. *Ge.* 37: 3.

Thou shalt make a vail of blue, and purple, and scarlet. *Ex.* 26: 31.

Thou shalt make pomegranates of blue, and of purple, and of scarlet, round about the hem thereof; and bells of gold between them round about. *Ex.* 28: 33.

Them hath he filled with wisdom of heart, to work all manner of work, . . . of the embroiderer, in blue, and in purple, in scarlet, and in fine linen. *Ex.* 35: 35.

She had a garment of divers colours upon her: for with such robes were the king's daughters that were virgins apparelled. *2 S.* 13: 18.

Send me now therefore a man cunning to work in gold, and in silver, and in brass, and in iron, and in purple, and crimson, and blue. *2 Ch.* 2: 7.

He pursueth them with words. *Pr.* 19: 7.

I will lay thy stones with fair colours. *Is.* 54: 11.

All Jerusalem was in an uproar. *Ac.* 21: 31.

See also

Clamor; Color.

Humaneness

If a bird's nest chance to be before thee in the way in any tree, or on the ground, whether they be young ones, or eggs, and the dam sitting upon the young, or upon the eggs, thou shalt not take the dam with the young. *De.* 22: 6.

When thou buildest a new house, then thou shalt make a battlement for thy roof, that thou bring not blood upon thy house, if any man fall from thence. *De.* 22: 8.

The beasts of the field shall be at peace with thee. *Jb.* 5: 23.

A righteous man regardeth the life of his beast: but the tender mercies of the wicked are cruel. *Pr.* 12: 10.

He was moved with compassion on them, because they fainted, and were scattered abroad, as sheep having no shepherd. *Mat.* 9: 36.

If a man have an hundred sheep, and one

of them be gone astray, doth he not leave the ninety and nine, and goeth into the mountains, and seeketh that which is gone astray? *Mat.* 18: 12.

Yet the dogs under the table eat of the children's crumbs. *Mk.* 7: 28.

See also

Animal; Beast; Benevolence; Clemency; Gentleness; Humanity; Kindness; Mercy; Tenderness.

Humanity

When thou cuttest down thine harvest in thy field, and hast forgot a sheaf in the field, thou shalt not go again to fetch it: it shall be for the stranger, for the fatherless, and for the widow. *De.* 24: 19.

Thou shalt heap coals of fire upon his head, and the Lord shall reward thee. *Pr.* 25: 22.

I will not turn away the punishment thereof; because they . . . remembered not the brotherly covenant. *Am.* 1: 9.

Inasmuch as ye have done it unto one of the least of these my brethren, ye have done it unto me. *Mat.* 25: 40.

They that are whole have no need of the physician, but they that are sick. *Mk.* 2: 17.

Above all these things put on charity, which is the bond of perfectness. *Col.* 3: 14.

Love the brotherhood. *1 Pe.* 2: 17.

Be pitiful. *1 Pe.* 3: 8.

He that loveth his brother abideth in the light. *1 Jn.* 2: 10.

He that loveth not his brother abideth in death. *1 Jn.* 3: 14.

See also

Beneficence; Benevolence; Clemency; Compassion; Gentleness; Goodness; Grace; Humaneness; Pity; Tenderness.

Humility

I am not worthy of the least of all the mercies, and of all the truth, which thou hast shewed unto thy servant. *Ge.* 32: 10.

Moses wist not that the skin of his face shone. *Ex.* 34: 29.

They fell upon their faces: and the glory of the Lord appeared unto them. *Nu.* 20: 6.

Am not I a Benjamite, of the smallest of the tribes of Israel? and my family the least of all the families of the tribe of Benjamin? wherefore then speakest thou so to me? *1 S.* 9: 21.

Who am I, O Lord God? and what is my house, that thou hast brought me hitherto? *2 S.* 7: 18.

Thou hast made thy servant king instead of David my father: and I am but a little child: I know not how to go out or come in. *1 K.* 3: 7.

Before honour is humility. *Pr.* 15: 33.

I dwell in the high and holy place, with him also that is of a contrite and humble spirit. *Is.* 57: 15.

Then answered Amos, . . . I was no prophet, neither was I a prophet's son; but I was an herdman, and a gatherer of sycomore fruit. *Am.* 7: 14.

I have need to be baptized of thee, and comest thou to me? *Mat.* 3: 14.

Let your light so shine before men, that they may see your good works, and glorify your Father which is in heaven. *Mat.* 5: 16.

I am not worthy that thou shouldest come under my roof: but speak the word only, and my servant shall be healed. *Mat.* 8: 8.

When thou art bidden, go and sit down in the lowest room. *Lu.* 14: 10.

We are unprofitable servants: we have done that which was our duty to do. *Lu.* 17: 10.

The publican, standing afar off, would not lift up so much as his eyes unto heaven, but smote upon his breast, saying, God be merciful to me a sinner. *Lu.* 18: 13.

He must increase, but I must decrease. *Jn.* 3: 30.

A damsel came to hearken, named Rhoda. *Ac.* 12: 13.

I say, through the grace given unto me, to every man that is among you, not to think of himself more highly than he ought to think. *Ro.* 12: 3.

Mind not high things, but condescend to men of low estate. *Ro.* 12: 16.

Who maketh thee to differ from another? and what hast thou that thou didst not receive? now if thou didst receive it, why dost thou glory, as if thou hadst not received it? *1 Co.* 4: 7.

We are made a spectacle unto the world, and to angels, and to men. *1 Co.* 4: 9.

God forbid that I should glory, save in the cross of our Lord Jesus Christ. *Ga.* 6: 14.

Whatsoever ye do in word or deed, do all in the name of the Lord Jesus, giving thanks to God and the Father by him. *Col.* 3: 17.

Christ Jesus came into the world to save sinners; of whom I am chief. *1 Ti.* 1: 15.

Charge them that are rich in this world, that they be not highminded, nor trust in uncertain riches, but in the living God, who giveth us richly all things to enjoy. *1 Ti.* 6: 17.

God . . . giveth grace unto the humble. *Ja.* 4: 6.

See also

Attitude; Lowliness; Meekness; Modesty.

Hundred

Shall a child be born unto him that is an hundred years old? *Ge.* 17: 17.

Though a sinner do evil an hundred times, and his days be prolonged, yet surely I know that it shall be well with them that fear God, which fear before him. *Ec.* 8: 12.

The child shall die an hundred years old. *Is.* 65: 20.

The city that went out by a thousand shall leave an hundred, and that which went forth by an hundred shall leave ten. *Am.* 5: 3.

Other fell into good ground, and brought forth fruit, some an hundredfold, some sixtyfold, some thirtyfold. *Mat.* 13: 8.

If a man have an hundred sheep, and one of them be gone astray, doth he not leave the ninety and nine, and goeth into the mountains, and seeketh that which is gone astray? *Mat.* 18: 12.

Every one that hath forsaken houses, or brethren, or sisters, or father, or mother, or wife, or children, or lands, for my name's sake, shall receive an hundredfold. *Mat.* 19: 29.

They sat down in ranks, by hundreds, and by fifties. *Mk.* 6: 40.

Hunger

There was a famine in the land. *Ru.* 1: 1.

He . . . filleth the hungry soul with goodness. *Ps.* 107: 9.

The full soul loatheth a honeycomb; but to the hungry soul every bitter thing is sweet. *Pr.* 27: 7.

They shall not hunger nor thirst. *Is.* 49: 10.

They shall eat, and not have enough. *Ho.* 4: 10.

I will send a famine in the land, not a famine of bread, nor a thirst for water, but of hearing the words of the Lord. *Am.* 8: 11.

Blessed are ye that hunger now: for ye shall be filled. *Lu.* 6: 21.

Woe unto you that are full! for ye shall hunger. *Lu.* 6: 25.

I perish with hunger! *Lu.* 15: 17.

Every where and in all things I am instructed both to be full and to be hungry. *Ph.* 4: 12.

To him that overcometh will I give to eat of the hidden manna. *Re.* 2: 17.

See also

Destitution; Drought; Famine; Starvation; Stomach.

Hunting

He was a mighty hunter before the Lord. *Ge.* 10: 9.

Thou huntest my soul to take it. *1 S.* 24: 11.

Thou huntest me as a fierce lion. *Jb.* 10: 16.

Wilt thou hunt the prey for the lion? or fill the appetite of the young lions? *Jb.* 38: 39.

Evil shall hunt the violent man to overthrow him. *Ps.* 140: 11.

Behold, I will send for many fishers, saith the Lord, and they shall fish them: and after will I send for many hunters, and they shall hunt them. *Je.* 16: 16.

They hunt every man his brother with a net. *Mi.* 7: 2.

See also

Search; Sport.

Hurry

Send me good speed this day. *Ge.* 24: 12.

Swift as the eagle flieth. *De.* 28: 49.

Swift as the roes upon the mountains. *1 Ch.* 12: 8.

God commanded me to make haste. *2 Ch.* 35: 21.

O Lord, make haste to help me. *Ps.* 40: 13.

Hear me speedily. *Ps.* 69: 17.

His word runneth very swiftly. *Ps.* 147: 15.

Feet that be swift in running to mischief. *Pr.* 6: 18.

The race is not to the swift. *Ec.* 9: 11.

Thou art a swift dromedary traversing her ways. *Je.* 2: 23.

As horsemen, so shall they run. *Jo.* 2: 4.

He that is swift of foot shall not deliver himself. *Am.* 2: 15.

They shall run like the lightnings. *Na.* 2: 4.

They shall fly as the eagle that hasteth to eat. *Hab.* 1: 8.

Go out quickly into the streets and lanes of the city, and bring in hither the poor, and the maimed, and the halt, and the blind. *Lu.* 14: 21.

Then she runneth. *Jn.* 20: 2.

He which testifieth these things saith, Surely I come quickly. Amen. Even so, come, Lord

Jesus. *Re.* **22: 20.**
See also
Haste; Quickness; Speed; Swiftness.

Hurt

Let them be ashamed and brought to confusion together that rejoice at mine hurt. *Ps.* **35: 26.**
There is a sore evil which I have seen under the sun, namely, riches kept for the owners thereof to their hurt. *Ec.* **5: 13.**
They shall not hurt nor destroy in all my holy mountain. *Is.* **11: 9.**
For the hurt of the daughter of my people am I hurt. *Je.* **8: 21.**
If they drink any deadly thing, it shall not hurt them. *Mk.* **16: 18.**
Nothing shall by any means hurt you. *Lu.* **10: 19.**
Love worketh no ill to his neighbour. *Ro.* **13: 10.**
Thrice was I beaten with rods, once was I stoned. *2 Co.* **11: 25.**
They were stoned, they were sawn asunder, were tempted, were slain with the sword. *He.* **11: 37.**
Who is he that will harm you, if ye be followers of that which is good? *1 Pe.* **3: 13.**
See also
Bruise; Harm; Injury; Loss; Mischief; Wound.

Husband

When a man hath taken a new wife, he shall not go out to war, neither shall he be charged with any business: but he shall be free at home one year, and shall cheer up his wife which he hath taken. *De.* **24: 5.**
A virtuous woman is a crown to her husband. *Pr.* **12: 4.**
Live joyfully with the wife whom thou lovest all the days of the life of thy vanity. *Ec.* **9: 9.**
Thy Maker is thine husband. *Is.* **54: 5.**
If any man come to me, and hate not his . . . wife, . . . yea, and his own life also, he cannot be my disciple. *Lu.* **14: 26.**
The head of the woman is the man. *1 Co.* **11: 3.**
The husband is the head of the wife, even as Christ is the head of the church. *Ep.* **5: 23.**
Husbands, love your wives, even as Christ also loved the church, and gave himself for it. *Ep.* **5: 25.**
See also
Marriage; Wedding.

Hymn

In the night his song shall be with me. *Ps.* **42: 8.**
They shout for joy, they also sing. *Ps.* **65: 13.**
They that wasted us required of us mirth, saying, Sing us one of the songs of Zion. *Ps.* **137: 3.**
How shall we sing the Lord's song in a strange land? *Ps.* **137: 4.**
The ransomed of the Lord shall return, and come to Zion with songs and everlasting joy upon their heads. *Is.* **35: 10.**
When they had sung an hymn, they went out. *Mat.* **26: 30.**
I will sing with the spirit, and I will sing with the understanding also. *1 Co.* **14: 15.**
Speaking to yourselves in psalms and hymns and spiritual songs, singing and making melody in your heart to the Lord. *Ep.* **5: 19.**
They sing the song of Moses the servant of God, and the song of the Lamb. *Re.* **15: 3.**
See also
Melody; Music; Psalm; Song.

Hypocrisy

The hypocrite's hope shall perish. *Jb.* **8: 13.**
They bless with their mouth, but they curse inwardly. *Ps.* **62: 4.**
An hypocrite with his mouth destroyeth his neighbour. *Pr.* **11: 9.**
The kisses of an enemy are deceitful. *Pr.* **27: 6.**
Every one is an hypocrite. *Is.* **9: 17.**
I will send him against an hypocritical nation, and against the people of my wrath will I give him a charge. *Is.* **10: 6.**
When ye fast, be not, as the hypocrites, of a sad countenance. *Mat.* **6: 16.**
My house shall be called the house of prayer; but ye have made it a den of thieves. *Mat.* **21: 13.**
Woe unto you, scribes and Pharisees, hypocrites! for ye are like unto whited sepulchres, which indeed appear beautiful outward, but are within full of dead men's bones, and of all uncleanness. *Mat.* **23: 27.**
Satan himself is transformed into an angel of light. *2 Co.* **11: 14.**
Thou hast a name that thou livest, and art dead. *Re.* **3: 1.**
See also
Affectation; Craftiness; Deceit; Duplicity; Faithlessness; Falsehood; Fraud; Inconsistency; Lie; Treachery.

I

Ideal

I am the Almighty God; walk before me, and be thou perfect. *Ge.* **17: 1.**
The Lord is able to give thee much more than this. *2 Ch.* **25: 9.**
This God is our God for ever and ever: he will be our guide even unto death. *Ps.* **48: 14.**

Where there is no vision, the people perish. *Pr.* **29: 18.**
Out of the abundance of the heart the mouth speaketh. *Mat.* **12: 34.**
I, if I be lifted up from the earth, will draw all men unto me. *Jn.* **12: 32.**
This also we wish, even your perfection. . . . Be perfect. *2 Co.* **13: 9, 11.**

A perfect man, . . . the measure of the stature of the fulness of Christ. *Ep.* 4: 13.

After Christ. *Col.* 2: 8.

See, saith he, that thou make all things according to the pattern shewed to thee in the mount. *He.* 8: 5.

These all died in faith, not having received the promises. *He.* 11: 13.

Leaving us an example, that ye should follow his steps. *1 Pe.* 2: 21.

Hereby we know that he abideth in us, by the Spirit which he hath given us. *1 Jn.* 3: 24.

See also
Completion; Example; Form; Fulness; Model; Pattern; Perfection; Standard.

Idleness

How long wilt thou sleep, O sluggard? when wilt thou arise out of thy sleep? *Pr.* 6: 9.

As vinegar to the teeth, and as smoke to the eyes, so is the sluggard to them that send him. *Pr.* 10: 26.

He also that is slothful in his work is brother to him that is a great waster. *Pr.* 18: 9.

She . . . eateth not the bread of idleness. *Pr.* 31: 27.

Through idleness of the hands the house droppeth through. *Ec.* 10: 18.

Every idle word that men shall speak, they shall give account thereof in the day of judgment. *Mat.* 12: 36.

Ye men of Galilee, why stand ye gazing up into heaven? *Ac.* 1: 11.

Not slothful in business; fervent in spirit, serving the Lord. *Ro.* 12: 11.

See also
Indolence; Inertia; Laziness; Sloth.

Idol

They sacrificed unto devils, not to God; to gods whom they knew not, to new gods that came newly up, whom your fathers feared not. *De.* 32: 17.

They have moved me to jealousy with that which is not God. *De.* 32: 21.

They . . . corrupted themselves . . . in following other gods to serve them, and to bow down unto them. *Ju.* 2: 19.

They . . . called on the name of Baal from morning even until noon, saying, O Baal, hear us. But there was no voice, nor any that answered. *1 K.* 18: 26.

Every nation made gods of their own, and put them in the houses of the high places. *2 K.* 17: 29.

If we have forgotten the name of our God, or stretched out our hands to a strange god; Shall not God search this out? for he knoweth the secrets of the heart. *Ps.* 44: 20, 21.

And the residue thereof he maketh a god. *Is.* 44: 17.

Before it came to pass I shewed it thee: lest thou shouldest say, Mine idol hath done them. *Is.* 48: 5.

Turn away your faces from all your abominations. *Eze.* 14: 6.

Woe unto him that saith to the wood, Awake; to the dumb stone, Arise, it shall teach! *Hab.* 2: 19.

The people gave a shout, saying, It is the voice of a god, and not of a man. *Ac.* 12: 22.

When they heard these sayings, they were full of wrath, and cried out, saying, Great is Diana of the Ephesians. *Ac.* 19: 28.

Flee from idolatry. *1 Co.* 10: 14.

No . . . man, who is an idolater, hath any inheritance in the kingdom of Christ and of God. *Ep.* 5: 5.

See also
Gods.

Ignominy

I was a reproach among all mine enemies, but especially among my neighbours, and a fear to mine acquaintance. *Ps.* 31: 11.

Thou hast known my reproach, and my shame, and my dishonour. *Ps.* 69: 19.

Reproach hath broken my heart. *Ps.* 69: 20.

When the wicked cometh, then cometh also contempt, and with ignominy reproach. *Pr.* 18: 3.

I will bring an everlasting reproach upon you, and a perpetual shame. *Je.* 23: 40.

Ye . . . are an infamy of the people. *Eze.* 36: 3.

The resurrection of the dead . . . is sown in dishonour; it is raised in glory. *1 Co.* 15: 42, 43.

See also
Christ, Humiliation of; Disgrace; Dishonor; Rebuke; Reproach; Scorn; Shame.

Ignorance

I know not the day of my death. *Ge.* 27: 2.

It shall be forgiven them; for it is ignorance. *Nu.* 15: 25.

O that they were wise, that they understood this, that they would consider their latter end! *De.* 32: 29.

There arose another generation after them, which knew not the Lord, nor yet the works which he had done for Israel. *Ju.* 2: 10.

We are but of yesterday, and know nothing. *Jb.* 8: 9.

He multiplieth words without knowledge. *Jb.* 35: 16.

Can any understand the spreadings of the clouds? *Jb.* 36: 29.

Who is this that darkeneth counsel by words without knowledge? *Jb.* 38: 2.

God is not in all his thoughts. *Ps.* 10: 4.

So foolish was I, and ignorant. *Ps.* 73: 22.

Such knowledge is too wonderful for me. *Ps.* 139: 6.

Fools hate knowledge. *Pr.* 1: 22.

He knoweth not that which shall be: for who can tell him when it shall be? *Ec.* 8: 7.

Man also knoweth not his time. *Ec.* 9: 12.

The lips of a fool will swallow up himself. *Ec.* 10: 12.

A man cannot tell what shall be; and what shall be after him, who can tell him? *Ec.* 10: 14.

Thou knowest not the works of God who maketh all. *Ec.* 11: 5.

My people are gone into captivity, because they have no knowledge. *Is.* 5: 13.

His watchmen are blind: they are all ignorant, they are all dumb dogs, they cannot bark; sleeping, lying down, loving to slumber. *Is.* 56: 10.

The way of peace they know not; and there is no judgment in their goings. *Is.* 59: 8.

They are wise to do evil, but to do good they have no knowledge. *Je. 4: 22.*

Surely these are poor; they are foolish: for they know not the way of the Lord, nor the judgment of their God. *Je. 5: 4.*

My people are destroyed for lack of knowledge. *Ho. 4: 6.*

Because thou hast rejected knowledge, I will also reject thee. *Ho. 4: 6.*

They know not the thoughts of the Lord. *Mi. 4: 12.*

Ye do err, not knowing the scriptures, nor the power of God. *Mat. 22: 29.*

Of that day and that hour knoweth no man. *Mk. 13: 32.*

Father, forgive them; for they know not what they do. *Lu. 23: 34.*

The world knew him not. *Jn. 1: 10.*

The wind bloweth where it listeth, and thou hearest the sound thereof, but canst not tell whence it cometh, and whither it goeth: so is every one that is born of the Spirit. *Jn. 3: 8.*

Herein is a marvellous thing, that ye know not from whence he is, and yet he hath opened mine eyes. *Jn. 9: 30.*

We know not whither thou goest; and how can we know the way? *Jn. 14: 5.*

They have not known the Father, nor me. *Jn. 16: 3.*

As yet they knew not the scriptures. *Jn. 20: 9.*

Whom therefore ye ignorantly worship, him declare I unto you. *Ac. 17: 23.*

The times of this ignorance God winked at; but now commandeth all men every where to repent. *Ac. 17: 30.*

Have ye received the Holy Ghost since ye believed? And they said unto him, We have not so much as heard whether there be any Holy Ghost. *Ac. 19: 2.*

Ignorant of God's righteousness. *Ro. 10: 3.*

Charity never faileth: but whether there be . . . knowledge, it shall vanish away. *1 Co. 13: 8.*

If any man be ignorant, let him be ignorant. *1 Co. 14: 38.*

Even unto this day, when Moses is read, the vail is upon their heart. *2 Co. 3: 15.*

Having the understanding darkened, being alienated from the life of God through the ignorance that is in them, because of the blindness of their heart. *Ep. 4: 18.*

I did it ignorantly in unbelief. *1 Ti. 1: 13.*

With well doing ye may put to silence the ignorance of foolish men. *1 Pe. 2: 15.*

See also
Folly.

Illness

Who forgiveth all thine iniquities; who healeth all thy diseases. *Ps. 103: 3.*

I am poor and needy, and my heart is wounded within me. *Ps. 109: 22.*

The spirit of man will sustain his infirmity. *Pr. 18: 14.*

They brought unto him all sick people that were taken with diverse diseases and torments, . . . and he healed them. *Mat. 4: 24.*

We then that are strong ought to bear the infirmities of the weak. *Ro. 15: 1.*

I take pleasure in infirmities, . . . for Christ's sake. *2 Co. 12: 10.*

The prayer of faith shall save the sick. *Ja. 5: 15.*

See also
Ailment; Disease; Disorder; Faith-Healing; Healing; Infirmity; Sickness.

Illumination

The Lord make his face shine upon thee, and be gracious unto thee. *Nu. 6: 25.*

Lighten mine eyes, lest I sleep the sleep of death. *Ps. 13: 3.*

The Lord is my light and my salvation. *Ps. 27: 1.*

In thy light shall we see light. *Ps. 36: 9.*

O send out thy light and thy truth: let them lead me. *Ps. 43: 3.*

Out of Zion, the perfection of beauty, God hath shined. *Ps. 50: 2.*

Thy word is a lamp unto my feet, and a light unto my path. *Ps. 119: 105.*

A man's wisdom maketh his face to shine. *Ec. 8: 1.*

The earth shined with his glory. *Eze. 43: 2.*

They that be wise shall shine as the brightness of the firmament. *Da. 12: 3.*

Let your light so shine before men that they may see your good works. *Mat. 5: 16.*

Then shall the righteous shine forth as the sun in the kingdom of their Father. *Mat. 13: 43.*

He put his hands again upon his eyes, and made him look up: and he was restored, and saw every man clearly. *Mk. 8: 25.*

His raiment became shining, exceeding white as snow; so as no fuller on earth can white them. *Mk. 9: 3.*

A light to lighten the Gentiles. *Lu. 2: 32.*

Full of light, having no part dark. *Lu. 11: 36.*

In him was life; and the life was the light of men. *Jn. 1: 4.*

After ye were illuminated, ye endured a great fight of afflictions. *He. 10: 32.*

See also
Brightness; Candle; Christ, the Light; Day; God, the Light; Inspiration; Lamp; Light; Light, the Inner; Lightning; Sun.

Image

God said, Let us make man in our image. *Ge. 1: 26.*

I shall be satisfied, when I awake, with thy likeness. *Ps. 17: 15.*

They have mouths, but they speak not: eyes have they, but they see not: They have ears, but they hear not: noses have they, but they smell not: They have hands, but they handle not: feet have they, but they walk not. *Ps. 115: 5–7.*

He maketh a god, and worshippeth it; he maketh it a graven image, and falleth down thereto. *Is. 44: 15.*

They have no knowledge that set up the wood of their graven image, and pray unto a god that cannot save. *Is. 45: 20.*

He saith unto them, Whose is this image and superscription? *Mat. 22: 20.*

They be no gods, which are made with hands. *Ac. 19: 26.*

The city of the Ephesians is a worshipper of the great goddess Diana, and of the image which fell down from Jupiter. *Ac.* 19: 35.

We know that an idol is nothing in the world, and that there is none other God but one. *1 Co.* 8: 4.

As we have borne the image of the earthy, we shall also bear the image of the heavenly. *1 Co.* 15: 49.

We all . . . are changed into the same image from glory to glory, even as by the Spirit of the Lord. *2 Co.* 3: 18.

Christ, who is the image of God. *2 Co.* 4: 4.
See also

Form; God, Image of; Gods; Idol; Imitation; Likeness; Model; Pattern; Resemblance; Symbol.

Imagination

The imagination of man's heart is evil from his youth. *Ge.* 8: 21.

The Lord searcheth all hearts, and understandeth all the imaginations of the thoughts. *1 Ch.* 28: 9.

I know your thoughts, and the devices which ye wrongfully imagine against me. *Jb.* 21: 27.

Why do the heathen rage, and the people imagine a vain thing? *Ps.* 2: 1.

They . . . imagine deceits all the day long. *Ps.* 38: 12.

How long will ye imagine mischief against a man? *Ps.* 62: 3.

These . . . things doth the Lord hate; . . . a lying tongue, . . . An heart that deviseth wicked imaginations. *Pr.* 6: 16–18.

The eye is not satisfied with seeing. *Ec.* 1: 8.

A dream cometh through the multitude of business. *Ec.* 5: 3.

They speak a vision out of their own heart, and not out of the mouth of the Lord. *Je.* 23: 16.

They say unto every one that walketh after the imagination of his own heart, No evil shall come upon you. *Je.* 23: 17.

Son of man, hast thou seen what the ancients of the house of Israel do in the dark, every man in the chambers of his imagery? *Eze.* 8: 12.

They imagine mischief against me. *Ho.* 7: 15.

They . . . became vain in their imaginations, and their foolish heart was darkened. *Ro.* 1: 21.

Casting down imaginations. *2 Co.* 10: 5.

Imitation

They followed vanity, and became vain, and went after the heathen that were round about them. *2 K.* 17: 15.

Be not ye therefore like unto them. *Mat.* 6: 8.

Jesus called a little child unto him, and set him in the midst of them. *Mat.* 18: 2.

Do not ye after their works: for they say, and do not. *Mat.* 23: 3.

Go, and do thou likewise. *Lu.* 10: 37.

Be . . . followers of them who through faith and patience inherit the promises. *He.* 6: 12.

See . . . that thou make all things according to the pattern shewed to thee in the mount. *He.* 8: 5.

Take, my brethren, the prophets, who have spoken in the name of the Lord, for an example. *Ja.* 5: 10.

Who is he that will harm you, if ye be followers of that which is good? *1 Pe.* 3: 13.
See also

God, Image of; Idol; Image; Likeness; Pattern; Resemblance; Sham.

Immanence

Surely the Lord is in this place; and I knew it not. *Ge.* 28: 16.

Because the Lord was with him, and that which he did, the Lord made it to prosper. *Ge.* 39: 23.

Can we find such a one as this is, a man in whom the Spirit of God is? *Ge.* 41: 38.

Certainly I will be with thee. *Ex.* 3: 12.

The soul of my lord shall be bound in the bundle of life with the Lord thy God. *1 S.* 25: 29.

He that dwelleth in the secret place of the most High shall abide under the shadow of the Almighty. *Ps.* 91: 1.

This is my rest for ever: here will I dwell *Ps.* 132: 14.

A virgin shall conceive, and bear a son, and shall call his name Immanuel. *Is.* 7: 14.

Thus saith the high and lofty One that inhabiteth eternity, whose name is Holy: I dwell in the high and holy place, with him also that is of a contrite and humble spirit. *Is.* 57: 15.

The glory of the Lord came into the house. *Eze.* 43: 4.

I will dwell in the midst of the children of Israel for ever. *Eze.* 43: 7.

In him dwelleth all the fulness of the Godhead bodily. *Col.* 2: 9.

Whosoever shall confess that Jesus is the Son of God, God dwelleth in him, and he in God. *1 Jn.* 4: 15.

He that dwelleth in love dwelleth in God, and God dwelleth in him. *1 Jn.* 4: 16.

He that sitteth on the throne shall dwell among them. *Re.* 7: 15.
See also

Immanuel; God, Immanence of; God, Presence of; Transcendence.

Immanuel

Behold, a virgin shall conceive, and bear a son, and shall call his name Immanuel. *Is.* 7: 14.

Butter and honey shall he eat, that he may know to refuse the evil, and choose the good. *Is.* 7: 15.

Before the child shall know to refuse the evil, and choose the good, the land that thou abhorrest shall be forsaken of both her kings. *Is.* 7: 16.

The stretching out of his wings shall fill the breadth of thy land, O Immanuel. *Is.* 8: 8.

They shall call his name Emmanuel, which being interpreted is, God with us. *Mat.* 1: 23.

Immaturity

The wheat and the rie were not smitten: for they were not grown up. *Ex.* 9: 32.

Would ye tarry for them till they were grown? *Ru.* 1: 13.

The child Samuel grew before the Lord. *1 S.* 2: 21.

Saul said to David, Thou art not able to go against this Philistine to fight with him: for thou art but a youth, and he a man of war from his youth. *1 S.* 17: 33.

Deal gently for my sake with the young man. *2 S.* 18: 5.

I am but a little child: I know not how to go out or come in. *1 K.* 3: 7.

While it is yet in his greenness, and not cut down, it withereth before any other herb. *Jb.* 8: 12.

He shall shake off his unripe grape as the vine. *Jb.* 15: 33.

Remember not the sins of my youth. *Ps.* 25: 7.

Rejoice, O young man, in thy youth. *Ec.* 11: 9.

Childhood and youth are vanity. *Ec.* 11: 10.

I was ashamed, yea, even confounded, because I did bear the reproach of my youth. *Je.* 31: 19.

Ephraim is a cake not turned. *Ho.* 7: 8.

Neither do men put new wine into old bottles. *Mat.* 9: 17.

When I became a man, I put away childish things. *1 Co.* 13: 11.

Flee also youthful lusts. *2 Ti.* 2: 22.

See also
Maturity; Youth.

Immensity
Let them grow into a multitude in the midst of the earth. *Ge.* 48: 16.

Ye are this day the stars of heaven for multitude. *De.* 1: 10.

Is not thy wickedness great? and thine iniquities infinite? *Pr.* 22: 5.

His going forth is from the end of the heaven, and his circuit unto the ends of it. *Ps.* 19: 6.

The Lord is upon many waters. *Ps.* 29: 3.

Thy way is in the sea, and thy path in the great waters. *Ps.* 77: 19.

As the heaven is high above the earth, so great is his mercy toward them that fear him. *Ps.* 103: 11.

O Lord my God, thou art very great; thou art clothed with honour and majesty. *Ps.* 104: 1.

His greatness is unsearchable. *Ps.* 145: 3.

God . . . Which made heaven, and earth, the sea, and all that therein is. *Ps.* 146: 5, 6.

He telleth the number of the stars: he calleth them all by their names. *Ps.* 147: 4.

His understanding is infinite. *Ps.* 147: 5.

Thy greatness is grown, and reacheth unto heaven, and thy dominion to the ends of the earth. *Da.* 4: 22.

Now shall he be great unto the end of the earth. *Mi.* 5: 4.

Seeing we also are compassed about with so great a cloud of witnesses. *He.* 12: 1.

Lo, a great multitude, which no man could number, of all nations, and kindreds, and people, and tongues. *Re.* 7: 9.

See also
Bigness; Greatness; Infinity.

Immersion
He that is to be cleansed shall wash his clothes, and shave off all his hair, and wash himself in water, that he may be clean. *Le.* 14: 8.

Go and wash in Jordan seven times, and thy flesh shall come again to thee, and thou shalt be clean. *2 K.* 5: 10.

Are not Abana and Pharpar, rivers of Damascus, better than all the waters of Israel? may I not wash in them, and be clean? *2 K.* 5: 12.

If I wash myself with snow water, and make my hands never so clean; Yet shalt thou plunge me in the ditch, and mine own clothes shall abhor me. *Jb.* 10: 30, 31.

Wash me throughly from mine iniquity, and cleanse me from my sin. *Ps.* 51: 2.

Wash me, and I shall be whiter than snow *Ps.* 51: 7.

Wash you, make you clean. *Is.* 1: 16.

Lord, if thou wilt, thou canst make me clean. *Mat.* 8: 2.

It came to pass in those days, that Jesus came from Nazareth of Galilee, and was baptized of John in Jordan. *Mk.* 1: 9.

John also was baptizing in Aenon near to Salim, because there was much water there. *Jn.* 3: 23.

They went down both into the water, both Philip and the eunuch; and he baptized him. *Ac.* 8: 38.

Be baptized, and wash away thy sins. *Ac.* 22: 16.

Christ sent me not to baptize, but to preach the gospel. *1 Co.* 1: 17.

Let us draw near with a true heart in full assurance of faith, having our hearts sprinkled from an evil conscience, and our bodies washed with pure water. *He.* 10: 22.

See also
Baptism.

Immigration
I have been a stranger in a strange land. *Ex.* 2: 22.

The stranger that dwelleth with you shall be unto you as one born among you, and thou shalt love him as thyself. *Le.* 19: 34.

Ye shall have one manner of law, as well for the stranger, as for one of your own country. *Le.* 24: 22.

The land, which we passed through to search it, is an excellent good land. *Nu.* 14: 7.

He shall enter also into the glorious land. *Da.* 11: 41.

I was a stranger, and ye took me in. *Mat.* 25: 35.

Moses . . . was a stranger in the land of Madian. *Ac.* 7: 29.

Let us labour therefore to enter into that rest. *He.* 4: 11.

By faith, he sojourned in the land of promise, as in a strange country. *He.* 11: 9.

They that say such things declare plainly that they seek a country. *He.* 11: 14.

He hath prepared for them a city. *He.* 11: 16.

See also
Alien; Foreigner; Repatriation; Stranger.

Immorality
Remember not the sins of my youth, nor my transgressions. *Ps.* 25: 7.

Lust not after her beauty in thine heart; neither let her take thee with her eyelids. *Pr.* 6: 25.

Ye have plowed wickedness, ye have reaped iniquity. *Ho.* 10: 13.

Whosoever looketh on a woman to lust after her hath committed adultery with her already in his heart. *Mat.* 5: 28.

The men . . . burned in their lust one toward another. *Ro.* 1: 27.

Sin shall not have dominion over you. *Ro.* 6: 14.

God hath not called us unto uncleanness, but unto holiness. *1 Th.* 4: 7.

Serving divers lusts and pleasures. *Tit.* 3: 3.

To enjoy the pleasures of sin for a season. *He.* 11: 25.

I beseech you as strangers and pilgrims, abstain from fleshly lusts which war against the soul. *1 Pe.* 2: 11.

All that is in the world, the lust of the flesh, and the lust of the eyes, and the pride of life is not of the Father, but is of the world. *1 Jn.* 2: 16.

See also

Evil; Flesh; Guile; Iniquity; Lust; Sin; Transgression; Ungodliness; Unrighteousness; Wickedness; Wrong.

Immortality

If a man die, shall he live again? *Jb.* 14: 14.

I know that my redeemer liveth. *Jb.* 19: 25.

His leaf also shall not wither. *Ps.* 1: 3.

Yea, though I walk through the valley of the shadow of death, I will fear no evil. *Ps.* 23: 4.

Shall the dust praise thee? *Ps.* 30: 9.

God will redeem my soul from the power of the grave. *Ps.* 49: 15.

I shall not die, but live, and declare the works of the Lord. *Ps.* 118: 17.

Then shall the dust return to the earth as it was: and the spirit shall return unto God who gave it. *Ec.* 12: 7.

Give place: for the maid is not dead, but sleepeth. *Mat.* 9: 24.

Neither can they die any more: for they are equal unto the angels. *Lu.* 20: 36.

The water that I shall give him shall be in him a well of water springing up into everlasting life. *Jn.* 4: 14.

Verily, verily, I say unto you, If a man keep my saying, he shall never see death. *Jn.* 8: 51.

Your father Abraham rejoiced to see my day: and he saw it, and was glad. *Jn.* 8: 56.

I am the resurrection. *Jn.* 11: 25.

He that believeth on me, the works that I do shall he do also; and greater works than these shall he do. *Jn.* 14: 12.

Because I live, ye shall live also. *Jn.* 14: 19.

We shall also bear the image of the heavenly. *1 Co.* 15: 49.

Our Saviour Jesus Christ, who hath abolished death, and hath brought life and immortality to light through the gospel. *2 Ti.* 1: 10.

He being dead yet speaketh. *He.* 11: 4.

By faith Enoch was translated. *He.* 11: 5.

The grass withereth, and the flower thereof falleth away: But the word of the Lord endureth for ever. *1 Pe.* 1: 24, 25.

This is the promise that he hath promised us, even eternal life. *1 Jn.* 2: 25.

See also

Christ, Resurrection of; Easter; Eternity; Life, the Eternal; Resurrection.

Immunity

Surely he shall deliver thee from the snare of the fowler, and from the noisome pestilence. *Ps.* 91: 3.

Thou shalt not be afraid for the terror by night; nor for the arrow that flieth by day. *Ps.* 91: 5.

Thou shalt not be afraid . . . for the pestilence that walketh in darkness. *Ps.* 91: 5, 6.

There shall no evil befall thee, neither shall any plague come nigh thy dwelling. *Ps.* 91: 10.

Thou shalt tread upon the lion and adder: the young lion and the dragon shalt thou trample under feet. *Ps.* 91: 13.

They shall not hurt nor destroy in all my holy mountain. *Is.* 11: 9.

When thou walkest through the fire, thou shalt not be burned; neither shall the flame kindle upon thee. *Is.* 43: 2.

The princes, governors, and captains, and the king's counsellors, being gathered together, saw these men, upon whose bodies the fire had no power, nor was an hair of their head singed, neither were their coats changed, nor the smell of fire had passed on them. *Da.* 3: 27.

There came a viper out of the heat, and fastened on his hand. . . . And he shook off the beast into the fire, and felt no harm. *Ac.* 28: 3, 5.

Being then made free from sin, ye became the servants of righteousness. *Ro.* 6: 18.

The law of the Spirit of life in Christ Jesus hath made me free from the law of sin and death. *Ro.* 8: 2.

He that overcometh shall not be hurt of the second death. *Re.* 2: 11.

See also

Contagion.

Impartiality

Ye shall hear the small as well as the great. *De.* 1: 17.

Is it fit to say to a king, Thou art wicked? and to princes, Ye are ungodly? *Jb.* 34: 18.

He maketh his sun to rise on the evil and on the good, and sendeth rain on the just and on the unjust. *Mat.* 5: 45.

God is no respecter of persons. *Ac.* 10: 34.

There is no difference between the Jew and the Greek. *Ro.* 10: 12.

Observe these things without preferring one before another. *1 Ti.* 5: 21.

See also

Bias; Equality; Equality, Racial; Fairness; God, Fairness of; God, Impartiality of; Justice; Justice, Social; Persons, Respect of.

Impatience

When the people saw that Moses delayed to come down out of the mount, the people gathered themselves together unto Aaron, and said unto him, Up, make us gods, . . . for as for this Moses, . . . we wot not what is become of him. *Ex.* 32: 1.

Now Joshua was old and stricken in years; and the Lord said unto him, Thou art old and stricken in years, and there remaineth yet very much land to be possessed. *Jos.* 13: 1.

Oh that I knew where I might find him! *Jb.* 23: 3.

My soul breaketh for the longing that it

hath unto thy judgments. *Ps.* **119: 20.**

He that is hasty of spirit exalteth folly. *Pr.* **14: 29.**

He that hasteth with his feet sinneth. *Pr.* **19: 2.**

His heart fretteth against the Lord. *Pr.* **19: 3.**

He that hasteth to be rich hath an evil eye. *Pr.* **28: 22.**

Oh that thou wouldest rend the heavens, that thou wouldest come down! *Is.* **64: 1.**

I have a baptism to be baptized with; and how am I straitened till it be accomplished! *Lu.* **12: 50.**

Then Martha, as soon as she heard that Jesus was coming, went and met him: but Mary sat still in the house. *Jn.* **11: 20.**

See also
Fretfulness; Haste.

Impediment

The angel of the Lord went further, and stood in a narrow place, where was no way to turn either to the right hand or to the left. *Nu.* **22: 26.**

Mephibosheth . . . did eat continually at the king's table; and was lame on both his feet. **2** *S.* **9: 13.**

The snare is laid for him in the ground, and a trap for him in the way. *Jb.* **18: 10.**

I, as a deaf man, heard not; and I was as a dumb man that openeth not his mouth. *Ps.* **38: 13.**

The slothful man saith, There is a lion in the way; a lion is in the streets. *Pr.* **26: 13.**

Their Saviour . . . led them through the deep, as an horse in the wilderness, that they should not stumble. *Is.* **63: 8, 13.**

Give glory to the Lord your God, before he cause darkness, and before your feet stumble upon the dark mountains. *Je.* **13: 16.**

I will cause them to walk by the rivers of waters in a straight way, wherein they shall not stumble. *Je.* **31: 9.**

They stumble upon their corpses. *Na.* **3: 3.**

They bring unto him one that was deaf, and had an impediment in his speech. *Mk.* **7: 32.**

If any man walk in the day, he stumbleth not, because he seeth the light of this world. *Jn.* **11: 9.**

I say then, Have they stumbled that they should fall? God forbid. *Ro.* **11: 11.**

I have been much hindered from coming to you. *Ro.* **15: 22.**

There was given to me a thorn in the flesh. **2** *Co.* **12: 7.**

See also
Difficulty; Encumbrance; Hindrance; Obstacle; Obstruction; Stumbling-block.

Impenitence

Harden not your heart, as in the provocation, and as in the day of temptation in the wilderness. *Ps.* **95: 8.**

He, that being often reproved hardeneth his neck, shall suddenly be destroyed, and that without remedy. *Pr.* **29: 1.**

Because sentence against an evil work is not executed speedily, therefore the heart of the sons of men is fully set in them to do evil. *Ec.* **8: 11.**

O Lord, . . . thou hast stricken them, but they have not grieved. *Je.* **5: 3.**

They have made their faces harder than a rock; they have refused to return. *Je.* **5: 3.**

I called you, but ye answered not. *Je.* **7: 13.**

Yet have ye not returned unto me, saith the Lord. *Am.* **4: 6.**

Then began he to upbraid the cities wherein most of his mighty works were done, because they repented not. *Mat.* **11: 20.**

Exhort one another daily, while it is called To day; lest any of you be hardened through the deceitfulness of sin. *He.* **3: 13.**

See also
Blindness; Hardness; Stubbornness.

Imperfection

If I justify myself, my own mouth shall condemn me. *Jb.* **9: 20.**

Cleanse thou me from secret faults. *Ps.* **19: 12.**

There is not a just man upon earth, that doeth good, and sinneth not. *Ec.* **7: 20.**

If thy right eye offend thee, pluck it out, and cast it from thee. *Mat.* **5: 29.**

They bring unto him one that was deaf, and had an impediment in his speech. *Mk.* **7: 32.**

It is better for thee to enter into life maimed. *Mk.* **9: 43.**

Pilate . . . went out again unto the Jews, and saith unto them, I find in him no fault at all. *Jn.* **18: 38.**

Herein do I exercise myself, to have a conscience void of offence toward God, and toward men. *Ac.* **24: 16.**

That ye may be blameless in the day of our Lord Jesus Christ. *1 Co.* **1: 8.**

I will not glory, but in mine infirmities. **2** *Co.* **12: 5.**

He hath chosen us in him before the foundation of the world, that we should be holy and without blame before him in love. *Ep.* **1: 4.**

Whosoever shall keep the whole law, and yet offend in one point, he is guilty of all. *Ja.* **2: 10.**

In many things we offend all. *Ja.* **3: 2.**

Confess your faults one to another. *Ja.* **5: 16.**

As of a lamb without blemish and without spot. *1 Pe.* **1: 19.**

These are spots in your feasts of charity. *Jude* **1: 12.**

I have not found thy works perfect before God. *Re.* **3: 2.**

See also
Blemish; Defect; Failure; Fault; Incompleteness; Lack; Spot; Vice; Want; Weakness.

Impermanence

My days . . . are passed away as the swift ships. *Jb.* **9: 25, 26.**

As for man, his days are as grass. *Ps.* **103: 15.**

The wind passeth over it, and it is gone. *Ps.* **103: 16.**

Man is like to vanity: his days are as a shadow that passeth away. *Ps.* **144: 4.**

One generation passeth away, and another generation cometh. *Ec.* **1: 4.**

All flesh is grass, and all the goodliness thereof is as the flower of the field: The grass withereth, the flower fadeth. *Is.* 40: 6, 7.

Therefore will I scatter them as the stubble that passeth away by the wind of the wilderness. *Je.* 13: 24.

They shall be as the morning cloud, and as the early dew that passeth away, as the chaff that is driven with the whirlwind out of the floor, and as the smoke out of the chimney. *Ho.* 13: 3.

Lay up for yourselves treasures in heaven, where neither moth nor rust doth corrupt, and where thieves do not break through nor steal. *Mat.* 6: 20.

Heaven and earth shall pass away: but my words shall not pass away. *Lu.* 21: 33.

We . . . have no certain dwellingplace. *1 Co.* 4: 11.

The fashion of this world passeth away. *1 Co.* 7: 31.

Charity never faileth: but whether there be prophecies, they shall fail; whether there be tongues, they shall cease; whether there be knowledge, it shall vanish away. *1 Co.* 13: 8.

We shall all be changed. *1 Co.* 15: 51.

We look not at the things which are seen, but at the things which are not seen: for the things which are seen are temporal; but the things which are not seen are eternal. *2 Co.* 4: 18.

Yet once more I shake not the earth only, but also heaven. *He.* 12: 26.

See also

Decay; Inconstancy; Life, the Short; Withering.

Impetus

Send me good speed this day. *Ge.* 24: 12.

Speak unto the children of Israel, that they go forward. *Ex.* 14: 15.

The Lord said unto me, Arise, get thee down quickly from hence. *De.* 9: 12.

The Spirit of the Lord began to move him at times. *Ju.* 13: 25.

Make speed, haste, stay not. *1 S.* 20: 38.

Go, do all that is in thine heart; for the Lord is with thee. *2 S.* 7: 3.

By my God have I leaped over a wall. *2 S.* 22: 30.

Quicken thou me in thy way. *Ps.* 119: 37.

Importance

As a prince hast thou power with God and with men, and hast prevailed. *Ge.* 32: 28.

Every valley shall be exalted. *Is.* 40: 4.

Seek ye first the kingdom of God, and his righteousness; and all these things shall be added unto you. *Mat.* 6: 33.

Who is the greatest in the kingdom of heaven? *Mat.* 18: 1.

The power of the Highest shall overshadow thee. *Lu.* 1: 35.

One thing is needful. *Lu.* 10: 42.

When thou art bidden of any man to a wedding, sit not down in the highest room. *Lu.* 14: 8.

He that is greatest among you, let him be as the younger; and he that is chief, as he that doth serve. *Lu.* 22: 26.

The voices of them and of the chief priests prevailed. *Lu.* 23: 23.

Jesus answered and said unto him, Art thou a master of Israel, and knowest not these things? *Jn.* 3: 10.

Have any of the rulers or of the Pharisees believed on him? *Jn.* 7: 48.

See also

Bigness; Distinction; Eminence; Excellence; Fame; Gravity; Greatness; Influence; Prominence; Superiority; Weight.

Importunity

Oh let not the Lord be angry, and I will speak yet but this once: Peradventure ten shall be found there. And he said, I will not destroy it for ten's sake. *Ge.* 18: 32.

He pressed upon them greatly. *Ge.* 19: 3.

I will not let thee go, except thou bless me. *Ge.* 32: 26.

I fell down before the Lord, as at the first, forty days and forty nights: I did neither eat bread nor drink water, because of all your sins which ye sinned. *De.* 9: 18.

Cease not to cry unto the Lord our God for us. *1 S.* 7: 8.

Art thou he that troubleth Israel? *1 K.* 18: 17.

They urged him till he was ashamed. *2 K.* 2: 17.

Lord, how are they increased that trouble me! *Ps.* 3: 1.

Because of his importunity. *Lu.* 11: 8.

Though I fear not God, nor regard man; Yet because this widow troubleth me, I will avenge her, lest by her continual coming she weary me. *Lu.* 18: 4, 5.

And being in an agony he prayed more earnestly. *Lu.* 22: 44.

Prayer was made without ceasing of the church unto God for him. *Ac.* 12: 5.

Impossibility

O Lord, I know that the way of man is not in himself: it is not in man that walketh to direct his steps. *Je.* 10: 23.

No man can serve two masters. *Mat.* 6: 24.

How can ye, being evil, speak good things? *Mat.* 12: 34.

Nothing shall be impossible unto you. *Mat.* 17: 20.

With men this is impossible; but with God all things are possible. *Mat.* 19: 26.

With God nothing shall be impossible. *Lu.* 1: 37.

It is impossible but that offences will come: but woe unto him, through whom they come! *Lu.* 17: 1.

The things which are impossible with men are possible with God. *Lu.* 18: 27.

It is impossible for those who were once enlightened, . . . If they shall fall away, to renew them again unto repentance. *He.* 6: 4, 6.

It was impossible for God to lie. *He.* 6: 18.

Without faith it is impossible to please him. *He.* 11: 6.

He that loveth not his brother whom he hath seen, how can he love God whom he hath not seen? *1 Jn.* 4: 20.

Impotence

Ye shall have no power to stand before your enemies. *Le.* 26: 37.

If I be shaven, then my strength will go from me, and I shall become weak. *Ju.* 16: 17.

His strength went from him. *Ju.* 16: 19.

There was no strength in him. *1 S.* 28: 20.

I am this day fourscore years old: and can I discern between good and evil? can thy servant taste what I eat or what I drink? can I hear any more the voice of singing men and women? *2 S.* 19: 35.

Lord, it is nothing with thee to help, whether with many, or with them that have no power. *2 Ch.* 14: 11.

How hast thou helped him that is without power? how savest thou the arm that hath no strength? *Jb.* 26: 2.

I am as a man that hath no strength. *Ps.* 88: 4.

Is my hand shortened at all, that it cannot redeem? or have I no power to deliver? *Is.* 50: 2.

I was left alone, and saw this great vision, and there remained no strength in me. *Da.* 10: 8.

Now there is at Jerusalem . . . a pool, . . . having five porches. In these lay a great multitude of impotent folk, of blind, halt, withered, waiting for the moving of the water. *Jn.* 5: 2, 3.

Thou couldest have no power at all against me, except it were given thee from above. *Jn.* 19: 11.

There is no power but of God. *Ro.* 13: 1.

We are glad, when we are weak, and ye are strong. *2 Co.* 13: 9.

Blessed and holy is he that hath part in the first resurrection: on such the second death hath no power. *Re.* 20: 6.

See also

Feebleness; Inability; Weakness.

Imprisonment

The Lord . . . despiseth not his prisoners. *Ps.* 69: 33.

Bring my soul out of prison. *Ps.* 142: 7.

He hath sent me to bind up the broken-hearted, to proclaim liberty to the captives, and the opening of the prison to them that are bound. *Is.* 61: 1.

Turn you to the strong hold, ye prisoners of hope. *Zch.* 9: 12.

I was in prison, and ye came unto me. *Mat.* 25: 36.

They shall lay their hands on you, and persecute you, delivering you up to the synagogues, and into prisons. *Lu.* 21: 12.

The angel of the Lord by night opened the prison doors, and brought them forth. *Ac.* 5: 19.

Many of the saints did I shut up in prison. *Ac.* 26: 10.

For the hope of Israel I am bound with this chain. *Ac.* 28: 20.

In prisons more frequent. *2 Co.* 11: 23.

See also

Arrest; Band; Bond; Bondage; Captivity; Capture; Chain; Prison; Restraint; Yoke.

Improvement

Behold, I go forward. *Jb.* 23: 8.

Better is the end of a thing than the beginning thereof. *Ec.* 7: 8.

For brass I will bring gold, and for iron I will bring silver, and for wood brass, and for stones iron. *Is.* 60: 17.

Seek that ye may excel to the edifying of the church. *1 Co.* 14: 12.

Let all things be done unto edifying. *1 Co.* 14: 26.

According to the power which the Lord hath given me to edification, and not to destruction. *2 Co.* 13: 10.

For the perfecting of the saints, for the work of the ministry, for the edifying of the body of Christ. *Ep.* 4: 12.

Bring them up in the nurture and admonition of the Lord. *Ep.* 6: 4.

Comfort yourselves together, and edify one another. *1 Th.* 5: 11.

It became him, . . . to make the captain of their salvation perfect through sufferings. *He.* 2: 10.

That ye may grow thereby. *1 Pe.* 2: 2.

Building up yourselves on your most holy faith. *Jude* 1: 20.

See also

Advance; Amendment; Betterment; Development; Education; Enlargement; Evolution; Growth; Increase; Progress.

Impurity

Thy way is perverse before me. *Nu.* 22: 32.

They have defiled by casting down the dwelling place of thy name to the ground. *Ps.* 74: 7.

I am a man of unclean lips, and I dwell in the midst of a people of unclean lips. *Is.* 6: 5.

Touch no unclean thing. *Is.* 52: 11.

All our righteousnesses are as filthy rags. *Is.* 64: 6.

See, O Lord, and consider; for I am become vile. *La.* 1: 11.

For this cause God gave them up unto vile affections. *Ro.* 1: 26.

There is nothing unclean in itself: but to him that esteemeth any thing to be unclean, to him it is unclean. *Ro.* 14: 14.

We are made as the filth of the world, and are the offscouring of all things unto this day. *1 Co.* 4: 13.

Put off . . . the old man, which is corrupt according to the deceitful lusts. *Ep.* 4: 22.

Unto them that are defiled and unbelieving is nothing pure; but even their mind and conscience is defiled. *Tit.* 1: 15.

Lay apart all filthiness and superfluity of naughtiness, and receive with meekness the engrafted word. *Ja.* 1: 21.

See also

Corruption; Defilement; Depravity; Evil; Iniquity; Lust; Pollution; Sin; Sinner; Uncleanness; Ungodliness; Unrighteousness; Vileness; Wickedness.

Inability

Who am I, that I should go unto Pharaoh? *Ex.* 3: 11.

I am not eloquent, neither heretofore, nor since thou hast spoken unto thy servant. *Ex.* 4: 10.

My family is poor in Manasseh, and I am the least in my father's house. *Ju.* 6: 15.

The slothful man saith, There is a lion without, I shall be slain in the streets. *Pr.* 22: 13.

Behold, I cannot speak: for I am a child. *Je.* 1: 6.

I was afraid, and went and hid thy talent in the earth. *Mat.* 25: 25.

They all with one consent began to make excuse. *Lu.* 14: 18.

See also

Feebleness; Frailty; Impotence; Infirmity; Taint; Weakness.

Inauguration

See, I have set thee over all the land of Egypt. *Ge.* 41: 41.

Sanctify yourselves against to morrow. *Jos.* 7: 13.

The trees went forth on a time to anoint a king over them; and they said unto the olive tree. Reign thou over us. *Ju.* 9: 8.

All the people shouted, and said, God save the king. *1 S.* 10: 24.

Behold, the Lord hath set a king over you. *1 S.* 12: 13.

The Lord sent me to anoint thee to be king over his people. *1 S.* 15: 1.

Thou shalt feed my people Israel, and thou shalt be a captain over Israel.. *2 S.* 5: 2.

They anointed David king over Israel. *2 S.* 5: 3.

The Lord . . . chose me, . . . to appoint me ruler over the people of the Lord. *2 S.* 6: 21.

I took thee from the sheepcote, from following the sheep, to be ruler over my people, over Israel. *2 S.* 7: 8.

Because the Lord loved Israel for ever, therefore made he thee king, to do judgment and justice. *1 K.* 10: 9.

I exalted thee from among the people, and made thee prince over my people Israel. *1 K.* 14: 7.

They . . . set the king upon the throne of the kingdom. *2 Ch.* 23: 20.

By me kings reign, and princes decree justice. By me princes rule, and nobles, even all the judges of the earth. *Pr.* 8: 15, 16.

Behold, a king shall reign in righteousness. *Is.* 32: 1.

He that shall rise to reign over the Gentiles; in him shall the Gentiles trust. *Ro.* 15: 12.

See also

Beginning; Commencement; Consecration; Coronation; Initiation; Installation; Ordination.

Incarnation

They shall call his name Emmanuel, which being interpreted is, God with us. *Mat.* 1: 23.

That he should be made manifest to Israel, therefore am I come baptizing with water. *Jn.* 1: 31.

God sending his own Son in the likeness of sinful flesh, and for sin, condemned sin in the flesh. *Ro.* 8: 3.

The last Adam was made a quickening spirit. *1 Co.* 15: 45.

He that descended is the same also that ascended up far above all heavens, that he might fill all things. *Ep.* 4: 10.

Christ Jesus . . . took upon him the form of a servant, and was made in the likeness of men. *Ph.* 2: 5, 7.

Every spirit that confesseth that Jesus Christ is come in the flesh is of God. *1 Jn.* 4: 2.

See also

Christ, Incarnation of; Flesh; God, Incarnation of.

Incense

The Lord smelled a sweet savour. *Ge.* 8: 21.

When Aaron lighteth the lamps at even, he shall burn incense upon it, a perpetual incense before the Lord throughout your generations. *Ex.* 30: 8.

Ye shall offer no strange incense. *Ex.* 30: 9.

Let my prayer be set forth before thee as incense; and the lifting up of my hands as the evening sacrifice. *Ps.* 141: 2.

Incense is an abomination to me. *Is.* 1: 13.

Christ also hath loved us, and hath given himself for us an offering and a sacrifice to God for a sweetsmelling savour. *Ep.* 5: 2.

The smoke of the incense, which came with the prayers of the saints, ascended up before God out of the angel's hand. *Re.* 8: 4.

See also

Offering; Perfume; Sacrifice; Savor; Scent; Smell; Worship.

Inclination

Incline your heart unto the Lord God of Israel. *Jos.* 24: 23.

The Lord our God be with us, . . . That he may incline our hearts unto him. *1 K.* 8: 57, 58.

I waited patiently for the Lord; and he inclined unto me, and heard my cry. *Ps.* 40: 1.

I delight to do thy will, O my God. *Ps.* 40: 8.

Incline not my heart to any evil thing. *Ps.* 141: 4.

The Lord hath sent unto you all his servants the prophets, rising early and sending them; but ye have not hearkened, nor inclined your ear to hear. *Je.* 25: 4.

If any man will do his will, he shall know of the doctrine, whether it be of God, or whether I speak of myself. *Jn.* 7: 17.

See also

Aspiration; Desire; Longing; Yearning.

Inclusion

The Lord shut him in. *Ge.* 7: 16.

The Lord did not set his love upon you, nor choose you, because ye were more in number than any people; for ye were the fewest of all people. *De.* 7: 7.

Is Saul also among the prophets? *1 S.* 10: 11.

The soul of my lord shall be bound in the bundle of life with the Lord thy God. *1 S.* 25: 29.

The heaven and heaven of heavens cannot contain thee: how much less this house that I have builded? *1 K.* 8: 27.

Thy law is within my heart. *Ps.* 40: 8.

Peace be within thy walls, and prosperity within thy palaces. *Ps.* 122: 7.

Then shall two be in the field; the one shall be taken, and the other left. *Mat.* 24: 40.

The kingdom of God is within you. *Lu.* 17: 21.

If thou hadst known, even thou, at least in this thy day, the things which belong unto thy peace! *Lu.* 19: 42.

Why seek ye the living among the dead? *Lu.* 24: 5.

I will come again, and receive you unto myself; that where I am, there ye may be also. *Jn.* 14: 3.

The Father that dwelleth in me, he doeth the works. *Jn.* 14: 10.

Believe me that I am in the Father, and the Father in me. *Jn.* **14: 11.**

There are also many other things which Jesus did, the which, if they should be written every one, I suppose that even the world itself could not contain the books that should be written. *Jn.* **21: 25.**

When the Gentiles, which have not the law, do by nature the things contained in the law, these, having not the law, are a law unto themselves. *Ro.* **2: 14.**

It is contained in the scripture, Behold, I lay in Sion a chief corner stone. *1 Pe.* **2: 6.**

Incompleteness

Wherefore have ye not fulfilled your task in making brick both yesterday and to day, as heretofore? *Ex.* **5: 14.**

This thing is too heavy for thee; thou art not able to perform it thyself alone. *Ex.* **18: 18.**

He is turned back from following me, and hath not performed my commandments. *1 S.* **15: 11.**

Joab . . . began to number, but he finished not. *1 Ch.* **27: 24.**

Since that time even until now hath it been in building, and yet it is not finished. *Ezr.* **5: 16.**

He disappointeth the devices of the crafty, so that their hands cannot perform their enterprise. *Jb.* **5: 12.**

They imagined a mischievous device, which they are not able to perform. *Ps.* **21: 11.**

I said, O my God, take me not away in the midst of my days. *Ps.* **102: 24.**

Lest haply, after he hath laid the foundation, and is not able to finish it, all that behold it begin to mock him. *Lu.* **14: 29.**

This man began to build, and was not able to finish. *Lu.* **14: 30.**

My Father worketh hitherto, and I work. *Jn.* **5: 17.**

See also

Blemish; Defect; Failure; Fault; Imperfection; Lack; Want; Weakness.

Inconsistency

Why beholdest thou the mote that is in thy brother's eye, but considerest not the beam that is in thine own eye? *Mat.* **7: 3.**

Why call ye me, Lord, Lord, and do not the things which I say? *Lu.* **6: 46.**

Wherein thou judgest another, thou condemnest thyself; for thou that judgest doest the same things. *Ro.* **2: 1.**

Thou therefore which teachest another, teachest thou not thyself? thou that preachest a man should not steal, dost thou steal? *Ro.* **2: 21.**

Thou that makest thy boast of the law, through breaking the law dishonourest thou God? *Ro.* **2: 23.**

They profess that they know God; but in works they deny him. *Tit.* **1: 16.**

Out of the same mouth proceedeth blessing and cursing. *Ja.* **3: 10.**

See also

Duplicity; Hypocrisy; Treachery.

Inconstancy

Unstable as water, thou shalt not excel. *Ge.* **49: 4.**

My friends scorn me. *Jb.* **16: 20.**

All my inward friends abhorred me: and they whom I loved are turned against me. *Jb.* **19: 19.**

I was a reproach . . . among my neighbours, and a fear to mine acquaintance. *Ps.* **31: 11.**

Lover and friend hast thou put far from me, and mine acquaintance into darkness. *Ps.* **88: 18.**

There was no man that would know me. *Ps.* **142: 4.**

They sinned against me: therefore will I change their glory into shame. *Ho.* **4: 7.**

They all forsook him, and fled. *Mk.* **14: 50.**

A reed shaken with the wind? *Lu.* **7: 24.**

We . . . have no certain dwellingplace. *1 Co.* **4: 11.**

Carried about with every wind of doctrine. *Ep.* **4: 14.**

Demas hath forsaken me. *2 Ti.* **4: 10.**

Doth a fountain send forth at the same place sweet water and bitter? *Ja.* **3: 11.**

They cannot cease from sin; beguiling unstable souls. *2 Pe.* **2: 14.**

Unlearned and unstable. *2 Pe.* **3: 16.**

See also

Alteration; Change; Fickleness; Impermanence.

Incorruption

They . . . changed the glory of the uncorruptible God into an image made like to corruptible man, and to birds, and fourfooted beasts, and creeping things. *Ro.* **1: 22, 23.**

They do it to obtain a corruptible crown; but we an incorruptible. *1 Co.* **9: 25.**

The resurrection of the dead . . . is sown in corruption; it is raised in incorruption. *1 Co.* **15: 42.**

Neither doth corruption inherit incorruption. *1 Co.* **15: 50.**

The trumpet shall sound, and the dead shall be raised incorruptible. *1 Co.* **15: 52.**

This corruptible must put on incorruption, and this mortal must put on immortality. *1 Co.* **15: 53.**

In doctrine shewing uncorruptness, gravity, sincerity. *Tit.* **2: 7.**

An inheritance incorruptible, and undefiled, and that fadeth not away, reserved in heaven for you. *1 Pe.* **1: 4.**

Being born again, not of corruptible seed, but of incorruptible, by the word of God. *1 Pe.* **1: 23.**

See also

Cleanness; Innocence; Piety; Purity; Righteousness; Saint; Sanctification.

Increase

I . . . will multiply thee exceedingly. *Ge.* **17: 2.**

If riches increase, set not your heart upon them. *Ps.* **62: 10.**

When all the workers of iniquity do flourish; it is that they shall be destroyed for ever. *Ps.* **92: 7.**

Those that be planted in the house of the Lord shall flourish in the courts of our God. *Ps.* **92: 13.**

There is that scattereth, and yet increaseth. *Pr.* **11: 24.**

With the increase of his lips shall he be filled. *Pr.* 18: 20.

In much wisdom is much grief: and he that increaseth knowledge increaseth sorrow. *Ec.* 1: 18.

Ye . . . have multiplied your words against me. *Eze.* 35: 13.

She did not know that I . . . multiplied her silver and gold. *Ho.* 2: 8.

Whosoever hath, to him shall be given. *Lu.* 8: 18.

He must increase, but I must decrease. *Jn.* 3: 30.

I have planted, Apollos watered; but God gave the increase. *1 Co.* 3: 6.

Christ: From whom the whole body fitly joined together and compacted by that which every joint supplieth, according to the effectual working in the measure of every part, maketh increase of the body unto the edifying of itself in love. *Ep.* 4: 15, 16.

Fruitful in every good work, and increasing in the knowledge of God. *Col.* 1: 10.

Add to your faith virtue. *2 Pe.* 1: 5.

Mercy unto you, and peace, and love, be multiplied. *Jude* 1: 2.

See also

Addition; Development; Education; Enlargement; Evolution; Expansion; Gain; Growth; Harvest; Multiplication; Progress; Yield.

Indebtedness

The borrower is servant to the lender. *Pr.* 22: 7.

We also forgive every one that is indebted to us. *Lu.* 11: 4.

We receive the due reward of our deeds. *Lu.* 23: 41.

I am debtor both to the Greeks and to the Barbarians; both to the wise, and to the unwise. *Ro.* 1: 14.

To him that worketh is the reward not reckoned of grace, but of debt. *Ro.* 4: 4.

Render therefore to all their dues. *Ro.* 13: 7.

Who maketh thee to differ from another? and what hast thou that thou didst not receive? *1 Co.* 4: 7.

I testify again to every man that is circumcised, that he is a debtor to do the whole law. *Ga.* 5: 3.

See also

Debt; Duty; Loan; Obligation; Trespass.

Indecision

How long halt ye between two opinions? *1 K.* 18: 21.

Lord, suffer me first to go and bury my father. *Mat.* 8: 21.

Lord, I will follow thee; but let me first go bid them farewell, which are at home at my house. *Lu.* 9: 61.

No man, having put his hand to the plow, and looking back, is fit for the kingdom of God. *Lu.* 9: 62.

He that wavereth is like a wave of the sea driven with the wind and tossed. *Ja.* 1: 6.

A double minded man is unstable in all his ways. *Ja.* 1: 8.

Purify your hearts, ye double minded. *Ja.* 4: 8.

See also

Doubt; Half-Heartedness; Hesitancy; In-

difference; Loyalty, Divided; Reluctance; Scepticism; Uncertainty.

Independence

Proclaim liberty throughout all the land unto all the inhabitants thereof. *Le.* 25: 10.

He looseth the bond of kings. *Jb.* 12: 18.

I will walk at liberty. *Ps.* 119: 45.

They have set up kings, but not by me: they have made princes, and I knew it not. *Ho.* 8:4.

Trust ye not in a friend, put ye not confidence in a guide. *Mi.* 7: 5.

If the Son therefore shall make you free, ye shall be free indeed. *Jn.* 8: 36.

The glorious liberty of the children of God. *Ro.* 8: 21.

So have I strived to preach the gospel, not where Christ was named, lest I should build upon another man's foundation. *Ro.* 15: 20.

Ye are bought with a price; be not ye the servants of men. *1 Co.* 7: 23.

Take heed lest by any means this liberty of yours become a stumblingblock to them that are weak. *1 Co.* 8: 9.

Labouring night and day, because we would not be chargeable unto any of you, we preached unto you the gospel of God. *1 Th.* 2: 9.

See also

Democracy; Emancipation; Freedom; Liberty.

Indifference

Shall your brethren go to war, and shall ye sit here? *Nu.* 32: 6.

How long are ye slack to go to possess the land, which the Lord God of your fathers hath given you? *Jos.* 18: 3.

They came not to the help of the Lord, to the help of the Lord against the mighty. *Ju.* 5: 23.

See that ye hasten the matter. Howbeit the Levites hastened it not. *2 Ch.* 24: 5.

Their nobles put not their necks to the work of their Lord. *Ne.* 3: 5.

Harden not your heart, . . . as in the day of temptation in the wilderness. *Ps.* 95: 8.

Our soul is exceedingly filled with the scorning of those that are at ease, and with the contempt of the proud. *Ps.* 123: 4.

They made me the keeper of the vineyard; but mine own vineyard have I not kept. *S. of S.* 1: 6.

They regard not the work of the Lord, neither consider the operation of his hands. *Is.* 5: 12.

Rise up, ye women that are at ease; hear my voice, ye careless daughters. *Is.* 32: 9.

Yea, the stork in the heaven knoweth her appointed times; and the turtle and the crane and the swallow observe the time of their coming; but my people know not the judgment of the Lord. *Je.* 8: 7.

O thou seer, go, flee thee away into the land of Judah, and there eat bread, and prophesy there. *Am.* 7: 12.

In the day that thou stoodest on the other side, . . . and foreigners entered into his gates, . . . even thou wast as one of them. *Ob.* 1: 11.

Offer it now unto thy governor; will he be pleased with thee, or accept thy person? *Mal.* 1: 8.

They made light of it, and went their ways, one to his farm, another to his merchandise. *Mat.* 22: 5.

Because iniquity shall abound, the love of many shall wax cold. *Mat.* 24: 12.

He took water, and washed his hands before the multitude. *Mat.* 27: 24.

They considered not the miracle of the loaves: for their heart was hardened. *Mk.* 6: 52.

Lest coming suddenly he find you sleeping. *Mk.* 13: 36.

There was in a city a judge, which feared not God, neither regarded man. *Lu.* 18: 2.

Gallio cared for none of those things. *Ac.* 18: 17.

Awake thou that sleepest, and arise from the dead, and Christ shall give you light. *Ep.* 5: 14.

Thou hast a name that thou livest, and art dead. *Re.* 3: 1.

See also

Apathy; Carelessness; Christ, Indifference toward; Half-heartedness; Heedlessness; Loyalty, Divided; Lukewarmness; Neglect; Stoicism; Worldliness.

Indignation

How long will ye vex my soul, and break me in pieces with words? *Jb.* 19: 2.

Cast abroad the rage of thy wrath: and behold every one that is proud, and abase him. *Jb.* 40: 11.

Pour out thine indignation upon them, and let thy wrathful anger take hold of them. *Ps.* 69: 24.

How long, O Lord? wilt thou hide thyself for ever? shall thy wrath burn like fire? *Ps.* 89: 46.

I have eaten ashes like bread, . . . Because of thine indignation and thy wrath. *Ps.* 102: 9, 10.

The fool rageth, and is confident. *Pr.* 14: 16.

At his wrath the earth shall tremble, and the nations shall not be able to abide his indignation. *Je.* 10: 10.

Who can stand before his indignation? and who can abide in the fierceness of his anger? *Na.* 1: 6.

See also

Anger; Christ, Wrath of; Displeasure; God, Anger of; God, Wrath of; Passion; Rage; Resentment; Vexation; Wrath.

Individual

The Lord shall count, when he writeth up the people, that this man was born there. *Ps.* 87: 6.

Ye shall be gathered one by one, O ye children of Israel. *Is.* 27: 12.

Master, the multitude throng thee and press thee, and sayest thou, Who touched me? *Lu.* 8: 45.

Are not five sparrows sold for two farthings, and not one of them is forgotten before God? . . . Ye are of more value than many sparrows. *Lu.* 12: 6, 7.

If he lose one of them. *Lu.* 15: 4.

Joy shall be in heaven over one sinner. *Lu.* 15: 7.

To day shalt thou be with me. *Lu.* 23: 43.

I seek not yours, but you. 2 *Co.* 12: 14.

See also

Person.

Indolence

He said, Ye are idle, ye are idle: therefore ye say, Let us go and do sacrifice to the Lord. *Ex.* 5: 17.

Be not slothful to go, and to enter to possess the land. *Ju.* 18: 9.

The Lord will perfect that which concerneth me. *Ps.* 138: 8.

He that sleepeth in harvest is a son that causeth shame. *Pr.* 10: 5.

By much slothfulness the building decayeth; and through idleness of the hands the house droppeth through. *Ec.* 10: 18.

Pride, fulness of bread, and abundance of idleness was in her. *Eze.* 16: 49.

Why stand ye here all the day idle? *Mat.* 20: 6.

See also

Idleness; Inertia; Laziness; Sloth.

Indulgence

We sat by the flesh pots, and . . . we did eat bread to the full. *Ex.* 16: 3.

This our son is . . . a glutton, and a drunkard. *De.* 21: 20.

In those days there was no king in Israel, but every man did that which was right in his own eyes. *Ju.* 17: 6.

Deal gently for my sake with the young man. 2 *S.* 18: 5.

He that laboureth laboureth for himself; for his mouth craveth it of him. *Pr.* 16: 26.

Put a knife to thy throat, if thou be a man given to appetite. *Pr.* 23: 2.

When shall I awake? I will seek it yet again. *Pr.* 23: 35.

To morrow shall be as this day, and much more abundant. *Is.* 56: 12.

He hath filled his belly with my delicates. *Je.* 51: 34.

Let us walk honestly, as in the day; not in rioting and drunkenness, not in chambering and wantonness. *Ro.* 13: 13.

They that are such serve not our Lord Jesus Christ, but their own belly. *Ro.* 16: 18.

Use not liberty for an occasion to the flesh. *Ga.* 5: 13.

Be not drunk with wine, wherein is excess: but be filled with the Spirit. *Ep.* 5: 18.

Whose God is their belly, and whose glory is in their shame. *Ph.* 3: 19.

The satisfying of the flesh. *Col.* 2: 23.

Ye have lived in pleasure on the earth, and been wanton. *Ja.* 5: 5.

See also

Dissipation; Drunkenness; Flesh; Gluttony; Intoxication; Lust; Passion; Tolerance.

Industry

Solomon seeing the young man that he was industrious, he made him ruler. *1 K.* 11: 28.

Go to the ant, thou sluggard; consider her ways, and be wise. *Pr.* 6: 6.

The hand of the diligent maketh rich. *Pr.* 10: 4.

He that gathereth in summer is a wise son: but he that sleepeth in harvest is a son that causeth shame. *Pr.* 10: 5.

He that tilleth his land shall be satisfied with bread. *Pr.* 12: 11.

The soul of the diligent shall be made fat. *Pr.* 13: 4.

Wealth gotten by vanity shall be diminished: but he that gathereth by labour shall increase. *Pr.* 13: 11.

In all labour there is profit. *Pr.* 14: 23.

Love not sleep, lest thou come to poverty: open thine eyes, and thou shalt be 'satisfied with bread. *Pr.* 20: 13.

The thoughts of the diligent tend only to plenteousness. *Pr.* 21: 5.

Seest thou a man diligent in his business? he shall stand before kings. *Pr.* 22: 29.

Be thou diligent to know the state of thy flocks, and look well to thy herds. *Pr.* 27: 23.

Not slothful in business; fervent in spirit; serving the Lord. *Ro.* 12: 11.

Let him labour, working with his hands the thing which is good. *Ep.* 4: 28.

A workman that needeth not to be ashamed. *2 Ti.* 2: 15.

I know thy works, and thy labour, and thy patience. *Re.* 2: 2.

See also

Activity; Attention; Business; Diligence; Earnestness; Heed; Occupation; Perseverance; Profession; Trade; Zeal.

Inequality

As his part is that goeth down to the battle, so shall his part be that tarrieth by the stuff: they shall part alike. *1 S.* 30: 24.

Let me not, I pray you, accept any man's person, neither let me give flattering titles unto man. *Jb.* 32: 21.

The legs of the lame are not equal. *Pr.* 26: 7.

To whom then will ye liken me, or shall I be equal? saith the Holy One. *Is.* 40: 25.

One basket had very good figs, even like the figs that are first ripe: and the other basket had very naughty figs, which could not be eaten, they were so bad. *Je.* 24: 2.

Ye say, The way of the Lord is not equal. Hear now, O house of Israel; Is not my way equal? are not your ways unequal? *Eze.* 18: 25.

The children of thy people say, The way of the Lord is not equal: but as for them, their way is not equal. *Eze.* 33: 17.

Neither do men put new wine into old bottles: else the bottles break, and the wine runneth out, and the bottles perish. *Mat.* 9: 17.

They supposed that they should have received more; and they likewise received every man a penny. *Mat.* 20: 10.

Hath not the potter power over the clay, of the same lump to make one vessel unto honour, and another unto dishonour? *Ro.* 9: 21.

God hath tempered the body together, having given more abundant honour to that part which lacked. *1 Co.* 12: 24.

Be ye not unequally yoked together with unbelievers. *2 Co.* 6: 14.

Masters, give unto your servants that which is just and equal; knowing that ye also have a Master in heaven. *Col.* 4: 1.

Inertia

Are ye still? be not slothful to go, and to enter to possess the land. *Ju.* 18: 9.

How long wilt thou sleep, O sluggard? *Pr.* 6: 9.

Yet a little sleep, a little slumber, a little folding of the hands to sleep: So shall thy poverty come as one that travelleth, and thy want as an armed man. *Pr.* 6: 10, 11.

He that sleepeth in harvest is a son that causeth shame. *Pr.* 10: 5.

As vinegar to the teeth, and as smoke to the eyes, so is the sluggard to them that send him. *Pr.* 10: 26.

The slothful man roasteth not that which he took in hunting. *Pr.* 12: 27.

A slothful man hideth his hand in his bosom, and will not so much as bring it to his mouth again. *Pr.* 19: 24.

Love not sleep, lest thou come to poverty. *Pr.* 20: 13.

The desire of the slothful killeth him; for his hands refuse to labour. *Pr.* 21: 25.

Drowsiness shall clothe a man with rags. *Pr.* 23: 21.

The sluggard is wiser in his own conceit than seven men that can render a reason. *Pr.* 26: 16.

I have been still, and refrained myself. *Is.* 42: 14.

His watchmen are blind: they are all ignorant, they are all dumb dogs, they cannot bark; sleeping, lying down, loving to slumber. *Is.* 56: 10.

Thy shepherds slumber, O king. *Na.* 3: 18.

They bind heavy burdens and grievous to be borne, and lay them on men's shoulders; but they themselves will not move them with one of their fingers. *Mat.* 23: 4.

I was afraid, and went and hid thy talent in the earth. *Mat.* 25: 25.

See also

Idleness; Indolence; Laziness; Sloth.

Inevitableness

We must needs die, and are as water spilt on the ground, which cannot be gathered up again. *2 S.* 14: 14.

It must needs be that offences come; but woe to that man by whom the offence cometh! *Mat.* 18: 7.

When ye shall hear of wars and rumours of wars, be ye not troubled: for such things must needs be; but the end shall not be yet. *Mk.* 13: 7.

I say unto you, that this that is written must yet be accomplished in me. *Lk.* 22: 37.

The Son of man must be delivered into the hands of sinful man, and be crucified, and the third day rise again. *Lu.* 24: 7.

He must increase, but I must decrease. *Jn.* 3: 30.

Men and brethren, this scripture must needs have been fulfilled. *Ac.* 1: 16.

Christ must needs have suffered. *Ac.* 17: 3.

Necessity is laid upon me. *1 Co.* 9: 16.

He must reign, till he hath put all enemies under his feet. *1 Co.* 15: 25.

We must all appear before the judgment seat of Christ. *2 Co.* 5: 10.

If I must needs glory I will glory of the things which concern mine infirmities. *2 Co.* 11: 30.

The Revelation of Jesus Christ, which God gave unto him, to shew unto his servants things which must shortly come to pass. *Re.* 1: 1.

The Lord God of the holy prophets sent his angel to shew unto his servants the things which must shortly be done. *Re.* 22: 6.

Infallibility

No doubt but ye are the people, and wisdom shall die with you. *Jb.* **12: 2.**

Upon this rock I will build my church; and the gates of hell shall not prevail against it. *Mat.* **16: 18.**

Ye do err, not knowing the scriptures. *Mat.* **22: 29.**

To whom also he shewed himself alive after his passion by many infallible proofs. *Ac.* **1: 3.**

The house of God . . . is the church of the living God, the pillar and ground of the truth. *1 Ti.* **3: 15.**

All scripture is given by inspiration of God, and is profitable for doctrine, for reproof, for correction, for instruction in righteousness. *2 Ti.* **3: 16.**

God . . . cannot lie. *Tit.* **1: 2.**

See also

Certainty; God, Certainty of; Inspiration; Truth.

Infant

He was a goodly child. *Ex.* **2: 2.**

Thy sons and thy daughters shall be given unto another people, and thine eyes shall look, and fail with longing for them all the day long. *De.* **28: 32.**

Thy seed shall be great, and thine offspring as the grass of the earth. *Jb.* **5: 25.**

That our sons may be as plants grown up in their youth; that our daughters may be as corner stones. *Ps.* **144: 12.**

O that thou wert as my brother, that sucked the breasts of my mother! *S. of S.* **8: 1.**

Thy sons shall come from far, and thy daughters shall be nursed at thy side. *Is.* **60: 4.**

They shall fall by the sword: their infants shall be dashed in pieces. *Ho.* **13: 16.**

Whosoever shall give to drink unto one of these little ones a cup of cold water only in the name of a disciple, verily I say unto you, he shall in no wise lose his reward. *Mat.* **10: 42.**

Except ye be converted, and become as little children, ye shall not enter into the kingdom of heaven. *Mat.* **18: 3.**

Take heed that ye despise not one of these little ones; for I say unto you, That in heaven their angels do always behold the face of my Father which is in heaven. *Mat.* **18: 10.**

They came with haste, and found Mary and Joseph, and the babe lying in a manger. *Lu.* **2: 16.**

When I was a child, I spake as a child, I understood as a child, I thought as a child. *1 Co.* **13: 11.**

We were gentle among you, even as a nurse cherisheth her children. *1 Th.* **2: 7.**

See also

Babe; Birth; Child; Childhood; Childlikeness.

Inferiority

I am not worthy of the least of all the mercies. *Ge.* **32: 10.**

I am the least in my father's house. *Ju.* **6: 15.**

I have understanding as well as you; I am not inferior to you. *Jb.* **12: 3.**

He shall save the humble person. *Jb.* **22: 29.**

Lord, thou hast heard the desire of the humble. *Ps.* **10: 17.**

My soul shall make her boast in the Lord: the humble shall hear thereof, and be glad. *Ps.* **34: 2.**

The evil bow before the good. *Pr.* **14: 19.**

Better is it to be of an humble spirit with the lowly, than to divide the spoil with the proud. *Pr.* **16: 19.**

Why callest thou me good? there is none good but one, that is, God. *Mat.* **19: 17.**

There cometh one mightier than I after me, the latchet of whose shoes I am not worthy to stoop down and unloose. *Mk.* **1: 7.**

I . . . am no more worthy to be called thy son. *Lu.* **15: 21.**

He must increase, but I must decrease. *Jn.* **3: 30.**

Base things of the world, and things which are despised, hath God chosen, yea, and things which are not, to bring to nought things that are. *1 Co.* **1: 28.**

Though I have the gift of prophecy . . . I am nothing. *1 Co.* **13: 2.**

I am the least of the apostles, that am not meet to be called an apostle. *1 Co.* **15: 9.**

Unto me, who am less than the least of all the saints, is this grace given. *Eph.* **3: 8.**

Thou madest him a little lower than the angels. *He.* **2: 7.**

See also

Humility; Superiority.

Infidel

There must be also heresies among you, that they which are approved may be made manifest among you. *1 Co.* **11: 19.**

What part hath he that believeth with an infidel? *2 Co.* **6: 15.**

Doctrines of devils. *1 Ti.* **4: 1.**

If any provide not for his own, and specially for those of his own house, he hath denied the faith, and is worse than an infidel. *1 Ti.* **5: 8.**

The time will come when they will not endure sound doctrine. *2 Ti.* **4: 3.**

A man that is an heretick after the first and second admonition reject. *Tit.* **3: 10.**

There shall be false teachers among you, who privily shall bring in damnable heresies, even denying the Lord that bought them. *2 Pe.* **2: 1.**

See also

Agnosticism; Atheism; Christ, Denial of; Christ, Doubt of; Denial; Doubt; Faithlessness; God, Denial of; Godlessness; Heathen; Heresy; Pagan; Unbelief.

Infinity

Is not thy wickedness great? and thine iniquities infinite? *Jb.* **22: 5.**

The Lord shall endure for ever. *Ps.* **9: 7.**

At thy right hand there are pleasures for evermore. *Ps.* **16: 11.**

The Lord shall preserve thy going out and thy coming in from this time forth, and even for evermore. *Ps.* **121: 8.**

Thine is the kingdom, and the power, and the glory, for ever. Amen. *Mat.* **6: 13.**

In the world to come life everlasting. *Lu.* **18: 30.**

In hope of eternal life, which God, that cannot lie, promised before the world began. *Tit.* **1: 2.**

See also

Eternity; God, the Infinite; Immensity; Immortality; Life, the Eternal.

Infirmity

The spirit of a man will sustain his infirmity. *Pr.* 18: 14.

Himself took our infirmities, and bare our sicknesses. *Mat.* 8: 17.

There was a woman which had a spirit of infirmity eighteen years, and was bowed together, and could in no wise lift up herself. *Lu.* 13: 11.

The Spirit also helpeth our infirmities. *Ro.* 8: 26.

We then that are strong ought to bear the infirmities of the weak. *Ro.* 15: 1.

If I must needs glory, I will glory of the things which concern mine infirmities. *2 Co.* 11: 30.

Lest I should be exalted above measure, . . . there was given to me a thorn in the flesh. *2 Co.* 12: 7.

See also

Ailment; Disease; Disorder; Faintness; Faith-Healing; Feebleness; Frailty; Healing; Illness; Sickness; Weakness.

Influence

What man is there that is fearful and faint-hearted? let him go and return unto his house, lest his brethren's heart faint as well as his heart. *De.* 20: 8.

Canst thou bind the sweet influences of the Pleiades? *Jb.* 38: 31.

There shall be, like people, like priest. *Ho.* 4: 9.

Let your light so shine before men, that they may see your good works, and glorify your Father which is in heaven. *Mat.* 5: 16.

The kingdom of heaven is like unto leaven, which a woman took, and hid in three measures of meal, till the whole was leavened. *Mat.* 13: 33.

Take heed, beware of the leaven of the Pharisees. *Mk.* 8: 15.

He was a burning and a shining light. *Jn.* 5: 35.

Then went in also that other disciple. *Jn.* 20: 8.

They brought forth the sick into the streets, and laid them on beds and couches, that at the least the shadow of Peter passing by might overshadow some of them. *Ac.* 5: 15.

None of us liveth to himself, and no man dieth to himself. *Ro.* 14: 7.

Know ye not that a little leaven leaveneth the whole lump? *1 Co.* 5: 6.

That ye may be blameless and harmless, the sons of God, without rebuke, in the midst of a crooked and perverse nation, among whom ye shine as lights in the world. *Ph.* 2: 15.

Those things, which ye have both learned, and received, and heard, and seen in me, do. *Ph.* 4: 9.

Be thou an example of the believers, in word, in conversation, in charity, in spirit, in faith, in purity. *1 Ti.* 4: 12.

See also

Authority; Example; Leaven.

Ingratitude

Yet did not the chief butler remember Joseph, but forgat him. *Ge.* 40: 23.

Beware lest thou forget the Lord, which brought thee forth out of the land of Egypt. *De.* 6: 12.

Do ye thus requite the Lord, O foolish people and unwise? is not he thy father that hath bought thee? *De.* 32: 6.

He hath requited me evil for good. *1 S.* 25: 21.

They were disobedient, and rebelled against thee, and cast thy law behind their backs, and slew thy prophets which testified against them to turn them to thee. *Ne.* 9: 26.

Whoso rewardeth evil for good, evil shall not depart from his house. *Pr.* 17: 13.

Now there was found in it a poor wise man, and he by his wisdom delivered the city; yet no man remembered that same poor man. *Ec.* 9: 15.

Thou hast forgotten the God of thy salvation, and hast not been mindful of the rock of thy strength. *Is.* 17: 10.

Though I have redeemed them, yet they have spoken lies against me. *Ho.* 7: 13.

Israel hath forgotten his Maker. *Ho.* 8: 14.

What thank have ye? *Lu.* 6: 32.

Were there not ten cleansed? but where are the nine? *Lu.* 17: 17.

There are not found that returned to give glory to God, save this stranger. *Lu.* 17: 18.

Many good works have I shewed you from my Father; for which of those works do ye stone me? *Jn.* 10: 32.

When they knew God, they glorified him not as God, neither were thankful. *Ro.* 1: 21.

See also

Carelessness; Forgetfulness; Heedlessness; Thanklessness.

Inhabitant

Proclaim liberty throughout all the land unto all the inhabitants thereof. *Le.* 25: 10.

Ye shall rejoice . . . within your gates. *De.* 12: 12.

Let all the inhabitants of the world stand in awe of him. *Ps.* 33: 8.

Blessed are they that dwell in thy house. *Ps.* 84: 4.

He blesseth the habitation of the just. *Pr.* 3: 33.

The wicked shall not inhabit the earth. *Pr.* 10: 30.

My people shall dwell in a peaceable habitation, and in sure dwellings. *Is.* 32: 18.

They shall build houses and inhabit them. *Is.* 65: 21.

Build ye houses, and dwell in them; and plant gardens, and eat the fruit of them. *Je.* 29: 5.

I will cause them to dwell safely. *Je.* 32: 37.

I will also cause you to dwell in the cities. *Eze.* 36: 33.

They shall build the waste cities, and inhabit them. *Am.* 9: 14.

Into whatsoever house ye enter, first say, Peace be to this house. *Lu.* 10: 5.

See also

Citizenship; Country; Dwelling.

Inheritance

I have a goodly heritage. *Ps.* 16: 6.

The meek shall inherit the earth. *Ps.* **37:** **11.**

Thou hast given me the heritage of those that fear thy name. *Ps.* **61: 5.**

Thy testimonies have I taken as an heritage for ever. *Ps.* **119: 111.**

All things are yours; . . . ye are Christ's; and Christ is God's. *1 Co.* **3: 21, 23.**

Our inheritance. *Ep.* **1: 14.**

The riches of the glory of his inheritance in the saints. *Ep.* **1: 18.**

The inheritance of the saints in light. *Col.* **1: 12.**

Of the Lord ye shall receive the reward of the inheritance. *Col.* **3: 24.**

Hath not God chosen the poor of this world rich in faith, and heirs of the kingdom? *Ja.* **2: 5.**

An inheritance incorruptible, and undefiled, and that fadeth not away. *1 Pe.* **1: 4.**

He that overcometh shall inherit all things. *Re.* **21: 7.**

See also

Ancestor; Bequest; Birthright; Descent; Father; Genealogy; Generation; Heir; Heredity; Heritage; Legacy.

Inhumanity

Instruments of cruelty are in their habitations. *Ge.* **49: 5.**

Wherefore then do ye harden your hearts, as the Egyptians and Pharaoh hardened their hearts? *1 S.* **6: 6.**

They turn the needy out of the way: the poor of the earth hide themselves together. *Jb.* **24: 4.**

The merciful man doeth good to his own soul: but he that is cruel troubleth his own flesh. *Pr.* **11: 17.**

Harden not your hearts. *He.* **3: 8.**

Others were tortured, not accepting deliverance. *He.* **11: 35.**

Others had trial of cruel mockings and scourgings. *He.* **11: 36.**

See also

Bondage; Cruelty; Hardness; Harshness; Oppression; Persecution; Rod; Severity; Tyranny.

Iniquity

I hear of your evil dealings by all this people. *1 S.* **2: 23.**

What evil thing is this that ye do, and profane the sabbath day. *Ne.* **13: 17.**

Let not wickedness dwell in thy tabernacles. *Jb.* **11: 14.**

I have hated the congregation of the evil doers; and I will not sit with the wicked. *Ps.* **26: 5.**

The workers of iniquity . . . are cast down, and shall not be able to rise. *Ps.* **36: 12.**

Fret not thyself because of evil-doers. *Ps.* **37: 1.**

Wash me thoroughly from mine iniquity, and cleanse me from my sin. *Ps.* **51: 2.**

My sin is ever before me. *Ps.* **51: 3.**

Add iniquity unto their iniquity: and let them not come into thy righteousness. *Ps.* **69: 27.**

Ye that love the Lord, hate evil. *Ps.* **97: 10.**

A righteous man falling down before the wicked is as a troubled fountain, and a corrupt spring. *Pr.* **25: 26.**

Wash you, make you clean; put away the evil of your doings from before mine eyes. *Is.* **1: 16.**

Hate the evil, and love the good. *Am.* **5: 15.**

I testify of it, that the works thereof are evil. *Jn.* **7: 7.**

The wages of sin is death. *Ro.* **6: 23.**

Charity . . . Rejoiceth not in iniquity, but rejoiceth in the truth. *1 Co.* **13: 4, 6.**

See also

Crime; Error; Evil; Fault; Guile; Injustice; Sin; Sinner; Transgression; Trespass; Unrighteousness; Wickedness; Wrong.

Initiation

Oh that God would speak, and open his lips against thee; And that he would shew thee the secrets of wisdom. *Jb.* **11: 5, 6.**

God, thy God, hath anointed thee with the oil of gladness above thy fellows. *Ps.* **45: 7.**

He revealeth the deep and secret things: he knoweth what is in the darkness, and the light dwelleth with him. *Da.* **2: 22.**

There is a God in heaven that revealeth secrets. *Da.* **2: 28.**

The Lord God . . . revealeth his secret unto his servants the prophets. *Am.* **3: 7.**

Unto you it is given to know the mysteries of the kingdom of God. *Lu.* **8: 10.**

According to the revelation of the mystery, which was kept secret since the world began. *Ro.* **16: 25.**

Stewards of the mysteries of God. *1 Co.* **4: 1.**

Though I have the gift of prophecy, and understand all mysteries, and all knowledge, . . . and have not charity, I am nothing. *1 Co.* **13: 2.**

In the spirit he speaketh mysteries. *1 Co.* **14: 2.**

By revelation he made known unto me the mystery. *Ep.* **3: 3.**

See also

Consecration; Introduction.

Injury

Men groan from out of the city, and the soul of the wounded crieth out. *Jb.* **24: 12.**

Who hath wounds without cause? . . . They that tarry long at the wine. *Pr.* **23: 29, 30.**

They shall not hurt nor destroy in all my holy mountain. *Is.* **11: 9.**

He was wounded for our transgressions. *Is.* **53: 5.**

I will heal thee of thy wounds. *Je.* **30: 17.**

My God hath sent his angel, and hath shut the lions' mouths, that they have not hurt me. *Da.* **6: 22.**

A certain man . . . fell among thieves, which stripped him of his raiment, and wounded him. *Lu.* **10: 30.**

A certain Samaritan . . . went to him, and bound up his wounds. *Lu.* **10: 33, 34.**

Of the Jews five times received I forty stripes save one. *2 Co.* **11: 24.**

They were stoned, they were sawn asunder, were tempted, were slain with the sword. *He.* **11: 37.**

See also

Abuse; Bane; Bruise; Evil; Harm; Hurt; Injustice; Loss; Mischief; Misfortune; Wound.

Injustice

Thou shalt not pervert the judgment of

the stranger, nor of the fatherless. *De.* 24: 17.

Cursed be he that perverteth the judgment of the stranger, fatherless, and widow. *De.* 27: 19.

They gather themselves together against the soul of the righteous, and condemn the innocent blood. *Ps.* 94: 21.

He looked for judgment, but behold oppression; for righteousness, but behold a cry. *Is.* 5: 7.

Woe unto them that decree unrighteous decrees, and that write grievousness which they have prescribed. *Is.* 10: 1.

Woe unto them that . . . turn aside the needy from judgment. *Is.* 10: 1, 2.

Hear this, I pray you, ye . . . that abhor judgment, and pervert all equity. *Mi.* 3: 9.

The judge asketh. for a reward. *Mi.* 7: 3.

If ye had known what this meaneth, I will have mercy, and not sacrifice, ye would not have condemned the guiltless. *Mat.* 12: 7.

Recompense to no man evil for evil. *Ro.* 12: 17.

See also

Faithlessness; Fraud; Hardship; Iniquity; Injury; Unfairness; Unrighteousness; Wickedness; Wrong.

Injustice, Social

They did set over them taskmasters to afflict them with their burdens. *Ex.* 1: 11.

All their service, wherein they made them serve, was with rigour. *Ex.* 1: 14.

We have mortgaged our lands, vineyards, and houses, that we might buy corn, because of the dearth. *Ne.* 5: 3.

We have borrowed money for the king's tribute, and that upon our lands and vineyards. *Ne.* 5: 4.

We bring into bondage our sons and our daughters to be servants. *Ne.* 5: 5.

Some of our daughters are brought unto bondage already: neither is it in our power to redeem them, for other men have our lands and vineyards. *Ne.* 5: 5.

Rob not the poor, because he is poor. *Pr.* 22: 22.

To turn aside the needy from judgment, and to take away the right from the poor of my people, that widows may be their prey, and that they may rob the fatherless: *Is.* 10: 2.

Truth is fallen in the street, and equity cannot enter. *Is.* 59: 14.

The city full of perverseness. *Eze.* 9: 9.

Forasmuch therefore as your treading is upon the poor, . . . ye have built houses of hewn stone, but ye shall not dwell in them. *Am.* 5: 11.

They afflict the just, they take a bribe, and they turn aside the poor in the gate from their right. *Am.* 5: 12.

That we may buy the poor for silver, and the needy for a pair of shoes. *Am.* 8: 6.

Shall I count them pure with the wicked balances? *Mi.* 6: 11.

We have toiled all the night, and have taken nothing. *Lu.* 5: 5.

There was in a city a judge, which feared not God, neither regarded man. *Lu.* 18: 2.

See also

Equality, Racial; Injury; Injustice; Unfairness.

Innocence

The innocent and the righteous slay thou not. *Ex.* 23: 7.

Who ever perished, being innocent? *Jb.* 4: 7.

I am afraid of all my sorrows, I know thou wilt not hold me innocent. *Jb.* 9: 28.

Then shalt thou lift up thy face without spot; yea, thou shalt be stedfast, and shalt not fear. *Jb.* 11: 15.

He shall deliver the island of the innocent: and it is delivered by the pureness of thine hands. *Jb.* 22: 30.

Keep back thy servant also from presumptuous sins; . . . then . . . shall I be innocent from the great transgression. *Ps.* 19: 13.

I will wash mine hands in innocency: so will I compass thine altar, O Lord. *Ps.* 26: 6.

Blessed is the man unto whom the Lord imputeth not iniquity, and in whose spirit there is no guile. *Ps.* 32: 2.

Who can say, I have made my heart clean, I am pure from my sin? *Pr.* 20: 9.

Thou art all fair, my love; there is no spot in thee. *S. of S.* 4: 7.

How long will it be ere they attain to innocency? *Ho.* 8: 5.

All the children that were in Bethlehem. *Mat.* 2: 16.

Blessed are the pure in heart: for they shall see God. *Mat.* 5: 8.

The end of the commandment is charity out of a pure heart, and of a good conscience. *1 Ti.* 1: 5.

Yet without sin. *He.* 4: 15.

To keep himself unspotted from the world. *Ja.* 1: 27.

In their mouth was found no guile: for they are without fault before the throne of God. *Re.* 14: 5.

See also

Acquittal; Blamelessness; Childlikeness; Guilelessness; Holiness; Purity; Saint; Sanctification; Simplicity; Sinlessness.

Inquiry

Take heed to thyself that . . . thou inquire not after their gods. *De.* 12: 30.

They inquired of the Lord further. *1 S.* 10: 22.

Is it not because there is no God in Israel to inquire of his word? *2 K.* 1: 16.

One thing have I desired of the Lord, that will I seek after; that I may dwell in the house of the Lord all the days of my life, to behold the beauty of the Lord, and to inquire in his temple. *Ps.* 27: 4.

They returned and inquired early after God. *Ps.* 78: 34.

Say not thou, What is the cause that the former days were better than these? for thou dost not inquire wisely concerning this. *Ec.* 7: 10.

The watchman said, The morning cometh, and also the night: if ye will inquire, inquire ye: return, come. *Is.* 21: 12.

Inquire, I pray thee, of the Lord for us. *Je.* 21: 2.

I will cut off . . . them that are turned

back from the Lord; and those that have not sought the Lord, nor inquired for him. *Zph.* **1: 3, 6.**

Asking them questions. *Lu.* **2: 46.**

See also

Christ, Quest for; Examination; God, Quest for; God, Search for; Quest; Question; Search; Seeker.

Inquisition

The judges shall make diligent inquisition. *De.* **19: 18.**

When inquisition was made of the matter, it was found out. *Es.* **2: 23.**

Thou enquirest after mine iniquity, and searchest after my sin. *Jb.* **10: 6.**

When he maketh inquisition for blood, he remembereth them. *Ps.* **9: 12.**

Examine me, O Lord, and prove me. *Ps.* **26: 2.**

They search out iniquities; they accomplish a diligent search. *Ps.* **64: 6.**

I, having examined him before you, have found no fault in this man touching those things whereof ye accuse him. *Lu.* **23: 14.**

The chief captain . . . bade that he should be examined by scourging. *Ac.* **22: 24.**

Mine answer to them that do examine me is this. *1 Co.* **9: 3.**

Insanity

Thou lovest thine enemies, and hatest thy friends. *2 S.* **19: 6.**

Folly is joy to him that is destitute of wisdom. *Pr.* **15: 21.**

The man that wandereth out of the way of understanding shall remain in the congregation of the dead. *Pr.* **21: 16.**

In the day when . . . those that look out of the windows be darkened. *Ec.* **12: 3.**

They say, He hath a devil. *Mat.* **11: 18.**

If a man walk in the night, he stumbleth, because there is no light in him. *Jn.* **11: 10.**

Their minds were blinded. *2 Co.* **3: 14.**

Having the understanding darkened. *Ep.* **4: 18.**

Comfort the feebleminded. *1 Th.* **5: 14.**

See also

Bedlam; Delusion; Devil; Madness; Sanity.

Insecurity

Surely thou didst set them in slippery places: thou castedst them down into destruction. *Ps.* **73: 18.**

Thou shalt be as he that lieth down in the midst of the sea, or as he that lieth upon the top of a mast. *Pr.* **23: 34.**

Their ways shall be unto them as slippery ways in the darkness. *Je.* **23: 12.**

The rain descended, and the floods came, and the winds blew, and beat upon that house; and it fell: and great was the fall of it. *Mat.* **7: 27.**

See also

Danger; Instability; Peril; Trial.

Insensibility

Harden not your heart. *Ps.* **95: 8.**

They have beaten me, and I felt it not. *Pr.* **23: 35.**

It hath set him on fire round about, yet he knew not; and it burned him, yet he laid it not to heart. *Is.* **42: 25.**

Thou hast stricken them, but they have not grieved; thou hast consumed them, but they have refused to receive correction: they have made their faces harder than a rock. *Je.* **5: 3.**

The heart of this people is waxed gross, and their ears are dull of hearing, and their eyes have they closed. *Ac.* **28: 27.**

Who being past feeling have given themselves over unto lasciviousness, to work all uncleanness with greediness. *Ep.* **4: 19.**

Having their conscience seared with a hot iron. *1 Ti.* **4: 2.**

See also

Blindness; Deafness; Dullness; Hardness; Impenitence; Stubbornness.

Inside

Give therefore thy servant an understanding heart. *1 K.* **3: 9.**

I have not hid thy righteousness within my heart. *Ps.* **40: 10.**

He knoweth the secrets of the heart. *Ps.* **44: 21.**

Peace be within thy walls, and prosperity within thy palaces. *Ps.* **122: 7.**

I will now say, Peace be within thee. *Ps.* **122: 8.**

A sound heart is the life of the flesh. *Pr.* **14: 30.**

I the Lord search the heart. *Je.* **17: 10.**

Cleanse first that which is within the cup and platter, that the outside of them may be clean also. *Mat.* **23: 26.**

From within, out of the heart of men, proceed evil thoughts. *Mk.* **7: 21.**

With the heart man believeth unto righteousness. *Ro.* **10: 10.**

Them which glory in appearance, and not in heart. *2 Co.* **5: 12.**

See also

Appearance; Exterior; Heart; Inside; Interior; Outside.

Insight

Give therefore thy servant an understanding heart to judge thy people, that I may discern between good and bad. *1 K.* **3: 9.**

I have given thee a wise and an understanding heart. *1 K.* **3: 12.**

Wisdom is the principal thing; therefore get wisdom: and with all thy getting get understanding. *Pr.* **4: 7.**

A wise man's heart discerneth both time and judgment. *Ec.* **8: 5.**

Your old men shall dream dreams, your young men shall see visions. *Jo.* **2: 28.**

Ye can discern the face of the sky; but can ye not discern the signs of the times? *Mat.* **16: 3.**

I was not disobedient unto the heavenly vision. *Ac.* **26: 19.**

The natural man receiveth not the things of the Spirit of God: for they are foolishness unto him: neither can he know them, because they are spiritually discerned. *1 Co.* **2: 14.**

Seeing him who is invisible. *He.* **11: 27.**

He that lacketh these things is blind. *2 Pe.* **1: 9.**

See also

Discernment; Discrimination; Judgment; Knowledge; Perception; Understanding; Vision; Wisdom.

Insincerity

The congregation of hypocrites shall be desolate. *Jb.* 15: 34.

O deliver me from the deceitful and unjust man. *Ps.* 43: 1.

An hypocrite with his mouth destroyeth his neighbour. *Pr.* 11: 9.

When ye fast, be not, as the hypocrites, of a sad countenance. *Mat.* 6: 16.

If . . . the light that is in thee be darkness, how great is that darkness. *Mat.* 6: 23.

Thou hypocrite, first cast out the beam out of thine own eye; and then shalt thou see clearly to cast out the mote out of thy brother's eye. *Mat.* 7: 5.

Let love be without dissimulation. *Ro.* 12: 9.

My little children, let us not love in word, neither in tongue; but in deed and in truth. *1 Jn.* 3: 18.

See also

Affectation; Craftiness; Deceit; Duplicity; Falsehood; Flattery; Fraud; Hypocrisy; Treachery.

Inspiration

I will be with thy mouth, and teach thee what thou shalt say. *Ex.* 4: 12.

When the spirit rested upon them, they prophesied, and did not cease. *Nu.* 11: 25.

These words, which I command thee this day, shall be in thine heart. *De.* 6: 6.

The Spirit of the Lord spake by me, and his word was in my tongue. *2 S.* 23: 2.

The word of the Lord is with him. *2 K.* 3: 12.

Yet many years didst thou forbear them, and testifiedst against them by thy spirit in thy prophets. *Ne.* 9: 30.

There is a spirit in man: and the inspiration of the Almighty giveth them understanding. *Jb.* 32: 8.

He wakeneth mine ear to hear as the learned. *Is.* 50: 4.

I have put my words in thy mouth, and I have covered thee in the shadow of mine hand. *Is.* 51: 16.

Then the Lord put forth his hand, and touched my mouth. *Je.* 1: 9.

Because ye speak this word, behold, I will make my words in thy mouth fire, and this people wood, and it shall devour them. *Je.* 5: 14.

The hand of the Lord was there upon him. *Eze.* 1: 3.

Hear the word at my mouth, and give them warning from me. *Eze.* 3: 17.

And the bones came together, bone to his bone. . . . but there was no breath in them. *Eze.* 37: 7, 8.

It shall come to pass afterward, that I will pour out my spirit upon all flesh. *Jo.* 2: 28.

Not by might, nor by power, but by my spirit, saith the Lord of hosts. *Zch.* 4: 6.

When they deliver you up, take no thought how or what ye shall speak: for it shall be given you in that same hour what ye shall speak. *Mat.* 10: 19.

Flesh and blood hath not revealed it unto thee, but my Father which is in heaven. *Mat.* 16: 17.

He saw the heavens opened, and the Spirit like a dove descending upon him. *Mk.* 1: 10.

I will give you a mouth and wisdom, which all your adversaries shall not be able to gainsay nor resist. *Lu.* 21: 15.

The wind bloweth where it listeth, and thou hearest the sound thereof, but canst not tell whence it cometh, and whither it goeth: so is every one that is born of the Spirit. *Jn.* 3: 8.

The word is nigh thee, even in thy mouth, and in thy heart: that is, the word of faith, which we preach. *Ro.* 10: 8.

Which things also we speak, not in the words which man's wisdom teacheth, but which the Holy Ghost teacheth; comparing spiritual things with spiritual. *1 Co.* 2: 13.

All these worketh that one and the selfsame Spirit, dividing to every man severally as he will. *1 Co.* 12: 11.

Be filled with the Spirit. *Ep.* 5: 18.

Let the word of Christ dwell in you richly in all wisdom. *Col.* 3: 16.

All scripture is given by inspiration of God. *2 Ti.* 3: 16.

No prophecy of the scripture is of any private interpretation. *2 Pe.* 1: 20.

The prophecy came not in old time by the will of man: but holy men of God spake as they were moved by the Holy Ghost. *2 Pe.* 1: 21.

I heard a voice from heaven saying unto me, Write, Blessed are the dead which die in the Lord from henceforth. *Re.* 14: 13.

See also

Christ, the Light; Conscience; God, the Light; Illumination; Light, the Inner; Vision.

Instability

How long halt ye between two opinions? *1 K.* 18: 21.

Meddle not with them that are given to change. *Pr.* 24: 21.

Why gaddest thou about so much to change thy way? *Je.* 2: 36.

Your goodness is as a morning cloud, and as the early dew it goeth away. *Ho.* 6: 4.

Their heart is divided. *Ho.* 10: 2.

No servant can serve two masters. *Lu.* 16: 13.

Tossed to and fro, and carried about with every wind of doctrine. *Ep.* 4: 14.

Be not carried about with divers and strange doctrines. *He.* 13: 9.

He that wavereth is like a wave of the sea driven with the wind and tossed. *Ja.* 1: 6.

A doubleminded man is unstable in all his ways. *Ja.* 1: 8.

See also

Fickleness; Insecurity; Loyalty, Divided.

Installation

Be thou for the people to God-ward. *Ex.* 18: 19.

I am the Lord that doth sanctify you. *Ex.* 31: 13.

Let the Lord . . . set a man over the congregation, Which may go out before them, and which may go in before them, and which may lead them out, and which may bring them in; that the congregation of the Lord be not as sheep which have no shepherd. *Nu.* 27: 16, 17.

Them the Lord thy God hath chosen to minister unto him. *De.* 21: 5.

See ye him whom the Lord hath chosen, that there is none like unto him among all the people? *1 S.* 10: 24.

Arise, anoint him: for this is he. *1 S.* 16: 12.

Let thy priests, O Lord God, be clothed with salvation, and let thy saints rejoice in goodness. *2 Ch.* 6: 41.

Blessed is the man whom thou choosest. *Ps.* 65: 4.

The Lord hath anointed me to preach good tidings unto the meek. *Is.* 61: 1.

I ordained thee a prophet unto the nations. *Je.* 1: 5.

I have even heard of thee, that the spirit of the gods is in thee, and that light and understanding and excellent wisdom is found in thee. *Da.* 5: 14.

I have chosen you out of the world. *Jn.* 15: 19.

God hath from the beginning chosen you to salvation through sanctification of the Spirit and belief of the truth. *1 Th.* 2: 13.

I am appointed a preacher, and an apostle. *2 Ti.* 1: 11.

See also

Consecration; Dedication; Ministration; Missionary; Ordination; Pastor; Priesthood.

Instruction

Out of heaven he made thee to hear his voice, that he might instruct thee. *De.* 4: 36.

Ask counsel, we pray thee, of God, that we may know whether our way which we go shall be prosperous. *Ju.* 18: 5.

Stand thou still a while, that I may shew thee the word of God. *1 S.* 9: 27.

One of the priests . . . taught them how they should fear the Lord. *2 K.* 17: 28.

Who is this that darkeneth counsel by words without knowledge? *Jb.* 38: 2.

His delight is in the law of the Lord. *Ps.* 1: 2.

I will bless the Lord, who hath given me counsel. *Ps.* 16: 7.

I will instruct thee and teach thee in the way which thou shalt go: I will guide thee with mine eye. *Ps.* 32: 8.

O God, thou hast taught me from my youth. *Ps.* 71: 17.

Wisdom . . . crieth in the chief place of concourse. *Pr.* 1: 20, 21.

My counsel shall stand. *Is.* 46: 10.

Though I taught them, rising up early and teaching them, yet they have not hearkened to receive instruction. *Je.* 32: 33.

He opened his mouth, and taught them, saying. *Mat.* 5: 2.

Every scribe which is instructed unto the kingdom of heaven . . . bringeth forth out of his treasure things new and old. *Mat.* 13: 52.

They shall be all taught of God. *Jn.* 6: 45.

Let us therefore follow after the things . . . wherewith one may edify another. *Ro.* 14: 19.

Whatsoever things were written aforetime were written for our learning. *Ro.* 15: 4.

Though ye have ten thousand instructors in Christ, yet have ye not many fathers: for in Christ Jesus I have begotten you through the gospel. *1 Co.* 4: 15.

He that speaketh in an unknown tongue edifieth himself; but he that prophesieth edifieth the church. *1 Co.* 14: 4.

The heir, as long as he is a child, . . . is under tutors and governors until the time appointed of the father. *Ga.* 4: 1, 2.

Everywhere and in all things I am instructed both to be full and to be hungry, both to abound and to suffer need. *Ph.* 4: 12.

Ye yourselves are taught of God to love one another. *1 Th.* 4: 9.

Study to be quiet, and to do your own business, and to work with your own hands, as we commanded you. *1 Th.* 4: 11.

See also

Admonition; Advice; Christ, the Teacher; Counsel; Education; Knowledge; Persuasion; Pupil; School; Study; Teaching; Teaching, False; Training.

Instrument

After him was Shamgar the son of Anath, which slew of the Philistines six hundred men with an ox goad. *Ju.* 3: 31.

By the three hundred men that lapped will I save thee. *Ju.* 7: 7.

David and all the house of Israel played before the Lord on all manner of instruments made of fir wood, even on harps and on psalteries, and on timbrels, and on cornets, and on cymbals. *2 S.* 6: 5.

Sing unto him with the psaltery. *Ps.* 33: 2.

Awake, psaltery and harp. *Ps.* 57: 8.

Take a psalm, and bring hither the timbrel the pleasant harp with the psaltery. *Ps.* 81: 2.

As well the singers as the players on instruments shall be there. *Ps.* 87: 7.

Praise him with stringed instruments and organs. *Ps.* 150: 4.

I gat me men singers and women singers, and the delights of the sons of men, as musical instruments, and that of all sorts. So I was great. *Ec.* 2: 8, 9.

The Lord was ready to save me: therefore we will sing my songs to the stringed instruments all the days of our life in the house of the Lord. *Is.* 38: 20.

I have created the smith that bloweth the coals in the fire, and that bringeth forth an instrument for his work. *Is.* 54: 16.

Neither yield ye your members as instruments of unrighteousness unto sin: but yield yourselves unto God, as those that are alive from the dead, and your members as instruments of righteousness unto God. *Ro.* 6: 13.

See also

Agent; Melody; Music; Psalm; Song; Symphony.

Integration

There is one event to the . . . clean, and to the unclean. *Ec.* 9: 2.

Blessed are ye that sow beside all waters. *Is.* 32: 20.

All souls are mine; as the soul of the father, so also the soul of the son is mine: the soul that sinneth it shall die. *Eze.* 18: 4.

Are ye not as children of the Ethiopians unto me, O children of Israel? saith the Lord *Am.* 9: 7.

Thou canst not make one hair white or black. *Mat.* 5: 36.

Not every one that saith unto me, Lord, Lord, shall enter into the kingdom of heaven;

but he that doeth the will of my Father which is in heaven. *Mat.* 7: 21.

Whosoever shall do the will of my Father which is in heaven, the same is my brother, and sister, and mother. *Mat.* 12: 50.

Master, we know that thou art true, and teachest the way of God in truth, neither carest thou for any man: for thou regardest not the person of men. *Mat.* 22: 16.

All ye are brethren. *Mat.* 23: 8.

This gospel of the kingdom shall be preached in all the world for a witness unto all nations. *Mat.* 24: 14.

Go ye therefore, and teach all nations. *Mat.* 28: 19.

Go ye into all the world, and preach the gospel to every creature. *Mk.* 16: 15.

Begin not to say within yourselves, We have Abraham to our father: for I say unto you, That God is able of these stones to raise up children unto Abraham. *Lu.* 3: 8.

He hath anointed me . . . to preach deliverance to the captives. *Lu.* 4: 18.

Blessed are ye, when men shall hate you, and when they shall separate you from their company. *Lu.* 6: 22.

God so loved the world, that he gave his only begotten Son, that whosoever believeth in him should not perish, but have everlasting life. *Jn.* 3: 16.

Ye shall be witnesses unto me . . . unto the uttermost part of the earth. *Ac.* 1: 8.

I will pour out of my Spirit upon all flesh. *Ac.* 2: 17.

Ye know how that it is an unlawful thing for a man that is a Jew to keep company, or come unto one of another nation; but God hath shewed me that I should not call any man common or unclean. *Ac.* 10: 28.

What God hath cleansed, that call not thou common. *Ac.* 11: 9.

There is no difference between the Jew and the Greek: for the same Lord over all is rich unto all that call upon him. *Ro.* 10: 12.

There is nothing unclean of itself. *Ro.* 14: 14.

That no one of you be puffed up for one against another. *1 Co.* 4: 6.

Who maketh thee to differ from another? and what hast thou that thou didst not receive? now if thou didst receive it, why dost thou glory? *1 Co.* 4: 7.

Now hath God set the members every one of them in the same body. *1 Co.* 12: 18.

Ye are all the children of God by faith in Christ Jesus. *Ga.* 3: 26.

Ye who sometimes were far off are made nigh by the blood of Christ. *Ep.* 2: 13.

He . . . hath broken down the middle wall of partition. *Ep.* 2: 14.

There is neither Greek nor Jew, circumcision nor uncircumcision, Barbarian, Scythian, bond nor free: but Christ is all, and in all. *Col.* 3: 11.

Remember them that are in bonds, as bound with them. *He.* 13: 3.

If a man say, I love God, and hateth his brother, he is a liar: for he that loveth not his brother whom he hath seen, how can he love God whom he hath not seen? *1 Jn.* 4: 20.

These be they who separate themselves, sensual, having not the Spirit. *Jude* 19.

I saw another angel fly in the midst of heaven, having the everlasting gospel to preach unto them that dwell on the earth, and to every nation, and kindred, and tongue, and people. *Re.* 14: 6.

See also

Brotherhood; Union; Unity; Segregation.

Integrity

I have not taken one ass from them, neither have I hurt one of them. *Nu.* 16: 15.

Thou shalt love the Lord thy God with all thine heart, and with all thy soul, and with all thy might. *De.* 6: 5.

Thou hast not defrauded us, nor oppressed us, neither hast thou taken aught of any man's hand. *1 S.* 12: 4.

Howbeit there was no reckoning made with them of the money that was delivered into their hand, because they dealt faithfully. *2 K.* 22: 7.

Then said his wife unto him, Dost thou still retain thine integrity? curse God, and die. *Jb.* 2: 9.

Till I die I will not remove mine integrity from me. *Jb.* 27: 5.

He that is perfect in knowledge is with thee. *Jb.* 36: 4.

As for me, I will walk in mine integrity. *Ps.* 26: 11.

Behold, thou desirest truth in the inward parts. *Ps.* 51: 6.

So he fed them according to the integrity of his heart. *Ps.* 78: 72.

No good thing will he withhold from them that walk uprightly. *Ps.* 84: 11.

Surely the righteous shall give thanks unto thy name: the upright shall dwell in thy presence. *Ps.* 140: 13.

The integrity of the upright shall guard them. *Pr.* 11: 3.

Better is the poor that walketh in his integrity, than he that is perverse in his lips, and is a fool. *Pr.* 19: 1.

Righteousness shall be the girdle of his loins. *Is.* 11: 5.

We have wronged no man, we have corrupted no man, we have defrauded no man. *2 Co.* 7: 2.

See also

Christ, Goodness of; Christ, Holiness of; Fairness; God, Righteousness of; Goodness; Holiness; Honesty; Honor; Justice; Rectitude; Righteousness; Uprightness; Virtue.

Intelligence

Wisdom crieth without; she uttereth her voice in the streets. *Pr.* 1: 20.

Wisdom is the principal thing; therefore get wisdom. *Pr.* 4: 7.

O ye simple, understand wisdom: and ye fools, be ye of an understanding heart. *Pr.* 8: 5.

The thoughts of the righteous are right. *Pr.* 12: 5.

Wisdom is justified of her children. *Mat.* 11: 19.

In his right mind. *Mk.* 5: 15.

The children of this world are in their generation wiser than the children of light. *Lu.* 16: 8.

The wisdom that is from above is first pure, then peaceable, gentle, and easy to be intreated, full of mercy and good fruits, without partiality, and without hypocrisy. *Ja.* 3: 17.

And to virtue knowledge. 2 *Pe.* 1: 5.

See also

Brain; Christ, Knowledge of; Christ, Mind of; Christ, Wisdom of; Comprehension; God, Knowledge of; God, Wisdom of; Knowledge; Learning; Mind; Perception; Reason; Sage; Thought; Wisdom.

Intemperance

To add drunkenness to thirst. *De.* 29: 19.

Be not among winebibbers. *Pr.* 23: 20.

Who hath woe? . . . They that tarry long at the wine. *Pr.* 23: 29, 30.

At the last it biteth like a serpent, and stingeth like an adder. *Pr.* 23: 32.

Lest they drink, and forget the law, and pervert the judgment. *Pr.* 31: 5.

I am like a drunken man, and like a man whom wine hath overcome. *Je.* 23: 9.

Be not drunk with wine, wherein is excess; but be filled with the Spirit. *Ep.* 5: 18.

See also

Drunkenness; Grape; Indulgence; Intoxication; Wine.

Intention

All that the Lord speaketh, that I must do. *Nu.* 23: 26.

Thou didst well that it was in thine heart. *1 K.* 8: 18.

They intended evil against thee. *Ps.* 21: 11.

The fierce anger of the Lord shall not return, until he have done it, and until he have performed the intents of his heart. *Je.* 30: 24.

He doth not afflict willingly nor grieve the children of men. *La.* 3: 33.

It is not the will of your Father which is in heaven, that one of these little ones should perish. *Mat.* 18: 14.

Which of you, intending to build a tower, sitteth not down first, and counteth the cost? *Lu.* 14: 28.

I came down from heaven not to do mine own will, but the will of him that sent me. *Jn.* 6: 38.

Ye . . . intend to bring this man's blood upon us. *Ac.* 5: 28.

The things that I purpose, do I purpose according to the flesh? 2 *Co.* 1: 17.

The word of God . . . is a discerner of the thoughts and intents of the heart. *He.* 4: 12.

Lo, I come (in the volume of the book it is written of me,) to do thy will, O God. *He.* 10: 7.

See also

Aim; Ambition; Aspiration; Christ, Purpose of; Determination; End; Goal; Plan; Purpose; Resolution.

Intercession

I stood between the Lord and you at that time, to shew you the word of the Lord. *De.* 5: 5.

He saw that there was no man, and wondered that there was no intercessor. *Is.* 59: 16.

I have prayed for thee, that thy faith fail not. *Lu.* 22: 32.

Father, forgive them; for they know not what they do. *Lu.* 23: 34.

I will pray the Father, and he shall give you another Comforter, that he may abide with you for ever. *Jn.* 14: 16.

The Spirit itself maketh intercession for us with groanings which cannot be uttered. *Ro.* 8: 26.

Praying always. . . . And for me. *Ep.* 6: 18, 19.

He ever liveth to make intercession for them. *He.* 7: 25.

Now to appear in the presence of God for us. *He.* 9: 24.

We have an advocate with the Father, Jesus Christ the righteous. *1 Jn.* 2: 1.

See also

Christ, the Mediator; Entreaty; Mediation; Petition; Prayer; Reconciliation.

Interest

Tell me now what thou hast done; hide it not from me. *Jos.* 7: 19.

Tell me, I pray thee, wherein thy great strength lieth. *Ju.* 16: 6.

Why camest thou down hither? and with whom hast thou left those few sheep in the wilderness? I know thy pride, and the naughtiness of thine heart; for thou art come down that thou mightest see the battle. *1 S.* 17: 28.

How went the matter? I pray thee, tell me. *2 S.* 1: 4.

Tell me, I pray thee, all the great things that Elisha hath done. *2 K.* 8: 4.

Be ye mindful always of his covenant. *1 Ch.* 16: 15.

They . . . refused to obey, neither were mindful of thy wonders that thou didst among them. *Ne.* 9: 16: 17.

What is man, that thou art mindful of him? *Ps.* 8: 4.

He will ever be mindful of his covenant. *Ps.* 111: 5.

The Lord hath been mindful of us. *Ps.* 115: 12.

Tell us, therefore, what thinkest thou? *Mat.* 22: 17.

Tell us, when shall these things be? and what shall be the sign of thy coming? *Mat.* 24: 3.

The Pharisees came forth, and began to question with him. *Mk.* 8: 11.

After three days they found him in the temple, sitting in the midst of the doctors, both hearing them, and asking them questions. *Lu.* 2: 46.

What is this thou hast to tell me? *Ac.* 23: 19.

Interior

Let us meet together in the house of God, within the temple. *Ne.* 6: 10.

The law of his God is in his heart. *Ps.* 37: 31.

The law is within my heart. *Ps.* 40: 8.

Behold, thou desirest truth in the inward parts. *Ps.* 51: 6.

Peace be within thy walls, and prosperity within thy palaces. *Ps.* 122: 7.

Wisdom resteth in the heart of him that hath understanding. *Pr.* 14: 33.

Out of the abundance of the heart the mouth speaketh. *Mat.* 12: 34.

Within they are full of extortion and excess. *Mat.* 23: 25.

Cleanse first that which is within the cup. *Mat.* 23: 26.

Evil things come from within, and defile the man. *Mk.* 7: 23.

Behold, the kingdom of God is within you. *Lu.* 17: 21.

Whose adorning . . . let it be the hidden man of the heart. *1 Pe.* 3: 3, 4.

A meek and quiet spirit, which is in the sight of God of great price. *1 Pe.* 3: 4.

See also

Appearance; Exterior; Heart; Inside; Outside.

Interlude

To every thing there is a season. *Ec.* 3: 1.

Mine eye trickleth down, and ceaseth not, without any intermission. *La.* 3: 49.

Their lives were prolonged for a season and time. *Da.* 7: 12.

Then Jesus said unto them, My time is not yet come. *Jn.* 7: 6.

The sufferings of this present time are not worthy to be compared with the glory that shall be revealed in us. *Ro.* 8: 18.

This I say, brethren, the time is short. *1 Co.* 7: 29.

We, brethren, being taken from you for a short time in presence, not in heart, endeavoured the more abundantly to see your face with great desire. *1 Th.* 2: 17.

What is your life? It is even a vapour, that appeareth for a little time, and then vanisheth away. *Ja.* 4: 14.

Internationalism

He will lift up an ensign to the nations from far. *Is.* 5: 26.

In that day shall there be a highway out of Egypt to Assyria, and the Assyrians shall come into Egypt, and the Egyptians into Assyria, and the Egyptians shall serve with the Assyrians. *Is.* 19: 23.

Blessed be Egypt my people, and Assyria the work of my hands, and Israel mine inheritance. *Is.* 19: 25.

Then said the Lord, Thou hast had pity on the gourd, . . . which came up in a night, and perished in a night: And should not I spare Nineveh? *Jon.* 4: 10, 11.

Many shall come from the east and west, and shall sit down with Abraham, and Isaac, and Jacob, in the kingdom of heaven. *Mat.* 8: 11.

God . . . hath made of one blood all nations of men. *Ac.* 17: 24, 26.

The Father, . . . Of whom the whole family in heaven and earth is named. *Ep.* 3: 14, 15.

I saw another angel fly in the midst of heaven, having the everlasting gospel to preach unto them that dwell on the earth, and to every nation, and kindred, and tongue, and people. *Re.* 14: 6.

See also

Alien; Equality, Racial; Foreigner; Nations, League of; Stranger.

Interpretation

Do not interpretations belong to God? *Ge.* 40: 8.

Who is as the wise man? and who knoweth the interpretation of a thing? *Ec.* 8: 1.

They shall call his name Emmanuel, which being interpreted is, God with us. *Mat.* 1: 23.

Ye can discern the face of the sky and of the earth; but how is it that ye do not discern this time? *Lu.* 12: 56.

He expounded unto them in all the scriptures the things concerning himself. *Lu.* 24: 27.

To one is given by the Spirit the word of wisdom; . . . to another the interpretation of tongues. *1 Co.* 12: 8, 10.

When ye come together, every one of you hath a psalm, hath a doctrine, hath a tongue, hath a revelation, hath an interpretation. Let all things be done unto edifying. *1 Co.* 14: 26.

If any man speak in an unknown tongue, . . . let one interpret. *1 Co.* 14: 27.

If there be no interpreter, let him keep silence in the church. *1 Co.* 14: 28.

No prophecy of the scripture is of any private interpretation. *2 Pe.* 1: 20.

In which are some things hard to be understood, which they that are unlearned and unstable wrest, as they do also the other scriptures, unto their own destruction. *2 Pe.* 3: 16.

See also

Language; Meaning.

Intolerance

Go not into the way of the Gentiles, and into any city of the Samaritans enter ye not. *Mat.* 10: 5.

I am not sent but unto the lost sheep of the house of Israel. *Mat.* 15: 24.

How is it that he eateth and drinketh with publicans and sinners? *Mk.* 2: 16.

This man, if he were a prophet, would have known who and what manner of woman this is that toucheth him: for she is a sinner. *Lu.* 7: 39.

The Jews have no dealings with the Samaritans. *Jn.* 4: 9.

Neither is there salvation in any other. *Ac.* 4: 12.

I have never eaten anything that is common or unclean. *Ac.* 10: 14.

It is an unlawful thing for a man that is a Jew to keep company, or come unto one of another nation. *Ac.* 10: 28.

God hath shewed me that I should not call any man common or unclean. *Ac.* 10: 28.

Of a truth I perceive that God is no respecter of persons. *Ac.* 10: 34.

In every nation he that feareth him, and worketh righteousness, is accepted with him. *Ac.* 10: 35.

Is he the God of the Jews only? is he not also of the Gentiles? Yes, of the Gentiles also. *Ro.* 3: 29.

See also

Bigotry; Persons, Respect of; Pharisaism; Strictness.

Intoxication

I was the song of the drunkards. *Ps.* 69: 12.

Who hath woe? who hath sorrow? who hath contentions? who hath babbling? who hath wounds without cause? who hath redness of eyes? They that tarry long at the wine. *Pr.* 23: 29, 30.

Look not thou upon the wine when it is red. *Pr.* 23: 31.

Strong drink shall be bitter to them that drink it. *Is.* 24: 9.

They are drunken. but not with wine; they stagger, but not with strong drink. *Is.* 29: 9.

Awake, ye drunkards, and weep; and howl, all ye drinkers of wine, because of the new wine. *Jo.* 1: 5.

Not in rioting and drunkenness. *Ro.* 13: 13.

Be not drunk with wine, wherein is excess. *Ep.* 5: 18.

See also

Dissipation, Drunkenness; Grape; Indulgence; Intemperance; Wine.

Intrigue

Thou knowest the people, that they are set on mischief. *Ex.* 32: 22.

Saul said unto him, Why have ye conspired against me? *1 S.* 22: 13.

The people of the land . . . hired counsellors against them, to frustrate their purpose. *Ezr.* 4: 4, 5.

They . . . conspired all of them together to come and to fight against Jerusalem. *Ne.* 4: 7, 8.

They thought to do me mischief. *Ne.* 6: 2.

They that plow iniquity, and sow wickedness, reap the same. *Jb.* 4: 8.

They conceive mischief, and bring forth vanity, and their belly prepareth deceit. *Jb.* 15: 35.

The wicked plotteth against the just. *Ps.* 37: 12.

Thy tongue deviseth mischiefs; like a sharp razor, working deceitfully. *Ps.* 52: 2.

He deviseth mischief continually; he soweth discord. *Pr.* 6: 14.

They trust in vanity and speak lies; they conceive mischief, and bring forth iniquity. *Is.* 59: 4.

Mischief shall come upon mischief. *Eze.* 7: 26.

Though I have bound and strengthened their arms, yet do they imagine mischief against me. *Ho.* 7: 15.

See also

Conspiracy; Mischief; Plot.

Introduction

Joseph made himself known unto his brethren. *Ge.* 45: 1.

I will bring you in unto the land, . . . and I will give it you for an heritage. *Ex.* 6: 8.

Mine Angel shall go before thee, and bring thee in. *Ex.* 23: 23.

Make me to go in the path of thy commandments. *Ps.* 119: 35.

We will go into his tabernacles: we will worship at his footstool. *Ps.* 132: 7.

I will pour out my spirit unto you, I will make known my words unto you. *Pr.* 1: 23.

I will make myself known among them. *Eze.* 35: 11.

So will I make my holy name known in the midst of my people. *Eze.* 39: 7.

Now, brethren, I commend you to God. *Ac.* 20: 32.

I commend unto you Phebe our sister, which is a servant of the church. *Ro.* 16: 1.

See also

Entrance; Initiation.

Invincibility

The Lord shall fight for you. *Ex.* 14: 14.

I will send my fear before thee, and will destroy all the people to whom thou shalt come. *Ex.* 23: 27.

There shall no man be able to stand before thee. *De.* 7: 24.

The Lord your God shall lay the fear of you and the dread of you upon all the land that ye shall tread upon, as he hath said unto you. *De.* 11: 25.

The Lord shall cause thine enemies that rise up against thee to be smitten before thy face: they shall come out against thee one way, and flee before thee seven ways. *De.* 28: 7.

As I was with Moses, so I will be with thee: I will not fail thee, nor forsake thee. *Jos.* 1: 5.

The Lord delivered all their enemies into their hand. *Jos.* 21: 44.

The Lord hath driven out from before you great nations and strong. *Jos.* 23: 9.

There is no restraint to the Lord to save by many or by few. *1 S.* 14: 6.

Terrible as an army with banners. *S. of S.* 6: 10.

In all these things we are more than conquerors through him that loved us. *Ro.* 8: 37.

Whatsoever is born of God overcometh the world. *1 Jn.* 5: 4.

He went forth conquering, and to conquer. *Re.* 6: 2.

See also

Christ, Triumph of; Success; Triumph; Victory.

Invisibility

My face shall not be seen. *Ex.* 33: 23.

No man hath seen God at any time. *Jn.* 1: 18.

The things which are not seen are eternal. *2 Co.* 4: 18.

The image of the invisible God. *Col.* 1: 15.

Now unto the King eternal, immortal, invisible. *1 Ti.* 1: 17.

He endured, as seeing him who is invisible. *He.* 11: 27.

He that loveth not his brother whom he hath seen, how can he love God whom he hath not seen? *1 Jn.* 4: 20.

See also

Christ, the Hidden; Christ, Mystery of; Cover; God, the Hiding; Mystery; Secrecy; Veil.

Invitation

Come thou and all thy house into the ark; for thee have I seen righteous before me in this generation. *Ge.* 7: 1.

Come thou with us, and we will do thee good. *Nu.* 10: 29.

Come now, and let us reason together. *Is.* 1: 18.

Ho, every one that thirsteth, come ye to the waters, and he that hath no money; come ye, buy, and eat. *Is.* 55: 1.

Come, and let us return unto the Lord: for he hath torn, and he will heal us. *Ho.* 6: 1.

Come unto me, all ye that labour and are heavy laden, and I will give you rest. *Mat.* 11: 28.

Come unto the marriage. *Mat.* 22: 4.

Come, ye blessed of my Father, inherit the kingdom prepared for you. *Mat.* 25: 34.

Be of good comfort, rise; he calleth thee. *Mk.* 10: 49.

Go, and do thou likewise. *Lu.* 10: 37.

When thou makest a feast, call the poor, the maimed, the lame, the blind: And thou shalt be blessed. *Lu.* 14: 13, 14.

Come; for all things are now ready. *Lu.* 14: 17.

Ye were called unto the fellowship of his Son. *1 Co.* 1: 9.

Lay hold on eternal life, whereunto thou art also called. *1 Ti.* 6: 12.

Who hath called you out of darkness into his marvellous light. *1 Pe.* 2: 9.

Whosoever will. *Re.* 22: 17.

See also

Allurement; Christ, Call of; Christ, Coming to; Christ, the Door; Enticement; God, Call of; Hospitality; Welcome.

Invocation

Then began men to call upon the name of the Lord. *Ge.* 4: 26.

I will call on the Lord, who is worthy to be praised. *2 S.* 22: 4.

Call ye on the name of your gods, and I will call on the name of the Lord. *1 K.* 18: 24.

Give thanks unto the Lord, call upon his name. *1 Ch.* 16: 8.

Call upon me in the day of trouble: I will deliver thee. *Ps.* 50: 15.

As for me, I will call upon God; and the Lord shall save me. *Ps.* 55: 16.

Quicken us, and we will call upon thy name. *Ps.* 80: 18.

Because he hath inclined his ear unto me, therefore will I call upon him as long as I live. *Ps.* 116: 2.

Then shall they call upon me, but I will not answer; they shall seek me early, but they shall not find me. *Pr.* 1: 28.

Then shall ye call upon me, and ye shall go and pray unto me, and I will hearken unto you. *Je.* 29: 12.

Whosoever shall call on the name of the Lord shall be delivered. *Jo.* 2: 32.

Iron

The Lord hath taken you, and brought you forth out of the iron furnace, even out of Egypt. *De.* 4: 20.

Thou shalt drive out the Canaanites, though they have iron chariots, and though they be strong. *Jos.* 17: 18.

Thou shalt break them with a rod of iron. *Ps.* 2: 9.

Such as sit in darkness and in the shadow of death, being bound in affliction and iron. *Ps.* 107: 10.

Iron sharpeneth iron; so a man sharpeneth the countenance of his friend. *Pr.* 27: 17.

If the iron be blunt, and he do not whet the edge, then must he put to more strength: but wisdom is profitable to direct. *Ec.* 10: 10.

I will break in pieces the gates of brass, and cut in sunder the bars of iron. *Is.* 45: 2.

For brass I will bring gold, and for iron I will bring silver, and for wood brass, and for stones iron. *Is.* 60: 17.

Speaking lies in hypocrisy; having their conscience seared with a hot iron. *1 Ti.* 4: 2.

See also

Firmness; Hardness; Power; Strength.

Irresolution

Solomon . . . went not fully after the Lord. *1 K.* 11: 6.

How long halt ye between two opinions? *1 K.* 18: 21.

Lord, I will follow thee; but . . . *Lu.* 9: 61.

No man, having put his hand to the plow, and looking back, is fit for the kingdom of God. *Lu.* 9: 62.

Almost thou persuadest me to be a Christian. *Ac.* 26: 28.

He that wavereth is like a wave of the sea driven with the wind and tossed. *Ja.* 1: 6.

See also

Doubt; Half-Heartedness; Hesitancy; Indecision; Indifference; Loyalty, Divided; Skepticism; Uncertainty.

Island

He shall deliver the island of the innocent. *Jb.* 22: 30.

The Lord reigneth; let the earth rejoice; let the multitude of isles be glad thereof. *Ps.* 97: 1.

Be still, ye inhabitants of the isle. *Is.* 23: 2.

Keep silence before me, O islands; and let the people renew their strength. *Is.* 41: 1.

The isles shall wait for his law. *Is.* 42: 4.

Let them give glory unto the Lord, and declare his praise in the islands. *Is.* 42: 12.

I will make the rivers islands, and I will dry up the pools. *Is.* 42: 15.

The heaven departed as a scroll when it is rolled together; and every mountain and island were moved out of their places. *Re.* 6: 14.

Isolation

Jacob was left alone; and there wrestled a man with him until the breaking of the day. *Ge.* 32: 24.

I, even I only, am left; and they seek my life, to take it away. *1 K.* 19: 10.

Let that night be solitary, let no joyful voice come therein. *Jb.* 3: 7.

For want and famine they were solitary. *Jb.* 30: 3.

My lovers and my friends stand aloof. *Ps.* 38: 11.

My kinsmen stand afar off. *Ps.* 38: 11.

I watch, and am as a sparrow alone upon the house top. *Ps.* 102: 7.

Behold, I was left alone. *Is.* 49: 21.

Feed thy people with thy rod, the flock of thine heritage, which dwell solitarily in the wood. *Mi.* 7: 14.

He was alone praying. *Lu.* 9: 18.

Except a corn of wheat fall into the ground and die, it abideth alone. *Jn.* 12: 24.

Even so faith, if it hath not works, is dead, being alone. *Ja.* 2: 17.

See also

Christ, Loneliness of; Loneliness; Privacy; Solitude.

Israel

Thy name shall be called no more Jacob, but Israel: for as a prince hast thou power with God and with men, and hast prevailed. *Ge.* 32: 28.

There shall come a Star out of Jacob, and a Sceptre shall rise out of Israel. *Nu.* 24: 17.

They shall teach Jacob thy judgments, and Israel thy law. *De.* 33: 10.

The Lord saw the affliction of Israel, that it was very bitter: for there was not any shut up, nor any left, nor any helper for Israel. *2 K.* 14: 26.

Israel would none of me. *Ps.* 81: 11.

Behold, he that keepeth Israel shall neither slumber nor sleep. *Ps.* 121: 4.

Let Israel hope in the Lord. *Ps.* 130: 7.

He gathereth together the outcasts of Israel. *Ps.* 147: 2.

Israel doth not know, my people doth not consider. *Is.* 1: 3.

Blessed be Egypt my people, and Assyria the work of my hands, and Israel mine inheritance. *Is.* 19: 25.

Israel is a scattered sheep; the lions have driven him away. *Je.* 50: 17.

Ye also shall sit upon twelve thrones, judging the twelve tribes of Israel. *Mat.* 19: 28.

Hath God cast away his people? God forbid. For I also am an Israelite. *Ro.* 11: 1.

Are they Hebrews? so am I. Are they Israelites? so am I. Are they the seed of Abraham? so am I. *2 Co.* 11: 22.

See also

Hebrew; Jew; Judah.

J

Jealousy

When his brethren saw that their father loved him more than all his brethren, they hated him, and could not speak peaceably unto him. *Ge.* 37: 4.

I the Lord thy God am a jealous God. *Ex.* 20: 5.

Thou shalt not avenge, nor bear any grudge against the children of thy people. *Le.* 19: 18.

There ran a young man, and told Moses and said, Eldad and Medad do prophesy in the camp. And Joshua . . . said, My Lord Moses, forbid them. *Nu.* 11: 27, 28.

They have ascribed unto David ten thousands, and to me they have ascribed but thousands: and what can he have more but the kingdom? *1 S.* 18: 8.

I have been very jealous for the Lord God of hosts. *1 K.* 19: 10.

Fret not thyself because of evildoers, neither be thou envious against the workers of iniquity. *Ps.* 37: 1.

A sound heart is the life of the flesh: but envy the rottenness of the bones. *Pr.* 14: 30.

I considered all travail, and every right work, that for this a man is envied of his neighbour. *Ec.* 4: 4.

Love is strong as death; jealousy is cruel as the grave. *S. of S.* 8: 6.

God repented of the evil, that he had said that he would do unto them. . . . But it displeased Jonah exceedingly. *Jon.* 3: 10; 4: 1.

I am jealous for Jerusalem and for Zion with a great jealousy. *Zch.* 1: 14.

Thou hast made them equal unto us, which have borne the burden and heat of the day. *Mat.* 20: 12.

He was angry, and would not go in. *Lu.* 15: 28.

There was also a strife among them, which of them should be accounted the greatest. *Lu.* 22: 24.

Full of envy. *Ro.* 1: 29.

Do we provoke the Lord to jealousy? are we stronger than he? *1 Co.* 10: 22.

Charity envieth not. *1 Co.* 13: 4.

I am jealous over you with godly jealousy. *2 Co.* 11: 2.

Where envying and strife is. *Ja.* 3: 16.

See also

Avarice; Competition; Covetousness; Envy; Rivalry.

Jerusalem

Do good in thy good pleasure unto Zion: build thou the walls of Jerusalem. *Ps.* 51: 18.

Our feet shall stand within thy gates, O Jerusalem. *Ps.* 122: 2.

Jerusalem is builded as a city that is compact together. *Ps.* 122: 3.

Pray for the peace of Jerusalem: they shall prosper that love thee. *Ps.* 122: 6.

As the mountains are round about Jerusalem, so the Lord is round about his people from henceforth even for ever. *Ps.* 125: 2.

If I forget thee, O Jerusalem, let my right hand forget her cunning. *Ps.* 137: 5.

The Lord doth build up Jerusalem. *Ps.* 147: 2.

Thine eyes shall see Jerusalem a quiet habitation. *Is.* 33: 20.

Speak ye comfortably to Jerusalem, and cry unto her, that her warfare is accomplished, that her iniquity is pardoned. *Is.* 40: 2.

O Jerusalem, that bringest good tidings, lift up thy voice with strength. *Is.* 40: 9.

I will rejoice in Jerusalem, and joy in my people. *Is.* 65: 19.

His windows being open in his chamber toward Jerusalem. *Da.* 6: 10.

The Lord shall yet comfort Zion, and shall yet choose Jerusalem. *Zch.* 1: 17.

I am returned unto Zion, and I will dwell in the midst of Jerusalem. *Zch.* 8: 3.

There came wise men from the east to Jerusalem. *Mat.* 2: 1.

O Jerusalem, Jerusalem, thou that killest the prophets, and stonest them which are sent unto thee, how often would I have gathered thy children together, even as a hen gathereth her chickens under her wings, and ye would not! *Mat.* 23: 37.

Jerusalem which is above is free, which is the mother of us all. *Ga.* 4: 26.

Ye are come unto mount Sion, and unto the city of the living God, the heavenly Jerusalem. *He.* 12: 22.

I John saw the holy city, new Jerusalem, coming down from God out of heaven. *Re.* 21: 2.
See also
City, the Holy; Civilization; Zion.

Jew
The Jews had light, and gladness, and joy, and honour. *Es.* 8: 16.
Truly God is good to Israel, even to such as are of a clean heart. *Ps.* 73: 1.
I will be as the dew unto Israel. *Ho.* 14: 5.
Many of the Jews . . . believed on Jesus. *Jn.* 12: 11.
Pilate answered, Am I a Jew? *Jn.* 18: 35.
Behold, thou art a Jew, and restest in the law, and makest thy boast of God. *Ro.* 2: 17.
There is no difference between the Jew and the Greek: for the same Lord over all is rich unto all that call upon him. *Ro.* 10: 12.
Unto the Jews I became as a Jew, that I might gain the Jews. *1 Co.* 9: 20.
Are they Hebrews? so am I. Are they Israelites? so am I. Are they the seed of Abraham? so am I. *2 Co.* 11: 22.
If thou, being a Jew, livest after the manner of Gentiles, and not as do the Jews, why compellest thou the Gentiles to live as do the Jews? *Ga.* 2: 14.
See also
Hebrew; Israel; Judah.

Journey
Abram journeyed, going on still toward the south. *Ge.* 12: 9.
Let us take our journey, and let us go. *Ge.* 33: 12.
I will depart to mine own land, and to my kindred. *Nu.* 10: 30.
The Son of man is as a man taking a far journey. *Mk.* 13: 34.
They departed, and went through the towns, preaching the gospel, and healing every where. *Lu.* 9: 6.
The younger son . . . took his journey into a far country. *Lu.* 15: 13.
Arise, let us go hence. *Jn.* 14: 31.
In journeyings often. *2 Co.* 11: 26.
See also
Pilgrim; Pioneer; Progress; Travel; Wandering.

Joy
The joy of the Lord is your strength. *Ne.* 8: 10.
Therefore will I offer in his tabernacle sacrifices of joy. *Ps.* 27: 6.
Beautiful for situation, the joy of the whole earth, is mount Zion. *Ps.* 48: 2.
O let the nations be glad and sing for joy: for thou shalt judge the people righteously. *Ps.* 67: 4.
Blessed is the man that feareth the Lord, that delighteth greatly in his commandments. *Ps.* 112: 1.
Therefore with joy shall ye draw water out of the wells of salvation. *Is.* 12: 3.
Is this your joyous city, whose antiquity is of ancient days? *Is.* 23: 7.
Upon the land of my people shall come up thorns and briers; yea, upon all the houses of joy in the joyous city. *Is.* 32: 13.
Break forth into singing, ye mountains:

. . . for the Lord hath redeemed Jacob. *Is.* 44: 23.
Ye shall go out with joy, and be led forth with peace. *Is.* 55: 12.
Thou shalt have joy and gladness; and many shall rejoice at his birth. *Lu.* 1: 14.
I . . . am sent to speak unto thee, and to shew thee these glad tidings. *Lu.* 1: 19.
This my joy therefore is fulfilled. *Jn.* 3: 29.
These things have I spoken unto you, that my joy might remain in you, and that your joy might be full. *Jn.* 15: 11.
That I might finish my course with joy. *Ac.* 20: 24.
Now the God of hope fill you with all joy and peace in believing. *Ro.* 15: 13.
I am exceeding joyful in all our tribulation. *2 Co.* 7: 4.
Strengthened with all might, according to his glorious power, unto all patience and long-suffering with joyfulness. *Col.* 1: 11.
Count it all joy when ye fall into divers temptations. *Ja.* 1: 2.
See also
Bliss; Christ, Joy in; Christ, Joy of; Contentment; Delight; Ecstasy; Exultation; Gaiety; Gladness; God, Joy in; Happiness; Merriment; Mirth; Pleasure; Rapture; Rejoicing; Satisfaction.

Jubilee
Then shalt thou cause the trumpet of the jubile to sound. *Le.* 25: 9.
Ye shall hallow the fiftieth year, and proclaim liberty throughout all the land unto all the inhabitants thereof. *Le.* 25: 10.
A jubile shall that fiftieth year be unto you. *Le.* 25: 11.
The people piped with pipes, and rejoiced with great joy, so that the earth rent with the sound of them. *1 K.* 1: 40.
All the sons of God shouted for joy. *Jb.* 38: 7.
Let us make a joyful noise to the rock of our salvation. *Ps.* 95: 1.
Her saints shall shout aloud for joy. *Ps.* 132: 16.
There was great joy in that city. *Ac.* 8: 8.
See also
Exultation; Joy.

Judah
Judah did evil in the sight of the Lord. *1 K.* 14: 22.
Judah is my lawgiver. *Ps.* 60: 7.
In Judah is God known: his name is great in Israel. *Ps.* 76: 1.
Judah was his sanctuary, and Israel his dominion. *Ps.* 114: 2.
Judah mourneth, and the gates thereof languish. *Je.* 14: 2.
O Judah, what shall I do unto thee? for your goodness is as a morning cloud, and as the early dew it goeth away. *Ho.* 6: 4.
Judah yet ruleth with God, and is faithful with the saints. *Ho.* 11: 12.
The Lord hath also a controversy with Judah; . . . according to his doings will he recompense him. *Ho.* 12: 2.
See also
Hebrew; Israel; Jew.

Judgment

Who made thee a prince and a judge over us? *Ex.* 2: 14.

The Lord raised up judges, which delivered them. *Ju.* 2: 16.

On the day thou goest out, and walkest abroad any whither, . . . thou shalt surely die. *1 K.* 2: 42.

Thou renderest to every man according to his work. *Ps.* 62: 12.

I will sing of mercy and judgment. *Ps.* 101: 1.

Teach me good judgment. *Ps.* 119: 66.

It is not good to have respect of persons in judgment. *Pr.* 24: 23.

Because sentence against an evil work is not executed speedily, therefore the heart of the sons of men is fully set in them to do evil. *Ec.* 8: 11.

He shall not judge after the sight of his eyes. *Is.* 11: 3.

I the Lord search the heart, I try the reins, even to give every man according to . . . the fruit of his doings. *Je.* 17: 10.

Execute judgment in the morning. *Je.* 21: 12.

Take thee a roll of a book, and write therein all the words that I have spoken unto thee against Israel, and against Judah, and against all the nations. *Je.* 36: 2.

Let judgment run down as waters, and righteousness as a mighty stream. *Am.* 5: 24.

I lifted up mine eyes again, and looked, and behold a man with a measuring line in his hand. Then said I, Whither goest thou? And he said unto me, To measure Jerusalem, to see what is the breadth thereof, and what is the length thereof. *Zch.* 2: 1, 2.

Agree with thine adversary quickly, whiles thou art in the way with him; lest at any time the adversary deliver thee to the judge. *Mat.* 5: 25.

Judge not, that ye be not judged. *Mat.* 7: 1.

With what judgment ye judge, ye shall be judged. *Mat.* 7: 2.

Who made me a judge or a divider over you? *Lu.* 12: 14.

Why even of yourselves judge ye not what is right? *Lu.* 12: 57.

Out of thine own mouth will I judge thee. *Lu.* 19: 22.

Judge not according to the appearance, but judge righteous judgment. *Jn.* 7: 24.

Now is the judgment of this world: now shall the prince of this world be cast out. *Jn.* 12: 31.

Who art thou that judgest another man's servant? to his own master he standeth or falleth. *Ro.* 14: 4.

So then every one of us shall give account of himself to God. *Ro.* 14: 12.

With me it is a very small thing that I should be judged of you, or of man's judgment: yea, I judge not mine own self. For I know nothing by myself; yet am I not hereby justified: but he that judgeth me is the Lord. *1 Co.* 4: 3, 4.

Behold, the judge standeth before the door. *Ja.* 5: 9.

My reward is with me, to give every man according as his work shall be. *Re.* 22: 12.

See also

Acquittal; Condemnation; Decision; Disapproval; Discernment; Discrimination; Insight; Judgment, the Last; Justice; Perception; Taste; Understanding; Wisdom.

Judgment, the Last

Many of them that sleep in the dust of the earth shall awake, some to everlasting life, and some to shame and everlasting contempt. *Da.* 12: 2.

The day of the Lord cometh, for it is nigh at hand. *Jo.* 2: 1.

The day cometh, that shall burn as an oven; and all the proud, yea, and all that do wickedly, shall be stubble: and the day that cometh shall burn them up, saith the Lord of hosts. *Mal.* 4: 1.

Every idle word that men shall speak, they shall give account thereof in the day of judgment. *Mat.* 12: 36.

To stand before the Son of man. *Lu.* 21: 36.

I know that he shall rise again in the resurrection at the last day. *Jn.* 11: 24.

The sun shall be turned into darkness, and the moon into blood, before that great and notable day of the Lord come. *Ac.* 2: 20.

He hath appointed a day, in the which he will judge the world in righteousness by that man whom he hath ordained; whereof he hath given assurance unto all men, in that he hath raised him from the dead. *Ac.* 17: 31.

Thinkest thou this, O man, . . . that thou shalt escape the judgment of God? *Ro.* 2: 3.

It is appointed unto men once to die, but after this the judgment. *He.* 9: 27.

Herein is our love made perfect, that we may have boldness in the day of judgment. *1 Jn.* 4: 17.

I was in the Spirit on the Lord's day, and heard behind me a great voice, as of a trumpet. *Re.* 1: 10.

The hour of his judgment is come. *Re.* 14: 7.

See also

Brimstone; Damnation; Hell.

Justice

That which is altogether just shalt thou follow. *De.* 16: 20.

He that ruleth over men must be just. *2 S.* 23: 3.

The Lord . . . blesseth the habitation of the just. *Pr.* 3: 33.

The path of the just is as the shining light, that shineth more and more unto the perfect day. *Pr.* 4: 18.

The memory of the just is blessed. *Pr.* 10: 7.

The tongue of the just is as choice silver. *Pr.* 10: 20.

To do justice and judgment is more acceptable to the Lord than sacrifice. *Pr.* 21: 3.

What doth the Lord require of thee, but to do justly, and to love mercy? *Mi.* 6: 8.

Masters, give unto your servants that which is just and equal. *Col.* 4: 1.

Christ also hath once suffered for sins, the just for the unjust. *1 Pe.* 3: 18.

See also

Christ, the Judge; Equality; Equality, Racial;

Fairness; God, Fairness of; God, Impartiality of; God, the Judge; Judgment; Justice, Social; Right; Truth; Uprightness.

Justice, Social

Just balances, just weights, . . . shall ye have. *Le.* 19: 36.

That there be no complaining in our streets. *Ps.* 144: 14.

A just weight and balance are the Lord's. *Pr.* 16: 11.

The profit of the earth is for all. *Ec.* 5: 9.

They shall not build, and another inhabit. *Is.* 65: 22.

Hate the evil, and love the good, and establish judgment in the gate. *Am.* 5: 15.

He walked with me in peace and equity, and did turn many away from iniquity. *Mal.* 2: 6.

Why stand ye here all the day idle? *Mat.* 20: 6.

Masters, give unto your servants that which is just and equal; knowing that ye also have a master in heaven. *Col.* 4: 1.

The husbandman that laboureth must be first partaker of the fruit. *2 Ti.* 2: 6.

See also

Equality; Equality, Racial; Fairness; Injustice; Injustice, Social; Judgment; Justice; Right.

Justification

There shall no evil happen to the just. *Pr.* 12: 21.

A just man falleth seven times, and riseth up again. *Pr.* 24: 16.

Why beholdest thou the mote that is in thy brother's eye, but considerest not the beam that is in thine own eye? *Mat.* 7: 3.

Wisdom is justified of her children. *Mat.* 11: 19.

Many that are first shall be last; and the last shall be first. *Mat.* 19: 30.

A man is justified by faith without the deeds of the law. *Ro.* 3: 28.

Jesus our Lord . . . was raised again for our justification. *Ro.* 4: 24, 25.

Being now justified by his blood, we shall be saved from wrath through him. *Ro.* 5: 9.

The free gift is of many offences unto justification. *Ro.* 5: 16.

Ye are justified in the name of the Lord Jesus. *1 Co.* 6: 11.

See also

Absolution; Defence; Deliverance; Forgiveness; Pardon; Remission.

K

Keeper

Am I my brother's keeper? *Ge.* 4: 9.

He is my shield, and the horn of my salvation, my high tower, and my refuge, my saviour; thou savest me from violence. *2 S.* 22: 3.

Hast thou not made an hedge about him? *Jb.* 1: 10.

Thou shalt be secure, because there is hope. *Jb.* 11: 18.

I had rather be a doorkeeper in the house of my God, than to dwell in the tents of wickedness. *Ps.* 84: 10.

The Lord shall preserve thee from all evil: he shall preserve thy soul. *Ps.* 121: 7.

In the day when the keepers of the house shall tremble. *Ec.* 12: 3.

See also

Defence; Fortress; God, the Keeper; God, Protection of; God, the Refuge; Preservation; Protection; Refuge; Safety; Security; Tower; Watch.

Key

He hath broken the gates of brass, and cut the bars of iron in sunder. *Ps.* 107: 16.

He hath strengthened the bars of thy gates. *Ps.* 147: 13.

The doors shall be shut in the streets. *Ec.* 12: 4.

The key of the house of David will I lay upon his shoulder; so he shall open, and none shall shut; and he shall shut, and none shall open. *Is.* 22: 22.

Come, my people, enter thou into thy chambers, and shut thy doors about thee. *Is.* 26: 20.

I will give unto thee the keys of the kingdom of heaven: and whatsoever thou shalt bind on earth shall be bound in heaven: and whatsoever thou shalt loose on earth shall be loosed in heaven. *Mat.* 16: 19.

They that were ready went in with him to the marriage: and the door was shut. *Mat.* 25: 10.

Woe unto you, lawyers! for ye have taken away the key of knowledge: ye entered not in yourselves, and them that were entering in ye hindered. *Lu.* 11: 52.

I . . . have the keys of hell and of death. *Re.* 1: 18.

These things saith he that is holy, he that is true, he that hath the key of David, he that openeth and no man shutteth; and shutteth, and no man openeth. *Re.* 3: 7.

To him was given the key of the bottomless pit. *Re.* 9: 1.

See also

Bar; Door.

Kindness

Thou shalt not cut off thy kindness from my house for ever. *1 S.* 20: 15.

I was eyes to the blind, and feet was I to the lame. *Jb.* 29: 15.

A word spoken in due season, how good it is! *Pr.* 15: 23.

Pleasant words are as a honeycomb, sweet to the soul, and health to the bones. *Pr.* 16: 24.

In her tongue is the law of kindness. *Pr.* 31: 26.

What doth the Lord require of thee, but to do justly, and to love mercy, and to walk humbly with thy God? *Mi.* 6: 8.

The King shall answer and say unto them,

Verily I say unto you, Inasmuch as ye have done it unto one of the least of these my brethren, ye have done it unto me. *Mat.* **25: 40.**

Let love be without dissimulation. *Ro.* **12: 9.**

Charity suffereth long, and is kind. *1 Co.* **13: 4.**

And to godliness brotherly kindness. *2 Pe.* **1: 7.**

See also

Beneficence; Benevolence; Benignity; Christ, Compassion of; Christ, Generosity of; Christ, Gentleness of; Christ, Goodness of; Christ, Grace of; Clemency; Compassion; Favor; Generosity; Gentleness; God, Beneficence of; God, Compassion of; God, Favor of; God, Gentleness of; God, Goodness of; God, Grace of; Goodness; Grace; Humanity; Tenderness.

King

The men of Israel said unto Gideon, Rule thou over us, both thou, and thy son, and thy son's son also. *Ju.* **8: 22.**

The Lord . . . shall give strength unto his king. *1 S.* **2: 10.**

All the people shouted, and said, God save the king. *1 S.* **10: 24.**

The king's business required haste. *1 S.* **21: 8.**

Give the king thy judgments, O God, and thy righteousness unto the king's son. *Ps.* **72: 1.**

The heaven for height, and the earth for depth, and the heart of kings is unsearchable. *Pr.* **25: 3.**

The king that faithfully judgeth the poor, his throne shall be established for ever. *Pr.* **29: 14.**

Thine eyes shall see the king in his beauty. *Is.* **33: 17.**

Kings shall see and arise, princes also shall worship, because of the Lord that is faithful. *Is.* **49: 7.**

The sons of strangers shall build up thy walls, and their kings shall minister unto thee. *Is.* **60: 10.**

The king's commandment was urgent. *Da.* **3: 22.**

Whosoever maketh himself a king speaketh against Cæsar. *Jn.* **19: 12.**

Another king arose, which knew not Joseph. *Ac.* **7: 18.**

Thou must prophesy again before many peoples, and nations, and tongues, and kings. *Re.* **10: 11.**

See also

Christ, the King; Christ, Reign of; Christ, Supremacy of; God, the King; God, Kingdom of; God, Sovereignty of; God, Supremacy of; Kingdom; Power; Reign; Rule; Sovereignty; Throne.

Kingdom

God hath numbered thy kingdom, and finished it. *Da.* **5: 26.**

Jesus went about, . . . preaching the gospel of the kingdom. *Mat.* **4: 23.**

Every kingdom divided against itself is brought to desolation. *Mat.* **12: 25.**

Then shall the righteous shine forth as the sun in the kingdom of their Father. *Mat.* **13: 43.**

Render therefore unto Cæsar the things which are Cæsar's and unto God the things that are God's. *Mat.* **22: 21.**

Come, ye blessed of my Father, inherit the kingdom prepared for you from the foundation of the world. *Mat.* **25: 34.**

It is your Father's good pleasure to give you the kingdom. *Lu.* **12: 32.**

Who through faith subdued kingdoms. *He.* **11: 33.**

See also

Christ, the King; Christ, Reign of; Christ, Supremacy of; Domain; Dominion; God, the King; God, Kingdom of; God, Sovereignty of; Heaven, Kingdom of; King; Kingdom, the Coming; Power; Realm; Reign; Rule; Throne.

Kingdom, the Coming

In that day shall the Lord of hosts be for a crown of glory, and for a diadem of beauty, unto the residue of his people. *Is.* **28: 5.**

The kingdom of heaven is at hand. *Mat.* **3: 2.**

Thy kingdom come. Thy will be done in earth, as it is in heaven. *Mat.* **6: 10.**

Seek ye first the kingdom of God. *Mat.* **6: 33.**

The kingdom of heaven is like unto leaven. *Mat.* **13: 33.**

I will not drink henceforth of this fruit of the vine, until that day when I drink it new with you in my Father's kingdom. *Mat.* **26: 29.**

There be some standing here, which shall not taste of death, till they see the kingdom of God. *Lu.* **9: 27.**

The kingdom of God cometh not with observation. *Lu.* **17: 20.**

Lord, remember me when thou comest into thy kingdom. *Lu.* **23: 42.**

Eye hath not seen, nor ear heard, neither have entered into the heart of man, the things which God hath prepared for them that love him. *1 Co.* **2: 9.**

See also

Age, the Golden; Climax; Day, the Coming; Future; God, Kingdom of; Heaven, Kingdom of; Land, the Promised; Millennium.

Kinship

They shall be one flesh. *Ge.* **2: 24.**

He is our brother and our flesh. *Ge.* **37: 27.**

A Prophet from the midst of thee, of thy brethren, like unto me. *De.* **18: 15.**

My kinsmen stand afar off. *Ps.* **38: 11.**

Call understanding thy kinswoman. *Pr.* **7: 4.**

Have we not all one father? hath not one God created us? *Mal.* **2: 10.**

He looked round about on them which sat about him, and said, Behold my mother and my brethren! *Mk.* **3: 34.**

Jesus said, Forbid him not: . . . For he that is not against us is on our part. *Mk.* **9: 39, 40.**

When thou makest a dinner or a supper, call not thy friends, nor thy brethren, neither thy kinsmen, nor thy rich neighbours. *Lu.* **14: 12.**

Ye shall be betrayed both by parents, and brethren, and kinsfolks, and friends. *Lu.* **21: 16.**

God . . . hath made of one blood all nations of men for to dwell on all the face of the earth. *Ac.* **17: 24, 26.**

See also

Brotherhood; Family; Home; House.

Kiss

Kiss the Son, lest he be angry, and ye perish from the way. *Ps.* **2: 12.**

Mercy and truth are met together; righteousness and peace have kissed each other. *Ps.* **85: 10.**

The kisses of an enemy are deceitful. *Pr.* **27: 6.**

Thou gavest me no kiss: but this woman since the time I came in hath not ceased to kiss my feet. *Lu.* **7: 45.**

Judas, betrayest thou the Son of man with a kiss? *Lu.* **22: 48.**

Greet all the brethren with an holy kiss. *1 Th.* **5: 26.**

Greet ye one another with a kiss of charity. *1 Pe.* **5: 14.**

See also

Affection; Attachment; Caress; Love.

Knee

Thou hast strengthened the feeble knees. *Jb.* **4: 4.**

Let us kneel before the Lord our maker. *Ps.* **95: 6.**

Strengthen ye the weak hands, and confirm the feeble knees. *Is.* **35: 3.**

He kneeled upon his knees three times a day, and prayed, and gave thanks before his God. *Da.* **6: 10.**

For this cause I bow my knees unto the Father of our Lord Jesus Christ. *Ep.* **3: 14.**

To know the love of Christ, which passeth knowledge. *Ep.* **3: 19.**

Lift up the hands which hang down, and the feeble knees. *He.* **12: 12.**

See also

Prayer.

Knowledge

Forsake her not, and she shall preserve thee: love her, and she shall keep thee. *Pr.* **4: 6.**

My mouth shall speak truth; and wickedness is an abomination to my lips. *Pr.* **8: 7.**

He that sinneth against me wrongeth his own soul: all they that hate me love death. *Pr.* **8: 36.**

In much wisdom is much grief: and he that increaseth knowledge increaseth sorrow. *Ec.* **1: 18.**

Because thou hast rejected knowledge, I will also reject thee. *Ho.* **4: 6.**

Then shall we know, if we follow on to know the Lord. *Ho.* **6: 3.**

The times of this ignorance God winked at. *Ac.* **17: 30.**

I determined not to know any thing among you, save Jesus Christ, and him crucified. *1 Co.* **2: 2.**

Knowledge puffeth up, but charity edifieth. *1 Co.* **8: 1.**

Now we see through a glass, darkly; but then face to face: now I know in part; but then shall I know even as also I am known. *1 Co.* **13: 12.**

Lest Satan should get an advantage of us: for we are not ignorant of his devices. *2 Co.* **2: 11.**

See also

Brain; Christ, Knowledge of; Christ, Mind of; Christ, Wisdom of; Comprehension; Doctor; Edification; Education; God, Knowledge of; God, Wisdom of; Intelligence; Learning; Mind; Perception; Reason; School; Science; Study; Teaching; Training; Understanding; Wisdom.

L

Labor

The Lord God took the man, and put him into the garden of Eden to dress it and to keep it. *Ge.* **2: 15.**

In the sweat of thy face shalt thou eat bread. *Ge.* **3: 19.**

Where hast thou gleaned to day? *Ru.* **2: 19.**

To strengthen their hands in the work of the house of God. *Ezr.* **6: 22.**

I am doing a great work, so that I cannot come down. *Ne.* **6: 3.**

Except the Lord build the house, they labour in vain that build it. *Ps.* **127: 1.**

Whatsoever thy hand findeth to do, do it with thy might. *Ec.* **9: 10.**

Be strong, all ye people of the land, saith the Lord, and work. *Hag.* **2: 4.**

Labour not for the meat which perisheth. *Jn.* **6: 27.**

I must work the works of him that sent me, while it is day: the night cometh, when no man can work. *Jn.* **9: 4.**

Ye know that your labour is not in vain in the Lord. *1 Co.* **15: 58.**

Wherefore we labour, that . . . we may be accepted of him. *2 Co.* **5: 9.**

These only are my fellow workers unto the kingdom of God. *Col.* **4: 11.**

If any would not work, neither should he eat. *2 Th.* **3: 10.**

We command and exhort by our Lord Jesus Christ, that with quietness they work, and eat their own bread. *2 Th.* **3: 12.**

Let us labour therefore to enter into that rest. *He.* **4: 11.**

See also

Christ, Work of; Drudgery; Duty; Effort; Employee; Employer; Endeavour; Exercise; God, Work of; Handiwork; Industry; Occupation; Service; Task; Toil; Travail; Work.

Lack

Who provideth for the raven his food? when his young ones cry unto God, they wander for lack of meat. *Jb.* **38: 41.**

There is no want to them that fear him. *Ps.* **34: 9.**

The young lions do lack, and suffer hunger: but they that seek the Lord shall not want any good thing. *Ps.* **34: 10.**

One thing thou lackest: go thy way, sell whatsoever thou hast, and give to the poor, and thou shalt have treasure in heaven. *Mk.* **10: 21.**

Ye lacked opportunity. *Ph.* **4: 10.**

That ye may have lack of nothing. *1 Th.* **4: 12.**

If any of you lack wisdom, let him ask of God. *Ja.* **1: 5.**

He that lacketh these things is blind, and cannot see afar off. *2 Pe.* **1: 9.**

Whoso hath this world's good, and seeth his brother have need, and shutteth up his bowels of compassion from him, how dwelleth the love of God in him? *1 Jn.* **3: 17.**

Because thou sayest, I am rich, and increased with goods, and have need of nothing; and knowest not that thou art wretched, and miserable, and poor, and blind, and naked: I counsel thee to buy of me . . . white raiment, that thou mayest be clothed. *Re.* **3: 17, 18.**

See also
Blemish; Charity; Defect; Destitution; Need; Philanthropy; Poor; Poverty; Want.

Laity

Would God that all the Lord's people were prophets, and that the Lord would put his spirit upon them! *Nu.* **11: 29.**

The child did minister unto the Lord. *1 S.* **2: 11.**

Let a man so account of us, as of the ministers of Christ, and stewards of the mysteries of God. Moreover it is required in stewards, that a man be found faithful. *1 Co.* **4: 1, 2.**

They which wait at the altar are partakers with the altar. *1 Co.* **9: 13.**

Ye are manifestly declared to be the epistle of Christ ministered by us, written not with ink, but with the Spirit of the living God. *2 Co.* **3: 3.**

In all things approving ourselves as the ministers of God. *2 Co.* **6: 4.**

Ye also, as lively stones, are built up a spiritual house, an holy priesthood. *1 Pe.* **2: 5.**

A royal priesthood. *1 Pe.* **2: 9.**

As every man hath received the gift, even so minister the same, one to another, as good stewards of the manifold grace of God. *1 Pe.* **4: 10.**

Jesus Christ . . . hath made us kings and priests unto God and his Father. *Re.* **1: 5, 6.**

They shall be priests of God and of Christ, and shall reign with him a thousand years. *Re.* **20: 6.**

Lamb

I delight not in the blood of bullocks, or of lambs. *Is.* **1: 11.**

The wolf also shall dwell with the lamb. *Is.* **11: 6.**

He is brought as a lamb to the slaughter. *Is.* **53: 7.**

The wolf and the lamb shall feed together. *Is.* **65: 25.**

The Lord will feed them as a lamb in a large place. *Ho.* **4: 16.**

I send you forth as lambs among wolves. *Lu.* **10: 3.**

Behold the Lamb of God, which taketh away the sin of the world. *Jn.* **1: 29.**

See also
Offering; Sacrifice; Sheep; Shepherd.

Lameness

Feet was I to the lame. *Jb.* **29: 15.**

Feet have they, but they walk not. *Ps.* **115: 7.**

The legs of the lame are not equal. *Pr.* **26: 7.**

Then shall the lame man leap as an hart, and the tongue of the dumb sing. *Is.* **35: 6.**

The lame walk. *Mat.* **11: 5.**

When thou makest a feast, call the poor, the maimed, the lame, the blind. *Lu.* **14: 13.**

Many taken with palsies, and that were lame, were healed. *Ac.* **8: 7.**

Make straight paths for your feet, lest that which is lame be turned out of the way. *He.* **12: 13.**

See also
Cripple; Foot; Halt.

Lamentation

The beauty of Israel is slain upon thy high places: how are the mighty fallen! *2 S.* **1: 19.**

I am distressed for thee, my brother Jonathan: very pleasant hast thou been unto me: thy love to me was wonderful, passing the love of women. *2 S.* **1: 26.**

How are the mighty fallen, and the weapons of war perished! *2 S.* **1: 27.**

Know ye not that there is a prince and a great man fallen this day in Israel? *2 S.* **3: 38.**

Now he is dead, wherefore should I fast? can I bring him back again? I shall go to him, but he shall not return to me. *2 S.* **12: 23.**

He requested for himself that he might die; and said, It is enough; now, O Lord, take away my life; for I am not better than my fathers. *1 K.* **19: 4.**

I have heard thy prayer, I have seen thy tears: behold, I will heal thee. *2 K.* **20: 5.**

By the waters of Babylon, there we sat down, yea, we wept, when we remembered Zion. *Ps.* **137: 1.**

A time to weep, and a time to laugh; a time to mourn, and a time to dance. *Ec.* **3: 4.**

The mourners go about the streets. *Ec.* **12: 5.**

We roar all like bears, and mourn sore like doves. *Is.* **59: 11.**

A voice was heard in Ramah, lamentation, and bitter weeping; Rahel weeping for her children refused to be comforted for her children, because they were not. *Je.* **31: 15.**

In that day shall one take up a parable against you, and lament with a doleful lamentation. *Mi.* **2: 4.**

We have mourned unto you, and ye have not lamented. *Mat.* **11: 17.**

Woe unto you that laugh now! for ye shall mourn and weep. *Lu.* **6: 25.**

When he was come near, he beheld the city, and wept over it. *Lu.* **19: 41.**

What mean ye to weep and to break mine heart? *Ac.* **21: 13.**

The time is short: it remaineth, that both they that have wives be as though they had none; And they that weep, as though they wept not. *1 Co.* **7: 29, 30.**

I wept much, because no man was found worthy to open and to read the book. *Re.* **5: 4.**

God shall wipe away all tears from their eyes; and there shall be no more death, neither

sorrow, nor crying. *Re.* 21: 4.
See also
Christ, Sorrow of; Grief; Mourning; Sadness; Sorrow; Tear; Unhappiness; Woe.

Lamp

Thou art my lamp, O Lord: and the Lord will lighten my darkness. *2 S.* 22: 29.
Thy word is a lamp unto my feet. *Ps.* 119: 105.
The commandment is a lamp; and the law is light. *Pr.* 6: 23.
The lamp of the wicked shall be put out. *Pr.* 13: 9.
For Zion's sake will I not hold my peace, . . . until the righteousness thereof go forth as brightness, and the salvation thereof as a lamp that burneth. *Is.* 62: 1.
Ye are the light of the world. *Mat.* 5: 14.
The light of the body is the eye. *Mat.* 6: 22.
The foolish said unto the wise, Give us of your oil; for our lamps are gone out. *Mat.* 25: 8.
No man, when he hath lighted a candle, covereth it with a vessel, or putteth it under a bed; but setteth it on a candlestick, that they which enter in may see the light. *Lu.* 8: 16.
Let your loins be girded about, and your lights burning. *Lu.* 12: 35.
A light that shineth in a dark place. *2 Pe.* 1: 19.
There fell a great star from heaven, burning as it were a lamp. *Re.* 8: 10.
See also
Candle; Christ, the Light; God, the Light; Light; Ray.

Land

God said, Let the waters under the heaven be gathered together unto one place, and let the dry land appear. *Ge.* 1: 9.
Ye shall eat the fat of the land. *Ge.* 45: 18.
Honour thy father and thy mother: that thy days may be long upon the land which the Lord thy God giveth thee. *Ex.* 20: 12.
The poor shall never cease out of the land. *De.* 15: 11.
Make a joyful noise unto God, all ye lands. *Ps.* 66: 1.
He that tilleth his land shall be satisfied with bread. *Pr.* 12: 11.
Thou shalt no more be termed Forsaken; neither shall thy land any more be termed Desolate. *Is.* 62: 4.
The land is as the garden of Eden before them, and behind them a desolate wilderness. *Jo.* 2: 3.
See also
Country; Earth; Ground; Nation; Nation, Decadence of; Nation, Greatness of; Nation, Prosperity of; Nations, League of; People; Race; Soil; State.

Land, the Promised

The Lord thy God bringeth thee into a good land, a land of brooks of water, of fountains and depths that spring out of valleys and hills. *De.* 8: 7.
A land which the Lord thy God careth for: the eyes of the Lord thy God are always upon it. *De.* 11: 12.
The Lord thy God . . . give thee all the land which he promised to give unto thy fathers. *De.* 19: 8.
I have given you a land for which ye did not labour, and cities which ye built not, and ye dwell in them. *Jos.* 24: 13.
Lead me into the land of uprightness. *Ps.* 143: 10.
I brought you into a plentiful country, to eat the fruit thereof and the goodness thereof. *Je.* 2: 7.
By faith he sojourned in the land of promise. *He.* 11: 9.
They desire a better country, that is, an heavenly. *He.* 11: 16.
See also
Age, the Golden; Civilization; Country, the Better; Day, the Coming; Future; Millennium; Pilgrim.

Landmark

Cursed be he that removeth his neighbour's landmark. *De.* 27: 17.
Some remove the landmarks; they violently take away flocks, and feed thereof. *Jb.* 24: 2.
Remove not the ancient landmark, which thy fathers have set. *Pr.* 22: 28.
I have removed the bounds of the people, and have robbed their treasures. *Is.* 10: 13.
The princes of Judah were like them that remove the bound. *Ho.* 5: 10.
God . . . hath determined . . . the bounds of their habitation. *Ac.* 17: 24, 26.
See also
Border; Bound.

Language

The whole earth was of one language, and of one speech. *Ge.* 11: 1.
Go to, let us go down, and there confound their language, that they may not understand one another's speech. *Ge.* 11: 7.
There is no speech nor language, where their voice is not heard. *Ps.* 19: 3.
In my name . . . they shall speak with new tongues. *Mk.* 16: 17.
They were all filled with the Holy Ghost, and began to speak with other tongues, as the Spirit gave them utterance. *Ac.* 2: 4.
How hear we every man in our own tongue, wherein we were born? *Ac.* 2: 8.
We do hear them speak in our tongues the wonderful works of God. *Ac.* 2: 11.
Though I speak with the tongues of men and of angels, and have not charity, I am become as sounding brass, or a tinkling cymbal. *1 Co.* 13: 1.
He that speaketh in an unknown tongue speaketh not unto men, but unto God. *1 Co.* 14: 2.
Greater is he that prophesieth than he that speaketh with tongues. *1 Co.* 14: 5.
Thou . . . hast redeemed us to God by thy blood out of every kindred, and tongue, and people, and nation. *Re.* 5: 9.
See also
Accent; Interpretation; Speech; Tongue; Utterance; Word.

Last

The end of the wicked shall be cut off. *Ps.* 37: 38.

Better is the end of a thing than the beginning thereof. *Ec.* 7: 8.

I the Lord, the first, and with the last; I am he. *Is.* 41: 4.

The last state of that man is worse than the first. *Mat.* 12: 45.

Many that are first shall be last; and the last shall be first. *Mat.* 19: 30.

I will give unto this last, even as unto thee. *Mat.* 20: 14.

If any man desire to be first, the same shall be last of all, and servant of all. *Mk.* 9: 35.

I think that God hath set forth us the apostles last, as it were appointed to death: for we are made a spectacle unto the world, and to angels, and to men. *1 Co.* 4: 9.

Last of all he was seen of me also, as of one born out of due time. *1 Co.* 15: 8.

In the last days perilous times shall come. *2 Ti.* 3: 1.

I am Alpha and Omega, the beginning and the end, the first and the last. *Re.* 22: 13.

See also

Christ, Finality of; Christ, the Goal; Death; End; Finality; Finish; Goal; Omega.

Lateness

It is vain for you to rise up early, to sit up late, to eat the bread of sorrows: for so he giveth his beloved sleep. *Ps.* 127: 2.

We wait for light, but behold obscurity; for brightness, but we walk in darkness. *Is.* 59: 9.

Blessed is he that waiteth. *Da.* 12: 12.

The vision is yet for an appointed time, but at the end it shall speak, and not lie: though it tarry, wait for it. *Hab.* 2: 3.

It shall come to pass, that at evening time it shall be light. *Zch.* 14: 7.

He answered and said, I will not: but afterward he repented, and went. *Mat.* 21: 29.

The stone which the builders rejected, the same is become the head of the corner. *Mat.* 21: 42.

Thy daughter is dead: why troublest thou the Master any further? *Mk.* 5: 35.

He hath been dead four days. *Jn.* 11: 39.

Thou shalt follow me afterwards. *Jn.* 13: 36.

Redeeming the time, because the days are evil. *Ep.* 5: 16.

See also

Tardiness.

Laughter

Therefore will I play before the Lord. *2 S.* 6: 21.

The innocent laugh them to scorn. *Jb.* 22: 19.

He that sitteth in the heavens shall laugh. *Ps.* 2: 4.

Thou, O Lord, shalt laugh at them; thou shalt have all the heathen in derision. *Ps.* 59: 8.

Then was our mouth filled with laughter, and our tongue with singing. *Ps.* 126: 2.

Even in laughter the heart is sorrowful; and the end of that mirth is heaviness. *Pr.* 14: 13.

A merry heart doeth good like a medicine. *Pr.* 17: 22.

Go to now, I will prove thee with mirth, therefore enjoy pleasure: and, behold, this also is vanity. *Ec.* 2: 1.

A time to weep, and a time to laugh; a time to mourn, and a time to dance. *Ec.* 3: 4.

Sorrow is better than laughter: for by the sadness of the countenance the heart is made better. *Ec.* 7: 3.

As the crackling of thorns under a pot, so is the laughter of the fool. *Ec.* 7: 6.

Blessed are ye that weep now: for ye shall laugh. *Lu.* 6: 21.

Woe unto you that laugh now. *Lu.* 6: 25.

Let your laughter be turned to mourning, and your joy to heaviness. *Ja.* 4: 9.

See also

Cheer; Gaiety; Merriment; Mirth; Smile.

Law

The law is light. *Pr.* 6: 23.

He that keepeth the law, happy is he. *Pr.* 29: 18.

In her tongue is the law of kindness. *Pr.* 31: 26.

The law of truth was in his mouth, and iniquity was not found in his lips. *Mal.* 2: 6.

By the deeds of the law there shall no flesh be justified in his sight. *Ro.* 3: 20.

The law worketh wrath: for where no law is, there is no transgression. *Ro.* 4: 15.

Ye are not under the law, but under grace. *Ro.* 6: 14.

Ye also are become dead to the law by the body of Christ. *Ro.* 7: 4.

We should serve in newness of spirit, and not in the oldness of the letter. *Ro.* 7: 6.

We know that the law is spiritual: but I am carnal, sold under sin. *Ro.* 7: 14.

Christ is the end of the law for righteousness to every one that believeth. *Ro.* 10: 4.

Love is the fulfilling of the law. *Ro.* 13: 10.

All things are lawful unto me, but all things are not expedient. *1 Co.* 6: 12.

A man is not justified by the works of the law, but by the faith of Jesus Christ. *Ga.* 2: 16.

The just shall live by faith. And the law is not of faith. *Ga.* 3: 11, 12.

Christ hath redeemed us from the curse of the law, being made a curse for us. *Ga.* 3: 13.

The law was our schoolmaster to bring us unto Christ. *Ga.* 3: 24.

Christ is become of no effect unto you, whosoever of you are justified by the law; ye are fallen from grace. *Ga.* 5: 4.

The law having a shadow of good things to come, and not the very image of the things, can never with those sacrifices which they offered year by year continually make the comers thereunto perfect. *He.* 10: 1.

If ye fulfil the royal law according to the scripture, Thou shalt love thy neighbour as thyself, ye do well. *Ja.* 2: 8.

So speak ye, and so do, as they that shall be judged by the law of liberty. *Ja.* 2: 12.

See also

Commandment; Decree; God, Commandment of; God, Law of; Justice; Lawyer; Order; Ordinance; Principle; Rule; Statute.

Lawfulness

The Lord is our lawgiver. *Is.* 33: 22.

If a man be just, and do that which is lawful and right, . . . he shall surely live, saith the Lord God. *Eze.* 18: 5, 9.

It is lawful to do well on the sabbath days. *Mat.* 12: 12.

All things are lawful unto me, but all things are not expedient. *1 Co. 6: 12.*

He was caught up into paradise, and heard unspeakable words, which it is not lawful for a man to utter. *2 Co. 12: 4.*

The law is good, if a man use it lawfully. *1 Ti. 1: 8.*

If a man also strive for masteries, yet is he not crowned, except he strive lawfully. *2 Ti. 2: 5.*

See also

Law; Lawlessness; Lawyer

Lawlessness

The children of Israel . . . walked in the statutes of the heathen. *2 K. 17: 7, 8.*

They were disobedient, and rebelled against thee, and cast thy law behind their backs. *Ne. 9: 26.*

They kept not the covenant of God, and refused to walk in his law. *Ps. 78: 10.*

If they break my statutes, and keep not my commandments; Then will I visit their transgression with the rod. *Ps. 89: 31, 32.*

Rivers of waters run down mine eyes, because they keep not thy law. *Ps. 119: 136.*

Salvation is far from the wicked: for they seek not thy statutes. *Ps. 119: 155.*

The law is no more; her prophets also find no vision from the Lord. *La. 2: 9.*

Seeing thou hast forsaken the law of thy God, I will also forget thy children. *Ho. 4: 6.*

Ye pay tithe of mint and anise and cummin, and have omitted the weightier matters of the law, judgment, mercy and faith. *Mat. 23: 23.*

Thou that makest thy boast of the law, through breaking the law dishonourest thou God? *Ro. 2: 23.*

See also

Anarchy; Chaos; Confusion; Lawfulness; Rebellion.

Lawyer

When they have a matter, they come unto me; . . . and I do make them know the statutes of God, and his laws. *Ex. 18: 16.*

The Lord is our judge, the Lord is our lawgiver, the Lord is our king. *Is. 33: 22.*

The Pharisees and lawyers rejected the counsel of God against themselves, being not baptized of him. *Lu. 7: 30.*

Woe unto you, lawyers! for ye have taken away the key of knowledge. *Lu. 11: 52.*

The letter killeth, but the spirit giveth life. *2 Co. 3: 6.*

We know that the law is good, if a man use it lawfully. *1 Ti. 1: 8.*

There is one lawgiver, who is able to save and to destroy. *Ja. 4: 12.*

See also

Advocate; Christ, the Judge; God, the Judge; Law.

Laziness

They be idle. *Ex. 5: 8.*

Go to the ant, thou sluggard; consider her ways, and be wise. *Pr. 6: 6.*

The slothful shall be under tribute. *Pr. 12: 24.*

The slothful man roasteth not that which he took in hunting. *Pr. 12: 27.*

The soul of the sluggard desireth, and hath nothing: but the soul of the diligent shall be made fat. *Pr. 13: 4.*

An idle soul shall suffer hunger. *Pr. 19: 15.*

The slothful man saith, There is a lion without, I shall be slain in the streets. *Pr. 22: 13.*

They learn to be idle, wandering about from house to house; and not only idle, but tattlers also and busybodies, ·speaking things which they ought not. *1 Ti. 5: 13.*

See also

Idleness; Indolence; Sloth.

Leadership

The Lord thy God, he it is that doth go with thee. *De. 31: 6.*

Have not I commanded thee? Be strong and of a good courage. *Jos. 1: 9.*

By the good hand of our God upon us, they brought us a man of understanding. *Ezr. 8: 18.*

The pillar of the cloud departed not from them by day, to lead them in the way; neither the pillar of fire by night, to shew them light, and the way wherein they should go. *Ne. 9: 19.*

Lead me, O Lord, in thy righteousness because of mine enemies. *Ps. 5: 8.*

Thou wilt shew me the path of life. *Ps. 16: 11.*

A man's heart deviseth his way: but the Lord directeth his steps. *Pr. 16: 9.*

He . . . shall gently lead those that are with young. *Is. 40: 11.*

Behold, I have given him for a witness to the people, a leader and commander to the people. *Is. 55: 4.*

I have set watchmen upon thy walls, O Jerusalem, which shall never hold their peace day nor night. *Is. 62: 6.*

My father, thou art the guide of my youth. *Je. 3: 4.*

I sent before thee Moses, Aaron, and Miriam. *Mi. 6: 4.*

I . . . will make thee as a signet: for I have chosen thee. *Hag. 2: 23.*

Not by might, nor by power, but by my spirit, saith the Lord of hosts. *Zch. 4: 6.*

If the blind lead the blind, both shall fall into the ditch. *Mat. 15: 14.*

Woe unto you, ye blind guides! *Mat. 23: 16.*

He calleth his own sheep by name, and leadeth them out. *Jn. 10: 3.*

He is a chosen vessel unto me, to bear my name before the Gentiles, and kings, and the children of Israel. *Ac. 9: 15.*

See also

Administration; Christ, the Leader; Commander; Commandment; Direction; Execution; Government; Guidance; Order; Prominence; Rule; Vanguard.

Leaf

The dove came in to him in the evening; and, lo, in her mouth was an olive leaf pluckt off. *Ge. 8: 11.*

His leaf also shall not wither. *Ps. 1: 3.*

Ye shall be as an oak whose leaf fadeth, and as a garden that hath no water. *Is. 1: 30.*

All the host of heaven shall be dissolved: . . . and all their host shall fall down, as the leaf falleth off from the vine, and as a falling fig from the fig tree. *Is. 34: 4.*

We all do fade as a leaf; and our iniquities, like the wind, have taken us away. *Is. 64: 6.*

When he saw a fig tree in the way, he came to it, and found nothing thereon, but leaves only. *Mat.* 21: 19.

Now learn a parable of the fig tree; when his branch is yet tender, and putteth forth leaves, ye know that summer is nigh. *Mat.* 24: 32.

The leaves of the tree were for the healing of the nations. *Re.* 22: 2.

See also

Tree; Verdure; Withering.

League

We be come from a far country: now therefore make ye a league with us. *Jos.* 9: 6.

Joshua made peace with them, and made a league with them, to let them live. *Jos.* 9: 15.

Make thy league with me, and, behold, my hand shall be with thee. 2 *S.* 3: 12.

There is a league between me and thee, and between my father and thy father. *1 K.* 15: 19.

Thou shalt be in league with the stones of the field: and the beasts of the field shall be at peace with thee. *Jb.* 5: 23.

They are confederate against thee. *Ps.* 83: 5.

Associate yourselves, O ye people, and ye shall be broken in pieces. *Is.* 8: 9.

Say ye not, A confederacy, to all them to whom this people shall say, A confederacy. *Is.* 8: 12.

See also

Alliance; Association; Covenant; Nations, League of.

Learning

The heart of him that hath understanding seeketh knowledge. *Pr.* 15: 14.

How much better is it to get wisdom than gold! *Pr.* 16: 16.

That the soul be without knowledge, it is not good. *Pr.* 19: 2.

By knowledge shall the chambers be filled with all precious and pleasant riches. *Pr.* 24: 4.

A man's wisdom maketh his face to shine. *Ec.* 8: 1.

The earth shall be filled with the knowledge of the glory of the Lord, as the waters cover the sea. *Hab.* 2: 14.

Paul, thou art beside thyself; much learning doth make thee mad. *Ac.* 26: 24.

To another the word of knowledge by the same Spirit. *1 Co.* 12: 8.

See also

Christ, Knowledge of; Christ, Mind of; Christ, Wisdom of; Education; Enlightenment; God, Knowledge of; God, Wisdom of; Intelligence; Knowledge; Mind; Perception; Reason; Sage; School; Study; Thought; Wisdom.

Least

Thou Bethlehem, in the land of Juda, art not the least among the princes of Juda: for out of thee shall come a Governor, that shall rule my people Israel. *Mat.* 2: 6.

Whosoever therefore shall break one of these least commandments, and shall teach men so, he shall be called the least in the kingdom of heaven. *Mat.* 5: 19.

Among them that are born of women there hath not risen a greater than John the Baptist: notwithstanding he that is least in the kingdom of heaven is greater than he. *Mat.* 11: 11.

The kingdom of heaven is like to a grain of mustard seed, . . . Which indeed is the least of all seeds. *Mat.* 13: 31, 32.

Inasmuch as ye have done it unto one of the least of these my brethren, ye have done it unto me. *Mat.* 25: 40.

He that is least among you all, the same shall be great. *Lu.* 9: 48.

He that is faithful in that which is least is faithful also in much: and he that is unjust in the least is unjust also in much. *Lu.* 16: 10.

I am the least of the apostles, that am not meet to be called an apostle, because I persecuted the church of God. *1 Co.* 15: 9.

Unto me, who am less than the least of all saints, is this grace given, that I should preach among the Gentiles the unsearchable riches of Christ. *Ep.* 3: 8.

See also

Humility; Little; Lowliness; Meekness; Modesty; Pettiness; Smallness; Thing, the Little; Trifle.

Leaven

Offer a sacrifice of thanksgiving with leaven. *Am.* 4: 5.

The kingdom of heaven is like unto leaven. *Mat.* 13: 33.

Till the whole was leavened. *Mat.* 13: 33.

Take heed and beware of the leaven of the Pharisees and of the Sadducees. *Mat.* 16: 6.

Know ye not that a little leaven leaveneth the whole lump? *1 Co.* 5: 6.

Purge out therefore the old leaven, that ye may be a new lump, as ye are unleavened. *1 Co.* 5: 7.

Therefore let us keep the feast not with old leaven, neither with the leaven of malice and wickedness; but with the unleavened bread of sincerity and truth. *1 Co.* 5: 8.

See also

Example; Ideal; Influence; Pattern.

Legacy

Elijah said unto Elisha, Ask what I shall do for thee, before I be taken away from thee. And Elisha said, I pray thee, let a double portion of thy spirit be upon me. 2 *K.* 2: 9.

He took up also the mantle of Elijah that fell from him. 2 *K.* 2: 13.

I have a goodly heritage. *Ps.* 16: 6.

Those that wait upon the Lord, they shall inherit the earth. *Ps.* 37: 9.

Thou hast given me the heritage of those that fear thy name. *Ps.* 61: 5.

I . . . will bring them again, every man to his heritage, and every man to his land. *Je.* 12: 15.

Peace I leave with you, my peace I give unto you: not as the world giveth, give I unto you. *Jn.* 14: 27.

The fathers have eaten a sour grape, and the children's teeth are set on edge. *Je.* 31: 29.

Giving thanks unto the Father, which hath made us meet to be partakers of the inheritance of the saints in light. *Col.* 1: 12.

See also

Bequest; Birthright; Heir; Heritage; Inheritance.

Leisure

Six days thou shalt do thy work, and on the seventh day thou shalt rest. *Ex.* 23: 12.

Man goeth forth unto his work and to his labour until the evening. *Ps.* 104: 23.

To every thing there is a season, and a time to every purpose under the heaven. *Ec.* 3: 1.

Every man should eat and drink, and enjoy the good of all his labour. *Ec.* 3: 13.

The sleep of a labouring man is sweet. *Ec.* 5: 12.

He said unto them, Come ye yourselves apart into a desert place, and rest a while: for there were many coming and going, and they had no leisure so much as to eat. *Mk.* 6: 31.

See also

Contentment; Ease; Quiet; Relief; Repose; Rest.

Length

Honour thy father and thy mother: that thy days may be long upon the land. *Ex.* 20: 12.

Man goeth to his long home. *Ec.* 12: 5.

Ye devour widows' houses, and for a pretence make long prayer. *Mat.* 23: 14.

Charity suffereth long. *I Co.* 13: 4.

That ye, being rooted and grounded in love, May be able to comprehend with all saints what is the breadth, and length, and depth, and height. *Ep.* 3: 17, 18.

The city lieth foursquare, and the length is as large as the breadth. *Re.* 21: 16.

Lent

Yet did not the chief butler remember Joseph, but forgat him. *Ge.* 40: 23.

Keep thy heart with all diligence; for out of it are the issues of life. *Pr.* 4: 23.

Thus saith the Lord; Shall they fall and not arise? shall he turn away, and not return? *Je.* 8: 4.

Jesus, moved with compassion, put forth his hand, and touched him, and saith unto him, I will; be thou clean. *Mk.* 1: 41.

Now we believe, not because of thy saying: for we have heard him ourselves, and know that this is indeed the Christ, the Saviour of the world. *Jn.* 4: 42.

Greater love hath no man than this, that a man lay down his life for his friends. *Jn.* 15: 13.

The Father himself loveth you, because ye have loved me, and have believed that I came out from God. *Jn.* 16: 27.

Be not overcome of evil, but overcome evil with good. *Ro.* 12: 21.

This one thing I do, forgetting those things which are behind, and reaching forth unto those things which are before, I press toward the mark for the prize of the high calling of God in Christ Jesus. *Ph.* 3: 13, 14.

I put thee in remembrance that thou stir up the gift of God, which is in thee. *2 Ti.* 1: 6.

God hath not given us the spirit of fear; but of power, and of love, and of a sound mind. *2 Ti.* 1: 7.

I . . . am persuaded that he is able to keep that which I have committed unto him against that day. *2 Ti.* 1: 12.

We love him, because he first loved us. *I Jn.* 4: 19.

The Spirit and the bride say, Come. And let him that heareth say, Come. And let him that is athirst come. And whosoever will, let him take the water of life freely. *Re.* 22: 17.

See also

Contrition; Conversion; Penance; Penitence; Purification; Reform; Regret; Remorse; Renewal; Revival.

Leprosy

He was also a mighty man in valour, but he was a leper. *2 K.* 5: 1.

He went out of his presence a leper as white as snow. *2 K.* 5: 27.

Uzziah the king was a leper unto the day of his death. *2 Ch.* 26: 21.

Jesus put forth his hand, and touched him, saying, I will; be thou clean. And immediately his leprosy was cleansed. *Mat.* 8: 3.

Heal the sick, cleanse the lepers, raise the dead, cast out devils: freely ye have received, freely give. *Mat.* 10: 8.

The lepers are cleansed. *Mat.* 11: 5.

Many lepers were in Israel in the time of Eliseus the prophet; and none of them was cleansed, saving Naaman the Syrian. *Lu.* 4: 27.

As he entered into a certain village, there met him ten men that were lepers. *Lu.* 17: 12.

Letter

We should serve in newness of spirit, and not in the oldness of the letter. *Ro.* 7: 6.

Need we, as some others, epistles of commendation to you, or letters of commendation from you? *2 Co.* 3: 1.

Ye are our epistle written in our hearts, known and read of all men. *2 Co.* 3: 2.

Forasmuch as ye are manifestly declared to be the epistle of Christ ministered by us, written not with ink, but with the Spirit of the living God; not in tables of stone, but in fleshy tables of the heart. *2 Co.* 3: 3.

The letter killeth, but the spirit giveth life. *2 Co.* 3: 6.

Such as we are in word by letters when we are absent, such will we be also in deed when we are present. *2 Co.* 10: 11.

Hold the traditions which ye have been taught, whether by word or our epistle. *2 Th.* 2: 15.

Brethren, I write no new commandment unto you. *I Jn.* 2: 7.

A new commandment I write unto you, which thing is true in him and in you. *I Jn.* 2: 8.

Having many things to write unto you, I would not write with paper and ink: but I trust to come unto you. *2 Jn.* 1: 12.

See also

Author; Epistle; Scripture; Writing.

Liberality

Every man that offered offered an offering of gold unto the Lord. *Ex.* 35: 22.

The people bring much more than enough for the service of the work. *Ex.* 36: 5.

The liberal soul shall be made fat: and he that watereth shall be watered also himself. *Pr.* 11: 25.

If thou wilt be perfect, go and sell that thou hast, and give to the poor. *Mat.* 19: 21.

Give, and it shall be given unto you; good measure, pressed down, and shaken together, and running over. *Lu.* 6: 38.

I give tithes of all that I possess. *Lu.* 18: 12.

God giveth not the Spirit by measure unto him. *Jn.* 3: 34.

Not as the world giveth, give I unto you. *Jn.* 14: 27.

Neither was there any among them that lacked: for as many as were possessors of lands or houses sold them, and brought the prices of the things that were sold. *Ac.* 4: 34.

It is more blessed to give than to receive. *Ac.* 20: 35.

How shall he not . . . freely give us all things? *Ro.* 8: 32.

That we might know the things that are freely given to us of God. *1 Co.* 2: 12.

Let him give; not grudgingly, or of necessity: for God loveth a cheerful giver. *2 Co.* 9: 7.

If any of you ask wisdom, let him ask of God, that giveth to all men liberally. *Ja.* 1: 5.

The wisdom that is from above is . . . full of mercy and good fruits. *Ja.* 3: 17.

Charity shall cover the multitude of sins. *1 Pe.* 4: 8.

And to brotherly kindness charity. *2 Pe.* 1: 7.

I know thy works, and charity, and service, and faith, and thy patience. *Re.* 2: 19.

See also

Almsgiving; Beneficence; Benevolence; Charity; Christ, Gift of; Generosity; Gift; God, Gift of; Philanthropy; Present; Unselfishness.

Liberty

Proclaim liberty throughout all the land unto all the inhabitants thereof. *Le.* 25: 10.

The angel of the Lord encampeth round about them that fear him, and delivereth them. *Ps.* 34: 7.

Thou hast ascended on high, thou hast led captivity captive. *Ps.* 68: 18.

I will walk at liberty: for I seek thy precepts. *Ps.* 119: 45.

The ransomed of the Lord shall return, and come to Zion with songs and everlasting joy upon their heads. *Is.* 35: 10.

Thus saith the Lord, In an acceptable time have I heard thee, and in a day of salvation have I helped thee. *Is.* 49: 8.

That thou mayest say to the prisoners, Go forth; to them that are in darkness, Shew yourselves. *Is.* 49: 9.

I was to them as they that take off the yoke on their jaws, and I laid meat unto them. *Ho.* 11: 4.

Behold, I will save my people from the east country, and from the west country. *Zch.* 8: 7.

Whom will ye that I release unto you? Barabbas, or Jesus which is called Christ? *Mat.* 27: 17.

Ye shall know the truth, and the truth shall make you free. *Jn.* 8: 32.

Being let go, they went to their own company. *Ac.* 4: 23.

With a great sum obtained I this freedom. *Ac.* 22: 28.

Now we are delivered from the law, . . . that we should serve in newness of spirit. *Ro.* 7: 6.

The glorious liberty of the children of God. *Ro.* 8: 21.

All things are lawful unto me, but all things are not expedient. *1 Co.* 6: 12.

Take heed lest by any means this liberty of yours become a stumblingblock to them that are weak. *1 Co.* 8: 9.

Stand fast therefore in the liberty wherewith Christ hath made us free, and be not entangled again with the yoke of bondage. *Ga.* 5: 1.

Whoso looketh into the perfect law of liberty, and continueth therein, . . . this man shall be blessed in his deed. *Ja.* 1: 25.

So speak ye, and so do, as they that shall be judged by the law of liberty. *Ja.* 2: 12.

As free, and not using your liberty for a cloke of maliciousness, but as the servants of God. *1 Pe.* 2: 16.

I will give unto him that is athirst of the fountain of the water of life freely. *Re.* 21: 6.

See also

Democracy; Emancipation; Freedom; Independence; Licence; Release.

Licence

In those days there was no king in Israel, but every man did that which was right in his own eyes. *Ju.* 17: 6.

The daughters of Zion are haughty, and walk with stretched forth necks and wanton eyes, walking and mincing as they go. *Is.* 3: 16.

Make not provision for the flesh, to fulfil the lusts thereof. *Ro.* 13: 14.

Use not liberty for an occasion to the flesh. *Ga.* 5: 13.

Flee also youthful lusts. *2 Ti.* 2: 22.

To enjoy the pleasures of sin for a season. *He.* 11: 25.

Ye have lived in pleasure on the earth, and been wanton. *Ja.* 5: 5.

As free . . . but as the servants of God. *1 Pe.* 2: 16.

They allure through the lusts of the flesh, through much wantonness. *2 Pe.* 2: 18.

See also

Emancipation; Flesh; Freedom; Independence; Liberty; Lust.

Lie

Keep thee far from a false matter. *Ex.* 23: 7.

All men are liars. *Ps.* 116: 11.

Their right hand is a right hand of falsehood. *Ps.* 144: 8.

The getting of treasures by a lying tongue is a vanity tossed to and fro of them that seek death. *Pr.* 21: 6.

Ephraim compasseth me about with lies. *Ho.* 11: 12.

Many bare false witness against him, but their witness agreed not together. *Mk.* 14: 56.

Thou hast not lied unto men, but unto God. *Ac.* 5: 4.

Who changed the truth of God into a lie. *Ro.* 1: 25.

In hope of eternal life, which God, that cannot lie, promised before the world began. *Tit.* 1: 2.

Lie not against the truth. *Ja.* 3: 14.

No lie is of the truth. *1 Jn.* 2: 21.

All liars shall have their part in the lake which burneth with fire and brimstone. *Re.* 21: 8.

See also

Calumny; Deceit; Dishonesty; Falsehood; Untruthfulness.

Life

The days of the years of my pilgrimage. *Ge.* 47: 9.

Now therefore hearken, O Israel, unto the statutes and unto the judgments, which I teach you, for to do them, that ye may live. *De.* 4: 1.

Choose life, that both thou and thy seed may live. *De.* 30: 19.

As thy days, so shall thy strength be. *De.* 33: 25.

No man is sure of life. *Jb.* 24: 22.

Men of the world . . . have their portion in this life. *Ps.* 17: 14.

The Lord . . . redeemeth thy life from destruction. *Ps.* 103: 2, 4.

To him that is joined to all the living there is hope. *Ec.* 9: 4.

A living dog is better than a dead lion. *Ec.* 9: 4.

By these things men live. *Is.* 38: 16.

This do, and thou shalt live. *Lu.* 10: 28.

None of these things move me, neither count I my life dear unto myself. *Ac.* 20: 24.

To be spiritually minded is life and peace. *Ro.* 8: 6.

None of us liveth to himself, and no man dieth to himself. *Ro.* 14: 7.

He that hath not the Son of God hath not life. *1 Jn.* 5: 12.

Whosoever will, let him take the water of life freely. *Re.* 22: 17.

See also

Existence; Life, Book of; Life, Bread of; Life, the Eternal; Life, Frontage of; Life, the Full; Life, the Long; Life, Love of; Life, the New; Life, Path of; Life, Prince of; Life, Quest of; Life, Reverence for; Life, the Short; Soul; Spirit.

Life, Book of

Rejoice, because your names are written in heaven. *Lu.* 10: 20.

My fellow labourers, whose names are in the book of life. *Ph.* 4: 3.

He that overcometh, the same shall be clothed in white raiment; and I will not blot out his name out of the book of life. *Re.* 3: 5.

All that dwell upon the earth shall worship him, whose names are not written in the book of life of the Lamb slain from the foundation of the world. *Re.* 13: 8.

Another book was opened, which is the book of life. *Re.* 20: 12.

Whosoever was not found written in the book of life was cast into the lake of fire. *Re.* 20: 15.

There shall in no wise enter into it any thing that defileth, . . . but they which are written in the Lamb's book of life. *Re.* 21: 27.

Life, Bread of

Man doth not live by bread only, but by every word that proceedeth out of the mouth of the Lord doth man live. *De.* 8: 3.

Thou openest thine hand, and satisfiest the desire of every living thing. *Ps.* 145: 16.

Ye shall eat in plenty, and be satisfied. *Jo.* 2: 26.

Take no thought for your life, what ye shall eat, or what ye shall drink; nor yet for your body, what ye shall put on. *Mat.* 6: 25.

A man's life consisteth not in the abundance of the things which he possesseth. *Lu.* 12: 15.

The life is more than meat, and the body is more than raiment. *Lu.* 12: 23.

Jesus said unto them, I am the bread of life. *Jn.* 6: 35.

I am the living bread which came down from heaven: if any man eat of this bread, he shall live for ever. *Jn.* 6: 51.

See also

Christ, the Bread of Life.

Life, the Eternal

The Lord be between thee and me for ever. *1 S.* 20: 23.

I know that my redeemer liveth. *Jb.* 19: 25.

The Lord knoweth the days of the upright: and their inheritance shall be for ever. *Ps.* 37: 18.

The righteous shall inherit the land, and dwell therein for ever. *Ps.* 37: 29.

The saints of the most High shall take the kingdom, and possess the kingdom for ever, even for ever and ever. *Da.* 7: 18.

God is not the God of the dead, but of the living. *Mat.* 22: 32.

What shall I do to inherit eternal life? *Lu.* 10: 25.

Why seek ye the living among the dead? *Lu.* 24: 5.

This is the will of him that sent me, that every one that seeth the Son, and believeth on him, may have everlasting life: and I will raise him up at the last day. *Jn.* 6: 40.

I give unto them eternal life. *Jn.* 10: 28.

Jesus said unto her, I am the resurrection, and the life. *Jn.* 11: 25.

Whosoever liveth and believeth in me shall never die. *Jn.* 11: 26.

This is life eternal, that they might know thee the only true God, and Jesus Christ whom thou hast sent. *Jn.* 17: 3.

As many as were ordained to eternal life believed. *Ac.* 13: 48.

This mortal must put on immortality. *1 Co.* 15: 53.

As dying, and, behold, we live. *2 Co.* 6: 9.

He that soweth to the Spirit shall of the Spirit reap life everlasting. *Ga.* 6: 8.

If ye then be risen with Christ, seek those things which are above. *Col.* 3: 1.

The power of an endless life. *He.* 7: 16.

Having obtained eternal redemption for us. *He.* 9: 12.

He that doeth the will of God abideth for ever. *1 Jn.* 2: 17.

They shall reign for ever and ever. *Re.* 22: 5.

See also

Christ, Resurrection of; Easter; Eternity; Immortality; Resurrection.

Life, Frontage of

His wife looked back from behind him, and she became a pillar of salt. *Ge.* 19: 26.

Thou Lord art seen face to face. *Nu.* 14: 14.

There arose not a prophet since in Israel like unto Moses, whom the Lord knew face to face. *De.* 34 :10.

They have turned unto me the back, and not the face. *Je.* 32: 33.

His windows being open in his chamber toward Jerusalem, he kneeled upon his knees three times a day, and prayed, and gave thanks before his God. *Da.* 6: 10.

Get thee behind me, Satan. *Mat.* 16: 23.

No man, having put his hand to the plow, and looking back, is fit for the kingdom of God. *Lu.* 10: 62.

Forgetting those things which are behind, and reaching forth unto those things which are before. *Ph.* 3: 13.

See also
Aspiration; Christ, Quest for; God, Aspiration for; God, Quest for; Longing; Yearning.

Life, the Full

I will run the way of thy commandments, when thou shalt enlarge my heart. *Ps.* 119: 32.

Thou openest thine hand, and satisfiest the desire of every living thing. *Ps.* 145: 16.

So shall thy barns be filled with plenty, and thy presses shall burst out with new wine. *Pr.* 3: 10.

The bed is shorter than that a man can stretch himself on it: and the covering narrower than that he can wrap himself in it. *Is.* 28: 20.

Full of wisdom, and perfect in beauty. *Eze.* 28: 12.

In him was life. *Jn.* 1: 4.

Jesus answered and said unto her, Whosoever drinketh of this water shall thirst again: But whosoever drinketh of the water that I shall give him shall never thirst; but the water that I shall give him shall be in him a well of water springing up into everlasting life. *Jn.* 4: 13, 14.

I am come that they might have life, and that they might have it more abundantly. *Jn.* 10: 10.

All things are yours; Whether . . . life, or death. *1 Co.* 3: 21, 22.

Be ye also enlarged. *2 Co.* 6: 13.

This I pray, that your love may abound yet more and more in knowledge and in all judgment; That ye may approve things that are excellent. *Ph.* 1: 9, 10.

See also
Christ, Fullness of; Christ, Perfection of; Completion; Fulfilment; Fullness; Perfection; Realization.

Life, the Long

If thou wilt walk in my ways, to keep my statutes and my commandments, . . . then I will lengthen thy days. *1 K.* 3: 14.

Thou shalt come to thy grave in a full age, like as a shock of corn cometh in in his season. *Jb.* 5: 26.

His leaf also shall not wither; and whatsoever he doeth shall prosper. *Ps.* 1: 3.

He asked life of thee, and thou gavest it him, even length of days for ever and ever. *Ps.* 21: 4.

What man is he that desireth life, and loveth many days, that he may see good? *Ps.* 34: 12.

I have been young, and now am old; yet have I not seen the righteous forsaken. *Ps.* 37: 25.

With long life will I satisfy him, and shew him my salvation. *Ps.* 91: 16.

They shall still bring forth fruit in old age. *Ps.* 92: 14.

The years of thy life shall be many. *Pr.* 4: 10.

The fear of the Lord prolongeth days. *Pr.* 10: 27.

If a man beget an hundred children, and live many years, so that the days of his years be many, and his soul be not filled with good, and also that he have no burial; I say, that an untimely birth is better than he. *Ec.* 6: 3.

There shall be no more thence an infant of days, nor an old man that hath not filled his days: for the child shall die an hundred years old. *Is.* 65: 20.

There shall yet old men and old women dwell in the streets of Jerusalem, and every man with his staff in his hand for very age. *Zch.* 8: 4.

Honour thy father and mother; . . . That it may be well with thee, and thou mayest live long on the earth. *Ep.* 6: 2, 3.

See also
Age; Length; Old.

Life, Love of

All that a man hath will he give for his life. *Jb.* 2: 4.

What man is he that desireth life, and loveth many days, that he may see good? Keep thy tongue from evil. *Ps.* 34: 12, 13.

A living dog is better than a dead lion. *Ec.* 9: 4.

He that loveth his life shall lose it. *Jn.* 12: 25.

Greater love hath no man than this, that a man lay down his life for his friends. *Jn.* 15: 13.

Neither count I my life dear unto myself. *Ac.* 20: 24.

He that will love life, and see good days, let him refrain his tongue from evil, and his lips that they speak no guile. *1 Pe.* 3: 10.

Life, the New

Man became a living soul. *Ge.* 2: 7.

And Moses made a serpent of brass, and put it upon a pole; and it came to pass, that if a serpent had bitten any man, when he beheld the serpent of brass, he lived. *Nu.* 21: 9.

He stretched himself upon the child three times, and cried unto the Lord. *1 K.* 17: 21.

For there is hope of a tree, if it be cut down, that it will sprout again, and that the tender branch thereof will not cease. *Jb.* 14: 7.

A new heart also will I give you, and a new spirit will I put within you: and I will take away the stony heart out of your flesh, and I will give you an heart of flesh. *Eze.* 36: 26.

He said unto me, Son of·man, can these bones live? And I answered, O Lord God, thou knowest. *Eze.* 37: 3.

These men are full of new wine. *Ac.* 2: 13.

As Christ was raised up from the dead by the glory of the Father, even so we also should walk in newness of life. *Ro.* 6: 4.

If any man be in Christ, he is a new creature. *2 Co.* 5: 17.

See also
Birth, the New; Conversion; Freshness; Immortality; Renascence.

Life, Path of

My presence shall go with thee, and I will give thee rest. *Ex.* 33: 14.

Thou wilt shew me the path of life. *Ps.* 16: 11.

Shew me thy ways, O Lord; teach me thy paths. *Ps.* 25: 4.

In all thy ways acknowledge him, and he shall direct thy paths. *Pr.* 3: 6.

The path of the just is as the shining light, that shineth more and more unto the perfect day. *Pr.* 4: 18.

I will bring the blind by a way that they knew not. *Is.* 42: 16.

I brought you into a plentiful country. *Je.* 2: 7.

Thus saith the Lord; Behold, I set before you the way of life, and the way of death. *Je.* 21: 8.

The ways of the Lord are right, and the just shall walk in them. *Ho.* 14: 9.

Narrow is the way, which leadeth unto life. *Mat.* 7: 14.

Yet shew I unto you a more excellent way. *1 Co.* 12: 31.

See also
Christ, Way of; God, Way of; Path; Way.

Life, Prince of

The Prince of life, whom God hath raised from the dead. *Ac.* 3: 15.

Him hath God exalted with his right hand to be a Prince and a Saviour, for to give repentance to Israel, and forgiveness of sins. *Ac.* 5: 31.

Jesus Christ, . . . the prince of the kings of the earth. *Re.* 1: 5.

Life, Quest of

The days of the years of my pilgrimage. *Ge.* 47: 9.

He asked life of thee, and thou gavest it him, even length of days for ever and ever. *Ps.* 21: 4.

One thing have I desired of the Lord, that will I seek after; that I may dwell in the house of the Lord all the days of my life. *Ps.* 27: 4.

Seek the Lord, and ye shall live. *Am.* 5: 6.

Seek good, and not evil, that ye may live. *Am.* 5: 14.

Seek ye the kingdom of God; and all these things shall be added unto you. *Lu.* 12: 31.

Be thou faithful unto death, and I will give thee a crown of life. *Rev.* 2: 10.

Blessed are they that do his commandments, that they may have right to the tree of life. *Re.* 22: 14.

See also
Christ, Quest for; God, Quest for.

Life, Reverence for

I establish my covenant with you, . . . And with every living creature that is with you, of the fowl, of the cattle, and of every beast of the earth with you. *Ge.* 9: 9, 10.

The seventh day is the sabbath . . . ; in it thou shalt not do any work, thou, nor thy son, nor thy daughter, thy manservant, nor thy maidservant, nor thy cattle, nor thy stranger that is within thy gates. *Ex.* 20: 10.

Thou shalt not seethe a kid in his mother's milk. *Ex.* 23: 19.

Balaam smote the ass. *Nu.* 22: 23.

Thou shalt not muzzle the ox when he treadeth out the corn. *De.* 25: 4.

Ask now the beasts, and they shall teach thee. *Jb.* 12: 7.

Deliver my soul from the sword; my darling from the power of the dog. *Ps.* 22: 20.

Rescue my soul from their destructions, my darling from the lions. *Ps.* 35: 17.

Every beast of the forest is mine. *Ps.* 50: 10.

I know all the fowls of the mountains. *Ps.* 50: 11.

The wild beasts of the field are mine. *Ps.* 50: 11.

His tender mercies are over all his works. *Ps.* 145: 9.

And also much cattle. *Jon.* 4: 11.

They saw the young child . . . , and fell down, and worshipped him. *Mat.* 2: 11.

He was there in the wilderness . . . with the wild beasts. *Mk.* 1: 13.

Preach the gospel to every creature. *Mk.* 16: 15.

She brought forth her firstborn son, . . . and laid him in a manger. *Lu.* 2: 7.

Doth not each one of you on the sabbath loose his ox or his ass from the stall, and lead him away to watering? *Lu.* 13: 15.

Doth God take care for oxen? *1 Co.* 9: 9.

See also
Life.

Life, the Short

Few and evil have the days of the years of my life been. *Ge.* 47: 9.

We are strangers before thee, and sojourners, as were all our fathers. *1 Ch.* 29: 15.

Our days on the earth are as a shadow, and there is none abiding. *1 Ch.* 29: 15.

Is there not an appointed time to man upon earth? *Jb.* 7: 1.

My days are swifter than a weaver's shuttle, and are spent without hope. *Jb.* 7: 6.

Remember that my life is wind. *Jb.* 7: 7.

I would not live alway: let me alone; for my days are vanity. *Jb.* 7: 16.

My days are swifter than a post: they flee away, they see no good. *Jb.* 9: 25.

Man that is born of a woman is of few days. *Jb.* 14: 1.

Behold, thou hast made my days as a handbreadth; and mine age is as nothing before thee. *Ps.* 39: 5.

Remember how short my time is. *Ps.* 89: 47.

A thousand years in thy sight are but as yesterday when it is past, and as a watch in the night. *Ps.* 90: 4.

The days of our years are threescore years and ten. *Ps.* 90: 10.

The living know that they shall die. *Ec.* 9: 5.

Brethren, the time is short. *1 Co.* 7: 29.

What is your life? It is even a vapour, that appeareth for a little time, and then vanisheth away. *Ja.* 4: 14.

See also
Abbreviation; Brevity; Shortness.

Light

God said, let there be light: and there was light. *Ge.* 1: 3.

God saw the light, that it was good. *Ge.* 1: 4.

Let them that love him be as the sun when he goeth forth in his might. *Ju.* 5: 31.

Light is sown for the righteous. *Ps.* 97: 11.

The sun to rule by day. *Ps.* 136: 8.

If I say, Surely the darkness shall cover me; even the night shall be light about me. *Ps.* 139: 11.

The path of the just is as the shining light, that shineth more and more unto the perfect day. *Pr.* 4: 18.

Truly the light is sweet, and a pleasant thing it is for the eyes to behold the sun. *Ec.* 11: 7.

The people that walked in darkness have seen a great light. *Is.* 9: 2.

They that dwell in the land of the shadow of death, upon them hath the light shined. *Is.* 9: 2.

When I fall, I shall arise; when I sit in darkness, the Lord shall be a light unto me. *Mi.* 7: 8.

At evening time it shall be light. *Zch.* 14: 7.

The people that sat in darkness saw a great light. *Mat.* 4: 16.

The children of this world are in their generation wiser than the children of light. *Lu.* 16: 8.

He was a burning and a shining light. *Jn.* 5: 35.

A light shined in the prison. *Ac.* 12: 7.

At midday, O king, I saw in the way a light from heaven, above the brightness of the sun, shining round about me. *Ac.* 26: 13.

Walk as children of light. *Ep.* 5: 8.

In the midst of a crooked and perverse nation . . . ye shine as lights in the world. *Ph.* 2: 15.

If we walk in the light, as he is in the light, we have fellowship one with another. *1 Jn.* 1: 7.

The nations of them which are saved shall walk in the light of it. *Re.* 21: 24.

See also
Brightness; Candle; Christ, the Light; Day; Gleam; God, the Light; Illumination; Inspiration; Lamp; Light, the Inner; Lightning; Radiance; Ray; Sun.

Light, the Inner

The light of the body is the eye: if therefore thine eye be single, thy whole body shall be full of light. *Mat.* 6: 22.

If therefore the light that is in thee be darkness, how great is that darkness! *Mat.* 6: 23.

Flesh and blood hath not revealed it unto thee, but my Father which is in heaven. *Mat.* 16: 17.

That was the true Light, which lighteth every man that cometh into the world. *Jn.* 1: 9.

While ye have light, believe in the light, that ye may be the children of light. *Jn.* 12: 36.

Let us therefore cast off the works of darkness, and let us put on the armour of light. *Ro.* 13: 12.

God, who commanded the light to shine out of darkness, hath shined in our hearts, to give the light of the knowledge of the glory of God in the face of Jesus Christ. *2 Co.* 4: 6.

For ye were sometimes darkness, but now are ye light in the Lord: walk as children of light; (For the fruit of the Spirit is in all goodness and righteousness and truth). *Ep.* 5: 8, 9.

Awake thou that sleepest, and arise from

the dead, and Christ shall give thee light. *Ep.* 5: 14.

Ye are all the children of light, and the children of the day. *1 Th.* 5: 5.

See also
Christ, the Light; Conscience; God, the Light; Illumination; Inspiration; Light; Vision.

Lightning

There were thunders and lightnings, and a thick cloud upon the mount. *Ex.* 19: 16.

Canst thou send lightnings, that they may go, and say unto thee, Here we are? *Jb.* 38: 35.

The voice of thy thunder was in the heaven: the lightnings lightened the world. *Ps.* 77: 18.

He maketh lightnings for the rain. *Ps.* 135: 7.

Cast forth lightning, and scatter them. *Ps.* 144: 6.

As the lightning cometh out of the east, and shineth even unto the west; so shall also the coming of the Son of man be. *Mat.* 24: 27.

I beheld Satan as lightning fall from heaven. *Lu.* 10: 18.

See also
Gleam; Ray.

Likeness

God said, Let us make man in our image. *Ge.* 1: 26.

Thou shalt not make unto thee any graven image, or any likeness of any thing that is in heaven above, or that is in the earth beneath, or that is in the water under the earth. *Ex.* 20: 4.

He set a carved image, the idol which he had made, in the house of God. *2 Ch.* 33: 7.

I shall be satisfied, when I awake, with thy likeness. *Ps.* 17: 15.

Be not ye therefore like unto them. *Mat.* 6: 8.

As we have borne the image of the earthy, we shall also bear the image of the heavenly. *1 Co.* 15: 49.

We all . . . are changed into the same image from glory to glory, even as by the Spirit of the Lord. *2 Co.* 3: 18.

Christ, who is the image of God. *2 Co.* 4: 4.

See . . . that thou make all things according to the pattern shewed to thee in the mount. *He.* 8: 5.

Take, my brethren, the prophets, who have spoken in the name of the Lord, for an example. *Ja.* 5: 10.

See also
Form; God, Image of; Image; Imitation; Pattern; Resemblance.

Limit

Unto the utmost bound of the everlasting hills. *Ge.* 49: 26.

Thou shalt not remove thy neighbour's landmark. *De.* 19: 14.

The place where we dwell with thee is too strait for us. *2 K.* 6: 1.

He looketh to the ends of the earth. *Jb.* 28: 24.

Hitherto shalt thou come, but no further: and here shall thy proud waves be stayed. *Jb.* 38: 11.

God shall bless us; and all the ends of the earth shall fear him. *Ps.* 67: 7.

They turned back and tempted God, and limited the Holy One of Israel. *Ps.* 78: 41.

The north and the south thou hast created them. *Ps.* 89: 12.

Thou hast set a bound that they may not pass over. *Ps.* 104: 9.

The Creator of the ends of the earth. *Is.* 40: 28.

From one end of heaven to the other. *Mat.* 24: 31.

He . . . hath made of one blood all nations of men for to dwell on all the face of the earth, and hath determined the times before appointed, and the bounds of their habitation. *Ac.* 17: 25, 26.

See also
Bound; Limitation; Margin.

Limitation

When ye are come to the brink of the water of Jordan, ye shall stand still in Jordan. *Jos.* 3: 8.

The Lord was with Judah; and he drave out the inhabitants of the mountain; but could not drive out the inhabitants of the valley, because they had chariots of iron. *Ju.* 1: 19.

Can the rush grow up without mire? can the flag grow without water? *Jb.* 8: 11.

Some remove the landmarks; they violently take away flocks, and feed thereof. *Jb.* 24: 2.

Hitherto shalt thou come, but no further. *Jb.* 38: 11.

Can God furnish a table in the wilderness? *Ps.* 78: 19.

Yea, they turned back and tempted God, and limited the Holy One of Israel. *Ps.* 78: 41.

Can one go upon hot coals, and his feet not be burned? *Pr.* 6: 28.

Man's goings are of the Lord; how can a man then understand his own way? *Pr.* 20: 24.

Which of you by taking thought can add one cubit unto his stature? *Mat.* 6: 27.

How can Satan cast out Satan? *Mk.* 3: 23.

Can the blind lead the blind? shall they not both fall into the ditch? *Lu.* 6: 39.

The Son can do nothing of himself, but what he seeth the Father do. *Jn.* 5: 19.

As the branch cannot bear fruit of itself, except it abide in the vine; no more can ye, except ye abide in me. *Jn.* 15: 4.

Ye are not straitened in us, but ye are straitened in your own bowels. *2 Co.* 6: 12.

He that loveth not his brother whom he hath seen, how can he love God whom he hath not seen? *1 Jn.* 4: 20.

See also
Bound; Confinement; Handicap; Hindrance; Limit; Restraint; Restriction.

Lincoln's Birthday

The Lord raised up a deliverer. *Ju.* 3: 9.

As the man is, so is his strength. *Ju.* 8: 21.

Seek peace, and pursue it. *Ps.* 34: 14.

I will hear what God the Lord will speak: for he will speak peace unto his people. *Ps.* 85: 8.

My soul hath long dwelt with him that hateth peace. I am for peace: but when I speak, they are for war. *Ps.* 120: 7.

The memory of the just is blessed. *Pr.* 10: 7.

I ordained thee a prophet unto the nations. *Je.* 1: 5.

Whosoever will be great among you, let him be your minister. *Mat.* 20: 26.

With a great sum obtained I this freedom. *Ac.* 22: 28.

Cast down, but not destroyed. *2 Co.* 4: 9.

See also
Washington's Birthday.

Line

Where wast thou when I laid the foundations of the earth? . . . who hath stretched the line upon it? *Jb.* 38: 4, 5.

The lines are fallen unto me in pleasant places. *Ps.* 16: 6.

Their line is gone out through all the earth, and their words to the end of the world. *Ps.* 19: 4.

He . . . divided them an inheritance by line. *Ps.* 78: 55.

Precept must be upon precept, precept upon precept; line upon line, line upon line. *Is.* 28: 10.

Not to boast in another man's line of things made ready to our hand. *2 Co.* 10: 16.

Lion

What is stronger than a lion? *Ju.* 14: 18.

He also that is valiant, whose heart is as the heart of a lion, shall utterly melt. *2 S.* 17: 10.

The young lion and the dragon shalt thou trample under feet. *Ps.* 91: 13.

The slothful man saith, There is a lion in the way; a lion is in the streets. *Pr.* 26: 13.

The righteous are bold as a lion. *Pr.* 28: 1.

A lion . . . is strongest among beasts, and turneth not away for any. *Pr.* 30: 30.

A living dog is better than a dead lion. *Ec.* 9: 4.

The lion shall eat straw like the ox. *Is.* 11: 7.

No lion shall be there, nor any ravenous beast shall go up thereon. *Is.* 35: 9.

Your adversary the devil, as a roaring lion, walketh about, seeking whom he may devour. *1 Pe.* 5: 8.

Lip

Give ear unto my prayer, that goeth not out of feigned lips. *Ps.* 17: 1.

Let the lying lips be put to silence. *Ps.* 31: 18.

He hath put a new song in my mouth. *Ps.* 40: 3.

O Lord, open thou my lips; and my mouth shall shew forth thy praise. *Ps.* 51: 15.

Swords are in their lips. *Ps.* 59: 7.

They have sharpened their tongues like a serpent; adders' poison is under their lips. *Ps.* 140: 3.

He that refraineth his lips is wise. *Pr.* 10: 19.

The lip of truth shall be established for ever. *Pr.* 12: 19.

Lying lips are an abomination to the Lord. *Pr.* 12: 22.

He that keepeth his mouth keepeth his life. *Pr.* 13: 3.

The talk of the lips tendeth only to penury. *Pr.* 14: 23.

Righteous lips are the delight of kings. *Pr.* 16: 13.

The sweetness of the lips increaseth learning. *Pr.* 16: 21.

The lips of knowledge are a precious jewel. *Pr.* 20: 15.

Let another man praise thee, and not thine own mouth. *Pr.* 27: 2.

The lips of a fool will swallow up himself. *Ec.* 10: 12.

I am a man of unclean lips, and I dwell in the midst of a people of unclean lips. *Is.* 6: 5.

Lo, this hath touched thy lips: and thine iniquity is taken away, and thy sin purged. *Is.* 6: 7.

This people draw near me with their mouth, and with their lips do honour me, but have removed their heart far from me. *Is.* 29: 13.

He that will love life, and see good days, let him refrain his tongue from evil, and his lips that they speak no guile. *1 Pe.* 3: 10.

See also
Language; Mouth; Speech; Tongue; Utterance; Word.

Listening

They and our fathers dealt proudly, and hardened their necks, and hearkened not to thy commandments. *Ne.* 9: 16.

Consider and hear me, O Lord my God: lighten mine eyes. *Ps.* 13: 3.

Come, ye children, hearken unto me: I will teach you the fear of the Lord. *Ps.* 34: 11.

Cause me to hear thy lovingkindness in the morning. *Ps.* 143: 8.

Opening the ears, but he heareth not. *Is.* 42: 20.

O that thou hadst hearkened to my commandments! then had thy peace been as a river, and thy righteousness as the waves of the sea. *Is.* 48: 18.

Listen, O isles, unto me; and hearken, ye people, from far. *Is.* 49: 1.

Incline your ear, and come unto me: hear, and your soul shall live. *Is.* 55: 3.

He that hath ears to hear, let him hear. *Mat.* 11: 15.

Of whom we have many things to say, and hard to be uttered, seeing ye are dull of hearing. *He.* 5: 11.

He that hath an ear, let him hear what the Spirit saith unto the churches. *Re.* 2: 7.

See also
Ear; Hearing; Heed.

Little

Are the consolations of God small with thee? *Jb.* 15: 11.

The mountains skipped like rams, and the little hills like lambs. *Ps.* 114: 4.

Yet a little sleep, a little slumber, a little folding of the hands to sleep: So shall thy poverty come as one that travelleth, and thy want as an armed man. *Pr.* 6: 10, 11.

Better is little with the fear of the Lord than great treasure and trouble therewith. *Pr.* 15: 16.

Better is a little with righteousness than great revenues without right. *Pr.* 16: 8.

If thou faint in the day of adversity, thy strength is small. *Pr.* 24: 10.

Here a little, and there a little. *Is.* 28: 10.

A little one shall become a thousand, and a small one a strong nation. *Is.* 60: 22.

Though thou be little among the thousands of Judah, yet out of thee shall he come forth unto me that is to be ruler in Israel. *Mi.* 5: 2.

To whom little is forgiven, the same loveth little. *Lu.* 7: 47.

Because thou hast been faithful in a very little, have thou authority over ten cities. *Lu.* 19: 17.

Do ye not know that the saints shall judge the world? and if the world shall be judged by you, are ye unworthy to judge the smallest matters? *1 Co.* 6: 2.

Behold also the ships, which though they be so great, and are driven of fierce winds, yet are they turned about with a very small helm. *Ja.* 3: 4.

The tongue is a little member, and boasteth great things. *Ja.* 3: 5.

Behold, how great a matter a little fire kindleth! *Ja.* 3: 5.

See also
Least; Pettiness; Smallness; Thing, the Little; Trifle.

Liturgy

Ye shall be unto me a kingdom of priests. *Ex.* 19: 6.

Let the children of Israel also keep the passover at his appointed season, . . . according to all the rites of it, and according to all the ceremonies thereof, shall ye keep it. *Nu.* 9: 2, 3.

Ezra blessed the Lord, the great God. And all the people answered, Amen, Amen, with lifting up their hands: and they bowed their heads, and worshipped the Lord with their faces to the ground. *Ne.* 8: 6.

O worship the Lord in the beauty of holiness. *Ps.* 96: 9.

We have heard him say that this Jesus of Nazareth shall destroy this place, and shall change the customs which Moses delivered us. *Ac.* 6: 14.

The first covenant had also ordinances of divine service. *He.* 9: 1.

See also
Ceremony; Formalism; Ritual.

Load

Ye have seen . . . how I bare you on eagles' wings. *Ex.* 19: 4.

As an eagle stirreth up her nest, fluttereth over her young, spreadeth abroad her wings, taketh them, beareth them on her wings: So the Lord alone did lead him. *De.* 32: 11, 12.

They shall bear the burden of the people with thee, that thou bear it not thyself alone. *Nu.* 11: 17.

Thy father made our yoke heavy, but make thou it lighter unto us. *1 K.* 12: 10.

My little finger shall be thicker than my father's loins. *1 K.* 12: 10.

Mine iniquities are gone over mine head: as an heavy burden they are too heavy for me. *Ps.* 38: 4.

Blessed be the Lord, who daily loadeth us with benefits. *Ps.* 68: 19.

The burden of the valley of vision. *Is.* 22: 1.

Behold, the name of the Lord cometh from far, burning with his anger, and the burden thereof is heavy. *Is.* 30: 27.

Upon the ancient thou hast very heavily laid thy yoke. *Is.* 47: 6.

When this people, or the prophet, or a priest shall ask thee, saying, What is the burden of the Lord? thou shalt then say unto them. What burden? *Je.* **23: 33.**

The burden of the Lord shall ye mention no more: for every man's word shall be his burden. *Je.* **23: 36.**

Come unto me, all ye that labour and are heavy laden, and I will give you rest. *Mat.* **11: 28.**

My burden is light. *Mat.* **11: 30.**

Bear ye one another's burdens. *Ga.* **6: 2.**

Let us lay aside every weight. *He.* **12: 1.**

See also
Burden; Charge; Heaviness; Weight.

Loaf

I will satisfy her poor with bread. *Ps.* **132: 15.**

Bread eaten in secret is pleasant. *Pr.* **9: 17.**

Go thy way, eat thy bread with joy. *Ec.* **9: 7.**

They that did eat of the loaves were about five thousand men. *Mk.* **6: 44.**

They considered not the miracle of the loaves: for their heart was hardened. *Mk.* **6: 52.**

Our fathers did eat manna in the desert; as it is written, He gave them bread from heaven to eat. *Jn.* **6: 31.**

I am the living bread which came down from heaven. *Jn.* **6: 51.**

The bread that I will give is my flesh, which I will give for the life of the world. *Jn.* **6: 51.**

See also
Bread.

Loan

He shall lend to thee, and thou shalt not lend to him. *De.* **28: 44.**

He is ever merciful, and lendeth. *Ps.* **37: 26.**

A good man sheweth favour and lendeth. *Ps.* **112: 5.**

The borrower is servant to the lender. *Pr.* **22: 7.**

It shall be, . . . as with the lender, so with the borrower. *Is.* **24: 2.**

If ye lend to them of whom ye hope to receive, what thank have ye? *Lu.* **6: 34.**

Love ye your enemies, and do good, and lend, hoping for nothing again. *Lu.* **6: 35.**

See also
Debt; Indebtedness; Obligation; Usury.

Locust

He spake, and the locusts came. *Ps.* **105: 34.**

The locusts have no king, yet go they forth all of them by bands. *Pr.* **30: 27.**

Your spoil shall be gathered like the gathering of the caterpiller: as the running to and fro of locusts shall he run upon them. *Is.* **33: 4.**

I will restore to you the years that the locust hath eaten. *Jo.* **2: 25.**

Thy crowned are as the locusts. *Na.* **3: 17.**

His meat was locusts and wild honey. *Mat.* **3: 4.**

Lodge

Where thou lodgest, I will lodge. *Ru.* **1: 16.**

Who shall dwell in thy holy hill? *Ps.* **15: 1.**

Lord, thou hast been our dwelling place in all generations. *Ps.* **90: 1.**

He that dwelleth in the secret place of the most High shall abide under the shadow of the Almighty. *Ps.* **91: 1.**

He blesseth the habitation of the just. *Pr.* **3: 33.**

The house of the righteous shall stand. *Pr.* **12: 7.**

Oh that I had in the wilderness a lodging place of wayfaring men; that I might leave my people, and go from them. *Je.* **9: 2.**

The foxes have holes, and the birds of the air have nests; but the Son of man hath not where to lay his head. *Mat.* **8: 20.**

The birds of the air come and lodge in the branches thereof. *Mat.* **13: 32.**

There was no room for them in the inn. *Lu.* **2: 7.**

He had compassion on him, . . . and brought him to an inn, and took care of him. *Lu.* **10: 33, 34.**

Rabbi, . . . where dwellest thou? *Jn.* **1: 38.**

See also
Abode; God, House of; Habitation; Home; House; Tent.

Loin

Gird up thy loins, and take my staff in thine hand, and go thy way. *2 K.* **4: 29.**

He looseth the bond of kings, and girdeth their loins with a girdle. *Jb.* **12: 18.**

Righteousness shall be the girdle of his loins, and faithfulness the girdle of his reins. *Is.* **11: 5.**

Stand therefore, having your loins girt about with truth, and having on the breastplate of righteousness. *Ep.* **6: 14.**

Wherefore gird up the loins of your mind. *1 Pe.* **1: 13.**

See also
Strength.

Loneliness

It is not good that the man should be alone; I will make him an help meet for him. *Ge.* **2: 18.**

Noah only remained alive, and they that were with him in the ark. *Ge.* **7: 23.**

Moses alone shall come near the Lord. *Ex.* **24: 2.**

I am not able to bear all this people alone, because it is too heavy for me. *Nu.* **11: 14.**

I, even I only, am left; and they seek my life, to take it away. *1 K.* **19: 10.**

I only am escaped alone to tell thee. *Jb.* **1: 15.**

My lovers and my friends stand aloof from my sore; and my kinsmen stand afar off. *Ps.* **38: 11.**

God setteth the solitary in families. *Ps.* **68: 6.**

I looked for some to take pity, but there was none; and for comforters, but I found none. *Ps.* **69: 20.**

I watch, and am as a sparrow alone upon the housetop. *Ps.* **102: 7.**

Refuge failed me; no man cared for my soul. *Ps.* **142: 4.**

Woe to him that is alone when he falleth; for he hath not another to help him up. *Ec.* **4: 10.**

How can one be warm alone? *Ec.* **4: 11.**

I have trodden the winepress alone. *Is.* **63: 3.**

He was alone praying. *Lu.* **9: 18.**

I have no man, when the water is troubled, to put me into the pool. *Jn.* **5: 7.**

Behold, the hour cometh, yea, is now come, that ye shall be scattered, every man to his own, and shall leave me alone: and yet I am not alone, because the Father is with me. *Jn.* 16: 32.

At my first answer no man stood with me, but all men forsook me. *2 Ti.* 4: 16.

See also

Christ, Loneliness of; Isolation; Seclusion; Solitude.

Longing

Thou hast given him his heart's desire. *Ps.* 21: 2.

He shall give thee the desires of thine heart. *Ps.* 37: 4.

My soul, wait thou only upon God; for my expectation is from him. *Ps.* 62: 5.

My soul longeth, yea, even fainteth for the courts of the Lord. *Ps.* 84: 2.

My soul breaketh for the longing that it hath unto thy judgments. *Ps.* 119: 20.

I have longed for thy salvation, O Lord. *Ps.* 119: 174.

The grasshopper shall be a burden, and desire shall fail. *Ec.* 12: 5.

We would see Jesus. *Jn.* 12: 21.

Now they desire a better country. *He.* 11: 16.

See also

Aspiration; Desire; God, Aspiration for; God, Hope in; God, Longing for; God, Thirst for; God, Yearning for; Hope; Hunger; Inclination; Wish; Yearning.

Long-Suffering

Rest in the Lord, and wait patiently for him. *Ps.* 37: 7.

For my name's sake will I defer mine anger, and for my praise will I refrain for thee, that I cut thee not off. *Is.* 48: 9.

He that shall endure unto the end, the same shall be saved. *Mat.* 24: 13.

Despisest thou the riches of his goodness and forbearance and longsuffering? *Ro.* 2: 4.

Charity suffereth long. *1 Co.* 13: 4.

Charity . . . Beareth all things, . . . endureth all things. *1 Co.* 13: 4, 7.

The fruit of the Spirit is . . . longsuffering. *Ga.* 5: 22.

In due season we shall reap, if we faint not. *Ga.* 6: 9.

After he had patiently endured, he obtained the promise. *He.* 6: 15.

Ye have need of patience. *He.* 10: 36.

The longsuffering of God waited. *1 Pe.* 3: 20.

See also

Endurance; Forbearance; Fortitude; Patience; Resignation; Suffering; Tolerance.

Look

God saw every thing that he had made, and, behold, it was very good. *Ge.* 1: 31.

God looked upon the earth, and, behold, it was corrupt. *Ge.* 6: 12.

Lift up now thine eyes, and look from the place where thou art. *Ge.* 13: 14.

Thou wilt save the afflicted people; but wilt bring down high looks. *Ps.* 18: 27.

They looked unto him, and were lightened. *Ps.* 34: 5.

As the eyes of servants look unto the hand of their masters, and as the eyes of a maiden unto the hand of her mistress; so our eyes wait upon the Lord our God. *Ps.* 123: 2.

An high look, and a proud heart, and the plowing of the wicked, is sin. *Pr.* 21: 4.

Truly the light is sweet, and a pleasant thing it is for the eyes to behold the sun. *Ec.* 11: 7.

The lofty looks of man shall be humbled, and the haughtiness of men shall be bowed down. *Is.* 2: 11.

Look unto the rock whence ye are hewn, and to the hole of the pit whence ye are digged. *Is.* 51: 1.

No man, having put his hand to the plow, and looking back, is fit for the kingdom of God. *Lu.* 9: 62.

Lift up your eyes, and look on the fields; for they are white already to harvest. *Jn.* 4: 35.

See also

Appearance; Christ, Vision of; Eye; God, Vision of; Sight; Spectator; Vision.

Lord

O Lord our God, other lords beside thee have had dominion over us: but by thee only will we make mention of thy name. *Is.* 26: 13.

Wherefore say my people, We are lords; we will come no more unto thee? *Je.* 2: 31.

The disciple is not above his master, nor the servant above his lord. *Mat.* 10: 24.

It is enough for the disciple that he be as his master, and the servant as his lord. *Mat.* 10: 25.

Enter thou into the joy of thy lord. *Mat.* 25: 21.

Ye know that they which are accounted to rule over the Gentiles exercise lordship over them; and their great ones exercise authority upon them. *Mk.* 10: 42.

Let your loins be girded about, and your lights burning; And ye yourselves like unto men that wait for their lord. *Lu.* 12: 35, 36.

The servant knoweth not what his lord doeth. *Jn.* 15: 15.

The servant is not greater than his lord. *Jn.* 15: 20.

To this end Christ both died, and rose, and revived, that he might be Lord both of the dead and living. *Ro.* 14: 9.

Though there be that are called gods, whether in heaven or in earth, (as there be gods many, and lords many,) But to us there is but one God. *1 Co.* 8: 5, 6.

Neither as being lords over God's heritage, but being ensamples to the flock. *1 Pe.* 5: 3.

See also

Authority; Christ, Supremacy of; Deity; Dominion; God, Supremacy of; Master; Power; Prince; Rule.

Lord, Day of the

The day of the Lord of hosts shall be upon every one that is proud and lofty. *Is.* 2: 12.

It is the day of the Lord's vengeance. *Is.* 34: 8.

Howl ye, Woe worth the day! *Eze.* 30: 2.

The day is near, even the day of the Lord is near, a cloudy day. *Eze.* 30: 3.

There shall be a time of trouble, such as never was since there was a nation even to that same time: and at that time thy people shall be delivered, every one that shall be found written in the book. *Da.* 12: 1.

Many of them that sleep in the dust of the earth shall awake, some to everlasting life, and some to shame and everlasting contempt. *Da.* 12: 2.

They shall say to the mountains, Cover us; and to the hills, Fall on us. *Ho.* 10: 8.

Blow ye the trumpet, . . . for the day of the Lord cometh. *Jo.* 2: 1.

The day of the Lord is great and very terrible; and who can abide it? *Jo.* 2: 11.

The sun shall be turned into darkness, and the moon into blood, before the great and the terrible day of the Lord come. *Jo.* 2: 31.

It shall come to pass, that whosoever shall call on the name of the Lord shall be delivered. *Jo.* 2: 32.

The day of the Lord is near in the valley of decision. *Jo.* 3: 14.

The day of the Lord is darkness, and not light. *Am.* 5: 18.

In the last days it shall come to pass, that the mountain of the house of the Lord shall be established in the top of the mountains, and it shall be exalted above the hills; and people shall flow unto it. *Mi.* 4: 1.

Many nations shall come, and say, Come, and let us go up to the mountain of the Lord. *Mi.* 4: 2.

The day of the Lord is at hand. *Zph.* 1: 7.

The great day of the Lord is near, it is near, and hasteth greatly. *Zph.* 1: 14.

Neither their silver nor their gold shall be able to deliver them in the day of the Lord's wrath. *Zph.* 1: 18.

They shall be mine, saith the Lord of hosts, in that day when I make up my jewels. *Mal.* 3: 17.

Behold, I will send you Elijah the prophet before the coming of the great and dreadful day of the Lord. *Mal.* 4: 5.

He shall turn the heart of the fathers to the children, and the heart of the children to their fathers, lest I come and smite the earth with a curse. *Mal.* 4: 6.

The day of the Lord will come as a thief in the night. *2 Pe.* 3: 10.

I was in the Spirit on the Lord's day, and heard behind me a great voice, as of a trumpet. *Re.* 1: 10.

The great day of his wrath is come; and who shall be able to stand? *Re.* 6: 17.

Fear God, and give glory to him; for the hour of his judgment is come. *Re.* 14: 7.

He gathered them together into a place called in the Hebrew tongue Armageddon. *Re.* 16: 16.

The cup of the wine of the fierceness of his wrath. *Re.* 16: 19.

Loss

Other men have our lands and vineyards. *Ne.* 5: 5.

The Lord gave, and the Lord hath taken away; blessed be the name of the Lord. *Jb.* 1: 21.

I have gone astray like a lost sheep. *Ps.* 119: 176.

There shall be no reward to the evil man; the candle of the wicked shall be put out. *Pr.* 24: 20.

Let us eat and drink; for to morrow we shall die. *Is.* 22: 13.

Your sins have withholden good things from you. *Je.* 5: 25.

They have sown wheat, but shall reap thorns: they have put themselves to pain, but shall not profit. *Je.* 12: 13.

If the salt have lost his savour, wherewith shall it be salted? *Mat.* 5: 13.

He that loseth his life for my sake shall find it. *Mat.* 10: 39.

I am not sent but unto the lost sheep of the house of Israel. *Mat.* 15: 24.

Every one that hath forsaken houses, or brethren, or sisters, or father, or mother, or wife, or children, or lands, for my name's sake, shall receive an hundredfold, and shall inherit everlasting life. *Mat.* 19: 29.

Take therefore the talent from him, and give it unto him which hath ten talents. *Mat.* 25: 28.

Unto every one that hath shall be given, and he shall have abundance: but from him that hath not shall be taken away even that which he hath. *Mat.* 25: 29.

What shall it profit a man, if he shall gain the whole world, and lose his own soul? *Mk.* 8: 36.

I have found the piece which I had lost. *Lu.* 15: 9.

He was lost, and is found. *Lu.* 15: 24.

If any man's work shall be burned, he shall suffer loss. *1 Co.* 3: 15.

If our gospel be hid, it is hid to them that are lost. *2 Co.* 4: 3.

He taketh away the first, that he may establish the second. *He.* 10: 9.

Lot

Thou maintainest my lot. *Ps.* 16: 5.

They part my garments among them, and cast lots upon my vesture. *Ps.* 22: 18.

The rod of the wicked shall not rest upon the lot of the righteous. *Ps.* 125: 3.

Cast in thy lot among us. *Pr.* 1: 14.

The lot is cast into the lap; but the whole disposing thereof is of the Lord. *Pr.* 16: 33.

Among the smooth stones of the stream is thy portion; they, they are thy lot. *Is.* 57: 6.

They have cast lots for my people; and have . . . sold a girl for wine, that they might drink. *Jo.* 3: 3.

Foreigners entered into his gates, and cast lots upon Jerusalem. *Ob.* 1: 11.

The lot fell upon Matthias. *Ac.* 1: .6.

Thou hast neither part nor lot in this matter. *Ac.* 8: 21.

He divided their land to them by lot. *Ac.* 13: 19.

Ye are a chosen generation. *1 Pe.* 2: 9.

Give diligence to make your calling and election sure. *2 Pe.* 1: 10.

See also

Calling; Chance; Destiny; Doom; Election; Fate; Fortune; Gambling; Predestination.

Love

They shall prosper that love thee. *Ps.* 122: 6.

Hatred stirreth up strifes: but love covereth all sins. *Pr.* 10: 12.

Better is a dinner of herbs where love is, than a stalled ox and hatred therewith. *Pr.* 15: 17.

His banner over me was love. *S. of S.* 2: 4.

Many waters cannot quench love, neither can the floods drown it. *S. of S.* 8: 7.

I the Lord love judgment. *Is.* 61: 8.

Hate the evil, and love the good. *Am.* 5: 15.

If ye love them which love you, what reward have ye? *Mat.* 5: 46.

He that loveth his life shall lose it. *Jn.* 12: 25.

By this shall all men know that ye are my disciples, if ye have love one to another. *Jn.* 13: 35.

If ye keep my commandments, ye shall abide in my love. *Jn.* 15: 10.

In all these things we are more than conquerors through him that loved us. *Ro.* 8: 37.

Thou shalt love thy neighbour as thyself. *Ro.* 13: 9.

Knowledge puffeth up, but charity edifieth. *1 Co.* 8: 1.

Yet shew I unto you a more excellent way. *1 Co.* 12: 31.

Though I speak with the tongues of men and of angels, and have not charity, I am become as sounding brass, or a tinkling cymbal. *1 Co.* 13: 1.

Though I have all faith, so that I could remove mountains, and have not charity, I am nothing. *1 Co.* 13: 2.

Charity . . . hopeth all things. *1 Co.* 13: 4, 7.

Now abideth faith, hope, charity, these three; but the greatest of these is charity. *1 Co.* 13: 13.

The God of love and peace shall be with you. *2 Co.* 13: 11.

The love of God . . . be with you all. *2 Co.* 13: 14.

Rooted and grounded in love. *Ep.* 3: 17.

The love of Christ, which passeth knowledge. *Ep.* 3: 19.

Speaking the truth in love. *Ep.* 4: 15.

This I pray, that your love may abound yet more and more in knowledge and in all judgment. *Ph.* 1: 9.

God hath not given us the spirit of fear; but of power, and of love. *2 Ti.* 1: 7.

Whoso keepeth his word, in him verily is the love of God perfected. *1 Jn.* 2: 5.

Every one that loveth is born of God. *1 Jn.* 4: 7.

There is no fear in love; but perfect love casteth out fear. *1 Jn.* 4: 18.

See also

Affection; Attachment; Caress; Christ, Love of; Devotion; God, Love of; God, Love to; Kiss; Life, Love of; Lovingkindness; Regard; Tenderness.

Loveliness

The sons of God saw the daughters of men that they were fair. *Ge.* 6: 2.

Upon the top of the pillars was lily work. *1 K.* 7: 22.

Deck thyself now with majesty and excellency; and array thyself with glory and beauty. *Jb.* 40: 10.

Thou art fairer than the children of men. *Ps.* 45: 2.

Let the beauty of the Lord our God be upon us. *Ps.* 90: 17.

The beauties of holiness from the womb of the morning. *Ps.* 110: 3.

Behold, thou art fair, my love; behold, thou art fair. *S. of S.* 1: 15.

Fair as the moon, clear as the sun. *S. of S.* 6: 10.

I will make thy windows of agates, and thy gates of carbuncles, and all thy borders of pleasant stones. *Is.* 54: 12.

Perfect in beauty. *Eze.* 28: 12.

Thine heart was lifted up because of thy beauty. *Eze.* 28: 17.

Lo, thou art unto them as a very lovely song of one that hath a pleasant voice. *Eze.* 33: 32.

The temple . . . was adorned with goodly stones and gifts. *Lu.* 21: 5.

My grace is sufficient for thee: for my strength is made perfect in weakness. *2 Co.* 12: 9.

Grow in grace, and in the knowledge of our Lord and Saviour Jesus Christ. *2 Pe.* 3: 18.

I John saw the holy city, the new Jerusalem, coming down from God out of heaven, prepared as a bride adorned for her husband. *Re.* 21: 2.

See also

Adornment; Allurement; Art; Attraction; Beauty; Charm; Christ, Grace of; Delight; Excellence; God, Grace of; Grace; Ornament.

Lovingkindness

Thou shalt be a blessing. *Ge.* 12: 2.

Thou shalt deal kindly with thy servant. *1 S.* 20: 8.

If thine enemy be hungry, give him bread to eat. *Pr.* 25: 21.

Having loved his own which were in the world, he loved them unto the end. *Jn.* 13: 1.

Lovest thou me? *Jn.* 21: 17.

The fruit of the Spirit is love. *Ga.* 5: 22.

Forbearing one another in love. *Ep.* 4: 2.

Let brotherly love continue. *He.* 13: 1.

Love the brotherhood. *1 Pe.* 2: 17.

Add . . . to godliness brotherly kindness. *2 Pe.* 1: 5, 7.

Now I beseech thee, lady, not as though I wrote a new commandment unto thee, but that which we had from the beginning, that we love one another. *2 Jn.* 1: 5.

See also

Beneficence; Benevolence; Christ, Compassion of; Christ, Goodness of; Christ, Grace of; Christ, Love of; Clemency; Compassion; Favor; God, Beneficence of; God, Compassion of; God, Favor of; God, Goodness of; God, Grace of; God, Love of; Goodness; Grace; Humanity; Kindness; Tenderness.

Lowliness

Who remembered us in our low estate. *Ps.* 136: 23.

He giveth grace unto the lowly. *Pr.* 3: 34.

With the lowly is wisdom. *Pr.* 11: 2.

Before honour is humility. *Pr.* 15: 33.

Better it is that it be said unto thee, Come up hither; than that thou shouldest be put lower in the presence of the prince whom thine eyes have seen. *Pr.* 25: 7.

I dwell in the high and holy place, with him also that is of a contrite and humble spirit, to revive the spirit of the humble, and to revive the heart of the contrite ones. *Is.* 57: 15.

The words of Amos, who was among the herdmen of Tekoa. *Am.* 1: 1.

Who hath despised the day of small things? *Zch.* 4: 10.

Rejoice greatly, O daughter of Zion; shout, O daughter of Jerusalem: behold, thy King cometh unto thee: he is just, and having salvation; lowly, and riding upon an ass, and upon a colt the foal of an ass. *Zch.* 9: 9.

Blessed are the poor in spirit: for theirs is the kingdom of heaven. *Mat.* 5: 3.

Lord, I am not worthy that thou shouldest come under my roof. *Mat.* 8: 8.

I thank thee, O Father, Lord of heaven and earth, because thou hast hid these things from the wise and prudent, and hast revealed them unto babes. *Mat.* 11: 25.

Whosoever exalteth himself shall be abased; and he that humbleth himself shall be exalted. *Lu.* 14: 11.

Be of the same mind one toward another. Mind not high things, but condescend to men of low estate. *Ro.* 12: 16.

Unto me, who am less than the least of all saints, is this grace given. *Ep.* 3: 8.

Let nothing be done through strife or vainglory; but in lowliness of mind let each esteem other better than himself. *Ph.* 2: 3.

See also

Humility; Meekness; Modesty.

Loyalty

Orpah kissed her mother in law; but Ruth clave unto her. *Ru.* 1: 14.

Surely in what place my lord the king will be, whether in death or life, even there also will thy servant be. *2 S.* 15: 21.

The faithful fail from among the children of men. *Ps.* 12: 1.

The Lord preserveth the faithful. *Ps.* 31: 23.

If I do not remember thee, let my tongue cleave to the roof of my mouth; if I prefer not Jerusalem above my chief joy. *Ps.* 137: 6.

A friend loveth at all times. *Pr.* 17: 17.

Faithful are the wounds of a friend. *Pr.* 27: 6.

Thou hast been faithful over a few things, I will make thee ruler over many things. *Mat.* 25: 23.

Now I stand and am judged for the hope of the promise made of God unto our fathers. *Ac.* 26: 6.

Moreover it is required in stewards, that a man be found faithful. *1 Co.* 4: 2.

Thou . . . hast not denied my faith. *Re.* 2: 13.

See also

Allegiance; Attachment; Christ, Loyalty to; Consecration; Constancy; Devotion; Faithfulness; Fidelity; God, Faithfulness of; God, Love to; God, Loyalty to.

Loyalty, Divided

How long halt ye between two opinions? *1 K.* 18: 21.

So these nations feared the Lord, and served their graven images. *2 K.* 17: 41.

Their heart is divided; now shall they be found faulty. *Ho.* 10: 2.

No man can serve two masters. *Mat.* 6: 24.

Ye cannot serve God and mammon. *Mat.* 6: 24.

Every city or house divided against itself shall not stand. *Mat.* 12: 25.

No man, having put his hand to the plow, and looking back, is fit for the kingdom of God. *Lu.* 9: 62.

No servant can serve two masters: for either he will hate the one, and love the other; or else he will hold to the one, and despise the other. *Lu.* 16: 13.

Ye cannot drink the cup of the Lord, and the cup of devils: ye cannot be partakers of the Lord's table, and of the table of devils. *1 Co.* 10: 21.

A double minded man is unstable in all his ways. *Ja.* 1: 8.

Purify your hearts, ye double minded. *Ja.* 4: 8.

See also

Half-Heartedness; Indifference; Lukewarmness.

Lucifer

How art thou fallen from heaven, O Lucifer, son of the morning! *Is.* 14: 12.

Then was Jesus led up of the spirit into the wilderness to be tempted of the devil. *Mat.* 4: 1.

Ye are of your father the devil, and the lusts of your father ye will do. *Jn.* 8: 44.

Jesus . . . went about doing good, and healing all that were oppressed of the devil. *Ac.* 10: 38.

Thou child of the devil, thou enemy of all righteousness, wilt thou not cease to pervert the right ways of the Lord? *Ac.* 13: 10.

Put on the whole armour of God, that ye may be able to stand against the wiles of the devil. *Ep.* 6: 11.

Resist the devil, and he will flee from you. *Ja.* 4: 7.

Your adversary the devil, as a roaring lion, walketh about, seeking whom he may devour. *1 Pe.* 5: 8.

He that committeth sin is of the devil; for the devil sinneth from the beginning. *1 Jn.* 3: 8.

The devil shall cast some of you into prison, that ye may be tried. *Re.* 2: 10.

See also

Devil; Fiend; Satan.

Luck

It was a chance that happened to us. *1 S.* 6: 9.

As I happened by chance upon mount Gilboa, behold, Saul leaned upon his spear. *2 S.* 1: 6.

The lot is cast into the lap; but the whole disposing thereof is of the Lord. *Pr.* 16: 33.

Time and chance happeneth to them all. *Ec.* 9: 11.

By chance there came down a certain priest that way. *Lu.* 10: 31.

See also

Accident; Chance; Fate; Fortune; Gambling; Lot.

Lukewarmness

Solomon . . . went not fully after the Lord. *1 K.* 11: 6.

How long halt ye between two opinions? *1 K.* 18: 21.

Ephraim is a cake not turned. *Ho.* 7: 8.

He that wavereth is like a wave of the sea driven with the wind and tossed. *Ja.* 1: 6.

A double minded man is unstable in all his ways. *Ja.* 1: 8.

I know thy works, that thou art neither cold nor hot: I would thou wert cold or hot. *Re.* 3: 15.

So then because thou art lukewarm, and neither cold nor hot, I will spue thee out of my mouth. *Re.* 3: 16.

See also

Half-Heartedness; Indifference; Loyalty, Divided.

Lust

The mixt multitude that was among them fell a lusting. *Nu.* 11: 4.

Neither shalt thou commit adultery. *De.* 5: 18.

His heart gathereth iniquity to itself. *Ps.* 41: 6.

He goeth after her straightway, as an ox goeth to the slaughter, or as a fool to the correction of the stocks. *Pr.* 7: 22.

From all your filthiness, and from all your idols, will I cleanse you. *Eze.* 36: 25.

Make not provision for the flesh, to fulfil the lusts thereof. *Ro.* 13: 14.

The flesh lusteth against the Spirit, and the Spirit against the flesh. *Ga.* 5: 17.

They that will be rich fall into temptation and a snare, and into many foolish and hurtful lusts. *1 Ti.* 6: 9.

Flee also youthful lusts. *2 Ti.* 2: 22.

To enjoy the pleasures of sin for a season. *He.* 11: 25.

When lust hath conceived, it bringeth forth sin: and sin, when it is finished, bringeth forth death. *Ja.* 1: 15.

Ye have lived in pleasure on the earth, and been wanton. *Ja.* 5: 5.

See also

Adultery; Brothel; Carnality; Debauchery; Desire; Dissipation; Flesh; Fornication; Obscenity; Prostitute; Sensuality.

Luxury

We sat by the flesh pots, and . . . we did eat bread to the full. *Ex.* 16: 3.

We remember the fish, which we did eat in Egypt freely; the cucumbers, and the melons, and the leeks, and the onions, and the garlick. *Nu.* 11: 5.

In the court of the garden of the king's palace; Where were white, green, and blue, hangings, fastened with cords of fine linen and purple to silver rings and pillars of marble: the beds were of gold and silver, upon a pavement of red and blue, and white, and black, marble. *Es.* 1: 5, 6.

All thy garments smell of myrrh, and aloes, and cassia, out of the ivory palaces, whereby they have made thee glad. *Ps.* 45: 8.

I have decked my bed with coverings of tapestry, with carved works, with fine linen of Egypt. *Pr.* 7: 16.

She maketh herself coverings of tapestry; her clothing is silk and purple. *Pr.* 31: 22.

Woe to them that are at ease in Zion. *Am.* 6: 1.

Ye that put far away the evil day, . . . That lie upon beds of ivory, . . . and eat the lambs out of the flock, . . . but they are not grieved for the affliction of Joseph. *Am.* 6: 3, 4, 6.

Even Solomon in all his glory was not arrayed like one of these. *Mat.* 6: 29.

There was a certain rich man, which was clothed in purple and fine linen, and fared sumptuously every day. *Lu.* 16: 19.

Not with broided hair, or gold, or pearls, or costly array. *1 Ti.* 2: 9.

See also

Comfort; Ease; Enjoyment; Gold; Goods; Mammon; Pleasure; Plenty; Riches; Wealth; Worldliness.

M

Machine

The Lord . . . took off their chariot wheels, that they drave them heavily. *Ex.* 14: 24, 25.

The Canaanites that dwell in the land of the valley have chariots of iron. *Jos.* 17: 16.

The work of the wheels was like the work of a chariot wheel. *1 K.* 7: 33.

Some trust in chariots, and some in horses. *Ps.* 20: 7.

The chariots of God are twenty thousand, even thousands of angels. *Ps.* 68: 17.

O my God, make them like a wheel. *Ps.* 83: 13.

The Lord . . . maketh the clouds his chariot. *Ps.* 104: 1, 3.

A wise king scattereth the wicked, and bringeth the wheel over them. *Pr.* 20: 26.

Iron sharpeneth iron. *Pr.* 27: 17.

Woe to them that . . . trust in chariots. *Is.* 31: 1.

Their work was as it were a wheel in the middle of a wheel. *Eze.* 1: 16.

His throne was like the fiery flame, and his wheels as burning fire. *Da.* 7: 9.

Madness

Mine enemies reproach me all the day; and they that are mad against me are sworn against me. *Ps.* 102: 8.

I gave my heart to know wisdom, and to know madness and folly: I perceived that this also is vexation of spirit. *Ec.* 1: 17.

I said of laughter, It is mad. *Ec.* 2: 2.

Surely oppression maketh a wise man mad. *Ec.* 7: 7.

The heart of the sons of men is full of evil, and madness is in their heart while they live, and after that they go to the dead. *Ec.* 9: 3.

The prophet is a fool, the spiritual man is mad. *Ho.* 9: 7.

They brought unto him . . . those which were possessed with devils; . . . and he healed them. *Mat.* 4: 24.

In my name shall they cast out devils. *Mk.* 16: 17.

Many of them said, He hath a devil, and is mad. *Jn.* 10: 20.

Paul, thou art beside thyself; much learning doth make thee mad. *Ac.* 26: 24.

I am not mad, most noble Festus; but speak forth the words of truth and soberness. *Ac.* 26: 25.

If therefore the whole church be come together into one place, and all speak with tongues, and there come in those that are unlearned, or unbelievers, will they not say that ye are mad? *1 Co.* 14: 23.

See also
Bedlam; Folly; Fool; Insanity.

Magic

I told this unto the magicians; but there was none that could declare it to me. *Ge.* 41: 24.

Is not this it in which my lord drinketh, and whereby indeed he divineth? *Ge.* 44: 5.

There shall not be found among you any one . . . that useth divination, or an observer of times, or an enchanter, or a witch, Or a charmer, or a consulter with familiar spirits, or a wizard, or a necromancer. For all that do these things are an abomination unto the Lord. *De.* 18: 10-12.

Blow ye the trumpets also on every side of all the camp, and say, The sword of the Lord, and of Gideon. *Ju.* 7: 18.

The deaf adder . . . will not hearken to the voice of charmers, charming never so wisely. *Ps.* 58: 4, 5.

Let now the astrologers, the stargazers, the monthly prognosticators, stand up, and save thee from these things that shall come upon thee. *Is.* 47: 13.

Hearken not ye to your prophets, nor to your diviners, nor to your dreamers, nor to your enchanters, nor to your sorcerers. *Je.* 27: 9.

Let not . . . your diviners, that be in the midst of you, deceive you. *Je.* 29: 8.

He found them ten times better than all the magicians and astrologers that were in all his realm. *Da.* 1: 20.

The prophets . . . divine for money. *Mi.* 3: 11.

I will be a swift witness against the sorcerers. *Mal.* 3: 5.

There was a certain man, called Simon, which beforetime in the same city used sorcery. *Ac.* 8: 9.

By thy sorceries were all nations deceived. *Re.* 18: 23.

See also
Charm; Science; Wonder.

Magnanimity

Let them that love him be as the sun when he goeth forth in his might. *Ju.* 5: 31.

The Lord turned the captivity of Job, when he prayed for his friends. *Jb.* 42: 10.

Love your enemies. *Mat.* 5: 44.

How often would I have gathered thy children together, even as a hen gathereth her chickens under her wings, and ye would not. *Mat.* 23: 37.

A new commandment I give unto you, That ye love one another; as I have loved you, that ye also love one another. *Jn.* 13: 34.

If thine enemy hunger, feed him; if he thirst, give him drink: for in so doing thou shalt heap coals of fire on his head. *Ro.* 12: 20.

Every man according as he purposeth in his heart, so let him give; not grudgingly, or of necessity. *2 Co.* 9: 7.

The charity of every one of you all toward each other aboundeth. *2 Th.* 1: 3.

The Lord direct your hearts into the love of God. *2 Th.* 3: 5.

We know that we have passed from death unto life, because we love the brethren. *1 Jn.* 3: 14.

See also
Beneficence; Benevolence; Generosity; Liberality; Love; Lovingkindness; Philanthropy; Unselfishness.

Magnetism

He draweth also the mighty with his power. *Jb.* 24: 22.

My heart hath been secretly enticed. *Jb.* 31: 27.

With lovingkindness have I drawn thee. *Je.* 31: 3.

Behold, I will allure her, and bring her into the wilderness, and speak comfortably unto her. *Ho.* 2: 14.

No man can come to me, except the Father which hath sent me draw him. *Jn.* 6: 44.

And I, if I be lifted up from the earth, will draw all men unto me. *Jn.* 12: 32.

Of your own selves shall men arise, speaking perverse things, to draw away disciples after them. *Ac.* 20: 30.

My speech and my preaching was not with enticing words of man's wisdom, but in demonstration of the Spirit and of power. *1 Co.* 2: 4.

Every man is tempted, when he is drawn away of his own lust. *Ja.* 1: 14.

See also
Allurement; Attraction; Charm; Enticement.

Magnificence

The house that is to be builded for the Lord must be exceeding magnifical, of fame and glory throughout all countries. *1 Ch.* 22: 5.

In the court of the garden of the king's palace; Where were white, green, and blue, hangings, fastened with cords of fine linen and purple to silver rings and pillars of marble: the beds were of gold and silver, upon a pavement of red, and blue, and white, and black, marble. *Es.* 1: 5, 6.

O magnify the Lord with me, and let us exalt his name together. *Ps.* 34: 3.

Let the Lord be magnified. *Ps.* 35: 27.

All thy garments smell of myrrh, and aloes, and cassia, out of the ivory palaces, whereby they have made thee glad. *Ps.* 45: 8.

I have decked my bed with coverings of tapestry, with carved works, with fine linen of Egypt. *Pr.* 7: 16.

I gathered me also silver and gold, and the peculiar treasure of kings and of the provinces. . . . So I was great. *Ec.* 2: 8, 9.

I saw also the Lord sitting upon a throne, high and lifted up, and his train filled the temple. *Is.* 6: 1.

Solomon in all his glory. *Mat.* 6: 29.

Mary said, My soul doth magnify the Lord. *Lu.* 1: 46.

Fear fell on them all, and the name of the Lord Jesus was magnified. *Ac.* 19: 17.

Not only this our craft is in danger to be set at nought; but also that the temple of the great goddess Diana should be despised, and her magnificence should be destroyed.*Ac.*19:27.

Christ shall be magnified in my body, whether it be by life, or by death. *Ph.* 1: 20.

See also

Christ, Glory of; Display; Distinction; Exaltation; Fame; Glory; God, Glory of; God, Majesty of; Grandeur; Honor; Majesty; Splendor; Sublimity.

Maiden

Thou shalt not covet thy neighbour's . . . maidservant. *Ex.* 20: 17.

The fire consumed their young men; and their maidens were not given to marriage. *Ps.* 78: 63.

Behold, as the eyes of servants look unto the hand of their masters, and as the eyes of a maiden unto the hand of her mistress; so our eyes wait upon the Lord our God. *Ps.* 123: 2.

Young men, and maidens; . . . Let them praise the name of the Lord. *Ps.* 148: 12, 13.

Wisdom . . . hath sent forth her maidens: she crieth upon the highest places of the city. *Pr.* 9: 1, 3.

I got me servants and maidens and had servants born in my house. . . . So I was great. *Ec.* 2: 7, 9.

Can a maid forget her ornaments? *Je.* 2: 32.

They have . . . sold a girl for wine. *Jo.* 3: 3.

Ye shall be my sons and daughters, saith the Lord Almighty. *2 Co.* 6: 18.

See also

Daughter; Girl; Virgin.

Majesty

Thine is the kingdom, O Lord, and thou art exalted as head above all. *1 Ch.* 29: 11.

The voice of the Lord is full of majesty. *Ps.* 29: 4.

Every beast of the forest is mine, and the cattle upon a thousand hills. *Ps.* 50: 10.

Sing forth the honour of his name: make his praise glorious. *Ps.* 66: 2.

All nations . . . shall glorify thy name. *Ps.* 86: 9.

Thou, Lord, art high above all the earth: thou art exalted far above all gods. *Ps.* 97: 9.

The Lord is high above all nations, and his glory above the heavens. *Ps.* 113: 4.

Who is like unto the Lord our God, who dwelleth on high?*Ps.* 113: 5.

According to the riches of his glory. *Ep.* 3: 16.

See also

Christ, Glory of; Dignity; Display; Distinction; Fame; Glory; God, Glory of; God, Majesty of; Grandeur; Honor; Magnificence; Splendor; Sublimity.

Majority

Behold, the people of the children of Israel are more and mightier than we. *Ex.* 1: 9.

Thou shalt not follow a multitude to do evil. *Ex.* 23: 2.

Who is on the Lord's side? *Ex.* 32: 26.

To the more ye shall give the more inheritance. *Nu.* 33: 54.

If thou shalt say in thine heart, These nations are more than I; how can I dispossess them? Thou shalt not be afraid of them. *De.* 7: 17, 18.

Fear not: for they that be with us are more than they that be with them. *2 K.* 6: 16.

They that hate me without a cause are more than the hairs of mine head. *Ps.* 69: 4.

A little one shall become a thousand. *Is.* 60: 22.

With God all things are possible. *Mat.* 19: 26.

Thinkest thou that I cannot now pray to my Father, and he shall presently give me more than twelve legions of angels? *Mat.* 26: 53.

The more part knew not wherefore they were come together. *Ac.* 19: 32.

The greater part remain unto this present, but some are fallen asleep. *1 Co.* 15: 6.

See also

Minority

Maker

Shall a man be more pure than his maker? *Jb.* 4: 17.

None saith, Where is God my maker, who giveth songs in the night. *Jb.* 35: 10.

Let us kneel before the Lord our maker. *Ps.* 95: 6.

The rich and poor meet together: the Lord is the maker of them all. *Pr.* 22: 2.

Woe unto him that striveth with his Maker! *Is.* 45: 9.

Thou . . . forgettest the Lord thy maker. *Is.* 51: 12, 13.

Thy Maker is thine husband; the Lord of hosts is his name. *Is.* 54: 5.

Israel hath forgotten his Maker, and buildeth temples. *Ho.* 8: 14.

He looked for a city which hath foundations, whose builder and maker is God. *He.* 11: 10.

See also

Architecture; Builder; Carpenter; Christ, the Creator; Creator; God, the Creator.

Male

It is not good that the man should be alone. *Ge.* 2: 18.

The Lord God said, Behold, the man is become as one of us, to know good and evil. *Ge.* 3: 22.

The sons of God came in unto the daughters of men. *Ge.* 6: 4.

We have seen this day that God doth talk with man, and he liveth. *De.* 5: 24.

As the man is, so is his strength. *Ju.* 8: 21.

The Lord seeth not as man seeth. *1 S.* 16: 7.

Man that is born of woman is of few days, and full of trouble. *Jb.* 14: 1.

What is man, that thou shouldest magnify him? *Jb.* 7: 17.

What is man, that thou art mindful of him? *Ps.* 8: 4.

Man did eat angels' food. *Ps.* 78: 25.

The way of a man with a maid. *Pr.* 30: 19.

Who knoweth what is good for man in this life, all the days of his vain life which he spendeth as a shadow? *Ec.* 6: 12.

Have ye not read, that he which made them at the beginning made them male and female? *Mat.* 19: 4.

Jesus . . . needed not that any should testify of man: for he knew what was in man. *Jn.* 2: 24, 25.

What man knoweth the things of a man, save the spirit of man which is in him? *1 Co.* 2: 11.

Neither was the man created for the woman; but the woman for the man. *1 Co.* 11: 9.

Ye shall be my sons and daughters, saith the Lord Almighty. *2 Co.* 6: 18.

There is neither male nor female: for ye are all one in Christ Jesus. *Ga.* 3: 28.

See also

Female; Man; Man, Divinity of; Man, Greatness of; Man, the New; Man, Spirit of; Manliness.

Malevolence

You only have I known of all the families of the earth: therefore I will punish you for all your iniquities. *Am.* 3: 2.

The kingdom of heaven suffereth violence, and the violent take it by force. *Mat.* 11: 12.

The servants did strike him with the palms of their hands. *Mk.* 14: 65.

We know that God heareth not sinners. *Jn.* 9: 31.

Thou hast not lied unto men, but unto God. *Ac.* 5: 4.

All have sinned, and come short of the glory of God. *Ro.* 3: 23.

Abstain from all appearance of evil. *1 Th.* 5: 22.

Unto them that are defiled and unbelieving is nothing pure. *Tit.* 1: 15.

Sin, when it is finished, bringeth forth death. *Ja.* 1: 15.

Let him eschew evil, and do good. *1 Pe.* 3: 11.

His own works were evil. *1 Jn.* 3: 12.

See also

Evil; Hatred; Malice.

Malice

Deliver me, O Lord, from the evil man. *Ps.* 140: 1.

Devise not evil against thy neighbour. *Pr.* 3: 29.

An ungodly man diggeth up evil: and in his lips there is as a burning fire. *Pr.* 16: 27.

He that is glad at calamities shall not be unpunished. *Pr.* 17: 5.

Every one that doeth evil hateth the light. *Jn.* 3: 20.

Being filled with all unrighteousness, . . . maliciousness, . . . malignity. *Ro.* 1: 29.

The leaven of malice and wickedness. *1 Co.* 5: 8.

Charity . . . thinketh no evil. *1 Co.* 13: 4, 5.

Howbeit in malice be ye children. *1 Co.* 14: 20.

Let all bitterness . . . be put away from you. *Ep.* 4: 31.

Let all . . . evil speaking, be put away from you, and all malice. *Ep.* 4: 31.

We ourselves also were sometimes foolish, . . . living in malice and envy, hateful, and hating one another. *Tit.* 3: 3.

Speak not evil one of another, brethren. *Ja.* 4: 11.

Not using your liberty for a cloak of maliciousness. *1 Pe.* 2: 16.

Prating against us with malicious words. *3 Jn.* 1: 10.

See also

Anger; Bitterness; Hatred. Indignation; Malevolence; Resentment.

Mammon

These are the ungodly, who prosper in the world; they increase in riches. *Ps.* 73: 12.

Where your treasure is, there will your heart be also. *Mat.* 6: 21.

Ye cannot serve God and mammon. *Mat.* 6: 24.

The children of this world are in their generation wiser than the children of light. *Lu.* 16: 8.

Make to yourselves friends of the mammon of unrighteousness; that, when ye fail, they may receive you into everlasting habitations. *Lu.* 16: 9.

If therefore ye have not been faithful in the unrighteous mammon, who will commit to your trust the true riches? *Lu.* 16: 11.

No servant can serve two masters. *Lu.* 16: 13.

Be not conformed to this world. *Ro.* 12: 2.

The god of this world hath blinded the minds of them which believe not. *2 Co.* 4: 4.

In time past ye walked according to the course of this world, according to the prince of the power of the air, the spirit that now worketh in the children of disobedience. *Ep.* 2: 2.

See also

Belongings; Gold; Goods; Luxury; Plenty; Riches; Wealth; Worldliness.

Man

God said, Let us make man in our image. *Ge.* 1: 26.

The Lord God formed man of the dust of the ground. *Ge.* 2: 7.

The Lord said, My spirit shall not always strive with man. *Ge.* 6: 3.

It repented the Lord that he had made man on the earth, and it grieved him at his heart. *Ge.* 6: 6.

The Lord said, I will destroy man whom I have created from the face of the earth. *Ge.* 6: 7.

Whoso sheddeth man's blood, by man shall his blood be shed. *Ge.* 9: 6.

Man doth not live by bread only. *De.* 8: 3.

As the man is, so is his strength. *Ju.* 8: 21.

The Lord seeth not as man seeth. *1 S.* 16: 7.

Nathan said to David, Thou art the man. *2 S.* 12: 7.

Man is born unto trouble, as the sparks fly upward. *Jb.* 5: 7.

Are thy days as the days of man? are thy years as man's days? *Jb.* 10: 5.

Help, Lord; for the godly man ceaseth. *Ps.* 12: 1.

Thou turnest man to destruction; and sayest, Return, ye children of men. *Ps.* 90: 3.

As for man, his days are as grass. *Ps.* 103: 15.

I am fearfully and wonderfully made. *Ps.* 139: 14.

Lord, what is man, that thou takest knowledge of him! or the son of man, that thou makest account of him! *Ps.* 144: 3.

Man's goings are of the Lord; how can a man then understand his own way? *Pr.* 20: 24.

That which befalleth the sons of men befalleth beasts; even one thing befalleth them: as the one dieth, so dieth the other. *Ec.* 3: 19.

God hath made man upright; but they have sought out many inventions. *Ec.* 7: 29.

Cursed be the man that trusteth in man. *Je.* 17: 5.

The natural man receiveth not the things of the Spirit of God: for they are foolishness unto him. *1 Co.* 2: 14.

When I was a child, I spake as a child, I understood as a child, I thought as a child: but when I became a man, I put away childish things. *1 Co.* 13: 11.

Quit you like men. *1 Co.* 16: 13.

See also

Adult; Male; Man, Divinity of; Man, Greatness of; Man, the New; Man, Spirit of; Manliness; Nature, Human.

Man, Divinity of

God created man in his own image. *Ge.* 1: 27.

Ye shall be as gods, knowing good and evil. *Ge.* 3: 5.

God hath made man upright; but they have sought out many inventions. *Ec.* 7: 29.

Jesus answered them, Is it not written in your law, I said, Ye are gods? *Jn.* 10: 34.

In him we live, and move, and have our being. *Ac.* 17: 28.

A man indeed ought not to cover his head, forasmuch as he is the image and glory of God. *1 Co.* 11: 7.

According to the power that worketh in us. *Ep.* 3: 20.

A perfect man. *Ep.* 4: 13.

Men, which are made after the similitude of God. *Ja.* 3: 9.

That . . . ye might be partakers of the divine nature. *2 Pe.* 1: 4.

According to the measure of a man, that is, of the angel. *Re.* 21: 17.

See also

Man, Greatness of; Man, the New; Man, Spirit of.

Man, Greatness of

Have dominion . . . over every living thing that moveth upon the earth. *Ge.* 1: 28.

What is man, that thou shouldest magnify him? *Jb.* 7: 17.

When I consider thy heavens, the work of thy fingers, the moon and the stars, which thou hast ordained; What is man, that thou art mindful of him? *Ps.* 8: 3, 4.

Thou hast made him a little lower than the angels, and hast crowned him with glory and honour. *Ps.* 8: 5.

Let another man praise thee, and not thine own mouth. *Pr.* 27: 2.

I will make a man more precious than fine gold. *Is.* 13: 12.

A man shall be as an hiding place from the wind, and a covert from the tempest; as rivers of water in a dry place, as the shadow of a great rock in a weary land. *Is.* 32: 2.

How much then is a man better than a sheep? *Mat.* 12: 12.

He knew what was in man. *Jn.* 2: 25.

All things are yours. *1 Co.* 3: 21.

All flesh is as grass, and all the glory of man as the flower of grass. *1 Pe.* 1: 24.

Honour all men. *1 Pe.* 2: 17.

See also

Man, Divinity of; Man, the New; Man, Spirit of; Manliness.

Man, the New

Create in me a clean heart, O God; and renew a right spirit within me. *Ps.* 51: 10.

Thou . . . shalt quicken me again, and shalt bring me up again from the depths of the earth. *Ps.* 71: 20.

They that wait upon the Lord shall renew their strength. *Is.* 40: 31.

Even unto them will I give in mine house and within my walls a place and a name better than of sons and of daughters. *Is.* 56: 5.

Thou shalt be called by a new name. *Is.* 62: 2.

I will put a new spirit within you. *Eze.* 11: 19.

This my son was dead, and is alive again. *Lu.* 15: 24.

Ye must be born again. *Jn.* 3: 7.

Be ye transformed by the renewing of your mind. *Ro.* 12: 2.

Though our outward man perish, yet the inward man is renewed day by day. *2 Co.* 4: 16.

If any man be in Christ, he is a new creature. *2 Co.* 5: 17.

He . . . hath raised us up together, and made us sit together in heavenly places in Christ Jesus. *Ep.* 2: 4, 6.

Put on the new man, which after God is created in righteousness and true holiness. *Ep.* 4: 24.

If ye then be risen with Christ, seek those things which are above. *Col.* 3: 1.

Ye have . . . put on the new man, which is renewed in knowledge after the image of him that created him. *Col.* 3: 9, 10.

See also

Birth, the New; Regeneration; Renewal; Restoration; Revival.

Man, Son of

He that soweth the good seed is the Son of man. *Mat.* 13: 37.

The Son of man shall send forth his angels, and they shall gather out of his kingdom all things that offend. *Mat.* 13: 41.

The Son of man is come to save that which is lost. *Mat.* 18: 11.

The Son of man came not to be ministered unto, but to minister, and to give his life a ransom for many. *Mat.* 20: 28.

The Son of man is as a man taking a far journey, who left his house, and gave authority to his servants, and to every man his work, and commanded the porter to watch. *Mk.* 13: 34.

Blessed are ye, when men shall hate you, . . . for the Son of man's sake. *Lu.* 6: 22.

The hour is come, that the Son of man should be glorified. *Jn.* 12: 23.

How sayest thou, The Son of man must be

lifted up? who is this Son of man? *Jn.* 12: 34.

Now is the Son of man glorified, and God is glorified in him. *Jn.* 13: 31.

Behold, I see the heavens opened, and the Son of man standing on the right hand of God. *Ac.* 7: 56.

See also
Christ, the Son of Man.

Man, Spirit of

There is a spirit in man, and the inspiration of the Almighty giveth them understanding. *Jb.* 32: 8.

Take not thy holy spirit from me. *Ps.* 51: 11.

The spirit of man will sustain his infirmity. *Pr.* 18: 14.

The spirit of man is the candle of the Lord. *Pr.* 20: 27.

Who knoweth the spirit of man that goeth upward, and the spirit of the beast that goeth downward to the earth? *Ec.* 3: 21.

There is no man that hath power over the spirit to retain the spirit. *Ec.* 8: 8.

The child grew, and waxed strong in spirit. *Lu.* 1: 80.

What man knoweth the things of a man, save the spirit of man which is in him? *1 Co.* 2: 11.

For which cause we faint not; but though our outward man perish, yet the inward man is renewed day by day. *2 Co.* 4: 16.

That he would grant you, according to the riches of his glory, to be strengthened with might by his Spirit in the inner man, *Ep.* 3: 16.

Put on the new man, which after God is created in righteousness and true holiness. *Ep.* 4: 24.

The hidden man of the heart. *1 Pe.* 3: 4.

See also
Man, Divinity of; Man, Greatness of; Man, the New; Man, Spirit of; Manliness; Nature, Human.

Manifestation

He that doeth truth cometh to the light, that his deeds may be made manifest, that they are wrought in God. *Jn.* 3: 21.

Neither hath this man sinned, nor his parents: but that the works of God should be made manifest in him. *Jn.* 9: 3.

The earnest expectation of the creature waiteth for the manifestation of the sons of God. *Ro.* 8: 19.

Every man's work shall be made manifest: for the day shall declare it, because it shall be revealed by fire. *1 Co.* 3: 13.

The manifestation of the Spirit is given to every man to profit withal. *1 Co.* 12: 7.

That the life also of Jesus might be made manifest in our mortal flesh. *2 Co.* 4: 11.

The grace of God that bringeth salvation hath appeared to all men. *Tit.* 2: 11.

The kindness and love of God our Saviour toward men appeared. *Tit.* 3: 4.

Thy judgments are made manifest. *Re.* 15: 4.

See also
Christ, Revelation of; Disclosure; Display; God, Revelation of; God, Vision of.

Manliness

Be of good courage, and let us play the men for our people, and for the cities of our God. *2 S.* 10: 12.

Be thou strong therefore, and shew thyself a man. *1 K.* 2: 2.

Gird up thy loins now like a man: I will demand of thee, and declare thou unto me. *Jb.* 40: 7.

The spirit of a man will sustain his infirmity. *Pr.* 18: 14.

Remember this, and shew yourselves men. *Is.* 46: 8.

I sought for a man among them, that should make up the hedge, and stand in the gap before me for the land, that I should not destroy it: but I found none. *Eze.* 22: 30.

Quit you like men. *1 Co.* 16: 13.

See also
Man; Man, Divinity of; Man, Greatness of; Man, the New; Man, Spirit of; Nature, Human.

Manna

The children of Israel did eat manna forty years, until they came to a land inhabited. *Ex.* 16: 35.

The manna was as coriander seed. *Nu.* 11: 7.

The taste of it was as the taste of fresh oil. *Nu.* 11: 8.

When the dew fell upon the camp in the night, the manna fell upon it. *Nu.* 11: 9.

He humbled thee, and suffered thee to hunger, and fed thee with manna. *De.* 8: 3.

Wherein was the golden pot that had manna. *He.* 9: 4.

To him that overcometh will I give to eat of the hidden manna. *Re.* 2: 17.

See also
Bread; Christ, the Bread of Life; God, Providence of; Hunger; Nourishment.

Manners

Ye shall not walk in the manners of the nation, which I cast out before you. *Le.* 20: 23.

Unto this day they do after the former manners. *2 K.* 17: 34.

Ye have not walked in my statutes, neither executed my judgments, but have done after the manners of the heathen that are round about you. *Eze.* 11: 12.

In eating every one taketh before other his own supper: and one is hungry, and another is drunken. *1 Co.* 11: 21.

Though I . . . have not charity, I am nothing. . . . Charity . . . Doth not behave itself unseemly. *1 Co.* 13: 2, 4, 5.

Good manners. *1 Co.* 15: 33.

Be courteous. *1 Pe.* 3: 8.

Use hospitality one to another without grudging. *1 Pe.* 4: 9.

See also
Behavior; Character; Conduct; Fashion; Politeness; Way.

Margin

I will cast out the nations before thee, and enlarge thy borders. *Ex.* 34: 24.

He bindeth the floods from overflowing. *Jb.* 28: 11.

Thou hast set all the borders of the earth. *Ps.* 74: 17.

He brought them to the border of his sanctuary. *Ps.* 78: 54.

He maketh peace in thy borders. *Ps.* 147: 14.

They shall call them, The border of wickedness. *Mal.* 1: 4.

The Lord will be magnified from the border
of Israel. *Mal.* 1: 5.

They . . . besought him that they might
only touch the hem of his garment: and as
many as were touched were made perfectly
whole. *Mat.* 14: 35, 36.

A certain householder . . . planted a vine-
yard, and hedged it round about. *Mat.* 21: 33.
See also
Border; Bound; Limit.

Mark

The Lord set a mark upon Cain. *Ge.* 4: 15.

If I sin, then thou markest me, and thou wilt
not acquit me from mine iniquity. *Jb.* 10: 14.

Mark the perfect man, and behold the upright: for the end of that man is peace. *Ps.*
37: 37.

Mark ye well her bulwarks, consider her
palaces. *Ps.* 48: 13.

Thine iniquity is marked before me, saith
the Lord God. *Je.* 2: 22.

He marked how they chose out the chief
rooms. *Lu.* 14: 7.

I bear in my body the marks of the Lord
Jesus. *Ga.* 6: 17.

I press toward the mark. *Ph.* 3: 14.
See also
Evidence; God, Evidence of; Proof; Sign;
Symbol; Testimony; Token.

Market

It is naught, it is naught, saith the buyer:
but when he is gone his way, then he
boasteth. *Pr.* 20: 14.

Buy the truth, and sell it not. *Pr.* 23: 23.

It shall be, . . . as with the buyer, so with
the seller. *Is.* 24: 2.

Come ye, buy, and eat; yea, come, buy wine
and milk without money and without price.
Is. 55: 1.

Let not the buyer rejoice, nor the seller
mourn: for wrath is upon all the multitude.
Eze. 7: 12.

Whereunto shall I liken this generation? It
is like unto children sitting in the markets.
Mat. 11: 16.

He . . . saw others standing idle in the
marketplace. *Mat.* 20: 3.

Go ye rather to them that sell, and buy for
yourselves. *Mat.* 25: 9.

Ye love . . . greetings in the markets. *Lu.*
11: 43.

Therefore disputed he . . . in the market
daily with them that met with him. *Ac.* 17: 17.

Go to now, ye that say, To day or to mor-
row we will go into such a city, and continue
there a year, and buy and sell, and get gain.
Ja. 4: 13.
See also
Business; Trade.

Marksman

God was with the lad; and he grew and
dwelt in the wilderness, and became an
archer. *Ge.* 21: 20.

His bow abode in strength, and the arms
of his hands were made strong by the hands
of the mighty God of Jacob. *Ge.* 49: 24.

I will shoot three arrows on the side thereof,
as though I shot at a mark. *1 S.* 20: 20.

The archers hit him. *1 S.* 31: 3.

The arrow cannot make him flee. *Jb.* 41: 28.

He breaketh the bow, and cutteth the spear
in sunder. *Ps.* 46: 9.

Who whet their tongue like a sword, and
bend their bows to shoot their arrows, even
bitter words. *Ps.* 64: 3.

Thou shalt not be afraid . . . for the arrow
that flieth by day. *Ps.* 91: 5.

Marriage

The Lord God said, It is not good that the
man should be alone; I will make him an
help meet for him. *Ge.* 2: 18.

Whoso findeth a wife findeth a good thing,
and obtaineth favour of the Lord. *Pr.* 18: 22.

Two are better than one. *Ec.* 4: 9.

I will betroth thee unto me for ever. *Ho.* 2:
19.

What therefore God hath joined together,
let not man put asunder. *Mat.* 19: 6.

In the resurrection they neither marry, nor
are given in marriage, but are as the angels
of God in heaven. *Mat.* 22: 30.

What therefore God hath joined together,
let not man put asunder. *Mk.* 10: 9.

The third day there was a marriage in Cana
of Galilee. . . . And both Jesus was called,
and his disciples, to the marriage. *Jn.* 2: 1, 2.

If they cannot contain, let them marry: for
it is better to marry than to burn. *1 Co.* 7: 9.

The unbelieving husband is sanctified by
the wife, and the unbelieving wife is sanctified
by the husband. *1 Co.* 7: 14.

They two shall be one flesh. *Ep.* 5: 31.

Blessed are they which are called unto the
marriage supper of the Lamb. *Re.* 19: 9.
See also
Bride; Bridegroom; Husband; Wedding;
Wife.

Martyr

The dead bodies of thy servants have they
given to be meat unto the fowls of the heaven,
the flesh of thy saints unto the beasts of the
earth. *Ps.* 79: 2.

They shall look upon me whom they have
pierced. *Zch.* 12: 10.

Men that have hazarded their lives for the
name of our Lord Jesus. *Ac.* 15: 26.

When the blood of thy martyr Stephen was
shed, I also was standing by, and consenting
unto his death. *Ac.* 22: 20.

For thy sake we are killed all the day long.
Ro. 8: 36.

Who have for my life laid down their own
necks. *Ro.* 16: 4.

He . . . became obedient unto death. *Ph.* 2:
8.

And what shall I more say? for the time
would fail me to tell. *He.* 11: 32.

Not accepting deliverance. *He.* 11: 35.

They wandered in deserts, and in mountains,
and in dens and caves of the earth. *He.* 11:
38.

They loved not their lives unto the death.
Re. 12: 11.

The blood of the martyrs of Jesus. *Re.* 17:
6.

I saw the souls of them that were beheaded
for the witness of Jesus, and for the word of

God, . . . and they lived and reigned with Christ a thousand years. *Re.* 20: 4.

See also

Cross; Persecution; Sacrifice; Self-Sacrifice; Suffering.

Marvel

Wilt thou shew wonders to the dead? shall the dead arise and praise thee? *Ps.* 88: 10.

Shall thy wonders be known in the dark? *Ps.* 88: 12.

Sing unto the Lord a new song; for he hath done marvellously. *Ps.* 98: 1.

Marvellous are thy works; and that my soul knoweth right well. *Ps.* 139: 14.

When they had heard these words, they marvelled, and left him. *Mat.* 22: 22.

He marvelled because of their unbelief. *Mk.* 6: 6.

There shall be signs in the sun, and in the moon, and in the stars. *Lu.* 21: 25.

That ye may marvel. *Jn.* 5: 20.

Why marvel ye at this? or why look ye so earnestly on us, as though by our own power or holiness we had made this man to walk? *Ac.* 3: 12.

Declaring what miracles and wonders God had wrought among the Gentiles by them. *Ac.* 15: 12.

I saw another sign in heaven, great and marvellous. *Re.* 15: 1.

See also

Amazement; Astonishment; Miracle; Sign; Wonder.

Mass

He gathered the waters of the sea together as an heap. *Ps.* 33: 7.

He heapeth up riches, and knoweth not who shall gather them. *Ps.* 39: 6.

Thou shalt heap coals of fire upon his head. *Pr.* 25: 22.

Jerusalem shall become heaps. *Mi.* 3: 12.

He took bread, and gave thanks, and brake it, and gave unto them, saying, This is my body which is given for you: this do in remembrance of me. Likewise also the cup after supper, saying, This cup is the new testament in my blood, which is shed for you. *Lu.* 22: 19, 20.

The bread which we break, is it not the communion of the body of Christ? *1 Co.* 10: 16.

Take, eat: this is my body, which is broken for you. *1 Co.* 11: 24.

This cup is the new testament in my blood. *1 Co.* 11: 25.

As often as ye eat this bread, and drink this cup, ye do shew the Lord's death till he come. *1 Co.* 11: 26.

We are made partakers of Christ. *He.* 3: 14.

See also

Accumulation; Christ, Blood of; Christ, Body of; Communion, Service of; Eucharist; Supper, the Last; Supper, the Lord's.

Master

Thy servants will do as my lord commandeth. *Nu.* 32: 25.

The ox knoweth his owner, and the ass his master's crib: but Israel doth not know. *Is.* 1: 3.

No man can serve two masters. *Mat.* 6: 24.

The disciple is not above the master, nor the servant above the lord. *Mat.* 10: 24.

Neither be ye called masters: for one is your Master, even Christ. *Mat.* 23: 10.

The Son of man is Lord also of the sabbath. *Mk.* 2: 28.

Every one that is perfect shall be as his master. *Lu.* 6: 40.

As a wise masterbuilder, I have laid the foundation. *1 Co.* 3: 10.

Your Master . . . is in heaven. *Ep.* 6: 9.

My brethren, be not many masters. *Ja.* 3: 1.

See also

Authority; Christ, the Master; Christ, Supremacy of; Dominion; God, Supremacy of; Lord; Mastery; Power; Prince; Rule.

Mastery

I will triumph in the works of thy hands. *Ps.* 92: 4.

His right hand, and his holy arm, hath gotten him the victory. *Ps.* 98: 1.

He that is slow to anger is better than the mighty; and he that ruleth his spirit than he that taketh a city. *Pr.* 16: 32.

He that hath no rule over his own spirit is like a city that is broken down, and without walls. *Pr.* 25: 28.

Behold, I give unto you power to tread on serpents and scorpions, and over all the power of the enemy. *Lu.* 10: 19.

Know ye not that they which run in a race run all, but one receiveth the prize? So run, that ye may obtain. *1 Co.* 9: 24.

Every man that striveth for the mastery is temperate in all things. *1 Co.* 9: 25.

See also

Adept; Christ, Triumph of; Continence; Control; Dominion; Preëminence; Restraint; Self-Control; Subjection; Success; Superiority; Supremacy; Triumph; Victory.

Materialism

The spirit of the living creature was in the wheels. *Eze.* 1: 20.

Neither will we say any more to the work of our hands, Ye are our gods. *Ho.* 14: 3.

He answered and said, It is written, Man shall not live by bread alone, but by every word that proceedeth out of the mouth of God. *Mat.* 4: 4.

Ye cannot serve God and mammon. *Mat.* 6: 24.

The Word was made flesh. *Jn.* 1: 14.

Be not conformed to this world. *Ro.* 12: 2.

The kingdom of God is not meat and drink; but righteousness, and peace, and joy in the Holy Ghost. *Ro.* 14: 17.

The god of this world hath blinded the minds of them which believe not. *2 Co.* 4: 4.

See also

Mammon; Money; Society; Ungodliness; Wealth.

Maturity

The Lord God said, Behold, the man is become as one of us, to know good and evil. *Ge.* 3: 22.

Let me die the death of the righteous, and let my last end be like his! *Nu.* 23: 10.

The flower of their age. *1 S.* 2: 33.

I go the way of all the earth: be thou strong therefore, and shew thyself a man. *1 K.* 2: 2.

Great men are not always wise: neither do the aged understand judgment. *Jb.* 32: 9.

In the morning it flourisheth, and groweth up. *Ps.* 90: 6.

He shall grow like a cedar in Lebanon. *Ps.* 92: 12.

As a flower of the field, so he flourisheth. *Ps.* 103: 15.

The sour grape is ripening in the flower. *Is.* 18: 5.

It is thou, O king, that art grown and become strong. *Da.* 4: 22.

Let both grow together until the harvest. *Mat.* 13: 30.

Gather the wheat into my barn. *Mat.* 13: 30.

When it is grown, it is the greatest among herbs. *Mat.* 13: 32.

Till the whole was leavened. *Mat.* 13: 33.

Jesus increased in wisdom and stature. *Lu.* 2: 52.

As many as received him, to them gave he power to become the sons of God. *Jn.* 1: 12.

Lift up your eyes, and look on the fields; for they are white already to harvest. *Jn.* 4: 35.

Unto the measure of the stature of the fulness of Christ. *Ep.* 4: 13.

Your faith groweth exceedingly. *2 Th.* 1: 3.

The harvest of the earth is ripe. *Re.* 14: 15.

See also

Adult; Immaturity.

Meaning

God meant it unto good. *Ge.* 50: 20.

What mean ye by this service? *Ex.* 12: 26.

What mean the testimonies, and the statutes, and the judgments, which the Lord our God hath commanded you? *De.* 6: 20.

This commandment which I command thee this day, it is not hidden from thee, neither is it far off. *De.* 30: 11.

So they read in the book of the law of God distinctly, and gave the sense, and caused them to understand the reading. *Ne.* 8: 8.

To understand a proverb, and the interpretation. *Pr.* 1: 6.

Know ye not what these things mean? *Eze.* 17: 12.

What meanest thou, O sleeper? *Jon.* 1: 6.

Go ye and learn what that meaneth, I will have mercy, and not sacrifice. *Mat.* 9: 13.

Hearing they hear not, neither do they understand. *Mat.* 13: 13.

Questioning one with another what the rising from the dead should mean. *Mk.* 9: 10.

Peter doubted in himself what this vision which he had seen should mean. *Ac.* 10: 17.

Whom therefore ye ignorantly worship, him declare I unto you. *Ac.* 17: 23.

Though I . . . understand all mysteries, and all knowledge; . . . and have not charity, I am nothing. *1 Co.* 13: 2.

How is it then, brethren? when ye come together, every one of you hath a psalm, hath a doctrine, hath a tongue, hath a revelation, hath an interpretation. Let all things be done unto edifying. *1 Co.* 14: 26.

These, as natural brute beasts, made to be taken and destroyed, speak evil of the things that they understand not. *2 Pe.* 2: 12.

Paul also according to the wisdom given unto him hath written unto you; As also in all his epistles, speaking in them of these things; in which are some things hard to be understood, which they that are unlearned and unstable wrest, as they do also the other scriptures, unto their own destruction. *2 Pe.* 3: 15, 16.

See also

Interpretation.

Measure

To make the weight for the winds; and he weigheth the waters by measure. *Jb.* 28: 25.

Lord, make me to know mine end, and the measure of my days, what it is; that I may know how frail I am. *Ps.* 39: 4.

Divers weights, and divers measures, both of them are alike abomination to the Lord. *Pr.* 20: 10.

Who hath measured the waters in the hollow of his hand, and meted out heaven with the span, and comprehended the dust of the earth in a measure, and weighed the mountains in scales, and the hills in a balance? *Is.* 40: 12.

The host of heaven cannot be numbered, neither the sand of the sea measured. *Je.* 33: 22.

Behold a man with a measuring line in his hand. *Zch.* 2: 1.

With what judgment ye judge, ye shall be judged: and with what measure ye mete, it shall be measured to you again. *Mat.* 7: 2.

Good measure, pressed down, and shaken together, and running over. *Lu.* 6: 38.

God giveth not the Spirit by measure unto him. *Jn.* 3: 34.

They measuring themselves by themselves, and comparing themselves among themselves, are not wise. *2 Co.* 10: 12.

Unto every one of us is given grace according to the measure of the gift of Christ. *Ep.* 4: 7.

See also

Accuracy; Balance; Survey; Weight.

Meat

I have esteemed the words of his mouth more than my necessary food. *Jb.* 23: 12.

My tears have been my meat day and night. *Ps.* 42: 3.

They gave me also gall for my meat; and in my thirst they gave me vinegar to drink. *Ps.* 69: 21.

The people asked, and he brought quails, and satisfied them with the bread of heaven. *Ps.* 105: 40.

Take no thought for your life, what ye shall eat, or what ye shall drink. *Mat.* 6: 25.

What man is there of you, whom if his son ask bread, will he give him a stone? Or if he ask a fish, will he give him a serpent? *Mat.* 7: 9, 10.

I have meat to eat that ye know not of. *Jn.* 4: 32.

My meat is to do the will of him that sent me. *Jn.* 4: 34.

Labour not for the meat which perisheth, but for that meat which endureth unto everlasting life. *Jn.* 6: 27.

If meat make my brother to offend, I will eat no flesh while the world standeth, lest I make my brother to offend. *1 Co.* 8: 13.

Who planteth a vineyard, and eateth not of the fruit thereof? or who feedeth a flock, and eateth not of the milk of the flock? *1 Co.* 9: 7.

Our fathers . . . did all eat the same spiritual meat. *1 Co.* 10: 1, 3.

Ye . . . are become such as have need of milk, and not of strong meat. *He.* 5: 12.
See also
Food; Hunger; Nourishment; Stomach.

Meddling

Why shouldest thou meddle to thy hurt? *2 K.* 14: 10.
Forbear thee from meddling with God, who is with me, that he destroy thee not. *2 Ch.* 35: 21.
The heart knoweth his own bitterness; and a stranger doth not intermeddle with his joy. *Pr.* 14: 10.
Through desire a man, having separated himself, seeketh and intermeddleth with all wisdom. *Pr.* 18: 1.
Every fool will be meddling. *Pr.* 20: 3.
Meddle not with him that flattereth with his lips. *Pr.* 20: 19.
Meddle not with them that are given to change. *Pr.* 24: 21.
We hear that there are some which walk among you disorderly, working not at all, but are busybodies. *2 Th.* 3: 11.
Let none of you suffer . . . as a busybody in other men's matters. *1 Pe.* 4: 15.
See also
Busybody.

Mediation

I stood between the Lord and you at that time, to shew you the word of the Lord. *De.* 5: 5.
He bare the sin of many, and made intercession for the transgressors. *Is.* 53: 12.
I exhort therefore, that, first of all, supplications, prayers, intercessions, and giving of thanks, be made for all men. *1 Ti.* 2: 1.
There is one mediator between God and men, the man Christ Jesus. *1 Ti.* 2: 5.
He ever liveth to make intercession for them. *He.* 7: 25.
Jesus the mediator of the new covenant. *He.* 12: 24.
See also
Christ, the Mediator; Intercession; Reconciliation.

Medicine

A merry heart doeth good like a medicine. *Pr.* 17: 22.
Is there no balm in Gilead; is there no physician there? *Je.* 8: 22.
There is none to plead thy cause, that thou mayest be bound up: thou hast no healing medicines. *Je.* 30: 13.
I will bring it health and cure, and I will cure them. *Je.* 33: 6.
In vain shalt thou use many medicines; for thou shalt not be cured. *Je.* 46: 11.
Howl for her; take balm for her pain, if so be she may be healed. *Je.* 51: 8.
The fruit thereof shall be for meat, and the leaf thereof for medicine. *Eze.* 47: 12.
Anoint thine eyes with eyesalve, that thou mayest see. *Re.* 3: 18.
The leaves of the tree were for the healing of the nations. *Re.* 22: 2.
See also
Antidote; Cure; Doctor; Healing; Physician; Remedy.

Mediocrity

I am a worm, and no man; a reproach of men. *Ps.* 22: 6.
I am small and despised: yet do not I forget thy precepts. *Ps.* 119: 141.
He shall not stand before mean men. *Pr.* 22: 29.
Give me neither poverty nor riches. *Pr.* 30: 8.
The poor man's wisdom is despised. *Ec.* 9: 16.
The mean man shall be brought down. *Is.* 5: 15.
He was despised and we esteemed him not. *Is.* 53: 3.
I will make thee small among the heathen, and despised among men. *Je.* 49: 15.
Who hath despised the day of small things. *Zch.* 4: 10.
The common people heard him gladly. *Mk.* 12: 37.
God hath shewed me that I should not call any man common. *Ac.* 10: 28.
I am . . . a citizen of no mean city. *Ac.* 21: 39.
Mind not high things, but condescend to men of low estate. *Ro.* 12: 16.
There is nothing unclean of itself: but to him that esteemeth any thing to be unclean, to him it is unclean. *Ro.* 14: 14.
Base things of the world, and things which are despised, hath God chosen. *1 Co.* 1: 28.
See also
Moderation.

Meditation

Thou shalt meditate therein day and night. *Jos.* 1: 8.
Commune with your own heart upon your bed, and be still. *Ps.* 4: 4.
My heart was hot within me; while I was musing the fire burned. *Ps.* 39: 3.
When I remember thee upon my bed, and meditate on thee in the night watches. *Ps.* 63: 6.
O how love I thy law! it is my meditation all the day. *Ps.* 119: 97.
Ponder the path of thy feet, and let all thy ways be established. *Pr.* 4: 26.
What think ye of Christ? *Mat.* 22: 42.
Mary kept all these things, and pondered them in her heart. *Lu.* 2: 19.
Whatsoever things are true, whatsoever things are honest, whatsoever things are just, whatsoever things are pure, whatsoever things are lovely, whatsoever things are of good report: if there be any virtue, and if there be any praise, think on these things. *Ph.* 4: 8.
See also
Consideration; Contemplation; God, Thought of; Reflection; Study; Thought.

Meekness

The man Moses was very meek. *Nu.* 12: 3.
The meek shall eat and be satisfied: they shall praise the Lord that seek him. *Ps.* 22: 26.
He will beautify the meek with salvation. *Ps.* 149: 4.
He giveth grace unto the lowly. *Pr.* 3: 34.
Better it is to be of an humble spirit with the lowly, than to divide the spoil with the proud. *Pr.* 16: 19.

As a sheep before her shearers is dumb, so he openeth not his mouth. *Is.* 53: 7.

Put up again thy sword into his place: for all they that take the sword shall perish with the sword. *Mat.* 26: 52.

Unto him that smiteth thee on the one cheek offer also the other; and him that taketh away thy cloke forbid not to take thy coat also. *Lu.* 6: 29.

Serving the Lord with all humility of mind. *Ac.* 20: 19.

I say, through the grace given unto me, to every man that is among you, not to think of himself more highly than he ought to think; but to think soberly, according as God hath dealt to every man the measure of faith. *Ro.* 12: 3.

The fruit of the Spirit is . . . Meekness. *Ga.* 5: 22, 23.

Brethren, if a man be overtaken in a fault, ye which are spiritual, restore such an one in the spirit of meekness; considering thyself, lest thou also be tempted. *Ga.* 6: 1.

With all lowliness and meekness. *Ep.* 4: 2.

Let nothing be done through strife or vainglory. *Ph.* 2: 3.

In lowliness of mind let each esteem other better than themselves. *Ph.* 2: 3.

Receive with meekness the engrafted word. *Ja.* 1: 21.

Who, when he was reviled, reviled not again; when he suffered, he threatened not. *1 Pe.* 2: 23.

God resisteth the proud, and giveth grace to the humble. *1 Pe.* 5: 5.

See also

Humility; Lowliness.

Meeting

The congregation was gathered together as one man. *Ju.* 20: 1.

In the midst of the congregation will I praise thee. *Ps.* 22: 22.

It is iniquity, even the solemn meeting. *Is.* 1: 13.

Gather the people, sanctify the congregation. *Jo.* 2: 16.

Many were gathered together praying. *Ac.* 12: 12.

Not forsaking the assembling of ourselves together. *He.* 10: 25.

See also

Audience; Church; Congregation; Congress; Rendezvous.

Melancholy

The bread of affliction. *De.* 16: 3.

To set up on high those that be low. *Jb.* 5: 11.

I bowed down heavily, as one that mourneth for his mother. *Ps.* 35: 14.

I am troubled; I am bowed down greatly; I go mourning all the day long. *Ps.* 38: 6.

Why art thou cast down, O my soul? and why art thou disquieted within me? hope thou in God: for I shall yet praise him, who is the health of my countenance, and my God. *Ps.* 42: 11.

I am poor and sorrowful: let thy salvation, O God, set me up on high. *Ps.* 69: 29.

Mine eye mourneth by reason of affliction. *Ps.* 88: 9.

The bread of sorrows. *Ps.* 127: 2.

How shall we sing the Lord's song in a strange land? *Ps.* 137: 4.

I went about to cause my heart to despair of all the labour which I took under the sun. *Ec.* 2: 20.

To give unto them . . . the garment of praise for the spirit of heaviness. *Is.* 61: 3.

What profit is it that we have kept his ordinance, and that we have walked mournfully before the Lord of hosts? *Mal.* 3: 14.

See also

Dejection; Depression; Despondency; Gloom; Mourning; Sadness; Sorrow.

Melody

They ministered before the dwelling place of the tabernacle of the congregation with singing. *1 Ch.* 6: 32.

When the morning stars sang together, and all the sons of God shouted for joy? *Jb.* 38: 7.

Praise ye the Lord. *Ps.* 150: 1.

Make sweet melody, sing many songs, that thou mayest be remembered. *Is.* 23: 16.

Joy and gladness shall be found therein, thanksgiving, and the voice of melody. *Is.* 51: 3.

Take thou away from me the noise of thy songs; for I will not hear the melody of thy viols. *Am.* 5: 23.

Singing and making melody in your heart to the Lord. *Ep.* 5: 19.

See also

Instrument; Music; Psalm; Song; Tune.

Member

All my members are as a shadow. *Jb.* 17: 7.

I am the vine, ye are the branches: He that abideth in me, and I in him, the sam bringeth forth much fruit: for without me ye can do nothing. *Jn.* 15: 5.

I see another law in my members, warring against the law of my mind, and bringing me into captivity to the law of sin which is in my members. *Ro.* 7: 23.

As we have many members in one body, and all members have not the same office: So we, being many, are one body in Christ, and every one members one of another. *Ro.* 12: 4, 5.

Know ye not that your bodies are the members of Christ? *1 Co.* 6: 15.

Whether one member suffer, all the members suffer with it; or one member be honoured, all the members rejoice with it. *1 Co.* 12: 26.

Now ye are the body of Christ, and members in particular. *1 Co.* 12: 27.

We are members one of another. *Ep.* 4: 25.

Mortify therefore your members which are upon the earth. *Col.* 3: 5.

See also

Part; Portion.

Memorial

This is my name for ever, and this is my memorial unto all generations. *Ex.* 3: 15.

Write this for a memorial in a book. *Ex.* 17: 14.

When they came unto the borders of Jordan, . . . the children of Reuben, and the children of Gad, and the half tribe of Manasseh built there an altar by Jordan, a great altar to see to. *Jos.* 22: 10.

Then Samuel took a stone, and set it between Mizpeh and Shen, and called the name of it Eben-ezer. *1 S.* 7: 12.

Thy name, O Lord, endureth for ever; and thy memorial, O Lord, throughout all generations. *Ps.* 135: 13.

The memory of the just is blessed. *Pr.* 10: 7.

Even the Lord God of hosts; the Lord is his memorial. *Ho.* 12: 5.

The kingdom of heaven is likened unto a man which sowed good seed in his field. *Mat.* 13: 24.

Wheresoever this gospel shall be preached in the whole world, there shall also this, that this woman hath done, be told for a memorial of her. *Mat.* 26: 13.

Thy prayers and thine alms are come up for a memorial before God *Ac.* 10: 4.

See also

Anniversary; Commemoration; Epitaph; History; Memory; Remembrance.

Memory

Remember the sabbath day, to keep it holy. *Ex.* 20: 8.

Remember all the way which the Lord thy God led thee. *De.* 8: 2.

Remember the day when thou camest forth out of the land of Egypt. *De.* 16: 3.

A Syrian ready to perish was my father, and he went down into Egypt. *De.* 26: 5.

Remember the days of old, consider the years of many generations. *De.* 32: 7.

O remember that my life is wind. *Jb.* 7: 7.

Remember ye not the former things, neither consider the things of old *Is.* 43: 18.

Remember the words of the Lord Jesus. *Ac.* 20: 35.

The Lord Jesus the same night in which he was betrayed took bread: And when he had given thanks, he brake it, and said, Take, eat: this is my body, which is broken for you: this do in remembrance of me. *1 Co.* 11: 23, 24.

Remember that Jesus Christ of the seed of David was raised from the dead. *2 Ti.* 2: 8.

He being dead yet speaketh. *He.* 11: 4.

I stir up your pure minds by way of remembrance. *2 Pe.* 3: 1.

Beloved, remember ye the words which were spoken before of the apostles of our Lord Jesus Christ. *Jude* 1: 17.

See also

Anniversary; Commemoration; Memorial; Remembrance.

Merchant

Her merchandise and her hire shall be holiness to the Lord. *Is.* 23: 18.

A city of merchants. *Eze.* 17: 4.

Tarshish was thy merchant by reason of the multitude of all kind of riches. *Eze.* 27: 12.

They of the house of Togarmah traded in thy fairs with horses and horsemen and mules. *Eze.* 27: 14.

When thy wares went forth out of the seas, thou filledst many people; thou didst enrich the kings of the earth with the multitude of thy riches and of thy merchandise. *Eze.* 27: 33.

Thou hast multiplied thy merchants above the stars of heaven. *Na.* 3: 16.

The kingdom of heaven is like unto a merchant man, seeking goodly pearls: Who, when he had found one pearl of great price, went and sold all that he had, and bought it. *Mat.* 13: 45, 46.

They . . . went their ways, one to his farm, another to his merchandise. *Mat.* 22: 5.

See also

Business; Commerce; Trade.

Mercy

Surely goodness and mercy shall follow me all the days of my life. *Ps.* 23: 6.

Remember, O Lord, thy tender mercies and thy lovingkindnesses. *Ps.* 25: 6.

Thy mercy, O Lord, is in the heavens; and thy faithfulness reacheth unto the clouds. *Ps.* 36: 5.

Is his mercy clean gone for ever? *Ps.* 77: 8.

Mercy and truth are met together. *Ps.* 85: 10.

I will sing of the mercies of the Lord for ever. *Ps.* 89: 1.

Who crowneth thee with lovingkindness and tender mercies. *Ps.* 103: 4.

The mercy of the Lord is from everlasting to everlasting upon them that fear him. *Ps.* 103: 17.

Let not mercy and truth forsake thee: bind them about thy neck; write them upon the table of thine heart. *Pr.* 3: 3.

A bruised reed shall he not break. *Is.* 42: 3.

I will have mercy upon her that had not obtained mercy. *Ho.* 2: 23.

I· desired mercy, and not sacrifice. *Ho.* 6: 6.

Blessed are the merciful: for they shall obtain mercy. *Mat.* 5: 7.

If a man have an hundred sheep, and one of them be gone astray, doth he not leave the ninety and nine, and goeth into the mountains, and seeketh that which is gone astray. *Mat.* 18: 12.

Put on therefore, as the elect of God, holy and beloved, bowels of mercies. *Col.* 3: 12.

See also

Charity; Christ, Compassion of; Clemency; God, Compassion of; God, Mercy of; Pity.

Merit

Ye shall serve the Lord your God, and he shall bless thy bread, and thy water. *Ex.* 23: 25.

The Lord give thee seed of this woman for the loan which is lent to the Lord *1 S.* 2: 20.

Behold, here I am: witness against me before the Lord, and before his anointed: whose ox have I taken? or whose ass have I taken? or whom have I defrauded? whom have I oppressed? or of whose hand have I received any bribe to blind mine eyes therewith? and I will restore it to you. *1 S.* 12: 3.

The Lord shall reward the doer of evil according to his wickedness. *2 S.* 3: 39.

Thou our God hast punished us less than our iniquities deserve. *Ezr.* 9: 13.

God will not cast away a perfect man, neither will he help the evil doers. *Jb.* 8: 20.

Know therefore that God exacteth of thee less than thine iniquity deserveth. *Jb.* 11: 6.

Judge me, O Lord: for I have walked in mine integrity. *Ps.* 26: 1.

Give them after the work of their hands; render to them their desert. *Ps.* 28: 4.

The heart of the wicked is little worth. *Pr.* 10: 20.

The great God that formed all things both rewardeth the fool, and rewardeth transgressors. *Pr.* **26: 10.**

Cast thy bread upon the waters: for thou shalt find it after many days. *Ec.* **11: 1.**

I will do unto them after their way, and according to their deserts will I judge them. *Eze.* **7: 27.**

Lord, I am not worthy. *Mat.* **8: 8.**

The workman is worthy of his meat. *Mat.* **10: 10.**

When I come again, I will repay thee. *Lu.* **10: 35.**

Who then is that faithful and wise steward, whom his lord shall make ruler over his household, to give them their portion of meat in due season? *Lu.* **12: 42.**

Rejoicing that they were counted worthy to suffer shame for his name. *Ac.* **5: 41.**

Every man shall receive his own reward according to his own labour. *1 Co.* **3: 8.**

I . . . beseech you that ye walk worthy of the vocation wherewith ye are called. *Ep.* **4: 1.**

Thou art worthy, O Lord, to receive glory and honour and power. *Re.* **4: 11.**

See also
Punishment; Reward; Worth.

Merriment

They drank, and were merry with him. *Ge.* **43: 34.**

All the people went their way . . . to make great mirth. *Ne.* **8: 12.**

Till he fill thy mouth with laughing, and thy lips with rejoicing. *Jb.* **8: 21.**

A merry heart maketh a cheerful countenance: but by sorrow of the heart the spirit is broken. *Pr.* **15: 13.**

I will prove thee with mirth. *Ec.* **2: 1.**

I know that there is no good in them, but for a man to rejoice, and to do good in his life. *Ec.* **3: 12.**

The heart of fools is in the house of mirth. *Ec.* **7: 4.**

A feast is made for laughter, and wine maketh merry. *Ec.* **10: 19.**

Let us eat, and be merry: For this my son was dead, and is alive again. *Lu.* **15: 23, 24.**

Is any merry? let him sing psalms. *Ja.* **5: 13.**

See also
Cheer; Gaiety; Laughter; Mirth; Smile.

Messenger

He shall send his angel before thee. *Ge.* **24: 7.**

I have a message from God unto thee. *Ju.* **3: 20.**

A faithful ambassador is health. *Pr.* **13: 17.**

He shall send them a saviour, and a great one, and he shall deliver them. *Is.* **19: 20.**

I send you forth as sheep in the midst of wolves. *Mat.* **10: 16.**

The Son of man shall send forth his angels. *Mat.* **13: 41.**

I send unto you prophets, and wise men, and scribes. *Mat.* **23: 34.**

Thou shalt go before the face of the Lord to prepare his ways. *Lu.* **1: 76.**

I will send my beloved son: it may be they will reverence him when they see him. *Lu.* **20: 13.**

They are the messengers of the churches,

and the glory of Christ. *2 Co.* **8: 23.**

There was given to me a thorn in the flesh, the messenger of Satan to buffet me. *2 Co.* **12: 7.**

Are they not all ministering spirits, sent forth to minister for them who shall be heirs of salvation? *He.* **1: 14.**

Whither the forerunner is for us entered, even Jesus. *He.* **6: 20.**

This then is the message which we have heard of him, and declare unto you, that God is light, and in him is no darkness at all. *1 Jn.* **1: 5.**

See also
Ambassador; Errand; Forerunner; God, Messenger of; Harbinger; Herald; Missionary; Prophet.

Messiah

Jesus, who is called Christ. *Mat.* **1: 16.**

Thou art the Christ, the Son of the living God. *Mat.* **16: 16.**

Art thou the Christ, the Son of the Blessed? *Mk.* **14: 61.**

We have found the Messias, which is, being interpreted, the Christ. *Jn.* **1: 41.**

I know that Messias cometh, which is called Christ: when he is come, he will tell us all things. *Jn.* **4: 25.**

He is Lord of all. *Ac.* **10: 36.**

This Jesus, whom I preach unto you, is Christ. *Ac.* **17: 3.**

See also
Christ; Christ, the Messiah.

Midday

Thine age shall be clearer than the noonday; thou shalt shine forth, thou shalt be as the morning. *Jb.* **11: 17.**

He shall bring forth thy righteousness as the light, and thy judgment as the noonday. *Ps.* **37: 6.**

Evening, and morning, and at noon, will I pray. *Ps.* **55: 17.**

Thou shalt not be afraid . . . for the destruction that wasteth at noonday. *Ps.* **91: 5, 6.**

We stumble at noon day as in the night. *Is.* **59: 10.**

At midday, O king, I saw in the way a light from heaven. *Ac.* **26: 13.**

See also
Noon.

Middle

God called unto him out of the midst of the bush. *Ex.* **3: 4.**

I stood between the Lord and you at that time. *De.* **5: 5.**

Ye sanctified me not in the midst of the children of Israel. *De.* **32: 51.**

God is in the midst of her; she shall not be moved. *Ps.* **46: 5.**

The destruction that wasteth at noonday. *Ps.* **91: 6.**

As the mountains are round about Jerusalem, so the Lord is round about his people from henceforth even for ever. *Ps.* **125: 2.**

I will gather you into the midst of Jerusalem. *Eze.* **22: 19.**

O Lord, revive thy work in the midst of the years. *Hab.* **3: 2.**

If he shall come in the second watch, or come in the third watch. *Lu.* **12: 38.**

They crucified him, and two other with him, on either side one, and Jesus in the midst. *Jn.* 19: 18.

There is one God, and one mediator between God and men, the man Christ Jesus. *1 Ti.* 2: 5.

See also

Center.

Midnight

Darkness . . . which may be felt. *Ex.* 10: 21.

At midnight the Lord smote all the firstborn. *Ex.* 12: 29.

Ye heard the voice out of the midst of the darkness. *De.* 5: 23.

The people shall be troubled at midnight. *Jb.* 34: 20.

Thou shalt not be afraid for the terror by night. *Ps.* 91: 5.

At midnight I will rise to give thanks unto thee. *Ps.* 119: 62.

Behold, the darkness shall cover the earth, and gross darkness the people. *Is.* 60: 2.

At midnight there was a cry made, Behold, the bridegroom cometh. *Mat.* 25: 6.

See also

Darkness; Night.

Might

Thy right hand, O Lord, is become glorious in power. *Ex.* 15: 6.

Blessed is the man whose strength is in thee. *Ps.* 84: 5.

Neither let the mighty man glory in his might. *Je.* 9: 23.

God hath chosen the weak things of the world to confound the things which are mighty. *1 Co.* 1: 27.

The kingdom of God is not in word, but in power. *1 Co.* 4: 20.

The love of Christ constraineth us. *2 Co.* 5: 14.

To be strengthened with might by his Spirit in the inner man. *Ep.* 3: 16.

Be strong in the Lord, and in the power of his might. *Ep.* 6: 10.

Strengthened with all might, according to his glorious power, unto all patience and longsuffering with joyfulness. *Col.* 1: 11.

We made known unto you the power and coming of our Lord Jesus Christ. *2 Pe.* 1: 16.

See also

Christ, Power of; Christ, Strength of; Coercion; Constraint; God, Omnipotence of; God, Power of; God, Strength of; Omnipotence; Power; Strength.

Migration

I will give unto thee, and to thy seed after thee, the land wherein thou art a stranger. *Ge.* 17: 8.

I have heard that there is corn in Egypt: get you down thither. *Ge.* 42: 2.

I have been a stranger in a strange land. *Ex.* 2: 22.

The Lord went before them by day in a pillar of cloud, to lead them the way; and by night in a pillar of fire, to give them light. *Ex.* 13: 21.

I am a stranger in the earth. *Ps.* 119: 19.

By the rivers of Babylon, there we sat down, yea, we wept, when we remembered Zion. *Ps.* 137: 1.

Hide the outcasts; bewray not him that wandereth. *Is.* 16: 3.

The younger son gathered all together, and took his journey into a far country. *Lu.* 15: 13.

Abraham . . . went out, not knowing whither he went. *He.* 11: 8.

Now they desire a better country, that is, an heavenly. *He.* 11: 16.

See also

Exile; Expatriation; Immigration; Refugee.

Milk

He asked water, and she gave him milk. *Ju.* 5: 25.

Hast thou not poured me out as milk, and curdled me as cheese? *Jb.* 10: 10.

Surely the churning of milk bringeth forth butter: . . . so the forcing of wrath bringeth forth strife. *Pr.* 30: 33.

Come, buy wine and milk without money and without price. *Is.* 55: 1.

They shall eat thy fruit, and they shall drink thy milk. *Eze.* 25: 4.

It shall come to pass in that day, that the mountains shall drop down new wine, and the hills shall flow with milk. *Jo.* 3: 18.

I have fed you with milk, and not with meat: for hitherto ye were not able to bear it. *1 Co.* 3: 2.

Ye . . . are become such as have need of milk, and not of strong meat. *He.* 5: 12.

Every one that useth milk is unskilful in the word of righteousness: for he is a babe. *He.* 5: 13.

Wherefore laying aside all malice, and all guile, and hypocrisies, and envies, and all evil speakings, As newborn babes, desire the sincere milk of the word, that ye may grow thereby. *1 Pe.* 2: 1, 2.

Millennium

Thine eyes shall see the king in his beauty: they shall behold the land that is very far off. *Is.* 33: 17.

The desert shall rejoice, and blossom as the rose. *Is.* 35: 1.

Then the eyes of the blind shall be opened, and the ears of the deaf shall be unstopped. *Is.* 35: 5.

They shall be mine, saith the Lord of hosts, in that day when I make up my jewels. *Mal.* 3: 17.

I reckon that the sufferings of this present time are not worthy to be compared with the glory which shall be revealed in us. *Ro.* 8: 18.

When that which is perfect is come, then that which is in part shall be done away. *1 Co.* 13: 10.

Nevertheless we, according to his promise, look for new heavens and a new earth, wherein dwelleth righteousness. *2 Pe.* 3: 13.

They lived and reigned with Christ a thousand years. *Re.* 20: 4.

They shall be priests of God and of Christ, and shall reign with him a thousand years. *Re.* 20: 6.

When the thousand years are expired, Satan shall be loosed out of his prison. *Re.* 20: 7.

See also

Age, the Golden;; Civilization; Climax; Day, the Coming; Future; Land, the Promised.

Mind

Behold, I know your thoughts. *Jb.* **21: 27.**

Thou shalt love the Lord thy God . . . with all thy mind. *Mk.* **12: 30.**

I see another law in my members, warring against the law of my mind. *Ro.* **7: 23.**

With the mind I myself serve the law of God; but with the flesh the law of sin. *Ro.* **7: 25.**

He that searcheth the hearts knoweth what is the mind of the Spirit. *Ro.* **8: 27.**

That ye may with one mind and one mouth glorify God. *Ro.* **15: 6.**

Humbleness of mind. *Col.* **3: 12.**

God hath not given us the spirit of fear; but of power, and of love, and of a sound mind. *2 Ti.* **1: 7.**

I will put my laws into their mind, and write them in their hearts. *He.* **8: 10.**

See also

Brain; Christ, Knowledge of; Christ, Mind of; Christ, Wisdom of; God, Knowledge of; God, Wisdom of; Intelligence, Knowledge; Learning; Perception; Reason; Sage; Thought; Wisdom.

Mind, the Closed

Therefore my people are gone into captivity, because they have no knowledge. *Is.* **5: 13.**

His mind hardened in pride. *Da.* **5: 20.**

Their eyes were holden that they should not know him. *Lu.* **24: 16.**

Because I tell you the truth, ye believe me not. *Jn.* **8: 45.**

Their minds were blinded. *2 Co.* **3: 14.**

Perverse disputings of men of corrupt minds, and destitute of the truth. *1 Ti.* **6: 5.**

Lest ye be wearied and faint in your minds. *He.* **12: 3.**

See also

Blindness.

Mind, the Open

Apply thine heart unto my knowledge. *Pr.* **22: 17.**

Their eyes were opened, and they knew him. *Lu.* **24: 31.**

These were more noble than those in Thessalonica, in that they received the word with all readiness of mind, and searched the scriptures daily. *Ac.* **17: 11.**

Be ye transformed by the renewing of your mind. *Ro.* **12: 2.**

I will pray with the spirit, and I will pray with the understanding also. *1 Co.* **14: 15.**

I know the forwardness of your mind. *2 Co.* **9: 2.**

The eyes of your understanding being enlightened. *Ep.* **1: 18.**

Be renewed in the spirit of your mind. *Ep.* **4: 23.**

Mind, Power of

A wise man scaleth the city of the mighty. *Pr.* **21: 22.**

As he thinketh in his heart, so is he. *Pr.* **23: 7.**

A wise man is strong; yea, a man of knowledge increaseth strength. *Pr.* **24: 5.**

Thou wilt keep him in perfect peace, whose mind is stayed on thee. *Is.* **26: 3.**

To be carnally minded is death; but to be spiritually minded is life and peace. *Ro.* **8: 6.**

We have the mind of Christ. *1 Co.* **2: 16.**

The peace of God . . . keep your hearts and minds. *Ph.* **4: 7.**

Gird up the loins of your mind. *1 Pe.* **1: 13.**

See also

Intelligence; Knowledge; Learning; Wisdom.

Ministry

Let the priests also, which come near to the Lord, sanctify themselves. *Ex.* **19: 22.**

The child did minister unto the Lord. *1 S.* **2: 11.**

He set the priests in their charges, and encouraged them to the service of the house of the Lord. *2 Ch.* **35: 2.**

The Lord put forth his hand, and touched my mouth. *Je.* **1: 9.**

The priests said not, Where is the Lord? and they that handle the law knew me not. *Je.* **2: 8.**

Angels came and ministered unto him. *Mat.* **4: 11.**

I am the good shepherd: the good shepherd giveth his life for the sheep. *Jn.* **10: 11.**

As my Father hath sent me, even so send I you. *Jn.* **20: 21.**

The ministry, which I have received of the Lord Jesus, to testify the gospel of the grace of God. *Ac.* **20: 24.**

I have appeared unto thee for this purpose, to make thee a minister and a witness both of these things which thou hast seen, and of those things in the which I will appear unto thee. *Ac.* **26: 16.**

I long to see you, that I may impart unto you some spiritual gift, to the end ye may be established. *Ro.* **1: 11.**

Woe is unto me, if I preach not the gospel! *1 Co.* **9: 16.**

Ye are manifestly declared to be the epistle of Christ ministered by us, written not with ink, but with the Spirit of the living God. *2 Co.* **3: 3.**

Approving ourselves as the ministers of God, . . . By pureness, by knowledge, by longsuffering, by kindness, by the Holy Ghost, by love unfeigned. *2 Co.* **6: 4, 6.**

He gave some, apostles; and some, prophets; and some, evangelists; and some, pastors and teachers; For the perfecting of the saints, for the work of the ministry, for the edifying of the body of Christ. *Ep.* **4: 11, 12.**

Do the work of an evangelist, make full proof of thy ministry. *2 Ti.* **4: 5.**

A minister of the sanctuary, . . . which the Lord pitched, and not man. *He.* **8: 2.**

Every priest standeth daily ministering and offering oftentimes the same sacrifices, which can never take away sins. *He.* **10: 11.**

As every man hath received the gift, even so minister the same one to another, as good stewards of the manifold grace of God. *1 Pe.* **4: 10.**

His servants shall serve him. *Re.* **22: 3.**

See also

Christ, Ministry of; Christ, the Servant; Clergy; Evangelism; Installation; Ordination; Pastor; Priesthood; Service.

Minority

I being few in number, they shall gather

themselves together against me, and slay me. *Ge.* 34: 30.

To the fewer ye shall give the less inheritance. *Nu.* 33: 54.

The Lord did not set his love upon you, nor choose you, because ye were more in number than any people: for ye were the fewest of all people. *De.* 7: 7.

The people that are with thee are too many for me. *Ju.* 7: 2.

There is no restraint to the Lord to save by many or by few. *1 S.* 14: 6.

I, even I only, am left; and they seek my life, to take it away. *1 K.* 19: 10.

Fear not, thou worm Jacob, and ye men of Israel; I will help thee, saith the Lord. *Is.* 41: 14.

Narrow is the way, which leadeth unto life, and few there be that find it. *Mat.* 7: 14.

The harvest truly is plenteous, but the labourers are few. *Mat.* 9: 37.

Many be called, but few chosen. *Mat.* 20: 16.

Not many wise men after the flesh, not many mighty, not many noble, are called. *1 Co.* 1: 26.

See also
Majority.

Miracle

Declare . . . his wonders among all people. *Ps.* 96: 3.

There shall arise false Christs, and false prophets, and shall shew great signs and wonders. *Mat.* 24: 24.

If thou be the Son of God, come down from the cross. *Mat.* 27: 40.

There is no man which shall do a miracle in my name, that can lightly speak evil of me. *Mk.* 9: 39.

And these signs shall follow them that believe. *Mk.* 16: 17.

Neither will they be persuaded, though one rose from the dead. *Lu.* 16: 31.

This beginning of miracles did Jesus in Cana of Galilee. *Jn.* 2: 11.

No man can do these miracles that thou doest, except God be with him. *Jn.* 3: 2.

A great multitude followed him, because they saw his miracles. *Jn.* 6: 2.

Those men, when they had seen the miracle that Jesus did, said, This is of a truth that prophet that should come into the world. *Jn.* 6: 14.

Ye seek me, not because ye saw the miracles, but because ye did eat of the loaves, and were filled. *Jn.* 6: 26.

John did no miracle: but all things that John spake of this man were true. *Jn.* 10: 41.

To another the working of miracles. *1 Co.* 12: 10.

He therefore that ministereth to you the Spirit, and worketh miracles among you, doeth he it by the works of the law, or by the hearing of faith? *Ga.* 3: 5.

God also bearing them witness, both with signs and wonders, and with divers miracles, and gifts of the Holy Ghost, according to his own will? *He.* 2: 4.

See also
Marvel; Sign; Wonder.

Mirth

Arise, and eat bread, and let thine heart be merry. *1 K.* 21: 7.

The end of that mirth is heaviness. *Pr.* 14: 13.

A merry heart maketh a cheerful countenance. *Pr.* 15: 13.

All the days of the afflicted are evil: but he that is of a merry heart hath a continual feast. *Pr.* 15: 15.

I will prove thee with mirth. *Ec.* 2: 1.

I said of laughter, It is mad: and of mirth, What doeth it? *Ec.* 2: 2.

As the crackling of thorns under a pot, so is the laughter of the fool. *Ec.* 7: 6.

The mirth of tabrets ceaseth, the noise of them that rejoice endeth, the joy of the harp ceaseth. *Is.* 24: 8.

All joy is darkened, the mirth of the land is gone. *Is.* 24: 11.

See also
Cheer; Gaiety; Laughter; Merriment; Smile.

Mischief

Thou art taken in thy mischief, because thou art a bloody man. *2 S.* 16: 8.

His mischief shall return upon his own head. *Ps.* 7: 16.

Under his tongue is mischief and vanity. *Ps.* 10: 7.

Fret not thyself because of evildoers. *Ps.* 37: 1.

How long will ye imagine mischief against a man? ye shall be slain all of you. *Ps.* 62: 3.

These . . . things doth the Lord hate; . . . feet that be swift in running to mischief. *Pr.* 6: 16, 18.

It is as sport to a fool to do mischief. *Pr.* 10: 23.

He that seeketh mischief, it shall come unto him. *Pr.* 11: 27.

The lips of a fool will swallow up himself. . . . the end of his talk is mischievous madness. *Ec.* 10: 12, 13.

Thou art my hope in the day of evil. *Je.* 17: 17.

O full of all subtilty and all mischief, thou child of the devil, thou enemy of all righteousness, wilt thou not cease to pervert the right ways of the Lord? *Ac.* 13: 10.

See also
Evil; Harm; Hurt; Iniquity; Plot.

Misery

In the morning thou shalt say, Would God it were even! and at even thou shalt say, Would God it were morning! *De.* 28: 67.

The wicked man travaileth with pain all his days, and the number of years is hidden to the oppressor. *Jb.* 15: 20.

Yet is their strength labour and sorrow. *Ps.* 90: 10.

They cried unto the Lord in their trouble, and he saved them out of their distresses. *Ps.* 107: 13.

The way of transgressors is hard. *Pr.* 13: 15.

The heart knoweth his own bitterness. *Pr.* 14: 10.

I hated life; because the work that is wrought under the sun is grievous unto me. *Ec.* 2: 17.

Joy is withered away from the sons of men. *Jo.* 1: 12.

He that endureth to the end shall be saved. *Mat.* 10: 22.

Tribulation and anguish, upon every soul of man that doeth evil, of the Jew first and also of the Gentile. *Ro.* 2: 9.

Destruction and misery are in their ways. *Ro.* 3: 16.

Wherein ye greatly rejoice, though now for a season, if need be, ye are in heaviness through manifold temptations. *1 Pe.* 1: 6, 7.

Thou . . . knowest not that thou art wretched, and miserable, and poor, and blind, and naked. *Re.* 3: 17.

See also

Affliction; Distress; Tribulation; Trouble; Wretchedness.

Misfortune

The famine was grievous in the land. *Ge.* 12: 10.

At destruction and famine thou shalt laugh: neither shalt thou be afraid of the beasts of the earth. *Jb.* 5: 22.

My heart is sore pained within me: and the terrors of death are fallen upon me. *Ps.* 55: 4.

I will early destroy all the wicked of the land. *Ps.* 101: 8.

Therefore shall his calamity come suddenly; suddenly shall he be broken without remedy. *Pr.* 6: 15.

If thou faint in the day of adversity, thy strength is small. *Pr.* 24: 10.

Thy depth closed me round about. *Jon.* 2: 5.

Some fell upon a rock. *Lu.* 8: 6.

I would ye should understand, brethren, that the things which happened unto me have fallen out rather unto the furtherance of the gospel. *Ph.* 1: 12.

See also

Accident; Adversity; Calamity; Disaster; Distress; Hardship; Trouble.

Mission

He shall send his angel before thee. *Ge.* 24: 7.

God did send me before you to preserve life. *Ge.* 45: 5.

I shall give thee the heathen for thine inheritance, and the uttermost parts of the earth for thy possession. *Ps.* 2: 8.

All the ends of the world shall remember and turn unto the Lord. *Ps.* 22: 27.

Ethiopia shall soon stretch out her hands unto God. *Ps.* 68: 31.

Declare his glory among the heathen, his wonders among all people. *Ps.* 96: 3.

Then said I, Here am I; send me. *Is.* 6: 8.

The people that walked in darkness have seen a great light: they that dwell in the land of the shadow of death, upon them hath the light shined. *Is.* 9: 2.

The earth shall be full of the knowledge of the Lord, as the waters cover the sea. *Is.* 11: 9.

He shall send them a saviour, and a great one, and he shall deliver them. *Is.* 19: 20.

Prepare ye the way of the Lord, make straight in the desert a highway for our God. *Is.* 40: 3.

I will say to them which were not my people, Thou art my people; and they shall say, Thou art my God. *Ho.* 2: 23.

From the rising of the sun even unto the going down of the same my name shall be great among the Gentiles. *Mal.* 1: 11.

I send you forth as sheep in the midst of wolves. *Mat.* 10: 16.

I send unto you prophets, and wise men, and scribes. *Mat.* 23: 34.

This gospel of the kingdom shall be preached in all the world for a witness unto all nations. *Mat.* 24: 14.

Go ye into all the world, and preach the gospel to every creature. *Mk.* 16: 15.

Thou shalt go before the face of the Lord to prepare his ways. *Lu.* 1: 76.

I will send my beloved son: it may be they will reverence him when they see him. *Lu.* 20: 13.

Repentance and remission of sins should be preached in his name among all nations. *Lu.* 24: 47.

God made choice among us, that the Gentiles by my mouth should hear the word of the gospel, and believe. *Ac.* 15: 7.

Come over into Macedonia, and help us. *Ac.* 16: 9.

To open their eyes, and to turn them from darkness to light, and from the power of Satan unto God. *Ac.* 26: 18.

The salvation of God is sent unto the Gentiles. *Ac.* 28: 28.

When he was called. *He.* 11: 8.

I saw another angel fly in the midst of heaven, having the everlasting gospel to preach unto them that dwell on the earth, and to every nation, and kindred, and tongue, and people. *Re.* 14: 6.

See also

Christ, Mission of; Commission; Errand; Messenger.

Missionary

He that winneth souls is wise. *Pr.* 11: 30.

I heard the voice of the Lord, saying, Whom shall I send, and who will go for us? Then said I, Here am I; send me. *Is.* 6: 8.

Son of man, I send thee to the children of Israel, to a rebellious nation that hath rebelled against me. *Eze.* 2: 3.

I will make you fishers of men. *Mat.* 4: 19.

Pray ye therefore the Lord of the harvest, that he will send forth labourers into his harvest. *Mat.* 9: 38.

These twelve Jesus sent forth, and commanded them, saying, Go not into the way of the Gentiles. *Mat.* 10: 5.

Then sent Jesus two disciples. *Mat.* 21: 1.

He ordained twelve, that . . . he might send them forth to preach. *Mk.* 3: 14.

Go thou and preach the kingdom of God. *Lu.* 9: 60.

After these things the Lord appointed other seventy also, and sent them two and two before his face into every city and place, whither he himself would come. *Lu.* 10: 1.

Repentance and remission of sins should be preached in his name among all nations, beginning at Jerusalem. *Lu.* 24: 47.

As thou hast sent me into the world, even so have I also sent them into the world. *Jn.* 17: 18.

As my Father hath sent me, even so send I you. *Jn.* 20: 21.

Unto whom now I send thee, To open their eyes, and to turn them from darkness to light, and from the power of Satan unto God. *Ac.* 26: 17, 18.

Approving ourselves as the ministers of God, in much patience, in afflictions, in necessities, in distresses. 2 *Co.* 6: 4.

God hath sent the Spirit of his Son into your hearts. *Ga.* 4: 6.

He went out, not knowing whither he went. *He.* 11: 8.

See also

Ambassador; Clergy; Consecration; Forerunner; God, Messenger of; Installation; Messenger; Ordination; Prophet.

Missions, Foreign

That thy way may be known upon earth, thy saving health among all nations. *Ps.* 67: 2.

Declare his glory among the heathen, his wonders among all people. *Ps.* 96: 3.

The isles shall wait for his law. *Is.* 42: 4.

Go ye therefore, and teach all nations. *Mat.* 28: 19.

Go ye into all the world, and preach the gospel to every creature. *Mk.* 16: 15.

Other sheep I have, which are not of this fold: them also I must bring, and they shall hear my voice; and there shall be one fold, and one shepherd. *Jn.* 10: 16.

That also he should gather together in one the children of God that were scattered abroad. *Jn.* 11: 52.

As my Father hath sent me, even so send I you. *Jn.* 20: 21.

God . . . opened the door of faith unto the Gentiles. *Ac.* 14: 27.

The Lord had called us for to preach the gospel unto them. *Ac.* 16: 10.

From henceforth I will go unto the Gentiles. *Ac.* 18: 6.

Depart: for I will send thee far hence unto the Gentiles. *Ac.* 22: 21.

By revelation he made known unto me the mystery; . . . That the Gentiles should be fellowheirs, and of the same body, and partakers of his promise in Christ by the gospel. *Ep.* 3: 3, 6.

Unto me, who am less than the least of all saints, is this grace given, that I should preach among the Gentiles the unsearchable riches of Christ. *Ep.* 3: 8.

No man taketh this honour unto himself, but he that is called of God. *He.* 5: 4.

As good stewards of the manifold grace of God. *1 Pe.* 4: 10.

See also

Foreigner; Gentile; Missionary; Stranger.

Mistake

Hold up my goings in thy paths, that my footsteps slip not. *Ps.* 17: 5.

Thou hast enlarged my steps under me, that my feet did not slip. *Ps.* 18: 36.

It is a people that do err in their heart. *Ps.* 95: 10.

In the greatness of his folly he shall go astray. *Pr.* 5: 23.

Go not astray in her paths. *Pr.* 7: 25.

Do they not err that devise evil? *Pr.* 14: 22.

Rejoice not when thine enemy falleth, and let not thine heart be glad when he stumbleth. *Pr.* 24: 17.

Suffer not thy mouth to cause thy flesh to sin; neither say thou before the angel, that it was an error. *Ec.* 5: 6.

They stumble in judgment. *Is.* 28: 7.

Ye were as sheep going astray. *1 Pe.* 2: 25.

See also

Blunder; Error; Fault.

Misunderstanding

Who can understand his errors? *Ps.* 19: 12.

Our fathers understood not thy wonders in Egypt. *Ps.* 106: 7.

Evil men understand not judgment. *Pr* 28: 5.

The ox knoweth his owner, and the ass his master's crib: but Israel doth not know, my people doth not consider. *Is.* 1: 3.

They are shepherds that cannot understand. *Is.* 56: 11.

By hearing ye shall hear, and shall not understand; and seeing ye shall see, and shall not perceive. *Mat.* 13: 14.

When they saw him walking upon the sea, they supposed it had been a spirit, and cried out. *Mk.* 6: 49.

They all saw him, and were troubled. *Mk.* 6: 50.

Some of them that stood by, when they heard it, said, Behold, he calleth Elias. *Mk.* 15: 35.

Ye can discern the face of the sky and of the earth; but how is it that ye do not discern this time? *Lu.* 12: 56.

This saying was hid from them, neither knew they the things which were spoken. *Lu.* 18: 34.

They understood not that he spake to them of the Father. *Jn.* 8: 27.

These things understood not the disciples at the first. *Jn.* 12: 16.

In which are some things hard to be understood. 2 *Pe.* 3: 16.

See also

Error; Ignorance; Interpretation.

Mixture

Thou shalt make it an oil of holy ointment compounded after the art of the apothecary. *Ex.* 30: 25.

In the hand of the Lord there is a cup, and the wine is red; it is full of mixture. *Ps.* 75: 8.

I have eaten ashes like bread, and mingled my drink with weeping. *Ps.* 102: 9.

They . . . were mingled among the heathen, and learned their works. *Ps.* 106: 34, 35.

Who hath woe? . . . They that tarry long at the wine; they that go to seek mixed wine. *Pr.* 23: 29, 30.

Thy silver is become dross, thy wine mixed with water. *Is.* 1: 22.

As the toes of the feet were part of iron, and part of clay, so the kingdom shall be partly strong, and partly broken. *Da.* 2: 42.

They gave him to drink wine mingled with myrrh. *Mk.* 15: 23.

The word preached did not profit them, not being mixed with faith in them that heard it. *He.* 4: 2.

Add to your faith virtue. 2 *Pe.* 1: 5.

If any man worship the beast and his image,

. . . The same shall drink of the wine of the wrath of God, which is poured out without mixture into the cup of his indignation. *Re.* 14: 9, 10.

Model

An image was before mine eyes. *Jb.* 4: 16.

Mark the perfect man, and behold the upright. *Ps.* 37: 37.

Out of Zion, the perfection of beauty, God hath shined. *Ps.* 50: 2.

Set up the standard toward Zion. *Je.* 4: 6.

Is this the city that men call The perfection of beauty, The joy of the whole earth? *La.* 2: 15.

Be ye therefore perfect, even as your Father which is in heaven is perfect. *Mat.* 5: 48.

The new man . . . is renewed in knowledge after the image of him that created him. *Col.* 3: 10.

The express image of his person. *He.* 1: 3.

There are priests . . . Who serve unto the example and shadow of heavenly things. *He.* 8: 4, 5.

See . . . that thou make all things according to the pattern shewed to thee in the mount. *He.* 8: 5.

Take, my brethren, the prophets, who have spoken in the name of the Lord, for an example of suffering affliction, and of patience. *Ja.* 5: 10.

See also
Form; Ideal; Image; Pattern; Perfection; Resemblance; Standard; Symbol.

Moderation

Give me neither poverty nor riches; feed me with food convenient for me. *Pr.* 30: 8.

Be not righteous over much; neither make thyself over wise: why shouldest thou destroy thyself? *Ec.* 7: 16.

He reasoned of righteousness, temperance. *Ac.* 24: 25.

Every man that striveth for the mastery is temperate in all things. *1 Co.* 9: 25.

The fruit of the Spirit is . . . temperance. *Ga.* 5: 22, 23.

Be not drunk with wine, wherein is excess. *Ep.* 5: 18.

Let your moderation be known unto all men. *Ph.* 4: 5.

Not given to much wine. *1 Ti.* 3: 8.

And to knowledge temperance. *2 Pe.* 1: 6.

See also
Alleviation; Appetite; Self-Control; Temperance.

Modesty

She took a vail, and covered herself. *Ge.* 24: 65.

A virtuous woman is a crown to her husband. *Pr.* 12: 4.

Put not forth thyself in the presence of the king, and stand not in the place of great men. *Pr.* 25: 6.

Thou art of purer eyes than to behold evil. *Hab.* 1: 13.

I will therefore, . . . that women adorn themselves in modest apparel, with shamefacedness and sobriety. *1 Ti.* 2: 8, 9.

Teach the young women to be sober. *Tit.* 2: 4.

To be discreet, chaste. *Tit.* 2: 5.

They behold your chaste conversation. *1 Pe.* 3: 2.

See also
Chastity; Purity; Virtue.

Moment

They spend their days in wealth, and in a moment go down to the grave. *Jb.* 21: 13.

His anger endureth but a moment. *Ps.* 30: 5.

I will water it every moment: lest any hurt it, I will keep it night and day. *Is.* 27: 3.

For a small moment have I forsaken thee; but with great mercies will I gather thee. *Is.* 54: 7.

In a moment, in the twinkling of an eye, at the last trump. *1 Co.* 15: 52.

Our light affliction . . . is but for a moment. *2 Co.* 4: 17.

Monasticism

He shall burn incense upon it, a perpetual incense before the Lord throughout your generations. *Ex.* 30: 8.

Seek the Lord and his strength, seek his face continually. *1 Ch.* 16: 11.

I give myself unto prayer. *Ps.* 109: 4.

Their strength is to sit still. *Is.* 30: 7.

Come, and let us join ourselves to the Lord in a perpetual covenant that shall not be forgotten. *Je.* 50: 5.

He went out, and departed into a solitary place, and there prayed. *Mk.* 1: 35.

Come ye yourselves apart into a desert place, and rest a while. *Mk.* 6: 31.

They are not of the world, even as I am not of the world. *Jn.* 17: 14.

For their sakes I sanctify myself. *Jn.* 17: 19.

These all continued with one accord in prayer and supplication. *Ac.* 1: 14.

Continuing instant in prayer. *Ro.* 12: 12.

Pray without ceasing. *1 Th.* 5: 17.

We pray always for you. *2 Th.* 1: 11.

The effectual fervent prayer of a righteous man availeth much. *Ja.* 5: 16.

Money

Come, buy wine and milk without money and without price. *Is.* 55: 1.

Wherefore do ye spend money for that which is not bread? *Is.* 55: 2.

He . . . commanded them that they should take . . . no money in their purse. *Mk.* 6: 7, 8.

Make to yourselves friends of the mammon of unrighteousness. *Lu.* 16: 9.

Ye cannot serve God and mammon. *Lu.* 16: 13.

Silver and gold have I none; but such as I have give I thee. *Ac.* 3: 6.

Thy money perish with thee, because thou hast thought that the gift of God may be purchased with money. *Ac.* 8: 20.

The love of money is the root of all evil. *1 Ti.* 6: 10.

Your riches are corrupt. *Ja.* 5: 2.

Not for filthy lucre. *1 Pe.* 5: 2.

See also
Bank; Gold; Mammon; Riches; Silver; Wealth.

Monotheism

Thou shalt have no other gods before me. *Ex.* 20: 3.

Know therefore this day, and consider it in thine heart, that the Lord he is God in heaven above, and upon the earth beneath: there is none else. *De.* 4: 39.

Hear, O Israel: the Lord our God is one Lord. *De.* 6: 4.

Before me there was no God formed, neither shall there be after me. *Is.* 43: 10.

I am the Lord, and there is none else, there is no God beside me: I girded thee, though thou hast not known me. *Is.* 45: 5.

There is none other God but one. *1 Co.* 8: 4.

One God and Father of all, who is above all, and through all, and in you all. *Ep.* 4: 6.

See also
God, Unity of.

Month

As for that night, let darkness seize upon it; let it not be joined unto the days of the year, let it not come into the number of the months. *Jb.* 3: 6.

The number of his months are with thee, thou hast appointed his bounds that he cannot pass. *Jb.* 14: 5.

What pleasure hath he in his house after him, when the number of his months is cut off in the midst? *Jb.* 21: 21.

Oh that I were as in months past, as in the days when God preserved me. *Jb.* 29: 2.

Canst thou number the months that they fulfil? *Jb.* 39: 2.

Ye observe days, and months, and times, and years. I am afraid of you, lest I have bestowed upon you labour in vain. *Ga.* 4: 10, 11.

The tree of life . . . yielded her fruit every month. *Re.* 22: 2.

Monument

This stone, which I have set for a pillar, shall be God's house. *Ge.* 28: 22.

What mean ye by these stones? *Jos.* 4: 6.

They . . . built there an altar by Jordan, a great altar to see to. *Jos.* 22: 10.

This stone shall be a witness unto us; for it hath heard all the words of the Lord which he spake unto us. *Jos.* 24: 27.

Samuel took a stone, and set it between Mizpeh and Shen, and called the name of it Eben-ezer, saying, Hitherto hath the Lord helped us. *1 S.* 7: 12.

The stone which the builders refused is become the head stone of the corner. *Ps.* 118: 22.

Behold, I lay in Zion for a foundation a stone, a tried stone, a precious corner stone, a sure foundation. *Is.* 28: 16.

See also
Epitaph; Memorial.

Moon

Let there be lights in the firmament of the heaven to divide the day from the night. *Ge.* 1: 14.

God made two great lights; the greater light to rule the day, and the lesser light to rule the night. *Ge.* 1: 16.

The moon walking in brightness. *Jb.* 31: 26.

They shall fear thee as long as the sun and moon endure. *Ps.* 72: 5.

It shall be established for ever as the moon. *Ps.* 89: 37.

He appointed the moon for seasons. *Ps.* 104: 19.

The sun shall not smite thee by day, nor the moon by night. *Ps.* 121: 6.

The moon and stars to rule by night. *Ps.* 136: 9.

Fair as the moon. *S. of S.* 6: 10.

Your new moons . . . my soul hateth. *Is.* 1: 14.

Neither for brightness shall the moon give light unto thee: but the Lord shall be unto thee an everlasting light. *Is.* 60: 19.

The Lord, which giveth the sun for a light by day, and the ordinances of the moon and of the stars for a light by night. *Je.* 31: 35.

There is one glory of the sun, and another glory of the moon, and another glory of the stars: for one star differeth from another star in glory. *1 Co.* 15: 41.

Morale

Be strong and of a good courage. *De.* 31: 6.

There is a spirit in man. *Jb.* 32: 8.

Though an host should encamp against me, my heart shall not fear. *Ps.* 27: 3.

Wait on the Lord: be of good courage, and he shall strengthen thine heart. *Ps.* 27: 14.

Renew a right spirit within me. *Ps.* 51: 10.

In the fear of the Lord is strong confidence. *Pr.* 14: 26.

The spirit of man is the candle of the Lord. *Pr.* 20: 27.

In quietness and confidence shall be your strength. *Is.* 30: 15.

There is a man in thy kingdom, in whom is the spirit of the holy gods. *Da.* 5: 11.

Every one shall be salted with fire. *Mk.* 9: 49.

The child grew, and waxed strong in spirit, filled with wisdom: and the grace of God was upon him. *Lu.* 2: 40.

He knew what was in man. *Jn.* 2: 25.

We are always confident. *2 Co.* 5: 6.

The fruit of the Spirit is love, joy, peace, longsuffering, gentleness, goodness, faith, meekness, temperance. *Ga.* 5: 22, 23.

Strengthened with might by his Spirit in the inner man. *Ep.* 3: 16.

Add to your faith virtue; and to virtue knowledge; And to knowledge temperance; and to temperance patience; and to patience godliness; And to godliness brotherly kindness; and to brotherly kindness charity. *2 Pe.* 1: 5-7.

Morality

Lighten mine eyes, lest I sleep the sleep of death. *Ps.* 13: 3.

I follow the thing that good is. *Ps.* 38: 20.

The righteous shall flourish like the palm tree: he shall grow like a cedar in Lebanon. *Ps.* 92: 12.

A virtuous woman is a crown to her husband. *Pr.* 12: 4.

The house of the righteous shall stand. *Pr.* 12: 7.

The just man walketh in his integrity. *Pr.* 20: 7.

I hate, I despise your feast days, and I will not smell in your solemn assemblies. . . . Let judgment run down as waters, and righteousness as a mighty stream. *Am.* 5: 21, 24.

What do ye more than others? *Mat.* 5: 47.

All these things have I kept from my youth up: what lack I yet? *Mat.* 19: 20.

Having a good conscience. *1 Pe.* 3: 16.

If ye know that he is righteous, ye know that every one that doeth righteousness is born of him. *1 Jn.* **2: 29.**

See also

Character; Christ, Goodness of; Christ, Holiness of; God, Goodness of; God, Righteousness of; Goodness; Holiness; Honor; Integrity; Justice; Purity; Quality; Rectitude; Righteousness; Virtue.

Morning

In the morning, then ye shall see the glory of the Lord. *Ex.* **16: 7.**

My voice shalt thou hear in the morning, O Lord; in the morning will I direct my prayer unto thee, and will look up. *Ps.* **5: 3.**

Weeping may endure for a night, but joy cometh in the morning. *Ps.* **30: 5.**

In the morning they are like grass which groweth up; . . . in the evening it is cut down, and withereth. *Ps.* **90: 5, 6.**

To shew forth thy lovingkindness in the morning. *Ps.* **92: 2.**

In the morning sow thy seed. *Ec.* **11: 6.**

The Lord's mercies . . . are new every morning. *La.* **3: 22, 23.**

His going forth is prepared as the morning. *Ho.* **6: 3.**

Seek him that . . . turneth the shadow of death into the morning. *Am.* **5: 8.**

They entered into the temple early in the morning. *Ac.* **5: 21.**

Ye are all the children of light, and the children of the day. *1 Th.* **5: 5.**

See also

Beginning; Day; Day, the Coming; Sunrise.

Morrow

Say not unto thy neighbour, Go, and come again, and to morrow I will give; when thou hast it by thee. *Pr.* **3: 28.**

Boast not thyself of to morrow: for thou knowest not what a day may bring forth. *Pr.* **27: 1.**

Let us eat and drink; for to morrow we shall die. *Is.* **22: 13.**

If God so clothe the grass of the field, which to day is, and to morrow is cast into the oven, shall he not much more clothe you, O ye of little faith? *Mat.* **6: 30.**

Take therefore no thought for the morrow. *Mat.* **6: 34.**

I do cures to day and to morrow, and the third day I shall be perfected. *Lu.* **13: 32.**

I must walk to day, and to morrow, and the day following: for it cannot be that a prophet perish out of Jerusalem. *Lu.* **13: 33.**

Ye know not what shall be on the morrow. *Ja.* **4: 14.**

See also

Future; Time, the Future; To-morrow.

Mortality

Shall mortal man be more just than God? *Jb.* **4: 17.**

Thou shalt come to thy grave in a full age, like as a shock of corn cometh in in his season. *Jb.* **5: 26.**

My soul chooseth . . . death rather than my life. *Jb.* **7: 15.**

Remember, I beseech thee, that thou hast made me as the clay; and wilt thou bring me into dust again? *Jb.* **10: 9.**

Unto God the Lord belong the issues from death. *Ps.* **68: 20.**

What man is he that liveth, and shall not see death? shall he deliver his soul from the hand of the grave? *Ps.* **89: 48.**

As for man, his days are as grass. *Ps.* **103: 15.**

All go into one place; all are of the dust, and all turn to dust again. *Ec.* **3: 20.**

Who art thou, that thou shouldest be afraid of a man that shall die, and of the son of man which shall be made as grass? *Is.* **51: 12.**

Thy daughter is dead. *Lu.* **8: 49.**

She is not dead, but sleepeth. *Lu.* **8: 52.**

He that heareth my word, and believeth on him that sent me, . . . is passed from death unto life. *Jn.* **5: 24.**

All that are in the graves shall hear his voice. *Jn.* **5: 28.**

Except a corn of wheat fall into the ground and die, it abideth alone: but if it die, it bringeth forth much fruit. *Jn.* **12: 24.**

Who shall deliver me from the body of this death? *Ro.* **7: 24.**

To be carnally minded is death. *Ro.* **8: 6.**

This mortal must put on immortality. *1 Co.* **15: 53.**

We have this treasure in earthen vessels. *2 Co.* **4: 7.**

That mortality might be swallowed up of life. *2 Co.* **5: 4.**

It is appointed unto man once to die. *He.* **9: 27.**

See also

Christ, Death of; Death; Decease; Grave; Immortality; Life, the Eternal.

Mother

She was the mother of all living. *Ge.* **3: 20.**

In sin did my mother conceive me. *Ps.* **51: 5.**

He maketh the barren woman to keep house, and to be a joyful mother of children. *Ps.* **113: 9.**

A foolish son is the heaviness of his mother. *Pr.* **10: 1.**

A foolish man despiseth his mother. *Pr.* **15: 20.**

Despise not thy mother when she is old. *Pr.* **23: 22.**

She looketh well to the ways of her household, and eateth not the bread of idleness. *Pr.* **31: 27.**

Her children arise up, and call her blessed; her husband also, and he praiseth her. *Pr.* **31: 28.**

They saw the young child with Mary his mother, and fell down, and worshipped him. *Mat.* **2: 11.**

Who is my mother? and who are my brethren? And he stretched forth his hand, . . . and said, Behold my mother and my brethren! *Mat.* **12: 48, 49.**

Is not his mother called Mary? *Mat.* **13: 55.**

His mother kept all these sayings in her heart. *Lu.* **2: 51.**

The mother of Jesus was there. *Jn.* **2: 1.**

Is not this Jesus, the son of Joseph, whose father and mother we know? *Jn.* **6: 42.**

There stood by the cross of Jesus his mother. *Jn.* **19: 25.**

Jerusalem which is above is free, which is the mother of us all. *Ga.* **4: 26.**

Teach the young women to be sober, to love their husbands, to love their children. *Tit.* 2: 4.
See also
Ancestor; Descent; Genealogy; Generation; Mother's Day; Parent.

Mother's Day

Take this child away, and nurse it for me. *Ex.* 2: 9.
My son . . . forsake not the law of thy mother. *Pr.* 1: 8.
Who can find a virtuous woman? for her price is far above rubies. *Pr.* 31: 10.
The heart of her husband doth safely trust in her. *Pr.* 31: 11.
Strength and honour are her clothing. *Pr.* 31: 25.
Behold king Solomon with the crown where with his mother crowned him. *S. of S.* 3: 11.
I and the children whom the Lord hath given me are for signs and for wonders. *Is.* 8: 18.
Can a woman forget her sucking child, that she should not have compassion on the son of her womb? *Is.* 49: 15.
God commanded, saying, Honour thy father and mother. *Mat.* 15: 4.
His mother saith unto the servants, Whatsoever he saith unto you, do it. *Jn.* 2: 5.
Then saith he to the disciple, Behold thy mother! *Jn.* 19: 27.
The unfeigned faith that is in thee . . . dwelt first in thy grandmother Lois, and thy mother Eunice. *2 Ti.* 1: 5.
From a child thou hast known the holy scriptures. *2 Ti.* 3: 15.
See also
Mother; Parent.

Motion

The Spirit of God moved upon the face of the waters. *Ge.* 1: 2.
God said unto them, . . . have dominion . . . over every living thing that moveth upon the earth. *Ge.* 1: 28.
The floods stood upright as an heap, and the depths were congealed in the heart of the sea. *Ex.* 15: 8.
The sun stood still, and the moon stayed. *Jos.* 10: 13.
The Spirit of the Lord began to move him. *Ju.* 13: 25.
The earth shook and trembled; the foundations of heaven moved and shook. *2 S.* 22: 8.
The world also shall be stable, that it be not moved. *1 Ch.* 16: 30.
He that doeth these things shall never be moved. *Ps.* 15: 5.
Therefore will not we fear, though the earth be removed, and though the mountains be carried into the midst of the sea. *Ps.* 46: 2.
He maketh the storm a calm, so that the waves thereof are still. *Ps.* 107: 29.
The mountains skipped like rams, and the little hills like lambs. *Ps.* 114: 4.
He will not suffer thy foot to be moved. *Ps.* 121: 3.
In these lay a great multitude of impotent folk, of blind, halt, withered, waiting for the moving of the water. *Jn.* 5: 3.
In him we live, and move, and have our being. *Ac.* 17: 28.

Every mountain and island were moved out of their places. *Re.* 6: 14.
See also
Action.

Motive

What reason ye in your hearts? *Lu.* 5: 22.
Present your bodies a living sacrifice, holy, acceptable unto God, which is your reasonable service. *Ro.* 12: 1.
For this cause I Paul, the prisoner of Jesus Christ for you Gentiles, . . . was made a minister. *Ep.* 3: 1, 7.
To me to live is Christ, and to die is gain. *Ph.* 1: 21.
For which cause I also suffer these things. *2 Ti.* 1: 12.
Be ready always to give an answer to every man that asketh you a reason of the hope that is in you. *1 Pe.* 3: 15.
For this cause was the gospel preached also to them that are dead. *1 Pe.* 4: 6.
For this purpose the Son of God was manifested, that he might destroy the works of the devil. *1 Jn.* 3: 8.
See also
End; Intention; Plan; Purpose; Reason.

Mountain

The Lord called unto him out of the mountain. *Ex.* 19: 3.
Moses went up into the mount, and a cloud covered the mount. *Ex.* 24: 15.
Moses was in the mount forty days and forty nights. *Ex.* 24: 18.
The Lord talked with you face to face in the mount out of the midst of the fire. *De.* 5: 4.
Go forth, and stand upon the mount before the Lord. *1 K.* 19: 11.
Thy righteousness is like the great mountains. *Ps.* 36: 6.
The mountains shall bring peace to the people, and the little hills, by righteousness. *Ps.* 72: 3.
The strength of the hills is his also. *Ps.* 95: 4.
I will lift up mine eyes unto the hills, from whence cometh my help. *Ps.* 121: 1.
It shall come to pass in the last days, that the mountain of the Lord's house shall be established in the top of the mountains. *Is.* 2: 2.
They shall come which were ready to perish, . . . and shall worship the Lord in the holy mount at Jerusalem. *Is.* 27: 13.
O Zion, that bringest good tidings, get thee up into the high mountain. *Is.* 40: 9.
The mountains and the hills shall break forth before you into singing. *Is.* 55: 12.
Thou son of man, prophesy unto the mountains of Israel. *Eze.* 36: 1.
He went out into a mountain to pray, and continued all night in prayer to God. *Lu.* 6: 12.
He came down with them, and stood in the plain. *Lu.* 6: 17.
Shewed to thee in the mount. *He.* 8: 5.
See also
Altitude; Ascension; Climbing; Elevation; Eminence; Hill; Summit; Top.

Mourning

As one that comforteth the mourners. *Jb.* 29: 25.

A time to mourn, and a time to dance. *Ec.* 3: 4.

It is better to go to the house of mourning, than to go to the house of feasting. *Ec.* 7: 2.

The heart of the wise is in the house of mourning. *Ec.* 7: 4.

The mourners go about the streets. *Ec.* 12: 5.

The redeemed of the Lord shall return; . . . and sorrow and mourning shall flee away. *Is.* 51: 11.

The Lord shall be thine everlasting light, and the days of thy mourning shall be ended. *Is.* 60: 20.

To comfort all that mourn. *Is.* 61: 2.

To give unto them beauty for ashes, the oil of joy for mourning. *Is.* 61: 3.

I will turn their mourning into joy, and will comfort them. *Je.* 31: 13.

The priests, the Lord's ministers, mourn. *Jo.* 1: 9.

Blessed are they that mourn: for they shall be comforted. *Mat.* 5: 4.

Can the children of the bridechamber mourn, as long as the bridegroom is with them? *Mat.* 9: 15.

We have mourned unto you, and ye have not lamented. *Mat.* 11: 17.

Woe unto you that laugh now! for ye shall mourn and weep. *Lu.* 6: 25.

Let your laughter be turned to mourning, and your joy to heaviness. *Ja.* 4: 9.

Therefore shall her plagues come in one day, death, and mourning, and famine. *Re.* 18: 8.

See also

Depression; Gloom; Lamentation; Melancholy; Sadness; Sorrow.

Mouth

Now therefore go, and I will be with thy mouth, and teach thee what thou shalt say. *Ex.* 4: 12.

Out of the mouths of babes and sucklings hast thou ordained strength. *Ps.* 8: 2.

His praise shall continually be in my mouth. *Ps.* 34: 1.

Set a watch, O Lord, before my mouth. *Ps.* 141: 3.

Keep the door of my lips. *Ps.* 141: 3.

The mouth of the just bringeth forth wisdom. *Pr.* 10: 31.

Whoso keepeth his mouth and his tongue keepeth his soul from trouble. *Pr.* 21: 23.

All the labour of man is for his mouth, and yet the appetite is not filled. *Ec.* 6: 7.

He laid it upon my mouth, and said, Lo, this hath touched thy lips; and thine iniquity is taken away. *Is.* 6: 7.

The law of truth was in his mouth. *Mal.* 2: 6.

Out of the abundance of the heart the mouth speaketh. *Mat.* 12: 34.

See also

Language; Lip; Speaker; Speech; Tongue; Utterance; Word.

Multiplication

God blessed them, saying, Be fruitful, and multiply, and fill the waters in the seas, and let fowl multiply in the earth. *Ge.* 1: 22.

That your days may be multiplied, and the days of your children, in the land which the Lord sware unto your fathers to give them, as the days of heaven upon the earth. *De.* 11: 21.

He . . . multiplieth my wounds without cause. *Jb.* 9: 17.

He multiplieth words without knowledge. *Jb.* 35: 16.

Their sorrows shall be multiplied that hasten after another god. *Ps.* 16: 4.

These are the ungodly, who prosper in the world; they increase in riches. *Ps.* 73: 12.

He blesseth them also, so that they are multiplied greatly. *Ps.* 107: 38.

Peace be multiplied unto you. *Da.* 4: 1.

She did not know that I . . . multiplied her silver and gold. *Ho.* 2: 8.

The churches, . . . walking in the fear of the Lord, and in the comfort of the Holy Ghost, were multiplied. *Ac.* 9: 31.

The word of God grew and multiplied. *Ac.* 12: 24.

I have planted, Apollos watered; but God gave the increase. *1 Co.* 3: 6.

See also

Enlargement; Expansion; Growth; Increase; Yield.

Multitude

Behold, ye are this day as the stars of heaven for multitude. *De.* 1: 10.

Much people, even as the sand that is upon the sea shore in multitude. *Jos.* 11: 4.

They came as grasshoppers for multitude. *Ju.* 6: 5.

Be not afraid . . . for all the multitude. *2 Ch.* 32: 7.

I had gone with the multitude, I went with them to the house of God. *Ps.* 42: 4.

I will praise him among the multitude. *Ps.* 109: 30.

Seeing the multitudes, he went up into a mountain. *Mat.* 5: 1.

All these things spake Jesus unto the multitude in parables. *Mat.* 13: 34.

I have compassion on the multitude. *Mat.* 15: 32.

Pilate . . . washed his hands before the multitude. *Mat.* 27: 24.

See also

Crowd; Host; Number; Rabble.

Murder

Whoso sheddeth man's blood, by man shall his blood be shed. *Ge.* 9: 6.

Thou shalt not kill. *Ex.* 20: 13.

Am I God, to kill and to make alive? *2 K.* 5: 7.

For thy sake are we killed all the day long. *Ps.* 44: 22.

They slay the widow and the stranger, and murder the fatherless. *Ps.* 94: 6.

A time to kill, and a time to heal. *Ec.* 3: 3.

Will ye steal, murder, and commit adultery, and swear falsely? *Je.* 7: 9.

Fear not them which kill the body, but are not able to kill the soul. *Mat.* 10: 28.

Out of the heart proceed evil thoughts, murders. *Mat.* 15: 19.

Jesus said, Thou shalt do no murder. *Mat.* 19: 18.

Your father the devil . . . was a murderer

from the beginning. *Jn.* 8: 44.

The time cometh, that whosoever killeth you will think that he doeth God service. *Jn.* 16: 2.

Let none of you suffer as a murderer, or as a thief, or as an evildoer. *1 Pe.* 4: 15.

Whosoever hateth his brother is a murderer. *1 Jn.* 3: 15.

Neither repented they of their murders. *Re.* 9: 21.

See also

Assassin; Blood; Slaughter.

Murmur

He heareth your murmurings. *Ex.* 16: 7.

I have heard the murmurings of the children of Israel, which they murmur against me. *Nu.* 14: 27.

All that hate me whisper together. *Ps.* 41: 7.

They . . . murmured in their tents, and hearkened not unto the voice of the Lord. *Ps.* 106: 24, 25.

Your tongue hath muttered perverseness. *Is.* 59: 3.

Lest there be debates, envyings, wraths, strifes, backbitings, whisperings, swellings, tumults. *2 Co.* 12: 20.

Do all things without murmurings and disputings. *Ph.* 2: 14.

See also

Complaint.

Music

Jubal . . . was the father of all such as handle the harp and organ. *Ge.* 4: 21.

Praise him with the sound of the trumpet. *Ps.* 150: 3.

All the daughters of musick shall be brought low. *Ec.* 12: 4.

The ransomed of the Lord shall return, and come to Zion with songs and everlasting joy upon their heads. *Is.* 35: 10.

I am their musick. *La.* 3: 63.

The elders have ceased from the gate, the young men from their musick. *La.* 5: 14.

Take thou away from me the noise of thy songs; for i will not hear the melody of thy viols. *Am.* 5: 23.

See also

Instrument; Melody; Psalm; Song; Symphony.

Mutability

The heavens are the work of thy hands. They shall perish, but thou shalt endure. *Ps.* 102: 25, 26.

The heavens shall be rolled together as a scroll. *Is.* 34: 4.

Can the Ethiopian change his skin, or the leopard his spots? *Je.* 13: 23.

The fashion of this world passeth away. *1 Co.* 7: 31.

The things which are seen are temporal. *2 Co.* 4: 18.

Who shall change our vile body, that it may be fashioned like unto his glorious body. *Ph.* 3: 21.

As a vesture shalt thou fold them up, and they shall be changed: but thou art the same. *He.* 1: 12.

The heavens shall pass away with a great noise, and the elements shall melt with fervent heat, the earth also and the works that are therein shall be burned up. *2 Pe.* 3: 10.

The first heaven and the first earth were passed away. *Re.* 21: 1.

See also

Alteration; Change; Transformation.

Myrrh

They presented unto him gifts; gold, and frankincense, and myrrh. *Mat.* 2: 11.

They gave him to drink wine mingled with myrrh: but he received it not. *Mk.* 15: 23.

There came also Nicodemus, . . . and brought a mixture of myrrh and aloes, about an hundred pound weight. Then took they the body of Jesus, and wound it in linen clothes with the spices. *Jn.* 19: 39, 40.

Mystery

Thou canst not see my face: for there shall no man see me, and live. *Ex.* 33: 20.

The secret things belong unto the Lord our God. *De.* 29: 29.

Which doeth great things and unsearchable; marvelous things without number. *Jb.* 5: 9.

Canst thou by searching find out God? *Jb.* 11: 7.

He . . . hangeth the earth upon nothing. *Jb.* 26: 7.

It is the glory of God to conceal a thing. *Pr.* 25: 2.

No man can find out the work that God maketh from the beginning to the end. *Ec.* 3: 11.

Unto you it is given to know the mystery of the kingdom of God. *Mk.* 4: 11.

Ye have neither heard his voice at any time, nor seen his shape. *Jn.* 5: 37.

O the depth of the riches both of the wisdom and knowledge of God! how unsearchable are his judgments, and his ways past finding out! *Ro.* 11: 33.

Neither have entered into the heart of man, the things which God hath prepared for them that love him. *1 Co.* 2: 9.

Who hath known the mind of the Lord? *1 Co.* 2: 16.

We know in part. *1 Co.* 13: 9.

Behold, I shew you a mystery: We shall not all sleep, but we shall all be changed. *1 Co.* 15: 51.

The mystery of Christ. *Ep.* 3: 4.

The mystery of the gospel. *Ep.* 6: 19.

Holding the mystery of the faith in a pure conscience. *1 Ti.* 3: 9.

Great is the mystery of godliness. *1 Ti.* 3: 16.

Who only hath immortality, dwelling in the light which no man can approach unto; whom no man hath seen, nor can see. *1 Ti.* 6: 16.

See also

Christ, the Hidden; Christ, Mystery of; Concealment; Cover; God, the Hiding; Mysticism; Sacrament; Secrecy; Veil.

Mysticism

There is a path which no fowl knoweth, and which the vulture's eye hath not seen. *Jb.* 28: 7.

Can any understand . . . the noise of his tabernacle? *Jb.* 36: 29.

The secret of the Lord is with them that fear him. *Ps.* 25: 14.

To understand a proverb, and the interpretation; the words of the wise, and their dark sayings. *Pr.* **1: 6.**

I will give thee the treasures of darkness, and the hidden riches of secret places. *Is.* **45: 3.**

I will utter things which have been kept secret from the foundation of the world. *Mat.* **13: 35.**

We speak the wisdom of God in a mystery, even the hidden wisdom. *1 Co.* **2: 7.**

The Spirit searcheth all things, yea, the deep things of God *1 Co.* **2: 10.**

The mystery of Christ Which in other ages was not made known unto the sons of men. *Ep.* **3: 4, 5.**

The mystery of God and of the Father, and of Christ. *Col.* **2: 2.**

Within the vail. *He.* **6: 19.**

See also

Christ, the Hidden; Christ, Mystery of; Concealment; Cover; God, the Hiding; Mystery; Secrecy; Veil.

N

Nakedness

They were both naked, the man and his wife, and were not ashamed. *Ge.* **2: 25.**

The eyes of them both were opened, and they knew that they were naked. *Ge.* **3: 7.**

Hell is naked before him, and destruction hath no covering. *Jb.* **26: 6.**

Strip you, and make you bare, and gird sackcloth upon your loins. *Is.* **32: 11.**

I was . . . Naked, and ye clothed me. *Mat.* **25: 35, 36.**

Who shall separate us from the love of Christ? shall . . . nakedness? *Ro.* **8: 35.**

Earnestly desiring to be clothed upon with our house which is from heaven: If so be that being clothed we shall not be found naked. *2 Co.* **5: 2, 3.**

In weariness and painfulness, in watchings often, in hunger and thirst, in fastings often, in cold and nakedness. *2 Co.* **11: 27.**

All things are naked and opened unto the eyes of him with whom we have to do. *He.* **4: 13.**

See also

Nudity.

Name

All people of the earth shall see that thou art called by the name of the Lord. *De.* **28: 10.**

Thy wisdom and prosperity exceedeth the fame which I heard. *1 K.* **10: 7.**

The name of the Lord is a strong tower: the righteous runneth into it, and is safe. *Pr.* **18: 10.**

A good name is rather to be chosen than great riches. *Pr.* **22: 1.**

A good name is better than precious ointment. *Ec.* **7: 1.**

From the rising of the sun even unto the going down of the same my name shall be great among the Gentiles. *Mal.* **1: 11.**

They . . . spread abroad his fame in all that country. *Mat.* **9: 31.**

His name was called Jesus. *Lu.* **2: 21.**

Rejoice, because your names are written in heaven. *Lu.* **10: 20.**

His name through faith in his name hath made this man strong, whom ye see and know. *Ac.* **3: 16.**

Of whom the whole family in heaven and earth is named. *Ep.* **3: 15.**

Whose names are in the book of life. *Ph.* **4: 3.**

He had a name written, that no man knew, but he himself. *Re.* **19: 12.**

See also

Auspices; Celebrity; Distinction; **Fame,** Glory; Honor; Renown; Report; Reputation; Title.

Narrowness

The angel of the Lord . . . stood in a narrow place. *Nu.* **22: 26.**

If thou be a great people, then get thee up to the wood country, . . . if mount Ephraim be too narrow for thee. *Jos.* **17: 15.**

The place where we dwell with thee is too strait for us. *2 K.* **6: 1.**

He enlargeth the nations, and straiteneth them again. *Jb.* **12: 23.**

Even so would he have removed thee out of the strait into a broad place, where there is no straitness. *Jb.* **36: 16.**

A strange woman is a narrow pit. *Pr.* **23: 27.**

The bed is shorter than that a man can stretch himself on it: and the covering narrower than that he can wrap himself in it. *Is.* **28: 20.**

Is the spirit of the Lord straitened? *Mi.* **2: 7.**

Enter ye in at the strait gate: for wide is the gate, and broad is the way, that leadeth to destruction. *Mat.* **7: 13.**

Strait is the gate, and narrow is the way, which leadeth unto life. *Mat.* **7: 14.**

See also

Restriction; Strait.

Nation

I am the Lord your God, which have separated you from other people. *Le.* **20: 24.**

Thou art an holy people unto the Lord thy God. *De.* **7: 6.**

Dwell in the land which the Lord your God giveth you to inherit. *De.* **12: 10.**

All nations shall serve him. *Ps.* **72: 11.**

Behold, the nations are as a drop of a bucket, and are counted as the small dust of the balance. *Is.* **40: 15.**

I will make them one nation in the land; . . . and one king shall be king to them all. *Eze.* **37: 22.**

He loveth our nation. *Lu.* **7: 5.**

He . . . hath made of one blood all nations for to dwell on all the face of the earth. *Ac.* **17: 26.**

We wrestle . . . against powers. *Ep.* **6: 12.**

See also

Civilization; Community; Country; Land; Nation, Decadence of; Nation, Greatness of;

Nation, Prosperity of; Nations, League of; People; Race; State.

Nation, Decadence of

Lest the land . . . become full of wickedness. *Le.* 19: 29.

It is a people that do err in their heart, and they have not known my ways. *Ps.* 95: 10.

Israel doth not know, my people doth not consider. *Is.* 1: 3.

This is a rebellious people. *Is.* 30: 9.

Ye defiled my land, and made mine heritage an abomination. *Je.* 2: 7.

My people hath forgotten me days without number. *Je.* 2: 32.

I have hid my face from this city. *Je.* 33: 5.

The land is full of bloody crimes. *Eze.* 7: 23.

They have filled the land with violence. *Eze.* 8: 17.

The land is full of blood, and the city full of perverseness. *Eze.* 9: 9.

In thee have they set light by father and mother. *Eze.* 22: 7.

In the midst of thee have they dealt by oppression with the stranger. *Eze.* 22: 7.

In thee have they vexed the fatherless and the widow. *Eze.* 22: 7.

There is no truth, nor mercy, nor knowledge of God in the land. *Ho.* 4: 1.

The kingdom of God shall be taken from you, and given to a nation bringing forth the fruits thereof. *Mat.* 21: 43.

See also
Corruption; Decay.

Nation, Greatness of

I will make of thee a great nation, and I will bless thee, and make thy name great. *Ge.* 12: 2.

Surely this great nation is a wise and understanding people. *De.* 4: 6.

What nation is there so great, who hath God so nigh unto them, as the Lord our God is in all things that we call upon him for? *De.* 4: 7.

What nation is there so great, that hath statutes and judgments so righteous as all this law, which I set before you this day? *De.* 4: 8.

The Lord did not set his love upon you, nor choose you, because ye were more in number than any people; for ye were the fewest of all people. *De.* 7: 7.

It shall come to pass, if thou shalt hearken diligently unto the voice of the Lord thy God, to observe and to do all his commandments which I command thee this day, that the Lord thy God will set thee on high above all nations of the earth. *De.* 28: 1.

Happy is that people, that is in such a case: yea, happy is that people, whose God is the Lord. *Ps.* 144: 15.

Righteousness exalteth a nation. *Pr.* 14: 34.

Therefore shall the strong people glorify thee. *Is.* 25: 3.

An holy nation. *1 Pe.* 2: 9.

See also
Civilization.

Nation, Prosperity of

He saw that rest was good, and the land that it was pleasant. *Ge.* 49: 15.

The land had rest from war. *Jos.* 14: 15.

They found fat pasture and good, and the land was wide, and quiet, and peaceable. *1 Ch.* 4: 40.

Our land shall yield her increase. *Ps.* 85: 12.

My people shall dwell in a peaceable habitation, and in sure dwellings, and in quiet resting places. *Is.* 32: 18.

The parched ground shall become a pool, and the thirsty land springs of water. *Is.* 35: 7.

Violence shall no more be heard in thy land, wasting nor destruction within thy borders. *Is.* 60: 18.

A little one shall become a thousand, and a small one a strong nation. *Is.* 60: 22.

All nations shall call you blessed: for ye shall be a delightsome land. *Mal.* 3: 12.

See also
Prosperity; Welfare.

Nations, League of

We be come from a far country: now therefore make ye a league with us. *Jos.* 9: 6.

Joshua made peace with them, and made a league with them, to let them live. *Jos.* 9: 15.

Make thy league with me, and, behold, my hand shall be with thee. *2 S.* 3: 12.

He is the governor among the nations. *Ps.* 22: 28.

Nation shall not lift up sword against nation, neither shall they learn war any more. *Is.* 2: 4.

Associate yourselves, O ye people, and ye shall be broken in pieces. *Is.* 8: 9.

Say ye not, A confederacy, to all them to whom this people shall say, A confederacy. *Is.* 8: 12.

I will gather all nations and tongues; and they shall come, and see my glory. *Is.* 66: 18.

This gospel of the kingdom shall be preached in all the world for a witness unto all nations. *Mat.* 24: 14.

God . . . hath made of one blood all nations of men for to dwell on all the face of the earth. *Ac.* 17: 24, 26.

God . . . hath determined the times before appointed, and the bounds of their habitation; That they should seek the Lord, if haply they might feel after him, and find him, though he be not far from every one of us. *Ac.* 17: 24, 26, 27.

The leaves of the tree were for the healing of the nations. *Re.* 22: 2.

See also
Alliance; Association; Civilization; League.

Nativity

Thou hast left thy father and thy mother, and the land of thy nativity, and art come unto a people which thou knewest not heretofore. *Ru.* 2: 11.

Sing, O barren, thou that didst not bear. *Is.* 54: 1.

Cursed be the day wherein I was born. *Je.* 20: 14.

Weep sore for him that goeth away: for he shall return no more, nor see his native country. *Je.* 22: 10.

Arise, and let us go again to our own people, and to the land of our nativity. *Je.* 46: 16.

Whence comest thou? what is thy country?

and of what people art thou? *Jon.* 1: 8.

She brought forth a man child, who was to rule all nations with a rod of iron. *Re.* 12: 5.

See also
Birth; Carol; Christ, Birth of.

Nature

Blessed of the Lord be his land, for the precious things of heaven, for the dew, and for the deep that coucheth beneath. *De.* 33: 13.

Blessed of the Lord be his land, . . . for the precious fruits brought forth by the sun, and for the precious things put forth by the moon. *De.* 33: 13, 14.

Blessed of the Lord be his land, . . . for the chief things of the ancient mountains, and for the precious things of the lasting hills. *De.* 33: 13, 15.

Blessed of the Lord be his land, . . . for the precious things of the earth and the fulness thereof, and for the good will of him that dwelt in the bush. *De.* 33: 13, 16.

Let the fields rejoice, and all that is therein. *1 Ch.* 16: 32.

Thou shalt be in league with the stones of the field. *Jb.* 5: 23.

Ask now the beasts, and they shall teach thee; and the fowls of the air, and they shall tell thee. *Jb.* 12: 7.

Speak to the earth, and it shall teach thee. *Jb.* 12: 8.

The pastures are clothed with flocks; the valleys also are covered over with corn. *Ps.* 65: 13.

Exalt ye the Lord our God, and worship at his footstool. *Ps.* 99: 5.

The earth is full of thy riches. *Ps.* 104: 24.

Open thou mine eyes, that I may behold wondrous things out of thy law. *Ps.* 119: 18.

I will lift up mine eyes unto the hills, from whence cometh my help. *Ps.* 121: 1.

He hath made every thing beautiful in his time. *Ec.* 3: 11.

Break forth into singing, ye mountains, O forest, and every tree therein. *Is.* 44: 23.

Consider the lilies of the field. *Mat.* 6: 28.

Doth not even nature itself teach you? *1 Co.* 11: 14.

That was not first which is spiritual, but that which is natural; and afterward that which is spiritual. *1 Co.* 15: 46.

See also
Earth; Flower; Moon; Plant; Sea; Sky; Star; Sun; Tree.

Nature, Human

God said, Let us make man in our image. *Ge.* 1: 26.

Ye shall be as gods, knowing good and evil. *Ge.* 3: 5.

Man doth not live by bread only. *De.* 8: 3.

Man is born unto trouble, as the sparks fly upward. *Jb.* 5: 7.

What is man, that thou art mindful of him? and the son of man, that thou visitest him? *Ps.* 8: 4.

Thou hast made him a little lower than the angels, and hast crowned him with glory and honour. *Ps.* 8: 5.

Honour and majesty hast thou laid upon him. *Ps.* 21: 5.

Lord, what is man, that thou takest knowl-

edge of him! or the son of man, that thou makest account of him! *Ps.* 144: 3.

A man hath no preëminence above a beast: for all is vanity. *Ec.* 3: 19.

Can the Ethiopian change his skin, or the leopard his spots? *Je.* 13: 23.

Cursed be the man that trusteth in man. *Je.* 17: 5.

For what man knoweth the things of a man, save the spirit of man which is in him? *1 Co.* 2: 11.

The natural man receiveth not the things of the Spirit of God: for they are foolishness unto him. *1 Co.* 2: 14.

A man . . . is the image and glory of God. *1 Co.* 11: 7.

Thou hast put all things in subjection under his feet. *He.* 2: 8.

The dog is turned to his own vomit again; and the sow that was washed to her wallowing in the mire. *2 Pe.* 2: 22.

According to the measure of a man, that is, of the angel. *Re.* 21: 17.

See also
Man; Man, Divinity of; Man, Greatness of; Man, the New; Man, Spirit of; Manliness.

Navigation

King Solomon made a navy of ships. *1 K.* 9: 26.

They are passed away as the swift ships: as the eagle that hasteth to the prey. *Jb.* 9: 26.

There go the ships. *Ps.* 104: 26.

They that go down to the sea in ships, that do business in great waters. *Ps.* 107: 23.

There the glorious Lord will be unto us a place of broad rivers and streams; wherein shall go no galley with oars, neither shall gallant ship pass thereby. *Is.* 33: 21.

Thy rowers have brought thee into great waters. *Eze.* 27: 26.

Jonah . . . found a ship going to Tarshish: so he paid his fare thereof, and went down into it. *Jon.* 1: 3.

See also
Pilot; Ship; Voyage.

Neck

I know thy rebellion, and thy stiff neck. *De.* 31: 27.

Joshua called for all the men of Israel, and said unto the captains of the men of war which went with him, Come near, put your feet upon the necks of these kings. *Jos.* 10: 24.

Let not mercy and truth forsake thee: bind them about thy neck. *Pr.* 3: 3.

I will break his yoke from off thy neck. *Je.* 30: 8.

Whoso shall offend one of these little ones which believe in me, it were better for him that a millstone were hanged about his neck, and that he were drowned in the depth of the sea. *Mat.* 18: 6.

Why tempt ye God, to put a yoke upon the neck of the disciples, which neither our fathers nor we were able to bear? *Ac.* 15: 10.

Who have for my life laid down their own necks. *Ro.* 16: 4.

Need

Can a man be profitable unto God? *Jb.* 22: 2.

I am poor and needy; yet the Lord thinketh upon me. *Ps.* **40: 17.**

He will regard the prayer of the destitute. *Ps.* **102: 17.**

Yet setteth he the poor on high from affliction. *Ps.* **107: 41.**

That we may buy the poor for silver, and the needy for a pair of shoes. *Am.* **8: 6.**

Your Father knoweth what things ye have need of, before ye ask him. *Mat.* **6: 8.**

They that be whole need not a physician, but they that are sick. *Mat.* **9: 12.**

The Lord hath need of them. *Mat.* **21: 3.**

My little daughter lieth at the point of death: I pray thee, come and lay thy hands on her. *Mk.* **5: 23.**

All they did cast in of their abundance; but she of her want did cast in all that she had. *Mk.* **12: 44.**

One thing is needful: and Mary hath chosen that good part. *Lu.* **10: 42.**

She of her penury hath cast in all the living that she had. *Lu.* **21: 4.**

Distribution was made unto every man according as he had need. *Ac.* **4: 35.**

God . . . dwelleth not in temples made with hands; Neither is worshipped with men's hands, as though he needed any thing. *Ac.* **17: 24, 25.**

Distributing to the necessity of saints. *Ro.* **12: 13.**

Necessity is laid upon me; yea, woe is unto me, if I preach not the gospel! *1 Co.* **9: 16.**

I mean not that other men be eased, and ye burdened: But by an equality, that now at this time your abundance may be a supply for their want, that their abundance also may be a supply for your want: that there may be equality. *2 Co.* **8: 13, 14.**

I take pleasure in . . . necessities . . . for Christ's sake. *2 Co.* **12: 10.**

My God shall supply all your need according to his riches in glory by Christ Jesus. *Ph.* **4: 19.**

Destitute, afflicted, tormented. *He.* **11: 37.**

They need no candle, neither light of the sun; for the Lord God giveth them light. *Re.* **22: 5.**

See also

Charity; Destitution; Lack; Philanthropy; Poor; Poverty; Want.

Neglect

Jehu took no heed to walk in the law of the Lord God of Israel with all his heart. *2 K.* **10: 31.**

My sons, be not now negligent: for the Lord hath chosen you to stand before him, to serve him. *2 Ch.* **29: 11.**

They have not served thee in their kingdom. *Ne.* **9: 35.**

The fear of the Lord is the beginning of knowledge: but fools despise wisdom and instruction. *Pr.* **1: 7.**

Whoso stoppeth his ears at the cry of the poor, he also shall cry himself, but shall not be heard. *Pr.* **21: 13.**

Israel doth not know, my people doth not consider. *Is.* **1: 3.**

There is none that calleth upon thy name,

that stirreth up himself to take hold of thee. *Is.* **64: 7.**

The diseased have ye not strengthened, neither have ye healed that which was sick, neither have ye bound up that which was broken, neither have ye brought again that which was driven away, neither have ye sought that which was lost. *Eze.* **34: 4.**

While men slept, his enemy came and sowed tares. *Mat.* **13: 25.**

I was a stranger, and ye took me not in. *Mat.* **25: 43.**

That servant, which knew his lord's will, and prepared not himself, neither did according to his will, shall be beaten with many stripes. *Lu.* **12: 47.**

They all with one consent began to make excuse. *Lu.* **14: 18.**

Their widows were neglected in the daily ministration. *Ac.* **6: 1.**

Neglect not the gift that is in thee, which was given thee by prophecy. *1 Ti.* **4: 14.**

Of these things put them in remembrance. *2 Ti.* **2: 14.**

Therefore we ought to give the more earnest heed to the things which we have heard, lest at any time we should let them slip. *He.* **2: 1.**

How shall we escape, if we neglect so great salvation? *He.* **2: 3.**

If they escaped not who refused him that spake on earth, much more shall not we escape, if we turn away from him that speaketh from heaven. *He.* **12: 25.**

What doth it profit, my brethren, though a man say he hath faith, and have not works? can faith save him? *Ja.* **2: 14.**

To him that knoweth to do good, and doeth it not, to him it is sin. *Ja.* **4: 17.**

I will not be negligent to put you always in remembrance of these things. *2 Pe.* **1: 12.**

See also

Carelessness; Heedlessness; Indifference.

Neighbor

Thou shalt not bear false witness against thy neighbour. *Ex.* **20: 16.**

Thou shalt not covet thy neighbour's house, thou shalt not covet thy neighbour's wife, nor his manservant, nor his maidservant, nor his ox, nor his ass, nor any thing that is thy neighbour's. *Ex.* **20: 17.**

Thou shalt love thy neighbour as thyself: I am the Lord. *Le.* **19: 18.**

He that is void of wisdom despiseth his neighbour. *Pr.* **11: 12.**

The righteous is more excellent than his neighbour. *Pr.* **12: 26.**

The poor is hated even of his own neighbour. *Pr.* **14: 20.**

Better is a neighbour that is near than a brother far off. *Pr.* **27: 10.**

They helped every one his neighbour. *Is.* **41: 6.**

Speak ye every man the truth to his neighbour. *Zch.* **8: 16.**

Let none of you imagine evil in your hearts against his neighbour. *Zch.* **8: 17.**

Thou shalt love thy neighbour as thyself. *Mk.* **12: 31.**

Who is my neighbour? *Lu.* **10: 29.**

Which now of these three, thinkest thou, was

neighbour unto him that fell among the thieves? And he said, He that shewed mercy on him. Then said Jesus unto him, Go, and do thou likewise. *Lu.* **10: 36, 37.**

There standeth one among you, whom ye know not. *Jn.* **1: 26.**

They, . . . breaking bread from house to house, did eat their meat with gladness and singleness of heart. *Ac.* **2: 46.**

Love worketh no ill to his neighbour. *Ro.* **13: 10.**

Let every one of us please his neighbour for his good to edification. *Ro.* **15: 2.**

We are members one of another. *Ep.* **4: 25.**

Look not every man on his own things, but every man also on the things of others. *Ph.* **2: 4.**

That ye may walk honestly toward them that are without. *1 Th.* **4: 12.**

See also
Brotherhood, Fraternity.

Nest

As an eagle stirreth up her nest, fluttereth over her young, spreadeth abroad her wings, taketh them, beareth them on her wings: So the Lord alone did lead him. *De.* **32: 11, 12.**

The sparrow hath found an house, and the swallow a nest for herself, where she may lay her young, even thine altars, O Lord of hosts. *Ps.* **84: 3.**

The trees of the Lord are full of sap; . . . Where the birds make their nests. *Ps.* **104: 16, 17.**

As a bird that wandereth from her nest, so is a man that wandereth from his place. *Pr.* **27: 8.**

Though thou shouldest make thy nest as high as the eagle. I will bring thee down from thence, saith the Lord. *Je.* **49: 16.**

Though thou set thy nest among the stars, thence will I bring thee down, saith the Lord. *Ob.* **1: 4.**

The foxes have holes, and the birds of the air have nests; but the Son of man hath not where to lay his head. *Mat.* **8: 20.**

See also
Bird; Brood.

Net

Know now that God hath overthrown me, and hath compassed me with his net. *Jb.* **19: 6.**

He shall pluck my feet out of the net. *Ps.* **25: 15.**

They have prepared a net for my steps. *Ps.* **57: 6.**

Let the wicked fall into their own nets, whilst that I withal escape. *Ps.* **141: 10.**

The wicked desireth the net of evil men. *Pr.* **12: 12.**

A man that flattereth his neighbour spreadeth a net for his feet. *Pr.* **29: 5.**

As the fishes that are taken in an evil net, and as the birds that are caught in the snare; so are the sons of men snared in an evil time, when it falleth suddenly upon them. *Ec.* **9: 12.**

Thus saith the Lord God: I will therefore spread out my net over thee. *Eze.* **32: 3.**

The kingdom of heaven is like unto a net, that was cast into the sea, and gathered of every kind. *Mat.* **13: 47.**

They forsook their nets, and followed him. *Mk.* **1: 18.**

Launch out into the deep, and let down your nets for a draught. *Lu.* **5: 4.**

Neutrality

Am I my brother's keeper? *Ge.* **4: 9.**

How long halt ye between two opinions? *1 K.* **18: 21.**

In the day that thou stoodest on the other side. *Ob.* **1: 11.**

He took water, and washed his hands before the multitude. *Mat.* **27: 24.**

He passed by on the other side. *Lu.* **10: 31.**

He that is not with me is against me. *Lu.* **11: 23.**

Who made me a judge or a divider over you? *Lu.* **12: 14.**

I know thy works, that thou art neither cold nor hot: I would thou wert cold or hot. So then because thou art lukewarm, and neither cold nor hot, I will spue thee out of my mouth. *Re.* **3: 15, 16.**

See also
Indifference.

Newness

They chose new gods. *Ju.* **5: 8.**

There is no new thing under the sun. *Ec.* **1: 9.**

The Lord's mercies . . . are new every morning: great is thy faithfulness. *La.* **3: 22, 23.**

I will put a new spirit within you. *Eze.* **11: 19.**

Make you a new heart and a new spirit: for why will ye die? *Eze.* **18: 31.**

I will not drink henceforth of this fruit of the vine, until that day when I drink it new with you in my Father's kingdom. *Mat.* **26: 29.**

They shall speak with new tongues. *Mk.* **16: 17.**

Put on the new man. *Ep.* **4: 24.**

By a new and living way, which he hath consecrated for us, through the veil, that is to say, his flesh. *He.* **10: 20.**

Behold, I make all things new. *Re.* **21: 5.**

See also
Birth, the New; Freshness; Life, the New; Novelty.

News, Good

As cold water to a thirsty soul, so is good news from a far country. *Pr.* **25: 25.**

How beautiful upon the mountains are the feet of him that bringeth good tidings. *Is.* **52: 7.**

The Lord hath anointed me to preach good tidings. *Is.* **61: 1.**

How beautiful are the feet of them that preach the gospel of peace! *Ro.* **10: 15.**

The light of the glorious gospel of Christ. *2 Co.* **4: 4.**

Timotheus . . . brought us good tidings of your faith and charity. *1 Th.* **3: 6.**

According to the glorious gospel of the blessed God. *1 Ti.* **1: 11.**

See also
Announcement; Evangelism; Gospel; Herald; Tidings.

Night

Darkness was upon the face of the deep. *Ge.* **1: 2.**

God called . . . the darkness . . . night. *Ge.* 1: 5.

God spake unto Israel in the visions of the night. *Ge.* 46: 2.

It gave light by night. *Ex.* 14: 20.

He made darkness pavilions round about him. *2 S.* 22: 12.

None saith, Where is God my maker, who giveth songs in the night? *Jb.* 35: 10.

Thou hast visited me in the night. *Ps.* 17: 3.

Night unto night sheweth knowledge. *Ps.* 19: 2.

Weeping may endure for a night, but joy cometh in the morning. *Ps.* 30: 5.

In the night his song shall be with me. *Ps.* 42: 8.

When I remember thee upon my bed, and meditate on thee in the night watches. *Ps.* 63: 6.

He led them . . . all the night with a light of fire. *Ps.* 78: 14.

To shew forth . . . thy faithfulness every night. *Ps.* 92: 2.

Even the night shall be light about me. *Ps.* 139: 11.

Yea, the darkness hideth not from thee. *Ps.* 139: 12.

Watchman, what of the night? *Is.* 21: 11.

I will give thee the treasures of darkness, and hidden riches of secret places. *Is.* 45: 3.

The same night in which he was betrayed. *1 Co.* 11: 23.

There shall be no night there. *Re.* 21: 25.

See also

Darkness; **Midnight; Obscurity.**

Nobility

In thy majesty ride prosperously because of truth and meekness and righteousness. *Ps.* 45: 4.

By me princes rule, and nobles, even all the judges of the earth. *Pr.* 8: 16.

It is an abomination to kings to commit wickedness: for the throne is established by righteousness. *Pr.* 16: 12.

Excellent speech becometh not a fool: much less do lying lips a prince. *Pr.* 17: 7.

Lo, I am come to great estate. *Ec.* 1: 16.

Blessed art thou, O land, when thy king is the son of nobles. *Ec.* 10: 17. ‹

The loftiness of man shall be bowed down. *Is.* 2: 17.

Upon a lofty and high mountain hast thou set thy bed. *Is.* 57: 7.

Yet I had planted thee a noble vine, wholly a right seed: how then art thou turned into the degenerate plant of a strange vine unto me? *Je.* 2: 21.

Thy nobles shall dwell in the dust. *Na.* 3: 18.

Not many wise men after the flesh, not many mighty, not many noble, are called. *1 Co.* 1: 26.

See also

Dignity; Gentleman; Honor; Superiority.

Noise

When thou hearest the sound of a going in the tops of the mulberry trees, . . . then shall the Lord go out before thee. *2 S.* 5: 24.

Get thee up, eat and drink; for there is a sound of abundance of rain. *1 K.* 18: 41.

God is gone up with a shout, the Lord with the sound of a trumpet. *Ps.* 47: 5.

Which stilleth the noise of the seas, the noise of their waves, and the tumult of the people. *Ps.* 65: 7.

Sing . . . upon the harp with a solemn sound. *Ps.* 92: 1, 3.

The Lord on high is mightier than the noise of many waters, yea, than the mighty waves of the sea. *Ps.* 93: 4.

The heavens shall pass away with a great noise. *2 Pe.* 3: 10.

His voice as the sound of many waters. *Re.* 1: 15.

I saw when the Lamb opened one of the seals, and I heard, as it were the noise of thunder. *Re.* 6: 1.

See also

Clamor; Confusion; Cry; Disorder; **Disturbance; Shout; Storm; Tumult.**

Nonresistance

Thou art more righteous than I: for thou hast rewarded me good, whereas I have rewarded thee evil. *1 S.* 24: 17.

Rejoice not when thine enemy falleth. *Pr.* 24: 17.

I gave my back to the smiters, and my cheeks to them that plucked off the hair. *Is.* 50: 6.

I say unto you, That ye resist not evil. *Mat.* 5: 39.

Whosoever shall smite thee on thy right cheek, turn to him the other also. *Mat.* 5: 39.

If any man will sue thee at the law, and take away thy coat, let him have thy cloke also. *Mat.* 5: 40.

Whosoever shall compel thee to go a mile, go with him twain. *Mat.* 5: 41.

Love ye your enemies, and do good. *Lu.* 6: 35.

If thine enemy hunger, feed him; if he thirst, give him drink: for in so doing thou shalt heap coals of fire on his head. *Ro.* 12: 20.

See also

Pacifism; Peace.

Nonsense

He multiplieth words without knowledge. *Jb.* 35: 16.

The fool hath said in his heart, There is no God. *Ps.* 14: 1.

A prating fool shall fall. *Pr.* 10: 8.

The foolishness of fools is folly. *Pr.* 14: 24.

The mouth of fools poureth out foolishness. *Pr.* 15: 2.

The instruction of fools is folly. *Pr.* 16: 22.

He that answereth a matter before he heareth it, it is folly and shame unto him. *Pr.* 18: 13.

Answer not a fool according to his folly. *Pr.* 26: 4.

A fool uttereth all his mind. *Pr.* 29: 11.

I sought in mine heart . . . to lay hold on folly. *Ec.* 2: 3.

The lips of a fool will swallow up himself. *Ec.* 10: 12.

Every mouth speaketh folly. *Is.* 9: 17.

That we may delivered from unreasonable . . . men. *2 Th.* 3: 2.

See also

Folly; Fool.

Noon

Thou shalt grope at noonday, as the blind gropeth in darkness. *De.* 28: 29.

Thine age shall be clearer than the noon-day. *Jb.* 11: 17.

He shall bring forth . . . thy judgment as the noonday. *Ps.* 37: 6.

At noon, will I pray. *Ps.* 55: 17.

Thou shalt not be afraid . . . for the arrow that flieth by day; . . . the destruction that wasteth at noonday. *Ps.* 91: 5, 6.

The sun shall not smite thee by day. *Ps.* 121: 6.

The path of the just is as the shining light, that shineth more and more unto the perfect day. *Pr.* 4: 18.

Thou makest thy flock to rest at noon. *S. of S.* 1: 7.

Then shall . . . thy darkness be as the noonday. *Is.* 58: 10.

The burden and heat of the day. *Mat.* 20: 12.

About noon, suddenly there shone from heaven a great light. *Ac.* 22: 6.

At midday, O king, I saw in the way a light from heaven, above the brightness of the sun. *Ac.* 26: 13.

See also
Midday.

North

He stretcheth out the north over the empty place. *Jb.* 26: 7.

Out of the south cometh the whirlwind: and cold out of the north. *Jb.* 37: 9.

Fair weather cometh out of the north: with God is terrible majesty. *Jb.* 37: 22.

Beautiful for situation, the joy of the whole earth, is mount Zion, on the sides of the north, the city of the great King. *Ps.* 48: 2.

He hath . . . gathered them out of the lands, from the east, and from the west, from the north, and from the south. *Ps.* 107: 2, 3.

They shall come from the east, and from the west, and from the north, and from the south, and shall sit down in the kingdom of God. *Lu.* 13: 29.

Nose

The Lord God . . . breathed into his nostrils the breath of life. *Ge.* 2: 7.

All in whose nostrils was the breath of life . . . died. *Ge.* 7: 22.

The Lord smelled a sweet savour. *Ge.* 8: 21.

The spirit of God is in my nostrils. *Jb.* 27: 3.

Noses have they, but they smell not. *Ps.* 115: 6.

If the whole body were . . . hearing, where were the smelling? *1 Co.* 12: 17.

See also
Smell.

Nothing

The earth was without form, and void. *Ge.* 1: 2.

The paths of their way are turned aside; they go to nothing, and perish. *Jb.* 6: 18.

Man is like to vanity: his days are as a shadow that passeth away. *Ps.* 144: 4.

There is that maketh himself rich, yet hath nothing: there is that maketh himself poor, yet hath great riches. *Pr.* 13: 7.

Behold, the Lord maketh the world empty, and maketh it waste, and turneth it upside down. *Is.* 24: 1.

All nations before him are as nothing; and

they are counted to him less than nothing, and vanity. *Is.* 40: 17.

Behold, ye are of nothing, and your work of nought. *Is.* 41: 24.

Behold, they are all vanity; their works are nothing. *Is.* 41: 29.

Ye have sold yourselves for nought. *Is.* 52: 3.

Nothing shall be impossible unto you. *Mat.* 17: 20.

The rich he hath sent empty away. *Lu.* 1: 53.

It is the spirit that quickeneth; the flesh profiteth nothing. *Jn.* 6: 63.

If I honour myself, my honour is nothing. *Jn.* 8: 54.

Without me ye can do nothing. *Jn.* 15: 5.

Why dost thou set at nought thy brother? *Ro.* 14: 10.

Base things of the world, and things which are despised, hath God chosen, yea, and things which are not, to bring to nought things that are. *1 Co.* 1: 28.

Though I have all faith, so that I could remove mountains, and have not charity, I am nothing. *1 Co.* 13: 2.

What is your life? It is even a vapour, that appeareth for a little time, and then vanisheth away. *Ja.* 4: 14.

See also
Emptiness; Vanity; Void.

Nourishment

Behold, I will rain bread from heaven for you. *Ex.* 16: 4.

The Lord had visited his people in giving them bread. *Ru.* 1: 6.

The ravens brought him bread and flesh in the morning, and bread and flesh in the evening; and he drank of the brook. *1 K.* 17: 6.

Man did eat angels' food: he sent them meat to the full. *Ps.* 78: 25.

I have nourished and brought up children, and they have rebelled against me. *Is.* 1: 2.

The stay and the staff, the whole stay of bread, and the whole stay of water. *Is.* 3: 1.

Wherefore do ye spend money for that which is not bread? and your labour for that which satisfieth not? hearken diligently unto me, and eat ye that which is good. *Is.* 55: 2.

The workman is worthy of his meat. *Mat.* 10: 10.

If any man eat of this bread, he shall live for ever. *Jn.* 6: 51.

He did good, and gave us rain from heaven, and fruitful seasons, filling our hearts with food and gladness. *Ac.* 14: 17.

No man ever yet hated his own flesh; but nourisheth and cherisheth it. *Ep.* 5: 29.

Having food and raiment let us be therewith content. *1 Ti.* 6: 8.

Such as have need of milk, and not of strong meat. *He.* 5: 12.

Ye have nourished your hearts, as in a day of slaughter. *Ja.* 5: 5.

See also
Bread; Christ, the Bread of Life; Food; Hunger; Manna; Meat; Stomach; Sustenance.

Novelty

There is no new thing under the sun. *Ec.* 1: 9.

Is there any thing whereof it may be said, See, this is new? it hath been already of old time, which was before us. *Ec.* 1: 10.

Behold, I will do a new thing; now it shall spring forth. *Is.* 43: 19.

Thou shalt be called by a new name. *Is.* 62: 2.

Every scribe which is instructed unto the kingdom of heaven is like unto a man that is an householder, which bringeth forth out of his treasure things new and old. *Mat.* 13: 52.

They questioned among themselves, saying, What thing is this? what new doctrine is this? *Mk.* 1: 27.

All the Athenians and strangers which were there spent their time in nothing else, but either to tell, or to hear some new thing. *Ac.* 17: 21.

See also

Birth, the New; Life, the New; Newness.

Nudity

Naked came I out of my mother's womb, and naked shall I return thither. *Jb.* 1: 21.

Thou hast . . . stripped the naked of their clothing. *Jb.* 22: 6.

They shall strip thee also of thy clothes, and shall take thy fair jewels, and leave thee naked and bare. *Eze.* 16: 39.

He that is courageous among the mighty shall flee away naked in that day, saith the Lord. *Am.* 2: 16.

Behold, I am against thee, saith the Lord of hosts; . . . and I will shew the nations thy nakedness. *Na.* 3: 5.

Even unto this present hour we both hunger, and thirst, and are naked, and are buffeted. *1 Co.* 4: 11.

Thou . . . knowest not that thou art wretched, and miserable, and poor, and blind, and naked. *Re.* 3: 17.

See also

Nakedness.

Number

If a man can number the dust of the earth, then shall thy seed also be numbered. *Ge.* 13: 16.

Ye shall be left few in number among the heathen. *De.* 4: 27.

Even as the sand that is upon the sea shore in multitude. *Jos.* 11: 4.

As grasshoppers for multitude. *Ju.* 6: 5.

Satan stood up against Israel, and provoked David to number Israel. *1 Ch.* 21: 1.

Their children also multipliedst thou as the stars of heaven. *Ne.* 9: 23.

God . . . doeth . . . marvellous things without number. *Jb.* 5: 8, 9.

For now thou numberest my steps: dost thou not watch over my sin? *Jb.* 14: 16.

Who can number the clouds in wisdom? *Jb.* 38: 37.

So teach us to number our days, that we may apply our hearts unto wisdom. *Ps.* 90: 12.

God hath numbered thy kingdom, and finished it. *Da.* 5: 26.

A great multitude, which no man could number, . . . stood before the throne. *Re.* 7: 9.

See also

Calculation; Count.

O

Oak

There came an angel of the Lord, and sat under an oak. *Ju.* 6: 11.

He . . . went after the man of God, and found him sitting under an oak. *1 K.* 13: 13, 14.

Ye shall be as an oak whose leaf fadeth, and as a garden that hath no water. *Is.* 1: 30.

He was strong as the oaks. *Am.* 2: 9.

Howl, O ye oaks of Bashan; for the forest of the vintage is come down. *Zch.* 11: 2.

Oath

I will perform the oath which I sware. *Ge.* 26: 3.

Let there be now an oath betwixt us, even betwixt us and thee, and let us make a covenant with thee. *Ge.* 26: 28.

Neither shall ye profane my holy name. *Le.* 22: 32.

His mouth is full of cursing. *Ps.* 10: 7.

Who shall ascend into the hill of the Lord? . . . He that . . . hath not lifted up his soul unto vanity, nor sworn deceitfully. *Ps.* 24: 3, 4.

They shall vow a vow unto the Lord, and perform it. *Is.* 19: 21.

The Lord hath sworn by his right hand, and by the arm of his strength. *Is.* 62: 8.

Thou shalt swear, The Lord liveth, in truth, in judgment, and in righteousness. *Je.* 4: 2.

Love no false oath. *Zch.* 8: 17.

Thou shalt not forswear thyself, but shalt perform unto the Lord thine oaths. *Mat.* 5: 33.

The Lord sware and will not repent. *He.* 7: 21.

Above all things, my brethren, swear not, neither by heaven, neither by the earth, neither by any other oath: but let your yea be yea; and your nay, nay; lest ye fall into condemnation. *Ja.* 5: 12.

See also

Covenant; Pledge; Profanity; Promise; Vow; Yea.

Obedience

Remember all the commandments of the Lord, and do them. *Nu.* 15: 39.

This day the Lord thy God hath commanded thee to do these statutes and judgments. *De.* 26: 16.

Take diligent heed to do the commandment and the law. *Jos.* 22: 5.

To obey is better than sacrifice, and to hearken than the fat of rams. *1 S.* 15: 22.

Hear, and your soul shall live. *Is.* 55: 3.

Obey my voice, . . . and ye shall be my people. *Je.* 7: 23.

Not every one that saith unto me, Lord, Lord, shall enter into the kingdom of heaven; but he that doeth the will of my Father which is in heaven. *Mat.* 7: 21.

Whosoever shall do the will of my Father which is in heaven, the same is my brother, and sister, and mother. *Mat.* 12: 50.

If any man will do his will, he shall know of the doctrine, whether it be of God, or whether I speak of myself. *Jn.* 7: 17.

I was not disobedient unto the heavenly vision. *Ac.* 26: 19.

Women . . . are commanded to be under obedience, as also saith the law. *1 Co.* 14: 34.

Children, obey your parents in the Lord: for this is right. *Ep.* 6: 1.

Servants, be obedient to them that are your masters according to the flesh. *Ep.* 6: 5.

Having confidence in thy obedience. *Phm.* 1: 21.

Though he were a Son, yet learned he obedience. *He.* 5: 8.

Then said he, Lo, I come to do thy will, O God. *He.* 10: 9.

As obedient children. *1 Pe.* 1: 14.

Ye have purified your souls in obeying the truth. *1 Pe.* 1: 22.

Blessed are they that do his commandments, that they may have right to the tree of life, and may enter in through the gates into the city. *Re.* 22: 14.

See also

Christ, Obedience to; Commandment; God, Obedience to; Subjection; Submission; Subordination.

Obligation

These ought ye to have done, and not to leave the other undone. *Mat.* 23: 23.

Ought not Christ to have suffered these things, and to enter into his glory? *Lu.* 24: 26.

We ought to obey God rather than men. *Ac.* 5: 29.

Ye ought to support the weak. *Ac.* 20: 35.

We then that are strong ought to bear the infirmities of the weak, and not to please ourselves. *Ro.* 15: 1.

He that saith he abideth in him ought himself also so to walk, even as he walked. *1 Jn.* 2: 6.

We ought to lay down our lives for the brethren. *1 Jn.* 3: 16.

If God so loved us, we ought also to love one another. *1 Jn.* 4: 11.

See also

Debt; Duty; Indebtedness; Loan; Requirement; Responsibility; Tribute.

Oblivion

I said, . . . I would make the remembrance of them to cease from among men. *De.* 32: 26.

His remembrance shall perish from the earth, and he shall have no name in the street. *Jb.* 18: 17.

In death there is no remembrance of thee. *Ps.* 6: 5.

Their memorial is perished with them. *Ps.* 9: 6.

The face of the Lord is against them that do evil, to cut off the remembrance of them from the earth. *Ps.* 34: 16.

Blot out all mine iniquities. *Ps.* 51: 9.

Shall thy wonders be known in the dark? and thy righteousness in the land of forgetfulness? *Ps.* 88: 12.

Let his posterity be cut off; and in the generation following let their name be blotted out. *Ps.* 109: 13.

Let him drink, and forget his poverty, and remember his misery no more. *Pr.* 31: 7.

His name shall be covered with darkness. *Ec.* 6: 4.

The wicked . . . were forgotten in the city. *Ec.* 8: 10.

The dead know not any thing, neither have they any more a reward; for the memory of them is forgotten. *Ec.* 9: 5.

There is no work, nor device, nor knowledge, nor wisdom, in the grave, whither thou goest. *Ec.* 9: 10.

I will not blot out his name out of the book of life. *Re.* 3: 5.

See also

Forgetfulness.

Obscenity

A wicked man is loathsome. *Pr.* 13: 5.

I am a man of unclean lips and I dwell in the midst of a people of unclean lips. *Is.* 6: 5.

In thy filthiness is lewdness. *Eze.* 24: 13.

Thou shalt not be purged from thy filthiness any more, till I have caused my fury to rest upon thee. *Eze.* 24: 13.

From all your filthiness . . . will I cleanse you. *Eze.* 36: 25.

Other Gentiles . . . have given themselves over unto lasciviousness. *Ep.* 4: 17, 19.

Put off . . . filthy communication out of your mouth. *Col.* 3: 8.

God hath not called us unto uncleanness. *1 Th.* 4: 7.

God . . . delivered just Lot, vexed with the filthy conversation of the wicked. *2 Pe.* 2: 4, 7.

He which is filthy, let him be filthy still. *Re.* 22: 11.

See also

Lust; Profanity.

Obscurity

He knoweth thy walking through this great wilderness. *De.* 2: 7.

Let that day be darkness; . . . neither let the light shine upon it. *Jb.* 3: 4.

A land of darkness, as darkness itself; and of the shadow of death, without any order, and where the light is as darkness. *Jb.* 10: 22.

On my eyelids is the shadow of death. *Jb.* 16: 16.

They are of those that rebel against the light. *Jb.* 24: 13.

Behold even to the moon, and it shineth not. *Jb.* 25: 5.

There is no darkness, nor shadow of death, where the workers of iniquity may hide themselves. *Jb.* 34: 22.

The light of mine eyes . . . also is gone from me. *Ps.* 38: 10.

In the night his song shall be with me. *Ps.* 42: 8.

Whoso curseth his father or his mother, his lamp shall be put out in obscure darkness. *Pr.* 20: 20.

The eyes of the blind shall see out of obscurity. *Is.* 29: 18.

Then shall thy light rise in obscurity. *Is.* **58: 10.**

We wait for light, but behold obscurity. *Is.* **59: 9.**

A day of darkness and of gloominess, a day of clouds and of thick darkness. *Jo.* **2: 2.**

Is a candle brought to be put under a bushel, or under a bed? and not to be set on a candlestick? *Mk.* **4: 21.**

The night cometh, when no man can work. *Jn.* **9: 4.**

Walk while ye have the light, lest darkness come upon you; for he that walketh in darkness knoweth not whither he goeth. *Jn.* **12: 35.**

Be ye not unequally yoked together with unbelievers: for what fellowship hath righteousness with unrighteousness? and what communion hath light with darkness? *2 Co.* **6: 14.**

Wandering stars, to whom is reserved the blackness of darkness for ever. *Jude* **13.**

The light of a candle shall shine no more at all in thee. *Re.* **18: 23.**

See also

Darkness; Dimness; Gloom; Night.

Observance

These are my feasts. *Le.* **23: 2.**

My offering . . . shall ye observe to offer unto me. *Nu.* **28: 2.**

I humbled my soul with fasting. *Ps.* **35: 13.**

Your new moons and your appointed feasts my soul hateth: they are a trouble unto me; I am weary to bear them. *Is.* **1: 14.**

The ways of Zion do mourn, because none come to the solemn feasts. *La.* **1: 4.**

I will also cause her all her mirth to cease, her feast days, her new moons, and her sabbaths, and all her solemn feasts. *Ho.* **2: 11.**

When ye fast, be not, as the hypocrites, of a sad countenance, for they disfigure their faces, that they may appear unto men to fast. *Mat.* **6: 16.**

The scribes and the Pharisees sit in Moses' seat: All therefore whatsoever they bid you observe, that observe and do; but do not ye after their works: for they say, and do not. *Mat.* **23: 2, 3.**

Go ye therefore, and teach all nations, . . . Teaching them to observe all things whatsoever I have commanded you. *Mat.* **28: 19, 20.**

Master, all these things have I observed from my youth. *Mk.* **10: 20.**

One man esteemeth one day above another: another esteemeth every day alike. Let every man be fully persuaded in his own m?nd. *Ro.* **14: 5.**

Let us keep the feast, not with old leaven, neither with the leaven of malice and wickedness; but with the unleavened bread of sincerity and truth. *1 Co.* **5: 8.**

Ye observe days, and months, and times, and years. I am afraid of you, lest I have bestowed upon you labour in vain. *Ga.* **4: 10, 11.**

See also

Celebration; Ceremony; Feast; Form; Formalism; Obedience; Ritual.

Obstacle

Hinder me not, seeing the Lord hath prospered my way. *Ge.* **24: 56.**

The crooked shall be made straight, and the rough places plain. *Is.* **40: 4.**

I will break in pieces the gates of brass, and cut in sunder the bars of iron. *Is.* **45: 2.**

Behold, I will lay stumblingblocks before this people, and the fathers and the sons together shall fall upon them. *Je.* **6: 21.**

Therefore, behold, I will hedge up thy way with thorns, and make a wall, that she shall not find her paths. *Ho.* **2: 6.**

Who art thou, O great mountain? before Zerubbabel thou shalt become a plain. *Zch.* **4: 7.**

Ye have caused many to stumble at the law. *Mal.* **2: 8.**

If ye shall say unto this mountain, Be thou removed, and be thou cast into the sea; it shall be done. *Mat.* **21: 21.**

How hard is it for them that trust in riches to enter into the kingdom of God! *Mk.* **10: 24.**

Take ye away the stone. *Jn.* **11: 39.**

Then came Jesus, the doors being shut. *Jn.* **20: 26.**

Who shall separate us from the love of Christ? shall tribulation, or distress, or persecution, or famine, or nakedness, or peril, or sword? . . . Nay, in all these things we are more than conquerors through him that loved us. *Ro.* **8: 35, 37.**

Who did hinder you that ye should not obey the truth? *Ga.* **5: 7.**

There is none occasion of stumbling in him. *1 Jn.* **2: 10.**

See also

Bar; Difficulty; Hindrance; Impediment; Obstruction; Opposition; Prevention; Stumblingblock.

Obstruction

Thou shalt not . . . put a stumblingblock before the blind. *Le.* **19: 14.**

Samson . . . took the doors of the gate of the city, and the two posts, and went away with them, bar and all. *Ju.* **16: 3.**

Let them shut the doors, and bar them. *Ne.* **7: 3.**

A brother offended is harder to be won than a strong city: and their contentions are like the bars of a castle. *Pr.* **18: 19.**

He that hath no rule over his own spirit is like a city that is broken down, and without walls. *Pr.* **25: 28.**

Let us break their bands asunder. *Ps.* **2: 3.**

Lift up your heads, O ye gates. *Ps.* **24: 7.**

He hath broken the gates of brass, and cut the bars of iron in sunder. *Ps.* **107: 16.**

He hath strengthened the bars of thy gates. *Ps.* **147: 9.**

Open ye the gates, that the righteous nation which keepeth the truth may enter in. *Is.* **26: 2.**

Take up the stumblingblock out of the way of my people. *Is.* **57: 14.**

I will go up to the land of unwalled villages. *Eze.* **38: 11.**

This gate shall be shut, it shall not be opened, and no man shall enter in by it. *Eze.* **44: 2.**

I will break also the bar of Damascus. *Am.* **1: 5.**

If a man walk in the night, he stumbleth, because there is no light in him. *Jn.* **11: 10.**

They stumbled at that stumblingstone. *Ro.* **9: 32.**

By faith they passed through the Red sea

as by dry land. *He.* **11: 29.**

By faith the walls of Jericho fell down. *He.* **11: 30.**

See also

Difficulty; Hindrance; Impediment; Obstacle; Stumbling-Block.

Occasion

Who knoweth whether thou art come to the kingdom for such a time as this? *Es.* **4: 14.**

To every thing there is a season, and a time to every purpose under the heaven. *Ec.* **3: 1.**

From that time he sought opportunity to betray him. *Mat.* **26: 16.**

Judge this rather, that no man put a stumblingblock or an occasion to fall in his brother's way. *Ro.* **14: 13.**

We . . . give you occasion to glory on our behalf. *2 Co.* **5: 12.**

Use not liberty for an occasion to the flesh. *Ga.* **5: 13.**

Give none occasion to the adversary to speak reproachfully. *1 Ti.* **5: 14.**

He that loveth his brother abideth in the light, and there is none occasion of stumbling in him. *1 Jn.* **2: 10.**

See also

Cause; Chance; Chance, the Second; Opportunity; Season; Time.

Occupation

What is thine occupation? *Jon.* **1: 8.**

Occupy till I come. *Lu.* **19: 13.**

And he trembling and astonished said, Lord, what wilt thou have me to do? *Ac.* **9: 6.**

The Holy Ghost said, Separate me Barnabas and Saul for the work whereunto I have called them. *Ac.* **13: 2.**

Because he was of the same craft, he abode with them, and wrought: for by their occupation they were tentmakers. *Ac.* **18: 3.**

As the Lord hath called every one, so let him walk. *1 Co.* **7: 17.**

Brethren, let every man, wherein he is called, therein abide with God. *1 Co.* **7: 24.**

He gave some, apostles; and some, prophets; and some, evangelists; and some, pastors and teachers. *Ep.* **4: 11.**

See also

Business; Calling; Profession; Trade; Vocation.

Ocean

The gathering together of the waters called he Seas. *Ge.* **1: 10.**

When the waves of death compassed me, the floods of ungodly men made me afraid. *2 S.* **22: 5.**

He hath founded it upon the seas, and established it upon the floods. *Ps.* **24: 2.**

The voice of the Lord is upon the waters. *Ps.* **29: 3.**

All thy waves and thy billows are gone over me. *Ps.* **42: 7.**

The Lord on high is mightier than the noise of many waters. *Ps.* **93: 4.**

The sea is his, and he made it. *Ps.* **95: 5.**

So is this great and wide sea, wherein are things creeping innumerable. *Ps.* **104: 25.**

All the rivers run into the sea; yet the sea is not full; unto the place from whence the rivers come, thither they return again. *Ec.* **1: 7.**

Sing unto the Lord a new song, . . . ye that go down to the sea. *Is.* **42: 10.**

Launch out into the deep. *Lu.* **5: 4.**

In perils of waters. *2 Co.* **11: 26.**

See also

Deep; Flood; Sea; Voyage; Water; Wave.

Odor

Aaron shall burn thereon sweet incense every morning: when he dresseth the lamps, he shall burn incense upon it. *Ex.* **30: 7.**

I will . . . bring your sanctuaries unto desolation, and I will not smell the savour of your sweet odours. *Le.* **26: 31.**

All thy garments smell of myrrh, and aloes and cassia. *Ps.* **45: 8.**

The vines with the tender grape give a good smell. *S. of S.* **2: 13.**

Incense is an abomination unto me. *Is.* **1: 13.**

His beauty shall be as the olive tree, and his smell as Lebanon. *Ho.* **14: 6.**

The house was filled with the odour of the ointment. *Jn.* **12: 3.**

See also

Fragrance; Nose; Perfume; Savor; Scent; Smell.

Offence

How long shall I bear with this evil congregation, which murmur against me? *Nu.* **14: 27.**

I have borne chastisement, I will not offend any more. *Jb.* **34: 31.**

If I say, I will speak thus; behold, I should offend against the generation of thy children. *Ps.* **73: 15.**

Blessed is he, whosoever shall not be offended in me. *Mat.* **11: 6.**

Whoso shall offend one of these little ones which believe in me, it were better for him that a millstone were hanged about his neck, and that he were drowned in the depth of the sea. *Mat.* **18: 6.**

Woe unto the world because of offences! for it must needs be that offences come; but woe to that man by whom the offence cometh! *Mat.* **18: 7.**

A conscience void of offence toward God, and toward men. *Ac.* **24: 16.**

Jesus our Lord . . . was delivered for our offences, and was raised again for our justification. *Ro.* **4: 24, 25.**

If meat make my brother to offend, I will eat no flesh while the world standeth, lest I make my brother to offend. *1 Co.* **8: 13.**

Give none offence, neither to the Jews, nor to the Gentiles, nor to the church of God. *1 Co.* **10: 32.**

Have I committed an offence in abasing myself that ye might be exalted? *2 Co.* **11: 7.**

That ye may be sincere and without offence till the day of Christ. *Ph.* **1: 10.**

See also

Affront; Annoyance; Corruption; Crime; Depravity; Evil; Fault; Guile; Harm; Hurt; Iniquity; Mischief; Provocation; Sin; Transgression; Trespass; Ungodliness, Unrighteousness; Wickedness; Wrong.

Offering

They shall take to them every man a lamb, according to the house of their fathers, a lamb for an house. *Ex.* 12: 3.

The rich shall not give more, and the poor shall not give less than half a shekel, when they give an offering unto the Lord, to make an atonement for your souls. *Ex.* 30: 15.

The children of Israel brought a willing offering unto the Lord, every man and woman, whose heart made them willing to bring for all manner of work, which the Lord had commanded. *Ex.* 35: 29.

Every man shall give as he is able. *De.* 16:17.

Hath the Lord as great delight in burnt offerings and sacrifices, as in obeying the voice of the Lord? *1 S.* 15: 22.

Then the people rejoiced, for that they offered willingly. *1 Ch.* 29: 9.

Offer the sacrifices of righteousness. *Ps.* 4: 5.

Sacrifice and offering thou didst not desire. *Ps.* 40: 6.

Thou desirest not sacrifice; else would I give it. *Ps.* 51: 16.

The sacrifices of God are a broken heart. *Ps.* 51: 17.

To do justice and judgment is more acceptable to the Lord than sacrifice. *Pr.* 21: 3.

I desired mercy, and not sacrifice. *Ho.* 6: 6.

Wherewith shall I come before the Lord, and bow myself before the high God? shall I come before him with burnt offerings? *Mi.* 6: 6.

He shall . . . purge them as gold and silver, that they may offer unto the Lord an offering in righteousness. *Mal.* 3: 3.

Will a man rob God? Yet ye have robbed me. But ye say, Wherein have we robbed thee? In tithes and offerings. *Mal.* 3: 8.

Go ye and learn what that meaneth, I will have mercy, and not sacrifice. *Mat.* 9: 13.

To love him with all the heart . . . is more than all whole burnt offerings and sacrifices. *Mk.* 12: 33.

Jesus sat over against the treasury, and beheld how the people cast money into the treasury. *Mk.* 12: 41.

Then took Mary a pound of ointment of spikenard, very costly, and anointed the feet of Jesus, and wiped his feet with her hair. *Jn.* 12: 3.

He that giveth, let him do it with simplicity. *Ro.* 12: 8.

If there be first a willing mind, it is accepted according to that a man hath, and not according to that he hath not. *2 Co.* 8: 12.

Christ . . . hath given himself for us an offering and a sacrifice to God for a sweet smelling savour. *Ep.* 5: 2.

I am now ready to be offered. *2 Ti.* 4: 6.

By one offering he hath perfected for ever them that are sanctified. *He.* 10: 14.

Offer up spiritual sacrifices. *1 Pe.* 2: 5.

See also

Christ, Cross of; Christ, Gift of; Christ, Sacrifice of; Christ, Suffering of; Cross; Donation; Gift; God, Gift of; Present; Sacrifice; Self-Sacrifice; Tithe.

Office

That he may minister unto me in the priest's office. *Ex.* 28: 1.

I took the chief of your tribes, wise men, and known, and made them heads over you. *De.* 1: 15.

Should I leave my fatness, wherewith by me they honour God and man, and go to be promoted over the trees? *Ju.* 9: 9.

I will also make thy officers' peace, and thine exactors righteousness. *Is.* 60: 17.

Officers in the house of the Lord. *Je.* 29: 26.

I magnify mine office. *Ro.* 11: 13.

All members have not the same office. *Ro.* 12: 4.

See also

Calling; Ministry; Occupation; Priesthood; Profession; Vocation.

Offspring

In sorrow thou shalt bring forth children. *Ge.* 3: 16.

Visiting the iniquity of the fathers upon the children, and upon the children's children, unto the third and to the fourth generation. *Ex.* 34: 7.

These words, which I command thee this day, shall be in thine heart: And thou shalt teach them diligently unto thy children. *De.* 6: 6, 7.

Thy seed shall be great, and thine offspring as the grass of the earth. *Jb.* 5: 25.

The Lord shall increase you more and more, you and your children. *Ps.* 115: 14.

As arrows are in the hand of a mighty man; so are children of the youth. Happy is the man that hath his quiver full of them. *Ps.* 127: 4, 5.

A good man leaveth an inheritance to his children's children. *Pr.* 13: 22.

Children's children are the crown of old men. *Pr.* 17: 6.

Their young ones shall lie down together. *Is.* 11: 7.

I will pour my spirit upon thy seed, and my blessing upon thine offspring: And they shall spring up as among the grass, as willows by the water courses. *Is.* 44: 3, 4.

The fathers have eaten a sour grape, and the children's teeth are set on edge. *Je.* 31: 29.

We are also his offspring. *Ac.* 17: 28.

I am the root and the offspring of David. *Re.* 22: 16.

See also

Babe; Child; Daughter; Descent; Genealogy; Generation; Son.

Oil

The rock poured me out rivers of oil. *Jb.* 29: 6.

Thou anointest my head with oil. *Ps.* 23: 5.

God, thy God, hath anointed thee with the oil of gladness above thy fellows. *Ps.* 45: 7.

His words were softer than oil, yet were they drawn swords. *Ps.* 55: 21.

With my holy oil have I anointed him. *Ps.* 89: 20.

He that loveth wine and oil shall not be rich. *Pr.* 21: 17.

I will plant in the wilderness . . . the oil tree. *Is.* 41: 19.

To give unto them beauty for ashes, the oil of joy for mourning. *Is.* 61: 3.

The wise took oil in their vessels with their lamps. *Mat.* 25: 4.

He . . . went to him, and bound up his wounds, pouring in oil and wine. *Lu.* 10: 33, 34.

Ointment

It is like the precious ointment upon the head. *Ps.* 133: 2.

Ointment and perfume rejoice the heart. *Pr.* 27: 9.

A good name is better than precious ointment. *Ec.* 7: 1.

Thy name is as ointment poured forth. *S. of S.* 1: 3.

This ointment might have been sold for much, and given to the poor. *Mat.* 26: 9.

In that she hath poured this ointment on my body, she did it for my burial. *Mat.* 26: 12.

Anoint thine eyes with eyesalve, that thou mayest see. *Re.* 3: 18.

See also
Anointing; Remedy.

Oldness

Thou shalt rise up before the hoary head, and honour the face of the old man. *Le.* 19: 32.

He forsook the counsel of the old men. *1 K.* 12: 8.

I have been young, and now am old; yet have I not seen the righteous forsaken. *Ps.* 37: 25.

Mark the perfect man, and behold the upright: for the end of that man is peace. *Ps.* 37: 37.

They shall still bring forth fruit in old age. *Ps.* 92: 14.

Praise him in the assembly of the elders. *Ps.* 107: 32.

The hoary head is a crown of glory, if it be found in the way of righteousness. *Pr.* 16: 31.

Say not thou, What is the cause that the former days were better than these? for thou dost not enquire wisely concerning this. *Ec.* 7: 10.

There shall be no more thence an infant of days, nor an old man that hath not filled his days: for the child shall die an hundred years old. *Is.* 65: 20.

No man also having drunk old wine straightway desireth new: for he saith, The old is better. *Lu.* 5: 39.

Old things are passed away; behold, all things are become new. *2 Co.* 5: 17.

That the aged men be sober, grave, temperate, sound in faith, in charity, in patience. *Tit.* 2: 2.

See also
Age; Ancestor; Elder; Generation; Life, the Long; Senior; Time, Past.

Olive

The dove came in to him in the evening; and, lo, in her mouth was an olive leaf pluckt off. *Ge.* 8: 11.

Vineyards and olive trees, which thou plantedst not. *De.* 6: 11.

The trees . . . said unto the olive tree, Reign thou over us. *Ju.* 9: 8.

He . . . shall cast off his flower as the olive. *Jb.* 15: 33.

I am like a green olive tree in the house of God. *Ps.* 52: 8.

Thy wife shall be as a fruitful vine: . . . thy children like olive plants round about thy table. *Ps.* 128: 3.

The Lord called thy name, A green olive tree, fair, and of goodly fruit. *Je.* 11: 16.

Although . . . the labour of the olive shall fail, . . . Yet I will rejoice in the Lord. *Hab.* 3: 17, 18.

Can the fig tree, my brethren, bear olive berries? *Ja.* 3: 12.

Omega

Better is the end of a thing than the beginning thereof. *Ec.* 7: 8.

Who hath wrought and done it, calling the generations from the beginning? I the Lord, the first, and with the last; I am he. *Is.* 41: 4.

Christ is the end of the law. *Ro.* 10: 4.

I am Alpha and Omega, the beginning and the ending, saith the Lord. *Re.* 1: 8.

These things saith the first and the last, which was dead, and is alive. *Re.* 2: 8.

See also
Alpha; End; Last.

Omission

He left nothing undone. *Jos.* 11: 15.

My sons, be not now negligent. *2 Ch.* 29: 11.

He hath left off to be wise, and to do good. *Ps.* 36: 3.

We have not wrought any deliverance in the earth. *Is.* 26: 18.

They say, and do not. *Mat.* 23: 3.

Ye pay tithe of mint and anise and cummin, and have omitted the weightier matters of the law, judgment, mercy and faith. *Mat.* 23: 23.

Inasmuch as ye did it not. *Mat.* 25: 45.

The good that I would I do not. *Ro.* 7: 19.

Though I . . . understand . . . all knowledge; . . . and have not charity, I am nothing. *1 Co.* 13: 2.

To him that knoweth to do good, and doeth it not, to him it is sin. *Ja.* 4: 17.

See also
Failure; Neglect.

Omnipotence

In thine hand it is to make great, and to give strength unto all. *1 Ch.* 29: 12.

Lord, it is nothing with thee to help. *2 Ch.* 14: 11.

Power belongeth unto God. *Ps.* 62: 11.

Above all that we ask or think. *Ep.* 3: 20.

Strengthened with all might, according to his glorious power. *Col.* 1: 11.

The power of an endless life. *He.* 7: 16.

I heard as it were the voice of a great multitude, and as the voice of many waters, and as the voice of mighty thunderings, saying, Alleluia: for the Lord God omnipotent reigneth. *Re.* 19: 6.

See also
Christ, Power of; Christ, Strength of; God, Omnipotence of; God, Power of; God, Strength of; Might; Power; Strength.

Omnipresence

Thou God seest me. *Ge.* 16: 13.

Bless the Lord, all his works in all places of his dominion: bless the Lord, O my soul. *Ps.* 103: 22.

Whither shall I go from thy spirit? or whither shall I flee from thy presence? *Ps.* 139: 7.

The eyes of the Lord are in every place, beholding the evil and the good. *Pr.* 15: 3.

His train filled the temple. *Is.* 6: 1.

Do not I fill heaven and earth? saith the Lord. *Je.* 23: 24.

In every place incense shall be offered unto my name. *Mal.* 1: 11.

Now thanks be unto God, which always causeth us to triumph in Christ, and maketh manifest the savour of his knowledge by us in every place. *2 Co.* 2: 14.

In every place your faith to God-ward is spread abroad. *1 Th.* 1: 8.

See also

God, Omnipresence of; God, Presence of.

Omniscience

He looketh to the ends of the earth, and seeth under the whole heaven. *Jb.* 28: 24.

Thou understandest my thought afar off. *Ps.* 139: 2.

The ways of man are before the eyes of the Lord, and he pondereth all his goings. *Pr.* 5: 21.

I know thy abode, and thy going out, and thy coming in, and thy rage against me. *Is.* 37: 28.

Your Father knoweth what things ye have need of, before ye ask him. *Mat.* 6: 8.

Thou, Lord, . . . knowest the hearts of all men. *Ac.* 1: 24.

The manifold wisdom of God. *Ep.* 3: 10.

See also

God, Knowledge of; God, Omniscience of; God, Wisdom of.

Oneness

They shall be one flesh. *Ge.* 2: 24.

Hear, O Israel: the Lord our God is one Lord. *De.* 6: 4.

One thing have I desired of the Lord. *Ps.* 27: 4.

One thing I know. *Jn.* 9: 25.

To us there is but . . . one Lord Jesus Christ. *1 Co.* 8: 6.

Ye are all the children of God by faith in Christ Jesus. *Ga.* 3: 26.

Endeavouring to keep the unity of the Spirit in the bond of peace. *Ep.* 4: 3.

One Lord, one faith, one baptism, One God and Father of all, who is above all, and through all, and in you all. *Ep.* 4: 5, 6.

The unity of the faith. *Ep.* 4: 13.

This one thing I do. *Ph.* 3: 13.

See also

Agreement; Concord; God, Unity of; Harmony; Integration; Monotheism; Unanimity; Uniformity; Unity.

Opening

They lodged round about the house of God, because . . . the opening thereof every morning pertained to them. *1 Ch.* 9: 27.

He shutteth up a man, and there can be no opening. *Jb.* 12: 14.

Lift up your heads, O ye gates; even lift them up, ye everlasting doors; and the King of glory shall come in. *Ps.* 24: 9.

Wisdom crieth . . . in the openings of the gates. *Pr.* 1: 20, 21.

I will speak of excellent things; and the opening of my lips shall be right things. *Pr.* 8: 6.

The windows from on high are open. *Is.* 24: 18.

Open ye the gates, that the righteous nation which keepeth the truth may enter in. *Is.* 26: 2.

He hath sent me . . . to proclaim liberty to the captives, and the opening of the prison to them that are bound. *Is.* 61: 1.

His windows being open in his chamber toward Jerusalem, he kneeled upon his knees three times a day, and prayed. *Da.* 6: 10.

Prove me now herewith, saith the Lord of hosts, if I will not open you the windows of heaven, and pour you out a blessing, that there shall not be room enough to receive it. *Mal.* 3: 10.

Knock, and it shall be opened unto you. *Mat.* 7: 7.

Hereafter ye shall see heaven open. *Jn.* 1: 51.

Behold, I have set before thee an open door, and no man can shut it. *Re.* 3: 8.

See also

Christ, the Door; Door; Entrance; Gate.

Operation

The Lord is a God of knowledge, and by him actions are weighed. *1 S.* 2: 3.

I have performed the commandment of the Lord. *1 S.* 15: 13.

They regard not the works of the Lord, nor the operation of his hands. *Ps.* 28: 5.

The Lord . . . shall be wroth as in the valley of Gibeon, that he may do his work, his strange work; and bring to pass his act, his strange act. *Is.* 28: 21.

Execute true judgments, and shew mercy and compassion every man to his brother. *Zch.* 7: 9.

Speak ye every man the truth to his neighbour; execute the judgment of truth and peace in your gates. *Zch.* 8: 16.

Blessed is she that believed: for there shall be a performance of those things which were told her from the Lord. *Lk.* 1: 45.

What shall we do, that we might work the works of God? *Jn.* 6: 28.

All things work together for good to them that love God. *Ro.* 8: 28.

There are differences of administrations, but the same Lord. *1 Co.* 12: 5.

There are diversities of operations, but it is the same God which worketh all in all. *1 Co.* 12: 6.

Now therefore perform the doing of it; that as there was a readiness to will, so there may be a performance also out of that which ye have. *2 Co.* 8: 11.

I also labour, striving according to his working, which worketh in me mightily. *Col.* 1: 29.

Ye are risen with him through the faith of the operation of God. *Col.* 2: 12.

See also

Action; Administration; Christ, Work of; Deed; Execution; Performance; Work.

Opponent

What are we, that ye murmur against us? *Ex.* 16: 7.

I will be an enemy unto thine enemies, and an adversary unto thine adversaries. *Ex.* 23: 22.

Behold, every man's sword was against his fellow, and there was a very great discomfiture. *1 S.* 14: 20.

We will be with thee in the war. *2 Ch.* **18: 3**

Thou art become cruel to me: with thy strong hand thou opposest thyself against me. *Jb.* **30: 21.**

O God, how long shall the adversary reproach? shall the enemy blaspheme thy name for ever? *Ps.* **74: 10.**

They compassed me about also with words of hatred; and fought against me without a cause. *Ps.* **109: 3.**

They have rewarded me evil for good, and hatred for my love. *Ps.* **109: 5.**

I am for peace: but when I speak, they are for war. *Ps.* **120: 7.**

He that is not with me is against me. *Lu.* **11: 23.**

When they opposed themselves, and blasphemed, he shook his raiment, and said unto them, Your blood be upon your own heads. *Ac.* **18: 6.**

We can do nothing against the truth, but for the truth. *2 Co.* **13: 8.**

The flesh lusteth against the Spirit, and the Spirit against the flesh: and these are contrary the one to the other. *Ga.* **5: 17.**

We wrestle not against flesh and blood, but against principalities, against powers, against the rulers of the darkness of this world, against spiritual wickedness in high places. *Ep.* **6: 12.**

That man of sin . . . opposeth and exalteth himself above all that is called God, or that is worshipped. *2 Th.* **2: 3, 4.**

Keep that which is committed to thy trust, avoiding . . . oppositions of science, falsely so called. *1 Ti.* **6: 20.**

Consider him that endured such contradiction of sinners against himself, lest ye be wearied and faint in your minds. *He.* **12: 3.**

Even now are there many antichrists. *1 Jn.* **2: 18.**

See also
Adversary; Antagonism; Enemy; Foe; God, Antagonism to; God, Rebellion against; Opposition; Resistance.

Opportunity

As thy servant was busy here and there, he was gone. *1 K.* **20: 40.**

Thou shouldest have smitten five or six times; then hadst thou smitten Syria till thou hadst consumed it. *2 K.* **13: 19.**

Who knoweth whether thou art come to the kingdom for such a time as this? *Es.* **4: 14.**

At our gates are all manner of pleasant fruits, new and old. *S of S.* **7: 13.**

What could have been done more to my vineyard, that I have not done in it? wherefore, when I looked that it should bring forth grapes, brought it forth wild grapes? *Is.* **5: 4.**

The harvest is past, the summer is ended, and we are not saved. *Je.* **8: 20.**

What meanest thou, O sleeper? arise, call upon thy God. *Jon.* **1: 6.**

Watch therefore: for ye know not what hour your Lord cometh. *Mat.* **24: 42.**

While they went to buy, the bridegroom came; and they that were ready went in with him to the marriage: and the door was shut. *Mat.* **25: 10.**

Inasmuch as ye did it not to one of the least of these, ye did it not to me. *Mat.* **25: 45.**

Unto none of them was Elias sent, save unto Sarepta, a city of Sidon. *Lu.* **4: 26.**

It shall be more tolerable in that day for Sodom. *Lu.* **10: 12.**

He called his ten servants, and delivered them ten pounds, and said unto them, Occupy till I come. *Lu.* **19: 13.**

Lift up your eyes, and look on the fields; for they are white already to harvest. *Jn.* **4: 35.**

I must work the works of him that sent me, while it is day: the night cometh, when no man can work. *Jn.* **9: 4.**

Jesus . . . lifted his eyes to heaven, and said, Father, the hour is come. *Jn.* **17: 1.**

Almost thou persuadest me to be a Christian. *Ac.* **26: 28.**

Sin, taking occasion by the commandment, wrought in me. *Ro.* **7: 8.**

Now it is high time to awake out of sleep. *Ro.* **13: 11.**

Now is our salvation nearer than when we believed. *Ro.* **13: 11.**

Behold, now is the accepted time; behold, now is the day of salvation. *2 Co.* **6: 2.**

As we have therefore opportunity, let us do good unto all men. *Ga.* **6: 10.**

Ye lacked opportunity. *Ph.* **4: 10.**

Walk in wisdom toward them that are without, redeeming the time. *Col.* **4: 5.**

The Holy Ghost saith, To day. *He.* **3: 7.**

If they had been mindful of that country from whence they came out, they might have had opportunity to have returned. *He.* **11: 15.**

Let him that is athirst come. And whosoever will, let him take the water of life freely. *Re.* **22: 17.**

See also
Chance; Chance, the Second; Occasion.

Opposition

I will beat down his foes before his face, and plague them that hate him. *Ps.* **89: 23.**

Prophesy not unto us right things, speak unto us smooth things, prophesy deceits. *Is.* **30: 10.**

Prophesy not in the name of the Lord, that thou die not by our hand. *Je.* **11: 21.**

I say unto you, Love your enemies, bless them that curse you, do good to them that hate you, and pray for them which despitefully use you, and persecute you. *Mat.* **5: 44.**

I give you power to tread on serpents and scorpions, and over all the power of the enemy: and nothing shall by any means hurt you. *Lu.* **10: 19.**

Ye do always resist the Holy Ghost: as your fathers did, so do ye. *Ac.* **7: 51.**

It is hard for thee to kick against the pricks. *Ac.* **26: 14.**

For we wrestle not against flesh and blood, but against principalities, against powers, against the rulers of the darkness of this world, against spiritual wickedness in high places. *Ep.* **6: 12.**

That ye may be able to withstand in the evil day. *Ep.* **6: 13.**

The son of perdition; Who opposeth and exalteth himself above all that is called God, or that is worshipped. *2 Th.* **2: 3, 4.**

Keep that which is committed to thy trust, avoiding . . . oppositions of science falsely so called. *1 Ti.* **6: 20.**

So do these also resist the truth: men of corrupt minds, reprobate concerning the faith. *2 Ti.* **3: 8.**

Consider him that endured such contradiction of sinners against himself. *He.* **12: 3.**

Whom resist stedfast in the faith. *1 Pe.* **5: 9.**

See also

Animosity; Antagonism; Antipathy; Antithesis; Bar; Contradiction; Difficulty; Enemy; Foe; Frustration; Hostility; **Obstruction;** Opposition; Resistance.

Oppression

Ye shall not oppress one another. *Le.* **25: 14.**

The Lord heard our voice, and looked on our affliction, and our labour, and our oppression. *De.* **26: 7.**

The Lord also will be a refuge for the oppressed, a refuge in times of trouble. *Ps.* **9: 9.**

To judge the fatherless and the oppressed, that the man of the earth may no more oppress. *Ps.* **10: 18.**

He shall judge the poor of the people, he shall save the children of the needy, and shall break in pieces the oppressor. *Ps.* **72: 4.**

Let not the proud oppress me. *Ps.* **119: 122.**

Deliver me from the oppression of man. *Ps.* **119: 134.**

Envy thou not the oppressor. *Pr.* **3: 31.**

He that oppresseth the poor reproacheth his Maker. *Pr.* **14: 31.**

On the side of their oppressors there was power; but they had no comforter. *Ec.* **4: 1.**

Seek judgment, relieve the oppressed, judge the fatherless, plead for the widow. *Is.* **1: 17.**

Thou shalt be far from oppression; for thou shalt not fear. *Is.* **54: 14.**

Blessed are they which are persecuted for righteousness' sake. *Mat.* **5: 10.**

If they have persecuted me, they will also persecute you; if they have kept my saying, they will keep yours also. *Jn.* **15: 20.**

Jesus . . . went about doing good, and healing all that were oppressed of the devil. *Ac.* **10: 38.**

See also

Autocrat; Bondage; Burden; Care; Cruelty; Despot; Harshness; Melancholy; Repression; Sorrow; Suppression; Tyranny; Weight; Yoke.

Optimism

There be many that say, Who will shew us any good? Lord, lift thou up the light of thy countenance upon us. *Ps.* **4: 6.**

Thou shalt not be afraid for the terror by night; . . . the pestilence that walketh in darkness. *Ps.* **91: 5, 6.**

The people which sat in darkness saw great light. *Mat.* **4: 16.**

Great is thy faith: be it unto thee even as thou wilt. *Mat.* **15: 28.**

When these things begin to come to pass, then look up, and lift up your heads; for your redemption draweth nigh. *Lu.* **21: 28.**

Be of good cheer. *Jn.* **16: 33.**

Blessed are they that have not seen, and yet have believed. *Jn.* **20: 29.**

Rejoice in hope. *Ro.* **12: 12.**

I thank my God always on your behalf, for the grace of God which is given you by Jesus Christ. *1 Co.* **1: 4.**

Charity . . . Beareth all things, believeth all things, hopeth all things, endureth all things. *1 Co.* **13: 4, 7.**

Walk as children of light. *Ep.* **5: 8.**

Christ in you, the hope of glory. *Col.* **1: 27.**

Now faith is the substance of things hoped for, the evidence of things not seen. *He.* **11: 1.**

See also

Belief; Best; Faith; Hope.

Option

Behold, I set before you this day a blessing and a curse; A blessing, if ye obey the commandments of the Lord your God, which I command you this day: And a curse, if ye will not obey the commandments of the Lord your God. *De.* **11: 26-28.**

Choose you this day whom ye will serve. *Jos.* **24: 15.**

Ye are witnesses against yourselves that ye have chosen you the Lord, to serve him. *Jos.* **24: 22.**

A good name is rather to be chosen than great riches. *Pr.* **22: 1.**

He that is not with me is against me. *Mat.* **12: 30.**

Whom will ye that I release unto you? *Mat.* **27: 17.**

What I shall choose I wot not. *Ph.* **1: 22.**

I am in a strait betwixt two. *Ph.* **1: 23.**

As free, and not using your liberty for a cloke of maliciousness, but as the servants of God. *1 Pe.* **2: 16.**

Whosoever will, let him take the water of life freely. *Re.* **22: 17.**

See also

Choice.

Oracle

The priests brought in the ark of the covenant of the Lord unto his place, to the oracle of the house, into the most holy place, even under the wings of the cherubim. *2 Ch.* **5: 7.**

Hear the voice of my supplications, when I cry unto thee, when I lift up my hands toward thy holy oracle. *Ps.* **28: 2.**

Blessed be the name of God for ever and ever. . . . He revealeth the deep and secret things. *Da.* **2: 20, 22.**

Your God is . . . a revealer of secrets. *Da.* **2: 47.**

This is that Moses, . . . who received the lively oracles to give unto us. *Ac.* **7: 37, 38.**

Unto them were committed the oracles of God. *Ro.* **3: 2.**

Ye have need that one teach you again which be the first principles of the oracles of God. *He.* **5: 12.**

If any man speak, let him speak as the oracles of God. *1 Pe.* **4: 11.**

See also

God, House of; God, Revelation of; God, Word of; Revelation; Temple.

Orchard

God said, Let the earth bring forth . . . the fruit tree yielding fruit after his kind. *Ge.* **1: 11.**

Out of the ground made the Lord God to grow every tree that is pleasant to the sight, and good for food. *Ge.* **2: 9.**

When thou beatest thine olive tree, thou shalt not go over the boughs again: it shall be for the stranger, for the fatherless, and for the widow. *De.* 24: 20.

He shall be like a tree planted by the rivers of water. *Ps.* 1: 3.

Fruitful trees, . . . Let them praise the name of the Lord. *Ps.* 148: 9, 13.

I made me gardens and orchards, and I planted trees in them of all kind of fruits. *Ec.* 2: 5.

A time to plant, and a time to pluck up that which is planted. *Ec.* 3: 2.

Thy plants are an orchard of pomegranates, with pleasant fruits. *S. of S.* 4: 13.

Plant gardens, and eat the fruit of them. *Je.* 29: 5.

Every tree is known by his own fruit. *Lu.* 6: 44.

See also

Fruit; Garden; Tree.

Order

Thus saith the Lord, Set thine house in order; for thou shalt die, and not live. *2 K.* 20: 1.

A land of darkness, as darkness itself; and of the shadow of death, without any order, and where the light is as darkness. *Jb.* 10: 22.

Hast thou commanded the morning since thy days? *Jb.* 38: 12.

Doth the eagle mount up at thy command? *Jb.* 39: 27.

He spake, and it was done. *Ps.* 33: 9.

The steps of a good man are ordered by the Lord. *Ps.* 37: 23.

Order my steps in thy word. *Ps.* 119: 133.

If thou be the Son of God, command that these stones be made bread. *Mat.* 4: 3.

First the blade, then the ear, after that the full corn in the ear. *Mk.* 4: 28.

He had commanded the unclean spirit to come out of the man. *Lu.* 8: 29.

These things I command you, that ye love one another. *Jn.* 15: 17.

He commanded us to preach unto the people. *Ac.* 10: 42.

Peter rehearsed the matter from the beginning, and expounded it by order unto them. *Ac.* 11: 4.

The times of this ignorance God winked at; but now commandeth all men every where to repent. *Ac.* 17: 30.

Let all things be done decently and in order. *1 Co.* 14: 40.

That was not first which is spiritual, but that which is natural; and afterward that which is spiritual. *1 Co.* 15: 46.

I am with you in the spirit, joying and beholding your order, and the stedfastness of your faith in Christ. *Col.* 2: 5.

See also

Calm; Commandment; Decree; Law; Ordinance; Peace; Quiet; Rule; Statute; Stillness; Symmetry; Tranquillity.

Ordinance

O that there were such an heart in them, that they would fear me, and keep all my commandments always! *De.* 5: 29.

I command thee this day to love the Lord thy God, to walk in his ways, and to keep his commandments and his statutes and his judgments. *De.* 30: 16.

Knowest thou the ordinances of heaven? *Jb.* 38: 33.

The statutes of the Lord are right, rejoicing the heart: the commandment of the Lord is pure, enlightening the eyes. *Ps.* 19: 8.

Even from the days of your fathers ye are gone away from mine ordinances. *Mal.* 3: 7.

If thou wilt enter into life, keep the commandments. *Mat.* 19: 17.

They were both righteous before God, walking in all the commandments and ordinances of the Lord blameless. *Lu.* 1: 6.

All things must be fulfilled, which were written in the law of Moses, and in the prophets, and in the psalms, concerning me. *Lu.* 24: 44.

The law is holy, and the commandment holy, and just, and good. *Ro.* 7: 12.

Whosoever therefore resisteth the power, resisteth the ordinance of God. *Ro.* 13: 2.

No man is justified by the law in the sight of God. *Ga.* 3: 11.

The first covenant had also ordinances of divine service, and a worldly sanctuary. *He.* 9: 1.

Carnal ordinances, imposed on them until the time of reformation. *He.* 9: 10.

See also

Commandment; Decree; God, Commandment of; God, Law of; Law; Statute.

Ordination

The moon and the stars, which thou hast ordained. *Ps.* 8: 3.

I ordained thee a prophet unto the nations. *Je.* 1: 5.

I have this day set thee over the nations and over the kingdoms. *Je.* 1: 10.

So thou, O son of man, I have set thee a watchman unto the house of Israel. *Eze.* 33: 7.

He ordained twelve, that they should be with him. *Mk.* 3: 14.

The powers that be are ordained of God. *Ro.* 13: 1.

The hidden mystery, which God ordained before the world unto our glory. *1 Co.* 2: 7.

Even so hath the Lord ordained that they which preach the gospel should live of the gospel. *1 Co.* 9: 14.

I am ordained a preacher, and an apostle, . . . a teacher of the Gentiles in faith and verity. *1 Ti.* 2: 7.

That thou shouldest . . . ordain elders in every city, as I had appointed thee. *Tit.* 1: 5.

Every high priest taken from among men is ordained for men in things pertaining to God. *He.* 5: 1.

See also

Anointing; Consecration; Dedication; Inauguration; Installation; Ministry; Missionary; Pastor; Priesthood.

Origin

In the beginning God created the heaven and the earth. *Ge.* 1: 1.

God created man in his own image. *Ge.* 1: 27.

These are the generations of the heavens and of the earth when they were created. *Ge.* 2: 4.

God brought him forth out of Egypt. *Nu.* 24: 8.

Whence comest thou? what is thy country?

and of what people art thou? *Jon.* 1: 8.

I came down from heaven, not to do mine own will, but the will of him that sent me. *Jn.* 6: 38.

I came forth from the Father, and am come into the world. *Jn.* 16: 28.

We believe that thou camest forth from God. *Jn.* 16: 30.

The disciples were called Christians first in Antioch. *Ac.* 11: 26.

These are they which came out of great tribulation, and have washed their robes, and made them white in the blood of the Lamb. *Re.* 7: 14.

See also

Beginning; Christ, the Creator; Commencement; Creation; Creator; First; Foundation; Genesis; God, the Creator; Source.

Ornament

They shall be an ornament of grace unto thy head. *Pr.* 1: 9.

Wisdom . . . shall give to thine head an ornament of grace: a crown of glory shall she deliver to thee. *Pr.* 4: 7, 9.

As a jewel of gold in a swine's snout, so is a fair woman which is without discretion. *Pr.* 11: 22.

The lips of knowledge are a precious jewel. *Pr.* 20: 15.

As an earring of gold, and an ornament of fine gold, so is a wise reprover upon an obedient ear. *Pr.* 25: 12.

Thou shalt surely clothe thee with them all, as with an ornament, and bind them on thee, as a bride doeth. *Is.* 49: 18.

Can a maid forget her ornaments, or a bride her attire? yet my people have forgotten me days without number. *Je.* 2: 32.

They shall be mine, saith the Lord of hosts, in that day when I make up my jewels. *Mal.* 3: 17.

The ornament of a meek and quiet spirit, which is in the sight of God of great price. *1 Pe.* 3: 4.

I John saw the holy city, new Jerusalem, coming down from God out of heaven, prepared as a bride adorned for her husband. *Re.* 21: 2.

See also

Adornment; Beauty.

Orphan

Ye shall not afflict any . . . fatherless child. *Ex.* 22: 22.

The stranger, and the fatherless, and the widow, which are within thy gates, shall come, and shall eat and be satisfied. *De.* 14: 29.

If I have lifted up my hand against the fatherless, . . . Then let mine arm fall from my shoulder blade. *Jb.* 31: 21, 22.

Thou art the helper of the fatherless. *Ps.* 10: 14.

Enter not into the fields of the fatherless. *Pr.* 23: 10.

We are orphans and fatherless. *La.* 5: 3.

In thee the fatherless findeth mercy. *Ho.* 14: 3.

I will be a swift witness against . . . those that oppress . . . the fatherless. *Mal.* 3: 5.

Pure religion and undefiled before God and the Father is this, To visit the fatherless and widows in their affliction. *Ja.* 1: 27.

Orthodoxy

Thou hast said, My doctrine is pure. *Jb.* 11: 4.

Therefore I esteem all thy precepts concerning all things to be right. *Ps.* 119: 128.

I give you good doctrine. *Pr.* 4: 2.

When the Son of man cometh, shall he find faith on the earth? *Lu.* 18: 8.

Neither against the law of the Jews, neither against the temple, nor yet against Caesar, have I offended any thing at all. *Ac.* 25: 8.

That thou mightest charge some that they teach no other doctrine. *1 Ti.* 1: 3.

A teacher of the Gentiles in faith and verity. *Ti.* 2: 7.

Nourished up in the words of faith and of good doctrine. *1 Ti.* 4: 6.

Take heed unto thyself, and unto the doctrine. *1 Ti.* 4: 16.

Holding fast the faithful word as he hath been taught, that he may be able by sound doctrine both to exhort and to convince the gainsayers. *Tit.* 1: 9.

Speak thou the things which become sound doctrine. *Tit.* 2: 1.

That ye should earnestly contend for the faith which was once delivered unto the saints. *Jude* 1: 3.

See also

Christ, Truth of; Creed; Denomination; Doctrine; Dogma; God, Truth of; Heresy; Tenet; Truth; Unorthodoxy.

Ostentation

Let us make us a name. *Ge.* 11: 4.

I lift up my hand to heaven, and say, I live for ever. *De.* 32: 40.

Come thou, and reign over us. *Ju.* 9: 10.

How long will ye love vanity? *Ps.* 4: 2.

The wicked boasteth of his heart's desire. *Ps.* 10: 3.

Thou . . . wilt bring down high looks. *Ps.* 18: 27.

Every man walketh in a vain shew. *Ps.* 39: 6.

Their inward thought is, that their houses shall continue for ever, and their dwelling places to all generations; they call their lands after their own names. *Ps.* 49: 11.

Lift not up your horn on high. *Ps.* 75: 5.

Most men will proclaim every one his own goodness. *Pr.* 20: 6.

Thou saidst, I shall be a lady for ever. *Is.* 47: 7.

Neither do men light a candle, and put it under a bushel. *Mat.* 5: 15.

That which ye have spoken in the ear in closets shall be proclaimed upon the house tops. *Lu.* 12: 3.

I thank thee that I am not as other men are. *Lu.* 18: 11.

Every one that exalteth himself shall be abased. *Lu.* 18: 14.

The scribes . . . for a shew make long prayers. *Lu.* 20: 46, 47.

See also

Arrogance; Boasting; Braggart; Pomp; Pride.

Otherworldliness

The prince of this world cometh, and hath nothing in me. *Jn.* 14: 30.

Be not conformed to this world. *Ro.* 12: 2.

I knew such a man, . . . How that he was

caught up into paradise. *2 Co.* **12: 3, 4.**

In heavenly places. *Ep.* **1: 3.**

Set your affection on things above, not on things on the earth. *Col.* **3: 2.**

As obedient children, not fashioning yourselves according to the former lusts. *1 Pe.* **1: 14.**

If any man love the world, the love of the Father is not in him. *1 Jn.* **2: 15.**

The world passeth away, and the lust thereof: but he that doeth the will of God abideth for ever. *1 Jn.* **2: 17.**

See also

Devoutness; Godliness; Holiness; Piety; Saint; Sanctification; Worldliness.

Outcast

See that ye fall not out by the way. *Ge.* **45: 24.**

Ye were the fewest of all people. *De.* **7: 7.**

Why dost thou cast me off? *Ps.* **43: 2.**

Why sleepest thou, O Lord? arise, cast us not off for ever. *Ps.* **44: 23.**

The wicked is driven away in his wickedness. *Pr.* **14: 32.**

I will cast you out of my sight. *Je.* **7: 15.**

I will heal thee of thy wounds, saith the Lord: because they called thee an Outcast. *Je.* **30: 17.**

I am cast out of thy sight; yet I will look again toward thy holy temple. *Jon.* **2: 4.**

The children of the kingdom shall be cast out into outer darkness. *Mat.* **8: 12.**

Him that cometh to me I will in no wise cast out. *Jn.* **6: 37.**

Every branch in me that beareth not fruit he taketh away. *Jn.* **15: 2.**

If a man abide not in me, he is cast forth as a branch. *Jn.* **15: 6.**

The great day of his wrath is come; and who shall be able to stand? *Re.* **6: 17.**

See also

Banishment; Exile; Expatriation.

Outgrowth

Out of the earth shall others grow. *Jb.* **8: 19.**

He cometh forth like a flower, and is cut down. *Jb.* **14: 2.**

Thou washest away the things which grow out of the dust of the earth. *Jb.* **14: 19.**

There shall come forth a rod out of the stem of Jesse, and a Branch shall grow out of his roots. *Is.* **11: 1.**

I am the vine, ye are the branches. *Jn.* **15: 5.**

If the root be holy, so are the branches. *Ro.* **11: 16.**

See also

Branch.

Outlook

Lot lifted up his eyes, and beheld all the plain of Jordan, that it was well watered everywhere. *Ge.* **13: 10.**

Lift up now thine eyes, and look from the place where thou art. *Ge.* **13: 14.**

Moses went up from the plains of Moab unto the mountain of Nebo, to the top of Pisgah, . . . And the Lord shewed him all the land. *De.* **34: 1.**

I have caused thee to see it with thine eyes, but thou shalt not go over thither. *De.* **34: 4.**

Lord, I pray thee, open his eyes that he may see. *2 K.* **6: 17.**

Mine eyes are ever toward the Lord. *Ps.* **25: 15.**

I will lift up mine eyes unto the hills, from whence cometh my help. *Ps.* **121: 1.**

Looking unto Jesus. *He.* **12: 2.**

See also

Christ, Vision of; Eye; God, Vision of; Perception; Prospect; Sight; Spectator; Vision.

Outside

Wisdom crieth without; she uttereth her voice in the streets. *Pr.* **1: 20.**

Wisdom . . . crieth at the gates, at the entry of the city, at the coming in at the doors. *Pr.* **8: 1, 3.**

They that were ready went in with him to the marriage: and the door was shut. *Mat.* **25: 10.**

Jesus could no more openly enter into the city, but was without in desert places. *Mk.* **1: 45.**

There is nothing from without a man, that entering into him can defile him: but the things which come out of him, those are they that defile the man. *Mk.* **7: 15.**

Now do ye Pharisees make clean the outside of the cup and the platter; but your inward part is full of ravening and wickedness. *Lu.* **11: 39.**

Did not he that made that which is without make that which is within also? *Lu.* **11: 40.**

There is nothing covered, that shall not be revealed; neither hid, that shall not be known. *Lu.* **12: 2.**

Them that are without God judgeth. *1 Co.* **5: 13.**

Without were fightings, within were fears. *2 Co.* **7: 5.**

Jesus . . . suffered without the gate. *He.* **13: 12.**

See also

Exterior; Inside; Interior.

Overflow

The waters prevailed exceedingly upon the earth; and all the high hills, that were under the whole heaven, were covered. *Ge.* **7: 19.**

The Lord shall give you in the evening flesh to eat, and in the morning bread to the full. *Ex.* **16: 8.**

Jordan overfloweth all his banks all the time of harvest. *Jos.* **3: 15.**

He bindeth the floods from overflowing. *Jb.* **28: 11.**

My cup runneth over. *Ps.* **23: 5.**

Let not the waterflood overflow me. *Ps.* **69: 15.**

When thou passest through the waters, I will be with thee; and through the rivers, they shall not overflow thee: when thou walkest through the fire, thou shalt not be burned; neither shall the flame kindle upon thee. *Is.* **43: 2.**

The mountains saw thee and they trembled: the overflowing of the water passed by. *Hab.* **3: 10.**

Prove me now herewith, saith the Lord of hosts, if I will not open you the windows of heaven, and pour you out a blessing, that there shall not be room enough to receive it. *Mal.* **3: 10.**

Give, and it shall be given unto you; good measure, pressed down, and shaken together, and running over, shall men give into your bosom. *Lu.* 6: 37.

Overthrow

Ye shall overthrow their altars. *De.* 12: 3.

How are the mighty fallen! *2 S.* 1: 19.

He overturneth the mountains by the roots. *Jb.* 28: 9.

A thousand shall fall at thy side, and ten thousand at thy right hand; but it shall not come nigh thee. *Ps.* 91: 7.

The Lord upholdeth all that fall. *Ps.* 145: 14.

The way of the wicked he turneth upside down. *Ps.* 146: 9.

God overthroweth the wicked for their wickedness. *Pr.* 21: 12.

A just man falleth seven times, and riseth up again. *Pr.* 24: 16.

Rejoice not when thine enemy falleth, and let not thine heart be glad when he stumbleth. *Pr.* 24: 17.

Whosoever shall fall on this stone shall be broken: but on whomsoever it shall fall, it will grind him to powder. *Mat.* 21: 44.

I beheld Satan as lightning fall from heaven. *Lu.* 10: 18.

If it be of God ye cannot overthrow it. *Ac.* 5: 39.
See also
Collapse; Defeat; Destruction; Failure; Fall; Ruin.

Ownership

The land shall be before you; dwell and trade ye therein, and get you possessions therein. *Ge.* 34: 10.

Ye shall be a peculiar treasure unto me above all people: for all the earth is mine. *Ex.* 19: 5.

The land shall not be sold for ever: for the land is mine. *Le.* 25: 23.

Ye shall go over, and possess that good land. *De.* 4: 22.

All things come of thee, and of thine own have we given thee. *1 Ch.* 29: 14.

The earth is the Lord's, and the fulness thereof. *Ps.* 24: 1.

When goods increase, they are increased that eat them: and what good is there to the owners thereof. *Ec.* 5: 11.

The ox knoweth his owner, and the ass his master's crib: but Israel doth not know, my people doth not consider. *Is.* 1: 3.

He that putteth his trust in me shall possess the land, and shall inherit my holy mountain. *Is.* 57: 13.

Behold, all souls are mine. *Eze.* 18: 4.

The silver is mine, and the gold is mine, saith the Lord of hosts. *Hag.* 2: 8.

Soul, thou hast much goods laid up for many years. *Lu.* 12: 19.

Whether we live, we live unto the Lord; and whether we die, we die unto the Lord: whether we live therefore, or die, we are the Lord's. *Ro.* 14: 8.

All things are yours; Whether Paul, or Apollos, or Cephas, or the world, or life, or death, or things present, or things to come; all are yours; And ye are Christ's; and Christ is God's. *1 Co.* 3: 21–23.

As having nothing, and yet possessing all things. *2 Co.* 6: 10.

In whom we have . . . the forgiveness of sins. *Ep.* 1: 7.

Knowing in yourselves that ye have in heaven a better and an enduring substance. *He.* 10: 34.
See also
Possession.

Ox

Thou shalt not covet thy neighbour's . . . ox. *Ex.* 20: 17.

Thou hast put all things under his feet: All sheep and oxen. *Ps.* 8: 6, 7.

I will praise the name of God with a song. . . . This also shall please the Lord better than an ox. *Ps.* 69: 30, 31.

Better is a dinner of herbs where love is, than a stalled ox and hatred therewith. *Pr.* 15: 17.

The ox knoweth his owner. *Is.* 1: 3.

The lion shall eat straw like the ox. *Is.* 11: 7.

They shall make thee to eat grass as oxen. *Da.* 4: 25.

Doth God take care for oxen? *1 Co.* 9: 9.
See also
Cattle.

P

Pacifist

To the counsellors of peace is joy. *Pr.* 12: 20.

The wrath of a king is as messengers of death: but a wise man will pacify it. *Pr.* 16: 14.

A gift in secret pacifieth anger. *Pr.* 21: 14.

Yielding pacifieth great offences. *Ec.* 10: 4.

His name shall be called . . . The Prince of Peace. *Is.* 9: 6.

How beautiful upon the mountains are the feet of him that bringeth good tidings, that publisheth peace. *Is.* 52: 7.

Saying, Peace, peace; when there is no peace. *Je.* 6: 14.

I . . . will save them by the Lord their God, and will not save them by bow, nor by sword,

nor by battle, by horses, nor by horsemen. *Ho.* 1: 7.

Blessed are the peacemakers: for they shall be called the children of God. *Mat.* 5: 9.

Love ye your enemies, and do good, . . . and ye shall be the children of the Highest. *Lu.* 6: 35.

If thine enemy hunger, feed him; if he thirst, give him drink: for in so doing thou shalt heap coals of fire on his head. *Ro.* 12: 20.

Let us therefore follow after the things which make for peace. *Ro.* 14: 19.

God hath called us to peace. *1 Co.* 7: 15.

The weapons of our warfare are not carnal, but mighty through God to the pulling down

of strong holds. *2 Co.* 10: 4.
See also
Nonresistance; Peace; War.

Pagan

I will give thanks unto thee, O Lord, among the heathen. *2 S.* 22: 50.

Why do the heathen rage? *Ps.* 2: 1.

God reigneth over the heathen. *Ps.* 47: 8.

The heathen shall fear the name of the Lord. *Ps.* 102: 15.

They shall declare my glory among the Gentiles. *Is.* 66: 19.

Learn not the way of the heathen. *Je.* 10: 2.

Men shall worship him, every one from his place, even all the isles of the heathen. *Zph.* 2: 11.

There is no respect of persons with God. *Ro.* 2: 11.

Rejoice, ye Gentiles, with his people. *Ro.* 15: 10.

See also
Alien; Foreigner; Gentile; Heathen; Stranger.

Pain

The wicked man travaileth with pain all his days. *Jb.* 15: 20.

He is chastened also with pain upon his bed. *Jo.* 33: 19.

He hath torn, and he will heal us: he hath smitten, and he will bind us up. *Ho.* 6: 1.

They brought unto him all sick people that were taken with divers diseases and torments. *Mat.* 4: 24.

Him . . . God hath raised up, having loosed the pains of death. *Ac.* 2: 23, 24.

We know that the whole creation groaneth and travaileth in pain together unto now. *Ro.* 8: 22.

In weariness and painfulness. *2 Co.* 11: 27.

Yet learned he obedience by the things which he suffered. *He.* 5: 8.

There shall be no more death, neither sorrow, nor crying, neither shall there be any more pain. *Re.* 21: 4.

See also
Affliction; Agony; Anguish; Distress; Grief; Harm; Hurt; Injury; Misery; Torment; Wound.

Palace

Think not with thyself that thou shalt escape in the king's house, more than all the Jews. *Es.* 4: 13.

With gladness and rejoicing shall they be brought: they shall enter into the king's palace. *Ps.* 45: 15.

Mark ye well her bulwarks, consider her palaces. *Ps.* 48: 13.

Peace be within thy walls, and prosperity within thy palaces. *Ps.* 122: 7.

The spider taketh hold with her hands, and is in kings' palaces. *Pr.* 30: 28.

The palaces shall be forsaken. *Is.* 32: 14.

Thorns shall come up in her palaces, nettles and brambles in the fortresses thereof. *Is.* 35: 13.

Give ye ear, O house of the king; for judgment is toward you. *Ho.* 5: 1.

Prophesy not again any more at Bethel: for it is the king's chapel, and it is the king's court. *Am.* 7: 13.

They which are gorgeously apparelled, and live delicately, are in kings' courts. *Lu.* 7: 25.

When a strong man armed keepeth his palace, his goods are in peace. *Lu.* 11: 21.

My bonds in Christ are manifest in all the palace, and in all other places. *Ph.* 1: 13.

See also
Castle; Court; God, House of; King.

Palliation

He that justifieth the wicked, and he that condemneth the just, even they both are abomination to the Lord. *Pr.* 17: 15.

He that saith unto the wicked, Thou art righteous; him shall the people curse, nations shall abhor him. *Pr.* 24: 24.

They that forsake the law praise the wicked: but such as keep the law contend with them. *Pr.* 28: 4.

Woe unto them that call evil good, and good evil; that put darkness for light, and light for darkness; that put bitter for sweet, and sweet for bitter! *Is.* 5: 20.

Ye have made the heart of the righteous sad, whom I have not made sad; and strengthened the hands of the wicked, that he would not return from his wicked way, by promising him life. *Eze.* 13: 22.

Wherein have we wearied him? When ye say, Every one that doeth evil is good in the sight of the Lord, and he delighteth in them. *Mal.* 2: 17.

They all with one consent began to make excuse. *Lu.* 14: 18.

Their conscience also bearing witness, and their thoughts the mean while accusing or else excusing one another. *Ro.* 2: 15.

Think ye that we excuse ourselves unto you? *2 Co.* 12: 19.

See also
Excuse; Pardon.

Palm

The righteous shall flourish like the palm tree. *Ps.* 92: 12.

This thy stature is like to a palm tree. *S. of S.* 7: 7.

They are upright as the palm tree, but speak not. *Je.* 10: 5.

The palm tree also, and the apple tree, even all the trees of the field, are withered. *Jo.* 1: 12.

On the next day much people that were come to the feast, when they heard that Jesus was coming to Jerusalem, Took branches of palm trees, and went forth to meet him. *Jn.* 12: 12, 13.

Palm Sunday

Yet have I set my king upon my holy hill of Zion. *Ps.* 2: 6.

The desire of all nations shall come. *Hag.* 2: 7.

Thy kingdom come. *Mat.* 6: 10.

The multitude said, This is Jesus the prophet of Nazareth of Galilee. *Mat.* 21: 11.

When the Son of man shall come in his glory. *Mat.* 25: 31.

All power is given unto me in heaven and in earth. *Mat.* 28: 18.

The whole multitude of the disciples began to rejoice and praise God. *Lu.* 19: 37.

When he was come near, he beheld the city, and wept over it. *Lu.* **19: 41.**

Behold, the world is gone after him. *Jn.* **12: 19.**

Jesus of Nazareth the King of the Jews. *Jn.* **19: 19.**

Now unto the King eternal, immortal, invisible, the only wise God, be honour and glory for ever and ever. Amen. *1 Ti.* **1: 17.**

See also

Christ, Triumph of; Christ, Triumphant Entry of.

Parable

I will incline mine ear to a parable: I will open my dark saying upon the harp. *Ps.* **49: 4.**

I will open my mouth in a parable: I will utter dark sayings of old. *Ps.* **78: 2.**

The legs of the lame are not equal: so is a parable in the mouth of fools. *Pr.* **26: 7.**

Why speakest thou unto them in parables? *Mat.* **13: 10.**

Without a parable spake he not unto them. *Mat.* **13: 34.**

Unto you it is given to know the mystery of the kingdom of God: but unto them that are without, all these things are done in parables. *Mk.* **4: 11.**

To others in parables; that seeing they might not see, and hearing they might not understand. *Lu.* **8: 10.**

See also

Allegory; Christ, the Teacher; Fable.

Paradise

Come, ye blessed of my Father, inherit the kingdom prepared for you from the foundation of the world. *Mat.* **25: 34.**

Behold, your reward is great in heaven. *Lu.* **6: 23.**

Joy shall be in heaven over one sinner that repenteth. *Lu.* **15: 7.**

Carried by the angels into Abraham's bosom. *Lu.* **16: 22.**

To day shalt thou be with me in paradise. *Lu.* **23: 43.**

In my Father's house are many mansions. *Jn.* **14: 2.**

This same Jesus, which is taken up from you into heaven, shall so come in like manner as ye have seen him go into heaven. *Ac.* **1: 11.**

We know that if our earthly house of this tabernacle were dissolved, we have a building of God, a house not made with hands, eternal in the heavens. *2 Co.* **5: 1.**

I knew such a man, . . . How that he was caught up into paradise, and heard unspeakable words, which it is not lawful for a man to utter. *2 Co.* **12: 3, 4.**

Our conversation is in heaven. *Ph.* **3: 20.**

Now they desire a better country, that is, an heavenly. *He.* **11: 16.**

An inheritance incorruptible, and undefiled, and that fadeth not away, reserved in heaven for you. *1 Pe.* **1: 4.**

To him that overcometh will I give to eat of the tree of life, which is in the midst of the paradise of God. *Re.* **2: 7.**

See also

Country, the Better; Eden; Heaven.

Paradox

Ye . . . shall leave me alone: and yet I am not alone, because the Father is with me. *Jn.* **16: 32.**

We are troubled on every side, yet not distressed; we are perplexed, but not in despair; Persecuted, but not forsaken; cast down, but not destroyed. *2 Co.* **4: 8, 9.**

As deceivers, and yet true. *2 Co.* **6: 8.**

As unknown, and yet well known. *2 Co.* **6: 9.**

As dying, and, behold, we live. *2 Co.* **6: 9.**

As sorrowful, yet always rejoicing. *2 Co.* **6: 10.**

As poor, yet making many rich. *2 Co.* **6: 10.**

As having nothing, and yet possessing all things. *2 Co.* **6: 10.**

For your sakes he became poor, that ye through his poverty might be rich. *2 Co.* **8: 9.**

I am crucified with Christ: nevertheless I live; yet not I, but Christ liveth in me. *Ga.* **2: 20.**

Pardon

Who is a God like unto thee, that pardoneth iniquity? *Mi.* **7: 18.**

Forgive us our debts, as we forgive our debtors. *Mat.* **6: 12.**

If ye forgive men their trespasses, your heavenly Father will also forgive you. *Mat.* **6: 14.**

To give knowledge of salvation unto his people by the remission of their sins. *Lu.* **1: 77.**

Take heed to yourselves: If thy brother trespass against thee, rebuke him; and if he repent, forgive him. And if he trespass against thee seven times in a day, and seven times in a day turn again to thee, saying, I repent; thou shalt forgive him. *Lu.* **17: 3, 4.**

Repent ye therefore, and be converted, that your sins may be blotted out. *Ac.* **3: 19.**

If ye through the Spirit do mortify the deeds of the body, ye shall live. *Ro.* **8: 13.**

Forgiving one another, even as God for Christ's sake hath forgiven you. *Ep.* **4: 32.**

Without shedding of blood is no remission. *He.* **9: 22.**

Their sins and iniquities will I remember no more. Now where remission of these is, there is no more offering for sin. *He.* **10: 17, 18.**

See also

Christ, Forgiveness of; Deliverance; Forgiveness; God, Forgiveness of; Remission; Reprieve.

Parent

Honour thy father and thy mother. *Ex.* **20: 12.**

When my father and my mother forsake me, then the Lord will take me up. *Ps.* **27: 10.**

Whoso curseth his father or his mother, his lamp shall be put out in obscure darkness. *Pr.* **20: 20.**

Train up a child in the way he should go: and when he is old, he will not depart from it. *Pr.* **22: 6.**

Kings shall be thy nursing fathers, and their queens thy nursing mothers. *Is.* **49: 23.**

The children shall rise up against their parents, and cause them to be put to death. *Mat.* **10: 21.**

He that loveth father or mother more than me is not worthy of me. *Mat.* **10: 37.**

He went down with him, and came to Nazareth, and was subject unto them. *Lu.* **2: 51.**

There is no man that hath left house, or parents, or brethren, or wife, or children, for the kingdom of God's sake, Who shall not receive manifold more in this present time, and in the world to come life everlasting. *Lu.* **18: 29, 30.**

Ye shall be betrayed both by parents, and brethren, and kinsfolks, and friends; and some of you shall they cause to be put to death. *Lu.* **21: 16.**

Master, who did sin, this man, or his parents, that he was born blind? *Jn.* **9: 2.**

The children ought not to lay up for the parents, but the parents for the children. *2 Co.* **12: 14.**

Children, obey your parents in the Lord: for this is right. *Ep.* **6: 1.**

Men shall be . . . disobedient to parents. *2 Ti.* **3: 2.**

Having faithful children. *Tit.* **1: 6.**

I have no greater joy than to hear that my children walk in truth. *3 Jn.* **1: 4.**

See also

Ancestor; Descent; Father; Genealogy; Generation; Mother.

Parsimony

There is that scattereth, and yet increaseth; and there is that withholdeth more than is meet, but it tendeth to poverty. *Pr.* **11: 24.**

Whoso stoppeth his ears at the cry of the poor, he also shall cry himself, but shall not be heard. *Pr.* **21: 13.**

He that giveth unto the poor shall not lack: but he that hideth his eyes shall have many a curse. *Pr.* **28: 27.**

There is a sore evil which I have seen under the sun, namely, riches kept for the owners thereof to their hurt. *Ec.* **5: 13.**

Thou hast bought me no sweet cane with money, neither hast thou filled me with the fat of thy sacrifices. *Is.* **43: 24.**

Israel is an empty vine, he bringeth forth fruit unto himself. *Ho.* **10: 1.**

Will a man rob God? Yet ye say, Wherein have we robbed thee? In tithes and offerings. *Mal.* **3: 8.**

When his disciples saw it, they had indignation, saying, To what purpose is this waste? *Mat.* **26: 8.**

A certain man named Ananias, with Sapphira his wife, sold a possession, And kept back part of the price. *Ac.* **5: 1, 2.**

Look not every man on his own things. *Ph.* **2: 4.**

See also

Greed; Selfishness.

Part

Mary hath chosen that good part, which shall not be taken away from her. *Lu.* **10: 42.**

If thy whole body therefore be full of light, having no part dark, the whole shall be full of light. *Lu.* **11: 36.**

As the lightning, that lighteneth out of the one part under heaven, shineth unto the other part under heaven; so shall also the Son of man be in his day. *Lu.* **17: 24.**

Then the soldiers, when they had crucified Jesus, took his garments, and made four parts, to every soldier a part. *Jn.* **19: 23.**

The body is not one member, but many. *1 Co.* **12: 14.**

Ye are the body of Christ, and members in particular. *1 Co.* **12: 27.**

We know in part, and we prophesy in part. *1 Co.* **13: 9.**

See also

Allotment; Member; Piece; Portion.

Partaker

We are all partakers of that one bread. *1 Co.* **10: 17.**

Ye all are partakers of my grace. *Ph.* **1: 7.**

Work out your own salvation with fear and trembling. For it is God which worketh in you both to will and to do of his good pleasure. *Ph.* **2: 12, 13.**

Partakers of the inheritance of the saints in light. *Col.* **1: 12.**

Holy brethren, partakers of the heavenly calling. *He.* **3: 1.**

Partakers of the Holy Ghost. *He.* **6: 4.**

Rejoice, inasmuch as ye are partakers of Christ's sufferings. *1 Pe.* **4: 13.**

See also

Christ, Partnership with; God, Partnership with; Share.

Partiality

Isaac loved Esau, because he did eat of his venison: but Rebekah loved Jacob. *Ge.* **25: 28.**

Israel loved Joseph more than all his children, because he was the son of his old age. *Ge.* **37: 3.**

I have given to thee one portion above thy brethren. *Ge.* **48: 22.**

The Lord doth put a difference between the Egyptians and Israel. *Ex.* **11: 7.**

I will put none of these diseases upon thee, which I have brought upon the Egyptians. *Ex.* **15: 26.**

Thou shalt not respect the person of the poor, nor honour the person of the mighty: but in righteousness shalt thou judge thy neighbour. *Le.* **19: 15.**

Though he was not the firstborn, yet his father made him the chief. *1 Ch.* **26: 10.**

He will surely reprove you, if ye do secretly accept persons. *Jb.* **13: 10.**

Therefore have I also made you contemptible and base before all the people, according as ye have not kept my ways, but have been partial in the law. *Mal.* **2: 9.**

I charge thee before God . . . that thou observe these things without preferring one before another, doing nothing by partiality. *1 Ti.* **5: 21.**

Are ye not then partial in yourselves, and are become judges of evil thoughts? *Ja.* **2: 4.**

See also

Bias; God, Impartiality of; Impartiality; Inequality; Persons, Respect of; Regard.

Parting

Entreat me not to leave thee, or to return from following after thee: for whither thou goest, I will go. *Ru.* **1: 16.**

The Lord do so to me, and more also, if

ought but death part thee and me. *Ru.* 1: 17.

In their death they were not divided. *2 S.* 1: 23.

There appeared a chariot of fire, and horses of fire, and parted them both asunder. *2 K.* 2: 11.

It came to pass, as the angels were gone away from them into heaven, the shepherds said one to another, Let us now go even unto Bethlehem. *Lu.* 2: 15.

Lord, I will follow thee; but let me first go bid them farewell, which are at home at my house. *Lu.* 9: 61.

While he blessed them, he was parted from them, and carried up into heaven. *Lu.* 24: 51.

Whither I go, thou canst not follow me now; but thou shalt follow me afterwards. *Jn.* 13: 36.

The hour cometh, yea, is now come, that ye shall be scattered, every man to his own, and shall leave me alone. *Jn.* 16: 32.

Fare ye well. *Ac.* 15: 29.

Sorrowing most of all for the words which he spake, that they should see his face no more. *Ac.* 20: 38.

Finally, brethren, farewell. *2 Co.* 13: 11.

He hath said, I will never leave thee, nor forsake thee. *He.* 13: 5.

See also

Absence; Departure; Exit; Removal; Separation; Withdrawal.

Partition

Let there be lights in the firmament of the heaven to divide the day from the night; and let them be for signs, and for seasons, and for days, and years. *Ge.* 1: 14.

The vail shall divide unto you between the holy place and the most holy. *Ex.* 26: 33.

He shall besiege thee in all thy gates, until thy high and fenced walls come down, wherein thou trustedst. *De.* 28: 52.

They were a wall unto us both by night and day. *1 S.* 25: 16.

He that hath no rule over his own spirit is like a city that is broken down, and without walls. *Pr.* 25: 28.

Jerusalem shall be inhabited as towns without walls. *Zch.* 2: 4.

For I, saith the Lord, will be unto her a wall of fire round about. *Zch.* 2: 5.

He shall set the sheep on his right hand, but the goats on the left. *Mat.* 25: 33.

Distribution was made unto every man according as he had need. *Ac.* 4: 35.

He is our peace, who hath made both one, and hath broken down the middle wall of partition between us. *Ep.* 2: 14.

See also

Division; Separation.

Partner

Whoso is partner with a thief hateth his own soul. *Pr.* 29: 24.

Two are better than one. *Ec.* 4: 9.

Woe to him that is alone when he falleth. *Ec.* 4: 10.

They beckoned unto their partners, which were in the other ship, that they should come and help them. *Lu.* 5: 7.

I am not alone, because the Father is with me. *Jn.* 16: 32.

We are all partakers of that one bread. *1 Co.* 10: 17.

I entreat thee also, true yokefellow. *Ph.* 4: 3.

Partakers of the inheritance of the saints in light. *Col.* 1: 12.

If thou count me therefore a partner, receive him as myself. *Phm.* 1: 17.

Ye are partakers of Christ's sufferings. *1 Pe.* 4: 13.

Our fellowship is with the Father, and with his Son Jesus Christ. *1 Jn.* 1: 3.

See also

Alliance; Association; Christ, Fellowship with; Christ, Partnership with; Collaboration; Colleague; Companionship; Comradeship; Coöperation; Fellowship; God, Fellowship with; God, Partnership with; Partaker; Share.

Passion

Let not thine anger burn against thy servant. *Ge.* 44: 18.

A fire is kindled in mine anger, and shall burn unto the lowest hell, and shall consume the earth with her increase, and set on fire the foundations of the mountains. *De.* 32: 22.

How long, Lord? wilt thou be angry for ever? shall thy jealousy burn like fire? *Ps.* 79: 5.

Thy fierce wrath goeth over me; thy terrors have cut me off. *Ps.* 88: 16.

Thou shalt tread upon the lion and adder: the young lion and the dragon shalt thou trample under feet. *Ps.* 91: 13.

He that is slow to anger is better than the mighty; and he that ruleth his spirit than he that taketh a city. *Pr.* 16: 32.

We also are men of like passions with you. *Ac.* 14: 15.

I will very gladly spend and be spent for you. *2 Co.* 12: 15.

Elias was a man subject to like passions as we are. *Ja.* 5: 17.

See also

Anger; Anguish; Christ, Cross of; Christ, Sacrifice of; Christ, Suffering of; Christ, Wrath of; Cross; Emotion; Feeling; Fury; Pain; Rage; Resentment; Sentiment; Torment; Wrath.

Passover

I will pass over you, and the plague shall not be upon you to destroy you, when I smite the land of Egypt. *Ex.* 12: 13.

It is the sacrifice of the Lord's passover, who passed over the houses of the children of Israel in Egypt, when he smote the Egyptians, and delivered our houses. *Ex.* 12: 27.

They made ready the passover. *Mat.* 26: 19.

The feast of unleavened bread drew nigh, which is called the Passover. *Lu.* 22: 1.

Through faith he kept the passover. *He.* 11: 28.

See also

Christ, the Passover.

Past

There were giants in the earth in those days. *Ge.* 6: 4.

Ask now of the days that are past. *De.* 4: 32.

Remember what the Lord thy God did unto Pharaoh, and unto all Egypt. *De.* 7: 18.

Thou shalt remember all the way which the Lord thy God led thee. *De.* 8: 2.

The word of the Lord was precious in those days. *1 S.* 3: 1.

A thousand years in thy sight are but as yesterday when it is past. *Ps.* 90: 4.

That which hath been is now; and that which is to be hath already been; and God requireth that which is past. *Ec.* 3: 15.

Say not thou, What is the cause that the former days were better than these? for thou dost not inquire wisely concerning this. *Ec.* 7: 10.

Remember ye not the former things, neither consider the things of old. *Is.* 43: 18.

Remember the former things of old. *Is.* 46: 9.

Thus saith the Lord; I remember thee, the kindness of thy youth. *Je.* 2: 2.

Why seek ye the living among the dead? *Lu.* 24: 5.

Come, see a man, which told me all things that ever I did: is not this the Christ? *Jn.* 4: 29.

Old things are passed away; behold, all things are become new. *2 Co.* 5: 17.

In time past ye walked according to the course of this world. *Ep.* 2: 2.

At that time ye were without Christ, being aliens from the commonwealth of Israel, and strangers from the covenants of promise, having no hope, and without God in the world. *Ep.* 2: 12.

Avoid . . . genealogies, . . . for they are unprofitable and vain. *Tit.* 3: 9.

God . . . spake in time past unto the fathers by the prophets. *He.* 1: 1.

See also

Annals; Time, the Past; Yesterday.

Pastor

I will raise me up a faithful priest, that shall do according to that which is in mine heart and my mind. *1 S.* 2: 35.

The pastors are become brutish. *Je.* 10: 21.

Woe be unto the pastors that destroy and scatter the sheep of my pasture! *Je.* 23: 1.

I send you forth as sheep in the midst of wolves: be ye therefore wise as serpents, and harmless as doves. *Mat.* 10: 16.

The hireling fleeth, because he is an hireling, and careth not for the sheep. *Jn.* 10: 13.

We will give ourselves continually to prayer, and to the ministry of the word. *Ac.* 6: 4.

He is the minister of God to thee for good. *Ro.* 13: 4.

I was made a minister, according to the gift of the grace of God given unto me. *Ep.* 3: 7.

He gave some, . . . pastors. *Ep.* 4: 11.

If thou put the brethren in remembrance of these things, thou shalt be a good minister of Jesus Christ. *1 Ti.* 4: 6.

The servant of the Lord must not strive. *2 Ti.* 2: 24.

Feed the flock of God which is among you, taking the oversight thereof, not by constraint, but willingly; not for filthy lucre, but of a ready mind; Neither as being lords over God's heritage, but being ensamples to the flock. *1 Pe.* 5: 2, 3.

See also

Clergy; Installation; Keeper; Ministry; Missionary; Ordination; Preacher; Priesthood, Sermon; Shepherd.

Pasture

The range of the mountains is his pasture. *Jb.* 39: 8.

He maketh me to lie down in green pastures. *Ps.* 23: 2.

The pastures are clothed with flocks. *Ps.* 65: 13.

We are the people of his pasture. *Ps.* 95: 7.

In that day shall thy cattle feed in large pastures. *Is.* 30: 23.

The Lord hath spoiled their pasture. *Je.* 25: 36.

I will feed them in a good pasture: . . . there shall they lie in a good fold. *Eze.* 34: 14.

By me if any man enter in, he shall be saved, and shall go in and out, and find pasture. *Jn.* 10: 9.

See also

Cattle; Flock; Herd; Pastor; Shepherd.

Path

Thou wilt shew me the path of life. *Ps.* 16: 11.

Shew me thy ways, O Lord, teach me thy paths. *Ps.* 25: 4.

Thy way is in the sea, and thy path in the great waters, and thy footsteps are not known. *Ps.* 77: 19.

They wandered in the wilderness in a solitary way. *Ps.* 107: 4.

Thou compassest my path and my lying down, and art acquainted with all my ways. *Ps.* 139: 3.

In all thy ways acknowledge him, and he shall direct thy paths. *Pr.* 3: 6.

The path of the just is as the shining light, that shineth more and more unto the perfect day. *Pr.* 4: 18.

I will bring the blind by a way that they knew not. *Is.* 42: 16.

Let the wicked forsake his way. *Is.* 55: 7.

The ways of the Lord are right, and the just shall walk in them. *Ho.* 14: 9.

Strait is the gate, and narrow is the way, which leadeth unto life. *Mat.* 7: 14.

Yet shew I unto you a more excellent way. *1 Co.* 12: 31.

See also

Christ, Way of; God, Way of; Highway; Life, Path of; Road; Street; Track; Way.

Patience

I have waited for thy salvation, O Lord, *Ge.* 49: 18.

My hope is in thee. *Ps.* 39: 7.

Truly my soul waiteth upon God. *Ps.* 62: 1.

I wait for the Lord, my soul doth wait, and in his word do I hope. *Ps.* 130: 5.

My soul waiteth for the Lord more than they that watch for the morning: I say, more than they that watch for the morning. *Ps.* 130: 6.

The patient in spirit is better than the proud in spirit. *Ec.* 7: 8.

Blessed are all they that wait for him. *Is.* 30: 18.

Couldest not thou watch one hour? *Mk.* 14: 37.

The kingdom of God cometh not with observation. *Lu.* 17: 20.

Being assembled together with them, commanded them that they should not depart from Jerusalem, but wait for the promise of the Father, which, saith he, ye have heard of me. *Ac.* 1: 4.

The Lord direct your hearts into the love of God, and into the patient waiting for Christ. *2 Th.* **3: 5.**

Ye have need of patience. *He.* **10: 36.**

Let us run with patience the race that is set before us. *He.* **12: 1.**

Let patience have her perfect work, that ye may be perfect and entire, wanting nothing. *Ja.* **1: 4.**

Be patient therefore, brethren, unto the coming of the Lord. *Ja.* **5: 7.**

Behold, the husbandman waiteth for the precious fruit of the earth, and hath long patience for it, until he receive the early and latter rain. *Ja.* **5: 7.**

Be ye also patient; stablish your hearts: for the coming of the Lord draweth nigh. *Ja.* **5: 8.**

Ye have heard of the patience of Job. *Ja.* **5: 11.**

And to temperance patience. *2 Pe.* **1: 6.**

In the kingdom and patience of Jesus Christ. *Re.* **1: 9.**

I know thy works, and thy labour, and thy patience. *Re.* **2: 2.**

See also

Endurance; Forbearance; Fortitude; Long-Suffering; Resignation; Self-Control; Submission; Tolerance.

Patriotism

I am the Lord your God, which have separated you from other people. *Le.* **20: 24.**

Defile not therefore the land which ye shall inhabit, wherein I dwell. *Nu.* **35: 34.**

Thou art an holy people unto the Lord thy God. *De.* **7: 6.**

Dwell in the land which the Lord your God giveth you to inherit. *De.* **12: 10.**

Let us play the men for our people, and for the cities of our God. *2 S.* **10: 12.**

Let me depart, that I may go to mine own country. *1 K.* **11: 21.**

Why should not my countenance be sad, when the city, the place of my fathers' sepulchres, lieth waste? *Ne.* **2: 3.**

Blessed is the nation whose God is the Lord. *Ps.* **33: 12.**

Lord, thou hast been favourable unto thy land. *Ps.* **85: 1.**

If I forget thee, O Jerusalem, let my right hand forget her cunning. *Ps.* **137: 5.**

Righteousness exalteth a nation: but sin is a reproach to any people. *Pr.* **14: 34.**

Rejoice ye with Jerusalem, and be glad with her, all ye that love her. *Is.* **66: 10.**

He loveth our nation. *Lu.* **7: 5.**

Are they Israelites? so am I. *2 Co.* **11: 22.**

They seek a country. *He.* **11: 14.**

See also

Country; Nation; Nation, Greatness of; Nation, Prosperity of; State.

Pattern

God said, Let us make man in our image. *Ge.* **1: 26.**

Behold the pattern of the altar of the Lord, which our fathers made, not for burnt offerings, nor for sacrifices; but it is a witness between us and you. *Jos.* **22: 28.**

Let your light so shine before men, that they may see your good works, and glorify your father which is in heaven. *Mat.* **5: 16.**

I have given you an example, that ye should do as I have done to you. *Jn.* **13: 15.**

All these things happened unto them for ensamples. *1 Co.* **10: 11.**

Not because we have not power, but to make ourselves an ensample unto you to follow us. *2 Th.* **3: 9.**

In all things shewing thyself a pattern. *Tit.* **2: 7.**

The example and shadow of heavenly things. *He.* **8: 5.**

See . . . that thou make all things according to the pattern shewed to thee in the mount. *He.* **8: 5.**

The holy places made with hands . . . are the figures of the true. *He.* **9: 24.**

Make straight paths for your feet, lest that which is lame be turned out of the way. *He.* **12: 13.**

Take . . . the prophets, who have spoken in the name of the Lord, for an example of suffering affliction, and of patience. *Ja.* **5: 10.**

See also

Example; Form; Fullness; Ideal; Image; Model; Perfection; Resemblance; Standard.

Payment

Honour the Lord with thy substance, . . . So shall thy barns be filled with plenty, and thy presses shall burst out with new wine. *Pr.* **3: 9, 10.**

The recompence of a man's hands shall be rendered unto him. *Pr.* **12: 14.**

To the righteous good shall be repaid. *Pr.* **13: 21.**

Every man should eat and drink, and enjoy the good of all his labour, it is the gift of God. *Ec.* **3: 13.**

Thy reward shall return upon thine own head. *Ob.* **1: 15.**

There is no man that hath left house, or brethren, or sisters, or father, or mother, or wife, or children, or lands, for my sake, and the gospel's, But he shall receive an hundredfold now in this time. *Mk.* **10: 29, 30.**

Love ye your enemies, and do good, and lend, hoping for nothing again; and your reward shall be great, and ye shall be the children of the Highest. *Lu.* **6: 35.**

Give, and it shall be given unto you. *Lu.* **6: 38.**

With the same measure that ye mete withal it shall be measured to you again. *Lu.* **6: 38.**

The wages of sin is death. *Ro.* **6: 23.**

He which soweth bountifully shall reap also bountifully. *2 Co.* **9: 6.**

Whatsoever good thing any man doeth, the same shall he receive of the Lord. *Ep.* **6: 8.**

The labourer is worthy of his reward. *1 Ti.* **5: 18.**

Balaam . . . loved the wages of unrighteousness. *2 Pe.* **2: 15.**

See also

Amends; Compensation; God, Reward of; Obligation; Recompense; Restoration; Return; Reward.

Peace

The land rested from war. *Jos.* **11: 23.**

Better is little with the fear of the Lord than great treasure and trouble therewith. *Pr.* **15: 16.**

A time of war, and a time of peace. *Ec.* **3: 8.**

Yielding pacifieth great offences. *Ec.* **10: 4.**

They shall beat their swords into plowshares, and their spears into pruninghooks. *Is.* **2: 4.**

The work of righteousness shall be peace. *Is.* **32: 17.**

I will also make thy officers peace. *Is.* **60: 17.**

I will extend peace to her like a river. *Is.* **66: 12.**

Jerusalem shall be inhabited as towns without walls . . . For I, saith the Lord, will be unto her a wall of fire round about, and will be the glory in the midst of her. *Zch.* **2: 4, 5.**

Blessed are the peacemakers. *Mat.* **5: 9.**

On earth peace, good will toward men. *Lu.* **2: 14.**

If thou hadst known, even thou, at least in this thy day, the things which belong unto thy peace! *Lu.* **19: 42.**

I have learned in whatsoever state I am, therein to be content. *Ph.* **4: 11.**

Be at peace among yourselves. *1 Th.* **5: 13.**

See also

Amnesty; Armistice; Calm; Christ, Peace of; Compatibility; Conciliation; Concord; Disarmament; Ease; God, Peace of; God, Rest in; Harmony; Quiet; Repose, Rest; Stillness; Tranquillity.

Pearl

No mention shall be made of coral, or of pearls: for the price of wisdom is above rubies. *Jb.* **28: 18.**

Give not that which is holy unto the dogs, neither cast ye your pearls before swine. *Mat.* **7: 6.**

The kingdom of heaven is like unto a merchant man, seeking goodly pearls: Who, when he had found one pearl of great price, went and sold all that he had, and bought it. *Mat.* **13: 45, 46.**

The twelve gates were twelve pearls; every several gate was of one pearl. *Re.* **21: 21.**

See also

Adornment; Ornament.

Penance

Rend your heart, and not your garments, and turn unto the Lord your God. *Jo.* **2: 13.**

Shall I give my firstborn for my transgression? *Mi.* **6: 7.**

Bring forth therefore fruits meet for repentance. *Mat.* **3: 8.**

Mortify therefore your members which are upon the earth. *Col.* **3: 5.**

See also

Amends; Ash Wednesday; Lent; Penitence; Repentance.

Penitence

Hide thy face from my sins, and blot out all mine iniquities. Create in me a clean heart, O God; and renew a right spirit within me. *Ps.* **51: 9, 10.**

A broken and a contrite heart, O God, thou wilt not despise. *Ps.* **51: 17.**

To this man will I look, even to him that is poor and of a contrite spirit, and trembleth at my word. *Is.* **66: 2.**

No man repented him of his wickedness, saying, What have I done? *Je.* **8: 6.**

Thou hast forsaken me, saith the Lord, thou art gone backward; . . . I am weary with repenting. *Je.* **15: 6.**

Mine heart is turned within me, my repentings are kindled together. *Ho.* **11: 8.**

Except ye repent, ye shall all likewise perish. *Lu.* **13: 3.**

Joy shall be in heaven over one sinner that repenteth. *Lu.* **15: 7.**

Repent therefore of this thy wickedness. *Ac.* **8: 22.**

The goodness of God leadeth thee to repentance. *Ro.* **2: 4.**

Godly sorrow worketh repentance. *2 Co.* **7: 10.**

See also

Ash Wednesday; Contrition; Grief; Humility; Lent; Penance; Regret; Remorse; Repentance.

Pentecost

The God that answereth by fire, let him be God. *1 K.* **18: 24.**

I will pour out my spirit upon all flesh; and your sons and your daughters shall prophesy, your old men shall dream dreams, and your young men shall see visions. *Jo.* **2: 28.**

Also upon the servants and upon the handmaids in those days will I pour out my spirit. *Jo.* **2: 29.**

When the day of Pentecost was fully come, they were all with one accord in one place. *Ac.* **2: 1.**

Suddenly there came a sound from heaven as of a rushing mighty wind, . . . And there appeared unto them cloven tongues like as of fire, and it sat upon each of them. *Ac.* **2: 2, 3.**

They were all filled with the Holy Ghost. *Ac.* **2: 4.**

They . . . began to speak with other tongues, as the Spirit gave them utterance. *Ac.* **2: 4.**

When this was noised abroad, the multitude came together, and were confounded. *Ac.* **2: 6.**

How hear we every man in our own tongue, wherein we were born? *Ac.* **2: 8.**

We do hear them speak in our tongues the wonderful works of God. *Ac.* **2: 11.**

This is that which was spoken by the prophet Joel: And it shall come to pass in the last days, saith God, I will pour out of my Spirit upon all flesh. *Ac.* **2: 16, 17.**

Then they that gladly received his word were baptized: and the same day there were added unto them about three thousand souls. *Ac.* **2: 41.**

Fear came upon every soul: and many wonders and signs were done by the apostles. *Ac.* **2: 43.**

The Lord added to the church daily such as should be saved. *Ac.* **2: 47.**

See also

Whitsunday.

People

Let people serve thee, and nations bow down to thee. *Ge.* **27: 29.**

The Lord thy God hath chosen thee to be a special people unto himself, above all people that are upon the face of the earth. *De.* **7: 6.**

Yea, he loved the people. *De.* **33: 3.**

Thy people shall be my people, and thy

God my God. *Ru.* 1: 16.

Hearken unto the voice of the people in all that they say unto thee. *1 S.* 8: 7.

The Lord will not forsake his people. *1 S.* 12: 22.

I will not be afraid of ten thousands of people. *Ps.* 3: 6.

He is high above all the people. *Ps.* 99: 2.

Sin is a reproach to any people. *Pr.* 14: 34.

Prepare ye the way of the people. *Is.* 62: 10.

Be strong, all ye people of the land. *Hag.* 2: 4.

They were instant with loud voices, requiring that he might be crucified. And the voices of them and of the chief priests prevailed. *Lu.* 23: 23.

I will be to them a God, and they shall be to me a people. *He.* 8: 10.

See also

Community; Country; Land; Nation; Rabble; Race; State.

Perception

He passeth on also, but I perceive him not. *Jb.* 9: 11.

Behold, I go forward, but he is not there; and backward, but I cannot perceive him. *Jb.* 23: 8.

God speaketh once, yea twice, yet man perceiveth it not. *Jb.* 33: 14.

Hast thou perceived the breadth of the earth? declare if thou knowest it all. *Jb.* 38: 18.

The wise man's eyes are in his head; but the fool walketh in darkness: and I myself perceived also that one event happeneth to them all. *Ec.* 2: 14.

Since the beginning of the world men have not heard, nor perceived by the ear, neither hath the eye seen, O God, beside thee, what he hath prepared for him that waiteth for him. *Is.* 64: 4.

Seeing ye shall see, and shall not perceive. *Mat.* 13: 14.

Hereby perceive we the love of God, because he laid down his life for us. *1 Jn.* 3: 16.

See also

Discernment; Discrimination; Insight; Judgment; Knowledge; Sensitivity; Understanding; Wisdom.

Perfection

Mark the perfect man. *Ps.* 37: 37.

He that walketh in a perfect way, he shall serve me. *Ps.* 101: 6.

I have seen an end of all perfection: but thy commandment is exceeding broad. *Ps.* 119: 96.

He hath made every thing beautiful in his time. *Ec.* 3: 11.

Let us hear the conclusion of the whole matter: Fear God, and keep his commandments. *Ec.* 12: 13.

Thou wilt keep him in perfect peace, whose mind is stayed on thee. *Is.* 26: 3.

Who is blind as he that is perfect? *Is.* 42: 19.

If thou wilt be perfect, go and sell that thou hast, and give to the poor. *Mat.* 19: 21.

Jesus Christ maketh thee whole. *Ac.* 9: 34.

The breadth, and length, and depth, and height. *Ep.* 3: 18.

Charity . . . is the bond of perfectness. *Col.* 3: 14.

The God of peace. . . . Make you perfect in every good work to do his will. *He.* 13: 20, 21.

Whoso looketh into the perfect law of liberty, and continueth therein, . . . this man shall be blessed in his deed. *Ja.* 1: 25.

By works was faith made perfect. *Ja.* 2: 22.

If any man offend not in word, the same is a perfect man. *Ja.* 3: 2.

Perfect love casteth out fear. *1 Jn.* 4: 18.

See also

Christ, Preëminence of; Completion; Excellence; God, Primacy of; Goodness; Greatness; Life, the Full; Model; Preëminence; Superiority; Supremacy.

Perfidy

Thy brother came with subtilty, and hath taken away thy blessing. *Ge.* 27: 35.

Keep thee far from a false matter. *Ex.* 23: 7.

Ye shall not steal, neither deal falsely, neither lie one to another. *Le.* 19: 11.

If your soul abhor my judgments, so that ye will not do my commandments, but that ye break my covenant: I also will do this unto you; I will even appoint over you terror. *Le.* 26: 15, 16.

The deceived and the deceiver are his. *Jb.* 12: 16.

His mouth is full of cursing and deceit and fraud. *Ps.* 10: 7.

My covenant will I not break. *Ps.* 89: 34.

Their deceit is falsehood. *Ps.* 119: 118.

He that speaketh truth sheweth forth righteousness: but a false witness deceit. *Pr.* 12: 17.

As a mad man who casteth firebrands, arrows, and death, So is the man that deceiveth his neighbour. *Pr.* 26: 18, 19.

The treacherous dealer dealeth treacherously. *Is.* 21: 2.

Behold, I am against them that prophesy false dreams. *Je.* 23: 32.

Shall I count them pure with the wicked balances, and with the bag of deceitful weights? *Mi.* 6: 11.

He answered and said, I go, sir: and went not. *Mat.* 21: 30.

Judas Iscariot . . . was the traitor. *Lu.* 6: 16.

Such are false apostles, deceitful workers. *2 Co.* 11: 13.

In the last days . . . men shall be . . . Traitors. *2 Ti.* 3: 1, 2, 4.

See also

Deceit; Faithlessness; Fraud; Traitor; Treachery.

Performance

Wipe not out my good deeds that I have done for the house of my God. *Ne.* 13: 14.

I will cry unto God most high; unto God that performeth all things for me. *Ps.* 57: 2.

Her warfare is accomplished. *Is.* 40: 2.

My word . . . shall accomplish that which I please, and it shall prosper in the thing whereto I sent it. *Is.* 55: 11.

He is strong that executeth his word. *Jo.* 2: 11.

Why call ye me, Lord, Lord, and do not the things which I say? *Lu.* 6: 46.

I have a baptism to be baptized with; and how am I straitened till it be accomplished! *Lu.* 12: 50.

God . . . will render to every man according

to his deeds. *Ro.* 2: 5, 6.

To will is present with me; but how to perform that which is good I find not. *Ro.* 7: 18.

Now therefore perform the doing of it; that as there was a readiness to will, so there may be a performance also out of that which ye have. *2 Co.* 8: 11.

Being confident of this very thing, that he which hath begun a good work in you will perform it until the day of Jesus Christ. *Ph.* 1: 6.

Ye have put off the old man with his deeds. *Col.* 3: 9.

See also

Accomplishment; Achievement; Administration; Completion; Conduct; Deed; Execution; Fulfilment; Operation; Work.

Perfume

A sweet savour before the Lord. *Ex.* 29: 25.

As for the perfume which thou shalt make, ye shall not make to yourselves according to the composition thereof: it shall be unto thee holy for the Lord. *Ex.* 30: 37.

I will make your cities waste, and bring your sanctuaries unto desolation, and I will not smell the savour of your sweet odours. *Le.* 26: 31.

All thy garments smell of myrrh, and aloes, and cassia, out of the ivory palaces. *Ps.* 45: 8.

Ointment and perfume rejoice the heart. *Pr.* 27: 9.

The vines with the tender grape give a good smell. *S. of S.* 2: 13.

The smell of thy garments is like the smell of Lebanon. *S. of S.* 4: 11.

My hands dropped with myrrh, and my fingers with sweet smelling myrrh. *S. of S.* 5: 5.

I will accept you with your sweet savour. *Eze.* 20: 41.

They presented unto him gifts; gold, and frankincense, and myrrh. *Mat.* 2: 11.

There came a woman having an alabaster box of ointment of spikenard very precious; and she brake the box, and poured it on his head. *Mk.* 14: 3.

We are unto God a sweet savour of Christ. *2 Co.* 2: 15.

See also

Fragrance; Incense; Odor; Savor; Scent; Smell.

Peril

Is not this the blood of the men that went in jeopardy of their lives? *2 S.* 23: 17.

My soul is among lions. *Ps.* 57: 4.

Men that have hazarded their lives for the name of our Lord Jesus Christ. *Ac.* 15: 26.

For thy sake we are killed all the day long. *Ro.* 8: 36.

Why stand we in jeopardy every hour? *1 Co.* 15: 30.

In weariness and painfulness, in watchings often, in hunger and thirst, in fastings often, in cold and nakedness. *2 Co.* 11: 27.

In the last days perilous times shall come. *2 Ti.* 3: 1.

See also

Danger; Hardship; Hazard; Trial; Urgency.

Perjury

Thou shalt not bear false witness against thy neighbour. *Ex.* 20: 16.

Thou shalt not raise a false report. *Ex.* 23: 1.

God is not a man, that he should lie; neither the son of man, that he should repent. *Nu.* 23: 19.

A false witness will utter lies. *Pr.* 14: 5.

A false witness shall not be unpunished, and he that speaketh lies shall not escape. *Pr* 19: 5.

Though they say, The Lord liveth; surely they swear falsely. *Je.* 5: 2.

I will be a swift witness against . . . false swearers. *Mal.* 3: 5.

Blessed are ye, when men shall revile you, and persecute you, and shall say all manner of evil against you falsely, for my sake. *Mat.* 5: 11.

Many bare false witness against him, but their witness agreed not together. *Mk.* 14: 56.

The law is . . . for liars, for perjured persons. *1 Ti.* 1: 9, 10.

See also

Witness.

Permanence

I will abide in thy tabernacle for ever. *Ps.* 61: 4.

Thy kingdom is an everlasting kingdom, and thy dominion endureth throughout all generations. *Ps.* 145: 13.

The grass withereth, the flower fadeth: but the word of our God shall stand for ever. *Is.* 40: 8.

Thou, O Lord, remainest for ever; thy throne from generation to generation. *La.* 5: 19.

We know that if our earthly house of this tabernacle were dissolved, we have a building of God, an house not made with hands, eternal in the heavens. *2 Co.* 5: 1.

Jesus Christ the same yesterday, and to day, and for ever. *He.* 13: 8.

The word of the Lord endureth for ever. And this is the word which by the gospel is preached unto you. *1 Pe.* 1: 25.

See also

Christ, Permanence of; Constancy; Endurance; Eternity; Faithfulness; God, the Eternal; Security; Stability; Steadfastness.

Permission

Hinder me not, seeing the Lord hath prospered my way. *Ge.* 24: 56.

The Lord refuseth to give me leave to go with you. *Nu.* 22: 13.

Thou shalt see the land before thee; but thou shalt not go thither unto the land which I give the children of Israel. *De.* 32: 52.

Let me not wander from thy commandments. *Ps.* 119: 10.

By what authority doest thou these things?. *Mat.* 21: 23.

Jesus gave them leave. *Mk.* 5: 13.

If thou believest with all thine heart, thou mayest. *Ac.* 8: 37.

That which I do I allow not: for what I would, that do I not; but what I hate, that do I. *Ro.* 7: 15.

Happy is he that condemneth not himself in that thing which he alloweth. *Ro.* 14: 22.

I speak this by permission, and not of commandment. *1 Co.* 7: 6.

Where the Spirit of the Lord is, there is liberty. *2 Co.* 3: 17.

As we were allowed of God to be put in trust with the gospel, even so we speak. *1 Th.* **2: 4.**

This will we do, if God permit. *He.* **6: 3.**

Perplexity

It is a day of trouble, and of treading down, and of perplexity by the Lord God of hosts in the valley of vision. *Is.* **22: 5.**

The herds of cattle are perplexed, because they have no pasture; yea, the flocks of sheep are made desolate. *Jo.* **1: 18.**

Now shall be their perplexity. *Mi.* **7: 4.**

Art thou he that should come? or look we for another? *Lu.* **7: 19.**

Neither be ye of doubtful mind. *Lu.* **12: 29.**

Upon the earth distress of nations, with perplexity. *Lu.* **21: 25.**

They were all amazed, and were in doubt. *Ac.* **2: 12.**

We are perplexed, but not in despair. *2 Co.* **4: 8.**

See also

Bewilderment; Christ, Doubt of; Confusion; Doubt; Skepticism; Uncertainty.

Persecution

Deliver me from the hand of mine enemies, and from them that persecute me. *Ps.* **31: 15.**

We are counted as sheep for the slaughter. *Ps.* **44: 22.**

For thy sake I have borne reproach. *Ps.* **69: 7.**

Many a time have they afflicted me from my youth. *Ps.* **129: 1.**

The plowers plowed upon my back: they made long their furrows. *Ps.* **129: 3.**

Blessed are they which are persecuted for righteousness' sake: for theirs is the kingdom of heaven. *Mat.* **5: 10.**

Pray for them which despitefully use you, and persecute you. *Mat.* **5: 44.**

Ye build the sepulchres of the prophets, and your fathers killed them. *Lu.* **11: 47.**

They shall lay their hands on you, and persecute you. *Lu.* **21: 12.**

If they have persecuted me, they will also persecute you. *Jn.* **15: 20.**

Another shall gird thee, and carry thee whither thou wouldest not. *Jn.* **21: 18.**

Which of the prophets have not your fathers persecuted? *Ac.* **7: 52.**

Saul, Saul, why persecutest thou me? *Ac.* **9: 4.**

I am Jesus whom thou persecutest. *Ac.* **9: 5.**

The Jews . . . raised persecution against Paul and Barnabas, and expelled them out of their coasts. . . . And the disciples were filled with joy, and with the Holy Ghost. *Ac.* **13: 50, 52.**

Who shall separate us from the love of Christ? shall . . . persecution? *Ro.* **8: 35.**

Bless them which persecute you: bless, and curse not. *Ro.* **12: 14.**

Persecuted, but not forsaken; cast down, but not destroyed. *2 Co.* **4: 9.**

I take pleasure in . . . persecutions. *2 Co.* **12: 10.**

Let us go forth therefore unto him without the camp, bearing his reproach. *He.* **13: 13.**

See also

Affliction; Bondage; Cruelty; Despot; Hardness; Harshness; Inhumanity; Martyr; Oppression; Rod; Severity; Trial; Tribulation; Tyranny.

Perseverance

Gideon came to Jordan, and passed over, he, and the three hundred men that were with him, faint, yet pursuing them. *Ju.* **8: 4.**

It came to pass at the seventh time. *1 K.* **18: 44.**

Turn not to the right hand nor to the left: remove thy foot from evil. *Pr.* **4: 27.**

Jesus saith unto him, I say not unto thee, Until seven times: but, Until seventy times seven. *Mat.* **18: 22.**

He that shall endure unto the end, the same shall be saved. *Mk.* **13: 13.**

I must walk to day, and to morrow, and the day following. *Lu.* **13: 33.**

And again he sent another servant. *Lu.* **20: 11.**

The Holy Ghost witnesseth in every city, saying that bonds and afflictions abide me. But none of these things move me. *Ac.* **20: 23, 24.**

Let us not be weary in well doing: for in due season we shall reap, if we faint not. *Ga.* **6: 9.**

Watching thereunto with all perseverance. *Ep.* **6: 18.**

See also

Determination; Firmness; Persistence; Purpose; Resolution; Steadfastness.

Persistence

Evening, and morning, and at noon, will I pray. *Ps.* **55: 17.**

The Lord called Samuel again the third time. *1 S.* **3: 8.**

A just man falleth seven times, and riseth up again: but the wicked shall fall into mischief. *Pr.* **24: 16.**

Because of his importunity he will rise and give him as many as he needeth. *Lu.* **11: 8.**

He saith unto him the third time, Simon, son of Jonas, lovest thou me? *Jn.* **21: 17.**

And they continued stedfastly in the apostles' doctrine and fellowship, and in breaking of bread, and in prayer. *Ac.* **2: 42.**

But Peter continued knocking. *Ac.* **12: 16.**

For this thing I besought the Lord thrice. *2 Co.* **12: 8.**

Hold fast that which is good. *1 Th.* **5: 21.**

See also

Continuance; Determination; Firmness; Perseverance; Resolution; Steadfastness; Stubbornness.

Person

Joseph was a goodly person, and well favoured. *Ge.* **39: 6.**

There was not among the children of Israel a goodlier person than he. *1 S.* **9: 2.**

He shall save the humble person. *Jb.* **22: 29.**

I have not sat with vain persons. *Ps.* **26: 4.**

Will he regard your persons? *Mal.* **1: 9.**

For your sakes forgave I it in the person of Christ. *2 Co.* **2: 10.**

No . . . unclean person . . . hath any inheritance in the kingdom of Christ and of God. *Ep.* **5: 5.**

The express image of his person. *He.* **1: 3.**

What manner of persons ought ye to be in all holy conversation and godliness? *2 Pe.* **3: 11.**

See also
Individual; Trinity.

Persons, Respect of

He will surely reprove you, if ye do secretly accept persons. *Jb.* 13: 10.

To have respect of persons is not good: for, for a piece of bread that man will transgress. *Pr.* 28: 21.

Master, we know that thou art true, and carest for no man: for thou regardest not the person of men. *Mk.* 12: 14.

Of a truth I perceive that God is no respecter of persons. *Ac.* 10: 34.

Ye masters, do the same things unto them, forbearing threatening: knowing that your Master also is in heaven; neither is there respect of persons with him. *Ep.* 6: 9.

My brethren, have not the faith of our Lord Jesus Christ, the Lord of glory, with respect of persons. *Ja.* 2: 1.

If ye have respect to him that weareth the gay clothing, and say unto him, Sit thou here in a good place; and say to the poor, Stand thou there, or sit here under my footstool: Are ye not then partial in yourselves, and are become judges of evil thoughts? *Ja.* 2: 3, 4.

If ye have respect to persons, ye commit sin, and are convinced of the law as transgressors. *Ja.* 2: 9.

See also
Bias; Caste; Class; Equality; Fairness; God, Fairness of; God, Impartiality of; Impartiality; Justice; Partiality.

Persuasion

By long forbearing is a prince persuaded. *Pr.* 25: 15.

If they hear not Moses and the prophets, neither will they be persuaded, though one rose from the dead. *Lu.* 16: 31.

Almost thou persuadest me to be a Christian. *Ac.* 26: 28.

I am persuaded, that neither death, nor life, nor angels, nor principalities, nor powers, nor things present, nor things to come, . . . shall be able to separate us from the love of God, which is in Christ Jesus our Lord. *Ro.* 8: 38, 39.

Let every man be fully persuaded in his own mind. *Ro.* 14: 5.

Knowing therefore the terror of the Lord, we persuade men. *2 Co.* 5: 11.

This persuasion cometh not of him that calleth you. *Ga.* 5: 8.

I . . . am persuaded that he is able to keep that which I have committed unto him against that day. *2 Ti.* 1: 12.

Though I might be much bold in Christ to enjoin thee, . . . Yet for love's sake I rather beseech thee. *Phm.* 1: 8, 9.

These all died in faith, not having received the promises, but having seen them afar off, and were persuaded of them, and embraced them. *He.* 11: 13.

See also
Belief; Conviction; Influence.

Perversion

Thou lovest thine enemies, and hatest thy friends. *2 S.* 19: 6.

Doth the Almighty pervert justice? *Jb.* 8: 3.

A wicked man taketh a gift out of the bosom to pervert the ways of judgment. *Pr.* 17: 23.

Better is the poor that walketh in his uprightness, than he that is perverse in his ways, though he be rich. *Pr.* 28: 6.

That which is crooked cannot be made straight. *Ec.* 1: 15.

I saw under the sun the place of judgment, that wickedness was there; and the place of righteousness, that iniquity was there. *Ec.* 3: 16.

God hath made man upright; but they have sought out many inventions. *Ec.* 7: 29.

Folly is set in great dignity, and the rich sit in low place. *Ec.* 10: 6.

I have seen servants upon horses, and princes walking as servants upon the earth. *Ec.* 10: 7.

Woe unto them that call evil good, and good evil; that put darkness for light, and light for darkness; that put bitter for sweet, and sweet for bitter! *Is.* 5: 20.

The vile person shall be no more called liberal, nor the churl said to be bountiful. *Is.* 32: 5.

We found this fellow perverting the nation. *Lu.* 23: 2.

I fear, lest . . . your minds should be corrupted from the simplicity that is in Christ. *2 Co.* 11: 3.

There be some that trouble you, and would pervert the gospel of Christ. *Ga.* 1: 7.

See also
Apostasy; Backsliding; Corruption; Depravity; Impurity; Lust; Sin; Ungodliness; Vileness; Wickedness.

Pessimism

Where the light is as darkness. *Jb.* 10: 22.

Men see not the bright light which is in the clouds. *Jb.* 37: 21.

Clouds and darkness are round about him. *Ps.* 97: 2.

All is vanity and vexation of spirit. *Ec.* 1: 14.

I was great, and increased more than all that were before me in Jerusalem: . . . and, behold, all was vanity. *Ec.* 2: 9, 11.

All his days are sorrows, and his travail grief; yea, his heart taketh not rest in the night. *Ec.* 2: 23.

For whom do I labour, and bereave my soul of good? *Ec.* 4: 8.

What profit hath he that hath laboured for the wind? *Ec.* 5: 16.

He cometh in with vanity, and departeth in darkness, and his name shall be covered with darkness. *Ec.* 6: 4.

All the labour of man is for his mouth, and yet the appetite is not filled. *Ec.* 6: 7.

The Lord hath forsaken the earth, and the Lord seeth not. *Eze.* 9: 9.

See also
Cynicism; Depression; Despair; Evil; Gloom; Melancholy.

Pestilence

If there be in the land . . . pestilence; . . . whatsoever plague, whatsoever sickness there be; What prayer and supplication soever be made by any man, . . . Then hear thou in heaven thy dwelling place, and forgive. *1 K.* 8: 37–39.

He shall deliver thee . . . from the noisome pestilence. *Ps. 91: 3.*

Thou shalt not be afraid . . . for the pestilence that walketh in darkness. *Ps. 91: 5, 6.*

The sword is without, and the pestilence and the famine within. *Eze. 7: 15.*

I have sent among you the pestilence after the manner of Egypt. *Am. 4: 10.*

Before him went the pestilence, and burning coals went forth at his feet. *Hab. 3: 5.*

There shall be famines, and pestilences, and earthquakes, in divers places. *Mat. 24: 7.*

We have found this man a pestilent fellow. *Ac. 24: 5.*

Men . . . blasphemed the name of God, which hath power over these plagues: and they repented not to give him glory. *Re. 16: 9.*

I testify unto every man that heareth the words of the prophecy of this book, If any man shall add unto these things, God shall add unto him the plagues that are written in this book. *Re. 22: 18.*

See also

Bane; Contagion; Disease; Plague.

Pet

My lord knoweth that the children are tender. *Ge. 33: 13.*

The poor man had nothing, save one little ewe lamb, which he had bought and nourished up: and it grew up together with him, and with his children; it did eat of his own meat, and drank of his own cup, and lay in his bosom, and was unto him as a daughter. *2 S. 12: 3.*

They send forth their little ones like a flock, and their children dance. *Jb. 21: 11.*

Who provideth for the raven his food? *Jb. 38: 41.*

Thy children like olive plants round about thy table. *Ps. 128: 3.*

He giveth to the beast his food, and to the young ravens which cry. *Ps. 147: 9.*

The ox knoweth his owner, and the ass his master's crib. *Is. 1: 3.*

He shall gather the lambs with his arm, and carry them in his bosom. *Is. 40: 11.*

Thy daughters shall be nursed at thy side. *Is. 60: 4.*

Behold the fowls of the air: for they sow not, neither do they reap, nor gather into barns; yet your heavenly Father feedeth them. *Mat. 6: 26.*

The dogs eat of the crumbs which fall from their masters' table. *Mat. 15: 27.*

Rejoice with me; for I have found my sheep which was lost. *Lu. 15: 6.*

I know my sheep, and am known of mine. *Jn. 10: 14.*

See also

Favoritism.

Petition

The God of Israel grant thee thy petition that thou hast asked of him. *1 S. 1: 17.*

The Lord fulfil all thy petitions. *Ps. 20: 5.*

Evening, and morning, and at noon, will I pray. *Ps. 55: 17.*

From the end of the earth will I cry unto thee. *Ps. 61: 2.*

In the morning shall my prayer prevent thee. *Ps. 88: 13.*

Hear me speedily, O Lord. . . . Cause me to hear. *Ps. 143: 7, 8.*

It shall come to pass, that before they call, I will answer; and while they are yet speaking, I will hear. *Is. 65: 24.*

Daniel . . . maketh his petition three times a day. *Da. 6: 13.*

When ye pray, use not vain repetitions, as the heathen do. *Mat. 6: 7.*

Praying always with all prayer and supplication in the Spirit. *Ep. 6: 18.*

In every thing by prayer and supplication with thanksgiving let your requests be made known unto God. *Ph. 4: 6.*

This is the confidence that we have in him, that, if we ask any thing according to his will, he heareth us. *1 Jn. 5: 14.*

See also

Appeal; Entreaty; God, Prayer to; Plea; Prayer; Request; Supplication.

Pettiness

Take no thought, saying, What shall we eat? or, What shall we drink? or, Wherewithal shall we be clothed? *Mat. 6: 31.*

Seek ye first the kingdom of God, and his righteousness; and all these things shall be added unto you. *Mat. 6: 33.*

Ye blind guides, which strain at a gnat, and swallow a camel. *Mat. 23: 24.*

Ye make clean the outside of the cup and the platter, but within they are full of extortion and excess. *Mat. 23: 25.*

Martha was cumbered about much serving. *Lu. 10: 40.*

Jesus answered and said unto her, Martha, Martha, thou art careful and troubled about many things. *Lu. 10: 41.*

Ye tithe mint and rue and all manner of herbs, and pass over judgment and the love of God. *Lu. 11: 42.*

The tongue is a little member, and boasteth great things. *Ja. 3: 5.*

See also

Little; Thing, the Little; Smallness; Trifle.

Pharisaism

Except your righteousness shall exceed the righteousness of the scribes and Pharisees, ye shall in no case enter into the kingdom of heaven. *Mat. 5: 20.*

When the Pharisees saw it, they said unto his disciples, Why eateth your Master with publicans and sinners? *Mat. 9: 11.*

Beware of the leaven of the Pharisees and of the Sadducees. *Mat. 16: 6.*

Woe unto you, scribes and Pharisees, hypocrites! for ye shut up the kingdom of heaven against men. *Mat. 23: 13.*

Ye devour widows' houses, and for a pretence make long prayer. *Mat. 23: 14.*

Ye pay tithe of mint and anise and cummin, and have omitted the weightier matters of the law, judgment, mercy, and faith. *Mat. 23: 23.*

Ye blind guides, which strain at a gnat, and swallow a camel. *Mat. 23: 24.*

Ye make clean the outside of the cup and the platter, but within they are full of extortion and excess. *Mat. 23: 25.*

Woe unto you, scribes and Pharisees, hypocrites! for ye are like unto whited sepulchres, which indeed appear beautiful outward, but are within full of dead men's bones, and of all uncleanness. *Mat.* **23: 27.**

The Pharisee stood and prayed thus with himself, God, I thank thee, that I am not as other men are. *Lu.* **18: 11.**

Men and brethren, I am a Pharisee, the son of a Pharisee. *Ac.* **23: 6.**

After the most straitest sect of our religion I lived a Pharisee. *Ac.* **26: 5.**

See also

Bigotry; Formalism; Hypocrisy; Intolerance; Ritual; Strictness.

Philanthropy

Love ye . . . the stranger. *De.* **10: 19.**

Thou shalt open thine hand wide unto him. *De.* **15: 8.**

All things come of thee, and of thine own have we given thee. *1 Ch.* **29: 14.**

In the morning sow thy seed, and in the evening withhold not thine hand. *Ec.* **11: 6.**

Take heed that ye do not your alms before men, to be seen of them. *Mat.* **6: 1.**

When thou doest thine alms, do not sound a trumpet before thee. *Mat.* **6: 2.**

Whosoever shall give to drink unto one of these little ones a cup of cold water only in the name of a disciple, verily I say unto you, he shall in no wise lose his reward. *Mat.* **10: 42.**

If thou wilt be perfect, go and sell that thou hast, and give to the poor. *Mat.* **19: 21.**

Unto whomsoever much is given, of him shall be much required. *Lu.* **12: 48.**

This is my commandment, That ye love one another, as I have loved you. *Jn.* **15: 12.**

Remember the words of the Lord Jesus, how he said, It is more blessed to give than to receive. *Ac.* **20: 35.**

Owe no man any thing, but to love one another. *Ro.* **13: 8.**

He that loveth another hath fulfilled the law. *Ro.* **13: 8.**

Though I bestow all my goods to feed the poor, . . . and have not charity, it profiteth me nothing. *1 Co.* **13: 3.**

God loveth a cheerful giver. *2 Co.* **9: 7.**

The end of the commandment is charity out of a pure heart. *1 Ti.* **1: 5.**

This is the message that ye heard from the beginning, that we should love one another. *1 Jn.* **3: 11.**

This commandment have we from him, That he who loveth God love his brother also. *1 Jn.* **4: 21.**

See also

Almsgiving; Beneficence; Benevolence; Charity; Love.

Philosophy

With the ancient is wisdom. *Jb.* **12: 12.**

So teach us to number our days, that we may apply our hearts unto wisdom. *Ps.* **90: 12.**

Wisdom is the principal thing; therefore get wisdom. *Pr.* **4: 7.**

Wisdom hath builded her house, she hath hewn out her seven pillars. *Pr.* **9: 1.**

In the beginning was the Word, and the Word was with God, and the Word was God. *Jn.* **1: 1.**

Then certain philosophers of the Epicureans, and of the Stoicks, encountered him. *Ac.* **17: 18.**

We speak the wisdom of God in a mystery, even the hidden wisdom. *1 Co.* **2: 7.**

The wisdom of this world is foolishness with God. *1 Co.* **3: 19.**

Beware lest any man spoil you through philosophy and vain deceit. *Col.* **2: 8.**

See also

Knowledge; Learning; Wisdom.

Physician

Ye are all physicians of no value. *Jb.* **13: 4.**

Is there no balm in Gilead; is there no physician there? *Je.* **8: 22.**

They that be whole need not a physician, but they that are sick. *Mat.* **9: 12.**

I was sick, and ye visited me. *Mat.* **25: 36.**

A certain woman . . . had suffered many things of many physicians. *Mk.* **5: 25, 26.**

They shall lay hands on the sick, and they shall recover. *Mk.* **16: 18.**

Physician, heal thyself. *Lu.* **4: 23.**

Have all the gifts of healing? *1 Co.* **12: 30.**

Luke, the beloved physician. *Col.* **4: 14.**

See also

Antidote; Cure; Doctor; Healing; Medicine; Remedy.

Piece

He hath also. taken me by my neck, and shaken me to pieces. *Jb.* **16: 12.**

They part my garments among them, and cast lots upon my vesture. *Ps.* **22: 18.**

Consider this, ye that forget God, lest I tear you in pieces, and there be none to deliver. *Ps.* **50: 22.**

Thou art my portion, O Lord. *Ps.* **119: 57.**

No man putteth a piece of new cloth unto an old garment. *Mat.* **9: 16.**

They covenanted with him for thirty pieces of silver. *Mat.* **26: 15.**

I have bought a piece of ground, and I must needs go and see it: I pray thee have me excused. *Lu.* **14: 18.**

What woman having ten pieces of silver, if she lose one piece, doth not light a candle, and sweep the house, and seek diligently till she find it? *Lu.* **15: 8.**

See also

Member; Part; Portion.

Piety

Help, Lord; for the godly man ceaseth. *Ps.* **12: 1.**

That we may lead a quiet and peaceable life in all godliness and honesty. *1 Ti.* **2: 2.**

Let them learn first to shew piety at home. *1 Ti.* **5: 4.**

Godliness with contentment is great gain. *1 Ti.* **6: 6.**

All that will live godly in Christ Jesus shall suffer persecution. *2 Ti.* **3: 12.**

According as his divine power hath given unto us all things that pertain unto life and godliness. *2 Pe.* **1: 3.**

See also

Consecration; Dedication; Devoutness; Godliness; Holiness; Righteousness; Saint.

Pilgrim

I am with thee, and will keep thee in all places whither thou goest, and will bring thee again into this land. *Ge.* 28: 15.

The days of the years of my pilgrimage. *Ge.* 47: 9.

I have also established my covenant with them, to give them the land of Canaan, the land of their pilgrimage, wherein they were strangers. *Ex.* 6: 4.

My presence shall go with thee, and I will give thee rest. *Ex.* 33: 14.

According to the commandment of the Lord they journeyed. *Nu.* 9: 20.

The Lord sent thee on a journey. *1 S.* 15: 18.

The steps of a good man are ordered by the Lord. *Ps.* 37: 23.

He . . . made his own people to go forth like sheep, and guided them in the wilderness like a flock. *Ps.* 78: 50, 52.

Thy statutes have been my songs in the house of my pilgrimage. *Ps.* 119: 54.

Come ye, and let us go up to the mountain of the Lord. *Is.* 2: 3.

He went through the cities and villages, teaching, and journeying toward Jerusalem. *Lu.* 13: 22.

Having a desire to depart, and to be with Christ. *Ph.* 1: 23.

They were strangers and pilgrims on the earth. *He.* 11: 13.

I beseech you as strangers and pilgrims, abstain from fleshly lusts. *1 Pe.* 2: 11.

See also

City, the Holy; Country, the Better; Discovery; Land, the Promised; Pioneer; Progress; Travel; Wandering.

Pillar

His wife looked back from behind him, and she became a pillar of salt. *Ge.* 19: 26.

These words, which I command thee this day, shall be in thine heart. And thou shalt write them upon the posts of thy house. *De.* 6: 6, 9.

Samson said unto the lad that held him by the hand, Suffer me that I may feel the pillars whereupon the house standeth, that I may lean upon them. *Ju.* 16: 26.

The pillars of the earth are the Lord's, and he hath set the world upon them. *1 S.* 2: 8.

God . . . shaketh the earth out of her place, and the pillars thereof tremble. *Jb.* 9: 2, 6.

The earth and all the inhabitants thereof are dissolved: I bear up the pillars of it. *Ps.* 75: 3.

Blessed is the man that heareth me, watching daily at my gates, waiting at the posts of my doors. *Pr.* 8: 34.

Wisdom hath builded her house, she hath hewn out her seven pillars. *Pr.* 9: 1.

That thou mayest know how thou oughtest to behave thyself in the house of God, which is the church of the living God, the pillar and ground of truth. *1 Ti.* 3: 15.

Him that overcometh will I make a pillar in the temple of my God. *Re.* 3: 12.

Pilot

He leadeth me beside the still waters. *Ps.* 23: 2.

The way of a ship in the midst of the sea. *Pr.* 30: 19.

That led them through the deep. *Is.* 63: 13.

Thy wise men . . . were thy pilots. *Eze.* 27: 8.

Thy mariners, and thy pilots . . . shall fall into the midst of the seas in the day of thy ruin. *Eze.* 27: 27.

All that handle the oar, the mariners, and all the pilots of the sea, shall come down from their ships, they shall stand upon the land; And shall cause their voice to be heard against thee. *Eze.* 27: 29, 30.

The shipmaster came to him, and said unto him, What meanest thou, O sleeper? *Jon.* 1: 6.

See also

Navigation; Ship; Voyage.

Pinnacle

He shall set me up upon a rock. *Ps.* 27: 5.

Wisdom . . . standeth in the top of high places. *Pr.* 8: 1, 2.

I will cause thee to ride upon the high places of the earth. *Is.* 58: 14.

The devil taketh him up into an exceeding high mountain. *Mat.* 4: 8.

He . . . set him on a pinnacle of the temple. *Lu.* 4: 9.

He carried me away in the spirit to a great and high mountain. *Re.* 21: 10.

See also

Eminence; Summit; Top.

Pioneer

Speak unto the children of Israel, that they go forward. *Ex.* 14: 15.

We are journeying unto the place of which the Lord said, I will give it you. *Nu.* 10: 29.

Let us go up at once, and possess it. *Nu.* 13: 30.

Arise, go over this Jordan, thou, and all this people, unto the land which I do give to them. *Jos.* 1: 2.

Every place that the sole of your foot shall tread upon, that have I given unto you. *Jos.* 1: 3.

Let us go over unto the other side of the lake. And they launched forth. *Lu.* 8: 22.

The Lord . . . sent them two and two before his face into every city and place, whither he himself would come. *Lu.* 10: 1.

Go your ways: behold, I send you forth as lambs among wolves. *Lu.* 10: 3.

He went out, not knowing whither he went. *He.* 11: 8.

They were strangers and pilgrims on the earth. *He.* 11: 13.

See also

Country, the Better; Discovery; Forerunner; Land, the Promised; Pilgrim; Preparation; Progress.

Pit

They shall go down to the bars of the pit. *Jb.* 17: 16.

He keepeth back his soul from the pit, and his life from perishing by the sword. *Jb.* 33: 18.

Be not silent to me: lest, if thou be silent to me, I become like them that go down into the pit. *Ps.* 28: 1.

What profit is there in my blood, when I go down to the pit? Shall the dust praise thee? *Ps.* 30: 9.

He brought me up also out of an horrible pit, out of the miry clay, and set my feet upon a rock. *Ps.* 40: 2.

Let not the pit shut her mouth upon me. *Ps.* 69: 15.

Look unto the rock whence ye are hewn, and to the hole of the pit whence ye are digged. *Is.* 51: 1.

The anointed of the Lord was taken in their pits. *La.* 4: 20.

What man shall there be among you, that shall have one sheep, and if it fall into a pit on the sabbath day, will he not lay hold on it, and lift it out? *Mat.* 12: 11.

See also
Abyss; Deep; Depth.

Pity

The poor shall never cease out of the land. *De.* 15: 11.

Have pity upon me, have pity upon me, O ye my friends. *Jb.* 19: 21.

I looked for some to take pity, but there was none; and for comforters, but I found none. *Ps.* 69: 20.

Thou, Lord, art . . . plenteous in mercy unto all them that call upon thee. *Ps.* 86: 5.

Who redeemeth thy life from destruction; who crowneth thee with lovingkindness and tender mercies. *Ps.* 103: 4.

Like as a father pitieth his children, so the Lord pitieth them that fear him. *Ps.* 103: 13.

He that hath pity upon the poor lendeth unto the Lord. *Pr.* 19: 17.

Then will the Lord be jealous for his land, and pity his people. *Jo.* 2: 18.

For three transgressions of Edom, and for four, I will not turn away the punishment thereof; because he . . . did cast off all pity, and his anger did tear perpetually, and he kept his wrath for ever. *Am.* 1: 11.

Blessed are the merciful: for they shall obtain mercy. *Mat.* 5: 7.

Whosoever shall give to drink unto one of these little ones a cup of cold water only . . . he shall in no wise lose his reward. *Mat.* 10: 42.

Shouldest not thou also have had compassion on thy fellow servant, even as I had pity on thee? *Mat.* 18: 33.

Jesus . . . put forth his hand, and touched him. *Mk.* 1: 41.

God, who is rich in mercy. *Ep.* 2: 4.

Be ye all of one mind, having compassion one of another, love as brethren, be pitiful, be courteous. *1 Pe.* 3: 8.

See also
Charity; Christ, Compassion of; Christ, Sympathy of; Clemency; Compassion; God, Compassion of; God, Mercy of; Mercy; Sympathy.

Place

The place whereon thou standest is holy ground. *Ex.* 3: 5.

The situation of the city is pleasant. *2 K.* 2: 19.

He shall return no more to his house, neither shall his place know him any more. *Jb.* 7: 10.

Where is the place of understanding? *Jb.* 28: 12.

Even so would he have removed thee out of the strait into a broad place. *Jb.* 36: 16.

The lines are fallen unto me in pleasant places. *Ps.* 16: 6.

Thou hast set my feet in a large room. *Ps.* 31: 8.

Beautiful for situation, the joy of the whole earth, is mount Zion, on the sides of the north, the city of the great King. *Ps.* 48: 2.

Thou broughtest us out into a wealthy place. *Ps.* 66: 12.

Bless the Lord, all his works in all places of his dominion. *Ps.* 103: 22.

The eyes of the Lord are in every place. *Pr.* 15: 3.

The Lord shall comfort . . . all her waste places. *Is.* 51: 3.

Enlarge the place of thy tent. *Is.* 54: 2.

I will make the place of my feet glorious. *Is.* 60: 13.

He . . . treadeth upon the high places of the earth. *Am.* 4: 13.

They . . . love the uppermost rooms at feasts. *Mat.* 23: 5, 6.

Plague

I will stretch out my hand, that I may smite thee and thy people with pestilence. *Ex.* 9: 15.

The Lord sent a pestilence upon Israel. *2 S.* 24: 15.

All thy people Israel . . . shall know every man the plague of his own heart. *1 K.* 8: 38.

All the day long have I been plagued, and chastened every morning. *Ps.* 73: 14.

I will beat down his foes before his face, and plague them that hate him. *Ps.* 89: 23.

There shall no evil befall thee, neither shall any plague come nigh thy dwelling. *Ps.* 91: 10.

O death, I will be thy plagues. *Ho.* 13: 14.

Go in peace, and be whole of thy plague. *Mk.* 5: 34.

In that same hour he cured many of their infirmities and plagues, and of evil spirits. *Lu.* 7: 21.

See also
Blight; Contagion; Disease; Pestilence.

Plan

I purpose to build an house unto the name of the Lord my God. *1 K.* 5: 5.

Without counsel purposes are disappointed. *Pr.* 15: 22.

To every thing there is a season, and a time to every purpose under the heaven. *Ec.* 3: 1.

He hath anointed me to preach the gospel to the poor; he hath sent me to heal the brokenhearted, to preach deliverance to the captives, and recovering of sight to the blind, to set at liberty them that are bruised. *Lu.* 4: 18.

Which of you, intending to build a tower, sitteth not down first, and counteth the cost, whether he have sufficient to finish it? *Lu.* 14: 28.

What king, going to make war against another king, sitteth not down first, and consulteth whether he be able with ten thousand to meet him that cometh against him with twenty thousand? *Lu.* 14: 31.

God so loved the world, that he gave his only begotten Son, that whosoever believeth in him should not perish, but have everlasting life. *Jn.* 3: 16.

I have chosen you, and ordained you, that ye should go and bring forth fruit. *Jn.* 15: 16.

I have appeared unto thee for this purpose, to make thee a minister and a witness both of these things which thou hast seen, and of those things in the which I will appear unto thee. *Ac.* 26: 16.

Having made known unto us the mystery of his will, according to his good pleasure which he hath purposed in himself: That in the dispensation of the fulness of times he might gather together in one all tHings in Christ, both which are in heaven, and which are on earth; even in him. *Ep.* 1: 9, 10.

Who hath . . . called us with an holy calling, not according to our works, but according to his own purpose and grace. *2 Ti.* 1: 9.

Thou hast fully known my doctrine, manner of life, purpose. *2 Ti.* 3: 10.

See also

Aim; Ambition; Aspiration; Christ, Purpose of; Determination; End; Intention; Purpose.

Plant

The Lord God made . . . every plant of the field before it was in the earth, and every herb of the field before it grew. *Ge.* 2: 4, 5.

The Lord God planted a garden eastward in Eden. *Ge.* 2: 8.

He cometh forth like a flower, and is cut down. *Jb.* 14: 2.

Thy wife shall be as a fruitful vine by the sides of thine house: thy children like olive plants round about thy table. *Ps.* 128: 3.

A time to plant, and a time to pluck up that which is planted. *Ec.* 3: 2.

In the day shalt thou make thy plant to grow, and in the morning shalt thou make thy seed to flourish: but the harvest shall be a heap in the day of grief. *Is.* 17: 11.

He shall grow up before him as a tender plant. *Is.* 53: 2.

They shall inherit the land for ever, the branch of my planting, the work of my hands, that I may be glorified. *Is.* 60: 21.

That they might be called trees of righteousness, the planting of the Lord. *Is.* 61: 3.

They shall not plant, and another eat. *Is.* 65: 22.

Plant gardens, and eat the fruit of them. *Je.* 29: 5.

Every plant, which my heavenly Father hath not planted, shall be rooted up. *Mat.* 15: 13.

Where was a garden. *Jn.* 18: 1.

I have planted, Apollos watered; but God gave the increase. *1 Co.* 3: 6.

See also

Cultivation; Flower; Fruit; Garden; Grain; Harvest; Herb; Olive; Seed; Tree; Verdure; Vine.

Play

The people sat down to eat and to drink, and rose up to play. *Ex.* 32: 6.

It came to pass, when their hearts were merry, that they said, Call for Samson, that he may make us sport. And they called for Samson out of the prison house; and he made them sport. *Ju.* 16: 25.

Let the young men now arise, and play before us *2 S.* 2: 14.

Therefore will I play before the Lord. *2 S.* 6: 21.

Surely the mountains bring him forth food, where all the beasts of the field play. *Jb.* 40: 20.

Wilt thou play with him as with a bird? *Jb.* 41: 5.

It is as sport to a fool to do mischief. *Pr.* 10: 23.

The sucking child shall play on the hole of the asp. *Is.* 11: 8.

The streets of the city shall be full of boys and girls playing in the streets thereof. *Zch.* 8: 5.

Whereunto shall I liken this generation? It is like unto children sitting in the markets, and calling unto their fellows. *Mat.* 11: 16.

See also

Amusement; Dance; Festival; Game; Gaiety; Laughter; Merriment; Mirth; Recreation; Sport.

Plea

I will entreat the Lord. *Ex.* 8: 29.

Intreat me not to leave thee, or to return from following after thee: for whither thou goest, I will go. *Ru.* 1: 16.

O that one might plead for a man with God, as a man pleadeth for his neighbour! *Jb.* 16: 21.

He forgetteth not the cry of the humble. *Ps.* 9: 12.

I entreated thy favour with my whole heart. *Ps.* 119: 58.

The Lord is nigh unto all them that call upon him, to all that call upon him in truth. *Ps.* 145: 18.

The poor useth entreaties; but the rich answereth roughly. *Pr.* 18: 23.

Thus saith thy Lord the Lord, and thy God that pleadeth the cause of his people. *Is.* 51: 22.

Seek ye the Lord while he may be found, call ye upon him while he is near. *Is.* 55: 6.

I will yet plead with you, saith the Lord, and with your children's children will I plead. *Je.* 2: 9.

Like as I pleaded with your fathers in the wilderness of the land of Egypt, so will I plead with you, saith the Lord God. *Eze.* 20: 36.

I will also gather all nations, . . . and will plead with them there for my people. *Jo.* 3: 2.

Praying us with much entreaty. *2 Co.* 8: 4.

The wisdom that is from above is first pure, then peaceable, gentle, and easy to be entreated. *Ja.* 3: 17.

See also

Appeal; Entreaty; God, Prayer to; Petition; Prayer; Request; Supplication.

Pleasure

Thou art not a God that hath pleasure in wickedness. *Ps.* 5: 4.

The lines are fallen unto me in pleasant places. *Ps.* 16: 6.

At thy right hand there are pleasures for evermore. *Ps.* 16: 11.

Surely goodness and mercy shall follow me all the days of my life *Ps.* 23: 6.

Bless ye the Lord, all ye his hosts; ye ministers of his, that do his pleasure. *Ps.* 103: 21.

Behold, how good and how pleasant it is for brethren to dwell together in unity! *Ps.* 133: 1.

The Lord taketh pleasure in his people. *Ps.* 149: 4.

Her ways are ways of pleasantness, and all her paths are peace. *Pr.* 3: 17.

There is nothing better for a man, than that he should eat and drink, and that he should make his soul enjoy good in his labour. *Ec.* **2: 24.**

Go thy way, eat thy bread with joy, and drink thy wine with a merry heart; for God now accepteth thy works. *Ec.* **9: 7.**

Rejoice with me; for I have found my sheep which was lost. *Lu.* **15: 6.**

The younger son . . . wasted his substance with riotous living. *Lu.* **15: 13.**

He made haste, and came down, and received him joyfully. *Lu.* **19: 6.**

If ye know these things, happy are ye if ye do them. *Jn.* **13: 17.**

Therefore did my heart rejoice, and my tongue was glad. *Ac.* **2: 26.**

I take pleasure in infirmities, in reproaches, in necessities, in persecutions, in distresses for Christ's sake. *2 Co.* **12: 10.**

The fruit of the Spirit is . . . joy. *Ga.* **5: 22.**

It is God which worketh in you both to will and to do of his good pleasure. *Ph.* **2: 13.**

Receive him therefore in the Lord with all gladness. *Ph.* **2: 29.**

We ourselves also were sometimes foolish, disobedient, deceived, serving divers lusts and pleasures. *Tit.* **3: 3.**

Choosing rather to suffer affliction with the people of God, than to enjoy the pleasures of sin for a season. *He.* **11: 25.**

See also
Cheerfulness; Christ, Joy in; Christ, Joy of; Contentment; Delight; Enjoyment; Gaiety; Gladness; God, Joy in; Happiness; Joy; Merriment; Mirth; Rejoicing; Satisfaction.

Pledge

With thee will I establish my covenant. *Ge.* **6: 18.**

Now therefore, if ye will obey my voice indeed, and keep my covenant, then ye shall be a peculiar treasure unto me above all people. *Ex.* **19: 5.**

I will never break my covenant with you. *Ju.* **2: 1.**

He will shew them his covenant. *Ps.* **25: 14.**

He hath given meat unto them that fear him: he will ever be mindful of his covenant. *Ps.* **111: 5.**

Better is it that thou shouldest not vow, than that thou shouldest vow and not pay. *Ec.* **5: 5.**

Come, and let us join ourselves to the Lord in a perpetual covenant. *Je.* **50: 5.**

God . . . hath also sealed us, and given the earnest of the Spirit in our hearts. *2 Co.* **1: 21, 22.**

That Holy Spirit of promise, Which is the earnest of our inheritance. *Ep.* **1: 13, 14.**

This is the covenant that I will make with the house of Israel after those days. *He.* **8: 10.**

See also
Assurance; Covenant; Promise; Votary; Vow.

Plenty

Ye shall eat your bread to the full, and dwell in your land safely. *Le.* **26: 5.**

The Lord . . . plentifully rewardeth the proud doer. *Ps.* **31: 23.**

Thou, Lord, art . . . plenteous in mercy unto all them that call upon thee. *Ps.* **86: 5.**

With him is plenteous redemption. *Ps.* **130: 7.**

I will abundantly bless her provision: I will satisfy her poor with bread. *Ps.* **132: 15.**

Honour the Lord with thy substance: . . . So shall thy barns be filled with plenty. *Pr.* **3: 9, 10.**

The thoughts of the diligent tend only to plenteousness. *Pr.* **21: 5.**

He that tilleth his land shall have plenty of bread. *Pr.* **28: 19.**

I brought you into a plentiful country, to eat the fruit thereof and the goodness thereof. *Je.* **2: 7.**

Joy and gladness is taken from the plentiful field. *Je.* **48: 33.**

Ye shall eat in plenty, and be satisfied, and praise the name of the Lord your God. *Jo.* **2: 26.**

The harvest truly is plenteous, but the labourers are few. *Mat.* **9: 37.**

See also
Abundance; Adequacy; Ampleness; Fertility; God, Wealth of; Goods; Riches; Store; Substance; Sufficiency; Wealth.

Plot

All of you have conspired against me. *1 S.* **22: 8.**

The workers of iniquity . . . speak peace to their neighbours, but mischief is in their hearts. *Ps.* **28: 3.**

He deviseth mischief upon his bed. *Ps.* **36: 4.**

The wicked plotteth against the just. *Ps.* **37: 12.**

Every one that is proud in heart is an abomination to the Lord: though hand join in hand, he shall not be unpunished. *Pr.* **16: 5.**

There is a conspiracy of her prophets in the midst thereof, like a roaring lion ravening the prey; they have devoured souls. *Eze.* **22: 25.**

Though I have bound and strengthened their arms, yet do they imagine mischief against me. *Ho.* **7: 15.**

Amos hath conspired against thee in the midst of the house of Israel: the land is not able to bear all his words. *Am.* **7: 10.**

They were more than forty which had made this conspiracy. *Ac.* **23: 13.**

See also
Conspiracy; Evil; Iniquity; Intrigue; Mischief; Plan.

Plow

They that plow iniquity, and sow wickedness, reap the same. *Jb.* **4: 8.**

If my land cry against me, or that the furrows likewise thereof complain; . . . Let thistles grow instead of wheat, and cockle instead of barley. *Jb.* **31: 38, 40.**

Canst thou bind the unicorn with his band in the furrow? or will he harrow the valleys after thee? *Jb.* **39: 10.**

Thou waterest the ridges thereof abundantly: thou settlest the furrows thereof. *Ps.* **65: 10.**

The plowers plowed upon my back: they made long their furrows. *Ps.* **129: 3.**

The sluggard will not plow by reason of the cold; therefore shall he beg in harvest, and have nothing. *Pr.* **20: 4.**

The plowing of the wicked is sin. *Pr.* **21: 4.**

They shall beat their swords into plowshares. *Is.* 2: 4.

Doth the plowman plow all day to sow? doth he open and break the clods of his ground? *Is.* 28: 24.

Zion shall be plowed like a field, and Jerusalem shall become heaps. *Je.* 26: 18.

Ye have plowed wickedness, ye have reaped iniquity. *Ho.* 10: 13.

Beat your plowshares into swords. *Jo.* 3: 10.

He that ploweth should plow in hope. *1 Co.* 9: 10.

No man, having put his hand to the plow, and looking back, is fit for the kingdom of God. *Lu.* 9: 62.

See also

Cultivation; Plant; Seed.

Plunder

They borrowed of the Egyptians jewels of silver, and jewels of gold, and raiment. *Ex.* 12: 35.

They take the widow's ox for a pledge. *Jb.* 24: 3.

Lord, who is like unto thee, which deliverest the poor from him that is too strong for him, yea, the poor and the needy from him that spoileth him? *Ps.* 35: 10.

They which hate us spoil for themselves. *Ps.* 44: 10.

The Lord will plead their cause, and spoil the soul of those that spoiled them. *Pr.* 22: 23.

No man can enter into a strong man's house, and spoil his goods, except he will first bind the strong man; and then he will spoil his house. *Mk.* 3: 27.

Ye . . . took joyfully the spoiling of your goods, knowing in yourselves that ye have in heaven a better and an enduring substance. *He.* 10: 34.

See also

Booty; Spoil.

Poetry

Moses spake . . . the words of this song, until they were ended. *De.* 31: 30.

He spake three thousand proverbs: and his songs were a thousand and five. *1 K.* 4: 32.

Now am I their song, yea, I am their byword. *Jb.* 30: 9.

He hath put a new song in my mouth, even praise unto our God. *Ps.* 40: 3..

Make sweet melody, sing many songs, that thou mayest be remembered. *Is.* 23: 16.

Thou art unto them as a very lovely song. *Eze.* 33: 32.

It is also written in the second psalm, Thou art my Son, this day have I begotten thee. *Ac.* 13: 33.

He saith also in another psalm, Thou shalt not suffer thine Holy One to see corruption. *Ac.* 13: 35.

As certain also of your own poets have said, For we are also his offspring. *Ac.* 17: 28.

Speaking to yourselves in psalms and hymns and spiritual songs. *Ep.* 5: 19.

See also

Hymn; Psalm; Song.

Poise

The pillars of the earth are the Lord's, and he hath set the world upon them. *1 S.* 2: 8.

Because he is at my right hand, I shall not be moved. *Ps.* 16: 8.

Rest in the Lord. *Ps.* 37: 7.

The whole earth is at rest, and is quiet. *Is.* 14: 7.

As much as lieth in you, live peaceably with all men. *Ro.* 12: 18.

Let the peace of God rule in your hearts. *Col.* 3: 15.

Follow righteousness, faith, charity, peace. *2 Ti.* 2: 22.

The ornament of a meek and quiet spirit. *1 Pe.* 3: 4.

See also

Balance; Confidence; Firmness; Peace; Rest; Security; Serenity; Stability; Steadfastness.

Poison

Their wine is the poison of dragons. *De.* 32: 33.

The arrows of the Almighty are within me, the poison whereof drinketh up my spirit. *Jb.* 6: 4.

Their poison is like the poison of a serpent. *Ps.* 58: 4.

Adders' poison is under their lips. *Ps.* 140: 3.

The Lord our God hath put us to silence, and given us water of gall to drink, because we have sinned against the Lord. *Je.* 8: 14.

Ye have turned judgment into gall, and the fruit of righteousness into hemlock. *Am.* 6: 12.

If they drink any deadly thing, it shall not hurt them. *Mk.* 16: 18.

The tongue . . . is an unruly evil, full of deadly poison. *Ja* 3: 8.

See also

Bane.

Politeness

Thou shalt not curse the deaf. *Le.* 19: 14.

Thou shalt rise up before the hoary head, and honour the face of the old man. *Le.* 19: 32.

Ye shall not respect persons in judgment; but ye shall hear the small as well as the great. *De.* 1: 17.

Honour thy father and thy mother. *De.* 5: 16.

A time to embrace, and a time to refrain from embracing. *Ec.* 3: 5.

The child shall behave himself proudly against the ancient, and the base against the honourable. *Is.* 3: 5.

Charity . . . Doth not behave itself unseemly. *1 Co.* 13: 4, 5.

Evil communications corrupt good manners. *1 Co.* 15: 33.

The fruit of the Spirit is . . . gentleness. *Ga.* 5: 22.

Be ye kind one to another. *Ep.* 4: 32.

Brethren, be pitiful, be courteous. *1 Pe.* 3: 8.

See also

Manners.

Pollution

Neither wilt thou suffer thine Holy One to see corruption. *Ps.* 16: 10.

Blessed is the man that . . . keepeth the sabbath from polluting it, and keepeth his hand from doing any evil. *Is.* 56: 2.

O Jerusalem, wash thine heart from wickedness, that thou mayest be saved. How long shall thy vain thoughts lodge within thee? *Je.* 4: 14.

The Lord . . . hath polluted the kingdom

and the princes thereof. *La.* 2: 2.

Her prophets, and . . . priests . . . have wandered as blind men in the streets, they have polluted themselves with blood, so that men could not touch their garments. *La.* 4: 13, 14.

Ye pollute yourselves with all your idols. *Eze.* 20: 31.

They shall pollute the sanctuary of strength. *Da.* 11: 31.

Her priests have polluted the sanctuary, they have done violence to the law. *Zph.* 3: 4.

Not that which goeth into the mouth defileth a man; but that which cometh out of the mouth, this defileth a man. *Mat.* 15: 11.

This is the man, that . . . hath polluted this holy place. *Ac.* 21: 28.

God gave them over to a reprobate mind, to do those things which are not convenient. *Ro.* 1: 28.

Unto them that are defiled and unbelieving is nothing pure; but even their mind and conscience is defiled. *Tit.* 1: 15.

If after they have escaped the pollutions of the world, . . . they are again entangled therein, and overcome, the latter end is worse with them than the beginning. 2 *Pe.* 2: 20.

He which is filthy, let him be filthy still. *Re.* 22: 11.

See also
Corruption; Defilement; Depravity; Impurity; Iniquity; Lust; Sin; Uncleanness; Vileness.

Pomp

Thou, even thou, art Lord alone; thou hast made heaven, the heaven of heavens, with all their host, the earth, and all things that are therein, the seas, and all that is therein, and thou preservest them all; and the host of heaven worshippeth thee. *Ne.* 9: 6.

The God of glory thundereth: the Lord is upon many waters. *Ps.* 29: 3.

They . . . trust in their wealth, and boast themselves in the multitude of their riches. *Ps.* 49: 6.

Treasures of wickedness profit nothing. *Pr.* 10: 2.

Before honour is humility. *Pr.* 15: 33.

Thy pomp is brought down to the grave. *Is.* 14: 11.

Thou shalt no more be called, the lady of kingdoms. *Is.* 47: 5.

Though thou clothest thyself with crimson, though thou deckest thee with ornaments of gold, though thou rentest thy face with painting, in vain shalt thou make thyself fair. *Je.* 4: 30.

I will also make the pomp of the strong to cease. *Eze.* 7: 24.

Thou didst trust in thine own beauty. *Eze.* 16: 15.

The glory of the Lord filled the house. *Eze.* 43: 5.

Beware of the scribes, which desire to walk in long robes, and love greetings in the markets, and the highest seats in the synagogues, and the chief rooms at feasts. *Lu.* 20: 46.

The pride of life is not of the Father, but is of the world. *1 Jn.* 2: 16.

See also
Display; Haughtiness; Ostentation.

Pool

I made me pools of water, to water therewith the wood that bringeth forth trees. *Ec.* 2: 6.

The parched ground shall become a pool, *Is.* 35: 7.

I will make the wilderness a pool of water, and the dry land springs of water. *Is.* 41: 18.

I will make the rivers islands, and I will dry up the pools. *Is.* 42: 15.

An angel went down at a certain season into the pool, and troubled the water. *Jn.* 5: 4.

I have no man, when the water is troubled, to put me into the pool. *Jn.* 5: 7.

See also
Spring; Water; Well.

Poor

None might enter into the king's gate clothed with sackcloth. *Es.* 4: 2.

Thou, O God, hast prepared of thy goodness for the poor. *Ps.* 68: 10.

The poor is separated from his neighbour. *Pr.* 19: 4.

All the brethren of the poor do hate him: how much more do his friends go far from him? *Pr.* 19: 7.

The righteous considereth the cause of the poor. *Pr.* 29: 7.

The needy shall lie down in safety. *Is.* 14: 30.

Hear this, O ye that swallow up the needy, even to make the poor of the land to fail. *Am.* 8: 4.

The Spirit of the Lord is upon me, because he hath anointed me to preach the gospel to the poor. *Lu.* 4: 18.

Blessed be ye poor. *Lu.* 6: 20.

Woe unto you that are rich. *Lu.* 6: 24.

See also
Charity; Destitution; Lack; Need; Philanthropy; Poverty; Want.

Popularity

Let us make us a name. *Ge.* 11: 4.

A good name is rather to be chosen than great riches, and loving favour rather than silver and gold. *Pr.* 22: 1.

A prophet is not without honour, save in his own country, and in his own house. *Mat.* 13: 57.

Many were gathered together, insomuch that there was no room to receive them. *Mk.* 2: 2.

He had healed many; insomuch that they pressed upon him. *Mk.* 3: 10.

Much people followed him, and thronged him. *Mk.* 5: 24.

The common people heard him gladly. *Mk.* 12: 37.

Woe unto you, when all men shall speak well of you. *Lu.* 6: 26.

They loved the praise of men more than the praise of God. *Jn.* 12: 43.

They . . . did eat their meat with gladness and singleness of heart, Praising God, and having favour with all the people. *Ac.* 2: 46, 47.

Hold such in reputation. *Ph.* 2: 29.

Not with eyeservice, as menpleasers. *Col.* 3: 22.

See also
Distinction; Fame; Favor; Honor; Name; Renown; Report; Reputation.

Portion

Ye have no part in the Lord. *Jos.* 22: 25.

I pray thee, let a double portion of thy spirit be upon me. 2 *K.* 2: 9.

Upon the wicked he shall rain snares, fire and brimstone, and an horrible tempest: this shall be the portion of their cup. *Ps.* 11: 6.

The Lord is the portion of mine inheritance and of my cup: thou maintainest my lot. *Ps.* 16: 5.

They part my garments among them, and cast lots upon my vesture. *Ps.* 22: 18.

God is the strength of my heart, and my portion for ever. *Ps.* 73: 26.

A wise servant . . . shall have part of the inheritance among the brethren. *Pr.* 17: 2.

The younger of them said to his father, Father, give me the portion of goods that falleth to me. *Lu.* 15: 12.

See also

Allotment; Member; Part; Piece.

Possession

The Lord your God hath given you this land to possess it. *De.* 3: 18.

O God, thou art my God. *Ps.* 63: 1.

So are the ways of every one that is greedy of gain; which taketh away the life of the owners thereof. *Pr.* 1: 19.

The upright shall have good things in possession. *Pr.* 28: 10.

I made me great works; I builded me houses; I planted me vineyards: . . . I had great possessions. *Ec.* 2: 4, 7.

There is a sore evil which I have seen under the sun, namely, riches kept for the owners thereof to their hurt. *Ec.* 5: 13.

Ye shall give them no possession in Israel: I am their possession. *Eze.* 44: 28.

A man's life consisteth not in the abundance of the things which he possesseth. *Lu.* 12: 15.

I give tithes of all that I possess. *Lu.* 18: 12.

As many as were possessors of lands or houses sold them, and brought the prices of the things that were sold, And laid them down at the apostles' feet. *Ac.* 4: 34, 35.

All things are yours. *1 Co.* 3: 21.

See also

Belongings; God, Wealth of; Gold; Goods; Mammon; Ownership; Wealth; Worldliness.

Possibility

The Lord is with thee, thou mighty man of valor. *Ju.* 6: 12.

They that wait upon the Lord shall renew their strength. *Is.* 40: 31.

Be ye therefore perfect, even as your Father which is in heaven is perfect. *Mat.* 5: 48.

If ye have faith as a grain of mustard seed, . . . nothing shall be impossible unto you. *Mat.* 17: 20.

With men this is impossible; but with God all things are possible. *Mat.* 19: 26.

If thou canst believe, all things are possible to him that believeth. *Mk.* 9: 23.

Father, all things are possible unto thee. *Mk.* 14: 36.

He brought him to Jesus. And when Jesus beheld him, he said, Thou art Simon the son of Jona: thou shalt be called Cephas, which is by interpretation, A stone. *Jn.* 1: 42.

I can do all things through Christ which strengtheneth me. *Ph.* 4: 13.

The power of an endless life. *He.* 7: 16.

See also

Ability; Capacity; Endowment; Energy; Power; Skill; Strength; Talent.

Potter

Thou shalt dash them in pieces like a potter's vessel. *Ps.* 2: 9.

Arise, and go down to the potter's house, and there I will cause thee to hear my words. *Je.* 18: 2.

I went down to the potter's house, and, behold, he wrought a work on the wheels. *Je.* 18: 3.

The vessel that he made of clay was marred in the hand of the potter: so he made it again another vessel, as seemed good to the potter to make it. *Je.* 18: 4.

O house of Israel, cannot I do with you as this potter? saith the Lord. *Je.* 18: 6.

Behold, as the clay is in the potter's hand, so are ye in mine hand, O house of Israel. *Je.* 18: 6.

The precious sons of Zion, comparable to fine gold, how are they esteemed as earthen pitchers, the work of the hands of the potter! *La.* 4: 2.

See also

Clay.

Poverty

For the poor shall never cease out of the land. *De.* 15: 11.

The Lord maketh poor, and maketh rich: he bringeth low, and lifteth up. *1 S.* 2: 7.

A little that a righteous man hath is better than the riches of many wicked. *Ps.* 37: 16.

The needy shall lie down in safety. *Is.* 14: 30.

I will also leave in the midst of thee an afflicted and poor people, and they shall trust in the name of the Lord. *Zph.* 3: 12.

Blessed are the poor in spirit. *Mat.* 5: 3.

The poor have the gospel preached to them. *Mat.* 11: 5.

The Spirit of the Lord is upon me, because he hath anointed me to preach the gospel to the poor. *Lu.* 4: 18.

Blessed be ye poor: for yours is the kingdom of God. *Lu.* 6: 20.

As poor, yet making many rich; as having nothing, and yet possessing all things. *2 Co.* 6: 10.

Though he was rich, yet for your sakes he became poor. *2 Co.* 8: 9.

Hath not God chosen the poor of this world rich in faith? *Ja.* 2: 5.

I know thy works, and tribulation, and poverty, (but thou art rich). *Re.* 2: 9.

See also

Charity; Destitution; Lack; Need; Philanthropy; Poor; Want.

Power

Thou hast made him a little lower than the angels. *Ps.* 8: 5.

The Lord will give strength unto his people. *Ps.* 29: 11.

He giveth power to the faint. *Is.* 40: 29.

The people that do know their God shall be strong, and do exploits. *Da.* 11: 32.

Ye know that the princes of the Gentiles exercise dominion over them. *Mat.* **20: 25.**

They that are great exercise authority upon them. But it shall not be so among you. *Mat.* **20: 25, 26.**

Ye shall receive power, after that the Holy Ghost is come upon you. *Ac.* **1: 8.**

God wrought special miracles by the hands of Paul. *Ac.* **19: 11.**

So mightily grew the word of God and prevailed. *Ac.* **19: 20.**

In all these things we are more than conquerors through him that loved us. *Ro.* **8: 37.**

Above all that we ask or think. *Ep.* **3: 20.**

God hath not given us the spirit of fear; but of power, and of love, and of a sound mind. *2 Ti.* **1: 7.**

The word of God is quick, and powerful. *He.* **4: 12.**

The power of an endless life. *He.* **7: 16.**

See also

Christ, Power of; Christ, Strength of; Coercion; Compulsion; Force; God, Omnipotence of; God, Power of; God, Strength of; Might; Omnipotence; Strength; Vitality.

Practice

David knew that Saul secretly practised mischief against him. *1 S.* **23: 9.**

So will I sing praise unto thy name for ever, that I may daily perform my vows. *Ps.* **61: 8.**

I have inclined mine heart to perform thy statutes alway, even unto the end. *Ps.* **119: 112.**

Lord, mine heart is not haughty, . . . neither do I exercise myself in great matters. *Ps.* **131: 1.**

Incline not my heart to any evil thing, to practise wicked works with men that work iniquity. *Ps.* **141: 4.**

The vile person will speak villany, and his heart will work iniquity, to practise hypocrisy. *Is.* **32: 6.**

I am the Lord which exercise lovingkindness, judgment, and righteousness, in the earth. *Je.* **9: 24.**

The people of the land have used oppression, and exercised robbery. *Eze.* **22: 29.**

Woe to them that devise iniquity, and work evil upon their beds! when the morning is light, they practise it. *Mi.* **2: 1.**

Why call ye me, Lord, Lord, and do not the things which I say? *Lu.* **6: 46.**

Exercise thyself rather unto godliness. *1 Ti.* **4: 7.**

A doer of the work . . . shall be blessed in his deed. *Ja.* **1: 25.**

An heart they have exercised with covetous practices. *2 Pe.* **2: 14.**

See also

Custom; Discipline; Exercise; Habit; Manners; Performance; Test; Trial.

Praise

Praise is comely. *Ps.* **33: 1.**

So will I sing praise unto thy name for ever. *Ps.* **61: 8.**

All that is within me, bless his holy name. *Ps.* **103: 1.**

They shall speak of the glory of thy kingdom, and talk of thy power. *Ps.* **145: 11.**

Let another man praise thee, and not thine own mouth; a stranger, and not thine own lips. *Pr.* **27: 2.**

Thou shalt call thy walls Salvation, and thy gates Praise. *Is.* **60: 18.**

Suddenly there was with the angel a multitude of the heavenly host praising God. *Lu.* **2: 13.**

Were there not ten cleansed? but where are the nine? *Lu.* **17: 17.**

They loved the praise of men more than the praise of God. *Jn.* **12: 43.**

I praise you. . . . I praise you not. *1 Co.* **11: 2, 17.**

By him therefore let us offer the sacrifice of praise to God continually. *He.* **13: 15.**

See also

Admiration; Alleluia; Commendation; Doxology; Eulogy; God, Praise to; Honor; Renown; Reputation.

Prayer

Seek the Lord and his strength, seek his face continually. *1 Ch.* **16: 11.**

In the shadow of thy wings will I make my refuge. *Ps.* **57: 1.**

Lord, I have called daily upon thee, I have stretched out my hands unto thee. *Ps.* **88: 9.**

Blessed is the man that heareth me, watching daily at my gates, waiting at the posts of my doors. *Pr.* **8: 34.**

Be not rash with thy mouth, and let not thine heart be hasty to utter any thing before God: for God is in heaven, and thou upon earth: therefore let thy words be few. *Ec.* **5: 2.**

When ye make many prayers, I will not hear. *Is.* **1: 15.**

Thou hast not called upon me, O Jacob; but thou hast been weary of me, O Israel. *Is.* **43: 22.**

Daniel . . . kneeled upon his knees three times a day, and prayed, and gave thanks before his God, as he did aforetime. *Da.* **6: 10.**

When thou prayest, thou shalt not be as the hypocrites are. *Mat.* **6: 5.**

They think that they shall be heard for their much speaking. *Mat.* **6: 7.**

After this manner therefore pray ye. *Mat.* **6: 9.**

Where two or three are gathered together in my name, there am I in the midst of them. *Mat.* **18: 20.**

He . . . fell on his face, and prayed. *Mat.* **26: 39.**

Watch and pray, that ye enter not into temptation. *Mat.* **26: 41.**

He said unto them, This kind can come forth by nothing, but by prayer and fasting. *Mk.* **9: 29.**

Which devour widows' houses, and for a pretence make long prayers. *Mk.* **12: 40.**

As he prayed, the fashion of his countenance was altered. *Lu.* **9: 29.**

Lord, teach us to pray. *Lu.* **11: 1.**

When ye pray, say, Our Father which art in heaven. *Lu.* **11: 2.**

Men ought always to pray, and not to faint. *Lu.* **18: 1.**

When they had prayed, the place was shaken where they were assembled together. *Ac.* **4: 31.**

Peter went up upon the house top to pray. *Ac.* **10: 9.**

I will pray with the spirit, and I will pray with the understanding also. *1 Co.* 14: 15.

Pray without ceasing. *1 Th.* 5: 17.

It is sanctified by the word of God and prayer. *1 Ti.* 4: 5.

Golden vials full of odours, which are the prayers of saints. *Re.* 5: 8.

See also

Entreaty; God, Prayer to; Petition; Plea; Prayer, Answer to; Request; Supplication.

Prayer, Answer to

There was no day like that before it or after it, that the Lord hearkened unto the voice of a man. *Jos.* 10: 14.

The Lord hath given me my petition which I asked of him. *1 S.* 1: 27.

So we fasted and besought our God for this: and he was entreated of us. *Ezr.* 8: 23.

Let thine ear now be attentive. *Ne.* 1: 6.

In the time of their trouble when they cried unto thee, thou heardest them from heaven. *Ne.* 9: 27.

The Lord . . . heareth the prayer of the righteous. *Pr.* 15: 29.

Ye shall seek me, and find me, when ye shall search for me with all your heart. *Je.* 29: 13.

Ask, and it shall be given you; seek, and ye shall find; knock, and it shall be opened unto you. *Mat.* 7: 7.

If two of you shall agree on earth as touching any thing that they shall ask, it shall be done for them of my Father which is in heaven. *Mat.* 18: 19.

Therefore I say unto you, What things soever ye desire, when ye pray, believe that ye receive them, and ye shall have them. *Mk.* 11: 24.

If any man be a worshipper of God, and doeth his will, him he heareth. *Jn.* 9: 31.

If ye abide in me, and my words abide in you, ye shall ask what ye will, and it shall be done unto you. *Jn.* 15: 7.

The same Lord over all is rich unto all that call upon him. *Ro.* 10: 12.

Ye ask, and receive not, because ye ask amiss. *Ja.* 4: 3.

The prayer of faith shall save the sick. *Ja.* 5: 15.

The effectual fervent prayer of a righteous man availeth much. *Ja.* 5: 16.

His ears are open unto their prayers. *1 Pe.* 3: 12.

Whatsoever we ask, we receive of him, because we keep his commandments, and do those things that are pleasing in his sight. *1 Jn.* 3: 22.

If we know that he hear us, whatsoever we ask, we know that we have the petitions that we desired of him. *1 Jn.* 5: 15.

See also

Prayer.

Preaching

Behold, thou hast instructed many, and thou hast strengthened the weak hands. Thy words have upholden him that was falling, and thou hast strengthened the feeble knees. But now it is come upon thee, and thou faintest; it toucheth thee, and thou art troubled. *Jb.* 4: 3-5.

Vanity of vanities, saith the Preacher, vanity of vanities; all is vanity. *Ec.* 1: 2.

He laid it upon my mouth, and said, Lo, this hath touched thy lips. *Is.* 6: 7.

The voice of one that crieth. *Is.* 40: 3.

The Lord hath anointed me to preach good tidings. *Is.* 61: 1.

They that be wise shall shine as the brightness of the firmament; and they that turn many to righteousness as the stars for ever and ever. *Da.* 12: 3.

We cannot but speak the things which we have seen and heard. *Ac.* 4: 20.

As he reasoned of righteousness, temperance, and judgment to come, Felix trembled. *Ac.* 24: 25.

I would to God, that not only thou, but also all that hear me this day, were both almost, and altogether such as I am, except these bonds. *Ac.* 26: 29.

How shall they believe in him of whom they have not heard? and how shall they hear without a preacher? *Ro.* 10: 14.

Praying also for us, that God would open unto us a door of utterance. *Col.* 4: 3.

I give thee charge in the sight of God. *1 Ti.* 6: 13.

Preach the word; be instant in season, out of season; reprove, rebuke, exhort with all longsuffering and doctrine. *2 Ti.* 4: 2.

See also

Christ, Preaching of; Christ, the Teacher; Clergy; God, Preaching of; God, Word of; Ministry; Missionary; Pastor; Priesthood; Sermon; Teaching.

Precedence

First be reconciled to thy brother, and then come and offer thy gift. *Mat.* 5: 24.

Seek ye first the kingdom of God, and his righteousness; and all these things shall be added unto you. *Mat.* 6: 33.

Many shall come from the east and west, and shall sit down with Abraham, and Isaac, and Jacob, in the kingdom of heaven. But the children of the kingdom shall be cast out into outer darkness. *Mat.* 8: 11, 12.

Behold, I send my messenger before thy face, which shall prepare thy way before thee. *Mat.* 11: 10.

Many that are first shall be last; and the last shall be first. *Mat.* 19: 30.

The scribes and the Pharisees . . . love the uppermost rooms at feasts, and the chief seats in the synagogues. *Mat.* 23: 2, 6.

First the blade, then the ear, after that the full corn in the ear. *Mk.* 4: 28.

By the way they had disputed among themselves, who should be the greatest. *Mk.* 9: 34.

He marked how they chose out the chief rooms. *Lu.* 14: 7.

He that cometh after me is preferred before me: for he was before me. *Jn.* 1: 15.

That was not first which is spiritual, but that which is natural; and afterward that which is spiritual. *1 Co.* 15: 46.

Adam was first formed, then Eve. *1 Ti.* 2: 13.

See also

Advantage; Christ, Preëminence of; God,

Primacy of; Order; Preëminence; Preference;
Superiority; Supremacy; Vanguard.

Precept

They are written among the sayings of the
seers. *2 Ch.* 33: 19.
Thy law is within my heart. *Ps.* 40: 8.
Thou hast commanded us to keep thy precepts diligently. *Ps.* 119: 4.
I will meditate in thy precepts, and have
respect unto thy ways. *Ps.* 119: 15.
Behold, I have longed after thy precepts. *Ps.*
119: 40.
I . . . delayed not to keep thy commandments. *Ps.* 119: 60.
I am a companion of all them that fear
thee, and of them that keep thy precepts. *Ps.*
119: 63.
I am small and despised: yet I do not forget thy precepts. *Ps.* 119: 141.
Great peace have they which love thy law. *Ps*
119: 165.
A word fitly spoken is like apples of gold in
pictures of silver. *Pr.* 25: 11.
Precept upon precept; line upon line; . . .
here a little, and there a little. *Is.* 28: 10.
O that thou hadst hearkened to my commandments! then had thy peace been as a
river, and thy righteousness as the waves of
the sea. *Is.* 48: 18.
These are the true sayings of God. *Re.* 19: 9.
See also
Commandment; Law; Rule.

Predecessor

The Lord went before them by day in a
pillar of a cloud, to lead them the way. *Ex.*
13: 21.
He that is now called a Prophet was beforetime called a Seer. *1 S.* 9: 9.
I pray thee, let a double portion of thy
spirit be upon me. *2 K.* 2: 9.
Say not thou, What is the cause that the
former days were better than these? for thou
dost not enquire wisely concerning this. *Ec.*
7: 10.
I will send you Elijah the prophet before the
coming of the great and dreadful day of the
Lord. *Mal.* 4: 5.
Behold, I send my messenger before thy
face, which shall prepare thy way before thee.
Lu. 7: 27.
He it is, who coming after me is preferred
before me. *Jn.* 1: 27.
Jesus said unto them, Verily, verily, I say
unto you, Before Abraham was, I am. *Jn.*
8: 58.
I go to prepare a place for you. *Jn.* 14: 2.
I thank God, whom I serve from my fore-
fathers. *2 Ti.* 1: 3.
The forerunner is for us entered, even Jesus.
Heb. 6: 20.
See also
Forerunner; Harbinger; Herald.

Predestination

Thou lovedst me before the foundation of
the world. *Jn.* 17: 24.
Him, being delivered by the determinate
counsel and foreknowledge of God, ye have
taken, and by wicked hands have crucified and
slain. *Ac.* 2: 23.

Whom he did foreknow, he also did predestinate to be conformed to the image of
his Son. *Ro.* 8: 29.
Whom he did predestinate, them he also
called: and whom he called, them he also
justified: and whom he justified, them he also
glorified. *Ro.* 8: 30.
God hath not cast away his people which he
foreknew. *Ro.* 11: 2.
In whom also we have obtained an inheritance, being predestinated according to
the purpose of him who worketh all things
after the counsel of his own will. *Ep.* 1: 11.
Elect according to the foreknowledge of God
the Father. *1 Pe.* 1: 2.
See also
Destiny; Election; Fate; Foreordination;
God, Foreknowledge of.

Preëminence

The Lord thy God will set thee on high
above all nations of the earth. *De.* 28: 1.
The Lord shall make thee the head, and
not the tail. *De.* 28: 13.
A man hath no preeminence above a beast:
for all is vanity. *Ec.* 3: 19.
The chiefest among ten thousand. *S. of S.*
5: 10.
I the Lord, the first, and with the last; I
am he. *Is.* 41: 4.
Many that are first shall be last; and the
last shall be first. *Mat.* 19: 30.
If any man desire to be first, the same shall
be last of all, and servant of all. *Mk.* 9: 35.
Thou, child, shalt be called the prophet of
the Highest. *Lu.* 1: 76.
I was not a whit behind the very chiefest
apostles. *2 Co.* 11: 5.
That in all things he might have the pre-
eminence. *Col.* 1: 18.
Diotrephes . . . loveth to have preeminence.
3 Jn. 1: 9.
I am Alpha and Omega, the beginning and
the end, the first and the last. *Re.* 22: 13.
See also
Advantage; Christ, Finality of; Christ, Pre-
eminence of; Excellence; God, Primacy of;
Perfection; Superiority; Supremacy; Worth.

Preference

A day in thy courts is better than a thou-
sand. *Ps.* 84: 10.
Let my tongue cleave to the roof of my
mouth; if I prefer not Jerusalem above my
chief joy. *Ps.* 137: 6.
Better is a little with righteousness than
great revenues without right. *Pr.* 16: 8.
Better is a neighbour that is near than a
brother far off. *Pr.* 27: 10.
Wisdom is better than strength. *Ec.* 9: 16.
Thy love is better than wine. *S. of S.* 1: 2.
He that cometh after me is preferred before
me: for he was before me. *Jn.* 1: 15.
In honour preferring one another. *Ro.* 12:
10.
Without preferring one before another,
doing nothing by partiality. *1 Ti.* 5: 21.
See also
Choice; Favor; Precedence; Preëminence;
Priority; Selection.

Prejudice

Are not Abana and Pharpar, rivers of

Damascus, better than all the waters of Israel? *2 K.* 5: 12.

Why eateth your Master with publicans and sinners? *Mat.* 9: 11.

It is not meet to take the children's bread, and to cast it to dogs. *Mat.* 15: 26.

No prophet is accepted in his own country. *Lu.* 4: 24.

Nathanael said unto him, Can there any good thing come out of Nazareth? Philip saith unto him, Come and see. *Jn.* 1: 46.

Out of Galilee ariseth no prophet. *Jn.* 7: 52.

Men and brethren, I am a Pharisee, the son of a Pharisee. *Ac.* 23: 6.

See also

Bias; Persons, Respect of; Preference; Segregation.

Preordination

Thou madest him to have dominion over the works of thy hands. *Ps.* 8: 6.

Lord, thou wilt ordain peace for us. *Is.* 26: 12.

Since the beginning of the world men have not heard, nor perceived by the ear, neither hath the eye seen, O God, beside thee, what he hath prepared for him that waiteth for him. *Is.* 64: 4.

I ordained thee a prophet unto the nations *Je.* 1: 5.

Inherit the kingdom prepared for you from the foundation of the world. *Mat.* 25: 34.

It is he which was ordained of God to be the Judge of quick and dead. *Ac.* 10: 42.

As many as were ordained to eternal life believed. *Ac.* 13: 48.

He . . . hath determined the times before appointed. *Ac.* 17: 26.

He hath appointed a day, in the which he will judge the world in righteousness by that man whom he hath ordained. *Ac.* 17: 31.

Whom he did foreknow, he also did predestinate to be conformed to the image of his Son. *Ro.* 8: 29.

Whom he did predestinate, them he also called. *Ro.* 8: 30.

The law . . . was ordained by angels in the hand of a mediator. *Ga.* 3: 19.

He hath chosen us in him before the foundation of the world. *Ep.* 1: 4.

Having predestinated us unto the adoption of children by Jesus Christ to himself. *Ep.* 1: 5.

In whom also we have obtained an inheritance, being predestinated according to the purpose of him who worketh all things after the counsel of his own will. *Ep.* 1: 11.

According to the prophecies which went before. *1 Ti.* 1: 18.

See also

Christ, Foreknowledge of; Foreknowledge; Foreordination; God, Foreknowledge of; God, Omniscience of.

Preparation

When ye had girded on every man his weapons of war, ye were ready to go up into the hill. *De.* 1: 41.

Prepare your hearts unto the Lord, and serve him only. *1 S.* 7: 3.

Thus saith the Lord, Make this valley full of ditches. For thus saith the Lord, Ye shall not see wind, neither shall ye see rain; yet that

valley shall be filled with water, that ye may drink. *2 K.* 3: 16, 17.

Go, borrow thee vessels abroad of all thy neighbours. *2 K.* 4: 3.

Go and wash in Jordan seven times. *2 K.* 5: 10.

Herein thou hast done foolishly: therefore from henceforth thou shalt have wars. *2 Ch.* 16: 9.

Half of my servants wrought in the work, and the other half of them held both the spears, the shields, and the bows. *Ne.* 4: 16.

That they should be ready against that day. *Es.* 3: 14.

Enquire, I pray thee, of the former age, and prepare thyself to the search of their fathers. *Jb.* 8: 8.

He hath prepared his throne for judgment. *Ps.* 9: 7.

Thou preparest a table before me in the presence of mine enemies. *Ps.* 23: 5.

Thou preparest them corn. *Ps.* 65: 9.

There he maketh the hungry to dwell, that they may prepare a city for habitation. *Ps.* 107: 36.

The preparations of the heart in man, and the answer of the tongue, is from the Lord. *Pr.* 16: 1.

Prepare ye the way of the Lord, make straight in the desert a highway for our God. *Is.* 40: 3.

Go through, go through the gates; prepare ye the way of the people. *Is.* 62: 10.

Since the beginning of the world men have not heard, nor perceived by the ear, neither hath the eye seen, O God, beside thee, what he hath prepared for him that waiteth for him. *Is.* 64: 4.

His going forth is prepared as the morning. *Ho.* 6: 3.

Sow to yourselves in righteousness, reap in mercy; break up your fallow ground: for it is time to seek the Lord. *Ho.* 10: 12.

Prepare to meet thy God, O Israel. *Am.* 4: 12.

Behold, I will send my messenger, and he shall prepare the way before me. *Mal.* 3: 1.

A people prepared for the Lord. *Lu.* 1: 17.

Thou shalt go forth before the face of the Lord to prepare his ways. *Lu.* 1: 76.

Let your loins be girded about, and your lights burning; And ye yourselves like unto men that wait for their lord. *Lu.* 12: 35, 36.

I go to prepare a place for you. *Jn.* 14: 2.

When forty years were expired, . . . the voice of the Lord came unto him, Saying, . . . now come, I will send thee into Egypt. *Ac.* 7: 30–32, 34.

So, as much as in me is, I am ready to preach the gospel to you that are at Rome also. *Ro.* 1: 15.

Eye hath not seen, nor ear heard, neither have entered into the heart of man, the things which God hath prepared for them that love him. But God hath revealed them unto us by his Spirit. *1 Co.* 2: 9, 10.

Purge out therefore the old leaven. *1 Co.* 5: 7.

If a man therefore purge himself from these, he shall be a vessel unto honour, sanctified, and meet for the master's use, and prepared unto every good work. *2 Ti.* **2: 21.**

Put them in mind . . . to be ready to every good work. *Tit.* **3: 1.**

It is appointed unto men once to die. *He.* **9: 27.**

See also

Forerunner; Forethought; Prophet; Readiness; Scout; Unpreparedness.

Presence

Adam and his wife hid themselves from the presence of the Lord God. *Ge.* **3: 8.**

Cain went out from the presence of the Lord. *Ge.* **4: 16.**

My presence shall go with thee, and I will give thee rest. *Ex.* **33: 14.**

Glory and honour are in his presence. *1 Ch.* **16: 27.**

Then shall the trees of the wood sing out at the presence of the Lord. *1 Ch.* **16: 33.**

Thou preparest a table before me in the presence of mine enemies. *Ps.* **23: 5.**

Thou shalt hide them in the secret of thy presence from the pride of man. *Ps.* **31: 20.**

Even Sinai itself was moved at the presence of God. *Ps.* **68: 8.**

Come before his presence with singing. *Ps.* **100: 2.**

Tremble, thou earth, at the presence of the Lord. *Ps.* **114: 7.**

Go from the presence of a foolish man. *Pr.* **14: 7.**

Hold thy peace at the presence of the Lord God. *Zph.* **1: 7.**

There is joy in the presence of the angels of God over one sinner that repenteth. *Lu.* **15: 10.**

His letters, say they, are weighty and powerful; but his bodily presence is weak, and his speech contemptible. *2 Co.* **10: 10.**

As ye have always obeyed, not as in my presence only, but now much more in my absence, work out your own salvation with fear and trembling. *Ph.* **2: 12.**

Are not even ye in the presence of our Lord Jesus Christ at his coming? *1 Th.* **2: 19.**

See also

Attendance; Christ, Presence of; God, Presence of.

Present

I will appease him with the present that goeth before me. *Ge.* **32: 20.**

Consecrate yourselves to day to the Lord. *Ex.* **32: 29.**

Because of thy temple at Jerusalem shall kings bring presents unto thee. *Ps.* **68: 29.**

The kings of Tarshish and of the isles shall bring presents: the kings of Sheba and Seba shall offer gifts. *Ps.* **72: 10.**

Let all that be round about him bring presents unto him that ought to be feared. *Ps.* **76: 11.**

This is the day which the Lord hath made; we will rejoice and be glad in it. *Ps.* **118: 24.**

They presented unto him gifts: gold, and frankincense, and myrrh. *Mat.* **2: 11.**

Straightway he called them. *Mk.* **1: 20.**

Behold, now is the accepted time; behold, now is the day of salvation. *2 Co.* **6: 2.**

To day if ye will hear his voice. *He.* **3: 7.**

Thou art my Son, to day have I begotten thee. *He.* **5: 5.**

See also

Almsgiving; Beneficence; Benevolence; Boon; Charity; Christ, Gift of; Contribution; Generosity; God, Gift of; Philanthropy; Time, the Present; To-day; Unselfishness.

Presentation

Present thyself there to me in the top of the mount. *Ex.* **34: 2.**

There was a day when the sons of God came to present themselves before the Lord, and Satan came also among them. *Jb.* **1: 6.**

When the days of her purification according to the law of Moses were accomplished, they brought him to Jerusalem, to present him to the Lord. *Lu.* **2: 22.**

I beseech you therefore, brethren, by the mercies of God, that ye present your bodies a living sacrifice. *Ro.* **12: 1.**

He which raised up the Lord Jesus shall raise up us also by Jesus, and shall present us with you. *2 Co.* **4: 14.**

To present you holy and unblameable and unreprovable in his sight. *Col.* **1: 22.**

That we may present every man perfect in Christ Jesus. *Col.* **1: 28.**

Unto him that is able to keep you from falling, and to present you faultless before the presence of his glory with exceeding joy, . . . be glory and majesty. *Jude* **1: 24, 25.**

See also

Bestowal; Christ, Gift of; Donation; Gift; God, Gift of; Offering; Present.

Preservation

Let integrity and uprightness preserve me; for I wait on thee. *Ps.* **25: 21.**

The Lord preserveth the faithful, and plentifully rewardeth the proud doer. *Ps.* **31: 23.**

Our soul waiteth for the Lord: he is our help and our shield. *Ps.* **33: 20.**

O Lord, thou preservest man and beast. *Ps.* **36: 6.**

He shall give his angels charge over thee, to keep thee in all his ways. *Ps.* **91: 11.**

He preserveth the souls of his saints. *Ps.* **97: 10.**

The Lord preserveth the simple. *Ps.* **116: 6.**

The Lord of hosts shall defend them. *Zch.* **9: 15.**

Whosoever shall lose his life shall preserve it. *Lu.* **17: 33.**

He is on my right hand, that I should not be moved. *Ac.* **2: 25.**

I pray God your whole spirit and soul and body be preserved blameless unto the coming of our Lord Jesus Christ. *1 Th.* **5: 23.**

See also

Defence; Fortress; God, the Keeper; God, Protection of; God, the Refuge; Keeper; Protection; Refuge; Safety; Salvation; Security; Tower; Watch.

Presumption

The soul that doeth ought presumptuously, . . . the same reproacheth the Lord. *Nu.* **15: 30.**

All the people shall hear, and fear, and do no more presumptuously. *De.* **17: 13.**

The prophet, which shall presume to speak a

word in my name, which I have not commanded him to speak, or that shall speak in the name of other gods, even that prophet shall die. *De.* **18: 20.**

Though his excellency mount up to the heavens, and his head reach unto the clouds; Yet he shall perish for ever. *Jb.* **20: 6, 7.**

Keep back thy servant also from presumptuous sins. *Ps.* **19: 13.**

Pride goeth before destruction, and an haughty spirit before a fall. *Pr.* **16: 18.**

Boast not thyself of to morrow; for thou knowest not what a day may bring forth. *Pr.* **27: 1.**

There is a generation, O how lofty are their eyes! *Pr.* **30: 13.**

Their glory, and their multitude, and their pomp, and he that rejoiceth, shall descend into it. *Is.* **5: 14.**

To morrow shall be as this day, and much more abundant. *Is.* **56: 12.**

Because thou hast lifted up thyself in height, . . . and his heart is lifted up in his height; I have therefore delivered him into the hand of the mighty one of the heathen. *Eze.* **31: 10, 11.**

Though thou exalt thyself as the eagle, and though thou set thy nest among the stars, thence will I bring thee down, saith the Lord. *Ob.* **1: 4.**

I will say to my soul, Soul, thou hast much goods laid up for many years; take thine ease, eat, drink, and be merry. *Lu.* **12: 19.**

Presumptuous are they, selfwilled, they are not afraid to speak evil of dignities. *2 Pe.* **2: 10.**

See also

Arrogance; Boasting; Conceit; Disdain; Haughtiness; Pride; Self-Satisfaction.

Pretension

There is a generation that are pure in their own eyes, and yet is not washed from their filthiness. *Pr.* **30: 12.**

The vile person will speak villany, and his heart will work iniquity, to practise hypocrisy, and to utter error against the Lord. *Is.* **32: 6.**

Do not ye after their works: for they say, and do not. *Mat.* **23: 3.**

Ye devour widows' houses, and for a pretence make long prayer. *Mat.* **23: 14.**

There shall arise false Christs, and false prophets, and shall shew great signs and wonders. *Mat.* **24: 24.**

Beware ye of the leaven of the Pharisees, which is hypocrisy. *Lu.* **12: 1.**

Handling the word of God deceitfully. *2 Co.* **4: 2.**

What then? notwithstanding, every way, whether in pretence, or in truth, Christ is preached; and I therein do rejoice. *Ph.* **1: 18.**

They profess that they know God; but in works they deny him. *Tit.* **1: 16.**

See also

Affectation; Craftiness; Deceit; Duplicity; Faithlessness; Fraud; Hypocrisy; Presumption; Sham; Treachery.

Prevention

Hinder me not, seeing the Lord hath prospered my way. *Ge.* **24: 56.**

Prepare thy chariot, and get thee down, that

the rain stop thee not. *1 K.* **18: 44.**

Stop the way against them that persecute me. *Ps.* **35: 3.**

The mouth of them that speak lies shall be stopped. *Ps.* **63: 11.**

Let me not wander from thy commandments. *Ps.* **119: 10.**

Ye entered not in yourselves, and them that were entering in ye hindered. *Lu.* **11: 52.**

No man shall stop me of this boasting. *2 Co.* **11: 10.**

Who did hinder you that ye should not obey the truth? *Ga.* **5: 7.**

Satan hindered us. *1 Th.* **2: 18.**

Let us lay aside every weight. *He.* **12: 1.**

See also

Bar, Difficulty; Hindrance; Obstacle; Opposition; Prohibition; Stumbling-block.

Prey

He delivered them into the hands of spoilers that spoiled them. *Ju.* **2: 14.**

They are passed away as the swift ships: as the eagle that hasteth to the prey. *Jb.* **9: 26.**

They have now compassed us in our steps: . . . Like as a lion that is greedy of his prey. *Ps.* **17: 11, 12.**

The young lions roar after their prey, and seek their meat from God. *Ps.* **104: 21.**

Blessed be the Lord, who hath not given us as a prey to their teeth. *Ps.* **124: 6.**

She also lieth in wait as for a prey. *Pr.* **23: 28.**

Be thou a covert to them from the face of the spoiler. *Is.* **16: 4.**

All that prey upon thee will I give for a prey. *Je.* **30: 16.**

See also

Spoil.

Price

Neither will I offer burnt offerings unto the Lord my God of that which doth cost me nothing. *2 S.* **24: 24.**

Man knoweth not the price thereof. *Jb.* **28: 13.**

Thou sellest thy people for nought, and dost not increase thy wealth by their price. *Ps.* **44: 12.**

Who can find a virtuous woman? for her price is far above rubies. *Pr.* **31: 10.**

Buy wine and milk without money and without price. *Is.* **55: 1.**

A merchant man, seeking goodly pearls: . . . when he had found one pearl of great price, went and sold all that he had, and bought it. *Mat.* **14: 45, 46.**

Thy money perish with thee, because thou hast thought that the gift of God may be purchased with money. *Ac.* **8: 20.**

Feed the church of God, which he hath purchased with his own blood. *Ac.* **20: 28.**

With a great sum obtained I this freedom. *Ac.* **22: 28.**

Ye are bought with a price. *1 Co.* **6: 20.**

The ornament of a meek and quiet spirit . . . is in the sight of God of great price. *1 Pe.* **3: 4.**

Even denying the Lord that bought them. *2 Pe.* **2: 1.**

See also

Appraisal; Cost; Money; Sacrifice; Value; Worth.

Pride

Who is the Lord, that I should obey his voice to let Israel go? *Ex.* 5: 2.

Naaman was wroth, and went away, and said, Behold, I thought, He will surely come out to me, and stand, and call on the name of the Lord his God. 2 *K.* 5: 11.

When he was strong, his heart was lifted up to his destruction. 2 *Ch.* 26: 16.

His heart was lifted up: therefore there was wrath upon him. 2 *Ch.* 32: 25.

The wicked in his pride doth persecute the poor. *Ps.* 10: 2.

My soul shall make her boast in the Lord. *Ps.* 34: 2.

Be not wise in thine own eyes: fear the Lord, and depart from evil. *Pr.* 3: 7.

Only by pride cometh contention. *Pr.* 13: 10.

There is a generation, O how lofty are their eyes! *Pr.* 30: 13.

Thy pomp is brought down to the grave. *Is.* 14: 11.

Which say, Stand by thyself, come not near to me; for I am holier than thou. These are a smoke in my nose, a fire that burneth all the day. *Is.* 65: 5.

Is not this great Babylon, that I have built for the house of the kingdom by the might of my power, and for the honour of my majesty? *Da.* 4: 30.

He did according to his will, and became great. *Da.* 8: 4.

Though thou exalt thyself as the eagle, and though thou set thy nest among the stars, thence will I bring thee down, saith the Lord. *Ob.* 1: 4.

Think not to say within yourselves, We have Abraham to our father. *Mat.* 3: 9.

From within, out of the heart of men, proceed evil thoughts, . . . pride, foolishness. *Mk.* 7: 21, 22.

He . . . called the twelve, and saith unto them, If any man desire to be first, the same shall be last of all. *Mk.* 9: 35.

I thank thee, that I am not as other men are. *Lu.* 18: 11.

Then they reviled him, and said, Thou art his disciple; but we are Moses' disciples. *Jn.* 9: 28.

It is not reason that we should leave the word of God, and serve tables. *Ac.* 6: 2.

I am not ashamed of the gospel of Christ. *Ro.* 1: 16.

And art confident that thou thyself art a guide of the blind, a light of them which are in darkness. *Ro.* 2: 19.

Now some are puffed up, as though I would not come to you. *1 Co.* 4: 18.

As the truth of Christ is in me, no man shall stop me of this boasting. *2 Co.* 11: 10.

See also
Arrogance; Attitude; Conceit; Contempt; Disdain; Haughtiness; Ostentation; Presumption; Scorn; Self-Satisfaction.

Priesthood

The Lord hath sworn, and will not repent, Thou art a priest for ever after the order of Melchizedek. *Ps.* 110: 4.

Many pastors have destroyed my vineyard. *Je.* 12: 10.

The Lord hath made thee priest. *Je.* 29: 26.

I will also reject thee, that thou shalt be no priest to me: seeing thou hast forgotten the law of thy God, I will also forget thy children. *Ho.* 4: 6.

The priests thereof teach for hire. *Mi.* 3: 11.

The high priest asked him, and said unto him, Art thou the Christ, the Son of the Blessed? *Mk.* 14: 61.

The priests were obedient to the faith. *Ac.* 6: 7.

They which wait at the altar are partakers with the altar. *1 Co.* 9: 13.

In all things approving ourselves as the ministers of God. *2 Co.* 6: 4.

This man, because he continueth ever, hath an unchangeable priesthood. *He.* 7: 24.

Ye also, as lively stones, are built up a spiritual house, an holy priesthood. *1 Pe.* 2: 5.

Jesus Christ . . . hath made us kings and priests unto God and his Father. *Re.* 1: 5, 6.

They shall be priests of God and of Christ, and shall reign with him a thousand years. *Re.* 20: 6.

See also
Clergy; Ministry; Missionary; Ordination; Pastor; Sermon.

Prince

As a prince hast thou power with God and with men, and hast prevailed. *Ge.* 32: 28.

Ye shall die like men, and fall like one of the princes. *Ps.* 82: 7.

It is better to trust in the Lord than to put confidence in princes. *Ps.* 118: 9.

Put not your trust in princes, nor in the son of man, in whom there is no help. *Ps.* 146: 3.

Thou Bethlehem, in the land of Juda, art not the least among the princes of Juda. *Mat.* 2: 6.

The Pharisees said, He casteth out devils through the prince of the devils. *Mat.* 9: 34.

Now shall the prince of this world be cast out. *Jn.* 12: 31.

The prince of this world cometh, and hath nothing in me. *Jn.* 14: 30.

We speak wisdom: . . . yet not the wisdom of this world, nor of the princes of this world, that come to nought. *1 Co.* 2: 6.

In time past ye walked according to the course of this world, according to the prince of the power of the air, the spirit that now worketh in the children of disobedience. *Ep.* 2: 2.

See also
Authority; Christ, Reign of; Christ, Supremacy of; Dominion; God, Supremacy of; Lord; Master; Power; Reign; Rule; Sovereignty.

Principle

Make me to understand the way of thy precepts. *Ps.* 119: 27.

I seek thy precepts. *Ps.* 119: 45.

I will never forget thy precepts. *Ps.* 119: 93.

Precept must be upon precept, precept upon precept. *Is.* 28: 10.

We have sinned, . . . by departing from thy precepts. *Da.* 9: 5.

This man was instructed in the way of the Lord. *Ac.* 18: 25.

See then that ye walk circumspectly. *Ep.* 5: 15.

Follow righteousness, faith, charity, peace. *2 Ti.* 2: 22.

Ye have need that one teach you again which be the first principles of the oracles of God. *He.* 5: 12.

Therefore leaving the principles of the doctrine of Christ, let us go on unto perfection. *He.* 6: 1.

See also

Belief; Creed; Doctrine; Faith; Rule; Tenet; Truth.

Priority

Ye shall be a peculiar treasure unto me above all people. *Ex.* 19: 5.

There is no God like thee, in heaven above, or on earth beneath. *1 K.* 8: 23.

Are not Abana and Pharpar, rivers of Damascus, better than all the waters of Israel? *2 K.* 5: 12.

Thou liftest me up above those that rise up against me. *Ps.* 18: 48.

A good name is better than precious ointment. *Ec.* 7: 1.

I will make a man more precious than fine gold. *Is.* 13: 12.

Daniel was preferred above the presidents and princes, because an excellent spirit was in him. *Da.* 6: 3.

Grant that these my two sons may sit, the one on thy right hand, and the other on thy left, in thy kingdom. *Mat.* 20: 21.

Of them he chose twelve, whom also he named apostles. *Lu.* 6: 13.

After me cometh a man which is preferred before me. *Jn.* 1: 30.

He is a chosen vessel unto me. *Ac.* 9: 15.

God also hath highly exalted him, and given him a name which is above every name. *Ph.* 2: 9.

Adam was first formed, then Eve. *1 Ti.* 2: 13.

Chosen of God and precious. *1 Pe.* 2: 4.

See also

First; Preference.

Prison

The Lord looseth the prisoners. *Ps.* 146: 7.

To bring out the prisoners from the prison, and them that sit in darkness out of the prison house. *Is.* 42: 7.

To proclaim liberty to the captives, and the opening of the prison to them that are bound. *Is.* 61: 1.

Now, behold, I loose thee this day from the chains which were upon thine hand. *Je.* 40: 4.

Turn you to the strong hold, ye prisoners of hope. *Zch.* 9: 12.

At midnight Paul and Silas prayed, and sang praises unto God. *Ac.* 16: 25.

Many of the saints did I shut up in prison. *Ac.* 26: 10.

I am an ambassador in bonds. *Ep.* 6: 20.

He went and preached unto the spirits in prison. *1 Pe.* 3: 19.

Satan shall be loosed out of his prison. *Re.* 20: 7.

See also

Band; Bond; Bondage; Captivity; Chain; Imprisonment; Restraint; Yoke.

Privacy

Behold, I go forward, but he is not there; and backward, but I cannot perceive him: On the left hand, where he doth work, but I cannot behold him; he hideth himself on the right hand, that I cannot see him: But he knoweth the way that I take. *Jb.* 23: 8-10.

His eyes are privily set against the poor. *Ps.* 10: 8.

He lieth in wait secretly as a lion in his den. *Ps.* 10: 9.

The wicked bend their bow, they make ready their arrow upon the string, that they may privily shoot at the upright in heart. *Ps.* 11: 2.

Whoso privily slandereth his neighbour, him will I cut off. *Ps.* 101: 5.

It is better to dwell in a corner of the housetop, than with a brawling woman in a wide house. *Pr.* 21: 9.

Verily thou art a God that hidest thyself. *Is.* 45: 15.

The disciples came unto him privately. *Mat.* 24: 3.

Sit ye here, while I go and pray yonder. *Mat.* 26: 36.

He was withdrawn from them about a stone's cast. *Lu.* 22: 41.

No prophecy of the scripture is of any private interpretation. *2 Pe.* 1: 20.

There shall be false teachers among you, who privily shall bring in damnable heresies. *2 Pe.* 2: 1.

See also

Isolation; Seclusion; Secrecy; Solitude.

Prize

I am . . . thy exceeding great reward. *Ge.* 15: 1.

There is a reward for the righteous. *Ps.* 58: 11.

Thy Father, which seeth in secret, shall reward thee openly. *Mat.* 6: 18.

Know ye not that they which run in a race run all, but one receiveth the prize? *1 Co.* 9: 24.

So run, that ye may obtain. *1 Co.* 9: 24.

I press toward the mark for the prize of the high calling of God in Christ Jesus. *Ph.* 3: 14.

If a man also strive for masteries, yet is he not crowned, except he strive lawfully. *2 Ti.* 2: 5.

Henceforth there is laid up for me a crown of righteousness, which the Lord, the righteous judge, shall give me at that day. *2 Ti.* 4: 8.

See also

Award; Crown; Reward.

Proclamation

I will proclaim the name of the Lord before thee. *Ex.* 33: 19.

Thou shalt also decree a thing, and it shall be established unto thee. *Jb.* 22: 28.

I will declare the decree: the Lord hath said unto me, Thou art my Son. *Ps.* 2: 7.

Hitherto have I declared thy wondrous works. *Ps.* 71: 17.

The Lord hath anointed me. . . . To proclaim the acceptable year of the Lord. *Is.* 61: 1, 2.

Stand in the gate of the Lord's house, and proclaim there this word. *Je.* 7: 2.

Publish ye, praise ye, and say, O Lord, save thy people. *Je.* **31: 7.**

Ye were now turned, and had done right in my sight, in proclaiming liberty every man to his neighbour. *Je.* **34: 15.**

This is the decree of the most High. *Da.* **4: 24.**

Proclaim ye this among the Gentiles; Prepare war, wake up the mighty men. *Jo.* **3: 9.**

There went out a decree from Caesar Augustus. *Lu.* **2: 1.**

That which ye have spoken in the ear in closets shall be proclaimed upon the house tops. *Lu.* **12: 3.**

These all do contrary to the decrees of Caesar, saying that there is another king, one Jesus. *Ac.* **17: 7.**

See also
Annunciation.

Procrastination

While he lingered, the men laid hold upon his hand, and upon the hand of his wife, and upon the hand of his two daughters. *Ge.* **19: 16.**

The harvest is past, the summer is ended, and we are not saved. *Je.* **8: 20.**

Lord, suffer me first to go and bury my father. *Mat.* **8: 21.**

My lord delayeth his coming. *Mat.* **24: 48.**

The door was shut. *Mat.* **25: 10.**

Lord, I will follow thee; but let me first go bid them farewell, which are at home at my house. *Lu.* **9: 61.**

He would not for a while. *Lu.* **18: 4.**

When they heard of the resurrection of the dead, some mocked: and others said, We will hear thee again of this matter. *Ac.* **17: 32.**

Now why tarriest thou? arise, and be baptized. *Ac.* **22: 16.**

Go thy way for this time; when I have a convenient season, I will call for thee. *Ac.* **24: 25.**

Now is the accepted time. *2 Co.* **6: 2.**

Now is the day of salvation. *2 Co.* **6: 2.**

He found no place of repentance, though he sought it carefully with tears. *He.* **12: 17.**

See also
Delay; Hesitancy; Patience; Wait.

Prodigal

There is treasure to be desired and oil in the dwelling of the wise; but a foolish man spendeth it up. *Pr.* **21: 20.**

Be not among winebibbers; among riotous eaters of flesh. *Pr.* **23: 20.**

He that is a companion of riotous men shameth his father. *Pr.* **28: 7.**

He that keepeth company with harlots spendeth his substance. *Pr.* **29: 3.**

Wherefore do ye spend money for that which is not bread? *Is.* **55: 2.**

Give not that which is holy unto the dogs, neither cast ye your pearls before swine. *Mat.* **7: 6.**

The younger son . . . wasted his substance with riotous living. *Lu.* **15: 13.**

When he had spent all, there arose a mighty famine in that land; and he began to be in want. *Lu.* **15: 14.**

He would fain have filled his belly with the husks that the swine did eat. *Lu.* **15: 16.**

Father, I have sinned against heaven, and in thy sight, and am no more worthy to be called thy son. *Lu.* **15: 21.**

As soon as this thy son was come, which hath devoured thy living with harlots, thou hast killed for him the fatted calf. *Lu.* **15: 30.**

This thy brother was dead, and is alive again; and was lost, and is found. *Lu.* **15: 32.**

See also
Liberality; Waste.

Productivity

The tree of life also in the midst of the garden. *Ge.* **2: 9.**

They . . . cut down . . . a branch with one cluster of grapes, and they bare it between two upon a staff. *Nu.* **13: 23.**

Blessed of the Lord be his land, . . . for the precious things of the earth and fulness thereof, and for the good will of him that dwelt in the bush. *De.* **33: 13, 16.**

He shall not see the rivers, the floods, the brooks of honey and butter. *Jb.* **20: 17.**

Wilt thou believe him, that he will bring home thy seed, and gather it into thy barn? *Jb.* **39: 12.**

He shall be like a tree planted by the rivers of water. *Ps.* **1: 3.**

My cup runneth over. *Ps.* **23: 5.**

That our garners may be full, affording all manner of store. *Ps.* **144: 13.**

Every bottle shall be filled with wine. *Je.* **13: 12.**

He shall be as a tree planted by the waters, and that spreadeth out her roots by the river, and shall not see when heat cometh, but her leaf shall be green; and shall not be careful in the year of drought, neither shall cease from yielding fruit. *Je.* **17: 8.**

Then will I . . . cause their rivers to run like oil. *Eze.* **32: 14.**

I will multiply the fruit of the tree, and the increase of the field. *Eze.* **36: 30.**

He shall grow as the lily. *Ho.* **14: 5.**

The floors shall be full of wheat. *Jo.* **2: 24.**

Is the seed yet in the barn? *Hag.* **2: 19.**

He will . . . gather his wheat into the garner. *Mat.* **3: 12.**

Gather the wheat into my barn. *Mat.* **13: 30.**

Good measure, pressed down, and shaken together, and running over. *Lu.* **6: 38.**

I will pull down my barns, and build greater. *Lu.* **12: 18.**

Consider the ravens: for they neither sow nor reap; which neither have storehouse nor barn. *Lu.* **12: 24.**

See also
Abundance; Fertility; Fruitfulness; Harvest; Plenty; Yield.

Profanity

Thou shalt not take the name of the Lord thy God in vain. *Ex.* **20: 7.**

He will curse thee to thy face. *Jb.* **1: 11.**

As he clothed himself with cursing like as with his garment, so let it come into his bowels like water, and like oil into his bones. *Ps.* **109: 18.**

Let them curse, but bless thou. *Ps.* **109: 28.**

Every one of them doth curse me. *Je.* **15: 10.**

Her priests have violated my law, and have profaned mine holy things. *Eze.* **22: 26.**

They profaned my holy name. *Eze.* **36: 20.**

They shall teach my people the difference between the holy and profane. *Eze.* 44: 23.

By swearing, and lying, and killing, and stealing, and committing adultery, they break out, and blood toucheth blood. *Ho.* 4: 2.

I say unto you, Swear not at all; neither by heaven; for it is God's throne: Nor by the earth; for it is his footstool. *Mat.* 5: 34, 35.

Then began he to curse and to swear, saying, I know not the man. *Mat.* 26: 74.

Bless them which persecute you: bless, and curse not. *Ro.* 12: 14.

Avoiding profane and vain babblings. *1 Ti.* 6: 20.

Men . . . blasphemed the name of God. *Re.* 16: 9.

There shall be no more curse. *Re.* 22: 3.

See also

Anathema; Blasphemy; Curse; Sacrilege.

Profession

Ye shall be named the Priests of the Lord: men shall call you the Ministers of our God. *Is.* 61: 6.

Then will I profess unto them, I never knew you: depart from me, ye that work iniquity. *Mat.* 7: 23.

Called to be saints. *Ro.* 1: 7.

Professing themselves to be wise, they became fools. *Ro.* 1: 22.

Not many wise men after the flesh, not many mighty, not many noble, are called. *1 Co.* 1: 26.

As the Lord hath called every one, so let him walk. *1 Co.* 7: 17.

Let every man abide in the same calling wherein he was called. *1 Co.* 7: 20.

He gave some, apostles; and some, prophets; and some, evangelists; and some, pastors and teachers. *Ep.* 4: 11.

Thou . . . hast professed a good profession before many witnesses. *1 Ti.* 6: 12.

They profess that they know God; but in works they deny him. *Tit.* 1: 16.

Wherefore, holy brethren, partakers of the heavenly calling, consider the Apostle and High Priest of our profession, Christ Jesus; Who was faithful to him that appointed him. *He.* 3: 1, 2.

Seeing then that we have a great high priest, that is passed into the heavens, Jesus the Son of God, let us hold fast our profession. *He.* 4: 14.

See also

Affirmation; Business; Calling; Occupation; Trade; Vocation.

Profit

Thou shalt keep therefore his statutes, and his commandments, which I command thee this day, that it may go well with thee, and with thy children after thee. *De.* 4: 40.

Turn ye not aside: for then should ye go after vain things, which cannot profit nor deliver; for they are vain. *1 S.* 12: 21.

I pray you, let us leave off this usury. *Ne.* 5: 10.

What profit should we have, if we pray unto him? *Jb.* 21: 15.

Can a man be profitable unto God? *Jb.* 22: 2.

Treasures of wickedness profit nothing. *Pr.* 10: 2.

He that withholdeth corn, the people shall curse him. *Pr.* 11: 26.

In all labour there is profit. *Pr.* 14: 23.

What profit hath a man of all his labour which he taketh under the sun? *Ec.* 1: 3.

All was vanity and vexation of spirit, and there was no profit under the sun. *Ec.* 2: 11.

The profit of the earth is for all. *Ec.* 5: 9.

Surely I know that it shall be well with them that fear God, which fear before him. *Ec.* 8: 12.

Say ye to the righteous, that it shall be well with him: for they shall eat the fruit of their doings. *Is.* 3: 10.

Their delectable things shall not profit. *Is.* 44: 9.

Mine elect shall long enjoy the work of their hands. *Is.* 65: 22.

It is profitable for thee that one of thy members should perish, and not that thy whole body should be cast into hell. *Mat.* 5: 29.

What shall it profit a man, if he shall gain the whole world, and lose his own soul? *Mk.* 8: 36.

It is the spirit that quickeneth; the flesh profiteth nothing. *Jn.* 6: 63.

A certain man named Ananias, with Sapphira his wife, sold a possession, And kept back part of the price, his wife also being privy to it, and brought a certain part, and laid it at the apostles' feet. *Ac.* 5: 1, 2.

This I speak for your own profit. *1 Co.* 7: 35.

The manifestation of the Spirit is given to every man to profit withal. *1 Co.* 12: 7.

I . . . profited in the Jews' religion above many my equals in mine own nation. *Ga.* 1: 13, 14.

Godliness is profitable unto all things. *1 Ti.* 4: 8.

Godliness with contentment is great gain. *1 Ti.* 6: 6.

These things are good and profitable unto men. *Tit.* 3: 8.

They verily for a few days chastened us after their own pleasure; but he for our profit, that we might be partakers of his holiness. *He.* 12: 10.

That ye may grow thereby. *1 Pe.* 2: 2.

See also

Abundance; Addition; Gain; Growth; Harvest; Increase; Progress; Riches; Yield.

Progress

Speak unto the children of Israel, that they go forward. *Ex.* 14: 15.

Let us go up at once, and possess it; for we are well able to overcome it. *Nu.* 13: 30.

Possess thou the west. *De.* 33: 23.

The word of the Lord was precious in those days; there was no open vision. *1 S.* 3: 1.

Thou hast enlarged my steps under me; so that my feet did not slip. *2 S.* 22: 37.

The place where we dwell with thee is too strait for us. Let us go, we pray thee, unto Jordan, and take thence every man a beam, and let us make us a place there, where we may dwell. And he answered, Go ye. *2 K.* 6: 1, 2.

The righteous also shall hold on his way, and he that hath clean hands shall be stronger and stronger. *Jb.* 17: 9.

They go from strength to strength, every one of them in Zion appeareth before God. *Ps.* **84: 7.**

The path of the just is as the shining light, that shineth more and more unto the perfect day. *Pr.* **4: 18.**

An highway shall be there, and a way, and it shall be called The way of holiness; the unclean shall not pass over it. *Is.* **35: 8.**

Instead of the thorn shall come up the fir tree, and instead of the brier shall come up the myrtle tree. *Is.* **55: 13.**

The Lord shall guide thee continually. *Is.* **58: 11.**

Many shall run to and fro, and knowledge shall be increased. *Da.* **12: 4.**

They shall build the waste cities, and inhabit them; and they shall plant vineyards, and drink the wine thereof; they shall also make gardens, and eat the fruit of them. *Am.* **9: 14.**

In that day shall the Lord defend the inhabitants of Jerusalem; and he that is feeble among them at that day shall be as David; and the house of David shall be as God, as the angel of the Lord before them. *Zch.* **12: 8.**

Be ye therefore perfect, even as your Father which is in heaven is perfect. *Mat.* **5: 48.**

Friend, go up higher. *Lu.* **14: 10.**

He made as though he would have gone further. *Lu.* **24: 28.**

Thou shalt see greater things than these. *Jn.* **1: 50.**

Greater works than these shall he do; because I go unto my Father. *Jn.* **14: 12.**

I have yet many things to say unto you, but ye cannot bear them now. *Jn.* **16: 12.**

I have planted, Apollos watered; but God gave the increase. *1 Co.* **3: 6.**

Now I know in part; but then shall I know even as also I am known. *1 Co.* **13: 12.**

I pray, that your love may abound yet more and more in knowledge and in all judgment; That ye may approve things that are excellent. *Ph.* **1: 9, 10.**

Meditate upon these things; give thyself wholly to them; that thy profiting may appear to all. *1 Ti.* **4: 15.**

Let us go on unto perfection. *He.* **6: 1.**

And have tasted . . . the powers of the world to come. *He.* **6: 5.**

Dwelling in tabernacles . . . he looked for a city. *He.* **11: 9, 10.**

Here have we no continuing city, but we seek one to come. *He.* **13: 14.**

Which in time past were not a people, but are now the people of God. *1 Pe.* **2: 10.**

Beloved, now are we the sons of God, and it doth not yet appear what we shall be. *1 Jn.* **3: 2.**

We know that, when he shall appear, we shall be like him. *1 Jn.* **3: 2.**

See also

Advance; Civilization; Development; Evolution; Growth; Increase; Unfolding.

Prohibition

Thou shalt not make unto thee any graven image. *Ex.* **20: 4.**

Thou shalt not take the name of the Lord thy God in vain. *Ex.* **20: 7.**

Thou shalt not kill. *Ex.* **20: 13.**

Thou shalt not commit adultery. *Ex.* **20: 14.**

Thou shalt not steal. *Ex.* **20: 15.**

Thou shalt not bear false witness. *Ex.* **20: 16.**

Thou shalt not covet. *Ex.* **20: 17.**

Ye shall not steal, neither deal falsely, neither lie one to another. *Le.* **19: 11.**

Thou shalt not hate thy brother in thine heart. *Le.* **19: 17.**

Stolen waters are sweet, and bread eaten in secret is pleasant. *Pr.* **9: 17.**

Look not thou upon the wine when it is red. *Pr.* **23: 31.**

They essayed to go into Bithynia: but the Spirit suffered them not. *Ac.* **16: 7.**

Be not drunk with wine, wherein is **excess.** *Ep.* **5: 18.**

See also

Ban; Bar; Hindrance; Opposition; Prevention.

Prominence

What nation is there so great, that hath statutes and judgments so righteous as all this law, which I set before you this day? *De.* **4: 8.**

There shall no man be able to stand before you. *De.* **11: 25.**

There arose not a prophet since in Israel like unto Moses, whom the Lord knew face to face. *De.* **34: 10.**

The Lord his God was with him, and magnified him exceedingly. *2 Ch.* **1: 1.**

I was the king's cupbearer. *Ne.* **1: 11.**

There is none like him in the earth, a perfect and an upright man, one that feareth God, and escheweth evil. *Jb.* **1: 8.**

My beloved is . . . the chiefest among ten thousand. *S. of S.* **5: 10.**

The Lord took me as I followed the flock, and the Lord said unto me, Go, prophesy unto my people. *Am.* **7: 15.**

All their works they do for to be seen of men. *Mat.* **23: 5.**

Be not ye called Rabbi: for one is your Master, even Christ; and all ye are brethren. *Mat.* **23: 8.**

Whosoever shall exalt himself shall be abased. *Mat.* **23: 12.**

They . . . love the uppermost rooms at feasts, and the chief seats in the synagogues. *Mat.* **23: 5, 6.**

Whosoever of you will be the chiefest, shall be servant of all. *Mk.* **10: 44.**

When thou art bidden of any man to a wedding, sit not down in the highest room. *Lu.* **14: 8.**

In nothing am I behind the very chiefest apostles, though I be nothing. *2 Co.* **12: 11.**

See also

Chief; Distinction; Eminence; First; Head; Importance; Leadership.

Promise

I do set my bow in the cloud, and it shall be for a token of a covenant between me and the earth. *Ge.* **9: 13.**

My covenant shall be in your flesh for an everlasting covenant. *Ge.* **17: 13.**

Sanctify yourselves: for to morrow the Lord will do wonders among you. *Jos.* **3: 5.**

I will never break my covenant with you. *Ju.* 2: 1.

Pay thy vows unto the most High. *Ps.* 50: 14.

Thou art snared with the words of thy mouth, thou art taken with the words of thy mouth. *Pr.* 6: 2.

When thou vowest a vow unto God, defer not to pay it. *Ec.* 5: 4.

Better is it that thou shouldest not vow, than that thou shouldest vow and not pay. *Ec.* 5: 5.

Even unto them will I give in mine house and within my walls a place and a name better than of sons and of daughters. *Is.* 56: 5.

See also

Agreement; Assurance; Covenant; Pledge; Vow.

Promptitude

Come up to us quickly, and save us, and help us. *Jos.* 10: 6.

He hath bent his bow, and made it ready. *Ps.* 7: 12.

Thou, Lord, art good, and ready to forgive. *Ps.* 86: 5.

Agree with thine adversary quickly. *Mat.* 5: 25.

I say to this man, Go, and he goeth. *Mat.* 8: 9.

Follow me; and let the dead bury their dead. *Mat.* 8: 22.

Straightway they forsook their nets, and followed him. *Mk.* 1: 18.

Immediately she arose and ministered unto them. *Lu.* 4: 39.

God shall . . . straightway glorify him. *Jn.* 13: 32.

They received the word with all readiness of mind. *Ac.* 17: 11.

There was a readiness to will. *2 Co.* 8: 11.

Be ready to every good work. *Tit.* 3: 1.

He beholdeth himself, and goeth his way, and straightway forgetteth what manner of man he was. *Ja.* 1: 24.

Be ready always to give an answer to every man that asketh you a reason of the hope that is in you. *1 Pe.* 3: 15.

Proof

The ear trieth words, as the mouth tasteth meat. *Jb.* 34: 3.

The Lord himself shall give you a sign: Behold, a virgin shall conceive, and bear a son. *Is.* 7: 14.

By their fruits ye shall know them. *Mat.* 7: 20.

When he had thus spoken, he shewed them his hands and his feet. *Lu.* 24: 40.

Except ye see signs and wonders, ye will not believe. *Jn.* 4: 48.

Beholding the man which was healed standing with them, they could say nothing against it. *Ac.* 4: 14.

The Jews require a sign, and the Greeks seek after wisdom. *1 Co.* 1: 22.

Shew ye to them, and before the churches, the proof of your love. *2 Co.* 8: 24.

Ye seek a proof of Christ speaking in me. *2 Co.* 13: 3.

Proving what is acceptable unto the Lord. *Ep.* 5: 10.

Make full proof of thy ministry. *2 Ti.* 4: 5.

Believe not every spirit, but try the spirits whether they are of God. *1 Jn.* 4: 1.

See also

Christ, Witness of; Evidence; God, Evidence of; God, Witness of; Testimony; Witness.

Prophet

Would God that all the Lord's people were prophets, and that the Lord would put his spirit upon them! *Nu.* 11: 29.

Is Saul also among the prophets? *1 S.* 10: 12.

Behold now, the words of the prophets declare good unto the king with one mouth: let thy word, I pray thee, be like the word of one of them, and speak that which is good. *1 K.* 22: 13.

I have heard what the prophets said, that prophesy lies in my name, saying, I have dreamed, I have dreamed. *Je.* 23: 25.

I am against them that prophesy false dreams, saith the Lord. *Je.* 23: 32.

The prophet is a fool, the spiritual man is mad. *Ho.* 9: 7.

I have multiplied visions and used similitudes, by the ministry of the prophets. *Ho.* 12: 10.

By a prophet the Lord brought Israel out of Egypt, and by a prophet was he preserved. *Ho.* 12: 13.

Ye . . . commanded the prophets, saying, Prophesy not. *Am.* 2: 12.

The Lord God hath spoken, who can but prophesy? *Am.* 3: 8.

O thou seer, go, flee thee away into the land of Judah, and there eat bread, and prophesy there. *Am.* 7: 12.

The diviners have seen a lie, and have told false dreams; they comfort in vain. *Zch.* 10: 2.

Many will say to me in that day, Lord, Lord, have we not prophesied in thy name? *Mat.* 7: 22.

He that receiveth a prophet in the name of a prophet shall receive a prophet's reward. *Mat.* 10: 41.

What went ye out for to see? A prophet? yea, I say unto you, and more than a prophet. *Mat.* 11: 9.

A prophet is not without honour, save in his own country, and in his own house. *Mat.* 13: 57.

Hypocrites! because ye build the tombs of the prophets. *Mat.* 23: 29.

Ye are the children of them which killed the prophets. *Mat.* 23: 31.

O Jerusalem, Jerusalem, thou that killest the prophets, and stonest them which are sent unto thee, how often would I have gathered thy children together! *Mat.* 23: 37.

Thou, child, shalt be called the prophet of the Highest. *Lu.* 1: 76.

Nathanael said unto him, Can there any good thing come out of Nazareth? Philip saith unto him, Come and see. *Jn.* 1: 46.

Had ye believed Moses, ye would have believed me: for he wrote of me. *Jn.* 5: 46.

Search, and look: for out of Galilee ariseth no prophet. *Jn.* 7: 52.

Ye are the children of the prophets. *Ac.* 3: 25.

Which of the prophets have not your fathers

persecuted? *Ac.* 7: 52.

Whether prophecy, let us prophesy according to the proportion of faith. *Ro.* 12: 6.

Though I have the gift of prophecy, . . . and have not charity, I am nothing. *1 Co.* 13: 2.

We know in part, and we prophesy in part. *1 Co.* 13: 9.

Greater is he that prophesieth than he that speaketh with tongues. *1 Co.* 14: 5.

Despise not prophesyings. *1 Th.* 5: 20.

Neglect not the gift that is in thee, which was given thee by prophecy. *1 Ti.* 4: 14.

By the prophets. *He.* 1: 1.

Of which salvation the prophets have inquired and searched diligently. *1 Pe.* 1: 10.

The prophecy came not in old time by the will of man: but holy men of God spake as they were moved by the Holy Ghost. *2 Pe.* 1: 21.

Thou must prophesy again before many peoples, and nations, and tongues, and kings. *Re.* 10: 11.

The testimony of Jesus is the spirit of prophecy. *Re.* 19: 10.

See also

Ambassador; Forerunner; God, Messenger of; Messenger; Missionary.

Propitiation

I will appease him with the present that goeth before me. *Ge.* 32: 20.

A gift in secret pacifieth anger. *Pr.* 21: 14.

That thou mayest remember, and be confounded, . . . when I am pacified toward thee for all that thou hast done, saith the Lord God. *Eze.* 16: 63.

He prophesied that Jesus should die for that nation. *Jn.* 11: 51.

Present your bodies a living sacrifice, holy, acceptable unto God. *Ro.* 12: 1.

Christ died for our sins. *1 Co.* 15: 3.

That he might reconcile both unto God in one body by the cross. *Ep.* 2: 16.

It pleased the Father . . . to reconcile all things unto himself. *Col.* 1: 19, 20.

To make reconciliation for the sins of the people. *He.* 2: 17.

He is the propitiation for our sins. *1 Jn.* 2: 2.

Hereby perceive we the love of God, because he laid down his life for us. *1 Jn.* 3: 16.

Herein is love, not that we loved God, but that he loved us, and sent his Son to be the propitiation for our sins. *1 Jn.* 4: 10.

See also

Atonement; Christ, the Mediator; Expiation; Intercession; Reconciliation; Satisfaction.

Proportion

According to the proportion of every one. *1 K.* 7: 36.

According to his substance shall the restitution be. *Jb.* 20: 18.

Answer not a fool according to his folly. *Pr.* 26: 4.

It shall be more tolerable in that day for Sodom. *Lu.* 10: 12.

Having then gifts differing according to the grace that is given to us, whether prophecy, let us prophesy according to the proportion of faith. *Ro.* 12: 6.

As ye have therefore received Christ Jesus the Lord, so walk ye in him. *Col.* 2: 6.

As every man hath received the gift. *1 Pe.* 4: 10.

See also

Dispersion; Distribution; Symmetry.

Proselyte

Sinners shall be converted unto thee. *Ps.* 51: 13.

He that winneth souls is wise. *Pr.* 11: 30.

They that be wise shall shine as the brightness of the firmament; and they that turn many to righteousness as the stars for ever and ever. *Da.* 12: 3.

Except ye be converted, and become as little children, ye shall not enter into the kingdom of heaven. *Mat.* 18: 3.

Ye compass sea and land to make one proselyte. *Mat.* 23: 15.

Go ye into all the world, and preach the gospel to every creature. *Mk.* 16: 15.

Repent ye, therefore, and be converted. *Ac.* 3: 19.

Many of them which heard the word believed. *Ac.* 4: 4.

The multitude of them that believed were of one heart and of one soul. *Ac.* 4: 32.

To the weak became I as weak, that I might gain the weak. *1 Co.* 9: 22.

I am made all things to all men, that I might by all means save some. *1 Co.* 9: 22.

He which converteth the sinner from the error of his way shall save a soul from death, and shall hide a multitude of sins. *Ja.* 5: 20.

See also

Conversion; Evangelism.

Prospect

Look from the place where thou art. *Ge.* 13: 14.

Look not behind thee. *Ge.* 19: 17.

His wife looked back from behind him, and she became a pillar of salt. *Ge.* 19: 26.

The Lord . . . will send his angel with thee, and prosper thy way. *Ge.* 24: 40.

Stand still, and see the salvation of the Lord. *Ex.* 14: 13.

Speak unto the children of Israel, that they go forward. *Ex.* 14: 15.

If from thence thou shalt seek the Lord thy God, thou shalt find him, if thou seek him with all thy heart and with all thy soul. *De.* 4: 29.

See, I have set before thee this day life and good, and death and evil. *De.* 30: 15.

The Lord opened the eyes of the young man; and he saw: and, behold, the mountain was full of horses and chariots of fire. *2 K.* 6: 17.

My soul, wait thou only upon God; for my expectation is from him. *Ps.* 62: 5.

I will lift up mine eyes unto the hills. *Ps.* 121: 1.

Thine eyes shall see the king in his beauty: they shall behold the land that is very far off. *Is.* 33: 17.

Behold, I will do a new thing. *Is.* 43: 19.

His windows being open in his chamber toward Jerusalem, he kneeled upon his knees three times a day, and prayed. *Da.* 6: 10.

The land is as the garden of Eden before them. *Jo.* 2: 3.

There be some standing here, which shall not taste of death, till they see the Son of man coming in his kingdom. *Mat.* 16: 28.

We are saved by hope: but hope that is seen is not hope: for what a man seeth, why doth he yet hope for? *Ro.* 8: 24.

See also

Outlook; Vision.

Prosperity

The Lord maketh poor, and maketh rich. *1 S.* 2: 7.

Shall I then take my bread, and my water, and my flesh that I have killed for my shearers, and give it unto men, whom I know not whence they be? *1 S.* 25: 11.

The Lord was with him; and he prospered whithersoever he went forth. *2 K.* 18: 7.

If thou wert pure and upright; surely now he would . . . make the habitation of thy righteousness prosperous. *Jb.* 8: 6.

If they obey and serve him, they shall spend their days in prosperity, and their years in pleasures. *Jb.* 36: 11.

His leaf also shall not wither; and whatsoever he doeth shall prosper. *Ps.* 1: 3.

Fret not thyself because of him that prospereth in his way. *Ps.* 37: 7.

They that trust in their wealth, and boast themselves in the multitude of their riches. *Ps.* 49: 6.

This is the man that . . . trusted in the abundance of his riches. *Ps.* 52: 7.

If riches increase, set not your heart upon them. *Ps.* 62: 10.

Their eyes stand out with fatness. *Ps.* 73: 7.

These are the ungodly, who prosper in the world; they increase in riches. *Ps.* 73: 12.

Wealth and riches shall be in his house. *Ps.* 112: 3.

Save now, I beseech thee, O Lord: O Lord I beseech thee, send now prosperity. *Ps.* 118: 25.

They shall prosper that love thee. *Ps.* 122: 6.

The liberal soul shall be made fat. *Pr.* 11: 25.

In the day of prosperity be joyful, but in the day of adversity consider. *Ec.* 7: 14.

O that thou hadst hearkened to my commandments! then had thy peace been as a river, and thy righteousness as the waves of the sea. *Is.* 48: 18.

No weapon that is formed against thee shall prosper. *Is.* 54: 17.

The floors shall be full of wheat, and the fats shall overflow with wine and oil. *Jo.* 2: 24.

Where your treasure is, there will your heart be also. *Mat.* 6: 21.

The rich he hath sent empty away. *Lu.* 1: 53.

Soul, thou hast much goods laid up for many years; take thine ease. *Lu.* 12: 19.

See also

Happiness; Nation, Prosperity of; Success; Welfare.

Prostitute

Do not prostitute thy daughter. *Le.* 19: 29.

King Solomon loved many strange women. *1 K.* 11: 1.

Understanding shall . . . deliver thee from the strange woman. *Pr.* 2: 11, 16.

The lips of a strange woman drop as an honeycomb, and her mouth is smoother than oil. *Pr.* 5: 3.

Her feet go down to death: her steps take hold on hell. *Pr.* 5: 5.

Remove thy way far from her, and come not nigh the door of her house. *Pr.* 5: 8.

Rejoice with the wife of thy youth. *Pr.* 5: 18.

Why wilt thou, my son, be ravished with a strange woman, and embrace the bosom of a stranger? *Pr.* 5: 20.

By means of a whorish woman a man is brought to a piece of bread. *Pr.* 6: 26.

The adultress will hunt for the precious life. *Pr.* 6: 26.

Keep thee from the strange woman. *Pr.* 7: 5.

The mouth of strange women is a deep pit. *Pr.* 22: 14.

The Lord hath created a new thing in the earth, A woman shall compass a man. *Je.* 31: 22.

Make not provision for the flesh, to fulfil the lusts thereof. *Ro.* 13: 14.

The body is not for fornication, but for the Lord. *1 Co.* 6: 13.

Ye should abstain from fornication. *1 Th.* 4: 3.

See also

Brothel; Carnality; Debauchery; Flesh; Fornication; Harlot; Lust.

Protection

Appoint out for you cities of refuge. *Jos.* 20: 2.

The Lord sent an angel, which cut off all the mighty men of valour, and the leaders and captains in the camp of the king of Assyria. *2 Ch.* 32: 21.

Let all those that put their trust in thee rejoice: let them ever shout for joy, because thou defendest them. *Ps.* 5: 11.

Let integrity and uprightness preserve me; for I wait on thee. *Ps.* 25: 21.

He shall give his angels charge over thee, to keep thee in all thy ways. *Ps.* 91: 11.

The Lord is thy shade upon thy right hand. *Ps.* 121: 5.

He is a shield unto them that put their trust in him. *Pr.* 30: 5.

He is on my right hand, that I should not be moved. *Ac.* 2: 25.

See also

Asylum; Auspices, Buckler; Defence; Fortress; God, the Keeper; God, Protection of; God, Providence of; Preservation; Refuge; Safety; Security; Shelter; Tower; Wall; Watch.

Protest

How long refuse ye to keep my commandments and my laws? *Ex.* 16: 28.

How long halt ye between two opinions? if the Lord be God, follow him. *1 K.* 18: 21.

Turn ye from your evil ways. *2 K.* 17: 13.

O ye sons of men, how long will ye turn my glory into shame? *Ps.* 4: 2.

Lord, how long shall the wicked, how long shall the wicked triumph? *Ps.* 94: 3.

How long wilt thou sleep, O sluggard? *Pr.* 6: 9.

Behold, I am against them that prophesy false dreams. *Je.* 23: 32.

Thus saith the Lord; Behold, I am against thee. *Eze.* 21: 3.

Turn ye, turn ye from your evil ways; for why will ye die? *Eze.* **33: 11.**

O Lord, how long shall I cry, and thou wilt not hear! *Hab.* **1: 2.**

The world cannot hate you; but me it hateth, because I testify of it, that the works thereof are evil. *Jn.* **7: 7.**

I protest by your rejoicing which I have in Christ Jesus our Lord, I die daily. *1 Co.* **15: 31.**

They speak against you as evildoers. *1 Pe.* **2: 12.**

See also

Affirmation; Dissent.

Proverb

Thou shalt become an astonishment, a proverb, and a byword. among all nations whither the Lord shall lead thee. *De.* **28: 37.**

It became a proverb, Is Saul also among the prophets? *1 S.* **10: 12.**

As saith the proverb of the ancients, Wickedness proceedeth from the wicked. *1 S.* **24: 13.**

Solomon . . . spake three thousand proverbs: and his songs were a thousand and five. *1 K.* **4: 29, 32.**

To understand a proverb, and the interpretation. *Pr.* **1: 6.**

Every one that useth proverbs shall use this proverb against thee, saying, As is the mother, so is her daughter. *Eze.* **16: 44.**

Ye will surely say unto me this proverb, Physician, heal thyself. *Lu.* **4: 23.**

The time cometh when I shall no more speak unto you in proverbs, but I shall shew you plainly of the Father. *Jn.* **16: 25.**

See also

Byword; Fable; Parable; Saying; Word.

Providence

God will provide. *Ge.* **22: 8.**

When shall I provide for mine own house also? *Ge.* **30: 30.**

Forty years didst thou sustain them in the wilderness, so that they lacked nothing. *Ne.* **9: 21.**

I laid me down and slept; I awaked; for the Lord sustained me. *Ps.* **3: 5.**

Cast thy burden upon the Lord, and he shall sustain thee. *Ps.* **55: 22.**

Can he give bread also? can he provide flesh for his people? *Ps.* **78: 20.**

The spirit of man will sustain his infirmity. *Pr.* **18: 14.**

His arm brought salvation unto him; and his righteousness, it sustained him. *Is.* **59: 16.**

Provide neither gold, nor silver, nor brass in your purses. *Mat.* **10: 9.**

I will pull down my barns, and build greater; and there will I bestow all my fruits and my goods. *Lu.* **12: 18.**

I will say to my soul, Soul, thou hast much goods laid up for many years; take thine ease, eat, drink, and be merry. *Lu.* **12: 19.**

This night thy soul shall be required of thee: then whose shall those things be, which thou hast provided? *Lu.* **12: 20.**

Take no thought for your life, what ye shall eat. *Lu.* **12: 22.**

Provide yourselves bags which wax not old, a treasure in the heavens that faileth not, where no thief approacheth, neither moth corrupteth. *Lu.* **12: 33.**

By thee we enjoy great quietness, and that very worthy deeds are done unto this nation by thy providence. *Ac.* **24: 2.**

If any provide not for his own, and specially for those of his own house, he hath denied the faith, and is worse than an infidel. *1 Ti.* **5: 8.**

See also

Care; Defence; God, the Keeper; God, Protection of; God, Providence of; Preservation; Protection; Refuge; Safety; Salvation; Security.

Provocation

Obey his voice, provoke him not. *Ex.* **23: 21.**

Then will they turn unto other gods, and serve them. and provoke me, and break my covenant. *De.* **31: 20.**

The tabernacles of robbers prosper, and they that provoke God are secure. *Jb.* **12: 6.**

Harden not your heart, as in the provocation, and as in the day of temptation in the wilderness. *Ps.* **95: 8.**

They provoked him to anger with their inventions. *Ps.* **106: 29.**

This city hath been to me as a provocation of mine anger and of my fury from the day that they built it even unto this day. *Je.* **32: 31.**

Charity . . . is not easily provoked. *1 Co.* **13: 4, 5.**

Your zeal hath provoked very many. *2 Co.* **9: 2.**

Let us not be desirous of vain glory, provoking one another, envying one another. *Ga.* **5: 26.**

Let us consider one another to provoke unto love and to good works. *He.* **10: 24.**

See also

Affront; Offence.

Prudence

I wisdom dwell with prudence. *Pr.* **8: 12.**

As a jewel of gold in a swine's snout, so is a fair woman which is without discretion. *Pr.* **11: 22.**

The prudent are crowned with knowledge. *Pr.* **14: 18.**

He that regardeth reproof is prudent. *Pr.* **15: 5.**

The heart of the prudent getteth knowledge. *Pr.* **18: 15.**

A prudent man foreseeth the evil, and hideth himself: but the simple pass on, and are punished. *Pr. 22: 3.*

Who is wise, and he shall understand these things? prudent, and he shall know them? *Ho.* **14: 9.**

Thou hast hid these things from the wise and prudent. *Lu.* **10: 21.**

The Lord commended the unjust steward, because he had done wisely: for the children of this world are in their generation wiser than the children of light. *Lu.* **16: 8.**

He hath abounded toward us in all wisdom and prudence. *Ep.* **1: 8.**

See also

Calculation; Care; Caution; Discretion; Discrimination; Heed; Judgment.

Psalm

David, . . . the sweet psalmist of Israel. *2 S.* **23: 1.**

Sing unto him, sing psalms unto him. *1 Ch.* **16: 9.**

None saith, Where is God my maker, who giveth songs in the night. *Jb.* 35: 10.

Sing forth the honour of his name. *Ps.* 66: 2.

Let us come before his presence with thanksgiving, and make a joyful noise unto him with psalms. *Ps.* 95: 2.

Sing unto the Lord with the harp; with the harp, and the voice of a psalm. *Ps.* 98: 5.

Thy statutes have been my songs in the house of my pilgrimage. *Ps.* 119: 54.

How is it then, brethren? when ye come together, every one of you hath a psalm. *1 Co.* 14: 26.

Teaching and admonishing one another in psalms and hymns and spiritual songs, singing with grace in your hearts to the Lord. *Col.* 3: 16.

Is any merry? let him sing psalms. *Ja.* 5: 13.

See also

Anthem; Chorus; Instrument; Melody; Music; Poetry; Song.

Publican

If ye love them which love you, what reward have ye? do not even the publicans the same? *Mat.* 5: 46.

Why eateth your Master with publicans and sinners? *Mat.* 9: 11.

The Son of man came eating and drinking, and they say, Behold a man gluttonous, and a winebibber, a friend of publicans and sinners. *Mat.* 11: 19.

Let him be unto thee as an heathen man and a publican. *Mat.* 18: 17.

The publicans and the harlots go into the kingdom of God before you. *Mat.* 21: 31.

The publicans and the harlots believed him. *Mat.* 21: 32.

I thank thee, that I am not . . . as this publican. *Lu.* 18: 11.

The publican, standing afar off, would not lift up so much as his eyes unto heaven, but smote upon his breast, saying, God be merciful to me a sinner. *Lu.* 18: 13.

Publicity

The heart of fools proclaimeth foolishness. *Pr.* 12: 23.

How beautiful upon the mountains are the feet of him that bringeth good tidings, that publisheth peace; that bringeth good tidings of good, that publisheth salvation. *Is.* 52: 7.

See thou say nothing to any man. *Mk.* 1: 44.

He went out, and began to publish it much, and to blaze abroad the matter. *Mk.* 1: 45.

The gospel must first be published among all nations. *Mk.* 13: 10.

He went his way, and published throughout the whole city how great things Jesus had done unto him. *Lu.* 8: 39.

We declare unto you glad tidings. *Ac.* 13: 32.

The word of the Lord was published throughout all the region. *Ac.* 13: 49.

Every man's work shall be made manifest: for the day shall declare it. *1 Co.* 3: 13.

That which we have seen and heard declare we unto you. *1 Jn.* 1: 3.

See also

Announcement; Annunciation; Evangelism; Gospel; News, Good; Proclamation; Tidings.

Punishment

My father hath chastised you with whips, but I will chastise you with scorpions. *1 K.* 12: 11.

Though hand join in hand, the wicked shall not be unpunished. *Pr.* 11: 21.

He that spareth his rod hateth his son: but he that loveth him chasteneth him betimes. *Pr.* 13: 24.

The backslider in heart shall be filled with his own ways. *Pr.* 14: 14.

A reproof entereth more into a wise man than a hundred stripes into a fool. *Pr.* 17: 10.

Chasten thy son while there is hope, and let not thy soul spare for his crying. *Pr.* 19: 18.

A whip for the horse, a bridle for the ass, and a rod for the fool's back. *Pr.* 26: 3.

He that diggeth a pit shall fall into it. *Ec.* 10: 8.

I will bring evil upon them, which they shall not be able to escape. *Je.* 11: 11.

Woe unto you that desire the day of the Lord! to what end is it for you? the day of the Lord is darkness, and not light. *Am.* 5: 18.

Though they dig into hell, thence shall mine hand take them; though they climb up to heaven, thence will I bring them down. *Am.* 9: 2.

They shall deliver you up to councils; and in the synagogues ye shall be beaten: and ye shall be brought before rulers and kings for my sake. *Mk.* 13: 9.

That the blood of all the prophets, which was shed from the foundation of the world, may be required of this generation. *Lu.* 11: 50.

That servant, which knew not his lord's will, . . . shall be beaten with many stripes. *Lu.* 12: 47.

If they have persecuted me, they will also persecute you. *Jn.* 15: 20.

Of the Jews five times received I forty stripes save one. *2 Co.* 11: 24.

When they shall say, Peace and safety; then sudden destruction cometh upon them. *1 Th.* 5: 3.

How shall we escape, if we neglect so great salvation? *He.* 2: 3.

He shall rule them with a rod of iron. *Re.* 2: 27.

See also

Chastisement; Correction; Discipline; God, Chastisement of; God, Punishment of; Reward; Rod; Scourge; Stripe; Trial.

Pupil

Thou gavest also thy good spirit to instruct them. *Ne.* 9: 20.

Happy is the man whom God correcteth. *Jb.* 5: 17.

Ask now the beasts, and they shall teach thee; and the fowls of the air, and they shall tell thee. *Jb.* 12: 7.

Speak to the earth, and it shall teach thee: and the fishes of the sea shall declare unto thee. *Jb.* 12: 8.

O God, thou hast taught me from my youth. *Ps.* 71: 17.

Blessed is the man whom thou . . . teachest. *Ps.* 94: 12.

Say unto wisdom, Thou art my sister; and call understanding thy kinswoman. *Pr.* 7: 4.

Much study is a weariness of the flesh. *Ec.* 12: 12.

All thy children shall be taught of the Lord; and great shall be the peace of thy children. *Is.* **54: 13.**

Lord, teach us to pray. *Lu.* **11: 1.**

They shall be all taught of God. *Jn.* **6: 45.**

I long to see you, that I may impart unto you some spiritual gift. *Ro.* **1: 11.**

Thou therefore which teachest another, teachest thou not thyself? *Ro.* **2: 21.**

The law was our schoolmaster to bring us unto Christ. *Ga.* **3: 24.**

After that faith is come, we are no longer under a schoolmaster. *Ga.* **3: 25.**

Ye yourselves are taught of God to love one another. *1 Th.* **4: 9.**

Study to be quiet. *1 Th.* **4: 11.**

See also

Christ, the Teacher; Education; Instruction; School; Study; Teaching; Training.

Puppet

I will be with thy mouth, and teach thee what thou shalt say. *Ex.* **4: 12.**

He shall be to thee instead of a mouth. *Ex.* **4: 16.**

I will raise them up a Prophet from among their brethren, . . . and will put my words in his mouth. *De.* **18: 18.**

We are the clay, and thou our potter. *Is.* **64: 8.**

The Lord said unto me, Behold, I have put my words in thy mouth. *Je.* **1: 9.**

Purification

This shall be the law of the leper in the day of his cleansing. *Le.* **14: 2.**

The words of the Lord are . . . as silver tried in a furnace of earth, purified seven times. *Ps.* **12: 6.**

Purge me with hyssop, and I shall be clean: wash me, and I shall be whiter than snow. *Ps.* **51: 7.**

Iniquities prevail against me: as for our transgressions, thou shalt purge them away. *Ps.* **65: 3.**

Verily I have cleansed my heart in vain, and washed my hands in innocency. *Ps.* **73: 13.**

Take away all the dross from the silver, and there shall come forth a vessel for the finer. *Pr.* **25: 4.**

Wash ye, make you clean. *Is.* **1: 16.**

He shall sit as a refiner and purifier of silver. *Mal.* **3: 3.**

He will throughly purge his floor, and gather his wheat into the garner; but he will burn up the chaff with unquenchable fire. *Mat.* **3: 12.**

Cleanse first that which is within the cup and platter, that the outside of them may be clean also. *Mat.* **23: 26.**

When the days of her purification according to the law of Moses were accomplished, they brought him to Jerusalem. *Lu.* **2: 22.**

Lord, not my feet only, but also my hands and my head. *Jn.* **13: 9.**

Every branch that beareth fruit, he purgeth it, that it may bring forth more fruit. *Jn.* **15: 2.**

Purge out therefore the old leaven, that ye may be a new lump, as ye are unleavened. *1 Co.* **5: 7.**

If the blood of bulls and of goats, . . . sanctifieth to the purifying of the flesh: How

much more shall the blood of Christ. *He.* **9: 13, 14.**

Seeing that ye have purified your souls, . . . see that ye love one another with a pure heart fervently. *1 Pe.* **1: 22.**

He . . . hath forgotten that he was purged from his old sins. *2 Pe.* **1: 9.**

The blood of Jesus Christ his Son cleanseth us from all sin. *1 Jn.* **1: 7.**

Every man that hath this hope in him purifieth himself, even as he is pure. *1 Jn.* **3: 3.**

See also

Cleansing; Consecration; Lent; Refinement; Sanctification; Wash.

Purity

Be ye clean, that bear the vessels of the Lord. *Is.* **52: 11.**

Blessed are the pure in heart: for they shall see God. *Mat.* **5: 8.**

And entering into the sepulchre, they saw a young man sitting on the right side, clothed in a long white garment. *Mk.* **16: 5.**

In the midst of a crooked and perverse nation, among whom ye shine as lights in the world. *Ph.* **2: 15.**

Whatsoever things are pure, whatsoever things are lovely, whatsoever things are of good report: . . . think on these things. *Ph.* **4: 8.**

A good conscience. *1 Ti.* **1: 19.**

Follow righteousness, faith, charity, peace, with them that call on the Lord out of a pure heart. *2 Ti.* **2: 22.**

Unto the pure all things are pure: but unto them that are defiled and unbelieving is nothing pure; but even their mind and conscience is defiled. *Tit.* **1: 15.**

Pure religion and undefiled before God and the Father. *Ja.* **1: 27.**

To keep himself unspotted from the world. *Ja.* **1: 27.**

The wisdom that is from above is first pure. *Ja.* **3: 17.**

See that ye love one another with a pure heart fervently. *1 Pe.* **1: 22.**

He shewed me a pure river of water of life, clear as crystal, proceeding out of the throne of God and of the Lamb. *Re.* **22: 1.**

See also

Chastity; Childlikeness; Cleanness; Holiness; Innocence; Piety; Righteousness; Saint; Sanctification.

Purpose

I am purposed. *Ps.* **17: 3.**

I will dwell in the house of the Lord for ever. *Ps.* **23: 6.**

The Spirit of the Lord is upon me, because he hath anointed me to preach the gospel to the poor; he hath sent me to heal the brokenhearted, to preach deliverance to the captives, and recovering of sight to the blind, to set at liberty them that are bruised. *Lu.* **4: 18.**

I am come that they might have life. *Jn.* **10: 10.**

Barnabas . . . exhorted them all, that with purpose of heart they would cleave unto the Lord. *Ac.* **11: 22, 23.**

I have appeared unto thee for this purpose, to make thee a minister and a witness both of these things which thou hast seen, and of those things in the which I will appear unto thee. *Ac.* 26: 16.

For which cause we faint not. *2 Co.* 4: 16.

Every man according as he purposeth in his heart, so let him give. *2 Co.* 9: 7.

The eternal purpose. *Ep.* 3: 11.

For this cause I bow my knees unto the Father of our Lord Jesus Christ. *Ep.* 3: 14.

This one thing I do, forgetting those things which are behind, . . . I press toward the mark. *Ph.* 3: 13, 14.

To the end he may stablish your hearts unblameable in holiness before God. *1 Th.* 3: 13.

Who hath saved us, and called us with an holy calling, not according to our works, but according to his own purpose and grace. *2 Ti.* 1: 9.

See also

Aim; Determination; End; Firmness; Intention; Motive; Plan; Resolution; Steadfastness.

Pursuit

Ye shall chase your enemies, and they shall fall before you by the sword. *Le.* 26: 7.

Ye shall flee when none pursueth. *Le.* 26: 17.

I will send a faintness into their hearts; . . . and the sound of a shaken leaf shall chase them; and they shall flee, as fleeing from the sword. *Le.* 26: 36.

How should one chase a thousand, and two put ten thousand to flight, except their Rock had sold them. *De.* 32: 30.

Terrors are turned upon me: they pursue my soul as the wind. *Jb.* 30: 15.

Seek peace, and pursue it. *Ps.* 34: 14.

Let them be as chaff before the wind: and let the angel of the Lord chase them. *Ps.* 35: 5.

As righteousness tendeth to life: so he that pursueth evil pursueth it to his own death. *Pr.* 11: 19.

Evil pursueth sinners. *Pr.* 13: 21.

All the brethren of the poor do hate him: how much more do his friends go far from him? he pursueth them with words, yet they are wanting to him. *Pr.* 19: 7.

The wicked flee when no man pursueth. *Pr.* 28: 1.

Follow after charity. *1 Co.* 14: 1.

See also

Christ, Follower of; Christ, Quest for; Flight; Follower; God, Quest for; God, Search for; Life, Quest for; Occupation; Perseverance; Search.

Q

Quality

Let me die the death of the righteous, and let my last end be like his! *Nu.* 23: 10.

Except your righteousness shall exceed the righteousness of the scribes and Pharisees, ye shall in no case enter into the kingdom of heaven. *Mat.* 5: 20.

Salt is good: but if the salt have lost its saltness, wherewith will ye season it? *Mk.* 9: 50.

Of thorns men do not gather figs, nor of a bramble bush gather they grapes. *Lu.* 6: 44.

If thou wert cut out of the olive tree which is wild by nature, and wert graffed contrary to nature into a good olive tree: how much more shall these, which be the natural branches, be graffed into their own olive tree? *Ro.* 11: 24.

Abstain from all appearance of evil. *1 Th.* 5: 22.

Your garments are motheaten. *Ja.* 5: 2.

Besides this, giving all diligence, add to your faith virtue; and to virtue knowledge; And to knowledge temperance; and to temperance patience; and to patience godliness; And to godliness brotherly kindness; and to brotherly kindness charity. *2 Pe.* 1: 5–7.

See also

Character; Trait.

Quarrel

See how he seeketh a quarrel against me. *2 K.* 5: 7.

A man of understanding holdeth his peace. *Pr.* 11: 12.

Who hath contentions? . . . They that tarry long at the wine. *Pr.* 23: 29, 30.

Full of envy, murder, debate, deceit. *Ro.* 1: 29.

If any man seem to be contentious, we have no such custom, neither the churches of God. *1 Co.* 11: 16.

Lest there be debates, envyings, wraths, strifes, backbitings, whisperings, swellings, tumults. *2 Co.* 12: 20.

Do all things without murmurings and disputings. *Ph.* 2: 14.

Forgiving one another, if any man have a quarrel against any. *Col.* 3: 13.

See also

Argument; Conflict; Contention; Controversy; Dispute; Fight; Strife; Tumult.

Quest

Faint, yet pursuing. *Ju.* 8: 4.

The Lord searcheth all hearts, and understandeth all the imaginations of the thoughts. *1 Ch.* 28: 9.

One thing have I desired of the Lord, that will I seek after; that I may dwell in the house of the Lord all the days of my life. *Ps.* 27: 4.

Seek peace, and pursue it. *Ps.* 34: 14.

O Lord, thou hast searched me, and known me. *Ps.* 139: 1.

Seek good, and not evil, that ye may live. *Am.* 5: 14.

Seek, and ye shall find. *Mat.* 7: 7.

The kingdom of heaven is like unto a merchant man, seeking goodly pearls. *Mat.* 13: 45.

The Son of man is come to seek and to save

that which was lost. *Mat.* 18: 11.

There cometh a woman of Samaria to draw water. *Jn.* 4: 7.

We would see Jesus. *Jn.* 12: 21.

See also

Christ, Quest for; Examination; God, Quest for; God, Search for; Inquiry; Life, Quest of; Question; Search; Seeker.

Question

No man after that durst ask him any question. *Mk.* 12: 34.

Ask, and it shall be given you. *Lu.* 11: 9.

He questioned with him in many words; but he answered him nothing. *Lu.* 23: 9.

There arose a question between some of John's disciples and the Jews about purifying. *Jn.* 3: 25.

I know thee to be expert in all customs and questions which are among the Jews. *Ac.* 26: 3.

Whatsoever is sold in the shambles, that eat, asking no question for conscience' sake. *1 Co.* 10: 25.

We know in part. *1 Co.* 13: 9.

Neither give heed to fables and endless genealogies, which minister questions, rather than godly edifying. *1 Ti.* 1: 4.

He is proud, knowing nothing, but doting about questions and strifes of words. *1 Ti.* 6: 4.

Foolish and unlearned questions avoid, knowing that they do gender strifes. *2 Ti.* 2: 23.

See also

Christ, Quest for; Curiosity; Examination; God, Quest for; God, Search for; Inquiry; Quest.

Quickening

Thou . . . shalt quicken me again, and shalt bring me up again from the depths of the earth. *Ps.* 71: 20.

Quicken thou me according to thy word. *Ps.* 119: 25.

Turn away mine eyes from beholding vanity; and quicken thou me in thy way. *Ps.* 119: 37.

Quicken me in thy righteousness. *Ps.* 119: 40.

Quicken me after thy lovingkindness. *Ps.* 119: 88.

Thus saith the Lord God unto these bones; Behold, I will cause breath to enter into you, and ye shall live. *Eze.* 37: 5.

I prophesied as he commanded me, and the breath came into them, and they lived. *Eze.* 37: 10.

It is the spirit that quickeneth; the flesh profiteth nothing. *Jn.* 6: 63.

I am the resurrection, and the life. *Jn.* 11: 25.

God . . . quickeneth the dead, and calleth those things which be not as though they were. *Ro.* 4: 17.

That which thou sowest is not quickened, except it die. *1 Co.* 15: 36.

The first man Adam was made a living soul; the last Adam was made a quickening spirit. *1 Co.* 15: 45.

The letter killeth, but the spirit giveth life. *2 Co.* 3: 6.

God, . . . Even when we were dead in sins, hath quickened us together with Christ. *Ep.* 2: 4, 5.

I charge thee therefore before God, and the Lord Jesus Christ, who shall judge the quick and the dead. *2 Ti.* 4: 1.

See also

Birth, the New; Confirmation; Man, the New; Refreshment; Regeneration; Renewal; Restoration; Resurrection; Revival; Spring.

Quickness

Bow down thine ear to me; deliver me speedily. *Ps.* 31: 2.

In the day when I call answer me speedily. *Ps.* 102: 2.

And shall make him of quick understanding in the fear of the Lord. *Is.* 11: 3.

I will hasten my word to perform it. *Je.* 1: 12.

The great day of the Lord is near, it is near, and hasteth greatly. *Zph.* 1: 14.

I tell you that he will avenge them speedily. *Lu.* 18: 8.

Repent, and do the first works; or else I will come unto thee quickly, and will remove thy candlestick out of his place. *Re.* 2: 5.

He which testifieth these things saith, Surely I come quickly. Amen. Even so, come, Lord Jesus. *Re.* 22: 20.

See also

Haste; Hurry; Speed; Swiftness.

Quiet

On the seventh day God ended his work which he had made; and he rested on the seventh day. *Ge.* 2: 2.

I will both lay me down in peace, and sleep. *Ps.* 4: 8.

Which stilleth the noise of the seas, the noise of their waves, and the tumult of the people. *Ps.* 65: 7.

Better is an handful with quietness, than both the hands full with travail and vexation of spirit. *Ec.* 4: 6.

The race is not to the swift, nor the battle to the strong. *Ec.* 9: 11.

In returning and rest shall ye be saved; in quietness and in confidence shall be your strength. *Is.* 30: 15.

The work of righteousness shall be peace; and the effect of righteousness quietness and assurance for ever. *Is.* 32: 17.

Thine eyes shall see Jerusalem a quiet habitation. *Is.* 33: 20.

I shall go softly all my years. *Is.* 38: 15.

He shall not strive, nor cry; neither shall any man hear his voice in the streets. *Mat.* 12: 19.

He arose, and rebuked the wind, and said unto the sea, Peace, be still. *Mk.* 4: 39.

Jesus answered and said unto her, Martha, Martha, thou art careful and troubled about many things: But one thing is needful: and Mary hath chosen that good part, which shall not be taken away from her. *Lu.* 10: 41, 42.

He answered him nothing. *Lu.* 23: 9.

There remaineth therefore a rest to the people of God. *He.* 4: 9.

See also

Calm; Christ, Peace of; Concord; Ease; God, Peace of; God, Rest in; Harmony; Peace; Repose; Rest; Security; Stillness; Tranquillity.

R

Rabbi

They . . . love . . . to be called of men, Rabbi, Rabbi. *Mat.* **23: 5–7.**

Be not ye called Rabbi: for one is your Master, even Christ; and all ye are brethren. *Mat.* **23: 8.**

Rabbi, . . . where dwellest thou? *Jn.* **1: 38.**

Rabbi, thou art the Son of God; thou art the King of Israel. *Jn.* **1: 49.**

Rabbi, we know that thou art a teacher come from God. *Jn.* **3: 2.**

Rabbi, when camest thou hither? *Jn.* **6: 25.**

See also

Christ, the Master; Master; Teacher.

Rabble

Thou shalt not curse the people: for they are blessed. *Nu.* **22: 12.**

Ye shall not be afraid of the face of man; for the judgment is God's. *De.* **1: 17**

One man of you shall chase a thousand: for the Lord your God, he it is that fighteth for you. *Jos.* **23: 10.**

The people that are with thee are too many for me. *Ju.* **7: 2.**

Be not afraid nor dismayed by reason of this great multitude; for the battle is not your's, but God's. *2 Ch.* **20: 15.**

He scorneth the multitude of the city. *Jb.* **39: 7.**

Woe to the multitude of many people, which make a noise like the noise of the seas. *Is.* **17: 12.**

The common people heard him gladly. *Mk.* **12: 37.**

They cried, saying, Crucify him, crucify him. *Lu.* **23: 21.**

The people stood beholding. *Lu.* **23: 35.**

They stoned Stephen. *Ac.* **7: 59.**

Some cried one thing, some another, among the multitude. *Ac.* **21: 34.**

The multitude of the people followed after, crying, Away with him. *Ac.* **21: 36.**

All the multitude of the Jews have dealt with me, both at Jerusalem, and also here, crying that he ought not to live any longer. *Ac.* **25: 24.**

They were stoned, they were sawn asunder, were tempted, were slain with the sword. *He.* **11: 37.**

See also

Crowd; Multitude; People.

Race

I am the Lord your God, which have separated you from other people. *Le.* **20: 24.**

Rejoiceth as a strong man to run a race. *Ps.* **19: 5.**

When thou runnest, thou shalt not stumble. *Pr.* **4: 12.**

The race is not to the swift. *Ec.* **9: 11.**

They that wait upon the Lord shall renew their strength; . . . they shall run, and not be weary. *Is.* **40: 31.**

Our fathers worshipped in this mountain; and ye say, that in Jerusalem is the place where men ought to worship. *Jn.* **4: 20.**

God hath shewed me that I should not call any man common or unclean. *Ac.* **10: 28.**

He . . . hath made of one blood all nations for to dwell on all the face of the earth. *Ac.* **17: 25, 26.**

Know ye not that they which run in a race run all, but one receiveth the prize? So run, that ye may obtain. *1 Co.* **9: 24.**

I therefore so run, not as uncertainly; so fight I, not as one that beateth the air. *1 Co.* **9: 26.**

There is neither Greek nor Jew, circumcision nor uncircumcision, Barbarian, Scythian, bond nor free: but Christ is all, and in all. *Col.* **3: 11.**

Let us lay aside every weight, and the sin which doth so easily beset us, and let us run with patience the race that is set before us. *He.* **12: 1.**

See also

Athlete; Competition; Contest; Emulation; Equality, Racial; Game; Nation; Offspring; People; Sport.

Radiance

Moses wist not that the skin of his face shone. *Ex.* **34: 29.**

The moon walking in brightness. *Jb.* **31: 26.**

He scattereth his bright cloud. *Jb.* **37: 11.**

Now men see not the bright light which is in the clouds. *Jb.* **37: 21.**

They looked unto him, and were lightened. *Ps.* **34: 5.**

The night shineth as the day. *Ps.* **139: 12.**

Gentiles shall come to thy light, and kings to the brightness of thy rising. *Is.* **60: 3.**

The Lord shall be unto thee an everlasting light. *Is.* **60: 19.**

All the bright lights of heaven will I make dark over thee. *Eze.* **32: 8.**

They that be wise shall shine as the brightness of the firmament; and they that turn many to righteousness as the stars for ever and ever. *Da.* **12: 3.**

While he yet spake, behold, a bright cloud overshadowed them. *Mat.* **17: 5.**

The glory of the Lord shone round about them: and they were sore afraid. *Lu.* **2: 9.**

His raiment was white and glistering. *Lu.* **9: 29.**

I prayed in my house, and, behold, a man stood before me in bright clothing. *Ac.* **10: 30.**

At midday, O king, I saw in the way a light from heaven, above the brightness of the sun, shining round about me. *Ac.* **26: 13.**

I am . . . the bright and morning star. *Re.* **22: 16.**

See also

Brightness; Christ, the Light; Gleam; God, the Light; Light; Splendor.

Rage

Wrath killeth the foolish man, and envy slayeth the silly one. *Jb.* **5: 2.**

The hypocrites in heart heap up wrath. *Jb.* **36: 13.**

Why do the heathen rage, and the people imagine a vain thing? *Ps.* **2: 1.**

Cease from anger, and forsake wrath. *Ps.* 37: 8.

Surely the wrath of man shall praise thee. *Ps.* 76: 10.

He that is slow to wrath is of great understanding. *Pr.* 14: 29.

The indignation of the Lord is upon all nations, and his fury upon all their armies. *Is.* 34: 2.

I am full of the fury of the Lord. *Je.* 6: 11.

But now ye also put off all these; anger, wrath, malice. *Col.* 3: 8.

Let every man be swift to hear, slow to speak, slow to wrath: For the wrath of man worketh not the righteousness of God. *Ja.* 1: 19, 20.

See also

Anger; Christ, Wrath of; Fury; God, Anger of; God, Wrath of; Passion; Wrath.

Raiment

Thy raiment waxed not old upon thee. *De.* 8: 4.

The Lord reigneth, he is clothed with majesty. *Ps.* 93: 1.

John had his raiment of camel's hair. *Mat.* 3: 4.

Consider the lilies of the field, how they grow; they toil not, neither do they spin: And yet I say unto you, That even Solomon in all his glory was not arrayed like one of these. *Mat.* 6: 28, 29.

A woman . . . came behind him, and touched the hem of his garment. *Mat.* 9: 20.

They which are gorgeously apparelled, and live delicately, are in kings' courts. *Lu.* 7: 25.

They parted my raiment among them, and for my vesture they did cast lots. *Jn.* 19: 24.

I have coveted no man's silver, or gold, or apparel. *Ac.* 20: 33.

He that overcometh, the same shall be clothed in white raiment. *Re.* 3: 5.

Lo, a great multitude, which no man could number, . . . clothed with white robes, and palms in their hands. *Re.* 7: 9.

See also

Apparel; Attire; Clothes; Garment; Robe.

Rain

The rain was upon the earth forty days and forty nights. *Ge.* 7: 12.

Behold, I will rain bread from heaven for you. *Ex.* 16: 4.

He shall be . . . as the tender grass springing out of the earth by clear shining after rain. *2 S.* 23: 4.

God . . . giveth rain upon the earth, and sendeth waters upon the fields. *Jb.* 5: 8, 10.

Hath the rain a father? or who hath begotten the drops of dew? *Jb.* 38: 28.

He shall come down like rain upon the mown grass: as showers that water the earth. *Ps.* 72: 6.

Who covereth the heaven with clouds, who prepareth rain for the earth. *Ps.* 147: 8.

Whoso boasteth himself of a false gift is like clouds and wind without rain. *Pr.* 25: 14.

As snow in summer, and as rain in harvest, so honour is not seemly for a fool. *Pr.* 26: 1.

A continual dropping in a very rainy day and a contentious woman are alike. *Pr.* 27: 15.

As the rain cometh down, and the snow from heaven, and returneth not thither, but watereth the earth, and maketh it bring forth and bud, . . . So shall my word be that goeth forth out of my mouth. *Is.* 55: 10, 11.

I will cause the shower to come down in his season; there shall be showers of blessing. *Eze.* 34: 26.

He shall come unto us as the rain, as the latter and former rain unto the earth. *Ho.* 6: 3.

It is time to seek the Lord, till he come and rain righteousness upon you. *Ho.* 10: 12.

He . . . sendeth rain on the just and on the unjust. *Mat.* 5: 45.

The rain descended, and the floods came, and the winds blew, and beat upon that house; and it fell not. *Mat.* 7: 25.

See also

Weather.

Rainbow

This is the token of the covenant which I make between me and you and every living creature that is with you, for perpetual generations: I do set my bow in the cloud, and it shall be for a token of a covenant between me and the earth. *Ge.* 9: 12, 13.

It shall come to pass, when I bring a cloud over the earth, that the bow shall be seen in the cloud. *Ge.* 9: 14.

I will remember my covenant, which is between me and you and every living creature of all flesh; and the waters shall no more become a flood to destroy all flesh. *Ge.* 9: 15.

The bow shall be in the cloud; and I will look upon it, that I may remember the everlasting covenant. *Ge.* 9: 16.

As the appearance of the bow that is in the cloud in the day of rain, so was the appearance of the brightness round about. *Eze.* 1: 28.

There was a rainbow round about the throne, in sight like unto an emerald. *Re.* 4: 3.

I saw another mighty angel come down from heaven, clothed with a cloud: and a rainbow was upon his head. *Re.* 10: 1.

Ransom

The ransomed of the Lord shall return, and come to Zion with songs and everlasting joy upon their heads. *Is.* 35: 10.

I will ransom them from the power of the grave. *Ho.* 13: 14.

Even the Son of man came not to be ministered unto, but to minister, and to give his life a ransom for many. *Mk.* 10: 45.

Through the redemption that is in Christ Jesus. *Ro.* 3: 24.

God commendeth his love toward us, in that, while we were yet sinners, Christ died for us. *Ro.* 5: 8.

God sending his own Son in the likeness of sinful flesh, and for sin, condemned sin in the flesh. *Ro.* 8: 3.

Christ Jesus . . . gave himself a ransom for all. *1 Ti.* 2: 5, 6.

Ye were not redeemed with corruptible things, as silver and gold, . . . But with the precious blood of Christ, as of a lamb without blemish and without spot. *1 Pe.* 1: 18, 19.

By whose stripes ye were healed. *1 Pe.* 2: 24.

See also

Christ, the Redeemer; Christ, Sacrifice of; Redemption; Suffering, Vicarious.

Rapture

Behold the angels of God ascending and descending. *Ge.* 28: 12

This is the gate of heaven. *Ge.* 28: 17.

The Almighty . . . shall bless thee with blessings of heaven. *Ge.* 49: 25.

Moses wist not that the skin of his face shone. *Ex.* 34: 29.

He . . . saw the vision of the Almighty, falling into a trance, but having his eyes open. *Nu.* 24: 16.

God had made them rejoice with great joy. *Ne.* 12: 43.

Let all those that seek thee rejoice and be glad in thee. *Ps.* 40: 16.

He . . . opened the doors of heaven. *Ps.* 78: 23.

Let thy saints shout for joy. *Ps.* 132: 9.

If I ascend up into heaven, thou art there. *Ps.* 139. 8.

I will . . . open you the windows of heaven, and pour you out a blessing. *Mal.* 3: 10.

They were all filled with the Holy Ghost. *Ac.* 2: 4.

Suddenly there shined round about him a light from heaven. *Ac.* 9: 3.

I knew a man in Christ . . . caught up to the third heaven. *2 Co.* 12: 2.

See also

Christ, Joy in; Delight; Ecstasy; Exaltation; Exultation; Joy.

Rashness

If my foot hath hasted to deceit; Let me be weighed in an even balance. *Jb.* 31: 5, 6.

I said in my haste, All men are liars. *Ps.* 116: 11.

He that is hasty of spirit exalteth folly. *Pr.* 14: 29.

He that hasteth with his feet sinneth. *Pr.* 19: 2.

He that hasteth to be rich hath an evil eye. *Pr.* 28: 22.

Be not rash with thy mouth, and let not thine heart be hasty to utter any thing before God. *Ec.* 5: 2.

Be not hasty in thy spirit to be angry. *Ec.* 7: 9.

The heart also of the rash shall understand knowledge. *Is.* 32: 4.

Ye ought to be quiet, and to do nothing rashly. *Ac.* 19: 36.

Raven

He sent forth a raven, which went forth to and fro, until the waters were dried up from off the earth. *Ge.* 8: 7.

I have commanded the ravens to feed thee there. *1 K.* 17: 4.

The ravens brought him bread and flesh in the morning, and bread and flesh in the evening. *1 K.* 17: 6.

Who provideth for the raven his food? when his young ones cry unto God, they wander for lack of meat. *Jb.* 38: 41.

He giveth to the beast his food, and to the young ravens which cry. *Ps.* 147: 9.

The owl also and the raven shall dwell in it. *Is.* 34: 11.

Consider the ravens: for they neither sow nor reap; which neither have storehouse nor barn; and God feedeth them. *Lu.* 12: 24.

Ray

God made two great lights; the greater light to rule the day, and the lesser light to rule the night. *Ge.* 1: 16.

Thou art my lamp, O Lord. *2 S.* 22: 29.

He shall be as the light of the morning, when the sun riseth, even a morning without clouds. *2 S.* 23: 4.

As the tender grass springing out of the earth by clear shining after rain. *2 S.* 23: 4.

The light shall shine upon thy ways. *Jb.* 22: 28.

Oh that I were as in months past, as in the days when God preserved me; When his candle shined upon my head, and when by his light I walked through darkness. *Jb.* 29: 2, 3.

Thou wilt light my candle. *Ps.* 18: 28.

All the bright lights of heaven will I make dark over thee. *Eze.* 32: 8.

Cause thy face to shine upon thy sanctuary that is desolate. *Da.* 9: 17.

The stars shall withdraw their shining. *Jo.* 2: 10.

His brightness was as the light. *Hab.* 3: 4.

As the lightning cometh out of the east, and shineth even unto the west; so shall also the coming of the Son of man be. *Mat.* 24: 27.

As when the bright shining of a candle doth give thee light. *Lu.* 11: 36.

Ye do well that ye take heed, as unto a light that shineth in a dark place. *2 Pe.* 1: 19.

The light of a candle shall shine no more at all in thee. *Re.* 18: 23.

See also

Brightness; Candle; Gleam; Lamp; Light; Lightning.

Reach

Let us build us a city and a tower, whose top may reach unto heaven. *Ge.* 11: 4.

He dreamed, and behold a ladder set up on the earth, and the top of it reached to heaven. *Ge.* 28: 12.

Though his excellency mount up to the heavens, . . . Yet he shall perish for ever. *Jb.* 20: 6, 7.

Thy faithfulness reacheth unto the clouds. *Ps.* 36: 5.

Thy truth reacheth unto the clouds. *Ps.* 108: 4.

Reach hither thy hand, and thrust it into my side. *Jn.* 20: 27.

We will not boast of things without our measure, but according to the measure of the rule which God hath distributed to us, a measure to reach even unto you. *2 Co.* 10: 13.

Forgetting those things which are behind, and reaching forth unto those things which are before, I press toward the mark. *Ph.* 3: 13, 14.

Her sins have reached unto heaven, and God hath remembered her iniquities. *Re.* 18: 5.

See also

Ambition; Aspiration.

Readiness

Set thine house in order; for thou shalt die, and not live. *2 K.* 20: 1.

He knoweth that the day of darkness is ready at his hand. *Jb.* 15: 23.

My tongue is the pen of a ready writer. *Ps.* 45: 1.

Thou, Lord, art good, and ready to forgive. *Ps.* 86: 5.

I am afflicted and ready to die from my youth up. *Ps.* 88: 15.

Thy people shall be willing in the day of thy power. *Ps.* 110: 3.

Keep thy foot when thou goest to the house of God, and be more ready to hear, than to give the sacrifice of fools. *Ec.* 5: 1.

Be ye also ready: for in such an hour as ye think not the Son of man cometh. *Mat.* 24: 44.

They that were ready went in with him to the marriage. *Mat.* 25: 10.

Watch ye therefore: for ye know not when the master of the house cometh, at even, or at midnight, or at the cockcrowing, or in the morning. *Mk.* 13: 35.

The spirit truly is ready, but the flesh is weak. *Mk.* 14: 38.

Let your loins be girded about, and your lights burning. *Lu.* 12: 35.

Lord, I am ready to go with thee, both into prison, and to death. *Lu.* 22: 33.

My time is not yet come: but your time is alway ready. *Jn.* 7: 6.

They received the word with all readiness of mind. *Ac.* 17: 11.

Perform the doing of it; that as there was a readiness to will, so there may be a performance also out of that which ye have. *2 Co.* 8: 11.

Your feet shod with the preparation of the gospel of peace. *Ep.* 6: 15.

I am now ready to be offered. *2 Ti.* 4: 6.

Ready always to give an answer to every man that asketh you a reason of the hope that is in you. *1 Pe.* 3: 15.

Let us be glad and rejoice, and give honour to him: for the marriage of the Lamb is come, and his wife hath made herself ready. *Re.* 19: 7.

See also

Expert; Preparation; Quickness; Skill; Unpreparedness; Willingness.

Reading

How sweet are thy words unto my taste! yea, sweeter than honey to my mouth! *Ps.* 119: 103.

Seek ye out of the book of the Lord, and read. *Is.* 34: 16.

Write the vision, and make it plain upon tables, that he may run that readeth it. *Hab.* 2: 2.

Did ye never read in the scriptures, The stone which the builders rejected, the same is become the head of the corner. *Mat.* 21: 42.

As his custom was, he went into the synagogue on the sabbath day, and stood up for to read. *Lu.* 4: 16.

He said unto him, What is written in the law? how readest thou? *Lu.* 10: 26.

The Jews marvelled, saying, How knoweth this man letters, having never learned? *Jn.* 7: 15.

Understandest thou what thou readest? *Ac.* 8: 30.

Ye are our epistle written in our hearts,

known and read of all men. *2 Co.* 3: 2.

Till I come, give attendance to reading. *1 Ti.* 4: 13.

Blessed is he that readeth, and they that hear the words of this prophecy. *Re.* 1: 3.

No man was found worthy to open and to read the book. *Re.* 5: 4.

See also

Book; Scripture; Writing.

Realism

The night of my pleasure hath he turned into fear unto me. *Is.* 21: 4.

The watchman said, The morning cometh, and also the night. *Is.* 21: 12.

Whosoever hath not, from him shall be taken even that which he seemeth to have. *Lu.* 8: 18.

And he confessed, and denied not; but confessed, I am not the Christ. *Jn.* 1: 20.

And needed not that any should testify of man: for he knew what was in man. *Jn.* 2: 25.

The people therefore, that stood by, and heard it, said that it thundered: others said, An angel spake to him. *Jn.* 12: 29.

Things which are not, to bring to nought things that are. *1 Co.* 1: 28.

Realization

God . . . maketh my way perfect. *2 S.* 22: 33.

The harvest is the end of the world. *Mat.* 13: 39.

O woman, great is thy faith: be it unto thee even as thou wilt. *Mat.* 15: 28.

If thou wilt be perfect, go and sell that thou hast, and give to the poor, and thou shalt have treasure in heaven. *Mat.* 19: 21.

For this cause came I unto this hour. *Jn.* 12: 27.

I have finished the work which thou gavest me to do. *Jn.* 17: 4.

When that which is perfect is come, then that which is in part shall be done away. *1 Co.* 13: 10.

Not as though I had already attained, either were already perfect: but I follow after. *Ph.* 3: 12.

We desire that every one of you do shew the same diligence to the full assurance of hope unto the end. *He.* 6: 11.

The God of all grace, . . . after that ye have suffered a while, make you perfect. *1 Pe.* 5: 10.

See also

Christ, Fullness of; Christ, the Goal; Christ, Perfection of; Completion; End; Fulfilment; Harvest; Life, the Full; Perfection.

Realm

The Lord shall reign for ever and ever. *Ex.* 15: 18.

What nation is there so great, who hath God so nigh unto them, as the Lord our God is in all things that we call upon him for? *De.* 4: 7.

Blessed of the Lord be his land, . . . for the chief things of the ancient mountains, and for the precious things of the lasting hills. *De.* 33: 13, 15.

All the people shouted, and said, God save the king. *1 S.* 10: 24.

Who knoweth whether thou art come to the kingdom for such a time as this? *Es.* 4: 14.

Thou settest a crown of pure gold on his head. *Ps.* 21: 3.

The kingdom is the Lord's. *Ps.* 22: 28.

God reigneth over the heathen. *Ps.* 47: 8.

God sitteth upon the throne of his holiness. *Ps.* 47: 8.

Sing unto God, ye kingdoms of the earth. *Ps.* 68: 32.

The moon shall be confounded, and the sun ashamed, when the Lord of hosts shall reign . . . before his ancients gloriously. *Is.* 24: 23.

Thus saith the Lord God; Remove the diadem, and take off the crown: this shall not be the same: exalt him that is low, and abase him that is high. *Eze.* 21: 26.

The kingdom and dominion, and the greatness of the kingdom under the whole heaven, shall be given to the people of the saints of the most High, whose kingdom is an everlasting kingdom, and all dominions shall serve and obey him. *Da.* 7: 27.

Thy kingdom come. *Mat.* 6: 10.

Of his kingdom there shall be no end. *Lu.* 1: 33.

My kingdom is not of this world. *Jn.* 18: 36.

By him were all things created, that are in heaven, and that are in earth, visible and invisible, whether they be thrones, or dominions, or principalities, or powers; all things were created by him, and for him. *Col.* 1: 16.

They lived and reigned with Christ a thousand years. *Re.* 20: 4.

See also

Christ, the King; Christ, Reign of; Dominion; God, the King; God, Kingdom of; Heaven, Kingdom of; Kingdom; Reign; Rule.

Reaping

They shall still bring forth fruit in old age. *Ps.* 92: 14.

They that sow in tears shall reap in joy. *Ps.* 126: 5.

He that regardeth the clouds shall not reap. *Ec.* 11: 4.

They joy before thee according to the joy in harvest. *Is.* 9: 3.

Yet a little while, and the time of her harvest shall come. *Je.* 51: 33.

Sow to yourselves in righteousness, reap in mercy. *Ho.* 10: 12.

The plowman shall overtake the reaper, and the treader of grapes him that soweth seed. *Am.* 9: 13.

Say not ye, There are yet four months, and then cometh harvest? behold, I say unto you, Lift up your eyes, and look on the fields; for they are white already to harvest. *Jn.* 4: 35.

Herein is that saying true, One soweth, and another reapeth. *Jn.* 4: 37.

I sent you to reap that whereon ye bestowed no labour. *Jn.* 4: 38.

He which soweth sparingly shall reap also sparingly; and he which soweth bountifully shall reap also bountifully. *2 Co.* 9: 6.

He that soweth to his flesh shall of the flesh reap corruption; but he that soweth to the Spirit shall of the Spirit reap life everlasting. *Ga.* 6: 8.

Thrust in thy sickle, and reap: for the time is come for thee to reap; for the harvest of the earth is ripe. *Re.* 14: 15.

See also

Consequence; Cultivation; Fruit; Fruitfulness; Fruits, First; Harvest; Yield.

Reason

Hear now my reasoning, and hearken to the pleadings of my lips. *Jb.* 13: 6.

Come now, and let us reason together, saith the Lord. *Is.* 1: 18.

One of the scribes came, and having heard them reasoning together, and perceiving that he had answered them well, asked him, Which is the first commandment of all? *Mk.* 12: 28.

What is the cause wherefore ye are come. *Ac.* 10: 21.

I will pray with the spirit, and I will pray with the understanding also: I will sing with the spirit, and I will sing with the understanding also. *1 Co.* 14: 15.

For this cause also thank we God without ceasing. *1 Th.* 2: 13.

For which cause he is not ashamed to call them brethren. *He.* 2: 11.

Be ready always to give an answer to every man that asketh you a reason of the hope that is in you. *1 Pe.* 3: 15.

See also

Cause; Mind; Thought; Understanding.

Rebellion

I will break the pride of your power. *Le.* 26: 19.

He wist not that the Lord was departed from him. *Ju.* 16: 20.

There be many servants now a days that break away every man from his master. *1 S.* 25: 10.

They are of those that rebel against the light. *Jb.* 24: 13.

He addeth rebellion unto his sin. *Jb.* 34: 37.

Why should ye be stricken any more? ye will revolt more and more: the whole head is sick, and the whole heart faint. *Is.* 1: 5.

They rebelled, and vexed his holy Spirit: therefore he was turned to be their enemy, and he fought against them. *Is.* 63: 10.

The Lord is righteous; for I have rebelled against his commandment. *La.* 1: 18.

Now they shall say, We have no king, because we feared not the Lord. *Ho.* 10: 3.

Neither could any man tame him. *Mk.* 5: 4.

See also

God, Rebellion against; Revolution.

Rebuke

O Lord, rebuke me not in thine anger. *Ps.* 6: 1.

They perish at the rebuke of thy countenance. *Ps.* 80: 16.

He v.ill not always chide. *Ps.* 103: 9.

He rebuked the Red sea also, and it was dried up. *Ps.* 106: 9.

Let the righteous smite me; it shall be a kindness: and let him reprove me; it shall be an excellent oil, which shall not break my head. *Ps.* 141: 5.

Turn you at my reproof. *Pr.* 1: 23.

A scorner heareth not rebuke. *Pr.* 13: 1.

Reprove one that hath understanding, and he will understand knowledge. *Pr.* 19: 25.

It is better to hear the rebuke of the wise, than for a man to hear the song of fools. *Ec.* 7: 5.

He shall not judge after the sight of his eyes, neither reprove after the hearing of his ears. *Is.* **11: 3.**

Then he arose, and rebuked the winds and the sea; and there was a great calm. *Mat.* **8: 26.**

If thy brother trespass against thee, rebuke him; and if he repent, forgive him. *Lu.* **17: 3.**

When he is come, he will reprove the world of sin. *Jn.* **16: 8.**

I myself also am persuaded of you, my brethren, that ye also are full of goodness, filled with all knowledge, able also to admonish one another. *Ro.* **15: 14.**

See also

Chastisement; Disapproval; God, Chastisement of; God, Punishment of; Reprimand; Reproach; Reproof.

Reception

Shall we receive good at the hand of God, and shall we not receive evil? *Jb.* **2: 10.**

The Lord will receive my prayer. *Ps.* **6: 9.**

He shall receive the blessing from the Lord. *Ps.* **24: 5.**

Ye shall receive power, after that the Holy Ghost is come upon you. *Ac.* **1: 8.**

Every man shall receive his own reward according to his own labour. *1 Co.* **3: 8.**

What hast thou that thou didst not receive? *1 Co.* **4: 7.**

Receive with meekness the engrafted word, which is able to save your souls. *Ja.* **1: 21.**

See also

Acceptance; Admission.

Receptivity

The wise in heart will receive commandments. *Pr.* **10: 8.**

The hearing ear, and the seeing eye, the Lord hath made even both of them. *Pr.* **20: 12.**

Son of man, all my words that I shall speak unto thee receive in thine heart, and hear with thine ears. *Eze.* **3: 10.**

He that receiveth you receiveth me, and he that receiveth me receiveth him that sent me. *Mat.* **10: 40.**

Blessed are your eyes, for they see: and your ears, for they hear. *Mat.* **13: 16.**

He that received seed into the good ground is he that heareth the word, and understandeth it. *Mat.* **13: 23.**

He that is able to receive it, let him receive it. *Mat.* **19: 12.**

Whatsoever ye shall ask in prayer, believing, ye shall receive. *Mat.* **21: 22.**

Whosoever shall not receive the kingdom of God as a little child, he shall not enter therein. *Mk.* **10: 15.**

Other fell on good ground. *Lu.* **8: 8.**

That on the good ground are they, which in an honest and good heart, having heard the word, keep it, and bring forth fruit with patience. *Lu.* **8: 15.**

The people gladly received him. *Lu.* **8: 40.**

They that gladly received his word were baptized: and the same day there were added unto them about three thousand souls. *Ac.* **2: 41.**

They received the word with all readiness of mind. *Ac.* **17: 11.**

Ye received it not as the word of men, but as it is in truth, the word of God. *1 Th.* **2: 13.**

The word preached did not profit them, not being mixed with faith in them that heard it. *He.* **4: 2.**

Ye ask, and receive not, because ye ask amiss. *Ja.* **4: 3.**

Whatsoever we ask, we receive of him, because we keep his commandments. *1 Jn.* **3: 22.**

Recognition

I have seen God face to face, and my life is preserved. *Ge.* **32: 30.**

I have seen thy face, as though I had seen the face of God. *Ge.* **33: 10.**

I will make there an altar unto God, who answered me in the day of my distress. *Ge.* **35: 3.**

The Lord spake unto Moses face to face, as a man speaketh unto his friend. *Ex.* **33: 11.**

I pray thee, open his eyes, that he may see. *2 K.* **6: 17.**

Acquaint now thyself with him, and be at peace. *Jb.* **22: 21.**

In all thy ways acknowledge him. *Pr.* **3: 6.**

Thus saith the Lord, Let not the wise man glory in his wisdom, neither let the mighty man glory in his might, let not the rich man glory in his riches: But let him that glorieth glory in this, that he understandeth and knoweth me. *Je.* **9: 23, 24.**

They shall teach no more every man his neighbour, and every man his brother, saying, Know the Lord: for they shall all know me, from the least of them unto the greatest of them, saith the Lord. *Je.* **31: 34.**

Whosoever therefore shall confess me before men, him will I confess also before my Father which is in heaven. *Mat.* **10: 32.**

Their eyes were holden that they should not know him. *Lu.* **24: 16.**

Their eyes were opened, and they knew him. *Lu.* **24: 31.**

Behold my hands and my feet, that it is I myself: handle me, and see; for a spirit hath not flesh and bones, as ye see me have. *Lu.* **24: 39.**

She . . . saw Jesus standing, and knew not that it was Jesus. *Jn* **20: 14.**

Except I shall see in his hands the print of the nails, and put my finger into the print of the nails, and thrust my hand into his side, I will not believe. *Jn.* **20: 25.**

Whom therefore ye ignorantly worship, him declare I unto you. *Ac.* **17: 23.**

Every tongue should confess that Jesus Christ is Lord. *Ph.* **2: 11.**

Recollection

We remember the fish, which we did eat in Egypt freely; the cucumbers, and the melons, and the leeks, and the onions, and the garlick. *Nu.* **11: 5.**

Remember that thou wast a servant in the land of Egypt. *De.* **5: 15.**

I have remembered thy name, O Lord, in the night. *Ps.* **119: 55.**

Remember the former things of old. *Is.* **46: 9.**

Peter remembered the word of Jesus. . . . And he went out, and wept bitterly. *Mat.* **26: 75.**

Do ye not remember? *Mk.* **8: 18.**

Remember how he spake unto you when he

was yet in Galilee. *Lu.* 24: 6.

When Jesus was glorified, then remembered they that these things were written of him. *Jn.* 12: 16.

Then remembered I the word of the Lord. *Ac.* 11: 16.

See also

God, Memory of; Memorial; Memory; Remembrance.

Recommendation

The poor committeth himself unto thee. *Ps.* 10: 14.

Let another man praise thee, and not thine own mouth. *Pr.* 27: 2.

I commended mirth. *Ec.* 8: 15.

I have not found so great faith, no, not in Israel. *Lu.* 7: 9.

The lord commended the unjust steward. *Lu.* 16. 8.

Into thy hands I commend my spirit. *Lu.* 23: 46.

Recommended to the grace of God for the work which they fulfilled. *Ac.* 14: 26.

Recommended by the brethren unto the grace of God. *Ac.* 15: 40.

God commendeth his love toward us. *Ro.* 5: 8.

Need we, as some others, epistles of commendation to you, or letters of commendation from you? *2 Co.* 3: 1.

We commend not ourselves again unto you. *2 Co.* 5: 12.

Not he that commendeth himself is approved, but whom the Lord commendeth. *2 Co.* 10: 18.

Recompense

Their sword shall enter into their own heart. *Ps.* 37: 15.

What shall I render unto the Lord for all his benefits toward me? *Ps.* 116: 12.

Therefore shall they eat of the fruit of their own way, and be filled with their own devices. *Pr.* 1: 31.

Say not thou, I will recompense evil; but wait on the Lord. *Pr.* 20: 22.

Shall not he render to every man according to his works? *Pr.* 24: 12.

Whoso diggeth a pit shall fall therein: and he that rolleth a stone, it will return upon him. *Pr.* 26: 27.

Cast thy bread upon the waters: for thou shalt find it after many days. *Ec.* 11: 1.

He shall see of the travail of his soul, and shall be satisfied. *Is.* 53: 11.

Wherefore do ye spend money for that which is not bread? and your labour for that which satisfieth not? *Is.* 55: 2.

Their own doings have beset them about. *Ho.* 7: 2.

They have sown the wind, and they shall reap the whirlwind. *Ho.* 8: 7.

Ye have plowed wickedness, ye have reaped iniquity. *Ho.* 10: 13.

As thou hast done, it shall be done unto thee. *Ob.* 1: 15.

Thy reward shall return upon thine own head. *Ob.* 1: 15.

If I have taken any thing from any man by false accusation, I restore him fourfold. *Lu.* 19: 8.

Who hath first given to him, and it shall be recompensed unto him again? *Ro.* 11; 35.

Recompense to no man evil for evil. *Ro.* 12: 17.

See that none render evil for evil unto any man. *1 Th.* 5: 15.

Cast not away therefore your confidence, which hath great recompence of reward. *He.* 10: 35.

Draw nigh to God, and he will draw nigh to you. *Ja.* 4: 8.

We love him, because he first loved us. *1 Jn.* 4: 19.

See also

Amends; Compensation; God, Reward of; Payment; Reparation; Restoration; Reward.

Reconciliation

Thou shalt forget the shame of thy youth. *Is.* 54: 4.

He shall turn the heart of the fathers to the children, and the heart of the children to their fathers. *Mal.* 4: 6.

If thou bring thy gift to the altar, and there rememberest that thy brother hath ought against thee; Leave there thy gift before the altar, and go thy way; first be reconciled to thy brother, and then come and offer thy gift. *Mat.* 5: 23, 24.

If, when we were enemies, we were reconciled to God by the death of his Son, much more, being reconciled, we shall be saved by his life. *Ro.* 5: 10.

Christ died for our sins. *1 Co.* 15: 3.

God . . . hath committed unto us the word of reconciliation. *2 Co.* 5: 19.

We pray you in Christ's stead, be ye reconciled to God. *2 Co.* 5: 20.

That he might reconcile both unto God in one body by the cross. *Ep.* 2: 16.

For it pleased the Father . . . to reconcile all things unto himself. *Col.* 1: 19, 20.

You, that were sometime alienated and enemies in your mind by wicked works, yet now hath he reconciled. *Col.* 1: 21.

To make reconciliation for the sins of the people. *He.* 2: 17.

See also

Atonement; Christ, the Mediator; Conciliation; Intercession; Propitiation; Reunion.

Reconstruction

It shall be an heap for ever; it shall not be built again. *De.* 13: 16.

The bricks are fallen down, but we will build with hewn stones: the sycomores are cut down, but we will change them into cedars. *Is.* 9: 10.

They that shall be of thee shall build the old waste places. *Is.* 58: 12.

Thou shalt be called, The repairer of the breach, The restorer of paths to dwell in. *Is.* 58: 12.

They shall repair the waste cities. *Is.* 61: 4.

The street shall be built again, and the wall, even in troublous times. *Da.* 9: 25.

In that day will I raise up the tabernacle of David that is fallen, and close up the breaches thereof; and I will raise up his ruins, and I will build it as in the days of old. *Am.* 9: 11.

Thou that destroyest the temple, and buildest

it in three days, save thyself. *Mat.* **27: 40.**

I will pull down my barns, and build greater; and there will I bestow all my fruits and my goods. *Lu.* **12: 18.**

If I build again the things which I destroyed, I make myself a transgressor. *Ga.* **2: 18.**

See also
Redemption; Restoration.

Recovery

God . . . hath made me forget all my toil. *Ge.* **41: 51.**

There is hope of a tree, if it be cut down, that it will sprout again, and that the tender branch thereof will not cease. *Jb.* **14: 7.**

When men are cast down, then thou shalt say, There is lifting up. *Jb.* **22: 29.**

Thou hast visited me in the night. *Ps.* **17: 3.**

O spare me, that I may recover strength, before I go hence, and be no more. *Ps.* **39: 13.**

He maketh the storm a calm. *Ps.* **107: 29.**

If thou faint in the day of adversity, thy strength is small. *Pr.* **24: 10.**

The bricks are fallen down, but we will build with hewn stones. *Is.* **9: 10.**

The Lord God will wipe away tears from off all faces. *Is.* **25: 8.**

Thou shalt be called, The repairer of the breach, The restorer of paths to dwell in. *Is.* **58: 12.**

All the trees of the field shall know that I the Lord have brought down the high tree, have exalted the low tree, have dried up the green tree, and have made the dry tree to flourish. *Eze.* **17: 24.**

Behold, I, even I, will both search my sheep, and seek them out. *Eze.* **34: 11.**

I will seek that which was lost, and bring again that which was driven away, and will bind up that which was broken, and will strengthen that which was sick. *Eze.* **34: 16.**

A new heart also will I give you, and a new spirit will I put within you: and I will take away the stony heart out of your flesh, and I will give you an heart of flesh. *Eze.* **36: 26.**

This land that was desolate is become like the garden of Eden. *Eze.* **36: 35.**

I the Lord build the ruined places, and plant that that was desolate. *Eze.* **36: 36.**

Thus saith the Lord God unto these bones; Behold, I will cause breath to enter into you, and ye shall live. *Eze.* **37: 5.**

Thus saith the Lord God; Come from the four winds, O breath, and breathe upon these slain, that they may live. *Eze.* **37: 9.**

Ye shall know that I am the Lord, when I have opened your graves, O my people, and brought you up out of your graves. *Eze.* **37: 13.**

They shall lay hands on the sick, and they shall recover. *Mk.* **16: 18.**

The Spirit of the Lord is upon me, because he hath anointed me to preach . . . recovering of sight to the blind. *Lu.* **4: 18.**

See also
Renewal; Restoration.

Recreation

Six days shalt thou labour, and do all thy work: But the seventh day is the sabbath. *Ex.* **20: 9, 10.**

On the seventh day thou shalt rest: that

thine ox and thine ass may rest, and the son of thy handmaid, and the stranger, may be refreshed. *Ex.* **23: 12.**

David took an harp, and played with his hand: so Saul was refreshed. *1 S.* **16: 23.**

Come now with me, and refresh thyself. *1 K.* **13: 7.**

The mountains bring him forth food, where all the beasts of the field play. *Jb.* **40: 20.**

Renew a right spirit within me. *Ps.* **51: 10.**

Thy youth is renewed like the eagle's. *Ps.* **103: 5.**

He that loveth pleasure shall be a poor man. *Pr.* **21: 17.**

A faithful messenger . . . refresheth the soul of his masters. *Pr.* **25: 13.**

I commended mirth, because a man hath no better thing under the sun, than to eat, and to drink, and to be merry. *Ec.* **8: 15.**

The sucking child shall play on the hole of the asp. *Is.* **11: 8.**

In returning and rest shall ye be saved. *Is.* **30: 15.**

They that wait upon the Lord shall renew their strength. *Is.* **40: 31.**

The streets of the city shall be full of boys and girls playing in the streets thereof. *Zch.* **8: 5.**

Refresh my bowels in the Lord. *Phm.* **20.**

See also
Play; Refreshment; Renewal; Sport.

Rectitude

Judge me, O Lord, according to my righteousness, and according to mine integrity that is in me. *Ps.* **7: 8.**

Thy righteousness is like the great mountains. *Ps.* **36: 6.**

Open to me the gates of righteousness: I will go into them. *Ps.* **118: 19.**

Teach me to do thy will; for thou art my God: thy spirit is good; lead me into the land of uprightness. *Ps.* **143: 10.**

The upright shall dwell in the land, and the perfect shall remain in it. *Pr.* **2: 21.**

The work of righteousness shall be peace; and the effect of righteousness quietness and assurance for ever. *Is.* **32: 17.**

In every nation he that feareth him, and worketh righteousness, is accepted with him. *Ac.* **10: 35.**

Abhor that which is evil; cleave to that which is good. *Ro.* **12: 9.**

Henceforth there is laid up for me a crown of righteousness. *2 Ti.* **4: 8.**

See also
Christ, Goodness of; Christ, Holiness of; Fairness; God, Righteousness of; Goodness; Holiness; Honesty; Honor; Integrity; Justice; Righteousness; Uprightness; Virtue.

Red

Look not thou upon the wine when it is red. *Pr.* **23: 31.**

Though your sins be as scarlet, they shall be as white as snow; though they be red like crimson, they shall be as wool. *Is.* **1: 18.**

When it is evening, ye say, It will be fair weather: for the sky is red. *Mat.* **16: 2.**

He brought them out, after that he had shewed wonders and signs in the land of Egypt, and in the Red sea. *Ac.* **7: 36.**

By faith they passed through the Red sea as by dry land. *He.* 11: 29.

Redemption

I know that my redeemer liveth. *Jb.* 19: 25.
Preserve me, O God. *Ps.* 16: 1.
Redeem us for thy mercies' sake. *Ps.* 44: 26.
God will redeem my soul from the power of the grave. *Ps.* 49: 15.
Let the redeemed of the Lord say so, whom he hath redeemed from the hand of the enemy. *Ps.* 107: 2.
Therefore with joy shall ye draw water out of the wells of salvation. *Is.* 12: 3.
Is my hand shortened at all, that it cannot redeem? *Is.* 50: 2.
The redeemed of the Lord shall return, and come with singing unto Zion; and everlasting joy shall be upon their head. *Is.* 51: 11.
Thou shalt call thy walls Salvation, and thy gates Praise. *Is.* 60: 18.
In his love and his pity he redeemed them. *Is.* 63: 9.
I am with thee to save thee and to deliver thee, saith the Lord. *Je.* 15: 20.
What man of you, having an hundred sheep, if he lose one of them, doth not leave the ninety and nine in the wilderness, and go after that which is lost, until he find it? *Lu.* 15: 4.
Verily, verily, I say unto thee, Except a man be born again, he cannot see the kingdom of God. *Jn.* 3: 3.
Likewise reckon ye also yourselves to be dead indeed unto sin. *Ro.* 6: 11.
In whom we have redemption through his blood. *Ep.* 1: 7.
God, who is rich in mercy, for his great love wherewith he loved us, . . . hath raised us up together, and made us sit together in heavenly places in Christ Jesus. *Ep.* 2: 4, 6.
Take the helmet of salvation. *Ep.* 6: 17.
God hath from the beginning chosen you to salvation. *2 Th.* 2: 13.
How shall we escape, if we neglect so great salvation? *He.* 2: 3.
The salvation of your souls. *1 Pe.* 1: 9.
Now is come salvation, and strength, and the kingdom of our God. *Re.* 12: 10.
Whosoever will, let him take the water of life freely. *Re.* 22: 17.
See also
Christ, the Redeemer; Christ, the Saviour; Deliverance; God, Deliverance of; God, the Redeemer; God, Salvation of; Ransom; Rescue; Restoration; Salvation; Succor.

Refinement

When he hath tried me, I shall come forth as gold. *Jb.* 23: 10.
The words of the Lord are pure words: as silver tried in a furnace of earth, purified seven times. *Ps.* 12: 6.
Every word of God is pure. *Pr.* 30: 5.
I have refined thee, but not with silver. *Is.* 48: 10.
I will refine them as silver is refined. *Zch.* 13: 9.
Who shall stand when he appeareth? he is like a refiner's fire. *Mal.* 3: 2.
He shall sit as a refiner and purifier of silver. *Mal.* 3: 3.

Evil communications corrupt good manners. *1 Co.* 15: 33.
See also
Civilization; Culture; Purification; Cultivation.

Reflection

Let the words of my mouth, and the meditation of my heart, be acceptable in thy sight. *Ps.* 19: 14.
My meditation of him shall be sweet. *Ps.* 104: 34.
As he thinketh in his heart, so is he. *Pr.* 23: 7.
My thoughts are not your thoughts. *Is.* 55: 8.
We desire to hear of thee what thou thinkest. *Ac.* 28: 22.
The Lord knoweth the thoughts of the wise, that they are vain. *1 Co.* 3: 20.
Meditate upon these things; give thyself wholly to them. *1 Ti.* 4: 15.
He is like unto a man beholding his natural face in a glass. *Ja.* 1: 23.
We love him, because he first loved us. *1 Jn.* 4: 19.
See also
Consideration; Contemplation; God, Thought of; Meditation; Study; Thought.

Reform

If ye will not be reformed by me by these things, but will walk contrary unto me; Then will I also walk contrary unto you. *Le.* 26: 23, 24.
He . . . removed all the idols that his fathers had made. *1 K.* 15: 12.
They brake down the image of Baal, and brake down the house of Baal, and made it a draught house unto this day. *2 K.* 10: 27.
All the people of the land went into the house of Baal, and brake it down. *2 K.* 11: 18.
Nevertheless, there are good things found in thee, in that thou hast taken away the groves out of the land, and hast prepared thine heart to seek God. *2 Ch.* 19: 3.
They gathered their brethren, and sanctified themselves, and came, according to the commandment of the king, by the words of the Lord, to cleanse the house of the Lord. *2 Ch.* 29: 15.
He took away the strange gods, and the idol out of the house of the Lord, and all the altars that he had built in the mount of the house of the Lord, and in Jerusalem, and cast them out of the city. *2 Ch.* 33: 15.
They cleansed the chambers: and thither brought I again the vessels of the house of God. *Ne.* 13: 9.
Amend your ways and your doings, and I will cause you to dwell in this place. *Je.* 7: 3.
If ye throughly amend your ways and your doings; if ye throughly execute judgment between a man and his neighbour; . . . Then will I cause you to dwell in this place. *Je.* 7: 5, 7.
Let us search and try our ways, and turn again to the Lord. *La.* 3: 40.
A new heart also will I give you, and a new spirit will I put into you. *Eze.* 36: 26.
Ye were as a firebrand plucked out of the burning. *Am.* 4: 11.
From that time Jesus began to preach, and

to say, Repent: for the kingdom of heaven is at hand. *Mat.* **4: 17.**

Ye cannot serve God and mammon. *Mat.* **6: 24.**

Jesus went into the temple of God, and cast out all them that sold and bought in the temple, and overthrew the tables of the money-changers, and the seats of them that sold doves. *Mat.* **21: 12.**

From within, out of the heart of men, proceed evil thoughts, adulteries, fornications, murders, . . . All these evil things come from within. *Mk.* **7: 21, 23.**

I will arise and go to my father, and will say unto him, Father, I have sinned against heaven, and before thee. *Lu.* **15: 18.**

This my son was dead, and is alive again. *Lu.* **15: 24.**

Meats and drinks, and divers washings, and carnal ordinances, imposed on them until the time of reformation. *He.* **9: 10.**

I saw a new heaven and a new earth: for the first heaven and the first earth were passed away. *Re.* **21: 1.**

See also
Amendment; Amends; Conversion; Lent; Penance; Penitence; Remorse; Repentance; Turn.

Refreshment

On the seventh day he rested, and was refreshed. *Ex.* **31: 17.**

David took an harp, and played with his hand: so Saul was refreshed, and was well, and the evil spirit departed from him. *1 S.* **16: 23.**

The king, and all the people that were with him, came weary, and refreshed themselves there. *2 S.* **16: 14.**

Come home with me, and refresh thyself. *1 K.* **13: 7.**

And the people rested themselves upon the words of Hezekiah king of Judah. *2 Ch.* **32: 8.**

I will speak, that I may be refreshed *Jb.* **32: 20.**

He restoreth my soul. *Ps.* **23: 3.**

Thou preparest a table before me in the presence of mine enemies. *Ps.* **23: 5.**

Wine that maketh glad the heart of man, and oil to make his face to shine, and bread which strengtheneth man's heart. *Ps.* **104: 15.**

A faithful messenger . . . refresheth the soul of his masters. *Pr.* **25: 13.**

This is the rest wherewith ye may cause the weary to rest; and this is the refreshing. *Is.* **28: 12.**

He said unto them, Come ye yourselves apart into a desert place, and rest a while. *Mk.* **6: 31.**

Repent ye therefore, and be converted, that your sins may be blotted out, when the times of refreshing shall come from the presence of the Lord. *Ac.* **3: 19.**

That I may come unto you with joy by the will of God, and may with you be refreshed. *Ro.* **15: 32.**

They have refreshed my spirit and yours. *1 Co.* **16: 18.**

The bowels of the saints are refreshed by thee, brother. *Phm.* **1: 7.**

See also
Drink; Food; Recreation; Restoration; Revival.

Refuge

Then shall ye appoint you cities to be cities of refuge for you. *Nu.* **35: 11.**

He is my shield, and the horn of my salvation, my high tower, and my refuge. *2 S.* **22: 3.**

They are wet with the showers of the mountains, and embrace the rock for want of a shelter. *Jb.* **24: 8.**

The Lord is our defence; the Holy One of Israel is our king. *Ps.* **89: 18.**

We have made lies our refuge, and under falsehood have we hid ourselves. *Is.* **28: 15.**

A man shall be as an hiding place from the wind, and a covert from the tempest; as rivers of water in a dry place, as the shadow of a great rock in a weary land. *Is.* **32: 2.**

They shall say to the mountains, Cover us; and to the hills, Fall on us. *Ho.* **10: 8.**

We have fled for refuge to lay hold upon the hope set before us. *He.* **6: 18.**

See also
Asylum; Cover; God, the Refuge; Shelter.

Refugee

Thou shalt neither vex a stranger, nor oppress him: for ye were strangers in the land of Egypt. *Ex.* **22: 21.**

There shall be six cities for refuge. *Nu.* **35: 6.**

Thou art a stranger, and also an exile. *2 S.* **15: 19.**

God is known in her palaces for a refuge. *Ps.* **48: 3.**

The high hills are a refuge for the wild goats. *Ps.* **104: 18.**

By the rivers of Babylon, there we sat down, yea, we wept, when we remembered Zion. *Ps.* **137: 1.**

How shall we sing the Lord's song in a strange land? *Ps.* **137: 4.**

His children shall have a place of refuge. *Pr.* **14: 26.**

They shall flee far off, and shall be chased as the chaff of the mountains before the wind, and like a rolling thing before the whirlwind. *Is.* **17: 13.**

They called thee an Outcast. *Je.* **30: 17.**

Though they dig into hell, thence shall mine hand take them; though they climb up to heaven, thence will I bring them down. *Am.* **9: 2.**

We . . . have fled for refuge to lay hold upon the hope set before us. *He.* **6: 18.**

See also
Exile; Expatriation; Fugitive; Immigration; Migration.

Refusal

How long wilt thou refuse to humble thyself before me? *Ex.* **10: 3.**

Blessed is the man that walketh not in the counsel of the ungodly, nor standeth in the way of sinners. *Ps.* **1: 1.**

In the day of my trouble I sought the Lord: . . . my soul refused to be comforted. *Ps.* **77: 2.**

I have called, and ye refused. *Pr.* **1: 24.**

Poverty and shame shall be to him that refuseth instruction. *Pr.* 13: 18.

They refuse to do judgment. *Pr.* 21: 7.

The desire of the slothful killeth him; for his hands refuse to labour. *Pr.* 21: 25.

The stone which the builders rejected, the same is become the head of the corner. *Mat.* 21: 42.

He was sad at that saying, and went away grieved: for he had great possessions. *Mk.* 10: 22.

Ye would not! *Lu.* 13: 34.

This is the stone that was set at naught of you builders, which is become the head of the corner. *Ac.* 4: 11.

See also

Christ, Denial of; Denial; God, Denial of; Rejection.

Regard

Let them not regard vain words. *Ex.* 5: 9.

Take heed, regard not iniquity. *Jb.* 36: 21.

Because they regard not the works of the Lord, . . . he shall destroy them. *Ps.* 28: 5.

If I regard iniquity in my heart, the Lord will not hear me. *Ps.* 66: 18.

He will regard the prayer of the destitute, and not despise their prayer. *Ps.* 102: 17.

I shall keep thy law; yea, I shall observe it with my whole heart. *Ps.* 119: 34.

I have stretched out my hand, and no man regarded. *Pr.* 1: 24.

He that regardeth the clouds shall not reap. *Ec.* 11: 4.

Keep thy solemn feasts, perform thy vows. *Na.* 1: 15.

Thou regardest not the person of men. *Mat.* 22: 16.

He hath regarded the low estate of his handmaiden. *Lu.* 1: 48.

I fear not God, nor regard man. *Lu.* 18: 4.

He that regardeth the day, regardeth it unto the Lord; and he that regardeth not the day, to the Lord he doth not regard it. *Ro.* 14: 6.

See also

Admiration; Affection; Heed; Observance; Respect; Sight.

Regeneration

Thy youth is renewed like the eagle's. *Ps.* 103: 5.

A new heart also will I give you, and a new spirit will I put within you. *Eze.* 36: 26.

Ye which have followed me, in the regeneration when the Son of man shall sit in the throne of his glory, ye also shall sit upon twelve thrones, judging the twelve tribes of Israel. *Mat.* 19: 28.

Which were born, not of blood, nor of the will of the flesh, nor of the will of man, but of God. *Jn.* 1: 13.

Except a man be born again, he cannot see the kingdom of God. *Jn.* 3: 3.

I say unto thee, Except a man be born of water and of the Spirit, he cannot enter into the kingdom of God. *Jn.* 3: 5.

Marvel not that I said unto thee, Ye must be born again. *Jn.* 3: 7.

Be not conformed to this world: but be ye transformed by the renewing of your mind, that ye may prove what is that good, and acceptable, and perfect, will of God. *Ro.* 12: 2.

Ye have . . . put on the new man, which is

renewed in knowledge after the image of him that created him. *Col.* 3: 10.

According to his mercy he saved us, by the washing of regeneration, and renewing of the Holy Ghost. *Tit.* 3: 5.

Being born again, not of corruptible seed, but of incorruptible, by the word of God. *1 Pe.* 1: 23.

See also

Birth, New; Man, the New; Reform; Renewal; Restoration; Revival.

Regret

We remember the fish, which we did eat in Egypt freely. *Nu.* 11: 5.

When I remember I am afraid. *Jb.* 21: 6.

Against thee, thee only, have I sinned, and done this evil in thy sight. *Ps.* 51: 4.

I remembered God, and was troubled. *Ps.* 77: 3.

We have sinned, we have done wickedly. *Da.* 9: 15.

Then Judas . . . repented himself, and brought again the thirty pieces of silver. *Mat.* 27: 3.

No man, having put his hand to the plow, and looking back, is fit for the kingdom of God. *Lu.* 9: 62.

Remember Lot's wife. *Lu.* 17: 32.

God be merciful to me a sinner. *Lu.* 18: 13.

Then said Martha unto Jesus, Lord, if thou hadst been here, my brother had not died. *Jn.* 11: 21.

See also

Ash Wednesday; Contrition; Grief; Lent; Penitence; Remorse; Repentance; Sorrow.

Reign

Rule thou over us, both thou, and thy son, and thy son's sons also: for thou hast delivered us from the hand of Midian. *Ju.* 8: 22.

They said, Give us a king to judge us. *1 S.* 8: 6.

By me kings reign, and princes decree justice. *Pr.* 8: 15.

The Lord shall reign over them in Mount Zion from henceforth, even for ever. *Mi.* 4: 7.

If by one man's offence death reigned by one; much more they which receive abundance of grace and of the gift of righteousness shall reign in life by one. *Ro.* 5: 17.

Let not sin therefore reign in your mortal body. *Ro.* 6: 12.

If we suffer, we shall also reign with him. *2 Ti.* 2: 12.

The Lord God omnipotent reigneth. *Re.* 19: 6.

They shall be priests of God and of Christ, and shall reign with him a thousand years. *Re.* 20: 6.

See also

Authority; Christ, the King; Christ, Reign of; Dominion; God, the King; God, Kingdom of; Kingdom; Power; Realm; Rule; Sovereignty.

Rejection

They have not rejected thee, but they have rejected me. *1 S.* 8: 7.

Ye have this day rejected your God. *1 S.* 10: 19.

The stone which the builders refused is become the head stone of the corner. *Ps.* 118: 22.

Hear instruction, and be wise, and refuse it not. *Pr.* 8: 33.

He is despised and rejected of men; a man of sorrows and acquainted with grief. *Is.* 53: 3.

Lo, they have rejected the word of the Lord; and what wisdom is in them? *Je.* 8: 9.

Because thou hast rejected knowledge, I will also reject thee. *Ho.* 4: 6.

Full well ye reject the commandment of God, that ye may keep your own tradition. *Mk.* 7: 9.

The Son of man must suffer many things, and be rejected of the elders, and of the chief priests, and scribes, and be killed. *Mk.* 8: 31.

The Pharisees and lawyers rejected the counsel of God against themselves, being not baptized of him. *Lu.* 7: 30.

He that rejecteth me, and receiveth not my words, hath one that judgeth him. *Jn.* 12: 48.

If any man have not the Spirit of Christ, he is none of his. *Ro.* 8: 9.

Refuse profane and old wives' tales. *1 Ti.* 4: 7.

See also
Abregation; Christ, Denial of; Denial; God, Denial of; Refusal; Repulsion.

Rejoicing

As a bridegroom coming out of his chamber, and rejoiceth as a strong man to run a race. *Ps.* 19: 5.

The statutes of the Lord are right, rejoicing the heart. *Ps.* 19: 8.

We will rejoice in thy salvation, and in the name of our God we will set up our banners. *Ps.* 20: 5.

Thou makest the outgoings of the morning and evening to rejoice. *Ps.* 65: 8.

He that goeth forth and weepeth, bearing precious seed, shall doubtless come again with rejoicing, bringing his sheaves with him. *Ps.* 126: 6.

The desert shall rejoice, and blossom as the rose. *Is.* 35: 1.

As the bridegroom rejoiceth over the bride, so shall thy God rejoice over thee. *Is.* 62: 5.

Be ye glad and rejoice for ever in that which I create. *Is.* 65: 18.

Rejoice greatly, O daughter of Zion; shout, O daughter of Jerusalem: behold, thy King cometh. *Zch.* 9: 9.

When they saw the star, they rejoiced with exceeding great joy. *Mat.* 2: 10.

He saith unto him, Friend, how camest thou in hither not having a wedding garment? *Mat.* 22: 12.

I say unto you, that likewise joy shall be in heaven over one sinner that repenteth, more than over ninety and nine just persons, which need no repentance. *Lu.* 15: 7.

If ye loved me, ye would rejoice, because I said, I go unto the Father: for my Father is greater than I. *Jn.* 14: 28.

When the Gentiles heard this, they were glad, and glorified the word of the Lord. *Ac.* 13: 48.

Rejoicing in hope. *Ro.* 12: 12.

Charity. . . . Rejoiceth not in iniquity, but rejoiceth in the truth. *1 Co.* 13: 4, 6.

As sorrowful, yet always rejoicing. *2 Co.* 6: 10.

See also
Bliss: Christ, Joy in; Christ, Joy of; Contentment; Delight; Ecstasy; Exaltation; Exultation; Gladness; God, Joy in; Happiness; Joy; Pleasure; Rapture; Satisfaction.

Release

At the end of every seven years thou shalt make a release. *De.* 15: 1.

The servant is free from his master. *Jb.* 3: 19.

I have found a ransom. *Jb.* 33: 24.

Who hath loosed the bands of the wild ass? *Jb.* 39: 5.

The king sent and loosed him; even the ruler of the people, and let him go free. *Ps.* 105: 20.

Is not this the fast that I have chosen? . . . to let the oppressed go free, and that ye break every yoke? *Is.* 58: 6.

Our God whom we serve is able to deliver us from the burning fiery furnace. *Da.* 3: 17.

I will ransom them from the power of the grave; I will redeem them from death: O death, I will be thy plagues; O grave, I will be thy destruction. *Ho.* 13: 14.

I will bring again the captivity of my people of Israel, and they shall build the waste cities, and inhabit them; and they shall plant vineyards, and drink the wine thereof: they shall also make gardens, and eat the fruit of them. *Am.* 9: 14.

Turn you to the strong hold, ye prisoners of hope. *Zch.* 9: 12.

The truth shall make you free. *Jn.* 8: 32.

Knowest thou not that I have power to crucify thee, and have power to release thee? *Jn.* 19: 10.

Where the Spirit of the Lord is, there is liberty. *2 Co.* 3: 17.

See also
Emancipation; Freedom; Liberty; Relief.

Reliance

The Lord shall fight for you, and ye shall hold your peace. *Ex.* 14: 14.

The Lord recompense thy work, . . . under whose wings thou art come to trust. *Ru.* 2: 12.

With him is an arm of flesh; but with us is the Lord our God to help us. *2 Ch.* 32: 8.

Wilt thou trust him, because his strength is great? or wilt thou leave thy labour to him? *Jb.* 39: 11.

It is better to trust in the Lord than to put confidence in man. *Ps.* 118: 8.

Thou didst trust in thine own beauty. *Eze.* 16: 15.

He knoweth them that trust in him. *Na.* 1: 7.

Believe ye that I am able to do this? They said unto him, Yea, Lord. *Mat.* 9: 28.

If ye have faith as a grain of mustard seed, ye shall say unto this mountain, Remove hence to yonder place; and it shall be removed. *Mat.* 17: 20.

Why are ye so fearful? how is it that ye have no faith. *Mk.* 4: 40.

Let not your heart be troubled: ye believe in God, believe also in me. *Jn.* 14: 1.

See also
Confidence; Dependence; God, Confidence in; God, Reliance on; God, Trust in; Trust.

Relief

If thy brother be waxen poor, and fallen in decay with thee; then thou shalt relieve him: yea, though he be a stranger, or a sojourner; that he may live with thee. *Le.* 25: 35.

Blessed is he that considereth the poor. *Ps.* 41: 1.

The Lord . . . relieveth the fatherless and widow. *Ps.* 146: 9.

Relieve the oppressed, judge the fatherless, plead for the widow. *Is.* 1: 17.

The comforter that should relieve my soul is far from me. *La.* 1: 16.

When thou doest alms, let not thy left hand know what thy right hand doeth. *Mat.* 6: 3.

Give alms of such things as ye have. *Lu.* 11: 41.

Then the disciples, every man according to his ability, determined to send relief unto the brethren which dwelt in Judaea. *Ac.* 11: 29.

Charity never faileth. *1 Co.* 13: 8.

If she have lodged strangers, if she have washed the saints' feet, if she have relieved the afflicted, if she have diligently followed every good work. *1 Ti.* 5: 10.

See also
Aid; Alleviation; Almsgiving; Charity; Help; Philanthropy; Poor; Poverty; Release; Succor.

Religion

Fear God, and keep his commandments: for this is the whole duty of man. *Ec.* 12: 13.

I desired mercy, and not sacrifice; and the knowledge of God more than burnt offerings. *Ho.* 6: 6.

What doth the Lord require of thee, but to do justly, and to love mercy, and to walk humbly with thy God? *Mi.* 6: 8.

To love him with all the heart, and with all the understanding, and with all the soul, and with all the strength, and to love his neighbour as himself, is more than all whole burnt offerings and sacrifices. *Mk.* 12: 33.

This day is salvation come to this house, forsomuch as he also is a son of Abraham. *Lu.* 19: 9.

After the most straitest sect of our religion I lived a Pharisee. *Ac.* 26: 5.

Love is the fulfilling of the law. *Ro.* 13: 10.

Examine yourselves, whether ye be in the faith; prove your own selves. *2 Co.* 13: 5.

I . . . profited in the Jews' religion. *Ga.* 1: 14.

The mystery of faith. *1 Ti.* 3: 9.

I have fought a good fight, I have finished my course, I have kept the faith. *2 Ti.* 4: 7.

Let us hold fast the profession of our faith without wavering. *He.* 10: 23.

If any man among you seem to be religious, and bridleth not his tongue, but deceiveth his own heart, this man's religion is vain. *Ja.* 1: 26.

Pure religion and undefiled before God and the Father is this, To visit the fatherless and widows in their affliction, and to keep himself unspotted from the world. *Ja.* 1: 27.

To them that have attained like precious faith with us. *2 Pe.* 1: 1.

Ye should earnestly contend for the faith which was once delivered unto the saints. *Jude* 1: 3.

See also
Belief; Christ, Belief in; Christ, Faith in; Christ, Faith of; Faith; God, Belief in; God, Faith in.

Reluctance

Ye have dwelt long enough in this mount: Turn you, and take your journey. *De.* 1: 6, 7.

Are not Abana and Pharpar, rivers of Damascus, better than all the waters of Israel? *2 K.* 5: 12.

Ah, Lord God, behold, I cannot speak: for I am a child. *Je.* 1: 6.

The Lord said unto me, Say not, I am a child: for thou shalt go to all that I shall send thee, and whatsoever I command thee thou shalt speak. *Je.* 1: 7.

I have need to be baptized of thee, and comest thou to me? *Mat.* 3: 14.

The spirit truly is ready, but the flesh is weak. *Mk.* 14: 38.

Neither be ye of doubtful mind. *Lu.* 12: 29.

They all with one consent began to make excuse. *Lu.* 14: 18.

Almost thou persuadest me to be a Christian. *Ac.* 26: 28.

See also
Hesitancy; Indecision; Uncertainty.

Remainder

While the earth remaineth, seedtime and harvest . . . shall not cease. *Ge.* 8: 22.

By the three hundred men that lapped will I save you: . . . let all the other people go every man unto his place. *Ju.* 7: 7.

He shall neither have son nor nephew among his people, nor any remaining in his dwelling. *Jb.* 18: 19.

I will gather the remnant of my flock out of all countries whither I have driven them, and will bring them again to their folds. *Je.* 23: 3.

Thou, O Lord, remainest for ever. *La.* 5: 19.

That which the palmerworm hath left hath the locust eaten; and that which the locust hath left hath the cankerworm eaten; and that which the cankerworm hath left hath the caterpiller eaten. *Jo.* 1: 4.

Who is left among you that saw this house in her first glory? *Hag.* 2: 3.

When they were filled, he said unto his disciples, Gather up the fragments that remain, that nothing be lost. *Jn.* 6: 12.

That which remaineth is glorious. *2 Co.* 3: 11.

He hath dispersed abroad; he hath given to the poor: his righteousness remaineth for ever. *2 Co.* 9: 9.

There remaineth therefore a rest to the people of God. *He.* 4: 9.

See also
Remnant.

Remedy

I will put none of these diseases upon thee: . . . for I am the Lord that healeth thee. *Ex.* 15: 26.

A merry heart doeth good like a medicine. *Pr.* 17: 22.

There is no healing for us. *Je.* 14: 19.

Thou hast no healing medicines. *Je.* 30: 13.

Behold, I will bring it health and cure, and I will cure them. *Je.* 33: 6.

In vain shalt thou use many medicines; for

thou shalt not be cured. *Je.* 46: 11.

Then will I sprinkle clean water upon you, and ye shall be clean. *Eze.* 36: 25.

Come, and let us return unto the Lord: for he hath torn, and he will heal us; he hath smitten, and he will bind us up. *Ho.* 6: 1.

In that day, saith the Lord, will I assemble her that halteth, and I will gather her that is driven out, and her that I have afflicted. *Mi.* 4: 6.

Not by might, nor by power, but by my spirit, saith the Lord of hosts. *Zch.* 4: 6.

They laid the sick in the streets, and besought him that they might touch if it were but the border of his garment. *Mk.* 6: 56.

I do cures to day and to morrow. *Lu.* 13: 32.

See also

Balm; Cure; Doctor; Medicine; Ointment; Physician.

Remembrance

Jacob set up a pillar in the place where he talked with him, even a pillar of stone. *Ge.* 35: 14.

Thou shalt remember all the way which the Lord thy God led thee these forty years in the wilderness. *De.* 8: 2.

All the ends of the world shall remember and turn unto the Lord. *Ps.* 22: 27.

The righteous shall be in everlasting remembrance. *Ps.* 112: 6.

The Lord hath forsaken me, and my Lord hath forgotten me. *Is.* 49: 14.

They may forget, yet will I not forget thee. *Is.* 49: 15.

Behold, I have graven thee upon the palms of my hands; thy walls are continually before me. *Is.* 49: 16.

A book of remembrance was written before him for them that feared the Lord, and that thought upon his name. *Mal.* 3: 16.

Verily, I say unto you, Wheresoever this gospel shall be preached in the whole world, there shall also this, that this woman hath done be told as a memorial of her. *Mat.* 26: 13.

This do in remembrance of me. *1 Co.* 11: 24.

I will not be negligent to put you always in remembrance of these things, though ye know them. *2 Pe.* 1: 12.

See also

Commemoration; Memorial; Memory; Recollection; Retrospect.

Remission

Blessed is he whose transgression is forgiven. *Ps.* 32: 1.

If ye forgive not men their trespasses, neither will your Father forgive your trespasses. *Mat.* 6: 15.

This is my blood of the new testament, which is shed for many for the remission of sins. *Mat.* 26: 28.

John did baptize in the wilderness, and preach the baptism of repentance for the remission of sins. *Mk.* 1: 4.

Behold the Lamb of God, which taketh away the sin of the world. *Jn.* 1: 29.

Receive ye the Holy Ghost; whose soever sins ye remit, they are remitted unto them; and whose soever sins ye retain, they are retained. *Jn.* 20: 22, 23.

Repent, and be baptized every one of you in the name of Jesus Christ for the remission of sins. *Ac.* 2: 38.

Through his name whosoever believeth in him shall receive remission of sins. *Ac.* 10: 43.

The redemption that is in Christ Jesus: Whom God hath set forth to be a propitiation through faith in his blood, to declare his righteousness for the remission of sins that are past, through the forbearance of God. *Ro.* 3: 24, 25.

If we confess our sins, he is faithful and just to forgive us our sins. *1 Jn.* 1: 9.

See also

Christ, Forgiveness of; Deliverance; Forgiveness; God, Forgiveness of; Pardon; Reprieve.

Remnant

The Lord shall scatter you among the nations, and ye shall be left few in number among the heathen. *De.* 4: 27.

I, even I only, am left; and they seek my life, to take it away. *1 K.* 19: 10.

Yet I have left me seven thousand in Israel, all the knees which have not bowed unto Baal. *1 K.* 19: 18.

Except the Lord of hosts had left unto us a very small remnant, we should have been as Sodom. *Is.* 1: 9.

Lift up thy prayer for the remnant that is left. *Is.* 37: 4.

Verily it shall be well with thy remnant. *Je.* 15: 11.

It may be that the Lord God of hosts will be gracious unto the remnant of Joseph. *Am.* 5: 15.

I will surely gather the remnant of Israel; I will put them together . . . as the flock in the midst of their fold. *Mi.* 2: 12.

I will bring the third part through the fire, and will refine them as silver is refined, and will try them as gold is tried. *Zch.* 13: 9.

See also

Remainder.

Remorse

The Lord . . . saveth such as be of a contrite spirit. *Ps.* 34: 18.

I said, Lord, be merciful unto me: heal my soul; for I have sinned against thee. *Ps.* 41: 4.

My sin is ever before me. *Ps.* 51: 3.

The sacrifices of God are a broken spirit. *Ps.* 51: 17.

I remembered God, and was troubled. *Ps.* 77: 3.

He said unto them, Take me up, and cast me forth into the sea; so shall the sea be calm unto you: for I know that for my sake this great tempest is upon you. *Jon.* 1: 12.

I have sinned in that I have betrayed innocent blood. *Mat.* 27: 4.

I have sinned against heaven, and before thee, And am no more worthy to be called thy son. *Lu.* 15: 18, 19.

When thou art converted, strengthen thy brethren. *Lu.* 22: 32.

Peter went out, and wept bitterly. *Lu.* 22: 62.

They shall look on him whom they pierced. *Jn.* 19: 37.

He found no place of repentance, though he sought it carefully with tears. *He.* 12: 17.

Remember therefore from whence thou art fallen. *Re.* **2: 5.**

See also

Ash Wednesday; Contrition; Grief; Lent; Penitence; Regret; Repentance; Sorrow.

Removal

Depart, I pray you, from the tents of these wicked men. *Nu.* **16: 26.**

Therefore will not we fear, though the earth be removed, and though the mountains be carried into the midst of the sea. *Ps.* **46: 2.**

As far as the east is from the west, so far hath he removed our transgressions from us. *Ps.* **103: 12.**

Remove thy foot from evil. *Pr.* **4: 27.**

The righteous shall never be removed. *Pr.* **10: 30.**

Remove not the ancient landmark, which thy fathers have set. *Pr.* **22: 28.**

Remove far from me vanity and lies. *Pr.* **30: 8.**

Remove sorrow from thy heart. *Ec.* **11: 10.**

Depart ye, depart ye, go ye out from thence. *Is.* **52: 11.**

The mountains shall depart, and the hills be removed; but my kindness shall not depart from thee. *Is.* **54: 10.**

If ye have faith as a grain of mustard seed, ye shall say unto this mountain, Remove hence to yonder place; and it shall remove. *Mat.* **17: 20.**

Father, if thou be willing, remove this cup from me. *Lu.* **22: 42.**

Depart, and go in peace. *Ac.* **16: 36.**

Though I have all faith, so that I could remove mountains, and have not charity, I am nothing. *1 Co.* **13: 2.**

I will come unto thee quickly, and will remove thy candlestick out of his place, except thou repent. *Re.* **2: 5.**

See also

Absence; Departure; Subtraction.

Renascence

Remember the former things of old *Is.* **46: 9.**

Behold, I create new heavens and a new earth: and the former shall not be remembered, nor come into mind. *Is.* **65: 17.**

A new heart also will I give you, and a new spirit will I put within you. *Eze.* **36: 26.**

O ye dry bones, hear the word of the Lord. *Eze.* **37: 4.**

They that dwell under his shadow shall return; they shall revive as the corn, and grow as the vine. *Ho.* **14: 7.**

They shall beat their swords into plowshares, and their spears into pruning hooks. *Mi.* **4: 3.**

This my son was dead, and is alive again. *Lu.* **15: 24.**

Except a man be born again, he cannot see the kingdom of God. *Jn.* **3: 3.**

How can a man be born when he is old? can he enter the second time into his mother's womb, and be born? *Jn.* **3: 4.**

Except a man be born of water and of the Spirit, he cannot enter into the kingdom of God. *Jn.* **3: 5.**

That which is born of the flesh is flesh; and that which is born of the Spirit is spirit. *Jn.* **3: 6.**

Marvel not that I said unto thee, Ye must be born again. *Jn.* **3: 7.**

As Christ was raised up from the dead by the glory of the Father, even so we also should walk in newness of life. *Ro.* **6: 4.**

We should serve in newness of spirit, and not in the oldness of the letter. *Ro.* **7: 6.**

My little children, of whom I travail in birth again until Christ be formed in you. *Ga.* **4: 19.**

Being born again, not of the corruptible seed, but of incorruptible, by the word of God, which liveth and abideth for ever. *1 Pe.* **1: 23.**

As newborn babes, desire the sincere milk of the word, that ye may grow thereby. *1 Pe.* **2: 2.**

See also

Birth, New; Conversion; Life, the New.

Rendezvous

The angels of God met him. *Ge.* **32: 1.**

Gather my saints together unto me. *Ps.* **50: 5.**

Mercy and truth are met together. *Ps.* **85: 10.**

The rich and poor meet together: the Lord is the maker of them all. *Pr.* **22: 2.**

Thou meetest him that rejoiceth and worketh righteousness, those that remember thee in thy ways. *Is.* **64: 5.**

Prepare to meet thy God. *Am.* **4: 12.**

Behold Jesus met them. *Mat.* **28: 9.**

Jesus himself drew near, and went with them. *Lu.* **24: 15.**

Much people that were come to the feast, when they heard that Jesus was coming to Jerusalem, Took branches of palm trees, and went forth to meet him. *Jn.* **12: 12, 13.**

Brother Saul, the Lord, even Jesus, that appeared unto thee in the way as thou camest, hath sent me. *Ac.* **9: 17.**

Certain philosophers of the Epicureans, and of the Stoicks, encountered him. *Ac.* **17: 18.**

We which are alive and remain shall be caught up together with them in the clouds, to meet the Lord in the air. *1 Th.* **4: 17.**

Come and gather yourselves together unto the supper of the great God. *Re.* **19: 17.**

See also

Meeting.

Renewal

That our God may lighten our eyes, and give us a little reviving in our bondage. *Ezr.* **9: 8.**

He restoreth my soul. *Ps.* **23: 3.**

Thou renewest the face of the earth. *Ps.* **104: 30.**

They that wait upon the Lord shall renew their strength. *Is.* **40: 31.**

I dwell in the high and holy place, with him also that is of a contrite and humble spirit, to revive the spirit of the humble, and to revive the heart of the contrite ones. *Is.* **57: 15.**

Thou shalt be called, The repairer of the breach, The restorer of paths to dwell in. *Is.* **58: 12.**

They that dwell under his shadow shall return; they shall revive as the corn, and grow as the vine. *Ho.* **14: 7.**

O Lord, revive thy work in the midst of the years. *Hab.* **3: 2.**

Be not conformed to this world: but be ye transformed by the renewing of your mind. *Ro. 12: 2.*

Though our outward man perish, yet the inward man is renewed day by day. *2 Co. 4: 16.*

Be renewed in the spirit of your mind. *Ep. 4: 23.*

See also

Birth, New; Confirmation; Lent; Recovery; Recreation; Refreshment; Regeneration; Restoration; Revival.

Renown

The same became mighty men which were of old, men of renown. *Ge. 6: 4.*

Let us make us a name. *Ge. 11: 4.*

We have heard the fame of him, and all that he did in Egypt. *Jos. 9: 9.*

His name shall be continued as long as the sun. *Ps. 72: 17.*

Thou art more glorious and excellent than the mountains of prey. *Ps. 76: 4.*

That men may know that thou, whose name alone is JEHOVAH, art the most high over all the earth. *Ps. 83: 18.*

Glorious things are spoken of thee, O city of God. *Ps. 87: 3.*

His work is honourable and glorious. *Ps. 111: 3.*

From thy state shall he pull thee down. *Is. 22: 19.*

A prophet is not without honour, save in his own country, and in his own house. *Mat. 13: 57.*

See also

Celebrity; Distinction; Fame; Glory; Honor; Report; Reputation.

Rent

I will tear your flesh with the thorns of the wilderness and with briers. *Ju. 8: 7.*

Then David took hold on his clothes, and rent them. *2 S. 1: 11.*

He teareth me in his wrath, who hateth me. *Jb. 16: 9.*

He teareth himself in his anger. *Jb. 18: 4.*

Deliver me: Lest he tear my soul like a lion, rending it in pieces. *Ps. 7: 1, 2.*

A time to rend, and a time to sew. *Ec. 3: 7.*

Rend your heart, and not your garments. *Jo. 2: 13.*

Give not that which is holy unto the dogs, . . . lest they . . . turn again and rend you. *Mat. 7: 6.*

Behold, the vail of the temple was rent in twain. *Mat. 27: 51.*

Renunciation

He shall give Israel up because of the sins of Jeroboam. *1 K. 14: 16.*

Put away the evil of your doings from before mine eyes. *Is. 1: 16.*

I will say to the north, Give up; and to the south, Keep not back: bring my sons from far, and my daughters from the ends of the earth. *Is. 43: 6.*

Let the wicked forsake his way. *Is. 55: 7.*

How shall I give thee up, Ephraim? *Ho. 11: 8.*

Shall I give my firstborn for my transgression? *Mi. 6: 7.*

Whosoever will come after me, let him deny himself, and take up his cross. *Mk. 8: 34.*

If thy hand offend thee, cut it off. *Mk. 9: 43.*

I must decrease. *Jn. 3: 30.*

I will lay down my life for thy sake. *Jn. 13: 37.*

Greater love hath no man than this, that a man lay down his life for his friends. *Jn. 15: 13.*

We . . . have renounced the hidden things of dishonesty. *2 Co. 4: 1, 2.*

They that are Christ's have crucified the flesh with the affections and lusts. *Ga. 5: 24.*

Put off . . . the old man. *Ep. 4: 22.*

Love not the world, neither the things that are in the world. *1 Jn. 2: 15.*

Hereby perceive we the love of God, because he laid down his life for us: and we ought to lay down our lives for the brethren. *1 Jn. 3: 16.*

See also

Abandonment; Christ, Denial of; Christ, Humiliation of; Christ, Sacrifice of; Denial; God, Denial of; Refusal; Rejection; Sacrifice; Surrender.

Reparation

He shall make amends for the harm that he hath done. *Le. 5: 16.*

Then they shall confess their sin which they have done: and he shall recompense his trespass. *Nu. 5: 7.*

To me belongeth . . . recompense. *De. 32: 35.*

Joash was minded to repair the house of the Lord. *2 Ch. 24: 4.*

I have sinned; what shall I do unto thee, O thou preserver of men? *Jb. 7: 20.*

Say not thou, I will recompense evil; but wait on the Lord, and he shall save thee. *Pr. 20: 22.*

Behold, I will lay thy stones with fair colours. *Is. 54: 11.*

Thou shalt be called, The repairer of the breach, The restorer of paths to dwell in. *Is. 58: 12.*

They shall repair the waste cities. *Is. 61: 4.*

If ye thoroughly amend your ways and your doings; . . . Then will I cause you to dwell in this place, in the land that I gave to your fathers. *Je. 7: 5, 7.*

The days of recompense are come. *Ho. 9: 7.*

He said unto them, Take me up, and cast me forth into the sea; so shall the sea be calm unto you: for I know that for my sake this great tempest is upon you. *Jon. 1: 12.*

When I come again, I will repay thee. *Lu. 10: 35.*

Father, I have sinned against heaven, and before thee, And am no more worthy to be called thy son: make me as one of thy hired servants. *Lu. 15: 18, 19.*

In the place where he was crucified there was a garden. *Jn. 19: 41.*

Vengeance is mine; I will repay, saith the Lord. *Ro. 12: 19.*

Every transgression and disobedience received a just recompense of reward. *He. 2: 2.*

See also

Amends; Expiation; Recompense; Restitution; Restoration.

Repatriation

I will bring my people again from the depths of the sea. *Ps. 68: 22.*

His people return hither. *Ps.* **73: 10.**

The Lord doth build up Jerusalem: he gathereth together the outcasts of Israel. *Ps.* **147: 2.**

He shall set up an ensign for the nations, and shall assemble the outcasts of Israel, and gather together the dispersed of Judah from the four corners of the earth. *Is.* **11: 12.**

It shall come to pass in that day, that the great trumpet shall be blown, and they shall come which were ready to perish in the land of Assyria, and the outcasts in the land of Egypt, and shall worship the Lord in the holy mount at Jerusalem. *Is.* **27: 13.**

I will bring thy seed from the east, and gather thee from the west; I will say to the north, Give up; and to the south, Keep not back: bring my sons from far, and my daughters from the ends of the earth. *Is.* **43: 5, 6.**

Again I will build thee, and thou shalt be built, O virgin of Israel. *Je.* **31: 4.**

Behold, I will bring them from the north country, and gather them from the coasts of the earth, and with them the blind and the lame, the woman with child and her that travaileth with child together: a great company shall return thither. *Je.* **31: 8.**

He that scattered Israel will gather him, and keep him, as a shepherd doth his flock. *Je.* **31: 10.**

They shall come again from the land of the enemy. *Je.* **31: 16.**

I shall bring again their captivity. *Je.* **31: 23.**

I will bring them again unto this place, and I will cause them to dwell safely. *Je.* **32: 37.**

I will arise and go to my father. *Lu.* **15: 18.**
See also
Expatriation; Immigration; Restoration; Return.

Repentance
Because thine heart was tender, and thou hast humbled thyself before the Lord, . . . and hast rent thy clothes, and wept before me; I also have heard thee, saith the Lord. *2 K.* **22: 19.**

The Lord is nigh unto them that are of a broken heart. *Ps.* **34: 18.**

In that day did the Lord God of hosts call to weeping, and to mourning, and to baldness, and the girding with sackcloth. *Is.* **22: 12.**

Let the wicked forsake his way, and the unrighteous man his thoughts: and let him return unto the Lord. *Is.* **55: 7.**

If the wicked will turn from all his sins that he hath committed, and keep all my statutes, and do that which is lawful and right, he shall surely live, he shall not die. *Eze.* **18: 21.**

Cast away from you all your transgressions, whereby ye have transgressed; and make you a new heart and a new spirit: for why will ye die, O house of Israel? *Eze.* **18: 31.**

Take with you words, and turn to the Lord: say unto him, Take away all iniquity, and receive us graciously. *Ho.* **14: 2.**

Turn ye even to me with all your heart, and with fasting, and with weeping, and with mourning. *Jo.* **2: 12.**

Is not this a brand plucked out of the fire? *Zch.* **3: 2.**

Repent ye: for the kingdom of heaven is at hand. *Mat.* **3: 2.**

I came not to call the righteous, but sinners to repentance. *Mk.* **2: 17.**

Bring forth therefore fruits worthy of repentance. *Lu.* **3: 8.**

They that are whole need not a physician: but they that are sick. *Lu.* **5: 31.**

Joy shall be in heaven over one sinner that repenteth. *Lu.* **15: 7.**

When he came to himself. *Lu.* **15: 17.**

Father, I have sinned against heaven, and in thy sight, and am no more worthy to be called thy son. *Lu.* **15: 21.**

If thy brother trespass against thee, rebuke him; and if he repent, forgive him. *Lu.* **17: 3.**

God be merciful to me a sinner. *Lu.* **18: 13.**

That repentance and remission of sins should be preached in his name among all nations, beginning at Jerusalem. *Lu.* **24: 47.**

Repentance toward God, and faith toward our Lord Jesus Christ. *Ac.* **20: 21.**

I rejoice, not that ye were made sorry, but that ye sorrowed to repentance. *2 Co.* **7: 9.**

Godly sorrow worketh repentance to salvation not to be repented of. *2 Co.* **7: 10.**

It is impossible for those who were once enlightened, . . . If they shall fall away, to renew them again unto repentance. *He.* **6: 4, 6.**

Remember therefore from whence thou art fallen, and repent, and do the first works. *Re.* **2: 5.**
See also
Ash Wednesday; Contrition; Lent; Penance; Penitence; Regret; Remorse.

Repetition
The Lord called Samuel again the third time. *1 S.* **3: 8.**

David enquired of the Lord yet again. *1 S.* **23: 4.**

Many times didst thou deliver them according to thy mercies. *Ne.* **9: 28.**

He that repeateth a matter separateth very friends. *Pr.* **17: 9.**

The word of the Lord came unto me the second time. *Je.* **1: 13.**

Their transgressions are many, and their backslidings are increased. *Je.* **5: 6.**

When ye pray, use not vain repetitions, as the heathen do: for they think that they shall be heard for their much speaking. *Mat.* **6: 7.**

I say not unto thee, Until seven times: but, Until seventy times seven. *Mat.* **18: 22.**

Before the cock crow, thou shalt deny me thrice. *Mat.* **26: 75.**

As we said before, so say I now again, If any man preach any other gospel unto you than that ye have received, let him be accursed. *Ga.* **1: 9.**

Again I say, Rejoice. *Ph.* **4: 4.**

Reply
So shall my righteousness answer for me in time to come. *Ge.* **30: 33.**

God is departed from me, and answereth me no more, neither by prophets, nor by dreams. *1 S.* **28: 15.**

There was no voice, nor any that answered. *1 K.* **18: 26.**

Have mercy also upon me, and answer me. *Ps.* **27: 7.**

In thy faithfulness answer me. *Ps.* 143: 1.

Then shall they call upon me, but I will not answer. *Pr.* 1: 28.

A soft answer turneth away wrath. *Pr.* 15: 1.

Answer a fool according to his folly. *Pr.* 26: 5.

It shall come to pass, that before they call, I will answer; and while they are yet speaking, I will hear. *Is.* 65: 24.

There is no answer of God. *Mi.* 3: 7.

They shall call on my name, and I will hear them: I will say, It is my people: and they shall say, The Lord is my God. *Zch.* 13: 9.

Take ye no thought how or what thing ye shall answer, or what ye shall say: For the Holy Ghost shall teach you. *Lu.* 12: 11, 12.

They marvelled at his answer, and held their peace. *Lu.* 20: 26.

Who art thou that repliest against God? *Ro.* 9: 20.

Be ready always to give an answer to every man that asketh you a reason of the hope that is in you. *1 Pe.* 3: 15.

See also

Answer.

Report

A good report maketh the bones fat. *Pr.* 15: 30.

Who hath believed our report? *Is.* 53: 1.

Falling down on his face he will worship God, and report that God is in you of a truth. *1 Co.* 14: 25.

Approving ourselves as the ministers of God, . . . By honour and dishonour, by evil report and good report. *2 Co.* 6: 4, 8.

Whatsoever things are of good report: . . . think on these things. *Ph.* 4: 8.

A bishop . . . must have a good report of them which are without. *1 Ti.* 3: 2, 7.

See also

Account; Fame; Hearsay; Renown; Reputation; Tale; Talebearing.

Repose

He took of the stones of that place, and put them for his pillows, and lay down in that place to sleep. *Ge.* 28: 11.

I will give peace in the land, and ye shall lie down, and none shall make you afraid. *Le.* 26: 6.

As he lay and slept under a juniper tree, behold, then an angel touched him. *1 K.* 19: 5.

I laid me down and slept; I awaked; for the Lord sustained me. *Ps.* 3: 5.

He giveth his beloved sleep. *Ps.* 127: 2.

How long wilt thou sleep, O sluggard? when wilt thou arise out of thy sleep? *Pr.* 6: 9.

I will feed my flock, and I will cause them to lie down, saith the Lord God. *Eze.* 34: 15.

I . . . will make them to lie down safely. *Ho.* 2: 18.

Awake thou that sleepest, and arise from the dead, and Christ shall give thee light. *Ep.* 5: 14.

We which have believed do enter into rest. *He.* 4: 3.

There remaineth therefore a rest to the people of God. *He.* 4: 9.

See also

Calm; Christ, Peace of; Ease; God, Peace of; God, Rest in; Peace; Quiet; Rest; Stillness; Tranquillity.

Repression

Let the lying lips be put to silence. *Ps.* 31: 18.

They did set over them taskmasters to afflict them with their burdens. *Ex.* 1: 11.

I have surely seen the affliction of my people which are in Egypt. *Ex.* 3: 7.

Ye shall not therefore oppress one another. *Le.* 25: 17.

The Lord also will be a refuge for the oppressed. *Ps* 9: 9.

Oppressors seek after my soul. *Ps.* 54: 3.

Envy thou not the oppressor, and choose none of his ways. *Pr.* 3: 31.

On the side of their oppressors there was power; but they had no comforter. *Ec.* 4: 1.

Seek judgment, relieve the oppressed. *Is.* 1: 17.

They shall rule over their oppressors. *Is.* 14: 2.

Our God hath put us to silence. *Je.* 8: 14.

I will punish all that oppress them. *Je.* 30: 20.

Woe to . . . the oppressing city! *Zph.* 3: 1.

At that time I will undo all that afflict thee. *Zph.* 3: 19.

No oppressor shall pass through them any more. *Zch.* 9: 8.

So is the will of God, that with well doing ye may put to silence the ignorance of foolish men. *1 Pe.* 2: 15.

See also

Bondage; Oppression; Suppression; Tyranny; Yoke.

Reprieve

Neither will I again smite any more every thing living, as I have done. *Ge.* 8: 21.

The Lord repented of the evil which he thought to do unto his people. *Ex.* 32: 14.

The Lord also hath put away thy sin; thou shalt not die. *2 S.* 12: 13.

Hear thou from thy dwelling place, even from heaven; and when thou hearest, forgive. *2 Ch.* 6: 21.

The Lord . . . will repent himself concerning his servants. *Ps.* 135: 14.

If the wicked restore the pledge, give again that he had robbed, walk in the statutes of life, without committing iniquity; he shall surely live, he shall not die. *Eze.* 33: 15.

If the wicked turn from his wickedness, and do that which is lawful and right, he shall live thereby. *Eze.* 33: 19.

I will heal their backsliding, I will love them freely: for mine anger is turned away from him. *Ho.* 14: 4.

Hate the evil, and love the good, and establish judgment in the gate: it may be that the Lord God of hosts will be gracious. *Am.* 5: 15.

God repented of the evil, that he had said that he would do unto them; and he did it not. *Jon.* 3: 10.

He retaineth not his anger for ever, because he delighteth in mercy. *Mi.* 7: 18.

Blessed are they whose iniquities are forgiven, and whose sins are covered. *Ro.* 4: 7.

See also

Forgiveness; Pardon, Remission.

Reprimand

Why chide ye with me? wherefore do ye tempt the Lord? *Ex.* 17: 2.

Nathan said to David, Thou art the man. 2 *S.* 12: 7.

He will not always chide: neither will he keep his anger for ever. *Ps.* 103. 9.

I et the righteous . . . reprove me; it shall be an excellent oil, which shall not break my head. *Ps.* 141: 5.

How have I hated instruction, and my heart despised reproof. *Pr.* 5: 12.

A reproof entereth more into a wise man than an hundred stripes into a fool. *Pr.* 17: 10.

When the wicked cometh, then cometh also contempt, and with ignominy reproach. *Pr.* 18: 3.

He, that being often reproved hardeneth his neck, shall suddenly be destroyed. *Pr.* 29: 1.

I et no man strive, nor reprove another. *Ho.* 4: 4.

I will no more make you a reproach among the heathen. *Jo.* 2: 19.

I withstood him to the face, because he was to be blamed. *Ga.* 2: 11.

See also
Blame; Rebuke; Reproach; Reproof.

Reproach

He that reproveth God, let him answer it. *Jb.* 40: 2.

Reproach hath broken my heart. *Ps.* 69: 20.

Remove from me reproach and contempt. *Ps.* 119: 22.

Ye have set at nought all my counsel, and would none of my reproof. *Pr.* 1: 25.

Reprove not a scorner, lest he hate thee. *Pr.* 9: 8.

He that regardeth reproof shall be honoured. *Pr.* 13: 18.

He that oppresseth the poor reproacheth his Maker. *Pr.* 14: 31.

He that hateth reproof shall die. *Pr.* 15: 10.

He that rebuketh a man afterwards shall find more favour than he that flattereth with the tongue. *Pr.* 28: 23.

Fear ye not the reproach of men, neither be ye afraid of their revilings. *Is.* 51: 7.

So have I sworn that I would not be wroth with thee, nor rebuke thee. *Is.* 54: 9.

Rejoicing that they were counted worthy to suffer shame for his name. *Ac.* 5: 41.

Give none occasion to the adversary to speak reproachfully. *1 Ti.* 5: 14.

Jesus . . . for the joy that was set before him endured the cross, despising the shame. *He.* 12: 2.

See also
Christ, Humiliation of; Contempt; Disapproval; Dishonor; Ignominy; Rebuke; Reprimand; Reproof; Scorn; Shame.

Reproof

At thy rebuke they fled; at the voice of thy thunder they hasted away. *Ps.* 104: 7.

Rebuke a wise man, and he will love thee. *Pr.* 9: 8.

He that heareth reproof getteth understanding. *Pr.* 15: 32.

Open rebuke is better than secret love. *Pr.* 27: 5.

The rod and reproof give wisdom. *Pr.* 29: 15.

Thou shalt be dumb, and shalt not be to them a reprover. *Eze.* 3: 26.

Let no man strive, nor reprove another. *Ho.* 4: 4.

Every one that doeth evil hateth the light, neither cometh to the light, lest his deeds should be reproved. *Jn.* 3: 20.

Reprove, rebuke, exhort with all longsuffering. *2 Ti.* 4: 2.

My son, despise not thou the chastening of the Lord, nor faint when thou art rebuked of him. *He.* 12: 5.

As many as I love, I rebuke and chasten. *Re.* 3: 19.

See also
Chastisement; Disapproval; God, Chastisement of; God, Punishment of; Punishment; Reprimand; Reproach.

Repulsion

Then will the Lord drive out all these nations from before you. *De.* 11: 23.

Many years didst thou forbear them, and testifiedest against them by thy spirit in thy prophets: yet would they not give ear. *Ne.* 9: 30.

With thy strong hand thou opposest thyself against me. *Jb.* 30: 21.

The ungodly . . . are like the chaff which the wind driveth away. *Ps.* 1: 4.

How thou didst drive out the heathen with thy hand. *Ps.* 44: 2.

This is the rest wherewith ye may cause the weary to rest; and this is the refreshing: yet they would not hear. *Is.* 28: 12.

Thus saith the Lord God, the Holy One of Israel; In returning and rest shall ye be saved; in quietness and in confidence shall be your strength: and ye would not. *Is.* 30: 15.

They refuse to know me, saith the Lord. *Je.* 9: 6.

Thou hast utterly rejected us; thou art very wroth against us. *La.* 5: 22.

He turned, and said unto Peter, Get thee behind me, Satan. *Mat.* 16: 23.

O Jerusalem, Jerusalem, thou that killest the prophets, and stonest them which are sent unto thee, how often would I have gathered thy children together, even as a hen gathereth her chickens under her wings, and ye would not! *Mat.* 23: 37.

Ye stiffnecked and uncircumcised in heart and ears, ye do always resist the Holy Ghost. *Ac.* 7: 51.

He therefore that despiseth, despiseth not man, but God. *1 Th.* 4: 8.

That which beareth thorns and briers is rejected. *He.* 6: 8.

Resist the devil, and he will flee from you. *Ja.* 4: 7.

God resisteth the proud. *1 Pe.* 5: 5.

See also
Refusal; Rejection.

Reputation

Thy wisdom and prosperity exceedeth the fame which I heard. *1 K.* 10: 7.

David my servant may have a light alway before me in Jerusalem. *1 K.* 11: 36.

Wherefore are we counted as beasts, and reputed vile in your sight? *Jb.* 18: 3.

Of Zion it shall be said, This and that man

was born in her. *Ps.* **87: 5.**

The name of the wicked shall rot. *Pr.* **10: 7.**

The name of the Lord is a strong tower: the righteous runneth into it, and is safe. *Pr.* **18: 10.**

A good name is rather to be chosen than great riches. *Pr.* **22: 1.**

Thy name is as ointment poured forth. *S. of S.* **1: 3.**

They . . . spread abroad his fame in all that country. *Mat.* **9: 31.**

The fame of Jesus. *Mat.* **14: 1.**

Notwithstanding in this rejoice not, that the spirits are subject unto you; but rather rejoice, because your names are written in heaven. *Lu.* **10: 20.**

We know that God spake unto Moses: as for this fellow, we know not from whence he is. *Jn.* **9: 29.**

Your faith is spoken of throughout the whole world. *Ro.* **1: 8.**

He that in these things serveth Christ is acceptable to God, and approved of men. *Ro.* **14: 18.**

Christ Jesus . . . made himself of no reputation, and took upon him the form of a servant. *Ph.* **2: 5, 7.**

See also

Celebrity; Distinction; Fame; Glory; Honor; Renown; Report.

Request

Jabez called on the God of Israel, saying, Oh that thou wouldest bless me indeed, and enlarge my coast, and that thine hand might be with me, and that thou wouldest keep me from evil, that it may not grieve me! And God granted him that which he requested. *1 Ch.* **4: 10.**

Oh that I might have my request; and that God would grant me the thing that I long for! *Jb.* **6: 8.**

Thou hast given him his heart's desire, and hast not withholden the request of his lips. *Ps.* **21: 2.**

He gave them their request; but sent leanness into their soul. *Ps.* **106: 15.**

Ask, and it shall be given you; seek, and ye shall find; knock, and it shall be opened unto you. *Mat.* **7: 7.**

Thy prayer is heard. *Lu.* **1: 13.**

If thou knewest, . . . thou wouldest have asked, . . . and he would have given thee. *Jn.* **4: 10.**

Whatsoever ye shall ask in my name, that will I do. *Jn.* **14: 13.**

We know not what we should pray for as we ought. *Ro.* **8: 26.**

I thank my God upon every remembrance of you, Always in every prayer of mine for you all making request with joy. *Ph.* **1: 3, 4.**

In everything by prayer and supplication with thanksgiving let your requests be made known unto God. *Ph.* **4: 6.**

Ye ask, and receive not, because ye ask amiss. *Ja.* **4: 3.**

See also

Appeal; Entreaty; God, Prayer to; Petition; Prayer; Supplication.

Requirement

I desired mercy, and not sacrifice; and the knowledge of God more than burnt offerings. *Ho.* **6: 6.**

What doth the Lord require of thee, but to do justly, and to love mercy, and to walk humbly with thy God? *Mi.* **6: 8.**

Except your righteousness shall exceed the righteousness of the scribes and Pharisees, ye shall in no case enter into the kingdom of heaven. *Mat.* **5: 20.**

Except ye be converted, and become as little children, ye shall not enter into the kingdom of heaven. *Mat.* **18: 3.**

Except ye repent, ye shall all likewise perish. *Lu.* **13: 3.**

They that worship him must worship him in spirit and in truth. *Jn.* **4: 24.**

Except ye eat the flesh of the Son of man, and drink his blood, ye have no life in you. *Jn.* **6: 53.**

If ye believe not that I am he, ye shall die in your sins. *Jn.* **8: 24.**

See also

Duty; Obligation; Religion.

Rescue

Rescue my soul from their destructions. *Ps.* **35: 17.**

He brought me up also out of an horrible pit. *Ps.* **40: 2.**

Save with thy right hand, and hear me. *Ps.* **60: 5.**

Surely he shall deliver thee from the snare of the fowler, and from the noisome pestilence. *Ps.* **91: 3.**

Then they cried unto the Lord in their trouble, and he delivered them out of their distresses. *Ps.* **107: 6.**

My soul fainteth for thy salvation. *Ps.* **119: 81.**

Bring my soul out of prison. *Ps.* **142: 7.**

Our God, whom we serve is able to deliver us, . . . and he will deliver us. *Da.* **3: 17.**

See also

Christ, the Redeemer; Christ, the Saviour; Deliverance; God, Deliverance of; God, the Redeemer; God, Salvation of; Ransom; Redemption; Restoration; Salvation; Succor.

Resemblance

God said, Let us make man in our image, after our likeness. *Ge.* **1: 26.**

Thou shalt be to him instead of God. *Ex.* **4: 16.**

Who among the sons of the mighty can be likened unto the Lord? *Ps.* **89: 6.**

As cold waters to a thirsty soul, so is good news from a far country. *Pr.* **25: 25.**

The precious sons of Zion, comparable to fine gold. *La.* **4: 2.**

As the appearance of the bow that is in the cloud in the day of rain, so was the appearance . . . of the likeness of the glory of the Lord. *Eze.* **1: 28.**

As is the mother, so is her daughter. *Eze.* **16: 44.**

I will liken him unto a wise man, which built his house upon a rock. *Mat.* **7: 24.**

Whereunto shall I liken this generation? It is like unto children sitting in the markets. *Mat.* **11: 16.**

Whereunto shall we liken the kingdom of God? *Mk.* **4: 30.**

The kingdom of God . . . is like leaven. *Lu.* 13: 20, 21.

The gods are come down to us in the likeness of men. *Ac.* 14: 11.

Conformed to the image of his Son. *Ro.* 8: 29.

Be not conformed to this world. *Ro.* 12: 2.

Comparing spiritual things with spiritual. *1 Co.* 2: 13.

What agreement hath the temple of God with idols? *2 Co.* 6: 16.

Abstain from all appearance of evil. *1 Th.* 5: 22.

If any be a hearer of the word, and not a doer, he is like unto a man beholding his natural face in a glass. *Ja.* 1: 23.

See also

Image; Imitation; Likeness; Model; Pattern.

Resentment

O Lord, rebuke me not in thine anger, neither chasten me in thy hot displeasure. *Ps.* 6: 1.

A soft answer turneth away wrath: but grievous words stir up anger. *Pr.* 15: 1.

The discretion of a man deferreth his anger; and it is his glory to pass over a transgression. *Pr.* 19: 11.

This people hath a revolting and a rebellious heart. *Je.* 5: 23.

All they in the synagogue, when they heard these things, were filled with wrath. *Lu.* 4: 28.

See also

Anger; Christ, Wrath of; God, Anger of; God, Wrath of; Hatred; Indignation; Malice.

Reserve

Hast thou not reserved a blessing for me? *Ge.* 27: 36.

David . . . chose him five smooth stones out of the brook. *1 S.* 17: 39, 40.

The wicked is reserved to the day of destruction. *Jb.* 21: 30.

He holdeth back the face of his throne. *Jb.* 26: 9.

Hast thou seen the treasures of the hail, Which I have reserved against the time of trouble, against the day of battle and war? *Jb.* 38: 22, 23.

How great is thy goodness, which thou hast laid up for them that fear thee. *Ps.* 31: 19.

A fool uttereth all his mind: but a wise man keepeth it in till afterwards. *Pr.* 29: 11.

Will he reserve his anger for ever? *Je.* 3: 5.

He reserveth unto us the appointed weeks of the harvest. *Je.* 5: 24.

Every man at the beginning doth set forth good wine; and when men have well drunk, then that which is worse: but thou hast kept the good wine until now. *Jn.* 2: 10.

An inheritance incorruptible, and undefiled, and that fadeth not away, reserved in heaven for you. *1 Pe.* 1: 4.

The Lord knoweth how . . . to reserve the unjust unto the day of judgment to be punished. *2 Pe.* 2: 9.

See also

Modesty; Restraint; Self-Control; Store.

Residence

He sent letters into all the king's provinces, . . . to every people after their language,

that every man should bear rule in his own house. *Es.* 1: 22.

Wisdom hath builded her house, she hath hewn out her seven pillars. *Pr.* 9: 1.

Every wise woman buildeth her house. *Pr.* 14: 1.

Through wisdom is an house builded. *Pr.* 24: 3.

They shall not build, and another inhabit; they shall not plant, and another eat. *Is.* 65: 22.

Thus saith the Lord, The heaven is my throne, and the earth my footstool: where is the house that ye build unto me? *Is.* 66: 1.

Ye have built houses of hewn stone, but ye shall not dwell in them; ye have planted pleasant vineyards, but ye shall not drink wine of them. *Am.* 5: 11.

He is like a man which built an house, and digged deep, and laid the foundation on a rock. *Lu.* 6: 48.

He hath laid the foundation, and is not able to finish it. *Lu.* 14: 29.

See also

Dwelling; Habitation; Home; House; Roof; Shelter.

Resignation

The Lord gave, and the Lord hath taken away; blessed be the name of the Lord. *Jb.* 1: 21.

What? shall we receive good at the hand of God, and shall we not receive evil? *Jb.* 2: 10.

Though he slay me, yet will I trust in him. *Jb.* 13: 15.

Rest in the Lord, and wait patiently for him. *Ps.* 37: 7.

Thy will be done on earth, as it is in heaven. *Mat.* 6: 10.

If it be possible, let this cup pass from me: nevertheless not as I will, but as thou wilt. *Mat.* 26: 39.

When he would not be persuaded, we ceased saying, The will of the Lord be done. *Ac.* 21: 14.

I have learned, in whatsoever state I am therewith to be content. *Ph.* 4: 11.

We ought to say, If the Lord will, we shall live, and do this, or that. *Ja.* 4: 15.

Beloved, think it not strange concerning the fiery trial which is to try you. *1 Pe.* 4: 12.

See also

Abandonment; Contentment; Endurance; God, Will of; Patience; Renunciation; Stoicism; Surrender.

Resistance

I say unto you, That ye resist not evil. *Mat.* 5: 39.

I will give you a mouth and wisdom, which all your adversaries shall not be able to gainsay nor resist. *Lu.* 21: 15.

They were not able to resist the wisdom and the spirit by which he spake. *Ac.* 6: 10.

O man, who art thou that repliest against God? *Ro.* 9: 20.

Whosoever therefore resisteth the power, resisteth the ordinance of God. *Ro.* 13: 2.

If . . . I have fought with beasts. *1 Co.* 15: 32.

Ye have not yet resisted unto blood, striving against sin. *He.* 12: 4.

God resisteth the proud. *Ja.* 4: **6.**
Resist the devil, and he will flee from you. *Ja.* 4: **7.**
See also
Frustration; God, Antagonism to; God, Rebellion against; Hindrance; Opponent; Opposition; Rebellion; Revolution.

Resolution

As for me and my house, we will serve the Lord. *Jos.* 24: **15.**
For the divisions of Reuben there were great thoughts of heart. *Ju.* 5: **15.**
All the congregation said, Amen, and praised the Lord. And the people did according 'to this promise. *Ne.* 5: **13.**
I am purposed. *Ps.* 17: **3.**
Multitudes, multitudes in the valley of decision: for the day of the Lord is near in the valley of decision. *Jo.* 3: **14.**
My determination is to gather the nations, that I may assemble the kingdoms, to pour upon them mine indignation. *Zph.* 3: **8.**
Lord, I will follow thee whithersoever thou goest. *Lu.* 9: **57.**
I am resolved what to do. *Lu.* 16: **4.**
Arise therefore, and get thee down, and go with them, doubting nothing: for I have sent them. *Ac.* 10: **20.**
I must also see Rome. *Ac.* 19: **21.**
None of these things move me. *Ac.* 20: **24.**
I determined not to know any thing among you, save Jesus Christ, and him crucified. *1 Co.* 2: **2.**
Having done all, to stand. *Ep.* 6: **13.**
This one thing I do, forgetting those things which are behind, . . . I press toward the mark. *Ph.* 3: **13, 14.**
See also
Decision; Firmness; Fortitude; Perseverance; Purpose; Steadfastness.

Resort

The congregation was gathered together as one man. *Ju.* 20: **1.**
Let us meet together in the house of God, within the temple. *Ne.* 6: **10.**
Be thou my strong habitation, whereunto I may continually resort. *Ps.* 71: **3.**
Mine house shall be called an house of prayer for all people. *Is.* 56: **7.**
Where two or three are gathered together in my name, there am I in the midst of them. *Mat.* 18: **20.**
All the multitude resorted unto him. *Mk.* 2: **13.**
The people resort unto him again. *Mk.* 10: **1.**
Many were gathered together praying. *Ac.* 12: **12.**
Therefore disputed he in the synagogue with the Jews, and with the devout persons, and in the market daily with them that met with him. *Ac.* 17: **17.**
See also
Assembly; Congregation; Meeting.

Respect

Neither doth God respect any person. *2 S.* 14: **14.**
Have thou respect unto the prayer of thy servant, and to his supplication, O Lord my God. *1 K.* 8: **28.**

He respecteth not any that are wise of heart. *Jb.* 37: **24.**
Blessed is that man that maketh the Lord his trust, and respecteth not the proud. *Ps.* 40: **4.**
Then shall I not be ashamed, when I have respect unto all thy commandments. *Ps.* 119: **6.**
I will . . . have respect unto thy ways. *Ps.* 119: **15.**
It is not good to have respect of persons in judgment. *Pr.* 24: **23.**
Curse not the king, no not in thy thought. *Ec.* 10: **20.**
I fear not God, nor regard men. *Lu.* 18: **4.**
Of a truth I perceive that God is no respecter of persons. *Ac.* 10: **34.**
Children, obey your parents in the Lord. *Ep.* 6: **1.**
Honour thy father and mother. *Ep.* 6: **2.**
Honour all men. *1 Pe.* 2: **17.**
See also
Esteem; Honor; Persons, Respect of; Regard.

Responsibility

Am I my brother's keeper? *Ge.* 4: **9.**
All that the Lord speaketh, that I must do. *Nu.* 23: **26.**
Every man shall be put to death for his own sin. *De.* 24: **16.**
Thus saith the whole congregation of the Lord, What trespass is this that ye have committed? *Jos.* 22: **16.**
His sons made themselves vile, and he restrained them not. *1 S.* 3: **13.**
The shield of the mighty is vilely cast away, the shield of Saul, as though he had not been anointed with oil. *2 S.* 1: **21.**
Be it indeed that I have erred, mine error remaineth with myself. *Jb.* 19: **4.**
The heaven, even the heavens, are the Lord's: but the earth hath he given to the children of men. *Ps.* 115: **16.**
Every one shall die for his own iniquity. *Je.* 31: **30.**
You only have I known of all the families of the earth: therefore I will punish you for all your iniquities. *Am.* 3: **2.**
What shall we do unto thee, that the sea may be calm unto us? *Jon.* 1: **11.**
The harvest truly is plenteous, but the labourers are few. *Mat.* 9: **37.**
Take heed what ye hear. *Mk.* 4: **24.**
Thou, Capernaum, which art exalted to heaven, shalt be thrust down to hell. *Lu.* 10: **15.**
He that knew not, and did commit things worthy of stripes, shall be beaten with few stripes. *Lu.* 12: **48.**
It is impossible but that offences will come: but woe unto him, through whom they come! *Lu.* 17: **1.**
If ye were blind, ye should have no sin: but now ye say, We see; therefore your sin remaineth. *Jn.* 9: **41.**
If I had not come and spoken unto them, they had not had sin; but now they have no cloke for their sin. *Jn.* 15: **22.**
Ye . . . intend to bring this man's blood upon us. *Ac.* 5: **28.**
Lord, lay not this sin to their charge. *Ac.* 7: **60.**
So then every one of us shall give account of himself to God. *Ro.* 14: **12.**

Let us not therefore judge one another any more: but judge this rather, that no man put a stumblingblock or an occasion to fall in his brother's way. *Ro.* 14: 13.

We then that are strong ought to bear the infirmities of the weak, and not to please ourselves. *Ro.* 15: 1.

Through thy knowledge shall the weak brother perish, for whom Christ died? *1 Co.* 8: 11.

Ye fathers, provoke not your children to wrath. *Ep.* 6: 4.

How shall we escape, if we neglect so great salvation. *He.* 2: 3.

Let no man say when he is tempted, I am tempted of God: for God cannot be tempted with evil, neither tempteth he any man. *Ja.* 1: 13.

God spared not the angels that sinned. *2 Pe.* 2: 4.

We ought to lay down our lives for the brethren. *1 Jn.* 3: 16.

If God so loved us, we ought also to love one another. *1 Jn.* 4: 11.

See also

Account; Christ, the Judge; Duty; God, the Judge; Judgment; Judgment, the Last; Obligation.

Responsiveness

As I have done, so God hath requited me. *Ju.* 1: 7.

With the pure thou wilt shew thyself pure; and with the froward thou wilt shew thyself froward. *Ps.* 18: 26.

When thou saidst, Seek ye my face; my heart said unto thee, Thy face, Lord, will I seek. *Ps.* 27: 8.

What shall I render unto the Lord for all his benefits toward me? *Ps.* 116: 12.

He that tilleth his land shall be satisfied with bread. *Pr.* 12: 11.

A man that hath friends must shew himself friendly. *Pr.* 18: 24.

As in water face answereth to face, so the heart of man to man. *Pr.* 27: 19.

Cast thy bread upon the waters: for thou shalt find it after many days. *Ec.* 11: 1.

Shall evil be recompensed for good? *Je.* 18: 20.

Their own doings have beset them about. *Ho.* 7: 2.

Whatsoever a man soweth, that shall he also reap. *Ga.* 6: 7.

He is like unto a man beholding his natural face in a glass. *Ja.* 1: 23.

Draw nigh to God, and he will draw nigh to you. *Ja.* 4: 8.

We love him, because he first loved us. *1 Jn.* 4: 19.

See also

Answer; Obedience; Prayer, Answer to.

Rest

Six days shalt thou do thy work, and on the seventh day thou shalt rest. *Ex.* 23: 12.

There the wicked cease from troubling; and there the weary be at rest. *Jb.* 3: 17.

He maketh me to lie down in green pastures. *Ps.* 23: 2.

Rest in the Lord. *Ps.* 37: 7.

And I said, Oh that I had wings like a dove! for then would I fly away, and be at rest. *Ps.* 55: 6.

Man goeth forth unto his work and to his labour until the evening. *Ps.* 104: 23.

Return unto thy rest, O my soul. *Ps.* 116: 7.

Come unto me, all ye that labour and are heavy laden, and I will give you rest. *Mat.* 11: 28.

There remaineth therefore a rest to the people of God. *He.* 4: 9.

That they may rest from their labours. *Re.* 14: 13.

See also

Calm; Christ, Peace of; Ease; God, Peace of; God, Rest in; Peace; Quiet; Repose; Serenity; Stillness; Tranquillity.

Restitution

He should make full restitution. *Ex.* 22: 3.

If a man have no kinsman to recompense the trespass unto, let the trespass be recompensed unto the Lord, even to the priest. *Nu.* 5: 8.

He hath swallowed down riches, and he shall vomit them up again. *Jb.* 20: 15.

According to his substance shall the restitution be. *Jb.* 20: 18.

Return ye now every man from his evil way, and amend your doings. *Je.* 35: 15.

If the wicked restore the pledge, give again that he had robbed, walk in the statutes of life, without committing iniquity; he shall surely live, he shall not die. *Eze.* 33: 15.

He shall send Jesus Christ, which before was preached unto you: Whom the heaven must receive until the times of restitution of all things. *Ac.* 3: 20. 21.

See also

Amends; Compensation; Man, the New; Recompense; Reparation; Restoration; Return.

Restoration

He shall be unto thee a restorer of thy life, and a nourisher of thine old age. *Ru.* 4: 15.

Go and wash in Jordan seven times, and thy flesh shall come again to thee. *2 K.* 5: 10.

His children shall seek to please the poor, and his hands shall restore their goods. *Jb.* 20: 10.

He restoreth my soul. *Ps.* 23: 3.

Restore unto me the joy of thy salvation. *Ps.* 51: 12.

I restored that which I took not away. *Ps.* 69: 4.

He . . . bindeth up their wounds. *Ps.* 147: 3.

They that wait upon the Lord shall renew their strength. *Is.* 40: 31.

Thou shalt be called, The repairer of the breach, The restorer of paths to dwell in. *Is.* 58: 12.

I will restore health unto thee, and I will heal thee of thy wounds, saith the Lord. *Je.* 30: 17.

I will restore to you the years that the locust hath eaten. *Jo.* 2: 25.

He was restored, and saw every man clearly. *Mk.* 8: 25.

They shall lay hands on the sick, and they shall recover. *Mk.* 16: 18.

If I have taken any thing from any man by

false accusation, I restore him fourfold. *Lu.*
19: 8.

Wilt thou at this time restore again the
kingdom to Israel? *Ac.* 1: 6.

God . . . hath reconciled us to himself by
Jesus Christ. *2 Co.* 5: 18.

If a man be overtaken in a fault, ye which
are spiritual, restore such an one in the spirit
of meekness. *Ga.* 6: 1.

See also

Amends; Compensation; Man, the New;
Recompense; Recovery; Refreshment; Renewal;
Reparation; Restitution; Return; Revival.

Restraint

There is no restraint to the Lord to save by
many or by few. *1 S.* 14: 6.

Thou castest off fear, and restrainest prayer
before God. *Jb.* 15: 4.

Be ye not as the horse, or as the mule,
which have no understanding: whose mouth
must be held in with bit and bridle. *Ps.* 32: 9.

The remainder of wrath shalt thou restrain.
Ps. 76: 10.

Set a watch, O Lord, before my mouth;
keep the door of my lips. *Ps.* 141: 3.

In the multitude of words there wanteth not
sin: but he that refraineth his lips is wise.
Pr. 10: 19.

He that is slow to anger is better than the
mighty; and he that ruleth his spirit than
he that taketh a city. *Pr.* 16: 32.

He that hath no rule over his own spirit
is like a city that is broken down, and without walls. *Pr.* 25: 28.

Where is thy zeal and thy strength? . . .
are they restrained? *Is.* 63: 15.

I covered the deep for him, and I restrained
the floods thereof, and the great waters were
stayed. *Eze.* 31: 15.

The Lord . . . reserveth wrath for his enemies. *Na.* 1: 2.

Every man that striveth for the mastery is
temperate in all things. *1 Co.* 9: 25.

The fruit of the Spirit is . . . temperance.
Ga. 5: 22, 23.

See also

Coercion; Compulsion; Constraint; Force;
Hindrance; Imprisonment; Limitation; Reserve; Restriction.

Restriction

Can I bring him back again? I shall go to
him, but he shall not return to me. *2 S.* 12: 23.

Can the rush grow up without mire? can the
flag grow without water? *Jb.* 8: 11.

Hitherto shalt thou come, but no further.
Jb. 38: 11.

Yea, they turned back and tempted God, and
limited the Holy One of Israel. *Ps.* 78: 41.

Can a man take fire in his bosom, and his
clothes not be burned? *Pr.* 6: 27.

How can ye, being evil, speak good things?
Mat. 12: 34.

Without me ye can do nothing. *Jn.* 15: 5.

We can do nothing against the truth, but for
the truth. *2 Co.* 13: 8.

Can the fig tree, my brethren, bear olive
berries? either a vine, figs? *Ja.* 3: 12.

See also

Bound; Coercion; Compulsion; Constraint;
Hindrance; Limitation; Restraint.

Result

Their sorrows shall be multiplied that hasten
after another God. *Ps.* 16: 4.

He gave them their request; but sent leanness into their soul. *Ps.* 106: 15.

The work of righteousness shall be peace.
Is. 32: 17.

The effect of righteousness quietness and
assurance for ever. *Is.* 32: 17.

Ye shall know them by their fruits. Do men
gather grapes of thorns, or figs of thistles? *Mat.*
7: 16.

Thus have ye made the commandment of
God of none effect by your tradition. *Mat.* 15:
6.

Shall their unbelief make the faith of God
without effect? *Ro.* 3: 3.

If they which are of the law be heirs, faith
is made void, and the promise made of none
effect. *Ro.* 4: 14.

Lest the cross of Christ should be made of
none effect. *1 Co.* 1: 17.

Christ is become of no effect unto you. *Ga.*
5: 4.

The fruit of the Spirit is love, joy, peace,
longsuffering, gentleness, goodness, faith, Meekness, temperance. *Ga.* 5: 22, 23.

See also

Consequence; Fruit; Fruitfulness; Fruits.
First; Harvest; Reaping; Yield.

Resurrection

God will redeem my soul from the power of
the grave: for he shall receive me. *Ps.* 49: 15.

Son of man, can these bones live? *Eze.* 37:
3.

Many of them that sleep in the dust of the
earth shall awake, some to everlasting life,
and some to shame and everlasting contempt.
Da. 12: 2.

The Sadducees . . . say that there is no
resurrection. *Mat.* 22: 23.

In the resurrection they neither marry, nor
are given in marriage. *Mat.* 22: 30.

He is not here: he is risen, as he said. *Mat.*
28: 6.

Thou shalt be recompensed at the resurrection of the just. *Lu.* 14: 14.

This thy brother was dead, and is alive
again; and was lost, and is found. *Lu.* 15:
32.

The children of the resurrection. *Lu.* 20: 36.

Destroy this temple, and in three days I will
raise it up. *Jn.* 2: 19.

The dead shall hear the voice of the Son
of God: and they that hear shall live. *Jn.*
5: 25.

Marvel not at this: for the hour is coming,
in the which all that are in the graves shall
hear his voice, And shall come forth. *Jn.* 5: 28,
29.

I am the resurrection. *Jn.* 11: 25.

Lazarus, come forth. *Jn.* 11: 43.

When they heard of the resurrection of the
dead, some mocked. *Ac.* 17: 32.

Why should it be thought a thing incredible
with you, that God should raise the dead?
Ac. 26: 8.

Like as Christ was raised up from the dead
by the glory of the Father, even so we also
should walk in newness of life. *Ro.* 6: 4.

God hath both raised up the Lord, and will also raise up us by his own power. *1 Co.* 6: 14.

How are the dead raised up? and with what body do they come? *1 Co.* 15: 35.

So also is the resurrection of the dead. . . . It is sown a natural body; it is raised a spiritual body. *1 Co.* 15: 42, 44.

We should not trust in ourselves, but in God which raiseth the dead. *2 Co.* 1: 9.

He which raised up the Lord Jesus shall raise up us also by Jesus. *2 Co.* 4: 14.

You hath he quickened. *Ep.* 2: 1.

God . . . hath raised us up together, and made us sit together in heavenly places in Christ Jesus. *Ep.* 2: 4, 6.

That I may know him, and the power of his resurrection, and the fellowship of his sufferings. *Ph.* 3: 10.

If ye then be risen with Christ. *Col.* 3: 1.

Of resurrection of the dead, and of eternal judgment. *He.* 6: 2.

God was able to raise him up, even from the dead. *He.* 11: 19.

Others were tortured, not accepting deliverance; that they might obtain a better resurrection. *He.* 11: 35.

And I saw the dead, small and great, stand before God. *Re.* 20: 12.

See also

Christ, Resurrection of; Easter; Quickening; Revival.

Retaliation

My wrath shall wax hot, and I will kill you with the sword. *Ex.* 22: 24.

Thou shalt not avenge, nor bear any grudge against the children of thy people. *Le.* 19: 18.

I will render vengeance to mine enemies, and will reward them that hate me. *De.* 32: 41.

So let the gods do to me, and more also, if I make not thy life as the life of one of them by to morrow about this time. *1 K.* 19: 2.

Jealousy is the rage of a man: therefore he will not spare in the day of his vengeance. *Pr.* 6: 34.

Say not thou, I will recompense evil; but wait on the Lord, and he shall save thee. *Pr.* 20: 22.

Say not, I will do so to him as he hath done to me: I will render to the man according to his work. *Pr.* 24: 29.

We shall take our revenge on him. *Je.* 20: 10.

The Philistines have dealt by revenge, and have taken vengeance with a despiteful heart, to destroy it for the old hatred. *Eze.* 25: 15.

Resist not evil. *Mat.* 5: 39.

Whosoever shall smite thee on thy right cheek, turn to him the other also. *Mat.* 5: 39.

Certain of the Jews banded together, and bound themselves under a curse, saying that they would neither eat nor drink till they had killed Paul. *Ac.* 23: 12.

Recompense to no man evil for evil. *Ro.* 12: 17.

He is the minister of God, a revenger to execute wrath upon him that doeth evil. *Ro.* 13: 4.

Not rendering evil for evil, or railing for railing: but contrariwise blessing. *1 Pe.* 3: 9.

See also

Revenge; Vengeance; Vindictiveness.

Retreat

Lest peradventure the people repent when they see war, and they return to Egypt. *Ex.* 13: 17.

What man is there that is fearful and fainthearted? let him go and return unto his house, lest his brethren's heart faint as well as his heart. *De.* 20: 8.

The people are fled from the battle, and many of the people also are fallen and dead. *2 S.* 1: 4.

Let them be driven backward and put to shame that wish me evil. *Ps.* 40: 14.

Thou makest us to turn back from the enemy. *Ps.* 44: 10.

When I cry unto thee, then shall mine enemies turn back: this I know; for God is for me. *Ps.* 56: 9.

They have provoked the Holy One of Israel unto anger, they are gone away backward. *Is.* 1: 4.

They . . . went backward, and not forward. *Je.* 7: 24.

And they have turned unto me the back, and not the face. *Je.* 32: 33.

Behold, Pharaoh's army, which is come forth to help you, shall return to Egypt into their own land. *Je.* 37: 7.

She sigheth, and turneth backward. *La.* 1: 8.

Jonah rose up to flee unto Tarshish from the presence of the Lord. *Jon.* 1: 3.

I went into Arabia. *Ga.* 1: 17.

For if after they have escaped the pollutions of the world through the knowledge of the Lord and Saviour Jesus Christ, they are again entangled therein, and overcome, the latter end is worse with them than the beginning. *2 Pe.* 2: 20.

See also

Asylum; Backsliding; Cowardice; Departure; God, the Refuge; Refuge; Solitude.

Retribution

An evil spirit from the Lord troubled him. *1 S.* 16: 14.

Thou . . . makest me to possess the iniquities of my youth. *Jb.* 13: 26.

Their sword shall enter their own heart. *Ps.* 37: 15.

His own iniquities shall take the wicked himself, and he shall be holden with the cords of his sins. *Pr.* 5: 22.

Whoso diggeth a pit shall fall therein. *Pr.* 26: 27.

He that rolleth a stone, it will return upon him. *Pr.* 26: 27.

They have sown the wind, and they shall reap the whirlwind. *Ho.* 8: 7.

Ye have plowed wickedness, ye have reaped iniquity. *Ho.* 10: 13.

With what measure ye mete, it shall be measured to you again. *Mat.* 7: 2.

Every idle word that men shall speak, they shall give account thereof in the day of judgment. *Mat.* 12: 36.

Thinkest thou, O man, . . . that thou shalt escape the judgment of God? *Ro.* 2: 3.

Whatsoever a man soweth, that shall he also reap. *Ga.* 6: 7.

He that soweth to his flesh shall of the flesh reap corruption. *Ga.* 6: 8.

Every transgression and disobedience received a just recompence of reward. *He.* **2: 2.**
See also
Chastisement; Christ, the Judge; Compensation; God, Chastisement of; God, the Judge; God, Punishment of; Judgment; Judgment, the Last; Punishment; Recompense.

Retrospect

Look not behind thee. *Ge.* **19: 17.**
Thou shalt remember all the way which the Lord thy God led thee these forty years in the wilderness. *De.* **8: 2.**
Remember the day when thou camest forth out of the land of Egypt. *De.* **16: 3.**
Remember the days of old, consider the years of many generations. *De.* **32: 7.**
Stand, stand, shall they cry; but none shall look back. *Na.* **2: 8.**
They shall remember me in far countries. *Zch.* **10: 9.**
No man, having put his hand to the plow, and looking back, is fit for the kingdom of God. *Lu.* **9: 62.**
See also
Memorial; Memory; Recollection; Remembrance.

Return

Dust thou art, and unto dust shalt thou return. *Ge.* **3: 19.**
Thou turnest man to destruction; and sayest, Return, ye children of men. *Ps.* **90: 3.**
Return unto thy rest, O my soul; for the Lord hath dealt bountifully with thee. *Ps.* **116: 7.**
He that rolleth a stone, it will return upon him. *Pr.* **26: 27.**
In returning and rest shall ye be saved. *Is.* **30: 15.**
The ransomed of the Lord shall return, and come to Zion with songs and everlasting joy upon their heads. *Is.* **35: 10.**
So shall my word be that goeth forth out of my mouth: it shall not return unto me void. *Is.* **55: 11.**
Who are these that fly as a cloud, and as the doves to their windows? *Is.* **60: 8.**
Jesus returned in the power of the Spirit into Galilee. *Lu.* **4: 14.**
See also
Homesickness; Prodigal; Repatriation; Restoration; Retreat; Reunion.

Reunion

The Lord your God is gracious and merciful, and will not turn away his face from you, if ye return unto him. *2 Ch.* **30: 9.**
God setteth the solitary in families. *Ps.* **68: 6.**
He . . . will come home at the day appointed. *Pr.* **7: 20.**
The ransomed of the Lord shall return. *Is.* **35: 10.**
I will go and return to my first husband. *Ho.* **2: 7.**
He delivered him to his mother. *Lu.* **7: 15.**
Return to thine own house, and shew how great things God hath done unto thee. *Lu.* **8: 39.**
When he cometh home, he calleth together his friends and neighbours, saying unto them,

Rejoice with me; for I have found my sheep which was lost. *Lu.* **15: 6.**
When he was yet a great way off, his father saw him, and had compassion, and ran, and fell on his neck, and kissed him. *Lu.* **15: 20.**
It was meet that we should make merry, and be glad: for this thy brother was dead, and is alive again; and was lost, and is found. *Lu.* **15: 32.**
If I go and prepare a place for you, I will come again, and receive you unto myself; that where I am, there ye may be also. *Jn.* **14: 3.**
See also
Homesickness; Prodigal; Restoration; Return.

Revel

He that is of a merry heart hath a continual feast. *Pr.* **15: 15.**
A feast is made for laughter, and wine maketh merry. *Ec.* **10: 19.**
He brought me to the banqueting house. *S. of S.* **2: 4.**
Behold joy and gladness, slaying oxen, and killing sheep, eating flesh, and drinking wine. *Is.* **22: 13.**
The Son of man came eating and drinking, and they say, Behold a man gluttonous, and a winebibber. *Mat.* **11: 19.**
Take thine ease, eat, drink, and be merry. *Lu.* **12: 19.**
The works of the flesh are manifest, which are these; . . . drunkenness, revellings, and such like. *Ga.* **5: 19, 21.**
When we walked in . . . excess of wine, revellings, banqueting. *1 Pe.* **4: 3.**
See also
Banquet; Drunkenness; Feast; Festival; Gluttony; Rejoicing; Wine.

Revelation

I will raise them up a Prophet from among their brethren, like unto thee, and will put my words in his mouth. *De.* **18: 18.**
Lo, these are parts of his ways: but how little a portion is heard of him? *Jb.* **26: 14.**
There is nothing covered, that shall not be revealed. *Mat.* **10: 26.**
There is nothing hid, which shall not be manifested; neither was any thing kept secret, but that it should come abroad. *Mk.* **4: 22.**
That the thoughts of many hearts may be revealed. *Lu.* **2: 35.**
What I do thou knowest not now; but thou shalt know hereafter. *Jn.* **13: 7.**
All things that I have heard of my Father I have made known unto you. *Jn.* **15: 15.**
I have yet many things to say unto you, but ye cannot bear them now. *Jn.* **16: 12.**
The Spirit of truth . . . will guide you into all truth. *Jn.* **16: 13.**
The sufferings of this present time are not worthy to be compared with the glory which shall be revealed in us. *Ro.* **8: 18.**
God hath revealed them unto us by his Spirit. *1 Co.* **2: 10.**
Every man's work shall be made manifest. *1 Co.* **3: 13.**
We all, with open face beholding as in a glass the glory of the Lord, are changed into the same image from glory to glory, even as by the Spirit of the Lord. *2 Co.* **3: 18.**

Having made known unto us the mystery of his will, according to his good pleasure which he hath purposed in himself. *Ep.* 1: 9.

At sundry times and in divers manners. *He.* 1: 1.

See also

Christ, Revelation of; Disclosure; Exposure; God, Revelation of; God, Vision of; God, Voice of; God. Word of; Manifestation; Scripture.

Revenge

If I whet my glittering sword, and mine hand take hold on judgment; I will render vengeance to mine enemies, and will reward them that hate me. *De.* 32: 41.

Out of the mouth of babes and sucklings hast thou ordained strength because of mine enemies, that thou mightest still the enemy and the avenger. *Ps.* 8: 2.

Say not thou, I will recompense evil; but wait on the Lord, and he shall save thee. *Pr.* 20: 22.

Behold, your God will come with vengeance, even God with a recompence. *Is.* 35: 4.

They shall be drunken with their own blood, as with sweet wine. *Is.* 49: 26.

He put on the garments of vengeance for clothing. *Is.* 59: 17.

We shall take our revenge on him. *Je.* 20: 10.

Avenge not yourselves, but rather give place unto wrath: for it is written, Vengeance is mine; I will repay, saith the Lord. *Ro.* 12: 19.

He is the minister of God, a revenger to execute wrath upon him that doeth evil. *Ro.* 13: 4.

Behold this selfsame thing, that ye sorrowed after a godly sort, what carefulness it wrought in you, yea, what clearing of yourselves, yea, what indignation, yea, what fear, yea, what vehement desire, yea, what zeal, yea, what revenge! *2 Co.* 7: 11.

In flaming fire taking vengeance on them that know not God. *2 Th.* 1: 8.

See also

Christ, Wrath of; God, Anger of; God, Wrath of; Recompense; Retaliation; Vengeance.

Reverence

The place whereon thou standest is holy ground. *Ex.* 3: 5.

Ye shall keep my sabbaths, and reverence my sanctuary. *Le.* 19: 30.

He also is to be feared above all gods. *1 Ch.* 16: 25.

Behold, God is great, and we know him not. *Jb.* 36: 26.

Stand in awe, and sin not: commune with your own heart upon your bed, and be still. *Ps.* 4: 4.

Let my prayer be set before thee as incense; and the lifting up of my hands as the evening sacrifice. *Ps.* 141: 2.

Sanctify the Lord of hosts himself. *Is.* 8: 13.

The Lord is in his holy temple: let all the earth keep silence before him. *Hab.* 2: 20.

Make not my Father's house an house of merchandise. *Jn.* 2: 16.

For to me to live is Christ. *Ph.* 1: 21.

We have had fathers of our flesh which corrected us, and we gave them reverence. *He.* 12: 9.

See also

Adoration; Awe; Christ, Worship of; God, Adoration of; God, Worship of; Veneration; Worship.

Reviling

Thou shalt not take the name of the Lord thy God in vain. *Ex.* 20: 7.

Thou shalt not revile the gods. *Ex.* 22: 28.

Thou shalt not . . . curse the ruler of thy people. *Ex.* 22: 28.

How shall I curse, whom God hath not cursed? or how shall I defy, whom the Lord hath not defied? *Nu.* 23: 8.

The Lord will not hold him guiltless that taketh his name in vain. *De.* 5: 11.

Fear ye not the reproach of men, neither be ye afraid of their revilings. *Is.* 51: 7.

Both prophet and priest are profane. *Je.* 23: 11.

They profaned my holy name. *Eze.* 36: 20.

Blessed are ye, when men shall revile you. *Mat.* 5: 11.

Pray for them which despitefully use you, and persecute you. *Mat.* 5: 44.

They that passed by reviled him, wagging their heads. *Mat.* 27: 39.

They that were crucified with him reviled him. *Mk.* 15: 32.

Being reviled, we bless. *1 Co.* 4: 12.

Avoiding profane and vain babblings. *1 Ti.* 6: 20.

Who, when he was reviled reviled not again. *Mat.* 2: 23.

See also

Abuse; Curse; Insult.

Revival

Renew a right spirit within me. *Ps.* 51: 10.

Restore unto me the joy of thy salvation. *Ps.* 51: 12.

Then will I teach transgressors thy ways. *Ps.* 51: 13.

Turn us again, O God of hosts, and cause thy face to shine; and we shall be saved. *Ps.* 80: 7.

Wilt thou not revive us again? *Ps.* 85: 6.

He shall drink of the brook in the way: therefore shall he lift up the head. *Ps.* 110: 7.

Though I walk in the midst of trouble, thou wilt revive me. *Ps.* 138: 7.

Until the spirit be poured upon us from on high, and the wilderness be a fruitful field, and the fruitful field be counted for a forest. *Is.* 32: 15.

Let the people renew their strength. *Is.* 41: 1.

Turn thou us unto thee, O Lord, and we shall be turned; renew our days as of old. *La.* 5: 21.

After two days will he revive us: in the third day he will raise us up, and we shall live in his sight. *Ho.* 6: 2.

O Lord, revive thy work in the midst of the years, in the midst of the years make known. *Hab.* 3: 2.

The angel . . . came again, and waked me, as a man that is wakened out of his sleep. *Zch.* 4: 1.

Repent ye. *Mk.* 1: 15.

He said unto them, Come ye yourselves apart into a desert place, and rest a while. *Mk.* 6: 31.

It is the spirit that quickeneth; the flesh profiteth nothing: the words that I speak unto you, they are spirit, and they are life. *Jn.* 6: 63.

When the commandment came, sin revived, and I died. *Ro.* 7: 9.

Christ both died, and rose, and revived, that he might be Lord both of the dead and living. *Ro.* 14: 9.

See also

Birth, New; Confirmation; Lent; Quickening; Refreshment: Regeneration; Renewal; Restoration; Return; Revival.

Revolution

Ye have been rebellious against the Lord. *De.* 9: 7.

Rebellion is as the sin of witchcraft. *1 S.* 15: 23.

The kings of the earth set themselves, and the rulers take counsel together, against the Lord. *Ps.* 2: 2.

An evil man seeketh only rebellion. *Pr.* 17: 11.

Woe to the rebellious children, saith the Lord, that take counsel, but not of me. *Is.* 30: 1.

This people hath a revolting and a rebellious heart; they are revolted and gone. *Je.* 5: 23.

They are all grievous revolters, walking with slanders. *Je.* 6: 28.

I will purge out from among you the rebels. *Eze.* 20: 38.

Seest thou these great buildings? there shall not be left one stone upon another, that shall not be thrown down. *Mk.* 13: 2.

See also

God, Rebellion against; Rebellion.

Reward

I gave unto Esau mount Seir, to possess it; but Jacob and his children went down into Egypt. *Jos.* 24: 4.

They gave Hebron unto Caleb, as Moses said: and he expelled thence the three sons of Anak. *Ju.* 1: 20.

In keeping of them there is great reward. *Ps.* 19: 11.

Say not, I will do so to him as he hath done to me: I will render to the man according to his work. *Pr.* 24: 29.

Cast thy bread upon the waters: for thou shalt find it after many days. *Ec.* 11: 1.

Every one loveth gifts, and followeth after rewards. *Is.* 1: 23.

His reward is with him, and his work before him. *Is.* 62: 11.

They shall plant vineyards, and eat the fruit of them. *Is.* 65: 21.

Thus saith the Lord unto the house of Israel, Seek ye me, and ye shall live. *Am.* 5: 4.

If ye love them which love you, what reward have ye? do not even the publicans the same? *Mat.* 5: 46.

Whosoever shall give to drink unto one of these little ones a cup of cold water only in the name of a disciple, verily I say unto you, he shall in no wise lose his reward. *Mat.* 10: 42.

And he said unto Jesus, Lord, remember me when thou comest into thy kingdom. *Lu.* 23: 42.

Glory, honour, and peace, to every man that worketh good. *Ro.* 2: 10.

Whatsoever good thing any man doeth, the same shall he receive of the Lord, whether he be bond or free. *Ep.* 6: 8.

I press toward the mark for the prize of the high calling of God in Christ Jesus. *Ph.* 3: 14.

If we suffer, we shall also reign with him. *2 Ti.* 2: 12.

Henceforth there is laid up for me a crown of righteousness, which the Lord, the righteous judge, shall give me at that day. *2 Ti.* 4: 8.

Let us labour therefore to enter into that rest. *He.* 4: 11.

He had respect unto the recompence of the reward. *He.* 11: 26.

Blessed is the man that endureth temptation: for when he is tried, he shall receive the crown of life. *Ja.* 1: 12.

Ye have . . . seen the end of the Lord. *Ja.* 5: 11.

Their works do follow them. *Re.* 14: 13.

See also

Award; Compensation; God, Reward of; Merit; Payment; Prize; Punishment; Recompense; Restoration; Retribution.

Riches

Thou shalt remember the Lord thy God: for it is he that giveth thee power to get wealth. *De.* 8: 18.

The increase of his house shall depart, and his goods shall flow away in the day of his wrath. *Jb.* 20: 28.

Will he esteem thy riches? no, not gold, nor all the forces of strength. *Jb.* 36: 19.

Wise men die, likewise the fool and the brutish person perish, and leave their wealth to others. *Ps.* 49: 10.

The rich and poor meet together. *Pr.* 22: 2.

Riches certainly make themselves wings. *Pr.* 23: 5.

A faithful man shall abound with blessings. *Pr.* 28: 20.

He that maketh haste to be rich shall not be innocent. *Pr.* 28: 20.

Give me neither poverty nor riches. *Pr.* 30: 8.

I gathered me also silver and gold. *Ec.* 2: 8.

He that loveth silver shall not be satisfied with silver; nor he that loveth abundance with increase. *Ec.* 5: 10.

The abundance of the rich will not suffer him to sleep. *Ec.* 5: 12.

She did not know that I gave her corn, and wine, and oil, and multiplied her silver and gold. *Ho.* 2: 8.

Lay not up for yourselves treasures upon earth. *Mat.* 6: 19.

How hard is it for them that trust in riches to enter into the kingdom of God! *Mk.* 10: 24.

Woe unto you that are rich! *Lu.* 6: 24.

God said unto him, Thou fool, this night thy soul shall be required of thee: then whose shall those things be, which thou hast provided? *Lu.* 12: 20.

Provide yourselves bags which wax not old, a treasure in the heavens that faileth not. *Lu.* 12: 33.

It came to pass, that the beggar died, and was carried by the angels into Abraham's bosom: the rich man also died, and was buried. *Lu.* 16: 22.

It is easier for a camel to go through a needle's eye, than for a rich man to enter into the kingdom of God. *Lu.* 18: 25.

Silver and gold have I none; but such as I have give I thee. *Ac.* 3: 6.

As poor, yet making many rich. *2 Co.* 6: 10.

Unto me, who am less than the least of all saints, is this grace given, that I should preach among the Gentiles the unsearchable riches of Christ. *Ep.* 3: 8.

We brought nothing into this world, and it is certain we can carry nothing out. *1 Ti.* 6: 7.

The sun is no sooner risen with a burning heat, but it withereth the grass, and the flower thereof falleth, and the grace of the fashion of it perisheth: so also shall the rich man fade away in his ways. *Ja.* 1: 11.

See also

Accumulation; Acquisition; Ampleness; Enrichment; God, Wealth of; Gold; Goods; Mammon; Money; Wealth; Worldliness.

Riddle

I will incline mine ear to a parable: I will open my dark sayings upon the harp. *Ps.* 49: 4.

There are three things that are never satisfied, yea, four things say not, It is enough. *Pr.* 30: 15.

There be three things which are too wonderful for me, yea, four things which I know not. *Pr.* 30: 18.

There be four things which are little upon the earth, but they are exceeding wise. *Pr.* 30: 24.

There be three things which go well, yea; four are comely in going. *Pr.* 30: 29.

Son of man, put forth a riddle, and speak a parable unto the house of Israel. *Eze.* 17: 2.

A king of fierce countenance, and understanding dark sentences, shall stand up. *Da.* 8: 23.

Why speakest thou unto them in parables? *Mat.* 13: 10.

It is given unto you to know the mysteries of the kingdom of heaven, but to them it is not given. *Mat.* 13: 11.

These things have I spoken unto you in proverbs: but the time cometh, when I shall no more speak unto you in proverbs. *Jn.* 16: 25.

Now we see through a glass, darkly. *1 Co.* 13: 12.

See also

Enigma.

Ride

I will sing unto the Lord, for he hath triumphed gloriously: the horse and his rider hath he thrown into the sea. *Ex.* 15: 1.

There is none like unto the God of Jeshurun, who rideth upon the heaven in thy help, and in his excellency on the sky. *De.* 33: 26.

Thou liftest me up to the wind; thou causest me to ride upon it. *Jb.* 30: 22.

In thy majesty ride prosperously because of truth and meekness and righteousness. *Ps.* 45: 4.

Extol him that rideth upon the heavens. *Ps.* 68: 4.

Behold, the Lord rideth upon a swift cloud. *Is.* 19: 1.

Ye said, No; for we will flee upon horses; therefore shall ye flee: and, We will ride upon the swift; therefore shall they that pursue you be swift. *Is.* 30: 16.

Right

Thou shalt do that which is right and good in the sight of the Lord: that it may be well with thee. *De.* 6: 18.

In those days there was no king in Israel, but every man did that which was right in his own eyes. *Ju.* 17: 6.

I will teach you the good and the right way. *1 S.* 12: 23.

Shall even he that hateth right govern? *Jb.* 34: 17.

Hear the right, O Lord, attend unto my cry. *Ps.* 17: 1.

The statutes of the Lord are right, rejoicing the heart. *Ps.* 19: 8.

The word of the Lord is right; and all his works are done in truth. *Ps.* 33: 4.

Renew a right spirit within me. *Ps.* 51: 10.

Their heart was not right with him, neither were they stedfast in his covenant. *Ps.* 78: 37.

Why even of yourselves judge ye not what is right? *Lu.* 12: 57.

Blessed are they that do his commandments, that they may have right to the tree of life. *Re.* 22: 14.

See also

Goodness; Righteousness.

Righteousness

Let me die the death of the righteous, and let my last end be like his! *Nu.* 23: 10.

He leadeth me in the paths of righteousness for his name's sake. *Ps.* 23: 3.

The Lord knoweth the days of the upright. *Ps.* 37: 18.

He shall judge thy people with righteousness, and thy poor with judgment. *Ps.* 72: 2.

Do good, O Lord, unto those that be good, and to them that are upright in their hearts. *Ps.* 125: 4.

Righteousness exalteth a nation. *Pr.* 14: 34.

Better is a little with righteousness than great revenues without right. *Pr.* 16: 8.

Be not righteous over much; neither make thyself over wise: why shouldest thou destroy thyself? *Ec.* 7: 16.

All things come alike to all: there is one event to the righteous, and to the wicked. *Ec.* 9: 2.

Open ye the gates, that the righteous nation which keepeth the truth may enter in. *Is.* 26: 2.

In righteousness shalt thou be established: thou shalt be far from oppression; for thou shalt not fear. *Is.* 54: 14.

We are all as an unclean thing, and all our righteousnesses are as filthy rags. *Is.* 64: 6.

They that be wise shall shine as the brightness of the firmament; and they that turn many to righteousness as the stars for ever and ever. *Da.* 12: 3.

It is time to seek the Lord, till he come and

rain righteousness upon you. *Ho.* 10: 12.

Suffer it to be so now: for thus it becometh us to fulfil all righteousness. *Mat.* 3: 15.

Blessed are they which are persecuted for righteousness' sake: for theirs is the kingdom of heaven. *Mat.* 5: 10.

Except your righteousness shall exceed the righteousness of the scribes and Pharisees, ye shall in no case enter into the kingdom of heaven. *Mat.* 5: 20.

I am not come to call the righteous, but sinners to repentance. *Mat.* 9: 13.

There is none righteous, no, not one. *Ro.* 3: 10.

The kingdom of God is not meat and drink; but righteousness, and peace, and joy in the Holy Ghost. *Ro.* 14: 17.

Watch ye, stand fast in the faith, quit you like men, be strong. *1 Co.* 16: 13.

A sceptre of righteousness is the sceptre of thy kingdom. *He.* 1: 8.

Nevertheless we, according to his promise, look for new heavens and a new earth, wherein dwelleth righteousness. *2 Pe.* 3: 13.

See also

Christ, Goodness of; Christ, Holiness of; Fairness; God, Righteousness of; Godliness; Goodness; Holiness; Integrity; Rectitude; Uprightness; Virtue.

Rise

Rise up, Lord, and let thine enemies be scattered. *Nu.* 10: 35.

He shall be as the light of the morning, when the sun riseth. *2 S.* 23: 4.

Many are they that rise up against me. *Ps.* 3: 1.

Though war should rise against me, in this will I be confident. *Ps.* 27: 3.

The Lord, hath spoken, and called the earth from the rising of the sun unto the going down thereof. *Ps.* 50: 1.

From the rising of the sun unto the going down of the same the Lord's name is to be praised. *Ps.* 113: 3.

At midnight I will rise to give thanks unto thee. *Ps.* 119: 62.

It is vain for you to rise up early, to sit up late, to eat the bread of sorrows: for so he giveth his beloved sleep. *Ps.* 127: 2.

A just man falleth seven times, and riseth up again. *Pr.* 24: 16.

If thou draw out thy soul to the hungry, and satisfy the afflicted soul; then shall thy light rise in obscurity, and thy darkness be as the noon day. *Is.* 58: 10.

Arise, shine; for thy light is come, and the glory of the Lord is risen upon thee. *Is.* 60: 1.

Gentiles shall come to thy light, and kings to the brightness of thy rising. *Is.* 60: 3.

He maketh his sun to rise on the evil and on the good. *Mat.* 5: 45.

Children shall rise up against their parents *Mat.* 10: 21.

The third day he shall rise again. *Mat.* 20: 19.

Nation shall rise against nation. *Mat.* 24: 7.

He is not here: for he is risen. *Mat.* 28: 6.

If the dead rise not, then is not Christ raised: And if Christ be not raised, your faith is vain. *1 Co.* 15: 16, 17.

Now is Christ risen from the dead. *1 Co.* 15: 20.

If ye then be risen with Christ, seek those things which are above, where Christ sitteth on the right hand of God. *Col.* 3: 1.

The dead in Christ shall rise first. *1 Th.* 4: 16.

The sun is no sooner risen with a burning heat, but it withereth the grass, and the flower thereof falleth. *Ja.* 1: 11.

See also

Ambition; Ascension; Aspiration; Climbing.

Ritual

Every oblation of theirs, . . . which they shall render unto me, shall be most holy for thee and for thy sons. *Nu.* 18: 9.

My offering, and my bread for my sacrifices made by fire, for a sweet savour unto me, shall ye observe to offer unto me in their due season. *Nu.* 28: 2.

To what purpose is the multitude of your sacrifices unto me? *Is.* 1: 11.

Bring no more vain oblations. *Is.* 1: 13.

Incense is an abomination unto me. *Is.* 1: 13.

To what purpose cometh there to me incense from Sheba, and the sweet cane from a far country? *Je.* 6: 20.

Your burnt offerings are not acceptable, nor your sacrifices sweet unto me. *Je.* 6: 20.

Can the children of the bridechamber fast, while the bridegroom is with them? *Mk.* 2: 19.

The Pharisees, and all the Jews, except they wash their hands oft, eat not, holding the tradition of the elders. *Mk.* 7: 3.

The Pharisee . . . marvelled that he had not washed before dinner. *Lu.* 11: 38.

This do in remembrance of me. *Lu.* 22: 19.

He which baptizeth with the Holy Ghost. *Jn.* 1: 33.

John truly baptized with water; but ye shall be baptized with the Holy Ghost. *Ac.* 1: 5.

Circumcision is nothing, and uncircumcision is nothing, but the keeping of the commandments of God. *1 Co.* 7: 19.

See also

Celebration; Ceremony; Formalism; Liturgy; Observance; Ordinance.

Rivalry

They shall fight every one against his brother, and every one against his neighbour. *Is.* 19: 2.

There was also a strife among them, which of them should be accounted the greatest. *Lu.* 22: 24.

I fear, lest . . . there be debates, envyings, wraths, strifes. *2 Co.* 12: 20.

Let nothing be done through strife or vainglory. *Ph.* 2: 3.

See also

Competition; Contest; Emulation; Envy; Jealousy.

River

As gardens by the river's side. *Nu.* 24: 6.

Are not Abana and Pharpar, rivers of Damascus, better than all the waters of Israel? *2 K.* 5: 12.

He shall be like a tree planted by the rivers of water. *Ps.* 1: 3.

There is a river, the streams whereof shall make glad the city of God. *Ps.* **46: 4.**

The stream had gone over our soul. *Ps.* **124: 4.**

All the rivers run into the sea; yet the sea is not full; unto the place from whence the rivers come, thither they return again. *Ec.* **1: 7.**

The harvest of the river. *Is.* **23: 3.**

There the glorious Lord will be unto us a place of broad rivers and streams. *Is.* **33: 21.**

In the wilderness shall waters break out, and streams in the desert. *Is.* **35: 6.**

I will extend peace to her like a river. *Is.* **66: 12.**

He shewed me a pure river. *Re.* **22: 1.**

See also

Stream; Water.

Road

Ye shall walk in all the ways which the Lord your God hath commanded you, that ye may live. *De.* **5: 33.**

Thou shalt remember all the way which the Lord thy God led thee these forty years in the wilderness. *De.* **8: 2.**

I will teach you the good and the right way. *1 S.* **12: 23.**

He knoweth the way that I take. *Jb.* **23: 10.**

Then will I teach transgressors thy ways. *Ps.* **51: 13.**

Blessed is every one that feareth the Lord; that walketh in his ways. *Ps.* **128: 1.**

To guide our feet into the way of peace. *Lu.* **1: 79.**

Jesus saith unto them, I am the way, the truth, and the life: no man cometh unto the Father but by me. *Jn.* **14: 6.**

Make straight paths for your feet. *He.* **12: 13.**

See also

Christ, Way of; God, Way of; Highway; Life, Path of; Path; Street; Way.

Roar

Why art thou so far from helping me, and from the words of my roaring? *Ps.* **22: 1.**

When I kept silence, my bones waxed old through my roaring all the day long. *Ps.* **32: 3.**

Though the waters thereof roar and be troubled. *Ps.* **46: 3.**

The young lions roar after their prey, and seek their meat from God. *Ps.* **104: 21.**

Their voice roareth like the sea. *Je.* **6: 23.**

Will a lion roar in the forest, when he hath no prey? *Am.* **3: 4.**

Your adversary the devil, as a roaring lion, walketh about, seeking whom he may devour. *1 Pe.* **5: 8.**

Robbery

Thou shalt not steal. *Ex.* **20: 15.**

Thou shalt not defraud thy neighbour, neither rob him. *Le.* **19: 13.**

Trust not in oppression, and become not vain in robbery. *Ps.* **62: 10.**

Rob not the poor, because he is poor. *Pr.* **22: 22.**

Is this house, which is called by my name, become a den of robbers in your eyes? *Je.* **7: 11.**

The robbers of thy people shall exalt themselves. *Da.* **11: 14.**

Woe to the bloody city! it is all full of lies and robbery. *Na.* **3: 1.**

A certain man went down from Jerusalem to Jericho, and fell among thieves. *Lu.* **10: 30.**

All that ever came before me are thieves and robbers. *Jn.* **10: 8.**

The thief cometh not, but for to steal, and to kill, and to destroy. *Jn.* **10: 10.**

See also

Burglar; Theft.

Robe

I put on righteousness, and it clothed me: my judgment was as a robe and a diadem. *Jb.* **29: 14.**

The Lord reigneth, he is clothed with majesty. *Ps.* **93: 1.**

He hath clothed me with the garments of salvation, he hath covered me with the robe of righteousness. *Is.* **61: 10.**

Even Solomon in all his glory was not arrayed like one of these. *Mat.* **6: 29.**

Bring forth the best robe, and put it on him. *Lu.* **15: 22.**

They put on him a purple robe. *Jn.* **19: 2.**

He that overcometh, the same shall be clothed in white raiment. *Re.* **3: 5.**

These are they which came out of great tribulation, and have washed their robes, and made them white in the blood of the Lamb. *Re.* **7: 14.**

See also

Apparel; Attire; Clothes; Garment; Raiment.

Rock

He took of the stones of that place, and put them for his pillows. *Ge.* **28: 11.**

He shall set me up upon a rock. *Ps.* **27: 5.**

A man shall be . . . as the shadow of a great rock in a weary land. *Is.* **32: 2.**

He caused the waters to flow out of the rock for them. *Is.* **48: 21.**

Look unto the rock whence ye are hewn. *Is.* **51: 1.**

What man is there of you, whom if his son ask bread, will he give him a stone? *Mat.* **7: 9.**

I will liken him unto a wise man, which built his house upon a rock. *Mat.* **7: 24.**

Thou art Peter, and upon this rock I will build my church. *Mat.* **16: 18.**

There shall not be left here one stone upon another, that shall not be thrown down. *Mat.* **24: 2.**

The angel . . . rolled back the stone from the door. *Mat.* **28: 2.**

Some fell upon a rock; and . . . it withered away. *Lu.* **8: 6.**

If these should hold their peace, the stones would immediately cry out. *Lu.* **19: 40.**

They drank of that spiritual Rock that followed them: and that Rock was Christ. *1 Co.* **10: 4.**

Ye also, as lively stones, are built up a spiritual house. *1 Pe.* **2: 5.**

See also

Christ, the Rock; Defence; Fortress; Stone.

Rod

I will be his father, and he shall be my son. If he commit iniquity, I will chasten him with the rod of men, and with the stripes of the children of men. *2 S.* **7: 14.**

Thy rod and thy staff they comfort me. *Ps.* **23: 4.**

Then will I visit their transgressions with
the rod. *Ps.* **89: 32.**

A rod is for the back of him that is void
of understanding. *Pr.* **10: 13.**

He that spareth his rod hateth his son. *Pr.*
13: 24.

Be not afraid of the Assyrian: he shall smite
thee with a rod, and shall lift up his staff
against thee. *Is.* **10: 24.**

The Lord hath broken the staff of the
wicked, and the sceptre of the rulers. *Is.* **14: 5.**

What will ye? shall I come unto you with
a rod, or in love, and in the spirit of meekness? *1 Co.* **4: 21.**

Thrice was I beaten with rods. *2 Co.* **11: 25.**

He shall rule them with a rod of iron. *Re.*
2: 27.

See also

Chastisement; Discipline; God, Chastisement
of; God, Punishment of; Punishment; Scourge;
Staff; Stripe; Tribulation.

Rome

These men . . . teach customs, which are
not lawful for us to receive, neither to observe,
being Romans. *Ac.* **16: 20, 21.**

The magistrates . . . feared, when they
heard that they were Romans. *Ac.* **16: 38.**

After I have been there I must also see
Rome. *Ac.* **19: 21.**

Is it lawful for you to scourge a man that is
a Roman, and uncondemned? *Ac.* **22: 25.**

The Lord stood by him, and said. Be of good
cheer, Paul: for as thou hast testified to me in
Jerusalem, so must thou bear witness also at
Rome. *Ac.* **23: 11.**

Yet was I delivered prisoner from Jerusalem
into the hands of the Romans. *Ac.* **28: 17.**

As much as in me is, I am ready to preach
the gospel to you that are at Rome also. *Ro.*
1: 15.

Roof

Under the shadow of my roof. *Ge.* **19: 8.**

Thou shalt make a battlement for thy roof,
that thou bring not blood upon thine house,
if any fall from thence. *De.* **22: 8.**

He built . . . the walls of the cieling. *1 K.*
6: 15.

The greater house he cieled with fir tree.
2 Ch. **3: 5.**

Hide me under the shadow of thy wings. *Ps.*
17: 8.

Who layeth the beams of his chambers in
the waters. *Ps.* **104: 3.**

If I do not remember thee, let my tongue
cleave to the roof of my mouth. *Ps.* **137: 6.**

Is it time for you, O ye, to dwell in your
cieled houses, and this house lie waste? *Hag.*
1: 4.

I am not worthy that thou shouldest come
under my roof. *Mat.* **8: 8.**

They uncovered the roof where he was. *Mk.*
2: 4.

Under the mighty hand of God. *1 Pe.* **5: 6.**

See also

Dwelling; Habitation; Home; House; Residence; Shelter.

Room

The sun . . . is as a bridegroom coming out
of his chamber, and rejoiceth as a strong man
to run a race. *Ps.* **19: 4, 5.**

Thou hast brought a vine out of Egypt.
. . . Thou preparedst room before it. *Ps.* **80:
8, 9.**

The Lord answered me, and set me in a large
place. *Ps.* **118: 5.**

By knowledge shall the chambers be filled
with all precious and pleasant riches. *Pr.* **24:
4.**

The place is too strait for me: give place
to me that I may dwell. *Is.* **49: 20.**

Enlarge the place of thy tent, and let them
stretch forth the curtains of thine habitations.
Is. **54: 2.**

His windows being open in his chamber
toward Jerusalem, he kneeled upon his knees
three times a day, and prayed. *Da.* **6: 10.**

Prove me now herewith, saith the Lord of
hosts, if I will not open you the windows of
heaven, and pour you out a blessing, that
there shall not be room enough to receive it.
Mal. **3: 10.**

He will shew you a large upper room furnished and prepared; there make ready for us.
Mk. **14: 15.**

There was no room for them in the inn. *Lu.*
2: 7.

Lord, it is done as thou hast commanded,
and yet there is room. *Lu.* **14: 22.**

See also

Chamber; Narrowness; Place; Strait.

Root

The root of the righteous shall not be moved.
Pr. **12: 3.**

The root of the righteous yieldeth fruit. *Pr.*
12: 12.

There shall come forth a rod out of the
stem of Jesse, and a branch shall grow out of
his roots. *Is.* **11: 1.**

He shall be as a tree planted by the waters,
and that spreadeth out her roots by the river.
Je. **17: 8.**

The ax is laid unto the root of the trees.
Mat. **3: 10.**

Because they had no root, they withered
away. *Mat.* **13: 6.**

If the root be holy, so are the branches. *Ro.*
11: 16.

Rooted and grounded in love. *Ep.* **3: 17.**

Rooted and built up in him, and stablished
in the faith, as ye have been taught, abounding
therein with thanksgiving. *Col.* **2: 7.**

The love of money is the root of all evil. *1
Ti.* **6: 10.**

Trees whose fruit withereth, without fruit,
twice dead, plucked up by the roots. *Jude* **1:
12.**

See also

Ground.

Ruin

Ye shall overthrow their altars, and break
their pillars, and burn their groves with fire.
De. **12: 3.**

Thou turnest man to destruction. *Ps.* **90: 3.**

Damascus is taken away from being a city,
and it shall be a ruinous heap. *Is.* **17: 1.**

Thou hast made of a city an heap; of a
defenced city a ruin: a palace of strangers to
be no city; it shall never be built. *Is.* **25: 2.**

The Lord God will help me; therefore shall
I not be confounded. *Is.* **50: 7.**

I the Lord build the ruined places, and plant that that was desolate. *Eze.* 36: 36.

I will overthrow the throne of kingdoms, and I will destroy the strength of the kingdoms of the heathen; and I will overthrow the chariots, and those that ride in them. *Hag.* 2: 22.

The ruin of that house was great. *Lu.* 6: 49.

I will build again the ruins thereof, and I will set it up. *Ac.* 15: 16.

Turning the cities of Sodom and Gomorrah into ashes condemned them with an overthrow. *2 Pe.* 2: 6.

See also

Annihilation; Collapse; Defeat; Desolation; Destruction; Fall; Overthrow; Wreck.

Rule

God made two great lights; the greater light to rule the day, and the lesser light to rule the night. *Ge.* 1: 16.

Let them have dominion. *Ge.* 1: 26.

Look out a man discreet and wise, and set him over the land of Egypt. *Ge.* 41: 33.

Moreover thou shalt provide out of all the people able men, such as fear God, men of truth, hating covetousness; and place such over them, to be rulers. *Ex.* 18: 21.

The men of Israel said unto Gideon, Rule thou over us. *Ju.* 8: 22.

Thou art the God, even thou alone, of all the kingdoms of the earth. *2 K.* 19: 15.

Yet have I set my King upon my holy hill of Zion. *Ps.* 2: 6.

Thou rulest the raging of the sea. *Ps.* 89: 9.

Mercy and truth preserve the king: and his throne is upholden by mercy. *Pr.* 20: 28.

The king that faithfully judgeth the poor, his throne shall be established for ever. *Pr.* 29: 14.

The government shall be upon his shoulder. *Is.* 9: 6.

The Lord shall reign over them in mount Zion from henceforth, even for ever. *Mi.* 4: 7.

Ye know not when the master of the house cometh. *Mk.* 13: 35.

Who made thee a ruler and a judge over us? *Ac.* 7: 27.

Death reigned from Adam to Moses. *Ro.* 5: 14.

As sin hath reigned unto death, even so might grace reign through righteousness unto eternal life by Jesus Christ our Lord. *Ro.* 5: 21.

Let not sin therefore reign in your mortal body. *Ro.* 6: 12.

So ordain I in all churches. *1 Co.* 7: 17.

As many as walk according to this rule, peace be on them. *Ga.* 6: 16.

We wrestle . . . against the rulers of the darkness of this world. *Ep.* 6: 12.

Whereto we have already attained, let us walk by the same rule. *Ph.* 3: 16.

Let the peace of God rule in your hearts. *Col.* 3: 15.

We shall reign on the earth. *Re.* 5: 10.

See also

Christ, the King; Commandment; Dominion; God, Commandment of; God, the King; God, Kingdom of; God, Law of; Government; Law; Order; Precept; Principle; Realm; Reign.

Rule, Golden

Thou shalt love thy neighbour as thyself: I am the Lord. *Le.* 19: 18.

As thou hast done, it shall be done unto thee. *Ob.* 1: 15.

Therefore all things whatsoever ye would that men should do to you, do ye even so to them: for this is the law and the prophets. *Mat.* 7: 12.

As ye would that men should do to you, do ye also to them likewise. *Lu.* 6: 31.

Give, and it shall be given unto you. *Lu.* 6: 38.

All the law is fulfilled in one word, even in this; Thou shalt love thy neighbour as thyself. *Ga.* 5: 14.

See that none render evil for evil unto any man; but ever follow that which is good, both among yourselves, and to all men. *1 Th.* 5: 15.

The end of the commandment is charity out of a pure heart. *1 Ti.* 1: 5.

Rust

Lay not up for yourselves treasures upon earth, where moth and rust doth corrupt. *Mat.* 6: 19.

Your gold and silver is cankered; and the rust of them shall be a witness against you. *Ja.* 5: 3.

S

Sabbath

Remember the sabbath day, to keep it holy. *Ex.* 20: 8.

My sabbaths ye shall keep: for it is a sign between me and you throughout your generations. *Ex.* 31: 13.

It shall be a sabbath of rest unto you. *Le.* 16: 31.

This is the day which the Lord hath made; we will rejoice and be glad in it. *Ps.* 118: 24.

Blessèd is the man . . . that keepeth the sabbath from polluting it. *Is.* 56: 2.

If thou . . . call the sabbath a delight, the holy of the Lord, honourable; and shalt

honour him, not doing thine own ways, nor finding thine own pleasure, nor speaking thine own words: Then shalt thou delight thyself in the Lord; and I will cause thee to ride upon the high places of the earth. *Is.* 58: 13, 14.

It shall come to pass, that from one new moon to another, and from one sabbath to another, shall all flesh come to worship before me, saith the Lord. *Is.* 66: 23.

Take heed to yourselves, and bear no burden on the sabbath day. *Je.* 17: 21.

Thou hast . . . profaned my sabbaths. *Eze.* 22: 8.

I will also cause all her mirth to cease, her

feast days, her new moons, and her sabbaths, and all her solemn feasts. *Ho.* 2: 11.

The Son of man is Lord even of the sabbath day. *Mat.* 12: 8.

The sabbath was made for man. *Mk.* 2: 27.

See also

Church, Attendance at; Sunday.

Sacrament

It is the Lord's passover. *Ex.* 12: 11.

They shall teach my people the difference between the holy and profane, and cause them to discern between the unclean and the clean. *Eze.* 44: 23.

It is given unto you to know the mysteries of the kingdom of heaven. *Mat.* 13: 11.

He that believeth and is baptized shall be saved. *Mk.* 16: 16.

He went into the house of God, and did take and eat the shewbread. *Lu.* 6: 4.

The Son of man is Lord also of the sabbath. *Lu.* 6: 5.

Except ye repent, ye shall all likewise perish. *Lu.* 13: 3.

This cup is the new testament in my blood: this do ye, as oft as ye drink it, in remembrance of me. *1 Co.* 11: 25.

See also

Celebration; Ceremony; Formalism; Observance; Ritual; Sacredness.

Sacredness

Speak unto all the congregation of the children of Israel, and say unto them, Ye shall be holy: for I the Lord your God am holy. *Le.* 19: 2.

The beauty of holiness. *2 Ch.* 20: 21.

Holiness becometh thine house, O Lord, for ever. *Ps.* 93: 5.

He preserveth the souls of his saints. *Ps.* 97: 10.

Let them praise thy great and terrible name; for it is holy. *Ps.* 99: 3.

The Lord is righteous in all his ways, and holy in all his works. *Ps.* 145: 17.

Hallowed be thy name. *Mat.* 6: 9.

Glorify God in your body, and in your spirit, which are God's. *1 Co.* 6: 20.

Sanctify the Lord God in your hearts. *1 Pe.* 3: 15.

See also

Christ, Holiness of; God, Holiness of; Ground, Holy; Holiness; Sacrament; Saint; Sanctification; Sanctuary.

Sacrifice

To what purpose is the multitude of your sacrifices unto me? *Is.* 1: 11.

Bring your sacrifices every morning. *Am.* 4: 4.

If thy right hand offend thee, cut it off, and cast it from thee. *Mat.* 5: 30.

Whosoever will come after me, let him deny himself, and take up his cross, and follow me. *Mk.* 8: 34.

If thy hand offend thee, cut it off: it is better for thee to enter into life maimed, than having two hands to go into hell. *Mk.* 9: 43.

To love him with all the heart, . . . and to love his neighbour as himself, is more than all whole burnt offerings and sacrifices. *Mk.* 12: 33.

He saved others; himself he cannot save. *Mk.* 15: 31.

Of a truth I say unto you, that this poor widow hath cast in more than they all: For all these have of their abundance cast in unto the offerings of God: but she of her penury hath cast in all the living that she had. *Lu.* 21: 3, 4.

He must increase, but I must decrease. *Jn.* 3: 30.

He prophesied that Jesus should die for that nation; And not for that nation only, but that also he should gather together in one the children of God that were scattered abroad. *Jn.* 11: 51, 52.

Peter said unto him, Lord, why cannot I follow thee now? I will lay down my life for thy sake. *Jn.* 13: 37.

Greater love hath no man than this, that a man lay down his life for his friends. *Jn.* 15: 13.

I beseech you therefore, brethren, by the mercies of God, that ye present your bodies a living sacrifice, holy, acceptable unto God, which is your reasonable service. *Ro.* 12: 1.

Though I give my body to be burned, and have not charity, it profiteth me nothing. *1 Co.* 13: 3.

Christ died for our sins according to the scriptures. *1 Co.* 15: 3.

I will very gladly spend and be spent for you. *2 Co.* 12: 15.

They that are Christ's have crucified the flesh with the affections and lusts. *Ga.* 5: 24.

I am now ready to be offered, and the time of my departure is at hand. I have fought a good fight, I have finished my course, I have kept the faith. *2 Ti.* 4: 6, 7.

Sacrifice and offering thou wouldest not, but a body hast thou prepared me. *He.* 10: 5.

By faith Abraham, when he was tried, offered up Isaac. *He.* 11: 17.

Choosing rather to suffer affliction with the people of God, than to enjoy the pleasures of sin for a season. *He.* 11: 25.

Esteeming the reproach of Christ greater riches than the treasures of Egypt. *He.* 11: 26.

See also

Christ, Cross of; Christ, Sacrifice of; Christ, Suffering of; Cross; Offering; Self-Forgetfulness; Self-Sacrifice; Victim.

Sacrilege

He hath profaned the hallowed thing of the Lord. *Le.* 19: 8.

They shall therefore keep mine ordinance, lest they bear sin for it, and die therefore, if they profane it. *Le.* 22: 9.

They shall not profane the holy things. *Le.* 22: 15.

Blessed is the man that . . . keepeth the sabbath from polluting it. *Is.* 56: 2.

Ye pollute yourselves with all your idols. *Eze.* 20: 31.

They profaned my holy name. *Eze.* 36: 20.

They shall pollute the sanctuary of strength. *Da.* 11: 31.

The thorn and the thistle shall come up on their altars. *Ho.* 10: 8.

Her priests have polluted the sanctuary, they have done violence to the law. *Zph.* 3: 4.

Judah hath profaned the holiness of the Lord. *Mal.* 2: 11.

On the sabbath days the priests in the temple profane the sabbath, and are blameless. *Mat.* 12: 5.

See also

Defilement; Pollution; Profanity.

Sadness

The bread of affliction. *De.* 16: 3.

Her countenance was no more sad. *1 S.* 1: 18.

Why is thy countenance sad, seeing thou art not sick? this is nothing else but sorrow of heart. *Ne.* 2: 2.

I am poor and sorrowful: let thy salvation, O God, set me up on high. *Ps.* 69: 29.

By the sadness of the countenance the heart is made better. *Ec.* 7: 3.

Blessed are ye that weep now: for ye shall laugh. *Lu.* 6: 21.

Ye shall weep and lament, but the world shall rejoice. *Jn.* 16: 20.

Ye shall be sorrowful, but your sorrow shall be turned into joy. *Jn.* 16: 20.

I would not have you to be ignorant, brethren, concerning them which are asleep, that ye sorrow not, even as others which have no hope. *1 Th.* 4: 13.

God shall wipe away all tears from their eyes. *Re.* 7: 17.

See also

Christ, Sorrow of; Dejection; Depression; Grief; Lamentation; Melancholy; Mourning; Sorrow; Tear.

Safety

His children are far from safety, and they are crushed in the gate, neither is there any to deliver them. *Jb.* 5: 4.

I laid me down and slept; I awaked; for the Lord sustained me. *Ps.* 3: 5.

Thou preparest a table before me in the presence of mine enemies. *Ps.* 23: 5.

Fret not thyself because of evildoers. *Ps.* 37: 1.

Hold thou me up, and I shall be safe. *Ps.* 119: 117.

The horse is prepared against the day of battle: but safety is of the Lord. *Pr.* 21: 31.

Whoso putteth his trust in the Lord shall be safe. *Pr.* 29: 25.

The firstborn of the poor shall feed, and the needy shall lie down in safety. *Is.* 14: 30.

Thou wilt keep him in perfect peace, whose mind is stayed on thee: because he trusteth in thee. *Is.* 26: 3.

I will break the bow and the sword and the battle out of the earth, and will make them to lie down safely. *Ho.* 2: 18.

They shall sit every man under his vine and under his fig tree; and none shall make them afraid. *Mi.* 4: 4.

When they shall say, Peace and safety; then sudden destruction cometh upon them. *1 Th.* 5: 3.

Who is he that will harm you, if ye be followers of that which is good? *1 Pe.* 3: 13.

See also

Christ, the Saviour; God, Salvation of; God, Security of; Salvation; Security; Shelter.

Sage

Should a wise man utter vain knowledge? *Jb.* 15: 2.

It [wisdom] cannot be gotten for gold, neither shall silver be weighed for the price thereof. *Jb.* 28: 15.

Where shall wisdom be found? and where is the place of understanding? *Jb.* 28 :12.

I cannot find one wise man among you. *Jb.* 17: 10.

A wise man will hear, and will increase learning. *Pr.* 1: 5.

A man of understanding shall attain unto wise counsels. *Pr.* 1: 5.

Rebuke a wise man, and he will love thee. *Pr.* 9: 8.

Give instruction to a wise man, and he will be yet wiser. *Pr.* 9: 9.

Seest thou a man wise in his own conceit? there is more hope of a fool than of him. *Pr.* 26: 12.

A fool uttereth all his mind: but a wise man keepeth it in till afterwards. *Pr.* 29: 11.

The wise man's eyes are in his head; but the fool walketh in darkness. *Ec.* 2: 14.

How dieth the wise man? as the fool. *Ec.* 2: 16.

The heart of the wise is in the house of mourning; but the heart of fools is in the house of mirth. *Ec.* 7: 4.

It is better to hear the rebuke of the wise, than for a man to hear the song of fools. *Ec.* 7: 5.

A poor wise man . . . by his wisdom delivered the city; yet no man remembered that same poor man. *Ec.* 9: 15.

The words of wise men are heard in quiet more than the cry of him that ruleth among fools. *Ec.* 9: 17.

Wisdom is better than weapons of war. *Ec.* 9: 18.

Let not the wise man glory in his wisdom. *Je.* 9: 23.

God gave them knowledge and skill in all learning and wisdom. *Da.* 1: 17.

They that be wise shall shine as the brightness of the firmament. *Da.* 12: 3.

My people are destroyed for lack of knowledge. *Ho.* 4: 6.

Whence hath this man this wisdom, and these mighty works? *Mat.* 13: 54.

See also

Intelligence; Knowledge; Learning; Mind; Sanity; Understanding; Wisdom.

Sailor

They that go down to the sea in ships, that do business in great waters; These see the works of the Lord, and his wonders in the deep. *Ps.* 107: 23, 24.

Thy tacklings are loosed; they could not well strengthen their mast, they could not spread their sail. *Is.* 33: 23.

Fine linen with broidered work from Egypt was that which thou spreadest forth to be thy sail. *Eze.* 27: 7.

As they sailed he fell asleep: and there came down a storm of wind on the lake. *Lu.* 8: 23.

When sailing was now dangerous, . . . Paul admonished them, And said unto them, Sirs, I perceive that this voyage will be with hurt and much damage, not only of the lading and ship, but also of our lives. *Ac.* 27: 9, 10.

Lo, God hath given thee all them that sail with thee. *Ac.* 27: 24.

Every shipmaster, and all the company in ships, and sailors, and as many as trade by sea, stood afar off. *Re.* 18: 17.

See also

Ocean; Sea; Ship; Voyage.

Saint

Sanctify yourselves: for to morrow the Lord will do wonders among you. *Jos.* 3: 5.

He will keep the feet of his saints. *1 S.* 2: 9.

Our fathers trusted in thee: they trusted, and thou didst deliver them. *Ps.* 22: 4.

The Lord loveth judgment, and forsaketh not his saints. *Ps.* 37: 28.

Then shall the righteous shine forth as the sun in the kingdom of their Father. *Mat.* 13: 43.

He was a just man and a holy. *Mk.* 6: 20.

Called to be saints. *Ro.* 1: 7.

Fellowcitizens with the saints, and of the household of God. *Ep.* 2: 19.

With all saints. *Ep.* 3: 18.

All the saints salute you, chiefly they that are of Caesar's household. *Ph.* 4: 22.

When Christ, who is our life, shall appear, then shall ye also appear with him in glory. *Col.* 3: 4.

Are they not all ministering spirits. *He.* 1: 14.

See also

Godliness; Holiness; Sanctification; Sanctuary.

Salt

His wife looked back from behind him, and she became a pillar of salt. *Ge.* 19: 26.

He took the city, and slew the people that was therein, and beat down the city, and sowed it with salt. *Ju.* 9: 45.

Can that which is unsavoury be eaten without salt? or is there any taste in the white of an egg? *Jb.* 6: 6.

In the day thou wast born, . . . thou wast not salted at all, nor swaddled at all. *Eze.* 16: 4.

Ye are the salt of the earth. *Mat.* 5: 13.

Every one shall be salted with fire, and every sacrifice shall be salted with salt. *Mk.* 9: 49.

Have salt in yourselves, and have peace one with another. *Mk.* 9: 50.

Salt is good: but if the salt have lost his savour, wherewith shall it be seasoned? *Lu.* 14: 34.

Let your speech be always with grace, seasoned with salt, that ye may know how ye ought to answer every man. *Col.* 4: 6.

So can no fountain both yield salt water and fresh. *Ja.* 3: 12.

See also

Savor; Taste.

Salutation

He hath clothed me with the garments of salvation, he hath covered me with the robe of righteousness. *Is.* 61: 10.

If ye salute your brethren only, what do ye more than others? *Mat.* 5: 47.

They . . . love . . . greetings in the markets, and to be called of men, Rabbi, Rabbi. *Mat.* 23: 5-7.

Salute one another with an holy kiss. The churches of Christ salute you. *Ro.* 16: 16.

All the brethren greet you. Greet ye one another with an holy kiss. *1 Co.* 16: 20.

The grace of our Lord Jesus Christ be with you. *1 Co.* 16: 23.

All the saints salute you. *2 Co.* 13: 13.

Grace be to you, and peace. *Ep.* 1: 2.

Our friends salute thee. *3 Jn.* 1: 14.

Salvation

Let us make a joyful noise to the rock of our salvation. *Ps.* 95: 1.

I will take the cup of salvation, and call upon the name of the Lord. *Ps.* 116: 13.

The harvest is past, the summer is ended, and we are not saved. *Je.* 8: 20.

The Lord thy God in the midst of thee is mighty; he will save, he will rejoice over thee with joy; he will rest in his love, he will joy over thee with singing. *Zph.* 3: 17.

Whosoever will lose his life for my sake shall find it. *Mat.* 16: 25.

Thy faith hath saved thee; go in peace. *Lu.* 7: 50.

Strive to enter in at the strait gate. *Lu.* 13: 24.

Many, I say unto you, will seek to enter in, and shall not be able. *Lu.* 13: 24.

This thy brother was dead, and is alive again; and was lost, and is found. *Lu.* 15: 32.

By the righteousness of one the free gift came upon all men unto justification of life. *Ro.* 5: 18.

The gift of God is eternal life through Jesus Christ our Lord. *Ro.* 6: 23.

He that spared not his own Son, but delivered him up for us all, how shall he not with him also freely give us all things? *Ro.* 8: 32.

Now is our salvation nearer than when we believed. *Ro.* 13: 11.

He himself shall be saved; yet so as by fire. *1 Co.* 3: 15.

Thanks be unto God for his unspeakable gift. *2 Co.* 9: 15.

By grace are ye saved through faith. *Ep.* 2: 8.

Work out your own salvation with fear and trembling. *Ph.* 2: 12.

If the righteous scarcely be saved, where shall the ungodly and the sinner appear? *1 Pe.* 4: 18.

An entrance shall be ministered unto you abundantly into the everlasting kingdom of our Lord and Saviour Jesus Christ. *2 Pe.* 1: 11.

The Lord is not slack concerning his promise, as some men count slackness; but is long-suffering to us-ward, not willing that any should perish, but that all should come to repentance. *2 Pe.* 3: 9.

The common salvation. *Jude* 1: 3.

See also

Christ, the Redeemer; Christ, the Saviour; Deliverance; God, Deliverance of; God, the Redeemer; God, Salvation of; Ransom; Redemption; Rescue; Restoration; Safety; Security; Succor.

Samaritan

Into any city of the Samaritans enter ye not. *Mat.* 10: 5.

A certain Samaritan, as he journeyed, came

where he was. *Lu.* 10: 33.

Which now of these three, thinkest thou, was neighbour unto him that fell among the thieves? *Lu.* 10: 36.

Go, and do thou likewise. *Lu.* 10: 37.

One of them . . . fell down on his face at his feet, giving him thanks: and he was a Samaritan. *Lu.* 17: 15, 16.

How is it that thou, being a Jew, askest drink of me, which am a woman of Samaria? *Jn.* 4: 9.

The Jews have no dealings with the Samaritans. *Jn.* 4: 9.

Many of the Samaritans of that city believed on him. *Jn.* 4: 39.

The Samaritans . . . besought him that he would tarry with them. *Jn.* 4: 40.

Say we not well that thou art a Samaritan, and hast a devil? *Jn.* 8: 48.

They . . . preached the gospel in many villages of the Samaritans. *Ac.* 8: 25.

Sanctification

Ye shall be holy: for I the Lord your God am holy. *Le.* 19: 2.

Sanctify yourselves therefore, and be ye holy: for I am the Lord your God. *Le.* 20: 7.

I am the Lord which hallow you. *Le.* 22: 32.

For their sakes I sanctify myself, that they also might be sanctified through the truth. *Jn.* 17: 19.

That they may receive forgiveness of sins, and inheritance among them which are sanctified by faith that is in me. *Ac.* 26: 18.

To them that are sanctified in Christ Jesus, called to be saints. *1 Co.* 1: 2.

Who of God is made unto us wisdom, and righteousness, and sanctification, and redemption. *1 Co.* 1: 30.

But ye are washed, but ye are sanctified, but ye are justified in the name of the Lord Jesus, and by the Spirit of our God. *1 Co.* 6: 11.

Put on the new man, which after God is created in righteousness and true holiness. *Ep.* 4: 24.

Who shall change our vile body, that it may be fashioned like unto his glorious body. *Ph.* 3: 21.

This is the will of God, even your sanctification. *1 Th.* 4: 3.

God hath not called us unto uncleanness, but unto holiness. *1 Th.* 4: 7.

By one offering he hath perfected for ever them that are sanctified. *He.* 10: 14.

Jesus also, that he might sanctify the people with his own blood, suffered without the gate. *He.* 13: 12.

Through sanctification of the Spirit. *1 Pe.* 1: 2.

See also

Consecration; Dedication; Purification; Saint.

Sanctuary

Surely the Lord is in this place; and I knew it not. *Ge.* 28: 16.

This is none other but the house of God, and this is the gate of heaven. *Ge.* 28: 17.

Ye shall keep my sabbaths, and reverence my sanctuary. *Le.* 19: 30.

The Lord hath chosen thee to build an house for the sanctuary: be strong, and do it. *1 Ch.* 28: 10.

The Lord is in his holy temple. *Ps.* 11: 4.

Lord, I have loved the habitation of thy house. *Ps.* 26: 8.

Until I went into the sanctuary. *Ps.* 73: 17.

He that dwelleth in the secret place of the most High shall abide under the shadow of the Almighty. *Ps.* 91: 1.

Strength and beauty are in his sanctuary. *Ps.* 96: 6.

Cause thy face to shine upon thy sanctuary that is desolate. *Da.* 9: 17.

Peter answered and said to Jesus, Master, it is good for us to be here. *Mk.* 9: 5.

Take these things hence; make not my Father's house an house of merchandise. *Jn.* 2: 16.

Put off thy shoes from thy feet: for the place where thou standest is holy ground. *Ac.* 7: 33.

The temple of God is holy, which temple ye are. *1 Co.* 3: 17.

They . . . serve him day and night in his temple. *Re.* 7: 15.

I John saw the holy city. *Re.* 21: 2.

See also

Church; God, the Refuge; Ground, Holy; Refuge; Synagogue; Temple.

Sand

I will multiply thy seed as the stars of the heaven, and as the sand which is upon the sea shore. *Ge.* 22: 17.

Oh that my grief were throughly weighed, and my calamity laid in the balances together! For now it would be heavier than the sand of the sea. *Jb.* 6: 2, 3.

He rained flesh also upon them as dust, and feathered fowls like as the sand of the sea. *Ps.* 78: 27.

If I should count them, they are more in number than the sand. *Ps.* 139: 18.

A stone is heavy, and the sand weighty; but a fool's wrath is heavier than them both. *Pr.* 27: 3.

Fear ye not me? saith the Lord: will ye not tremble at my presence, which have placed the sand for the bound of the sea by a perpetual decree, that it cannot pass it: and though the waves thereof toss themselves, yet can they not prevail; though they roar, yet can they not pass over it? *Je.* 5: 22.

A foolish man . . . built his house upon the sand. *Mat.* 7: 26.

I stood upon the sand of the sea, and saw a beast rise up out of the sea. *Re.* 13: 1.

See also

Aridity; Desert; Dryness.

Sanity

Let Pharaoh look out a man discreet and wise. *Ge.* 41: 33.

Should a wise man . . . reason with unprofitable talk? *Jb.* 15: 2, 3.

God . . . hath taken away my judgment. *Jb.* 27: 2.

A good man . . . will guide his affairs with discretion. *Ps.* 112: 5.

Discretion shall preserve thee, understanding shall keep thee. *Pr.* 2: 11.

My son, . . . keep sound wisdom and discretion. *Pr.* 3: 21.

I applied mine heart to know, and to search,

and to seek out wisdom, and the reason of things, and to know the wickedness of folly. *Ec.* 7: 25.

A wise man's heart discerneth both time and judgment. *Ec.* 8: 5.

At the same time my reason returned unto me. *Da.* 4: 36.

Think soberly. *Ro.* 12: 3.

Young men likewise exhort to be sober minded. *Tit.* 2: 6.

Gird up the loins of your mind. *1 Pe.* 1: 13.

See also

Insanity; Sage.

Satan

The serpent said unto the woman, Ye shall not surely die. *Ge.* 3: 4.

Satan went forth from the presence of the Lord. *Jb.* 1: 12.

Let Satan stand at his right hand. *Ps.* 109: 6.

The Lord rebuke thee, O Satan. *Zch.* 3: 2.

If Satan cast out Satan, he is divided against himself. *Mat.* 12: 26.

Then cometh the wicked one, and catcheth away that which was sown in his heart. *Mat.* 13: 19.

The tares are the children of the wicked one. *Mat.* 13: 38.

He was there in the wilderness forty days, tempted of Satan. *Mk.* 1: 13.

If thou therefore wilt worship me, all shall be thine. *Lu.* 4: 7.

I beheld Satan as lightning fall from heaven. *Lu.* 10: 18.

From the power of Satan unto God. *Ac.* 26: 18.

The god of this world hath blinded the minds of them which believe not. *2 Co.* 4: 4.

Then shall that Wicked be revealed, whom the Lord shall consume with the spirit of his mouth, and shall destroy with the brightness of his coming. *2 Th.* 2: 8.

That through death he might destroy him that had the power of death, that is, the devil. *He.* 2: 14.

Be vigilant; because your adversary the devil, as a roaring lion, walketh about, seeking whom he may devour. *1 Pe.* 5: 8.

Contending with the devil. *Jude* 1: 9.

I know thy works, and' where thou dwellest, even where Satan's seat is. *Re.* 2: 13.

The synagogue of Satan. *Re.* 3: 9.

When the thousand years are expired, Satan shall be loosed out of his prison. *Re.* 20: 7.

See also

Devil; Fiend; Lucifer.

Satiety

The meek shall eat and be satisfied. *Ps.* 22: 26.

Thou shalt make them drink of the river of thy pleasures. *Ps.* 36: 8.

In the days of famine they shall be satisfied. *Ps.* 37: 19.

He watereth the hills from his chambers. *Ps.* 104: 13.

The righteous eateth to the satisfying of his soul. *Pr.* 13: 25.

A good man shall be satisfied from himself. *Pr.* 14: 14.

The eyes of man are never satisfied. *Pr.* 27: 20.

The eye is not satisfied with seeing, nor the ear filled with hearing. *Ec.* 1: 8.

He shall snatch on the right hand, and be hungry; and he shall eat on the left hand, and they shall not be satisfied. *Is.* 9: 20.

It shall even be as when an hungry man dreameth, and, behold, he eateth; but he awaketh, and his soul is empty: or as when a thirsty man dreameth, and, behold, he drinketh; but he awaketh, and, behold, he is faint, and his soul hath appetite. *Is.* 29: 8.

My people shall be satisfied with my goodness, saith the Lord. *Je.* 31: 14.

I have satiated the weary soul, and I have replenished every sorrowful soul. *Je.* 31: 25.

They shall eat, and not have enough. *Ho.* 4: 10.

Behold, I will send you corn, and wine, and oil, and ye shall be satisfied therewith. *Jo.* 2: 19.

See also

Insanity; Sage Satisfaction.

Satisfaction

The Lord recompense thy work, and a full reward be given thee. *Ru.* 2: 12.

The Lord gave them rest round about. *2 Ch.* 15: 15.

I shall be satisfied, when I awake, with thy likeness. *Ps.* 17: 15.

Thou hatest instruction, and castest my words behind thee. *Ps.* 50: 17.

With long life will I satisfy him. *Ps.* 91: 16.

Bless the Lord, . . . Who satisfieth thy mouth with good things. *Ps.* 103: 2, 5.

Thou openest thine hand, and satisfiest the desire of every living thing. *Ps.* 145: 16.

When the desire cometh, it is a tree of life. *Pr.* 13: 12.

As cold waters to a thirsty soul, so is good news from a far country. *Pr.* 25: 25.

Better is an handful with quietness, than both the hands full with travail and vexation of spirit. *Ec.* 4: 6.

Ho, every one that thirsteth, come ye to the waters, and he that hath no money; come ye, buy, and eat; yea, come, buy wine and milk without money and without price. *Is.* 55: 1.

The floors shall be full of wheat, and the fats shall overflow with wine and oil. *Jo.* 2: 24.

Blessed are ye that hunger now: for ye shall be filled. *Lu.* 6: 21.

It is your Father's good pleasure to give you the kingdom. *Lu.* 12: 32.

Whosoever drinketh of the water that I shall give him shall never thirst. *Jn.* 4: 14.

I have learned, in whatsoever state I' am, therewith to be content. *Ph.* 4: 11.

They shall hunger no more, neither thirst any more; neither shall the sun light on them, nor any heat. *Re.* 7: 16.

See also

Adequacy; Amends; Atonement; Compensation; Contentment; Pleasure; Plenty; Propitiation; Recompense; Satiety; Sufficiency.

Savage

He will be a wild man; his hand will be against every man, and every man's hand against him. *Ge.* 16: 12.

He grew, and dwelt in the wilderness. *Ge.* 21: 20.

Cursed be their anger, for it was fierce; and

their wrath, for it was cruel. *Ge.* 49: 7.

They that dwell in the wilderness shall bow before him. *Ps.* 72: 9.

I am like a pelican of the wilderness. *Ps.* 102: 6.

They wandered through the wilderness. *Is.* 16: 8.

There met him two possessed with devils, coming out of the tombs, exceeding fierce. *Mat.* 8: 28.

See also
Ferocity.

Savior

The Lord . . . saveth such as be of contrite spirit. *Ps.* 34: 18.

The Lord redeemeth the soul of his servants. *Ps.* 34: 22.

My soul shall be joyful in the Lord: it shall rejoice in his salvation. *Ps.* 35: 9.

They cry unto the Lord in their trouble, and he saveth them out of their distresses. *Ps.* 107: 19.

My salvation is gone forth, and mine arms shall judge the people. *Is.* 51: 5.

Thou, O Lord, art our father, our redeemer. *Is.* 63: 16.

The Son of man is come to seek and to save that which was lost. *Lu.* 19: 10.

Behold the Lamb of God, which taketh away the sin of the world. *Jn.* 1: 29.

Believe on the Lord Jesus Christ, and thou shalt be saved, and thy house. *Ac.* 16: 31.

According to his mercy he saved us. *Tit.* 3: 5.

He is able also to save them to the uttermost. *He.* 7: 25.

Salvation ready to be revealed in the last time. *1 Pe.* 1: 5.

The Father sent the Son to be the Saviour of the world. *1 Jn.* 4: 14.

See also
Christ, the Redeemer; Christ, the Saviour; Deliverance; God, Deliverance of; God, the Redeemer; God, Salvation of; Redemption; Rescue; Restoration.

Savor

The Lord smelled a sweet savour; and the Lord said in his heart, I will not again curse the ground. *Ge.* 8: 21.

Make me savoury meat, such as I love, and bring it to me, that I may eat. *Ge.* 27: 4.

I will not smell the savour of your sweet odours. *Le.* 26: 31.

Ye are the salt of the earth. *Mat.* 5: 13.

Thou savourest not the things that be of God, but those that be of men. *Mat.* 16: 23.

Thanks be unto God, which . . . maketh manifest the savour of his knowledge by us in every place. *2 Co.* 2: 14.

We are unto God a sweet savour of Christ, in them that are saved, and in them that perish. *2 Co.* 2: 15.

To the one we are the savour of death unto death; and to the other the savour of life unto life. *2 Co.* 2: 16.

Christ also hath loved us, and hath given himself for us an offering and a sacrifice to God for a sweetsmelling savour. *Ep.* 5: 2.

See also
Perfume; Salt; Scent; Smell; Taste.

Saying

This their way is their folly: yet their posterity approve their sayings. *Ps.* 49: 13.

A man of understanding shall attain unto wise counsels: To understand a proverb, and the interpretation; the words of the wise, and their dark sayings. *Pr.* 1: 5, 6.

My son, attend to my words; incline thine ear unto my sayings. *Pr.* 4: 20.

Let these sayings sink down into your ears: for the Son of man shall be delivered into the hands of men. *Lu.* 9: 44.

He that loveth me not keepeth not my sayings. *Jn.* 14: 24.

These are the true sayings of God. *Re.* 19: 9.

These sayings are faithful and true. *Re.* 22: 6.

See also
Byword; Fable; Parable; Proverb; Word.

Scandal

Be sure your sin will find you out. *Nu.* 32: 23.

Why do ye such things? for I hear of your evil dealings by all this people. *1 S.* 2: 23.

I have heard the slander of many. *Ps.* 31: 13.

He that hideth hatred with lying lips, and he that uttereth a slander, is a fool. *Pr.* 10: 18.

In thee are men that carry tales to shed blood. *Eze.* 22: 9.

I know your manifold transgressions and your mighty sins: they afflict the just, they take a bribe, and they turn aside the poor in the gate from their right. *Am.* 5: 12.

The Son of man shall send forth his angels, and they shall gather out of his kingdom all things that offend, and them which do iniquity. *Mat.* 13: 41.

If thine eye offend thee, pluck it out. *Mk.* 9: 47.

That which ye have spoken in the ear in closets shall be proclaimed upon the housetops. *Lu.* 12: 3.

It is impossible but that offences will come: but woe unto him, through whom they come! *Lu.* 17: 1.

We be slanderously reported. *Ro.* 3: 8.

Mark them which cause divisions and offences. *Ro.* 16: 17.

Even so must their wives be grave, not slanderers. *1 Ti.* 3: 11.

There is none occasion of stumbling in him. *1 Jn.* 2: 10.

See also
Calumny; Gossip; Slander.

Scapegoat

I the Lord thy God am a jealous God, visiting the iniquity of the fathers upon the children unto the third and fourth generation of them that hate me. *Ex.* 20: 5.

Let him go for a scapegoat into the wilderness. *Le.* 16: 10.

The goat shall bear upon him all their iniquities unto a land not inhabited. *Le.* 16: 22.

For thy sake I have borne reproach. *Ps.* 69: 7.

Surely he hath borne our griefs, and carried our sorrows. *Is.* 53: 4.

He was wounded for our transgressions, he was bruised for our iniquities: the chastisement of our peace was upon him; and with his stripes we are healed. *Is.* 53: 5.

My righteous servant . . . shall bear their iniquities. *Is.* 53: 11.

He shall not die for the iniquity of his father, he shall surely live. *Eze.* 18: 17.

The son shall not bear the iniquity of the father, neither shall the father bear the iniquity of the son: the righteousness of the righteous shall be upon him, and the wickedness of the wicked shall be upon him. *Eze.* 18: 20.

I, if I be lifted up from the earth, will draw all men unto me. *Jn.* 12: 32.

God hath not appointed us to wrath, but to obtain salvation by our Lord Jesus Christ, Who died for us. *1 Th.* 5: 9, 10.

Christ was once offered to bear the sins of many. *He.* 9: 28.

See also

Christ, Cross of; Christ, the Lamb of God; Christ, Sacrifice of; Christ, Suffering of.

Scarlet

Bind this line of scarlet thread in the window which thou didst let us down by. *Jos.* 2: 18.

She is not afraid of the snow for her household: for all her household are clothed with scarlet. *Pr.* 31: 21.

Though your sins be as scarlet, they shall be as white as snow. *Is.* 1: 18.

They stripped him, and put on him a scarlet robe. *Mat.* 27: 28.

Scent

Through the scent of water it will bud, and bring forth boughs like a plant. *Jb.* 14: 9.

Noses have they, but they smell not. *Ps.* 115: 6.

Thy name is as ointment poured forth. *S. of S.* 1: 3.

A bundle of myrrh is my well-beloved unto me. *S. of S.* 1: 13.

Perfumed with myrrh and frankincense. *S. of S.* 3: 6.

His taste remained in him, and his scent is not changed. *Je.* 48: 11.

The scent thereof shall be as the wine of Lebanon. *Ho.* 14: 7.

They . . . prepared spices and ointments. *Lu.* 23: 56.

We are unto God a sweet savour of Christ. *2 Co.* 2: 15.

See also

Fragrance; Incense; Odor; Perfume; Savor; Smell; Tasted.

Schism

Suppose ye that I am come to give peace on earth? I tell you, Nay; but rather division. *Lu.* 12: 51.

Mark them which cause divisions; . . . and avoid them. *Ro.* 16: 17.

Every one of you saith, I am of Paul; and I of Apollos; and I of Cephas; and I of Christ. *1 Co.* 1: 12.

Whereas there is among you envying, and strife, and divisions, are ye not carnal, and walk as men? *1 Co.* 3: 3.

I hear that there be divisions among you; and I partly believe it. *1 Co.* 11: 18.

As the body is one, and hath many members, and all the members of that one body, being many, are one body: so also is Christ. *1 Co.* 12: 12.

That there should be no schism in the body. *1 Co.* 12: 25.

What part hath he that believeth with an infidel? *2 Co.* 6: 15.

See also

Denomination; Division; Heresy; Orthodoxy; Sect; Separation; Teaching, False.

School

As well the small as the great, the teacher as the scholar. *1 Ch.* 25: 8.

Blessed is the man whom thou chastenest, O Lord, and teachest him out of thy law. *Ps.* 94: 12.

I am the Lord thy God which teacheth thee to profit. *Is.* 48: 17.

The Lord will cut off the man that doeth this, the master and the scholar. *Mal.* 2: 12.

Take my yoke upon you, and learn of me; for I am meek and lowly in heart; and ye shall find rest unto your souls. *Mat.* 11: 29.

Disputing daily in the school of one Tyrannus. *Ac.* 19: 9.

The law was our schoolmaster to bring us unto Christ. *Ga.* 3: 24.

After that faith is come, we are no longer under a schoolmaster. *Ga.* 3: 25.

See also

Christ, the Teacher; Education; Instruction; Knowledge; Pupil; Study; Teaching; Training.

Science

The tree of knowledge of good and evil. *Ge.* 2: 9.

Keep sound wisdom: . . . Then shalt thou walk in thy way safely, and thy foot shall not stumble. *Pr.* 3: 21, 23.

Say unto wisdom, Thou art my sister; and call understanding thy kinswoman. *Pr.* 7: 4.

I wisdom dwell with prudence, and find out knowledge of witty inventions. *Pr.* 8: 12.

Wise men lay up knowledge. *Pr.* 10: 14.

Wisdom strengtheneth the wise more than ten mighty men which are in the city. *Ec.* 7: 19.

I applied mine heart to know, and to search, and to seek out wisdom, and the reason of things. *Ec.* 7: 25.

If the iron be blunt, and he do not whet the edge, then must he put to more strength: but wisdom is profitable to direct. *Ec.* 10: 10.

Thy wisdom and thy knowledge, it hath perverted thee. *Is.* 47: 10.

Children . . . skilful in wisdom, and cunning in knowledge, and understanding science. *Da.* 1: 4.

Filled with all knowledge. *Ro.* 15: 14.

The natural man receiveth not the things of the Spirit of God: for they are foolishness unto him: neither can he know them, because they are spiritually discerned. *1 Co.* 2: 14.

Avoiding profane and vain babblings, and oppositions of science falsely so called. *1 Ti.* 6: 20.

See also

Knowledge; Learning; Wisdom.

Scorn

Wherefore hast thou despised the commandment of the Lord, to do evil in his sight? *2 S. 12: 9.*

They mocked the messengers of God, and despised his words, and misused his prophets, until the wrath of the Lord arose against his people, till there was no remedy. *2 Ch. 36: 16.*

They laughed us to scorn, and despised us, and said, What is this thing that ye do? *Ne. 2: 19.*

Blessed is the man that walketh not in the counsel of the ungodly, nor standeth in the way of sinners, nor sitteth in the seat of the scornful. *Ps. 1: 1.*

Let the lying lips be put to silence; which speak grievous things proudly and contemptuously against the righteous. *Ps. 31: 18.*

Our soul is exceedingly filled with the scorning of those that are at ease, and with the contempt of the proud. *Ps. 123: 4.*

Fools despise wisdom and instruction. *Pr. 1: 7.*

How have I hated instruction, and my heart despised reproof. *Pr. 5: 12.*

He that is void of wisdom despiseth his neighbour. *Pr. 11: 12.*

Whoso mocketh the poor reproacheth his Maker. *Pr. 17: 5.*

He was despised, and we esteemed him not. *Is. 53: 3.*

They despised my judgments, which if a man do, he shall even live in them. *Eze. 20: 13.*

They shall scoff at the kings, and the princes shall be a scorn unto them: they shall deride every strong hold. *Hab. 1: 10.*

Take heed that ye despise not one of these little ones. *Mat. 18: 10.*

They shall mock him, and shall scourge him, and shall spit upon him, and shall kill him. *Mk. 10: 34.*

They laughed him to scorn, knowing that she was dead. *Lu. 8: 53.*

He therefore that despiseth, despiseth not man, but God. *1 Th. 4: 8.*

Others had trial of cruel mockings and scourgings. *He. 11: 36.*

See also

Contempt; Disdain; Dishonor; Haughtiness; Pride.

Scourge

Beware of men: for they will deliver you up to the councils, and they will scourge you in their synagogues. *Mat. 10: 17.*

When he had scourged Jesus, he delivered him to be crucified. *Mat. 27: 26.*

When he had made a scourge of small cords, he drove them all out of the temple. *Jn. 2: 15.*

Is it lawful for you to scourge a man that is a Roman, and uncondemned? *Ac. 22: 25.*

Others had trial of cruel mockings and scourgings. *He. 11: 36.*

Whom the Lord loveth he chasteneth, and scourgeth every son whom he receiveth. *He. 12: 6.*

See also

Chastisement; Discipline; God, Chastisement of; God, Punishment of; Punishment; Rod; Stripe; Tribulation.

Scout

The Lord went before them . . . to search out a resting place for them. *Nu. 10: 33.*

Moses sent them to spy out the land of Canaan. *Nu. 13: 17.*

See . . . what the land is that they dwell in, whether it be good or bad; and what cities they be that they dwell in, whether in tents, or in strong holds. *Nu. 13: 18, 19.*

Be ye of good courage, and bring of the fruit of the land. *Nu. 13: 20.*

They went up, and searched the land. *Nu. 13: 21.*

The land, which we passed through to search it, is an exceeding good land. *Nu. 14: 7.*

Thou shalt prepare thee a way. *De. 19: 3.*

The ants are a people not strong, yet they prepare their meat in the summer. *Pr. 30: 25.*

Be thou prepared. *Eze. 38: 7.*

Prepare ye the way of the Lord, make his paths straight. *Mat. 3: 3.*

That servant, which knew his lord's will, and prepared not himself, neither did according to his will, shall be beaten with many stripes. *Lu. 12: 47.*

If I go and prepare a place for you, I will come again. *Jn. 14: 3.*

He hath prepared for them a city. *He. 11: 16.*

The four angels were loosed, which were prepared for an hour, and a day, and a month, and a year. *Re. 9: 15.*

See also

Exploration; Preparation; Search; Spy; Survey.

Scribe

Except your righteousness shall exceed the righteousness of the scribes and Pharisees, ye shall in no case enter into the kingdom of heaven. *Mat. 5: 20.*

He taught them as one having authority, and not as the scribes. *Mat. 7: 29.*

Every scribe which is instructed unto the kingdom of heaven is like unto a man that is an householder, which bringeth forth out of his treasure things new and old. *Mat. 13: 52.*

From that time forth began Jesus to shew unto his disciples, how that he must . . . suffer many things of the elders and chief priests and scribes. *Mat. 16: 21.*

The Son of man shall be betrayed unto the chief priests and unto the scribes, and they shall condemn him to death. *Mat. 20: 18.*

The Son of man must suffer many things, and be rejected of the elders, and of the chief priests, and scribes. *Mk. 8: 31.*

The scribes and the chief priests heard it, and sought how they might destroy him. *Mk. 11: 18.*

Beware of the scribes, which love to go in long clothing, and love salutations in the marketplaces. *Mk. 12: 38.*

Immediately, while he yet spake, cometh Judas, one of the twelve, and with him a great multitude with swords and staves, from the chief priests and the scribes and the elders. *Mk. 14: 43.*

Where is the wise? where is the scribe? where is the disputer of this world? hath not God made foolish the wisdom of this world? *1 Co. 1: 20.*

See also

Author; Teaching; Writing.

Scripture

The writing was the writing of God, graven upon the tables. *Ex.* **32: 16.**

Ye shall not add unto the word which I command you, neither shall ye diminish aught from it. *De.* **4: 2.**

Man doth not live by bread only, but by every word that proceedeth out of the mouth of the Lord doth man live. *De.* **8: 3.**

Neither have I gone back from the commandment of his lips; I have esteemed the words of his mouth more than my necessary food. *Jb.* **23: 12.**

How sweet are thy words unto my taste! yea, sweeter than honey to my mouth. *Ps.* **119: 103.**

Seek ye out of the book of the Lord, and read. *Is.* **34: 16.**

Thy words were found, and I did eat them; and thy word was unto me the joy and rejoicing of mine heart. *Je.* **15: 16.**

Ye do err, not knowing the scriptures, nor the power of God. *Mat.* **22: 29.**

Did not our heart burn within us, while he talked with us by the way, and while he opened to us the scriptures? *Lu.* **24: 32.**

Search the scriptures; for in them ye think ye have eternal life. *Jn.* **5: 39.**

As yet they knew not the scripture, that he must rise again from the dead. *Jn.* **20: 9.**

What saith the scripture? *Ro.* **4: 3.**

Whatsoever things were written aforetime were written for our learning, that we through patience and comfort of the scriptures might have hope. *Ro.* **15: 4.**

Christ died for our sins according to the scriptures; . . . he was buried, and . . . rose again according to the scriptures. *1 Co.* **15: 3, 4.**

From a child thou hast known the holy scriptures. *2 Ti.* **3: 15.**

All scripture is given by inspiration of God, and is profitable for doctrine, for reproof, for correction, for instruction in righteousness. *2 Ti.* **3: 16.**

The word of God is quick, and powerful, and sharper than any twoedged sword, . . . and is a discerner of the thoughts and intents of the heart. *He.* **4: 12.**

Receive with meekness the engrafted word, which is able to save your souls. *Ja.* **1: 21.**

The word of God *1 Pe.* **1: 23.**

No prophecy of the scripture is of private interpretation. *2 Pe.* **1: 20.**

If any man shall take away from the words of the book of this prophecy, God shall take away his part out of the book of life, and out of the holy city, and from the things which are written in this book. *Re.* **22: 19.**

See also

Author; Bible; God, Word of; Life, Book of; Testament, New; Testament, Old; Scroll; Writing.

Scroll

Let them be blotted out of the book of the living, and not be written with the righteous. *Ps.* **69: 28.**

Of making many books there is no end. *Ec.* **12: 12.**

Take thee a great roll, and write in it with a man's pen. *Is.* **8: 1.**

The heavens shall be rolled together as a scroll. *Is.* **34: 4.**

Go thou, and read in the roll, which thou hast written from my mouth, the words of the Lord. *Je.* **36: 6.**

When I looked, behold, an hand was sent unto me; and, lo, a roll of a book was therein; And he spread it before me; and it was written within and without: and there was written therein lamentations, and mourning, and woe. *Eze.* **2: 9, 10.**

I suppose that even the world itself could not contain the books that should be written. *Jn.* **21: 25.**

Whose names are in the book of life. *Ph.* **4: 3.**

What thou seest, write in a book. *Re.* **1: 11.**

The heaven departed as a scroll when it is rolled together; and every mountain and island were moved out of their places. *Re.* **6: 14.**

Another book was opened, which is the book of life. *Re.* **20: 12.**

See also

Book; Scripture; Writing.

Sea

God gave Solomon . . . largeness of heart, even as the sand that is on the sea shore. *1 K.* **4: 29.**

He hath compassed the waters with bounds. *Jb.* **26: 10.**

Hitherto shalt thou come, but no further: and here shall thy proud waves be stayed. *Jb.* **38: 11.**

Deep calleth unto deep. *Ps.* **42: 7.**

He shall have dominion also from sea to sea. *Ps.* **72: 8.**

The sea is his, and he made it: and his hands formed the dry land. *Ps.* **95: 5.**

They that go down to the sea in ships, that do business in great waters; These see the works of the Lord, and his wonders in the deep. *Ps.* **107: 23, 24.**

Out of the depths have I cried unto thee, O Lord. *Ps.* **130: 1.**

The earth shall be full of the knowledge of the Lord, as the waters cover the sea. *Is.* **11: 9.**

How art thou destroyed, that wast inhabited of seafaring men. *Eze.* **26: 17.**

Thou wilt cast all their sins into the depths of the sea. *Mi.* **7: 19.**

He arose, and rebuked the winds and the sea. *Mat.* **8: 26.**

All our fathers . . . passed through the sea. *1 Co.* **10: 1.**

The sea gave up the dead which were in it. *Re.* **20: 13.**

There was no more sea. *Re.* **21: 1.**

See also

Ocean; Sailor; Voyage; Water; Wave.

Seal

The vision of all is become unto you as the words of a book that is sealed. *Is.* **29: 11.**

He that hath received his testimony hath set to his seal that God is true. *Jn.* **3: 33.**

Labour not for the meat which perisheth, but for that meat which endureth unto everlasting life, which the Son of man shall give unto you: for him hath God the Father sealed. *Jn.* **6: 27.**

He received the sign of circumcision, a seal

of the righteousness of the faith. *Ro.* 4: 11.

The seal of mine apostleship are ye in the Lord. *1 Co.* 9: 2.

God . . . hath also sealed us, and given the earnest of the Spirit in our hearts. *2 Co.* 1: 21, 22.

In whom also after that ye believed, ye were sealed with that Holy Spirit of promise. *Ep.* 1: 13.

Grieve not the Holy Spirit of God, whereby ye are sealed unto the day of redemption. *Ep.* 4: 30.

The foundation of God standeth sure, having this seal, The Lord knoweth them that are his. *2 Ti.* 2: 19.

I saw in the right hand of him that sat on the throne a book, . . . sealed with seven seals. *Re.* 5: 1.

Thou art worthy to take the book, and to open the seals thereof. *Re.* 5: 9.

Seal not the sayings of the prophecy in this book: for the time is at hand. *Re.* 22: 10.

See also

Assurance; Pledge; Sign.

Search

Canst thou by searching find out God? *Jb.* 11: 7.

Search me, O God, and know my heart. *Ps.* 139: 23.

There came wise men from the east to Jerusalem, Saying, Where is he that is born King of the Jews? for we have seen his star in the east, and are come to worship him. *Mat.* 2: 1, 2.

Seek ye first the kingdom of God. *Mat.* 6: 33.

All men seek for thee. *Mk.* 1: 37.

Seek, and ye shall find. *Lu.* 11: 9.

The Father seeketh such to worship him. *Jn.* 4: 23.

The Spirit searcheth all things, yea, the deep things of God. *1 Co.* 2: 10.

Seek that ye may excel to the edifying of the church. *1 Co.* 14: 12.

I follow after, if that I may apprehend that for which also I am apprehended of Christ Jesus. *Ph.* 3: 12.

They seek a country. *He.* 11: 14.

See also

Christ, Quest for; Examination; Exploration; God, Quest for; God, Search for; Hunt; Life, Quest of; Quest; Scout; Seeker.

Season

Let there be lights in the firmament of the heaven to divide the day from the night; and let them be for signs, and for seasons, and for days, and years. *Ge.* 1: 14.

A tree . . . bringeth forth his fruit in his season. *Ps.* 1: 3.

He appointed the moon for seasons. *Ps.* 104: 19.

To every thing there is a season, and a time to every purpose under the heaven. *Ec.* 3: 1.

A time to get, and a time to lose; a time to keep, and a time to cast away. *Ec.* 3: 6.

Thrust in thy sharp sickle, and gather the clusters of the vine of the earth; for her grapes are fully ripe. *Re.* 14: 18.

See also

Autumn; Harvest; Spring; Summer; Time; Winter.

Seat

Oh that I knew where I might find him! that I might come even to his seat! *Jb.* 23: 3.

Blessed is the man that walketh not in the counsel of the ungodly, . . . nor sitteth in the seat of the scornful. *Ps.* 1: 1.

A foolish woman . . . sitteth at the door of her house, on a seat in the high places of the city. *Pr.* 9: 13, 14.

Thine heart is lifted up, and thou hast said, I am a god, I sit in the seat of God, in the midst of the seas; yet thou art a man, and not God. *Eze.* 28: 2.

The scribes and the Pharisees sit in Moses' seat. *Mat.* 23: 2.

They . . . love the uppermost rooms at feasts, and the chief seats in the synagogues. *Mat.* 23: 5, 6.

He hath put down the mighty from their seats, and exalted them of low degree. *Lu.* 1: 52.

See also

Place.

Seclusion

Israel then shall dwell in safety alone. *De.* 33: 28.

He himself went a day's journey into the wilderness. *1 K.* 19: 4.

Thou shalt keep them secretly in a pavilion from the strife of tongues. *Ps.* 31: 20.

They wandered in the wilderness in a solitary way. *Ps.* 107: 4.

Thy sleep shall be sweet. *Pr.* 3: 24.

Bread eaten in secret is pleasant. *Pr.* 9: 17.

They shall sit every man under his vine and under his fig tree; and none shall make them afraid. *Mi.* 4: 4.

Then was Jesus led up of the spirit into the wilderness. *Mat.* 4: 1.

What went ye out into the wilderness to see? *Mat.* 11: 7.

When Jesus therefore perceived that they would come and take him by force, to make him a king, he departed again into a mountain himself alone. *Jn.* 6: 15.

This thing was not done in a corner. *Ac.* 26: 26.

He carried me away in the spirit into the wilderness. *Re.* 17: 3.

See also

Christ, Loneliness of; Isolation; Loneliness; Privacy.

Second

And of every living thing of all flesh, two of every sort shalt thou bring into the ark. *Ge.* 6: 19.

There is one alone, and there is not a second. *Ec.* 4: 8.

The word of the Lord came unto Jonah the second time. *Jon.* 3: 1.

The second is like unto it, Thou shalt love thy neighbour as thyself. *Mat.* 22: 39.

This is again the second miracle that Jesus did, when he was come out of Judæa into Galilee. *Jn.* 4: 54.

The second man is the Lord from heaven. *1 Co.* 15: 47.

Death and hell were cast into the lake of fire. This is the second death. *Re.* 20: 14.

Secrecy

The secret things belong unto the Lord our God: but those things which are revealed belong unto us and to our children for ever. *De.* 29: 29.

The children of Israel did secretly those things that were not right against the Lord their God. *2 K.* 17: 9.

The murderer rising with the light killeth the poor and needy, and in the night is as a thief. *Jb.* 24: 14.

In the dark they dig through houses, which they had marked for themselves in the day-time: they know not the light. *Jb.* 24: 16.

He made darkness his secret place. *Ps.* 18: 11.

Thou shalt keep them secretly in a pavilion from the strife of tongues. *Ps.* 31: 20.

He knoweth the secrets of the heart. *Ps.* 44: 21.

Thou hast set our iniquities before thee, our secret sins in the light of thy countenance. *Ps.* 90: 8.

He that dwelleth in the secret place of the most High shall abide under the shadow of the Almighty. *Ps.* 91: 1.

God shall bring every work into judgment, with every secret thing, whether it be good, or whether it be evil. *Ec.* 12: 14.

Then said he unto me, Son of man, hast thou seen what the ancients of the house of Israel do in the dark, every man in the chambers of his imagery? for they say, The Lord seeth us not; the Lord hath forsaken the earth. *Eze.* 8: 12.

There is nothing covered, that shall not be revealed; neither hid, that shall not be known. *Lu.* 12: 2.

Every one that doeth evil hateth the light, neither cometh to the light, lest his deeds should be reproved. *Jn.* 3: 20.

Howbeit no man spake openly of him for fear of the Jews. *Jn.* 7: 13.

This thing was not done in a corner. *Ac.* 26: 26.

God shall judge the secrets of man. *Ro.* 2: 16.

Let us therefore cast off the works of darkness, and let us put on the armour of light. *Ro.* 13: 12.

Thus are the secrets of his heart made manifest. *1 Co.* 14: 25.

Have no fellowship with the unfruitful works of darkness, but rather reprove them. *Ep.* 5: 11.

They that be drunken are drunken in the night. *1 Th.* 5: 7.

See also

Apocrypha; Christ, the Hidden; Christ, Mystery of; Cloud; God, the Hiding; Mystery; Privacy; Stealth; Veil.

Sect

The sect of the Sadducees. *Ac.* 5: 17.

The sect of the Pharisees. *Ac.* 15: 5.

A ringleader of the sect of the Nazarenes. *Ac.* 24: 5.

After the most straitest sect of our religion I lived a Pharisee. *Ac.* 26: 5.

As concerning this sect, we know that every where it is spoken against. *Ac.* 28: 22.

Mark them which cause divisions and offences contrary to the doctrine which ye have learned; and avoid them. *Ro.* 16: 17.

I beseech you, brethren, . . . that ye all speak the same thing, and that there be no divisions among you. *1 Co.* 1: 10.

Is Christ divided? was Paul crucified for you? or were ye baptized in the name of Paul? *1 Co.* 1: 13.

There are diversities of administrations, but the same Lord. *1 Co.* 12: 5.

See also

Church, Divisions of; Denomination; Division; Heresy; Orthodoxy; Schism; Separation.

Secularism

Money answereth all things. *Ec.* 10: 19.

A wonderful and horrible thing is committed in the land; The prophets prophesy falsely, and the priests bear rule by their means; and my people love to have it so. *Je.* 5: 30, 31.

This is the rejoicing city that dwelt carelessly, that said in her heart, I am, and there is none beside me: how is she become a desolation, a place for beasts to lie down in! every one that passeth by her shall hiss, and wag his hand. *Zph.* 2: 15.

They were troubled, because there was no shepherd. *Zch.* 10: 2.

The care of this world, and the deceitfulness of riches, choke the word. *Mat.* 13: 22.

They made light of it, and went their ways, one to his farm, another to his merchandise. *Mat.* 22: 5.

It might have been sold for more than three hundred pence. *Mk.* 14: 5.

Martha was cumbered about much serving. *Lu.* 10: 40.

Ye are of this world; I am not of this world. *Jn.* 8: 23.

Be not conformed to this world. *Ro.* 12: 2.

The wisdom of this world is foolishness with God. *1 Co.* 3: 19.

Jesus Christ . . . gave himself for our sins, that he might deliver us from this present evil world. *Ga.* 1: 3, 4.

The love of money is the root of all evil. *1 Ti.* 6: 10.

Charge them that are rich in this world, that they be not highminded. *1 Ti.* 6: 17.

Denying ungodliness and worldly lusts, we should live soberly. *Tit.* 2: 12.

The first covenant had . . . a worldly sanctuary. *He.* 9: 1.

See also

Worldliness.

Security

We will build sheepfolds here for our cattle, and cities for our little ones. *Nu.* 32: 16.

With me thou shalt be in safeguard. *1 S.* 22: 23.

The Lord preserved David whithersoever he went. *2 S.* 8: 6.

Their houses are safe from fear. *Jb.* 21: 9.

Thou, Lord, only makest me dwell in safety. *Ps.* 4: 8.

Thou shalt guide me with thy counsel, and afterward receive me to glory. *Ps.* 73: 24.

He led them on safely, so that they feared not. *Ps.* 78: 53.

His heart is fixed, trusting in the Lord. *Ps.* 112: 7.

Then shalt thou walk in thy way safely, and

thy foot shall not stumble. *Pr.* 3: 23.

Thou shalt lie down, and thy sleep shall be sweet. *Pr.* 3: 24.

Devise not evil against thy neighbour, seeing he dwelleth securely by thee. *Pr.* 3: 29.

The wolf also shall dwell with the lamb. *Is.* 11: 6.

My people shall dwell in . . . sure dwellings. *Is.* 32: 18.

We have a building of God, an house not made with hands. *2 Co.* 5: 1.

When they shall say, Peace and safety; then sudden destruction cometh upon them, as travail upon a woman with child. *1 Th.* 5: 3.

Which hope we have as an anchor of the soul, both sure and stedfast. *He.* 6: 19.

The Lord is my helper, and I will not fear what man shall do unto me. *He.* 13: 6.

Who is he that will harm you, if ye be followers of that which is good? *1 Pe.* 3: 13.

Peace be with you all that are in Christ Jesus. *1 Pe.* 5: 14.

See also

Asylum; Certainty; Christ, the Saviour; Defence; Ease; Fortress; God, Salvation of; God, Security of; Protection; Safety; Salvation; Shelter.

Seduction

The serpent beguiled me, and I did eat. *Ge.* 3: 13.

Entice him, and see wherein his great strength lieth. *Ju.* 16: 5.

They flatter with their tongue. *Ps.* 5: 9.

If sinners entice thee, consent thou not. *Pr.* 1: 10.

That they may keep thee from the strange woman, from the stranger which flattereth with her words. *Pr.* 7: 5.

With her much fair speech she caused him to yield, with the flattering of her lips she forced him. *Pr.* 7: 21.

The righteous is more excellent than his neighbour: but the way of the wicked seduceth them. *Pr.* 12: 26.

A violent man enticeth his neighbour. *Pr.* 16: 29.

A man that flattereth his neighbour spreadeth a net for his feet. *Pr.* 29: 5.

As the fishes that are taken in an evil net, and as the birds that are caught in the snare; so are the sons of men snared in an evil time. *Ec.* 9: 12.

Peradventure he will be enticed, and we shall prevail against him. *Je.* 20: 10.

They have seduced my people, saying, Peace; and there was no peace. *Eze.* 13: 10.

Such as do wickedly against the covenant shall he corrupt by flatteries. *Da.* 11: 32.

The days shall come upon you, that he will take you away with hooks, and your posterity with fishhooks. *Am.* 4: 2.

This I say, lest any man should beguile you with enticing words. *Col.* 2: 4.

Some shall depart from the faith, giving heed to seducing spirits. *1 Ti.* 4: 1.

Evil men and seducers shall wax worse and worse. *2 Ti.* 3: 13.

They allure through the lusts of the flesh. *2 Pe.* 2: 18.

See also

Allurement; Temptation.

Seed

While the earth remaineth, seedtime and harvest . . . shall not cease. *Ge.* 8: 22.

I will make thy seed as the dust of the earth. *Ge.* 13: 16.

In thy seed shall all the nations of the earth be blessed. *Ge.* 22: 18.

His soul shall dwell at ease; and his seed shall inherit the earth. *Ps.* 25: 13.

I have been young, and now am old; yet have I not seen the righteous forsaken, nor his seed begging bread. *Ps.* 37: 25.

The children of thy servants shall continue, and their seed shall be established before thee. *Ps.* 102: 28.

He that goeth forth and weepeth, bearing precious seed, shall doubtless come again with rejoicing, bringing his sheaves with him. *Ps.* 126: 6.

To him that soweth righteousness shall be a sure reward. *Pr.* 11: 18.

The seed of the righteous shall be delivered. *Pr.* 11: 21.

There is that scattereth, and yet increaseth. *Pr.* 11: 24.

In the morning sow thy seed, and in the evening withhold not thine hand. *Ec.* 11: 6.

Blessed are ye that sow beside all waters. *Is.* 32: 20.

I had planted thee a noble vine, wholly a right seed: how then art thou turned into the degenerate plant of a strange vine unto me? *Je.* 2: 21.

Ye shall know them by their fruits. *Mat.* 7: 16.

So is the kingdom of God, as if a man should cast seed into the ground; And should sleep, and rise night and day, and the seed should spring and grow up, he knoweth not how. *Mk.* 4: 26, 27.

A sower went out to sow his seed. *Lu.* 8: 5.

The seed is the word of God. *Lu.* 8: 11.

Of this man's seed hath God according to his promise raised unto Israel a Saviour, Jesus. *Ac.* 13: 23.

To every seed his own body. *1 Co.* 15: 38.

It is sown a natural body; it is raised a spiritual body. *1 Co.* 15: 44.

He which soweth bountifully shall reap also bountifully. *2 Co.* 9: 6.

Whatsoever a man soweth, that shall he also reap. *Ga.* 6: 7.

He that soweth to the Spirit shall of the Spirit reap life everlasting. *Ga.* 6: 8.

See also

Child; Cultivation; Descent; Generation; Grain; Offspring; Plant.

Seeker

Enquire, I pray thee, of the former age. *Jb.* 8: 8.

My spirit made diligent search. *Ps.* 77: 6.

They . . . enquired early after God. *Ps.* 78: 34.

Search me, O God, and know my heart: try me, and know my thoughts. *Ps.* 139: 23.

The Lord is nigh unto all them that call upon him, to all that call upon him in truth. *Ps.* 145: 18.

If thou criest after knowledge, and liftest up thy voice for understanding; If thou seekest her as silver, and searchest for her as for hid treasures; Then shalt thou understand the fear of the Lord. *Pr. 2: 3-5.*

There is no searching of his understanding. *Is. 40: 28.*

Seek ye the Lord while he may be found, call ye upon him while he is near. *Is. 55: 6.*

I the Lord search the heart. *Je. 17: 10.*

Ye shall seek me, and find me, when ye shall search for me with all your heart. *Je. 29: 13.*

Seek good, and not evil, that ye may live. *Am. 5: 14.*

They shall wander from sea to sea, and from the north even to the east, they shall run to and fro to seek the word of the Lord, and shall not find it. *Am. 8: 12.*

All men seek for thee. *Mk. 1: 37.*

What woman having ten pieces of silver, if she lose one piece, doth not light a candle, and sweep the house, and seek diligently till she find it? *Lu. 15: 8.*

Search the scriptures; for in them ye think ye have eternal life: and they are they which testify of me. *Jn. 5: 39.*

He that searcheth the hearts knoweth what is the mind of the Spirit. *Ro. 8: 27.*

See also

Christ, Quest for; God, Quest for; God, Search for; Inquiry; Life, Quest of; Quest; Search.

Segregation

Cursed be Canaan; a servant of servants shall he be unto his brethren. *Ge. 9: 25.*

Thou shalt not let thy cattle gender with a diverse kind. *Le. 19: 19.*

Ye shall therefore put difference between clean beasts and unclean. *Le. 20: 25.*

Ye shall be holy unto me: for I the Lord am holy, and have severed you from other people, that ye should be mine. *Le. 20: 26.*

Ye have transgressed, and have taken strange wives. *Ezr. 10: 10.*

The Lord hath utterly separated me from his people. *Is. 56: 3.*

Her priests . . . have put no difference between the holy and profane, neither have they shewed difference between the unclean and the clean. *Eze. 22: 26.*

Thou wentest in to men uncircumcised, and didst eat with them. *Ac. 11: 3.*

Come out from among them, and be ye separate, saith the Lord, and touch not the unclean thing. *2 Co. 6: 17.*

See also

Integration; Prejudice; Separation.

Selection

Choose us out men, and go out. *Ex. 17: 9.*

The Lord thy God hath chosen thee to be a special people unto himself, above all people that are upon the face of the earth. *De. 7: 6.*

Choose life, that both thou and thy seed may live. *De. 30: 19.*

Choose you this day whom ye will serve. *Jos. 24: 15.*

The Lord said unto Gideon, By the three hundred men that lapped will I save you, and deliver the Midianites into thine hand. *Ju. 7: 7.*

Blessed is the man whom thou choosest, and causest to approach unto thee. *Ps. 65: 4.*

I have chosen thee, and not cast thee away. *Is. 41: 9.*

Behold my servant, whom I uphold; mine elect, in whom my soul delighteth. *Is. 42: 1.*

And many lepers were in Israel in the time of Eliseus the prophet; and none of them was cleansed, saving Naaman the Syrian. *Lu. 4: 27.*

Mary hath chosen that good part, which shall not be taken away from her. *Lu. 10: 42.*

Ye have not chosen me, but I have chosen you, and ordained you, that ye should go and bring forth fruit, and that your fruit should remain. *Jn. 15: 16.*

I have chosen you out of the world, therefore the world hateth you. *Jn. 15: 19.*

He is a chosen vessel unto me. *Ac. 9: 15.*

The God of this people of Israel chose our fathers. *Ac. 13: 17.*

The God of our fathers hath chosen thee. *Ac. 22: 14.*

God hath chosen the foolish things of the world to confound the wise; and God hath chosen the weak things of the world to confound the things which are mighty. *1 Co. 1: 27.*

He hath chosen us in him before the foundation of the world, that we should be holy and without blame before him in love. *Ep. 1: 4.*

Knowing, brethren beloved, your election of God. *1 Th. 1: 4.*

According to the faith of God's elect. *Tit. 1: 1.*

Give diligence to make your calling and election sure. *2 Pe. 1: 10.*

See also

Choice; Election; Foreordination; Predestination.

Self-Confidence

The Spirit of the Lord came upon Gideon, and he blew a trumpet. *Ju. 6: 34.*

The Spirit of the Lord will come upon thee, and thou shalt prophesy with them, and shalt be turned into another man. *1 S. 10: 6.*

Adonijah the son of Haggith exalted himself, saying, I will be king. *1 K. 1: 5.*

Let not him that is deceived trust in vanity. *Jb. 15: 31.*

His confidence shall be rooted out of his tabernacle. *Jb. 18: 14.*

In quietness and in confidence shall be your strength. *Is. 30: 15.*

Thou hast trusted in thy wickedness: thou hast said, None seeth me. *Is. 47: 10.*

They shall dwell safely therein, and shall build houses, and plant vineyards; yea, they shall dwell with confidence. *Eze. 28: 26.*

If he trust to his own righteousness, and commit iniquity, all his righteousnesses shall not be remembered. *Eze. 33: 13.*

Let the weak say, I am strong. *Jo. 3: 10.*

If the trumpet give an uncertain sound, who shall prepare himself to the battle? *1 Co 14: 8.*

We are always confident. *2 Co. 5: 6.*

Every man shall bear his own burden. *Ga. 6: 5.*

Cast not away therefore your confidence. *He. 10: 35.*

A double minded man is unstable in all his ways. *Ja. 1: 8.*

See also

Assurance; Boldness; Confidence.

Self-Control

Set a watch, O Lord, before my mouth; keep the door of my lips. *Ps.* 141: 3.

He that keepeth his mouth keepeth his life: but he that openeth wide his lips shall have destruction. *Pr.* 13: 3.

He that is slow to anger is better than the mighty; and he that ruleth his spirit than he that taketh a city. *Pr.* 16: 32.

He that hath no rule over his own spirit is like a city that is broken down, and without walls. *Pr.* 25: 28.

I know that the way of man is not in himself: it is not in man that walketh to direct his steps. *Je.* 10: 23.

Strait is the gate, and narrow is the way, which leadeth unto life. *Mat.* 7: 14.

Herein do I exercise myself, to have always a conscience void of offence toward God, and toward men. *Ac.* 24: 16.

Let not sin therefore reign in your mortal body. *Ro.* 6: 12.

Every man that striveth for the mastery is temperate in all things. *1 Co.* 9: 25.

The fruit of the Spirit is . . . temperance. *Ga.* 5: 22, 23.

We wrestle . . . against the rulers of the darkness of this world. *Ep.* 6: 12.

I will put my laws into their mind, and write them in their hearts. *He.* 8: 10.

If any man among you seem to be religious, and bridleth not his tongue, but deceiveth his own heart, this man's religion is vain. *Ja.* 1: 26.

If any man offend not in word, the same is a perfect man, and able also to bridle the whole body. *Ja.* 3: 2.

He that overcometh shall inherit all things; and I will be his God, and he shall be my son. *Re.* 21: 7.

See also

Abstinence; Continence; Control; Mastery; Restraint; Self-Sacrifice; Temperance.

Self-Expression

In those days there was no king in Israel, but every man did that which was right in his own eyes. *Ju.* 17: 6.

I will speak in the bitterness of my soul. *Jb.* 10: 1.

Hear diligently my speech, and my declaration with your ears. *Jb.* 13: 17.

Thy mouth uttereth thine iniquity. *Jb.* 15: 5.

Hearken to me; I also will shew mine opinion. *Jb.* 32: 10.

Most men will proclaim every one his own goodness. *Pr.* 20: 6.

A fool uttereth all his mind. *Pr.* 29: 11.

The vile person will speak villany. *Is.* 32: 6.

Set the trumpet to thy mouth. *Ho.* 8: 1.

They think that they shall be heard for their much speaking. *Mat.* 6: 7.

Those things which proceed out of the mouth come forth from the heart. *Mat.* 15: 18.

Out of the heart proceed evil thoughts. *Mat.* 15: 19.

Thy speech bewrayeth thee. *Mat.* 26: 73.

The wind bloweth where it listeth. *Jn.* 3: 8.

Though I speak with the tongues of men and of angels, and have not charity, I am become as sounding brass, or a tinkling cymbal. *1 Co.* 13: 1.

See also

Speech; Tongue; Utterance; Word.

Self-Forgetfulness

Now I know that thou fearest God, seeing that thou hast not withheld thy son, thine only son from me. *Ge.* 22: 12.

Not unto us, O Lord, not unto us, but unto thy name give glory. *Ps.* 115: 1.

He saved others; himself he cannot save. *Mat.* 27: 42.

He that hath two coats, let him impart to him that hath none. *Lu.* 3: 11.

Lend, hoping for nothing again. *Lu.* 6: 35.

Whosoever doth not bear his cross, and come after me, cannot be my disciple. *Lu.* 14: 27.

This poor widow hath cast in more than they all. *Lu.* 21: 3.

For their sakes I sanctify myself *Jn.* 17: 19.

I beseech you therefore, brethren, by the mercies of God, that ye present your bodies a living sacrifice. *Ro.* 12: 1.

For though I be free from all men, yet have I made myself servant unto all. *1 Co.* 9: 19.

I am nothing. *1 Co.* 13: 2.

Of myself I will not glory. *2 Co.* 12: 5.

Christ Jesus . . . made himself of no reputation, and took upon him the form of a servant. *Ph.* 2: 5, 7.

Christ Jesus . . . gave himself a ransom for all. *1 Ti.* 2: 5, 6.

See also

Christ, Cross of; Christ, Sacrifice of; Cross; Sacrifice; Self-Sacrifice.

Self-Realization

Ye shall be as gods, knowing good and evil. *Ge.* 3: 5.

There is a spirit in man, and the inspiration of the Almighty giveth them understanding. *Jb.* 32: 8.

Who knoweth the spirit of man that goeth upward? *Ec.* 3: 21.

When he came to himself. *Lu.* 15: 17.

He knew what was in man. *Jn.* 2: 25.

Know ye not that ye are the temple of God, and that the Spirit of God dwelleth in you? *1 Co.* 3: 16.

All things are yours. *1 Co.* 3: 21.

According to the power that worketh in us. *Ep.* 3: 20.

Put on the new man, which after God is created in righteousness and true holiness. *Ep.* 4: 24.

The hidden man of the heart. *1 Pe.* 3: 4.

That . . . ye might be partakers of the divine nature. *2 Pe.* 1: 4.

See also

Achievement; Completion; Fulfilment; Man, Greatness of; Perfection.

Self-Sacrifice

Bring an offering, and come into his courts. *Ps.* 96: 8.

He that cometh after me is mightier than I, whose shoes I am not worthy to bear. *Mat.* 3: 11.

He that loseth his life for my sake shall find it. *Mat.* 10: 39.

Lo, we have left all, and have followed thee. *Mk.* 10: 28.

There came a woman having an alabaster box of ointment of spikenard very precious; and she brake the box, and poured it on his head. *Mk.* 14: 3.

If any man will come after me, let him deny himself, and take up his cross daily, and follow me. *Lu.* 9: 23.

If any man come to me, and hate not his father, and mother, and wife, and children, and brethren. and sisters, . . . he cannot be my disciple. *Lu.* 14: 26.

He must increase, but I must decrease. *Jn.* 3: 30.

If it die, it bringeth forth much fruit. *Jn.* 12: 24.

He that loveth his life shall lose it. *Jn.* 12: 25.

Knowing this, that our old man is crucified with him, that the body of sin might be destroyed. *Ro.* 6: 6.

We then that are strong ought to bear the infirmities of the weak, and not to please ourselves. *Ro.* 15: 1.

Even Christ pleased not himself. *Ro.* 15: 3.

I keep under my body, and bring it into subjection: lest that by any means, when I have preached to others, I myself should be a castaway. *1 Co.* 9: 27.

I will very gladly spend and be spent for you; though the more abundantly I love you, the less I be loved. *2 Co.* 12: 15.

We are glad, when we are weak, and ye are strong: and this also we wish, even your perfection. *2 Co.* 13: 9.

They that are Christ's have crucified the flesh with the affections and lusts. *Ga.* 5: 24.

A bishop must be blameless, as the steward of God; not selfwilled. *Tit.* 1: 7.

By faith Moses, when he was come to years, refused to be called the son of Pharaoh's daughter. *He.* 11: 24.

That he no longer should live the rest of his time in the flesh to the lusts of men, but to the will of God. *1 Pe.* 4: 2.

Hereby perceive we the love of God, because he laid down his life for us: and we ought to lay down our lives for the brethren. *1 Jn.* 3: 16.

See also

Abasement; Abnegation; Cross; Denial; Humility; Sacrifice; Self-Forgetfulness; Suffering.

Self-Satisfaction

Talk no more so exceeding proudly; let not arrogancy come out of your mouth. *1 S.* 2: 3.

If I justify myself, mine own mouth shall condemn me. *Jb.* 9: 20.

Who can bring a clean thing out of an unclean? not one. *Jb.* 14: 4.

How long will ye love vanity? *Ps.* 4: 2.

He hath said in his heart, I shall not be moved: for I shall never be in adversity. *Ps.* 10: 6.

They speak loftily. *Ps.* 73: 8.

The way of a fool is right in his own eyes. *Pr.* 12: 15.

Most men will proclaim every one his own goodness. *Pr.* 20: 6.

Every way of a man is right in his own eyes. *Pr.* 21: 2.

Seest thou a man wise in his own conceit? there is more hope of a fool than of him. *Pr.* 26: 12.

He that trusteth in his own heart is a fool: but whoso walketh wisely, he shall be delivered. *Pr.* 28: 26.

Remove far from me vanity and lies. *Pr.* 30: 8.

There is a generation that are pure in their own eyes. *Pr.* 30: 12.

There is not a just man upon earth, that doeth good, and sinneth not. *Ec.* 7: 20.

The haughtiness of men shall be made low. *Is.* 2: 17.

Thou hast said in thine heart, I will ascend into heaven, I will exalt my throne above the stars of God. *Is.* 14: 13.

He shall bring down their pride together with the spoils of their hands. *Is.* 25: 11.

My people have committed two evils; they have forsaken me, the fountain of living waters, and hewed them out cisterns, broken cisterns, that can hold no water. *Je.* 2: 13.

Because I am innocent, surely his anger shall turn from me. *Je.* 2: 35.

Thou didst trust in thy way, in the multitude of thy mighty men. *Ho.* 10: 13.

They were filled, and their heart was exalted; therefore have they forgotten me. *Ho.* 13: 6.

The pride of thine heart hath deceived thee. *Ob.* 1: 3.

Think not to say within yourselves, We have Abraham to our father. *Mat.* 3: 9.

Grant that these my two sons may sit, the one on thy right hand, and the other on the left. in thy kingdom. But Jesus answered and said, Ye know not what ye ask. *Mat.* 20: 21, 22.

He, willing to justify himself, said unto Jesus. *Lu.* 10: 29.

Whosoever exalteth himself shall be abased. *Lu.* 14: 11.

God, I thank thee, that I am not as other men are. *Lu.* 18: 11.

They made a calf in those days, and offered sacrifice unto the idol, and rejoiced in the works of their own hands. *Ac.* 7: 41.

Giving out that himself was some great one. *Ac.* 8: 9.

That every mouth may be stopped, and all the world may become guilty before God. *Ro.* 3: 19.

Be not highminded. *Ro.* 11: 20.

I say, . . . to every man that is among you, not to think of himself more highly than he ought to think; but to think soberly. *Ro.* 12: 3.

Be not wise in your own conceits. *Ro.* 12: 16.

I know nothing by myself; yet am I not hereby justified: but he that judgeth me is the Lord. *1 Co.* 4: 4.

Who maketh thee to differ from another? and what hast thou that thou didst not receive? *1 Co.* 4: 7.

Let him that thinketh he standeth take heed lest he fall. *1 Co.* 10: 12.

Not that we are sufficient of ourselves to think any thing as of ourselves; but our sufficiency is of God. *2 Co.* 3: 5.

We dare not make ourselves of the number, or compare ourselves with some that commend themselves. *2 Co.* 10: 12.

Let us not be desirous of vainglory. *Ga.* **5: 26.**

God resisteth the proud. *1 Pe.* **5: 5.**

Presumptuous are they, selfwilled, they are not afraid to speak evil of dignities. *2 Pe.* **2: 10.**

See also

Arrogance; Boasting; Complacency; Conceit; Egotism; Haughtiness; Pride; Selfishness.

Selfishness

Doth Job fear God for nought? Hast thou not made an hedge about him, and about his house, and about all that he hath on every side? *Jb.* **1: 9, 10.**

Satan answered the Lord, and said, Skin for skin, yea, all that a man hath will he give for his life. *Jb.* **2: 4.**

He that withholdeth corn, the people shall curse him. *Pr.* **11: 26.**

I made me great works; I builded me houses; . . . and, behold, all was vanity. *Ec.* **2: 4, 11.**

Seemeth it a small thing unto you to have eaten up the good pasture, but ye must tread down with your feet the residue of your pastures? *Eze.* **34: 18.**

Israel is an empty vine, he bringeth forth fruit unto himself. *Ho.* **10: 1.**

I was a stranger, and ye took me not in. *Mat.* **25: 43.**

Ye entered not in yourselves, and them that were entering in ye hindered. *Lu.* **11: 52.**

Not only this our craft is in danger to be set at nought; but also that the temple of the great goddess Diana should be despised. *Ac.* **19: 27.**

Charity . . . seeketh not her own. *1 Co.* **13: 4, 5.**

Look not every man on his own things. *Ph.* **2: 4.**

See also

Complacency; Egotism; Parsimony; Self-Satisfaction.

Senility

Then shall ye bring down my gray hairs with sorrow to the grave. *Ge.* **42: 38.**

Moses was an hundred and twenty years old when he died: his eye was not dim, nor his natural force abated. *De.* **34: 7.**

The king . . . had no compassion upon young man or maiden, old man, or him that stooped for age. *2 Ch.* **36: 17.**

We are but of yesterday, and know nothing. *Jb.* **8: 9.**

Cast me not off in the time of old age; forsake me not when my strength faileth. *Ps.* **71: 9.**

While the evil days come not, nor the years draw nigh, when thou shalt say, I have no pleasure in them. *Ec.* **12: 1.**

In the day when the keepers of the house shall tremble, and the strong men shall bow themselves, and the grinders cease because they are few, and those that look out of the windows be darkened. *Ec.* **12: 3.**

The grasshopper shall be a burden, and desire shall fail: because man goeth to his long home. *Ec.* **12: 5.**

Strangers have devoured his strength, and he knoweth it not. *Ho.* **7: 9.**

Gray hairs are here and there upon him, yet he knoweth not. *Ho.* **7: 9.**

See also

Age; Oldness.

Senior

The elder shall serve the younger. *Ge.* **25: 23.**

Thou shalt rise up before the hoary head, and honour the face of the old man. *Le.* **19: 32.**

I will make him my firstborn, higher than the kings of the earth. *Ps.* **89: 27.**

A man hath no preëminence above a beast. *Ec.* **3: 19.**

Even to your old age I am he; and even to hoar hairs will I carry you. *Is.* **46: 4.**

Your sons and your daughters shall prophesy, your old men shall dream dreams, your young men shall see visions. *Jo.* **2: 28.**

The scribes . . . love . . . the chief seats in the synagogues. *Mk.* **12: 38, 39.**

He is the head of the body, the church: who is the beginning, the firstborn from the dead; that in all things he might have the preeminence. *Col.* **1: 18.**

Rebuke not an elder, but intreat him as a father. *1 Ti.* **5: 1.**

Against an elder receive not an accusation, but before two or three witnesses. *1 Ti.* **5: 19.**

Ye younger, submit yourselves unto the elder. *1 Pe.* **5: 5.**

Round about the throne were four and twenty seats: and upon the seats I saw four and twenty elders sitting, clothed in white raiment; and they had on their heads crowns of gold. *Re.* **4: 4.**

The four and twenty elders fell down and worshipped him that liveth for ever and ever. *Re.* **5: 14.**

See also

Age; Chief; Christ, the Leader; Elder; First; Head; Oldness; Superiority.

Sensationalism

Behold, I will put a fleece of wool in the floor; and if the dew be on the fleece only, and it be dry upon all the earth beside, then shall I know that thou wilt save Israel by mine hand, as thou hast said. *Ju.* **6: 37.**

The devil . . . setteth him on the pinnacle of the temple, And saith, . . . If thou be the Son of God, cast thyself down: for it is written, He shall give his angels charge concerning thee. *Mat.* **4: 5, 6.**

There shall arise false Christs, and false prophets, and shall shew great signs and wonders. *Mat.* **24: 24.**

Come down from the cross. *Mat.* **27: 40.**

This is an evil generation: they seek a sign; and there shall no sign be given it, but the sign of Jonas the prophet. *Lu.* **11: 29.**

Neither will they be persuaded, though one rose from the dead. *Lu.* **16: 31.**

A great multitude followed him, because they saw his miracles. *Jn.* **6: 2.**

Ye seek me, . . . because ye did eat of the loaves, and were filled. *Jn.* **6: 26.**

See also

Miracle; Sign; Wonder.

Sensitivity

The Lord hath not given you an heart to perceive, and eyes to see, and ears to hear. *De.* 29: 4.

Thy gentleness hath made me great. *2 S.* 22: 36.

Surely he shall not feel quietness. *Jb.* 20: 20.

God speaketh once, yea twice, yet man perceiveth it not. *Jb.* 33: 14.

As many as touched him were made whole. *Mk.* 6: 56.

Why beholdest thou the mote that is in thy brother's eye, but perceivest not the beam that is in thine own eye? *Lu.* 6: 41.

I perceive that virtue is gone out of me. *Lu.* 8: 46.

God hath tempered the body together. *1 Co.* 12: 24.

We have not an high priest which cannot be touched with the feeling of our infirmities. *He.* 4: 15.

Strong meat belongeth to them that are of full age, even those who by reason of use have their senses exercised to discern both good and evil. *He.* 5: 14.

Hereby perceive we the love of God, because he laid down his life for us. *1 Jn.* 3: 16.

See also

Feeling; Perception.

Sensuality

The mixt multitude that was among them fell a lusting. *Nu.* 11: 4.

He goeth after her straightway, as an ox goeth to the slaughter, or as a fool to the correction of the stocks. *Pr.* 7: 22.

Make no provision for the flesh, to fulfil the lusts thereof. *Ro.* 13: 14.

The flesh lusteth against the Spirit, and the Spirit against the flesh. *Ga.* 5: 17.

To enjoy the pleasures of sin for a season. *He.* 11: 25.

This wisdom descendeth not from above, but is earthly, sensual, devilish. *Ja.* 3: 15.

Ye have lived in pleasure on the earth, and been wanton. *Ja.* 5: 5.

These be they who separate themselves, sensual, having not the Spirit. *Jude* 1: 19.

See also

Adultery; Brothel; Carnality; Debauchery; Flesh; Fornication; Lust; Prostitute; Sin.

Sentiment

The children of Israel also wept again, and said, Who shall give us flesh to eat? We remember the fish, which we did eat in Egypt freely; the cucumbers, and the melons, and the leeks, and the onions, and the garlick. *Nu.* 11: 4, 5.

David and the people that were with him lifted up their voice and wept, until they had no more power to weep. *1 S.* 30: 4.

David longed, and said, Oh that one would give me drink of the water of the well of Bethlehem, which is by the gate! *2 S.* 23: 15.

Happy are thy men, happy are these thy servants, which stand continually before thee. *1 K.* 10: 8.

Why is thy countenance sad, seeing thou art not sick? this is nothing else but sorrow of heart. *Ne.* 2: 2.

Thy love is better than wine. *S. of S.* 1: 2.

Lovest thou me? *Jn.* 21: 17.

Being past feeling. *Ep.* 4: 19.

See that ye love one another with a pure heart fervently. *1 Pe.* 1: 22.

I have somewhat against thee, because thou hast left thy first love. *Re.* 2: 4.

See also

Emotion; Feeling.

Separation

Let there be a firmament in the midst of the waters, and let it divide the waters from the waters. *Ge.* 1: 6.

Is not the whole land before thee? separate thyself, I pray thee, from me. *Ge.* 13: 9.

The Lord do so to me, and more also, if ought but death part thee and me. *Ru.* 1: 17.

In their death they were not divided. *2 S.* 1: 23.

Depart ye, depart ye, go ye out from thence; . . . go ye out of the midst of her. *Is.* 52: 11.

Your iniquities have separated between you and your God. *Is.* 59: 2.

The anger of the Lord hath divided them. *La.* 4: 16.

Gather ye together first the tares, and bind them in bundles to burn them: but gather the wheat into my barn. *Mat.* 13: 30.

So shall it be at the end of the world: the angels shall come forth, and sever the wicked from among the just. *Mat.* 13: 49.

He shall separate them one from another, as a shepherd divideth his sheep from the goats. *Mat.* 25: 32.

Blessed are ye, when men shall hate you, and when they shall separate you from their company. *Lu.* 6: 22.

Between us and you there is a great gulf fixed. *Lu.* 16: 26.

In that night there shall be two men in one bed; the one shall be taken, and the other shall be left. *Lu.* 17: 34.

Whither I go, thou canst not follow me now; but thou shalt follow me afterwards. *Jn.* 13: 36.

Because ye are not of the world, but I have chosen you out of the world, therefore the world hateth you. *Jn.* 15: 19.

Save yourselves from this untoward generation. *Ac.* 2: 40.

Who shall separate us from the love of Christ? *Ro.* 8: 35.

Come out from among them, and be ye separate. *2 Co.* 6: 17.

Have no fellowship with the unfruitful works of darkness, but rather reprove them. *Ep.* 5: 11.

See also

Departure; Division; Heresy; Parting; Partition; Schism; Sect; Segregation.

Serenity

Which stilleth the noise of the seas, the noise of their waves, and the tumult of the people. *Ps.* 65: 7.

Return unto thy rest, O my soul. *Ps.* 116: 7.

When thou liest down, thou shalt not be afraid: yea, thou shalt lie down, and thy sleep shall be sweet. *Pr.* 3: 24.

The whole earth is at rest, and is quiet. *Is.* 14: 7.

To guide our feet into the way of peace. *Lu.* 1: 79.

Lord, now lettest thou thy servant depart in peace. *Lu.* **2: 29.**

If it be possible, as much as lieth in you, live peaceably with all men. *Ro.* **12: 18.**

The kingdom of God is not meat and drink; but righteousness, and peace. *Ro.* **14: 17.**

He is our peace. *Ep.* **2: 14.**

The peace of God, which passeth all understanding, shall keep your hearts and minds through Christ Jesus. *Ph.* **4: 7.**

See also

Calm; Christ, Peace of; Contentment; God, Peace of; God, Rest of; Peace; Quiet; Repose; Rest; Stillness; Tranquillity.

Sermon

I the Preacher was king over Israel. *Ec.* **1: 12.**

The pastors are become brutish, and have not sought the Lord: therefore they shall not prosper. *Je.* **10: 21.**

The Spirit of the Lord fell upon me, and said unto me, Speak. *Eze.* **11: 5.**

Preach . . . the preaching that I bid thee. *Jon.* **3: 2.**

The men of Nineveh shall rise in judgment with this generation, and shall condemn it: because they repented at the preaching of Jonas; and, behold, a greater than Jonas is here. *Mat.* **12: 41.**

He hath anointed me to preach the gospel to the poor. *Lu.* **4: 18.**

He went throughout every city and village, preaching and shewing the glad tidings of the kingdom of God. *Lu.* **8: 1.**

They . . . preached the word of the Lord. *Ac.* **8: 25.**

This Jesus, whom I preach unto you, is Christ. *Ac.* **17: 3.**

Thou therefore which teachest another, teachest thou not thyself? *Ro.* **2: 21.**

Thou that preachest a man should not steal, dost thou steal? *Ro.* **2: 21.**

How shall they hear without a preacher? *Ro.* **10: 14.**

How shall they preach, except they be sent? *Ro.* **10: 15.**

How beautiful are the feet of them that preach the gospel of peace. *Ro.* **10: 15.**

The preaching of the cross is to them that perish foolishness. *1 Co.* **1: 18.**

We preach Christ crucified . . . unto the Greeks foolishness. *1 Co.* **1: 23.**

They which preach the gospel should live of the gospel. *1 Co.* **9: 14.**

Woe is unto me, if I preach not the gospel! *1 Co.* **9: 16.**

If Christ be not risen, then is our preaching vain, and your faith is also vain. *1 Co.* **15: 14.**

In the sight of God speak we in Christ. *2 Co.* **2: 17.**

We preach not ourselves, but Christ Jesus the Lord. *2 Co.* **4: 5.**

I went up by revelation, and communicated unto them that gospel which I preach among the Gentiles. *Ga.* **2: 2.**

Let him that is taught in the word communicate unto him that teacheth in all good things. *Ga.* **6: 6.**

To make known the mystery of the gospel. *Ep.* **6: 19.**

The gospel . . . was preached to every creature which is under heaven. *Col.* **1: 23.**

Preach the word. *2 Ti.* **4: 2.**

Exhort with all longsuffering and doctrine. *2 Ti.* **4: 2.**

Having the everlasting gospel to preach unto them that dwell on the earth, and to every nation, and kindred, and tongue, and people. *Re.* **14: 6.**

See also

Christ, Preaching of; Clergy; God, Preaching of; God, Word of; Ministry; Pastor; Preaching; Priesthood.

Serpent

The serpent was more subtil than any beast of the field. *Ge.* **3: 1.**

The woman said, The serpent beguiled me, and I did eat. *Ge.* **3: 13.**

The Lord sent fiery serpents among the people, and they bit the people. *Nu.* **21: 6.**

Moses made a serpent of brass, and put it upon a pole, and it came to pass, that if a serpent had bitten any man, when he beheld the serpent of brass, he lived. *Nu.* **21: 9.**

Their poison is like the poison of a serpent: they are like the deaf adder that stoppeth her ear. *Ps.* **58: 4.**

Thou shalt tread upon the lion and adder. *Ps.* **91: 13.**

They have sharpened their tongues like a serpent; adders' poison is under their lips. *Ps.* **140: 3.**

At the last it biteth like a serpent, and stingeth like an adder. *Pr.* **23: 32.**

The sucking child shall play on the hole of the asp, and the weaned child shall put his hand on the cockatrice's den. *Is.* **11: 8.**

If he ask a fish, will he give him a serpent? *Mat.* **7: 10.**

Be ye therefore wise as serpents, and harmless as doves. *Mat.* **10: 16.**

Ye serpents, ye generation of vipers, how can ye escape the damnation of hell? *Mat.* **23: 33.**

Behold, I give unto you power to tread on serpents and scorpions, and over all the power of the enemy: and nothing shall by any means hurt you. *Lu.* **10: 19.**

As Moses lifted up the serpent in the wilderness, even so must the Son of man be lifted up. *Jn.* **3: 14.**

The great dragon was cast out, that old serpent, called the Devil, and Satan, which deceiveth the whole world. *Re.* **12: 9.**

Servant

It had been better for us to serve the Egyptians, than that we should die in the wilderness. *Ex.* **14: 12.**

The king of Israel answered and said, My Lord, O king, according to thy saying, I am thine, and all that I have. *1 K.* **20: 4.**

The fool shall be servant to the wise of heart. *Pr.* **11: 29.**

Upon the servants and upon the handmaids in those days will I pour out my spirit. *Jo.* **2: 29.**

A son honoureth his father, and a servant his master. *Mal.* **1: 6.**

It is enough for the disciple that he be as his master, and the servant as his lord. *Mat.* **10: 25.**

Whosoever will be chief among you, let him be your servant. *Mat.* **20: 27.**

Well done, thou good and faithful servant. *Mat.* 25: 21.

Who then is a faithful and wise servant? *Mat.* 24: 45.

We are unprofitable servants: we have done that which was our duty to do. *Lu.* 17: 10.

Where I am, there shall also my servant be. *Jn.* 12: 26.

The servant is not greater than his lord; neither he that is sent greater than he that sent him. *Jn.* 13: 16.

Who art thou that judgest another man's servant? to his own master he standeth or falleth. *Ro.* 14: 4.

Though I be free from all men, yet have I made myself servant unto all. *1 Co.* 9: 19.

Do I seek to please men? for if I yet pleased men, I should not be the servant of Christ. *Ga.* 1: 10.

Thou art no more a servant, but a son. *Ga.* 4: 7.

Servants, be obedient to them that are your masters according to the flesh, with fear and trembling, in singleness of your heart, as unto Christ. *Ep.* 6: 5.

Not with eyeservice, as menpleasers; but as the servants of Christ, doing the will of God from the heart. *Ep.* 6: 6.

James, a servant of God and of the Lord Jesus Christ. *Ja.* 1: 1.

As good stewards. *1 Pe.* 4: 10.

See also

Christ, the Servant; Fidelity; God, Servant of; Help; Labor; Ministry; Service; Toil; Work.

Service

The poor shall never cease out of the land. *De.* 15: 11.

Trust in the Lord, and do good. *Ps.* 37: 3.

Here am I; send me. *Is.* 6: 8.

Take up the stumblingblock out of the way of my people. *Is.* 57: 14.

Verily I say unto you, Inasmuch as ye have done it unto one of the least of these my brethren, ye have done it unto me. *Mat.* 25: 40.

If any man desire to be first, the same shall be last of all, and servant of all. *Mk.* 9: 35.

That he would grant unto us, that we being delivered out of the hand of our enemies might serve him without fear, In holiness and righteousness before him, all the days of our life. *Lu.* 1: 74, 75.

Whosoever will save his life shall lose it. *Lu.* 9: 24.

Lo, these many years do I serve thee. *Lu.* 15: 29.

He that is greatest among you, let him be as the younger; and he that is chief, as he that doth serve. *Lu.* 22: 26.

Whether is greater, he that sitteth at meat, or he that serveth? *Lu.* 22: 27.

Jesus knowing that the Father had given all things into his hands . . . laid aside his garments; and took a towel, and girded himself. *Jn.* 13: 3, 4.

So labouring ye ought to support the weak. *Ac.* 20: 35.

I beseech you therefore. . . . that ye present your bodies a living sacrifice, holy, acceptable unto God, which is your reasonable service. *Ro.* 12: 1.

Fervent in spirit; serving the Lord. *Ro.* 12: 11.

We then that are strong ought to bear the infirmities of the weak, and not to please ourselves. *Ro.* 15: 1.

Even Christ pleased not himself. *Ro.* 15: 3.

Bringing into captivity every thought to the obedience of Christ. *2 Co.* 10: 5.

By love serve one another. *Ga.* 5: 13.

With good will doing service, as to the Lord, and not to men. *Ep.* 6: 7.

Lift up the hands which hang down, and the feeble knees. *He.* 12: 12.

If a brother or sister be naked, and destitute of daily food, And one of you say unto them, Depart in peace, be ye warmed and filled; notwithstanding ye give them not those things which are needful to the body; what doth it profit? *Ja.* 2: 15, 16.

See also

Aid; Allegiance; Assistance; Charity; Christ, the Servant; Duty; God, Servant of; Help; Labor; Ministry; Philanthropy; Succor; Support.

Severity

The Egyptians made the children of Israel to serve with rigour. *Ex.* 1: 13.

I will harden the hearts of the Egyptians. *Ex.* 14: 17.

Thou art become cruel to me: with thy strong hand thou opposest thyself against me. *Jb.* 30: 21.

What mean ye that ye beat my people to pieces, and grind the faces of the poor? *Is.* 3: 15.

Because he cruelly oppressed, . . . even he shall die in his iniquity. *Eze.* 18: 18.

Hear this, O ye that swallow up the needy, even to make the poor of the land to fail. *Am.* 8: 4.

Pilate . . . washed his hands, . . . saying, I am innocent. . . . When he had scourged Jesus, he delivered him to be crucified. *Mat.* 27: 24, 26.

If any man come to me, and hate not his father, and mother, and wife, and children, and brethren, and sisters, yea, and his own life also, he cannot be my disciple. *Lu.* 14: 26.

Whosoever he be of you that forsaketh not all that he hath, he cannot be my disciple. *Lu.* 14: 33.

Behold therefore the goodness and severity of God: on them which fell, severity; but toward thee, goodness. *Ro.* 11: 22.

See also

Austerity; Cruelty; Hardness; Harshness.

Sex

God created man in his own image, in the image of God created he him; male and female created he them. *Ge.* 1: 27.

Adam said, This is now bone of my bones, and flesh of my flesh: she shall be called Woman, because she was taken out of man. *Ge.* 2: 23.

Therefore shall a man leave his father and his mother, and shall cleave unto his wife: and they shall be one flesh. *Ge.* 2: 24.

Of every living thing of all flesh, two of every sort shalt thou bring into the ark, to keep them alive with thee; they shall be male and female. *Ge.* 6: 19.

Of every clean beast thou shalt take to thee by sevens, the male and his female: and of beasts that are not clean by two, the male and his female. *Ge.* 7: 2.

Have ye not read, that he which made them at the beginning made them male and female. *Mat.* 19: 4.

Therefore glorify God in your body. *I Co.* 6: 20.

There is neither male nor female, for ye are all one in Christ Jesus. *Ga.* 3: 28.

See also

Flesh; Man; Sensuality; Woman.

Shadow

Hide me under the shadow of thy wings. *Ps.* 17: 8.

In the shadow of thy wings will I make my refuge. *Ps.* 57: 1.

Because thou hast been my help, therefore in the shadow of thy wings will I rejoice. *Ps.* 63: 7.

He that dwelleth in the secret place of the most High shall abide under the shadow of the Almighty. *Ps.* 91: 1.

My days are like a shadow that declineth. *Ps.* 102: 11.

The Lord is thy shade upon thy right hand. *Ps.* 121: 5.

Who knoweth what is good for man in this life, all the days of his vain life which he spendeth as a shadow? *Ec.* 6: 12.

A man shall be . . . as the shadow of a great rock in a weary land. *Is.* 32: 2.

That at the least the shadow of Peter passing by might overshadow some of them. *Ac.* 5: 15.

A shadow of things to come; but the body is of Christ. *Col.* 2: 17.

There are priests that offer gifts according to the law: Who serve unto the example and shadow of heavenly things. *He.* 8: 4, 5.

The law having a shadow of good things to come. *He.* 10: 1.

Every good gift and every perfect gift is from above, and cometh down from the Father of lights. with whom is no variableness, neither shadow of turning. *Ja.* 1: 17.

See also

Cloud; Darkness; Night; Veil.

Shallowness

My strength is dried up like a potsherd. *Ps.* 22: 15.

Thou driedst up mighty rivers. *Ps.* 74: 15.

When there were no depths, I was brought forth. *Pr.* 8: 24.

If thou faint in the day of adversity, thy strength is small. *Pr.* 24: 10.

I will dry up her sea, and make her springs dry. *Je.* 51: 36.

I will make the rivers dry. *Eze.* 30: 12.

Your goodness is as a morning cloud, and as the early dew it goeth away. *Ho.* 6: 4.

They shall be as the morning cloud, and as the early dew that passeth away, as the chaff that is driven with the whirlwind out of the floor, and as the smoke out of the chimney. *Ho.* 13: 3.

Some fell on stony ground, where it had not much earth; and immediately it sprang up, because it had no depth of earth. *Mk.* 4: 5.

See also

Depth; Superficiality.

Sham

We are but of yesterday, and know nothing, because our days upon earth are a shadow. *Jb.* 8: 9.

The triumphing of the wicked is short, and the joy of the hypocrite but for a moment. *Jb.* 20: 5.

The hypocrite . . . shall fly away as a dream, and shall not be found. *Jb.* 20: 8.

His mouth is full of cursing and deceit and fraud. *Ps.* 10: 7.

The counsels of the wicked are deceit. *Pr.* 12: 5.

All our righteousnesses are as filthy rags. *Is.* 64: 6.

As a cage is full of birds, so are their houses full of deceit. *Je.* 5: 27.

Trust ye not in lying words, saying, The temple of the Lord, The temple of the Lord, The temple of the Lord, are these. *Je.* 7: 4.

Though ye offer me burnt offerings and your meat offerings, I will not accept them. *Am.* 5: 22.

The pride of thine heart hath deceived thee. *Ob.* 1: 3.

The heads . . . judge for reward, and the priests . . . teach for hire, and the prophets . . . divine for money. *Mi.* 3: 11.

He answered and said, I go, sir: and went not. *Mat.* 21: 30.

Do not ye after their works: for they say, and do not. *Mat.* 23: 3.

They bind heavy burdens and grievous to be borne, and lay them on men's shoulders; but they themselves will not move them with one of their fingers. *Mat.* 23: 4.

Beware of the scribes, which . . . for a pretence make long prayers. *Mk.* 12: 38, 40.

False Christs and false prophets shall rise. *Mk.* 13: 22.

Ye tithe mint and rue and all manner of herbs, and pass over judgment and the love of God. *Lu.* 11: 42.

See also

Counterfeit; Fraud; Imitation; Pretension.

Shame

I was naked; and I hid myself. *Ge.* 3: 10.

O my God, I am ashamed and blush to lift up my face to thee, my God: for our iniquities are increased over our head. *Ezr.* 9: 6.

Let them be clothed in shame and dishonour that magnify themselves against me. *Ps.* 35: 26.

As with a sword in my bones, mine enemies reproach me. *Ps.* 42: 10.

My confusion is continually before me, and the shame of my face hath covered me. *Ps.* 44: 15.

Let mine adversaries be clothed with shame. *Ps.* 109: 29.

Hell hath enlarged herself, and opened her mouth without measure: and their glory, and their multitude, and their pomp, and he that rejoiceth, shall descend into it. *Is.* 5: 14.

I will bring an everlasting reproach upon you, and a perpetual shame, which shall not be forgotten. *Je.* 23: 40.

As they were increased, so they sinned against me: therefore will I change their glory into shame. *Ho.* 4: 7.

Their glory shall fly away like a bird. *Ho.* 9: 11.

Whosoever shall be ashamed of me and of my words, of him shall the Son of man be ashamed. *Lu.* 9: 26.

I am not ashamed of the gospel of Christ: for it is the power of God unto salvation. *Ro.* 1: 16.

In all things approving ourselves as the ministers of God . . . By honour and dishonour. *2 Co.* 6: 4, 8.

Therefore we both labour and suffer reproach, because we trust in the living God. *1 Ti.* 4: 10.

All flesh is as grass, and all the glory of man as the flower of grass. *1 Pe.* 1: 24.

See also

Christ, Humiliation of; Disgrace; Dishonor; Ignominy; Reproach.

Shape

The earth was without form. *Ge.* 1: 2.

Thou art unmindful, and hast forgotten God that formed thee. *De.* 32: 18.

I was shapen in iniquity. *Ps.* 51: 5.

Or ever thou hadst formed the earth and the world, even from everlasting to everlasting, thou art God. *Ps.* 90: 2.

The Holy Ghost descended in a bodily shape like a dove upon him. *Lu.* 3: 22.

Ye have neither heard his voice at any time, nor seen his shape. *Jn.* 5: 37.

Thou . . . hast the form of knowledge. *Ro.* 2: 19, 20.

In whom all the building fitly framed together groweth unto an holy temple in the Lord. *Ep.* 2: 21.

Who, being in the form of God, thought it not robbery to be equal to God. *Ph.* 2: 6.

Having a form of godliness, but denying the power thereof. *2 Ti.* 3: 5.

See also

Fashion; Form.

Share

A man shall sanctify unto the Lord some part of a field of his possession. *Le.* 27: 16.

The Lord's portion is his people. *De.* 32: 9.

I pray thee, let a double portion of thy spirit be upon me. *2 K.* 2: 9.

Who then is that faithful and wise steward, whom his lord shall make ruler over his household, to give them their portion of meat in due season? *Lu.* 12: 42.

The younger of them said to his father, Father, give me the portion of goods that falleth to me. *Lu.* 15: 12.

If I wash thee not, thou hast no part with me. *Jn.* 13: 8.

Thou hast neither part nor lot in this matter. *Ac.* 8: 21.

See also

Allotment; Division; Part; Piece; Portion.

Sharpness

He gnasheth upon me with his teeth; mine enemy sharpeneth his eyes upon me. *Jb.* 16: 9.

Thy tongue deviseth mischiefs; like a sharp razor, working deceitfully. *Ps.* 52: 2.

They have sharpened their tongues like a serpent. *Ps.* 140: 3.

Iron sharpeneth iron; so a man sharpeneth the countenance of his friend. *Pr.* 27: 17.

The best of them is as a brier: the most upright is sharper than a thorn hedge. *Mi.* 7: 4.

The contention was so sharp between them, that they departed asunder one from the other. *Ac.* 15: 39.

I write these things being absent, lest being present I should use sharpness. *2 Co.* 13: 10.

The word of God is quick, and powerful, and sharper than any twoedged sword. *He.* 4: 12.

Sheep

That the congregation of the Lord be not as sheep which have no shepherd. *Nu.* 27: 17.

I have gone astray like a lost sheep. *Ps.* 119: 176.

Will the Lord be pleased with thousands of rams, or with ten thousands of rivers of oil? *Mi.* 6: 7.

Beware of false prophets, which come to you in sheep's clothing. *Mat.* 7: 15.

They . . . were scattered abroad, as sheep having no shepherd. *Mat.* 9: 36.

How much then is a man better than a sheep? *Mat.* 12: 12.

He . . . shall go in and out and find pasture. *Jn.* 10: 9.

See also

Christ, the Shepherd; Pastor; Pasture; Shepherd.

Shelter

Their houses are safe from fear. *Jb.* 21: 9.

They . . . embrace the rock for want of a shelter. *Jb.* 24: 8.

In the Lord put I my trust: how say ye to my soul, Flee as a bird to your mountain? *Ps.* 11: 1.

The sparrow hath found an house, and the swallow a nest for herself, . . . even thine altars. *Ps.* 84: 3.

As for the stork, the fir trees are her house. *Ps.* 104: 17.

The high hills are a refuge for the wild goats. *Ps.* 104: 18.

He blesseth the habitation of the just. *Pr.* 3: 33.

Under falsehood have we hid ourselves. *Is.* 28: 15.

A man shall be as an hiding place from the wind. *Is.* 32: 2.

Be like the dove that maketh her nest in the sides of the hole's mouth. *Je.* 48: 28.

They shall sit every man under his . . . fig tree. *Mi.* 4: 4.

The foxes have holes, and the birds of the air have nests; but the Son of man hath not where to lay his head. *Mat.* 8: 20.

The birds of the air come and lodge in the branches. *Mat.* 13: 32.

If they drink any deadly thing, it shall not hurt them. *Mk.* 16: 18.

Nothing shall by any means hurt you. *Lu.* 10: 19.

I pray not that thou shouldest take them out of the world, but that thou shouldest keep them from the evil. *Jn.* 17: 15.

See also

Asylum; Booth; Dwelling; Habitation; Home; House; Protection; Refuge; Residence; Retreat; Roof; Safety; Security; Tenant.

Shepherd

Abel was a keeper of sheep. *Ge.* 4: 2.

Ye have scattered my flock, and driven them away, and have not visited them: behold, I will visit upon you the evil of your doings, saith the Lord. *Je.* 23: 2.

I will set up shepherds over them which shall feed them. *Je.* 23: 4.

Woe be to the shepherds of Israel that do feed themselves! should not the shepherds feed the flocks? *Eze.* 34: 2.

Ye eat the fat, and ye clothe you with the wool, ye kill them that are fed: but ye feed not the flock. *Eze.* 34: 3.

The shepherds fed themselves, and fed not my flock. *Eze.* 34: 8.

Smite the shepherd, and the sheep shall be scattered. *Zch.* 13: 7.

There were in the same country shepherds abiding in the field, keeping watch over their flock by night. *Lu.* 2: 8.

The shepherds returned, glorifying and praising God for all the things that they had heard. *Lu.* 2: 20.

He that entereth in by the door is the shepherd of the sheep. *Jn.* 10: 2.

I am the good shepherd. *Jn.* 10: 11.

The good shepherd giveth his life for the sheep. *Jn.* 10: 11.

Take heed therefore unto yourselves, and to all the flock, over the which the Holy Ghost hath made you overseers. *Ac.* 20: 28.

See also

Christ, the Shepherd; Pastor; Pasture; Sheep.

Shield

With favour wilt thou compass him as with a shield. *Ps.* 5: 12.

The shields of the earth belong unto God. *Ps.* 47: 9.

God is my defence. *Ps.* 59: 9.

The Lord God is a sun and shield. *Ps.* 84: 11.

His truth shall be thy shield and buckler. *Ps.* 91: 4.

The Lord . . . is their help and their shield. *Ps.* 115: 9.

Take unto you the whole armour of God. *Ep.* 6: 13.

Having on the breastplate of righteousness. *Ep.* 6: 14.

Above all, taking the shield of faith, wherewith ye shall be able to quench all the fiery darts of the wicked. *Ep.* 6: 16.

See also

Armor; Breastplate; Buckler; Defence; Protection.

Ship

My days . . . are passed away as the swift ships. *Jb.* 9: 25, 26.

There go the ships. *Ps.* 104: 26.

They that go down to the sea in ships, that do business in great waters; These see the works of the Lord, and his wonders in the deep. *Ps.* 107: 23, 24.

There be three things which are too wonderful for me, yea, four which I know not: The way of an eagle in the air; the way of a serpent upon a rock; the way of a ship in the midst of the sea; and the way of a man with a maid. *Pr.* 30: 18, 19.

There the glorious Lord will be unto us a place of broad rivers and streams; wherein shall go no galley with oars, neither shall gallant ship pass thereby. *Is.* 33: 21.

When they had sent away the multitude, they took him even as he was in the ship. And there were also with him other little ships. *Mk.* 4: 36.

There arose a great storm of wind, and the waves beat into the ship, so that it was now full. *Mk.* 4: 37.

He was in the hinder part of the ship, asleep on a pillow. *Mk.* 4: 38.

He went up unto them into the ship; and the wind ceased. *Mk.* 6: 51.

He sat down, and taught the people out of the ship. *Lu.* 5: 3.

See also

Navigation; Ocean; Pilot; Sailor; Sea; Voyage.

Shoe

Put off thy shoes from off thy feet, for the place whereon thou standest is holy ground. *Ex.* 3: 5.

How beautiful are thy feet with shoes, O prince's daughter! *S. of S.* 7: 1.

They sold . . . the poor for a pair of shoes. *Am.* 2: 6.

He that cometh after me is mightier than I, whose shoes I am not worthy to bear. *Mat.* 3: 11.

Provide . . . neither shoes, nor yet staves. *Mat.* 10: 9, 10.

Put a ring on his hand, and shoes on his feet. *Lu.* 15: 22.

When I sent you without purse, and scrip, and shoes, lacked ye any thing? And they said, Nothing. *Lu.* 22: 35.

Whose shoe's latchet I am not worthy to unloose. *Jn.* 1: 27.

See also

Foot.

Shore

I will multiply thy seed . . . as the sand which is upon the sea shore. *Ge.* 22: 17.

Unto the uttermost sea shall your coast be. *De.* 11: 24.

God gave Solomon wisdom and understanding exceeding much, and largeness of heart, even as the sand that is on the sea shore. *1 K.* 4: 29.

Oh that thou wouldest bless me indeed, and enlarge my coast. *1 Ch.* 4: 10.

Herod . . . slew all the children that were in Bethlehem, and in all the coasts thereof. *Mat.* 2: 16.

The same day went Jesus out of the house, and sat by the sea side. *Mat.* 13: 1.

The whole multitude stood on the shore. *Mat.* 13: 2.

He began again to teach by the sea side. *Mk.* 4: 1.

They began to pray him to depart out of their coasts. *Mk.* 5: 17.

A great multitude of people out of all Judæa and Jerusalem, and from the sea coast of Tyre and Sidon . . . came to hear him, and to be healed of their diseases. *Lu.* 6: 17.

When the morning was now come, Jesus stood on the shore. *Jn.* 21: 4.

We kneeled down on the shore, and prayed. *Ac.* 21: 5.

See also
Bank.

Shortness

Is the Lord's hand waxed short? *Nu.* 11: 23.

The triumphing of the wicked is short. *Jb.* 20: 5.

The days of his youth hast thou shortened. *Ps.* 89: 45.

Remember how short my time is. *Ps.* 89: 47.

The years of the wicked shall be shortened. *Pr.* 10: 27.

The bed is shorter than that a man can stretch himself on it. *Is.* 28: 20.

Brethren, the time is short. *1 Co.* 7: 29.

See also
Brevity; Life, the Short.

Shoulder

Surely I would take it upon my shoulder, and bind it as a crown to me. *Jb.* 31: 36.

I removed his shoulder from the burden: his hands were delivered from the pots. *Ps.* 81: 6.

Then shall his yoke depart from off them, and his burden depart from off their shoulders. *Is.* 14: 25.

They bind heavy burdens and grievous to be borne, and lay them on men's shoulders; but they themselves will not move them with one of their fingers. *Mat.* 23: 4.

When he hath found it, he layeth it upon his shoulders, rejoicing. *Lu.* 15: 5.

Shout

When ye hear the sound of the trumpet, all the people shall shout with a great shout. *Jos.* 6: 5.

Shout; for the Lord hath given you the city. *Jos.* 6: 16.

What meaneth the noise of this great shout in the camp of the Hebrews? *1 S.* 4: 6.

God is gone up with a shout. *Ps.* 47: 5.

Break forth into singing, and cry aloud. *Is.* 54: 1.

Shout, O daughter of Jerusalem: behold thy King cometh unto thee. *Zch.* 9: 9.

At midnight there was a cry made, Behold, the bridegroom cometh. *Mat.* 25: 6.

Ye have received the Spirit of adoption, whereby we cry, Abba, Father. *Ro.* 8: 15.

See also
Acclamation; Call; Christ, Call of; Cry; God, Call of.

Shrine

Draw not nigh hither: put off thy shoes from off thy feet, for the place whereon thou standest is holy ground. *Ex.* 3: 5.

Take heed now; for the Lord hath chosen thee to build an house for the sanctuary: be strong, and do it. *1 Ch.* 28: 10.

Who is able to build him an house, seeing the heaven and heaven of heavens cannot contain him? *2 Ch.* 2: 6.

Will God in very deed dwell with men on the earth? behold, heaven and the heaven of heavens cannot contain thee; how much less this house which I have built! *2 Ch.* 6: 18.

The glory of the Lord filled the house. *2 Ch.* 7: 1.

They praised the Lord, because the foundation of the house of the Lord was laid. *Ezr.* 3: 11.

We . . . walked unto the house of God in company. *Ps.* 55: 14.

It was too painful for me; Until I went into the sanctuary of God. *Ps.* 73: 16, 17.

A day in thy courts is better than a thousand. *Ps.* 84: 10.

The glory of Lebanon shall come unto thee, the fir tree, the pine tree, and the box together, to beautify the place of my sanctuary. *Is.* 60: 13.

They shall not hurt nor destroy in all my holy mountain. *Is.* 65: 25.

My tabernacle also shall be with them: yea, I will be their God, and they shall be my people. *Eze.* 37: 27.

It is the king's chapel. *Am.* 7: 13.

The Lord is in his holy temple: let all the earth keep silence before him. *Hab.* 2: 20.

The veil of the temple was rent in twain. *Mat.* 27: 51.

He hath built us a synagogue. *Lu.* 7: 5.

The house of God . . . is the church of the living God, the pillar and ground of the truth. *1 Ti.* 3: 15.

Him that overcometh will I make a pillar in the temple of my God. *Re.* 3: 12.

See also
Church; Church, Building the; Church, the House of God; Tabernacle; Temple.

Sickness

I will even appoint over you terror, consumption, and the burning ague, that shall consume the eyes, and cause sorrow of heart. *Le.* 26: 16.

Every sickness, and every plague, which is not written in the book of this law, them will the Lord bring upon thee, until thou be destroyed. *De.* 28: 61.

Fools because of their transgression, and because of their iniquities, are afflicted. *Ps.* 107: 17.

I am poor and needy, and my heart is wounded within me. *Ps.* 109: 22.

Why should ye be stricken any more? ye will revolt more and more: the whole head is sick, and the whole heart faint. *Is.* 1: 5.

He shall see of the travail of his soul, and shall be satisfied. *Is.* 53: 11.

Is there no balm in Gilead; is there no physician there? *Je.* 8: 22.

Thy bruise is incurable, and thy wound is grievous. *Je.* 30: 12.

Therefore also will I make thee sick in smiting thee, in making thee desolate because of thy sins. *Mi.* 6: 13.

They brought unto him all sick people that were taken with divers diseases and torments, . . . and he healed them. *Mat.* 4: 24.

They that are whole have no need of the physician, but they that are sick. *Mk.* 2: 17.

Thy faith hath saved thee. *Lu.* 18: 42.

This sickness is not unto death, but for the glory of God, that the Son of God might be glorified thereby. *Jn.* 11: 4.

I take pleasure in infirmities, . . . for

Christ's sake: for when I am weak, then am I strong. *2 Co.* 12: 10.

Through infirmity of the flesh I preached the gospel unto you. *Ga.* 4: 13.

The prayer of faith shall save the sick. *Ja.* 5: 15.

See also

Ailment; Disease; Faith-Healing; Healing; Illness; Infirmity.

Side

Who is on the Lord's side? let him come unto me. *Ex.* 32: 26.

We have sought the Lord our God, we have sought him, and he hath given us rest on every side. *2 Ch.* 14: 7.

Hast not thou made an hedge about him, and about his house, and about all that he hath on every side? *Jb.* 1: 10.

The wicked walk on every side, when the vilest men are exalted. *Ps.* 12: 8.

Beautiful for situation, the joy of the whole earth, is mount Zion, on the sides of the north, the city of the great King. *Ps.* 48: 2.

The little hills rejoice on every side. *Ps.* 65: 12.

Thou shalt increase my greatness, and comfort me on every side. *Ps.* 71: 21.

A thousand shall fall at thy side, and ten thousand at thy right hand; but it shall not come nigh thee. *Ps.* 91: 7.

The Lord is on my side; I will not fear. *Ps.* 118: 6.

If it had not been the Lord who was on our side, when men rose up against us: Then they had swallowed us up quick. *Ps.* 124: 2, 3.

On the side of their oppressors there was power. *Ec.* 4: 1.

Thou stoodest on the other side, . . . thou wast as one of them. *Ob.* 1: 11.

They crucified him, and two other with him, on either side one, and Jesus in the midst. *Jn.* 19: 18.

Reach hither thy hand, and thrust it into my side: and be not faithless, but believing. *Jn.* 20: 27.

We are troubled on every side, yet not distressed. *2 Co.* 4: 8.

See also

Border.

Sigh

The children of Israel sighed by reason of the bondage. *Ex.* 2: 23.

For the oppression of the poor, for the sighing of the needy, now will I arise. *Ps.* 12: 5.

My life is spent with grief, and my years with sighing. *Ps.* 31: 10.

Let the sighing of the prisoner come before thee. *Ps.* 79: 11.

All the merryhearted do sigh. *Is.* 24: 7.

The ransomed of the Lord shall return, . . . they shall obtain joy and gladness, and sorrow and sighing shall flee away. *Is.* 35: 10.

My sighs are many, and my heart is faint. *La.* 1: 22.

See also

Grief; Sadness; Sorrow; Tear.

Sight

The Lord opened the eyes of the young man; and he saw. *2 K.* 6: 17.

I was eyes to the blind. *Jb.* 29: 15.

I will behold thy face in righteousness. *Ps.* 17: 15.

Eyes have they, but they see not. *Ps.* 115: 5.

Open thou mine eyes, that I may behold wondrous things out of thy law. *Ps.* 119: 18.

Our eyes wait upon the Lord our God. *Ps.* 123: 2.

The Lord openeth the eyes of the blind. *Ps.* 146: 8.

Better is the sight of the eyes than the wandering of the desire. *Ec.* 6: 9.

He shall not judge after the sight of his eyes. *Is.* 11: 3.

In that day . . . the eyes of the blind shall see out of obscurity. *Is.* 29: 18.

Look, ye blind, that ye may see. *Is.* 42: 18.

Blessed are the pure in heart: for they shall see God. *Mat.* 5: 8.

The blind receive their sight. *Mat.* 11: 5.

The blind man said unto him, Lord, that I might receive my sight. *Mk.* 10: 51.

Jesus said unto him, Receive thy sight. *Lu.* 18: 42.

We walk by faith, not by sight. *2 Co.* 5: 7.

Behold, he cometh with clouds; and every eye shall see him. *Re.* 1: 7.

See also

Christ, Vision of; Eye; God, Vision of; Spectator; Vision.

Sign

Let there be lights in the firmament of the heaven to divide the day from the night; and let them be for signs. *Ge.* 1: 14.

I do set my bow in the cloud, and it shall be for a token of a covenant between me and the earth. *Ge.* 9: 13.

My sabbaths ye shall keep: for it is a sign between me and you throughout your generations. *Ex.* 31: 13.

Thou shalt bind this line of scarlet thread in the window. *Jos.* 2: 18.

Behold, I will put a fleece of wool in the floor; and if the dew be on the fleece only, and it be dry upon all the earth beside, then shall I know that thou wilt save Israel by mine hand, as thou hast said. *Ju.* 6: 37.

Declare his glory among the heathen, his wonders among all people. *Ps.* 96: 3.

Ye hypocrites, ye can discern the face of the sky; but can ye not discern the signs of the times? *Mat.* 16: 3.

What shall be the sign of thy coming, and of the end of the world? *Mat.* 24: 3.

There shall arise false Christs, and false prophets, and shall shew great signs and wonders. *Mat.* 24: 24.

If thou be the Son of God, come down from the cross. *Mat.* 27: 40.

What shall be the sign when all these things shall be fulfilled? *Mk.* 13: 4.

This shall be a sign unto you; Ye shall find the babe. *Lu.* 2: 12.

This is an evil generation: they seek a sign; and there shall no sign be given it, but the sign of Jonas the prophet. *Lu.* 11: 29.

See also

Marvel; Miracle; Symbol; Token; Wonder.

Silence

Ye shall not shout, nor make any noise with

your voice, . . . until the day I bid you shout. *Jos.* 6: 10.

Hold your peace, for the day is holy. *Ne.* 8: 11.

There was silence, and I heard a voice. *Jb.* 4: 16.

I was dumb with silence. *Ps.* 39: 2.

Unless the Lord had been my help, my soul had almost dwelt in silence. *Ps.* 94: 17.

A man of understanding holdeth his peace. *Pr.* 11: 12.

He that hath knowledge spareth his words. *Pr.* 17: 27.

Even a fool, when he holdeth his peace, is counted wise: and he that shutteth his lips is esteemed a man of understanding. *Pr.* 17: 28.

A time to keep silence, and a time to speak. *Ec.* 3: 7.

He shall not cry, nor lift up, nor cause his voice to be heard in the street. *Is.* 42: 2.

Hold thy peace at the presence of the Lord God. *Zph.* 1: 7.

He answered him to never a word; insomuch that the governor marvelled greatly. *Mat.* 27: 14.

They held their peace. *Lu.* 14: 4.

If these should hold their peace, the stones would immediately cry out. *Lu.* 19: 40.

Hereafter I will not talk much with you. *Jn.* 14: 30.

The men which journeyed with him stood speechless, hearing a voice, but seeing no man. *Ac.* 9: 7.

I conferred not with flesh and blood. *Ga.* 1: 16.

So is the will of God, that with well doing ye may put to silence the ignorance of foolish men. *1 Pe.* 2: 15.

There was silence in heaven about the space of half an hour. *Re.* 8: 1.

See also

Calm; Christ, Silence of; God, Silence of; Peace; Quiet; Repose; Stillness; Tranquillity.

Silver

Ye shall not make with me gods of silver, neither shall ye make unto you gods of gold. *Ex.* 20: 23.

The words of the Lord are pure words: as silver tried in a furnace of earth, purified seven times. *Ps.* 12: 6.

Thou, O God, hast proved us: thou hast tried us, as silver is tried. *Ps.* 66: 10.

The merchandise of it is better than the merchandise of silver. *Pr.* 3: 14.

Receive my instruction, and not silver; and knowledge rather than choice gold. *Pr.* 8: 10.

The tongue of the just is as choice silver. *Pr.* 10: 20.

How much better is it to get wisdom than gold! and to get understanding rather to be chosen than silver! *Pr.* 16: 16.

He that loveth silver shall not be satisfied with silver. *Ec.* 5: 10.

Or ever the silver cord be loosed. *Ec.* 12: 6.

Thy silver is become dross, thy wine mixed with water. *Is.* 1: 22.

They sold the righteous for silver. *Am.* 2: 6.

He shall sit as a refiner and purifier of silver. *Mal.* 3: 3.

See also

Money; Riches; Wealth.

Simplicity

The testimony of the Lord is sure, making wise the simple. *Ps.* 19: 7.

The Lord preserveth the simple. *Ps.* 116: 6.

The entrance of thy words giveth light; it giveth understanding unto the simple. *Ps.* 119: 130.

To give subtilty to the simple. *Pr.* 1: 4.

How long, ye simple ones, will ye love simplicity? *Pr.* 1: 22.

If therefore thine eye be single, thy whole body shall be full of light. *Mat.* 6: 22.

There were in the same country shepherds abiding in the field, keeping watch over their flock by night. *Lu.* 2: 8.

He that giveth, let him do it with simplicity. *Ro.* 12: 8.

In simplicity and godly sincerity, not with fleshly wisdom, we have had our conversation in the world. *2 Co.* 1: 12.

The simplicity that is in Christ. *2 Co.* 11: 3.

See also

Christ, Simplicity of; Clearness; Single-Mindedness.

Sin

The stars in their courses fought against Sisera. *Ju.* 5: 20.

How much more abominable and filthy is man, which drinketh iniquity like water? *Jb.* 15: 16.

Blessed is he whose transgression is forgiven, whose sin is covered. *Ps.* 32: 1.

Thou lovest evil more than good. *Ps.* 52: 3.

Every one of them is gone back: they are altogether become filthy; there is none that doeth good, no, not one. *Ps.* 53: 3.

If thou, Lord, shouldest mark iniquities, O Lord, who shall stand? *Ps.* 130: 3.

The perverseness of transgressors shall destroy them. *Pr.* 11: 3.

Fools make a mock at sin. *Pr.* 14: 9.

God hath made man upright; but they have sought out many inventions. *Ec.* 7: 29.

Though your sins be as scarlet, they shall be as white as snow; though they be red like crimson, they shall be as wool. *Is.* 1: 18.

Your iniquities have separated between you and your God. *Is.* 59: 2.

Thus have they loved to wander, they have not refrained their feet. *Je.* 14: 10.

They shall go with their flocks and with their herds to seek the Lord; but they shall not find him; he hath withdrawn himself from them. *Ho.* 5: 6.

O Israel, thou hast destroyed thyself. *Ho.* 13: 9.

Shall I give . . . the fruit of my body for the sin of my soul? *Mi.* 6: 7.

He that shall blaspheme against the Holy Ghost hath never forgiveness. *Mk.* 3: 29.

He fell down at Jesus' knees, saying, Depart from me; for I am a sinful man. *Lu.* 5: 8.

Forgive us our sins. *Lu.* 11: 4.

He that is without sin among you, let him first cast a stone at her. *Jn.* 8: 7.

If I had not come and spoken unto them they had not had sin. *Jn.* 15: 22.

Be not overcome of evil, but overcome evil with good. *Ro.* 12: 21.

That ye put off concerning the former conversation the old man, which is corrupt according to the deceitful lusts. *Ep.* 4: 22.

The Lord shall deliver me from every evil work. *2 Ti.* 4: 18.

The sin which doth so easily beset us. *He.* 12: 1.

The blood of Jesus Christ his Son cleanseth us from all sin. *1 Jn.* 1: 7.

See also

Corruption; Crime; Depravity; Evil; Fault; Guile; Iniquity; Lust; Sinner; Transgression; Trespass; Ungodliness; Unrighteousness; Wickedness; Wrong.

Sin, Original

There is not a just man upon earth, that doeth good, and sinneth not. *Ec.* 7: 20.

Ye are of your father the devil, and the lusts of your father ye will do. *Jn.* 8: 44.

If by one man's offence death reigned by one; much more they which receive abundance of grace and of the gift of righteousness shall reign in life by one. *Ro.* 5: 17.

For as by one man's disobedience many were made sinners, so by the obedience of one shall many be made righteous. *Ro.* 5: 19.

The evil which I would not, that I do. *Ro.* 7: 19.

O wretched man that I am! who shall deliver me from the body of this death? *Ro.* 7: 24.

As in Adam all die, even so in Christ shall all be made alive. *1 Co.* 15: 22.

You hath he quickened, who were dead in trespasses and sins; Wherein in time past ye walked according to the course of this world. *Ep.* 2: 1, 2.

Sin, when it is finished, bringeth forth death. *Ja.* 1: 15.

See also

Corruption; Depravity.

Sincerity

Fear the Lord, and serve him in sincerity and in truth. *Jos.* 24: 14.

Let love be without dissimulation. *Ro.* 12: 9.

Let us keep the feast . . . with the unleavened bread of sincerity. *1 Co.* 5: 8.

As of sincerity, . . . in the sight of God speak we in Christ. *2 Co.* 2: 17.

The sincerity of your love. *2 Co.* 8: 8.

Doing the will of God from the heart. *Ep.* 6: 6.

That ye may be sincere and without offence till the day of Christ. *Ph.* 1: 10.

In doctrine shewing uncorruptness, gravity, sincerity. *Tit.* 2: 7.

Neither was guile found in his mouth. *1 Pe.* 2: 22.

See also

Frankness; Honesty; Truthfulness; Uprightness.

Single-Mindedness

How long halt ye between two opinions? *1 K.* 18: 21.

Their heart is divided; now shall they be found faulty. *Ho.* 10: 2.

The light of the body is the eye: if therefore thine eye be single, thy whole body shall be full of light. But if thine eye be evil, thy

whole body shall be full of darkness. *Mat.* 6: 22, 23.

No man can serve two masters. *Mat.* 6: 24.

One thing is needful. *Lu.* 10: 42.

If I will that he tarry till I come, what is that to thee? follow thou me. *Jn.* 21: 22.

They . . . did eat their meat with gladness and singleness of heart. *Ac.* 2: 46.

I determined not to know any thing among you, save Jesus Christ, and him crucified. *1 Co.* 2: 2.

Ye cannot drink the cup of the Lord, and the cup of devils. *1 Co.* 10: 21.

In singleness of your heart, as unto Christ. *Ep.* 6: 5.

In singleness of heart, fearing God. *Col.* 3: 22.

See also

Guilelessness; Oneness; Unity.

Sinlessness

In the integrity of my heart and innocency of my hands have I done this. *Ge.* 20: 5.

The Lord rewarded me according to my righteousness: according to the cleanness of my hands hath he recompensed me. *2 S.* 22: 21.

Shall a man be more pure than his maker? *Jb.* 4: 17.

Thou hast said, My doctrine is pure, and I am clean in thine eyes. *Jb.* 11: 4.

I am clean without transgression, I am innocent; neither is there iniquity in me. *Jb.* 33: 9.

It shall be called The way of holiness; the unclean shall not pass over it. *Is.* 35: 8.

Before him innocency was found in me. *Da.* 6: 22.

I would have you wise unto that which is good, and simple concerning evil. *Ro.* 16: 19.

By pureness. *2 Co.* 6: 6.

That ye may be blameless and harmless, the sons of God, without rebuke, in the midst of a crooked and perverse nation, among whom ye shine as lights in the world. *Ph.* 2: 15.

I pray God your whole spirit and soul and body be preserved blameless. *1 Th.* 5: 23.

I thank God, whom I serve from my forefathers with pure conscience. *2 Ti.* 1: 3.

See also

Acquittal; Christ, Holiness of; Christ, Sinlessness of; God, Righteousness of; Godliness; Holiness; Righteousness; Uprightness.

Sinner

They forsook the Lord. *Ju.* 2: 13.

Thou art the man. *2 S.* 12: 7.

They that plow iniquity, and sow wickedness, reap the same. *Jb.* 4: 8.

My son, if sinners entice thee, consent thou not. *Pr.* 1: 10.

The candle of the wicked shall be put out. *Pr.* 24: 20.

One sinner destroyeth much good. *Ec.* 9: 18.

There is no peace, saith the Lord, unto the wicked. *Is.* 48: 22.

They say, The Lord seeth us not. *Eze.* 8: 12.

Israel hath cast off the thing that is good. *Ho.* 8: 3.

Let them turn every one from his evil way. *Jon.* 3: 8.

The last state of that man is worse than the first. *Mat.* 12: 45.

How is it that he eateth and drinketh with publicans and sinners? *Mk.* 2: 16.

He was reckoned among the transgressors. *Lu.* 22: 37.

The evil which I would not, that I do. *Ro.* 7: 19.

Ye were sometimes darkness. *Ep.* 5: 8.

Christ Jesus came into the world to save sinners. *1 Ti.* 1: 15.

If any man sin. *1 Jn.* 2: 1.

Whosoever committeth sin transgresseth also the law. *1 Jn.* 3: 4.

See also

Crime; Evil; Guile; Iniquity; Sin; Transgression; Wickedness; Wrong.

Sister

And his sisters, are they not all with us? *Mat.* 13: 56.

Every one that hath forsaken houses, or brethren, or sisters, or father, or mother, or wife, or children, or lands, for my name's sake, shall receive an hundredfold, and shall inherit everlasting life. *Mat.* 19: 29.

Whosoever shall do the will of God, the same is my brother, and my sister, and mother. *Mk.* 3: 35.

Dost thou not care that my sister hath left me to serve alone? *Lu.* 10: 40.

If the unbelieving depart, let him depart. A brother or a sister is not under bondage in such cases: but God hath called us to peace. *1 Co.* 7: 15.

Have we not power to lead about a sister, a wife, as well as other apostles? *1 Co.* 9: 5.

Entreat . . . The elder women as mothers; the younger as sisters, with all purity. *1 Ti.* 5: 1, 2.

If a brother or sister be naked, and destitute of daily food, And one of you say unto them, Depart in peace, be ye warmed and filled; notwithstanding ye give them not those things which are needful to the body; what doth it profit? *Ja.* 2: 15, 16.

Skepticism

Who is the Lord, that I should obey his voice? *Ex.* 5: 2.

If the Lord be with us, why then is all this befallen us? *Ju.* 6: 13.

If I say, I will speak thus; behold, I should offend against the generation of thy children. *Ps.* 73: 15.

The men . . . say in their hearts, The Lord will not do good, neither will he do evil. *Zph.* 1: 12.

Whereby shall I know this? *Lu.* 1: 18.

Neither be ye of doubtful mind. *Lu.* 12: 29.

Take heed, brethren, lest there be in any of you an evil heart of unbelief. *He.* 3: 12.

See also

Agnosticism; Christ, Doubt of; Doubt; Unbelief.

Skill

A man of Tyre, skilful to work in gold, and in silver, in brass, in iron, in stone, and in timber, in purple, in blue, and in fine linen,

and in crimson; also to grave any manner of graving. *2 Ch.* 2: 14.

He . . . guided them by the skilfulness of his hands. *Ps.* 78: 72.

If I forget thee, O Jerusalem, let my right hand forget her cunning. *Ps.* 137: 5.

She . . . worketh willingly with her hands. *Pr.* 31: 13.

She layeth her hands to the spindle, and her hands hold the distaff. *Pr.* 31: 19.

She maketh fine linen, and selleth it. *Pr.* 31: 24.

The race is not to the swift, or the battle to the strong, neither yet bread to the wise, nor yet riches to men of understanding, nor yet favour to men of skill. *Ec.* 9: 11.

Hath not the potter power over the clay? *Ro.* 9: 21.

Who also hath made us able ministers. *2 Co.* 3: 6.

See also

Ability; Adept; Aptitude; Cunning; Expert; Handiwork; Workmanship.

Skin

Moses wist not that the skin of his face shone. *Ex.* 34: 29.

Skin for skin, yea, all that a man hath will he give for his life. *Jb.* 2: 4.

By reason of the voice of my groaning my bones cleave to my skin. *Ps.* 102: 5.

Can the Ethiopian change his skin, or the leopard his spots? *Je.* 13: 23.

Thus saith the Lord God unto these bones; Behold, I . . . will lay sinews upon you, and will bring up flesh upon you, and will cover you with skin, and put breath in you, and ye shall live. *Eze.* 37: 5, 6.

John was clothed with camel's hair, and with a girdle of a skin about his loins. *Mk.* 1: 6.

They wandered about in sheepskins and goatskins; being destitute. *He.* 11: 37.

Sky

Let there be lights in the firmament of the heaven to divide the day from the night. *Ge.* 1: 14.

This is none other but the house of God, and this is the gate of heaven. *Ge.* 28: 17.

God . . . rideth upon the heaven in thy help, and in his excellency on the sky. *De.* 33: 26.

Is not God in the height of heaven? and behold the height of the stars how high they are! *Jb.* 22: 12.

Hast thou with him spread out the sky, which is strong, and as a molten looking glass? *Jb.* 37: 18.

The firmament sheweth his handywork. *Ps.* 19: 1.

The heavens are thine, the earth also is thine. *Ps.* 89: 11.

The host of heaven cannot be numbered. *Je.* 33: 22.

They that be wise shall shine as the brightness of the firmament. *Da.* 12: 3.

Prove me now herewith, saith the Lord of hosts, if I will not open you the windows of heaven, and pour you out a blessing, that there shall not be room enough to receive it. *Mal.* 3: 10.

When it is evening, ye say, It will be fair weather: for the sky is red. *Mat.* 16: 2.

O ye hypocrites, ye can discern the face of the sky; but can ye not discern the signs of the times? *Mat.* 16: 3.

Hereafter ye shall see heaven open, and the angels of God ascending and descending upon the Son of man. *Jn.* 1: 51.

There are also celestial bodies, and bodies terrestrial: but the glory of the celestial is one, and the glory of the terrestrial is another. *1 Co.* 15: 40.

See also

Constellation; Firmament; Heaven.

Slackness

He will not be slack to him that hateth him, he will repay him to his face. *De.* 7: 10.

When thou shalt vow a vow unto the Lord thy God, thou shalt not slack to pay it. *De.* 23: 21.

How long are ye slack to go to possess the land, which the Lord God of your fathers hath given you? *Jos.* 18: 3.

I am as a man that hath no strength. *Ps.* 88: 4.

He becometh poor that dealeth with a slack hand: but the hand of the diligent maketh rich. *Pr.* 10: 4.

The law is slacked, and judgment doth never go forth. *Hab.* 1: 4.

Let not thine hands be slack. *Zph.* 3: 16.

We ought to give the more earnest heed to the things which we have heard, lest at any time we should let them slip. *He.* 2: 1.

The Lord is not slack concerning his promise, as some men count slackness. *2 Pe.* 3: 9.

See also

Carelessness; Weakness.

Slander

He hath slandered thy servant unto my lord the king. *2 S.* 19: 27.

I have heard the slander of many. *Ps.* 31: 13.

Thou sittest and speakest against thy brother; thou slanderest thine own mother's son. *Ps.* 50: 20.

Whoso privily slandereth his neighbour, him will I cut off. *Ps.* 101: 5.

He that uttereth a slander is a fool. *Pr.* 10: 18.

An hypocrite with his mouth destroyeth his neighbour. *Pr.* 11: 9.

There is that speaketh like the piercings of a sword: but the tongue of the wise is health. *Pr.* 12: 18.

A froward man soweth strife: and a whisperer separateth chief friends. *Pr.* 16: 28.

He that repeateth a matter separateth very friends. *Pr.* 17: 9.

Whisperers, Backbiters, . . . inventors of evil things. *Ro.* 1: 29, 30.

Even so must their wives be grave, not slanderers. *1 Ti.* 3: 11.

Presumptuous are they, selfwilled, they are not afraid to speak evil of dignities. *2 Pe.* 2: 10.

See also

Backbiting; Gossip; Talebearing.

Slaughter

Wrath killeth the foolish man, and envy slayeth the silly one. *Jb.* 5: 2.

Though he slay me, yet will I trust in him. *Jb.* 13: 15.

Evil shall slay the wicked. *Ps.* 34: 21.

We are counted as sheep for the slaughter. *Ps.* 44: 22.

They slay the widow and the stranger, and murder the fatherless. *Ps.* 94: 6.

Surely thou wilt slay the wicked, O God: depart from me therefore, ye bloody men. *Ps.* 139: 19.

He goeth after her straightway, as an ox goeth to the slaughter. *Pr.* 7: 22.

He is brought as a lamb to the slaughter, and as a sheep before her shearers is dumb, so he openeth not his mouth. *Is.* 53: 7.

For thy sake we are killed all the day long. *Ro.* 8: 36.

See also

Assassin; Blood; Ferocity; Murder.

Slavery

I will bring you out from under the burdens of the Egyptians. *Ex.* 6: 6.

Now therefore ease thou somewhat the grievous servitude of thy father. *2 Ch.* 10: 4.

Our God hath not forsaken us in our bondage. *Ezr.* 9: 9.

Will ye even sell your brethren? *Ne.* 5: 8.

Thou sellest thy people for nought. *Ps.* 44: 12.

Seeing I . . . am desolate, a captive. *Is.* 49: 21.

Is Israel a servant? is he a homeborn slave? *Je.* 2: 14.

I was among the captives by the river of Chebar. *Eze.* 1: 1.

We be Abraham's seed, and were never in bondage to any man. *Jn.* 8: 33.

I perceive that thou art . . . in the bond of iniquity. *Ac.* 8: 23.

Remember them that are in bonds, as bound with them. *He.* 13: 3.

See also

Bondage; Captivity; Capture; Imprisonment; Prison; Subjection.

Sleep

God speaketh . . . in slumberings upon the bed. *Jb.* 33: 14, 15.

I will both lay me down in peace, and sleep. *Ps.* 4: 8.

He that keepeth Israel shall neither slumber nor sleep. *Ps.* 121: 4.

It is vain for you to rise up early, to sit up late, to eat the bread of sorrows: for so he giveth his beloved sleep. *Ps.* 127: 2.

When thou liest down, thou shalt not be afraid. *Pr.* 3: 24.

Yet a little sleep, a little slumber, a little folding of the hands to sleep: So shall thy poverty come. *Pr.* 6: 10, 11.

Love not sleep, lest thou come to poverty. *Pr.* 20: 13.

Drowsiness shall clothe a man with rags. *Pr.* 23: 21.

I sleep, but my heart waketh. *S. of S.* 5: 2.

Awake, awake, stand up, O Jerusalem, which hast drunk at the hand of the Lord the cup of his fury. *Is.* 51: 17.

My sleep was sweet unto me. *Je.* 31: 26.

Watch ye therefore: . . . Lest coming suddenly he find you sleeping. *Mk.* 13: 35, 36.

Sleeping for sorrow. *Lu.* 22: 45.

Why sleep ye? rise and pray, lest ye enter into temptation. *Lu.* 22: 46.

God hath given them the spirit of slumber. *Ro.* 11: 8.

Now it is high time to awake out of sleep. *Ro.* 13: 11.

Even so them also which sleep in Jesus will God bring with him. *1 Th.* 4: 14.

There remaineth therefore a rest to the people of God. *He.* 4: 9.

See also

Dream; Repose; Rest.

Slide

Hold up my goings in thy paths, that my footsteps slip not. *Ps.* 17: 5.

I have trusted also in the Lord; therefore I shall not slide. *Ps.* 26: 1.

Let their way be dark and slippery. *Ps.* 35: 6.

The law of his God is in his heart; none of his steps shall slide. *Ps.* 37: 31.

As for me, my feet were almost gone; my steps had well nigh slipped. *Ps.* 73: 2.

Surely thou didst set them in slippery places. *Ps.* 73: 18.

When I said, My foot slippeth; thy mercy, O Lord, held me up. *Ps.* 94: 18.

Why then is this people of Jerusalem slidden back by a perpetual backsliding? *Je.* 8: 5.

Israel slideth back as a backsliding heifer. *Ho.* 4: 16.

See also

Backsliding.

Sloth

The way of the slothful man is as an hedge of thorns. *Pr.* 15: 19.

Slothfulness casteth into a deep sleep; and an idle soul shall suffer hunger. *Pr.* 19: 15.

The sluggard will not plow by reason of the cold; therefore shall he beg in harvest, and have nothing. *Pr.* 20: 4.

I went by the field of the slothful, . . . And, lo, it was all grown over with thorns, and nettles had covered the face thereof, and the stone wall thereof was broken down. *Pr.* 24: 30, 31.

As the door turneth upon his hinges, so doth the slothful upon his bed. *Pr.* 26: 14.

We desire that . . . ye be not slothful. *He.* 6: 11, 12.

See also

Idleness; Indolence; Inertia; Laziness

Slowness

Thou art a God ready to pardon, gracious and merciful, slow to anger, and of great kindness. *Ne.* 9: 17.

He that is slow to wrath is of great understanding. *Pr.* 14: 29.

He that is slow to anger appeaseth strife. *Pr.* 15: 18.

He that is slow to anger is better than the mighty. *Pr.* 16: 32.

The Lord is slow to anger, and great in power. *Na.* 1: 3.

Let every man be swift to hear, slow to speak, slow to wrath. *Ja.* 1: 19.

See also

Delay; Deliberation; Procrastination.

Smallness

The Lord was not in the wind: and after the wind an earthquake; but the Lord was not in the earthquake: And after the earthquake a fire; But the Lord was not in the fire: and after the fire a still small voice. *1 K.* 19: 11, 12.

A little that a righteous man hath is better than the riches of many wicked. *Ps.* 37: 16.

I am small and despised: yet do not I forget thy precepts. *Ps.* 119: 141.

Better is little with the fear of the Lord than great treasure and trouble therewith. *Pr.* 15: 16.

Better is a little with righteousness than great revenues without right. *Pr.* 16: 8.

The ants are a people not strong, yet they prepare their meat in the summer. *Pr.* 30: 25.

The conies are but a feeble folk, yet make they their houses in the rocks. *Pr.* 30: 26.

The locusts have no king, yet go they forth all of them by bands. *Pr.* 30: 27.

The spider taketh hold with her hands, and is in kings' palaces. *Pr.* 30: 28.

There was a little city, and few men within it. *Ec.* 9: 14.

Two or three berries in the top of the uppermost bough. *Is.* 17: 6.

Behold, the nations are as a drop of a bucket. *Is.* 40: 15.

The place is too strait for me: give place to me that I may dwell. *Is.* 49: 20.

I was no prophet, neither was I a prophet's son; but I was an herdman, and a gatherer of sycomore fruit. *Am.* 7: 14.

Thou, Beth-lehem Ephratah, though thou be little among the thousands of Judah, yet out of thee shall he come forth unto me that is to be ruler in Israel; whose goings forth have been from old, from everlasting. *Mi.* 5: 2.

How many loaves have ye? And they said, Seven, and a few little fishes. *Mat.* 15: 34.

Except ye be converted, and become as little children, ye shall not enter into the kingdom of heaven. *Mat.* 18: 3.

There were also with him other little ships. *Mk.* 4: 36.

Even so then at this present time also there is a remnant according to the election of grace. *Ro.* 11: 5.

A little leaven leaveneth the whole lump. *Ga.* 5: 9.

We put bits in the horses' mouths, that they may obey us; and we turn about their whole body. *Ja.* 3: 3.

Behold also the ships, which though they be so great, and are driven of fierce winds, yet are they turned about with a very small helm, whithersoever the governor listeth. *Ja.* 3: 4.

The tongue is a little member, and boasteth great things. *Ja.* 3: 5.

Behold, how great a matter a little fire kindleth! *Ja.* 3: 5.

See also

Least; Little; Pettiness; Trifle; Thing, the Little.

Smell

The Lord smelled a sweet savour. *Ge.* 8: 21.

Ye shall serve gods, . . . which neither see, nor hear, nor eat, nor smell. *De.* 4: 28.

He smelleth the battle afar off. *Jb.* 39: 25.

Noses have they, but they smell not. *Ps.* 115: 6.

His beauty shall be as the olive tree, and his smell as Lebanon. *Ho.* **14: 6.**

Thou savourest not the things that be of God. *Mat.* **16: 23.**

If the whole were hearing, where were the smelling? *1 Co.* **12: 17.**

We are unto God a sweet savour of Christ. *2 Co.* **2: 15.**

See also

Fragrance; Nose; Odor; Perfume; Savor; Scent.

Smile

Let thine heart be merry. *1 K.* **21: 7.**

The lines are fallen unto me in pleasant places. *Ps.* **16: 6.**

I commended mirth, because a man hath no better thing under the sun, than to eat, and to drink, and to be merry. *Ec.* **8: 15.**

A feast is made for laughter. *Ec.* **10: 19.**

Is any merry? let him sing psalms. *Ja.* **5: 13.**

See also

Cheer; Gaiety; Laughter; Merriment; Mirth.

Smoke

Mount Sinai was altogether on a smoke. *Ex.* **19: 18.**

The wicked shall perish: . . . they shall consume; into smoke shall they consume away. *Ps.* **37: 20.**

My days are consumed like smoke. *Ps.* **102: 3.**

He toucheth the hills, and they smoke. *Ps.* **104: 32.**

As smoke to the eyes, so is the sluggard to them that send him. *Pr.* **10: 26.**

The house was filled with smoke. *Is.* **6: 4.**

The smoking flax shall he not quench. *Is.* **42: 3.**

The heavens shall vanish away like smoke, and the earth shall wax old like a garment. *Is.* **51: 6.**

Smoothness

My foot standeth in an even place. *Ps.* **26: 12.**

The words of his mouth were smoother than butter, but war was in his heart. *Ps.* **55: 21.**

Her mouth is smoother than oil. *Pr.* **5: 3.**

Speak unto us smooth things, prophesy deceits. *Is.* **30: 10.**

The crooked shall be made straight, and the rough places plain. *Is.* **40: 4.**

The carpenter encouraged the goldsmith, and he that smootheth with the hammer him that smote the anvil. *Is.* **41: 7.**

The rough ways shall be made smooth. *Lu.* **3: 5.**

Snare

The sorrows of hell compassed me about; the snares of death prevented me. *2 S.* **22: 6.**

They also that seek after my life lay snares for me. *Ps.* **38: 12.**

Let their table become a snare before them: and that which should have been for their welfare, let it become a trap. *Ps.* **69: 22.**

Surely he shall deliver thee from the snare of the fowler, and from the noisome pestilence. *Ps.* **91: 3.**

The wicked have laid a snare for me. *Ps.* **119: 110.**

Our soul is escaped as a bird out of the snare of the fowlers: the snare is broken, and we are escaped. *Ps.* **124: 7.**

The law of the wise is a fountain of life, to depart from the snares of death. *Pr.* **13: 14.**

A fool's mouth is his destruction, and his lips are the snare of his soul. *Pr.* **18: 7.**

As the fishes that are taken in an evil net, and as the birds that are caught in the snare; so are the sons of men snared in an evil time, when it falleth suddenly upon them. *Ec.* **9: 12.**

Lest he fall into reproach and the snare of the devil. *1 Ti.* **3: 7.**

They that will be rich fall into temptation and a snare. *1 Ti.* **6: 9.**

Snow

Summer and winter . . . shall not cease. *Ge.* **8: 22.**

He saith to the snow, Be thou on the earth. *Jb.* **37: 6.**

By the breath of God frost is given. *Jb.* **37: 10.**

Hast thou entered into the treasures of the snow? *Jb.* **38: 22.**

Wash me, and I shall be whiter than snow. *Ps.* **51: 7.**

He giveth snow like wool: he scattereth the hoarfrost like ashes. *Ps.* **147: 16.**

As snow in summer, and as rain in harvest, so honour is not seemly for a fool. *Pr.* **26: 1.**

Though your sins be as scarlet, they shall be as white as snow. *Is.* **1: 18.**

As the rain cometh down, and the snow from heaven, and returneth not thither, . . . So shall my word be that goeth forth. *Is.* **55: 10, 11.**

See also

Frost; Weather; Winter.

Sobriety

Speak forth the words of truth and soberness. *Ac.* **26: 25.**

I say, through the grace given unto me, to every man that is among you, not to think of himself more highly than he ought to think; but to think soberly, according as God hath dealt to every man the measure of faith. *Ro.* **12: 3.**

Every man that striveth for the mastery is temperate in all things. *1 Co.* **9: 25.**

Let us, who are of the day, be sober. *1 Th.* **5: 8.**

Teach the young women to be sober. *Tit.* **2: 4.**

Young men likewise exhort to be sober minded. *Tit.* **2: 6.**

We should live soberly, righteously, and godly, in this present world. *Tit.* **2: 12.**

Be sober. *1 Pe.* **1: 13.**

The end of all things is at hand: be ye therefore sober, and watch unto prayer. *1 Pe.* **4: 7.**

Be sober, be vigilant; because your adversary the devil, as a roaring lion, walketh about, seeking whom he may devour. *1 Pe.* **5: 8.**

See also

Abstinence; Moderation; Self-Control; Temperance.

Socialism

How good and how pleasant it is for brethren to dwell together in unity! *Ps.* **133: 1.**

All ye are brethren. *Mat.* **23: 8.**

They . . . sold their possessions and goods, and parted them to all men, as every man had need. *Ac.* **2: 42, 45.**

All that believed were together, and had all things common. *Ac.* **2: 44.**

The multitude of them that believed were of one heart and of one soul: neither said any of them that ought of the things which he possessed was his own; but they had all things common. *Ac.* **4: 32.**

Then the disciples, every man according to his ability, determined to send relief unto the brethren which dwelt in Jerusalem. *Ac.* **11: 29.**

I mean not that other men be eased, and ye burdened: But by an equality, that now at this time your abundance may be a supply for their want, that their abundance also may be a supply for your want: that there may be equality. *2 Co.* **8: 13, 14.**

He that had gathered much had nothing over; and he that had gathered little had no lack. *2 Co.* **8: 15.**

Whoso hath this world's good, and seeth his brother have need, and shutteth up his bowels of compassion from him, how dwelleth the love of God in him? *1 Jn.* **3: 17.**

See also

Brother; Equality; Communism, Christian.

Society

That man perished not alone in his iniquity. *Jos.* **22: 20.**

Wealth gotten by vanity shall be diminished: but he that gathereth by labour shall increase. *Pr.* **13: 11.**

Behold, all souls are mine; as the soul of the father, so also the soul of the son is mine. *Eze.* **18: 4.**

Lay not up for yourselves treasures upon earth. *Mat.* **6: 19.**

Levi made him a great feast in his own house: and there was a great company of publicans and of others that sat down with them. *Lu.* **5: 29.**

The body is not one member, but many. *1 Co.* **12: 14.**

Whether one member suffer, all the members suffer with it. *1 Co.* **12: 26.**

Whether . . . one member be honoured, all the members rejoice with it. *1 Co.* **12: 26.**

Now ye are the body of Christ, and members in particular. *1 Co.* **12: 27.**

In time past ye walked according to the course of this world. *Ep.* **2: 2.**

We are members one of another. *Ep.* **4: 25.**

Lovers of pleasures more than lovers of God. *2 Ti.* **3: 4.**

We are compassed about. *He.* **12: 1.**

Your brethren that are in the world. *1 Pe.* **5: 9.**

They are of the world: therefore speak they of the world, and the world heareth them. *1 Jn.* **4: 5.**

See also

Association; Christ, Companionship of; Christ, Fellowship with; Christ, the Friend; Communism, Christian; Community; Companionship; Companionship, Evil; Fellowship; God, Companionship of; God, the Friend; Wealth; Worldliness.

Softness

God maketh my heart soft, and the Almighty troubleth me. *Jb.* **23: 16.**

The meek shall inherit the earth. *Ps.* **37: 11.**

Thou visitest the earth, and waterest it: . . . thou makest it soft with showers. *Ps.* **65: 9, 10.**

A soft answer turneth away wrath. *Pr.* **15: 1.**

A soft tongue breaketh the bone. *Pr.* **25: 15.**

I shall go softly all my years in the bitterness of my soul. *Is.* **38: 15.**

He . . . shall gently lead those that are with young. *Is.* **40: 11.**

When the south wind blew softly, . . . they sailed close by Crete. *Ac.* **27: 13.**

Know ye not that the unrighteous shall not inherit the kingdom of God? . . . nor effeminate. *1 Co.* **6: 9.**

The fruit of the Spirit is . . . gentleness. *Ga.* **5: 22.**

See also

Gentleness; Meekness; Tenderness.

Soil

While the earth remaineth, seedtime and harvest . . . shall not cease. *Ge.* **8: 22.**

Blessed shall be . . . the fruit of thy ground. *De.* **28: 4.**

As for the earth, out of it cometh bread. *Jb.* **28: 5.**

Then shall the earth yield her increase. *Ps.* **67: 6.**

To him that soweth righteousness shall be a sure reward. *Pr.* **11: 18.**

It was planted in a good soil by great waters, that it might bring forth branches, and that it might bear fruit, that it might be a goodly vine. *Eze.* **17: 8.**

Behold, a sower went forth to sow: And when he sowed, some seeds fell . . . upon stony places, where they had not much earth: and forthwith they sprung up, because they had no deepness of earth: and when the sun was up, they were scorched; and because they had no root, they withered away. *Mat.* **13: 3–5.**

He that received seed into the good ground is he that heareth the word, and understandeth it. *Mat.* **13: 23.**

Except a corn of wheat fall into the ground and die, it abideth alone: but if it die, it bringeth forth much fruit. *Jn.* **12: 24.**

See also

Earth; Ground; Land.

Sojourn

Sojourn in this land, and I will be with thee. *Ge.* **26: 3.**

They found no city to dwell in. *Ps.* **107: 4.**

Thy statutes have been my songs in the house of my pilgrimage. *Ps.* **119: 54.**

He himself stayed in Asia for a season. *Ac.* **19: 22.**

Even unto this present hour we . . . have no certain dwellingplace. *1 Co.* **4: 11.**

Ye are no more strangers and foreigners, but fellowcitizens with the saints, and of the household of God. *Ep.* **2: 19.**

By faith he sojourned in the land of promise, as in a strange country. *He.* **11: 9.**

Pass the time of your sojourning here in fear. *1 Pe.* **1: 17.**

See also
Pilgrim; Pioneer; Stranger; Travel.

Solace

Job's three friends . . . had made an appointment together to come to mourn with him and to comfort him. *Jb.* **2: 11.**

None spake a word unto him: for they saw that his grief was very great. *Jb.* **2: 13.**

Cast thy burden upon the Lord. *Ps.* **55: 22.**

Thou, Lord, hast holpen me, and comforted me. *Ps.* **86: 17.**

Mine eyes fail for thy word, saying, When wilt thou comfort me? *Ps.* **119: 82.**

That we through patience and comfort of the scriptures might have hope. *Ro.* **15: 4.**

Blessed be God, . . . Who comforteth us in all our tribulation, that we may be able to comfort them which are in any trouble, by the comfort wherewith we ourselves are comforted of God. *2 Co.* **1: 3, 4.**

We were comforted in your comfort. *2 Co.* **7: 13.**

We were comforted over you in all our affliction and distress by your faith. *1 Th.* **3: 7.**

See also
Christ, the Comforter; Comfort; Consolation; God, Comfort of; Relief.

Soldier

The Lord is a man of war. *Ex.* **15: 3.**

When the host goeth forth against thine enemies, then keep thee from every wicked thing. *De.* **23: 9.**

Mighty men of valour, . . . soldiers, fit to go out for war and battle. *1 Ch.* **7: 11.**

The battle is not yours, but God's. *2 Ch.* **20: 15.**

Scatter thou the people that delight in war. *Ps.* **68: 30.**

Neither shall they learn war any more. *Is.* **2: 4.**

I will break the bow and the sword and the battle out of the earth. *Ho.* **2: 18.**

I am a man under authority, having soldiers under me; and I say to this man, Go, and he goeth; and to another, Come, and he cometh. *Mat.* **8: 9.**

Thou therefore endure hardness as a good soldier of Jesus Christ. *2 Ti.* **2: 3.**

No man that warreth entangleth himself with the affairs of this life; that he may please him who hath chosen him to be a soldier. *2 Ti.* **2: 4.**

See also
Armor; Army; Attack; Battle; Belligerent; Fight; War.

Solemnity

It is a good thing to give thanks unto the Lord, and to sing praises unto thy name, O most High; . . . upon the harp with a solemn sound. *Ps.* **92: 1, 3.**

The new moons and sabbaths, the calling of assemblies, I cannot away with; it is iniquity, even the solemn meeting. *Is.* **1: 13.**

Ye shall have a song, as in the night when a holy solemnity is kept. *Is.* **30: 29.**

Look upon Zion, the city of our solemnities. *Is.* **33: 20.**

None come to the solemn feasts. *La.* **1: 4.**

Thou hast called as in a solemn day my terrors round about. *La.* **2: 22.**

What will ye do in the solemn day? *Ho.* **9: 5.**

Sanctify ye a fast, call a solemn assembly. *Jo.* **1: 14.**

Whether we be beside ourselves, it is to God: or whether we be sober, it is for your cause. *2 Co.* **5: 13.**

Let us watch and be sober. *1 Th.* **5: 6.**

Let us, who are of the day, be sober. *1 Th.* **5: 8.**

Young men likewise exhort to be sober minded. *Tit.* **2: 6.**

Be ye therefore sober, and watch unto prayer. *1 Pe.* **4: 7.**

See also
Dignity; Gravity.

Solicitude

Rivers of waters run down mine eyes, because they keep not thy law. *Ps.* **119: 136.**

I will weep bitterly, labour not to comfort me, because of the spoiling of the daughter of my people. *Is.* **22: 4.**

My soul shall weep in secret places for your pride. *Je.* **13: 17.**

Their soul was poured out into their mothers' bosom. *La.* **2: 12.**

How often would I have gathered thy children together, even as a hen gathereth her chickens under her wings, and ye would not! *Mat.* **23: 37.**

By the space of three years I ceased not to warn every one night and day with tears. *Ac.* **20: 31.**

I have great heaviness and continual sorrow in my heart. *Ro.* **9: 2.**

Many walk of whom I have told you often, and now tell you even weeping, that they are the enemies of the cross of Christ. *Ph.* **3: 18.**

See also
Anxiety; Care; Concern; Worry.

Solitude

It is not good that the man should be alone. *Ge.* **2: 18.**

Get thee hence, . . . and hide thyself by the brook Cherith. *1 K.* **17: 3.**

I, even I only, am left; and they seek my life, to take it away. *1 K.* **19: 10.**

He went in therefore, and shut the door upon them twain, and prayed unto the Lord. *2 K.* **4: 33.**

God setteth the solitary in families. *Ps.* **68: 6.**

They wandered in the wilderness in a solitary way; they found no city to dwell in. *Ps.* **107: 4.**

The wilderness and the solitary place shall be glad for them; and the desert shall rejoice, and blossom as the rose. *Is.* **35: 1.**

How doth the city sit solitary, that was full of people! *La.* **1: 1.**

A wild ass alone by himself. *Ho.* **8: 9.**

When the evening was come, he was there alone. *Mat.* **14: 23.**

Jesus departed from thence, . . . and went up into a mountain, and sat down there. *Mat.* **15: 29.**

In the morning, rising up a great while before day, he went out, and departed into a solitary place, and there prayed. *Mk.* **1: 35.**

He . . . entered into an house, and would have no man know it: but he could not be hid. *Mk.* **7: 24.**

He was alone praying. *Lu.* 9: 18.

He was withdrawn from them about a stone's cast, and kneeled down, and prayed. *Lu.* 22: 41.

Jesus . . . departed again into a mountain himself alone. *Jn.* 6: 15.

Peter put them all forth, and kneeled down, and prayed. *Ac.* 9: 40.

I went into Arabia. *Ga.* 1: 17.

See also

Christ, Loneliness of; Isolation; Loneliness; Privacy.

Son

God . . . hath also heard my voice, and hath given me a son. *Ge.* 30: 6.

Teach them thy sons, and thy sons' sons. *De.* 4: 9.

Thou shalt beget sons and daughters, but thou shalt not enjoy them. *De.* 28: 41.

I raised up your sons for prophets. *Am.* 2: 11.

I will spare them, as a man spareth his own son that serveth him. *Mal.* 3: 17.

He that loveth son or daughter more than me is not worthy of me. *Mat.* 10: 37.

Last of all he sent unto them his son, saying, They will reverence my son. *Mat* 21: 37.

If a son shall ask bread of any of you that is a father, will he give him a stone? *Lu.* 11: 11.

The father shall be divided against the son, and the son against the father. *Lu.* 12: 53.

I . . . am no more worthy to be called thy son: make me as one of thy hired servants. *Lu.* 15: 18, 19.

This my son was dead, and is alive again; he was lost, and is found. *Lu.* 15: 24.

Woman, behold thy son! . . . Behold thy mother! *Jn.* 19: 26, 27.

As my beloved sons I warn you. *1 Co.* 4: 14.

Song

The Lord is my strength and song. *Ex.* 15: 2.

His songs were a thousand and five. *1 K.* 4: 32.

Thou shalt compass me about with songs of deliverance. *Ps.* 32: 7.

Sing unto him a new song. *Ps.* 33: 3.

I call to remembrance my song in the night. *Ps.* 77: 6.

Serve the Lord with gladness: come before his presence with singing. *Ps.* 100: 2.

As he that taketh away a garment in cold weather, and as vinegar upon nitre, so is he that singeth songs to an heavy heart. *Pr.* 25: 20.

The song of songs, which is Solomon's. *S. of S.* 1: 1.

Then shall the lame man leap as an hart, and the tongue of the dumb sing. *Is.* 35: 6.

My servants shall sing for joy of heart. *Is.* 65: 14.

When they had sung an hymn, they went out into the mount of Olives. *Mat.* 26: 30.

See also

Chorus; Hymn; Melody; Music; Poetry; Psalm; Tune.

Sorrow

Many sorrows shall be to the wicked. *Ps.* 32: 10.

The bread of sorrows. *Ps.* 127: 2.

Even in laughter the heart is sorrowful; and the end of that mirth is heaviness. *Pr.* 14: 13.

Sorrow is better than laughter: for by the sadness of the countenance the heart is made better. *Ec.* 7: 3.

He hath sent me . . . to comfort all that mourn; To appoint unto them that mourn in Zion, to give unto them beauty for ashes, the oil of joy for mourning. the garment of praise for the spirit of heaviness. *Is.* 61: 1–3.

Their soul shall be as a watered garden; and they shall not sorrow any more at all. *Je.* 31: 12.

Thy father and I have sought thee sorrowing. *Lu.* 2: 48.

Now we see through a glass darkly; but then face to face: now I know in part; but then shall I know even as also I am known. *1 Co.* 13: 12.

As sorrowful, yet always rejoicing. *2 Co.* 6: 10.

The sorrow of the world worketh death. *2 Co.* 7: 10.

Be afflicted, and mourn, and weep: let your laughter be turned to mourning, and your joy to heaviness. *Ja.* 4: 9.

See also

Christ, Sorrow of; Dejection; Depression; Gloom; Grief; Lamentation; Melancholy; Mourning; Sadness; Tear; Unhappiness; Weeping; Woe.

Soul

Man became a living soul. *Ge.* 2: 7.

Thou shalt love the Lord thy God with all thine heart, and with all thy soul, and with all thy might. *De.* 6: 5.

Serve him with all your heart and with all your soul. *De.* 11: 13.

Return, O Lord, deliver my soul. *Ps.* 6: 4.

Thou wilt not leave my soul in hell. *Ps.* 16: 10.

The law of the Lord is perfect, converting the soul. *Ps.* 19: 7.

He restoreth my soul. *Ps.* 23: 3.

Who shall ascend into the hill of the Lord? . . . He that . . . hath not lifted up his soul unto vanity. *Ps.* 24: 3, 4.

Unto thee, O Lord, do I lift up my soul. *Ps.* 25: 1.

The Lord redeemeth the soul of his servants. *Ps.* 34: 22.

My soul shall be joyful in the Lord. *Ps.* 35: 9.

As the hart panteth after the water brooks, so panteth my soul after thee, O God. *Ps.* 42: 1.

My soul thirsteth for God, for the living God. *Ps.* 42: 2.

Why art thou cast down, O my soul? and why art thou disquieted in me? hope thou in God. *Ps.* 42: 5.

My soul followeth hard after thee: thy right hand upholdeth me. *Ps.* 63: 8.

Bless the Lord, O my soul: and all that is within me, bless his holy name. *Ps.* 103: 1.

He satisfieth the longing soul, and filleth the hungry soul with goodness. *Ps.* 107: 9.

The Lord shall preserve thee from all evil: he shall preserve thy soul. *Ps.* 121: 7.

The liberal soul shall be made fat. *Pr.* 11: 25.

He that winneth souls is wise. *Pr.* **11: 30.**

The desire accomplished is sweet to the soul. *Pr.* **13: 19.**

A true witness delivereth souls. *Pr.* **14: 25.**

He that keepeth the commandments keepeth his own soul. *Pr.* **19: 16.**

Whoso keepeth his mouth and his tongue keepeth his soul from troubles. *Pr.* **21: 23.**

Behold, all souls are mine. *Eze.* **18: 4.**

Fear not them which kill the body, but are not able to kill the soul: but rather fear him which is able to destroy both soul and body in hell. *Mat.* **10: 28.**

What shall a man give in exchange for his soul? *Mat.* **16: 26.**

What shall it profit a man, if he shall gain the whole world, and lose his own soul? *Mk.* **8: 36.**

Mary said, My soul doth magnify the Lord. *Lu.* **1: 46.**

Soul, thou hast much goods laid up for many years; take thine ease, eat, drink, and be merry. *Lu.* **12: 19.**

Thou fool, this night thy soul shall be required of thee. *Lu.* **12: 20.**

The first Adam was made a living soul; the last Adam was made a quickening spirit. *1 Co.* **15: 45.**

The inward man is renewed day by day. *2 Co.* **4: 16.**

The end of your faith, even the salvation of your souls. *1 Pe.* **1: 9.**

Abstain from fleshly lusts, which war against the soul. *1 Pe.* **2: 11.**

Ye were as sheep going astray; but are now returned unto the Shepherd and Bishop of your souls. *1 Pe.* **2: 25.**

Let them that suffer according to the will of God commit the keeping of their souls to him in well doing, as unto a faithful Creator. *1 Pe.* **4: 19.**

See also

Heart; Man, Spirit of; Spirit.

Sound

Play skilfully with a loud noise. *Ps.* **33: 3.**

Deep calleth unto deep at the noise of thy waterspouts. *Ps.* **42: 7.**

Make a joyful noise unto God, all ye lands. *Ps.* **66: 1.**

I heard the noise of their wings, like the noise of great waters, as the voice of the Almighty, the voice of speech, as the noise of an host. *Eze.* **1: 24.**

Suddenly there came a sound from heaven as of a rushing mighty wind, and it filled all the house where they were sitting. *Ac.* **2: 2.**

Though I speak with the tongues of men and of angels, and have not charity, I am become as sounding brass, or a tinkling cymbal. *1 Co.* **13: 1.**

If the trumpet give an uncertain sound, who shall prepare himself to the battle? *1 Co.* **14: 8.**

The trumpet shall sound, and the dead shall be raised incorruptible, and we shall be changed. *1 Co.* **15: 52.**

Let all . . . anger, and clamour, . . . be put away from you. *Ep.* **4: 31.**

See also

Cry; Noise; Shout; Tumult.

Source

Some trust in chariots, and some in horses: but we will remember the name of the Lord our God. *Ps.* **20: 7.**

Promotion cometh neither from the east, nor from the west, nor from the south. But God is the judge. *Ps.* **75: 6, 7.**

Unto the place from whence the rivers come, thither they return again. *Ec.* **1: 7.**

Look unto the rock whence ye are hewn, and to the hole of the pit whence ye are digged. *Is.* **51: 1.**

Thou shalt be like a watered garden, and like a spring of water, whose waters fail not. *Is.* **58: 11.**

Prove me now herewith, saith the Lord of hosts, if I will not open you the windows of heaven, and pour you out a blessing, that there shall not be room enough to receive it. *Mal.* **3: 10.**

The baptism of John, whence was it? from heaven, or of men? *Mat.* **21 25.**

Salvation is of the Jews. *Jn.* **4: 22.**

How can ye believe, which receive honour one of another, and seek not the honour that cometh from God only? *Jn.* **5: 44.**

Out of Galilee ariseth no prophet. *Jn.* **7: 52.**

As for this fellow, we know not from whence he is. *Jn.* **9: 29.**

If this man were not of God, he could do nothing. *Jn.* **9: 33.**

My kingdom is not of this world. *Jn.* **18: 36.**

Whence come wars and fightings among you? come they not hence, even of your lusts that war in your members? *Ja.* **4: 1.**

See also

Genesis; Origin; Spring.

South

God, . . . Which maketh Arcturus, Orion, and Pleiades, and the chambers of the south. *Jb.* **9: 2, 9.**

Out of the south cometh the whirlwind: and cold out of the north. *Jb.* **37: 9.**

How thy garments are warm, when he quieteth the earth by the south wind? *Jb.* **37: 17.**

The north and the south thou hast created them. *Ps.* **89: 12.**

He hath . . . gathered them out of the lands, from the east, and from the west, from the north, and from the south. *Ps.* **107: 2, 3.**

The wind goeth toward the south, and turneth about unto the north. *Ec.* **1: 6.**

Awake, O north wind; and come, thou south; blow upon my garden, that the spices thereof may flow out. *S. of S.* **4: 16.**

The queen of the south shall rise up in the judgment with this generation, and shall condemn it. *Mat.* **12: 42.**

When ye see the south wind blow, ye say, There will be heat; and it cometh to pass. *Lu.* **12: 55.**

They shall come from the east, and from the west, and from the north, and from the south, and shall sit down in the kingdom of God. *Lu.* **13: 29.**

Sovereignty

The trees went forth on a time to anoint a king to reign over them. *Ju.* **9: 8.**

Samuel also said unto Saul, The Lord sent me to anoint thee to be king over his people. *1 S.* 15: 1.

The kingdom is the Lord's: and he is the governor among the nations. *Ps.* 22: 28.

The Lord reigneth, he is clothed with majesty. *Ps.* 93: 1.

The king . . . shall exalt himself, and magnify himself above every god, and shall speak marvellous things against the God of gods. *Da.* 11: 36.

The devil taketh him up into an exceeding high mountain, and sheweth him all the kingdoms of the world, and the glory of them. *Mat.* 4: 8.

If we suffer, we shall also reign with him. *2 Ti.* 2: 12.

Remember them which have the rule over you. *He.* 13: 7.

Honour the king. *1 Pe.* 2: 17.

The kingdoms of this world are become the kingdoms of our Lord, and of his Christ; and he shall reign for ever and ever. *Re.* 11: 15.

See also
Authority; Christ, the King; Christ, Reign of; Christ, Supremacy of; Dominion; Empire; God, the King; God, Kingdom of; God, Sovereignty of; God, Supremacy of; Kingdom; Power; Reign; Rule; Throne.

Speaker

Let it suffice thee; speak no more unto me of this matter. *De.* 3: 26.

We have seen this day that God doth talk with man, and he liveth. *De.* 5: 24.

The word is very nigh unto thee, in thy mouth, and in thy heart, that thou mayest do it. *De.* 30: 14.

Speak, Lord; for thy servant heareth. *1 S.* 3: 9.

Who can withhold himself from speaking? *Jb.* 4: 2.

Hear diligently my speech, and my declaration with your ears. *Jb.* 13: 17.

Should a wise man utter vain knowledge? *Jb.* 15: 2.

Should he reason with unprofitable talk? *Jb.* 15: 3.

The ear trieth words, as the mouth tasteth meat. *Jb.* 34: 3.

Keep thy tongue from evil, and thy lips from speaking guile. *Ps.* 34: 13.

Let not an evil speaker be established in the earth. *Ps.* 140: 11.

He speaketh with his feet. *Pr.* 6: 13.

O earth, earth, earth, hear the word of the Lord. *Je.* 22: 29.

I have seen folly in the prophets. *Je.* 23: 13.

Son of man, stand upon thy feet, and I will speak unto thee. *Eze.* 2: 1.

I will send a famine in the land, not a famine of bread, nor a thirst for water, but of hearing the words of the Lord. *Am.* 8: 11.

Let your communication be, Yea, yea; Nay, nay: for whatsoever is more than these cometh of evil. *Mat.* 5: 37.

They think that they shall be heard for their much speaking. *Mat.* 6: 7.

Every idle word that men shall speak, they shall give account thereof in the day of judgment. *Mat.* 12: 36.

By thy words thou shalt be justified, and by thy words thou shalt be condemned. *Mat.* 12: 37.

Blessed are they that hear the word of God, and keep it. *Lu.* 11: 28.

What manner of communications are these that ye have one to another, as ye walk, and are sad? *Lu.* 24: 17.

When I was a child, I spake as a child. *1 Co.* 13: 11.

Let all . . . evil speaking be put away from you. *Ep.* 4: 31.

Let your speech be alway with grace, seasoned with salt. *Col.* 4: 6.

The tongue is a fire, a world of iniquity. *Ja.* 3: 6.

Their mouth speaketh great swelling words. *Jude* 16.

I was in the Spirit on the Lord's day, and heard behind me a great voice, as of a trumpet. *Re.* 1: 10.

They heard a great voice from heaven saying unto them, Come up hither. And they ascended up to heaven in a cloud; and their enemies beheld them. *Re.* 11: 12.

See also
Mouth; Speech; Utterance; Word.

Spear

Draw out also the spear, and stop the way against them that persecute me. *Ps.* 35: 3.

He breaketh the bow, and cutteth the spear in sunder. *Ps.* 46: 9.

They shall beat . . . their spears into pruninghooks. *Is.* 2: 4.

Beat . . . your pruninghooks into spears. *Jo.* 3: 10.

The sun and the moon stood still in their habitation: at the light of thine arrows they went, and at the shining of thy glittering spear. *Hab.* 3: 11.

One of the soldiers with a spear pierced his side. *Jn.* 19: 34.

Spectator

From the top of the rocks I see him, and from the hills I behold him. *Nu.* 23: 9.

I shall behold him, but not nigh. *Nu.* 24: 17.

I shall see for myself, and mine eyes shall behold. *Jb.* 19: 27.

Every man may see it; man may behold it afar off. *Jb.* 36: 25.

Mark the perfect man, and behold the upright. *Ps.* 37: 37.

Look down from heaven, and behold. *Ps.* 80: 14.

He hath looked down from the height of his sanctuary; from heaven did the Lord behold the earth. *Ps.* 102: 19.

The eyes of the Lord are in every place, beholding the evil and the good. *Pr.* 15: 3.

Many women were there beholding afar off. *Mat.* 27: 55.

The people stood beholding. *Lu.* 23: 35.

We . . . were eyewitnesses of his majesty. *2 Pe.* 1: 16.

See also
Eye; Sight; Vision; Witness.

Speech

Should he reason with unprofitable talk? or with speeches wherewith he can do no good? *Jb.* 15: 3.

Day unto day uttereth speech. *Ps.* 19: 2.

Let the words of my mouth, and the meditation of my heart, be acceptable in thy sight, O Lord, my strength, and my redeemer. *Ps.* 19: 14.

Keep the door of my lips. *Ps.* 141: 3.

Pleasant words are as an honeycomb, sweet to the soul, and health to the bones. *Pr.* 16: 24.

Death and life are in the power of the tongue. *Pr.* 18: 21.

Let your communication be, Yea, yea; Nay, nay: for whatsoever is more than these cometh of evil. *Mat.* 5: 37.

They think that they shall be heard for their much speaking. *Mat.* 6: 7.

Out of the abundance of the heart the mouth speaketh. *Mat.* 12: 34.

I . . . will know, not the speech of them which are puffed up, but the power. *1 Co.* 4: 19.

We use great plainness of speech. *2 Co.* 3:12.

Let your speech be always with grace, seasoned with salt, that ye may know how ye ought to answer every man. *Col.* 4: 6.

Hold fast the form of sound words, which thou hast heard of me. *2 Ti.* 1: 13.

Sound speech, that cannot be condemned. *Tit.* 2: 8.

Slow to speak. *Ja.* 1: 19.

See also

Accent; Christ, Word of; Eloquence; God, Voice of; God, Word of; Lip; Mouth; Self-Expression, Speaker; Tongue; Utterance; Word.

Speed

Whosoever will not do the law of thy God, and the law of the king, let judgment be executed speedily upon him. *Ezr.* 7: 26.

Let thy tender mercies speedily prevent us. *Ps.* 79: 8.

Because sentence against an evil work is not executed speedily, therefore the heart of the sons of men is fully set in them to do evil. *Ec.* 8: 11.

I the Lord will hasten it in his time. *Is.* 60: 22.

The flight shall perish from the swift. *Am.* 2: 14.

Then said Jesus unto him, That thou doest, do quickly. *Jn.* 13: 27.

Hasting unto the coming of the day of the Lord. *2 Pe.* 3: 12.

Behold, I come quickly. *Re.* 3: 11.

See also

Haste; Hurry; Quickness; Swiftness.

Spirit

Man doth not live by bread only. *De.* 8: 3.

The spirit of man is the candle of the Lord. *Pr.* 20: 27.

Then shall the dust return to the earth as it was: and the spirit shall return unto God who gave it. *Ec.* 12: 7.

Blessed are the poor in spirit. *Mat.* 5: 3.

The spirit indeed is willing, but the flesh is weak. *Mat.* 26: 41.

It is the spirit that quickeneth; the flesh profiteth nothing: the words that I speak unto you, they are spirit, and they are life. *Jn.* 6: 63.

Now if any man have not the Spirit of Christ, he is none of his. *Ro.* 8: 9.

The Spirit searcheth all things, yea, the deep things of God. *1 Co.* 2: 10.

Comparing spiritual things with spiritual. *1 Co.* 2: 13.

It is sown a natural body; it is raised a spiritual body. There is a natural body, and there is a spiritual body. *1 Co.* 15: 44.

Flesh and blood cannot inherit the kingdom of God. *1 Co.* 15: 50.

How shall not the ministration of the spirit be rather glorious? *2 Co.* 3: 8.

For though we walk in the flesh, we do not war after the flesh. *2 Co.* 10: 3.

The flesh lusteth against the Spirit, and the Spirit against the flesh: and these are contrary the one to the other. *Ga.* 5: 17.

If ye be led of the Spirit, ye are not under the law. *Ga.* 5: 18.

If we live in the Spirit, let us also walk in the Spirit. *Ga.* 5: 25.

There is one body, and one Spirit. *Ep.* 4: 4.

Quench not the Spirit. . . . Faithful is he that calleth you. *1 Th.* 5: 19, 24.

The angels of God. *He.* 1: 6.

Are they not all ministering spirits, sent forth to minister for them who shall be heirs of salvation? *He.* 1: 14.

Try the spirits whether they are of God. *1 Jn.* 4: 1.

See also

Ardor; Christ, Spirit of; Courage; Energy; Fire; Ghost; Ghost, Holy; God, Spirit of; Life; Soul; Spirit, Holy.

Spirit, Fruit of

The spirit of the Lord shall rest upon him, the spirit of wisdom and understanding, the spirit of counsel and might, the spirit of knowledge and of the fear of the Lord. *Is.* 11: 2.

A corrupt tree bringeth forth evil fruit. *Mat.* 7: 17.

By their fruits ye shall know them. *Mat.* 7: 20.

To be spiritually minded is life and peace. *Ro.* 8: 6.

Walk in the Spirit, and ye shall not fulfil the lust of the flesh. *Ga.* 5: 16.

The fruit of the Spirit is love, joy, peace, longsuffering, gentleness, goodness, faith, Meekness, temperance. *Ga.* 5: 22, 23.

He that soweth to the Spirit shall of the Spirit reap life everlasting. *Ga.* 6: 8.

I bow my knees unto the Father, . . . That he would grant you, according to the riches of his glory, to be strengthened with might by his Spirit in the inner man. *Ep.* 3: 14, 16.

The fruit of the Spirit is in all goodness and righteousness and peace. *Ep.* 5: 9.

See also

Abundance; Fruitfulness; Fulfilment; Harvest; Reaping.

Spirit, Holy

When the spirit rested upon them, they prophesied, and did not cease. *Nu.* 11: 25.

The Spirit of the Lord came upon Gideon, and he blew a trumpet. *Ju.* 6: 34.

The Spirit of God came upon him, and he prophesied among them. *1 S.* 10: 10.

The Spirit of God was upon the messengers of Saul, and they also prophesied. *1 S.* **19: 20.**

Thou gavest also thy good Spirit to instruct them, and withheldest not thy manna from their mouth, and gavest them water for their thirst. *Ne.* **9: 20.**

They rebelled, and vexed his Holy Spirit: therefore he was turned to be their enemy, and he fought against them. *Is.* **63: 10.**

The wind bloweth where it listeth, and thou hearest the sound thereof, but canst not tell whence it cometh, and whither it goeth: so is every one that is born of the Spirit. *Jn.* **3: 8.**

I will pray the Father, and he shall give you another Comforter, that he may abide with you for ever. *Jn.* **14: 16.**

The Comforter, which is the Holy Ghost, . . . he shall teach you all things. *Jn.* **14: 26.**

When he, the Spirit of truth, is come, he will guide you into all truth. *Jn.* **16: 13.**

They were all filled with the Holy Ghost. *Ac.* **2: 4.**

He said unto them, Have ye received the Holy Ghost since ye believed? And they said unto him, We have not so much as heard whether there be any Holy Ghost. *Ac.* **19: 2.**

The Spirit itself beareth witness with our spirit, that we are the children of God. *Ro.* **8: 16.**

The kingdom of God is . . . joy in the Holy Ghost. *Ro.* **14: 17.**

Sanctified by the Holy Ghost. *Ro.* **15: 16.**

The manifestation of the Spirit is given to every man to profit withal. *1 Co.* **12: 7.**

Holy men of God spake as they were moved by the Holy Ghost. *2 Pe.* **1: 21.**

It is the Spirit that beareth witness, because the Spirit is truth. *1 Jn.* **5: 6.**

Praying in the Holy Ghost. *Jude* **1: 20.**

See also

Christ, Spirit of; Ghost, Holy; God, Spirit of.

Splendor

The glory of the Lord abode upon mount Sinai. *Ex.* **24: 16.**

All the earth shall be filled with the glory of the Lord. *Nu.* **14: 21.**

Thine, O Lord, is the greatness, and the power, and the glory, and the victory, and the majesty. *1 Ch.* **29: 11.**

The God of glory thundereth: the Lord is upon many waters. *Ps.* **29: 3.**

In his temple doth every one speak of his glory. *Ps.* **29: 9.**

The Lord God is a sun and shield. *Ps.* **84: 11.**

The Lord reigneth, he is clothed with majesty; the Lord is clothed with strength, wherewith he hath girded himself. *Ps.* **93: 1.**

Who maketh his angels spirits; his ministers a flaming fire. *Ps.* **104: 4.**

I saw also the Lord sitting upon a throne, high and lifted up, and his train filled the temple. *Is.* **6: 1.**

For as the heavens are higher than the earth, so are my ways higher than your ways, and my thoughts than your thoughts. *Is.* **55: 9.**

Arise, shine; for thy light is come, and the glory of the Lord is risen upon thee. *Is.* **60: 1.**

The glory of the Lord went up from the midst of the city, and stood upon the mountain. *Eze.* **11: 23.**

The city had no need of the sun, neither of the moon, to shine in it: for the glory of God did lighten it. *Re.* **21: 23.**

See also

Brightness; Christ, Glory of; Display; Glory; God, Glory of; God, Majesty of; Grandeur; Magnificence; Sublimity.

Spoil

He delivered them into the hands of spoilers that spoiled them, and he sold them into the hands of their enemies round about. *Ju.* **2: 14.**

They have now compassed us in our steps: . . . Like as a lion that is greedy of his prey. *Ps.* **17: 11, 12.**

I rejoice at thy word, as one that findeth great spoil. *Ps.* **119: 162.**

We shall find all precious substance, we shall fill our houses with spoil. *Pr.* **1: 13.**

Better it is to be of an humble spirit with the lowly, than to divide the spoil with the proud. *Pr.* **16: 19.**

Ye have eaten up the vineyard; the spoil of the poor is in your houses. *Is.* **3: 14.**

Be thou a covert to them from the face of the spoiler. *Is.* **16: 4.**

All that prey upon thee will I give for a prey. *Je.* **30: 16.**

Behold, therefore I will stretch out mine hand upon thee, and will deliver thee for a spoil to the heathen. *Eze.* **25: 7.**

How can one enter into a strong man's house, and spoil his goods, except he first bind the strong man? and then he will spoil his house. *Mat.* **12: 29.**

See also

Booty; Plunder; Prey.

Sport

He was a mighty hunter before the Lord. *Ge.* **10: 9.**

Take, I pray thee, thy weapons, thy quiver and thy bow, and go out to the field, and take me some venison. *Ge.* **27: 3.**

They called for Samson out of the prison house; and he made them sport. *Ju.* **16: 25.**

As when one doth hunt a partridge in the mountains. *1 S.* **26: 20.**

Rejoiceth as a strong man to run a race. *Ps.* **19: 5.**

It is as sport to a fool to do mischief. *Pr.* **10: 23.**

The slothful man roasteth not that which he took in hunting. *Pr.* **12: 27.**

He that loveth pleasure shall be a poor man. *Pr.* **21: 17.**

Simon Peter saith unto them, I go a fishing. *Jn.* **21: 3.**

Know ye not that they which run in a race run all, but one receiveth the prize? *1 Co.* **9: 24.**

See also

Athlete; Fisher; Game; Hunter; Play; Race; Recreation.

Spot

Then shalt thou lift up thy face without spot. *Jb.* **11: 15.**

Cleanse thou me from secret faults. *Ps.* **19: 12.**

There is no spot in thee. *S. of S.* **4: 7.**

Can the Ethiopian change his skin, or the leopard his spots? *Je.* **13: 23.**

That he might present it to himself a glorious church, not having spot, or wrinkle, or any such thing; but that it should be holy and without blemish. *Ep.* 5: 27.

That thou keep this commandment without spot, unrebukeable. *1 Ti.* 6: 14.

Christ . . . offered himself without spot to God. *He.* 9: 14.

Confess your faults one to another. *Ja.* 5: 16.

With the precious blood of Christ, as of a lamb without blemish and without spot. *1 Pe.* 1: 19.

Spots they are and blemishes, sporting themselves with their own deceivings. *2 Pe.* 2: 13.

Be diligent that ye may be found of him in peace, without spot, and blameless. *2 Pe.* 3: 14.

See also

Blemish; Blot; Disgrace; Fault; Reproach; Taint.

Spring

Thou hast given me a south land; give me also springs of water. And he gave her the upper springs and the nether springs. *Jos.* 15: 19.

Thou visitest the earth, and waterest it: . . . thou blessest the springing thereof. *Ps.* 65: 9, 10.

Wilt thou not revive us again: that thy people may rejoice in thee? *Ps.* 85: 6.

Truth shall spring out of the earth; and righteousness shall look down from heaven. *Ps.* 85: 11.

Sing unto the Lord, all the earth. *Ps.* 96: 1.

Let the heavens rejoice, and let the earth be glad. *Ps.* 96: 11.

Let the field be joyful, and all that is therein: then shall all the trees of the wood rejoice. *Ps.* 96: 12.

He sendeth the springs into the valleys, which run among the hills. *Ps.* 104: 10.

Thou renewest the face of the earth. *Ps.* 104: 30.

A time to plant, and a time to pluck up that which is planted. *Ec.* 3: 2.

Lo, the winter is past, the rain is over and gone. *S. of S.* 2: 11.

The flowers appear on the earth; the time of the singing of birds is come. *S. of S.* 2: 12.

The voice of the turtle is heard in our land. *S. of S.* 2: 12.

The parched ground shall become a pool, and the thirsty land springs of water. *Is.* 35: 7.

Lift up your eyes on high, and behold who hath created these things. *Is.* 40: 26.

I will make the wilderness a pool of water, and the dry land springs of water. *Is.* 41: 18.

Let the earth open, and let them bring forth salvation, and let righteousness spring up together; I the Lord have created it. *Is.* 45: 8.

He that hath mercy on them shall lead them, even by the springs of water shall he guide them. *Is.* 49: 10.

The earth bringeth forth her bud, and . . . the garden causeth the things that are sown in it to spring forth. *Is.* 61: 11.

I create new heavens and a new earth. *Is.* 65: 17.

Whosoever drinketh of the water that I shall give him shall never thirst. *Jn.* 4: 14.

The water that I shall give him shall be in

him a well of water springing up into everlasting life. *Jn.* 4: 14.

Be ye transformed by the renewing of your mind. *Ro.* 12: 2.

God, who is rich in mercy, for his great love wherewith he loved us, Even when we were dead in sins, hath quickened us together with Christ. *Ep.* 2: 4, 5.

See also

Pool; Refreshment; Renewal; Revival; Source; Water; Well.

Spy

Send thou men, that they may search the land of Canaan. *Nu.* 13: 2.

See the land, what it is; and the people that dwelleth therein, whether they be strong or weak, few or many. *Nu.* 13: 18.

See . . . what the land is, whether it be fat or lean, whether there be wood therein, or not. *Nu.* 13: 18, 20.

We came unto the land whither thou sentest us, and surely it floweth with milk and honey. *Nu.* 13: 27.

Go, I pray you, prepare yet, and know and see his place where his haunt is. *1 S.* 23: 22.

See therefore, and take knowledge of all the lurking places where he hideth himself, and come ye again to me with the certainty. *1 S.* 23: 23.

David . . . sent his servants unto thee, to search the city, and to spy it out. *2 S.* 10: 3.

Go and spy where he is, that I may send and fetch him. *2 K.* 6: 13.

False brethren . . . came in privily to spy out our liberty which we have in Christ Jesus. *Ga.* 2: 4.

See also

Scout; Survey.

Stability

His hands were steady until the going down of the sun. *Ex.* 17: 12.

Because he is at my right hand, I shall not be moved. *Ps.* 16: 8.

Lengthen thy cords, and strengthen thy stakes. *Is.* 54: 2.

According to the law of the Medes and Persians, which altereth not. *Da.* 6: 8.

Till heaven and earth pass, one jot or one tittle shall in no wise pass from the law, till all be fulfilled. *Mat.* 5: 18.

Our hope of you is stedfast. *2 Co.* 1: 7.

Stand therefore, having your loins girt about with truth. *Ep.* 6: 14.

Nevertheless the foundation of God standeth sure. *2 Ti.* 2: 19.

This is a faithful saying, and these things I will that thou affirm constantly. *Tit.* 3: 8.

Hope we have as an anchor of the soul, both sure and stedfast. *He.* 6: 19.

See also

Constancy; Firmness; Security; Steadfastness.

Staff

Thy rod and thy staff they comfort me. *Ps.* 23: 4.

He called for a famine upon the land: he brake the whole staff of bread. *Ps.* 105: 16.

The rod of mine anger, and the staff in their hand is mine indignation. *Is.* 10: 5.

Shall the ax boast itself against him that heweth therewith? or shall the saw magnify itself against him that shaketh it? as if the rod should shake itself against them that lift it up, or as if the staff should lift up itself, as if it were no wood. *Is.* 10: 15.

There shall yet old men and old women dwell in the streets of Jerusalem, and every man with his staff in his hand for very age. *Zch.* 8: 4.

I took my staff, even Beauty, and cut it asunder, that I might break my covenant which I had made with all the people. *Zch.* 11: 10.

He . . . commanded them that they should take nothing for their journey, save a staff only. *Mk.* 6: 7, 8.
See also
Rod.

Standard

The children of Israel shall pitch their tents, every man by his own camp, and every man by his own standard. *Nu.* 1: 52.

They shall be as when a standardbearer fainteth. *Is.* 10: 18.

I will . . . set up my standard to the people. *Is.* 49: 22.

When the enemy shall come in like a flood, the Spirit of the Lord shall lift up a standard against him. *Is.* 59: 19.

Lift up a standard for the people. *Is.* 62: 10.

Publish, and set up a standard. *Je.* 50: 2.

They measuring themselves by themselves, and comparing themselves among themselves, are not wise. *2 Co.* 10: 12.

In all things shewing thyself a pattern. *Tit.* 2: 7.

See . . . that thou make all things according to the pattern shewed to thee in the mount. *He.* 8: 5.
See also
Example; Form; Ideal; Model; Perfection; Symbol.

Star

He made the stars also. *Ge.* 1: 16.

God set them in the firmament of the heaven to give light upon the earth. *Ge.* 1: 17.

There shall come a Star out of Jacob. *Nu.* 24: 17.

The stars in their courses fought against Sisera. *Ju.* 5: 20.

The host of heaven worshippeth thee. *Ne.* 9: 6.

Which commandeth the sun, and it riseth not; and sealeth up the stars. *Jb.* 9: 7.

Which maketh Arcturus, Orion, and Pleiades, and the chambers of the south. *Jb.* 9: 9.

When the morning stars sang together, and all the sons of God shouted for joy. *Jb.* 38: 7.

Canst thou bind the sweet influences of Pleiades, or loose the bands of Orion? *Jb.* 38: 31.

He telleth the number of the stars. *Ps.* 147: 4.

Praise ye him, sun and moon: praise him, all ye stars of light. *Ps.* 148: 3.

They that be wise shall shine as the brightness of the firmament; and they that turn many to righteousness as the stars for ever and ever. *Da.* 12: 3.

Seek him that maketh the seven stars and Orion. *Am.* 5: 8.

We have seen his star in the east, and have come to worship him. *Mat.* 2: 2.

When they saw the star, they rejoiced with exceeding great joy. *Mat.* 2: 10.

One star differeth from another star in glory. *1 Co.* 15: 41.

I will give him the morning star. *Re.* 2: 28.

There fell a great star from heaven. *Re.* 8: 10.

I am . . . the bright and morning star. *Re.* 22: 16.
See also
Constellation; Firmament; Heaven; Sky.

Starvation

There was no bread in all the land; for the famine was very sore. *Ge.* 47: 13.

In famine he shall redeem thee from death. *Jb.* 5: 20.

In the days of famine they shall be satisfied. *Ps.* 37: 19.

I will increase the famine upon you, and will break your staff of bread. *Eze.* 5: 16.

I also have given you cleanness of teeth in all your cities, and want of bread in all your places: yet have ye not returned unto me. *Am.* 4: 6.

Blessed are they which do hunger and thirst after righteousness: for they shall be filled. *Mat.* 5: 6.

There arose a mighty famine in that land; and he began to be in want. *Lu.* 15: 14.

They shall hunger no more, neither thirst any more. *Re.* 7: 16.
See also
Famine; Hunger.

State

Lord, wilt thou slay also a righteous nation? *Ge.* 20: 4.

All the ends of the world shall remember and turn unto the Lord. *Ps.* 22: 27.

Blessed is the nation whose God is the Lord. *Ps.* 33: 12.

Open ye the gates, that the righteous nation which keepeth the truth may enter in. *Is.* 26: 2.

Yea, many people and strong nations shall come to seek the Lord. *Zch.* 8: 22.

Before him shall be gathered all nations. *Mat.* 25: 32.

Render to Caesar the things that are Caesar's, and to God the things that are God's. *Mk.* 12: 17.

In every nation he that feareth him, and worketh righteousness, is accepted with him. *Ac.* 10: 35.

Render therefore to all their dues: tribute to whom tribute is due; custom to whom custom. *Ro.* 13: 7.
See also
Community; Country; Empire; Nation; Nation, Decadence of; Nation, Greatness of; Nation, Prosperity of; Nations, League of; People; Race.

Statesmanship

Look out a man discreet and wise, and set him over the land of Egypt. *Ge.* 41: 33.

Ye shall be unto me a kingdom of priests, and an holy nation. *Ex.* 19: 6.

By the good hand of our God upon us, they brought us a man of understanding. *Ezr.* 8: 18.

Righteousness exalteth a nation. *Pr.* **14: 34.**
Where there is no vision, the people perish.
Pr. **29: 18.**
I will commit thy government into his hand.
Is. **22: 21.**
Behold, I have given him for a witness to
the people, a leader and commander to the
people. *Is.* **55: 4.**
Lift up a standard for the people. *Is.* **62: 10.**
He shall execute judgment and righteousness
in the land. *Je.* **33: 15.**
It is required in stewards, that a man be
found faithful. *1 Co.* **4: 2.**
See also
Citizenship; Government; Leadership.

Stature
Saul, a choice young man, and a goodly:
. . . from his shoulders and upward he was
higher than any of the people. *1 S.* **9: 2.**
Look not on his countenance, or on the
height of his stature; because I have refused
him. *1 S.* **16: 7.**
There went out a champion out of the camp
of the Philistines, named Goliath, of Gath,
whose height was six cubits and a span. *1 S.*
17: 4.
Men of stature shall come over unto thee, and
they shall be thine. *Is.* **45: 14.**
Which of you by taking thought can add
one cubit unto his stature? *Mat.* **6: 27.**
Jesus increased in wisdom and stature. *Lu.*
2: 52.
Unto the measure of the stature of the fulness of Christ. *Ep.* **4: 13.**
See also
Growth; Height.

Statute
In his law doth he meditate day and night.
Ps. **1: 2.**
The statutes of the Lord are right, re-
joicing the heart: the commandment of the
Lord is pure, enlightening the eyes. *Ps.* **19: 8.**
The law of his God is in his heart; none of
his steps shall slide. *Ps.* **37: 31.**
Thy statutes have been my songs in the
house of my pilgrimage. *Ps.* **119: 54.**
Thy commandment is exceeding broad. *Ps.*
119: 96.
The thing is true, according to the law of
the Medes and Persians, which altereth not.
Da. **6: 12.**
Think not that I am come to destroy the
law, or the prophets: I am not come to destroy,
but to fulfil. *Mat.* **5: 17.**
If thou wilt enter into life, keep the commandments. *Mat.* **19: 17.**
Master, which is the great commandment in
the law? *Mat.* **22: 36.**
Now we are delivered from the law, that
being dead wherein we were held; that we
should serve in newness of spirit, and not in
the oldness of the letter. *Ro.* **7: 6.**
This is the love of God, that we keep his
commandments. *1 Jn.* **5: 3.**
See also
Commandment; Decree; God, Commandment
of; God, Law of; Law; Ordinance.

Steadfastness
Cleave unto the Lord your God, as ye have
done unto this day. *Jos.* **23: 8.**

The man of God said unto the king, If thou
wilt give me half thine house, I will not go
in with thee. *1 K.* **13: 8.**
Then shalt thou lift up thy face without spot;
yea, thou shalt be stedfast, and shalt not fear.
Jb. **11: 15.**
The righteous also shall hold on his way,
and he that hath clean hands shall be
stronger and stronger. *Jb.* **17: 9.**
My foot hath held his steps, his way have I
kept, and not declined. *Jb.* **23: 11.**
Who shall dwell in thy holy hill? . . . He
that sweareth to his own hurt, and changeth
not. *Ps.* **15: 1, 4.**
My covenant will I not break, nor alter the
thing that has gone out of my lips. *Ps.* **89: 34.**
He that endureth to the end shall be saved.
Mat. **10: 22.**
He that shall endure unto the end, the same
shall be saved. *Mat.* **24: 13.**
He stedfastly set his face to go to Jerusalem.
Lu. **9: 51.**
If ye continue in my word, then are ye my
disciples indeed. *Jn.* **8: 31.**
Continue ye in my love. *Jn.* **15: 9.**
Ye shall abide in my love. *Jn.* **15: 10.**
We cannot but speak the things which we
have seen and heard. *Ac.* **4: 20.**
Watch ye, stand fast in the faith, quit you
like men, be strong. *1 Co.* **16: 13.**
Stand fast therefore in the liberty where-
with Christ hath made us free. *Ga.* **5: 1.**
Let us not be weary in well doing. *Ga.* **6: 9.**
Stand therefore. *Ep.* **6: 14.**
Stand fast in one spirit, with one mind striv-
ing together for the faith of the gospel. *Ph.* **1:27.**
I am with you in the spirit, joying and be-
holding your order, and the stedfastness of
your faith in Christ. *Col.* **2: 5.**
Which hope we have as an anchor of the
soul. *He.* **6: 19.**
Beware lest ye also, being led away with
the error of the wicked, fall from your own
stedfastness. *2 Pe.* **3: 17.**
Hold that fast which thou hast, that no man
take thy crown. *Re.* **3: 11.**
See also
Constancy; Faithfulness; Firmness; Security;
Stability.

Stealth
Lay thee an ambush for the city. *Jos.* **8: 2.**
Behold, ye shall lie in wait against the city.
Jos. **8: 4.**
He taketh the wise in their own craftiness.
Jb. **5: 13.**
The murderer rising with the light killeth
the poor and needy, and in the night is as
a thief. *Jb.* **24: 14.**
The eye also of the adulterer waiteth for
the twilight, saying, No eye shall see me: and
disguiseth his face. *Jb.* **24: 15.**
He sitteth in the lurking places of the vil-
lages: in the secret places doth he murder the
innocent. *Ps.* **10: 8.**
He lieth in wait secretly as a lion in his den.
Ps. **10: 9.**
The scribes sought how they might take him
by craft. *Mk.* **14: 1.**
They lie in wait to deceive. *Ep.* **4: 14.**
See also
Secrecy.

Step

They heard the voice of the Lord God walking in the garden in the cool of the day. *Ge.* 3: 8.

Enoch walked with God. *Ge.* 5: 22.

There is but a step between me and death. *S.* 20: 3.

Thou numberest my steps. *Jb.* 14: 16.

Doth not he see my ways, and count all my steps? *Jb.* 31: 4.

If my step hath turned out of the way, . . . Then let me sow, and let another eat. *Jb.* 31: 7, 8.

Thou hast enlarged my steps under me, that my feet did not slip. *Ps.* 18: 36.

Though I walk through the valley of the shadow of death, I will fear no evil. *Ps.* 23: 4.

The steps of a good man are ordered by the Lord. *Ps.* 37: 23.

I will walk at liberty. *Ps.* 119: 45.

Order my steps in thy word. *Ps.* 119: 133.

Thy foot shall not stumble. *Pr.* 3: 23.

A man's heart deviseth his way: but the Lord directeth his steps. *Pr.* 16: 9.

They shall walk, and not faint. *Is.* 40: 31.

O Lord, I know that the way of man is not in himself: it is not in man that walketh to direct his steps. *Je.* 10: 23.

Go thou thy way till the end be. *Da.* 12: 13.

They shall walk every one in his path. *Jo.* 2: 8.

He will teach us of his ways, and we will walk in his paths. *Mi.* 4: 2.

All people will walk every one in the name of his god, and we will walk in the name of the Lord our God for ever and ever. *Mi.* 4: 5.

He hath shewed thee, O man, what is good; and what doth the Lord require of thee, but to do justly, and to love mercy, and to walk humbly with thy God? *Mi.* 6: 8.

They followed him on foot. *Mat.* 14: 13.

I must walk to day, and to morrow, and the day following. *Lu.* 13: 33.

We also should walk in newness of life. *Ro.* 6: 4.

If we live in the Spirit, let us also walk in the Spirit. *Ga.* 5: 25.

Christ also suffered for us, leaving us an example, that ye should follow his steps. *1 Pe.* 2: 21.

See also

Foot; Footstep; Walk.

Steward

My sons, be not now negligent: for the Lord hath chosen you to stand before him, to serve him. *2 Ch.* 29: 11.

Well done, thou good and faithful servant. *Mat.* 25: 21.

Who then is that faithful and wise steward, whom his lord shall make ruler over his household? *Lu.* 12: 42.

Unto whomsoever much is given, of him shall be much required: and to whom men have committed much, of him they will ask the more. *Lu.* 12: 48.

Give an account of thy stewardship. *Lu.* 16: 2.

The Lord commended the unjust steward, because he had done wisely: for the children of this world are in their generation wiser than the children of light. *Lu.* 16: 8.

The servant is not greater than his lord; neither he that is sent greater than he that sent him. *Jn.* 13: 16.

Every one of us shall give account of himself to God. *Ro.* 14: 12.

Let a man so account of us, as of the ministers of Christ, and stewards of the mysteries of God. *1 Co.* 4: 1.

Moreover it is required in stewards, that a man be found faithful. *1 Co.* 4: 2.

Keep that which is committed to thy trust. *1 Ti.* 6: 20.

A bishop must be blameless, as the steward of God. *Tit.* 1: 7.

As every man hath received the gift, even so minister the same one to another, as good stewards of the manifold grace of God. *1 Pe.* 4: 10.

See also

God, Servant of; Ministry; Servant; Service.

Stillness

The Lord lift up his countenance upon thee, and give thee peace. *Nu.* 6: 26.

He leadeth me beside the still waters. *Ps.* 23: 2.

Be still, and know that I am God. *Ps.* 46: 10.

I will hear what God the Lord will speak: for he will speak peace unto his people. *Ps.* 85: 8.

Thou wilt keep him in perfect peace, whose mind is stayed on thee: because he trusteth in thee. *Is.* 26: 3.

Ye shall go out with joy, and be led forth with peace. *Is.* 55: 12.

Ye shall find rest unto your souls. *Mat.* 11: 29.

Being justified by faith, we have peace with God through our Lord Jesus Christ. *Ro.* 5: 1.

That ye study to be quiet. *1 Th.* 4: 11.

Now the Lord of peace himself give you peace always by all means. *2 Th.* 3: 16.

See also

Calm; Christ, Silence of; God, Silence of; Peace; Quiet; Repose; Tranquillity.

Stoicism

If I perish, I perish. *Es.* 4: 16.

The Lord gave, and the Lord hath taken away; blessed be the name of the Lord. *Jb.* 1: 21.

Shall we receive good at the hand of God, and shall we not receive evil? *Jb.* 2: 10.

Though he slay me, yet will I trust in him. *Jb.* 13: 15.

Though I walk through the valley of the shadow of death, I will fear no evil. *Ps.* 23: 4.

If thou faint in the day of adversity, thy strength is small. *Pr.* 24: 10.

I said in mine heart, Go to now, I will prove thee with mirth, therefore enjoy pleasure: and, behold, this also is vanity. *Ec.* 2: 1.

I said of laughter, It is mad; and of mirth, What doeth it? *Ec.* 2: 2.

It shall be well with them that fear God. *Ec.* 8: 12.

When thou walkest through the fire, thou shalt not be burned; neither shall the flame kindle upon thee. *Is.* 43: 2.

Although the fig tree shall not blossom, neither shall fruit be in the vines; the labour of the olive shall fail, and the fields shall yield no meat; the flock shall be cut off from the

fold, and there shall be no herd in the stalls:
Yet I will rejoice in the Lord. *Hab.* 3: 17, 18.

O my Father, if this cup may not pass away
from me, except I drink it, thy will be done.
Mat. 26: 42.

In a great trial of affliction the abundance
of their joy and their deep poverty abounded.
2 *Co.* 8: 2.

I have learned, in whatsoever state I am,
therewith to be content. *Ph.* 4: 11.

See also

Endurance; God, Will of; Indifference;
Patience; Resignation.

Stomach

Upon thy belly shalt thou go, and dust shalt
thou eat. *Ge.* 3: 14.

They conceive mischief, and bring forth
vanity, and their belly prepareth deceit. *Jb.*
15: 35.

I have eaten ashes like bread. *Ps.* 102: 9.

The belly of the wicked shall want. *Pr.* 13:
25.

Out of the belly of hell cried I. *Jon.* 2: 2.

As in the days that were before the flood
they were eating and drinking, marrying and
giving in marriage. *Mat.* 24: 38.

Man shall not live by bread alone, but by
every word of God. *Lu.* 4: 4.

The life is more than meat, and the body
is more than raiment. *Lu.* 12: 23.

I have meat to eat that ye know not of. *Jn.*
4: 32.

My meat is to do the will of him that sent
me, and to finish his work. *Jn.* 4: 34.

Labour not for the meat which perisheth,
but for that meat which endureth unto everlasting life. *Jn.* 6: 27.

My Father giveth you the true bread from
heaven. *Jn.* 6: 32.

Jesus said unto them, I am the bread of life.
Jn. 6: 35.

My flesh is meat indeed, and my blood is
drink indeed. *Jn.* 6: 55.

Jesus saith unto them, Come and dine. *Jn.*
21: 12.

The kingdom of God is not meat and drink;
but righteousness, and peace, and joy in the
Holy Ghost. *Ro.* 14: 17.

They that are such serve not our Lord Jesus
Christ, but their own belly. *Ro.* 16: 18.

Meats for the belly, and the belly for meats:
but God shall destroy both it and them. *1 Co.*
6: 13.

Whose God is their belly. *Ph.* 3: 19.

Drink no longer water, but use a little wine
for thy stomach's sake. *1 Ti.* 5: 23.

See also

Bread; Food; Hunger; Meat; Nourishment.

Stone

Jacob set up a pillar in the place where he
talked with him, even a pillar of stone. *Ge.* 35:
14.

Thou shalt be in league with the stones of
the field: and the beasts of the field shall be at
peace with thee. *Jb.* 5: 23.

Is my strength the strength of stones? or
is my flesh of brass? *Jb.* 6: 12.

The waters wear the stones. *Jb.* 14: 19.

His heart is as firm as a stone; yea, as hard
as a piece of the nether millstone. *Jb.* 41: 24.

He shall set me up upon a rock. *Ps.* 27: 5.

They shall bear thee up in their hands, lest
thou dash thy foot against a stone. *Ps.* 91: 12.

Happy shall he be, that taketh and dasheth
thy little ones against the stones. *Ps.* 137: 9.

He that rolleth a stone, it will return upon
him. *Pr.* 26: 27.

A stone is heavy, and the sand weighty;
but a fool's wrath is heavier than them both.
Pr. 27: 3.

A time to cast away stones, and a time to
gather stones together. *Ec.* 3: 5.

Behold, I lay in Zion for a foundation a
stone, a tried stone, a precious corner stone, a
sure foundation. *Is.* 28: 16.

Look unto the rock whence ye are hewn. *Is.*
51: 1.

I will take the stony heart out of their
flesh, and will give them an heart of flesh. *Eze.*
11: 19.

What man is there of you, whom if his son
ask bread, will he give him a stone? *Mat.* 7: 9.

Some fell upon stony places. *Mat.* 13: 5.

Whosoever shall fall on this stone shall be
broken: but on whomsoever it shall fall, it
will grind him to powder. *Mat.* 21: 44.

O Jerusalem, Jerusalem, thou that killest
the prophets, and stonest them which are sent
unto thee, how often would I have gathered
thy children together, . . . and ye would not!
Mat. 23: 37.

There shall not be left here one stone upon
another, that shall not be thrown down. *Mat.*
24: 2.

The angel of the Lord descended from
heaven, and came and rolled back the stone
from the door, and sat upon it. *Mat.* 28: 2.

If thou be the Son of God, command this
stone that it be made bread. *Lu.* 4: 3.

I tell you that, if these should hold their
peace, the stones would immediately cry out.
Lu. 19: 40.

Once was I stoned. 2 *Co.* 11: 25.

They were stoned. *He.* 11: 37.

Ye also, as lively stones, are built up a
spiritual house. *1 Pe.* 2: 5.

See also

Christ, the Rock; Cornerstone; Memorial;
Rock.

Store

The Lord shall command the blessing upon
thee in thy storehouses, and in all that thou
settest thine hand unto. *De.* 28: 8.

He gathereth the waters of the sea together
as an heap: he layeth up the depth in storehouses. *Ps.* 33: 7.

That our garners may be full, affording all
manner of store. *Ps.* 144: 13.

We shall find all precious substance, we shall
fill our houses with spoil. *Pr.* 1: 13.

Come against her from the utmost border,
open her storehouses: cast her up as heaps,
and destroy her utterly. *Je.* 50: 26.

They know not to do right, saith the Lord,
who store up violence and robbery in their
palaces. *Am.* 3: 10.

Consider the ravens: for they neither sow nor
reap; which neither have storehouse nor barn;
and God feedeth them. *Lu.* 12: 24.

Laying up in store for themselves a good

foundation against the time to come, that they may lay hold on eternal life. *1 Ti.* 6: 19.

See also

Abundance; Accumulation; Goods; Substance.

Storm

Here shall thy proud waves be stayed. *Jb.* 38: 11.

The floods lift up their waves. *Ps.* 93: 3.

He maketh the storm a calm, so that the waves thereof are still. *Ps.* 107: 29.

Thou hast been a . . . refuge from the storm. *Is.* 25: 4.

A man shall be as an hiding place from the wind, and a covert from the tempest. *Is.* 32: 2.

The Lord hath his way in the whirlwind and in the storm. *Na.* 1: 3.

The rain descended, and the floods came, and the winds blew, and beat upon that house; and it fell not: for it was founded upon a rock. *Mat.* 7: 25.

The ship was now in the midst of the sea, tossed with waves. *Mat.* 14: 24.

He that wavereth is like a wave of the sea driven with the wind and tossed. *Ja.* 1: 6.

See also

Tempest; Wind.

Strait

I am in a great strait. *2 S.* 24: 14.

The place where we dwell with thee is too strait for us. *2 K.* 6: 1.

He enlargeth the nations, and straiteneth them again. *Jb.* 12: 23.

In the fulness of his sufficiency he shall be in straits. *Jb.* 20: 22.

Even so would he have removed thee out of the strait into a broad place, where there is no straitness. *Jb.* 36: 16.

The place is too strait for me: give place to me that I may dwell. *Is.* 49: 20.

I will cause them to eat the flesh of their sons and the flesh of their daughters, and they shall eat every one the flesh of his friend in the siege and straitness. *Je.* 19: 9.

Is the spirit of the Lord straitened? *Mi.* 2: 7.

Enter ye in at the strait gate. *Mat.* 7: 13.

I have a baptism to be baptized with; and how am I straitened till it be accomplished! *Lu.* 12: 50.

I am in a strait betwixt two, having a desire to depart, and to be with Christ; which is far better: Nevertheless to abide in the flesh is more needful for you. *Ph.* 1: 23, 24.

See also

Difficulty; Distress; Narrowness; Need.

Strangeness

Put away the strange gods that are among you, and be clean. *Ge.* 35: 2.

I have been a stranger in a strange land. *Ex.* 2: 22.

How shall we sing the Lord's song in a strange land? *Ps.* 137: 4.

Why have they provoked me to anger with their graven images, and with strange vanities? *Je.* 8: 19.

We have seen strange things to day. *Lu.* 5: 26.

His seed should sojourn in a strange land. *Ac.* 7: 6.

He seemeth to be a setter forth of strange gods. *Ac.* 17: 18.

Thou bringest certain strange things to our ears. *Ac.* 17: 20.

By faith he sojourned in the land of promise, as in a strange country. *He.* 11: 9.

Be not carried about with divers and strange doctrines. *He.* 13: 9.

Beloved, think it not strange concerning the fiery trial which is to try you, as though some strange thing happened to you. *1 Pe.* 4: 12.

See also

Abnormality; Abomination; Stranger; Unnaturalness.

Stranger

Thou art a stranger, and also an exile. *2 S.* 15: 19.

We are strangers before thee, and sojourners, as were all our fathers. *1 Ch.* 29: 15.

I am a stranger in the earth. *Ps.* 119: 19.

The Lord preserveth the strangers. *Ps.* 146: 9.

Even them will I bring to my holy mountain, and make them joyful in my house of prayer. *Is.* 56: 7.

Art thou only a stranger in Jerusalem, and hast not known the things which are come to pass there in these days? *Lu.* 24: 18.

Aliens from the commonwealth of Israel. *Ep.* 2: 12.

Now in Christ Jesus ye who sometimes were far off are made nigh by the blood of Christ. *Ep.* 2: 13.

Now therefore ye are no more strangers and foreigners, but fellowcitizens with the saints, and of the household of God. *Ep.* 2: 19.

These all . . . confessed that they were strangers and pilgrims on the earth. *He.* 11: 13.

Peter, an apostle of Jesus Christ, to the strangers scattered throughout Pontus, Galatia, Cappadocia, Asia, and Bithynia. *1 Pe.* 1: 1.

I beseech you as strangers and pilgrims. *1 Pe.* 2: 11.

See also

Alien; Foreigner; Gentile; Immigration; Strangeness.

Stream

A river went out of Eden to water the garden. *Ge.* 2: 10.

Are not Abana and Pharpar, rivers of Damascus, better than all the waters of Israel? may I not wash in them, and be clean? *2 K.* 5: 12.

As the hart panteth after the water brooks, so panteth my soul after thee, O God. *Ps.* 42: 1.

There is a river, the streams whereof shall make glad the city of God, the holy place of the tabernacles of the most High. *Ps.* 46: 4.

Thou visitest the earth, and waterest it: thou greatly enrichest it with the river of God. *Ps.* 65: 9.

He shall drink of the brook in the way: therefore shall he lift up the head. *Ps.* 110: 7.

By the rivers of Babylon, there we sat down, yea, we wept. *Ps.* 137: 1.

A fountain of gardens, a well of living waters, and streams from Lebanon. *S. of S.* 4: 15.

A man shall be . . . as rivers of water in a dry place. *Is.* 32: 2.

When thou passest through the waters, I will be with thee; and through the rivers, they shall not overflow thee. *Is.* 43: 2.

Every thing that liveth, which moveth, whithersoever the river shall come, shall live. *Eze.* 47: 9.

He that believeth on me, as the scripture hath said, out of his belly shall flow rivers of living water. *Jn.* 7: 38.

He shewed me a pure river of water of life, clear as crystal. *Re.* 22: 1.

See also
River; Water.

Street

I made their streets waste, that none passeth by. *Zph.* 3: 6.

The streets of the city shall be full of boys and girls playing in the streets thereof. *Zch.* 8: 5.

They love to pray standing in the synagogues and in the corners of the streets. *Mat.* 6: 5.

Arise, and go into the street which is called Straight. *Ac.* 9: 11.

The street of the city was pure gold, as it were transparent glass. *Re.* 21: 21.

In the midst of the street of it, . . . was there the tree of life. *Re.* 22: 2.

See also
Christ, Way of; God, Way of; Highway; Life, Path of; Path; Road; Way.

Strength

Out of the strong came forth sweetness. *Ju.* 14: 14.

Tell me, I pray thee, wherein thy great strength lieth. *Ju.* 16: 6.

Howbeit the hair of his head began to grow again after he was shaven. *Ju.* 16: 22.

How are the mighty fallen! *2 S.* 1: 19.

Be strong and courageous, be not afraid nor dismayed for . . . all the multitude. *2 Ch.* 32: 7.

The Lord is the strength of my life. *Ps.* 27: 1.

Cast thy burden upon the Lord, and he shall sustain thee. *Ps.* 55: 22.

I will lift up mine eyes unto the hills, from whence cometh my help. *Ps.* 121: 1.

Their strength is to sit still. *Is.* 30: 7.

Strengthen ye the weak hands, and confirm the feeble knees. *Is.* 35: 3.

Awake, awake, put on strength, O arm of the Lord. *Is.* 51: 9.

Awake, awake; put on thy strength, O Zion. *Is.* 52: 1.

The floods came, and the winds blew, and beat upon that house; and it fell not: for it was founded upon a rock. *Mat.* 7: 25.

Thou shalt love the Lord thy God . . . with all thy strength. *Mk.* 12: 30.

The stream beat vehemently upon that house, and could not shake it: for it was founded upon a rock. *Lu.* 6: 48.

Be strong. *1 Co.* 16: 13.

When I am weak, then am I strong. *2 Co.* 12: 10.

The signs of an apostle were wrought among you in all patience, in signs, and wonders, and mighty deeds. *2 Co.* 12: 12.

Out of weakness were made strong. *He.* 11: 34.

See also
Christ, Power of; Christ, Strength of; Coer-

cion; Energy; Firmness; Force; Fortitude; God, Omnipotence of; God, Power of; God, Strength of; Might; Omnipotence; Power; Vigor; Vitality.

Strictness

Thou . . . lookest narrowly unto all my paths. *Jb.* 13: 27.

The place is too strait for me: give place to me that I may dwell. *Is.* 49: 20.

Strait is the gate, and narrow is the way, which leadeth unto life. *Mat.* 7: 14.

All these things have I kept from my youth up: what lack I yet? *Mat.* 19: 20.

Ye pay tithes of mint and anise and cummin, and have omitted the weightier matters of the law. *Mat.* 23: 23.

I fast twice in the week, I give tithes of all that I possess. *Lu.* 18: 12.

After the most straitest sect of our religion I lived a Pharisee. *Ac.* 26: 5.

We should serve in newness of spirit, and not in the oldness of the letter. *Ro.* 7: 6.

See also
Harshness; Restraint; Restriction; Severity.

Strife

He lifted up his eyes and looked, and, behold, there stood a man over against him with his sword drawn in his hand. *Jos.* 5: 13.

Men of war fit for the battle. *1 Ch.* 12: 8.

Nation was destroyed of nation, and city of city. *2 Ch.* 15: 6.

The battle is not yours, but God's. *2 Ch.* 20: 15.

Blessed be the Lord my strength, which teacheth my hands to war, and my fingers to fight. *Ps.* 144: 1.

These . . . things doth the Lord hate; . . . A false witness that speaketh lies, and he that soweth discord among brethren. *Pr.* 6: 19.

It is an honour for a man to cease from strife. *Pr.* 20: 3.

He that is of a proud heart stirreth up strife. *Pr.* 28: 25.

Violence in the land, ruler against ruler. *Je.* 51: 46.

Nation shall rise against nation, and kingdom against kingdom. *Lu.* 21: 10.

Lest haply ye be found even to fight against God. *Ac.* 5: 39.

So fight I, not as one that beateth the air. *1 Co.* 9: 26.

Quit you like men, be strong. *1 Co.* 16: 13.

We wrestle not against flesh and blood. *Ep.* 6: 12.

There was war in heaven. *Re.* 12: 7.

See also
Attack; Battle; Contention; Fight; Quarrel; Struggle; War.

Stripe

Thou shalt give life for life, . . . Burning for burning, wound for wound, stripe for stripe. *Ex.* 21: 23, 25.

If he commit iniquity, I will chasten him with the rod of men, and with the stripes of the children of men. *2 S.* 7: 14.

Then will I visit their transgression with the rod, and their iniquity with stripes. *Ps.* 89: 32.

A rod is for the back of him that is void of understanding. *Pr.* 10: 13.

Judgments are prepared for scorners, and

stripes for the back of fools. *Pr.* 19: 29.

The chastisement of our peace was upon him; and with his stripes we are healed. *Is.* 53: 5.

In stripes, in imprisonments, in tumults, in labours, in watchings, in fastings. 2 *Co.* 6: 5.

In labours more abundant, in stripes above measure, in prisons more frequent, in deaths oft. 2 *Co.* 11: 23.

Of the Jews five times received I forty stripes save one. 2 *Co.* 11: 24.

Thrice was I beaten with rods. 2 *Co.* 11: 25.

See also

Chastisement; Discipline; God, Chastisement of; God, Punishment of; Punishment; Rod; Scourge; Tribulation.

Struggle

There wrestled a man with him until the breaking of the day. *Ge.* 32: 24.

They be many that fight against me. *Ps.* 56: 2.

Ye shall hear of wars and rumours of wars. *Mat.* 24: 6.

So fight I, not as one that beateth the air. *1 Co.* 9: 26.

We wrestle not against flesh and blood, but against principalities, against powers. *Ep.* 6: 12.

Whence come wars and fightings among you? *Ja.* 4: 1.

Ye fight and war, yet ye have not, because ye ask not. *Ja.* 4: 2.

See also

Battle; Contention; Fight; Quarrel; Strife; War.

Stubbornness

It is a stiffnecked people. *Ex.* 32: 9.

I spake unto you; and ye would not hear, but rebelled against the commandment of the Lord, and went presumptuously up into the hill. *De.* 1: 43.

Look not unto the stubbornness of this people, nor to their wickedness, nor to their sin. *De.* 9: 27.

This our son is stubborn and rebellious, he will not obey our voice. *De.* 21: 20.

The people refused to obey the voice of Samuel; and they said, Nay; but we will have a king over us. *1 S.* 8: 19.

He stiffened his neck, and hardened his heart from turning unto the Lord God of Israel. *2 Ch.* 36: 13.

That they . . . might not be as their fathers, a stubborn and rebellious generation. *Ps.* 78: 7, 8.

She is loud and stubborn; her feet abide not in her house. *Pr.* 7: 11.

A threefold cord is not quickly broken. *Ec.* 4: 12.

The bricks are fallen down, but we will build with hewn stones. *Is.* 9: 10.

They have turned unto me the back, and not the face. *Je.* 32: 33.

As for the word that thou hast spoken unto us in the name of the Lord, we will not hearken unto thee. *Je.* 44: 16

They are impudent children and stiffhearted. *Eze.* 2: 4.

They refused to hearken, and pulled away

the shoulder, and stopped their ears. *Zch.* 7: 11.

Ye stiffnecked and uncircumcised in heart and ears, ye do always resist the Holy Ghost: as your fathers did, so do ye. *Ac.* 7: 51.

See also

Firmness; Hardness; Impenitence; Steadfastness.

Study

In his law doth he meditate day and night. *Ps.* 1: 2.

I will meditate in thy statutes. *Ps.* 119: 48.

I meditate on all thy works; I muse on the work of thy hands. *Ps.* 143: 5.

Wisdom is the principal thing; therefore get wisdom. *Pr.* 4: 7.

Whoso loveth instruction loveth knowledge. *Pr.* 12: 1.

In much wisdom is much grief: and he that increaseth knowledge increaseth sorrow. *Ec.* 1: 18.

Of making many books there is no end; and much study is a weariness of the flesh. *Ec.* 12: 12.

Study to be quiet, and to do your own business, and to work with your own hands. *1 Th.* 4: 11.

Study to shew thyself approved unto God. *2 Ti.* 2: 15.

See also

Brain; Consideration; Contemplation; Meditation; Pupil; School; Teacher; Thought.

Stumbling-Block

Thou shalt not . . . put a stumblingblock before the blind. *Le.* 19: 14.

The way of the wicked is as darkness: they know not at what they stumble. *Pr.* 4: 19.

None shall be weary nor stumble among them. *Is.* 5: 27.

Take up the stumblingblock out of the way of my people. *Is.* 57: 14.

We grope as if we had no eyes: we stumble at noon day as in the night. *Is.* 59: 10.

Gather out the stones. *Is.* 62: 10.

If any man walk in the day, he stumbleth not. *Jn.* 11: 9.

I lay in Sion a stumblingstone and rock of offence: and whosoever believeth on him shall not be ashamed. *Ro.* 9: 33.

Judge this rather, that no man put a stumblingblock or an occasion to fall in his brother's way. *Ro.* 14: 13.

We preach Christ crucified, unto the Jews a stumblingblock, and unto the Greeks foolishness. *1 Co.* 1: 23.

Take heed lest by any means this liberty of yours become a stumblingblock to them that are weak. *1 Co.* 8: 9.

A stone of stumbling, and a rock of offence, even to them which stumble at the word, being disobedient. *1 Pe.* 2: 8.

He that loveth his brother abideth in the light, and there is none occasion of stumbling in him. *1 Jn.* 2: 10.

See also

Hindrance; Impediment; Obstacle; Obstruction.

Stupidity

Behold, I have played the fool, and have erred exceedingly. *1 S.* **26: 21.**

In the greatness of his folly he shall go astray. *Pr.* **5: 23.**

He that followeth vain persons is void of understanding. *Pr.* **12: 11.**

The way of a fool is right in his own eyes. *Pr.* **12: 15.**

The foolishness of fools is folly. *Pr.* **14: 24.**

Folly is joy to him that is destitute of wisdom. *Pr.* **15: 21.**

Let a bear robbed of her whelps meet a man, rather than a fool in his folly. *Pr.* **17: 12.**

A fool's mouth is his destruction. *Pr.* **18: 7.**

I went by . . . the vineyard of the man void of understanding; And, lo, it was all grown over with thorns. *Pr.* **24: 30, 31.**

Seest thou a man wise in his own conceit? there is more hope of a fool than of him. *Pr.* **26: 12.**

Whoso causeth the righteous to go astray in an evil way, he shall fall himself into his own pit. *Pr.* **28: 10.**

A fool uttereth all his mind. *Pr.* **29: 11.**

I saw that wisdom excelleth folly, as far as light excelleth darkness. *Ec.* **2: 13.**

O my people, they which lead thee cause thee to err. *Is.* **3: 12.**

They err in vision, they stumble in judgment. *Is.* **28: 7.**

He that getteth riches, and not by right, shall leave them in the midst of his days, and at his end shall be a fool. *Je.* **17: 11.**

O fools, and slow of heart to believe. *Lu.* **24: 25.**

Their foolish heart was darkened. *Ro.* **1: 21.**

Having the understanding darkened. *Ep.* **4: 18.**

Ye were as sheep going astray. *1 Pe.* **2: 25.**

See also

Folly; Fool.

Subjection

It is God that avengeth me, and subdueth the people under me. *Ps.* **18: 47.**

Through thy name will we tread them under that rise up against us. *Ps.* **44: 5.**

He shall subdue the people under us, and the nations under our feet. *Ps.* **47: 3.**

Their enemies also oppressed them, and they were brought into subjection under their hand. *Ps.* **106: 42.**

We are not under the law, but under grace. *Ro.* **6: 15.**

Let every soul be subject unto the higher powers. *Ro.* **13: 1.**

I keep under my body, and bring it into subjection. *1 Co.* **9: 27.**

The spirits of the prophets are subject to the prophets. *1 Co.* **14: 32.**

When all things shall be subdued unto him, then shall the Son also himself be subject unto him that put all things under him, that God may be all in all. *1 Co.* **15: 28.**

As the church is subject unto Christ, so let the wives be to their own husbands. *Ep.* **5: 24.**

According to the working whereby he is able even to subdue all things unto himself. *Ph.* **3: 21.**

Unto the angels hath he not put in subjection the world to come. *He.* **2: 5.**

Thou hast put all things in subjection under his feet. For in that he put all in subjection under him, he left nothing that is not put under him. *He.* **2: 8.**

Who through faith subdued kingdoms. *He.* **11: 33.**

We have had fathers of our flesh which corrected us, and we gave them reverence: shall we not much rather be in subjection unto the Father of spirits, and live? *He.* **12: 9.**

Angels and authorities and powers being made subject unto him. *1 Pe.* **3: 22.**

See also

Bondage; Captivity; Imprisonment; Prison; Slavery; Subordination.

Sublimity

God said, Let us make man in our image. *Ge.* **1: 26.**

A man of God came unto me, and his countenance was like the countenance of an angel of God, very terrible. *Ju.* **13: 6.**

There appeared a chariot of fire, and horses of fire, and . . . Elijah went up by a whirlwind into heaven. *2 K.* **2: 11.**

The Lord most high is terrible. *Ps.* **47: 2.**

He telleth the number of the stars; he calleth them all by their names. *Ps.* **147: 4.**

Thine eyes shall see the king in his beauty. *Is.* **33: 17.**

I will make the place of my feet glorious. *Is.* **60: 13.**

The heavens were opened, and I saw visions of God. *Eze.* **1: 1.**

Seek him that maketh the seven stars and Orion, and turneth the shadow of death into the morning, and maketh the day dark with night: that calleth for the waters of the sea, and poureth them out upon the face of the earth: The Lord is his name. *Am.* **5: 8.**

For I, saith the Lord, will be unto her a wall of fire round about, and will be the glory in the midst of her. *Zch.* **2: 5.**

All that sat in the council, looking stedfastly on him, saw his face as it had been the face of an angel. *Ac.* **6: 15.**

O the depth of the riches both of the wisdom and knowledge of God! how unsearchable are his judgments, and his ways past finding out! *Ro.* **11: 33.**

God, who commanded the light to shine out of darkness, hath shined in our hearts, to give the light of the knowledge of the glory of God in the face of Jesus Christ. *2 Co.* **4: 6.**

Thanks be unto God for his unspeakable gift. *2 Co.* **9: 15.**

See alo

Christ, Glory of; Glory; God, Glory of; God, Majesty of; Grandeur; Magnificence; Majesty; Splendor.

Submission

It is the Lord: let him do what seemeth him good. *1 S.* **3: 18.**

The Lord gave, and the Lord hath taken away; blessed be the name of the Lord. *Jb.* **1: 21.**

Teach me to do thy will; for thou art my God. *Ps.* **143: 10.**

Thy kingdom come. *Mat.* **6: 10.**

Thy will be done in earth, as it is in heaven. *Mat.* **6: 10.**

Nevertheless not as I will, but as thou wilt. *Mat.* **26: 39.**

So Pilate, willing to content the people, released Barabbas unto them, and delivered Jesus, when he had scourged him, to be crucified. *Mk.* **15: 15.**

Be it unto me according to thy word. *Lu.* **1: 38.**

The cup which my Father hath given me, shall I not drink it? *Jn.* **18: 11.**

Yield yourselves unto God. *Ro.* **6: 13.**

Let every soul be subject unto the higher powers. *Ro.* **13: 1.**

Submitting yourselves one to another in the fear of God. *Ep.* **5: 21.**

Submit yourselves therefore to God. *Ja.* **4: 7.**

Submit yourselves to every ordinance of man for the Lord's sake: whether it be to the king, as supreme; Or unto governors, as unto them that are sent by him for the punishment of evildoers, and for the praise of them that do well. *1 Pe.* **2: 13, 14.**

Likewise, ye younger, submit yourselves unto the elder. *1 Pe.* **5: 5.**

Yea, all of you be subject one to another, and be clothed with humility. *1 Pe.* **5: 5.**

See also

Acquiescence; Christ, Obedience to; God, Obedience to; Humility; Meekness; Modesty; Obedience; Subjection; Subordination.

Subordination

If Balak would give me his house full of silver and gold, I cannot go beyond the word of the Lord my God. *Nu.* **22: 18.**

Fear the Lord, and serve him in sincerity and in truth. *Jos.* **24: 14.**

It is the Lord: let him do what seemeth him good. *1 S.* **3: 18.**

To obey is better than sacrifice, and to hearken than the fat of rams. *1 S.* **15: 22.**

Shall mortal man be more just than God? shall a man be more pure than his maker? *Jb.* **4: 17.**

When the righteous are in authority, the people rejoice. *Pr.* **29: 2.**

Fear God, and keep his commandments: for this is the whole duty of man. *Ec.* **12: 13.**

Stand by thyself, come not near to me; for I am holier than thou. *Is.* **65: 5.**

Amend your ways and your doings, and obey the voice of the Lord your God. *Je.* **26: 13.**

Ye my flock, the flock of my pasture, are men, and I am your God, saith the Lord God. *Eze.* **34: 31.**

Be not ye called Rabbi: for one is your Master, even Christ; and all ye are brethren. *Mat.* **23: 8.**

Call no man your father upon the earth: for one is your Father, which is in heaven. *Mat.* **23: 9.**

Neither be ye called masters: for one is your Master, even Christ. *Mat.* **23: 10.**

Not as I will, but as thou wilt. *Mat.* **26: 39.**

Thy will be done. *Lu.* **11: 2.**

I was not disobedient unto the heavenly vision. *Ac.* **26: 19.**

By the obedience of one shall many be made righteous. *Ro.* **5: 19.**

Yield yourselves unto God. *Ro.* **6: 13.**

They . . . have not submitted themselves unto the righteousness of God. *Ro.* **10: 3.**

Let every soul be subject unto the higher powers. *Ro.* **13: 1.**

A man indeed ought not to cover his head, forasmuch as he is the image and glory of God: but the woman is the glory of the man. *1 Co.* **11: 7.**

Let your women keep silence in the churches: for it is not permitted unto them to speak; but they are commanded to be under obedience. *1 Co.* **14: 34.**

He hath put all things under his feet. *1 Co.* **15: 27.**

He that glorieth, let him glory in the Lord. *2 Co.* **10: 17.**

We are glad, when we are weak, and ye are strong. *2 Co.* **13: 9.**

If I yet pleased men, I should not be the servant of Christ. *Ga.* **1: 10.**

Children, obey your parents in the Lord: for this is right. *Ep.* **6: 1.**

He is able even to subdue all things unto himself. *Ph.* **3: 21.**

As obedient children. *1 Pe.* **1: 14.**

See also

Christ, Obedience to; God, Obedience to; Obedience; Subjection; Submission.

Substance

Every living substance that I have made will I destroy from off the face of the earth. *Ge.* **7: 4.**

The Lord shall make thee plenteous in goods. *De.* **28: 11.**

Thou hast blessed the work of his hands, and his substance is increased in the land. *Jb.* **1: 10.**

We shall find all precious substance, we shall fill our houses with spoil. *Pr.* **1: 13.**

So are the ways of every one that is greedy of gain; which taketh away the life of the owners thereof. *Pr.* **1: 19.**

That I may cause those that love me to inherit substance; and I will fill their treasures. *Pr.* **8: 21.**

The substance of a diligent man is precious. *Pr.* **12: 27.**

If a man would give all the substance of his house for love, it would utterly be contemned. *S. of S.* **8: 7.**

I will consecrate their gain unto the Lord, and their substance unto the Lord of the whole earth. *Mi.* **4: 13.**

Many others . . . ministered unto him of their substance. *Lu.* **8: 3.**

A man's life consisteth not in the abundance of the things which he possesseth. *Lu.* **12: 15.**

The younger son . . . wasted his substance with riotous living. *Lu.* **15: 13.**

Faith is the substance of things hoped for. *He.* **11: 1.**

See also

Goods; Possessions; Store; Wealth.

Substitution

Skin for skin, yea, all that a man hath will he give for his life. *Jb.* **2: 4.**

They change the night into day. *Jb.* **17: 12.**

The exchange of it shall not be for jewels of fine gold. *Jb.* **28: 17.**

I delight not in the blood of bullocks, or of lambs, or of he goats. *Is.* **1: 11.**

He was bruised for our iniquities. *Is.* **53: 5.**

To give unto them beauty for ashes, the oil

of joy for mourning, the garment of praise for the spirit of heaviness. *Is.* 61: 3.

Can the Ethiopian change his skin, or the leopard his spots? *Je.* 13: 23.

I desired mercy, and not sacrifice; and the knowledge of God more than burnt offerings. *Ho.* 6: 6.

Wherewith shall I come before the Lord, and bow myself before the high God? shall I come before him with burnt offerings, with calves of a year old? *Mi.* 6: 6.

Will the Lord be pleased with thousands of rams, or with ten thousands of rivers of oil? shall I give my firstborn for my transgression, the fruit of my body for the sin of my soul? *Mi.* 6: 7.

What shall a man give in exchange for his soul? *Mk.* 8: 37.

From henceforth thou shalt catch men. *Lu.* 5: 10.

The ruler of the feast . . . tasted the water that was made wine. *Jn.* 2: 9.

For which cause we faint not; but though our outward man perish, yet the inward man is renewed day by day. *2 Co.* 4: 16.

Who shall change our vile body, that it may be fashioned like unto his glorious body. *Ph.* 3: 21.

See also

Change.

Subtraction

Take not thy holy spirit from me. *Ps.* 51: 11.

Remove not the ancient landmark, which thy fathers have set. *Pr.* 22: 28.

Take away the dross from the silver, and there shall come forth a vessel for the finer. *Pr.* 25: 4.

Whosoever hath not, from him shall be taken even that he hath. *Mat.* 13: 12.

He called every one of his lord's debtors unto him, and said unto the first, How much owest thou unto my lord? And he said, An hundred measures of oil. And he said unto him, Take thy bill, and sit down quickly, and write fifty. *Lu.* 16: 5, 6.

Take from him the pound, and give it to him that hath ten pounds. *Lu.* 19: 24.

From him that hath not, even that he hath shall be taken away from him. *Lu.* 19: 26.

Your joy no man taketh from you. *Jn.* 16: 22.

If any man shall take away from the words of the book of this prophecy, God shall take away his part out of the book of life, and out of the holy city, and from the things which are written in this book. *Re.* 22: 19.

See also

Removal; Withdrawal.

Success

Then thou shalt have good success. *Jos.* 1: 8.

Within three days ye shall pass over this Jordan, to go in to possess the land, which the Lord your God giveth you to possess it. *Jos.* 1: 11.

The righteous also shall hold on his way, and he that hath clean hands shall be stronger and stronger. *Jb.* 17: 9.

If they obey and serve him, they shall spend their days in prosperity, and their years in pleasures. *Jb.* 36: 11.

As the rain cometh down, and the snow from heaven, and returneth not thither, but watereth the earth, and maketh it bring forth and bud, that it may give seed to the sower, and bread to the eater: So shall my word be that goeth forth out of my mouth: it shall not return unto me void, but it shall accomplish that which I please, and it shall prosper in the thing whereto I sent it. *Is.* 55: 10, 11.

We are more than conquerors through him that loved us. *Ro.* 8: 37.

I have not run in vain, neither laboured in vain. *Ph.* 2: 16.

The effectual fervent prayer of a righteous man availeth much. *Ja.* 5: 16.

Him that overcometh will I make a pillar in the temple of my God, and he shall go no more out. *Re.* 3: 12.

See also

Accomplishment; Achievement; Attainment; Christ, Triumph of; God, Victory of; Triumph; Victory.

Successor

There arose up a new king over Egypt, which knew not Joseph. *Ex.* 1: 8.

Moses my servant is dead; now therefore arise, go over this Jordan, thou, and all this people. *Jos.* 1: 2.

The spirit of Elijah doth rest on Elisha. *2 K.* 2: 15.

When David was old and full of days, he made Solomon his son king over Israel. *1 Ch.* 23: 1.

Hath Israel no sons? hath he no heir? *Je.* 49: 1.

He that cometh after me is preferred before me: for he was before me. *Jn.* 1: 15.

I will pray the Father, and he shall give you another Comforter, that he may abide with you for ever. *Jn.* 14: 16.

When the Comforter is come, whom I will send unto you from the Father, even the Spirit of truth, which proceedeth from the Father, he shall testify of me. *Jn.* 15: 26.

We are the children of God: And if children, then heirs. *Ro.* 8: 16, 17.

Blessed are the dead which die in the Lord from henceforth: Yea, saith the Spirit, that they may rest from their labours; and their works do follow them. *Re.* 14: 13.

See also

Follower; Heir.

Succor

Then began men to call upon the name of the Lord. *Ge.* 4: 26.

Stand still, and see the salvation of the Lord. *Ex.* 14: 13.

The Lord that delivered me out of the paw of the lion, and out of the paw of the bear, he will deliver me out of the hand of this Philistine. *1 S.* 17: 37.

Ye shall not need to fight in this battle: set yourselves, stand ye still, and see the salvation of the Lord with you. *2 Ch.* 20: 17.

With him is an arm of flesh; but with us is the Lord our God to help us, and to fight our battles. *2 Ch.* 32: 8.

An horse is a vain thing for safety. *Ps.* 33: 17.

I will not trust in my bow, neither shall my sword save me. *Ps.* 44: 6.

Wilt not thou deliver my feet from falling? *Ps.* **56: 13.**

I will bring my people again from the depths of the sea. *Ps.* **68: 22.**

Lo, this is our God; we have waited for him, and he will save us: this is the Lord. *Is.* **25: 9.**

When I called, was there none to answer? Is my hand shortened at all, that it cannot redeem? *Is.* **50: 2.**

I . . . will save them by the Lord their God, and will not save them by bow, nor by sword, nor by battle, by horses, nor by horsemen. *Ho.* **1: 7.**

Come over into Macedonia, and help us. *Ac.* **16: 9.**

I am with thee, and no man shall set on thee to hurt thee: for I have much people in this city. *Ac.* **18: 10.**

She hath been a succourer of many, and of myself also. *Ro.* **16: 2.**

In the day of salvation, have I succoured thee. *2 Co.* **6: 2.**

In that he himself hath suffered being tempted, he is able to succour them that are tempted. *He.* **2: 18.**

See also
Aid; Christ, the Savior; Deliverance; God, Deliverance of; God, Salvation of; Help; Redemption; Relief; Rescue; Salvation; Support.

Suffering

If any man will come after me, let him deny himself, and take up his cross, and follow me. *Mat.* **16: 24.**

Are ye able to drink of the cup that I shall drink of, and to be baptized with the baptism that I am baptized with? *Mat.* **20: 22.**

I will shew him how great things he must suffer for my name's sake. *Ac.* **9: 16.**

I reckon that the sufferings of this present time are not worthy to be compared with the glory which shall be revealed in us. *Ro.* **8: 18.**

Being reviled, we bless; being persecuted, we suffer it. *1 Co.* **4: 12.**

Charity suffereth long. *1 Co.* **13: 4.**

Our light affliction, which is but for a moment, worketh for us a far more exceeding and eternal weight of glory. *2 Co.* **4: 17.**

Unto you it is given in the behalf of Christ, not only to believe on him, but also to suffer for his sake. *Ph.* **1: 29.**

If we suffer, we shall also reign with him. *2 Ti.* **2: 12.**

Choosing rather to suffer affliction with the people of God, than to enjoy the pleasures of sin for a season. *He.* **11: 25.**

Is any among you afflicted? let him pray. *Ja.* **5: 13.**

If ye suffer for righteousness' sake, happy are ye. *1 Pe.* **3: 14.**

He that hath suffered in the flesh hath ceased from sin. *1 Pe.* **4: 1.**

Wherefore let them that suffer according to the will of God commit the keeping of their souls to him in well doing, as unto a faithful Creator. *1 Pe.* **4: 19.**

The God of all grace, . . . after that ye have suffered a while, make you perfect, stablish, strengthen, settle you. *1 Pe.* **5: 10.**

Fear none of those things which thou shalt suffer. *Re.* **2: 10.**

See also
Agony; Anguish; Christ, Cross of; Christ, Sacrifice of; Christ, Suffering of; Cross; Distress; Pain; Torment.

Suffering, Vicarious

All we like sheep have gone astray; we have turned every one to his own way; and the Lord hath laid on him the iniquity of us all. *Is.* **53: 6.**

I will shew him how great things he must suffer for my name's sake. *Ac.* **9: 16.**

Being now justified by his blood, we shall be saved from wrath through him. *Ro.* **5: 9.**

Whether one member suffer, all the members suffer with it. *1 Co.* **12: 26.**

We have redemption through his blood. *Ep.* **1: 7.**

Unto you it is given in the behalf of Christ, not only to believe on him, but also to suffer for his sake. *Ph.* **1: 29.**

That he by the grace of God should taste death for every man. *He.* **2: 9.**

It became him, . . . to make the captain of their salvation perfect through sufferings. *He.* **2: 10.**

How much more shall the blood of Christ, who through the eternal Spirit offered himself without spot to God, purge your conscience from dead works to serve the living God. *He.* **9: 14.**

Christ was once offered to bear the sins of many. *He.* **9: 28.**

Suffering wrongfully. *1 Pe.* **2: 19.**

Christ also suffered for us, leaving us an example, that we should follow his steps. *1 Pe.* **2: 21.**

The just for the unjust. *1 Pe.* **3: 18.**

The blood of Jesus Christ his Son cleanseth us from all sin. *1 Jn.* **1: 7.**

See also
Atonement; Christ, Cross of; Christ, the Lamb of God; Christ, Sacrifice of; Christ, Suffering of; Cross; Offering; Propitiation; Scapegoat; Self-Sacrifice.

Sufficiency

God give thee of the dew of heaven, and the fatness of the earth, and plenty of corn and wine. *Ge.* **27: 28.**

Ye shall eat your bread to the full, and dwell in your land safely. *Le.* **26: 5.**

The barrel of meal shall not waste, neither shall the cruse of oil fail, until the day that the Lord sendeth rain upon the earth. *1 K.* **17: 14.**

In the fulness of his sufficiency he shall be in straits. *Jb.* **20: 22.**

My soul shall be satisfied as with marrow and fatness. *Ps.* **63: 5.**

I will satisfy her poor with bread. *Ps.* **132: 15.**

A man's belly shall be satisfied with the fruit of his mouth. *Pr.* **18: 20.**

Open thine eyes, and thou shalt be satisfied with bread. *Pr.* **20: 13.**

The Lord shall . . . satisfy thy soul in drought. *Is.* **58: 11.**

Thou shalt be like a watered garden, and like a spring of water, whose waters fail not. *Is.* **58: 11.**

Sufficient unto the day is the evil thereof. *Mat.* **6: 34.**

The harvest truly is plenteous, but the labourers are few. *Mat.* 9: 37.

Lord, shew us the Father, and it sufficeth us. *Jn.* 14: 8.

Our sufficiency is of God. 2 *Co.* 3: 5.

My grace is sufficient for thee. 2 *Co.* 12: 9.
See also
Abundance; Adequacy; Ampleness; Fullness; Plenty; Satiety; Satisfaction.

Suicide

Saul took a sword, and fell upon it. *1 S.* 31: 4.

When his armourbearer saw that Saul was dead, he fell likewise upon his sword, and died with him. *1 S.* 31: 5.

Their sword shall enter into their own heart. *Ps.* 37: 15.

All they that hate me love death. *Pr.* 8: 36.

He cast down the pieces of silver in the temple, and departed, and went and hanged himself. *Mat.* 27: 5.

Then said the Jews, Will he kill himself? because he saith, Whither I go, ye cannot come. *Jn.* 8: 22.

He drew out his sword and would have killed himself, supposing that the prisoners had been fled. *Ac.* 16: 27.

Summer

While the earth remaineth, seedtime and harvest, and cold and heat, and summer and winter, and day and night shall not cease. *Ge.* 8: 22.

Thou hast made summer and winter. *Ps.* 74: 17.

The ant . . . Provideth her meat in the summer. *Pr.* 6: 6, 8.

He that gathereth in summer is a wise son. *Pr.* 10: 5.

As snow in summer, and as rain in harvest, so honour is not seemly for a fool. *Pr.* 26: 1.

The harvest is past, the summer is ended, and we are not saved. *Je.* 8: 20.

Like the chaff of the summer threshing-floors. *Da.* 2: 35.

Behold the fig tree, and all the trees: When they now shoot forth, ye see and know of your own selves that summer is now nigh at hand. *Lu.* 21: 29, 30.
See also
Heat; Season.

Summit

The Lord came down upon mount Sinai, on the top of the mount: and the Lord called Moses up to the top of the mount. *Ex.* 19: 20.

The sight of the glory of the Lord was like devouring fire on the top of the mount. *Ex.* 24: 17.

Wisdom . . . standeth in the top of high places. *Pr.* 8: 1, 2.

Lift ye up a banner upon the high mountain. *Is.* 13: 2.

Get thee up into the high mountain. *Is.* 40: 9.

In the visions of God brought he me into the land of Israel, and set me upon a very high mountain. *Eze.* 40: 2.

He carried me away in the spirit to a great and high mountain. *Re.* 21: 10.
See also
Christ, Transfiguration of; Climbing; Eminence; Hill; Mountain; Pinnacle; Top.

Summons

I call heaven and earth to witness against you this day, that ye shall soon utterly perish from off the land. *De.* 4: 26.

Who will rise up for me against the evildoers? or who will stand up for me against the workers of iniquity? *Ps.* 94: 16.

I the Lord have called thee in righteousness. *Is.* 42: 6.

Follow me, and I will make you fishers of men. *Mat.* 4: 19.

I am not come to call the righteous, but sinners to repentance. *Mat.* 9: 13.

Come; for all things are now ready. *Lu.* 14: 17.

A vision appeared to Paul in the night; There stood a man of Macedonia, and prayed him, saying, Come over into Macedonia, and help us. *Ac.* 16: 9.

Come up hither, and I will shew thee things which must be hereafter. *Re.* 4: 1.

I heard, as it were the noise of thunder, one of the four beasts saying, Come and see. *Re.* 6: 1.
See also
Call; Invitation; Warning.

Sun

God made two great lights; the greater light to rule the day, and the lesser light to rule the night. *Ge.* 1: 16.

The sun stood still. *Jos.* 10: 13.

In them hath he set a tabernacle for the sun. *Ps.* 19: 4.

Thou hast prepared the light and the sun. *Ps.* 74: 16.

The Lord God is a sun. *Ps.* 84: 11.

The sun shall not smite thee by day. *Ps.* 121: 6.

The sun to rule by day. *Ps.* 136: 8.

A pleasant thing it is for the eyes to behold the sun. *Ec.* 11: 7.

Clear as the sun. *S. of S.* 6: 10.

Then shall the righteous shine forth as the sun. *Mat.* 13: 43.

His face did shine as the sun. *Mat.* 17: 2.

There is one glory of the sun, and another glory of the moon, and another glory of the stars: for one star differeth from another star in glory. *1 Co.* 15: 41.

The city had no need of the sun. *Re.* 21: 23.
See also
Day; Light; Weather.

Sunday

Six days shalt thou labour, and do all thy work: But the seventh is the sabbath of the Lord thy God: in it thou shalt not do any work. *Ex.* 20: 9, 10.

The Lord blessed the sabbath day, and hallowed it. *Ex.* 20: 11.

He maketh me to lie down in green pastures: he leadeth me beside the still waters. *Ps.* 23: 2.

This is the day which the Lord hath made; we will rejoice and be glad in it. *Ps.* 118: 24.

Therefore the Son of man is Lord also of the sabbath. *Mk.* 2: 28.

Is it lawful to do good on the sabbath days, or to do evil? to save life, or to kill? *Mk.* 3: 4.

Very early in the morning the first day of the week, they came unto the sepulchre at the rising of the sun. *Mk.* 16: 2.

Is it lawful on the sabbath days to do good, or to do evil? to save life, or to destroy it? *Lu.* **6: 9.**

One man esteemeth one day above another: another esteemeth every day alike. Let every man be fully persuaded in his own mind. *Ro.* **14: 5.**

He that regardeth the day, regardeth it unto the Lord; and he that regardeth not the day, to the Lord he doth not regard it. *Ro.* **14: 6.**
See also
Church, Attendance at; Sabbath.

Sunday, Palm

Behold, thy King cometh unto thee, meek, and sitting upon an ass, and a colt the foal of an ass. *Mat.* **21: 5.**

When he was come into Jerusalem, all the city was moved, saying, Who is this? *Mat.* **21: 10.**

And the multitude said, This is Jesus the prophet of Nazareth of Galilee. *Mat.* **21: 11.**

Many spread their garments in the way. *Mk.* **11: 8.**

They that went before, and they that followed, cried, saying, Hosanna; Blessed is he that cometh in the name of the Lord. *Mk.* **11: 9.**

When he was come nigh, even now at the descent of the mount of Olives, the whole multitude of the disciples began to rejoice and praise God with a loud voice for all the mighty works that they had seen. *Lu.* **19: 37.**

He answered and said unto them, I tell you that, if these should hold their peace, the stones would immediately cry out. *Lu.* **19: 40.**

When he was come near, he beheld the city, and wept over it, Saying, If thou hadst known, even thou, at least in this thy day, the things which belong unto thy peace! but now they are hid from thine eyes. *Lu.* **19: 41, 42.**

Because thou knewest not the time of thy visitation. *Lu.* **19: 44.**

On the next day much people that were come to the feast, when they heard that Jesus was coming to Jerusalem, Took branches of palm trees, and went forth to meet him, and cried, Hosanna: Blessed is the King of Israel that cometh in the name of the Lord. *Jn.* **12: 12, 13.**

Sunrise

I am full of tossings to and fro unto the dawning of the day. *Jb.* **7: 4.**

Hast thou commanded the morning? *Jb.* **38: 12.**

I prevented the dawning of the morning. *Ps.* **119: 147.**

If I take the wings of the morning, . . . Even there shall thy hand lead me. *Ps.* **139: 9, 10.**

Until the day break, and the shadows flee away. *S. of S.* **2: 17.**

So shall they fear the name of the Lord from the west, and his glory from the rising of the sun. *Is.* **59: 19.**

They worshipped the sun toward the east. *Eze.* **8: 16.**

From the rising of the sun even unto the going down of the same my name shall be great. *Mal.* **1: 11.**

Unto you that fear my name shall the Sun of righteousness arise with healing in his wings. *Mal.* **4: 2.**

The night is far spent, the day is at hand: let us therefore cast off the works of darkness. *Ro.* **13: 12.**

Until the day dawn, and the day star arise in your hearts. *2 Pe.* **1: 19.**
See also
Dawn; Day, the Coming.

Sunset

Now the day draweth toward evening. *Ju.* **19: 9.**

The mighty God, even the Lord, hath spoken, and called the earth from the rising of the sun unto the going down thereof. *Ps.* **50: 1.**

From the rising of the sun unto the going down of the same the Lord's name is to be praised. *Ps.* **113: 3.**

The sun also ariseth, and the sun goeth down. *Ec.* **1: 5.**

Thy sun shall no more go down; neither shall thy moon withdraw itself: for the Lord shall be thine everlasting light. *Is.* **60: 20.**

The night cometh, when no man can work. *Jn.* **9: 4.**

Let not the sun go down upon your wrath. *Ep.* **4: 26.**
See also
Sunrise; Twilight.

Superficiality

My days are swifter than a post; they flee away, they see no good. *Jb.* **9: 25.**

Where is thy zeal and thy strength? *Is.* **63: 15.**

Ephraim . . . is like a silly dove without heart. *Ho.* **7: 11.**

Israel is an empty vine, he bringeth forth fruit unto himself. *Ho.* **10: 1.**

Why are ye fearful, O ye of little faith? *Mat.* **8: 26.**

He saw a fig tree in the way, . . . and found nothing thereon, but leaves only. *Mat.* **21: 19.**

Ye pay tithe of mint and anise and cummin, and have omitted the weightier matters of the law, judgment, mercy, and faith. *Mat.* **23: 23.**

Ye blind guides, which strain at a gnat, and swallow a camel. *Mat.* **23: 24.**

They are not all Israel, which are of Israel. *Ro.* **9: 6.**

Ye are manifestly declared to be the epistle of Christ ministered by us, written not with ink, but with the Spirit of the living God; not in tables of stone, but in fleshy tables of the heart. *2 Co.* **3: 3.**

We look not at the things which are seen, but at the things which are not seen. *2 Co.* **4: 18.**
See also
Shallowness.

Superfluity

Joseph gathered corn as the sand of the sea, very much, until he left numbering; for it was without number. *Ge.* **41: 49.**

The barrel of meal shall not waste, neither shall the cruse of oil fail, until the day that the Lord sendeth rain upon the earth. *1 K.* **17: 14.**

My cup runneth over. *Ps.* **23: 5.**

Many, O Lord my God, are thy wonderful works which thou hast done, and thy thoughts which are to us-ward: . . . if I would declare and speak of them, they are more than can be numbered. *Ps.* 40: 5.

Prove me now herewith, saith the Lord of hosts, if I will not open you the windows of heaven, and pour you out a blessing, that there shall not be room enough to receive it. *Mal.* 3: 10.

They took up of the fragments that remained twelve baskets full. *Mat.* 14: 20.

Give, and it shall be given unto you; good measure, pressed down, and shaken together, and running over. *Lu.* 6: 38.

Where sin abounded, grace did much more abound. *Ro.* 5: 20.

Lay apart all filthiness and superfluity of naughtiness. *Ja.* 1: 21.

See also

Abundance; Excess; Fullness.

Superiority

The excellency of dignity, and the excellency of power. *Ge.* 49: 3.

The Lord thy God will set thee on high above all nations of the earth. *De.* 28: 1.

The Lord shall make thee the head, and not the tail. *De.* 28: 13.

The chiefest among ten thousand. *S. of S.* 5: 10.

Thou, child, shalt be called the prophet of the Highest. *Lu.* 1: 76.

Seek that ye may excel. *1 Co.* 14: 12.

I was not a whit behind the very chiefest apostles. *2 Co.* 11: 5.

That in all things he might have the preeminence. *Col.* 1: 18.

He hath by inheritance obtained a more excellent name than they. *He.* 1: 4.

See also

Advantage; Christ, Finality of; Christ, Preeminence of; Elevation; Eminence; Exaltation; Excellence; God, Primacy of; Inferiority; Preeminence; Senior; Supremacy.

Superstition

They sacrificed unto devils, not to God; to gods whom they knew not, to new gods that come newly up, whom your fathers feared not. *De.* 32: 17.

Where are their gods, their rock in whom they trusted? *De.* 32: 37.

Ye have taken away my gods which I made. *Ju.* 18: 24.

They . . . called on the name of Baal from morning even until noon, saying, O Baal, hear us. But there was no voice, nor any that answered. *1 K.* 18: 26.

They served idols, whereof the Lord had said unto them, Ye shall not do this thing. *2 K.* 17: 12.

Their land also is full of idols; they worship the work of their own hands. *Is.* 2: 8.

The residue thereof he maketh a god. *Is.* 44: 17.

Woe unto him that saith to the wood, Awake; to the dumb stone, Arise, it shall teach! *Hab.* 2: 19.

Ye men of Athens, I perceive that in all things ye are too superstitious. *Ac.* 17: 22.

They . . . had certain questions against him of their own superstition. *Ac.* 25: 18, 19.

See also

Gods; Idol.

Supervision

The Lord watch between me and thee, when we are absent one from another. *Ge.* 31: 49.

These forty years the Lord thy God hath been with thee; thou hast lacked nothing. *De.* 2: 7.

As the Lord liveth, and as thy soul liveth, I will not leave thee. *2 K.* 2: 4.

In all thy ways acknowledge him, and he shall direct thy paths. *Pr.* 3: 6.

The ant, . . . having no guide, overseer, or ruler, Provideth her meat in the summer. *Pr.* 6: 6-8.

A man's heart deviseth his way: but the Lord directeth his steps. *Pr.* 16: 9.

I have raised him up in righteousness, and I will direct all his ways. *Is.* 45: 13.

They thirsted not when he led them through the deserts. *Is.* 48: 21.

He that hath mercy on them shall lead them, even by the springs of water shall he guide them. *Is.* 49: 10.

Thou, O Lord, art in the midst of us, and we are called by thy name; leave us not. *Je.* 14: 9.

The most High ruleth in the kingdom of men, and giveth it to whomsoever he will. *Da.* 4: 25.

Take heed therefore unto yourselves, and to all the flock, over the which the Holy Ghost hath made you overseers, to feed the church of God. *Ac.* 20: 28.

Feed the flock of God which is among you, taking the oversight thereof. *1 Pe.* 5: 2.

See also

Administration; Christ, the Leader; Direction; Guidance.

Supper, the Last

The Master saith, My time is at hand; I will keep the passover at thy house with my disciples. *Mat.* 26: 18.

Now when the even was come, he sat down with the twelve. *Mat.* 26: 20.

Jesus took bread, and blessed it, and brake it, and gave it to the disciples, and said, Take, eat; this is my body. *Mat.* 26: 26.

He took the cup, and gave thanks, and gave it to them, saying, Drink ye all of it. *Mat.* 26: 27.

This is my blood of the new testament, which is shed for many for the remission of sins. *Mat.* 26: 28.

I will not drink henceforth of this fruit of the vine, until that day when I drink it new with you in my Father's kingdom. *Mat.* 26: 29.

He took bread, and gave thanks. *Lu.* 22: 19.

This do in remembrance of me. *Lu.* 22: 19.

The hand of him that betrayeth me is with me on the table. *Lu.* 22: 21.

I am that bread of life. *Jn.* 6: 48.

See also

Communion, Service of; Eucharist; Mass; Supper, the Lord's.

Supper, the Lord's

Jesus said unto them, I am the bread of

life: he that cometh to me shall never hunger. *Jn.* **6: 35.**

I am the living bread which came down from heaven. *Jn.* **6: 51.**

Except ye eat the flesh of the Son of man, and drink his blood, ye have no life in you. *Jn.* **6: 53.**

The kingdom of God is not meat and drink; but righteousness, and peace, and joy in the Holy Ghost. *Ro.* **14: 17.**

When ye come together therefore into one place, this is not to eat the Lord's supper. *1 Co.* **11: 20.**

The Lord Jesus the same night in which he was betrayed took bread: And when he had given thanks, he brake it, and said, Take, eat: this is my body, which is broken for you. *1 Co.* **11: 23, 24.**

This cup is the new testament in my blood: this do ye, as oft as ye drink it, in remembrance of me. *1 Co.* **11: 25.**

As often as ye eat this bread, and drink this cup, ye do shew the Lord's death till he come. *1 Co.* **11: 26.**

Let a man examine himself, and so let him eat of that bread, and drink of that cup. *1 Co.* **11: 28.**

He that eateth and drinketh unworthily, eateth and drinketh damnation to himself, not discerning the Lord's body. *1 Co.* **11: 29.**

Blessed are they which are called unto the marriage supper of the Lamb. *Re.* **19: 9.**

See also

Communion, Service of; Eucharist; Mass; Supper, the Last.

Supplication

Hearken thou to the supplication of thy servant. *1 K.* **8: 30.**

The Lord hath heard my supplication. *Ps.* **6: 9.**

He forgetteth not the cry of the humble. *Ps.* **9: 12.**

Unto the Lord I made supplication. *Ps.* **30: 8.**

Give ear to my prayer, O God; and hide not thyself from my supplication. *Ps.* **55: 1.**

Pray for the peace of Jerusalem. *Ps.* **122: 6.**

Let thine ears be attentive to the voice of my supplications. *Ps.* **130: 2.**

I will pour upon . . . the inhabitants of Jerusalem, the spirit of grace and of supplications. *Zch.* **12: 10.**

Lord, teach us to pray. *Lu.* **11: 1.**

These all continued with one accord in prayer and supplication. *Ac.* **1: 14.**

I make mention of you always in my prayers. *Ro.* **1: 9.**

Praying always with all prayer and supplication in the Spirit. *Ep.* **6: 18.**

In every thing by prayer and supplication with thanksgiving let your requests be made known unto God. *Ph.* **4: 6.**

I exhort therefore, that, first of all, supplications, prayers, intercessions, and giving of thanks, be made for all men. *1 Ti.* **2: 1.**

The effectual fervent prayer of a righteous man availeth much. *Ja.* **5: 16.**

Watch unto prayer. *1 Pe.* **4: 7.**

See also

Appeal; Entreaty; God, Prayer to; Petition; Prayer; Request.

Support

My presence shall go with thee, and I will give thee rest. *Ex.* **33: 14.**

Come thou with us, and we will do thee good. *Nu.* **10: 29.**

The land, whither ye go to possess it, is a land . . . which the Lord thy God careth for. *De.* **11: 11, 12.**

Ye know in all your hearts and in all your souls, that not one thing hath failed of all the good things which the Lord your God spake concerning you. *Jos.* **23: 14.**

The Lord saveth not with sword and spear: for the battle is the Lord's, and he will give you into our hands. *1 S.* **17: 47.**

David behaved himself wisely in all his ways; and the Lord was with him. *1 S.* **18: 14.**

The hand of the Lord was on Elijah; and he girded up his loins. *1 K.* **18: 46.**

God hath power to help, and to cast down. *2 Ch.* **25: 8.**

The Lord . . . Send thee help from the sanctuary. *Ps.* **20: 1, 2.**

Though an host should encamp against me, my heart shall not fear. *Ps.* **27: 3.**

There is no king saved by the multitude of an host. *Ps.* **33: 16.**

What time I am afraid, I will trust in thee. *Ps.* **56: 3.**

They shall bear thee up in their hands, lest thou dash thy foot against a stone. *Ps.* **91: 12.**

A brother is born for adversity. *Pr.* **17: 7.**

Better is a neighbour that is near than a brother far off. *Pr.* **27: 10.**

They helped every one his neighbour; and every one said to his brother, Be of good courage. *Is.* **41: 6.**

They shall dwell safely, and none shall make them afraid. *Eze.* **34: 28.**

Wherefore, if God so clothe the grass of the field, which to day is, and to morrow is cast into the oven, shall he not much more clothe you, O ye of little faith? *Mat.* **6: 30.**

Be not afraid, but speak, and hold not thy peace: For I am with thee. *Ac.* **18: 9, 10.**

Support the weak, be patient toward all men. *1 Th.* **5: 14.**

See also

Aid; Help; Succor.

Suppression

I have . . . heard their cry by reason of their taskmasters. *Ex.* **3: 7.**

Is it good unto thee that thou shouldest oppress? *Jb.* **10: 3.**

Because he hath oppressed and hath forsaken the poor; . . . Surely he shall not feel quietness. *Jb.* **20: 19, 20.**

This is . . . the heritage of oppressors, which they shall receive of the Almighty. If his children be multiplied, it is for the sword. *Jb.* **27: 13, 14.**

Tread down the wicked in their place. *Jb.* **40: 12.**

Lord, thou hast heard the desire of the humble: . . . that the man of the earth may no more oppress. *Ps.* **10: 17, 18.**

The young lion and the dragon shalt thou trample under feet. *Ps.* **91: 13.**

Leave me not to mine oppressors. *Ps.* **119: 121.**

He that oppresseth the poor to increase his

riches, and he that giveth to the rich, shall surely come to want. *Pr.* 22: 16.

So I . . . considered all the oppressions that are done under the sun: and behold the tears of such as were oppressed, and they had no comforter. *Ec.* 4: 1.

He was oppressed, and he was afflicted, yet he opened not his mouth. *Is.* 53: 7.

Thou shalt be far from oppression; for thou shalt not fear. *Is.* 54: 14.

I will tread them in mine anger, and trample them in my fury. *Is.* 63: 3.

Jerusalem shall be trodden down of the Gentiles. *Lu.* 21: 24.

See also

Bondage; Oppression; Repression; Tyranny; Yoke.

Supremacy

Let men say among the nations, The Lord reigneth. *1 Ch.* 16: 31.

Yet have I set my king upon my holy hill of Zion. *Ps.* 2: 6.

Let us exalt his name together. *Ps.* 34: 3.

He ruleth by his power for ever; his eyes behold the nations. *Ps.* 66: 7.

The Lord said unto my Lord, Sit thou at my right hand, until I make thine enemies thy footstool. *Ps.* 110: 1.

All the kings of the earth shall praise thee. *Ps.* 138: 4.

Of a truth it is, that your God is a God of gods, and a Lord of kings. *Da.* 2: 47.

Thy greatness is grown, and reacheth unto heaven, and thy dominion to the end of the earth. *Da.* 4: 22.

Whosoever will be chief among you, let him be your servant. *Mat.* 20: 27.

He is above all things, and by him all things consist. *Col.* 1: 17.

The kingdoms of this world are become the kingdoms of our Lord, and of his Christ. *Re.* 11: 15.

On his head were many crowns. *Re.* 19: 12.

See also

Christ, Finality of; Christ, Preëminence of; Christ, Supremacy of; Excellence; God, Primacy of; God, Supremacy of; Preëminence; Superiority.

Surprise

Thou hast shewed thy people hard things: thou hast made us to drink the wine of astonishment. *Ps.* 60: 3.

The sinners in Zion are afraid; fearfulness hath surprised the hypocrites. *Is.* 33: 14.

The strong holds are surprised. *Je.* 48: 41.

They were astonished with a great astonishment. *Mk.* 5: 42.

They wondered every one at all things which Jesus did. *Lu.* 9: 43.

The Son of man cometh at an hour when ye think not. *Lu.* 12: 40.

They were filled with wonder and amazement at that which had happened unto him. *Ac.* 3: 10.

Marvel not, my brethren, if the world hate you. *1 Jn.* 3: 13.

See also

Amazement; Astonishment; Marvel; Wonder.

Surrender

The Lord thy God walketh in the midst of thy camp, to deliver thee, and to give up thine enemies before thee. *De.* 23: 14.

Be ye not stiffnecked, as your fathers were, but yield yourselves unto the Lord. *2 Ch.* 30: 8.

What shall I render unto the Lord for all his benefits toward me? *Ps.* 116: 12.

Yielding pacifieth great offences. *Ec.* 10: 4.

I will say to the north, Give up; and to the south, Keep not back. *Is.* 43: 6.

All things are delivered unto me of my Father. *Mat.* 11: 27.

They shall condemn him to death, And shall deliver him to the Gentiles to mock, and to scourge, and to crucify him. *Mat.* 20: 18, 19.

Render therefore unto Caesar the things which are Caesar's; and unto God the things that are God's. *Mat.* 22: 21.

There is joy in the presence of the angels of God over one sinner that repenteth. *Lu.* 15: 10.

I seek not mine own will, but the will of the Father which hath sent me. *Jn.* 5: 30.

I am ready not to be bound only, but also to die at Jerusalem for the name of the Lord Jesus. *Ac.* 21: 13.

The will of the Lord be done. *Ac.* 21: 14.

Yield yourselves unto God. *Ro.* 6: 13.

Know ye not, that to whom ye yield yourselves servants to obey, his servants ye are to whom ye obey? *Ro.* 6: 16.

Yield your members servants to righteousness unto holiness. *Ro.* 6: 19.

The sea gave up the dead which were in it; and death and hell delivered up the dead which were in them. *Re.* 20: 13.

See also

Abandonment; Desertion; Renunciation; Resignation.

Surroundings

After the doings of the land of Egypt, wherein ye dwelt, shall ye not do: and after the doings of the land of Canaan, whither I bring you, shall ye not do. . . . Ye shall . . . keep mine ordinances. *Le.* 18: 3, 4.

He giveth you rest from your enemies round about. *De.* 12: 10.

The Lord opened the eyes of the young man; and he saw: and, behold, the mountain was full of horses and chariots of fire round about Elisha. *2 K.* 6: 17.

Snares are round about thee, and sudden fear troubleth thee. *Jb.* 22: 10.

Lift up thine eyes round about, and behold: all these gather themselves together, and come to thee. *Is.* 49: 18.

I will encamp about mine house. *Zch.* 9: 8.

Choked with cares and riches and pleasures of this life. *Lu.* 8: 14.

To the saints and faithful brethren in Christ which are at Colosse. *Col.* 1: 2.

For that righteous man dwelling among them, in seeing and hearing, vexed his righteous soul from day to day with their unlawful deeds. *2 Pe.* 2: 8.

See also

Environment.

Survey

Go view the land. *Jos.* 2: 1.

Go up and view the country. *Jos.* 7: 2.

I went out by night . . . and viewed the walls of Jerusalem. *Ne.* 2: 13.

The measure thereof is longer than the earth, and broader than the sea. *Jb.* 11: 9.

Make me to know mine end, and the measure of my days. *Ps.* 39: 4.

Where there is no vision, the people perish. *Pr.* 29: 18.

Behold, I will set a plumbline in the midst of my people. *Am.* 7: 8.

He stood, and measured the earth. *Hab.* 3: 6.

Rise, and measure the temple of God. *Re.* 11: 1.

The city lieth foursquare, and the length is as large as the breadth . . . The length and the breadth and the height of it are equal. *Re.* 21: 16.

See also

Exploration; Measure; Scout; Spy.

Suspicion

On whom dost thou trust, that thou rebellest against me? *2 K.* 18: 20.

He putteth no trust in his saints. *Jb.* 15: 15.

His confidence shall be rooted out. *Jb.* 18: 14.

I will not trust in my bow, neither shall my sword save me. *Ps.* 44: 6.

Behold, ye trust in lying words, that cannot profit. *Je.* 7: 8.

Take ye heed every one of his neighbour, and trust ye not in any brother. *Je.* 9: 4.

Trust ye not in a friend, put ye not confidence in a guide: keep the doors of thy mouth from her that lieth in thy bosom. *Mi.* 7: 5.

By what authority doest thou these things? and who gave thee this authority? *Mat.* 21: 23.

The governor asked him, saying, Art thou the King of the Jews? *Mat.* 27: 11.

I desire to be present with you now, and to change my voice; for I stand in doubt of you. *Ga.* 4: 20.

Cast not away therefore your confidence. *He.* 10: 35.

See also

Disbelief; Distrust; Doubt; Skepticism.

Sustenance

With corn and wine have I sustained him. *Ge.* 27: 37.

When shall I provide for mine own house also? *Ge.* 30: 30.

She had heard in the country of Moab how that the Lord had visited his people in giving them bread. *Ru.* 1: 6.

Forty years didst thou sustain them in the wilderness, so that they lacked nothing. *Ne.* 9: 21.

I laid me down and slept; I awaked; for the Lord sustained me. *Ps.* 3: 5.

Cast thy burden upon the Lord, and he shall sustain thee. *Ps.* 55: 22.

Thou preparest them corn, when thou hast so provided for it. *Ps.* 65: 9.

Can God furnish a table in the wilderness? *Ps.* 78: 19.

The spirit of a man will sustain his infirmity. *Pr.* 18: 14.

His arm brought salvation unto him; and his righteousness, it sustained him. *Is.* 59: 16.

Take no thought for your life, what ye shall eat. *Lu.* 12: 22.

There came a dearth over all the land of Egypt and Chanaan, and great affliction: and our fathers found no sustenance. *Ac.* 7: 11.

See also

Bread; Christ, Bread of; Food; God, the Sustainer; Manna; Nourishment.

Sweetness

He made him to suck honey out of the rock. *De.* 32: 13.

The fig tree said unto them, Should I forsake my sweetness, and my good fruit, and go to be promoted over the trees? *Ju.* 9: 11.

Out of the eater came forth meat, and out of the strong came forth sweetness. *Ju.* 14: 14.

What is sweeter than honey? *Ju.* 14: 18.

The sweet psalmist of Israel. *2 S.* 23: 1.

Canst thou bind the sweet influences of Pleiades? *Jb.* 38: 31.

The judgments of the Lord are true and righteous altogether. . . . Sweeter also than honey and the honeycomb. *Ps.* 19: 9, 10.

My meditation of him shall be sweet. *Ps.* 104: 34.

How sweet are thy words unto my taste! yea, sweeter than honey to my mouth! *Ps.* 119: 103.

Stolen waters are sweet, and bread eaten in secret is pleasant. *Pr.* 9: 17.

The desire accomplished is sweet to the soul. *Pr.* 13: 19.

The sweetness of the lips increaseth learning. *Pr.* 16: 21.

The sleep of a labouring man is sweet. *Ec.* 5: 12.

Woe unto them that . . . put bitter for sweet, and sweet for bitter! *Is.* 5: 20.

See also

Honey.

Swiftness

My days are swifter than a weaver's shuttle, and are spent without hope. *Jb.* 7: 6.

His word runneth very swiftly. *Ps.* 147: 15.

Feet that be swift in running to mischief. *Pr.* 6: 18.

The race is not to the swift, or the battle to the strong. *Ec.* 9: 11.

The Lord rideth upon a swift cloud. *Is.* 19: 1.

Their feet are swift to shed blood. *Ro.* 3: 15.

Let every man be swift to hear, slow to speak. *Ja.* 1: 19.

There shall be false teachers among you, who privily shall bring in damnable heresies, even denying the Lord that bought them, and bring upon themselves swift destruction. *2 Pe.* 2: 1.

See also

Haste; Hurry; Quickness; Speed.

Swine

The swine . . . is unclean to you. *Le.* 11: 7.

As a jewel of gold in a swine's snout, so is a fair woman which is without discretion. *Pr.* 11: 22.

Give not that which is holy unto the dogs, neither cast ye your pearls before swine, lest they trample them under their feet, and turn again and rend you. *Mat.* 7: 6.

The devils besought him, saying, If thou

cast us out, suffer us to go away into the herd of swine. *Mat.* 8: 31.

He sent him into the fields to feed swine. *Lu.* 15: 15.

He would fain have filled his belly with the husks that the swine did eat. *Lu.* 15: 16.

Sword

Not with thy sword, nor with thy bow. *Jos.* 24: 12.

The sword of the Lord, and of Gideon. *Ju.* 7: 18.

Deliver my soul from the sword. *Ps.* 22: 20.

They shall beat their swords into plowshares, and their spears into pruninghooks. *Is.* 2: 4.

Nation shall not lift up a sword against nation. *Mi.* 4: 3.

Then said Jesus unto him, Put up again thy sword into his place: for all they that take the sword shall perish with the sword. *Mat.* 26: 52.

Yea, a sword shall pierce through thy own soul also. *Lu.* 2: 35.

He that hath no sword, let him sell his garment, and buy one. *Lu.* 22: 36.

The sword . . . which is the word. *Ep.* 6: 17.

He that killeth with the sword must be killed with the sword. *Re.* 13: 10.

See also
Battle; Contention; Fight; War; Weapon.

Symbol

The Lord set a mark upon Cain. *Ge.* 4: 15.

Thou shalt not make unto thee any graven image. *Ex.* 20: 4.

Take ye therefore good heed unto yourselves; for ye saw no manner of similitude on the day that the Lord spake unto you in Horeb out of the midst of the fire. *De.* 4: 15.

In the name of our God we will set up our banners. *Ps.* 20: 5.

His banner over me was love. *S. of S.* 2: 4.

Thou art . . . terrible as an army with banners. *S. of S.* 6: 4.

A wicked and adulterous generation seeketh after a sign; and there shall no sign be given unto it, but the sign of the prophet Jonas. *Mat.* 16: 4.

What shall be the sign of thy coming, and of the end of the world? *Mat.* 24: 3.

This shall be a sign unto you; Ye shall find the babe wrapped in swaddling clothes, lying in a manger. *Lu.* 2: 12.

Shew me a penny. Whose image and superscription hath it? *Lu.* 20: 24.

Ye took up . . . figures which ye made to worship them. *Ac.* 7: 43.

He is a Jew, which is one inwardly; and circumcision is that of the heart, in the spirit, and not in the letter. *Ro.* 2: 29.

Circumcision is nothing, and uncircumcision is nothing, but the keeping of the commandments of God. *1 Co.* 7: 19.

He is the image and glory of God. *1 Co.* 11: 7.

Christ . . . is the image of God. *2 Co.* 4: 4.

I bear in my body the marks of the Lord Jesus. *Ga.* 6: 17.

His dear Son . . . is the image of the invisible God, the firstborn of every creature. *Col.* 1: 13, 15.

The first tabernacle . . . was a figure for the time then present. *He.* 9: 8, 9.

Christ is not entered into the holy places made with hands, which are the figures of the true; but into heaven itself. *He.* 9: 24.

See also
Banner; Image; Mark; Sign; Standard.

Symmetry

Thou shalt be perfect with the Lord thy God. *De.* 18: 13.

According to the proportion of every one. *1 K.* 7: 36.

Let me be weighed in an even balance. *Jb.* 31: 6.

Dost thou know the balancings of the clouds, the wondrous works of him which is perfect in knowledge? *Jb.* 37: 16.

I will not conceal his parts, nor his power, nor his comely proportion. *Jb.* 41: 12.

I will praise thee; for I am fearfully and wonderfully made. *Ps.* 139: 14.

Thy neck is like the tower of David builded for an armoury. *S. of S.* 4: 4.

This thy stature is like to a palm tree. *S. of S.* 7: 7.

As the body is one, and hath many members, and all the members of that one body, being many, are one body: so also is Christ. *1 Co.* 12: 12.

Now hath God set the members every one of them in the body, as it hath pleased him. *1 Co.* 12: 18.

See also
Balance; Harmony; Order; Proportion.

Sympathy

When Moses held up his hand, Israel prevailed: and when he let down his hand, Amalek prevailed. But Moses' hands were heavy; and they took a stone and put it under him, and he sat thereon; and Aaron and Hur stayed up his hands. *Ex.* 17: 11, 12.

I am distressed for thee, my brother Jonathan. *2 S.* 1: 26.

What, could ye not watch with me one hour? *Mat.* 26: 40.

Jesus wept. *Jn.* 11: 35.

When the brethren heard of us, they came to meet us: . . . whom when Paul saw, he thanked God, and took courage. *Ac.* 28: 15.

Rejoice with them that do rejoice, and weep with them that weep. *Ro.* 12: 15.

Who is weak, and I am not weak? who is offended, and I burn not? *2 Co.* 11: 29.

Let brotherly love continue. *He.* 13: 1.

Remember them that are in bonds, as bound with them. *He.* 13: 3.

To visit the fatherless and widows in their affliction. *Ja.* 1: 27.

Having compassion one of another. *1 Pe.* 3: 8.

Some have compassion, making a difference. *Jude* 1: 22.

See also
Christ, Compassion of; Christ, Sympathy of; Compassion; God, Compassion of; God, Sympathy of; Pity; Tenderness.

Symphony

David and all the house of Israel played before the Lord on all manner of instruments made of fir wood, even on harps, and on psalteries, and on timbrels, and on cornets, and on cymbals. *2 S.* 6: 5.

The priests praised the Lord day by day. singing with loud instruments unto the Lord. *2 Ch.* 30: 21.

They take the timbrel and harp, and rejoice at the sound of the organ. *Jb.* 21: 12.

Awake up, my glory; awake, psaltery and harp. *Ps.* 57: 8.

Praise him with the sound of the trumpet: praise him with the psaltery and harp. *Ps.* 150: 3.

Praise him with the timbrel and dance: praise him with stringed instruments and organs. *Ps.* 150: 4.

Praise him upon the loud cymbals: praise him upon the high sounding cymbals. *Ps.* 150: 5.

The harp, and the viol, the tabret, and pipe. and wine, are in their feasts: but they regard not the work of the Lord. *Is.* 5: 12.

The Lord was ready to save me: therefore we will sing my songs to the stringed instruments all the days of our life. *Is.* 38: 20.

When all the people heard the sound of the cornet, flute, harp, sackbut, psaltery, and all kinds of musick, all the people, the nations, and the languages, fell down and worshipped the golden image. *Da.* 3: 7.

I in them, and thou in me, that they may be made perfect in one. *Jn.* 17: 23.

I beseech you . . . that ye be perfectly joined together in the same mind and in the same judgment. *1 Co.* 1: 10.

Even things without life giving sound, whether pipe or harp, except they give a distinction in the sounds, how shall it be known what is piped or harped? *1 Co.* 14: 7.

I heard the voice of harpers harping with their harps. *Re.* 14: 2.

See also

Instrument; Music.

Synagogue

They have burned up all the synagogues of God in the land. *Ps.* 74: 8.

When thou doest thine alms, do not sound a trumpet before thee, as the hypocrites do in the synagogues. *Mat.* 6: 2.

The hypocrites . . . love to pray standing in the synagogues. *Mat.* 6: 5.

They . . . love the uppermost rooms at feasts, and the chief seats in the synagogues. *Mat.* 23: 5, 6.

In the synagogues ye shall be beaten. *Mk.* 13: 9.

As his custom was, he went into the synagogue on the sabbath day, and stood up for to read. *Lu.* 4: 16.

The eyes of all them that were in the synagogue were fastened on him. *Lu.* 4: 20.

I know the blasphemy of them which say they are Jews, and are not, but are the synagogue of Satan. *Re.* 2: 9.

See also

Church; Congregation; Meeting; Temple.

T

Tabernacle

How goodly are thy tents, O Jacob, and thy tabernacles, O Israel! *Nu.* 24: 5.

The light shall be dark in his tabernacle. *Jb.* 18: 6.

Lord, who shall abide in thy tabernacle? *Ps.* 15: 1.

In them hath he set a tabernacle for the sun. *Ps.* 19: 4.

In the secret of his tabernacle shall he hide me; he shall set me up upon a rock. *Ps.* 27: 5.

Send out thy light and thy truth: let them lead me; let them bring me unto thy holy hill, and to thy tabernacles. *Ps.* 43: 3.

Let their habitation be desolate; and let none dwell in their tents. *Ps.* 69: 25.

He . . . made the tribes of Israel to dwell in their tents. *Ps.* 78: 55.

God . . . forsook the tabernacle of Shiloh, the tent which he placed among men. *Ps.* 78: 59, 60.

How amiable are thy tabernacles, O Lord of hosts! *Ps.* 84: 1.

Mine age is departed, and is removed from me as a shepherd's tent. *Is.* 38: 12.

Lord, it is good for us to be here: if thou wilt, let us make here three tabernacles; one for thee, and one for Moses, and one for Elias. *Mat.* 17: 4.

If our earthly house of this tabernacle were dissolved, we have a building of God, an house not made with hands, eternal in the heavens. *2 Co.* 5: 1.

Shortly I must put off this my tabernacle. *2 Pe.* 1: 14.

The tabernacle of God is with men, and he will dwell with them. *Re.* 21: 3.

See also

Church, Building the; Church, the House of God; Dwelling; Habitation; House; Shrine; Temple; Tent.

Table

It came to pass, as they sat at the table, that the word of the Lord came unto the prophet. *1 K.* 13: 20.

Thou preparest a table before me. *Ps.* 23: 5.

Can God furnish a table in the wilderness? *Ps.* 78: 19.

This is the table that is before the Lord. *Eze.* 41: 22.

The dogs eat of the crumbs which fall from their masters' table. *Mat.* 15: 27.

Jesus went into the temple of God, . . . and overthrew the tables of the moneychangers. *Mat.* 21: 12.

There they made him a supper; and Martha served. *Jn.* 12: 2.

Taint

The imagination of man's heart is evil from his youth. *Ge.* 8: 21.

I the Lord thy God am a jealous God, visiting the iniquity of the fathers upon the children unto the third and fourth generation of them that hate me. *Ex.* 20: 5.

Let darkness and the shadow of death stain it. *Jb.* 3: 5.

Then shalt thou lift up thy face without spot. *Jb.* 11: 15.

Cleanse thou me from secret faults. *Ps.* 19: 12.

There is no spot in thee. *S. of S.* 4: 7.

The Lord of hosts hath purposed it, to stain the pride of all glory, and to bring into contempt all the honourable of the earth. *Is.* 23: 9.

I will curse your blessings. *Mal.* 2: 2.

An evil man out of the evil treasure of his heart bringeth forth that which is evil. *Lu.* 6: 45.

Evil communications corrupt good manners. *1 Co.* 15: 33.

Born again, not of corruptible seed, but of incorruptible. *1 Pe.* 1: 23.

They are without fault before the throne of God. *Re.* 14: 5.

See also

Adulteration; Blemish; Blot; Corruption; Defect; Defilement; Fault; Impurity; Spot.

Tale

A proverb and a byword. *1 K.* 9: 7.

I have heard the slander of many. *Ps.* 31: 13.

We spend our years as a tale that is told. *Ps.* 90: 9.

Whoso privily slandereth his neighbour, him will I cut off. *Ps.* 101: 5.

He that repeateth a matter separateth very friends. *Pr.* 17: 9.

In thee are men that carry tales to shed blood. *Eze.* 22: 9.

Their words seemed to them as idle tales, and they believed them not. *Lu.* 24: 11.

See also

Account; Fable; Gossip; Parable; Slander; Talebearing

Talebearing

Thou shalt not go up and down as a talebearer among thy people. *Le.* 19: 16.

All that hate me whisper together against me. *Ps.* 41: 7.

He spake unadvisedly with his lips. *Ps.* 106: 33.

He that uttereth a slander is a fool. *Pr.* 10: 18.

A talebearer revealeth secrets. *Pr.* 11: 13.

The words of a talebearer are as wounds. *Pr.* 18: 8.

Where no wood is, there the fire goeth out: 30 where there is no talebearer, the strife ceaseth. *Pr.* 26: 20.

See also

Calumny; Gossip; Slander; Tale.

Talent

Moses chose able men out of all Israel, and made them heads over the people. *Ex.* 18: 25.

Every man shall give as he is able. *De.* 16: 17.

Unto one he gave five talents, to another two, and to another one; to every man according to his several ability. *Mat.* 25: 15.

Having then gifts differing according to the grace that is given to us. *Ro.* 12: 6.

There are diversities of gifts, but the same Spirit. *1 Co.* 12: 4.

Covet earnestly the best gifts. *1 Co.* 12: 31.

Neglect not the gift that is in thee. *1 Ti.* 4: 14.

See also

Ability; Aptitude; Endowment; Gift; Skill; Workmanship.

Talk

The Lord spake unto Moses, face to face, as a man speaketh unto his friend. *Ex.* 33: 11.

Moses wist not that the skin of his face shone while he talked with him. *Ex.* 34: 29.

Should a man full of talk be justified? *Jb.* 11: 2.

To slay such as be of upright conversation. *Ps.* 37: 14.

To him that ordereth his conversation aright will I shew the salvation of God. *Ps.* 50: 23.

So shall I talk of thy wondrous works. *Ps.* 119: 27.

The talk of the lips tendeth only to penury. *Pr.* 14: 23.

A wholesome tongue is a tree of life. *Pr.* 15: 4.

Did not our heart burn within us, while he talked with us by the way? *Lu.* 24: 32.

Jesus said unto him, Thou hast both seen him, and it is he that talketh with thee. *Jn.* 9: 37.

I came . . . not with excellency of speech. *1 Co.* 2: 1.

Neither filthiness, nor foolish talking, nor jesting, which are not convenient. *Ep.* 5: 4.

There are many unruly and vain talkers. *Tit.* 1: 10.

The tongue is a fire. *Ja.* 3: 6.

Let your yea be yea; and your nay, nay. *Ja.* 5: 12.

See also

Christ, Word of; Conversation; God, Voice of; God, Word of; Gossip; Lip; Mouth; Slander; Tale; Talebearing; Tongue; Word.

Tardiness

My days are swifter than a weaver's shuttle, and are spent without hope. *Jb.* 7: 6.

It is vain for you . . . to sit up late. *Ps.* 127: 2.

The harvest is passed, the summer is ended, and we are not saved. *Je.* 8: 20.

O Jerusalem! wilt thou not be made clean? when shall it once be? *Je.* 13: 27.

It shall come to pass, that at evening time it shall be light. *Zch.* 14: 7.

Give us of your oil; for our lamps are gone out. *Mat.* 25: 8.

Afterward came also the other virgins, saying, Lord, Lord, open to us. But he answered and said, Verily I say unto you, I know you not. *Mat.* 25: 11, 12.

When the day was now far spent, his disciples came unto him. *Mk.* 6: 35.

Now the time is far passed. *Mk.* 6: 35.

Ye know not when the master of the house cometh, at even, or at midnight, or at the cockcrowing, or in the morning. *Mk.* 13: 35.

Abide with us: for it is toward evening. *Lu.* 24: 29.

The night is far spent, the day is at hand. *Ro.* 13: 12.

To day, after so long a time. *He.* 4: 7.

See also
Lateness.

Task

They did set over them taskmasters to afflict them with their burdens. *Ex.* 1: 11.

The Lord said, I have surely seen the affliction of my people which are in Egypt, and have heard their cry by reason of their taskmasters. *Ex.* 3: 7.

Fulfil your works, your daily tasks, as when there was straw. *Ex.* 5: 13.

Wherefore have ye not fulfilled your task? *Ex.* 5: 14.

Ye shall not minish ought from your bricks of your daily task. *Ex.* 5: 19.

The men did the work faithfully. *2 Ch.* 34: 12.

Establish thou the work of our hands upon us. *Ps.* 90: 17.

Thou shalt eat the labour of thine hands. *Ps.* 128: 2.

Whatsoever thy hand findeth to do, do it with thy might. *Ec.* 9: 10.

Be strong, all ye people of the land, saith the Lord, and work. *Hag.* 2: 4.

Wist ye not that I must be about my Father's business? *Lu.* 2: 49.

We are labourers together with God. *1 Co.* 3: 9.

See also
Chore; Christ, Purpose of; Christ, Work of; Duty; Employee; Employer; God, Work of; Labor; Service; Toil; Undertaking; Work.

Taste

Can that which is unsavoury be eaten without salt? or is there any taste in the white of an egg? *Jb.* 6: 6.

Doth not the ear try words? and the mouth taste his meat? *Jb.* 12: 11.

O taste and see that the Lord is good: blessed is the man that trusteth in him. *Ps.* 34: 8.

How sweet are thy words unto my taste! *Ps.* 119: 103.

Eat thou honey, because it is good; and the honeycomb, which is sweet to thy taste. *Pr.* 24: 13.

There be some standing here, which shall not taste of death, till they see the Son of man coming in his kingdom. *Mat.* 16: 28.

Salt is good. *Lu.* 14: 34.

Why, as though living in the world, are ye subject to ordinances, (Touch not; taste not; handle not)? *Col.* 2: 20, 21.

That he by the grace of God should taste death for every man. *He.* 2: 9.

It is impossible for those who were once enlightened, and have tasted of the heavenly gift, . . . And have tasted the good word of God, . . . If they shall fall away, to renew them again unto repentance. *He.* 6: 4–6.

Desire the sincere milk of the word, that ye may grow thereby: If so be ye have tasted that the Lord is gracious. *1 Pe.* 2: 2, 3.

See also
Salt; Savor; Tongue.

Teaching

God is with thee in all that thou doest. *Ge.* 21: 22.

He led him about, he instructed him, he kept him as the apple of his eye. *De.* 32: 10.

I will teach you the good and the right way. *1 S.* 12: 23.

Behold, thou hast instructed many, and thou hast strengthened the weak hands. *Jb.* 4: 3.

Ask now the beasts, and they shall teach thee; and the fowls of the air, and they shall tell thee: Or speak to the earth, and it shall teach thee: and the fishes of the sea shall declare unto thee. *Jb.* 12: 7, 8.

Hear counsel, and receive instruction, that thou mayest be wise in thy latter end. *Pr.* 19: 20.

Though the Lord give you the bread of adversity, and the water of affliction, yet shall not thy teachers be removed into a corner any more, but thine eyes shall see thy teachers. *Is.* 30: 20.

By these things men live. *Is.* 38: 16.

With whom took he counsel, and who instructed him, and taught him in the path of judgment, and taught him knowledge, and shewed to him the way of understanding? *Is.* 40: 14.

Behold, there went out a sower to sow. *Mk.* 4: 3.

Thou therefore which teachest another, teachest thou not thyself? *Ro.* 2: 21.

The servant of the Lord must . . . be gentle unto all men, apt to teach, patient, In meekness instructing those that oppose themselves. *2 Ti.* 2: 24, 25.

When for the time ye ought to be teachers. *He.* 5: 12.

See also
Christ, the Teacher; Education; Instruction; Knowledge; Precept; Pupil; School; Study; Teaching, False; Training.

Teaching, False

His watchmen are blind: they are all ignorant, they are all dumb dogs, they cannot bark; sleeping, lying down, loving to slumber. *Is.* 56: 10.

They are shepherds that cannot understand: they all look to their own way, every one for his gain, from his quarter. *Is.* 56: 11.

Believe them not, though they speak fair words unto thee. *Je.* 12: 6.

Thou hast taught rebellion against the Lord. *Je.* 28: 16.

Teaching for doctrines the commandments of men. *Mat.* 15: 9.

Such are false apostles, deceitful workers, transforming themselves into the apostles of Christ. *2 Co.* 11: 13.

There be some that trouble you, and would pervert the gospel of Christ. *Ga.* 1: 7.

Some indeed preach Christ of envy and strife. *Ph.* 1: 15.

There are many unruly and vain talkers and deceivers, . . . teaching things which they ought not, for filthy lucre's sake. *Tit.* 1: 10, 11.

Be not carried about with divers and strange doctrines. *He.* 13: 9.

There were false prophets also among the

people, even as there shall be false teachers among you. *2 Pe.* **2: 1.**

See also

Division; Heresy; Schism; Sect; Separation; Unorthodoxy.

Tear

Did not I weep for him that was in trouble? *Jb.* **30: 25.**

My tears have been my meat day and night. *Ps.* **42: 3.**

They that sow in tears shall reap in joy. *Ps.* **126: 5.**

The voice of weeping shall be no more heard in her, nor the voice of crying. *Is.* **65: 19.**

My soul shall weep in secret places for your pride; and mine eye shall weep sore, and run down with tears. *Je.* **13: 17.**

Weep ye not for the dead, neither bemoan him: but weep sore for him that goeth away. *Je.* **22: 10.**

There shall be weeping and gnashing of teeth. *Mat.* **8: 12.**

She hath washed my feet with tears, and wiped them with the hairs of her head. *Lu.* **7: 44.**

Ye shall weep and lament, but the world shall rejoice: and ye shall be sorrowful, but your sorrow shall be turned into joy. *Jn.* **16: 20.**

They say unto her, Woman, why weepest thou? *Jn.* **20: 13.**

Be afflicted, and mourn, and weep: let your laughter be turned to mourning, and your joy to heaviness. *Ja.* **4: 9.**

God shall wipe away all tears from their eyes. *Re.* **7: 17.**

See also

Christ, Sorrow of; Grief; Lamentation; Mourning; Sadness; Sorrow; Unhappiness; Weeping.

Tedium

Let the day perish wherein I was born, and the night in which it was said, There is a man child conceived. *Jb.* **3: 3.**

When I lie down, I say, When shall I arise, and the night be gone? and I am full of tossings to and fro unto the dawning of the day. *Jb.* **7: 4.**

My days are swifter than a weaver's shuttle, and are spent without hope. *Jb.* **7: 6.**

O my God, I cry in the daytime, but thou hearest not; and in the night season, and am not silent. *Ps.* **22: 2.**

My flesh longeth for thee in a dry and thirsty land, where no water is. *Ps.* **63: 1.**

Mine eyes fail while I wait for my God. *Ps.* **69: 3.**

My soul breaketh for the longing that it hath. *Ps.* **119: 20.**

Withdraw thy foot from thy neighbour's house; lest he be weary of thee, and so hate thee. *Pr.* **25: 17.**

Is it a small thing for you to weary men, but will ye weary my God also? *Is.* **7: 13.**

Even the youths shall faint and be weary. *Is.* **40: 30.**

Thou hast been weary of me, O Israel. *Is.* **43: 22.**

O my people, what have I done unto thee? and wherein have I wearied thee? *Mi.* **6: 3.**

Notwithstanding, that I be not further tedious unto thee, I pray thee that thou

wouldest hear us of thy clemency a few words. *Ac.* **24: 4.**

See also

Weariness.

Temper

The driving is like the driving of Jehu the son of Nimshi; for he driveth furiously. *2 K.* **9: 20.**

He teareth me in his wrath; . . . mine enemy sharpeneth his eyes upon me. *Jb.* **16: 9.**

The fool rageth, and is confident. *Pr.* **14: 16.**

Make no friendship with an angry man. *Pr.* **22: 24.**

Anger resteth in the bosom of fools. *Ec.* **7: 9.**

Be ye angry, and sin not. *Ep.* **4: 26.**

Fathers, provoke not your children to anger, lest they be discouraged. *Col.* **3: 21.**

A bishop must be blameless, as the steward of God; not self-willed, not soon angry. *Tit.* **1: 7.**

See also

Anger; Christ, Wrath of; God, Anger of; God, Wrath of; Passion; Rage; Wrath.

Temperance

Who hath woe? who hath sorrow? who hath contentions? who hath babbling? who hath wounds without cause? who hath redness of eyes? They that tarry long at the wine. *Pr.* **23: 29, 30.**

Give me neither poverty nor riches. *Pr.* **30: 8.**

Let them give us pulse to eat and water to drink. *Da.* **1: 12.**

He reasoned of righteousness, temperance. *Ac.* **24: 25.**

To think soberly. *Ro.* **12: 3.**

It is good neither to eat flesh, nor to drink wine, nor any thing whereby thy brother stumbleth. *Ro.* **14: 21.**

The fruit of the Spirit is . . . temperance. *Ga.* **5: 22, 23.**

Not given to much wine. *1 Ti.* **3: 8.**

A bishop must be . . . sober, just, holy, temperate. *Tit.* **1: 7, 8.**

That the aged men be sober, grave, temperate. *Tit.* **2: 2.**

And to knowledge temperance. *2 Pe.* **1: 6.**

See also

Abstinence; Appetite; Continence; Control; Moderation; Self-Control; Sobriety.

Tempest

I would hasten my escape from the windy storm and tempest. *Ps.* **55: 8.**

Make them afraid with thy storm. *Ps.* **83: 15.**

He commandeth, and raiseth the stormy wind, which lifteth up the waves thereof. *Ps.* **107: 25.**

Stormy wind fulfilling his word. *Ps.* **148: 8.**

The wind . . . whirleth about continually, and the wind returneth again according to his circuits. *Ec.* **1: 6.**

A man shall be as an hiding place from the wind, and a covert from the tempest. *Is.* **32: 2.**

O thou afflicted, tossed with tempest, and not comforted, behold, I will lay thy stones with fair colours, and lay thy foundations with sapphires. *Is.* **54: 11.**

They have sown the wind, and they shall reap the whirlwind. *Ho.* **8: 7.**

What manner of man is this, that even the winds and the sea obey him! *Mat.* **8: 27.**

He arose, and rebuked the wind, and said unto the sea, Peace, be still. *Mk.* **4: 39.**

A sound from heaven as of a rushing mighty wind. *Ac.* **2: 2.**

Ye are not come unto the mount that might be touched, and that burned with fire, nor unto blackness, and darkness, and tempest. *He.* **12: 18.**

These are . . . clouds that are carried with a tempest. *2 Pe.* **2: 17.**

See also

Storm; Whirlwind; Wind.

Temple

Let the house of God be builded in his place. *Ezr.* **5: 15.**

His train filled the temple. *Is.* **6: 1.**

Mine house shall be called an house of prayer for all people. *Is.* **56: 7.**

Trust ye not in lying words, saying, The temple of the Lord, The temple of the Lord, The temple of the Lord, are these. *Je.* **7: 4.**

Israel hath forgotten his Maker, and buildeth temples. *Ho.* **8: 14.**

They found him in the temple, sitting in the midst of the doctors. *Lu.* **2: 46.**

The vail of the temple was rent in the midst. *Lu.* **23: 45.**

God . . . dwelleth not in temples made with hands. *Ac.* **17: 24.**

Know ye not that ye are the temple of God, and that the Spirit of God dwelleth in you? *1 Co.* **3: 16.**

If any man defile the temple of God, him shall God destroy. *1 Co.* **3: 17.**

Know ye not that your body is the temple of the Holy Ghost? *1 Co.* **6: 19.**

What agreement hath the temple of God with idols? *2 Co.* **6: 16.**

All the building fitly framed together groweth into an holy temple in the Lord. *Ep.* **2: 21.**

Ye also, as lively stones, are built up a spiritual house. *1 Pe.* **2: 5.**

There was given me a reed like unto a rod: and the angel stood saying, Rise, and measure the temple of God, and the altar, and them that worship therein. *Re.* **11: 1.**

I saw no temple therein: for the Lord God Almighty and the Lamb are the temple of it. *Re.* **21: 22.**

See also

Bethel; Church; Church, Building the; Church, the House of God; Congregation; God, House of; Meeting; Shrine; Synagogue; Tabernacle.

Temptation

Now the serpent was more subtil than any beast of the field. *Ge.* **3: 1.**

Thou shalt not desire the silver or gold that is on them. *De.* **7: 25.**

Satan . . . provoked David to number Israel. *1 Ch.* **21: 1.**

If sinners entice thee, consent thou not. *Pr.* **1: 10.**

Can a man take fire in his bosom, and his clothes not be burned? *Pr.* **6: 27.**

He knoweth not that the dead are there; and that her guests are in the depths of hell. *Pr.* **9: 18.**

A violent man enticeth his neighbour, and leadeth him into the way that is not good. *Pr.* **16: 29.**

Then was Jesus led up of the spirit into the wilderness to be tempted of the devil. *Mat.* **4: 1.**

Lead us not into temptation, but deliver us from evil. *Mat.* **6: 13.**

Watch ye and pray, lest ye enter into temptation. *Mk.* **14: 38.**

If thou be the Son of God, command this stone that it be made bread. *Lu.* **4: 3.**

Pray that ye enter not into temptation. *Lu.* **22: 40.**

I pray not that thou shouldest take them out of the world. *Jn.* **17: 15.**

There hath no temptation taken you but such as is common to man: but God is faithful, who will not suffer you to be tempted above that ye are able; but will with the temptation also make a way to escape, that ye may be able to bear it. *1 Co.* **10: 13.**

Lest Satan should get an advantage of us. *2 Co.* **2: 11.**

Take unto you the whole armour of God, that ye may be able to withstand in the evil day. *Ep.* **6: 13.**

They that will be rich fall into temptation and a snare, and into many foolish and hurtful lusts. *1 Ti.* **6: 9.**

Count it all joy when ye fall into divers temptations: Knowing this, that the trying of your faith worketh patience. *Ja.* **1: 2, 3.**

Blessed is the man that endureth temptation. *Ja.* **1: 12.**

Let no man say when he is tempted, I am tempted of God, for God cannot be tempted of evil, neither tempteth he any man. *Ja.* **1: 13.**

Every man is tempted, when he is drawn away of his own lust, and enticed. *Ja.* **1: 14.**

Beware lest ye also, being led away with the error of the wicked, fall from your own stedfastness. *2 Pe.* **3: 17.**

Because thou hast kept the word of my patience, I also will keep thee from the hour of temptation, which shall come upon all the world, to try them that dwell upon the earth. *Re.* **3: 10.**

See also

Allurement; Christ. Temptation of; Enticement; Proof; Seduction; Test; Trial.

Tenant

Thus saith the Lord, Shalt thou build me an house for me to dwell in? *2 S.* **7: 5.**

I will settle him in mine house and in my kingdom for ever. *1 Ch.* **17: 14.**

I will dwell in the house of the Lord for ever. *Ps.* **23: 6.**

Blessed are they that dwell in thy house. *Ps.* **84: 4.**

He blesseth the habitation of the just. *Pr.* **3: 33.**

They shall build houses, and inhabit them. *Is.* **65: 21.**

In my Father's house are many mansions. *Jn.* **14: 2.**

We know that if our earthly house of this tabernacle were dissolved, we have a building of God, an house not made with hands, eternal in the heavens. *2 Co.* 5: 1.

In this we groan, earnestly desiring to be clothed upon with our house which is from heaven. *2 Co.* 5: 2.

See also

Dwelling; Habitation; Home; House; Shelter.

Tenderness

Whose hearts God had touched. *1 S.* 10: 26.

Because thine heart was tender, . . . I also have heard thee, saith the Lord. *2 K.* 22: 19.

Great are thy tender mercies, O Lord. *Ps.* 119: 156.

He . . . shall gently lead those that are with young. *Is.* 40: 11.

A bruised reed shall he not break, and the smoking flax shall he not quench. *Is.* 42: 3.

He shall grow up before him as a tender plant. *Is.* 53: 2.

Continue ye in my love. *Jn.* 15: 9.

Be ye kind one to another, tenderhearted. *Ep.* 4: 32.

Husbands, love your wives, even as Christ also loved the church. *Ep.* 5: 25.

He that loveth not his brother abideth in death. *1 Jn.* 3: 14.

See also

Benignity; Caress; Christ, Compassion of; Christ, Gentleness of; Christ, Sympathy of; Compassion; Gentleness; God, Compassion of; God, Gentleness of; God, Kindness of; God, Mercy of; God, Sympathy of; Humaneness; Kindness; Lovingkindness; Mercy; Pity; Softness; Sympathy.

Tenet

Thou . . . commandedst them precepts, statutes, and laws. *Ne.* 9: 13, 14.

Through thy precepts I get understanding. *Ps.* 119: 104.

What thing is this? what new doctrine is this? *Mk.* 1: 27.

Ye have obeyed from the heart that form of doctrine which was delivered you. *Ro.* 6: 17.

Till I come, give attendance to reading, to exhortation, to doctrine. *1 Ti.* 4: 13.

Thou hast fully known my doctrine. *2 Ti.* 3: 10.

The doctrine of baptisms, and of laying on of hands, and of resurrection of the dead, and of eternal judgment. *He.* 6: 2.

See also

Belief; Doctrine; Dogma; Faith; Principle.

Tension

When he giveth quietness, who then can make trouble? *Jb.* 34: 29.

Many bulls have compassed me: strong bulls of Bashan have beset me round. *Ps.* 22: 12.

Hatred stirreth up strifes: but love covereth all sins. *Pr.* 10: 12.

It is better to dwell in the corner of the housetop, than with a brawling woman and in a wide house. *Pr.* 25: 24.

The churning of milk bringeth forth butter, and the wringing of the nose bringeth forth blood: so the forcing of wrath bringeth forth strife. *Pr.* 30: 33.

There is no peace, saith the Lord, unto the wicked. *Is.* 48: 22.

The wicked are like the troubled sea, when it cannot rest. *Is.* 57: 20.

He hath . . . pulled me in pieces. *La.* 3: 11.

Ye blind guides, which strain at a gnat, and swallow a camel. *Mat.* 23: 24.

The cares of this world . . . choke the word. *Mk.* 4: 19.

The contention was so sharp between them, that they departed asunder one from the other. *Ac.* 15: 39.

I beseech you, brethren, . . . that there be no divisions among you. *1 Co.* 1: 10.

Whereas there is among you envying, and strife, and divisions, are ye not carnal, and walk as men? *1 Co.* 3: 3.

Without were fightings, within were fears. *2 Co.* 7: 5.

Let us lay aside every weight. *He.* 12: 1.

See also

Anxiety; Discontent.

Tent

How goodly are thy tents, O Jacob, and thy tabernacles, O Israel! *Nu.* 24: 5.

Every man to his tents, O Israel. *2 S.* 20: 1.

Thou shalt know that thy tabernacle shall be in peace. *Jb.* 5: 24.

Let not wickedness dwell in thy tabernacles. *Jb.* 11: 14.

The secret of God was upon my tabernacle. *Jb.* 29: 4.

I had rather be a doorkeeper in the house of my God, than to dwell in the tents of wickedness. *Ps.* 84: 10.

They . . . murmured in their tents, and hearkened not unto the voice of the Lord. *Ps.* 106: 24, 25.

The tabernacle of the upright shall flourish. *Pr.* 14: 11.

It is he . . . that stretcheth out the heavens as a curtain, and spreadeth them out as a tent to dwell in. *Is.* 40: 22.

Enlarge the place of thy tent, and let them stretch forth the curtains of thine habitations: spare not, lengthen thy cords, and strengthen thy stakes. *Is.* 54: 2.

I think it meet, as long as I am in this tabernacle, to stir you up by putting you in remembrance. *2 Pe.* 1: 13.

See also

Habitation; Tabernacle.

Termination

Shall the sword devour for ever? knowest thou not that it will be bitterness in the latter end? *2 S.* 2: 26.

Is there not an appointed time to man upon earth? *Jb.* 7: 1.

Thou art the same, and thy years shall have no end. *Ps.* 102: 27.

There is a way which seemeth right unto a man, but the end thereof are the ways of death. *Pr.* 14: 12.

Our end is near, our days are fulfilled; for our end is come. *La.* 4: 18.

Go thou thy way till the end be: for thou shalt rest, and stand in thy lot at the end of the days. *Da.* 12: 13.

The great houses shall have an end, saith the Lord. *Am.* 3: 15.

This gospel of the kingdom shall be preached in all the world for a witness unto all nations; and then shall the end come. *Mat.* 24: 14.

What fruit had ye then in those things

whereof ye are now ashamed? for the end of those things is death. *Ro.* 6: 21.

Finally, my brethren, be strong in the Lord. *Ep.* 6: 10.

The end of the commandment is charity out of a pure heart. *1 Ti.* 1: 5.

The latter end is worse with them than the beginning. *2 Pe.* 2: 20.

See also

Climax; Conclusion; End; Finality; Finish.

Terror

An horror of great darkness fell upon him. *Ge.* 15: 12.

The terror of God was upon the cities that were round about them. *Ge.* 35: 5.

By the greatness of thine arm they shall be as still as a stone. *Ex.* 15: 16.

As soon as we had heard these things, our hearts did melt, neither did there remain any more courage in any man. *Jos.* 2: 11.

They are in the terrors of the shadow of death. *Jb.* 24: 17.

Fearfulness and trembling are come upon me, and horror hath overwhelmed me. *Ps.* 55: 5.

They are utterly consumed with terrors. *Ps.* 73: 19.

Thou shalt not be afraid for the terror by night. *Ps.* 91: 5.

Horror hath taken hold upon me. *Ps.* 119: 53.

Your fear cometh as desolation, and your destruction cometh as a whirlwind. *Pr.* 1: 27.

Thou shalt be far from oppression; for thou shalt not fear: and from terror; for it shall not come near thee. *Is.* 54: 14.

See also

Alarm; Awe; Dread; Fear; Horror; Trembling.

Test

God is come to prove you. *Ex.* 20: 20.

The people are yet too many; bring them down unto the water, and I will try them for thee there. *Ju.* 7: 4.

David said unto Saul, I cannot go with these; for I have not proved them. *1 S.* 17: 39.

Doth not the ear try words? and the mouth taste his meat? *Jb.* 12: 11.

Thou hast proved mine heart; thou hast visited me in the night. *Ps.* 17: 3.

Examine me, O Lord, and prove me; try my reins and my heart. *Ps.* 26: 2.

I proved thee at the waters of Meribah. *Ps.* 81: 7.

All the ways of a man are clean in his own eyes; but the Lord weigheth the spirits. *Pr.* 16: 2.

I said in mine heart, Go to now, I will prove thee with mirth. *Ec.* 2: 1.

God shall bring every work into judgment. *Ec.* 12: 14.

Behold, I will set a plumbline in the midst of my people Israel. *Am.* 7: 8.

Then was Jesus led up of the spirit into the wilderness to be tempted of the devil. *Mat.* 4: 1.

The stream beat vehemently upon that house, and could not shake it: for it was founded upon a rock. *Lu.* 6: 48.

This he said to prove him. *Jn.* 6: 6.

I have glorified thee on the earth. . . . I am glorified in them. *Jn.* 17: 4, 10.

They . . . searched the scriptures daily, whether those things were so. *Ac.* 17: 11.

Prove what is that good, and acceptable, and perfect, will of God. *Ro.* 12: 2.

Prove all things; hold fast that which is good. *1 Th.* 5: 21.

Your fathers tempted me, proved me, and saw my works forty years. *He.* 3: 9.

Try the spirits whether they are of God. *1 Jn.* 4: 1.

See also

Christ, Temptation of; Experiment; Fire; Furnace; Pattern; Proof; Standard; Temptation; Trial.

Testament, New

The days come, saith the Lord, that I will make a new covenant with the house of Israel. *Je.* 31: 31.

This is my blood of the new testament. *Mat.* 26: 28.

This cup is the new testament in my blood. *Lu.* 22: 20.

Who also hath made us able ministers of the new testament. *2 Co.* 3: 6.

At that time ye were without Christ, being aliens from the commonwealth of Israel, and strangers from the covenants of promise. *Ep.* 2: 12.

By so much was Jesus made a surety of a better testament. *He.* 7: 22.

He is the mediator of a better covenant. *He.* 8: 6.

In that he saith, A new covenant, he hath made the first old. *He.* 8: 13.

Jesus the mediator of the new covenant. *He.* 12: 24.

See also

Bible; Covenant; God, Word of; Text.

Testament, Old

With thee will I establish my covenant. *Ge.* 6: 18.

I do set my bow in the cloud, and it shall be for a token of a covenant between me and the earth. *Ge.* 9: 13.

My covenant shall be in your flesh for an everlasting covenant. *Ge.* 17: 13.

Seek ye out the book of the Lord, and read. *Is.* 34: 16.

Thy words were found, and I did eat them; and thy word was unto me the joy and rejoicing of mine heart. *Je.* 15: 16.

Come, and let us join ourselves to the Lord in a perpetual covenant. *Je.* 50: 5.

As it is also written in the second psalm. *Ac.* 13: 33.

Whatsoever things were written aforetime were written for our learning, that we through patience and comfort of the scriptures might have hope. *Ro.* 15: 4.

If that first covenant had been faultless, then should no place have been sought for the second. *He.* 8: 7.

This is the blood of the testament which God hath enjoined unto you. *He.* 9: 20.

See also

Bible; Covenant; God, Word of; Promise; Testament, New; Text.

Testimony

Come and hear, all ye that fear God, and I will declare what he hath done for my soul. *Ps.* 66: 16.

Thy testimonies are very sure. *Ps.* 93: 5.

Blessed are they that keep his testimonies. *Ps.* 119: 2.

Thy testimonies are wonderful. *Ps.* 119: 129.

I said, I will not make mention of him, nor speak any more in his name. But his word was in mine heart as a burning fire shut up in my bones, and I was weary with forbearing, and I could not stay. *Je.* 20: 9.

The centurion . . . said, Truly this man was the Son of God. *Mk.* 15: 39.

Unto us, which from the beginning were eyewitnesses. *Lu.* 1: 2.

Whosoever shall confess me before men, him shall the Son of man also confess before the angels of God. *Lu.* 12: 8.

Ye are witnesses of these things. *Lu.* 24: 48.

Jesus himself testified, that a prophet hath no honour in his own country. *Jn.* 4: 44.

John did no miracle: but all things that John spake of this man were true. *Jn.* 10: 41.

He shall testify of me: And ye also shall bear witness. *Jn.* 15: 26, 27.

They were all filled with the Holy Ghost, and began to speak with other tongues. *Ac.* 2: 4.

We cannot but speak the things which we have seen and heard. *Ac.* 4: 20.

To testify the gospel of the grace of God. *Ac.* 20: 24.

Thou shalt be his witness unto all men of what thou hast seen and heard. *Ac.* 22: 15.

The Lord stood by him, and said, Be of good cheer, Paul: for as thou hast testified of me in Jerusalem, so must thou bear witness also at Rome. *Ac.* 23: 11.

We also believe, and therefore speak. *2 Co.* 4: 13.

The brethren came and testified of the truth that is in thee. *3 Jn.* 1: 3.

See also

Christ, Witness of; Evidence; God, Evidence of; God, Witness of; Proof; Witness.

Text

The scripture was fulfilled. *Mk.* 15: 28.

There was delivered unto him the book of the prophet Esaias. And when he had opened the book, he found the place where it was written, The spirit of the Lord is upon me. *Lu.* 4: 17, 18.

This day is this scripture fulfilled in your ears. *Lu.* 4: 21.

Then opened he their understanding, that they might understand the scriptures. *Lu.* 24: 45.

He that believeth on me, as the scripture hath said, out of his belly shall flow rivers of living water. *Jn.* 7: 38.

Understandest thou what thou readest? *Ac.* 8: 30.

What saith the scripture? *Ga.* 4: 30.

The word of God is quick, and powerful, and sharper than any twoedged sword. *He.* 4: 12.

Blessed is he that readeth, and they that hear the words of this prophecy, and keep those things which are written therein. *Re.* 1: 3.

His name is called The Word of God. *Re.* 19: 13.

If any man shall take away from the words of the book of this prophecy, God shall take away his part out of the book of life. *Re.* 22: 19.

See also

Bible; God, Word of; Life, Book of; Testament, New; Testament, Old.

Thanklessness

Esau despised his birthright. *Ge.* 25: 34.

Yet did not the chief butler remember Joseph, but forgat him. *Ge.* 40: 23.

Because thou servedst not the Lord thy God with joyfulness, and with gladness of heart, for the abundance of all things; Therefore shalt thou serve thine enemies. *De.* 28: 47, 48.

Shall thy wonders be known in the dark? and thy righteousness in the land of forgetfulness? *Ps.* 88: 12.

Bless the Lord, O my soul, and forget not all his benefits. *Ps.* 103: 2.

If I forget thee, O Jerusalem, let my right hand forget her cunning. *Ps.* 137: 5.

Thou hast forgotten the God of thy salvation, and hast not been mindful of the rock of thy strength. *Is.* 17: 10.

Israel hath forgotten his Maker. *Ho.* 8: 14.

Were there not ten cleansed? but where are the nine? *Lu.* 17: 17.

There are not found that returned to give glory to God, save this stranger. *Lu.* 17: 18.

See also

Forgetfulness; Ingratitude; Unthankfulness.

Thanksgiving

The Lord thy God bringeth thee into a good land. *De.* 8: 7.

Let the people praise thee, O God; let all the people praise thee. *Ps.* 67: 3.

It is a good thing to give thanks unto the Lord, and to sing praises unto thy name, O most High. *Ps.* 92: 1.

Let us come before his presence with thanksgiving. *Ps.* 95: 2.

Praise ye the Lord. Praise, O ye servants of the Lord, praise the name of the Lord. *Ps.* 113: 1.

Praise the Lord, O Jerusalem; praise thy God, O Zion. *Ps.* 147: 12.

Jesus answering said, Were there not ten cleansed? but where are the nine? There are not found that returned to give glory to God, save this stranger. *Lu.* 17: 17, 18.

He took bread, and gave thanks, and brake it. *Lu.* 22: 19.

Giving thanks always for all things. *Ep.* 5: 20.

He that eateth, eateth to the Lord, for he giveth God thanks; and he that eateth not, to the Lord he eateth not, and giveth God thanks. *Ro.* 14: 6.

See also

Christ, Gratitude to; God, Gratitude to; God, Praise to; God, Thankfulness to; Gratitude; Praise.

Theft

Whoso robbeth his father or his mother, and saith, It is no transgression; the same is the companion of a destroyer. *Pr.* 28: 24.

Whoso is partner with a thief hateth his own soul. *Pr.* **29: 24.**

Thy princes are rebellious, and companions of thieves. *Is.* **1: 23.**

Will a man rob God? Yet ye have robbed me. *Mal.* **3: 8.**

Lay not up for yourselves treasures upon earth, . . . where thieves break through and steal. *Mat.* **6: 19.**

Then were there two thieves crucified with him. *Mat.* **27: 38.**

Ye have taken away the key of knowledge. *Lu.* **11: 52.**

He that entereth not by the door into the sheepfold, but climbeth up some other way, the same is a thief and a robber. *Jn.* **10: 1.**

Let him that stole steal no more: but rather let him labour, working with his hands the thing which is good, that he may have to give to him that needeth. *Ep.* **4: 28.**

The day of the Lord so cometh as a thief in the night. *1 Th.* **5: 2.**

Not purloining, but shewing all good fidelity. *Tit.* **2: 10.**

See also
Burglar; Robbery.

Theocracy

Shall not the Judge of all the earth do right? *Ge.* **18: 25.**

The Lord searcheth all hearts, and understandeth all the imaginations of the thoughts. *1 Ch.* **28: 9.**

In the name of our God we will set up our banners. *Ps.* **20: 5.**

Let them know that God ruleth. *Ps.* **59: 13.**

He ruleth by his power for ever. *Ps.* **66: 7.**

Thou rulest the raging of the sea. *Ps.* **89: 9.**

The Lord hath prepared his throne in the heavens; and his kingdom ruleth over all. *Ps.* **103: 19.**

For ever, O Lord, thy word is settled in heaven. *Ps.* **119: 89.**

Thy kingdom is an everlasting kingdom, and thy dominion endureth throughout all generations. *Ps.* **145: 13.**

By me kings reign, and princes decree justice. By me princes rule, and nobles, even all the judges of the earth. *Pr.* **8: 15, 16.**

The most High ruleth in the kingdom of men. *Da.* **4: 17.**

He shall judge among many people, and rebuke strong nations afar off. *Mi.* **4: 3.**

From the rising of the sun even unto the going down of the same my name shall be great. *Mal.* **1: 11.**

With God nothing shall be impossible. *Lu.* **1: 37.**

Before Abraham was, I am. *Jn.* **8: 58.**

See also
Dominion; God, the King; God, Kingdom of; God, Sovereignty of; God, Supremacy of.

Theology

The Lord, he is the God; the Lord, he is the God. *1 K.* **18: 39.**

Canst thou by searching find out God? canst thou find out the Almighty unto perfection? *Jb.* **11: 7.**

Touching the Almighty, we cannot find him out: he is excellent in power, and in judgment, and in plenty of justice. *Jb.* **37: 23.**

There is no searching of his understanding. *Is.* **40: 28.**

Is there a God beside me? yea, there is no God; I know not any. *Is.* **44: 8.**

I am God, and there is none else. *Is.* **45: 22.**

There is no . . . knowledge of God in the land. *Ho.* **4: 1.**

I desired . . . the knowledge of God more than burnt offerings. *Ho.* **6: 6.**

In the beginning was the Word, and the Word was with God, and the Word was God. *Jn.* **1: 1.**

Whom therefore ye ignorantly worship, him declare I unto you. *Ac.* **17: 23.**

O the depth of the riches both of the wisdom and knowledge of God! how unsearchable are his judgments, and his ways past finding out! *Ro.* **11: 33.**

Some have not the knowledge of God. *1 Co.* **15: 34.**

Grace and peace be multiplied unto you through the knowledge of God. *2 Pe.* **1: 2.**

God is light, and in him is no darkness at all. *1 Jn.* **1: 5.**

No man hath seen God at any time. *1 Jn.* **4: 12.**

See also
God, Knowledge of.

Thickness

These words the Lord spake unto all your assembly in the mount out of the midst of the fire, of the cloud, and of the thick darkness, with a great voice. *De.* **5: 22.**

Thou art waxen fat, thou art grown thick, thou art covered with fatness. *De.* **32: 15.**

My little finger shall be thicker than my father's loins. *1 K.* **12: 10.**

He bindeth up the waters in his thick clouds. *Jb.* **26: 8.**

His pavilion round about him were dark waters and thick clouds of the skies. *Ps.* **18: 11.**

The glory of Jacob shall be made thin, and the fatness of his flesh shall wax lean. *Is.* **17: 4.**

I have blotted out, as a thick cloud, thy transgressions, and, as a cloud, thy sins. *Is.* **44: 22.**

A thick cloud of incense went up. *Eze.* **8: 11.**

See also
Fat.

Thing

Is any thing too hard for the Lord? *Ge.* **18: 14.**

All things come of thee, and of thine own have we given thee. *1 Ch.* **29: 14.**

I know that thou canst do every thing. *Jb.* **42: 2.**

Thou hast put all things under his feet. *Ps.* **8: 6.**

My covenant will I not break, nor alter the thing that is gone out of my lips. *Ps.* **89: 34.**

It is the glory of God to conceal a thing. *Pr.* **25: 2.**

There is no new thing under the sun. *Ec.* **1: 9.**

Thou savourest not the things that be of God, but those that be of men. *Mat.* **16: 23.**

Render therefore unto Caesar the things which are Caesar's; and unto God the things that are God's. *Mat.* **22: 21.**

All things are possible to him that believeth. *Mk.* 9: 23.

Martha, Martha, thou art careful and troubled about many things. *Lu.* 10: 41.

Shall the thing formed say to him that formed it, Why hast thou made me thus? *Ro.* 9: 20.

Thing, the Common

Better is a dinner of herbs where love is, than a stalled ox and hatred therewith. *Pr.* 15: 17.

He hath made every thing beautiful in his time. *Ec.* 3: 11.

Yea, every pot in Jerusalem and in Judah shall be holiness unto the Lord of hosts. *Zch.* 14: 21.

A colt . . . whereon never man sat. *Mk.* 11: 2.

He commanded to give her meat. *Lu.* 8: 55.

He took bread. *Lu.* 22: 19.

As soon then as they were come to land, they saw a fire of coals there, and fish laid thereon, and bread. Jesus saith unto them, Come and dine. *Jn.* 21: 9, 12.

All that believed were together, and had all things common. *Ac.* 2: 44.

Mind not high things, but condescend to men of low estate. *Ro.* 12: 16.

God hath chosen the weak things of the world to confound the things which are mighty. *1 Co.* 1: 27.

And base things of the world, and things which are despised, hath God chosen. *1 Co.* 1: 28.

This is the message that ye heard from the beginning, that we should love one another. *1 Jn.* 3: 11.

See also

Commonplace; Equality; Importance.

Thing, the Little

Are the consolations of God small with thee? is there any secret thing with thee? *Jb.* 15: 11.

There be four things which are little upon the earth, but they are exceeding wise: The ants, . . . The conies, . . . The locusts, . . . The spider. *Pr.* 30: 24–28.

Behold, the nations are as a drop of a bucket, and are counted as the small dust of the balance: behold, he taketh up the isles as a very little thing. *Is.* 40: 15.

Thou, Bethlehem Ephratah, though thou be little among the thousands of Judah. *Mi.* 5: 2.

Who hath despised the day of small things? *Zch.* 4: 10.

Thou hast been faithful over a few things, I will make thee ruler over many things. *Mat.* 25: 21.

He that is faithful in that which is least is faithful also in much. *Lu.* 16: 10.

Because thou hast been faithful in a very little, have thou authority over ten cities. *Lu.* 19: 17.

He saw also a certain poor widow casting in thither two mites. *Lu.* 21: 2.

There is a lad here, which hath five barley loaves, and two small fishes. *Jn.* 6: 9.

Gather up the fragments that remain, that nothing be lost. *Jn.* 6: 12.

God hath chosen the foolish things of the world to confound the wise; and God hath chosen the weak things of the world to confound the things which are mighty. *1 Co.* 1: 27.

Know ye not that a little leaven leaveneth the whole lump? *1 Co.* 5: 6.

All things are of God. *2 Co.* 5: 18.

Behold also the ships, which though they be so great, and are driven of fierce winds, yet are they turned about with a very small helm. *Ja.* 3: 4.

See also

Commonplace; Little; Pettiness; Smallness; Trifle.

Thirst

My soul thirsteth for God. *Ps.* 42: 2.

Hungry and thirsty, their soul fainted in them. *Ps.* 107: 5.

The God of Jacob . . . turned the rock into a standing water, the flint into a fountain of water. *Ps.* 114: 7, 8.

Ho, every one that thirsteth, come ye to the waters. *Is.* 55: 1.

The beasts of the field cry also unto thee: for the rivers of waters are dried up. *Jo.* 1: 20.

Blessed are they which do hunger and thirst after righteousness. *Mat.* 5: 6.

Whosoever drinketh of the water that I shall give him shall never thirst. *Jn.* 4: 14.

In the last day, that great day of the feast, Jesus stood and cried, saying, If any man thirst, let him come unto me, and drink. *Jn.* 7: 37.

If thine enemy hunger, feed him; if he thirst, give him drink. *Ro.* 12: 20.

Even unto this present hour we both hunger, and thirst. *1 Co.* 4: 11.

In hunger and thirst, in fastings often. *2 Co.* 11: 27.

See also

Desire; Drink; God, Longing for; God, Thirst for; God, Yearning for; Longing; Milk; Water; Wine; Yearning.

Thorn

Instead of the thorn shall come up the fir tree. *Is.* 55: 13.

They have sown wheat, but shall reap thorns. *Je.* 12: 13.

I will hedge up thy way with thorns, and make a wall, that she shall not find her paths. *Ho.* 2: 6.

The thorn and the thistle shall come up on their altars. *Ho.* 10: 8.

Do men gather grapes of thorns, or figs of thistles? *Mat.* 7: 16.

When they had platted a crown of thorns, they put it upon his head. *Mat.* 27: 29.

Some fell among thorns; and the thorns sprang up with it, and choked it. *Lu.* 8: 7.

There was given to me a thorn in the flesh, the messenger of Satan to buffet me, lest I should be exalted above measure. *2 Co.* 12: 7.

See also

Brier.

Thought

Try me, and know my thoughts. *Ps.* 139: 23.

Through wisdom is an house builded; and by understanding it is established. *Pr.* 24: 3.

A fool uttereth all his mind. *Pr.* 29: 11.

Let the wicked forsake his way, and the unrighteous man his thoughts. *Is.* 55: 7.

I know the thoughts that I think toward you, saith the Lord, thoughts of peace, and not of evil. *Je.* 29: 11.

Out of the heart proceed evil thoughts. *Mat.* 15: 19.

Bringing into captivity every thought to the obedience of Christ. *2 Co.* 10: 5.

See also

Brain; Consideration; Contemplation; Intelligence; Meditation; Mind; Study.

Thousand

Shewing mercy unto thousands of them that love me, and keep my commandments. *Ex.* 20: 6.

The Lord God of your fathers make you a thousand times so many more as ye are, and bless you! *De.* 1: 11.

Know therefore that the Lord thy God, he is God, the faithful God, which keepeth covenant and mercy with them that love him and keep his commandments to a thousand generations. *De.* 7: 9.

How should one chase a thousand, and two put ten thousand to flight, except their Rock had sold them? *De.* 32: 30.

Every beast of the forest is mine, and the cattle upon a thousand hills. *Ps.* 50: 10.

A day in thy courts is better than a thousand. *Ps.* 84: 10.

A thousand years in thy sight are but as yesterday when it is past, and as a watch in the night. *Ps.* 90: 4.

A thousand shall fall at thy side, and ten thousand at thy right hand; but it shall not come nigh thee. *Ps.* 91: 7.

The law of thy mouth is better unto me than thousands of gold and silver. *Ps.* 119: 72.

One man among a thousand have I found; but a woman among all those have I not found. *Ec.* 7: 28.

A little one. shall become a thousand, and a small one a strong nation. *Is.* 60: 22.

Thou shewest lovingkindness unto thousands. *Je.* 32: 18.

Will the Lord be pleased with thousands of rams? *Mi.* 6: 7.

Be not ignorant of this one thing, that one day is with the Lord as a thousand years, and a thousand years as one day. *2 Pe.* 3: 8.

They shall be priests of God and of Christ, and shall reign with him a thousand years. *Re.* 20: 6.

See also

Millennium.

Three

Where two or three are gathered together in my name, there am I in the midst of them. *Mat.* 18: 20.

Which now of these three, thinkest thou, was neighbour unto him that fell among the thieves? *Lu.* 10: 36.

From henceforth there shall be five in one house divided, three against two, and two against three. *Lu.* 12: 52.

Now abideth faith, hope, charity, these three. *1 Co.* 13: 13.

If any man speak in an unknown tongue, let it be by two, or at the most by three, and that by course; and let one interpret. *1 Co.* 14: 27.

There are three that bear record in heaven, the Father, the Word, and the Holy Ghost: and these three are one. *1 Jn.* 5: 7.

There are three that bear witness in earth, the spirit, and the water, and the blood: and these agree in one. *1 Jn.* 5: 8.

See also

Trinity.

Threshing-Floor

Your threshing shall reach unto the vintage, and the vintage shall reach unto the sowing time: and ye shall eat your bread to the full, and dwell in your land safely. *Le.* 26: 5.

O my threshing, and the corn of my floor: that which I have heard of the Lord of hosts, the God of Israel, have I declared unto you. *Is.* 21: 10.

Then was the iron, the clay, the brass, the silver, and the gold, broken to pieces together, and became like the chaff of the summer threshingfloors. *Da.* 2: 35.

He that thresheth in hope should be partaker of his hope. *1 Co.* 9: 10.

See also

Chaff; Harvest.

Throat

Their throat is an open sepulchre; they flatter with their tongue. *Ps.* 5: 9.

I am weary of my crying: my throat is dried: mine eyes fail while I wait for my God. *Ps.* 69: 3.

They have hands, but they handle not: feet have they, but they walk not: neither speak they through their throat. *Ps.* 115: 7.

Put a knife to thy throat, if thou be a man given to appetite. *Pr.* 23: 2.

Withhold thy foot from being unshod, and thy throat from thirst. *Je.* 2: 25.

Throne

I will stablish the throne of his kingdom for ever. *2 S.* 7: 13.

The Lord is in his holy temple, the Lord's throne is in heaven. *Ps.* 11: 4.

Thy throne, O God, is for ever and ever. *Ps.* 45: 6.

Justice and judgment are the habitation of thy throne. *Ps.* 89: 14.

Shall the throne of iniquity have fellowship with thee? *Ps.* 94: 20.

The Lord hath prepared his throne in the heavens. *Ps.* 103: 19.

There are set thrones of judgment. *Ps.* 122: 5.

His throne is upholden by mercy. *Pr.* 20: 28.

Swear not at all; neither by heaven; for it is God's throne. *Mat.* 5: 34.

The Lord God shall give unto him the throne of his father David. *Lu.* 1: 32.

Let us therefore come boldly unto the throne of grace, that we may obtain mercy, and find grace to help in time of need. *He.* 4: 16.

Out of the throne proceeded lightnings and thunderings and voices. *Re.* 4: 5.

I saw a great white throne, and him that sat on it, from whose face the earth and the heaven fled away. *Re.* 20: 11.

See also

Authority; Christ, the King; Christ, Reign of; Christ, Supremacy of; Dominion; God, the King; God, Kingdom of; God, Sovereignty of;

God, Supremacy of; Heaven, Kingdom of; Kingdom; Power; Reign; Rule; Sovereignty.

Thunder

The Lord thundered with a great thunder on that day upon the Philistines, and discomfited them. *1 S.* 7: 10.

The thunder of his power who can understand? *Jb.* 26: 14.

He thundereth with the voice of his excellency. *Jb.* 37: 4.

God thundereth marvellously with his voice. *Jb.* 37: 5.

Hast thou an arm like God? or canst thou thunder with a voice like him? *Jb.* 40: 9.

The voice of the Lord is upon the waters: the God of glory thundereth. *Ps.* 29: 3.

The voice of thy thunder was in the heaven: the lightnings lightened the world: the earth trembled and shook. *Ps.* 77: 18.

He gave up their cattle also to the hail, and their flocks to hot thunderbolts. *Ps.* 78: 48.

I answered thee in the secret place of thunder. *Ps.* 81: 7.

At the voice of thy thunder they hasted away. *Ps.* 104: 7.

The people therefore, that stood by, and heard it, said that it thundered: others said, An angel spake to him. *Jn.* 12: 29.

Out of the throne proceeded lightnings and thunderings and voices. *Re.* 4: 5.

I heard a voice from heaven, as the voice of many waters, and as the voice of a great thunder. *Re.* 14: 2.

See also
Lightning.

Tidings

He shall not be afraid of evil tidings: his heart is fixed, trusting in the Lord. *Ps.* 112: 7.

As cold waters to a thirsty soul, so is good news from a far country. *Pr.* 25: 25.

O Zion, that bringest good tidings, get thee up into the high mountain; O Jerusalem, that bringest good tidings, lift up thy voice with strength. *Is.* 40: 9.

The Lord hath anointed me to preach good tidings unto the meek. *Is.* 61: 1.

Cursed be the man who brought tidings to my father, saying, A man child is born unto thee; making him very glad. *Je.* 20: 15.

I am Gabriel, that stand in the presence of God; and am sent to speak unto thee, and to shew thee these glad tidings. *Lu.* 1: 19.

Fear not: for, behold, I bring you good tidings of great joy, which shall be to all people. *Lu.* 2: 10.

He went throughout every city and village, preaching and shewing the glad tidings of the kingdom of God. *Lu.* 8: 1.

We declare unto you glad tidings, how that the promise which was made unto the fathers, God hath fulfilled the same unto us their children. *Ac.* 13: 32, 33.

How beautiful are the feet of them that preach the gospel of peace, and bring glad tidings of good things! *Ro.* 10: 15.

Timotheus . . . brought us good tidings of your faith and charity. *1 Th.* 3: 6.

The glorious gospel of the blessed God. *1 Ti.* 1: 11.

See also
Announcement; Evangelism; Gospel; Herald; News, Good.

Time

Ye shall not . . . observe times. *Le.* 19: 26.

Is there not an appointed time to man upon earth? *Jb.* 7: 1.

Seeing times are not hidden from the Almighty, do they that know him not see his days? *Jb.* 24: 1.

The Lord also will be a refuge for the oppressed, a refuge in times of trouble. *Ps.* 9: 9.

I will bless the Lord at all times. *Ps.* 34: 1.

My prayer is unto thee, O Lord, in an acceptable time. *Ps.* 69: 13.

Cast me not off in the time of old age. *Ps.* 71: 9.

So teach us to number our days, that we may apply our hearts unto wisdom. *Ps.* 90: 12.

It is time for thee, Lord, to work. *Ps.* 119: 126.

To every thing there is a season, and a time to every purpose under the heaven. *Ec.* 3: 1.

A time to break down, and a time to build up. *Ec.* 3: 3.

A time of war, and a time of peace. *Ec.* 3: 8.

He hath made every thing beautiful in his time. *Ec.* 3: 11.

Time and chance happeneth to them all. *Ec.* 9: 11.

Man also knoweth not his time. *Ec.* 9: 12.

He changeth the times and the seasons. *Da.* 2: 21.

The signs of the times. *Mat.* 16: 3.

No man hath seen God at any time. *Jn.* 1: 18.

The fashion of this world passeth away. *1 Co.* 7: 31.

The heir . . . is under tutors and governors until the time appointed of the father. *Ga.* 4: 1, 2.

Ye observe days, and months, and times, and years. *Ga.* 4: 10.

Let us therefore come boldly unto the throne of grace, that we may obtain mercy, and find grace to help in time of need. *He.* 4: 16.

One day is with the Lord as a thousand years, and a thousand years as one day. *2 Pe.* 3: 8.

See also
Age; Day; Duration; Epoch; Era; Month; Season; Year.

Time, Future

He prophesieth of the times that are far off. *Eze.* 12: 27.

At the time appointed the end shall be. *Da.* 8: 19.

The vision is yet for an appointed time, but at the end it shall speak, and not lie: though it tarry, wait for it. *Hab.* 2: 3.

Take ye heed, watch and pray: for ye know not when the time is. *Mk.* 13: 33.

It is not for you to know the times or the seasons, which the Father hath put in his own power. *Ac.* 1: 7.

In the last days perilous times shall come. *2 Ti.* 3: 1.

Kept by the power of God through faith

unto salvation ready to be revealed in the last time. *1 Pe.* 1: 5.

See also

Age, Golden; Epoch; Era; Future; Millenium; To-morrow.

Time, Past

There were giants in the earth in those days. *Ge.* 6: 4.

In those times there was no peace. *2 Ch.* 15: 5.

The wise men, which knew the times. *Es.* 1: 13.

Our fathers have told us, what work thou didst in their days, in the times of old. *Ps.* 44: 1.

I have considered the days of old, the years of ancient times. *Ps.* 77: 5.

When the time of the promise drew nigh. *Ac.* 7: 17.

He . . . hath determined the times before appointed. *Ac.* 17: 25, 26.

The times of this ignorance God winked at. *Ac.* 17: 30.

God . . . at sundry times and in divers manners spake in time past unto the fathers by the prophets. *He.* 1: 1.

See also

Age, Golden; Epoch; Era; Past; Yesterday.

Time, Present

Who knoweth whether thou art come to the kingdom for such a time as this? *Es.* 4: 14.

My days are swifter than a weaver's shuttle. *Jb.* 7: 6.

Remember how short my time is: wherefore hast thou made all men in vain? *Ps.* 89: 47.

This is the time of the Lord's vengeance. *Je.* 51: 6.

The Master saith, My time is at hand. *Mat.* 26: 18.

The time is fulfilled, and the kingdom of God is at hand. *Mk.* 1: 15.

Ye can discern the face of the sky and of the earth; but how is it that ye do not discern this time? *Lu.* 12: 56.

My time is not yet come: but your time is alway ready. *Jn.* 7: 6.

The time is short: it remaineth, that both they that have wives be as though they had none; And they that weep, as though they wept not; and they that rejoice, as though they rejoiced not; and they that buy, as though they possessed not; And they that use this world, as not abusing it: for the fashion of this world passeth away. *1 Co.* 7: 29–31.

I have heard thee in a time accepted, and in the day of salvation have I succoured thee: behold, now is the accepted time; behold, now is the day of salvation. *2 Co.* 6: 2.

Redeeming the time, because the days are evil. *Ep.* 5: 16.

The time of my departure is at hand. *2 Ti.* 4: 6.

See also

To-day.

Timidity

Fear came upon me, and trembling. *Jb.* 4: 14.

What time I am afraid, I will trust in thee. *Ps.* 56: 3.

The wicked flee when no man pursueth. *Pr.* 28: 1.

He that observeth the wind shall not sow; and he that regardeth the clouds shall not reap. *Ec.* 11: 4.

Be not dismayed at their faces, lest I confound thee before them. *Je.* 1: 17.

Fear is on every side. *Je.* 6: 25.

Why are ye so fearful? how is it that ye have no faith? *Mk.* 4: 40.

They understood not that saying, and were afraid to ask him. *Mk.* 9: 32.

They all forsook him, and fled. *Mk.* 14: 50.

Peter followed afar off. *Lu.* 22: 54.

If ye suffer for righteousness' sake, happy are ye: and be not afraid of their terror, neither be troubled. *1 Pe.* 3: 14.

See also

Alarm; Caution; Cowardice; Fear; Terror; Trembling.

Tithe

Of all that thou shalt give me I will surely give the tenth unto thee. *Ge.* 28: 22.

All the tithe of the land, whether of the seed of the land, or of the fruit of the tree, is the Lord's: it is holy unto the Lord. *Le.* 27: 30.

The tenth shall be holy unto the Lord. *Le.* 27: 32.

Will a man rob God? Yet ye have robbed me. But ye say, Wherein have we robbed thee? In tithes and offerings. *Mal.* 3: 8.

Ye pay tithe of mint and anise and cummin, and have omitted the weightier matters of the law, judgment, mercy and faith. *Mat.* 23: 23.

Woe unto you, Pharisees! for ye tithe mint and rue and all manner of herbs, and pass over judgment and the love of God: these ought ye to have done, and not to leave the other undone. *Lu.* 11: 42.

I give tithes of all that I possess. *Lu.* 18: 12.

Title

She shall be called Woman, because she was taken out of Man. *Ge.* 2: 23.

This glorious and fearful name, THE LORD THY GOD. *De.* 28: 58.

Let me not, I pray you, accept any man's person, neither let me give flattering titles unto man. *Jb.* 32: 21.

I know not to give flattering titles; in so doing my maker would soon take me away. *Jb.* 32: 22.

His name shall be called Wonderful, Counsellor, The mighty God, The everlasting Father, The Prince of Peace. *Is.* 9: 6.

The Lord of hosts is his name. *Je.* 10: 16.

This is his name whereby he shall be called, THE LORD OUR RIGHTEOUSNESS. *Je.* 23: 6.

The Lord is his name. *Am.* 5: 8.

Jerusalem shall be called a city of truth. *Zch.* 8: 3.

They shall call his name Emmanuel, which being interpreted is, God with us. *Mat.* 1: 23.

He shall be great, and shall be called the Son of the Highest. *Lu.* 1: 32.

That holy thing which shall be born of thee shall be called the Son of God. *Lu.* 1: 35.

Pilate wrote a title, and put it on the cross. And the writing was, JESUS OF NAZARETH

THE KING OF THE JEWS. *Jn.* 19: 19.

Then said the chief priests of the Jews to Pilate, Write not, The King of the Jews; but that he said, I am King of the Jews. *Jn.* 19: 21.

He was called the Friend of God. *Ja.* 2: 23.

Upon her forehead was a name written, MYSTERY, BABYLON THE GREAT, THE MOTHER OF HARLOTS AND ABOMINATIONS OF THE EARTH. *Re.* 17: 5.

I saw heaven opened, and behold a white horse; and he that sat upon him was called Faithful and True, and in righteousness he doth judge. *Re.* 19: 11.

See also
Name.

To-day

Consecrate yourselves to day to the Lord. *Ex.* 32: 29.

To day if ye will hear his voice, Harden not your heart. *Ps.* 95: 7, 8.

This is the day which the Lord hath made; we will rejoice and be glad in it. *Ps.* 118: 24.

When I awake, I am still with thee. *Ps.* 139: 18.

Give us this day. *Mat.* 6: 11.

If God so clothe the grass of the field, which to day is, and to morrow is cast into the oven, shall he not much more clothe you, O ye of little faith? *Mat.* 6: 30.

Sufficient unto the day is the evil thereof. *Mat.* 6: 34.

I must walk to day, and to morrow, and the day following: for it cannot be that a prophet perish out of Jerusalem. *Lu.* 13: 33.

To day shalt thou be with me in paradise. *Lu.* 23: 43.

Now is the accepted time; behold, now is the day of salvation. *2 Co.* 6: 2.

Exhort one another daily, while it is called To day. *He.* 3: 13.

Thou art my Son, to day have I begotten thee. *He.* 5: 5.

See also
Time, Present.

Toil

In the sweat of thy face shalt thou eat bread, till thou return unto the ground; for out of it wast thou taken. *Ge.* 3: 19.

God, said he, hath made me forget all my toil. *Ge.* 41: 51.

Is it good unto thee that thou . . . shouldest despise the work of thine hands? *Jb.* 10: 3.

He that tilleth his land shall be satisfied with bread. *Pr.* 12: 11.

All things are full of labour. *Ec.* 1: 8.

Whatsoever thy hand findeth to do, do it with thy might. *Ec.* 9: 10.

If ye be willing and obedient, ye shall eat the good of the land. *Is.* 1: 19.

They shall not labour in vain, nor bring forth for trouble. *Is.* 65: 23.

Be strong, all ye people of the land, saith the Lord, and work. *Hag.* 2: 4.

Consider the lilies of the field, how they grow; they toil not, neither do they spin. *Mat.* 6: 28.

Master, we have toiled all the night, and have taken nothing. *Lu.* 5: 5.

We are labourers together with God. *1 Co.* 3: 9.

Let every man take heed how he buildeth. *1 Co.* 3: 10.

Every man's work shall be made manifest. *1 Co.* 3: 13.

Remembering without ceasing your . . . labour of love. *1 Th.* 1: 3.

See also
Christ, Work of; Drudgery; Duty; Employee; Employer; God, Work of; Labor; Occupation; Service; Task; Travail; Undertaking; Work.

Token

This is the token of the covenant which I make between me and you and every living creature that is with you, for perpetual generations: I do set my bow in the cloud. *Ge.* 9: 12, 13.

Do ye not know their tokens, That the wicked is reserved to the day of destruction? *Jb.* 21: 29, 30.

They also that dwell in the uttermost parts are afraid at thy tokens: thou makest the outgoings of the morning and evening to rejoice. *Ps.* 65: 8.

The Lord . . . sent tokens and wonders into the midst of thee. *Ps.* 135: 6, 9.

What shall be the sign of thy coming, and of the end of the world? *Mat.* 24: 3.

What shall be the sign when all these things shall be fulfilled? *Mk.* 13: 4.

This shall be a sign unto you; Ye shall find the babe. *Lu.* 2: 12.

We ourselves glory in you in the churches of God for your patience and faith in all your persecutions and tribulations that ye endure: Which is a manifest token of the righteous judgment of God. *2 Th.* 1: 4, 5.

See also
Evidence; Proof; Sign.

Tolerance

He shall not judge after the sight of his eyes. *Is.* 11: 3.

Judge not, that ye be not judged. *Mat.* 7: 1.

He that is not against us is on our part. *Mk.* 9: 40.

He loveth our nation, and he hath built us a synagogue. *Lu.* 7: 5.

When his disciples James and John saw this, they said, Lord, wilt thou that we command fire to come down from heaven, and consume them? . . . But he turned, and rebuked them. *Lu.* 9: 54, 55.

Who made me a judge or a divider over you? *Lu.* 12: 14.

Judge not according to the appearance, but judge righteous judgment. *Jn.* 7: 24.

Refrain from these men, and let them alone: for if this counsel or this work be of men, it will come to nought: But if it be of God, ye cannot overthrow it. *Ac.* 5: 38, 39.

I will be no judge of such matters. *Ac.* 18: 15.

Above all things have fervent charity among yourselves: for charity shall cover the multitude of sins. *1 Pe.* 4: 8.

See also
Charity; Forbearance; Judgment.

Tomb

No man knoweth of his sepulchre unto this day. *De.* 34: 6.

As the cloud is consumed and vanisheth away: so he that goeth down to the grave shall come up no more. *Jb.* 7: 9.

Yet shall he be brought to the grave, and shall remain in the tomb. *Jb.* 21: 32.

In the grave who shall give thee thanks? *Ps.* 6: 5.

Let the wicked be ashamed, and let them be silent in the grave. *Ps.* 31: 17.

It shall come to pass, that at evening time it shall be light. *Zch.* 14: 7.

Ye are like unto whited sepulchres, which indeed appear beautiful outward, but are within full of dead men's bones, and of all uncleanness. *Mat.* 23: 27.

Woe unto you, scribes and Pharisees, hypocrites! because ye build the tombs of the prophets, and garnish the sepulchres of the righteous. *Mat.* 23: 29.

When Joseph had taken the body, he wrapped it in a clean linen cloth, And laid it in his own new tomb. *Mat.* 27: 59, 60.

The people therefore that was with him when he called Lazarus out of his grave, and raised him from the dead, bare record. *Jn.* 12: 17.

Now in the place where he was crucified there was a garden; and in the garden a new sepulchre, wherein was never man yet laid. *Jn.* 19: 41.

Let me freely speak unto you of the patriarch David, that he is both dead and buried, and his sepulchre is with us unto this day. *Ac.* 2: 29.

Why should it be thought a thing incredible with you, that God should raise the dead? *Ac.* 26: 8.

By faith Enoch was translated that he should not see death. *He.* 11: 5.

See also

Burial; Death; Funeral; Grave.

To-morrow

Boast not thyself of to morrow: for thou knowest not what a day may bring forth. *Pr.* 27: 1.

Let us eat and drink; for to morrow we shall die. *Is.* 22: 13.

To-morrow shall be as this day, and much more abundant. *Is.* 56: 12.

Take therefore no thought for the morrow. *Mat.* 6: 34.

Go to now, ye that say, To day or to morrow we will go into such a city, and continue there a year, and buy and sell, and get gain: Whereas ye know not what shall be on the morrow. *Ja.* 4: 13, 14.

Ye ought to say, If the Lord will. *Ja.* 4: 15.

See also

Future; Morrow; Time, the Future.

Tongue

I said, I will take heed to my ways, that I sin not with my tongue. *Ps.* 39: 1.

My tongue is the pen of a ready writer. *Ps.* 45: 1.

The tongue of the wise useth knowledge aright. *Pr.* 15: 2.

A wholesome tongue is a tree of life. *Pr.* 15: 4.

A word spoken in due season, how good is it! *Pr.* 15: 23.

The words of the pure are pleasant words. *Pr.* 15: 26.

Death and life are in the power of the tongue. *Pr.* 18: 21.

Her tongue is the law of kindness. *Pr.* 31: 26.

They helped every one his neighbour; and every one said to his brother, Be of good courage. *Is.* 41: 6.

The Lord God hath given me the tongue of the learned, that I should know how to speak a word in season to him that is weary. *Is.* 50: 4.

Let your speech be alway with grace, seasoned with salt, that ye may know how ye ought to answer every man. *Col.* 4: 6.

The tongue is a little member, and boasteth great things. Behold, how great a matter a little fire kindleth! *Ja.* 3: 5.

The tongue is a fire. *Ja.* 3: 6.

The tongue can no man tame. *Ja.* 3: 8.

See also

Accent; Language; Lip; Mouth; Self-Expression; Speech; Utterance; Word.

Tooth

Eye for eye, tooth for tooth, hand for hand, foot for foot. *Ex.* 21: 24.

Thou hast broken the teeth of the ungodly. *Ps.* 3: 7.

Break their teeth, O God, in their mouth. *Ps.* 58: 6.

Blessed be the Lord, who hath not given us as a prey to their teeth. *Ps.* 124: 6.

As vinegar to the teeth, and as smoke to the eyes, so is the sluggard to them that send him. *Pr.* 10: 26.

Confidence in an unfaithful man in time of trouble is like a broken tooth, and a foot out of joint. *Pr.* 25: 19.

There is a generation, whose teeth are as swords, and their jaw teeth as knives, to devour the poor from off the earth, and the needy from among men. *Pr.* 30: 14.

The fathers have eaten a sour grape, and the children's teeth are set on edge. *Je.* 31: 29.

I also have given you cleanness of teeth in all your cities, and want of bread in all your places. *Am.* 4: 6.

Top

Behold a ladder set up on the earth, and the top of it reached to heaven. *Ge.* 28: 12.

To morrow I will stand on the top of the hill with the rod of God in mine hand. *Ex.* 17: 9.

When thou hearest the sound of a going in the tops of the mulberry trees, . . . then shall the Lord go out before thee. *2 S.* 5: 24.

They are . . . cut off as the tops of the ears of corn. *Jb.* 24: 24.

Thou shalt be as he that lieth down in the midst of the sea, or as he that lieth upon the top of a mast. *Pr.* 23: 34.

The mountain of the Lord's house shall be established in the top of the mountains. *Is.* 2: 2.

They sacrifice upon the tops of the mountains, and burn incense upon the hills. *Ho.* 4: 13.

See also

Climbing; Hill; Mountain; Pinnacle; Summit.

Torch

He placed at the east of the garden of Eden Cherubims, and a flaming sword which turned every way, to keep the way of the tree of life. *Ge.* 3: 24.

The Lord went before them by day in a pillar of a cloud, to lead them the way; and by night in a pillar of fire, to give them light. *Ex.* 13: 21.

He put a trumpet in every man's hand, with empty pitchers, and lamps within the pitchers. *Ju.* 7: 16.

Samson went and caught three hundred foxes, and took firebrands, and turned tail to tail, and put a firebrand in the midst between two tails. *Ju.* 15: 4.

As a mad man who casteth firebrands. *Pr.* 26: 18.

The chariots shall be with flaming torches in the day of his preparation. *Na.* 2: 3.

Let your loins be girded about, and your lights burning. *Lu.* 12: 35.

He was a burning and a shining light: and ye were willing for a season to rejoice in his light. *Jn.* 5: 35.

Judas then . . . cometh thither with lanterns and torches and weapons. *Jn.* 18: 3.

Torment

My heart is sore pained within me: and the terrors of death are fallen upon me. *Ps.* 55: 4.

The pains of hell gat hold upon me. *Ps.* 116: 3.

Why is my pain perpetual, and my wound incurable, which refuseth to be healed? *Je.* 15: 18.

In hell he lift up his eyes, being in torment. *Lu.* 16: 23.

We which live are alway delivered unto death for Jesus' sake. *2 Co.* 4: 11.

I . . . fill up that which is behind of the afflictions of Christ. *Col.* 1: 23, 24.

Perfect love casteth out fear: because fear hath torment. *1 Jn.* 4: 18.

The smoke of their torment ascendeth up for ever and ever. *Re.* 14: 11.

See also
Affliction; Agony; Anguish; Distress; Hell; Pain.

Touch

Jesus put forth his hand, and touched him, saying, I will; be thou clean. *Mat.* 8: 3.

He touched her hand, and the fever left her. *Mat.* 8: 15.

If I may but touch his garment, I shall be whole. *Mat.* 9: 21.

As many as touched were made perfectly whole. *Mat.* 14: 36.

They pressed upon him for to touch him. *Mk.* 3: 10.

A woman . . . Came behind him, and touched the border of his garment. *Lu.* 8: 43, 44.

Jesus said, Somebody hath touched me. *Lu.* 8: 46.

He touched his ear. *Lu.* 22: 51.

Behold my hands and my feet, that it is myself: handle me, and see. *Lu.* 24: 39.

Touch not; taste not; handle not. *Col.* 2: 21.

See also
Hand.

Tower

Let us build us a city and a tower, whose top may reach unto heaven. *Ge.* 11: 4.

He is my shield, and the horn of my salvation, my high tower, and my refuge. *2 S.* 22: 3.

Walk about Zion, and go round about her: tell the towers thereof. *Ps.* 48: 12.

Thou hast been a shelter for me, and a strong tower from the enemy. *Ps.* 61: 3.

The name of the Lord is a strong tower. *Pr.* 18: 10.

I have set thee for a tower and a fortress among my people. *Je.* 6: 27.

Which of you, intending to build a tower, sitteth not down first, and counteth the cost, whether he have sufficient to finish it? *Lu.* 14: 28.

See also
Castle; Fortress; Protection; Refuge.

Town

Woe to him that buildeth a town with blood. *Hab.* 2: 12.

Jerusalem shall be inhabited as towns without walls for the multitude of men and cattle therein. *Zch.* 2: 4.

Into whatsoever city or town ye shall enter, enquire who in it is worthy; and there abide till ye go thence. *Mat.* 10: 11.

They departed, and went through the towns, preaching the gospel, and healing every where. *Lu.* 9: 6.

Christ cometh of the seed of David, and out of the town of Bethlehem, where David was? *Jn.* 7: 42.

Jesus was not yet come into the town. *Jn.* 11: 30.

See also
City; Village.

Track

So are the paths of all that forget God; and the hypocrite's hope shall perish. *Jb.* 8: 13.

There is a path which no fowl knoweth. *Jb.* 28: 7.

They wandered in the wilderness in a solitary way. *Ps.* 107: 4.

Make me to go in the path of thy commandments. *Ps.* 119: 35.

Enter not into the path of the wicked. *Pr.* 4: 14.

The way of an eagle in the air; the way of a serpent upon a rock; the way of a ship in the midst of the sea. *Pr.* 30: 19.

An highway shall be there, and a way, and it shall be called The way of holiness. *Is.* 35: 8.

The Lord . . . maketh a way in the sea, and a path in the mighty waters. *Is.* 43: 16.

See also
Path; Way.

Trade

Tubal-cain, an instructor of every artificer in brass and iron. *Ge.* 4: 22.

In all the business of the Lord. *1 Ch.* 26: 30.

He had much business in the cities of Judah. *2 Ch.* 17: 13.

Buy the truth, and sell it not. *Pr.* 23: 23.

Tyre, the crowning city, whose merchants are princes, whose traffickers are the honourable of the earth. *Is.* 23: 8.

Javan, Tubal, and Meshech, they were thy

merchants: they traded the persons of men. *Eze.* 27: 13.

The ships of Tarshish did sing of thee in thy market: and thou wast replenished, and made very glorious in the midst of the seas. *Eze.* 27: 25.

He that had received the five talents went and traded with the same, and made them other five talents. *Mat.* 25: 16.

Go to now, ye that say, To day or to morrow we will go into such a city, and continue there a year, and buy and sell, and get gain. *Ja.* 4: 13.

See also

Business; Commerce; Industry; Market; Merchant; Occupation.

Tradition

He shall not alter it, nor change it, a good for a bad, or a bad for a good. *Le.* 27: 10.

Remove not the old landmark. *Pr.* 23: 10.

They have caused them to stumble in their ways from the ancient paths. *Je.* 18: 15.

Ye have heard that it was said by them of old time . . . But I say unto you. *Mat.* 5: 21, 22.

Why do thy disciples transgress the tradition of the elders? *Mat.* 15: 2.

Ye made the commandment of God of none effect by your tradition. *Mat.* 15: 6.

Laying aside the commandment of God, ye hold the tradition of men. *Mk.* 7: 8.

Our fathers worshipped in this mountain; and ye say, that in Jerusalem is the place where men ought to worship. *Jn.* 4: 20.

These men, being Jews, do exceedingly trouble our city, And teach customs, which are not lawful for us to . . . observe, being Romans. *Ac.* 16: 20, 21.

Thou teachest all the Jews . . . not to circumcise their children, neither to walk after the customs. *Ac.* 21: 21.

I have committed nothing against the people, or customs of our fathers. *Ac.* 28: 17.

Zealous of the traditions of my fathers. *Ga.* 1: 14.

See also

Conformity; Conservatism; Custom.

Tragedy

The day of their calamity is at hand. *De.* 32: 35.

Oh that my grief were throughly weighed, and my calamity laid in the balances together! *Jb.* 6: 2.

Can the rush grow up without mire? *Jb.* 8: 11.

Deep calleth unto deep at the noise of thy waterspouts: all thy waves and thy billows are gone over me. *Ps.* 42: 7.

They that sow in tears shall reap in joy. He that goeth forth and weepeth, bearing precious seed, shall doubtless come again with rejoicing, bringing his sheaves with him. *Ps.* 126: 5, 6.

Their calamity shall rise suddenly. *Pr.* 24: 22.

The harvest shall be a heap in the day of grief and of desperate sorrow. *Is.* 17: 11.

The mirth of the land is gone. *Is.* 24: 11.

Therefore shall her plagues come in one day, death, and mourning, and famine. *Re.* 18: 8.

God shall wipe away all tears from their eyes; and there shall be no more death. *Re.* 21: 4.

See also

Calamity; Catastrophe; Disaster; Evil.

Training

Thou shalt teach them diligently unto thy children. *De.* 6: 7.

How shall we order the child and how shall we do unto him? *Ju.* 13: 12.

Train up a child in the way he should go: and when he is old, he will not depart from it. *Pr.* 22: 6.

Precept must be upon precept, precept upon precept; line upon line, line upon line; here a little, and there a little. *Is.* 28: 10.

The heir, as long as he is a child, . . . is under tutors and governors until the time appointed of the father. *Ga.* 4: 1, 2.

Ye fathers, provoke not your children to wrath: but bring them up in the nurture and admonition of the Lord. *Ep.* 6: 4.

Exercise thyself rather unto godliness. *1 Ti.* 4: 7.

Bodily exercise profiteth little: but godliness is profitable unto all things. *1 Ti.* 4: 8.

See also

Christ, the Teacher; Discipline; Education; Exercise; Instruction; Study; Teaching.

Trait

Let integrity and uprightness preserve me. *Ps.* 25: 21.

Salt is good: but if the salt have lost his saltness, wherewith will ye season it? *Mk.* 9: 50.

A good man, and a just. *Lu.* 23: 50.

But thou, O man of God, flee these things; and follow after righteousness, godliness, faith, love, patience, meekness. *1 Ti.* 6: 11.

God hath not given us the spirit of fear; but of power, and of love, and of a sound mind. *2 Ti.* 1: 7.

Follow righteousness, faith, charity, peace, with them that call on the Lord out of a pure heart. *2 Ti.* 2: 22.

Add to your faith virtue; and to virtue knowledge; And to knowledge temperance; and to temperance patience; and to patience godliness; And to godliness brotherly kindness; and to brotherly kindness charity. *2 Pe.* 1: 5–7.

See also

Character; Quality.

Traitor

Athaliah rent her clothes, and cried, Treason, Treason. *2 K.* 11: 14.

If ye be come to betray me to mine enemies, seeing there is no wrong in mine hands, the God of our fathers look thereon, and rebuke it. *1 Ch.* 12: 17.

Confidence in an unfaithful man in time of trouble is like a broken tooth. *Pr.* 25: 19.

The brother shall betray the brother to death, and the father the son; and children shall rise up against their parents, and shall cause them to be put to death. *Mk.* 13: 12.

Judas Iscariot . . . was the traitor. *Lu.* 6: 16.

He that is not with me is against me: and he that gathereth not with me scattereth. *Lu.* 11: 23.

Ye shall be betrayed both by parents, and

brethren, and kinsfolks, and friends. *Lu.* **21: 16.**

The hand of him that betrayeth me is with me on the table. *Lu.* **22: 21.**

The Lord turned, and looked upon Peter. And Peter remembered the word of the Lord. *Lu.* **22: 61.**

Jesus knew from the beginning who they were that believed not, and who should betray him. *Jn.* **6: 64.**

He that eateth bread with me hath lifted up his heel against me. *Jn.* **13: 18.**

They that are such serve not our Lord Jesus Christ, but their own belly. *Ro.* **16: 18.**

Men shall be . . . Traitors. *2 Ti.* **3: 2, 4.**

See also

Betrayal; Perfidy; Treachery; Unfaithfulness.

Tranquillity

The land was wide, and quiet, and peaceable. *1 Ch.* **4: 40.**

Thou shalt take thy rest in safety. *Jb.* **11: 18.**

And I said, Oh that I had wings like a dove! for then would I fly away, and be at rest. *Ps.* **55: 6.**

Pray for the peace of Jerusalem: for they shall prosper that love thee. *Ps.* **122: 6.**

Peace be within thy walls, and prosperity within thy palaces. *Ps.* **122: 7.**

My people shall dwell in a peaceable habitation, and in sure dwellings, and in quiet resting places. *Is.* **32: 18.**

Peace I leave with you, my peace I give unto you: not as the world giveth, give I unto you. *Jn.* **14: 27.**

To be spiritually minded is life and peace *Ro.* **8: 6.**

The peace of God, which passeth all understanding, shall keep your hearts and minds through Christ Jesus. *Ph.* **4: 7.**

That we may lead a quiet and peaceable life in all godliness and honesty. *1 Ti.* **2: 2.**

See also

Calm; Christ, Peace of; Ease; God, Peace of; God, Rest in; Peace; Quiet; Repose; Rest; Stillness.

Transcendence

Will God indeed dwell on the earth? behold the heaven and heaven of heavens cannot contain thee; how much less this house that I have builded? *1 K.* **8: 27.**

Hear thou in heaven thy dwelling place. *1 K.* **8: 30.**

O Lord God of Israel, which dwellest between the cherubims, thou art the God, even thou alone, of all the kingdoms of the earth. *2 K.* **19: 15.**

Canst thou by searching find out God? canst thou find out the Almighty unto perfection? It is as high as heaven; what canst thou do? *Jb.* **11: 7, 8.**

O God, thou art terrible out of thy holy places. *Ps.* **68: 35.**

Thou, Lord, art high above all the earth: thou art exalted far above all gods. *Ps.* **97: 9.**

Who is like unto the Lord our God, who dwelleth on high? *Ps.* **113: 5.**

Unto thee lift I up mine eyes, O thou that dwellest in the heavens. *Ps.* **123: 1.**

I saw also the Lord sitting upon a throne, high and lifted up. *Is.* **6: 1.**

The Lord is exalted, for he dwelleth on high. *Is.* **33: 5.**

As the heavens are higher than the earth, so are my ways higher than your ways, and my thoughts than your thoughts. *Is.* **55: 9.**

The most High dwelleth not in temples made with hands. *Ac.* **7: 48.**

Heaven is my throne, and earth is my footstool: what house will ye build me? *Ac.* **7: 49.**

See also

God, Transcendence of; Immanence.

Transformation

Behold, the rod of Aaron for the house of Levi was budded, and brought forth buds, and bloomed blossoms, and yielded almonds. *Nu.* **17: 8.**

Who passing through the valley of Baca make it a well. *Ps.* **84: 6.**

He that goeth forth and weepeth, bearing precious seed, shall doubtless come again with rejoicing, bringing his sheaves with him. *Ps.* **126: 6.**

The wilderness and the solitary place shall be glad for them; and the desert shall rejoice, and blossom as the rose. *Is.* **35: 1.**

They shall beat their swords into plowshares, and their spears into pruninghooks. *Mi.* **4: 3.**

I will make you to become fishers of men, *Mk.* **1: 17.**

Thou art Simon the son of Jona: thou shalt be called Cephas, which is by interpretation, A stone. *Jn.* **1: 42.**

Your sorrow shall be turned into joy. *Jn.* **16: 20.**

Be not conformed to this world: but be ye transformed by the renewing of your mind, that ye may prove what is that good, and acceptable, and perfect, will of God. *Ro.* **12: 2.**

We all, with open face beholding as in a glass the glory of the Lord, are changed into the same image from glory to glory, even as by the Spirit of the Lord. *2 Co.* **3: 18.**

Without Christ, . . . But now in Christ Jesus. *Ep.* **2: 12, 13.**

The Lord Jesus Christ . . . shall change our vile body, that it may be fashioned like unto his glorious body. *Ph.* **3: 20, 21.**

He which converteth the sinner from the error of his way shall save a soul from death, and shall hide a multitude of sins. *Ja.* **5: 20.**

We know that we have passed from death unto life, because we love the brethren. *1 Jn.* **3: 14.**

See also

Alteration; Change; Conversion; Mutability.

Transgression

God saw that the wickedness of man was great in the earth, and that every imagination of the thoughts of his heart was only evil continually. *Ge.* **6: 5.**

All that do unrighteously, are an abomination unto the Lord thy God. *De.* **25: 16.**

I shall be innocent from the great transgression. *Ps.* **19: 13.**

Remember not the sins of my youth, nor my transgressions. *Ps.* **25: 7.**

Blessed is he whose transgression is forgiven, whose sin is covered. *Ps.* **32: 1.**

Then will I teach transgressors thy ways. *Ps.* **51: 13.**

The way of the wicked is as darkness. *Pr.* 4: 19.

The way of transgressors is hard. *Pr.* 13: 15.

I have blotted out, as a thick cloud, thy transgressions. *Is.* 44: 22.

He was wounded for our transgressions. *Is.* 53: 5.

Why do thy disciples transgress the tradition of the elders? *Mat.* 15: 2.

He was numbered with the transgressors. *Mk.* 15: 28.

Sin is the transgression of the law. *1 Jn.* 3: 4.

See also

Crime; Evil; Fault; Guile; Iniquity; Sin; Sinner; Unrighteousness; Wickedness; Wrong.

Travail

The wicked man travaileth with pain all his days. *Jb.* 15: 20.

He travaileth with iniquity, and hath conceived mischief, and brought forth falsehood. *Ps.* 7: 14.

Fear took hold upon them there, and pain, as of a woman in travail. *Ps.* 48: 6.

This sore travail hath God given to the sons of man to be exercised therewith. *Ec.* 1: 13.

All his days are sorrows, and his travail grief; yea, his heart taketh not rest in the night. *Ec.* 2: 23.

To the sinner he giveth travail. *Ec.* 2: 26.

I have seen the travail, which God hath given to the sons of men to be exercised in it. *Ec.* 3: 10.

He shall see of the travail of his soul, and shall be satisfied. *Is.* 53: 11.

A woman when she is in travail hath sorrow, because her hour is come: but as soon as she is delivered of the child, she remembereth no more the anguish, for joy that a man is born into the world. *Jn.* 16: 21.

The whole creation groaneth and travaileth in pain together until now. *Ro.* 8: 22.

Ye remember, brethren, our labour and travail. *1 Th.* 2: 9.

See also

Agony; Birth; Pain; Toil; Trial; Tribulation.

Travel

Abram journeyed, going on still toward the south. *Ge.* 12: 9.

God caused me to wander from my father's house. *Ge.* 20: 13.

Let us take our journey, and let us go. *Ge.* 33: 12.

I have been a stranger in a strange land. *Ex.* 2: 22.

The highways were unoccupied, and the travellers walked through byways. *Ju.* 5: 6.

There came a traveller unto the rich man, and he . . . took the poor man's lamb, and dressed it for the man that was come to him. *2 S.* 12: 4.

I opened my doors to the traveller. *Jb.* 31: 32.

My heart is fixed. *Ps.* 57: 7.

So shall thy poverty come as one that travelleth, and thy want as an armed man. *Pr.* 6: 11.

As a bird that wandereth from her nest, so is a man that wandereth from his place. *Pr.* 27: 8.

They shall be wanderers among the nations. *Ho.* 9: 17.

They shall wander from sea to sea, and from the north even to the east, they shall run to and fro to seek the word of the Lord. *Am.* 8: 12.

The Son of man is as a man taking a far journey. *Mk.* 13: 34.

In journeyings often. *2 Co.* 11: 26.

See also

Journey; Pilgrim; Pioneer; Progress; Wandering.

Treachery

Thou shalt not bear false witness against thy neighbour. *Ex.* 20: 16.

His words were softer than oil, yet were they drawn swords. *Ps.* 55: 21.

From the prophet even unto the priest every one dealeth falsely. *Je.* 6: 13.

Her prophets are light and treacherous persons. *Zph.* 3: 4.

Have we not all one father? hath not one God created us? why do we deal treacherously every man against his brother? *Mal.* 2: 10.

Take heed to your spirit, that ye deal not treacherously. *Mal.* 2: 16.

Judas, one of the twelve. *Mat.* 26: 47.

He then having received the sop went immediately out: and it was night. *Jn.* 13: 30.

Judas . . . was guide to them that took Jesus. *Ac.* 1: 16.

In perils among false brethren. *2 Co.* 11: 26.

In the last days perilous times shall come. For men shall be . . . Traitors. *2 Ti.* 3: 1, 2, 4.

See also

Assassin; Betrayal; Deceit; Faithlessness; Fraud; Perfidy; Traitor.

Treasure

Wisdom . . . cannot be gotten for gold, neither shall silver be weighed for the price thereof. *Jb.* 28: 12, 15.

I have made gold my hope. *Jb.* 31: 24.

Whatsoever he doeth shall prosper. *Ps.* 1: 3.

Treasures of wickedness profit nothing. *Pr.* 10: 2.

The blessing of the Lord, it maketh rich. *Pr.* 10: 22.

Riches profit not in the day of wrath: but righteousness delivereth from death. *Pr.* 11: 4.

Better is little with the fear of the Lord than great treasure and trouble therewith. *Pr.* 15: 16.

Riches are not for ever. *Pr.* 27: 24.

There is a sore evil which I have seen under the sun, namely, riches kept for the owners thereof to their hurt. *Ec.* 5: 13.

Lay not up for yourselves treasures upon earth. *Mat.* 6: 19.

Where your treasure is, there will your heart be also. *Lu.* 12: 34.

He looked up, and saw the rich men casting their gifts into the treasury. *Lu.* 21: 1.

Keep that which is committed to thy trust. *1 Ti.* 6: 20.

See also

God, Wealth of; Gold; Goods; Mammon; Money; Riches; Store; Substance; Worldliness.

Treaty

Let there be now an oath betwixt us, even

betwixt us and thee, and let us make a covenant with thee. *Ge.* 26: 28.

Behold, I give unto him my covenant of peace. *Nu.* 25: 12.

The children of Israel have forsaken thy covenant, thrown down thine altars, and slain thy prophets with the sword. *1 K.* 19: 10.

Come, and let us join ourselves to the Lord in a perpetual covenant that shall not be forgotten. *Je.* 50: 5.

I will establish unto thee an everlasting covenant. *Eze.* 16: 60.

Behold, the days come, saith the Lord, when I will make a new covenant with the house of Israel. *He.* 8: 8.

This is the covenant that I will make with the house of Israel after those days, saith the Lord; I will put my laws into their mind, and write them in their hearts: and I will be to them a God, and they shall be to me a people. *He.* 8: 10.

See also

Accord; Compact; Contract; Covenant.

Tree

Out of the ground made the Lord God to grow every tree that is pleasant to the sight, and good for food. *Ge.* 2: 9.

Lest he put forth his hand, and take also of the tree of life, and eat, and live for ever. *Ge.* 3: 22.

Thou shalt not destroy the trees. *De.* 20: 19.

Then shall the trees of the wood sing out at the presence of the Lord. *1 Ch.* 16: 33.

He shall be like a tree planted by the rivers of water. *Ps.* 1: 3.

As the apple tree among the trees of the wood, so is my beloved among the sons. *S. of S.* 2: 3.

As the days of a tree are the days of my people. *Is.* 65: 22.

All the trees of the field shall know that I the Lord have brought down the high tree, have exalted the low tree, have dried up the green tree, and have made the dry tree to flourish. *Eze.* 17: 24.

Every good tree bringeth forth good fruit; but a corrupt tree bringeth forth evil fruit. *Mat.* 7: 17.

It is written, Cursed is every one that hangeth on a tree. *Ga.* 3: 13.

Who his own self bare our sins in his own body on the tree, that we, being dead to sins, should live unto righteousness. *1 Pe.* 2: 24.

Trees whose fruit withereth, without fruit. *Jude* 1: 12.

To him that overcometh will I give to eat of the tree of life, which is in the midst of the paradise of God. *Re.* 2: 7.

The leaves of the tree were for the healing of the nations. *Re.* 22: 2.

See also

Forest; Orchard; Verdure; Wood.

Trembling

The Lord shall give thee there a trembling heart, and failing of eyes, and sorrow of mind. *De.* 28: 65.

The earth trembled, and the heavens dropped. *Ju.* 5: 4.

Fear came upon me, and trembling, which made all my bones to shake. *Jb.* 4: 14.

Serve the Lord with fear, and rejoice with trembling. *Ps.* 2: 11.

Thou hast made the earth to tremble. *Ps.* 60: 2.

The Lord reigneth; let the people tremble. *Ps.* 99: 1.

He looketh on the earth, and it trembleth: he toucheth the hills, and they smoke. *Ps.* 104: 32.

My flesh trembleth for fear of thee; and I am afraid of thy judgments. *Ps.* 119: 120.

In the day when the keepers of the house shall tremble. *Ec.* 12: 3.

I was with you in weakness, and in fear, and in much trembling. *1 Co.* 2: 3.

Work out your salvation with fear and trembling. *Ph.* 2: 12.

See also

Alarm; Awe; Fear; Terror.

Trespass

Your iniquities have separated between you and your God. *Is.* 59: 2.

Forgive us our debts, as we forgive our debtors. *Mat.* 6: 12.

If ye forgive men their trespasses, your heavenly Father will also forgive you. *Mat.* 6: 14.

If thy brother shall trespass against thee, go and tell him his fault between thee and him alone: if he shall hear thee, thou hast gained thy brother. *Mat.* 18: 15.

Forgive us our sins. *Lu.* 11: 4.

Be not overcome of evil, but overcome evil with good. *Ro.* 12: 21.

God was in Christ, reconciling the world unto himself, not imputing their trespasses unto them. *2 Co.* 5: 19.

You hath he quickened, who were dead in trespasses and sins. *Ep.* 2: 1.

You, being dead in your sins and the uncircumcision of your flesh, hath he quickened together with him, having forgiven you all trespasses. *Col.* 2: 13.

The sin which doth so easily beset us. *He.* 12: 1.

See also

Crime; Evil; Fault; Guile; Iniquity; Sin; Sinner; Transgression; Unrighteousness; Wickedness; Wrong.

Trial

When he hath tried me, I shall come forth as gold. *Jb.* 23: 10.

He setteth an end to darkness. *Jb.* 28: 3.

It is God that girdeth me with strength. *Ps.* 18: 32.

The Lord is good, a strong hold in the day of trouble. *Na.* 1: 7.

Then was Jesus led up of the spirit into the wilderness to be tempted of the devil. *Mat.* 4: 1.

When the tempter came to him, he said, If thou be the Son of God. *Mat.* 4: 3.

When they persecute you. *Mat.* 10: 23.

Many devils were entered into him. *Lu.* 8: 30.

Lead us not into temptation. *Lu.* 11: 4.

In the world ye shall have tribulation: but be of good cheer; I have overcome the world. *Jn.* 16: 33.

After ye were illuminated, ye endured a great fight of afflictions. *He.* **10: 32.**

Blessed is the man that endureth temptation: for when he is tried, he shall receive the crown of life. *Ja.* **1: 12.**

That the trial of your faith, being much more precious than of gold that perisheth, though it be tried with fire, might be found unto praise and honour and glory at the appearing of Jesus Christ. *1 Pe.* **1: 7.**

Think it not strange concerning the fiery trial which is to try you. *1 Pe.* **4: 12.**

Wherefore let them that suffer according to the will of God commit the keeping of their souls to him in well doing, as unto a faithful Creator. *1 Pe.* **4: 19.**

See also

Calamity; Catastrophe; Christ, Sorrow of; Disaster; Effort; Evil; Experiment; Proof; Sorrow; Test; Tribulation.

Tribulation

The name of that place was called, The valley of Achor, unto this day. *Jos.* **7: 26.**

They have slain the servants with the edge of the sword; and I only am escaped alone to tell thee. *Jb.* **1: 15.**

Now men see not the bright light which is in the clouds: but the wind passeth, and cleanseth them. *Jb.* **37: 21.**

Then the Lord answered Job out of the whirlwind. *Jb.* **38: 1.**

Fret not. *Ps.* **37: 1.**

I will be with him in trouble; I will deliver him, and honour him. *Ps.* **91: 15.**

I hated life; because the work that is wrought under the sun is grievous unto me. *Ec.* **2: 17.**

Every one that hath forsaken houses, or brethren, or sisters, or father, or mother, or wife, or children, or lands, for my name's sake, shall receive an hundredfold, and shall inherit everlasting life. *Mat.* **19: 29.**

Nation shall rise against nation, and kingdom against kingdom: and there shall be famines, and pestilences, and earthquakes, in divers places. *Mat.* **24: 7.**

We must through much tribulation enter into the kingdom of God. *Ac.* **14: 22.**

But thanks be to God, which giveth us the victory through our Lord Jesus Christ. *1 Co.* **15: 57.**

Cast down, but not destroyed. *2 Co.* **4: 9.**

Our light affliction . . . worketh for us a far more exceeding and eternal weight of glory. *2 Co.* **4: 17.**

Beloved, think it not strange concerning the fiery trial which is to try you. *1 Pe.* **4: 12.**

See also

Calamity; Catastrophe; Christ, Sorrow of; Depression; Disaster; Gloom; Melancholy; Mourning; Sadness; Tear; Trouble; Weeping.

Tribute

The slothful shall be under tribute. *Pr.* **12: 24.**

She that was great among the nations, and princess among the provinces, how is she become tributary! *La.* **1: 1.**

Is it lawful to give tribute unto Caesar, or not? *Mat.* **22: 17.**

Render therefore unto Caesar the things which are Caesar's; and unto God the things that are God's. *Mat.* **22: 21.**

Render therefore to all their dues: tribute to whom tribute is due; custom to whom custom; fear to whom fear; honour to whom honour. *Ro.* **13: 7.**

See also

Duty; Praise; Service.

Trifle

Take no thought, saying, What shall we eat? or, What shall we drink? or, Wherewithal shall we be clothed? *Mat.* **6: 31.**

Seek ye first the kingdom of God, . . . and all these things shall be added unto you. *Mat.* **6: 33.**

Ye pay tithe of mint and anise and cummin, and have omitted the weightier matters of the law. *Mat.* **23: 23.**

Ye blind guides, which strain at a gnat, and swallow a camel. *Mat.* **23: 24.**

Ye make clean the outside of the cup and of the platter, but within they are full of extortion and excess. *Mat.* **23: 25.**

Martha was cumbered about much serving. *Lu.* **10: 40.**

Jesus answered and said unto her, Martha, Martha, thou art careful and troubled about many things. *Lu.* **10: 41.**

The tongue is a little member, and boasteth great things. *Ja.* **3: 5.**

See also

Little; Pettiness; Smallness; Thing, the Little.

Trinity

The grace of the Lord Jesus Christ, and the love of God, and the communion of the Holy Ghost, be with you all. *2 Co.* **13: 14.**

Through him we both have access by one Spirit unto the Father. *Ep.* **2: 18.**

There are three that bear record in heaven, the Father, the Word, and the Holy Ghost: and these three are one. *1 Jn.* **5: 7.**

There are three that bear witness in earth, the spirit, and the water, and the blood: and these three agree in one. *1 Jn.* **5: 8.**

See also

Three.

Triumph

Thou hast enlarged me when I was in distress. *Ps.* **4: 1.**

Thou settest a crown of pure gold on his head. *Ps.* **21: 3.**

Shout unto God with the voice of triumph. *Ps.* **47: 1.**

Lord, how long shall the wicked . . . triumph? *Ps.* **94: 3.**

O death, where is thy sting? O grave, where is thy victory? *1 Co.* **15: 55.**

Thanks be unto God, which always causeth us to triumph in Christ, and maketh manifest the savour of his knowledge by us in every place. *2 Co.* **2: 14.**

This is the victory that overcometh the world, even our faith. *1 Jn.* **5: 4.**

I beheld, and, lo, a great multitude, which no man could number, of all nations, and kindreds, and people, and tongues, stood before the throne, and before the Lamb, clothed with white robes, and palms in their hands. *Re.* **7: 9.**

See also

Christ, Triumph of; Invincibility; Success; Victory.

Trouble

Are not these evils come upon us, because our God is not among us? *De. 31: 17.*

He drew me out of many waters. *Ps. 18: 16.*

God is our refuge and strength, a very present help in trouble. *Ps. 46: 1.*

God prepared a worm when the morning rose the next day, and it smote the gourd that it withered. *Jon. 4: 7.*

He shall sit as a refiner and purifier of silver: and he shall . . . purge them as gold and silver. *Mal. 3: 3.*

Let not your heart be troubled: ye believe in God, believe also in me. *Jn. 14: 1.*

We glory in tribulations also. *Ro. 5: 3.*

Our light affliction, which is but for a moment, worketh for us a far more exceeding and eternal weight of glory. *2 Co. 4: 17.*

Be thou partaker of the afflictions of the gospel according to the power of God. *2 Ti. 1: 8.*

Call to remembrance the former days, in which, after ye were illuminated, ye endured a great fight of afflictions. *He. 10: 32.*

Casting all your care upon him. *1 Pe. 5: 7.*
See also
Adversity; Affliction; Agitation; Annoyance; Anxiety; Calamity; Chagrin; Christ, Sorrow of; Concern; Depression; Disaster; Gloom; Grief; Melancholy; Misery; Misfortune; Mourning; Sadness; Tear; Tribulation; Tumult; Turmoil; Weeping.

Trumpet

With trumpets and sound of cornet make a joyful noise before the Lord, the King. *Ps. 98: 6.*

Cry aloud, spare not, lift up thy voice like a trumpet. *Is. 58: 1.*

The Lord God shall blow the trumpet, and shall go with whirlwinds of the south. *Zch. 9: 14.*

If the trumpet give an uncertain sound, who shall prepare himself to the battle? *1 Co. 14: 8.*

We shall all be changed, In a moment, in the twinkling of an eye, at the last trump. *1 Co. 15: 51, 52.*

The trumpet shall sound, and the dead shall be raised. *1 Co. 15: 52.*

The Lord himself shall descend from heaven with a shout, with the voice of the archangel, and with the trump of God. *1 Th. 4: 16.*

The voice of harpers, and musicians, and of pipers, and trumpeters, shall be heard no more at all in thee. *Re. 18: 22.*
See also
Instrument; Music.

Trust

Trust in him at all times. *Ps. 62: 8.*

I will trust, and not be afraid. *Is. 12: 2.*

Thine eyes shall see the king in his beauty: they shall behold the land that is very far off. *Is. 33: 17.*

Whatsoever ye shall ask in prayer, believing, ye shall receive. *Mat. 21: 22.*

How is it that ye have no faith? *Mk. 4: 40.*

Be not faithless, but believing. *Jn. 20: 27.*

Let a man so account of us, as of the ministers of Christ, and stewards of the mysteries of God. *1 Co. 4: 1.*

Such trust have we through Christ to God-ward. *2 Co. 3: 4.*

I rejoice therefore that I have confidence in you in all things. *2 Co. 7: 16.*

Fight the good fight of faith. *1 Ti. 6: 12.*

Keep that which is committed to thy trust. *1 Ti. 6: 20.*

Who through faith and patience inherit the promises. *He. 6: 12.*

Now faith is the substance of things hoped for. *He. 11: 1.*
See also
Assurance; Belief; Christ, Belief in; Christ, Faith in; Confidence; Dependence; God, Confidence in; God, Faith in; God, Reliance on; God, Trust in.

Truth

Fear the Lord, and serve him in sincerity and in truth. *Jos. 24: 14.*

He that walketh uprightly, and worketh righteousness, and speaketh the truth in his heart. *Ps. 15: 2.*

Send out thy light and thy truth: let them lead me. *Ps. 43: 3.*

Thou desirest truth in the inward parts. *Ps. 51: 6.*

Mercy and truth are met together. *Ps. 85: 10.*

I have chosen the way of truth. *Ps. 119: 30.*

Take not the word of truth utterly out of my mouth. *Ps. 119: 43.*

The law of thy mouth is better unto me than thousands of gold and silver. *Ps. 119: 72.*

The Lord is nigh unto all them that call upon him, to all that call upon him in truth. *Ps. 145: 18.*

Speak ye every man the truth to his neighbour. *Zch. 8: 16.*

The law of truth was in his mouth. *Mal. 2: 6.*

Let your communication be, Yea, yea; Nay, nay: for whatsoever is more than these cometh of evil. *Mat. 5: 37.*

Ye shall know the truth, and the truth shall make you free. *Jn. 8: 32.*

Pilate saith unto him, What is truth? *Jn. 18: 38.*

Charity . . . Rejoiceth not in iniquity, but rejoiceth in the truth. *1 Co. 13: 4, 6.*

We can do nothing against the truth, but for the truth. *2 Co. 13: 8.*

They walked not uprightly according to the truth of the gospel. *Ga. 2: 14.*

Am I therefore become your enemy, because I tell you the truth? *Ga. 4: 16.*

Speaking the truth in love. *Ep. 4: 15.*

Stand therefore, having your loins girt about with truth. *Ep. 6: 14.*

The house of God . . . is the church of the living God, the pillar and ground of the truth. *1 Ti. 3: 15.*

I rejoiced greatly that I found of thy children walking in truth. *2 Jn. 1: 4.*

Thou walkest in the truth. *3 Jn. 1: 3.*
See also
Accuracy; Authenticity; Christ, Truth of; God, Truth of; Honesty; Sincerity; Uprightness; Validity; Veracity; Verity.

Truth, Search for

Buy the truth, and sell it not. *Pr. 23: 23.*

There was a man of the Pharisees, named

Nicodemus, a ruler of the Jews: The same came to Jesus by night. *Jn.* 3: 1, 2.

Search the scriptures. *Jn.* 5: 39.

Prove all things; hold fast that which is good. *1 Th.* 5: 21.

See also

Experiment; Inquiry; Proof; Test; Veracity; Verity.

Truth, Spirit of

Even the Spirit of truth; whom the world cannot receive, because it seeth him not, neither knoweth him: but ye know him; for he dwelleth with you, and shall be in you. *Jn.* 14: 17.

The Spirit of truth, which proceedeth from the Father, . . . shall testify of me. *Jn.* 15: 26.

When he, the Spirit of truth, is come, he will guide you into all truth. *Jn.* 16: 13.

Not in the words which man's wisdom teacheth, but which the Holy Ghost teacheth. *1 Co.* 2: 13.

It is the Spirit that beareth witness, because the Spirit is truth. *1 Jn.* 5: 6.

See also

Ghost, Holy; Spirit, Holy; Veracity; Verity.

Tumult

Which stilleth the noise of the seas, the noise of their waves, and the tumult of the people. *Ps.* 65: 7.

Every battle of the warrior is with confused noise. *Is.* 9: 5.

Thou that art full of stirs, a tumultuous city, a joyous city. *Is.* 22: 2.

Behold, the noise of the bruit is come, and a great commotion out of the north country. *Je.* 10: 22.

Therefore shall a tumult arise among thy people. *Ho.* 10: 14.

When ye shall hear of wars and commotions, be not terrified. *Lu.* 21: 9.

The multitude came together, and were confounded, because that every man heard them speak in his own language. *Ac.* 2: 6.

See also

Agitation; Bedlam; Clamor; Confusion; Din; Disorder; Disturbance; Noise; Storm; Turmoil.

Tune

I will sing unto the Lord, for he hath triumphed gloriously. *Ex.* 15: 1.

The Lord is my strength and song. *Ex.* 15: 2.

He spake three thousand proverbs: and his songs were a thousand and five. *1 K.* 4: 32.

With my song will I praise him. *Ps.* 28: 7.

Unto thee will I sing with the harp. *Ps.* 71: 22.

O sing unto the Lord a new song. *Ps.* 96: 1.

The song of songs, which is Solomon's. *S. of S.* 1: 1.

Thou art unto them as a very lovely song of one that hath a pleasant voice, and can play well on an instrument: for they hear thy words, but they do them not. *Eze.* 33: 32.

Take thou away from me the noise of thy songs; for I will not hear the melody of thy viols. *Am.* 5: 23.

I will turn your feasts into mourning, and all your songs into lamentation. *Am.* 8: 10.

See also

Hymn; Melody; Song.

Turmoil

Why do the heathen rage . . . ? *Ps.* 2: 1.

Like a mighty man that shouteth by reason of wine. *Ps.* 78: 65.

A foolish woman is clamorous. *Pr.* 9: 13.

Their contentions are like the bars of a castle. *Pr.* 18: 19.

Better is an handful with quietness, than both the hands full with travail and vexation of spirit. *Ec.* 4: 6.

Woe to the multitude of many people, which make a noise like the noise of the seas; and to the rushing of nations, that make a rushing like the rushing of mighty waters! *Is.* 17: 12.

There is sorrow on the sea; it cannot be quiet. *Je.* 49: 23.

His voice was like a noise of many waters. *Eze.* 43: 2.

Lest there be an uproar among the people. *Mat.* 26: 5.

The Jews . . . set all the city on an uproar. *Ac.* 17: 5.

These that have turned the world upside down are come hither also. *Ac.* 17: 6.

Art not thou that Egyptian, which before these days madest an uproar? *Ac.* 21: 38.

We have found this man a pestilent fellow, and a mover of sedition. *Ac.* 24: 5.

Lest there be debates, envyings, wraths, strifes, backbitings, whisperings, swellings, tumults. *2 Co.* 12: 20.

Let all bitterness, and wrath, and anger, and clamour, and evil speaking, be put away from you. *Ep.* 4: 31.

Where envying and strife is, there is confusion and every evil work. *Ja.* 3: 16.

The heavens shall pass away with a great noise. *2 Pe.* 3: 10.

I heard, as it were the noise of thunder. *Re.* 6: 1.

See also

Agitation; Bedlam; Clamor; Din; Trouble; Tumult.

Turn

Call now, if there be any that will answer thee; and to which of the saints wilt thou turn? *Jb.* 5: 1.

How long will ye turn my glory into shame? *Ps.* 4: 2.

All the ends of the world shall remember and turn unto the Lord. *Ps.* 22: 27.

O turn thyself to us again. *Ps.* 60: 1.

He turned the sea into dry land. *Ps.* 66: 6.

Blessed be God, which hath not turned away my prayer, nor his mercy from me. *Ps.* 66: 20.

Thou turnest man to destruction; and sayest, Return, ye children of men. *Ps.* 90: 3.

God . . . turned the rock into a standing water, the flint into a fountain of waters. *Ps.* 114: 7, 8.

The way of the wicked he turneth upside down. *Ps.* 146: 9.

Turn not to the right hand nor to the left: remove thy foot from evil. *Pr.* 4: 27.

A soft answer turneth away wrath. *Pr.* 15: 1.

All are of the dust, and all turn to dust again. *Ec.* 3: 20.

Turn ye again now every one from his evil way, and from the evil of your doings. *Je.* 25: 5.

I will turn their mourning into joy. *Je.* 31: 13.

Let us search and try our ways, and turn again to the Lord. *La.* 3: 40.

Ephraim is a cake not turned. *Ho.* 7: 8.

Turn you to the strong hold, ye prisoners of hope. *Zch.* 9: 12.

He shall turn the heart of the fathers to the children, and the heart of the children to their fathers, lest I come and smite the earth with a curse. *Mal.* 4: 6.

Whosoever shall smite thee on thy right cheek, turn to him the other also. *Mat.* 5: 39.

Except ye be converted, and become as little children, ye shall not enter into the kingdom of heaven. *Mat.* 18: 3.

See also

Conversion; Revolution; Transformation.

Twilight

They heard the voice of the Lord God walking in the garden in the cool of the day. *Ge.* 3: 8.

At even thou shalt say, Would God it were morning! *De.* 28: 67.

Let the stars of the twilight thereof be dark; let it look for light, but have none. *Jb.* 3: 9.

The eye also of the adulterer waiteth for the twilight, saying, No eye shall see me. *Jb.* 24: 15.

He went the way to her house, In the twilight, in the evening, in the black and dark night. *Pr.* 7: 8, 9.

The shadows of the evening are stretched out. *Je.* 6: 4.

Abide with us: for it is toward evening. *Lu.* 24: 29.

See also

Evening.

Twin

Two are better than one. *Ec.* 4: 9.

Every one bear twins, and none is barren among them. *S. of S.* 4: 2.

Thy two breasts are like two young roes that are twins, which feed among the lilies. *S. of S.* 4: 5.

See also

Double; Two.

Two

There went in two and two unto Noah into the ark. *Ge.* 7: 9.

Two are better than one. *Ec.* 4: 9.

If two lie together, then they have heat: but how can one be warm alone? *Ec.* 4: 11.

If one prevail against him, two shall withstand him. *Ec.* 4: 12.

Can two walk together, except they be agreed? *Am.* 3: 3.

Whosoever shall compel thee to go a mile, go with him twain. *Mat.* 5: 41.

If two of you shall agree on earth as touching any thing that they shall ask, it shall be done for them of my Father which is in heaven. *Mat.* 18: 19.

He called unto him the twelve, and began to send them forth by two and two. *Mk.* 6: 7.

Two, saith he, shall be one flesh. *1 Co.* 6: 16.

To make in himself of twain one new man, so making peace. *Ep.* 2: 15.

The word of God is quick, and powerful and sharper than any twoedged sword. *He.* 4: 12.

Tyranny

The Egyptians made the children of Israel to serve with rigour. *Ex.* 1: 13.

I will harden his heart, that he shall not let the people go. *Ex.* 4: 21.

Is it good unto thee that thou shouldest oppress? *Jb.* 10: 3.

By reason of the multitude of oppressions they make the oppressed to cry. *Jb.* 35: 9.

Keep me . . . From the wicked that oppress me, from my deadly enemies. *Ps.* 17: 8, 9.

Trust not in oppression. *Ps.* 62: 10.

Envy thou not the oppressor, and choose none of his ways. *Pr.* 3: 31.

What mean ye that ye beat my people to pieces, and grind the faces of the poor? *Is.* 3: 15.

He looked for judgment, but behold oppression. *Is.* 5: 7.

They oppress a man and his house, even a man and his heritage. *Mi.* 2: 2.

He shall rule them with a rod of iron. *Re.* 2: 27.

See also

Autocrat; Cruelty; Despot; Hardness; Harshness; Repression; Severity; Suppression.

U

Ugliness

The ill favoured and leanfleshed kine did eat up the seven well favoured and fat kine. *Ge.* 41: 4.

The beauty of Israel is slain upon thy high places. *2 S.* 1: 19.

So went Satan forth from the presence of the Lord, and smote Job with sore boils from the sole of his foot unto his crown. *Jb.* 2: 7.

My skin is broken, and become loathsome. *Jb.* 7: 5.

Their beauty shall consume in the grave. *Ps.* 49: 14.

A wicked man is loathsome. *Pr.* 13: 5.

There is no beauty that we should desire him. *Is.* 53: 2.

Unanimity

Behold, how good and how pleasant it is for brethren to dwell together in unity! *Ps.* 133: 1.

My beloved is mine, and I am his. *S. of S.* 2: 16.

They shall see eye to eye, when the Lord shall bring again Zion. *Is.* 52: 8.

Come, and let us join ourselves to the Lord. *Je.* 50: 5.

They twain shall be one flesh. *Mat.* 19: 5.

All ye are brethren. *Mat.* 23: 8.

Have peace one with another. *Mk.* 9: 50.

There shall be one fold, and one shepherd. *Jn.* 10: 16.

When the day of Pentecost was fully come,

they were all with one accord in one place. *Ac.* 2: 1.

The multitude of them that believed were of one heart and of one soul. *Ac.* 4: 32.

So we, being many, are one body in Christ. *Ro.* 12: 5.

He that is joined unto the Lord is one spirit. *1 Co.* 6: 17.

There is neither Jew nor Greek, there is neither bond nor free, there is neither male nor female: for ye are all one in Christ Jesus. *Ga.* 3: 28.

He is our peace, who hath made both one, and hath broken down the middle wall of partition between us. *Ep.* 2: 14.

Till we all come in the unity of the faith, and of the knowledge of the Son of God, unto a perfect man. *Ep.* 4: 13.

They two shall be one flesh. *Ep.* 5: 31.

Fulfil ye my joy, that ye be like-minded, having the same love, being of one accord, of one mind. *Ph.* 2: 2.

Both he that sanctifieth and they who are sanctified are all of one. *He.* 2: 11.

If we walk in the light, as he is in the light, we have fellowship one with another. *1 Jn.* 1: 7.

See also

Accord; Agreement; Concord; Harmony; Oneness; Unity.

Unbelief

Who is the Lord, that I should obey his voice? *Ex.* 5: 2.

Ye believed me not. *Nu.* 20: 12.

They are a very froward generation, children in whom is no faith. *De.* 32: 20.

Behold, if the Lord would make windows in heaven, might this thing be? And he said, Behold, thou shalt see it with thine eyes, but shalt not eat thereof. *2 K.* 7: 2.

They continually say unto me, Where is thy God? *Ps.* 42: 3.

He did not many mighty works there because of their unbelief. *Mat.* 13: 58.

He could there do no mighty work. . . . And he marvelled because of their unbelief. *Mk.* 6: 5, 6.

Lord, I believe; help thou mine unbelief. *Mk.* 9: 24.

He . . . upbraided them with their unbelief and hardness of heart. *Mk.* 16: 14.

Thou shalt be dumb, and not able to speak, until the day that these things shall be performed, because thou believest not my words. *Lu.* 1: 20.

He said unto them, If I tell you, ye will not believe. *Lu.* 22: 67.

Their words seemed to them as idle tales, and they believed them not. *Lu.* 24: 11.

Ye receive not our witness. *Jn.* 3: 11.

If ye believe not that I am he, ye shall die in your sins. *Jn.* 8: 24.

Be not faithless, but believing. *Jn.* 20: 27.

Why should it be thought a thing incredible with you, that God should raise the dead? *Ac.* 26: 8.

Some believed the things which were spoken, and some believed not. *Ac.* 28: 24.

What if some did not believe? shall their unbelief make the faith of God without effect? *Ro.* 3: 3.

Be ye not unequally yoked together with unbelievers. *2 Co.* 6: 14.

I obtained mercy, because I did it ignorantly in unbelief. *1 Ti.* 1: 13.

Unto them that are defiled and unbelieving is nothing pure. *Tit.* 1: 15.

Take heed, brethren, lest there be in any of you an evil heart of unbelief, in departing from the living God. *He.* 3: 12.

See also

Christ, Denial of; Christ, Doubt of; Denial; Disbelief; Dissent; Doubt; Faithlessness; God, Denial of; Heresy; Skepticism.

Uncertainty

How long halt ye between two opinions? *1 K.* 18: 21.

Their heart is divided. *Ho.* 10: 2.

No man can serve two masters. *Mat.* 6: 24.

Every city or house divided against itself shall not stand. *Mat.* 12: 25.

He looked up, and said, I see men as trees, walking. *Mk.* 8: 24.

No man, having put his hand to the plow, and looking back, is fit for the kingdom of God. *Lu.* 9: 62.

I go bound in the spirit unto Jerusalem, not knowing the things that shall befall me there. *Ac.* 20: 22.

I therefore so run, not as uncertainly; so fight I, not as one that beateth the air. *1 Co.* 9: 26.

If the trumpet give an uncertain sound, who shall prepare himself to the battle? *1 Co.* 14: 8.

Charge them that are rich in this world, that they be not highminded, nor trust in uncertain riches. *1 Ti.* 6: 17.

A double minded man is unstable in all his ways. *Ja.* 1: 8.

Purify your hearts, ye double minded. *Ja.* 4: 8.

What is your life? It is even a vapour, that appeareth for a little time, and then vanisheth away. *Ja.* 4: 14.

See also

Christ, Doubt of; Doubt; Loyalty, Divided; Reluctance; Skepticism.

Uncleanness

I did cast them out as the dirt in the streets. *Ps.* 18: 42.

Who can understand his errors? Cleanse thou me from secret faults. *Ps.* 19: 12.

They . . . lusted exceedingly in the wilderness, and tempted God in the desert. *Ps.* 106: 13, 14.

Wickedness is an abomination to my lips. *Pr.* 8: 7.

Be ye clean, that bear the vessels of the Lord. *Is.* 52: 11.

Your hands are defiled with blood. *Is.* 59: 3.

To eat with unwashen hands defileth not a man. *Mat.* 15: 20.

God hath shewed me that I should not call any man common or unclean. *Ac.* 10: 28.

Let us cleanse ourselves from all filthiness of the flesh and spirit. *2 Co.* 7: 1.

This ye know, that no . . . unclean person . . . hath any inheritance in the kingdom of Christ and of God. *Ep.* 5: 5.

The tongue . . . defileth the whole body. *Ja.* 3: 6.

See also

Corruption; Defilement; Depravity; Evil; Iniquity; Lust; Pollution; Sin; Sinner; Ungodliness; Unrighteousness; Vileness; Wickedness.

Unconsciousness

Let not your hearts faint, fear not, and do not tremble. *De.* 20: 3.

I had fainted, unless I had believed to see the goodness of the Lord in the land of the living. *Ps.* 27: 13.

The everlasting God, the Lord, the Creator of the ends of the earth, fainteth not, neither is weary. *Is.* 40: 28.

They shall run, and not be weary; and they shall walk and not faint. *Is.* 40: 31.

Thy sons have fainted, they lie at the head of all the streets. *Is.* 51: 20.

The children and the sucklings swoon in the streets of the city. *La.* 2: 11.

He was moved with compassion on them, because they fainted. *Mat.* 9: 36.

Thou . . . for my name's sake hast laboured, and hast not fainted. *Re.* 2: 2, 3.

See also

Faintness.

Understanding

Wisdom is the principal thing; therefore get wisdom: and with all thy getting get understanding. *Pr.* 4: 7.

Exalt her, and she shall promote thee: she shall bring thee to honour, when thou dost embrace her. *Pr.* 4: 8.

She standeth in the top of high places, by the way in the places of the paths. *Pr.* 8: 2.

By me kings reign, and princes decree justice. *Pr.* 8: 15.

I was set up from everlasting, from the beginning, or ever the earth was. *Pr.* 8: 23.

The man that wandereth out of the way of understanding shall remain in the congregation of the dead. *Pr.* 21: 16.

Unto the Greeks foolishness. *1 Co.* 1: 23.

In malice be ye children, but in understanding be men. *1 Co.* 14: 20.

Through faith we understand. *He.* 11: 3.

See also

Christ, Knowledge of; Christ, Mind of; Christ, Wisdom of; Comprehension; Enlightenment; God, Knowledge of; God, Wisdom of; Intelligence; Knowledge; Learning; Mind; Perception; Reason; Sage; Wisdom.

Undertaking

Go therefore now, and work. *Ex.* 5: 18.

That the Lord thy God may bless thee in all the work of thine hand which thou doest. *De.* 14: 29.

These things did these three mighty men. *2 S.* 23: 17.

So built we the wall . . . for the people had a mind to work. *Ne.* 4: 6.

So we laboured in the work. *Ne.* 4: 21.

I am doing a great work, so that I cannot come down: why should the work cease, whilst I leave it? *Ne.* 6: 3.

Thou hast blessed the work of his hands. *Jb.* 1: 10.

A good man . . . will guide his affairs with discretion. *Ps.* 112: 5.

I will run the way of thy commandments, when thou shalt enlarge my heart. *Ps.* 119: 32.

All this have I seen, and applied my heart unto every work that is done under the sun. *Ec.* 8: 9.

I will work a work in your days, which ye will not believe, though it be told you. *Hab.* 1: 5.

I must work the works of Him that sent me, while it is day. *Jn.* 9: 4.

Work out your own salvation with fear and trembling. *Ph.* 2: 12.

Study to be quiet, and to do your own business, and to work with your own hands, as we commanded you. *1 Th.* 4: 11.

See also

Task; Toil; Work.

Unemployment

An idle soul shall suffer hunger. *Pr.* 19: 15.

The desire of the slothful killeth him; for his hands refuse to labour. *Pr.* 21: 25.

She . . . eateth not the bread of idleness. *Pr.* 31: 27.

Through idleness of the hands the house droppeth through. *Ec.* 10: 18.

The harvest truly is plenteous, but the labourers are few. *Mat.* 9: 37.

He went out about the third hour, and saw others standing idle in the marketplace. *Mat.* 20: 3.

No man hath hired us. *Mat.* 20: 7.

Mark . . . went not with them to the work. *Ac.* 15: 37, 38.

We commanded you, that if any would not work, neither should he eat. *2 Th.* 3: 10.

There are some which walk among you disorderly, working not at all, but are busybodies. *2 Th.* 3: 11.

Unfairness

Wilt thou also destroy the righteous with the wicked? *Ge.* 18: 23.

Deliver me from the deceitful and unjust man. *Ps.* 43: 1.

The hope of unjust men perisheth. *Pr.* 11: 7.

An unjust man is an abomination to the just. *Pr.* 29: 27.

Wherefore doth the way of the wicked prosper? wherefore are all they happy that deal very treacherously? *Je.* 12: 1.

What mean ye, that ye use this proverb, . . . saying, The fathers have eaten sour grapes, and the children's teeth are set on edge? *Eze.* 18: 2.

They know not to do right, saith the Lord, who store up violence and robbery in their palaces. *Am.* 3: 10.

The unjust knoweth no shame. *Zph.* 3: 5.

The lord commended the unjust steward. *Lu.* 16: 8.

He that is unjust in the least is unjust also in much. *Lu.* 16: 10.

Dare any of you, having a matter against another, go to law before the unjust? *1 Co.* 6: 1.

The Lord knoweth how . . . to reserve the unjust unto the day of judgment to be punished. *2 Pe.* 2: 9.

He that is unjust, let him be unjust still. *Re.* 22: 11.

See also

Injustice; Injustice, Social.

Unfaithfulness

They are a very froward generation, children in whom is no faith. *De.* 32: 20.

They . . . turned back, and dealt unfaithfully like their fathers. *Ps.* 78: 56, 57.

Confidence in an unfaithful man in time of trouble is like a broken tooth, and a foot out of joint. *Pr.* 25: 19.

Mine own vineyard have I not kept. *S. of S.* 1: 6.

They be all . . . an assembly of treacherous men. *Je.* 9: 2.

All her friends have dealt treacherously with her. *La.* 1: 2.

They like men have transgressed the covenant: there have they dealt treacherously against me. *Ho.* 6: 7.

Have we not all one father? hath not one God created us? why do we deal treacherously every man against his brother? *Mal.* 2: 10.

Take heed to your spirit, that ye deal not treacherously. *Mal.* 2: 16.

O faithless and perverse generation, how long shall I be with you? *Mat.* 17: 17.

The kingdom of God shall be taken from you, and given to a nation bringing forth the fruits thereof. *Mat.* 21: 43.

In the last days . . . men shall be . . . trucebreakers. *2 Ti.* 3: 1–3.

See also
Deceit; Faithlessness; Traitor; Treachery.

Unfitness

I am not worthy of the least of all the mercies, and of all the truth, which thou hast shewed unto thy servant. *Ge.* 32: 10.

I hear of your evil dealings by all this people. *1 S.* 2: 23.

The ungodly are . . . like the chaff which the wind driveth away. *Ps.* 1: 4.

Their heart is divided. *Ho.* 10: 2.

My people are bent to backsliding from me. *Ho.* 11: 7.

He that cometh after me is mightier than I, whose shoes I am not worthy to bear. *Mat.* 3: 11.

The centurion answered and said, Lord, I am not worthy that thou shouldest come under my roof. *Mat.* 8: 8.

He that loveth father or mother more than me is not worthy of me: and he that loveth son or daughter more than me is not worthy of me. *Mat.* 10: 37.

He that taketh not his cross, and followeth after me, is not worthy of me. *Mat.* 10: 38.

It is not meet to take the children's bread, and to cast it to dogs. *Mat.* 15: 26.

The wedding is ready, but they which were bidden were not worthy. *Mat.* 22: 8.

Depart from me, ye cursed, into everlasting fire. *Mat.* 25: 41.

Whosoever shall be ashamed of me and of my words, of him shall the Son of man be ashamed. *Lu.* 9: 26.

No man, having put his hand to the plow, and looking back, is fit for the kingdom of God. *Lu.* 9: 62.

If the salt have lost his savour, . . . It is neither fit for the land, nor yet for the dunghill; but men cast it out. *Lu.* 14: 34, 35.

I . . . am no more worthy to be called thy son. *Lu.* 15: 18, 19.

Away with such a fellow from the earth: for it is not fit that he should live. *Ac.* 22: 22.

Whosoever shall eat this bread, and drink this cup of the Lord, unworthily, shall be guilty of the body and blood of the Lord. *1 Co.* 11: 27.

No man was found worthy to open and to read the book, neither to look thereon. *Re.* 5: 4.

See also
Unworthiness.

Unfolding

The child Samuel grew before the Lord. *1 S.* 2: 21.

David went on, and grew great, and the Lord God of hosts was with him. *2 S.* 5: 10.

The righteous shall grow like the palm tree: he shall flourish like a cedar in Lebanon. *Ps.* 92: 12.

As a flower of the field, so he flourisheth. *Ps.* 103: 15.

The flowers appear on the earth; the time of the singing of birds is come, and the voice of the turtle is heard in our land. *S. of S.* 2: 12.

The fig tree putteth forth her green figs, and the vines with the tender grape give a good smell. *S. of S.* 2: 13.

When the bud is perfect, and the sour grape is ripening in the flower. *Is.* 18: 5.

It became a vine, and brought forth branches, and shot forth sprigs. *Eze.* 17: 6.

The tree grew, and was strong, and the height thereof reached unto heaven, and the sight thereof to the end of all the earth: The leaves thereof were fair, and the fruit thereof much. *Da.* 4: 11, 12.

He shall grow as the lily. *Ho.* 14: 5.

Put ye in the sickle, for the harvest is ripe. *Jo.* 3: 13.

First the blade, then the ear, after that the full corn in the ear. *Mk.* 4: 28.

Thou art not far from the kingdom of God. *Mk.* 12: 34.

Jesus increased in wisdom and stature, and in favour with God and man. *Lu.* 2: 52.

It is like a grain of mustard seed, which a man took, and cast into his garden; and it grew, and waxed a great tree. *Lu.* 13: 19.

Mightily grew the word of God and prevailed. *Ac.* 19: 20.

All the building fitly framed together groweth unto an holy temple in the Lord. *Ep.* 2: 21.

Your faith groweth exceedingly. *2 Th.* 1: 3.

Stir up the gift of God, which is in thee. *2 Ti.* 1: 6.

Grow in grace, and in the knowledge of our Lord and Saviour Jesus Christ. *2 Pe.* 3: 18.

See also
Development; Evolution; Growth; Progress.

Ungodliness

When the waves of death compassed me, the floods of ungodly men made me afraid. *2 S.* 22: 5.

God hath delivered me to the ungodly, and turned me over into the hands of the wicked. *Jb.* 16: 11.

How oft is the candle of the wicked put out! . . . They are as stubble before the wind, and as chaff that the storm carrieth away. *Jb.* 21: 17, 18.

Blessed is the man that walketh not in the counsel of the ungodly. *Ps.* 1: 1.

The ungodly are not so. *Ps.* 1: 4.

The Lord knoweth the way of the righteous: but the way of the ungodly shall perish. *Ps.* 1: 6.

These are the ungodly, who prosper in the world; they increase in riches. *Ps.* 73: 12.

Enter not into the path of the wicked. *Pr.* 4: 14.

An ungodly man diggeth up evil. *Pr.* 16: 27.

The tares are children of the wicked one. *Mat.* 13: 38.

Ye are of your father the devil. *Jn.* 8: 44.

Thou child of the devil, thou enemy of all righteousness, wilt thou not cease to pervert the right ways of the Lord? *Ac.* 13: 10.

The wrath of God is revealed from heaven against all ungodliness and unrighteousness of men. *Ro.* 1: 18.

When we were yet without strength, in due time Christ died for the ungodly. *Ro.* 5: 6.

Shun profane and vain babblings: for they will increase unto more ungodliness. *2 Ti.* 2:16.

Denying ungodliness and worldly lusts, we should live soberly, righteously, and godly, in this present world. *Tit.* 2: 12.

Whosoever doeth not righteousness is not of God, neither he that loveth not his brother. *1 Jn.* 3: 10.

See also

Crime; Evil; Guile; Iniquity; Sin; Sinner; Transgression; Trespass; Unrighteousness; Wickedness; Wrong.

Unhappiness

They were in evil case. *Ex.* 5: 19.

Why should not my countenance be sad, when the city, the place of my fathers' sepulchres, lieth waste? *Ne.* 2: 3.

Man is born unto trouble, as the sparks fly upward. *Jb.* 5: 7.

The wicked man travaileth with pain all his days. *Jb.* 15: 20.

My harp also is turned to mourning, and my organ into the voice of them that weep. *Jb.* 30: 31.

Sorrow is better than laughter: for by the sadness of the countenance the heart is made better. *Ec.* 7: 3.

Behold, my servants shall eat, but ye shall be hungry: behold my servants shall drink, but ye shall be thirsty: behold, my servants shall rejoice, but ye shall be ashamed: Behold, my servants shall sing for joy of heart, but ye shall cry for sorrow of heart. *Is.* 65: 13, 14.

Her tears are on her cheeks. *La.* 1: 2.

Is it nothing to you, all ye that pass by? behold, and see if there be any sorrow like unto my sorrow. *La.* 1: 12.

The priests, the Lord's ministers, mourn. *Jo.* 1: 9.

Joy is withered away from the sons of men. *Jo.* 1: 12.

Ye shall be sorrowful, but your sorrow shall be turned into joy. *Jn.* 16: 20.

The God of all comfort . . . comforteth us in all our tribulation. *2 Co.* 1: 3, 4.

If I make you sorry, who is he then that maketh me glad? *2 Co.* 2: 2.

See also

Christ, Sorrow of; Dejection; Depression; Despondency; Grief; Lamentation; Sadness; Sorrow; Tear; Woe.

Uniformity

Thou art the same, and thy years shall have no end. *Ps.* 102: 27.

The thing that hath been, it is that which shall be; and that which is done is that which shall be done: and there is no new thing under the sun. *Ec.* 1: 9.

That which befalleth the sons of man befalleth beasts; even one thing befalleth them: as the one dieth, so dieth the other; yea, they have all one breath; so that a man hath no preëminence above a beast: for all is vanity. *Ec.* 3: 19.

All things come alike to all: there is one event to the righteous, and to the wicked; to the good and to the clean, and to the unclean. *Ec.* 9: 2.

There is one event unto all. *Ec.* 9: 3.

Can the Ethiopian change his skin, or the leopard his spots? *Je.* 13: 23.

No decree nor statute which the king establisheth may be changed. *Da.* 6: 15.

I am the Lord, I change not. *Mal.* 3: 6.

Jesus Christ the same yesterday, and to day, and for ever. *He.* 13: 8.

With whom is no variableness, neither shadow of turning. *Ja.* 1: 17.

The word of God . . . liveth and abideth for ever. *1 Pe.* 1: 23.

See also

Oneness.

Uniqueness

Ye shall be a peculiar treasure unto me above all people. *Ex.* 19: 5.

The Lord he is God; there is none else beside him. *De.* 4: 35.

He only is my rock and my salvation. *Ps.* 62: 2.

You only have I known of all the families of the earth. *Am.* 3: 2.

The Lord shall be king over all the earth: in that day shall there be one Lord, and his name one. *Zch.* 14: 9.

Who can forgive sins, but God alone? *Lu.* 5: 21.

None is good, save one, that is, God. *Lu.* 18: 19.

This is life eternal, that they might know thee the only true God. *Jn.* 17: 3.

There is none other name under heaven given among men, whereby we must be saved. *Ac.* 4: 12.

To God only wise, be glory. *Ro.* 16: 27.

There is one God, and one mediator between God and men, the man Christ Jesus. *1 Ti.* 2: 5.

Jesus Christ . . . Who only hath immortality, dwelling in the light which no man can approach unto; whom no man hath seen, nor can see: to whom be honour and power everlasting. *1 Ti.* 6: 14, 16.

The blessed and only Potentate, the King of kings, and Lord of lords. *1 Ti.* 6: 15.

I am Alpha and Omega, the beginning and the ending, saith the Lord, which is, and which was, and which is to come, the Almighty. *Re.* 1: 8.

Thou only art holy. *Re.* 15: 4.

See also

Chief; First; Head.

Unity

The Lord our God is one Lord. *De.* 6: 4.

Unite my heart to fear thy name. *Ps.* 86: 11.

I will praise the Lord with my whole heart. *Ps.* 111: 1.

I will make them one nation. *Eze.* 37: 22.

All that believed were together, and had all things common. *Ac.* 2: 44.

The multitude of them that believed were of one heart and of one soul. *Ac.* 4: 32.

God . . . hath made of one blood all nations of men for to dwell on all the face of the earth. *Ac.* 17: 24, 26.

Is Christ divided? *1 Co.* 1: 13.

Whether one member suffer, all the members suffer with it. *1 Co.* 12: 26.

They gave to me and Barnabas the right hands of fellowship; that we should go unto the heathen, and they unto the circumcision. *Ga.* 2: 9.

To make in himself of twain one new man, so making peace. *Ep.* 2: 15.

Endeavouring to keep the unity of the Spirit. *Ep.* 4: 3.

There is one body, and one Spirit, even as ye are called in one hope of your calling. *Ep.* 4: 4.

The unity of the faith. *Ep.* 4: 13.

By him all things consist. *Col.* 1: 17.

See also

Agreement; Concord; God, Unity of; Harmony; Integration; Monotheism; Oneness; Unanimity.

Universality

All the nations of the earth shall be blessed in him. *Ge.* 18: 18.

Their line is gone out through all the earth, and their words to the end of the world. *Ps.* 19: 4.

I will pour out my spirit upon all flesh: and your sons and your daughters shall prophesy, your old men shall dream dreams, your young men shall see visions. *Jo.* 2: 28.

This gospel of the kingdom shall be preached in all the world. *Mat.* 24: 14.

Go ye into all the world, and preach the gospel to every creature. *Mk.* 16: 15.

Good tidings of great joy, which shall be to all people. *Lu.* 2: 10.

All bear him witness, and wondered at the gracious words which proceeded out of his mouth. *Lu.* 4: 22.

Other sheep I have, which are not of this fold: them also I must bring, and they shall hear my voice; and there shall be one fold, and one shepherd. *Jn.* 10: 16.

It was written in Hebrew, and Greek, and Latin. *Jn.* 19: 20.

The world, or life, or death, or things present, or things to come; all are yours. *1 Co.* 3: 22.

The everlasting gospel to preach unto them that dwell on the earth, and to every nation, and kindred, and tongue, and people. *Re.* 14: 6.

See also

Catholicity; Creation; Creator; Universe; World.

Universe

In the beginning God created the heaven and the earth. *Ge.* 1: 1.

Thus the heavens and the earth were finished, and all the host of them. *Ge.* 2: 1.

The heaven and the heaven of heavens is the Lord's thy God, the earth also, with all that therein is. *De.* 10: 14.

The stars in their courses fought against Sisera. *Ju.* 5: 20.

The heaven and the heaven of heavens cannot contain thee. *1 K.* 8: 27.

Let thy glory be above all the earth. *Ps.* 57: 5.

Look unto me, and be ye saved, all the ends of the earth. *Is.* 45: 22.

Mine hand also hath laid the foundation of the earth, and my right hand hath spanned the heavens. *Is.* 48: 13.

The God of the whole earth shall he be called. *Is.* 54: 5.

See also

Christ, the Creator; Creation; Creator; Earth; Globe; God the Creator; Universality.

Unkindness

Thou hast not given water to the weary to drink, and thou hast withholden bread from the hungry. *Jb.* 22: 7.

Thou art become cruel to me. *Jb.* 30: 21.

Hath God forgotten to be gracious? hath he in anger shut up his tender mercies? *Ps.* 77: 9.

Say not unto thy neighbour, Go, and come again, and to morrow I will give; when thou hast it by thee. *Pr.* 3: 28.

As a roaring lion, and a ranging bear; so is a wicked ruler over the poor people. *Pr.* 28: 15.

Woe unto them that . . . turn aside the needy from judgment. *Is.* 10: 1, 2.

He that made them will not have mercy on them, and he that formed them will shew them no favour. *Is.* 27: 11.

Thou didst shew them no mercy; upon the ancient hast thou very heavily laid thy yoke. *Is.* 47: 6.

They are cruel, and will not shew mercy. *Je.* 50: 42.

There is no truth, nor mercy, . . . in the land. *Ho.* 4: 1.

Execute true judgment, and shew mercy and compassions every man to his brother. *Zch.* 7: 9.

Thou shalt love thy neighbour as thyself. *Mk.* 12: 31.

There was no room for them in the inn. *Lu.* 2: 7.

Sir, I have no man, when the water is troubled, to put me into the pool. *Jn.* 5: 7.

He shall have judgment without mercy, that hath shewed no mercy. *Ja.* 2: 13.

See also

Cruelty; Harshness, Inhumanity; Unmercifulness.

Unmercifulness

Thou hast sent widows away empty, and the arms of the fatherless have been broken. *Jb.* 22: 9.

The needy shall not alway be forgotten. *Ps.* 9: 18.

He remembered not to shew mercy. *Ps.* 109: 16.

The tender mercies of the wicked are cruel. *Pr.* 12: 10.

Wrath is cruel, and anger is outrageous. *Pr.* 27: 4.

The Lord shall have no joy in their young men, neither shall have mercy on their fatherless and widows. *Is.* 9: 17.

I will no more have mercy upon the house of Israel. *Ho.* 1: 6.

I will not turn away the punishment thereof; because he did pursue his brother with the sword, and did cast off all pity, and his anger did tear perpetually, and he kept his wrath for ever. *Am.* 1: 11.

They sold the righteous for silver, and the poor for a pair of shoes. *Am.* 2: 6.

They turn aside the poor in the gate from their right. *Am.* 5: 12.

Ye . . . have omitted the weightier matters of the law, judgment, mercy, and faith. *Mat.* 23: 23.

I was an hungered, and ye gave me no meat: I was thirsty, and ye gave me no drink: I was a stranger, and ye took me not in: naked, and ye clothed me not: sick, and in prison, and ye visited me not. *Mat.* 25: 42, 43.

When he saw him, he passed by on the other side. *Lu.* 10: 31.

See also

Cruelty; Harshness; Inhumanity; Unkindness.

Unnaturalness

She is hardened against her young ones, as though they were not her's. *Jb.* 39: 16.

I have seen servants upon horses, and princes walking as servants upon the earth. *Ec.* 10: 7.

I will not turn away the punishment thereof; because they . . . remembered not the brotherly covenant. *Am.* 1: 9.

For thy violence against thy brother Jacob shame shall cover thee. *Ob.* 10.

They all lie in wait for blood; they hunt every man his brother with a net. *Mi.* 7: 2.

The son dishonoureth the father, the daughter riseth up against her mother, the daughter in law against her mother in law; a man's enemies are the men of his own house. *Mi.* 7: 6.

Let none of you imagine evil against his brother in your heart. *Zch.* 7: 10.

One shall say unto him, What are these wounds in thine hands? Then he shall answer, Those with which I was wounded in the house of my friends. *Zch.* 13: 6.

Have we not all one father? hath not one God created us? why do we deal treacherously every man against his brother? *Mal.* 2: 10.

It is not meet to take the children's bread, and to cast it to dogs. *Mat.* 15: 26.

They . . . changed the glory of the uncorruptible God into an image made like to corruptible man. *Ro.* 1: 22, 23.

They . . . changed the truth of God into a lie. *Ro.* 1: 22, 25.

Even their women did change the natural use into that which is against nature. *Ro.* 1: 26.

If thou wert cut out of the olive tree which is wild by nature, and were graffed contrary to nature into a good olive tree: how much more shall these, which be the natural branches, be graffed into their own olive tree? *Ro.* 11: 24.

See also

Abnormality; Abomination; Strangeness.

Unorthodoxy

In vain they do worship me, teaching for doctrines the commandments of men. *Mat.* 15: 9.

Beware . . . of the doctrine of the Pharisees and of the Sadducees. *Mat.* 16: 12.

There shall arise false Christs, and false prophets. *Mat.* 24: 24.

After the way which they call heresy, so worship I the God of my fathers. *Ac.* 24: 14.

I hear that there be divisions among you. *1 Co.* 11: 18.

There must be also heresies among you, that they which are approved may be made manifest among you. *1 Co.* 11: 19.

Henceforth be no more children tossed to and fro, and carried about with every wind of doctrine. *Ep.* 4: 14.

In the latter times some shall depart from the faith, giving heed to seducing spirits, and doctrines of devils. *1 Ti.* 4: 1.

A man that is an heretick after the first and second admonition reject. *Tit.* 3: 10.

They do always err in their hearts. *He.* 3: 10,

Be not carried about with divers and strange doctrines. *He.* 13: 9.

There were false prophets also among the people, even as there shall be false teachers among you, who privily shall bring in damnable heresies, even denying the Lord that bought them, and bring upon themselves swift destruction. *2 Pe.* 2: 1.

See also

Doctrine; Heresy; Orthodoxy; Teaching, False.

Unpreparedness

As yet the people had not prepared their hearts unto the God of their fathers. *2 Ch.* 20: 33.

Go to the ant, thou sluggard; consider her ways, and be wise. *Pr.* 6: 6.

Yet a little sleep, a little slumber, a little folding of the hands to sleep: So shall thy poverty come. *Pr.* 6: 10, 11.

The sluggard will not plow by reason of the cold; therefore shall he beg in harvest, and have nothing. *Pr.* 20: 4.

Woe to them . . . That lie upon beds of ivory, and stretch themselves upon their couches, and eat the lambs out of the flock. *Am.* 6: 1, 4.

The wedding is ready, but they which were bidden were not worthy. *Mat.* 22: 8.

They that were foolish took their lamps, and took no oil with them. *Mat.* 25: 3.

That servant, which knew his lord's will, and prepared not himself, neither did according to his will, shall be beaten with many stripes. *Lu.* 12: 47.

They all with one consent began to make excuse. *Lu.* 14: 18.

God hath given them the spirit of slumber, eyes that they should not see, and ears that they should not hear. *Ro.* 11: 8.

Lest haply if they of Macedonia come with me, and find you unprepared, we . . . should be ashamed. *2 Co.* 9: 4.

No man that warreth entangleth himself with the affairs of this life. *2 Ti.* 2: 4.

See also

Preparation; Readiness; Sloth.

Unreadiness

Man also knoweth not his time. *Ec.* 9: 12.

The lord of that servant shall come in a day when he looketh not for him, and in an hour that he is not aware of. *Mat.* 24: 50.

While they went to buy, the bridegroom came; and they that were ready went in with him to the marriage: and the door was shut. *Mat.* 25: 10.

Take heed to yourselves, lest at any time your hearts be overcharged with surfeiting, and drunkenness, and cares of this life, and so that day come upon you unawares. *Lu.* 21: 34.

Unreliability

The bramble said unto the trees, If in truth ye anoint me king over you, then come and put your trust in my shadow. *Ju.* 9: 15.

Behold, he put no trust in his servants; and his angels he charged with folly. *Jb.* 4: 18.

Behold, he putteth no trust in his saints. *Jb.* 15: 15.

I will not trust in my bow, neither shall my sword save me. *Ps.* 44: 6.

It is better to trust in the Lord than to put confidence in princes. *Ps.* 118: 9.

Therefore shall the strength of Pharaoh be your shame, and the trust in the shadow of Egypt your confusion. *Is.* 30: 3.

Woe to them that go down to Egypt for help; and stay on horses, and trust in chariots, because they are many; and in horsemen, because they are very strong. *Is.* 31: 1.

Lo, thou trustest in the staff of this broken reed, on Egypt; whereon if a man lean, it will go into his hand, and pierce it. *Is.* 36: 6.

Ye trust in lying words, that cannot profit. *Je.* 7: 8.

The prophets prophesy lies in my name: I sent them not, neither have I commanded them. *Je.* 14: 14.

Behold, I am against the prophets, saith the Lord, that use their tongues, and say, He saith. *Je.* 23: 31.

With their mouth they shew much love, but their heart goeth after their covetousness. *Eze.* 33: 31.

See also
Untrustworthiness.

Unrest

In the morning thou shalt say, Would God it were even! and at even thou shalt say, Would God it were morning! *De.* 28: 67.

In those times there was no peace to him that went out, nor to him that came in, but great vexations were upon all the inhabitants of the countries. *2 Ch.* 15: 5.

When he giveth quietness, who then can make trouble? *Jb.* 34: 29.

Why do the heathen rage, and the people imagine a vain thing? *Ps.* 2: 1.

Fret not thyself because of evildoers. *Ps.* 37: 1.

Why art thou cast down, O my soul? and why art thou disquieted within me? *Ps.* 43: 5.

Which stilleth the noise of the seas, the noise of their waves, and the tumult of the people. *Ps.* 65: 7.

All his days are sorrows, and his travail grief. *Ec.* 2: 23.

Thou that art full of stirs, a tumultuous city. *Is.* 22: 2.

There is no peace, saith the Lord, unto the wicked. *Is.* 48: 22.

The wicked are like the troubled sea, when it cannot rest. *Is.* 57: 20.

They have made them crooked paths: whosoever goeth therein shall not know peace. *Is.* 59: 8.

Our necks are under persecution: we labour, and have no rest. *La.* 5: 5.

They shall seek peace, and there shall be none. *Eze.* 7: 25.

They have seduced my people, saying, Peace; and there was no peace. *Eze.* 13: 10.

Come unto me, all ye that labour and are heavy laden, and I will give you rest. *Mat.* 11: 28.

Let not your heart be troubled. *Jn.* 14: 1.

Casting all your care upon him. *1 Pe.* 5: 7.

The smoke of their torment ascendeth up for ever and ever. *Re.* 14: 11.

See also
Confusion; Disorder; Disturbance; Fretfulness; Noise; Storm; Tumult.

Unrighteousness

Deliver me, O my God, out of the hand of the wicked, out of the hand of the unrighteous and cruel man. *Ps.* 71: 4.

He is my rock, and there is no unrighteousness in him. *Ps.* 92: 15.

Woe unto them that decree unrighteous decrees. *Is.* 10: 1.

Let the wicked forsake his way, and the unrighteous man his thoughts. *Is.* 55: 7.

Your iniquities have separated between you and your God. *Is.* 59: 2.

He fell down at Jesus' knees, saying, Depart from me; for I am a sinful man. *Lu.* 5: 8.

Forgive us our sins. *Lu.* 11: 4.

Filled with all unrighteousness, fornication, wickedness, covetousness, maliciousness. *Ro.* 1: 29.

What shall we say then? Is there unrighteousness with God? God forbid. *Ro.* 9: 14.

Be not overcome of evil, but overcome evil with good. *Ro.* 12: 21.

Know ye not that the unrighteous shall not inherit the kingdom of God? *1 Co.* 6: 9.

What fellowship hath righteousness with unrighteousness? *2 Co.* 6: 14.

God is not unrighteous to forget your work. *He.* 6: 10.

See also
Crime; Evil; Guile; Iniquity; Sin; Sinner; Transgression; Trespass; Ungodliness; Wickedness; Wrong.

Unselfishness

If thou wilt take the left hand, then I will go to the right; or if thou depart to the right hand, then I will go to the left. *Ge.* 13: 9.

Jonathan stripped himself of the robe that was upon him, and gave it to David, and his garments, even to his sword, and to his bow, and to his girdle. *1 S.* 18: 4.

His own new tomb. *Mat.* 27: 60.

And the second is like, namely this, Thou shalt love thy neighbour as thyself. *Mk.* 12: 31.

Father, forgive them; for they know not what they do. *Lu.* 23: 34.

The friend of the bridegroom, which standeth and heareth him, rejoiceth greatly because of the bridegroom's voice. *Jn.* 3: 29.

We then that are strong ought to bear the infirmities of the weak, and not to please ourselves. *Ro.* 15: 1.

Even Christ pleased not himself. *Ro.* 15: 3.

Let no man seek his own, but every man another's wealth. *I Co.* 10: 24.

Not seeking mine own profit, but the profit of many, that they may be saved. *I Co.* 10: 33.

Charity . . . seeketh not her own. *I Co.* 13: 4, 5.

For your sakes he became poor, that ye through his poverty might be rich. *2 Co.* 8: 9.

Look not every man on his own things, but every man also on the things of others. *Ph.* 2: 4.

Not unto themselves, but unto us. *I Pe.* 1: 12.

See also

Almsgiving; Altruism; Beneficence; Benevolence; Charity; Clemency; Generosity; Philanthropy; Will, Good.

Unthankfulness

Of the Rock that begat thee thou art unmindful, and hast forgotten God that formed thee. *De.* 32: 18.

Our fathers . . . refused to obey, neither were mindful of thy wonders that thou didst among them. *Ne.* 9: 16, 17.

I have nourished and brought up children, and they have rebelled against me. *Is.* 1: 2.

Thou hast forgotten the God of thy salvation, and hast not been mindful of the rock of thy strength. *Is.* 17: 10.

Can a woman forget her sucking child, that she should not have compassion on the son of her womb? yea, they may forget, yet will I not forget thee. *Is.* 49: 15.

Thou . . . forgettest the Lord thy maker. *Is.* 51: 12, 13.

They made light of it, and went their ways, one to his farm, another to his merchandise. *Mat.* 22: 5.

He is kind unto the unthankful. *Lu.* 6: 35.

Were there not ten cleansed? but where are the nine? *Lu.* 17: 17.

There are not found that returned to give glory to God, save this stranger. *Lu.* 17: 18.

When they knew God, they glorified him not as God, neither were thankful. *Ro.* 1: 21.

See also

Forgetfulness; Ingratitude; Thanklessness.

Untimeliness

Is it a time to receive money, and to receive garments, and oliveyards, and vineyards, and sheep, and oxen, and menservants, and maidservants? *2 K.* 5: 26.

As an untimely birth I had not been; as infants which never saw light. *Jb.* 3: 16.

As a snail which melteth, let every one of them pass away: like the untimely birth of a woman, that they may not see the sun. *Ps.* 58: 8.

As snow in summer, and as rain in harvest, so honour is not seemly for a fool. *Pr.* 26: 1.

If a man beget an hundred children, and live many years, so that the days of his years be many, and his soul be not filled with good, and also that he have no burial; I say, that

an untimely birth is better than he. *Ec.* 6: 3.

When he saw a fig tree in the way, he came to it, and found nothing thereon, but leaves only. *Mat.* 21: 19.

Go thy way for this time; when I have a convenient season.I will call for thee. *Ac.* 24: 25.

Judge nothing before the time, until the Lord come. *I Co.* 4: 5.

Last of all he was seen of me also, as of one born out of due time. *I Co.* 15: 8.

The stars of heaven fell unto the earth, even as a fig tree casteth her untimely figs, when she is shaken of a mighty wind. *Re.* 6: 13.

Untrustworthiness

How then wilt thou . . . put thy trust on Egypt for chariots and for horsemen? *2 K.* 18: 24.

If I have made gold my hope, or have said to the fine gold, Thou art my confidence; . . . I should have denied the God that is above. *Jb.* 31: 24, 28.

Some trust in chariots, and some in horses: but we will remember the name of the Lord our God. *Ps.* 20: 7.

They that trust in their wealth, and boast themselves in the multitude of their riches; None of them can by any means redeem his brother. *Ps.* 49: 6, 7.

It is better to trust in the Lord than to put confidence in man. *Ps.* 118: 8.

Put not your trust in princes, nor in the son of man, in whom there is no help. *Ps.* 146: 3.

Woe to the rebellious children, saith the Lord, that take counsel, but not of me. *Is.* 30: 1.

They shall be greatly ashamed, that trust in graven images, that say to the molten images, Ye are our gods. *Is.* 42: 17.

I have not spoken to them, yet they prophesied. *Je.* 23: 21.

The shepherds fed themselves, and fed not my flock. *Eze.* 34: 8.

How hard is it for them that trust in riches to enter into the kingdom of God! *Mk.* 10: 24.

Beloved, believe not every spirit, but try the spirits whether they are of God: because many false prophets are gone out into the world. *I Jn.* 4: 1.

See also

Unreliability.

Untruthfulness

Then Satan answered the Lord, and said, Doth Job fear God for nought? *Jb.* 1: 9.

I hate every false way. *Ps.* 119: 104.

A righteous man hateth lying. *Pr.* 13: 5.

Remove far from me vanity and lies. *Pr.* 30: 8.

Ye trust in lying words, that cannot profit. *Je.* 7: 8.

They are not valiant for the truth upon the earth. *Je.* 9: 3.

They have taught their tongue to speak lies. *Je.* 9: 5.

They have spoken words, swearing falsely in making a covenant. *Ho.* 10: 4.

Thou hast not lied unto men, but unto God. *Ac.* 5: 4.

Lie not against the truth. *Ja.* 3: 14.

No lie is of the truth. *I Jn.* 2: 21.

See also

Dishonesty; Falsehood; Lie.

Unworldliness

Man doth not live by bread only. *De.* 8: 3.

Let thy saints rejoice in goodness. *2 Ch.* 6: 41.

Holiness becometh thine house, O Lord, for ever. *Ps.* 93: 5.

I pray not that thou shouldest take them out of the world, but that thou shouldest keep them from the evil. *Jn.* 17: 15.

The fashion of this world passeth away. *1 Co.* 7: 31.

Flesh and blood cannot inherit the kingdom of God. *1 Co.* 15: 50.

Though we walk in the flesh, we do not war after the flesh. *2 Co.* 10: 3.

If ye be led of the Spirit, ye are not under the law. *Ga.* 5: 18.

If we live in the Spirit, let us also walk in the Spirit. *Ga.* 5: 25.

No man that warreth entangleth himself with the affairs of this life. *2 Ti.* 2: 4.

Choosing rather to suffer affliction with the people of God, than to enjoy the pleasures of sin for a season. *He.* 11: 25.

Love not the world, neither the things that are in the world. If any man love the world, the love of the Father is not in him. *1 Jn.* 2: 15.

See also

Godliness; Holiness; Sanctification; Spirit.

Unworthiness

No man, having put his hand to the plow, and looking back, is fit for the kingdom of God. *Lu.* 9: 62.

It was necessary that the word of God should first have been spoken to you: but seeing ye put it from you, and judge yourselves unworthy of everlasting life, lo, we turn to the Gentiles. *Ac.* 13: 46.

Do ye not know that the saints shall judge the world? and if the world shall be judged by you, are ye unworthy to judge the smallest matters? *1 Co.* 6: 2.

Whosoever shall eat this bread, and drink this cup of the Lord, unworthily, shall be guilty of the body and blood of the Lord. *1 Co.* 11: 27.

He that eateth and drinketh unworthily, eateth and drinketh damnation to himself, not discerning the Lord's body. *1 Co.* 11: 29.

Let your conversation be as it becometh the gospel of Christ. *Ph.* 1: 27.

No man was found worthy to open and to read the book, neither to look thereon. *Re.* 5: 4.

See also

Fitness; Unfitness; Uselessness; Worthiness.

Uprightness

With the merciful thou wilt shew thyself merciful, and with the upright man thou wilt shew thyself upright. *2 S.* 22: 26.

I know also, my God, that thou triest the heart, and hast pleasure in uprightness. *1 Ch.* 29: 17.

The Lord knoweth the way of the righteous: but the way of the ungodly shall perish. *Ps.* 1: 6.

Lord, who shall abide in thy tabernacle? who shall dwell in thy holy hill? He that walketh uprightly. *Ps.* 15: 1, 2.

Mark the perfect man, and behold the up-

right: for the end of that man is peace. *Ps.* 37: 37.

Mercy and truth are met together; righteousness and peace have kissed each other. *Ps.* 85: 10.

Unto the upright there ariseth light in the darkness: he is gracious, and full of compassion, and righteous. *Ps.* 112: 4.

In the way of righteousness is life; and in the pathway thereof there is no death. *Pr.* 12: 28.

The throne is established by righteousness. *Pr.* 16: 12.

The wicked flee when no man pursueth: but the righteous are bold as a lion. *Pr.* 28: 1.

When the righteous are in authority, the people rejoice: but when the wicked beareth rule, the people mourn. *Pr.* 29: 2.

Lo, this only have I found, that God hath made man upright; but they have sought out many inventions. *Ec.* 7: 29.

They are upright as the palm tree. *Je.* 10: 5.

Add to your faith virtue. *2 Pe.* 1: 5.

See also

Christ, Goodness of; Christ, Holiness of; Fairness; God, Righteousness of; Goodness; Holiness; Honesty; Honor; Integrity; Justice; Rectitude; Righteousness; Virtue.

Urgency

Every one with one of his hands wrought in the work, and with the other hand held a weapon. *Ne.* 4: 17.

Neither I, nor my brethren, nor my servants, nor the men of the guard which followed me, none of us put off our clothes, saving that every one put them off for washing. *Ne.* 4: 23.

Cry aloud, spare not, lift up thy voice like a trumpet. *Is.* 58: 1.

The king's commandment was urgent. *Da.* 3: 22.

The day of the Lord cometh, for it is nigh at hand. *Jo.* 2: 1.

The great day of the Lord is near, it is near, and hasteth greatly. *Zph.* 1: 14.

The Lord God shall blow the trumpet. *Zch.* 9: 14.

Because of his importunity he will rise and give him as many as he needeth. *Lu.* 11: 8.

Now is our salvation nearer than when we believed. *Ro.* 13: 11.

The night is far spent, the day is at hand. *Ro.* 13: 12.

This I say, brethren, the time is short. *1 Co.* 7: 29.

The Lord is at hand. *Ph.* 4: 5.

Thrust in thy sickle and reap: for the time is come for thee to reap; for the harvest of the earth is ripe. *Re.* 14: 15.

See also

Peril; Danger.

Usefulness

Now thou art worth ten thousand of us. *2 S.* 18: 3.

I was eyes to the blind, and feet was I to the lame. *Jb.* 29: 15.

Here am I; send me. *Is.* 6: 8.

They helped every one his neighbour. *Is.* 41: 6.

The workman is worthy of his meat. *Mat.* 10: 10.

Uselessness

Ye are of more value than many sparrows. *Mat.* 10: 31.

Salt is good. . . . Have salt in yourselves. *Mk.* 9: 50.

Lo, these many years do I serve thee. *Lu.* 15: 29.

As we have therefore opportunity, let us do good unto all men. *Ga.* 6: 10.

With good will doing service, as to the Lord, and not to men. *Ep.* 6: 7.

A vessel unto honour, sanctified, and meet for the master's use, and prepared unto every good work. *2 Ti.* 2: 21.

See also

Goodness; Helpfulness; Value; Worth.

Uselessness

Treasures of wickedness profit nothing. *Pr.* 10: 2.

Riches profit not in the day of wrath. *Pr.* 11: 4.

What profit hath a man of all his labour which he taketh under the sun? *Ec.* 1: 3.

I looked on all the works that my hands had wrought: . . . and, behold, all was vanity and vexation of spirit, and there was no profit under the sun. *Ec.* 2: 11.

The prophets . . . walked after things that do not profit. *Je.* 2: 8.

Their root is dried up, they shall bear no fruit. *Ho.* 9: 16.

Every tree which bringeth not forth good fruit is hewn down, and cast into the fire. *Mat.* 3: 10.

If the salt have lost his savour, wherewith shall it be salted? it is thenceforth good for nothing, but to be cast out, and to be trodden under foot of men. *Mat.* 5: 13.

The care of this world, and the deceitfulness of riches, choke the word, and he becometh unfruitful. *Mat.* 13: 22.

There was a man there which had a withered hand. *Mk.* 3: 1.

He passed by on the other side. *Lu.* 10: 31.

The flesh profiteth nothing. *Jn.* 6: 63.

Though I bestow all my goods to feed the poor, and though I give my body to be burned, and have not charity, it profiteth me nothing. *1 Co.* 13: 3.

See also

Fruitlessness; Worthlessness.

Usury

If thou lend money to any of my people that is poor by thee, thou shalt not be to him as an usurer. *Ex.* 22: 25.

Take thou no usury of him, or increase: but fear thy God. *Le.* 25: 36.

Unto a stranger thou mayest lend upon usury; but unto thy brother thou shalt not lend upon usury. *De.* 23: 20.

When thou dost lend thy brother any thing, thou shalt not go into his house to fetch his pledge. *De.* 24: 10.

He that putteth not out his money to usury, nor taketh reward against the innocent. He that doeth these things shall never be moved. *Ps.* 15: 5.

The borrower is servant to the lender. *Pr.* 22: 7.

Let thy gifts be to thyself, and give thy rewards to another. *Da.* 5: 17.

Thou oughtest therefore to have put my money to the exchangers, and then at my coming I should have received mine own with usury. *Mat.* 25: 27.

If ye lend to them of whom ye hope to receive, what thank have ye? for sinners also lend to sinners, to receive as much again. *Lu.* 6: 34.

Love ye your enemies, and do good, and lend, hoping for nothing again. *Lu.* 6: 35.

See also

Borrower; Debt; Loan.

Utterance

Should he reason with unprofitable talk? or with speeches wherewith he can do no good? *Jb.* 15: 3.

My lips shall utter knowledge clearly. *Jb.* 33: 3.

Day unto day uttereth speech. *Ps.* 19: 2.

My lips shall utter praise, when thou hast taught me thy statutes. *Ps.* 119: 171.

They shall abundantly utter the memory of thy great goodness, and shall sing of thy righteousness. *Ps.* 145: 7.

Death and life are in the power of the tongue. *Pr.* 18: 21.

I will utter things which have been kept secret from the foundation of the world. *Mat.* 13: 35.

They were all filled with the Holy Ghost, and began to speak with other tongues, as the Spirit gave them utterance. *Ac.* 2: 4.

In every thing ye are enriched by him, in all utterance, and in all knowledge. *1 Co.* 1: 5.

Ye abound in every thing, in faith, and utterance, and knowledge, and in all diligence, and in your love to us. *2 Co.* 8: 7.

He was caught up into paradise, and heard unspeakable words, which it is not lawful for a man to utter. *2 Co.* 12: 4.

Continue in prayer, . . . that God would open unto us a door of utterance, to speak the mystery of Christ. *Col.* 4: 2, 3.

See also

Christ, Word of; God, Voice of; God, Word of; Lip; Mouth; Self-Expression; Speaker; Speech; Tongue; Word.

V

Validity

The secret things belong unto the Lord our God: but those things which are revealed belong unto us and to our children for ever, that we may do all the words of this law. *De.* 29: 29.

All his commandments are sure. *Ps.* 11: 7.

The testimony of the Lord is sure, making wise the simple. *Ps.* 19: 7.

Concerning thy testimonies, I have known of old that thou hast founded them for ever. *Ps.* 119: 152.

Let not mercy and truth forsake thee: bind them about thy neck; write them upon the table of thine heart. *Pr.* 3: 3.

That which was written was upright, even words of truth. *Ec.* 12: 10.

Cursed be the man that obeyeth not the words of this covenant. *Je.* 11: 3.

Whatsoever thou shalt bind on earth shall be bound in heaven. *Mat.* 16: 19.

All things must be fulfilled, which were written in the law of Moses, and in the prophets, and in the psalms, concerning me. *Lu.* 24: 44.

I speak forth the words of truth and soberness. *Ac.* 26: 25.

Other foundation can no man lay than is laid, which is Jesus Christ. *1 Co.* 3: 11.

Ye are our epistle written in our hearts. *2 Co.* 3: 2.

Prove all things; hold fast that which is good. *1 Th.* 5: 21.

The foundation of God standeth sure, having this seal, The Lord knoweth them that are his. *2 Ti.* 2: 19.

Holding fast the faithful word as he hath been taught, that he may be able by sound doctrine both to exhort and to convince the gainsayers. *Tit.* 1: 9.

He looked for a city that hath foundations, whose builder and maker is God. *He.* 11: 10.

That those things which cannot be shaken may remain. *He.* 12: 27.

See also
Authenticity; Law; Truth.

Valley

The land, whither ye go to possess it, is a land of hills and valleys. *De.* 11: 11.

Because the Syrians have said, The Lord is God of the hills, but he is not God of the valleys, therefore will I deliver all this great multitude into thine hand, and ye shall know that I am the Lord. *1 K.* 20: 28.

Though I walk through the valley of the shadow of death, I will fear no evil. *Ps.* 23: 4.

The valleys also are covered over with corn. *Ps.* 65: 13.

He sendeth the springs into the valleys, which run among the hills. *Ps.* 104: 10.

I am the rose of Sharon, and the lily of the valley. *S. of S.* 2: 1.

The burden of the valley of vision. *Is.* 22: 1.

Every valley shall be exalted, and every mountain and hill shall be made low. *Is.* 40: 4.

See thy way in the valley. *Je.* 2: 23.

The hand of the Lord was upon me, and carried me out in the spirit of the Lord, and set me down in the midst of the valley which was full of bones. *Eze.* 37: 1.

Multitudes in the valley of decision. *Jo.* 3: 14.

Every valley shall be filled, and every mountain and hill shall be brought low. *Lu.* 3: 5.

Valor

The Lord is with thee, thou mighty man of valour. *Ju.* 6: 12.

Mighty men of valour. *Ne.* 11: 14.

Through God we shall do valiantly. *Ps.* 60: 12.

Ye shall die like men, and fall like one of the princes. *Ps.* 82: 7.

He shall give his angels charge over thee, to keep thee in all thy ways. *Ps.* 91: 11.

Thrice I suffered shipwreck. *2 Co.* 11: 25.

See also
Boldness; Bravery; Courage; Fearlessness; Fortitude; Heroism.

Value

Man knoweth not the price thereof. *Jb.* 28: 13.

It cannot be valued with the gold of Ophir. *Jb.* 28: 16.

Ye are of more value than many sparrows. *Mat.* 10: 31.

Again, the kingdom of heaven is like unto a merchant man, seeking goodly pearls: Who, when he had found one pearl of great price, went and sold all that he had, and bought it. *Mat.* 13: 45, 46.

What shall it profit a man, if he shall gain the whole world, and lose his own soul? Or what shall a man give in exchange for his soul? *Mk.* 8: 36, 37.

What man of you, having an hundred sheep, if he lose one of them, doth not . . . go after that which is lost? *Lu.* 15: 4.

The Son of man is come to seek and to save that which was lost. *Lu.* 19: 10.

The church of God, which he hath purchased with his own blood. *Ac.* 20: 28.

What things were gain to me, those I counted loss for Christ. *Ph.* 3: 7.

See also
Appraisal; Excellence; Goodness; Helpfulness; Importance; Price; Worth.

Vanguard

The Lord went before them by day in a pillar of cloud, to lead them the way; and by night in a pillar of fire, to give them light. *Ex.* 13: 21.

Moses sent them to spy out the land. *Nu.* 13: 17.

The armed men went before the priests. *Jos.* 6: 9.

He leadeth me. *Ps.* 23: 3.

If I ascend up into heaven, thou art there: if I make my bed in hell, behold, thou art there. *Ps.* 139: 8.

A little child shall lead them. *Is.* 11: 6.

I am the Lord thy God which . . . leadeth thee by the way that thou shouldest go. *Is.* 48: 17.

The Son of man shall send forth his angels. *Mat.* 13: 41.

The multitudes that went before . . . cried, saying, Hosanna. *Mat.* 21: 9.

In the beginning was the Word, and the Word was with God. *Jn.* 1: 1.

I am the voice of one crying in the wilderness, Make straight the way of the Lord. *Jn.* 1: 23.

I go to prepare a place for you. *Jn.* 14: 2.

Christ also suffered for us, leaving us an example, that ye should follow in his steps. *1 Pe.* 2: 21.

See also
Forerunner; Leadership; Precedence; Prophet.

Vanity

They have provoked me to anger with their vanities. *De.* 32: 21.

He . . . hath not lifted up his soul unto vanity. *Ps.* **24: 4.**

Surely men of low degree are vanity, and men of high degree are a lie: to be laid in the balance, they are altogether lighter than vanity. *Ps.* **62: 9.**

I hate vain thoughts. *Ps.* **119: 113.**

Beauty is vain. *Pr.* **31: 30.**

Vanity of vanities, saith the Preacher, vanity of vanities; all is vanity. *Ec.* **1: 2.**

All is vanity and vexation of spirit. *Ec.* **1: 14.**

What hath man of all his labour, and of the vexation of his heart, wherein he hath laboured under the sun? *Ec.* **2: 22.**

Childhood and youth are vanity. *Ec.* **11: 10.**

Israel is an empty vine, he bringeth forth fruit unto himself. *Ho.* **10: 1.**

We . . . preach unto you that ye should turn from these vanities unto the living God. *Ac.* **14: 15.**

Though I have the gift of prophecy, and understand all mysteries, and all knowledge; . . . and have not charity, I am nothing. *1 Co.* **13: 2.**

Great swelling words of vanity. *2 Pe.* **2: 18.**

See also

Braggart; Egotism; Emptiness; Haughtiness; Nothing; Pride; Self-Satisfaction.

Variety

I made me gardens and orchards, and I planted trees in them of all kind of fruits. *Ec.* **2: 5.**

Ye hear the sound of the cornet, flute, harp, sackbut, psaltery, dulcimer, and all kinds of musick. *Da.* **3: 5.**

The kingdom of heaven is like unto a net, that was cast into the sea, and gathered of every kind. *Mat.* **13: 47.**

There are diversities of gifts, but the same Spirit. *1 Co.* **12: 4.**

There are, it may be, so many kinds of voices in the world, and none of them is without signification. *1 Co.* **14: 10.**

God also bearing them witness, both with signs and wonders, and with divers miracles. *He.* **2: 4.**

With whom is no variableness, neither shadow of turning. *Ja.* **1: 17.**

Every kind of beasts, and of birds, and of serpents, and of things in the sea, is tamed, and hath been tamed of mankind. *Ja.* **3: 7.**

See also

Change; Diversity; Transformation.

Vastness

Unto the utmost bound of the everlasting hills. *Ge.* **49: 26.**

I am come down . . . to bring them up out of that land unto a good land and a large. *Ex.* **3: 8.**

My father . . . became there a nation, great, mighty, and populous. *De.* **26: 5.**

The Lord opened the eyes of the young man; and he saw: and, behold, the mountain was full of horses and chariots of fire round about Elisha. *2 K.* **6: 17.**

When I consider thy heavens, the work of thy fingers, the moon and the stars, which thou hast ordained. *Ps.* **8: 3.**

As the heaven is high above the earth, so great is his mercy toward them that fear him. *Ps.* **103: 11.**

As far as the east is from the west, so far hath he removed our transgressions from us. *Ps.* **103: 12.**

If I should count them, they are more in number than the sand. *Ps.* **139: 18.**

He telleth the number of the stars; he calleth them all by their names. *Ps.* **147: 4.**

His understanding is infinite. *Ps.* **147: 5.**

They shall gather together his elect from the four winds, from one end of heaven to the other. *Mat.* **24: 31.**

Of his kingdom there shall be no end. *Lu.* **1: 33.**

Without father, without mother, without descent, having neither beginning of days, nor end of life. *He.* **7: 3.**

The city lieth foursquare, and the length is as large as the breadth. *Re.* **21: 16.**

See also

Bigness: Greatness; Immensity.

Veil

The glory of the Lord abode upon mount Sinai, and the cloud covered it six days. *Ex.* **24: 16.**

I . . . will cover thee with my hand while I pass by. *Ex.* **33: 22.**

If I say, Surely the darkness shall cover me; even the night shall be light about me. *Ps.* **139: 11.**

Each one had six wings; with twain he covered his face. *Is.* **6: 2.**

I have covered thee in the shadow of mine hand. *Is.* **51: 16.**

Darkness shall cover the earth, and gross darkness the people. *Is.* **60: 2.**

There is nothing covered, that shall not be revealed; and hid, that shall not be known. *Mat.* **10: 26.**

The vail of the temple was rent in twain from the top to the bottom. *Mat.* **27: 51.**

When it shall turn to the Lord, the vail shall be taken away. *2 Co.* **3: 16.**

The mystery which hath been hid from ages and from generations, but now is made manifest to his saints. *Col.* **1: 26.**

See also

Christ, the Hidden; Concealment; Cover; Disguise; God, the Hiding; Secrecy.

Veneration

Behold, the sun and the moon and the eleven stars made obeisance to me. *Ge.* **37: 9.**

Ye shall keep my sabbaths, and reverence my sanctuary. *Le.* **26: 2.**

Bless ye God in the congregation. *Ps.* **68: 26.**

God is greatly to be feared in the assembly of the saints, and to be had in reverence of all them that are about him. *Ps.* **89: 7.**

Holy and reverend is his name. *Ps.* **111: 9.**

One cried unto another, and said, Holy, holy, holy, is the Lord of hosts: the whole earth is full of his glory. *Is.* **6: 3.**

Wherewith shall I come before the Lord, and bow myself before the high God? *Mi.* **6: 6.**

The perpetual hills did bow: his ways are everlasting. *Hab.* **3: 6.**

There came unto him a woman having an alabaster box of very precious ointment, and poured it on his head. *Mat.* **26: 7.**

The true worshippers shall worship the Father in spirit and in truth. *Jn.* **4: 23.**

I bow my knees unto the Father of our

Lord Jesus Christ. *Ep.* 3: 14.

At the name of Jesus every knee should bow. *Ph.* 2: 10.

Let all the angels of God worship him. *He.* 1: 6.

Holy, holy, holy, Lord God Almighty, which was, and is, and is to come. *Re.* 4: 8.

When those beasts give glory and honour and thanks to him that sat on the throne, who liveth for ever and ever, The four and twenty elders fall down before him that sat on the throne, and worship him that liveth for ever and ever. *Re.* 4: 9, 10.

The Lamb shall overcome them: for he is Lord of lords, and King of kings: and they that are within him are called, and chosen, and faithful. *Re.* 17: 14.

I fell at his feet to worship him. *Re.* 19: 10.

See also
Adoration; Adulation; Christ, Worship of; God, Adoration of; God, Worship of; Reverence.

Vengeance

To me belongeth vengeance, and recompence. *De.* 32: 35.

I will make mine arrows drunk with blood. *De.* 32: 42.

It is God that avengeth me. 2 *S.* 22: 48.

Jealousy is the rage of a man: therefore he will not spare in the day of vengeance. *Pr.* 6: 34.

O Lord, thou knowest: remember me, and visit me, and revenge me of my persecutors. *Je.* 15: 15.

God is jealous, and the Lord revengeth; the Lord revengeth, and is furious; the Lord will take vengeance on his adversaries. *Na.* 1: 2.

Is God unrighteous who taketh vengeance? *Ro.* 3: 5.

Dearly beloved, avenge not yourselves, but rather give place unto wrath: for it is written, Vengeance is mine; I will repay, saith the Lord. *Ro.* 12: 19.

If thine enemy hunger, feed him; if he thirst, give him drink: for in so doing thou shalt heap coals of fire on his head. *Ro.* 12: 20.

A readiness to revenge all disobedience. 2 *Co.* 10: 6.

Sodom and Gomorrah . . . are set forth for an example, suffering the vengeance of eternal fire. *Jude* 1: 7.

See also
Christ, Wrath of; God, Anger of; God, Wrath of; Recompense; Retaliation; Retribution; Revenge.

Veracity

Thou shalt provide out of all the people able men, such as fear God, men of truth. *Ex.* 18: 21.

My brethren have dealt deceitfully as a brook. *Jb.* 6: 15.

Shall I count them pure with the wicked balances, and with the bag of deceitful weights? *Mi.* 6: 11.

We know that thou art true, and teachest the way of God in truth, neither carest thou for any man: for thou regardest not the person of men. *Mat.* 22: 16.

There shall arise false Christs, and false prophets. *Mat.* 24: 24.

That on the good ground are they, which in an honest and good heart, having heard the word, keep it, and bring forth fruit with patience. *Lu.* 8: 15.

Look ye out among you seven men of honest report, full of the Holy Ghost and wisdom. *Ac.* 6: 3.

Provide things honest in the sight of all men. *Ro.* 12: 17.

That ye may walk honestly. *I Th.* 4: 12.

We trust we have a good conscience, in all things willing to live honestly. *He.* 13: 18.

See also
Christ, Truth of; God, Truth of; Honesty; Truth; Truth, Search for; Truth, Spirit of; Verity.

Verdure

Let the earth bring forth grass, the herb yielding seed, and the fruit tree yielding fruit after his kind. *Ge.* 1: 11.

The Lord God made . . . every plant of the field. *Ge.* 2: 4, 5.

Can the flag grow without water? Whilst it is yet in his greenness, and not cut down, it withereth before any other herb. *Jb.* 8: 11, 12.

The shady trees cover him with their shadow; the willows of the brook compass him about. *Jb.* 40: 22.

His leaf also shall not wither. *Ps.* 1: 3.

I am like a green olive tree in the house of God. *Ps.* 52: 8.

The righteous shall flourish like the palm tree: he shall grow like a cedar in Lebanon. *Ps.* 92: 12.

That our sons may be as plants. *Ps.* 144: 12.

The hay is withered away, the grass faileth, there is no green thing. *Is.* 15: 6.

He shall grow up before him as a tender plant. *Is.* 53: 2.

We all do fade as a leaf. *Is.* 64: 6.

I am like a green fir tree. From me is thy fruit found. *Ho.* 14: 8.

How soon is the fig tree withered away! *Mat.* 21: 20.

Now learn a parable of the fig tree; When her branch is yet tender, and putteth forth leaves, ye know that summer is near. *Mk.* 13: 28.

The leaves of the tree were for the healing of the nations. *Re.* 22: 2.

See also
Forest; Grass; Herb; Leaf; Plant; Tree.

Verity

Thou shalt not have in thy bag divers weights, a great and a small. *De.* 25: 13.

Lead me in thy truth, and teach me. *Ps.* 25: 5.

Thy mercy is great unto the heavens, and thy truth unto the clouds. *Ps.* 57: 10.

His truth shall be thy shield and buckler. *Ps.* 91: 4.

Thy word is true from the beginning. *Ps.* 119: 160.

Happy is he, . . . whose hope is in the Lord his God: . . . which keepeth truth for ever. *Ps.* 146: 5, 6.

Let not mercy and truth forsake thee. *Pr.* 3: 3.

The hail shall sweep away the refuge of lies. *Is.* 28: 17.

As a cage is full of birds, so are their houses full of deceit. *Je.* 5: 27.

The Lord hath a controversy with the inhabitants of the land, because there is no truth, nor mercy, nor knowledge of God in the land. *Ho.* 4: 1.

Jerusalem shall be called a city of truth. *Zch.* 8: 3.

John . . . bare witness unto the truth. *Jn.* 5: 33.

Ye shall know the truth, and the truth shall make you free. *Jn.* 8: 32.

O foolish Galatians, who hath bewitched you, that ye should not obey the truth? *Ga.* 3: 1.

Hereby know we the spirit of truth, and the spirit of error. *1 Jn.* 4: 6.

See also

Christ, Truth of; God, Truth of; Honesty; Truth; Truth, Search for; Truth, Spirit of; Veracity.

Vessel

Bring the ark of the covenant of the Lord, and the holy vessels of God, into the house that is to be built to the name of the Lord. *1 Ch.* 22: 19.

I am forgotten as a dead man out of mind: I am like a broken vessel. *Ps.* 31: 12.

Take away the dross from the silver, and there shall come forth a vessel for the finer. *Pr.* 25: 4.

The wise took oil in their vessels with their lamps. *Mat.* 25: 4.

No man, when he hath lighted a candle, covereth it with a vessel. *Lu.* 8: 16.

He is a chosen vessel unto me. *Ac.* 9: 15.

Peter . . . saw heaven opened, and a certain vessel descending unto him, as it had been a great sheet knit at the four corners. *Ac.* 10: 9, 11.

Hath not the potter power over the clay, of the same lump to make one vessel unto honour, and another unto dishonour? *Ro.* 9: 21.

We have this treasure in earthen vessels, that the excellency of the power may be of God, and not of us. *2 Co.* 4: 7.

He shall be a vessel unto honour, sanctified, and meet for the master's use, and prepared unto every good work. *2 Ti.* 2: 21.

Giving honour unto the wife, as unto the weaker vessel. *1 Pe.* 3: 7.

See also

Ship.

Vexation

The Lord shall send upon thee cursing, vexation, and rebuke. *De.* 28: 20.

God did vex them with all adversity. *2 Ch.* 15: 6.

Then shall he speak unto them in his wrath, and vex them in his sore displeasure. *Ps.* 2: 5.

My soul is also sore vexed: but thou, O Lord, how long? *Ps.* 6: 3.

I have seen all the works that are done under the sun; and, behold, all is vanity and vexation of spirit. *Ec.* 1: 14.

What hath man of all his labour, and of the vexation of his heart, wherein he hath laboured under the sun? *Ec.* 2: 22.

They rebelled, and vexed his holy Spirit. *Is.* 63: 10.

I will also vex the hearts of many people. *Eze.* 32: 9.

That righteous man dwelling among them, in seeing and hearing, vexed his righteous soul from day to day with their unlawful deeds. *2 Pe.* 2: 8.

See also

Affliction; Anger; Annoyance; Chagrin; Displeasure; Fretfulness; Trouble.

Vice

Thou shalt not commit adultery. *Ex.* 20: 14.

His heart gathered iniquity to itself. *Ps.* 41: 6.

Thou lovest evil more than good. *Ps.* 52: 3.

Come, let us take our fill of love until the morning: let us solace ourselves with loves. *Pr.* 7: 18.

It shall be called The way of holiness; the unclean shall not pass over it. *Is.* 35: 8.

Many devils were entered into him. *Lu.* 8: 30.

Walk in the Spirit, and ye shall not fulfil the lust of the flesh. *Ga.* 5: 16.

The spirit that dwelleth in us lusteth to envy. *Ja.* 4: 5.

Abstain from fleshly lusts, which war against the soul. *1 Pe.* 2: 11.

That he no longer should live the rest of his time in the flesh to the lusts of men, but to the will of God. *1 Pe.* 4: 2.

When we walked in lasciviousness, lusts, excess of wine, revelling, banquetings, and abominable idolatries. *1 Pe.* 4: 3.

See also

Corruption; Crime; Depravity; Evil; Fault; Guile; Iniquity; Lust; Sin; Sinner; Transgression; Ungodliness; Unrighteousness; Wickedness; Wrong.

Vicissitude

The land, whither ye go to possess it, is a land of hills and valleys. *De.* 11: 11.

Shall we receive good at the hand of God, and shall we not receive evil? *Jb.* 2: 10.

When he hath tried me, I shall come forth as gold. *Jb.* 23: 10.

Because they have no changes, therefore they fear not God. *Ps.* 55: 19.

It is good for me that I have been afflicted; that I might learn thy statutes. *Ps.* 119: 71.

I have seen servants upon horses, and princes walking as servants upon the earth. *Ec.* 10: 7.

All the merryhearted do sigh. *Is.* 24: 7.

For a small moment have I forsaken thee; but with great mercies will I gather thee. *Is.* 54: 7, 8.

Cast down, but not destroyed. *2 Co.* 4: 9.

Our light affliction . . . worketh for us a far more exceeding and eternal weight of glory. *2 Co.* 4: 17.

After ye were illuminated, ye endured a great fight of afflictions. *He.* 10: 32.

Whom the Lord loveth he chasteneth. *He.* 12: 6.

Think it not strange concerning the fiery trial which is to try you. *1 Pe.* 4: 12.

The God of all grace, . . . after that ye have suffered a while, make you perfect. *1 Pe.* 5: 10.

See also

Adversity; Affliction; Calamity; Change; Disaster; Discipline; Misfortune; Revolution; Transformation; Trial; Tribulation; Trouble; Variety.

Victim

God will provide himself a lamb for a burnt offering. *Ge.* **22: 8.**

Abraham built an altar there, and laid the wood in order, and bound Isaac his son, and laid him on the altar upon the wood. *Ge.* **22: 9.**

The murderer rising with the light killeth the poor and needy. *Jb.* **24: 14.**

For thy sake are we killed all the day long; we are counted as sheep for the slaughter. *Ps.* **44: 22.**

Whoso diggeth a pit shall fall therein: and he that rolleth a stone, it will return upon him. *Pr.* **26: 27.**

Surely he hath borne our griefs, and carried our sorrows. *Is.* **53: 4.**

He is brought as a lamb to the slaughter, and as a sheep before her shearers is dumb, so he openeth not his mouth. *Is.* **53: 7.**

He bare the sin of many, and made intercession for the transgressors. *Is.* **53: 12.**

He sent, and beheaded John in the prison. *Mat.* **14: 10.**

The Son of man came not to be ministered unto, but to minister, and to give his life a ransom for many. *Mat.* **20: 28.**

Let us kill him, and let us seize on his inheritance. *Mat.* **21: 38.**

Every sacrifice shall be salted with salt. *Mk.* **9: 49.**

Christ our passover is sacrificed for us. *1 Co.* **5: 7.**

The man Christ Jesus . . . gave himself a ransom for all. *1 Ti.* **2: 5, 6.**

Christ was once offered to bear the sins of many. *He.* **9: 28.**

The hire of the labourers who have reaped down your fields, which is of you kept back by fraud, crieth. *Ja.* **5: 4.**

Christ hath suffered for us in the flesh. *1 Pe.* **4: 1.**

See also

Christ, Cross of; Christ, Sacrifice of; Christ, Suffering of; Sacrifice.

Victory

The triumphing of the wicked is short. *Jb.* **20: 5.**

Through thee will we push down our enemies: through thy name will we tread them under that rise up against us. *Ps.* **44: 5.**

To give thanks unto thy holy name, and to triumph in thy praise. *Ps.* **106: 47.**

All nations compassed me about: but in the name of the Lord will I destroy them. *Ps.* **118: 10.**

He will swallow up death in victory. *Is.* **25: 8.**

When thou passest through the waters, I will be with thee; and through the rivers, they shall not overflow thee: when thou walkest through the fire, thou shalt not be burned; neither shall the flame kindle upon thee. *Is.* **43: 2.**

Therefore will I divide him a portion with the great, and he shall divide the spoil with the strong; because he hath poured out his soul unto death. *Is.* **53: 12.**

A bruised reed shall he not break, and smoking flax shall he not quench, till he send forth judgment unto victory. *Mat.* **12: 20.**

Nay, in all these things we are more than conquerors through him that loved us. *Ro.* **8: 37.**

Thanks be unto God, which always causeth us to triumph in Christ. *2 Co.* **2: 14.**

Be thou faithful unto death, and I will give thee a crown of life. *Re.* **2: 10.**

To him that overcometh will I give to eat of the hidden manna. *Re.* **2: 17.**

He went forth conquering, and to conquer. *Re.* **6: 2.**

These shall make war with the Lamb, and the Lamb shall overcome them: for he is Lord of lords, and King of kings. *Re.* **17: 14.**

See also

Christ, Triumph of; Invincibility; Success; Triumph.

Vigilance

God speaketh once, yea twice, yet man perceiveth it not. In a dream, in a vision of the night, when deep sleep falleth upon men, in slumberings upon the bed; Then he openeth the ears of men, and sealeth their instruction. *Jb.* **33: 14-16.**

I . . . meditate on thee in the night watches. *Ps.* **63: 6.**

Except the Lord build the house, they labour in vain that build it. *Ps.* **127: 1.**

My soul waiteth for the Lord more than they that watch for the morning: I say, more than they that watch for the morning. *Ps.* **130: 6.**

I stand continually upon the watchtower. *Is.* **21: 8.**

Thy watchmen shall lift up the voice. *Is.* **52: 8.**

Woe to them that are at ease in Zion. *Am.* **6: 1.**

Watch therefore: for ye know not what hour your Lord doth come. *Mat.* **24: 42.**

If the goodman of the house had known in what watch the thief would come, he would have watched. *Mat.* **24: 43.**

Tarry ye here, and watch with me. *Mat.* **26: 38.**

Watch ye therefore: for ye know not when the master of the house cometh, at even, or at midnight, or at the cockcrowing, or in the morning. *Mk.* **13: 35.**

What I say unto you I say unto all, Watch. *Mk.* **13: 37.**

There were in the same country shepherds abiding in the field, keeping watch over their flock by night. *Lu.* **2: 8.**

A bishop then must be . . . vigilant. *1 Ti.* **3: 2.**

Be sober, be vigilant; because your adversary the devil, as a roaring lion, walketh about, seeking whom he may devour. *1 Pe.* **5: 8.**

Blessed is he that watcheth. *Re.* **16: 15.**

See also

Alertness; Wakefulness; Watch.

Vigor

He was a mighty hunter before the Lord. *Ge.* **10: 9.**

Be strong. *Jos.* **1: 6.**

O Lord, my strength, and my redeemer. *Ps. 19: 14.*

They go from strength to strength. *Ps. 84: 7.*

Whatsoever thy hand findeth to do, do it with thy might. *Ec. 9: 10.*

Compel them to come in. *Lu. 14: 23.*

Stand therefore, having your loins girt about with truth. *Ep. 6: 14.*

If a man also strive for masteries, yet is he not crowned, except he strive lawfully. *2 Ti. 2: 5.*

See also

Christ, Power of; Christ, Strength of; Energy; Firmness; Force; Fortitude; God, Omnipotence of; God, Power of; God, Strength of; Might; Omnipotence; Power; Strength; Vitality.

Vileness

Thy way is perverse before me. *Nu. 22: 32.*

The shield of the mighty is vilely cast away, the shield of Saul, as though he had not been anointed with oil. *2 S. 1: 21.*

Wherefore are we counted as beasts, and reputed vile in your sight? *Jb. 18: 3.*

They were children of fools, yea, children of base men: they were viler than the earth. *Jb. 30: 8.*

Behold, I am vile; what shall I answer thee? I will lay mine hand upon my mouth. *Jb. 40: 4.*

The wicked walk on every side, when the vilest men are exalted. *Ps. 12: 8.*

All our righteousnesses are as filthy rags. *Is. 64: 6.*

I will . . . make them like vile figs, that cannot be eaten, they are so evil. *Je. 29: 17.*

We are made as the filth of the world, and are the offscouring of all things unto this day. *1 Co. 4: 13.*

Christ . . . shall change our vile body, . . . according to the working whereby he is able even to subdue all things unto himself. *Ph. 3: 20, 21.*

See also

Bestiality; Corruption; Crime; Defilement; Depravity; Evil; Impurity; Iniquity; Lust; Sin; Sinner; Ungodliness; Unrighteousness; Wickedness; Worthlessness.

Village

Let us lodge in the villages. *S. of S. 7: 11.*

Thou shalt say, I will go up to the land of unwalled villages; I will go to them that are at rest, that dwell safely, all of them dwelling without walls, and having neither bars nor gates, To take a spoil, and to take a prey. *Eze. 38: 11, 12.*

He went round about the villages, teaching. *Mk. 6: 6.*

He went throughout every city and village, preaching and shewing the glad tidings of the kingdom of God. *Lu. 8: 1.*

He entered into a certain village. *Lu. 10: 38.*

They . . . preached the gospel in many villages of the Samaritans. *Ac. 8: 25.*

See also

City; Town.

Vindictiveness

My wrath shall wax hot, and I will kill you with the sword. *Ex. 22: 24.*

Jealousy is the rage of a man: therefore he

will not spare in the day of vengeance. *Pr. 6: 34.*

The Lord will come with fire, and with his chariots like a whirlwind, to render his anger with fury. *Is. 66: 15.*

I will not turn away the punishment thereof; because . . . his anger did tear perpetually, and he kept his wrath for ever. *Am. 1: 11.*

Then said the Lord, Doest thou well to be angry? *Jon. 4: 4.*

The Lord revengeth, and is furious. *Na. 1: 2.*

Vengeance is mine; I will repay, saith the Lord. *Ro. 12: 19.*

See also

Retaliation; Revenge; Vengeance.

Vine

The angel of the Lord stood in a path of the vineyards. *Nu. 22: 24.*

Judah and Israel dwelt safely, every man under his vine and under his fig tree. *1 K. 4: 25.*

Eat ye every man of his own vine. *2 K. 18: 31.*

The fathers have eaten a sour grape, and the children's teeth are set on edge. *Je. 31: 29.*

Israel is an empty vine, he bringeth forth fruit unto himself. *Ho. 10: 1.*

They shall sit every man under his vine and under his fig tree; and none shall make them afraid. *Mi. 4: 4.*

Do men gather grapes of thorns? *Mat. 7: 16.*

I am the vine, ye are the branches. *Jn. 15: 5.*

Can the fig tree, my brethren, bear olive berries? either a vine, figs? *Ja. 3: 12.*

Thrust in thy sharp sickle, and gather the clusters of the vine of the earth; for her grapes are fully ripe. *Re. 14: 18.*

See also

Christ, the Vine; Drunkenness; Grape; Wine.

Violence

The earth was filled with violence. *Ge. 6: 11.*

Violence covereth them as a garment. *Ps. 73: 6.*

Violence shall no more be heard in thy land, wasting nor destruction within thy borders. *Is. 60: 18.*

They know not to do right, saith the Lord, who store up violence and robbery in their palaces. *Am. 3: 10.*

They covet fields, and take them by violence; and houses, and take them away. *Mi. 2: 2.*

The rich men thereof are full of violence. *Mi. 6: 12.*

The kingdom of heaven suffereth violence, and the violent take it by force. *Mat. 11: 12.*

Do violence to no man. *Lu. 3: 14.*

See also

Coercion; Compulsion; Constraint; Cruelty; Enforcement; Ferocity; Force; Harshness; Oppression; Persecution; Transgression; Vigor.

Virgin

The damsel was very fair to look upon, a virgin. *Ge. 24: 16.*

Behold, a virgin shall conceive, and bear a son, and shall call his name Immanuel. *Is. 7: 14.*

The virgins of Jerusalem hang down their heads to the ground. *La. 2: 10.*

Behold, a virgin shall be with child, and shall bring forth a son. *Mat. 1: 23.*

Then shall the kingdom of heaven be likened unto ten virgins. *Mat.* 25: 1.

There is difference also between a wife and a virgin. The unmarried woman careth for the things of the Lord, that she may be holy both in body and in spirit: but she that is married careth for the things of the world, how she may please her husband. *1 Co.* 7: 34.

I have espoused you to one husband, that I may present you as a chaste virgin to Christ. *2 Co.* 11: 2.

These are they which were not defiled with women; for they are virgins. *Re.* 14: 4.

See also

Chastity; Guilelessness; Innocence; Maiden; Purity.

Virtue

Keep my commandments: For length of days, and long life, and peace, shall they add to thee. *Pr.* 3: 1, 2.

Let not mercy and truth forsake thee: bind them about thy neck; write them upon the table of thine heart. *Pr.* 3: 3.

A virtuous woman is a crown to her husband. *Pr.* 12: 4.

Who can find a virtuous woman? for her price is far above rubies. *Pr.* 31: 10.

If there be any virtue, and if there be any praise, think on these things. *Ph.* 4: 8.

In all things shewing thyself a pattern of good works. *Tit.* 2: 7.

God . . . Make you perfect in every good work to do his will. *He.* 13: 20, 21.

Through the knowledge of him that hath called us to glory and virtue. *2 Pe.* 1: 3.

Add to your faith virtue; and to virtue knowledge. *2 Pe.* 1: 5.

He that lacketh these things is blind. *2 Pe.* 1: 9.

See also

Chastity; Christ, Goodness of; Christ, Holiness of; God, Righteousness of; Goodness; Holiness; Honor; Integrity; Justice; Purity; Rectitude; Righteousness; Value; Worth.

Vision

A man of God came unto me, and his countenance was like the countenance of an angel of God, very terrible. *Ju.* 13: 6.

Lord, I pray thee, open his eyes that he may see. *2 K.* 6: 17.

In a dream, in a vision of the night, when deep sleep falleth upon men, in slumberings upon the bed. *Jb.* 33: 15.

I have heard of thee by the hearing of the ear: but now mine eye seeth thee. *Jb.* 42: 5.

Let thine eyes look right on, and let thine eyelids look straight before thee. *Pr.* 4: 25.

The burden of the valley of vision. *Is.* 22: 1.

Thine eyes shall see the king in his beauty: they shall behold the land that is very far off. *Is.* 33: 17.

I saw in the night visions, and, behold, one like the Son of man came with the clouds of heaven. *Da.* 7: 13.

I Daniel alone saw the vision: for the men that were with me saw not the vision. *Da.* 10: 7.

Your young men shall see visions. *Jo.* 2: 28.

Tell the vision to no man, until the Son of man be risen again from the dead. *Mat.* 17: 9.

Coming up out of the water, he saw the heavens opened. *Mk.* 1: 10.

They perceived that he had seen a vision in the temple. *Lu.* 1: 22.

When they found not his body, they came, saying, that they had also seen a vision of angels, which said that he was alive. *Lu.* 24: 23.

He being full of the Holy Ghost, looked up stedfastly into heaven. *Ac.* 7: 55.

As he journeyed, he came near Damascus: and suddenly there shined round about him a light from heaven. *Ac.* 9: 3.

He saw in a vision. *Ac.* 10: 3.

A vision appeared to Paul in the night. *Ac.* 16: 9.

After he had seen the vision, immediately we endeavoured to go into Macedonia, assuredly gathering that the Lord had called us. *Ac.* 16: 10.

Whereupon, O king Agrippa, I was not disobedient unto the heavenly vision. *Ac.* 26: 19.

Have I not seen Jesus Christ our Lord? *1 Co.* 9: 1.

They shall see his face. *Re.* 22: 4.

See also

Christ, Vision of; Dream; God, Vision of; Perception; Prospect.

Visitation

God will surely visit you. *Ge.* 50: 24.

I the Lord thy God am a jealous God, visiting the iniquity of the fathers upon the children. *Ex.* 20: 5.

What is man, . . . that thou shouldest visit him every morning, and try him every moment? *Jb.* 7: 17, 18.

What is . . . the son of man, that thou visitest him? *Ps.* 8: 4.

Thou hast visited me in the night. *Ps.* 17: 3

O visit me with thy salvation. *Ps.* 106: 4.

Withdraw thy foot from thy neighbour's house; lest he be weary of thee, and so hate thee. *Pr.* 25: 17.

What will ye do in the day of visitation? *Is.* 10: 3.

The days of visitation are come, the days of recompence are come. *Ho.* 9: 7.

I was sick, and ye visited me: I was in prison, and ye came unto me. *Mat.* 25: 36.

Blessed be the Lord God of Israel; for he hath visited and redeemed his people. *Lu.* 1: 68.

Thou knewest not the time of thy visitation. *Lu.* 19: 44.

The Master saith unto thee, Where is the guestchamber? *Lu.* 22: 11.

Let us go again and visit our brethren in every city where we have preached. *Ac.* 15: 36.

Pure religion and undefiled before God and the Father is this, To visit the fatherless and widows in their affliction, and to keep himself unspotted from the world. *Ja.* 1: 27.

See also

Call; Chastisement; God, Chastisement of; God, Punishment of; Judgment; Judgment, the Last; Punishment; Recompense.

Vitality

Thou shalt no more be called tender and delicate. *Is.* 47: 1.

The people that do know their God shall be strong, and do exploits. *Da.* 11: 32.

They brought forth the sick into the streets, and laid them on beds and couches, that at the least the shadow of Peter passing by might overshadow some of them. *Ac.* 5: 15.

See also

Energy; Force; Power; Strength; Vigor.

Vocation

The Lord God of Israel chose me before all the house of my father to be king over Israel for ever. *1 Ch.* 28: 4.

He called unto him the twelve, and began to send them forth by two and two. *Mk.* 6: 7.

Paul, called to be an apostle of Jesus Christ. *1 Co.* 1: 1.

For ye see your calling, brethren, how that not many wise men after the flesh, not many mighty, not many noble, are called. *1 Co.* 1: 26.

Let every man abide in the same calling wherein he was called. *1 Co.* 7: 20.

That ye may know what is the hope of his calling. *Ep.* 1: 18.

I therefore, the prisoner of the Lord, beseech you that ye walk worthy of the vocation wherewith ye are called. *Ep.* 4: 1.

According to the power of God; Who hath saved us, and called us with an holy calling. *2 Ti.* 1: 8, 9.

Give diligence to make your calling and election sure. *2 Pe.* 1: 10.

See also

Business; Calling; Christ, Call of; God, Call of; Occupation; Profession; Trade.

Voice

The voice is Jacob's voice, but the hands are the hands of Esau. *Ge.* 27: 22.

After the fire a still small voice. *1 K.* 19: 12.

The voice of the Lord is upon the waters. *Ps.* 29: 3.

Lord, hear my voice. *Ps.* 130: 2.

The posts of the door moved at the voice of him that cried. *Is.* 6: 4.

Thou shalt be brought down, and shalt speak out of the ground, and thy speech shall be low out of the dust. *Is.* 29: 4.

The sheep follow him: for they know his voice. *Jn.* 10: 4.

There are, it may be, so many kinds of voices in the world, and none of them is without signification. *1 Co.* 14: 10.

Out of the throne proceeded lightnings and thunderings and voices. *Re.* 4: 5.

There were great voices in heaven. *Re.* 11: 15.

I heard a loud voice saying in heaven, Now is come salvation, and strength, and the kingdom of our God, and the power of his Christ. *Re.* 12: 10.

A voice came out of the throne, saying, Praise our God, all ye his servants. *Re.* 19: 5.

See also

Christ, Word of; Cry; God, Voice of; God, Word of; Lip; Mouth; Speaker; Speech; Tongue; Utterance; Whisper; Word.

Void

The earth was without form and void. *Ge.* 1: 2.

He that is void of wisdom despiseth his neighbour. *Pr.* 11: 12.

I went by . . . the vineyard of the man void of understanding; And, lo, it was all grown over with thorns, and nettles had covered the face thereof, and the stone wall thereof was broken down. *Pr.* 24: 30, 31.

Behold, the Lord maketh the earth empty, and maketh it waste. *Is.* 24: 1.

The land shall be utterly emptied, and utterly spoiled. *Is.* 24: 3.

My word . . . shall not return unto me void. *Is.* 55: 11.

Then he saith, I will return into my house from whence I came out; and when he is come, he findeth it empty, swept and garnished. *Mat.* 12: 44.

See also

Destitution; Emptiness; Nothingness; Space; Zero.

Volunteer

The children of Israel brought a willing offering unto the Lord, every man and woman, whose heart made them willing to bring for all manner of work, which the Lord had commanded. *Ex.* 35: 29.

He shall offer it of his own voluntary will at the door of the tabernacle. *Le.* 1: 3.

When the people willingly offered themselves. *Ju.* 5: 2.

The people had a mind to work. *Ne.* 4: 6.

The people blessed all the men, that willingly offered themselves to dwell at Jerusalem. *Ne.* 11: 2.

Thy people shall be willing in the day of thy power. *Ps.* 110: 3.

Then said I, Here am I; send me. *Is.* 6: 8.

Lord, what wilt thou have me to do? *Ac.* 9: 6.

Let no man beguile you of your reward in a voluntary humility and worshipping of angels. *Col.* 2: 18.

I am now ready to be offered. *2 Ti.* 4: 6.

When he offered up himself. *He.* 7: 27.

See also

Offering; Willingness.

Votary

Every devoted thing is most holy unto the Lord. *Le.* 27: 28.

Jephthah vowed a vow unto the Lord, and said, . . . Whatsoever cometh forth of the doors of my house to meet me . . . shall surely be the Lord's. *Ju.* 11: 30, 31.

The child shall be a Nazarite unto God. *Ju.* 13: 5.

She vowed a vow, and said, O Lord of hosts, if thou . . . wilt give unto thine handmaid a man child, then I will give him unto the Lord all the days of his life. *1 S.* 1: 11.

Thou shalt make thy prayer unto him, and he shall hear thee, and thou shalt pay thy vows. *Jb.* 22: 27.

She shall bring forth a son, and thou shalt call his name JESUS: for he shall save his people from their sins. *Mat.* 1: 21.

Thy wife Elisabeth shall bear thee a son, and thou shalt call his name John. And . . . many shall rejoice at his birth. *Lu.* 1: 13, 14.

The Son . . . is consecrated for evermore. *He.* 7: 28.

See also

Consecration; Dedication; Pledge; Vow.

Vow

Jephthah vowed a vow unto the Lord. *Ju.* **11: 30.**

Thou, O God, hast heard ,my vows. *Ps.* **61: 5.**

I will pay thee my vows, Which my lips have uttered, and my mouth hath spoken, when I was in trouble. *Ps.* **66: 13, 14.**

Lord, where are thy former lovingkindnesses, which thou swarest unto David in thy truth? *Ps.* **89: 49.**

I have sworn, and I will perform it. *Ps.* **119: 106.**

If thy children will keep my covenant, . . . their children shall also sit upon thy throne for evermore. *Ps.* **132: 12.**

I will make with them a covenant of peace. *Eze.* **34: 25.**

When God made promise to Abraham, because he could swear by no greater, he sware by himself. *He.* **6: 13.**

Above all things, my brethren, swear not, neither by heaven, neither by the earth, neither by any other oath: but let your yea be yea; and your nay, nay; lest ye fall into condemnation. *Ja.* **5: 12.**

See also

Covenant; Oath; Pledge; Promise; Votary.

Voyage

Who shall go over the sea for us, and bring it unto us, that we may hear it, and do ,it? *De.* **30: 13.**

There go the ships. *Ps.* **104: 26.**

They that go down to the sea in ships, that do business in great waters. *Ps.* **107: 23.**

The merchants . . . that pass over the sea. *Is.* **23: 2.**

They shall wander from sea to sea. *Am.* **8: 12.**

Jonah . . . found a ship going to Tarshish. *Jon.* **1: 3.**

When Jesus heard of it, he departed thence by ship into a desert place apart. *Mat.* **14: 13.**

He sent away the multitude, and took ship, and came into the coasts of Magdala. *Mat.* **15: 39.**

When Jesus was passed over again by ship unto the other side, much people gathered unto him. *Mk.* **5: 21.**

They departed into a desert place by ship privately. *Mk.* **6: 32.**

There came other boats from Tiberias. *Jn.* **6: 23.**

The other disciples came in a little ship. *Jn.* **21: 8.**

Sirs, I perceive that this voyage will be with hurt and much damage. *Ac.* **27: 10.**

We being exceedingly tossed with a tempest. *Ac.* **27: 18.**

Except these abide in the ship, ye cannot be saved. *Ac.* **27: 31.**

Behold also the ships, which though they be so great, and are driven of fierce winds, yet are they turned about with a very small helm. *Ja.* **3: 4.**

See also

Navigation; Ocean; Pilot; Sailor; Sea; Ship.

W

Wage

The recompence of a man's hands shall be rendered unto him. *Pr.* **12: 14.**

To the righteous good shall be repaid. *Pr.* **13: 21.**

He that earneth wages earneth wages to put it into a bag with holes. *Hag.* **1: 6.**

I will be a swift witness against . . . those that oppress the hireling in his wages. *Mal.* **3: 5.**

Do violence to no man, neither accuse any falsely; and be content with your wages. *Lu.* **3: 14.**

He that reapeth receiveth wages, and gathereth fruit unto life eternal. *Jn.* **4: 36.**

The wages of sin is death. *Ro.* **6: 23.**

I robbed other churches, taking wages of them, to do you service. *2 Co.* **11: 8.**

The labourer is worthy of his reward. *1 Ti.* **5: 18.**

Balaam . . . who loved the wages of unrighteousness. *2 Pe.* **2: 15.**

See also

Compensation; God, Reward of; Payment; Punishment; Recompense; Retribution; Reward.

Wait

Let none that wait on thee be ashamed. *Ps.* **25: 3.**

On thee do I wait all the day. *Ps.* **25: 5.**

Wait on the Lord. *Ps.* **27: 14.**

Those that wait upon the Lord, they shall inherit the earth. *Ps.* **37: 9.**

I waited patiently for the Lord. *Ps.* **40: 1.**

Make no tarrying, O my God. *Ps.* **40: 17.**

I made haste, and delayed not to keep thy commandments. *Ps.* **119: 60.**

Our eyes wait upon the Lord our God, until that he have mercy upon us. *Ps.* **123: 2.**

The eyes of all wait upon thee; and thou givest them their meat in due season. *Ps.* **145: 15.**

Therefore will the Lord wait, that he may be gracious unto you: . . . blessed are all they that wait for him. *Is.* **30: 18.**

They that wait upon the Lord shall renew their strength. *Is.* **40: 31.**

It is good that a man should both hope and quietly wait for the salvation of the Lord. *La.* **3: 26.**

The vision is yet for an appointed time: . . . though it tarry, wait for it. *Hab.* **2: 3.**

Tarry ye in the city of Jerusalem, until ye be endued with power from on high. *Lu.* **24: 49.**

He, . . . being assembled together with them, commanded them that they should not depart from Jerusalem, but wait for the promise of the Father, which, saith he, ye have heard of me. *Ac.* 1: 3, 4.

Even we ourselves groan within ourselves, waiting for the adoption, to wit, the redemption of our body. *Ro.* 8: 23.

If we hope for that we see not, then do we with patience wait for it. *Ro.* 8: 25.

We through the Spirit wait for the hope of righteousness by faith. *Ga.* 5: 5.

Ye turned to God from idols to serve the living and true God; And to wait for his Son from heaven, whom he raised from the dead. *1 Th.* 1: 9, 10.

See also

Abeyance; Delay; Patience; Procrastination; Wakefulness; Watch.

Wakefulness

On that night could not the king sleep. *Es.* 6: 1.

When I lie down, I say, When shall I arise, and the night be gone? and I am full of tossings to and fro unto the dawning of the day. *Jb.* 7: 4.

The abundance of the rich will not suffer him to sleep. *Ec.* 5: 12.

He shall rise up at the voice of the bird. *Ec.* 12: 4.

Awake, awake, stand up, O Jerusalem. *Is.* 51: 17.

His sleep went from him. *Da.* 6: 18.

Watch therefore, for ye know neither the day nor the hour wherein the Son of man cometh. *Mat.* 25: 13.

Awake to righteousness, and sin not. *1 Co.* 15: 34.

Awake thou that sleepest, and arise from the dead. *Ep.* 5: 14.

Let us not sleep, as do others; but let us watch and be sober. *1 Th.* 5: 6.

See also

Vigilance; Wait; Watch.

Walk

I am the Almighty God; walk before me, and be thou perfect. *Ge.* 17: 1.

I will walk among you and will be your God. *Le.* 26: 12.

He walketh in the circuit of heaven. *Jb.* 22: 14.

The moon walking in brightness. *Jb.* 31: 26.

Who walketh upon the wings of the wind. *Ps.* 104: 3.

Jesus went unto them, walking on the sea. *Mat.* 14: 25.

Jesus saith unto him, Rise, take up thy bed, and walk. *Jn.* 5: 8.

In the name of Jesus Christ of Nazareth rise up and walk. *Ac.* 3: 6.

Walk in love. *Ep.* 5: 2.

Walk as children of light. *Ep.* 5: 8.

See then that ye walk circumspectly. *Ep.* 5:15.

See also

Behavior; Conduct; Step.

Wall

Do good in thy good pleasure unto Zion: build thou the walls of Jerusalem. *Ps.* 51: 18.

Peace be within thy walls, and prosperity within thy palaces. *Ps.* 122: 7.

The rich man's wealth is his strong city, and as an high wall in his own conceit. *Pr.* 18: 11.

He that hath no rule over his own spirit is like a city that is broken down, and without walls. *Pr.* 25: 28.

Thou shalt call thy walls Salvation, and thy gates Praise. *Is.* 60: 18.

I have set watchmen upon thy walls, O Jerusalem, which shall never hold their peace day nor night. *Is.* 62: 6.

I, saith the Lord, will be unto her a wall of fire round about, and will be the glory in the midst of her. *Zch.* 2: 5.

God shall smite thee, thou whited wall. *Ac.* 23: 3.

He is our peace, who hath made both one, and hath broken down the middle wall of partition between us. *Ep.* 2: 14.

By faith the walls of Jericho fell down, after they were compassed about seven days. *He.* 11: 30.

The wall of the city had twelve foundations, and in them the names of the twelve apostles of the Lamb. *Re.* 21: 14.

See also

Defence; Fortress; Protection; Tower.

Wandering

He wandereth abroad for bread, saying, Where is it? *Jb.* 15: 23.

Thou tellest my wanderings. *Ps.* 56: 8.

Let them wander up and down for meat. *Ps.* 59: 15.

I have gone astray like a lost sheep; seek thy servant; for I do not forget thy commandments. *Ps.* 119: 176.

They have gone from mountain to hill, they have forgotten their restingplace. *Je.* 50: 6.

They have wandered as blind men in the streets. *La.* 4: 14.

My sheep wandered through all the mountains, and upon every high hill. *Eze.* 34: 6.

Many shall run to and fro, and knowledge shall be increased. *Da.* 12: 4.

The kingdom of heaven is as a man travelling into a far country. *Mat.* 25: 14.

They wandered about in sheepskins and goatskins. *He.* 11: 37.

They wandered in deserts, and in mountains, and in dens and caves of the earth. *He.* 11: 38.

Which have forsaken the right way, and are gone astray. *2 Pe.* 2: 15.

Wandering stars, to whom is reserved the blackness of darkness for ever. *Jude* 1: 13.

See also

Journey; Pilgrim; Pioneer; Progress; Sojourn; Travel.

Want

A land wherein thou shalt eat bread without scarceness, thou shalt not lack any thing in it. *De.* 8: 9.

Therefore shalt thou serve thine enemies which the Lord shall send against thee, in hunger, and in thirst, and in nakedness, and in want of all things. *De.* 28: 48.

The old lion perisheth for lack of prey. *Jb.* 4: 11.

He wandereth abroad for bread, saying, Where is it? *Jb.* 15: 23.

If I have seen any perish for want of clothing. . . . Then let mine arm fall from my shoulder blade. *Jb.* 31: 19, 22.

The Lord is my shepherd; I shall not want. *Ps.* **23: 1.**

They that seek the Lord shall not want any good thing. *Ps.* **34: 10.**

Thou desirest truth in the inward parts. *Ps.* **51: 6.**

For I am poor and needy. *Ps.* **86: 1.**

So shall thy poverty come as one that travelleth, and thy want as an armed man. *Pr.* **6: 11.**

The destruction of the poor is their poverty. *Pr.* **10: 15.**

The desire of the righteous shall be granted. *Pr.* **10: 24.**

Slothfulness casteth into a deep sleep; and an idle soul shall suffer hunger. *Pr.* **19: 15.**

The sluggard will not plow by reason of the cold; therefore shall he beg in harvest, and have nothing. *Pr.* **20: 4.**

He that giveth unto the poor shall not lack. *Pr.* **28: 27.**

He judged the cause of the poor and needy. *Je.* **22: 16.**

My people are destroyed for lack of knowledge. *Ho.* **4: 6.**

What lack I yet? *Mat.* **19: 20.**

Ye have the poor always with you; but me ye have not always. *Mat.* **26: 11.**

When he had spent all, there arose a mighty famine in that land; and he began to be in want. *Lu.* **15: 14.**

God hath tempered the body together, having given more abundant honour to that part which lacked. *1 Co.* **12: 24.**

Let him labour, working with his hands the thing which is good, that he may have to give to him that needeth. *Ep.* **4: 28.**

Every where and in all things I am instructed both to be full and to be hungry, both to abound and to suffer need. *Ph.* **4: 12.**

Night and day praying exceedingly that we might see your face, and might perfect that which is lacking in your faith. *1 Th.* **3: 10.**

See also

Charity; Destitution; Lack; Need; Philanthropy; Poor; Poverty.

War

The Lord is a man of war. *Ex.* **15: 3.**

When the host goeth forth against thine enemies, then keep thee from every wicked thing. *De.* **23: 9.**

The battle is not yours, but God's. *2 Ch.* **20: 15.**

He maketh wars to cease unto the end of the earth. *Ps.* **46: 9.**

Scatter thou the people that delight in war. *Ps.* **68: 30.**

Nation shall not lift up sword against nation, neither shall they learn war any more. *Is.* **2: 4.**

Her warfare is accomplished. *Is.* **40: 2.**

Thou sword of the Lord, how long will it be ere thou be quiet? put up thyself into thy scabbard, rest, and be still. *Je.* **47: 6.**

I will break the bow and the sword and the battle out of the earth, and will make them to lie down safely. *Ho.* **2: 18.**

Beat your plowshares into swords, and your pruninghooks into spears: let the weak say, I am strong. *Jo.* **3: 10.**

I came not to send peace, but a sword. *Mat.* **10: 34.**

Whence come wars and fightings among you? *Ja.* **4: 1.**

God is love. *1 Jn.* **4: 8.**

There was war in heaven. *Re.* **12: 7.**

See also

Attack; Battle; Belligerent; Conflict; Contention; Enemy; Fight; Soldier; Strife; Struggle; Weapon.

Warning

Thou shalt not follow a multitude to do evil. *Ex.* **23: 2.**

Take heed to thyself, lest thou make a covenant with the inhabitants of the land whither thou goest. *Ex.* **34: 12.**

How then wilt thou . . . put thy trust on Egypt for chariots and for horsemen? *2 K.* **18: 24.**

The judgments of the Lord are true. . . . By them is thy servant warned. *Ps.* **19: 9, 11.**

Enter not into the path of the wicked, and go not in the way of evil men. *Pr.* **4: 14.**

Cry aloud, spare not, lift up thy voice like a trumpet. *Is.* **58: 1.**

To whom shall I speak, and give warning, that they may hear? *Je.* **6: 10.**

Set the trumpet to thy mouth. *Ho.* **8: 1.**

Will a lion roar in the forest, when he hath no prey? *Am.* **3: 4.**

Shall a trumpet be blown in the city, and the people not be afraid? *Am.* **3: 6.**

Prepare to meet thy God, O Israel. *Am.* **4: 12.**

Let your loins be girded about, and your lights burning. *Lu.* **12: 35.**

I ceased not to warn every one night and day with tears. *Ac.* **20: 31.**

All these things happened unto them for ensamples: and they are written for our admonition, upon whom the ends of the world are come. *1 Co.* **10: 11.**

Watch ye. *1 Co.* **16: 13.**

Warning every man, and teaching every man in all wisdom. *Col.* **1: 28.**

Warn them that are unruly. *1 Th.* **5: 14.**

It is impossible . . . to renew them again unto repentance. *He.* **6: 4, 6.**

See also

Admonition; Caution.

Wash

If I wash myself with snow water, and make my hands never so clean; Yet shalt thou plunge me in the ditch. *Jb.* **9: 30, 31.**

I washed my steps in butter, and the rock poured me out rivers of oil. *Jb.* **29: 6.**

Cleanse thou me from secret faults. *Ps.* **19: 12.**

Wash me thoroughly from mine iniquity, and cleanse me from my sin. *Ps.* **51: 2.**

Wash me, and I shall be whiter than snow. *Ps.* **51: 7.**

Wash you, make you clean; put away the evil of your doings from before mine eyes. *Is.* **1: 16.**

Thou, when thou fastest, anoint thine head, and wash thy face. *Mat.* **6: 17.**

Ye make clean the outside of the cup and of the platter, but within they are full of extortion and excess. *Mat.* **23: 25.**

Arise, and be baptized, and wash away thy sins, calling on the name of the Lord. *Ac.* **22: 16.**

But ye are washed, but ye are sanctified, but ye are justified in the name of the Lord Jesus, and by the Spirit of our God. *1 Co.* **6: 11.**

He saved us, by the washing of regeneration. *Tit.* **3: 5.**

Let us draw near with a true heart in full assurance of faith, having our hearts sprinkled from an evil conscience, and our bodies washed with pure water. *He.* **10: 22.**

Cleanse your hands, ye sinners. *Ja.* **4: 8.**

See also

Cleansing; Purification.

Washington's Birthday

Moreover thou shalt provide out of all the people able men, such as fear God, men of truth, hating covetousness; and place such over them. *Ex.* **18: 21.**

The Lord spake unto Moses face to face. *Ex.* **33: 11.**

Be of good courage, and let us play the men for our people, and for the cities of our God. *2 S.* **10: 12.**

Think upon me, my God, for good, according to all that I have done for this people. *Ne.* **5: 19.**

The path of the just is as the shining light, that shineth more and more unto the perfect day. *Pr.* **4: 18.**

The memory of the just is blessed. *Pr.* **10: 7.**

He that is slow to anger is better than the mighty; and he that ruleth his spirit than he that taketh a city. *Pr.* **16: 32.**

Not by might, nor by power, but by my spirit, saith the Lord of hosts. *Zch.* **4: 6.**

The same did God send to be a ruler and a deliverer. *Ac.* **7: 35.**

Let this mind be in you, which was also in Christ Jesus. *Ph.* **2: 5.**

He endured, as seeing him who is invisible. *He.* **11: 27.**

See also

Lincoln's Birthday.

Waste

Take heed to thyself that thou offer not thy burnt offerings in every place that thou seest. *De.* **12: 13.**

The slothful man roasteth not that which he took in hunting. *Pr.* **12: 27.**

He also that is slothful in his work is brother to him that is a great waster. *Pr.* **18: 9.**

He that keepeth company with harlots spendeth his substance. *Pr.* **29: 3.**

Wherefore do ye spend money for that which is not bread? and your labour for that which satisfieth not? *Is.* **55: 2.**

Violence shall no more be heard in thy land, wasting nor destruction within thy borders. *Is.* **60: 18.**

The cities shall be inhabited, and the wastes shall be builded. *Eze.* **36: 10.**

Give not that which is holy unto the dogs, neither cast ye your pearls before swine, lest they trample them under their feet, and turn again and rend you. *Mat.* **7: 6.**

To what purpose is this waste? *Mat.* **26: 8.**

Why was this waste of the ointment made? *Mk.* **14: 4.**

The younger son . . . wasted his substance with riotous living. *Lu.* **15: 13.**

Gather up the fragments that remain, that nothing be lost. *Jn.* **6: 12.**

I will very gladly spend and be spent for you. *2 Co.* **12: 15.**

See also

Desolation; Destruction; Devastation; Loss; Prodigal.

Watch

The Lord watch between me and thee, when we are absent one from another. *Ge.* **31: 49.**

When I remember thee upon my bed, and meditate on thee in the night watches. *Ps.* **63: 6.**

A thousand years in thy sight are but as yesterday when it is past, and as a watch in the night. *Ps.* **90: 4.**

Except the Lord keep the city, the watchman waketh but in vain. *Ps.* **127: 1.**

My soul waiteth for the Lord more than they that watch for the morning. *Ps.* **130: 6.**

Set a watch, O Lord, before my mouth; keep the door of my lips. *Ps.* **141: 3.**

Watch in the watchtower. *Is.* **21: 5.**

The watchman said, The morning cometh, and also the night. *Is.* **21: 12.**

If the watchman see the sword come, and blow not the trumpet, and the people be not warned; if the sword come, and take any person from among them, he is taken away in his iniquity; but his blood will I require at the watchman's hands. *Eze.* **33: 6.**

I will stand upon my watch, and set me upon the tower, and will watch to see what he will say unto me. *Hab.* **2: 1.**

Watch therefore: for ye know not what hour your Lord doth come. *Mat.* **24: 42.**

If the goodman of the house had known in what watch the thief would come, he would have watched, and would not have suffered his house to be broken up. *Mat.* **24: 43.**

What, could ye not watch with me one hour? *Mat.* **26: 40.**

Watch and pray, that ye enter not into temptation. *Mat.* **26: 41.**

There were in the same country shepherds abiding in the field, keeping watch over their flock by night. *Lu.* **2: 8.**

Ye yourselves like unto men that wait for their lord. *Lu.* **12: 36.**

Blessed are those servants, whom the Lord when he cometh shall find watching. *Lu.* **12: 37.**

Be ye therefore ready also: for the Son of man cometh at an hour when ye think not. *Lu.* **12: 40.**

They watched him. *Lu.* **20: 20.**

My time is not yet come, but your time is alway ready. *Jn.* **7: 6.**

Watch ye, stand fast in the faith, quit you like men, be strong. *1 Co.* **16: 13.**

In stripes, in imprisonments, in tumults, in labours, in watchings. *2 Co.* **6: 5.**

Watching . . . with all perseverance and supplication for all saints. *Ep.* **6: 18.**

Therefore let us not sleep, as do others; but let us watch and be sober. *1 Th.* **5: 6.**

Watch thou in all things. *2 Ti.* **4: 5.**

Be ye therefore sober, and watch unto prayer. *1 Pe.* **4: 7.**

Be watchful, and strengthen the things which remain. *Re.* 3: 2.

Blessed is he that watcheth, and keepeth his garments, lest he walk naked, and they see his shame. *Re.* 16: 15.

See also

Vigilance; Wait; Wakefulness.

Water

Unstable as water, thou shalt not excel. *Ge.* 49: 4.

Thou shalt smite the rock, and there shall come water out of it. *Ex.* 17: 6.

The hearts of the people melted, and became as water. *Jos.* 7: 5.

Can the flag grow without water? *Jb.* 8: 11.

The waters wear the stones. *Jb.* 14: 19.

Who hath divided a watercourse for the overflowing of waters? *Jb.* 38: 25.

I am poured out like water. *Ps.* 22: 14.

He leadeth me beside the still waters. *Ps.* 23: 2.

We went through fire and through water: but thou broughtest us out into a wealthy place. *Ps.* 66: 12.

Stolen waters are sweet. *Pr.* 9: 17.

He that watereth shall be watered also himself. *Pr.* 11: 25.

Cast thy bread upon the waters: for thou shalt find it after many days. *Ec.* 11: 1.

Many waters cannot quench love. *S. of S.* 8: 7.

The stay and the staff, the whole stay of bread, and the whole stay of water. *Is.* 3: 1.

Blessed are ye that sow beside all waters. *Is.* 32: 20.

Ho, every one that thirsteth, come ye to the waters. *Is.* 55: 1.

Thou shalt be like a watered garden. *Is.* 58: 11.

Let judgment run down as waters, and righteousness as a mighty stream. *Am.* 5: 24.

Whosoever shall give to drink unto one of these little ones a cup of cold water only in the name of a disciple, verily I say unto you, he shall in no wise lose his reward. *Mat.* 10: 42.

Except a man be born of water and of the Spirit, he cannot enter into the kingdom of God. *Jn.* 3: 5.

Jesus answered and said unto her, If thou knewest the gift of God, and who it is that saith to thee, Give me to drink; thou wouldest have asked of him, and he would have given thee living water. *Jn.* 4: 10.

In these lay a great multitude of impotent folk, of blind, halt, withered, waiting for the moving of the waters. *Jn.* 5: 3.

Doth a fountain send forth at the same place sweet water and bitter? *Ja.* 3: 11.

Clouds they are without water, carried about of winds. *Jude* 1: 12.

The Lamb . . . shall lead them unto living fountains of waters. *Re.* 7: 17.

See also

Drink; Ocean; Sea; Spring; Wave.

Wave

The waves of death compassed me, the floods of ungodly men made me afraid. *2 S.* 22: 5.

Hitherto shalt thou come, but no further: and here shall thy proud waves be stayed. *Jb.* 38: 11.

All thy waves and thy billows are gone over me. *Ps.* 42: 7.

Thy wrath lieth hard upon me, and thou hast afflicted me with all thy waves. *Ps.* 88: 7.

The floods have lifted up, O Lord, the floods have lifted up their voice; the floods lift up their waves. *Ps.* 93: 3.

He maketh the storm a calm, so that the waves thereof are still. *Ps.* 107: 29.

He that wavereth is like a wave of the sea driven with the wind and tossed. *Ja.* 1: 6.

See also

Ocean; Sea.

Way

Jacob went on his way, and the angels of God met him. *Ge.* 32: 1.

He . . . causeth them to wander in a wilderness where there is no way. *Jb.* 12: 24.

The Lord knoweth the way of the righteous: but the way of the ungodly shall perish. *Ps.* 1: 6.

I will instruct thee and teach thee in the way which thou shalt go: I will guide thee with mine eye. *Ps.* 32: 8.

Commit thy way unto the Lord. *Ps.* 37: 5.

Thy word is a lamp unto my feet, and a light unto my path. *Ps.* 119: 105.

Her ways are ways of pleasantness, and all her paths are peace. *Pr.* 3: 17.

The path of the just is as the shining light, that shineth more and more unto the perfect day. *Pr.* 4: 18.

Ponder the path of thy feet, and let all thy ways be established. *Pr.* 4: 26.

Train up a child in the way he should go. *Pr.* 22: 6.

The Lord . . . maketh a way in the sea, and a path in the mighty waters. *Is.* 43: 16.

I will make all my mountains a way, and my highways shall be exalted. *Is.* 49: 11.

Thou shalt be called, The repairer of the breach, The restorer of paths to dwell in. *Is.* 58: 12.

Narrow is the way, which leadeth unto life. *Mat.* 7: 14.

See also

Christ, Way of; Fashion; God, Way of; Highway; Life, Path of; Path; Road.

Weakness

O our God, wilt thou not judge them? for we have no might against this great company that cometh against us. *2 Ch.* 20: 12.

Thou hast strengthened the weak hands. *Jb.* 4: 3.

Out of the mouth of babes and sucklings hast thou ordained strength. *Ps.* 8: 2.

Blessed is he that considereth the poor. *Ps.* 41: 1.

I was brought low, and he helped me. *Ps.* 116: 6.

It is not in man that walketh to direct his steps. *Je.* 10: 23.

The fathers shall not look back to their children for feebleness of hands. *Je.* 47: 3.

Let the weak say, I am strong. *Jo.* 3: 10.

He was moved with compassion on them, because they fainted, and were scattered abroad, as sheep having no shepherd. *Mat.* 9: 36.

He that heareth, and doeth not, is like a man that without a foundation built an house upon the earth. *Lu.* 6: 49.

I know that in me . . . dwelleth no good thing: for to will is present with me; but how to perform that which is good I find not. *Ro.* 7: 18.

Him that is weak in the faith receive ye. *Ro.* 14: 1.

Let us not therefore judge one another any more: but judge this rather, that no man put a stumblingblock or an occasion to fall in his brother's way. *Ro.* 14: 13.

God hath chosen the foolish things of the world to confound the wise; and God hath chosen the weak things of the world to confound the things which are mighty. *1 Co.* 1: 27.

We are weak, but ye are strong; ye are honourable, but we are despised. *1 Co.* 4: 10.

Take heed lest by any means this liberty of yours become a stumblingblock to them that are weak. *1 Co.* 8: 9.

The resurrection of the dead . . . is sown in dishonour; it is raised in glory: it is sown in weakness; it is raised in power. *1 Co.* 15: 42, 43.

Not that we are sufficient unto ourselves to think any thing as of ourselves. *2 Co.* 3: 5.

Therefore seeing we have this ministry, as we have received mercy, we faint not. *2 Co.* 4: 1.

Who is weak, and I am not weak? *2 Co.* 11: 29.

Of myself I will not glory, but in mine infirmities. *2 Co.* 12: 5.

My grace is sufficient for thee: for my strength is made perfect in weakness. *2 Co.* 12: 9.

We also are weak in him, but we shall live with him by the power of God toward you. *2 Co.* 13: 4.

Support the weak, be patient toward all men. *1 Th.* 5: 14.

Out of weakness were made strong. *He.* 11: 34.

Make straight paths for your feet, lest that which is lame be turned out of the way; but let it rather be healed. *He.* 12: 13.

See also

Ailment; Faintness; Feebleness; Frailty; Illness; Impotence; Inability; Infirmity.

Wealth

More to be desired are they than gold, yea, than much fine gold. *Ps.* 19: 10.

Wise men die, . . . and leave their wealth to others. *Ps.* 49: 10.

Thou broughtest us out into a wealthy place. *Ps.* 66: 12.

Wealth gotten by vanity shall be diminished. *Pr.* 13: 11.

A good name is rather to be chosen than great riches, and loving favour rather than silver and gold. *Pr.* 22: 1.

Labour not to be rich. *Pr.* 23: 4.

Riches certainly make themselves wings; they fly away as an eagle toward heaven. *Pr.* 23: 5.

He that hasteth to be rich hath an evil eye. *Pr.* 28: 22.

Every man also to whom God hath given riches and wealth, . . . this is the gift of God. *Ec.* 5: 19.

A man to whom God hath given riches, wealth, and honour, so that he wanteth nothing for his soul of all that he desireth, yet God giveth him not power to eat thereof, but a stranger eateth it: this is vanity, and it is an evil disease. *Ec.* 6: 2.

As the bridegroom rejoiceth over the bride, so shall thy God rejoice over thee. *Is.* 62: 5.

It is easier for a camel to go through the eye of a needle, than for a rich man to enter into the kingdom of God. *Mat.* 19: 24.

He looked up, and saw the rich men casting their gifts into the treasury. *Lu.* 21: 1.

I have coveted no man's silver, or gold, or apparel. *Ac.* 20: 33.

Unto me, who am less than the least of all saints, is this grace given, that I should preach among the Gentiles the unsearchable riches of Christ. *Ep.* 3: 8.

We brought nothing into this world, and it is certain we can carry nothing out. *1 Ti.* 6: 7.

Esteeming the reproach of Christ greater riches than the treasures in Egypt. *He.* 11: 26.

See also

Acquisition; Ampleness; Belongings; God, Wealth of; Gold; Goods; Mammon; Possessions; Worldliness.

Weapon

Not with thy sword, nor with thy bow. *Jos.* 24: 12.

How are the mighty fallen, and the weapons of war perished! *2 S.* 1: 27.

Deliver my soul from the sword. *Ps.* 22: 20.

He breaketh the bow, and cutteth the spear in sunder. *Ps.* 46: 9.

Wisdom is better than weapons of war: but one sinner destroyeth much good. *Ec.* 9: 18.

They come from a far country, from the end of heaven, even the Lord, and the weapons of his indignation, to destroy the whole land. *Is.* 13: 5.

No weapon that is formed against thee shall prosper. . . . This is the heritage of the servants of the Lord. *Is.* 54: 17.

Behold, I will turn back the weapons of war. *Je.* 21: 4.

Thou art my battle ax and weapons of war: for with thee will I break in pieces the nations. *Je.* 51: 20.

The mighty . . . are gone down to hell with their weapons of war. *Eze.* 32: 27.

Thou . . . shalt lie with them that are slain with the sword. *Eze.* 32: 28.

The weapons of our warfare are not carnal, but mighty through God to the pulling down of strong holds. *2 Co.* 10: 4.

They overcame him by the blood of the Lamb, and by the word of their testimony. *Re.* 12: 11.

He that killeth with the sword must be killed with the sword. *Re.* 13: 10.

See also

Armor; Battle; Fight; Spear; Sword; War.

Weariness

In the sweat of thy face shalt thou eat bread, till thou return unto the ground; for out of it wast thou taken. *Ge.* 3: 19.

There the wicked cease from troubling; and there the weary be at rest. *Jb.* 3: 17.

Wherefore is light given to him that is in misery, and life unto the bitter in soul? *Jb.* 3: 20.

Wearisome nights are appointed to me. *Jb.* 7: 3.

My soul is weary of my life. *Jb.* 10: 1.

I am weary with my groaning; all the night make I my bed to swim. *Ps.* 6: 6.

Cast thy burden upon the Lord, and he shall sustain thee. *Ps.* 55: 22.

The work that is wrought under the sun is grievous unto me. *Ec.* 2: 17.

So I returned, and considered all the oppressions that are done under the sun: and behold the tears of such as were oppressed, and they had no comforter. *Ec.* 4: 1.

I praised the dead which are already dead more than the living which are yet alive. *Ec.* 4: 2.

The sleep of a labouring man is sweet, whether he eat little or much. *Ec.* 5: 12.

The labour of the foolish wearieth every one of them, because he knoweth not how to go to the city. *Ec.* 10: 15.

None shall be weary nor stumble among them. *Is.* 5: 27.

As the shadow of a great rock in a weary land. *Is.* 32: 2.

Thou art wearied in the greatness of thy way. *Is.* 57: 10.

He fainted, and wished in himself to die, and said, It is better for me to die than to live. *Jon.* 4: 8.

I will avenge her, lest by her continual coming she weary me. *Lu.* 18: 5.

In weariness and painfulness, in watchings often. *2 Co.* 11: 27.

Let us not be weary in well doing: for in due season we shall reap, if we faint not. *Ga.* 6: 9.

Consider him that endured such contradiction of sinners against himself, lest ye be wearied and faint in your minds. *He.* 12: 3.

See also
Faintness; Tedium.

Weather

While the earth remaineth, seedtime and harvest, and cold and heat, and summer and winter, and day and night shall not cease. *Ge.* 8: 22.

Fair weather cometh out of the north. *Jb.* 37: 22.

Hast thou entered into the treasures of the snow? or hast thou seen the treasures of the hail? *Jb.* 38: 22.

Hath the rain a father? or who hath begotten the drops of dew? *Jb.* 38: 28.

The sun shall not smite thee by day. *Ps.* 121: 6.

He bringeth the wind out of his treasuries. *Ps.* 135: 7.

Fire, and hail; snow, and vapours; stormy wind fulfilling his word. *Ps.* 148: 8.

As the cold of snow in the time of harvest. *Pr.* 25: 13.

Like clouds and wind without rain. *Pr.* 25: 14.

As he that taketh away a garment in cold weather, . . . so is he that singeth songs to an heavy heart. *Pr.* 25: 20.

A pleasant thing it is for the eyes to behold the sun. *Ec.* 11: 7.

Lo, the winter is past, the rain is over and gone; The flowers appear on the earth; the time of the singing of birds is come. *S. of S.* 2: 11, 12.

He shall come unto us as the rain, as the latter and former rain unto the earth. *Ho.* 6: 3.

When it is evening, ye say, It will be fair weather: for the sky is red. *Mat.* 16: 2.

In the morning, [ye say], It will be foul weather to day: for the sky is red and lowring. *Mat.* 16: 3.

See also
Cold; Frost; Heat; Rain; Snow; Sun; Wind.

Wedding

Therefore shall a man leave his father and his mother, and shall cleave unto his wife: and they shall be one flesh. *Ge.* 2: 24.

Let thy fountain be blessed: and rejoice with the wife of thy youth. *Pr.* 5: 18.

Turn, O backsliding children, saith the Lord; for I am married unto you. *Je.* 3: 14.

I will betroth thee unto me for ever. *Ho.* 2: 19.

I have married a wife, and therefore I cannot come. *Lu.* 14: 20.

Jesus was called, and his disciples, to the marriage. *Jn.* 2: 2.

The wife hath not power of her own body, but the husband: and likewise also the husband hath not power of his own body, but the wife. *1 Co.* 7: 4.

He that is unmarried careth for the things that belong to the Lord, how he may please the Lord: But he that is married careth for the things that are of the world, how he may please his wife. *1 Co.* 7: 32, 33.

Wives, submit yourselves unto your own husbands, as it is fit in the Lord. Husbands, love your wives, and be not bitter against them. *Col.* 3: 18, 19.

Marriage is honourable in all. *He.* 13: 4.

See also
Anniversary; Bride; Bridegroom; Husband; Marriage; Wife.

Weeping

Mine eye poureth out tears unto God. *Jb.* 16: 20.

All the night make I my bed to swim; I water my couch with my tears. *Ps.* 6: 6.

The Lord hath heard the voice of my weeping. *Ps.* 6: 8.

Weeping may endure for a night, but joy cometh in the morning. *Ps.* 30: 5.

Thou tellest my wanderings: put thou my tears into thy bottle: are they not in thy book? *Ps.* 56: 8.

Thou feedest them with the bread of tears. *Ps.* 80: 5.

He that goeth forth and weepeth, bearing precious seed, shall doubtless come again with rejoicing, bringing his sheaves with him. *Ps.* 126: 6.

A time to weep, and a time to laugh. *Ec.* 3: 4.

The Lord God will wipe away tears from off all faces. *Is.* 25: 8.

Thou shalt weep no more: he will be very gracious unto thee at the voice of thy cry. *Is.* 30: 19.

Let tears run down like a river day and night: give thyself no rest; let not the apple of thine eye cease. *La.* 2: 18.

Blessed are ye that weep now: for ye shall laugh. *Lu.* 6: 21.

Daughters of Jerusalem, weep not for me, but weep for yourselves, and for your children. *Lu.* 23: 28.

See also

Christ, Sorrow of; Grief; Lamentation; Sadness; Sorrow; Tear.

Weight

Ye shall do no unrighteousness in judgment, in meteyard, in weight, or in measure. *Le.* 19: 35.

Just balances, just weights, a just ephah, a just hin, shall ye have. *Le.* 19: 36.

Thou shalt not have in thy bag divers weights, a great and a small. *De.* 25: 13.

Oh that my grief were thoroughly weighed, and my calamity laid in the balances together! *Jb.* 6: 2.

To make the weight for the winds; and he weigheth the waters by measure. *Jb.* 28: 25.

Let me be weighed in an even balance. *Jb.* 31: 6.

In heart ye work wickedness; ye weigh the violence of your hands in the earth. *Ps.* 58: 2.

A false balance is abomination to the Lord: but a just weight is his delight. *Pr.* 11: 1.

All the ways of a man are clean in his own eyes; but the Lord weigheth the spirits. *Pr.* 16: 2.

A just weight and balance are the Lord's: all the weights of the bag are his work. *Pr.* 16: 11.

Thou, most upright, dost weigh the path of the just. *Is.* 26: 7.

Who hath measured the waters in the hollow of his hand, and meted out heaven with the span, and comprehended the dust of the earth in a measure, and weighed the mountains in scales, and the hills in a balance? *Is.* 40: 12.

Thou art weighed in the balances, and art found wanting. *Da.* 5: 27.

Shall I count them pure with the wicked balances, and with the bag of deceitful weights? *Mi.* 6: 11.

Ye pay tithe of mint and anise and cummin, and have omitted the weightier matters of the law, judgment, mercy and faith. *Mat.* 23: 23.

Our light affliction, which is but for a moment, worketh for us a far more exceeding and eternal weight of glory. *2 Co.* 4: 17.

Let us lay aside every weight, and the sin which doth so easily beset us, and let us run with patience the race that is set before us. *He.* 12: 1.

See also

Accuracy; Burden; Heaviness; Importance; Load.

Welcome

Thy gates shall be open continually; they shall not be shut day or night. *Is.* 60: 11.

Say unto him, Take away all iniquity, and

receive us graciously. *Ho.* 14: 2.

He that receiveth you receiveth me, and he that receiveth me receiveth him that sent me. *Mat.* 10: 40.

He that receiveth a prophet in the name of a prophet shall receive a prophet's reward. *Mat.* 10: 41.

Whoso shall receive one such little child in my name receiveth me. *Mat.* 18: 5.

I was a stranger, and ye took me in. *Mat.* 25: 35.

Into whatsoever city ye enter, and they receive you, eat such things as are set before you. *Lu.* 10: 8.

Yet there is room. *Lu.* 14: 22.

He made haste, and came down, and received him joyfully. *Lu.* 19: 6.

He came unto his own, and his own received him not. *Jn.* 1: 11.

Receive ye one another, as Christ also received us to the glory of God. *Ro.* 15: 7.

Ye . . . received me as an angel of God, even as Christ Jesus. *Ga.* 4: 14.

A lover of hospitality. *Tit.* 1: 8.

See also

Cordiality; Guest; Hospitality; Reception.

Welfare

He asked them of their welfare, and said, Is your father well? *Ge.* 43: 27.

They asked each other of their welfare. *Ex.* 18: 7.

Thou shalt keep therefore his statutes, and his commandments, which I command thee this day, that it may go well with thee, and with thy children after thee. *De.* 4: 40.

The Lord was with him; and he prospered whithersoever he went forth. *2 K.* 18: 7.

Terrors are turned upon me: they pursue my soul as the wind: and my welfare passeth away as a cloud. *Jb.* 30: 15.

If they obey and serve him, they shall spend their days in prosperity, and their years in pleasures. *Jb.* 36: 11.

Let their table become a snare before them: and that which should have been for their welfare, let it become a trap. *Ps.* 69: 22.

They shall prosper that love thee. *Ps.* 122: 6.

Thou shalt eat the labour of thine hands: happy shalt thou be, and it shall be well with thee. *Ps.* 128: 2.

This man seeketh not the welfare of this people, but the hurt. *Je.* 38: 4.

See also

Happiness; Prosperity; Well-Being.

Well

Then Israel sang this song, Spring up, O well; sing ye unto it. *Nu.* 21: 17.

The princes digged the well, the nobles of the people digged it. *Nu.* 21: 18.

The three mighty men brake through the host of the Philistines, and drew water out of the well of Bethlehem. *2 S.* 23: 16.

Who passing through the valley of Baca make it a well. *Ps.* 84: 6.

Drink waters out of thine own cistern, and running waters out of thine own well. *Pr.* 5: 15.

The mouth of the righteous man is a well of life. *Pr.* 10: 11.

Understanding is a wellspring of life unto him that hath it. *Pr.* 16: 22.

The words of a man's mouth are as deep waters, and the wellspring of wisdom as a flowing brook. *Pr.* 18: 4.

With joy shall ye draw water out of the wells of salvation. *Is.* 12: 3.

The water that I shall give him shall be in him a well of water springing up into everlasting life. *Jn.* 4: 14.

These are wells without water, clouds that are carried with a tempest. *2 Pe.* 2: 17.

See also

Spring; Water.

Well-Being

Ye shall walk in all the ways which the Lord your God hath commanded you, that ye may live, and that it may be well with you. *De.* 5: 33.

Art thou in health, my brother? *2 S.* 20: 9.

Is it well with thee? is it well with thy husband? is it well with the child? And she answered, It is well. *2 K.* 4: 26.

The Jews had light, and gladness, and joy, and honour. *Es.* 8: 16.

God . . . is the health of my countenance. *Ps.* 42: 11.

That thy way may be known upon earth, thy saving health among all nations. *Ps.* 67: 2.

In the multitude of my thoughts within me thy comforts delight my soul. *Ps.* 94: 19.

The blessing of the Lord, it maketh rich, and he addeth no sorrow with it. *Pr.* 10: 22.

Whoso trusteth in the Lord, happy is he. *Pr.* 16: 20.

Pleasant words are as an honeycomb, sweet to the soul, and health to the bones. *Pr.* 16: 24.

I will extend peace to her like a river. *Is.* 66: 12.

As one whom his mother comforteth, so will I comfort you. *Is.* 66: 13.

I will restore health unto thee. *Je.* 30: 17.

This man seeketh not the welfare of this people. *Je.* 38: 4.

O man greatly beloved, fear not: peace be unto thee, be strong, yea, be strong. *Da.* 10: 19.

Then shall the righteous shine forth as the sun in the kingdom of their Father. *Mat.* 13: 43.

Have salt in yourselves, and have peace one with another. *Mk.* 9: 50.

Be content with your wages. *Lu.* 3: 14.

Having food and raiment let us be therewith content. *1 Ti.* 6: 8.

See also

Comfort; Happiness; Health, Welfare.

Well-Doing

According to the kindness that I have done unto thee, thou shalt do unto me. *Ge.* 21: 23.

He becometh poor that dealeth with a slack hand. *Pr.* 10: 4.

They helped every one his neighbour. *Is.* 41: 6.

Blessed are the merciful: for they shall obtain mercy. *Mat.* 5: 7.

Except your righteousness shall exceed the righteousness of the scribes and Pharisees, ye shall in no case enter into the kingdom of heaven. *Mat.* 5: 20.

God . . . will render to every man according to his deeds: To them who by patient continuance in well doing seek for glory and honour and immortality, eternal life. *Ro.* 2: 5–7.

Love worketh no ill to his neighbour. *Ro.* 13: 10.

Love is the fulfilling of the law. *Ro.* 13: 10.

Let all your things be done with charity. *1 Co.* 16: 14.

By love serve one another. *Ga.* 5: 13.

Let us not be weary in well doing: for in due season we shall reap, if we faint not. *Ga.* 6: 9.

Bowels of mercies, kindness, humbleness of mind, meekness, longsuffering. *Col.* 3: 12.

So is the will of God, that with well doing ye may put to silence the ignorance of foolish men. *1 Pe.* 2: 15.

It is better, if the will of God be so, that ye suffer for well doing, than for evil doing. *1 Pe.* 3: 17.

Above all things have fervent charity among yourselves. *1 Pe.* 4: 8.

See also

Beneficence; Benevolence; Charity; Lovingkindness; Philanthropy.

West

Lift up now thine eyes, and look from the place where thou art northward, and southward, and eastward, and westward. *Ge.* 13: 14.

As far as the east is from the west, so far hath he removed our transgressions from us. *Ps.* 103: 12.

That they may know from the rising of the sun, and from the west, that there is none beside me. *Is.* 45: 6.

So shall they fear the name of the Lord from the west, and his glory from the rising of the sun. *Is.* 59: 19.

Many shall come from the east and west, and shall sit down with Abraham, and Isaac, and Jacob, in the kingdom of heaven. *Mat.* 8: 11.

As the lightning cometh out of the east, and shineth even unto the west; so shall also the coming of the Son of man be. *Mat.* 24: 27.

Wheat

Let thistles grow instead of wheat, and cockle instead of barley. *Jb.* 31: 40.

He should have fed them also with the finest of the wheat. *Ps.* 81: 16.

He maketh peace in thy borders, and filleth thee with the finest of the wheat. *Ps.* 147: 14.

Though thou shouldest bray a fool in a mortar among wheat with a pestle, yet will not his foolishness depart from him. *Pr.* 27: 22.

They have sown wheat, but shall reap thorns. *Je.* 12: 13.

While men slept, his enemy came and sowed tares among the wheat. *Mat.* 13: 25.

Satan hath desired to have you, that he may sift you as wheat. *Lu.* 22: 31.

Except a corn of wheat fall into the ground and die, it abideth alone. *Jn.* 12: 24.

Whirlwind

Out of the south cometh the whirlwind: and cold out of the north. *Jb.* 37: 9.

The Lord answered Job out of the whirlwind. *Jb.* 38: 1.

He shall take them away as with a whirlwind, both living, and in his wrath. *Ps.* 58: 9.

Your destruction cometh as a whirlwind.
Pr. 1: 27.

The wind . . . whirleth about continually.
Ec. 1: 6.

The Lord will come with fire, and with his
chariots like a whirlwind, to render his anger
with fury. *Is.* 66: 15.

They have sown the wind, and they have
reaped the whirlwind. *Ho.* 8: 7.

The Lord hath his way in the whirlwind
and in the storm. *Na.* 1: 3.

See also
Storm; Tempest; Wind.

Whisper

All that hate me whisper together against
me. *Ps.* 41: 7.

A whisperer separateth chief friends. *Pr.* 16:
28.

Thy speech shall whisper out of the dust.
Is. 29: 4.

Whisperers, Backbiters, haters of God. *Ro.*
1: 29, 30.

Lest there be debates, envyings, wraths,
strifes, backbitings, whisperings, swellings,
tumults. *2 Co.* 12: 20.

See also
Gossip; Slander; Talebearing; Utterance.

White

Can that which is unsavoury be eaten without salt? or is there any taste in the white of
an egg? *Jb.* 6: 6.

Wash me, and I shall be whiter than snow.
Ps. 51: 7.

Let thy garments be always white; and let
thy head lack no ointment. *Ec.* 9: 8.

Thou canst not make one hair white or
black. *Mat.* 5: 36.

His raiment became shining, exceeding
white as snow. *Mk.* 9: 3.

Entering into the sepulchre, they saw a
young man sitting on the right side, clothed
in a long white garment. *Mk.* 16: 5.

Lift up your eyes, and look on the fields;
for they are white already to harvest. *Jn.* 4: 35.

I saw a great white throne. *Re.* 20: 11.

See also
Snow; Wool.

Whitsunday

I will pour out my spirit unto you. *Pr.* 1: 23.

Until the spirit be poured upon us from on
high. *Is.* 32: 15.

I will pour my spirit upon thy seed, and my
blessing upon thine offspring. *Is.* 44: 3.

I will pray the Father, and he shall give you
another Comforter, that he may abide with
you for ever. *Jn.* 14: 16.

When the Comforter is come, whom I will
send unto you from the Father, even the Spirit
of truth, which proceedeth from the Father,
he shall testify of me. *Jn.* 15: 26.

It is expedient for you that I go away: for
if I go not away, the Comforter will not come
unto you. *Jn.* 16: 7.

When he, the Spirit of truth, is come, he will
guide you into all truth. *Jn.* 16: 13.

Suddenly there came a sound from heaven
as of a rushing mighty wind, . . . And there
appeared unto them cloven tongues like as of

fire, and it sat upon each of them. *Ac.* 2: 2, 3.

They . . . began to speak with other tongues,
as the Spirit gave them utterance. *Ac.* 2: 4.

Repent, and be baptized every one of you
in the name of Jesus Christ for the remission
of sins, and ye shall receive the gift of the
Holy Ghost. *Ac.* 2: 38.

While Peter yet spake these words, the Holy
Ghost fell on all them which heard the word.
Ac. 10: 44.

On the Gentiles also was poured out the gift
of the Holy Ghost. *Ac.* 10: 45.

They heard them speak with tongues, and
magnify God. *Ac.* 10: 46.

See also
Pentecost.

Whole

Then shalt thou be pleased with the sacrifices of righteousness, with burnt offering and
whole burnt offering. *Ps.* 51: 19.

Let the whole earth be filled with his glory.
Ps. 72: 19.

The lot is cast into the lap; but the whole
disposing thereof is of the Lord. *Pr.* 16: 33.

Fear God, and keep his commandments: for
this is the whole duty of man. *Ec.* 12: 13.

The light of the body is the eye: if therefore thine eye be single, thy whole body shall
be full of light. *Mat.* 6: 22.

They that be whole need not a physician,
but they that are sick. *Mat.* 9: 12.

The kingdom of heaven is like unto leaven,
which a woman took, and hid in three measures of meal, till the whole was leavened. *Mat.*
13: 33.

As many as touched were made perfectly
whole. *Mat.* 14: 36.

Thy faith hath made thee whole; go in
peace, and be whole of thy plague. *Mk.* 5:
34.

If thy whole body therefore shall be full of
light, having no part dark, the whole shall
be full of light. *Lu.* 11: 36.

Wilt thou be made whole? *Jn.* 5: 6.

Jesus Christ maketh thee whole. *Ac.* 9: 34.

We know that the whole creation groaneth
and travaileth in pain together until now. *Ro.*
8: 22.

If the whole body were an eye, where were
the hearing? *1 Co.* 12: 17.

A perfect man. *Ep.* 4: 13.

Put on the whole armour of God, that ye
may be able to stand against the wiles of the
devil. *Ep.* 6: 11.

Ye are complete in him. *Col.* 2: 10.

The very God of peace sanctify you wholly;
and I pray God your whole spirit and soul
and body be preserved blameless. *1 Th.* 5: 23.

Meditate upon these things; give thyself
wholly to them. *1 Ti.* 4: 15.

Let patience have her perfect work, that ye
may be perfect and entire, wanting nothing.
Ja. 1: 4.

See also
All; Completion; Perfection.

Wickedness

So shalt thou put the evil away from the
midst of thee. *De.* 13: 5.

Keep thy tongue from evil, and thy lips
from speaking guile. *Ps.* 34: 13.

I have seen the wicked in great power, and spreading himself like a green bay tree. Yet he passed away, and, lo, he was not: yea, I sought him, but he could not be found. *Ps.* 37: 35, 36.

Depart from me, ye evil-doers. *Ps.* 119: 115.

Enter not into the path of the wicked, and go not in the way of evil men. Avoid it, pass not by it, turn from it, and pass away. *Pr.* 4: 14, 15.

Wickedness is an abomination to my lips. *Pr.* 8: 7.

Treasures of wickedness profit nothing. *Pr.* 10: 2.

As the whirlwind passeth, so is the wicked no more. *Pr.* 10: 25.

A wise man feareth, and departeth from evil. *Pr.* 14: 16.

There is no peace, saith the Lord, unto the wicked. *Is.* 48: 22.

Ye have plowed wickedness, ye have reaped iniquity. *Ho.* 10: 13.

Sufficient unto the day is the evil thereof. *Mat.* 6: 34.

Out of the heart proceed evil thoughts. *Mat.* 15: 19.

See also

Crime; Evil; Guile; Iniquity; Sin; Sinner; Transgression; Trespass; Ungodliness; Unrighteousness; Wrong.

Widow

Thou hast sent widows away empty, and the arms of the fatherless have been broken. *Jb.* 22: 9.

He evil entreateth the barren that beareth not: and doeth not good to the widow. *Jb.* 24: 21.

I caused the widow's heart to sing for joy. *Jb.* 29: 13.

If I . . . have caused the eyes of the widow to fail: . . . Then let mine arm fall from my shoulder blade. *Jb.* 31: 16, 22.

A father of the fatherless, and a judge of the widows, is God in his holy habitation. *Ps.* 68: 5.

The Lord . . . relieveth the fatherless and widow. *Ps.* 146: 9.

Ye devour widows' houses, and for a pretence make long prayers. *Mat.* 23: 14.

This poor widow hath cast more in, than all they which have cast into the treasury. *Mk.* 12: 43.

Honour widows that are widows indeed. *1 Ti.* 5: 3.

Pure religion and undefiled before God and the Father is this, To visit the fatherless and widows in their affliction, and to keep himself unspotted from the world. *Ja.* 1: 27.

Wife

The Lord God said, It is not good that the man should be alone; I will make him an help meet for him. *Ge.* 2: 18.

Thou shalt not covet thy neighbour's wife. *Ex.* 20: 17.

The wife of thy bosom. *De.* 13: 6.

Rejoice with the wife of thy youth. *Pr.* 5: 18.

Whoso findeth a wife findeth a good thing, and obtaineth favour of the Lord. *Pr.* 18: 22.

She will do him good and not evil all the days of her life. *Pr.* 31: 12.

Let none deal treacherously against the wife of his youth. *Mal.* 2: 15.

I have married a wife, and therefore I cannot come. *Lu.* 14: 20.

Art thou bound unto a wife? seek not to be loosed. Art thou loosed from a wife? seek not a wife. *1 Co.* 7: 27.

He that loveth his wife loveth himself. *Ep.* 5: 28.

So must their wives be grave, not slanderers, sober, faithful in all things. *1 Ti.* 3: 11.

Be in subjection to your own husbands; that, if any obey not the word, they also may without the word be won by the conversation of the wives. *1 Pe.* 3: 1.

Giving honour unto the wife, as unto the weaker vessel. *1 Pe.* 3: 7.

I John saw the holy city, new Jerusalem, coming down from God out of heaven, prepared as a bride adorned for her husband. *Re.* 21: 2.

Come hither, I will shew thee the bride, the Lamb's wife. *Re.* 21: 9.

See also

Marriage; Wedding.

Wilderness

We went through all that great and terrible wilderness. *De.* 1: 19.

He . . . causeth them to wander in a wilderness where there is no way. *Jb.* 12: 24.

He turneth rivers into a wilderness, and the watersprings into dry ground. *Ps.* 107: 33.

He turneth the wilderness into a standing water, and dry ground into watersprings. *Ps.* 107: 35.

Wild beasts of the desert shall lie there. *Is.* 13: 21.

Is this the man. . . . That made the world as a wilderness? *Is.* 14: 16, 17.

The wilderness and the solitary place shall be glad for them; and the desert shall rejoice, and blossom as the rose. *Is.* 35: 1.

The voice of him that crieth in the wilderness. *Is.* 40: 3.

Make straight in the desert a highway for our God. *Is.* 40: 3.

He will make her wilderness like Eden, and her desert like the garden of the Lord. *Is.* 51: 3.

O that I had in the wilderness a lodging place of wayfaring men; that I might leave my people, and go from them! for they be all adulterers, an assembly of treacherous men. *Je.* 9: 2.

Then was Jesus led up of the Spirit into the wilderness to be tempted of the devil. *Mat.* 4: 1.

What went ye out into the wilderness to see? *Mat.* 11: 7.

They wandered in deserts, and in mountains, and in dens and caves of the earth. *He.* 11: 38.

See also

Desert; Desolation; Solitude; Waste.

Will

Deliver me not over unto the will of mine enemies. *Ps.* 27: 12.

Thy will be done in earth as it is in heaven. *Mat.* 6: 10.

Father, if thou be willing, remove this cup

from me: nevertheless, not my will, but thine, be done. *Lu.* 22: 42.

My meat is to do the will of him that sent me, and to finish his work. *Jn.* 4: 34.

I seek not mine own will, but the will of the Father which hath sent me. *Jn.* 5: 30.

This is the Father's will which hath sent me, that of all which he hath given me I should lose nothing. *Jn.* 6: 39.

David . . . served his own generation by the will of God. *Ac.* 13: 36.

To will is present with me; but how to perform that which is good I find not. *Ro.* 7: 18.

It is not of him that willeth, nor of him that runneth, but of God that sheweth mercy. *Ro.* 9: 16.

According to the good pleasure of his will. *Ep.* 1: 5.

It is God which worketh in you both to will and to do of his good pleasure. *Ph.* 2: 13.

Which things have indeed a shew of wisdom in will worship, and humility, and neglecting of the body; not in any honour to the satisfying of the flesh. *Col.* 2: 23.

See also

Christ, Purpose of; Desire; Determination; God, Purpose of; God, Will of; Inclination; Purpose; Wish.

Will, Free

Why is light given to a man whose way is hid, and whom God hath hedged in? *Jb.* 3: 23.

Ho, every one that thirsteth, come ye to the waters, and he that hath no money; come ye, buy, and eat; yea, come, buy wine and milk without money and without price. *Is.* 55: 1.

Come unto me, all ye that labour and are heavy laden, and I will give you rest. *Mat.* 11: 28.

Him that cometh to me I will in no wise cast out. *Jn.* 6: 37.

Whosoever shall call on the name of the Lord shall be saved. *Ac.* 2: 21.

He that spared not his own Son, but delivered him up for us all, how shall he not with him also freely give us all things? *Ro.* 8: 32.

I will give unto him that is athirst of the fountain of the water of life freely. *Re.* 21: 6.

Let him that is athirst come. *Re.* 22: 17.

Whosoever will, let him take the water of life freely. *Re.* 22: 17.

See also

Freedom; Liberty.

Will, Good

Thou shalt love thy neighbour as thyself: I am the Lord. *Le.* 19: 18.

The good will of him that dwelt in the bush. *De.* 33: 16.

Teach me to do thy will; for thou art my God: thy spirit is good; lead me into the land of uprightness. *Ps.* 143: 10.

On earth peace, good will toward men. *Lu.* 2: 14.

The love of God is shed abroad in our hearts. *Ro.* 5: 5.

Be kindly affectioned one to another with brotherly love. *Ro.* 12: 10.

Now abideth faith, hope, charity, these three; but the greatest of these is charity. *1 Co.* 13: 13.

With good will doing service, as to the Lord, and not to men. *Ep.* 6: 7.

Some indeed preach Christ . . . of good will. *Ph.* 1: 15.

Let brotherly love continue. *He.* 13: 1.

Above all things have fervent charity among yourselves: for charity shall cover the multitude of sins. *1 Pe.* 4: 8.

He that loveth his brother abideth in the light. *1 Jn.* 2: 10.

This commandment have we from him, That he who loveth God love his brother also. *1 Jn.* 4: 21.

Mercy unto you, and peace, and love, be multiplied. *Jude* 1: 2.

See also

Beneficence; Benevolence; Charity; Christ, Compassion of; Christ, Goodness of; Christ, Grace of; Clemency; Compassion; Favor; Generosity; God, Compassion of; God, Favor of; God, Generosity of; God, Goodness of; God, Kindness of; Goodness; Grace; Humaneness; Humanity; Kindness.

Willingness

The people willingly offered themselves. *Ju.* 5: 2.

Know thou the God of thy father, and serve him with a perfect heart and with a willing mind. *1 Ch.* 28: 9.

Thy people shall be willing in the day of thy power. *Ps.* 110: 3.

She . . . worketh willingly with her hands. *Pr.* 31: 13.

The spirit indeed is willing, but the flesh is weak. *Mat.* 26: 41.

If I do this thing willingly, I have a reward: but if against my will, a dispensation of the gospel is committed unto me. *1 Co.* 9: 17.

We are . . . willing rather to be absent from the body, and to be present with the Lord. *2 Co.* 5: 8.

Feed the flock of God which is among you, taking the oversight thereof, not by constraint, but willingly. *1 Pe.* 5: 2.

See also

Readiness; Volunteer.

Wind

He was seen upon the wings of the wind. *2 S.* 22: 11.

The Lord was not in the wind. *1 K.* 19: 11.

O remember that my life is wind. *Jb.* 7: 7.

They are as . . . chaff that the storm carrieth away. *Jb.* 21: 18.

To make the weight for the winds. *Jb.* 28: 25.

Terrors are turned upon me: they pursue my soul as the wind. *Jb.* 30: 15.

The wind passeth, and cleanseth them. *Jb.* 37: 21.

He bringeth the wind out of his treasuries. *Ps.* 135: 7.

Who hath gathered the wind in his fists? *Pr.* 30: 4.

He that observeth the wind shall not sow. *Ec.* 11: 4.

A man shall be as an hiding place from the wind. *Is.* 32: 2.

Ephraim feedeth on wind, and followeth after the east wind. *Ho.* 12: 1.

What went ye out into the wilderness to see? A reed shaken with the wind? *Mat.* 11: 7.

The wind bloweth where it listeth: . . . so is every one that is born of the Spirit. *Jn.* 3: 8.

The prince of the power of the air. *Ep.* 2: 2.

That we henceforth be no more children, tossed to and fro, and carried about with every wind of doctrine. *Ep.* 4: 14.

See also

Air; Atmosphere; Storm; Tempest; Weather; Whirlwind.

Window

The same day were all the fountains of the great deep broken up, and the windows of heaven were opened. *Ge.* 7: 11.

He said, Open the window eastward. And he opened it. Then Elisha said, Shoot. And he shot. And he said, The arrow of the Lord's deliverance. *2 K.* 13: 17.

At the window of my house I looked through my casement. *Pr.* 7: 6.

Who are these that fly as a cloud, and as the doves to their windows? *Is.* 60: 8.

Death is come up into our windows. *Je.* 9: 21.

His windows being open in his chamber toward Jerusalem, he kneeled upon his knees three times a day, and prayed. *Da.* 6: 10.

Prove me now herewith, saith the Lord of hosts, if I will not open you the windows of heaven, and pour you out a blessing, that there shall not be room enough to receive it. *Mal.* 3: 10.

See also

Life, Frontage of.

Wine

Wine, which cheereth God and man. *Ju.* 9: 13.

Wine is a mocker, strong drink is raging. *Pr.* 20: 1.

Look not thou upon the wine when it is red. *Pr.* 23: 31.

Give strong drink unto him that is ready to perish, and wine unto those that be of heavy hearts. *Pr.* 31: 6.

Let him drink, and forget his poverty, and remember his misery no more. *Pr.* 31: 7.

Thy love is better than wine. *S. of S.* 1: 2.

No man putteth new wine into old bottles. *Lu.* 5: 37.

No man having drunk old wine straightway desireth new. *Lu.* 5: 39.

These men are full of new wine. *Ac.* 2: 13.

Drink no longer water, but use a little wine for thy stomach's sake and thine often infirmities. *1 Ti.* 5: 23.

When we walked in . . . excess of wine. *1 Pe.* 4: 3.

See also

Christ, the Vine; Drunkenness; Grape; Intoxication.

Wing

God created . . . every winged fowl after his kind. *Ge.* 1: 21.

I bare you on eagles' wings, and brought you unto myself. *Ex.* 19: 4.

As an eagle stirreth up her nest, fluttereth over her young, spreadeth abroad her wings, taketh them, beareth them on her wings: So the Lord alone did lead him. *De.* 32: 11, 12.

He was seen upon the wings of the wind. *2 S.* 22: 11.

Gavest thou the goodly wings unto the peacocks? or wings and feathers unto the ostrich? *Jb.* 39: 13.

Doth the hawk fly by thy wisdom? *Jb.* 39: 26.

Hide me under the shadow of thy wings. *Ps.* 17: 8.

He did fly upon the wings of the wind. *Ps.* 18: 10.

Oh that I had wings like a dove! for then would I fly away and be at rest. *Ps.* 55: 6.

In the shadow of thy wings will I make my refuge. *Ps.* 57: 1.

In the shadow of thy wings will I rejoice. *Ps.* 63: 7.

Yet is their strength labour and sorrow; for it is soon cut off, and we fly away. *Ps.* 90: 10.

If I take the wings of the morning, and dwell in the uttermost parts of the sea; Even there shall thy hand lead me. *Ps.* 139: 9, 10.

Riches certainly make themselves wings; they fly away as an eagle toward heaven. *Pr.* 23: 5.

They that wait upon the Lord shall renew their strength; they shall mount up with wings as eagles. *Is.* 40: 31.

Unto you that fear my name shall the Sun of righteousness arise with healing in his wings. *Mal.* 4: 2.

How often would I have gathered thy children together, even as a hen gathereth her chickens under her wings, and ye would not. *Mat.* 23: 37.

See also

Bird; Flight.

Winter

While the earth remaineth, seedtime and harvest, and cold and heat, and summer and winter, and day and night shall not cease. *Ge.* 8: 22.

He saith to the snow, Be thou on the earth. *Jb.* 37: 6.

Hast thou entered into the treasures of the snow? *Jb.* 38: 22.

Thou hast set all the borders of the earth: thou hast made summer and winter. *Ps.* 74: 17.

He giveth snow like wool: he scattereth the hoarfrost like ashes. He casteth forth his ice like morsels: who can stand before his cold? *Ps.* 147: 16, 17.

The winter is past. *S. of S.* 2: 11.

I will smite the winter house with the summer house. *Am.* 3: 15.

Pray ye that your flight be not in the winter. *Mat.* 24: 20.

It was winter. *Jn.* 10: 22.

It may be that I will abide, yea, and winter with you. *1 Co.* 16: 6.

Do thy diligence to come before winter. *2 Ti.* 4: 21.

See also

Cold; Snow.

Wisdom

So teach us to number our days, that we may apply our hearts unto wisdom. *Ps.* 90: 12.

The fear of the Lord is the beginning of wisdom. *Ps.* 111: 10.

Length of days is in her right hand; and in her left hand riches and honour. *Pr. 3: 16.*

Her ways are ways of pleasantness, and all her paths are peace. *Pr. 3: 17.*

She is a tree of life to them that lay hold upon her: and happy is every one that retaineth her. *Pr. 3: 18.*

The wise shall inherit glory. *Pr. 3: 35.*

She crieth at the gates, at the entry of the city, at the coming in at the doors. *Pr. 8: 3.*

Wisdom is better than rubies. *Pr. 8: 11.*

Blessed is the man that heareth me, watching daily at my gates, waiting at the posts of my doors. *Pr. 8: 34.*

Wisdom hath builded her house, she hath hewn out her seven pillars. *Pr. 9: 1.*

God hath chosen the foolish things of the world to confound the wise; and God hath chosen the weak things of the world to confound the things that are mighty. *1 Co. 1: 27.*

We speak the wisdom of God in a mystery, even the hidden wisdom, which God ordained before the world unto our glory: Which none of the princes of this world knew: for had they known it, they would not have crucified the Lord of glory. *1 Co. 2: 7, 8.*

The wisdom of this world is foolishness with God. *1 Co. 3: 19.*

If any of you lack wisdom, let him ask of God, that giveth to all men liberally, and upbraideth not; and it shall be given him. *Ja. 1: 5.*

See also

Brain; Christ, Knowledge of; Christ, Mind of; Christ, Wisdom of; Doctor; Enlightenment; God, Knowledge of; God, Wisdom of; Intelligence; Knowledge; Learning; Mind; Perception; Sage; Understanding.

Wish

My desire is, that the Almighty would answer me. *Jb. 31: 35.*

They have more than heart could wish. *Ps. 73: 7.*

He gave them their own desire. *Ps. 78: 29.*

The desire accomplished is sweet to the soul. *Pr. 13: 19.*

The eyes of a fool are in the ends of the earth. *Pr. 17: 24.*

The Son quickeneth whom he will. *Jn. 5: 21.*

This is the Father's will which hath sent me, that of all which he hath given me I should lose nothing. *Jn. 6: 39.*

If ye abide in me, and my words abide in you, ye shall ask what ye will, and it shall be done unto you. *Jn. 15: 7.*

This also we wish, even your perfection. *2 Co. 13: 9.*

Let us not be desirous of vain glory. *Ga. 5: 26.*

I wish above all things that thou mayest prosper and be in health, even as thy soul prospereth. *3 Jn. 1: 2.*

See also

Desire; Hope; Longing; Petition; Request; Yearning.

Withdrawal

Lest peradventure the people repent when they see war, and they return to Egypt. *Ex. 13: 17.*

What man is there that is fearful and faint-hearted? let him go and return unto his house. *De. 20: 8.*

If God will not withdraw his anger, the proud helpers do stoop under him. *Jb. 9: 13.*

Withdraw thine hand far from me: and let not thy dread make me afraid. *Jb. 13: 21.*

He withdraweth not his eyes from the righteous. *Jb. 36: 7.*

Remove thy foot from evil. *Pr. 4: 27.*

Withdraw thy foot from thy neighbour's house; lest he be weary of thee, and so hate thee. *Pr. 25: 17.*

From this withdraw not thine hand: for he that feareth God shall come forth of them all. *Ec. 7: 18.*

Thy sun shall no more go down; neither shall thy moon withdraw itself: for the Lord God shall be thine everlasting light, and the days of thy mourning shall be ended. *Is. 60: 20.*

The earth shall quake before them; the heavens shall tremble: the sun and the moon shall be dark, and the stars shall withdraw their shining. *Jo. 2: 10.*

Withdraw yourselves from every brother that walketh disorderly. *2 Th. 3: 6.*

Perverse disputings of men of corrupt minds, and destitute of the truth, supposing that gain is godliness: from such withdraw thyself. *1 Ti. 6: 5.*

See also

Departure; Parting; Removal; Retreat; Subtraction.

Withering

His leaf also shall not wither; and whatsoever he doeth shall prosper. *Ps. 1: 3.*

In the morning it flourisheth, and groweth up; in the evening it is cut down, and withereth. *Ps. 90: 6.*

My heart is smitten, and withered like grass; so that I forget to eat my bread. *Ps. 102: 4.*

My days are like a shadow that declineth; and I am withered like grass. *Ps. 102: 11.*

The hay is withered away, the grass faileth, there is no green thing. *Is. 15: 6.*

The grass withereth, the flower fadeth: because the spirit of the Lord bloweth upon it: surely the people is grass. *Is. 40: 7.*

The vine is dried up, and the fig tree languisheth; the pomegranate tree, the palm tree also, the apple tree, even all the trees of the field, are withered: because joy is withered away from the sons of men. *Jo. 1: 12.*

There was a man which had his hand withered. And they asked him, saying, Is it lawful to heal on the sabbath days? *Mat. 12: 10.*

Some fell upon a rock; and as soon as it was sprung up, it withered away, because it lacked moisture. *Lu. 8: 6.*

See also

Atrophy; Decay.

Withholding

I also withheld thee from sinning against me. *Ge. 20: 6.*

He withholdeth the waters, and they dry up. *Jb. 12: 15.*

Withhold not thou thy tender mercies from me, O Lord: let thy lovingkindness and thy truth continually preserve me. *Ps. 40: 11.*

No good thing will he withhold from them that walk uprightly. *Ps.* 84: 11.

Withhold not correction from the child: for if thou beatest him with the rod, he shall not die. *Pr.* 23: 13.

A fool uttereth all his mind: but a wise man keepeth it in till afterwards. *Pr.* 29: 11.

I withheld not my heart from any joy. *Ec.* 2: 10.

In the morning sow thy seed, and in the evening withhold not thine hand. *Ec.* 11: 6.

Will he reserve his anger for ever? *Je.* 3: 5.

Thou hast kept the good wine until now. *Jn.* 2: 10.

See also

Reserve; Store.

Witness

Thou shalt not bear false witness against thy neighbour. *Ex.* 20: 16.

Thou shalt not raise a false report. *Ex.* 23: 1.

My witness is in heaven, and my record is on high. *Jb.* 16: 19.

A faithful witness will not lie: but a false witness will utter lies. *Pr.* 14: 5.

Ye are my witnesses, saith the Lord. *Is.* 43: 10.

I have given him for a witness to the people. *Is.* 55: 4.

I have set watchmen upon thy walls, O Jerusalem, which shall never hold their peace day nor night. *Is.* 62: 6.

Go home to thy friends, and tell them how great things the Lord hath done for thee, and hath had compassion on thee. *Mk.* 5: 19.

The people stood beholding. *Lu.* 23: 35.

The Pharisees therefore said unto him, Thou bearest record of thyself; thy record is not true. *Jn.* 8: 13.

Though I bear record of myself, yet my record is true. *Jn.* 8: 14.

Ye shall be witnesses unto me. *Ac.* 1: 8.

Go, stand and speak in the temple to the people all the words of this life. *Ac.* 5: 20.

He left not himself without witness. *Ac.* 14: 17.

Be not afraid, but speak, and hold not thy peace. *Ac.* 18: 9.

I take you to record this day, that I am pure from the blood of all men. *Ac.* 20: 26.

I . . . came not with excellency of speech or of wisdom. *1 Co.* 2: 1.

There are, it may be, so many kinds of voices in the world, and none of them is without signification. *1 Co.* 14: 10.

Falling down on his face he will worship God, and report that God is in you of a truth. *1 Co.* 14: 25.

I call God for a record upon my soul. *2 Co.* 1: 23.

God is my record, how greatly I long after you. *Ph.* 1: 8.

Among whom ye shine as lights in the world. *Ph.* 2: 15.

This witness is true. *Tit.* 1: 13.

Adorn the doctrine of God our Saviour in all things. *Tit.* 2: 10.

These things speak, and exhort, and rebuke with all authority. *Tit.* 2: 15.

Wherefore, seeing we also are compassed about with so great a cloud of witnesses, let us lay aside every weight, and the sin which doth so easily beset us, and let us run with patience the race that is set before us. *He.* 12: 1.

Be ready always to give an answer to every man that asketh you a reason of the hope that is in you. *1 Pe.* 3: 15.

Testifying that this is the true grace of God wherein ye stand. *1 Pe.* 5: 12.

We . . . were eyewitnesses of his majesty. *2 Pe.* 1: 16.

The prophecy came not in old time by the will of man: but holy men of God spake as they were moved by the Holy Ghost. *2 Pe.* 1: 21.

There are three that bear record in heaven, the Father, the Word, and the Holy Ghost: and these three are one. *1 Jn.* 5: 7.

There are three that bear witness in earth, the spirit, and the water, and the blood: and these three agree in one. *1 Jn.* 5: 8.

See also

Christ, Witness of; Evidence; God, Evidence of; God, Witness of; Proof; Sign; Token.

Woe

The sorrows of hell compassed me about; the snares of death prevented me. *2 S.* 22: 6.

Woe unto them that call evil good, and good evil. *Is.* 5: 20.

Woe to them that go down to Egypt for help: and stay on horses, and trust in chariots, because they are many; and in horsemen, because they are very strong; but they look not unto the Holy One of Israel, neither seek the Lord! *Is.* 31: 1.

Woe to them that are at ease in Zion. *Am.* 6: 1.

Woe to them that devise iniquity! *Mi.* 2: 1.

Woe unto the world because of offences! for it must needs be that offences come; but woe to that man by whom the offence cometh! *Mat.* 18: 7.

Woe unto you, scribes and Pharisees, hypocrites! *Mat.* 23: 13.

Woe unto that man by whom the Son of man is betrayed! *Mat.* 26: 24.

Yea, a sword shall pierce through thy own soul. *Lu.* 2: 35.

Woe unto you, when all men speak well of you! *Lu.* 6: 26.

Daughters of Jerusalem, weep not for me, but weep for yourselves, and for your children. *Lu.* 23: 28.

Woe is unto me, if I preach not the gospel! *1 Co.* 9: 16.

See also

Christ, Sorrow of; Depression; Gloom; Grief; Lamentation; Melancholy; Mourning; Sadness; Sorrow; Tear; Unhappiness; Weeping.

Wolf

The wolf also shall dwell with the lamb. *Is.* 11: 6.

The wolf and the lamb shall feed together, and the lion shall eat straw like the bullock. *Is.* 65: 25.

Her princes in the midst thereof are like wolves ravening the prey, to shed blood, and to destroy souls, to get dishonest gain. *Eze.* 22: 27.

Her princes within her are roaring lions;
her judges are evening wolves. *Zph.* **3: 3.**

Beware of false prophets, which come to you
in sheep's clothing, but inwardly they are
ravening wolves. *Mat.* **7: 15.**

I send you forth as sheep in the midst of
wolves. *Mat.* **10: 16.**

He that is an hireling, and not the shepherd,
whose own the sheep are not, seeth the wolf
coming, and leaveth the sheep, and fleeth: and
the wolf catcheth them, and scattereth the
sheep. *Jn.* **10: 12.**

Woman

The rib, which the Lord God had taken
from man, made he a woman, and brought her
unto the man. *Ge.* **2: 22.**

This is now bone of my bones, and flesh of
my flesh: she shall be called Woman, because
she was taken out of Man. *Ge.* **2: 23.**

Eve . . . was the mother of all living. *Ge.*
3: 20.

I am weary of my life because of the daughters of Heth. *Ge.* **27: 46.**

Man that is born of a woman is of few
days, and full of trouble. *Jb.* **14: 1.**

Fear took hold upon them there, and pain,
as of a woman in travail. *Ps.* **48: 6.**

Keep thee from the evil woman, from the
flattery of the tongue of a strange woman. *Pr.*
6: 24.

It is better to dwell in the wilderness, than
with a contentious and an angry woman. *Pr.*
21: 19.

A strange woman is a narrow pit. *Pr.* **23: 27.**

A continual dropping in a very rainy day
and a contentious woman are alike. *Pr.* **27: 15.**

Favour is deceitful, and beauty is vain: but
a woman that feareth the Lord, she shall be
praised. *Pr.* **31: 30.**

Whosoever looketh on a woman to lust after
her hath committed adultery with her already in his heart. *Mat.* **5: 28.**

The head of every man is Christ; and the
head of the woman is the man; and the head
of Christ is God. *1 Co.* **11: 3.**

A man . . . is the image and glory of God:
but the woman is the glory of the man. *1 Co.*
11: 7.

The man is not of the woman; but the
woman of the man. *1 Co.* **11: 8.**

Neither was the man created for the woman;
but the woman for the man. *1 Co.* **11: 9.**

As the woman is of the man, even so is the
man also by the woman; but all things of God.
1 Co. **11: 12.**

Let your women keep silence in the churches:
for it is not permitted unto them to speak. *1
Co.* **14: 34.**

See also
Female; Sex; Woman, the Virtuous.

Woman, the Virtuous

All the city of my people doth know that
thou art a virtuous woman. *Ru.* **3: 11.**

A gracious woman retaineth honour. *Pr.*
11: 16.

A virtuous woman is a crown to her husband. *Pr.* **12: 4.**

Every wise woman buildeth her house. *Pr.*
14: 1.

Who can find a virtuous woman? for her

price is far above rubies. *Pr.* **31: 10.**

She will do him good and not evil all the
days of her life. *Pr.* **31: 12.**

She riseth also while it is yet night, and
giveth meat to her household, and a portion to
her maidens. *Pr.* **31: 15.**

She stretcheth out her hand to the poor;
yea, she reacheth forth her hands to the needy.
Pr. **31: 20.**

Her children arise up, and call her blessed;
her husband also, and he praiseth her. *Pr.* **31: 28.**

A woman that feareth the Lord, she shall
be praised. *Pr.* **31: 30.**

The Lord is with thee: blessed art thou
among women. *Lu.* **1: 28.**

This woman was full of good works and
almsdeeds which she did. *Ac.* **9: 36.**

See also
Woman.

Womb

Let the day perish wherein I was born, and
the night in which it was said, There is a
man child conceived. *Jb.* **3: 3.**

Did not he that made me in the womb make
him? and did not one fashion us in the womb?
Jb. **31: 15.**

Out of whose womb came the ice? and the
hoary frost of heaven, who hath gendered it?
Jb. **38: 29.**

He travaileth with iniquity, and hath conceived mischief, and brought forth falsehood. *Ps.* **7: 14.**

Thou art he that took me out of the womb.
Ps. **22: 9.**

I was shapen in iniquity; and in sin did
my mother conceive me. *Ps.* **51: 5.**

Thy people shall be willing in the day of
thy power, in the beauties of holiness from
the womb of the morning: thou hast the dew
of thy youth. *Ps.* **110: 3.**

There are three things that are never satisfied, yea, four things say not, It is enough:
The grave; and the barren womb; the earth
that is not filled with water; and the fire that
saith not, It is enough. *Pr.* **30: 15, 16.**

When lust hath conceived, it bringeth forth
sin: and sin, when it is finished, bringeth forth
death. *Ja.* **1: 15.**

See also
Birth.

Wonder

The great temptations which thine eyes have
seen, the signs, and those great miracles. *De.*
29: 3.

From him cometh my salvation. *Ps.* **62: 1.**

Open thou mine eyes, that I may behold
wondrous things out of thy law. *Ps.* **119: 18.**

Such knowledge is too wonderful for me; it
is high, I cannot attain unto it. *Ps.* **139: 6.**

There be three things which are too wonderful for me, yea, four which I know not:
The way of an eagle in the air; the way of a
serpent upon a rock; the way of a ship in the
midst of the sea; and the way of a man with a
maid. *Pr.* **30: 18, 19.**

Behold, I and the children whom the Lord
hath given me are for signs and for wonders
in Israel. *Is.* **8: 18.**

His name shall be called Wonderful. *Is.* **9: 6.**

All they that heard it wondered at those

things which were told them by the shepherds. *Lu.* 2: 18.

All bare him witness, and wondered at the gracious words which proceeded out of his mouth. *Lu.* 4: 22.

See also

Admiration; Amazement; Astonishment; Marvel; Miracle; Sign; Token.

Wood

Let them be hewers of wood and drawers of water unto all the congregation. *Jos.* 9: 21.

If thou be a great people, then get thee up to the wood country. *Jos.* 17: 15.

Then shall the trees of the wood sing out at the presence of the Lord, because he cometh to judge the earth. *1 Ch.* 16: 33.

He esteemeth iron as straw, and brass as rotten wood. *Jb.* 41: 27.

Then shall all the trees of the wood rejoice. *Ps.* 96: 12.

Where no wood is, there the fire goeth out: so where there is no talebearer, the strife ceaseth. *Pr.* 26: 20.

As coals are to burning coals, and wood to fire; so is a contentious man to kindle strife. *Pr.* 26: 21.

They shall dwell safely in the wilderness, and sleep in the woods. *Eze.* 34: 25.

Go up to the mountain, and bring wood, and build the house; and I will take pleasure in it, and I will be glorified. *Hag.* 1: 8.

If any man build upon this foundation gold, silver, precious stones, wood, hay, stubble; Every man's work shall be made manifest: for the day shall declare it, because it shall be revealed by fire. *1 Co.* 3: 12, 13.

See also

Forest; Tree.

Wool

He giveth snow like wool. *Ps.* 147: 16.

She seeketh wool, and flax, and worketh willingly with her hands. *Pr.* 31: 13.

Though your sins be as scarlet, they shall be as white as snow; though they be red like crimson, they shall be as wool. *Is.* 1: 18.

The moth shall eat them up like a garment, and the worm shall eat them like wool. *Is.* 51: 8.

Word

A word spoken in due season, how good is it! *Pr.* 15: 23.

The words of the pure are pleasant words. *Pr.* 15: 26.

The words of a man's mouth are as deep waters, and the wellspring of wisdom as a flowing brook. *Pr.* 18: 4.

Be not rash with thy mouth. *Ec.* 5: 2.

A fool's voice is known by multitude of words. *Ec.* 5: 3.

I am a man of unclean lips. *Is.* 6: 5.

Trust ye not in lying words. *Je.* 7: 4.

Take with you words. *Ho.* 14: 2.

Every idle word that men shall speak, they shall give account thereof in the day of judgment. *Mat.* 12: 36.

By thy words thou shalt be justified, and by thy words thou shalt be condemned. *Mat.* 12: 37.

Ministers of the word. *Lu.* 1: 2.

Blessed are they that hear the word of God, and keep it. *Lu.* 11: 28.

We will give ourselves continually to prayer, and to the ministry of the word. *Ac.* 6: 4.

Remember the words of the Lord Jesus. *Ac.* 20: 35.

The kingdom of God is not in word, but in power. *1 Co.* 4: 20.

I had rather speak five words with my understanding, that by my voice I might teach others also, than ten thousand words in an unknown tongue. *1 Co.* 14: 19.

God . . . hath committed unto us the word of reconciliation. *2 Co.* 5: 19.

Let no man deceive you with vain words. *Ep.* 5: 6.

Comfort your hearts, and stablish you in every good word and work. *2 Th.* 2: 17.

Be thou an example of the believers, in word, in conversation. *1 Ti.* 4: 12.

Hold fast the form of sound words. *2 Ti.* 1: 13.

Preach the word; be instant in season, out of season. *2 Ti.* 4: 2.

Receive with meekness the engrafted word. *Ja.* 1: 21.

Be ye doers of the word, and not hearers only. *Ja.* 1: 22.

See also

Christ, Word of; Commandment; Declaration; Expression; God, Voice of; God, Word of; Mouth; Order; Promise; Report; Tidings; Tongue; Utterance.

Work

The men did the work faithfully. *2 Ch.* 34: 12.

Establish thou the work of our hands upon us. *Ps.* 90: 17.

Thou shalt eat the labour of thine hands. *Ps.* 128: 2.

Wist ye not that I must be about my Father's business? *Lu.* 2: 49.

The labourer is worthy of his hire. *Lu.* 10: 7.

Therefore we conclude that a man is justified by faith without the deeds of the law. *Ro.* 3: 28.

Not slothful in business. *Ro.* 12: 11.

Workers together with him. *2 Co.* 6: 1.

In labours more abundant. *2 Co.* 11: 23.

When I am weak, then am I strong. *2 Co.* 12: 10.

Not according to our works, but according to his own purpose and grace. *2 Ti.* 1: 9.

Repentance from dead works. *He.* 6: 1.

What doth it profit, my brethren, though a man say he hath faith, and have not works? *Ja.* 2: 14.

Can faith save him? *Ja.* 2: 14.

I know thy works, and charity, and service, and faith, and thy patience, and thy works; and the last to be more than the first. *Re.* 2: 19.

Their works do follow them. *Re.* 14: 13.

See also

Chore; Christ, Work of; Drudgery; Duty; Employee; Employer; God, Work of; Labor; Occupation; Operation; Service; Task; Toil; Travail; Undertaking.

Workmanship

A man of Tyre, skilful to work in gold, and

in silver, in brass, in iron, in stone, and in timber, in purple, in blue, and in fine linen, and in crimson; also to grave any manner of graving. *2 Ch.* **2: 14.**

Their idols are silver and gold, the work of men's hands. *Ps.* **115: 4.**

She maketh fine linen, and selleth it. *Pr.* **31: 24.**

Whatsoever thy hand findeth to do, do it with thy might. *Ec.* **9: 10.**

The workman melteth a graven image, and the goldsmith spreadeth it over with gold. *Is.* **40: 19.**

Mine elect shall long enjoy the work of their hands. They shall not labour in vain. *Is.* **65: 22, 23.**

James the son of Zebedee, and John his brother, in a ship with Zebedee their father, mending their nets. *Mat.* **4: 21.**

Jesus answered them, My Father worketh hitherto, and I work. *Jn.* **5: 17.**

Simon Peter saith unto them, I go a fishing. They say unto him, We also go with thee. *Jn.* **21: 3.**

Hath not the potter power over the clay? *Ro.* **9: 21.**

We are labourers together with God. *1 Co.* **3: 9.**

We are his workmanship. *Ep.* **2: 10.**

Walk worthy of the vocation wherewith ye are called. *Ep.* **4: 1.**

Work out your own salvation with fear and trembling. *Ph.* **2: 12.**

Neglect not the gift that is in thee. *1 Ti.* **4: 14.**

See also
Ability; Adept; Expert; Handiwork; Skill.

World

The earth is full of the goodness of the Lord. *Ps.* **33: 5.**

Sing unto God, ye kingdoms of the earth. *Ps.* **68: 32.**

He hath set the world in their heart. *Ec.* **3: 11.**

Let all the earth keep silence before him. *Hab.* **2: 20.**

The care of this world, and the deceitfulness of riches, choke the word. *Mat.* **13: 22.**

The children of this world are in their generation wiser than the children of light. *Lu.* **16: 8.**

Ye are of this world; I am not of this world. *Jn.* **8: 23.**

If the world hate you, ye know that it hated me, before it hated you. *Jn.* **15: 18.**

I pray for them: I pray not for the world. *Jn.* **17: 9.**

They that use this world as not abusing it. *1 Co.* **7: 31.**

Love not the world, neither the things that are in the world. *1 Jn.* **2: 15.**

If any man love the world, the love of the Father is not in him. *1 Jn.* **2: 15.**

See also
Christ, the Creator; Creation; Creator; Earth; Globe; God, the Creator; Universality; Universe.

World, End of

All the ends of the world shall remember and turn unto the Lord. *Ps.* **22: 27.**

The harvest is the end of the world. *Mat.* **13: 39.**

He that shall endure unto the end, the same shall be saved. *Mat.* **24: 13.**

Be ye also ready: for in such an hour as ye think not the Son of man cometh. *Mat.* **24: 44.**

I am with you alway, even unto the end of the world. *Mat.* **28: 20.** ..

He shall receive . . . in the world to come eternal life. *Mk.* **10: 30.**

They . . . use this world, as not abusing it: for the fashion of this world passeth way. *1 Co.* **7: 31.**

Then cometh the end. *1 Co.* **15: 24.**

See also
Judgment, the Last; World, New.

World, New

The former things are come to pass, and new things do I declare. *Is.* **42: 9.**

For, behold, I create new heavens and a new earth: for the former shall not be remembered, nor come into mind. *Is.* **65: 17.**

I will not drink henceforth of this fruit of the vine, until that day when I drink it new with you in my Father's kingdom. *Mat.* **26: 29.**

Old things are passed away; behold, all things are become new. *2 Co.* **5: 17.**

Looking for and hasting unto the coming of the day of God. *2 Pe.* **3: 12.**

We, according to his promise, look for new heavens and a new earth, wherein dwelleth righteousness. *2 Pe.* **3: 13.**

New Jerusalem, which cometh down out of heaven from my God. *Re.* **3: 12.**

The kingdoms of this world are become the kingdoms of our Lord, and of his Christ. *Re.* **11: 15.**

I saw a new heaven and a new earth: for the first heaven and the first earth were passed away. *Re.* **21: 1.**

See also
Age, the Golden; Future; Kingdom, the Coming; Land, the Promised; Millennium; Newness; World, End of.

Worldliness

Thou shalt not follow a multitude to do evil. *Ex.* **23: 2.**

They are inclosed in their own fat: with their mouth they speak proudly. *Ps.* **17: 10.**

These are the ungodly, that prosper in the world; they increase in riches. *Ps.* **73: 12.**

They are wise to do evil, but to do good they have no knowledge. *Je.* **4: 22.**

Pride, fulness of bread, and abundance of idleness was in her and in her daughters, neither did she strengthen the hand of the poor and needy. *Eze.* **16: 49.**

For where your treasure is, there will your heart be also. *Mat.* **6: 21.**

The wisdom of this world is foolishness with God. *1 Co.* **3: 19.**

The god of this world hath blinded the minds of them which believe not. *2 Co.* **4: 4.**

In time past ye walked according to the course of this world, according to the prince of the power of the air. *Ep.* **2: 2.**

After the commandments and doctrines of men. *Col.* **2: 22.**

Set your attention on things above, not on things on the earth. *Col.* **3: 2.**

The love of money is the root of all evil. *1 Ti.* **6: 10.**

Lovers of pleasures more than lovers of God. *2 Ti.* **3: 4.**

Demas hath forsaken me, having loved this present world. *2 Ti.* **4: 10.**

This wisdom descendeth not from above, but is earthly, sensual, devilish. *Ja.* **3: 15.**

Know ye not that the friendship of the world is enmity with God? *Ja.* **4: 4.**

All that is in the world, the lust of the flesh, and the lust of the eyes, and the pride of life, is not of the Father, but is of the world. *1 Jn.* **2: 16.**

They are of the world: therefore speak they of the world, and the world heareth them. *1 Jn.* **4: 5.**

Thou sayest, I am rich, and increased with goods, and have need of nothing. *Re.* **3: 17.**
See also
Acquisition; Mammon; Money; Secularism; Society; Ungodliness; Wealth.

Worm

I have said to corruption, Thou art my father: to the worm, Thou art my mother, and my sister. *Jb.* **17: 14.**

Though after my skin worms destroy this body, yet in my flesh shall I see God. *Jb.* **19: 26.**

The worm shall feed sweetly on him; he shall be no more remembered. *Jb.* **24: 20.**

The stars are not pure in his sight. How much less man, that is a worm? and the son of man, which is a worm? *Jb.* **25: 5, 6.**

I am a worm, and no man: a reproach of men, and despised of the people. *Ps.* **22: 6.**

The worm shall eat them like wool. *Is.* **51: 8.**

Their worm shall not die, neither shall their fire be quenched. *Is.* **66: 24.**

God prepared a worm when the morning rose the next day, and it smote the gourd that it withered. *Jon.* **4: 7.**

Worry

When he giveth quietness, who then can make trouble? *Jb.* **34: 29.**

Fret not thyself because of· him who prospereth in his way. *Ps.* **37: 7.**

Cast thy burden upon the Lord, and he shall sustain thee. *Ps.* **55: 22.**

The wicked . . . are not in trouble as other men: neither are they plagued like other men. *Ps.* **73: 3, 5.**

Take no thought for your life. *Mat.* **6: 25.**

Take therefore no thought for the morrow: for the morrow shall take thought for the things of itself. *Mat.* **6: 34.**

That which cometh upon me daily, the care of all the churches. *2 Co.* **11: 28.**

I suffer trouble, as an evil doer, even unto bonds; but the word of God is not bound. *2 Ti.* **2: 9.**

Casting all your care upon him; for he careth for you. *1 Pe.* **5: 7.**
See also
Anxiety; Care; Chagrin; Concern; Solicitude; Torment; Trial; Trouble; Vexation.

Worsening

He, that being often reproved hardeneth his neck, shall suddenly be destroyed. *Pr.* **29: 1.**

I will increase the famine upon you. *Eze.* **5: 16.**

He daily increaseth lies and desolation. *Ho.* **12: 1.**

The good man is perished out of the earth: and there is none upright among men. *Mi.* **7: 2.**

The rent is made worse. *Mat.* **9: 16.**

The last state of that man is worse than the first. *Mat.* **12: 45.**

By one man's disobedience many were made sinners. *Ro.* **5: 19.**
See also
Decline; Degeneration.

Worship

We took sweet counsel together, and walked unto the house of God in company. *Ps.* **55: 14.**

So will we render the calves of our lips. *Ho.* **14: 2.**

Thy graven images also will I cut off, . . . and thou shalt no more worship the work of thine hands. *Mi.* **5: 13.**

God is a Spirit: and they that worship him must worship him in spirit and in truth. *Jn.* **4: 23, 24.**

After the way which they call heresy, so worship I the God of my fathers. *Ac.* **24: 14.**

Though there be that are called gods, whether in heaven or in earth, . . . to us there is but one God, the Father. *1 Co.* **8: 5, 6.**

I bow my knees unto the Father of our Lord Jesus Christ. *Ep.* **3: 14.**

Speaking to yourselves in psalms and hymns and spiritual songs, singing and making melody in your heart to the Lord. *Ep.* **5: 19.**

We have an altar. *He.* **13: 10.**

Spiritual sacrifices, acceptable to God by Jesus Christ. *1 Pe.* **2: 5.**

I fell at his feet to worship him. *Re.* **19: 10.**
See also
Adoration; Awe; Christ, Worship of; God, Adoration of; God, Worship of; Honor; Respect; Reverence.

Worth

Do thou worthily. *Ru.* **4: 11.**

Now thou art worth ten thousand of us. *2 S.* **18: 3.**

Who can find a virtuous woman? for her price is far above rubies. *Pr.* **31: 10.**

The workman is worthy of his meat. *Mat.* **10: 10.**

A prophet is not without honour, save in his own country. *Mat.* **13: 57.**

What shall a man give in exchange for his soul? *Mk.* **8: 37.**

He that loveth his life shall lose it. *Jn.* **12: 25.**

What things were gain to me, those I counted loss for Christ. *Ph.* **3: 7.**

That ye might walk worthy of the Lord unto all pleasing. *Col.* **1: 10.**

We pray always for you, that our God would count you worthy of this calling. *2 Th.* **1: 11.**
See also
Appraisal; Excellence; Goodness; Helpfulness; Importance; Merit; Price; Value.

Worthlessness

Now ye are nothing. *Jb.* 6: 21.

Ye are all physicians of no value. *Jb.* 13: 4.

He fleeth also as a shadow, and continueth not. *Jb.* 14: 2.

They were children of fools, yea, children of base men: they were viler than the earth. *Jb.* 30: 8.

The wicked walk on every side, when the vilest men are exalted. *Ps.* 12: 8.

When he dieth he shall carry nothing away. *Ps.* 49: 17.

The heart of the wicked is little worth. *Pr.* 10: 20.

Riches profit not in the day of wrath. *Pr.* 11: 4.

It is naught, it is naught, saith the buyer. *Pr.* 20: 14.

The mean man shall be brought down, and the mighty man shall be humbled. *Is.* 5: 15.

Behold, they are all vanity; their works are nothing. *Is.* 41: 29.

Ye have sold yourselves for nought; and ye shall be redeemed without money. *Is.* 52: 3.

Wherefore do ye spend money for that which is not bread? *Is.* 55: 2.

Let not the rich man glory in his riches. *Je.* 9: 23.

I . . . will make them like vile figs, that cannot be eaten, they are so evil. *Je.* 29: 17.

See, O Lord, and consider; for I am become vile. *La.* 1: 11.

God said unto him, Thou fool, this night thy soul shall be required of thee: then whose shall those things be? *Lu.* 12: 20.

Thy money perish with thee. *Ac.* 8: 20.

Thou sayest, I am rich, and increased with goods, and have need of nothing; and knowest not that thou art wretched, and miserable, and poor, and blind, and naked. *Re.* 3: 17.

No man was found worthy to open and to read the book. *Re.* 5: 4.

See also

Fruitlessness; Uselessness; Vileness.

Wound

I kill, and I make alive; I wound, and I heal. *De.* 32: 39.

My wound is incurable without transgression. *Jb.* 34: 6.

I am poor and needy, and my heart is wounded within me. *Ps.* 109: 22.

He healeth the broken in heart, and bindeth up their wounds. *Ps.* 147: 3.

The words of a talebearer are as wounds. *Pr.* 18: 8.

Who hath wounds without cause? who hath redness of eyes? They that tarry long at the wine. *Pr.* 23: 29, 30.

Faithful are the wounds of a friend. *Pr.* 27: 6.

He was wounded for our transgressions, he was bruised for our iniquities. *Is.* 53: 5.

I will restore health unto thee, and I will heal thee of thy wounds. *Je.* 30: 17.

One shall say unto him, What are these wounds in thine hands? Then he shall answer, Those with which I was wounded in the house of my friends. *Zch.* 13: 6.

A certain man . . . fell among thieves, which stripped him of his raiment, and wounded him, and departed, leaving him half dead. *Lu.* 10: 30.

He . . . went to him, and bound up his wounds, pouring in oil and wine, and set him on his own beast, and brought him to an inn, and took care of him. *Lu.* 10: 33, 34.

See also

Harm; Hurt; Injury.

Wrath

Wrath bringeth the punishments of the sword, that ye may know there is a judgment. *Jb.* 19: 29.

Surely the wrath of men shall praise thee. *Ps.* 76: 10.

He that is soon angry dealeth foolishly. *Pr.* 14: 17.

A soft answer turneth away wrath. *Pr.* 15: 1.

Herod . . . was exceeding wroth, and sent forth, and slew all the children that were in Bethlehem. *Mat.* 2: 16.

O generation of vipers, who hath warned you to flee from the wrath to come? *Mat.* 3: 7.

When he had looked round about on them with anger, being grieved for the hardness of their hearts. *Mk.* 3: 5.

When Jesus saw it, he was much displeased, and said unto them, Suffer the little children to come unto me. *Mk.* 10: 14.

We all . . . were by nature the children of wrath. *Ep.* 2: 3.

Ye fathers, provoke not your children to wrath. *Ep.* 6: 4.

God hath not appointed us to wrath, but to obtain salvation by our Lord Jesus Christ. *1 Th.* 5: 9.

I will therefore that men pray every where, lifting up holy hands, without wrath and doubting. *1 Ti.* 2: 8.

The wrath of the Lamb. *Re.* 6: 16.

See also

Anger; Christ, Wrath of; Displeasure; Fury; God, Anger of; God, Wrath of; Indignation; Passion; Rage.

Wreck

The Lord sent out a great wind into the sea, and there was a mighty tempest in the sea, so that the ship was like to be broken. *Jon.* 1: 4.

Thou hadst cast me into the deep, in the midst of the seas. *Jon.* 2: 3.

It fell: and great was the fall of it. *Mat.* 7: 27.

There arose a great tempest in the sea, insomuch that the ship was covered with the waves: but he was asleep. *Mat.* 8: 24.

Lord, save us: we perish. *Mat.* 8: 25.

The ruin of that house was great. *Lu.* 6: 49.

Sirs, I perceive that this voyage will be with hurt and much damage, not only of the lading and ship, but also of our lives. *Ac.* 27: 10.

They ran the ship aground; and the forepart stuck fast, and remained unmoveable, but the hinder part was broken with the violence of the waves. *Ac.* 27: 41.

Paul . . . commanded that they which could swim should cast themselves first into the sea, and get to land: and the rest, some on boards, and some on broken pieces of the ship. *Ac.* 27: 43, 44.

Thrice I suffered shipwreck. *2 Co.* 11: 25.

Holding faith, and a good conscience; which

some having put away concerning faith have made shipwreck. *I Ti.* 1: 19.
See also
Ruin.

Wrestling
And Rachel said, With great wrestlings have I wrestled with my sister, and I have prevailed. *Ge.* 30: 8.
Jacob was left alone; and there wrestled a man with him until the breaking of the day. *Ge.* 32: 24.
Every man that striveth for the mastery is temperate in all things. *I Co.* 9: 25.
We wrestle not against flesh and blood, but against principalities, against powers, against the rulers of the darkness of this world, against spiritual wickedness in high places. *Ep.* 6: 12.
If a man also strive for masteries, yet is he not crowned, except he strive lawfully. *2 Ti.* 2: 5.

Wretchedness
Although affliction cometh not forth of the dust, neither doth trouble spring out of the ground; Yet man is born unto trouble, as the sparks fly upward. *Jb.* 5: 6, 7.
My life is spent with grief, and my years with sighing. *Ps.* 31: 10.
The sorrows of death compassed me, and the pains of hell gat hold upon me. *Ps.* 116: 3.
All his days are sorrows, and his travail grief; yea, his heart taketh not rest in the night. *Ec.* 2: 23.
All thy billows and thy waves passed over me. *Jon.* 2: 3.
O wretched man that I am! who shall deliver me from the body of this death? *Ro.* 7: 24.
Thou . . . knowest not that thou art wretched, and miserable, and poor, and blind, and naked. *Re.* 3: 17.
See also
Adversity; Affliction; Calamity; Depression; Misery; Misfortune; Poor; Poverty; Sadness; Tribulation; Trouble; Weeping; Woe.

Writing
He gave unto Moses . . . two tables of testimony, tables of stone, written with the finger of God. *Ex.* 31: 18.
They that handle the pen of the writer. *Ju.* 5: 14.
In the volume of the book it is written of me. *Ps.* 40: 7.
Let not mercy and truth forsake thee: . . . write them upon the table of thine heart. *Pr.* 3: 3.

I will put my law in their inward parts, and write it in their hearts. *Je.* 31: 33.
Write the vision, and make it plain upon tables, that he may run that readeth it. *Hab.* 2: 2.
He answered and said, It is written. *Mat.* 4: 4.
Rejoice, because your names are written in heaven. *Lu.* 10: 20.
Search the scriptures; . . . they are they which testify of me. *Jn.* 5: 39.
If ye believe not his writings, how shall ye believe my words? *Jn.* 5: 47.
Pilate answered, What I have written I have written. *Jn.* 19: 22.
There are also many other things which Jesus did, the which, if they should be written every one, I suppose that even the world itself could not contain the books that should be written. *Jn.* 21: 25.
I will write upon him the name of my God. *Re.* 3: 12.
Write, Blessed are the dead which die in the Lord from henceforth. *Re.* 14: 13.
Write, Blessed are they which are called unto the marriage supper of the Lamb. *Re.* 19: 9.
He said unto me, Write: for these words are true and faithful. *Re.* 21: 5.
See also
Author; Book; Epistle; Letter; Life, Book of; Scripture; Scroll.

Wrong
Against thee, thee only, have I sinned, and done this evil in thy sight: that thou mightest be justified when thou speakest, and be clear when thou judgest. *Ps.* 51: 4.
He that sinneth against me wrongeth his own soul. *Pr.* 8: 36.
Among my people are found wicked men: they lay wait, as he that setteth snares; they set a trap, they catch men. *Je.* 5: 26.
Woe unto him that buildeth his house by unrighteousness, and his chambers by wrong. *Je.* 22: 13.
Sirs, ye are brethren; why do ye wrong one to another? *Ac.* 7: 26.
Charity . . . is not easily provoked, thinketh no evil; Rejoiceth not in iniquity. *I Co.* 13: 4–6.
He that doeth wrong shall receive for the wrong which he hath done: and there is no respect of persons. *Col.* 3: 25.
See also
Crime; Error; Evil; Fault; Guile; Iniquity; Injustice; Sin; Sinner; Transgression; Trespass; Unrighteousness; Wickedness.

Y

Yea
Let your communication be, Yea, yea; Nay, nay: for whatsoever is more than these cometh of evil. *Mat.* 5: 37.
The Son of God, Jesus Christ, who was preached among you by us, . . . was not yea and nay, but in him was yea. *2 Co.* 1: 19.

All the promises of God in him are yea, and in him Amen, unto the glory of God by us. *2 Co.* 1: 20.
Above all things, my brethren, swear not, neither by heaven, neither by the earth, neither by any other oath: but let your yea be yea; and your nay, nay. *Ja.* 5: 12.

I am he that liveth, and was dead; and, behold, I am alive for evermore, Amen. *Re.* 1: 18.

Amen: blessing, and glory, and wisdom, and thanksgiving, and honour, and power, and might, be unto our God for ever and ever. Amen. *Re.* 7: 12.

See also
Amen; Oath.

Year

Days should speak, and multitude of years should teach wisdom. *Jb.* 32: 7.

Thou crownest the year with thy goodness. *Ps.* 65: 11.

Make us glad according to . . . the years wherein we have seen evil. *Ps.* 90: 15.

Thy years are throughout all generations. *Ps.* 102: 24.

The years of thy life shall be many. *Pr.* 4: 10.

I shall go softly all my years. *Is.* 38: 15.

To proclaim the acceptable year of the Lord. *Is.* 61: 2.

The year of my redeemed is come. *Is.* 63: 4.

I will bring . . . the year of their visitation. *Je.* 11: 23.

Revive thy work in the midst of the years. *Hab.* 3: 2.

Thou art the same, and thy years shall not fail. *He.* 1: 12.

Year, End of

The eternal God is thy refuge, and underneath are the everlasting arms. *De.* 33: 27.

Ye have not passed this way heretofore. *Jos.* 3: 4.

Samuel took a stone, and set it between Mizpeh and Shen, . . . saying, Hitherto hath the Lord helped us. *1 S.* 7: 12.

The days of our years are threescore years and ten. *Ps.* 90: 10.

At midnight I will rise to give thanks unto thee. *Ps.* 119: 62.

All the rivers run into the sea. *Ec.* 1: 7.

Thine ears shall hear a word behind thee, saying, This is the way, walk ye in it. *Is.* 30: 21.

Let not your heart be troubled. *Jn.* 14: 1.

Brethren, the time is short. *1 Co.* 7: 29.

The fashion of this world passeth away. *1 Co.* 7: 31.

Then cometh the end. *1 Co.* 15: 24.

Ye know not what shall be on the morrow. *Ja.* 4: 14.

Year, New

How old art thou? *Ge.* 47: 8.

It came to pass at the end of the four hundred and thirty years, even the selfsame day it came to pass, that all the hosts of the Lord went out from the land of Egypt. *Ex.* 12: 41.

As the days of heaven upon the earth. *De.* 11: 21.

Ye shall henceforth return no more that way. *De.* 17: 16.

As thy days, so shall thy strength be. *De.* 33: 25.

Ye have not passed this way heretofore. *Jos.* 3: 4.

Choose you this day whom ye will serve. *Jos.* 24: 15.

Hitherto hath the Lord helped us. *1 S.* 7: 12.

Whereas it was in thine heart to build an house unto my name, thou didst well. *1 K.* 8: 18.

My times are in thy hand. *Ps.* 31: 15.

I will go in the strength of the Lord. *Ps.* 71: 16.

Seek the Lord, and his strength: seek his face evermore. *Ps.* 105: 4.

Happy is the man that findeth wisdom. *Pr.* 3: 13.

The Lord shall be thy confidence, and shall keep thy foot from being taken. *Pr.* 3: 26.

Thou wilt keep him in perfect peace, whose mind is stayed on thee: because he trusteth in thee. *Is.* 26: 3.

Every valley shall be exalted, and every mountain and hill shall be made low: and the crooked shall be made straight, and the rough places plain: And the glory of the Lord shall be revealed. *Is.* 40: 4, 5.

Behold, the former things are come to pass, and new things do I declare. *Is.* 42: 9.

He hath sent me . . . To proclaim the acceptable year of the Lord. *Is.* 61: 1, 2.

They went every one straight forward. *Eze.* 10: 22.

Ye have built houses of hewn stone, but ye shall not dwell in them. *Am.* 5: 11.

He stedfastly set his face to go to Jerusalem. *Lu.* 9: 51.

Old things are passed away; behold, all things are become new. *2 Co.* 5: 17.

Behold, now is the accepted time. *2 Co.* 6: 2.

Redeeming the time, because the days are evil. *Ep.* 5: 16.

Forgetting those things which are behind, and reaching forth unto those things which are before. *Ph.* 3: 13.

Set your affection on things above, not on things on the earth. *Col.* 3: 2.

Let us go on unto perfection. *He.* 6: 1.

Things not seen as yet. *He.* 11: 7.

Thou art worthy to take the book, and to open the seals thereof. *Re.* 5: 9.

The books were opened. *Re.* 20: 12.

He that sat upon the throne said, Behold, I make all things new. *Re.* 21: 5.

Yearning

Lord, thou hast heard the desire of the humble. *Ps.* 10: 17.

One thing have I desired of the Lord, that will I seek after; that I may dwell in the house of the Lord all the days of my life. *Ps.* 27: 4.

Lord, all my desire is before thee. *Ps.* 38: 9.

My soul thirsteth for thee, my flesh longeth for thee in a dry and thirsty land, where no water is. *Ps.* 63: 1.

There is none upon earth that I desire beside thee. *Ps.* 73: 25.

My heart and my flesh crieth out for the living God. *Ps.* 84: 2.

He satisfieth the longing soul. *Ps.* 107: 9.

I longed for thy commandments. *Ps.* 119: 131.

My soul desired the firstripe fruit. *Mi.* 7: 1.

What I do thou knowest not now; but thou shalt know hereafter. *Jn.* 13: 7.

See also
Desire; God, Longing for; God, Thirst for; God, Yearning for; Hope; Hunger; Longing; Thirst.

Yellow

Though ye have lien among the pots, yet shall ye be as the wings of a dove covered with silver, and her feathers with yellow gold. *Ps.* 68: 13.

Yesterday

The God of your father spake unto me yesternight. *Ge.* 31: 29.

Hitherto hath the Lord helped us. *1 S.* 7: 12.

We are but of yesterday, and know nothing, because our days upon earth are a shadow. *Jb.* 8: 9.

A thousand years in thy sight are but as yesterday when it is past, and as a watch in the night. *Ps.* 90: 4.

Some have entertained angels unawares. *He.* 13: 2.

Yesterday, and to day, and for ever. *He.* 13: 8.

See also
Past; Time, Past.

Yield

God said, Let the earth bring forth grass, the herb yielding seed, and the fruit tree yielding fruit after his kind. *Ge.* 1: 11.

Yield yourselves unto the Lord, and enter into his sanctuary. *2 Ch.* 30: 8.

The wilderness yieldeth food for them and for their children. *Jb.* 24: 5.

Yielding pacifieth great offences. *Ec.* 10: 4.

Every good tree bringeth forth good fruit; but a corrupt tree bringeth forth evil fruit. *Mat.* 7: 17.

Jesus, when he had cried again with a loud voice, yielded up the ghost. *Mat.* 27: 50.

Neither yield ye your members as instruments of unrighteousness unto sin: but yield yourselves unto God, as those that are alive from the dead, and your members as instruments of righteousness unto God. *Ro.* 6: 13.

Know ye not, that to whom ye yield yourselves servants to obey, his servants ye are to whom ye obey; whether of sin unto death, or of obedience unto righteousness? *Ro.* 6: 16.

Yield your members servants to righteousness unto holiness. *Ro.* 6: 19.

Whatsoever a man soweth, that shall he also reap. *Ga.* 6: 7.

The fruit of the Spirit is in all goodness and righteousness and truth. *Ep.* 5: 9.

So can no fountain both yield salt water and fresh. *Ja.* 3: 12.

See also
Acquiescence; Fruit; Fruitfulness; Harvest; Productivity; Reaping; Submission.

Yoke

Make the yoke which thy father did put upon us lighter. *1 K.* 12: 9.

The Lord laid this burden upon him. *2 K.* 9: 25.

Cast thy burden upon the Lord. *Ps.* 55: 22.

I am full of heaviness. *Ps.* 69: 20.

Thou hast broken the yoke of his burden, and the staff of his shoulder. *Is.* 9: 4.

I have broken thy yoke, and burst thy bands. *Je.* 2: 20.

The yoke of my transgressions is bound by his hand. *La.* 1: 14.

It is good for a man that he bear the yoke in his youth. *La.* 3: 27.

I was to them as they that take off the yoke on their jaws, and I laid meat unto them. *Ho.* 11: 4.

Now will I break this yoke from off thee. *Na.* 1: 13.

Take my yoke upon you, and learn of me. *Mat.* 11: 29.

My yoke is easy, and my burden is light. *Mat.* 11: 30.

Be not unequally yoked together with unbelievers. *2 Co.* 6: 14.

Stand fast therefore in the liberty wherewith Christ hath made us free, and be not entangled again with the yoke of bondage. *Ga.* 5: 1.

Every man shall bear his own burden. *Ga.* 6: 5.

See also
Autocrat; Bond; Bondage; Burden; Concern; Despot; Repression; Slavery; Suppression.

Youth

Deal gently for my sake with the young man. *2 S.* 18: 5.

The Lord opened the eyes of the young man; and he saw. *2 K.* 6: 17.

Thou art my trust from my youth. *Ps.* 71: 5.

Thy youth is renewed like the eagle's. *Ps.* 103: 5.

Wherewithal shall a young man cleanse his way? by taking heed thereto according to thy word. *Ps.* 119: 9.

The glory of young men is their strength: and the beauty of old men is the gray head. *Pr.* 20: 29.

Rejoice, O young man, in thy youth. *Ec.* 11: 9.

Childhood and youth are vanity. *Ec.* 11: 10.

Remember now thy Creator in the days of thy youth, while the evil days come not, nor the years draw nigh, when thou shalt say, I have no pleasure in them. *Ec.* 12: 1.

Even the youths shall faint and be weary, and the young men shall utterly fall. *Is.* 40: 30.

It is good for a man that he bear the yoke in his youth. *La.* 3: 27.

When Israel was a child, then I loved him. *Ho.* 11: 1.

There followed him a certain young man. *Mk.* 14: 51.

Young man, I say unto thee, Arise. *Lu.* 7: 14.

Your young men shall see visions, and your old men shall dream dreams. *Ac.* 2: 17.

Let no man despise thy youth. *1 Ti.* 4: 12.

Young men likewise exhort to be sober minded. *Tit.* 2: 6.

I write unto you, young men, because ye have overcome the wicked one. *1 Jn.* 2: 13.

See also
Immaturity.

Z

Zeal

The zeal of the Lord of hosts shall do this. *2 K.* 19: 31.

The zeal of thine house hath eaten me up. *Ps.* 69: 9.

Consider diligently what is before thee. *Pr.* 23: 1.

The zeal of the Lord of hosts will perform this. *Is.* 9: 7.

Look down from heaven, and behold from the habitation of thy holiness and of thy glory: where is thy zeal and thy strength? *Is.* 63: 15.

Simon called Zelotes. *Lu.* 6: 15.

They have a zeal of God, but not according to knowledge. *Ro.* 10: 2.

Being more exceedingly zealous of the traditions of my fathers. *Ga.* 1: 14.

Whatsoever ye do, do it heartily, as to the Lord, and not unto men. *Col.* 3: 23.

I bear him record, that he hath a great zeal for you. *Col.* 4: 13.

A peculiar people, zealous of good works. *Tit.* 2: 14.

That ye should earnestly contend for the faith which was once delivered unto the saints. *Jude* 1: 3.

See also

Ardor; Eagerness; Earnestness; Enthusiasm; Fervor; Zest.

Zero

They go to nothing, and perish. *Jb.* 6: 18.

For now ye are nothing. *Jb.* 6: 21.

We are but of yesterday, and know nothing, because our days upon earth are a shadow. *Jb.* 8: 9.

Thou hast tried me, and shalt find nothing. *Ps.* 17: 3.

There is that maketh himself rich, yet hath nothing. *Pr.* 13: 7.

It is naught, it is naught, saith the buyer: but when he is gone his way, then he boasteth. *Pr.* 20: 14.

All nations before him are as nothing; and they are counted to him less than nothing. *Is.* 40: 17.

Behold, ye are of nothing, and your work of nought. *Is.* 41: 24.

And commanded them that they should take nothing for their journey, . . . no money in their purse. *Mk.* 6: 8.

See also

Emptiness; Nothing; Void.

Zest

O taste and see that the Lord is good. *Ps.* 34: 8.

There is nothing better for a man, than that he should eat and drink, and that he should make his soul enjoy good in his labour. *Ec.* 2: 24.

Live joyfully with the wife whom thou lovest. *Ec.* 9: 9.

Mine elect shall long enjoy the work of their hands. *Is.* 65: 22.

Fervent in spirit; serving the Lord. *Ro.* 12: 11.

It is good to be zealously affected always in a good thing. *Ga.* 4: 18.

He hath a great zeal for you. *Col.* 4: 13.

Trust . . . in the living God, who giveth us richly all things to enjoy. *1 Ti.* 6: 17.

See that ye love one another with a pure heart fervently. *1 Pe.* 1: 22.

See also

Ardor; Eagerness; Enjoyment; Enthusiasm; Fervor; Passion; Zeal.

Zion

Sing praises to the Lord, which dwelleth in Zion. *Ps.* 9: 11.

Beautiful for situation, the joy of the whole earth, is mount Zion, on the sides of the north, the city of the great King. *Ps.* 48: 2.

Walk about Zion, and go round about her: tell the towers thereof. *Ps.* 48: 12.

Out of Zion, the perfection of beauty, God hath shined. *Ps.* 50: 2.

God will save Zion, and will build the cities of Judah. *Ps.* 69: 35.

The Lord loveth the gates of Zion more than all the dwellings of Jacob. *Ps.* 87: 2.

The Lord shall bless thee out of Zion. *Ps.* 128: 5.

The Lord hath chosen Zion; he hath desired it for his habitation. *Ps.* 132: 13.

They that carried us away captive required of us a song; . . . saying, Sing us one of the songs of Zion. *Ps.* 137: 3.

Praise the Lord, O Jerusalem; praise thy God, O Zion. *Ps.* 147: 12.

The Lord shall comfort Zion: he will comfort all her waste places. *Is.* 51: 3.

The redeemed of the Lord shall return, and come with singing unto Zion; and everlasting joy shall be upon their head. *Is.* 51: 11.

Woe to them that are at ease in Zion. *Am.* 6: 1.

I looked, and, lo, a Lamb stood on the mount Sion, and with him an hundred forty and four thousand, having his Father's name written in their foreheads. *Re.* 14: 1.

See also

Civilization; Jerusalem.